THE COMPLETE ENCYCLOPEDIA OF

WINE
BEER
AND
SPIRITS

THIS IS A CARLTON BOOK

First published in 2000 by Carlton Books Limited

10 9 8 7 6 5 4 3 2 1

UK ISBN 1 84222 118 3
USA ISBN 1 84222 063 2

Project editor: Martin Corteel
Project art direction: Brian Flynn
Production: Sarah Corteel
Designed by Dave Sutton

Carlton Books Limited
20 Mortimer Street
London W1N 7RD

Printed and bound in Indonesia

Publisher's Note

The sections of this book specified below were first published in the following titles:

Pages 10–219 – *The Ultimate Encyclopedia of Wine* by Robert Joseph (1996)
Pages 220–405 – *The Ultimate Encyclopedia of Beer* by Roger Protz (1995)
Pages 406–631 – *Spirits & Cocktails* and *Whisky: A Connoisseur's Guide* by Dave Broom (1997)

Pictures used in prelims

p.3 *Dean Stewart Distillery, Doune, Perthshire, Scotland*

p.4/5 *Vineyard at Little Karoo, Republic of South Africa*

p.6. *La Fortuna Lontue vineyards, Chile*

p.7 Top: *Whisky barrels stored at Speyside Cooperage, Scotland;* **Bottom:** *Royal Tokaji Vaults, Hungary*

p.8 *Pacific Vineyard, California, USA;* **Bottom:** *Cool, refreshing lager*

p.9 *Martini is probably the best-known cocktail in the world*

p.10 *Stained glass window in the Hudson Valley vineyards, New York, USA*

THE COMPLETE ENCYCLOPEDIA OF

WINE
BEER
AND
SPIRITS

Robert Joseph • Roger Protz • Dave Broom

CARLTON
BOOKS

CONTENTS

INTRODUCTION

What will you drink today? Or this week, or this year? If you're like most of us, you'll dip in and out of different lifestyles. One evening you'll drink tasty but inexpensive wine with supper at home; another evening you'll seek out a more expensive bottle and cook something special to share with friends. You might stop for a drink after work, and that might mean a country pub or a fashionable urban bar; it might mean locally produced bitter or imported lager, gin and tonic or premium tequila. At the weekend you might go to a barbecue or a smart party; you might be invited to help yourself from the fridge, or take Champagne from a waiter. After dinner you might pour yourself a Cognac or a malt whisky or glass of Vin Santo: we all of us, when it comes to drink, speak many, many languages.

We also expect to understand more than ever about what we consume. Thirty years ago it was commonplace for people who made wine or beer or spirits to have large gaps in their knowledge: wine producers, for example, might ascribe particular flavours to the soil of their vineyards when in reality those flavours came from bacterial infection. They made wine in the way that their grandfathers made it, but neither generation knew why they did things – or rather, the reasons they gave for doing them relied on tradition and folklore rather than on an understanding of the chemistry of winemaking.

In the whisky distilleries of Scotland, there was little experience 30 years ago of how the flavour of a malt might be fine-tuned by maturation in different sorts of wood, and indeed no idea at all that people at the turn of the new century would be keen to pay a premium for the rarest, most complex malt whiskies. Whisky used to be a commodity, with only a few single malts available for the enthusiast; now there are bottlings of different ages, finished in different sorts of oak barrel, with flavours that range from flowery to smoky to seaweedy. .

Beer, too, has undergone a revolution. Just as it looked as though lager would sweep aside everything in its path, real ale made a remarkable comeback in the UK in the late-1980s and 1990s – against all the odds. Indeed, in Britain around half the beer produced is still in ale form, while in Ireland, clever advertising and quality presentation have succeeded in converting young people to the delights of Irish stout.

But while Britain and Ireland can justifiably lay claim to being at the heart of the renaissance in real ale and stout, other countries are also experiencing renewed enthusiasm for traditional-style beers. Erstwhile wine strongholds such as France and Italy are seeing significant interest, while the bière de garde of Northern France and the specialist beers of Belgium are reaching an ever-wider audience outside their home territory. Even in the USA, where asking for a beer simply used to get you a glass of something cold, golden, fizzy and bland, the dramatic increase in small craft breweries has given new prominence to the beer world.

The drinks revolution has been brought about partly by technology and partly by

consumer demand. In wine, California and Australia burst upon the world with clean, fresh, fruity wines that tasted totally different from the wines that had always been made in Europe. Their flavours were more upfront, more exotic, more attention-grabbing. And we loved them: we fell for the Chardonnays with their tropical fruit flavours, their pineapple and butterscotch tastes. We loved the assertive plums and blackcurrants of the Cabernet Sauvignons; and the winemakers of Europe took note. Soon they, too, were experimenting with the same technology that was working such wonders in the New World, and soon they, too, were questioning the handed-down wisdom of generations, and reviewing their practices in the light of science.

Beer and spirits had less to learn from science – both industries have long been in the hands of large corporations rather than small father-and-son operations. Here there was a gradual realisation that what we wanted was diversity: we didn't just want to be restricted to a few big brands, however reliable they were. We wanted, in fact, the same variety that we had in wine – and in wine we wanted the same reliability that we had in beer and spirits.

It could all have ended in tears: we could have ended up with wine that tasted the same wherever it came from; beers with myriad different names, but all industrially tailored to fit a mythical consumer ideal; spirits that charged premium prices but delivered no real interest. Instead we live in something of a golden age. We have a better selection of good wines at affordable prices than has ever been seen in the history of the world: to find a really nasty wine now takes more work than finding a decent one. Beers are genuinely interesting, and attracting attention from the same consumers who drink fine wines; spirits can be good-value commodities or high-priced rarities.

But in order to appreciate all this wealth of flavours we have to do a little homework. Just as we buy better at the cheese or the fish counter if we know the

differences between the varieties displayed before us, so drink becomes more interesting, more rewarding and more fun if we know which wines will taste dry and lemony, which peachy and honeyed, and which juicy and plummy; which Armagnac will best suit our palate and budget; which malt whisky will be light and which heavy. It just so happens that drink is also one of the most fascinating subjects to read about; and the three authors behind this book have the lightest touch and the quickest wit. So find a comfortable chair, reach for your favourite bottle and a glass, and read on.

WINE

Twenty-five years ago, a trip to the local wine store wouldn't have taxed even the most indecisive of consumers. Such was the restricted fare fed to a hapless public that only the most avid of connoisseurs were sampling the delights of "new" wines from countries such as Australia, New Zealand, South Africa, South America and the USA. The rest of us rarely ventured beyond a bottle of Blue Nun.

How times – and tastes – change. Encouraged by a plethora of TV wine programmes, and "wine of the week" recommendations in newspapers and in major supermarkets – as well as more demanding consumers – today's wines stores present a bewildering sight. Shelves are stacked high with row upon row of fruity Chardonnays, light Colombards and Semillons, oaky Cabernet Sauvignons, spicy Shirazes – the list is endless. It can take longer to make your wine selection than to do the rest of your shopping.

Nor do these wines come only from the traditional producers. Back in those little-lamented Liebfraumilch-only days, who'd have thought that countries such as Argentina, Bulgaria, Chile, Hungary and Moldova would figure among the world's major wine regions?

Of course, interest in wine has also been boosted by the massive increase in worldwide travel. People take their holidays in unfamiliar locations, sample the local fare, and then want to recreate some of the atmosphere of their holiday when they return home.

Once your interest in wine has been kindled, it's hard to resist the urge to examine the labels on the myriad wines at your local store – carefully noting attributes such as the grape type and nose. But the enjoyment of wine isn't just about high-flown descriptions on a label and the elusive ability to identify the vineyard the wine came from just by its smell: tasting it is far more important (despite the continual warnings of the health risks associated with alcohol consumption).

Just like the beer connoisseur with his new-found choice of bottle-conditioned ales, it's time to shrug off the shackles of the nanny state and political correctness, and work your way steadily through the spectrum of affordable wines on offer at your local wine store. You're unlikely to be disappointed – these days, it's much harder to find a bad wine than a good one.

HOW WINE IS MADE

God, they say, helps those who help themselves. Well, help yourself to a handful of grapes, crush them, and leave them be for a few days in a reasonably warm place, remove the skins and pips and, hey presto, you'll have made an alcoholic liquid which could legally describe itself as wine. It makes life hard for all those religious anti-alcohol nuts: if God really didn't want us to drink wine, why did He create a self-contained wine-making kit in every grape?

The stuff you've made will probably taste quite foul, of course, but it's only your first attempt, after all, and you've not used much in the way of skill or equipment. All you've done is allow the liquid and the natural sugar within the grape to combine with the millions of yeast cells on the fruit surface which kicked off the natural process of fermentation.

There are all sorts of ways of managing this process to achieve a particular style of wine, but nothing the wine-maker does can ever influence the ultimate flavour of the stuff in the bottle as much as the raw materials: the type of grapes used, where and how they were grown and harvested, and, of course, the climate.

Grape Expectations

The grape variety (or varieties – wines are often blends of more than one) used for making any wine is as fundamental to its taste as the type of meat or fish will be to a particular dish. The differences in the flavour of freshly picked Riesling and Gewürztraminer grapes are even more apparent in the wines they are used to make.

Some varieties, such as Burgundy's Pinot Noir and Chardonnay, traditionally perform best as soloists; most, however, are ensemble players, and are more usually found in blends. Claret, for example, is almost always a mixture of two or more varieties, principally the Cabernet Sauvignon, Merlot and Cabernet Franc.

Old World countries' wine laws (Germany being a notable exception) prescribe and proscribe certain varieties for each of their designated quality wine areas, based on experience of what grows best there. Only certain grapes – or blends of grapes – may be used to produce a wine labelled with that appellation.

In the New World, rules like these are almost non-existent; producers are free to experiment with as many varieties as they like. The advantage of this approach lies in the way it allows the wine industry to develop new styles without the constraints of potentially irrelevant laws. On the other hand, as consumers have discovered in their high streets throughout the world, a wholly free market rarely favours the demanding, the small and the unfashionable.

Without some kind of appellation system, traditional but little-known grapes like the Gros and Petit Manseng, which are used to make the equally traditional and little-known wine of Jurançon in France, could disappear in the same way as the local butcher and fishmonger.

Some Like It Hot

Whatever the flavour or fashionability of the grape variety, it will never make decent wine unless it has enough sun to ripen properly. The climatic conditions demanded by wine-making vines are pretty precise.

Ideally, winters should be cold – cold enough for the vine to lie dormant and conserve all its growing energy until the spring when the vine flowers. From this moment until the harvest, the most important element is timely, well measured doses of sun. The all-important final ripening of the grapes should happen in the cooler months of autumn, not all in a rush in the blazing heat of high summer. Too long or hot a blast encourages growth to be too prolific and too rapid to concentrate the subtleties of flavour which can develop naturally through a slower ripening.

The wine-producing regions of the world lie in two

FLYING WINE-MAKERS

Imagine calling up your favourite Italian restaurant and asking if the chef would mind your sending a young friend into his kitchen to cook dinner for you on your next visit, and every time thereafter. Your friend – an Australian who doesn't even speak Italian – would use the restaurant's ingredients and equipment to prepare precisely the same dishes the chef has been making for years. But he's going to make them the way you want.

Well, hard though it may be to believe, that's the precise equivalent of the proposal Britain's biggest wine-retailers successfully made during the 1990s to dozens of wineries in France (including such classic regions as Bordeaux and Burgundy), Spain, Portugal, Italy, Germany and Eastern Europe, as well, more surprisingly, as such New-World countries as South Africa, Chile and California. Could they send in their own Antipodean "Flying Wine-makers" – young men and women, most of whom arrived shortly before the harvest and left shortly afterward?

What was the secret of these mercenaries of the wine world?

And why were they almost all Antipodean? The answer is one of philosophy: unlike many of their Old-World counterparts who tend to let nature and the climate decide on the style of wine produced in any given year, the New-World wine-makers start out with a pretty clear idea of the kind of wine they want to make.

Outsiders also acknowledge that the Flying Wine-makers are readier to work longer hours – no long lunches and week-ends off – and to pay greater attention to cleanliness and hygiene than the bosses of the Old-World co-operatives and larger commercial wineries in which they work.

Critics complain that Flying Wine-makers' wines all taste the same; supporters point out that, in blind tastings, and when British and Dutch consumers are allowed to vote with their wallets, it is the interlopers whose bottles regularly win the greatest favour. In 1995, there were over 100 Flying Wine-makers working in Europe – and few signs that their temporary hosts were learning enough from them to make their presence unnecessary.

Around the world vines are irrigated to avoid the effects of drought

phenomena as the Gulf Stream. To help to define particular local conditions, a Californian scale of "heat units" was devised, based on the average daily temperature during the growing season. This kind of scale tends to underestimate factors such as the difference in day and night-time temperatures – and just how hot and cold the weather tends to get. Grapes simply do not mature when it is too hot or cool, so high-altitude Idaho, which according to its average temperatures ought to ripen grapes well, cannot usually do so: after a chilly night, they get an hour or so of moderate warmth mid-morning before the noonday heat becomes intense enough to send the fruit off for a self-protective siesta. Elsewhere, on the other hand, in parts of Chile, and the Barossa Valley in Australia, for example, cool nights help to prevent the grapes from becoming over-ripe.

Handling The Rains

Like any other plant, vines need water to grow properly. If they don't get it, however ideal the rest of the weather, the grapes will be parched and their tough skins will make for hard, tannic red wine. Worse still, a vine which gets no water during crucial periods of its growing season will simply stop growing. On the other hand, what the vines don't need is an untimely storm just before or

quite sharply defined bands: the moderate, temperate zones between 50° and 30° latitude in the northern hemisphere, and 30° and 50° in the southern hemisphere. Within these bands, in general, fine wines are made in the cooler areas furthest removed from the Equator. Unless they are carefully handled, grapes from truly warm regions tend to produce large quantities of soft, jammy wine.

However, even within the same latitudes, the climate can vary widely, depending on altitude, distance from the sea and mountains and the influence of such

HOW WINE IS MADE TO SPARKLE

Sparkling wines are made by every wine-producing country in the world. The carbon dioxide which creates the bubbles in the wine is a natural by-product of fermentation.

If the wine-maker intends his product to be sparkling, he traps the gas in the wine. There it remains dissolved until the pressure is released, when it rapidly makes its way to the surface in the form of tiny bubbles.

There are various ways of capturing fizz in a wine. The best is the méthode champenoise, used not only in Champagne but throughout the wine-making world.

The way in which the gas is trapped can vary, from a highly skilled, labour-intensive science to a heavy-handed, mass-produced routine, as can the quality of the base wine itself. The best base wines for sparkling wine are those with high acidity and little character. That the soil (chalk) and climate (cool) of Champagne are ideally suited to producing wines of this type is a major factor in explaining Champagne's pre-eminence among sparkling wines.

The Champagne Method (AKA méthode classique or traditionelle)
Used for: Champagne; Cava; Crémant de Loire, de Bourgogne and d'Alsace; Blanquette de Limoux; quality New-World sparkling wines; Italian "Metodo Classico"; quality German Sekt.

After the blending of the base wines, a solution of wine and sugar is added, along with specially cultured yeasts, to provoke a secondary fermentation. The bottles are then stacked on their sides in a cool cellar and left for the second fermentation slowly to run its course.

Traditionally, the bottles were then placed, neck first, into specially designed sloping racks, called pupitres, where skilled rémueurs would, over the course of a few weeks, daily shake, rotate and tilt the bottle slightly to shift the sediment down so that it rested on the cork. Nowadays this job is generally done – many say – just as effectively by machines called giropalettes.

Finally the necks of the bottles are chilled, freezing the sediment into a solid plug. When the corks are removed, the plug pops out under the pressure of the carbon dioxide in the bottle. The wine remaining in the bottle is then topped up with more of the same wine and a little liquid sugar, known as the dosage, before being corked with the traditional Champagne cork tied down with wire.

The Transfer Method
Used for: more run-of-the-mill European wines such as Kriter from France; some New-World fizz. This is essentially a "second-best" cross between the Champagne and cuve close (see below) methods. The second fermentation takes place in the bottle and the wine is transferred under pressure to tanks for dosage, filtering and re-bottling.

The Cuve Close, Charmat or Tank Method
Used for: basic French sparklers; all but the best German Sekt; most Asti; Spanish "Granvas" fizz.

Invented by the Frenchman Charmat, this method can make tolerable sparkling wine – ideal, perhaps, for mixing a Buck's Fizz. The base wine is run into huge stainless steel tanks where secondary fermentation takes place at a controlled temperature, followed by dosage, filtering and bottling.

---

during the harvest, when the rain will simply dilute the juice of the grapes.

Sometimes these late storms spoil what might have been a fine vintage; sometimes, on the other hand, as in the early 1990s in Bordeaux, nature meanly subjects the vines to both drought and storms so that the end result is both watery and unripe.

In the New World, Southern France and – more recently – Spain, growers will irrigate the plants to avoid the effects of drought or "stress". French traditionalists in particular, however, dismiss even the most carefully measured irrigation as "industrialized" wine-making and ban it outright. Oddly, they take a more tolerant view when richer château owners hover over their vineyards in helicopters in an elaborate ploy to protect the vines from the ravages of the rain.

The French fear of irrigation per se is unreasonable, as the Bordelais who have gone to make wine in Chile where grapes cannot be grown without additional water would have to admit. But Chile, like Argentina and the more basic vineyards of Australia and California, does offer an object lesson in the dangers of over-irrigation. If your Bordeaux tastes dilute, it's God's fault; if your South American Cabernet Sauvignon is watery, blame the grape-grower.

Siting The Vineyard

The way in which the vines are selected, planted and looked after dictates the quality of the fruit they will yield. If the best vineyards are sited in relatively cool areas, to prevent the vine from over-stretching itself, maximum use must be made of the precious – sometimes elusive – summer sun. So the best location for a vineyard in the northern hemisphere is normally on a south-facing slope which, from dawn until dusk, catches as many of the sun's rays as possible.

Vines planted in flat land receive less sunshine, are badly drained, and are prone to frost. The lowest part of the slope is better off, but will suffer from any damp conditions prevailing on the flat land, particularly if there happens to be a stream or river running through it. Vines half-way up the hill receive the most direct sunlight and are well-drained. Higher up, altitude causes cooler temperatures which inhibit ripening. The top of the hill is thus no better than the bottom, suffering from cool temperatures, wind and reduced direct sunlight. In the best wine-growing areas of France, the hilltops are covered by trees.

You do not have to travel far to realize, though, that this recipe can vary enormously from one quality wine region to another. The vineyards on the banks of the Rhône, Rhine and Douro rivers, for example, often appear steep enough to call for the skills of an amateur mountaineer. The slopes in Beaujolais and Chianti are gentler while those in the Médoc are often hardly noticeable at all, and parts of the valley floors of the Napa and Marlborough Valleys, in California and New

METHODS OF FORTIFICATION

The other way to make sweet wines is to add alcohol to the fermenting juice. Those who fortify wine in this way can produce wines – varying in strength from under 16 per cent to as much as 25 per cent – such as port, Marsala, Madeira, the delicious fortified Muscats of Australia and the vins doux naturels of France: Muscat de Beaumes de Venise and Rivesaltes.

With a few exceptions, fortified wines tend to be sweet. This is either because the addition of alcohol was made whilst there was still sugar in the grapes, or because in a few cases – most notably certain sherries – the final result is sweetened.

The French distinguish between vins de liqueur, which are made by alcohol being added to the grape juice before it has begun to ferment, and vins doux naturels, in which it is added during the fermentation process. Least prestigious of the vins de liqueur are the mistelles. The best-known are Pineau des Charentes, made in Cognac, Ratafia de Champagne and Floc de Gascogne. Others are used as the base for branded aperitifs.

Of the vins doux naturels, the most popular are the Muscats from the Rhône, Roussillon and Languedoc regions, such as Beaumes de Venise, Rivesaltes and most notably Banyuls, made in Roussillon from the Grenache grape.

Of the other fortified wines, port and Madeira are made by the vin doux naturel method. Sherry is fermented to dryness, then fortified before oxygen and yeasts start to act on the wine.

THE VARIETIES OF SOIL

Gravel

A great number of vineyards are perched on the side of river valleys, in well-drained gravel deposits. Vines do better in poor, well-drained soils which make them plunge their roots deeper to find water and goodness. The great wines of Bordeaux come from gravel soils (Graves means gravel) which particularly suit the Cabernet Sauvignon. Much depends, however, on the other kinds of soil with which the gravel is combined. If it is over clay, the wine will have less acidity than if it is over limestone.

Granite

The granite vineyards of the southern Rhône, home of Châteauneuf-du-Pape and Tavel rosé, are littered with huge "pudding stones", making the cultivation of anything seem virtually impossible. Once vines are established, however, the stones act as reflectors, bouncing the heat from the sun back on to the grapes. The end result is that they produce big, high-in-alcohol reds and France's most famous dry rosé. In the Beaujolais, granite suits the Gamay; its chemical properties reduce the wine's natural acidity.

Chalk

Chalk, too, makes for very good drainage and forces the vines to work hard for a living. Not all vine varieties like predominantly alkaline soil. Those that do best on chalky hillsides produce white wines of unique character such as the Chardonnay, which forms part of the inimitable blend for Champagne. The keynote of wines made from grapes grown on chalky – limestone – soil is their acidity, a characteristic that links Champagne, Chablis and Sancerre.

Slate

The richer minerals found in slatey soils suit some vines admirably. The alluvial deposits on the banks beside the Rhine and Mosel rivers in Germany are responsible for the delicate fragrance of the gently fruity local wines, produced on the precipitous, barren-looking slopes. The locals say: "Where the plough may go, no great wines grow." The main advantage of slate in regions like the Mosel is its heat retention, which compensates for the low temperatures in which the grapes have to ripen. Slate is also credited with the quality of Rieslings from the far warmer region of Clare in South Australia.

Zealand respectively, have a billiard-table flatness.

If a vineyard is particularly prone to frost – as is the case in Chablis, Champagne and the Napa Valley – there are ways to combat it: water sprinklers, oil burners or wind machines to mix in warm air and dispel the cold air lying close to the vines. Over the years, however, man has ingeniously devised non-mechanical methods to improve the environment in which he wants to grow his grapes, draining the soil in Bordeaux and Ontario, for example, planting trees as a wind-break in Tasmania and chopping a few of them down in California to allow air to pass through and blow away the pools of cool air which can cause frost. The most dramatic example of this Godlike remodelling of the earth is the E & J Gallo estate in Sonoma where 800 hectares (2,000 acres) were totally re-landscaped before the vines were planted.

The Answer Lies In The Soil

Vine-growing is not unlike gardening: just as you can't grow roses in a garden with unsuitable soil, most varieties of vine have been historically proven to have strong preferences as to where they like growing. These preferences have led French traditionalists to build up a mystique surrounding what they call the *goût de terroir* of their better wines. Translated literally, this refers to the taste of the earth in which the grapes are grown; in fact the term includes other factors such as the physical situation of the vineyard and the climate.

Like most living things (ourselves included), grapes consist largely of water, and so, in turn, does wine. The water content of a grape will inevitably have passed through the soil in which the vine has planted its roots. Different soil types therefore affect the taste of wine as well. Around the world, the structure of the earth varies considerably. Conditions may repeat themselves, but often a particular region's geology is unique and accounts for the individuality of its wine.

The idea, however, that it is the specific minerals in the soil of a given plot of land, that actually contribute to the flavour of a wine made from vines grown there, has come in for increasingly sceptical treatment. Today, the general consensus is that the influence of the soil has far more to do with its natural acidity or alkalinity and its physical structure: the way it holds and reflects heat and its capacity for draining water. Vines, for example, as their growers say, have just as great a dislike of standing around with wet feet as they do of being thirsty.

Tending The Vines

Growing vines is farming, just as much as growing barley or rearing pigs, and demands long hours and dedicated attention if the harvest of grapes is to be worth waiting for. Before a vineyard can be planted, it must be prepared and the soil properly turned over and aired. In some instances, it may need to be fumigated; in others, growers may decide to correct its acidity or alkalinity.

Next, it is time to plant the vines – a less straightforward business than one might suppose. Unless your chosen site is in a place like Chile, Argentina or parts of the Antipodes that have yet to fall prey to the otherwise ubiquitous *phylloxera* louse, you are almost bound to have to graft your baby plants onto some kind of rootstock that is resistant to the louse.

Rootstock comes in a number of forms, most of which are distinguished by sets of letters or numbers. Until the mid-1980s, the identity of individual types of rootstock was of little interest to growers who merely noted that some were more productive than others. Then came the discovery that AXR, the particular rootstock recommended by the University of California to vine-growers throughout that state, proved – as French experts had predicted in vain – to be less than wholly resistant to new biotypes of *phylloxera*. During the late 1980s and early 1990s, the louse attacked well over three-quarters of the vineyards of the Napa Valley, allowing those who had disregarded the University's advice by planting other (reliably resistant) rootstocks to continue to harvest their crops while their neighbours had to replant their entire estates.

Having selected the rootstock, the next task is to choose a clone of the variety you want to grow (see opposite page), the number of vines you are going to plant per hectare and the way you are going to train and prune them.

In the Old World, the density of your vineyard and the method of training will often be pre-ordained by tradition and law. Elsewhere, your decision will depend on the grape variety, the climate – in warm regions you can have fewer vines per hectare – and the style, quality and quantity of wine you want to make.

Methods of training are traditionally adapted to the climates of the countries in which the vines are grown. In the late 1980s, though, vine-growers throughout the world began to acknowledge that they might have something to learn from systems of vine "canopy

SEND IN THE CLONES

Anyone who read or saw The Boys from Brazil will recall the idea of propagating human beings from cells taken from a particular individual. The ability to create clones of Adolf Hitler may still be the subject of fiction, but vine-growers throughout the world have, since the 1980s, been able to plant identical copies of, say, one of the healthiest, most reliable Chardonnay vines in the Le Montrachet vineyard of Burgundy.

The clone sold by their local nursery will have been reproduced by a process of taking cuttings of successive generations and rejecting any that do not have precisely the same characteristics as the original, until "dissident" examples simply cease to occur. Cuttings taken from the successful strain will always have the desirable features of that original Le Montrachet vine.

Critics of clones complain that planting an entire vineyard with the same clone makes for wines lacking in complexity; most quality-conscious growers recognize this and now opt for a "cocktail" of different clones.

management" developed in New Zealand and Australia by a man called Richard Smart.

In hot countries with limited rainfall, vines are likely to be trained to grow relatively close to the ground, so that the limited moisture available does not have to waste itself on producing too many shoots and leaves, but can be directed into the grapes. In cooler climates, with more rainfall and less sun, priorities are different. Here grapes are usually trained higher, to catch the limited sun more effectively, and reduce the risks of mildew and rot by permitting a free flow of air around the bunches of grapes.

Inevitably, this all paints a very simple picture of what is an extremely complicated subject, with innumerable methods of training and pruning vines. Among those frequently encountered are the Single and Double Guyot, Gobelet, Lenz Moser and the exotically named Geneva Double Curtain, which, needless to say, has nothing to do with Switzerland, but originated in New York State.

From Vineyard To Winery

Until quite recently, in the Old World at least, the emphasis has been on the vineyard rather than the winery or cellar. French wine-producers, for example, routinely describe themselves as *viticulteurs* and *vignerons* – both terms which refer to vine-growing – and rarely, if ever, as *vinificateurs*, the word which most accurately covers the job of converting the grapes into wine.

For many, in both the Old and New Worlds, the task does indeed stop with the harvest; they simply deliver their crop to the local co-operative or bigger winery. But for tens of thousands of smaller estates, picking the grapes only marks the end of a chapter. There's many a slip between the snip of the secateurs and the sip of the wine.

In the 1970s and 1980s, the traditionally conservative world of wine was shaken to its roots by the arrival of technology in the shape of stainless steel tanks to replace the old wooden vats, cooling and heating equipment for the fermentation vats and all manner of high-tech presses and filters – not to mention computers to save human beings from having to watch the gauges and flick the switches.

The wine chemists – the oenologists – and biologists were playing their part too, developing special enzymes and yeast strains to replace the unpredictable stuff found on the skins of the grapes or in the cellars. Taken together, these innovations removed much of the guess-work from the wine-making process, turning, as one Australian gleefully admitted, what was an art or a craft

Mechanical harvesting at the Robert Mondavi Vineyard, California

ROLL OUT THE BARREL

Wine-makers have been using oak barrels since the Romans became frustrated with the tendency of amphorae to break. The difference between then and now, however, is that, until the 1970s, the only time they brought in new oak barrels was when the old ones fell apart. This is not to say that no-one had realized that in the first three years of their working life, oak casks could add an extra note of sweet vanilla spice to the wines they contained – nor that certain forests produced wood with distinctive and attractive flavours. But the systematic use of oak as an ingredient did not begin until the best châteaux of Bordeaux used the newly acquired funds from the post-war vintages to replace tired casks and New-World wine-makers, eager not to miss a trick, followed in their footsteps...

There is no question that the flavour of oak can improve and add complexity to a wine – and that particular styles of wine work better with particular styles of oak (Rioja and Australian Shiraz do well in American oak while fine Chardonnay prefers wood from the forests of Nevers, Allier or Vosges in France). New barrels are expensive, however, and, even if "scraped" and re-fired, have a relatively short life. Flying Wine-makers (see p. 13) and others achieve something of the same effect by putting the oak – in the form of chips – in the wine rather than vice versa. For some odd reason, this practice is frowned on by Old-World authorities.

Traditionalists frequently complain about wines being "over-oaked" and even Professor Emile Peynaud, the so-called "father of modern Bordeaux" and the man often credited with and blamed for creating the fashion for new oak, believed that few wines are concentrated and complex enough to support the 100 per cent new oak they are often given.

Thirty years on, Professor Peynaud's suspicion of oak abuse is beginning to strike a chord with wine-makers. In 1995, Andrew Pirie's Pipers Brook winery in Tasmania won "White Wine of the Year" at the International Wine Challenge with an unoaked Chardonnay, while the first reds made in Chile by Paul Pontallier and Bruno Pratts of Bordeaux were bravely almost devoid of obvious oak flavour.

Barrels contribute their own "certain something" to the wine's ageing

into a science.

If wine-making is a natural process, certain refinements are necessary to make sure that the wine you make tastes good. Present in the white bloom on the skin of grapes are not only good wine yeasts, but tricky wild yeasts and bacteria as well. These are brought to the grapes by insects, or just carried in the air, and are fashionably aerobic – meaning they need plenty of oxygen to work.

If you were to leave fermentation to take place unaided in the open air, the wild yeasts would set to work in a furious rush until they were overcome by alcohol (at a strength of about 4 per cent). The slower-working, but more persistent, wine yeasts would then take over until they had completed the job, leaving the fruits of their labours exposed to the bacteria which feed on alcohol, turning it into vinegar.

Obviously, the bacteria must be prevented from getting a hold, along with the wild yeasts, which work too quickly for the good of the wine. There are two ways of doing this; one is to seal the tanks and starve them of oxygen, and the other is to add sulphur dioxide to the wine juice (or *must*), which feeds on oxygen and forms an oxygen-exclusive coating on top of the must. These precautions taken, vinification is quite straightforward.

Wine-making is rather like cooking. If the ingredients are fresh and of good quality, and if the basic rules are followed, the final result should be good wine. But just as each cook may have an individual touch, every quality wine-maker will aim to produce wines which bear his own stamp. This he can do by following the rules in his own way.

The temperature of the fermentation, the length of time it is allowed to carry on, the choice of wooden barrels or stainless steel tanks, the age and size of the casks, the period before bottling: all these are factors over which the wine-maker has complete control and which will influence the character of the finished wine.

Much of the fascination of wine-tasting lies in guessing exactly how each particular wine was made. Every glass of wine you drink will have gone through one of the processes described on these pages.

How Dry White Wine Is Made

1. Grapes are picked, possibly by mechanical harvesters which shake them from the vines. They may be sorted; rotten ones are removed. The rest are taken quickly back to the winery. The longer the journey, the greater the risk of oxidation by heat and air.

2. For heavier-bodied wines, grapes may be crushed and allowed to macerate for 24 hours in a cool tank. This "skin-contact" is particularly popular in the New World.

3. For crisp, fruity wines, grapes are lightly crushed and the solid matter passed straight into the press. Wine-makers may control the temperature, keeping it cool for enhanced crispness.

4. The more you press, the more bitter the result. Some pressed juice is generally added to the "free-run" juice drawn off from the crusher, and the mixture passed into vats. Sulphur is added to kill off bacteria and prevent oxidation.

5. In the vat, suspended matter will drop out of the juice, which can then be allowed to ferment – in vats or in wooden barrels. Modern wineries may use vacuum pumps or centrifuges to separate solids from liquid.

6. In Old-World wineries, the natural yeasts found in the cellars will be responsible for fermentation. New-World and Flying Wine-makers generally prefer to use enzymes and selected cultured yeasts which are more predictable and can, between them, help to give potentially dull wine more flavour, though in California there is a trend towards using "natural yeasts" as in Europe.

7. Fermentation may be fast or slow, warm or cool. "Warm" means between 18°C and 25°C; "cool", 18°C. The cooler the fermentation, the fruitier, but possibly less complex, the wine.

8. Barrel fermentation – particularly in small, new oak barrels, as in Burgundy – will give the wine an oaky, vanilla character and some longevity-bearing tannin. This is only appropriate for certain grapes, notably the Chardonnay and Sémillon, and not for more aromatic ones like Muscat and Gewürztraminer. Tank-fermented wine may then go into barrel, or stay in tank.

9. If there is insufficient grape sugar, (powdered) sugar or concentrated grape juice may be added to increase the final alcohol level in a process known as chaptalization. This procedure is banned in most warm regions and supposedly closely controlled in the cool ones. If there's too little acidity (as is often the case in warm regions), tartaric or citric acid can correct the balance; if there's too much, chalk will remove it.

10. Malolactic fermentation – the natural conversion of (appley) malic acid to (yoghurty) lactic – may take place partially or fully, either of its own accord or with the help of a specially developed innoculum, except where producers want to retain that acidity – as in some New-World styles and Vinho Verde.

11. The wine will then be fined, probably with bentonite, a powdery clay which drags any remaining solid matter, or "lees", to the bottom of the vat or barrel. It will then be "racked" – passed into another vat – before (usually but not invariably) filtering and bottling months or, in some cases, years after the harvest.

12. Some wines, notably Muscadet, are left "*sur lie*" – on their lees – and so taste slightly yeasty.

13. Inexpensive white wine is often "cold stabilized": chilled so that its tartaric acid forms harmless crystals which can be filtered out rather than be allowed to form in the bottle.

14. If barrels are used, there is the choice of how long the wine remains in them, and what kind and size of barrel to use. Chardonnay gains from being matured

in small new oak barrels. Old-fashioned white Dão tends to remain for a long time in large old ones which remove the little fruit flavour with which it was born.

15. Sulphur dioxide is added before bottling to protect the wine. The dose must be carefully judged, otherwise the wine will suffer from a "bad egg" smell.

How Red Wine Is Made

Red wine is made almost exclusively from black grapes, the colour coming from the skins.

1. In some regions – Burgundy, for example – grapes are left to macerate in a cool-room or beneath a coating of sulphur for 24 hours or longer before fermentation is allowed/encouraged to begin.

2. All or most of the freshly picked bunches of grapes are first put through a crusher (unless *macération carbonique* is being used – see stage 4, below), which just breaks the skins. Depending on the sort of wine to be made, and the amount of tannin required, the stalks may or may not be discarded at this stage.

3. From the crusher, the grapes go straight into the fermentation vats, skins and all. Fermentation can take a few days or up to four weeks or longer to complete, some wine-makers relying on natural yeasts while others prefer cultured ones. The higher the temperature, the more colour and tannin is extracted.

4. To produce youthful, soft, lighter reds, whole grapes are fermented in sealed vats in a process known as carbonic maceration or "whole berry" fermentation. Carbon dioxide trapped in the vat forces the grapes to ferment quickly – sometimes inside their skins – under pressure, and the whole process can be completed in as few as five days. Quite often, modern producers use a "semi-carbonic" system in which some of the grapes are crushed.

5. A wine's colour and tannin content are dictated partly by the length of time the fermenting must remains in contact with the skins and pips. Unless these are restrained under the surface of the must, by a mesh or other device, they will be carried to the surface of the vat by the carbon dioxide formed during fermentation, and form a "cap" there. If there is no such device, the must is pumped up and over the cap from time to time or dripped through a sprinkler, to break it up and extract colour.

6. To produce bigger, richer reds, the skins may be left in contact with the juice for days or even weeks once fermentation is complete. Paradoxically, this prolonged contact with the tannin-bearing solids can make for softer-tasting wine.

7. If necessary, the must will be chaptalized (see How White Wine is Made, stage 9, on previous page).

8. Some Australian wine-makers – unusually – transfer the liquid into barrel before fermentation is complete. This process, which maximizes the effect of new oak on the still-fermenting wine, seems to suit big red styles, though there have been successful, lighter Pinot Noirs made in this way too.

9. The weight of the mass of grapes is sufficient to squeeze the fermented juice out of the grapes, which is then allowed to run into a cask as free-run wine.

10. The rest of the bulk goes into a press and is crushed to produce a highly tannic, dark wine. This "press wine" may be added to the free-run wine to add structure to the blend. The wine from both vat and press is transferred to tanks or barrels where the malolactic fermentation (see p. 19) will occur.

11. Red wine generally needs more time to mature than white. The tannin mellows in time, while the other components of the wine have time to blend together harmoniously. Wood barrels are often used for the maturation of red wines, and the oak contributes not only additional flavour and complexity but also greater staying power to the wine.

12. In the case of Bordeaux and other blended wines, the "assemblage" will probably take place within a few months of the harvest. It is at this stage that particularly good or disappointing vats or barrels can be set aside for sale separately.

13. "Fine" wine almost always spends at least a year in barrels, large or small, new or old. During this time it must be "racked" (passed from one container to another, leaving the solids behind) to avoid growing stale and almost certainly "fined" with egg-white, which drags suspended yeasts and other solids in the wine downwards. Many quality-conscious producers now choose not to filter their wines to avoid removing flavour, but most commercial reds will pass through a filter before bottling.

14. Finally, time spent in bottle is important, but not every wine needs it. A complex (and expensive) bottle of red will almost certainly benefit from bottle ageing, as will whites with both body and high enough acidity. Simple wines, intended for prompt drinking, will lose colour, freshness and just about everything that makes wine enjoyable, if left for too long.

How Rosé Is Made

The classic way of making pink wines is to follow the red wine process until about 24 hours into stage 2, opposite. The wine is thus in contact with the black skins for just long enough to become delicately coloured. It is then racked off to complete fermentation on its own. Alternatively, the grapes may be allowed to macerate on the skins for a few hours before they are pressed and vinified like a white wine. The simple addition of red wine to white is illegal for quality still wines in Europe – but permitted for rosé Champagne, and customary for "white" or "blush" Zinfandel which is, in fact, often a blend of red Zinfandel and white Muscat.

Sweet And Fortified Wines

Sweet wines are the most difficult to make and yet can be the best value of any wines in the world. Out of fashion for many years – and still frowned upon by health fascists who would prefer us to consume neither alcohol nor sweetness – good, rich, honeyed white wine is beginning to enjoy a comeback. Quality sweet wine depends on using grape varieties which naturally contain a lot of sugar, picking them late to get all the sweetness of really ripe fruit.

The sugar contained in any grape will, given half a chance and a bit of yeast, ferment into alcohol. The sweeter the grape, the stronger the wine – in theory. In practice, once the strength rises to 15–16 per cent, the alcohol itself will kill off the yeast, leaving you with rather sweet, very alcoholic wine.

So, the key is to stop the fermentation before it gets to this stage. This can be achieved in one of two tricky ways. One method inevitably involves the use of the wine-maker's friend and, occasionally, wine-drinker's enemy – sulphur. Sulphur is needed for almost all white wines, but the sweeter examples need larger doses which, unless they are handled very carefully, give the wines an irritating throat-tickling character. Sadly, while wine-making skills have improved elsewhere, producers of sweet wines are often set in their sulphurous ways. Which is why cheap Sauternes and German late-harvest wines are often so poor – and why Austrian, New Zealand, South African, Australian and US wines, though rarely as complex as the best classic examples, are rapidly gaining in popularity.

Wherever a sweet wine is made, ideally it should be produced from grapes affected by "noble rot" – a fungus correctly known as *botrytis cinerea*. Mysteriously, and despite its name, the fungus doesn't actually rot the grapes as much as dehydrate them, breaking through their skins, allowing the water content to evaporate and thus concentrating the richness of the sugar which remains.

In California, where wine-makers have already learnt to master the yeasts which make wine ferment, the aim now is to create great sweet wine every year by *spraying* rot onto the grapes. Scientists are eagerly devising methods of duplicating exactly the effect of the mould as it creeps over the vines of Bordeaux, the Loire and the Rhine.

Purists believe that such pre-empting of nature is cheating, but there are plenty of producers in Sauternes who, in the all-too-frequent years when the *botrytis* fails to form, must feel very tempted to pre-empt nature too.

Grape juice flows into a tank ready for the next step in the process

FRANCE

Try listing the world's 10 best-known wine regions – without including Champagne, Bordeaux, Burgundy, Châteauneuf-du-Pape, Muscadet, Beaujolais, Sancerre, Sauternes, Chablis and Côtes du Rhône. Rioja, Chianti and the Mosel would obviously be fighting pretty hard to get on that list too, along with Barolo, California's Napa Valley, Australia's Coonawarra and Portugal's Douro – but so would Pouilly-Fumé, Hermitage and Alsace. In other words, France is rather like one of the Hollywood studios of the 1940s that somehow managed to sign up Garbo, Gable and Grable, cornering the market in the stars most people wanted to see.

Despite the explosion of exciting wines from the New World, the renaissance of run-down wine regions of Europe and an unprecedented international readiness to question France's pre-eminence in the wine world, this is still the one country that no-one interested in wine can possibly ignore.

And, as if France's innately chauvinist wine-makers needed it, their confidence has also been increasingly boosted by the sincerest of all forms of flattery. What kinds of grape do the wine-makers in California, Australia and Chile – and even such long-established wine-making countries as Spain, Italy and Greece – want to plant? The Chardonnay and Cabernet Sauvignon, the Pinot Noir, the Syrah and the Merlot: varieties historically most closely associated with France. And what styles of wine do they want to make? Those of Champagne, Bordeaux and Burgundy, the Loire and the Rhône.

But what separates French wine-makers today from many of the producers in the countries that have adopted their grapes is the way in which they have tended to plant them. In California and Australia, the Cabernet Sauvignon, Riesling and Chardonnay are often grown almost cheek-by-jowl in the same vineyards. In France, there have been centuries of natural selection to sort out what grows best where – and, for the last 50 years or so, strict legislation to ensure that no-one tries to experiment with Bordeaux grape varieties in Burgundy or *vice versa*.

Until the 1980s, when a few pioneers began to try their luck in what was once the wine morass of southern France, the Pinot Noir was only cultivated in a handful of regions, all of them in the northern, cooler half of the country; the Merlot was more or less restricted to Bordeaux; the Sauvignon Blanc rarely strayed beyond the Loire and Bordeaux and the Viognier was exclusively at home in a tiny region in the northern Rhône. Even now, the Riesling and the Gewürztraminer are grown almost nowhere outside Alsace.

Climate, Soils and Traditions

The variation in climate between France's wine regions is enormous. The climates of regions such as Muscadet and Bordeaux, for example, benefit from the moderating effect of the Atlantic Ocean; those further east, such as Burgundy, Alsace and the northern Rhône, are subject to the more continental heat-chill conditions associated with areas surrounded by a mass of land.

Soil types vary, too, from the sands of the Mediterranean in which the *vin de sable* vines are grown, to the "pudding stone" pebbles of Châteauneuf-du-Pape, the gravel of the Graves in Bordeaux and the chalk of Champagne. The vineyards in some regions – the Médoc, for example – appear at first glance to be boringly flat while those of Alsace and the northern Rhône are perched on improbably steep slopes.

Finally, there are the diverse styles of wine-making that have evolved region by region, over the centuries. Some areas make white wines with varying shades of sweetness; others restrict themselves to dry wine. Some produce little but sparkling or rosé; others concentrate exclusively on red. Some use new oak barrels; others would never dream of doing so.

History

If the French cannot claim to have invented wine, they can, through a combination of luck and judgement, boast of having been, with a little help from the Romans and subsequent settlers, the first to isolate some of the best sites and grape varieties.

It was the Dutch who helped to provide the Médoc with the drainage ditches that converted what was often a bog into land fit for vines; it was a German who first experimented with making Sauternes in the style we know today, and it was Scots, English and Irish merchants and estate-owners who, with châteaux like Lynch-Bages, Smith Haut-Lafitte and Cantenac-Brown, were instrumental in creating the prestige of Bordeaux.

The success of particular regions, however, often had as much to do with ease of access as the quality of their wines. Regions like Cahors saw their wines sold as Bordeaux – because that was the port from which they were shipped overseas. Likewise, wine made in Pommard bought at the market in Beaune might well have been sold as "Vin de Beaune". Areas close to Paris such as Chablis and Sancerre were far more heavily cultivated than they are today and, until a canal was opened linking Burgundy to the capital, there were sizeable areas of well-regarded vines in and around the city itself.

The first major change in the development of the French industry came with the French Revolution, which redistributed large tracts of land that were previously in the hands of the church, and introduced inheritance laws that divided property equally among a deceased owner's heirs. While well-established domaines in Bordeaux survived these changes, there and elsewhere, estates were split into tiny entities, most of which would rely on bigger merchants or, ultimately, co-operatives to handle their grapes or wine. Today, while California has a few hundred wineries, Bordeaux can boast some 20,000 individual producers, of whom just 4,000 ever get to see the name of their estate on the labels.

The second dramatic change came at the end of the nineteenth century with the arrival of the *phylloxera* louse which chomped its way through the roots of vineyards throughout Europe. After strenuous and fruitless efforts to combat the pest, the French finally acknowledged that the only solution was to graft traditional vines – or some of them at least – onto *phylloxera*-resistant rootstock imported from North America.

The *phylloxera* crisis provided France with the opportunity to tidy up its wine industry, reducing the size of Chablis' vineyards, for example, from 40,000 acres to 2,000, and the number of grape varieties grown in Bordeaux from 60 to fewer than a dozen.

Taking Contrôlée

Life for the newly replanted vineyards was not easy, however. In the financially strapped years between the two World Wars, wine was often hard to sell, and quality-conscious producers with vines in regions like Châteauneuf-du-Pape and Nuits-St-Georges increasingly found themselves competing against counterfeit versions of their wines.

The defence mechanism those disgruntled producers helped to invent was a quality hierarchy – the *Appellation Contrôlée* system – that has become the envy of wine-makers in other countries and, increasingly, the subject of heated debate. Almost from the outset, the system – usually referred to as AC or AOC – was based on the early discovery that certain pieces of land always seem to produce better wine, that particular climates and types of soil suit some grapes better than others and – this is the contentious part – that, given half a chance, wine-makers will cut corners and cheat.

There have been laws covering what could be planted and where for well over a millennium. The Emperor Charlemagne issued precise edicts in the ninth century; the English king Edward I defined the boundaries of St Emilion in 1289; and 100 years later, Philip the Bold, Duke of Burgundy, issued an ordinance banning the planting, in the region we now know as the Côte d'Or, of the heavy-cropping, easy-to-grow Gamay.

In the 1930s, a Gamay-packed Beaune or Nuits-St-Georges might have been distinctly preferable to some of the wines masquerading under the names of these and other classic regions. As one visitor to Sète in southern France noted at the time, unscrupulous companies shamelessly filled smartly labelled bottles with blends of all manner of liquids and solids, many of them wholly unrelated to grapes, and some most likely poisonous.

This was the background against which France's *Appellation* system was born. To understand how it evolved, and the role it now holds today, however, you have to know something about the Gallic character. The French may have a healthy Latin disrespect for law, but there is an ingrained reverence for qualifications and official rank.

Remember this when you are confronted by the confusing mass of qualifications to be found on French labels – *Appellation Contrôlée*, *VDQS*, *Vin de Pays*, *Grand* and *Premier Cru*, *Premier Grand Cru* and so on... To the French, these are all a cross between battle-medals, aristocratic pedigrees and professional qualifications. As such, they are not to be taken lightly.

At the foot of the quality pyramid, without even the faintest trace of blue blood, there are the *vins de table* – basic red and white wine made any old where from any old kinds of grapes and, usually, any old how. Traditionally, this was the stuff you got if you ordered *"un coup de rouge"* in a bar, that the sinew-stiffener old drunks would buy in supermarkets by the alcoholic degree, and the major part of the nearly two-thirds of a bottle of wine consumed daily by the average Frenchman during the years following World War Two.

Today, *vins de table* represent a steadily shrinking part of France's wine industry – even the internationally popular Piat d'Or has climbed out of this category – and regulations that bar producers from printing a vintage or a grape variety on the label of a *vin de table* hardly encourage producers to choose it.

These legislative handicaps, however, prevent French producers from competing on level terms against New-World companies such as Penfold's in Australia and Fetzer in California who unashamedly – and tastily – use blends of grapes grown in different regions to make highly successful wines whose labels include both vintage and grape. In France, when the Bordeaux firm of Dulong produced just such an innovative red blend called "Rebelle", its *vin de table* status ensured that no Gallic critic was even prepared to taste it.

Next come the 139 *vins de pays*, the country yeomanry which are supposedly representative of the region in which they are made and the varieties of grapes grown there. For the decade or so after the designation was created at the end of the 1960s, these wines were often produced by the same co-operatives as the *vins de table* and to the same low standards. Under the leadership of a few go-ahead co-ops, companies and estates, however, they underwent a quality revolution which leapfrogged a growing number into the international marketplace. These (to French tradition-alists) non-aristocratic, under-qualified wines are still little appreciated in France itself. Thanks, however, to the relatively relaxed rules covering the grape varieties which may be used for them, *vins de pays* have proved particularly popular with innovative producers seeking to compete on level terms with "varietal" wines from the New World. Ironically, in countries like the USA and Britain, *vin de pays* Chardonnay and Cabernet Sauvignon is often easier to sell, and at a higher price, than white Burgundy and red Bordeaux made from the same grapes.

Above the *vins de pays*, like the ornament nobody can quite find a way to get rid of, there are the VDQSs – *Vins Délimités de Qualité Supérieure*. Originally intended as a waiting-room between *vin de pays* and the heady peaks of *Appellation Contrôlée*, this has become a tiny anachronism, a limbo-land representing just 1.5 per cent of France's wines. No new VDQS has been created for a while. Some are indeed occasionally promoted, although others are more frequently bypassed by *vins de pays* like Limoux, which skip the waiting-room entirely to become instant *Appellations Contrôlées*.

This of course is the promotion to which the *vins de pays* and VDQSs are supposed to aspire. *Appellation Contrôlée* wines, like those in both "inferior" categories, come from tightly specified regions, some as small as a single vineyard, others as big as Bordeaux, of which, in a single vintage, nearly one thousand million bottles may be produced.

AC wines also have to comply with strict rules covering the grapes from which they can be made, yields per acre and methods of wine-making. They are also, theoretically, subject to tasting and analysis. All of which, when taken with the promotional campaigns for

AC regions and wines, could reasonably lead one to suppose that the words "*Appellation Contrôlée*" might provide some guarantee of quality.

Sadly, as even the more honest apologists for the system would concede, the only thing an *Appellation* is likely to guarantee – at best – is typicality. The supposedly rigorous tasting is frequently performed by friends and neighbours of the producer and takes place while the wine is still in barrel or tank. Perhaps unsurprisingly, only two per cent or so of the wines are rejected. Experienced wine enthusiasts know that anyone who orders a bottle of wine from even such well-known *Appellations* as Nuits-St-Georges, St Emilion, Sancerre or Champagne, without knowing the name of the producer, is flying as blind as if he asked for "Californian Chardonnay" or "Australian Cabernet".

Added to which, the authorities in France subject French producers to handicaps rarely suffered by their competitors. New-World wine-makers may blend in limited quantities of grapes from other regions; neighbouring countries such as Spain and Italy allow the addition of small amounts of wine from other harvests. In France these procedures – potentially invaluable in tricky vintages – are outlawed. As is irrigation, even when vines are dying of thirst.

First Among Equals

If France's *Appellations* form the tip of the quality pyramid, they are themselves often stratified with further sets of arcane mini-hierarchies. Within the regional *Appellation* of Burgundy – Bourgogne – for example, you should get better wine within the village *Appellation* of Gevrey-Chambertin, within whose boundaries you will find even finer stuff in one of the *Premier Cru* vineyards such as "les Cazetiers". "Premier" does not, however, as one might expect mean "first". For that, one has to look to a *Grand Cru* vineyard such as "le Chambertin" itself, whose wine really should be sublime.

But wander into the cellar of a less careful producer or of a less scrupulous merchant, and you could well taste a *Grand Cru* that's a lot less impressive than a good example of plain Bourgogne Rouge. The fault does not lie in the *Appellation* – time has proved that the *Grand Cru* vineyard is capable of yielding top class

– but in the way in which its grapes have been handled.

Once you have learned about those Burgundian Premiers and Grands Crus – and taken on board the fact that villages as well known as Meursault and Beaune don't actually have any Grands Crus – you can then turn to the even more confusing world of Bordeaux, most of whose regions have hierarchies of their own. So, St Emilion has its regularly revised Premier Grand Cru Classé and Grand Cru Classé wines; the Médoc its 140-year-old table of Premier, Deuxième, Troisième, Quatrième and Cinquième Crus and Sauternes its Grand Premier, Premier and Deuxième Crus, while Pomerol, home of Château Pétrus, priciest Bordeaux of them all, exists quite nicely without any classification at all.

After such a brutal exposé of its failings, it may come as a surprise to hear that *Appellation* of some kind makes sense – the same kind of sense as the preservation orders even some of the youngest countries in the world slap on to their more interesting buildings.

Unrestrained market forces would have the same effect on wines as on nineteenth- and early twentieth-century buildings. Little-known, uncommercial Appellations like Jurançon would most probably disappear, along with Pacherenc de Vic Bilh and Crépy, as the marketeers replaced the quirky grapes from which they are made with easier-to-sell Chardonnay, Cabernet and Merlot.

But stopping people from pulling down buildings and killing off traditional wine styles is the easy part. The real challenge lies in overseeing the way those bits of heritage are maintained. Allow them to fall into disrepair and disrepute and you simply make life easier for the developer and the marketeer.

In general, when considering Appellations in France or elsewhere, there are two essential rules. First, that Appellations are not all equal. Smaller ones like Meursault, Bergerac and Carneros in California generally make much more sense than larger, more diverse, ones such as Mâcon, Bordeaux and Napa. Second, that any Appellation refers to the potential quality of the piece of land, and not necessarily to the actual quality of the bottle in your hand. Remember these, and an Appellation system can serve as a useful guide from one style and quality level to another.

BORDEAUX

57 Varieties

Two glasses. The one on the left contains a paleish red liquid that tastes of unripe berries, green pepper – and water. The wine on the right is quite different: dark, almost black, with a rich, deep smell of plum, mulberry, pencil shavings and spice. The flavour goes even further, creamily blending all of these flavours with ripe blackcurrant and maybe a touch of violet. There's power here, but there's subtlety too, in a combination never quite attained in even the best efforts of the New World.

Two clarets: a pair of examples from some 750,000,000 bottles of wine produced per year from the nearly 250,000 acres (100,000 ha) of vineyards which comprise the 57 different *Appellations* of Bordeaux. The one on the right is a St Emilion from Château Pavie, packed with the ripeness of the 1985 vintage; as for the watery stuff, that was a basic Bordeaux Rouge from the rainy harvest of 1993. Unfortunately, there's a lot more of the latter than the former; bobbing along in the wake of the 100 or so big-name flagship châteaux, whose wines regularly feature in restaurant wine lists and auctioneers' catalogues, there are 4,000 or so lesser-known estates, not to mention the reds and whites made every year by some 15,000 producers whose names are never even seen on a label.

In warm vintages, most of these little wines are generally more or less acceptable, if often not as well made as they might be. In cooler wetter years, however, their failings – and the fundamental differences in quality between the soil and climate in which they are made, and that of the better-sited châteaux – become all too apparent. So, if there is one fundamental lesson to learn about Bordeaux it is: don't treat it as one region, but as several thousand variations on 57 themes.

The History

Serious wine-making began in Bordeaux with the Romans, whose contribution can be seen in archaeological remains – and on the labels of wines such as Château Ausone, named after the poet Ausonius who was born in St Emilion. Precisely what happened to the wines made in Bordeaux during the period between the days of the Roman occupation and the early twelfth century is unclear, but there are stories of eighth- and ninth-century exports to Ireland and the west of England.

Everything changed, however, when Henry II of England married Eleanor of Aquitaine, and Bordeaux became for 300 years what it sometimes still seems to be – a part of the British Isles. Richard *Coeur de Lion* regularly drank wine from Bordeaux and, under King John, the region's merchants were encouraged to send their barrels to England by an exemption from export tax. During the thirteenth and fourteenth centuries, thousands of casks of "Gascon wine" regularly crossed the Channel – six bottles per year for every English man, woman and child.

Most of the wine those early English Bordeaux drinkers would have enjoyed drinking at court, in inns and in their homes was of the style the French called *clairet,* a pale red made by leaving the skins in contact with the fermenting juice for only a day or so. It was from this name that the English took the term they still use for all red Bordeaux – "Claret".

In fact, though, much of that "Bordeaux" was actually produced nowhere near the city whose name it bore. At that time, Bordeaux was an internationally famous sea-port; its name was far more saleable than, say, that of a wine such as Cahors which was produced a long cart-ride inland.

Ironically, while Bordeaux seems itself to have been predestined to produce a number of great wines, the region owes much to the seventeenth-century Dutch engineers who laid down a system of invaluable drainage ditches in the Médoc without which much of the land would still regularly become a bog. If the Bordelais often ungratefully overlook the part played by the Dutch, they rarely make much of the contribution of the English and Irish château-owners and merchants who helped to bring Bordeaux its international renown. Today, the names of such Bordeaux châteaux as Cantenac-Brown, Smith Haut-Lafitte, Léoville-Barton and Lynch-Bages give them the lie.

The Pont du Pierre across the Garonne river in Bordeaux, a symbol of the wine-based wealth of his historic city

Surprisingly, for those who liken the French Revolution to its Russian counterpart, the grand estates of Bordeaux survived the removal of the monarchy surprisingly well: the Gallic revolutionaries harboured a far greater dislike of the church than of the similarly anti-clerical aristocracy. So, while the vineyards of Burgundy were redistributed among thousands of peasant-farmers, the great châteaux of Bordeaux continued to build their international reputation. During the nineteenth century, the market for their wines was sufficiently well established for the brokers and merchants of the city of Bordeaux periodically to draw up league tables to mark which wines regularly fetched the highest prices. For some reason, one such league table, drawn up for the Grand Exhibition of 1855, like that other supposedly temporary structure the Eiffel Tower, unexpectedly survived to become something of a national monument.

The arrival of *phylloxera* decimated the vineyards here, as elsewhere, but it also gave the owners the opportunity to plan which of the 60 or so uprooted red and white grape varieties were worth replanting. Henceforth, red Bordeaux would have the now recognizable flavours of Cabernet and Merlot, and the white would be made principally from Sémillon and Sauvignon.

Wine-making was, however, still quite unsophisticated. As recently as the 1960s, for example, there were many producers who completely misunderstood the natural process of malolactic fermentation; they would talk straightfacedly of the wine in the barrel reacting in sympathy with the sap rising in the vines. The man who helped to drag the region into the twentieth century was Professor Emile Peynaud of Bordeaux University.

In the late 1970s and early 1980s, money was invested in cleaning up the *cuveries* which, even in some of the more famous châteaux, often looked as though they had last been modernized at some time during the nineteenth century. Cooling equipment was brought in for the fermentation vats in order to avoid the problems of overheating in hot years and, where relevant, to allow the production of crisp, dry white wines. Throughout the region, dirty old casks were replaced, either by cleanable tanks or, in the best properties, by a greater number of 225-litre barrels, a proportion of which would be replaced every year, giving the wine a touch of the spicy vanilla which had helped to win friends for those New-World reds.

Despite the influence of Peynaud and his successors at the University of Bordeaux, and the more recent introduction of such high-tech devices as must-concentrators which freeze and remove the watery component of wines produced in rainy years – the methods used to make the more basic wines have often remained ... well, fairly basic.

Responsibility for the lack of progress can be blamed largely on the *négociants* – the merchants, who have been happy to buy in ready-made wines from producers and co-operatives – and on their customers, especially in France, who have been remarkably tolerant of the frequent shortcomings of Bordeaux. It is revealing that the producers of Mouton Cadet continued to buy in the white wine sold under their label until the early 1990s – which helps to explain the traditionally uninspiring quality of that commercially successful brand.

Bordeaux Today

There have been three recent key vintages in Bordeaux. The great 1945 – coming directly after the end of the war and 11 years after the last fine pre-hostility harvest – marked a triumphant return to normality. The 1961 vintage, for its part, changed the way top-class Bordeaux was bought. Traditionally the merchants of the region had routinely fixed a price per barrel "*sur souche*" – while the grapes were still on the vine. The method worked well enough until the agreements reached before the great, but woefully short crop of 1961 obliged them to sell the small quantities they had

made at far less than their value. Thereafter, they began instead to offer their wine "*en primeur*", in the spring following the vintage, by which time it was possible to assess its quality and quantity.

The next most significant moment came in 1982, which brought a happy coincidence of fine weather, the fruits of all that modernization in the wineries, and the arrival on the scene of a new generation of well-off wine-drinkers. Looking back at what is now acknowledged to be one of Bordeaux's great years, it is chastening to recall that when the 1982s were first tasted, traditionalists often found them too ripe, too approachable, too "New-World" in style. One man, however, disagreed. Robert Parker, a young American lawyer, waxed – highly – lyrical about their voluptuous flavour in his *Wine Advocate* newsletter. Parker's timing was impeccable. His recommendations were devoured by Americans with dollars to spend and a (readily admitted) lack of vinous experience.

Unlike their European counterparts, who still tended to rely for bespoke guidance on wine merchants and auctioneers, these novices wanted to be told precisely what they should and should not buy. This need was filled by Parker and subsequently by a glossy New York-based magazine called the *Wine Spectator*. Both employed a curious marking system adapted by the former lawyer from one used by US law schools. Erroneously known as the 100-point scale, it actually begins at 50 – the mark which would be given to a blend of pond water and sulphuric acid. Suddenly, a desirable new phenomenon was born, the "90+ point" wine.

The interest of the new wave of collectors and investors, not to mention the readiness of France's supermarket chains to sell off surplus stocks of even the grandest châteaux wines in their annual "*Foires aux Vins*", and a punitive system of death duties, were all instrumental in laying the ground for a change in the ownership of Bordeaux. To the horror of traditionalists, cash-strapped families sold out to insurance companies and industrial giants with a taste for diversification, including, *mon Dieu!*, Japanese whisky distillers.

Local traditionalists understandably and predictably bemoaned the disappearance of the families – conveniently forgetting that many of these had had little physically to do with their châteaux. When a subsidiary of the giant AXA insurance company took over Château Pichon-Longueville in the late 1980s, parts of the building were in the state in which they'd been abandoned by the German soldiers billeted there during a war which had ended nearly half a century earlier. The newcomers were under no illusion that a wine estate had to be run in as businesslike a way as any of their other investments. Almost without exception their wines tasted better than the ones made during the previous few vintages by their predecessors. And they were certainly to the taste of the increasingly influential US gurus.

Bordeaux is unquestionably making more fine red and white wine than ever before; despite a series of difficult harvests in the early 1990s, the top wines have reasserted their position securely atop the wine world. The lesser wines have improved too; unfortunately for their producers and fortunately for wine-drinkers, so – often far more dramatically – have their competitors and imitators from other regions.

What Gives Bordeaux Its Flavour?

Most New-World wine-makers would give the greatest credit to the grape varieties that are grown here. For the red wines, these consist of the blackcurranty, sun-loving Cabernet Sauvignon; its easier-to-please, lighter-bodied "kid brother" the Cabernet Franc; the plummier Merlot, which ripens a little earlier and is an invaluable softening ingredient in any Bordeaux blend; and the Petit Verdot, which only ripens in the best vintages but imparts a wonderfully spicy note, even when it makes up only two or three per cent of the wine. Also allowed are the now-unfashionable Malbec and the almost-impossible-to-fi nd Carmenère.

For the whites, the two key grapes are the rich, honeyed Sémillon, which can make great dry and sweet wines; and the tangier, more gooseberryish Sauvignon Blanc – better known as the variety used to make Sancerre in the Loire. The white counterpart to the Petit Verdot is the similarly spicy Muscadelle which, like that variety, is only ever used as a small component of a blend. The two also-rans here are the Colombard and, for some reason, the dull Ugni Blanc.

It is blending which sets Bordeaux apart from purely "varietal" wines produced elsewhere. There is, very rarely, no such thing as a 100 per cent Bordeaux Cabernet Sauvignon or 100 per cent Bordeaux Merlot; every top-quality claret you are ever likely to drink will be a blend of at least a couple of grape varieties. This tradition may have developed to enable the Bordelais to back two horses at once, so that in years when the Merlot fails to ripen (like 1986, say) or when rain hits the later-harvested Cabernet (as in 1994), they could still make good wine.

The Bordelais, however, would stress that it is not so much the grapes *per se* as the soil in which they grow – the well-drained gravel which covers clay or sand in the Médoc and Graves; the limestone and chalk of Sauternes and Barsac; and the clay and limestone in St Emilion and Pomerol – plus the way in which it nurtures the grape varieties that makes Bordeaux special. In fact, while the different soils clearly dictate the choice of which kind of grape to plant where, strenuous efforts to link quality to specific soil types have yet to bear fruit.

The Vintage

Even within these regional *Appellations*, wine-making styles – and skills – vary. When buying Bordeaux, you need to look for the commune – or region, in the case, for instance, of the Médoc, Haut-Médoc and Graves – and the château (and possibly château-owner – the owner of one good estate may also have others). And, of course, the vintage. Because of the size of the region and the range of soils and grapes, some vintages are more successful for some *Appellations* than they are for others. In 1964, for example, the pickers of St Emilion and Pomerol had already harvested their grapes when many of their neighbours in the Médoc (where the Cabernet Sauvignon ripens rather later) saw their crop washed out by torrential storms.

The reputation of Bordeaux vintages is often greatly affected by their investment – in other words, long-term – potential. Wines made by the best estates in years such as 1987, 1992 and 1993, which were generally light-bodied and for early drinking, are often underestimated by the experts. When fairly priced, these can be well worth buying, particularly by those waiting for wines from "better" vintages to reach their peak – or by those who would like a taste of great Bordeaux style at a more affordable price.

THE MEDOC

"That man," my friend whispered conspiratorially across the restaurant table, "is worth over a billion dollars". Looking across at this colossus among millionaires, I felt strangely let down; he looked resolutely unexceptional – just like the newsagent from whom I bought my paper every day. The only evidence of tycoonal prestige lay in the evident quality of the briefcase propped against his chair-leg and a discreet but decidedly stylish watch.

My first visit to the Médoc left me with pretty much the same feeling of disappointment – and for pretty much the same reasons. The flat, featureless landscape – the variation in altitude is no more than about 80 ft/25 metres – was like the unmemorable profile of the millionaire. And like the watch and briefcase, the occasional château did not somehow seem enough.

But there's no questioning the wealth and the potential of this region which easily outranks its neighbours, the Graves, St Emilion and Pomerol. This is the area that can boast Châteaux Lafite, Latour, Mouton Rothschild and Margaux, and in their wake a small fleet of other illustrious estates. When people think of Bordeaux this is the part most of them, consciously or unconsciously, have in mind.

So how do all those great wines come to be produced in a place that looks like a billiard table? Why don't they need the slopes of Burgundy and the Rhône? For the answer you have to look not at the lie of the land but at the land itself. As any Bordelais will tell you, the secret of the Médoc's success – and the particular level of success enjoyed by any specific château – has always come from the character of the soil in which its grapes are grown. While the Californian is often striving to express the flavour of the grape, the Bordeaux grower's aim is to convey the character of the *terroir* – the vineyard.

For around 1,300 years, while the Burgundians were busily cultivating vines and making wine in the Côte d'Or, most of the Médoc was no more than wild and lonely marshland. Even such now-illustrious estates as Margaux and Lafite were largely devoted to growing wheat. There wasn't even very much in the way of roads between the villages, and landowners travelled to their châteaux from Bordeaux by boat along the Garonne.

The grand classical facade of Château Margaux, source of one of the silkiest of all Médocs

But, at the end of the sixteenth century, the wine-growing potential of the Médoc was finally realized by the ingenuity of a team of Dutchmen, who drained the marshes and then introduced the novel idea of planting vines in rows instead of in the higgledy-piggledy way the Bordelais had been doing.

The following two centuries were Bordeaux's – and the Médoc's – heyday as virtually the world's only source of great wine, and much of this success was directly attributable to the Irish, English and Scots families – the Johnstons, Lynches, Bartons, Smiths and the rest – who settled here and produced and sold wine to the rest of Europe.

The key date for the Médoc, however, was 1855, the year of the Great Exhibition in Paris, and the year which saw the publication of an official classification which divided the red wines of the Médoc into first, second, third, fourth and fifth growths – the *Crus Classés*. The red and white wines of the Graves and the white wines of Sauternes and Barsac also received their own classifications with just two levels – *Premier* and *Deuxième Cru*.

It is often supposed that these league tables were specially produced for the exhibition; in fact, they were merely official versions of lists the brokers of Bordeaux had long been using among themselves to establish the prices for which wine might be sold to local customers and to such distinguished foreigners as Thomas Jefferson.

Even in the previous century Médoc first-growths such as Latour and Lafite had been worth twice as much as second-growths, three times as much as the thirds and so on. Over the years, various wine writers have acknowledged the fact that the 1855 classification was merely the last and most widely publicized in a series of such lists, by drawing up hierarchies of their own. In France, where restaurants that omit the producers' names from their list of Burgundies rarely fail to suffix a Bordeaux château with its 1855 classification, this lack of reverence is considered distinctly *infra dig*. Indeed when an American oil millionaire decided to hold a blind tasting in 1995 to reassess the *Crus Classés*, French commentators reacted as though he had pointed a howitzer at the palace of Versailles.

I suspect the people who would have the longest laugh at all this would be those 1855 brokers. After all, if they'd known their efforts were going to be taken quite this seriously close on a century and a half later, they might have laid down some rather tighter ground-rules. Back then, for instance, they took no account of the specific size and location of each château's vineyards. In other words, Château Margaux could sell off almost all of its best land and replace it with less good vineyards in the same commune, and still sell its wine with its First-Growth label. Château Margaux might not do that, but a former owner of Château Lascombes, for example, added substantial acreage of less-than-top-quality land without anyone suggesting that he might be jeopardizing the estate's second-growth status. (Revealingly, the current wine-maker, René Vanatelle, tastes all of the vats blind every year to decide which will go into the "*grand*," and which into the "*second*" *vin* – and almost invariably finds that the rejects contain the fruit of those additional vineyards.)

The Communes of the Médoc

Driving north from Bordeaux, you have barely left the outskirts of the city before you find yourself in the gravelly soil of the Haut-Médoc. This *Appellation* – literally "High Médoc" – confusingly comprises the lower part of the overall region and includes the six higher-quality communal *Appellations* of Margaux, St-Julien, Pauillac, St-Estèphe, Moulis and Listrac, while the Médoc *Appellation* itself includes the lesser-quality area mostly further north.

Haut-Médoc wines from land that falls outside those six communes can offer some of the best value in Bordeaux. Only five are classed – the delicious La Lagune and Cantemerle, de Camensac, La Tour-Carnet and Belgrave – but several unclassed châteaux, like Caronne-Ste-Gemme, Beaumont and Lanessan, are easily better than some fifth- and even fourth-growth wines.

The key words to look for on Haut-Médoc labels are, in descending order of quality, *Cru Grand Bourgeois Exceptionnel*, *Cru Grand Bourgeois* or *Cru Bourgeois*, all of which ought to indicate that the wine is a cut above the average. But a word of warning: there are two lists of *Crus Bourgeois* – one a 1932 classification, and the other a 1978 membership list of

Margaux

The first "classy" *Appellation* you reach after leaving Bordeaux is Margaux. The only one that shares its name with its best château, this, as countless hopelessly lost visitors have discovered to their exasperation, is actually more of a collection of villages than a single commune; wines from Arsac, Cantenac, Labarde, Soussans and Margaux itself can all call themselves Margaux. This occasionally raises a wry smile in the cafés of Labarde, Arsac and Cantenac – these quiet villages to the south of Margaux boast some of the juicier wines of the *Appellation*. Châteaux here such as Giscours, Siran, d'Angludet, du Tertre, d'Issan, Prieuré-Lichine, Kirwan and Brane-Cantenac can, and do, legitimately describe themselves as Margaux.

But it would be dangerous to overstate that juiciness; Margaux has a reputation for making the most delicate and perfumed wines of the Médoc, with a scent of violets and flavour of blackberries, rather than the more usual Bordeaux blackcurrant. The vines have to work hard for their nourishment, fighting their way through the gravelly soil, but, as the locals say, the plants never get their feet as wet here as they do in the clay soil of more northerly St-Estèphe.

Margaux is (relatively) big – the largest communal *Appellation* in the Médoc, and the most blessed with classed growths and top-quality *Crus Bourgeois*. Sadly, though, as some of its more forthright producers would admit, the quality of Margaux's land is often let down by some pretty poor wine-making. Apart from the glorious Château Margaux itself, and Château Palmer, its closest rival, the best classed wines are d'Issan, Lascombes, Rauzan-Segla, Malescot-St-Exupéry (the last two most particularly in recent vintages) and du Tertre. Prieuré-Lichine, which belonged to the great Russian-American wine-writer Alexis Lichine, is fairly priced, and good value can also be found in Château Notton and Pavillon Rouge du Château Margaux (the second wines respectively of Châteaux Brane-Cantenac and Margaux).

Among non-classed wines, seek out Château d'Angludet (made by Peter Sichel, who is also responsible for Château Palmer), La Gurgue, Labégorce-Zédé, Monbrison and Siran, all of which make wine of at least fourth-growth quality at far lower prices.

The barrel cellar at Château Lafite, one of the top wines in Pamillar.

the *Syndicat des Crus Bourgeois*. According to the Syndicat, there are just 127 wines that can describe themselves as any kind of *Cru Bourgeois*; a significant number of the better wines from the 1932 list, such as Labégorce-Zédé and Siran in Margaux, were excluded. In addition, some châteaux which could call themselves *Cru Bourgeois* prefer not to be included among the "middle class", perhaps fearing that to do so might jeopardize their chances of ever being considered for inclusion in a revised classification of the classed growths.

As for basic Médoc, the advice is to beware – especially of anything but a really ripe vintage. Wines carrying this *Appellation* are rarely better than basic Bordeaux Supérieur and may even be worse. At least a producer of the latter could blend together wine from throughout the region.

Before leaving Margaux, we have to mention the exception that proves the rule. The Médoc is emphatically not white-wine territory – but then there's Pavillon Blanc du Château Margaux, an extraordinary oaky, honeyed, tangy Sauvignon Blanc which has to be the ultimate "basic" Bordeaux Blanc (there is no *Appellation* for white Margaux or Médoc).

Moulis and Listrac

From Margaux the obvious next stop, quite a drive north, is St-Julien. Worth a diversion on the way, though, by turning off to the west into the forest, are two communes rarely mentioned in the old wine books – for the simple reason that neither includes any classed growths. But the villages of Moulis and Listrac-Médoc well repay a visit, because they both, in their different ways, can produce some very worthwhile wines.

Moulis and the village with which it shares its small *Appellation*, Grand Poujeaux, lie on gravelly soil, are bang next door to Margaux and have everything it takes to make wine of classed quality. Château Chasse-Spleen and, to a slightly lesser extent, Château Maucaillou prove what can be done here every year and Poujeaux and Gressier-Grand-Poujeaux are both good too. All these wines "come round" rather more quickly than Margaux, but good examples can last at least 15 years.

If Moulis wines can be enjoyed young, Listracs demand greater patience; they're much tougher, and much more closely related to those of St-Estèphe, a little further to the north. The Merlot grows well in the heavy soil here, but isn't used as much as it ought to be. Despite heavy investment at Château Clarke, these and wines like those of Châteaux Fonréaud, Fourcas-Hosten and Fourcas-Dupré remain daunting in all but the ripest vintages.

St-Julien

You know that you've got to St-Julien when you round the bend in the road and see the smart gates, statuary and gardens of Château Beychevelle. Before continuing north, turn right just beyond the château and drive down to enjoy the peaceful view from the river bank.

THE MEDOC

What to look for Complex, rich, yet subtle wines with flavours of blackcurrant and cedar. The iron fist in the velvet glove.

Official quality AOCs are Bordeaux, Bordeaux Supérieur, Haut-Médoc, Médoc, Moulis, Listrac, St-Estèphe, Pauillac, St-Julien and Margaux. Superimposed on these are the Cru Bourgeois and Cru Classé hierarchies, the latter in a strictly ranked league. No VDQS or vins de pays wines are produced, though there is talk of creating a Vin de Pays d'Aquitaine.

Style All Appellations, bar the first, are for red wine – the tiny amount of white made qualifies only as Bordeaux Blanc. Reds are blackcurranty/cedary and more or less tannic depending on the region and in proportion to the amount of Cabernet Sauvignon used. Styles are very site-specific, varying with each communal Appellation and with the care given to wine-making.

Climate Basically maritime, though the position, between two masses of water (the Atlantic and the estuary of the Gironde), moderates extremes of temperatures, creating a unique micro-climate. The Gulf Stream gives mild winters, warm summers and long autumns. The area is also fortunate in being shielded from westerly winds by the pine forest seaboard strip that runs parallel to the Gironde.

Cultivation Vineyards are planted on flattish land with occasional low, rolling hills. Soils are variable but principally composed of gravel over limestone and clay.

Grape varieties Reds: Cabernet Sauvignon, Cabernet Franc, Merlot, Malbec, Petit Verdot. Whites: (rare) Sauvignon, Sémillon.

Production/maturation Style of wine-making is very influential, the best wines being the most complex and concentrated, and those which have received the most new oak ageing – though use of new oak is dependent on the wine having sufficient concentration to handle it. Old oak is being gradually replaced, and stainless steel is now commonly used for fermentation.

Longevity Bordeaux Supérieur, Médoc and Haut-Médoc: 1–6 years; Crus Bourgeois, Moulis and Listrac 4–10 years (though good wines in good years can last longer); Crus Classés anything up to 25 years and sometimes more.

Vintage guide 78, 79, 82, 83, 85, 86, 88, 89, 90, 95, 96, 98.

Top 19 For lots of different reasons, and in no particular order: Châteaux Margaux, Cos d'Estournel, Léoville-Lascases, Palmer, Léoville-Barton, Pichon-Longueville-Lalande, Pichon-Longueville, Angludet, Haut-Marbuzet, Labégorce-Zédé, Latour, Monbrison, Lynch-Bages, la Lagune, Mouton Rothschild, Chasse-Spleen, Grand-Puy-Lacoste, Pontet-Canet, Sociando-Mallet.

This is where it is said that passing boats obeyed the command to lower their sails ("Basse-les-Voiles") issued by the then owner of the château, the Duc d'Epéron, one of France's best-known admirals. Sadly, neither the story that this command gave the château its name, nor the one that the sailors occasionally dropped their trousers instead of the sails, is actually true.

Château Beychevelle is as good an introduction to the commune as you are likely to need. This is a place for grand, big châteaux though, surprisingly, no first-growth wines. But, if there are no firsts, there are certainly two famous "super-seconds" – second growths that make wine as good as the firsts – in the shape of Léoville-Lascases and Ducru-Beaucaillou; Léoville-Barton, a château the equal of that pair; the almost as impressive Gruaud-Larose; and a clutch of other richly wonderful wines in recent vintages, particularly Beychevelle, Léoville-Poyferré, Branaire-Ducru, Talbot and Lagrange.

This is Bordeaux the way the British have always liked it: blackcurranty, but cedary too, with the unmistakable sweet scent traditionally described as "cigar-box". Despite its smaller size, St-Julien is a more reliable source of good, fairly priced wine than Margaux – such as Langoa-Barton, Léoville-Barton's slightly lighter-weight stable-mate, Lalande-Borie, Terrey-Gros-Caillou, St-Pierre and Clos du Marquis, the second wine of Château Léoville-Lascases.

Pauillac

The town of Pauillac is disconcertingly like a sleepy seaside resort, with café terraces and fish merchants lining the bank of the Gironde. This looks far more like the kind of place that couples run away to for illicit weekends in French films than the town whose name appears on some of the world's greatest red wine.

It's not easy to know that you've arrived in Pauillac's vineyards; they run into those of St-Julien almost seamlessly, with only one of those Dutch drainage ditches to mark the join. Léoville-Lascases is right next door to Latour; indeed, according to some old maps, the latter estate really ought to be situated in St-Julien, but it was Pauillac that drew the better hand.

It is easy to understand why these wines have made so many friends for themselves; they are magnificent in the way that they manage to combine the intense flavour of blackcurrant with those of cedar and honey. Taste these against the best Cabernet Sauvignon from California and you will understand just how brilliantly this variety shines here – and how far the complex flavours of Pauillac can go beyond the simple Cabernet flavour of most of those New-World wonders.

Apart from Latour, Lafite and Mouton Rothschild, there is a second row of wines chasing hard on their heels: Pichon-Longueville-Lalande is Pauillac's best-established "super-second", now rivalled by its neighbour Pichon-Longueville, which has recently been restored to its former prestige by Jean-Michel Cazes. Cazes' own Château Lynch-Bages, though on paper only a fourth growth, can also perform as well as many a second (and turn out an impressive white), while fine wines can be found at Clerc-Milon, Grand-Puy-Ducasse, Grand-Puy-Lacoste, Haut-Bages-Libéral, Haut-Batailley, d'Armailhac (the former Mouton Baron-Philippe) and Pontet-Canet. For a relatively affordable taste of Pauillac, try Reserve de la Comtesse, Haut-Bages-Averous and Les Forts de Latour, the second wines respectively of Châteaux Pichon-Longueville-Lalande, Lynch-Bages and Latour.

St-Estèphe

St-Estèphe is the most attractive town in the Médoc, but it feels like a distant outpost. And the wine is like that too – distant and forbidding stuff that suggests expressions like "austere" and "masculine" that one would normally avoid like the plague. It is distinctly cooler here and this, coupled with the generally less gravelly, more clayey, soil, makes for wines that can take forever to soften and become more friendly. One tends to think of these as "old-fashioned" wines, but many of them evidently failed to dazzle the drinkers of 1855 and their forebears; there are only five *Crus Classés*, a quarter of the number in Margaux which covers a similar amount of land.

The stars of the *Appellation* are Châteaux Calon-Ségur, Montrose and Cos d'Estournel. Of these, Calon-Ségur is the least immediately impressive, but in their different styles, Montrose and Cos d'Estournel are two of the finest wines in the Médoc. Montrose can be majestic stuff, more approachable in its youth than it used to be, but still packed with cedary, blackcurrant flavour.

It's a shame that so many Bordeaux lovers know

The gates of Château Cos d'Estournel: châteaux in the Médoc are every bit as imposing as their wines

what Cos (as it is known by aficionados, who pronounce it like the name of the lettuce) looks like – it is too easy to imagine that their descriptions of the wine as "spicy" are influenced by thoughts of the mock-oriental folly with its carved front door imported by its owner from Zanzibar.

In fact Cos benefits from its gravelly soil to make wines that are rather closer to Pauillac in style than they are to those of most of its neighbours. But their wonderful, spicy flavour is all their own. Of St-Estèphe's unclassed wines, the best are Marbuzet, Haut-Marbuzet, Andron-Blanquet, Beau-Site, Le Boscq, Meyney, Les Ormes-de-Pez, de Pez and Lafon-Rochet.

Beyond St-Estèphe, where the gravel gives way to clay and the Cabernet is supplanted by the Merlot, the wines can only be sold as Médoc; in theory, this northern counterpart to the Haut-Médoc really ought to be called the Bas (low) Médoc; it is where much of the wine that is sold as "Médoc" and "House Claret" is made.

There is very little of real class here, though there are occasional flashes of brilliance such as Château Potensac (made by the owner of Château Léoville-Lascases), La Tour Haut Caussin, La Tour-de-By, Castéra, Patache d'Aux, La Tour-St-Bonnet and Les Ormes-Sorbet. Most can be drunk young (thanks to their high Merlot content) but when well made they can be kept for a decade or longer. One that seems built to last is the St-Estèphe-like Château Cissac, but only in the ripest vintages. The pin-striped devotees of London's El Vino bars, however, relish even Cissac's toughest efforts; perhaps you have to have gone to the right school to appreciate its disciplinarian style.

ST EMILION AND POMEROL

The atmosphere of anticipation must have been extraordinary as the inhabitants of the little town of Libourne gathered on the platform of their newly built railway station in 1853 and listened for the whistle of the first train ever to stop there. For some, the excitement must have been caused by the possibility for the first time of travelling directly to Paris along the new iron path – the *chemin de fer*. Most, though, were most likely relishing the idea of using the new mode of transport to carry them across the two rivers that separated them from the city of Bordeaux just 20 miles (30 km) away.

It was not only human passengers who were going to benefit from the train; wine made in the nearby vineyards of St Emilion and Pomerol could make the journey too, and finally take its place alongside the already well known clarets of the Médoc and Graves in the Gironde.

But not, it transpired, among the estates featured in the classification drawn up two years later by Bordeaux merchants, who were far more used to selling wines from their back yard and allowing the produce of these more easterly regions to make its own way north to Brussels and Amsterdam, where it was highly appreciated. So, when the Great Exhibition opened in 1855, the best-known St Emilion châteaux – Cheval Blanc, Ausone and Figeac – and Château Petrus in Pomerol, were never directly ranked alongside Latour, Lafite, Margaux and Haut-Brion.

To a historian this might seem rather unfair; after all, good wine-making has been going on here for rather longer than it has in the Médoc. One of the best châteaux, Ausone, owes its name to the Roman poet Ausonius, who was born near St Emilion, and ownership of the vineyards of another top château, Figeac, can be traced back to the same era. The wines of the region were already known abroad as early as the twelfth century and it was Edward I of England who, as Duke of Gascony 700 years ago, drew up the boundaries of St Emilion.

Apart from the problems of transportation – until the early 1900s the only way across the two rivers was by ferry – there are two other possible explanations for the surprising second-class status the region as a whole retained until the 1950s. Firstly, there was the estates' lack of size; the average St Emilion château produces far less wine than its Médoc equivalent and those in Pomerol are often positively tiny: the annual harvest at Château Pétrus yields just 25,000 bottles, a tenth of the quantity Château Margaux might make. With limited production, it was hard for an estate to gain an international reputation. Secondly – and critically – there was the style of the wines.

The clay soil that covers most of the region does not suit the Cabernet Sauvignon; it simply doesn't ripen properly. Despite this, it was this variety and the uninspiring Malbec that were traditionally included in much of the wine. The St Emilions and Pomerols of the nineteenth century, and even of the first half of the twentieth, were often lean, unripe, rangy beasts.

The fortunes of the producers changed dramatically and unexpectedly in 1956, when vicious frosts wiped out large sections of the vineyards and obliged the growers to

St Emilion sits among the vineyards that produce its famous wines

replant. When they did so, it was largely with the clay-loving Merlot along with some Cabernet Franc for the areas with limestone. As for the Cabernet Sauvignon, that was restricted to the few patches of gravel on which it would thrive. The new improved blend in the vineyards brought what was for many a new style of wine: one that was not only softer and more approachable than it had been, but riper and easier than the wines of the Médoc.

There was another incidental effect which is not appreciated by people with credit-card sized vintage charts offering a single mark out of 10 for a Bordeaux of any given year. The Merlot flowers before the Cabernets. This can make for years like 1986 when it fails to develop properly – and the risk of increased damage from late frosts – but early flowering leads to earlier ripening and picking, with the chance as in 1964 of getting the grapes into the winery ahead of the storms that can spoil the harvest in the Médoc.

Chacun à Son Goût

Today, with the further refinement of modern wine-making, the made-in-heaven marriage of soil and grape has created what can be some of the world's most immediately appealing serious wines. It is no accident that British claret-drinkers, for whom drinking anything before its sixteenth birthday is only just this side of illegal, still cleave to their favourite Médocs while American drinkers who prefer more instant gratification opt for St Emilion and Pomerol.

The best way to appreciate the difference wrought by the change in grape varieties is to undertake what is in any case one of the most instructive tasting exercises of all: to compare a set of Bordeaux "blind" and to guess which side of the Gironde they come from. If the stuff in your glass is tannic and tastes of blackcurrant and cedar it's probably a Médoc; if its complex array of flavours make you think of ripe plums, honey and toffee, the likelihood is that it comes from St Emilion or maybe Pomerol.

Having determined that the wine is from the right rather than the left bank of the Dordogne, your next task is to decide in which of the two communes it was made. This is a great deal trickier; indeed, it can flummox experienced tasters. With practice, this too is an art you could master.

St Emilion

This is one of the few parts of Bordeaux that looks like a proper wine region. The land has some contours to it and

the vines run up and down slopes; the cosy old town is set right amongst the vineyards.

The vine-covered hillsides form one long south-facing slope, the Côtes, that contributes toward the quality of some of St Emilion's best, most long-lived wines: Ausone, Belair, Canon, Pavie, Pavie-Decesse and Magdelaine all include grapes grown on the Côtes. L'Arrosée is one of the very few châteaux to make good wine exclusively from the hillside. Much of the rest of St Emilion's vineyard area is planted in sandy soil – the *sables* – that results in lighter, young-drinking wine. In theory, young-drinking Merlot should be delicious – provided yields are kept low. When – often – they aren't, the Merlot's toffee can take over from the plum and make for wine that's downright dull.

But there are two top-class St Emilion châteaux that are on neither the Côtes nor the *sables*. Cheval Blanc and Figeac both sit on the same long outcrop of gravel, and compete with Ausone for the commune's crown. It's an unfair fight, really, because Cheval Blanc always wins; its big, sumptuous flavours simply eclipse the other wines. But give Figeac time, taste it beyond Cheval Blanc's shadow, and its gentler, more perfumed character could well seduce one into calling the whole thing a draw.

However, both these wines are atypical St Emilions; neither is predominantly Merlot-based, and Cheval Blanc is a true rarity in being largely made from the Cabernet Franc. Other good St Emilions grown on gravelly soil include La Tour Figeac, Dominique, Soutard and de Grand Corbin, all of which can be rather less costly than Figeac or Cheval Blanc.

Finally, a word of warning. If St Emilion's best châteaux produce some of the finest wines in the world, bottles from lesser estates – even ones with a *Grand Cru* to their name – are often woefully dull and horribly overpriced. Their only defence is that they may be a bit better than stuff that's simply labelled as St Emilion which is among the worst-value wine in France.

The St Emilion Satellites

Your money would be far better spent on a wine from Lussac, Montagne, Puisseguin or St Georges, a set of "satellite" villages which, until 1936, could sell their wine as St Emilion but now have to prefix it with their own names. The best of these more affordable *Appellations* is

St Georges-St Emilion, where Château St Georges makes wine of soft, classed St Emilion quality. Montagne-St Emilion partly overlaps this *Appellation* and some châteaux have the choice of which label they prefer to use. Of the wines labelled as Montagne-St Emilion, the nod goes to for Vieux-Château-St-André, made by the oenologist at Château Pétrus. Lussac-St Emilion can produce attractively plummy wine too (try Château Cap de Merle). Puisseguin has traditionally been the weakest of the quartet but Château des Laurets is helping to lead a drive toward quality.

Pomerol

If the Médoc has a small fleet of flagships, Pomerol – a fraction of its size at just 2,000 acres – has just one: Château Pétrus, the world's most expensive red wine. But even as recently as 50 years ago, mentioning Pétrus would have aroused very little response among even some of the keenest British wine-drinkers; as a Pomerol, it was firmly stuck in the shadow of its more famous neighbours in St Emilion. Uniquely in Bordeaux, there is no quality classification here and no separate *Grand Cru Appellation*, though any open-minded comparison between a set of Pomerols and supposed *Grands Crus*

from St Emilion provides a perfect justification for sticking all such questionable tags straight in the bin.

It was America that discovered Pétrus – and wine buffs there fell head-over-heels for its extraordinary spicy-fruity-gamey intensity. Of course, they couldn't all actually drink it – the château makes only 20 or 30,000 bottles in a good year – but they fell in love with the idea of it, and with the rich, plummy, chocolatey, berryish Merlot flavour of the other Pomerols they proceeded to seek out.

Heretical though it may sound, blind tastings of Pétrus have always been a touch disappointing, given its astronomical price. It's like being in a Ferrari and looking for a little extra acceleration. Even so, this is remarkable stuff, partly because of the careful way in which it is made, but more essentially because of the magic piece of clay soil in which its vines are planted. To look at, there doesn't appear to be anything special about Pétrus's soil – nor about the château itself, which could easily be a modestly successful Bordeaux merchant's weekend retreat. But that's Pomerol's style. The land here is flatter and less picturesque than St Emilion, but its very flatness helpfully allows you to see just how small the estates are – you could pack at least half a dozen into the vineyards of the average Médoc château.

The soil is far less variable here than it is in St Emilion, but there are parts of the commune where the clay does contain all kinds of minerals that help to give the best Pomerols an extra dimension, a minerally edge which balances what could all too easily be jammy sweet fruit.

As there is no Pomerol classification, the commune's estates can all compete for the role of prince to Pétrus's king. The strong field includes Le Pin, Vieux-Château-Certan, Certan-de-May, La Conseillante, La Fleur Pétrus, L'Evangile, Trotanoy, Bon-Pasteur, Petit-Village, Lafleur, Clos-René, Feytit-Clinet, Clos du Clocher, Franc-Maillet, l'Eglise-Clinet and Clinet, Latour-à-Pomerol and La Grave Trigant de Boisset.

Lalande-de-Pomerol

What's in a name? Well, in this case, there's the recognizable name of Pomerol which, particularly in the USA, has helped to boost prices of this once-inexpensive *Appellation*. Even so, the wines of Lalande-de-Pomerol can still be delicious, plummily ripe buys for drinking earlier. There are lots of good examples, but Châteaux Annereaux, Tournefeuille, Bel-Air and Siaurac are particularly recommended.

Fronsac

In the eighteenth century Fronsac was one of the classiest wines of Bordeaux and sold for a higher price than Pomerol. All that changed with the Revolution. From being scarce and good, Fronsac suddenly became plentiful and mediocre. Today, with the support of Christian Moueix who's best known for Château Pétrus, Fronsac is making a gradual comeback with wines that often outclass all but the best of St Emilion. Try a bottle from Château la Rivière; better still, go and taste the wine at the château – it's straight out of one of Polanski's more Gothic films. Other Fronsacs to look out for include Villars, Mayne-Vieil and La Valade.

Canon-Fronsac

This is a patch of hillside country within Fronsac itself. The style of the wines is somewhat similar to that of Pomerol, but rather more rustic, particularly when the wines are young. But give them time; they can be worth it. The best wine here is made by Christian Moueix at one of Bordeaux's several estates called Château Canon.

The vine-covered côte, or hillside, of St Emilion

Bordeaux-Cotes-de-Castillon

Castillon, almost hidden between St Emilion and the Dordogne river at Bergerac, seems such a sleepy little place that it is hard to imagine that, in 1453, it was here that Aquitaine and the vineyards of Bordeaux were snatched back by the French after 300 years in English hands. Today the town, or its hills, are known for Merlot-based, good-value reds from such châteaux as Robin, Belcier and Pitray.

Bordeaux-Cotes-des-Francs

A name that even the best-informed Bordelais would rarely have known – until recently. Today, as vineyard and wine prices in the rest of Bordeaux climb steadily higher, this warm, dry farmland area that was once part of St Emilion has suddenly attracted new interest – from some very keen and skilful young wine-makers who come with a fine pedigree. Château de Francs was bought by the owners of the top St Emilion property Château Cheval Blanc, while Châteaux Puygueraud and La Claverie belong to the Thienpont family, whose Château Vieux-Château-Certan is one of the finest estates in Pomerol. The Merlot-packed wines are impressive and not too dear.

GRAVES

The French have an expression mentioned elsewhere in this book: *le goût de terroir*, "the flavour of the soil". For those of us who, unlike His Holiness the Pope, have never even kissed the dirt, let alone chewed a mouthful of it, this kind of language seems either fanciful or downright unhelpful. Until, that is, you get to this area to the south of the city of Bordeaux – and discover that the free-draining qualities of the gravel here are important enough for them to have named the region after it.

Time and a regard for accuracy have, however, slightly rearranged matters. The metropolis – in the shape of an airport, industrial parks, housing and shopping centres – has eaten into some of the best, gravelliest land and displaced over 150 châteaux. In 1988, the owners of the surviving properties in the north of the region acknowledged that the southern part of the Graves has more sand and clay than gravel – and created a new *Appellation* for themselves, frankly naming it after two of Bordeaux's duller (but authentically gravelly) suburbs: Pessac and Léognan. So, paradoxically, if you want to find the best wines of the gravel – the *crus classés* – the Graves is no longer the place to look.

The Graves is the oldest of the regions around Bordeaux, the one that, in the thirteenth century, produced all the best wine. Today it is still recognized as being the only bit of Bordeaux to make quality red *and* white. Then, in the early 1980s, there was a revolution. Faced with the prospect of a major revision of the Classification of the Graves, and influenced by three men – Peter Vinding-Diers, a Dane who'd worked in Australia; Pierre Coste, a wine merchant; and Denis Dubordieu, an oenologist at Bordeaux University – a small but growing band of producers introduced a number of changes to the way in which they made their wine.

First, they gave up the practice of picking too early – and instantly did away with those raw flavours. Second, they cooled down their fermentation tanks – and increased the flavour of their wine. Third, in some cases, they left the juice in contact with its skins, fermented it with specially cultured yeasts and even in

oak barrels. And fourth, they cut down on the amount of sulphur dioxide they used, simultaneously casting out all those dirty dishrags.

The results were startling. Suddenly the Graves began to make wines that tasted ripe, buttery and peachy, with all the fascinating flavours of ripe Sémillon that had already dazzled visitors to Australia in the examples made there.

Today, as an increasing number of châteaux follow the revolutionaries' example, the only real debate concerns the choice of white grape. For some people, the Sémillon should be king; for others, including André Lurton, who makes great wine at several châteaux, including La Louvière and Couhins-Lurton (which, like Malartic-Lagravière and the fast-improving Smith-Haut-Lafite, is 100 per cent Sauvignon), the Sauvignon Blanc is essential. The authorities seem to have agreed with him, insisting that Pessac-Léognan whites contain at least 25 per cent Sauvignon Blanc.

But if the whites have been undergoing a revolution, the traditional focus of attention has remained on the reds. And the best place to discover how they should taste is more or less in the middle of a housing estate at Pessac, not far from Bordeaux's Mérignac airport.

On April 10, 1663, Samuel Pepys tasted "a sort of French wine, called Ho Bryan" and thought its flavour "good and most particular". Two centuries later, in 1855, Château Haut-Brion was the only Graves château to be ranked alongside Lafite, Latour and Margaux. Today, it is still quintessential Graves, combining the blackcurrant Cabernet fruit of the Médoc with the richer, softer approachability of Pomerol.

Haut-Brion is an easy wine to underestimate because, though dangerously easy to drink in its youth, it takes time to develop its host of complex flavours. Its next-door neighbour, La Mission-Haut-Brion, is tougher, as is Pape-Clément. All three can resemble top-class wines from Margaux, but with a honeyed, slightly minerally flavour of their own.

Down the road, in the commune of Léognan, there lies one of the most alluring Bordeaux estates, Domaine de Chevalier, a small property that produces wonderfully subtle, raspberryish red and rich, peachy white wine almost every year. Domaine de Chevalier's neighbour, Châteaux Fieuzal, though classified for its red, was never recognized for its whites. Today they are among the region's oaky superstars. Château Haut-Bailly, another underrated favourite, makes a deliciously soft, approachable red wine, but no white.

Further south, you move into the Graves, and into affordability, early-drinking reds and innovative whites. It was in this area that Peter Vinding-Diers, with a little help from such now-famous Australians as Brian Croser and Len Evans, first showed the region how good well made, carefully oaked Sémillon could be at the unclassified Château Rahoul. Vinding-Diers has moved on to make impressive wine at Domaine La Grave and Château de Landiras.

Other wines from the south that are certainly worth looking out for include the reds from Châteaux Ferrande and Cardaillan; both reds and whites from Pierre Coste's châteaux, Montalivet and l'Etoile; Domaine de Gaillat; and Châteaux Chicane and Chantegrive. Some of these estates may benefit as and when the authorities get around to reclassifying the region.

Cérons

Tucked away in the Graves, on the border with Barsac, Cérons is a sweet white *Appellation* that has largely switched its attention to making dry wine. It's a pity, really, because Cérons' sweet whites, which have to be made in the same way as Sauternes, can be a good cheap alternative to that wine; on the other hand, it's quite understandable because, unlike the Sauternais who can only call their dry white Bordeaux Blanc, producers of Cérons can call theirs Graves – and charge a higher price.

As for Graves Supérieur, this is a white wine *Appellation* that most wine-drinkers overlook – despite the fact that it applies to one in every five bottles of wine produced in this region. There are some reasonable dry examples made, but the best ones are sweet. Occasionally, examples like Clos St Georges can compete with Barsac – but not top-class Barsac.

The people who make real Sauternes, the stuff that only comes from a hilly corner of Bordeaux, have long been a dedicated and masochistic bunch. If their main aim in life had been to make wine for profit, they'd have switched their attention to red or dry white ages ago, either of which would have enabled them to produce at least a bottle of wine per vine instead of just a glass or two of Sauternes. Until recently, with the exception of a few big-name châteaux, they received little financial reward for their effort; in the 1980s, good Sauternes was famously undervalued. Today, happily for the producers and unhappily for the rest of us, this is a pleasure that has to be paid for. But it's worth it.

THE ESSENTIALS
GRAVES

What to look for Blackcurranty reds and peachy whites.

Official quality AOC Graves, Graves Supérieur, Pessac-Léognan and Cérons, with a cru classification for red and white Graves.

Style Reds are very much a cross between Médoc and Pomerol, with soft, blackcurranty fruit and raspberry and even floral notes. Dry whites vary in style depending on the grape varieties used and wine-making style (with or without new oak). Graves Supérieur and Cérons can be a little like a light Sauternes, though of lesser quality.

Climate Slightly warmer than the Médoc.

Cultivation The terrain is more undulating than the Médoc; soil varies from classic gravel in the north (the area recently granted its own AOC, Pessac-Léognan) to a more sandy gravel in the south.

Grape varieties As in the Médoc, Cabernet Sauvignon, Cabernet Franc, Merlot, Malbec and Petit Verdot are used for reds; Sémillon, Sauvignon Blanc and Muscadelle for whites.

Production/maturation New oak is increasingly used for fermenting white Graves by good châteaux, while mixtures of old and new small oak remain the preferred method of maturation for reds.

Longevity Red: 6–25 years; White: 3–10 years.

Vintage guide Red: 78, 79, 81, 82, 83, 85, 86, 88, 89, 90, 94, 95. White: 78, 79, 81, 82, 83, 85, 86, 88, 89, 90, 94, 95, 96, 98.

Top 20 Graves/Pessac-Léognan Red: Haut Bailly; White: Clos Floridène, Couhins-Lurton, Landiras, Domaine la Grave Clos St Georges; Red and white: Châteaux Haut-Brion, La Tour Haut-Brion, La Mission Haut-Brion, La Louvière, Fieuzal, Smith Haut-Lafite, Pape-Clément, Domaine de Chevalier, Malartic-Lagravière, Rochemorin, Rahoul; Cérons: Château d'Archambeau, Grand Enclos du Château de Cérons, Mayne-Binet.

SAUTERNES AND BARSAC

The History

The gently hilly region of Sauternes has been making wine since the Roman occupation – but the wine we know today is a recent innovation. The wine-makers of 400 years ago had to add alcohol to their light, dryish white wine to stabilize it for the journey to the Netherlands, where much of it was drunk. With or without the alcohol, the stuff they were making must have tasted pretty good because, in 1787, Thomas Jefferson described Sauternes as one of the three best white wines in France – along with Hermitage and Champagne – and bought some for his cellar.

The switch from the style Jefferson enjoyed to the Yquem came some time in the 1800s, though no-one is quite certain of precisely how or when. According to one story, it was a German called Focke who, in 1836, recognizing noble rot in the vineyards, tried to recreate a German-style botrytized wine in France. The Sauternais don't like giving credit to a foreigner; they prefer to fix the date of the first "modern" Sauternes vintage to 1847, when a delay in the harvest at Château d'Yquem allowed the rot to develop in the vineyards. It was the combination of that rot and the skill they developed at handling sulphur dioxide, an

THE ESSENTIALS

SAUTERNES AND BARSAC

Official quality AOC Sauternes and Barsac, which also share their own cru classification, drawn up in 1855 at the same time as that for the Médoc.

Style Very sweet, luscious whites, with tropical or marmalade aromas. The lusciousness and complexity depend upon the degree to which botrytis cinerea has affected the vintage and the care taken to restrict picking to nobly-rotten grapes. Barsac is perhaps lighter but can be of as high a quality as Sauternes. Barsac may be sold as Sauternes, but not vice versa. The little dry white produced may be sold only as Bordeaux Blanc, though it can be of high quality in its distinctive, nutty way.

Climate A warmer micro-climate within Bordeaux; the region is also peculiarly susceptible to morning mists rising from the Ciron river which, combined with warm afternoons, provide ideal conditions for the development and proliferation of botrytis.

Grape varieties Sémillon, plus Sauvignon Blanc and Muscadelle.

Cultivation Soil is of clay limestone to sandy gravel. The most experienced pickers are needed for the vintage here as, to make fine Sauternes, only the overripe and, when appropriate, botrytized grapes must be plucked from each bunch. Several sorties into the vineyard are made – at the best châteaux, as many as 10 – until all the grapes are harvested; these successive selective pickings are known as tries. In some years, though, noble rot never appears; when this happens, Château d'Yquem makes no vintage wine.

Production/maturation Grapes are whole-pressed and wood fermented and matured. New oak is increasingly being used.

Longevity Anything between 5 and 40 years.

Vintage guide 70, 75, 76, 78, 80, 81, 83, 85, 86, 88, 89, 90, 97.

Top 20 Château d'Yquem, Rieussec, Lafaurie-Peyraguey, Suduiraut, Coutet, Climens, Guiraud, Doisy- Daëne, Doisy-Védrines, D'Arche, de Malle, Nairac, Broustet, Raymond-Lafon, Gilette, Bastor-Lamontagne, Rabaud-Promis, Sigalas-Rabaud, Filhot, Rayne-Vigneau.

---

essential protection against bacteria, that allowed the Sauternais to establish their tradition of sweet, unfortified wine.

Unfortunately, that skill with the sulphur dioxide has still not been mastered as widely and consistently as most modern wine-drinkers might wish. In the past, when wines were left to age for decades in their owners' cellars, the sulphur overdose from which even some of the biggest names suffered would have been less apparent; today, with younger bottles being opened, it can remove a large amount of the pleasure from the wine, quite obscuring the fascinating, spicy flavour of grapes that have been subject to noble rot.

But the capricious *botrytis cinerea* will not appear to order. Everything depends on the weather – and on the wine-maker's preparedness to wait for the warm, humid fog from the River Ciron that encourages *pourriture noble* to grow on the grapes.

In some years – 1985 is a good example – when the weather has been perfect for red wines, the crucial blanket of mist does not appear. In vintages like these, all but the best producers will simply make wine with little or no *botrytis* character, while the harvesters

Opposite: Château d'Yquem, the most famous of all Sauternes. Its wines are the weightiest and most concentrated in the region

working with their more painstaking neighbours will wait patiently, making as many as six, eight or even more trips into the vineyards to pick only the *botrytis*-affected bunches.

If you are going to wait, though, Sauternes is a very pleasant place in which to do so. This is a far easier region to fall in love with than the flatlands of the Médoc or Pomerol. Even today, Sauternes itself is still small and makes no great effort to flaunt its fame: there are just 600 inhabitants, the odd church and a town hall – and the *Maison du Sauternes*, which looks as though it only opens once a year. The meandering tourist might well pass it by in favour of the comparatively bustling village of Barsac down the road.

Barsac

Barsac can produce wine under its own name which, when of the likes of Châteaux Coutet and Climens, can compete with the finest Sauternes, though with a slightly drier, less unctuous style. Other Barsac properties, however, often prefer to take advantage of the permission given to them and their wine-making neighbours, Fargues, Preignac and Bommes, to give their wines the better-known label. Which is perhaps a pity; Barsac certainly shouldn't be thought of as second-class Sauternes.

THE OTHER WINES OF BORDEAUX

In good vintages, vineyards throughout Bordeaux can make decent wine; the trick is to find the best value. In more difficult years, however, the region can be a minefield in which value for money sometimes seems no longer to exist. In both cases, it is worth looking to regions like Blaye, Bourg and the Premières Côtes – but don't forget to carry our list of recommendations (or a reliable mine detector).

Premières Côtes de Blaye

A brief ferry ride from the Médoc, the lovely, old, walled citadel of Blaye ought to be on every wine-tourist's list of places to visit. On paper, as a wine region, Blaye has a great deal to offer too: a handy set of no fewer than four red and white *Appellations*, clay soil for the Merlot and limestone for the Sauvignon (with a bit of the Colombard which grows well here). Unfortunately, this is an area that has suffered from neglect. In the last century its vineyards were used to produce acidic white wine for distillation into brandy. Replanting was often haphazard and, all too often, other forms of agriculture – this is great asparagus country – were allowed to take over.

But take another look at that limestone, at the clay, at the slopes and at the red and white wines Château Haut Bertinerie is making. What Blaye needs is love and investment; given both, it can give several better-known Bordeaux regions a serious run for their money.

Bourg

The wine-makers of Bourg are an enterprising lot; they did what many other regions ought to consider doing and employed a team of market researchers to find out what people thought of their wine. The answer came back that Bourg, which has been making wine since Roman times, was thought now to be producing "rustic", "country" wine that lacked the finesse most people look for in red Bordeaux. The solution, it seemed, was to learn a few lessons from their neighbours in Margaux, on the other side of the Gironde.

Today, the wines are decidedly classier in style than they used to be – and rather more so than those of the Blayais, which are produced all around them. Both the Cabernet and Merlot grow well here and styles vary depending on which of the two is used. The Tauriac co-operative is spear-heading the move toward quality, and Château de Barbe is a model for the region as a whole. Most of the wine is red and sold as Côtes de Bourg, but the Bourg and Bourgeais *Appellations* also exist and there is a tiny amount of white Bourg made.

Premières Côtes de Bordeaux

Like the Graves, this is a region where land tends to be valued in two ways – as vineyards and, for rather higher sums, as building plots. As the city of Bordeaux expands, there seems little hope for the vines – particularly because this 30-mile-long strip of riverside land has no great reputation for its wines. However, the Premières Côtes have tremendous potential; not for the sort of wines it has traditionally made – sweet and semi-sweet whites – but for its blackcurrant reds and *clairet rosés*. Among the best châteaux at present are Lamothe, Barreyres, Grand-Mouëys, Tanesse, Fayau and de Bouteilley.

Cadillac

Within the region of the Premières Côtes, Cadillac sits on the Garonne facing Sauternes. All the wine made here is sweet and semi-sweet white, and most is dull stuff – sales are difficult and there is little incentive for quality wine-making. One estate that is trying hard, though, is Château Fayau, which backs up its Yquem-style label with some pretty luscious wine – despite the evident absence of the *botrytis* that makes Sauternes special.

Loupiac

Making sweet white wine often referred to as "poor man's Sauternes", this island in the Premières Côtes perseveres, despite public indifference and the unwillingness of *botrytis* to visit its vineyards as often as it does Sauternes and Barsac. As those more famous sweet wines return to favour, hopefully the overall quality of Loupiac will rise too. Wines worth looking for now are the ones made by Château Loupiac-Gaudiet and de Ricaud.

Ste-Croix-du-Mont

This is the third and best of the Premières Côtes *Appellations*, producing sweet and very sweet white wines. There is a little more *botrytis* here, and even when the rot doesn't appear, the wines can be well made and well balanced. The top château is Loubens; la Rame and des Tastes are good too.

Entre-Deux-Mers

The name is misleading; there are no seas, only the rivers Garonne and Dordogne. In fact, it would make rather more sense to call this large region "Entre-Deux-Vins" in recognition of the way in which it separates the Graves from St Emilion and Pomerol. Once a name that was synonymous with the most awful cheap, sweet white wines, Entre-Deux-Mers has recently gone through a between-two-seas-change to become a region that can produce perfectly decent dry white and a red

and pink Bordeaux – but only when there is enough sun to ripen the grapes and low enough yields to provide concentrated flavours.

This is attractively varied country, where farmland competes with woods and vineyards and a growing number of small estates have to combat not only the frequent unwillingness of the grapes to ripen properly but also the readiness of some big customers to buy on price rather than quality. But quality is possible, as the Lurton family have proved at Château Bonnet, a property whose oaked white puts some famous Graves wines to shame.

Although it has been the whites that have put Entre-Deux-Mers back on the map, the suspicion is that the future stars of this region will be red. Just taste the wines of Châteaux La Tour Martines, Thieuley and Toutigeac, and you'll see what we mean. Unfortunately for the area, these, like all of the other reds made here, can only be sold as Bordeaux Rouge and Bordeaux Supérieur, names that can be used for red wine made anywhere in Bordeaux. Perhaps one day soon, the authorities will allow them to call themselves Entre-Deux-Mers Rouge.

BURGUNDY

You can always spot the true Burgundy lover in a wine shop. The claret fan relaxedly strolls across to pick up a bottle of Château This or That, pausing only to check the vintage. Back among the Burgundies, the enthusiast has pulled out his magnifying glass and his pocket guide, reading the small print on every label like a nervous householder examining an insurance certificate.

Every now and then, he probably glances across at the Bordeaux buyer, envying him the simplicity of his choice – but, until he's got to the last bottle on the shelf, he'll go on searching. He knows that, if he can find precisely the bottle he's looking for, it will give him far more pleasure and excitement than even the greatest Bordeaux. But if he gets it wrong, he'll end up with a few glasses of very expensive disappointment.

And that's it in a nutshell, really. Buying Bordeaux is a pretty simple process; all you have to do is remember the names of a few châteaux that make wine you enjoy and follow them faithfully from year to year. Château Lynch-Bages, Château La Louvière, Château Rieussec ... apart from vintage variations (and they're traditionally less severe in temperate Bordeaux than in inland Burgundy), the wines from any of these or a few hundred other estates should always taste recognizably the same.

At first glance, Burgundy ought to be just as simple; except that instead of the names of châteaux, it's villages you're looking for; villages like Nuits-St-Georges, Meursault and Gevrey-Chambertin. Unfortunately, it doesn't work like that. Every bottle of Château Lynch-Bages will taste the same for the simple reason that it was all made and bottled at the same place by the same person; a bottle labelled Gevrey-Chambertin could have been produced by any one of several hundred individual wine-growers, all of whom own their own little slices of land here.

Sometimes those growers bottle their own wine; sometimes they sell it to one of the region's *négociants*, or merchants, who will most likely blend it with other growers' wines from the same village in order to have enough wine to sell around the world.

Burgundy is a small-scale place. If you include Beaujolais, it produces around half as much wine as Bordeaux; if you exclude that sea of fruity young red, the figure drops to 25 per cent. And if you focus in on the tiny strip of the Côte d'Or, two dozen villages together produce less wine than only four – Margaux, Pauillac, St-Julien and St-Estèphe – do in the Médoc.

Visiting Burgundy cellars is very different from visiting ones in Bordeaux. And it takes longer. Even the tiniest estate probably makes at least five wines every year; some will produce a dozen – but in tiny quantities. In an average vintage, a Médoc château could easily produce 25,000 12-bottle cases of the same wine; an estate in Meursault might make just 250 cases each of 10 different ones.

The difference is all to do with eighteenth-century politics. Most Bordeaux estates escaped the wrath of the revolutionaries because they often belonged to anti-papist merchants with whom the new order had no quarrel. Burgundy, on the other hand, was church territory through and through.

The small plots into which the vineyards were divided among the gleeful villagers were made smaller still in subsequent generations, thanks to the new inheritance laws that guaranteed equal shares to all of a landowner's sons and daughters. The death of a man with 10 acres and 10 children could have resulted in 10 wine-makers, each with just an acre.

The only reason, apart from the ability of heirs to come to common-sense agreements among themselves, that estates did not shrink to the size of postage stamps was the propensity for sons of wine-growers to marry wine-growers' daughters from the next village, combining names and vineyards to create new estates with new ranges of wines. This process (which continues to this day) not only explains the diverse range of wines, but also the confusing plethora of neighbouring domaines with similar double-barrelled names, such as Coche-Debord and Coche-Dury.

The diversity of wines would be rather less broad if the Burgundians had not discovered over the centuries that the differences in quality and character between vineyards could be so significant that each of the best plots, or *climats* (micro-climates), deserved to be known by its own *lieu-dit* – place-name. By the 1330s, when the Cistercians were building the stone walls to enclose their Clos de Vougeot vineyard, they had already identified most of the *climats* that are best known today, including Clos de Tart, Clos de Bèze, the Chambertin (Bertin's field) and Montrachet. When these vineyards were taken back from the church and split up and distributed among the villagers, the new owners were often more than happy to perpetuate their fame.

Indeed, the vineyards were often so much more famous than the villages in which they were sited that the villagers eventually decided to reflect a little glory on to their other wines by adopting the best plots' names; the little-known village of Gevrey became the well-known village of Gevrey-Chambertin, Nuits became Nuits-St-Georges, and both Chassagne and Puligny added the name of the Montrachet to their own.

After the Revolution, marriages and inheritances, a grower might have ended up with small patches in three different *climats* of Gevrey, two in Morey-St-Denis, four in Vosne-Romanée and one in land that could only be called Bourgogne.

The problem with only making 10 barrels (3,000 bottles) each of 10 different wines is that it is hard not to frustrate one's customers – so the brighter growers began to buy in wine from the same village and to blend it with their own to produce a larger, more saleable amount. The *négociant-éleveur,* the merchant who literally "*élève*" or "brings up" the wine, was born.

For the following 200 years, the *négociants* more or less ran things, buying in barrel, blending and bottling. Some did the job shoddily, some did it well and honestly and some, caught between the frequent unwillingness of the Pinot Noir and Gamay to ripen and customers' demands for rich, alcoholic red, "helped" pallid wines along with judicious additions of beefier wine from further south.

Then, in the 1970s, a new generation of wine-drinkers decided that it was more *sympathique* to buy wine made by an individual in a little cellar rather than by a big company in a factory – only to discover that some of those little cellars were full of filthy barrels and filthier wine, and that some of the "factories" were

Château Corton-André in the commune of Aloxe-Corton. Geometrically patterned roofs like this are typical of the region

producing the best wine in the region.

Today, it is a rare wine-lover who would want categorically to declare himself for or against either growers, *négociants* or co-operatives; most would acknowledge the need to seek out the best in each category.

The Quality

So what makes one producer and his or her Burgundy better than the next one on the shelf? If there were no vines planted in France, and if a team of Californian experts were to visit on a mission to decide where to plant them, one thing is pretty certain; they wouldn't linger for long in Burgundy. Almost the entire region would be dismissed as being too cold, too damp, too frost-prone, too hail-prone, too variable... You can't grow the Cabernet Sauvignon here and even the Pinot Noir and Chardonnay rarely ripen sufficiently, so wine-growers have to unload sacks of sugar into their vats to boost the alcohol to an adequate level. The Californians would be just as dismissive of Burgundy, as many of them have been of the similarly cool, damp north-western state of Oregon where (just by coincidence?)

Burgundy in early summer. Every winter the vines are pruned right back to restrict the size of the crop

the Pinot Noir is beginning to achieve a little of the success it has in Burgundy.

The climatic conditions shared by Burgundy and Oregon are officially described as "marginal"; in other words, both regions are right on the northernmost boundary that defines where great red wine can be made. This closeness to the edge coupled, in the case of Burgundy, with the character of the Pinot Noir and Chardonnay and the region's extraordinary range of soil types, can make for sharply defined fruit flavours and complexity rarely achieved in warmer, easier climates where the Pinot Noir, at least, tends to produce duller, jammier wine.

But a marginal climate is no place for a lazy, greedy or even unlucky wine-grower. Even when the vines escape the attentions of frost, rot and hail, they have to be pruned tightly. If they are allowed to overproduce, the red wine in particular will be thin, flavourless and low in natural sugar. To rectify this, the producers who are now (in theory at least) denied the possibility of adding stronger wine from the Rhône or North Africa, resort to the sugar bag. They are allowed to use cane sugar to raise the strength of a wine – to *chaptalize* it –

by two per cent – for example, from a natural 10.5 per cent to 12.5 per cent. What they are not allowed to do is jack up a nine per cent wine to 13 per cent.

A lot of nonsense is talked about chaptalization, particularly by Californians who pat themselves on the back for not having to add sugar to their ripe grapes, while conveniently overlooking the doses of tartaric acid with which they routinely have to balance their wines. The only sensible thing to be said on the subject is that, while with rare exceptions most good and even great Burgundy is chaptalized to a certain extent, there are still too many thin wines whose mouth-burning alcohol reveals a very heavy hand with the sugar bag.

Then there is the question of new barrels – to oak or not to oak. The flavour of new oak, like that of alcohol, can be overdone. On the other hand, top-class red and white Burgundy can, like top-class Bordeaux, broaden its range of flavours extraordinarily if enough of the wine spends just enough time in new enough wood.

The Regions

Burgundy is a very disparate region, strung out like a series of lakes, beginning in Chablis, around 100 miles (160 km) south of Paris, and stretching down through the Côte d'Or (the heart and the greatest part of the region), the under-appreciated Côte Chalonnaise, the Mâconnais and Beaujolais, almost at the outskirts of Lyon and well within the southern half of France.

Today, it can be hard to imagine what Chablis has in common with Beaujolais. The answer in part is historical politics; both fell within the boundaries of what was once one of the most powerful states in the then-developed world. At its heyday in the fourteenth and fifteenth centuries, the Duchy of Burgundy extended all the way up to the coast of Flanders and the Duke of Burgundy was a major political player, who negotiated with the king of England and delivered him Joan of Arc.

But the style, the diminutive size of the estates and the varieties of grapes grown are common themes that run through all of Burgundy's regions. This is essentially a land of just four grape varieties; two greats – the Pinot Noir and Chardonnay – which are shared with Champagne and a growing number of wine regions throughout the world, and two – the red Gamay and the white Aligoté – which are allocated very specific roles. The former is used to make Beaujolais, a lot of red Mâcon and, in a two-thirds/one-third blend with the Pinot Noir, Bourgogne Passetoutgrains, traditionally most Burgundians' daily red in the days when they could afford to drink their own wines.

In the right hands, the Aligoté produces good, basic white that, at its rare ripest and best, can have a creaminess not unlike that of Chardonnay; more usually, its wines are light and acidic, and best drunk mixed with locally made *cassis* – blackcurrant – liqueur in a cocktail known as Kir. Apart from these four, there are a few Pinot Blanc and Pinot Gris vines around, as well as a few oddities such as the César and Tressot, grown in northern Burgundy, but wines made from these are very rare.

The Styles

Avoid anything labelled Bourgogne Grand Ordinaire; the odds are 250-to-one against it being any good and the only relevant part of its name is the "Ordinaire".

Bourgogne Rouge and Bourgogne Blanc, on the other hand, can range from basic to brilliant, depending on where they were made, how and by whom. Wine produced anywhere from the chilly hills of Chablis to the warm Mâconnais can bear these labels, provided that, in the case of the white, it has been made from the Chardonnay (or, in very rare instances, the Pinot Blanc or Pinot Gris, here called the Pinot Beurot), and in the case of the red that it has been produced from the Pinot Noir (or in the even rarer instances in the Chablis region, from the Tressot or César). There is one other peculiar exception; wines made in the Beaujolais *cru* villages, where only the Gamay is grown, may be declassified to Bourgogne Rouge.

The vineyards in which this basic red and white Burgundy are produced range from the flat land of the Côte d'Or to the hills of the Côte Chalonnaise. And then there are the "almost" wines made by top-class producers in the top-class villages of the Côte d'Or from grapes grown on vines that are just outside the legal limits of those villages. Occasionally, these producers may also decide to declassify some of their potentially higher-class wine that doesn't quite come up to scratch.

More tightly defined than Bourgogne are the *villages*

Appellations for areas within the overall region. These include Beaujolais-Villages as well as smaller *Appellations* such as the Côte de Beaune-Villages and Côte de Nuits-Villages in the Côte d'Or.

Next come the *Appellations* centred around villages and towns, such as Chablis, Fleurie, Beaune and Pouilly-Fuissé, and, in some cases, the best vineyards within those *Appellations*. Some villages – like Pouilly-Fuissé, St-Romain and Fleurie – have no official recognition for their best *climats*, but may include a vineyard name – such as Morgon "Le Py" – on their labels.

Other, more fortunate communes – including Beaune, Meursault and Nuits-St-Georges – have sets of *Premier Cru* vineyards, whose names also feature on labels, usually, but not always, with the additional words "*Premier Cru*" – such as Beaune Grèves *Premier Cru* or Meursault Charmes. Some producers whose *Premiers Crus* have little-known names, or who blend wine from two or more *Premiers Crus* vineyards together, may simply choose to label a wine Beaune *Premier Cru*.

A very few communes – Aloxe-Corton, Gevrey-Chambertin and Chassagne-Montrachet for example – have *Premiers Crus* and *Grands Crus*. *Grands Crus* are considered to be so important that their labels don't need to mention the name of the village in which the wine was made. So Le Corton labels say nothing about Aloxe-Corton, and Richebourg labels don't say that the wine is made in Vosne-Romanée.

These *Grands Crus* are all situated in the grand vineyards of the Côte d'Or. Chablis has *Premier* and *Grand Cru* plots of its own – but helpfully tacks them on to the region's name – "Chablis *Grand Cru* Grenouilles", for example. In theory, if they were all lined up in the same cellar, the *Grand Cru* would have more complex flavours and greater potential longevity than the *Premier Cru* from the next-door vineyard; the *Premier Cru* would be a notch above the wine made from a humbler piece of land in the same village, and the village wine would have a more characterful flavour than one simply labelled Bourgogne.

Life gets trickier when you compare wines made by different producers; one man's carefully made Bourgogne Rouge is most likely better than his careless cousin's Vosne-Romanée – and even his Richebourg.

CHABLIS

You'll recognize the town of Chablis, because you've already been there – every time you've watched one of those old French films; black and white even when they're in colour; brightly lit cafés in empty, rainswept streets; and quiet country folk of the kind who have affairs with and murder each other.

But raise your eyes, and you'll see the reason for Chablis' fame – in the shape of the vineyard-covered hillside that overlooks the town, home to the *Grand Cru* vineyards with their mysterious and evocative names: Vaudésir, Valmur, Grenouilles, Blanchot, Les Clos, Bougros and Les Preuses. These are the epitome of what Chablis can be, the "big wines", the ones most worth keeping. Beneath them on the scale of excellence, there are the *Premiers Crus;* beneath these, plain Chablis and, most humble of all, Petit Chablis. And all must be made from Chardonnay grapes grown in this 4,000-acre Burgundian oasis, almost precisely mid-way between Paris and Beaune.

During the summer months, the owner of the town's best café gets rather bored by the stream of tourists – even French tourists – who ask for "a glass of red Chablis". American visitors are more likely to order "blush Chablis". Neither exists. Chablis comes in one style: dry and white.

Until a quarter of a century or so ago, Chablis was often little more than a convenient, easy-to-pronounce (and remember) name for almost any old white wine. The lazy attitude of pre-EC Britain still prevails in the US, where producers on either coast cynically make "Chablis" out of any old grapes, any old where, any old how. These forgers (for that is what they are) defend themselves by saying that what they are selling is a style of wine – and then shamelessly continue to sell sweet white and pink wine under the name of one of the driest white wines in the world.

Ironically, the more this abuse is practised, the more famous Chablis becomes, and the more the price of the real thing rockets, leaving its aficionados to bemoan the fact that their favourite tipple does not hail from a Burgundian village with a less approachable name – like Auxey-Duresses.

The unique quality of good, typical, authentic Chablis isn't easy to describe. It is absolutely dry, but with a suppleness and a fatty fullness that you seldom find in the dry wines of Sancerre and Pouilly-Fumé,

---

THE ESSENTIALS
CHABLIS

What to look for Bone dry white – usually unoaked – wine which develops richness with age.
Location Centred on the town of Chablis, half-way between Paris and Beaune.
Official quality AOC Chablis, with a further hierarchy of Grands and Premiers Crus (see below). Also AOC Petit Chablis, Irancy, Epineuil, Crémant de Bourgogne, and VDQS Sauvignon de St Bris.
Style Flavours range from steely and austere to pineappley and rounded, usually with either no or little clearly detectable oak (although new oak is finding favour with modernists). Premier Cru wines should have a minerally acidity and the capacity to develop with age. Grands Crus are the biggest. richest, most complex wines, yet are lean and

restrained compared with white Burgundy from farther south. Sauvignon de St Bris is gooseberryish and Sancerre-like; Irancy and Epineuil are light reds though the latter can be white.
Climate Continental.
Cultivation Soils are of calcareous clay. Rivalry exists over the benefits of the classic Kimmeridgian versus the more recently allowed Portlandian limestone. All the Grands Crus are on one south-west-facing slope.
Grape varieties Chardonnay for Chablis; Sauvignon Blanc in St Bris, Pinot Noir, Tressot and César for reds; Sacy for Crémant de Bourgogne.
Production/maturation Stainless steel has largely replaced oak for both, but new oak still has some

fervent and successful supporters, notably William Fèvre.
Longevity Petit Chablis, Sauvignon de St Bris and red wines are intended to be drunk young. Chablis drinks from 1 to 8 years; Premiers Crus for up to 15; Grands Crus should be kept for 5 years, and can be drunk for a further 15.
Vintage guide 85, 86, 88, 89, 90, 92, 95, 96, 97.
Top 15 Chablis: Vincent and René Raveneau, William Fèvre, René Dauvissat, Domaine Laroche, Louis Pinson, Vocoret, Daniel Defaix, Joseph Drouhin, Louis Michel, Tremblay, Jean-Paul Droin, la Chablisienne Co-operative, Jean-Marc Brocard; Sauvignon de St Bris: Domaine Sorin, Jean-Marc Brocard.

both of which are little further away than Beaune or Nuits-St-Georges. But there's also a flinty flavour to Chablis, particularly when it is young, and the wine still has its characteristic green-tinged colour.

The flavour of Chablis has changed in recent years. The steely style has gradually given way to a softer, less demanding one, thanks to over-production, to a succession of ripe vintages, and to the decision of some wine-makers to allow their wine to undergo malolactic fermentation and, in a few cases, to ferment and age it in new oak barrels. To Chablisien purists, both techniques ought to be outlawed; in their view, producers who use them are merely trying to make Meursault-style wines 150 kilometres north of Meursault.

Also contributing to the change in style is the controversial authorization that transformed what was previously Petit Chablis land into Chablis and Chablis *Premier Cru* vineyards. The crucial difference between the "new" land and the area from which the original, most typical, Chablis comes lies in the soil. Or, more precisely, beneath it.

The limestone bedrock on which Chablis rests has been the subject of a violent squabble between two groups of Chablisien wine-growers. The traditionalists claim, with the vehemence of real-ale campaigners, that "real" Chablis can only be grown on the small area of Kimmeridgian limestone which takes its name from the village in Dorset where it is also found. The modernists, like keen urban planners, argue that the Portland limestone that sits beneath the rest of the region can produce wine that is just as good. Tasting the wines side by side, one tends to agree with the traditional line – but then again, the Portland faction are making wines that are certainly of good, if not great, quality. And, given the way that demand for this, the most famous white wine in the world, has forced its price through the roof, it's very tempting to allow the Chablisiens to expand their vineyards as much as they'd like.

Besides, a little over a century ago, the Chablis vineyard was perhaps 10 times its current size. The ravages of the *phylloxera* louse in the 1880s, then the depredations of two World Wars, took a heavy toll on the region's vines and vinegrowers. By the early 1960s, when thirsty Americans were already gulping back their version by the gallon, the area of Chablis vines had shrunk to less than 1,500 acres (600 he) – less than the size of a modest Texan farm.

In those days, few men could rely on making a living simply from their vines. One of their biggest problems was frost, which could – and can – destroy a whole year's crop in a single night. The reason why Chablis is so subject to frost – as late as May in some years – is because of the way that the sheltered valley of the Serein traps and holds cold air.

At the end of rows of vines one can still see the archaic oil burners which are lit as soon as the temperature falls below zero. Now, however, many growers prefer to rely on sprinklers that protect the vines from frost by, paradoxically, allowing a thin layer of ice to form on them.

The Chardonnay vine produces its steely, minerally white wine in the chilly northerly vineyards of Chablis

THE COTE D'OR

Set out from Dijon on the *route nationale* heading south, with the east-facing vine-covered hills on your right and the humbler, flatter land on your left, and read the village signs as you pass: you're driving down a restaurant wine list. Even if you stick rigorously to the speed limit, there they are: one every two or three minutes – Gevrey-Chambertin, Morey-St-Denis, Chambolle-Musigny, Clos de Vougeot, Vosne-Romanée and Nuits-St-Georges...

But for more than signposts, take one of the narrow tracks to your right and follow the *Route des Vins* – past the weather-worn archways that punctuate the rough stone walls and indicate the name of the vineyard or of the proprietor of that particular segment. If it's autumn, bask in the colours, from green to bronze via the gold after which these hills were named. At dusk, stroll slowly between the vineyards and you may even sense the fractional but influential variations in temperature which led the Burgundians to refer to each piece of land as a *"climat"* – a climate. Pick up a handful of soil from each of a couple of neighbouring vineyards and see how the way the earth was folded here aeons ago has packed one with fossils which are almost completely absent in the other.

The Côte d'Or is divided into two parts: the 3,500 acres (1,400 ha) of the more northerly Côte de Nuits, in which most of Burgundy's greatest reds are made and where there is scarcely a drop of white, and the 7,500 acres (3,000 ha) of the Côte de Beaune, where the Pinot Noir still covers 75 per cent of the land, but a handful of villages produce the white wine that turns owners of Chardonnay vineyards in other countries green with envy.

Both Côtes produce simpler wine labelled as Bourgogne Rouge, Bourgogne Blanc, Bourgogne Passetoutgrains and Aligoté, from land that cannot legally produce wine of a grander *Appellation*; some of these can be delicious, especially when made by a grower who also makes loftier wines.

The Côte de Nuits

Apart from the wines produced in the "big-name" villages and those more basic reds and whites, the Côte de Nuits has two other *Appellations*.

Côte de Nuits-Villages can come from the villages of Marsannay, Fixin and Brochon just north of Gevrey-Chambertin, and from the marble-quarrying country around Comblanchien, Corgoloin and Prissy, immediately to the south of Nuits-St-Georges. Little of the wine does actually come from Fixin, which has an *Appellation* of its own, but Brochon and the more southerly communes can produce good-quality, blackcurranty, plummy wine with a recognizable family resemblance to the wines of the better-known villages along the Côte. These are the country cousins, dressed up for a day in the town.

Rather more rustic wines are also produced high in the hills behind the Côte in the Hautes Côtes de Nuits. These definitely have wisps of straw poking out of their hats sometimes, but they can also be the closest thing to a bargain Burgundy has to offer. Stick to warm years; it can get quite chilly up here and lesser vintages tend to produce unripe-tasting wine. Almost all of the wine made here is red. The occasional white can make you wonder why they don't make more. Intriguingly, some of these whites don't taste quite like Burgundy, inspiring vinous know-it-alls to claim that they are made from Aligoté rather than Chardonnay. But the know-it-alls are wrong. If they used their tastebuds instead of regurgitating bits of half-digested information, they might just notice a resemblance between the stuff in their glass and white wine from Alsace – which is hardly surprising because dotted around there are still plantings of Pinot Blanc and Pinot Gris.

What was once called the Côte Dijonnaise is now largely full of the tyre-fitting operations, discount warehouses and *hypermarchés* that make Dijon's southern suburbs look like those of any medium-sized American town. Nowadays, the Côte d'Or officially begins with Marsannay, a village which is still celebrating its recent elevation to join its *Appellation Contrôlée* neighbours.

Marsannay's traditional reputation was for rosé, and that's arguably the one style it can claim as its own (pink Pinot Noir is a rarity). Its reds are still rather closer in quality to decent Bourgogne Rouge (the label they used to bear) than to the kind of stuff one might expect to find down the road in Fixin or Gevrey-Chambertin. One label to look out for (you're sure to notice it) is that from the "Montre Cul" vineyard, whose name – literally "show-arse" – refers to the steepness of the slope and the view male pickers got of their female companions' bloomers. Perversely, the authorities who oversee alcohol, firearms and tobacco in the USA forbade the importation of this wine because the vaguely bawdy cartoon on the label apparently created too strong a connection between sex and alcohol. Such a rigid ruling is put into perspective when you read of the innocent victims of legally imported firearms.

Back to the wine. As one might gather, Marsannay's a fairly jolly place and so is its wine. Fixin, the next-door neighbour, comes as a bit of a shock. Wine merchants have a description for the wines of this village: "Hard to say (it's pronounced *Fissan*), harder to drink and almost impossible to sell". This is as good a place as any to learn about the effects of Burgundian micro-climates. When Gevrey-Chambertin starts to pick its grapes, those in

Fixin across the track still need another week on the vine to ripen. Even when the grapes are ripe, they produce tough, uncompromising wine that seems to taste the way it must have done when the Cistercian monks first made it in the early twelfth century. Give it a decade or so and it can soften – a bit – but it's still Burgundy's answer to old-fashioned St-Estèphe.

Gevrey-Chambertin's much more fun. Or it ought to be. Sadly this, like Nuits-St-Georges, Beaujolais and Châteauneuf-du-Pape, has suffered from the fame syndrome. There are brilliant vineyards here – the *Grands Crus*, including the Chambertin itself, the more immediately appealing Charmes-Chambertin, the Chambertin-Clos de Bèze, Mazis-Chambertin and the Griotte-Chambertin (possibly named after, and certainly tasting of, bitter cherries), and the slightly lighter-weight but sometimes equally impressive *Premiers Crus* such as the Clos St Jacques and Cazetiers. But this is one of the region's biggest villages and its *Appellation* includes a huge tract of flat land, including some which is on the other side of the *route nationale*, the side that usually only makes Bourgogne Rouge. Dull wine-making and

Ancient bottles kept cool and dark in the underground cellars of the company of Joseph Drouhin in Beaune

over-production don't help either; Gevrey-Chambertin *should* be a rich cocktail of dark cherries and really ripe plums. Treat cheap examples with the respect you'd pay to the gold watches on offer from market stalls.

Morey-St-Denis is not a name that rings many bells with Burgundy fans, and nor is Clos-St-Denis, the *Grand Cru* that gave it its name, but here lovely village wines are vying for attention with often poorly made *Grands* and *Premiers Crus*. The best stuff from the Clos de la Roche *Grand Cru* can be majestic, deep wine – better than most Clos-St-Denis. The Clos Sorbès and Clos des Ormes are the best *Premiers Crus*.

Chambolle-Musigny provides your first chance to taste classy white Burgundy – of which a very few bottles are made in the primarily red *Grand Cru* Musigny vineyard – and a red from one of the most romantically named *Premiers Crus*, Les Amoureuses. Chambolle-Musigny's wines should taste more like Côte de Beaune than Côte de Nuits, with that area's more delicate style. Bonnes Mares is the other top *Grand Cru*.

Clos de Vougeot is Burgundy's nearest to a Bordeaux-style château – or that's what it used to be in the days when the Cistercian monks owned this 125-acre (50-ha) walled vineyard and made wine here, carefully separating the inferior grapes grown on the flatland from the best ones grown on the slopes. The French Revolution and inheritance laws changed all that; today there are seven dozen individual owners and seven dozen

---

THE ESSENTIALS

THE COTE D'OR

What to look for Fine examples of the Pinot Noir and rich, buttery Chardonnay.

Location In Burgundy, a narrow strip of land from Dijon in the north to Cheilly-les-Maranges 30 km south of Beaune.

Official quality Overall Côte d'Or AOCs: Bourgogne; Bourgogne Aligoté; Crémant de Bourgogne; Bourgogne Passetoutgrains. Principal Côte de Nuits AOCs:
Chambertin*; Chambertin Clos de Bèze*; Charmes Chambertin*; Chambolle-Musigny; Clos de la Roche*; Clos de Vougeot*; Côte de Nuits-Villages; Echézeaux*; Fixin; Gevrey-Chambertin; Grands-Echézeaux*; Hautes-Côtes de Nuits; Marsannay; Morey St Denis; Nuits-St-Georges; Richebourg*; Romanée*; Vosne-Romanée. Principal Côte de Beaune AOCs: Ladoix; Aloxe-Corton; Auxey-Duresses; Bâtard Montrachet*; Beaune; Blagny; Chassagne-Montrachet; Chorey-lès-Beaune; Corton*; Corton-Charlemagne*; Côte de Beaune; Côte de Beaune-Villages; Hautes-Côtes de Beaune; Maranges; Meursault; Monthélie; Montrachet*; Pernand-Vergelesses; Pommard; Puligny-Montrachet; St Aubin, St Romain; Santenay; Savigny-lès-Beaune; Volnay. Superimposed on most of the Appellations is a complex structure of named vineyards: the Grands and Premiers Crus. The AOCs marked (*) are in themselves Grands Crus.

Style Whites, at their best, have a dazzling array of enticing flavours, with rich, buttery fruit, a creamy/nutty texture and splendid overtones of honey, vanilla and toasty oak. The reds are more varied in quality but should have delicate strawberry/raspberry fruit in the Côte de Beaune and a finer character, with greater depth and a sumptuous silky texture, in the Côte de Nuits. With bottle age, the reds develop a gamey flavour. Because of the myriad small-plot owners, the producer's name is all-important and the best guide to quality. A general rule is that the wines are reasonably straightforward at village level, with greater complexity and depth of flavour to be expected from Premier and Grand Cru wines. Tiny quantities of dry rosé, packed with soft currant and berry fruit flavours, are also made.

Climate Temperate continental climate with hot, sunny summers and long, cold winters. Hail and heavy rain can cause rot and dilute wines.

Cultivation Subtly varying marl, clay and calcareous soils overlay a limestone subsoil which underpins the east-facing slopes of the region. Vines generally grow at 200–400 m above sea level and vineyards generally face north-east or south-east. Vines are trained low to maximize heat reflected from the soil during the day.

Grape varieties The dominant red is the Pinot Noir, though the Gamay is also grown. Principal white is the Chardonnay; secondary white the Aligoté.

Production/maturation Traditional methods are used. For red wines the grapes are at least partially de-stemmed and the juice receives 8–14 days' skin contact. Some producers leave the black grapes for a period of a few hours to a few days at low temperature or beneath SO_2 before fermentation begins. Top whites are cask-fermented although stainless steel is used for lesser wines. Both reds and whites are matured in oak.

Longevity Reds: Village wines and basic Bourgogne: 4–17 years; Premiers Crus: 8–25 years; Grands Crus: 10–30+ years. Whites: Village wines: 3–11 years; Premiers Crus: 6–15 years; Grands Crus: 10–30+ years. Rosés: Up to 4 years.

Vintage guide Reds: 71, 76, 78, 79, 83, 85, 88, 89, 90, 92, 95, 96, 97; Whites: 78, 79, 81, 82, 85, 86, 88, 89, 90, 92, 93, 95, 96, 97.

Top 32 Côte de Nuits: Jayer, Jayer-Gilles, Ponsot, Dujac, Patrice Rion, Méo-Camuset, Gros Frères, Mongeard-Mugneret, Domaine de la Romanée-Conti, Domaine Leroy, Jean Grivot, Alain Michelot, Henri Gouges, Joseph Drouhin, Jaffelin, Faiveley; Côte de Beaune: Bonneau du Martray, Lafarge, Mussy, Château de Chorey, Leflaive, Sauzet, Pothier Rieusset, Domaine de la Pousse d'Or, Domaine Bachelet, Ramonet, Comtes Lafon, Joseph Drouhin, Leroy, Chartron & Trébuchet, Michelot-Buisson, Louis Jadot.

different wines, ranging from the poor (badly made and/or from the flattest parts) to the sublime (well made, generally from the slopes). But every drop is *Grand Cru*. Confusingly, there is also an *Appellation* for Vougeot wine made outside the walls, 90 per cent of which is classified as *Premier Cru*. Good Clos de Vougeot ought to be soft and velvety with the flavours of ripe raspberries and plum. The château itself, which looks just like a ship sinking in a sea of vines, is worth visiting too, either by day to see its old presses, or by night when the local order of wine enthusiasts, the Chevaliers de Tastevin, dress up in mock medieval costumes for one of their banquets.

There isn't a lot of village at Flagey-Echézeaux – a few houses, a great café/restaurant and a church – and it's in the wrong place, down on the flat land, a fair distance from its *Grand Cru* Echézeaux and Grands Echézeaux vineyards up on the slopes. Both produce tiny amounts of gloriously rich, raspberryish, plum-flavoured wine with more than a hint of spice. They can be among the more affordable *Premiers Crus*, except when they are made by the Domaine de la Romanée-Conti, Burgundy's equivalent of Château Pétrus. Hidden away in a modest building in the heart of Vosne-Romanée, this is the shrine to which well-heeled Burgundy lovers flock to worship – and buy. Less-well-heeled enthusiasts merely stand and stare at the domaine's minuscule *Grand Cru* Romanée-Conti vineyard. If you want to taste that wine, you have to buy it from the domaine, where a bottle would cost you at least a week's wages. You can, however, discover the juicy, blackberryish flavour of Vosne-Romanée's wines a little more cheaply by going for a village wine, or one of the *Premier Crus* such as Beaux Monts, Suchots and Chaumes.

If you find yourself enjoying a glass of young Nuits-St-Georges, beware – it is unlikely to be a really good one. This is like Fixin with class; tough, broody wine that usually needs at least five years to soften. But when they do, the mulberry-and-plum wines of Nuits itself, or the ones made at Prémeaux just down the Côte – also sold as Nuits-St-Georges – are among the best buys in Burgundy. Nuits has no *Grands Crus*. This is an injustice; examples of Les St Georges, Les Vaucrains and Les Pruliers all regularly outclass plenty of *Grand Cru* Corton – about which more later.

As you leave Prémeaux, past the marble quarries which reveal the limestone lying beneath the soil, you leave the big-name villages of the Côte de Nuits and pass through a tract of Côte de Nuits-Villages before imperceptibly crossing the border into the Côte de Beaune, just south of the village of Corgoloin.

The Côte de Beaune

Like its Côte de Nuits counterpart, Côte de Beaune-Villages is a rag-bag *Appellation* for wine produced almost throughout this half of the Côte d'Or. Unlike the Côte de Nuits, however, it only covers red wines, despite the fact that this bit of Burgundy is where all of the best whites are made; white wines that ought to be sold as Côte de Beaune-Villages are stuck with plain Bourgogne Blanc. The hillside *Appellation*, Hautes-Côtes de Beaune, does include wines of both colours – or rather all three, because a little light, raspberryish *clairet* and *rosé* is made here. All are pleasant in warm years, and lean in cool ones.

The first Côte de Beaune village is Ladoix-Serrigny, whose unfamiliar wines are usually sold as Ladoix. They actually *taste* as though they are made on the border; they combine some of the gentle, raspberryish flavours of Beaune with the toughness of Nuits-St-Georges, but in rather a rustic way. With time they can, however, sometimes outclass some of the less impressive wines from its neighbour Aloxe-Corton.

A village that is quite literally in the shadow of its *Grands Crus*, grown in vineyards which extend rather too far around the hill of the Corton itself, Aloxe (pronounced "Aloss")-Corton makes red wines that, like those of Nuits-St-Georges, can take forever to come round. The better examples of the *Grands Crus* Corton, Corton-Vergennes, Corton Bressandes *et al* (there are 21 different bits of the Corton vineyard) do eventually develop glorious richness of flavour; others remain perpetually comatose. The more reliably exciting wine is the white Corton-Charlemagne – made in, it is implausibly said, vineyards that belonged to the emperor and were named after him, following his conversion from red to white wine by his wife who complained at the undignified red stains on his snowy imperial beard.

If Aloxe-Corton makes tough wine, the little-known *Appellation* of Chorey-lès-Beaune, (*lès*, by the way, is old

The town of Nuits-St-Georges, the centre of the Côte de Nuits

Burgundian for "near") produced from grapes grown on the flat land on the east of the *nationale,* is a place to look for lovely, soft, raspberryish Pinot Noir which, drunk young, is one of the region's classiest bargains.

Back in the hills, Pernand-Vergelesses also produces soft, approachable reds, some of which can be so soft that they taste a bit too much like damson jam and make you wonder if their makers are not over-compensating for the tough Cortons most of them produce from the part of that *Grand Cru* vineyard that strays into their village. The best wine here is the white, which can be very distinguished – hazelnutty and buttery, sometimes with a hint of the quality of the Corton-Charlemagne many of its producers make too. Les Vergelesses and Ile des Vergelesses are the best *Premiers Crus.*

The village of Savigny-lès-Beaune is just beneath Pernand-Vergelesses and has a good *Premier Cru,* Les Basses Vergelesses. Red Savigny can be – and often is – like a classier version of Chorey-lès-Beaune (several estates make both), with lovely, ripe, blackberryish, mulberryish sweetness, but some examples are rather too jammy for their price. There is very little white wine made here, but it's worth looking out for – and unusual in being made from the Pinot Blanc, a variety usually associated with Alsace.

From just above Savigny-lès-Beaune, you can see the old walled town of Beaune, its church and its most famous building, the Hospice at which, every November, wines of the most recent vintage from various Côte de Beaune vineyards (and one Côte de Nuits plot) are auctioned in aid of the town's hospital.

Like Nuits-St-Georges, Beaune has no *Grands Crus;* also like that *Appellation,* it has at least three contenders in Theurons, Grèves and Bressandes. None really fits the mould of *Grand Cru* Côte de Nuits wines, however, because these are far less "big" wines; they whisper rather than roar. A classic tasting note for a mature Beaune is of the smell of faded roses and the flavour of wild raspberries and honey.

Perhaps because most of Burgundy's best-known merchants have their cellars in a rabbit warren beneath the town, and more crucially because they almost all have large vineyard holdings here and so are often making wine from their own grapes, Beaune remains one of the most reliable labels in Burgundy. A tiny amount of white Beaune is made too; it tastes a little like a leaner version of Meursault.

Apart from the *Appellation* of Beaune itself, there is the tiny anomaly called simply Côte de Beaune that includes a small set of vineyards in the hills overlooking the town. Often quite understandably confused with Côte de Beaune-Villages, Côte de Beaune can be good value.

Pommard is a little like Gevrey-Chambertin, a well-known village too much of whose wine comes from the wrong side of the *nationale,* except that here any grapes that cross the road do so illegally. Good Pommard, like Aloxe-Corton, is sturdy stuff. Like Aloxe-Corton, these wines need time and sensitive wine-making to bring out the plummy fruit that's hiding behind all that muscle. The best *Premiers Crus* are Les Epenots, Les Rugiens and Les Arvelets.

Many of Pommard's growers produce prettier wine a few yards further south in Volnay, a village that can make some of the greatest red Burgundy of all. The *Premier Cru* Les Santenots – which, confusingly, is actually in Meursault – should be a *Grand Cru,* but it too rarely dazzles as most Côte de Nuits *Grands Crus* are expected to, because of a lightness of touch, attributable to its very, very shallow topsoil and deep limestone. The best Volnay combines ripe plums and violets; the Côte de Beaune's counterpart to Vosne-Romanée, with which it is often confused.

On the same hillside, you next arrive in the village of Monthélie, which makes little-known wines that used to be sold as Volnay. Tasting them, you can see why it was subsequently decided to sell these more rustic wines under their own name, but they still often offer good value. The rare whites can be tasty too.

Auxey-Duresses is a victim of its hard-to-pronounce name (as elsewhere round here the "x" sounds like "ss"). Prices are often lower for well-made whites than they are for fairly basic Meursault, but the quality is more variable, as much because of a lack of care by the wine-growers, as because of the poor siting of some of the vineyards. The reds, which make up a quarter of the wine, can be good and juicy, but rarely delicate.

Further up in the hills, among the Hautes-Côtes de Beaune, St Romain is a glorious place to picnic and watch hungry birds circling over the vines. The reds can be fruitily appealing, but only in warm years; in cool ones, the grapes don't ripen well. The whites are better, in their lean way – provided they aren't over-exposed to the new oak barrels made by the village success-story, Jean François, most of whose toasty casks end up being used for the Californian and Australian Chardonnays that are big enough to handle them.

The wine many of those New-World wine-makers really want to make is Meursault. They just love the fat, buttery, hazelnutty style of this wine, but sometimes miss the point that Meursault shouldn't just be buttered toast and oak; it should also be about subtlety and complexity. For these qualities, sidestep the obvious appeal of most village Meursault and the immediately seductive Charmes (these names do mean something) and try the *Premiers Crus* Genevrières, Goutte d'Or and Perrières, all of which could be *Grands Crus* if Meursault had any. Incidentally, if Meursault's *Premiers Crus* are undervalued, so are some of its village wines, many of which proudly print their non-*Premier Cru* names on their labels. Red Meursault is a rare oddity, but try some if you get the chance – it can be like drinking liquidized wild raspberries; pure Pinot Noir.

Puligny-Montrachet and Chassagne-Montrachet *do* have *Grands Crus* of their own – but they have to share the small plot of land that gave them their name. The 18.5-acre (7.5-ha) Le Montrachet vineyard, and its oddly named neighbours – Bâtard (bastard) Montrachet; Bienvenue Bâtard (welcome bastard) Montrachet; Criots Bâtard (cries of the bastard) Montrachet and Chevalier (Knight) Montrachet – can produce the greatest dry white wine in the world. The flavour is almost impossible to describe, an explosive marriage of ripe, peachy, appley, peary fruit, butter, roasted nuts, digestive biscuits and honey. Drink it when it's at least 10 years old.

Tasting village or *Premier Cru* wine from Puligny- or Chassagne-Montrachet alongside one of the *Grands Crus* is a little like looking at a black-and-white photograph next to a colour one, especially since worldwide popularity has allowed greedy *vignerons* to overproduce. Even given good examples, telling a Puligny-Montrachet from a Chassagne-Montrachet can be tricky; as a rule, the latter is toastier in style and the former is slightly more floral. Both tend to be ferociously priced.

Red Chassagne-Montrachet (around half the production) can be good, if rarely delicate, but beware disappointing examples forced on to merchants by producers who refuse to offer their white to anyone who won't take the red too.

Slightly off the beaten track, close to the village of Gamay – said to be the birthplace of the Beaujolais grape – St Aubin is one white-wine-producing village it may be unwise to mention. That is because the secret of this commune's nutty, buttery wines should not be spread too far. When well made, they can show up a Meursault, Chassagne or Puligny – for a far lower price. The reds (of which there are far more) are a little less impressive, but can still be good value.

Santenay is the last important commune on the Côte. The reds here from the *Premiers Crus* Clos Tavannes, Gravières and Commes can be good, straight-down-the-line wines, but too many Santenays are a bit dull and earthy. The whites are, if anything, less impressive, but Santenay is worth a visit – by anyone who fancies a flutter at the casino or a dip in the spa. Beyond Santenay, Dézize-les-Maranges, Sampigny-les-Maranges and Cheilly-les-Maranges unaccountably share their own Maranges *Appellation* and even some *Premiers Crus*. Sensible producers, however, sell their often rather basic wine as Côte de Beaune-Villages.

SOUTHERN BURGUNDY

As you drive away from the Côte d'Or and into the Côte Chalonnaise just outside the small town of Chagny, past the three-star Lameloise restaurant, you cross the invisible border that separates "smart" Burgundy from the rest.

But 'twas not ever thus. This is a region of might-have-been places. Tourists flock to the magnificent medieval abbey of Cluny – but it's a ruin; the town of Autun was intended, Brasilia-like, by the Romans to be a "Rome of the West"; today, all that remains is the Forum and bits of an amphitheatre. As for Chalon-sur-Saône itself, its industrial heyday is long past.

To an eighteenth-century Frenchman, though, names like Mercurey, Rully and Givry would have rung louder bells than some of today's superstar villages of the Côte d'Or. Henri IV, the French king who made the name of Sancerre's wines, was a particular fan of Givry; his mistress lived there. The *négociants* of Beaune, Nuits-St-Georges and Mâcon have always treated the Côte Chalonnaise rather as though it were their mistress: a region to be taken advantage of and not referred to in public. And their attitude was understandable. This area has always been a good minor source (20 per cent of the crop) of Chardonnay and Aligoté and more plentiful red Burgundy, almost all of which (even the humblest Bourgogne Rouge) is grown on hillsides.

In the mid-1980s, as prices rose for the wines of the Côte d'Or, bargain-hunters inevitably began to head south. Today, a decent bottle from the Côte Chalonnaise costs as much as many a bottle from smarter villages up north. There is, however, one style of Côte Chalonnaise wine with which the Côte d'Or cannot easily compete. The Aligoté, Burgundy's secondary white grape, has, since 1979, had its very own *Appellation* in the shape of Bourgogne Aligoté de Bouzeron. The village of Bouzeron, northernmost commune of the region, is a perfect place to discover how good this light, lemony variety can be.

Rully is not so much little-known as almost unknown outside the region. Which is a pity, because this village – whose vines were planted by the Romans – makes Chablis-like Chardonnay, pleasantly plummy and rather "pretty" Pinot Noir, and a large quantity of good

Crémant de Bourgogne fizz. Rully's wines used to be sold under the name of the far larger, more southerly commune of Mercurey, a quiet town whose historic credentials are confirmed by the presence of a Roman temple dedicated to the messenger of the gods from whom it took its name.

It was traditionally said that there were three types of Mercurey: for masters, for servants and for washing horses' hooves – and, until quite recently, the masters took little interest in it. Today, however, it is increasingly acknowledged that the tiny quantity of this buttery white can compete with Meursault, while the beefier red can put some Pommard to shame.

Givry used to be thought the equal of wines from the Côte d'Or. Well, perhaps... Its jammy, easy-drinking reds can match some of the less exciting stuff from Pernand-Vergelesses, but it's a far cry from Beaune or Volnay – but then again, so is the price. There is a tiny amount of white wine made; for the most part, nutty, up-market Bourgogne Blanc.

For good white, travel a little further to the hillside village of Montagny where they make nothing else. Of at least basic Chablis quality, though with a slightly nuttier, more buttery richness, this is another good buy. But don't get taken in by the words *"Premier Cru"* on the label; they only indicate a higher natural alcohol level. Montagny is the southernmost *Appellation* of the Côte Chalonnaise, but in the unrecognized village of Buxy, the go-ahead co-operative produces large quantities of good Bourgogne Rouge, including some that has been matured in new oak.

The Mâconnais

The Mâcon region has one of the longest-established wine traditions in Burgundy. Ausonius, the Roman poet who was born in Bordeaux, wrote about it in the fourth century and, in 1660, a grower called Claude Brosse travelled to Versailles and introduced it to the court. Brosse, it is said, was a giant who was noticed in church by the king when, because of his height, he appeared not to be kneeling.

In Brosse's day – and even in the last century – the region was three times as big as it is today. Now, it's very varied in its agriculture; the fields surrounding the savage

Château de Rully in the Côte Chalonnaise. Wines from this area can be bargains compared to the stars of the Côte d'Or

SOUTHERN BURGUNDY

What to look for From the Côte Chalonnaise, better than average "basic" Bourgogne Rouge and Blanc, and good if rarely complex village wines. From the Mâconnais: mostly run-of-the-mill whites and rustic reds, though the best village wines can be as good as some Côte de Beaune examples.

Official quality AOCs: Crémant de Bourgogne; Bourgogne Passetoutgrains; Bourgogne Aligoté de Bouzeron; Givry; Mercurey; Montagny; Mâcon; Mâcon-Villages; Mâcon + village name (may be used by 42 specified villages, e.g. Mâcon-Viré, Mâcon-Lugny, Mâcon-Clessé); Pouilly-Fuissé; Pouilly-Loché; Pouilly-Vinzelles; St-Véran; Rully.

Style Dry whites are soft, but with good acidity, and can achieve a fair degree of richness in good years and in the hands of the right producer. For example. the intense, richly flavoured Château Fuissé Vieilles Vignes, with its delicious creamy-vanilla and honey aromas, can match many whites from the Côte d'Or. Virtually no sweet

white is produced, though Jean Thevenet has made small quantities of a botrytized white at Mâcon in hot years. Reds are – at best – generally light-bodied with soft raspberry fruit; white Mâcons from named villages have greater depth and complexity and should, but often do not, offer excellent value.

Climate Drier than the Côte d'Or, these more southerly regions enjoy some Mediterranean influences.

Cultivation Gentle rolling hills with clay, alluvial and iron deposits covering a limestone subsoil. All the red vines of the Côte Chalonnaise are planted on hillsides.

Grape varieties Pinot Noir, Gamay, Aligoté and Chardonnay.

Production/maturation Similar to the Côte de Beaune in that the very top whites are barrel-fermented. Most, though, are fermented in stainless steel and bottled early to retain acidity and freshness. Reds are vinified using the

macération carbonique technique.

Longevity Whites: Mâcon-Villages and lesser wines: up to 4 years. Montagny, Mercurey, Rully, Pouilly-Fuissé: 4–12 years; Reds: Mâcon-Villages and lesser wines: up to 6 years. Mercurey, Rully, Mercurey Premiers Crus: 5–15 years.

Vintage guide Reds: 83, 85, 88, 89, 90, 92, 93. Whites: 85, 88, 89, 90, 91, 92, 93.

Top 29 Aligoté de Bouzeron: A & P Villaine, Chanzy; Mercurey: Faiveley, Antonin Rodet, Juillot, de Suremain;
Rully: Jadot, Antonin Rodet, Chanzy, Cogny, Domaine de la Folie; Givry: Joblot, Thénard; Montagny: Louis Latour, Michel, Vachet; Mâconnais: Jean Thevenet, Georges Duboeuf, Louis Latour, André Bonhomme, Henri Goyard, Château de Viré;
Pouilly-Fuissé: Château Fuissé/Marcel Vincent, Domaine Ferret, Luquet, Noblet, Guffens-Heynen, Léger-Plumet;
St Véran: Corsin, Lycée Viticole.

hill of Solutré, over which primitive man chased hundreds of horses in religious ritual, are now inhabited by goats and creamy-white Charolais cattle. The main style here used to be dull red, made from the Gamay, but without using the *macération carbonique* technique. Today, however, two-thirds of the vineyards have been given over to Chardonnay. Mâcon Blanc and the rather better Mâcon-Villages are many people's idea of affordable white Burgundy. Both these wines can be perfectly pleasant but, made in large quantities by 15 co-operatives, they are rarely exciting – and they still cost Burgundian prices.

Ignore the suffix "*Supérieur*" which merely refers to the wine's strength. Look instead for Mâcons from communes such as Lugny, Prissé and Viré and Chardonnay (the last thought to be the grape's birthplace), which can tack their names onto the Mâcon *Appellation*, and particularly Clessé, where the Domaine de la Bongran produces extraordinary Sauternes-style, late-harvest Chardonnay. The wines of St-Véran should be a cut above these Mâcon villages, but they're not.

A relatively recent *Appellation*, created as an alternative for wines which might otherwise call themselves Beaujolais Blanc, this is often seen as a cheaper alternative to Pouilly-Fuissé. It can indeed outclass poor Pouilly-Fuissé, but can't compete with one that's half-way good. Pouilly-Fuissé's problem (the inhabitants wouldn't call it a problem) is its inexplicable ease of pronunciation by Anglo-Saxons. At its best, made and oak-aged at the Château Fuissé or Domaine Ferret, its wines do deserve their international fame and Meursault-level prices; they can be wonderfully ripe, at once peachy and nuttily spicy – and quite "serious". Far too much, however, is made in bulk to be sold to people who don't notice that they are paying through the nose for stuff that tastes no better than Mâcon-Villages.

Bargain hunters are often pointed toward the wines of Pouilly-Vinzelles and Pouilly-Loché, but the harvest of both *Appellations* is unambitiously vinified by the Loché co-operative and sold as Pouilly-Vinzelles, whichever commune the grapes come from. The style and quality is like that of St-Véran.

Château Mâcon is almost hidden by the trees that surround it and the nearby buildings that are almost as tall

BEAUJOLAIS

I have a sure-fire way of spotting a wine snob – just ask him what he thinks of Beaujolais. If his nose turns up by as much as a millimetre, you know that you're talking to a label-lover, to someone who cares more about what the wine is called than about the way it tastes. Because that's what Beaujolais – and most especially Beaujolais Nouveau, the target of some of the sniffiest disdain – ought to be all about: taste. It should quite simply be the tastiest, fruitiest red wine of them all, stuff for gulping back by the chilled glassful and enjoying without snobbery or inhibitions.

But Beaujolais has been misunderstood for a long time. For over 200 years, from the time vines were first planted on the gentle hills of this region in the seventeenth century, this was a wine that rarely saw a bottle; it was driven up to Lyon in a cart and shipped up to Paris by river and canal, to be drawn directly from the barrel and served from jugs over the zinc-topped bars of cafés in both cities.

It was when it reached other countries that Beaujolais was found wanting; this purple-red cherry juice was nothing like what British, Belgian and Dutch wine-drinkers thought of as "real" wine. It wasn't alcoholic enough, it was too vibrantly fruity, and its colour was wrong.

So, they – or the merchants from whom they were buying the Beaujolais – turned it into "real" wine, quite simply by dosing it up with a good dollop of red from North Africa or the Rhône. Served at room temperature, from a bottle with a label, Beaujolais became just another soft, anonymous red.

Its proud producers quite naturally took exception to this "everyday" image. In the 1960s, the drum-beats of revolution were heard when the wine-makers, co-operatives and merchants of the region, led by pioneers like Georges Duboeuf, began to take control of their wine – and their destiny.

For many people, it took some time to get used to the new style, and to the idea that it was, and still is, best drunk young and chilled. It is quite possible that the flavour would never have really caught on, but for the invention of a marvellous marketing gimmick: Beaujolais Nouveau.

For around 20 years, this instant release of wine made from grapes picked a few weeks earlier has focused international attention on the region's wine and enabled producers to raise prices to levels way above those asked for basic Bordeaux. Today, thanks in part to those prices, the novelty of Nouveau has worn thin: at one time half the region's wine was sold in this form, now it's a still impressive one bottle in three.

The Styles

Beaujolais is the basic stuff, well over half of which is sold within weeks of the harvest as Beaujolais Nouveau or Primeur, which is exactly the same as any other kind of Beaujolais but made to be ready to drink early. After New Year's Eve, wine merchants and producers can legally relabel any unsold Nouveau or Primeur as plain Beaujolais. Wines labelled Beaujolais-Villages come from vineyards surrounding a select group of better-sited communes; they are usually worth their slightly higher price. Some Beaujolais-Villages Nouveau is also made and this, too, is usually a cut above plain Nouveau.

Beaujolais Blanc is very rare – for the simple reason that most is quite legally sold as St-Véran. Whatever the label, this is pleasant Chardonnay; a tad better than most Mâcon-Villages.

The Cru Villages

These 10 communes make better wine than the Beaujolais villages further north. There are no *Premiers Crus* within

An old mill in Beaujolais, where the wine is light, juicy red

these communes, but there are quite certainly vineyards with their own characteristics; just compare a Fleurie La Madone with one from the Pointe du Jour.

Similarly, wine-making styles vary, from wines that are light, fruity and made for immediate consumption to fuller-bodied, longer-vatted, traditionally fermented wines which seem to want to be taken as seriously as Burgundy.

Chiroubles is classically the lightest Beaujolais *cru* and the one to offer at any blind tasting as the best example of what young Beaujolais is supposed to be. But drink it young. Wonderfully named, Fleurie really can smell and taste the way you'd imagine a wine made from a bowlful of flowers immersed in plenty of cherry juice.

Another glorious name – taken from that of a Roman centurion – is St Amour, as romantic as it sounds, though it's a surprisingly little-known *cru*.

Brouilly is less exciting – up-market Beaujolais-Villages sold at Beaujolais *cru* prices. The vineyards are too big, too flat and too far south to compete with the best. Better to spend just a little more on Côte de Brouilly, produced on the volcanic hillside in the middle of the Brouilly vines; it's just as fruity, but richer and longer-lasting.

Regnié is controversial because it was only recently promoted to *cru* status. Some examples do support its case for promotion, but more taste like good Beaujolais-Villages, the label under which it was previously sold. Chénas has never been an easy sale – indeed much of the small amount of wine made here has, in the past, legally been sold by Beaune merchants as Bourgogne Rouge. Its style is – for a Beaujolais – rather tough, particularly when young.

Juliénas isn't immediately seductive but, like Chénas, can be an ugly duckling that needs three years or so to develop into a splendid swan.

There isn't a village of Moulin à Vent, but there is still a windmill. The vineyards make some of the richest, most "serious" wines in the region. Drink a bottle at two or three years old and you'll enjoy its cherryish, chocolatey flavour.

Another "big" Beaujolais, Morgon, has even given its name to a verb – *morgonner* – which describes the way the wine develops a cherry-ish flavour that, with time, really does vaguely resemble wine from the Côte de Nuits.

Just to the south of the Beaujolais, there are the Coteaux du Lyonnais, which produce lightweight versions of that region's wines and some pleasant, fruity rosé.

THE ESSENTIALS
BEAUJOLAIS

What to look for Fresh, fruity reds with vibrant cherry fruit.

Official quality AOCs: Beaujolais; Beaujolais Supérieur; Beaujolais-Villages; Coteaux du Lyonnais. There are 10 named cru villages – Brouilly; Chénas; Chiroubles; Côte de Brouilly; Fleurie; Juliénas; Morgon; Moulin-à-Vent, Regnié; St Amour.

Style Reds are soft, full of attractive, juicy raspberry fruit with smooth, supple character and fresh acidity. Generic Beaujolais, made by the macération carbonique method, has a characteristic "pear-drop" aroma. Cru wines are firmer, more complex and compact. White Beaujolais is rare; the best – often sold as St-Véran – is dry and peachy.

Climate A temperate continental climate with temperatures and rainfall that are ideal for wine-growing, although the influence of the Mediterranean leads to the occasional storm and problematic hail.

Cultivation Traditional, on rolling hills of granite-based soils. Vines are "spur-trained" following a single main branch for plain Beaujolais; villages and cru vines follow the "gobelet" bush pattern and the fruit is generally hand-harvested.

Grape varieties The dominant red grape is the Gamay; Pinot Noir may be used in cru wines, though it never does as well here as it does further north. Whites are from the Chardonnay.

Production/maturation The macération carbonique method is widely used although cru Beaujolais producers frequently employ traditional vinification methods. Experiments are now being carried out with new oak for the crus by go-ahead producers like Duboeuf.

Longevity Generic Beaujolais – including Nouveau – is intended for early consumption (within two years). Crus are capable of ageing for up to 10 years – up to 15 in great vintages like 1983 and 1985. With age, these wines become more Burgundian in style – but seldom, it must be said, like terribly good Burgundy.

Vintage guide 85, 88, 89, 90, 94, 95, 97, 98.

Top 22 Georges Duboeuf, Château de la Plume, Domaine Jambon, Domaine Labruyère, Louis Tête, Château des Jacques, Jacques Depagneux, Chanut, Sylvain Fessy, Eventail, André Large, Jean Garlon, Champagnon, Janodet, Foillard, Château du Moulin à Vent, La Tour du Bief, Trichard, Chauvet, Charvet, Hospices de Beaujeu, Château des Tours.

THE LOIRE

If someone were handing out prizes for Most Half-Understood Region in France, the Loire would get the nomination. How many diners in smart restaurants, ordering an obligatory Sancerre to go with their monkfish, know that they could have had the pigeon instead – and washed it down with a red Sancerre, made from the same grape as Nuits-St-Georges? How many Nouveau fans realize that there are wine-makers in the Loire using the Gamay to make red wines that could make some Beaujolais blush? How many restaurateurs offer sweet white Loires as alternatives to their Sauternes?

The best way to explore the Loire is to get in a car at Nantes in Muscadet country, and to head along the river toward Sancerre. At the end of a long and somewhat tortuous journey, you'd have tasted wines made from the Chardonnay, the improbably named Melon de Bourgogne, the Chenin Blanc, the Sauvignon Blanc, the Pinot Noir, the Gamay, the Cabernet Franc and the Malbec. In other words, you'd have discovered wines that are directly related to Champagne, to red and white Burgundy, to Bordeaux and Cahors, but all with their own distinctive styles. Some, like most of the Muscadet produced nowadays, are wines to be taken more or less for granted; others, like Savennières and dry Vouvray, can be among the most exciting – and demanding – in the world.

MUSCADET

If Muscadet has a red cousin, it has to be Beaujolais. Both are light, easy-going and perfect to drink within a few months of the harvest, and they've both come a

An old grape press in Muscadet, retired from active duty and doing a good job of advertising its owner's name

MUSCADET

What to look for Fresh, young, zingy white alternative to modern, "fruit-driven" Chardonnay and Sauvignon.

Location The Pays Nantais; a 40km sweep around Nantes encompassing the Loire estuary.

Official quality AOCs are: Muscadet; Muscadet Côtes de Grand Lieu; Muscadet de Sèvre et Maine (which, though officially the best part of the region, actually covers 85 per cent of its overall area); Muscadet des Coteaux de la Loire. All may be bottled, and bear the designation, sur lie. VDQSs are: Gros Plant du Pays Nantais; Coteaux d'Ancenis and Fiefs Vendéens.

Style Whites are crisp and dry, light-bodied and modestly fruity, occasionally slightly pétillant. The best are bone-dry (but not tart), lemony and fresh.

Sur lie wines should have a yeasty, more complex character; Muscadet de Sèvre et Maine should be better than straight Muscadet. Coteaux d'Ancenis and Fiefs Vendéens reds and rosés are dry, light-to-medium-bodied, lively and often grassy.

Climate Maritime.

Cultivation On the flat land around Nantes mechanical harvesting has been introduced with ease. The vineyard area stretches away to the gentle Sèvre et Maine hills; soils are mainly sandy overlying schist and volcanic subsoils.

Grape varieties Primarily the white Muscadet (Melon de Bourgogne) and Folle Blanche (Gros Plant). Coteaux d'Ancenis and the Fiefs Vendéens use a mix of Loire and classic Bordeaux and Burgundian varieties for reds, rosés and whites.

Production/maturation Stainless steel is increasingly used for fermentation. Sur lie wines are aged on their lees – yeasts – until, traditionally, the February 15 following the harvest; the process by which the yeasts affect the wine's character is known as autolysis. Bottling is direct from the tank; new oak is very occasionally found.

Longevity Most of these wines are best young or in their first 2 years.

Vintage guide 94, 95, 96, 97, 98.

My Top 10 Bossard, Sauvion et Fils, Donatien Bahuaud, Luneau, Chéreau-Carré, Louis Métaireau, Marquis de Goulaine, Domaines de la Dimerie, Chasseloir, des Dorices.

---

long way from where they started out. A hundred years ago neither wine would have found its way into a bottle; Muscadet's the stuff Brittany fishermen and poor Montmartre artists would have been given by the jugful as basic "house white".

Since then, like Beaujolais, Muscadet has become an international star. Sometimes it's difficult to understand why. New Beaujolais tastes of a bowlful of fresh fruit, while Muscadet tastes of ... well, it's rather difficult to define precisely what it does taste of. Eventually, it is all too easy to fall back on the description of it as prototypical "dry white wine".

But Muscadet matured in a certain way can have its own, distinctive character. Most newly fermented white wine is removed from its lees – solid yeasts – as quickly as possible; good, typical Muscadet is left to sit for several months on this yeast, picking up a nutty, biscuity flavour and a slight fizz in the process. Unfortunately, until the rules were tightened up in the early 1990s, there were far more bottles of Muscadet which claimed to have been "*mis en bouteilles sur lie*" – bottled on their lees – than had the biscuity flavour those words theoretically ought to promise.

Like Beaujolais, there are a few key villages that make better, more characterful wine than the surrounding area. Unlike Beaujolais, they don't feature helpfully on the labels as *crus*. So, as elsewhere in France, it is essential to look for the name of the producer. But if you've got a plate of fresh Atlantic oysters in prospect, it's worth taking the trouble; good, fresh, young Muscadet will do them far more justice than many a smarter Chardonnay or Sauvignon.

And if you're in France and you want something even simpler with which to wash down your seafood, you could always save a few francs by buying the Nantes region's lesser white, Gros Plant. This bone-dry VDQS, made from the Folle Blanche, is generally even less fruity than the Muscadet. When well made *sur lie*, however, it can give some stale Muscadets a run for their money.

Other regional VDQS wines include the light red, rosé and white Coteaux d'Ancenis, often made from the Gamay, the Pinot Gris (here called the Malvoisie) and the Chenin Blanc (or Pineau de la Loire), and the Fiefs Vendéens, with its attractive dry rosé, Cabernet-influenced red and less dazzling dry white.

THE MIDDLE LOIRE

Anjou

Following the river Loire eastwards through a vinous no-man's-land surrounding the village of Ancenis, within a few miles you will be deep in the heart of one of the most abused wine *Appellations* in France – Anjou, the area that helped to give the colour pink such a bad name that the Californians had to rename their rosé as "white" or "blush".

In fact, Anjou Rosé is also a relatively modern invention, created in the twentieth century by wine-makers who found they were unable to sell their dry red wines.

In the Loire, though, the change of style must have come as a shock to those used to the red and white wines Anjou had been producing for nearly 2,000 years. In the sixteenth and seventeenth centuries the Dutch had developed a taste for the region's sweet whites. As buyers, they were evidently more quality-conscious than

The Loire Valley is dotted with fairytale châteaux that overlook both vineyards and river

some of today's customers for Anjou Rosé; in those days, the region's wines were divided into *vins pour la mer* (the stuff that was considered good enough for foreigners) and *vins pour Paris* (the dregs, kept back for the easy-going domestic market).

The innovative Bordeaux-born wine-maker Jacques Lurton proved that it is possible to make interesting dry Anjou Rosé, but even that effort displayed the hard-edged shortcomings of the Groslot grape. Pay a little more for the potentially far better Cabernet d'Anjou (one of the few rosés which genuinely does age), or the slightly lighter Cabernet de Saumur from just along the river. At their best, these pink wines are crunchily blackcurranty, as is Anjou Rouge when it is made from the Cabernet varieties. When Anjou Rouge is made from the Gamay, however, and by the same method as Beaujolais, the effort to match that more southerly wine rarely quite works – because neither climate nor soil suits the grape so well here. Look instead for Anjou-Villages, which can only be made from the Cabernets and can taste like good summer-picnic claret.

From Pink To White

Anjou Blanc provides a good introduction to the often difficult character of the Chenin Blanc. Throughout the region, modern wine-makers are learning to work with the Chenin, allowing the skins to remain in contact with the juice before fermentation or, in Anjou, adding a proportion of Chardonnay or Sauvignon Blanc to the blend. These wines range from bone-dry to intensely sweet and from dire to delicious; they can be inexpensive, fresh and clean tasting and a good showcase for the Chenin hallmarks of apple and honey. Pure Chenin Blancs of slightly higher quality are labelled Anjou Coteaux de la Loire; these can be good, cheaper alternatives to Vouvray.

For top-class sweet wines, though, turn your back on the Loire and visit a set of villages that face each other across the River Layon, surrounded by vineyards that produce rich, honeyed, semi-sweet-to-luscious Chenin appropriately called Coteaux du Layon. The best of these villages, Rochefort-sur-Loire, has a micro-

THE MIDDLE LOIRE

What to look for Honeyed late-harvest and dry Chenin Blanc whites; crunchy young Cabernet-based reds, some of which age surprisingly well; sparkling wines.

Location Surrounding the Loire River and its tributaries, particularly the Cher, largely between Angers and Tours.

Official quality AOCs: Anjou; Anjou Coteaux de la Loire; Anjou Gamay; Anjou Mousseux; Cabernet d'Anjou and Cabernet d'Anjou-Val-de-Loire; Rosé d'Anjou and Rosé d'Anjou Pétillant; Bonnezeaux; Bourgueil; Chinon; Coteaux de l'Aubance, Coteaux du Loire; Coteaux du Layon and Coteaux du Layon-Chaume; Crémant de Loire; Jasnières; Montlouis; sparkling Montlouis; Quarts de Chaume; Rosé de Loire; Saumur, Saumur Champigny, sparkling Saumur; Cabernet de Saumur, Coteaux de Saumur; Savennières; Savennières-Coulée-de-Serrant and Savennières-Roche-aux-Moines; St-Nicolas-de-Bourgueil; Touraine; Touraine-Amboise; Touraine-Azay-le-Rideau; Touraine-Mesland; sparkling Touraine; Vouvray; sparkling Vouvray. VDQSs and vins de pays: Cheverny; Coteaux du Vendômois; Valençay; Vin du Haut Poitou; Vin du Thouarsais. Vin de pays du Jardin de la France.

Style The Cabernet Franc produces cool reds which have clean, blackcurrant fruit and an appealing herbaceous freshness. The best are undoubtedly Chinon, Bourgueil and Saumur-Champigny. Though pleasant when young, these tend to need ageing to lose their early earthiness. The dry and medium white wines are generally light, fresh and for early consumption. Savennières and Jasnières have a stark acidity in youth but open out with age into rich and honeyed, yet still dry wines; Vouvray, Quarts de Chaume and Bonnezeaux are the best sweet styles, and again need ageing, often lasting for decades. Rosés, both dry and medium, can be appealing and very fruity, though many are over-sweetened and dull. The best sparkling wines – Saumur, Vouvray and Crémant de Loire – are soft and approachable but with good acidity.

Climate Influenced by the Atlantic, though less maritime than Muscadet. Warm summers and autumns and little rain.

Cultivation Crammed between fields full of other crops in this agricultural region, the best sites are south-facing on gentle slopes or terraced on steeper slopes, as in the schist soils of the Layon valley. Elsewhere, soils vary from chalk to clay overlying sand and gravel.

Grape varieties Arbois, Aligoté, Cabernet Franc, Cabernet Sauvignon, Chambourcin, Chenin Blanc (Pineau de la Loire), Chardonnay, Gamay, Grolleau/Groslot, Gros Plant, Malbec, Meslier, Pineau d'Aunis, Pinot Blanc, Pinot Gris, Pinot Meunier, Pinot Noir, Plantet, Romorantin, Sauvignon Blanc.

Production/maturation Though old wood is still used for fermentation and maturation, stainless steel and new oak are becoming more common. To make Bonnezeaux and Quarts de Chaume, Chenin grapes are left on the vines until late October to await noble rot. Fermentation takes at least 3 months and the wines are bottled the following October.

Longevity Lesser reds, dry and medium whites and rosé should be drunk within 3 years. Chinon, Bourgueil and St-Nicolas-de-Bourgueil will last at least 5 years. Sweet Bonnezeaux, Chaume and Layon and the dry Savennières and Jasnières will develop over a decade and beyond.

Vintage guide White: 76, 78, 82, 83, 85, 88, 89, 90, 93, 94, 95, 96, 97; Red: 78, 82, 83, 85, 88, 89, 90, 95, 96, 97.

Top 25 Anjou: Richou, Cailleau, Daviau, Ackerman-Laurance;
Savennières: Clos de la Coulée-de-Serrant, Roche aux Moines, Domaine Bizolière, Château Chamboureau;
Vouvray: Huët, Domaines des Aubuisières, Champalou, Foreau, Mabille;
Chinon: Olga and Jean-Maurice Raffault, Couly-Dutheil, Joguet;
Bonnezeaux: Renou, Château de Fesles;
Quarts de Chaume: Domaine Echarderie;
Coteaux de Layon: Vincent Ogereau, Domaine Jolivet;
Saumur: Bouvet-Ladubay, Gratin-Meyer, Langlois-Château, Filliatreau.

---

climate that allows the grapes to ripen almost every year, and sometimes to develop noble rot, thus producing a pair of more intense wines: Coteaux du Layon Chaume and Quarts de Chaume, which owes its name to the local lord who used to extort a quarter of the tiny harvests.

At their best, these wines are at once apricoty, rich and floral, with a surprisingly attractive hint of zesty bitterness; they can keep for at least 10 – more like 20 – years. Bonnezeaux (disconcertingly pronounced "Bonzo"), though often as well thought of, is rarely quite as good. The few great examples, however, are extraordinary honey-and-spice cocktails that last for decades. For a lower price than any of these, and built on a lighter scale, Coteaux de l'Aubance provides good, cellarable, *demi-sec* Chenin Blanc – but in small and diminishing quantities.

The sweet style of these wines was once shared by Savennières which is now made dry or *demi-sec*. It's "difficult" wine that can often taste bitterly like unripe limes until it has been given a decade or so to soften; of 15 producers, only five survive by making and selling wine alone. One of these, Nicolas Joly, proves what can be done here using biodynamic methods with his fruit-and-flower, dry Sauternes-like *Grand Cru* Coulée de Serrant, which slightly outclasses Savennières' other larger *Grand Cru*, La Roche aux Moines.

Saumur

Saumur once enjoyed the same prestige as Vouvray, but today neither the white nor the red produced under this *Appellation* is inspiring, and sparkling wine has become the focus of attention. Links with Champagne go back to 1811, when a wine-maker called Jean Ackerman, who had worked there, decided to use its techniques on grapes grown in the similarly chalky soil of his native Saumur. His wine was sold as Champagne; today the rules are stricter, yet Champagne houses like Bollinger and Taittinger own sparkling Saumur houses here, making fizz labelled until very recently with the now-banned words "méthode champenoise".

Even at its best, sparkling Saumur never really matches even the most modestly successful of Champagnes, largely because the Chenin Blanc and the red Cabernet grapes simply aren't as good at the job as the Chardonnay and Pinots. On the other hand, the quality is rarely less than adequate, thanks to the combination of the Chenin, the chalky soil and the cool(ish) climate. Coteaux de Saumur, Saumur's *Appellation* for its sweet wines, was once the priciest in the Loire, partly thanks to the enthusiasm of Edward VII, a loyal customer, and partly to the reputation of the curious Clos des Murs, a set of 11 100-metre-long walls along which vines were trained to obtain as much sheltered sunshine as possible. Today, sadly, examples are very, very rare, but the vineyard is still worth a visit.

Apart from its sparkling and still whites and pinks, Saumur also produces two reds, Saumur Rouge and Saumur Champigny. The former is rarely impressive Cabernet Franc-dominated stuff. Champigny, however, is much classier – either young, or after five years or so (though not between the two), this can be gorgeously crunchy, black-curranty wine. To taste Saumur Champigny at its best, look out for Filliatreau's Vieilles Vignes, made from old vines.

South of Saumur, in stark contrast to the small scale of some of the region's estates, there stands the Loire's biggest modern co-operative, the Cave du Haut Poitou. The success here has been the Sauvignon Blanc, a wine that has on occasion shown the potential to fight its corner against pricier examples from Sancerre, but it still never rises above workaday levels. The Chardonnay is less impressive, but there is a reliable *méthode champenoise* sparkling wine.

The modest and little-known VDQS, Vin du Thouarsais, similar in style to basic Anjou, but slightly cheaper, certainly deserves a backward glance as one crosses the frontier into the next of the Loire's major regions.

Touraine

If Touraine had no other claim to vinous fame, it would have been sure of a place in the history books because it was here that, according to local legend, St Martin invented vine-pruning, after discovering that he made better wine from vines that had been partially nibbled away by his donkey.

Today, the region owes much of the success of its blanket *Appellation* to the Oisly et Thesée co-operative whose *directeur*, Jacques Choquet, took the rare and brave step of enforcing a quality test for his member-growers' grapes. His audacity was all the more impressive given the ever-present financial temptations to the producers to uproot their vines and replace them with other crops. Oisly et Thesée Sauvignon and Chenin (here called Pineau de la Loire) are among the most reliably affordable whites in the region, and the blended reds are also worthwhile, thanks to the way in which the Cabernet is allowed to make up for the failings of the Malbec (here known as the Cot) and the Gamay. Experiments with Pinot Noir and sparkling wine are interesting too.

The Touraine vineyards cover around a tenth of the land they would have occupied a century or so ago. It is a striking polyculture, with easy-to-grow, easy-to-sell strawberries, sun-flowers, asparagus and wheat all competing for space on level terms with vines. From a distance, the layers of gold, yellow and green crops make the countryside here look like nothing so much as a slice of vegetable terrine. The Touraine *Appellation* – and its three village *Appellations*, Azay-Le-Rideau, Amboise and Mesland – can produce fair to excellent dry and *demi-sec* Chenin Blanc and, in the case of Amboise, good, fruity Cabernet Franc.

Non-wine-buff visitors to the region are often unknowingly led by their guide books to the source of the Loire's best reds, Chinon, whose castle some readers may remember from the play or film of *The Lion in*

Winter. Almost all of Chinon's wines are red, combining – in ripe years – rich flavours of mulberry, blackberry and blackcurrant, with just a hint of earthiness. There is a little rosé and white, the latter made in a floral-spicy style said to have been popular with Rabelais.

Like Chinon, red Bourgueil is built to last and can take as long as a decade to soften. But in good vintages it's worth waiting for, delivering a real mouthful of wonderfully jammy damson and blackcurrant fruit. St-Nicolas-de-Bourgeuil is usually less impressive, less intense and less long-lived but can be more approachable than Bourgueil when young.

Vouvray

Before my first visit to Vouvray, I had never quite believed in the tales I had heard of the town's community of cave dwellers. But there they were – modern Frenchmen and women who not only make and store wine, but also live in homes burrowed deep into the sides of cliffs. Of course, these are twenty-first - century troglodytes, with video recorders, shiny new Citroëns and central heating flues channelled up through the chalk, but there is still something deeply traditional about their wines.

Vouvray comes in just about every white style you could want – and several you wouldn't. But whatever they are like – dry (*sec*), semi-sweet (*demi-sec*), sweet (*moëlleux*) or sparkling (*crémant*) – they provide an invaluable insight into what the Chenin Blanc is really like. And how difficult it is to get right. The dry style can have all the mean, cooking-apple character of the grape, while the *demi-sec* and *moëlleux* can be respectively honeyed and dull, and sweetly honeyed and dull. At its least successful, semi-sweet Vouvray can make you long for a glass of fairly basic Liebfraumilch.

Then, just as you decide to drive further west to Sancerre, you stop and have lunch at a little roadside restaurant, order a last bottle – and discover what the estate made famous by the mayor of the village, Gaston Huët (pronounced "wet"), or the Domaine des Aubuisiers can do with the Chenin Blanc. Suddenly both wine and grape make sense. These Vouvray *secs* have the rich, creamy texture of Chardonnay and the appley bite of the Chenin. The *demi-secs* are beautifully well balanced – sweet but

The Loire makes every style of wine, from red to sparkling

not cloyingly so – and the *moëlleux* have the luscious intensity of noble rot. All of these, but particularly the *moëlleux*, are made to last – "for 50 years or so" as they say in Vouvray.

Huët also makes great sparkling wine. Bubbles are very saleable around here – as the producers of nearby Montlouis have discovered to their delight. Turning their back on the still wines with which they made lighter, less acidic, less long-lived versions of Vouvray, they have switched to sparkling wine, so successfully that of the 4.2 million bottles of Montlouis made every year, only 700,000 come without bubbles.

Having come to terms with dry Chenin Blanc in Vouvray, you could put yourself to a further test with Jasnières, a wine that can be so bitingly acidic in cool years that only a masochist or a drinker with a palate lined with elephant hide could enjoy it. But, in warmer vintages, and – this is essential – given a decade or so in the bottle, Jasnières can be one of the most exciting, dry yet honeyed, wines of all.

Of the region's other wines, VDQS Chéverny can be good, lightly floral, still and sparkling white, despite the presence in the blend of the "characterful" Romarantin, which seems to work against the fresh appeal of the Sauvignon, Chenin and Chardonnay with which it shares the vat. Sales are growing fast, though this owes much to buyers confusing it with Chardonnay.

THE UPPER LOIRE

Wine can be as much of a victim of fashion as any reader of *Vogue* or *Vanity Fair*. It just takes a little longer. For most wine buffs, Sancerre and Pouilly are almost synonymous with the extraordinarily gooseberryish, blackcurranty, asparagusy Sauvignon Blanc. Wine-makers from around the world regularly make pilgrimages to this easternmost part of the Loire to marvel at the perfect marriage of grape, chalky soils and climate. A century or so ago, though, what they'd have found was a bulging rag-bag of red-wine grapes including lots of Pinot Noir – and a few acres of featureless Chasselas.

Today, Sancerre and Pouilly-Fumé have become world-famous, easy-option whites. But this newly acquired fashionability is already proving fragile. Over the last few years both wines have lost fans to the New World.

In the USA, people who find the Sauvignon's innate zinginess too "herbaceous" have opted for local efforts which often taste like understudy Chardonnays. Elsewhere, it has been the New Zealanders, South Africans, and cool-climate Australians that have become flavours of the month.

It's a pity because the best Loire Sauvignons ought to be packed with the same kind of zappy gooseberry fruit as the Sauvignons from New Zealand – but in a far less obvious way. Their steely backbone and complexity should make them more interesting to drink, long after the palate has tired of the simplicity of some of those New-World flavours.

The Loire classics have been handicapped by the readiness of the region's less commendable producers to produce dilute, over-sulphured, over-priced, soft, fat, dull versions of their wine – and by the authorities' preparedness to allow these travesties onto the market. The same authorities, mark you, who chose to obstruct one of Pouilly-Fumé's best producers, Didier Dagueneau, when he experimented with late-harvest versions of his organically produced wine. Perhaps they might have done well to read up a little of their local history and discover how well the Upper Loire has done out of the fashion pioneers of the past.

Sancerre

Sancerre is not so much a single *Appellation* as a collection of 14 villages with slightly differing versions of the same chalky soil, on varying slopes that surround the hill-top town itself. If this were Beaujolais, and if the inhabitants of these villages had their way, at least a few of them would be promoted to *cru* status. The strongest contenders for any such promotion are the village of Bué and a cluster of houses called Chavignol, locally famous for its little round goat's cheeses, Crottins de Chavignol, and for wines which would, it was said by the wine-loving French King Henri IV, if drunk by the entire populace, put an instant stop to religious wars. Chavignol's best wines come from its Les Monts Damnés, Clos Beaujeu and Clos du Paradis vineyards; Bué's finest vineyards are the Clos du Chêne Marchand and Le Grand Chemarin. Other villages worth looking out for include Champtin, Sury-en-Vaux, Reigny, Ménétréol and Verdigny.

Sancerre also makes small quantities of pink and red wines from its old mainstay, the Pinot Noir. The former are pleasant, raspberryish versions of the grape, but woefully overpriced, thanks – *again!* – to their fashionability in Paris restaurants; the latter have much of the style of good, basic Bourgogne Rouge, but with less stuffing.

Down on the Loire itself, the featureless town of Pouilly-sur-Loire still confuses even those wine-drinkers who know the difference between Pouilly-Fumé and Pouilly-Fuissé by using Chasselas grapes to produce an unmemorable wine called Pouilly-sur-Loire.

The "Fumé" in Pouilly-Fumé is said to come from the smoky dust from the grapes that hangs over the vineyards during the harvest or, more popularly, from the smoky flavour of the wine. The latter explanation is preferable; these wines really can taste as though they have spent a while in a salmon smokery. Some descriptions also refer to gun-flint and, even without having tasted any, you can see what they mean; this character is reckoned to come from the flintier, lighter clay content of some of Pouilly's best slopes. To taste the mixture of smoke and flint at its best, look for wines whose labels mention *silex*, the term for this kind of soil.

Pouilly-Fumé is said to be the Loire Sauvignon with the best potential for ageing – which really means that the wines here develop their flavours of asparagus rather more slowly. With rare exceptions, though this wine is better drunk, like Sancerre, within three years of the harvest.

The best of Pouilly's communes, and the ones you are most likely to see mentioned on labels, are Les Berthiers and Les Loges. For the quintessence of Pouilly-Fumé, splash out on a bottle of Didier Dagueneau's "Silex" or "Baron de L" from the Baron de Ladoucette's Château de Nozet. And remember their flavours the next time you taste a "Blanc-Fumé" from California or Australia; warm-climate Sauvignon Blanc plus new oak does not equal the sheer complexity of this variety grown in the cooler conditions and the best soil of the Loire.

Reuilly needs your support: its growers have to be encouraged to stop growing vegetables and to turn their attention back to the vines that used to cover this commune. Reuilly's soil is very similar to that of Sancerre or Pouilly-Fumé, and most of the vines are the same variety – the Sauvignon Blanc – so there seems little reason why its wines shouldn't be every bit as fine.

In fact, the slightly greater limestone content here makes for lighter, leaner wines that rarely have the richness of its more famous neighbours. What Reuilly can make, however, is that most unfashionable style, rosé, produced not (as in Sancerre) exclusively from the Pinot Noir, but with a generous dose of the pink-skinned grape known here as the Pinot Beurot and more readily found in Alsace, where it's called the Tokay-Pinot Gris.

The small (250-acre/l00-ha) *Appellation* of Menetou-Salon has the same *terre blanche* soil as Reuilly, and an even longer history; its growers proudly, yet wryly, point out that Menetou-Salon had its *Appellation* before any of its neighbours. Often, the wines taste rather rustic, but at their best they can be cheaper alternatives to good – but not great – Sancerre; the Pinot Noir reds are disappointing.

The wines of Orleans itself – the *vins de l'Orléanais* – were once thought equal to those of Beaune. Today they are less exalted, but the pale pink Pinot Meunier is a rare treat; the white Auvernat Blanc, however, is unimpressive. This is the local alias for the Chardonnay, though from tasting the wine you'd never guess.

Among the other lesser-known wines in this part of the Loire, the Côtes Roannaises and Côtes du Forez both make easy-going wines from the Gamay. St Pourcain Blanc is a weird blend of Chardonnay, Sauvignon and the oddly smoky Tressalier. It's very dry, and very much an acquired taste. Minuscule quantities of Gamay-Pinot Noir rosé are made too.

THE ESSENTIALS
THE UPPER LOIRE

What to look for Crisp, dry Sauvignons with the occasional light Pinot Noir red or rosé.
Location At the eastern end of the Loire Valley toward Burgundy: Sancerre and Pouilly-Fumé face each other across the river.
Official quality AOCs: Ménétou Salon; Pouilly-Fumé; Pouilly-sur-Loire; Quincy; Reuilly and Sancerre. VDQSs are: Châteaumeillant; Coteaux du Giennois; Côte Roannaise; Côtes d'Auvergne; Côtes du Forez; St-Pourçain-sur-Sioule; Vins d'Orléanais. Vins de pays: Coteaux du Cher et l'Arnon; Coteaux Charitois.
Style Classic Sancerre and Pouilly-Fumé rank among the most exciting Sauvignons in the world, with a smoky aroma and full of gooseberry and asparagus flavours. Bué, Chavignol, Les Loges,

Tracy and Les Berthiers are noted for quality. Lesser whites may capture a little of this style and are generally crisp, herbaceous and appealing. Do not confuse Pouilly-sur-Loire. a rather ordinary Chasselas, with Pouilly-Fumé. Red and rosé wines, from Sancerre, are quite Burgundian.
Climate Continental, with short, hot summers.
Cultivation Soils are mainly chalk and clay with a lot of limestone. The vineyards are on mainly south-facing, often steep, slopes, with other crops being grown on the opposite side of the valley. Picking is usually done by hand.
Grape varieties Aligoté, Cabernet Franc, Chardonnay, Chasselas, Chenin Blanc, Gamay Noir à Jus Blanc, Gamay, Pinot Gris, Pinot Meunier, Pinot Noir, Sauvignon Blanc, Tresallier.

Production/maturation Stainless steel is widely used, although some of the red wines spend up to 18 months in oak and Didier Dagueneau is experimenting with new oak for his whites.
Longevity Most wines are at their best within 3 years. Although the top wines will continue to develop. they may lose their initial freshness.
Vintage guide 95, 97, 98.
My Top 22 Sancerre: Vacheron, Alain and Pierre Dézat, Laporte, Jean Thomas, Bourgeois, Crochet, Gitton, Jean-Max Roger, Pinard, Jean Vatan, Henri Natter; Pouilly-Fumé: Didier Dagueneau, Château de Nozet (Ladoucette), Pabiot, Château de Tracy; Menetou-Salon: Domaine H Pellé, Teiller, de Chatenoy; Reuilly: Lafond, Beurdin; Quincy: Pichard, Rouzé.

THE RHONE

It's sometimes said that the French are a Latin people but, talking to some of the starchily mannered gentlemen of Bordeaux and Champagne, it's an idea that's very difficult to accept. And then you arrive back in the Rhône, the land of terracotta roof tiles, of fresh herbs growing at the roadside, of olive oil and garlic and ripe, tasty tomatoes, and you know you're in the land of the sun – savage country that must look just as it did when the Romans arrived.

The vineyards of the Rhône valley begin just beyond the southern suburbs of Lyon and follow the river south almost as far as the Mediterranean. But to talk of the Rhône as though it were a single region is misleading. Like the Loire, the river is more of a link between very different wine-making areas: in this instance, the northern and southern Rhône.

The essential differences between the two regions lie in the grape varieties, and the land in which they are planted. The north, like Burgundy, is a region in which wine-growers use just one kind of black grape – in this case, the smoky, brooding Syrah. With it they produce long-lived red wines such as Côte-Rôtie, Hermitage and Cornas, and their more approachable but still muscular neighbours, Crozes-Hermitage and St-Joseph.

If the wines are tough, so is making them; the vineyards are some of the most spectacular in the world, rivalling those of the Rhine and Douro in the way they cling to the perilously steep slopes that overlook the river as it snakes its way southward.

Down south, in the Côtes du Rhône-Villages (the more select area within the broad Côtes du Rhône *Appellation*), Gigondas and Châteauneuf-du-Pape, it is another grape, the peppery, berryish Grenache, that holds sway, but as the captain of a team that also includes the Mourvèdre, the Cinsault and, of course, the Syrah.

Here, as in Bordeaux, wine-makers have to be as skilled at the art of blending as they are at growing grapes. In some cases, for example in many Côtes du Rhônes, the Grenache is allowed to trumpet its presence in juicy-fruity reds that are almost indecently easy to drink. In Châteauneuf-du-Pape, on the other hand, the blender's art can be taken to absurd lengths, with a total of 13 permitted grapes to choose from. Very few producers use even half this number – one, Château Rayas, focuses almost exclusively on the Grenache – but, even with three or four to play with, they can make wonderful wine that takes you straight to the spice bazaar.

The flat vineyards of the south are different too, and they're a revelation. Until you see them, you would never believe that vines – or any plants for that matter – could grow in what looks just like the uncomfortable pebbles that cover some of Europe's least hospitable beaches.

But if the Rhône is best known for characterful reds (and for its readiness, in times gone by, to supply them to wine-growers in Burgundy and Bordeaux whose own wines needed a little body-building and "beefing-up"), it's also the place to find an extraordinary range of other styles. Muscat de Beaumes de Venise, now a favourite inexpensive alternative to Sauternes, comes from a village that makes good red Côtes du Rhône-Villages; Clairette de Die, a less pungently perfumed counterpart to Asti Spumante, comes from here too. So do the strange and wonderful creamy-spicy dry whites of Condrieu and the dry, peppery rosés of Lirac.

But ultimately the reds have always been the Rhône's strong suit. Unfortunately, in the past, too much of the wine was dull and disappointing; Châteauneuf-du-Pape, for example, once rivalled Beaujolais for the prize for best-known, worst-made red. The problem was that no one paid these wines much respect. Old-timers recalled the days when Hermitage sold for a higher price than the best Bordeaux, and when a dollop of their wine could raise the value of a barrel of Lafite – and shrugged their shoulders.

Today, though, the Rhône is back in fashion. The region's growers, merchants and co-operatives are tidying themselves up and, despite the size of the area – it's nearly 150 miles (240 km) long – and the amount it makes (over 200 million bottles of Côtes du Rhône each year), this has become one of the world's most reliable,

Harvesting Syrah grapes on perilously steep slopes in the northern Rhône. These vineyards are owned by Paul Jaboulet Aîné

good-value wine regions. And people have begun to notice.

America's wine guru, Robert Parker, is the author of what has been described as the "definitive" guide to Bordeaux. What would you find if you looked in his cellars – nothing but claret? No, they're packed wall-to-wall with Rhônes, red and white. And what kind of grape varieties are California's most pioneering wineries all falling over each other to plant? Yes, you guessed – Syrah, Viognier, Mourvèdre and Cinsault.

The prices of the best wines of the northern Rhône already reflect this growing success and popularity, but they're still rising fast. Buy now before everyone gets the taste for them. And stock up on a few dozen cheap bottles of Côtes du Rhône to enjoy while you wait for your brooding monsters to soften.

THE NORTHERN RHONE

It takes a couple of days to drive south from the quiet, riverside town of Vienne to the Mediterranean coast. Although it is probable that if you put your foot down on the *autoroute* you could do it in four or five hours. But if there's any romance in your soul, you won't be on the *autoroute*; you'll be following the broad Rhône on the old *route nationale* and you won't even be on that for long. No, you'll be forever heading off and up into the vineyards at almost every bend in the river.

The first temptation will strike on the west bank, on the sheer "roasted hillside" of Côte Rôtie. Only a masochist would ever have wanted to plant vines up here – but what else could anyone have done with this land? The men and women who prune the Syrah vines and harvest their grapes deserve every penny they can get for their wine, and not just for their talents as mountaineers. The 250 acres (100 ha) of vineyards here are very, very exposed. In the summer, as the sun blazes down, you soon learn how the Côte got its name – and then there's the 90 mph mistral wind and the winter frosts. But the efforts pay off. The flavour of the Syrah, tempered slightly by the addition of up to 20 per cent of the perfumed white Viognier grapes, is a cocktail of ripe, dark berries and wild flowers, with just a hint of woodsmoke.

The Viognier's role in red Côte Rôtie is generally unrecognized, but this curious variety gets the credit for the two white wines that are made, on similarly steep slopes, a little further down the river at Condrieu and Château-Grillet. The former *Appellation* is small at just 25 acres (10 ha), but the latter is tiny, with just six and a half acres (2.5 ha) of terraced vineyards. This diminutive size only partly explains Château-Grillet's astronomical price; the fact that there is only one producer (Château-Grillet) has some bearing too.

THE ESSENTIALS

NORTHERN RHONE

What to look for Big, rich, spicy, smoky Syrah reds and rich, perfumed whites.

What to buy Go for the big reds; they'll cost you but they're worth it. There are some good-value St-Josephs and Crozes-Hermitages too.

Location From Vienne, just below Lyons, to Valence in the south.

Official quality AOCs: Chatillon-en-Diois; Château Grillet; Clairette de Die; Condrieu; Cornas; Côtes du Rhône; Côtes du Rhône-Villages; Coteaux du Tricastin; Crozes-Hermitage; Hermitage; St-Joseph; St-Péray and St-Péray Mousseux.

Style Reds vary from the cheap and cheerful to the mighty – Hermitage and Côte Rôtie are two of France's greatest wines. Immensely tannic in youth, Hermitage matures into an approachable but serious wine, with a cocktail of rich fruit flavours and characteristic smokiness. Côte Rôtie is slightly softer but even smokier. (Look for wines from the best slopes, the Côtes Brune et Blonde.) More affordable, but still showing good Syrah character, are St-Joseph and Crozes-Hermitage. The white wines are dry and quite full in style. Condrieu, in particular, produces rich yet dry wines with an inviting tropical fruit aroma. Sweet, grapey sparkling Clairette de Die is infinitely superior to plain Crémant de Die.

Climate Continental, with hot summers and cold winters.

Cultivation Varied soil, but mainly granite. The vineyards are set into the steep slopes of the rocky hillsides, though some extend beyond.

Grape varieties Aligoté, Bourboulenc, Calitor, Camarèse, Carignan, Chardonnay, Cinsault, Clairette, Counoise, Gamay, Grenache, Marsanne, Mauzac, Mourvèdre, Muscardin, Muscat Blanc à Petits Grains, Pascal Blanc, Picardan, Picpoul, Pinot Blanc, Pinot Noir, Roussanne, Syrah, Terret Noir, Ugni Blanc, Vacarèse, Viognier.

Production/maturation Traditional methods prevail, with less emphasis on new oak.

Longevity Lesser whites should be drunk as young as possible and even the better white wines tend to peak before 5 years. Côtes du Rhône, Crozes-Hermitage and St-Joseph will be drinkable at 3 years but, as the quality of the wine increases, so does its ageing potential.

Vintage guide Reds: 78, 80, 82, 85, 88, 89, 90, 91, 95, 96; Whites: 78, 82, 83, 87, 88, 89, 90, 91, 96, 97.

Top 30 Hermitage: Jaboulet Aîné, Chapoutier, Guigal, Chave, Grippat, Delas, Sorrel, Desmeure, Gray;

Côte Rôtie: Jasmin, Jamet & Barge, Vidal-Fleury, Jaboulet Aîné, Guigal, Delas, Rostaing, Dervieux-Thaize, Georges Vernay, Burgaud, Champet;

Condrieu: de Rozay, Dumazet, Georges Vernay, Guigal;

St-Joseph: Chave, Coursodin, Grippat, Jaboulet Aîné, Co-op St-Désirat-Champagne;

Crozes-Hermitage: Guigal, Desmeure, Graillot, Tardy & Ange, Delas, Fayolle, Jaboulet Aîné;

Cornas: Clape, Juge, Guy de Barjac, Alain Voge, Colombo.

The advice would be to save some money and go for a Condrieu (particularly from Georges Vernay) which, judging by recent unimpressive vintages of Château-Grillet, will give you a better taste of the Viognier's weird aromatic perfume and peach, apple and cream cheese flavours. Try it, and you'll see just why all those Chardonnay-sated Californians are turning to it in their droves.

The *Appellation* of St-Joseph overlaps that of Condrieu or, to be more precise, runs along beneath it on the flat land by the river. Elsewhere, close to Tournon and Mauves, between Hermitage and Valence, it runs up into the hills on its way to Valence. It is in these hills that the best wines are made: spicy, peachy whites from Marsanne and Roussanne, and intensely blackcurranty, spicy ("spicy" can't help being an overworked word around here) reds from the Syrah. Most examples of St-Joseph are good; some are much more chunky and long-lived than others.

Hermitage

The next site of pilgrimage is Hermitage. Stand beside the huge statue of the Madonna in the hills here and you can see steep terraces dotted with long signs proclaiming the names of the region's biggest merchants: Jaboulet-Aîné, Chapoutier, Guigal... The tiny chapel high on the hill stands in the middle of Hermitage's most famous plot. Jaboulet-Aîné's "La Chapelle" vineyard produces one of the very best Hermitages. And the view from here at dusk is one of the most unforgettable sights in the vinous world.

Red Hermitage is usually made exclusively from the Syrah, though growers are allowed to add a little Marsanne and Roussanne, the grapes from which the *Appellation*'s white is made. Good red Hermitage is astonishing – classy, but raunchy too, combining just about every berry and spice you can imagine. There's tannin, but also a sweet ripeness; in all but the lightest years, you should allow these wines 10 or 15 years for flavours to develop.

White Hermitage is rarely as exciting an experience but, like the red, it too can need time. When young, it can taste dull and earthy but, given 10 years or so, the earthiness can miraculously turn into all kinds of floral, herby, peachy smells and flavours.

The easiest way to describe Crozes-Hermitage is that it is – usually – scaled-down Hermitage. The wine-making

Vines in Cornas, source of smoky, blackberryish reds

rules are the same, and so is the region, more or less, except that the Crozes *Appellation* extends eastward behind Hermitage and away from the river. The wine still has those flavours of berries and spice, but you can get at them earlier, and they don't usually last as long. For a taste of wines that give the lie to those "usuallys", try ones made by Alain Graillot. White Crozes-Hermitage is for early drinking.

Cornas

As outsiders have discovered Hermitage and Côte Rôtie, the last remaining semi-secret red of the northern Rhône is the tiny (165-acre/67-ha) region of Cornas. Critics complain that the wines here are more "rustic" than their northern neighbours, and that they take even longer to come round. Those critics obviously haven't tasted the smoky, blackberryish wines made by Auguste Clape, Guy de Barjac and Alain Voge.

South of Cornas, the interesting reds dry up and it's time to move on to fizz. St-Péray, whose vineyards rub shoulders with the suburbs of Valence, makes full-flavoured still wine and fizz from the Marsanne and Roussanne that sell well enough in local restaurants but are decidedly unfashionable elsewhere, so it's hard to blame the growers for selling out to house-builders.

More commercial stuff is produced down to the south-west, along the Drôme river, in Clairette de Die and Chatillon-en-Diois, close to the village of Bourdeaux. Avoid straight Crémant de Die itself; made from at least 75 per cent of the neutral Clairette, it's lighter than St-Péray, but with less fruit.

THE SOUTHERN RHONE

According to the *Appellation Contrôlée* maps, the area directly to the south of the northern Rhône is a grapeless no-vine's-land. In fact, although there is no AOC wine made here, there are two *vins de pays*: the Collines Rhodaniennes (easy red from the Gamay and Syrah) and the Coteaux de l'Ardèche which, apart from the reds it makes from the Gamay and from Rhône and Bordeaux varieties can, thanks to Louis Latour and his fellow Burgundians, now boast Chardonnay vines galore and, thanks to Georges Duboeuf, the world's biggest planting of Viognier. A little further south, there is the up-and-coming new *Appellation Contrôlée* of the Coteaux du Tricastin, source of some first-class, pure, smoky Syrah.

Wines labelled Côtes du Rhône can legally be made in a number of areas along the Rhône valley; in practice most come from the flat land on either side of the river south of Montélimar. This is a huge area, and quality and styles can vary enormously. The same *Appellation* can be used to label a Syrah that tastes just like Hermitage's kid brother and a blend of the Grenache, Cinsault and Carignan that's first cousin to Beaujolais Nouveau.

The key to knowing what you are going to find in the bottle is to look for wines from good individual estates, or to pay a little extra for a Côtes du Rhône-Villages, which legally has to come from one of 17 named villages, be made from grapes that come from lower-yielding vines and be a blend that includes at least 25 per cent of Syrah, Mourvèdre and Cinsault.

The wine-makers of the 17 villages are nothing if not individualists, and are active promoters of the wines of their communes, driven on by the example of Gigondas and Vacqueyras which have both been promoted from Côtes du Rhône-Villages to have their own *Appellation*. It is easy to understand why Gigondas was the first of the pair to get its *Appellation*; its red wines do taste a bit more "serious", and its (rare) rosés are first-class. Good examples are a much better buy than many a wine sold under the label of Châteauneuf-du-Pape.

Several villages, most notably Visan, Cairanne, Valréas and Seguret, take advantage of the rules that let them print their commune's name on the labels of their wines; each could make a case for the quality of its reds. Chusclan deserves an *Appellation* for the rosé made by its co-operative (better than a great deal of Tavel), and Laudun merits one for its white. Ironically, Beaumes de Venise and Rasteau, which make decent reds, have had *Appellations* of their own for nearly 50 years, but not for their unfortified wines; both make *vins doux naturels*, fortified wines made by adding pure grape spirit to partly fermented juice. Muscat de Beaumes de Venise is a world-famous success story; Rasteau's fortified Grenache is less immedi-ately appealing but has a plummy, port-like charm.

Chateauneuf-du-Pape

Châteauneuf-du-Pape is one of the world's famous wine names – but, until quite recently, despite their embossed keys and their price, the wines here were often a little like the Pope's castle itself; impressive from a distance and a hollow ruin when viewed at close range.

Châteauneuf should be brilliant stuff. The "pudding stones" covering the vineyards, which release heat during the night, help to ensure perfectly ripe grapes – and wines of up to 14.5 per cent alcohol. The local *Appellation* laws, the first to be drawn up in France, further guarantee the quality of the fruit (in a way unique to Châteauneuf) by obliging producers to use the least-ripe 5 to 20 per cent of the crop to make *vin de table*. The rules also strictly control yields and restrict the use of grape varieties to eight reds and five whites.

Valréas, one of the best villages in the southern Rhône

THE ESSENTIALS
SOUTHEN RHONE

What to look for Spicy reds, New Wave vins de pays de l'Ardèche.

Location South-eastern France, north of Avignon.

Official quality AOCs: Châteauneuf-du-Pape; Côtes du Rhône; Côtes du Rhône-Villages (named villages include Cairanne, Vacqueyras, Séguret, Visan, Valréas, Chusclan and Laudun); Côtes du Lubéron; Côtes du Ventoux; Gigondas; Lirac; Tavel. Côtes du Vivarais is the VDQS, while vins de pays include Coteaux de l'Ardèche, Vaucluse, Collines Rhodaniennes and Bouches-du-Rhône.

Style Ripe, full-bodied red wines are produced, warmer and softer than their northern Rhône neighbours, simple in style though with more depth and complexity in Gigondas, Châteauneuf-du-Pape and some of the better Côtes du Rhône-Villages, such as Cairanne and Séguret. There are also some soft, fresh and fragrant whites, most notably in Châteauneuf-du-Pape and Lirac. The

most famous rosé is Tavel, though neighbouring Lirac can be better. The now-famous sweet white Muscat de Beaumes de Venise is arguably the best and classiest of France's vins doux naturels, luscious yet elegant, while the area's other vdn, Rasteau, can be almost port-like.

Climate Mediterranean with very long, hot summers.

Cultivation Arid chalk and clay soils covered with large, round "pudding-stone" pebbles which reflect and intensify the heat. As the river widens the vineyard slopes become less steep.

Grape varieties As for northern Rhône; 13 varieties are designated for use in Châteauneuf-du-Pape, chiefly Carignan, Cinsault, Grenache, Mourvèdre and Syrah. Whites are principally from Muscat, Clairette, Picpoul and Bourboulenc.

Production/maturation Increasing use of stainless steel with old wood being used for maturation.

Longevity Reds, apart from the best village

Appellations and Châteauneuf-du-Pape, peak after about 3 years. Good village wines will last beyond 5 years, and the best Châteauneuf-du-Pape beyond a decade. White and rosé wines are for early consumption.

Vintage guide 81, 83, 85, 86, 88, 89, 90, 95.

Top 30 Châteauneuf-du-Pape: Rayas, Beaucastel, Font de Michelle, Fortia, Clos des Papes, Clos du Mont Olivet, Guigal, Vieux Télégraphe, Chante-Cigale, Bosquet des Papes, Sabon, Delas, Guigal, Jaboulet Aîné;

Gigondas: Gouberts, St Gayan, de Montmirail, Faraud, de Piaugier, Guigal;

Beaumes de Venise: Vidal-Fleury, Co-operative;

Côtes du Rhône: Jaboulet Aîné, Ste-Anne, Rabasse-Charavin, Ameillaud, Cru de Coudoulet, Grand Moulas, Guigal;

Ardèche: Georges Duboeuf, Louis Latour;

Lirac: Maby, Méjan.

The fact that these rules had to be drawn up as early as 1923 illustrates the well-established tradition of abusing the reputation of what has long been a household name. Today, fortunately, the merchants who were largely guilty of that abuse are prevented from doing so by the keenness of the individual estates to make and bottle their own wine. This has made for a huge improvement in quality, but today's Châteauneuf is still rather two-faced; some are big, packed with pizza herbs, bitter chocolate and oriental spice; others, made by the *macération carbonique* method, taste rather like peppered Beaujolais. There's nothing wrong with these lighter versions, but they don't really do justice to Châteauneuf. The biggest examples from the best estates are worth keeping for a decade or so but, unlike their counterparts from the northern Rhône, they can all be broached by the time they are 5 years old.

White Châteauneuf-du-Pape is very rare – two or three bottles in a hundred – but good modern examples can be worth looking for; their mixture of spice, flowers and lemon is delicious for the first few years after the harvest.

Tavel

The traditional claims for Tavel are first that it is one of the world's only rosés that can age, and second that it is a cut above its neighbour Lirac. However, both claims fail the taste test. Old Tavel tastes duller than young Tavel, and young Tavel often tastes duller than young Lirac. The trouble is that the producers at Tavel now try too hard to make "serious" pink wine. Sadly, the winemakers at Lirac, who do produce good rosé, are increasingly turning their attention to red instead.

Other Wines

There are several "lesser" *Appellations* and VDQSs in the region for which bargain-hunters ought to keep their eyes open. The Côtes du Ventoux benefit from limestone soil to make light, but still quite spicy, red which can outclass many a basic Côtes du Rhône. The Côtes du Lubéron, between Avignon and Aix-en-Provence, got their brand new AOC largely through the efforts of vegetable-oil millionaire Jean-Louis Chancel of Château Val Joanis, where he makes pleasant, if unexceptional, early-drinking red, white and rosé. Still VDQS, the Côtes du Vivarais behave as if they were AOC by having a set of *crus* – serve you a jugful of refreshing rosé.

ALSACE

As wine-makers everywhere else have seemingly given up naming their wines after places and begun to call them after the grape varieties from which they are made, the Alsatians smile knowingly to themselves. They invented "varietal" labels long before the Californians and Australians; indeed, in Alsace more or less the only way wine is sold is by its grape variety, be it the Riesling, the Pinot Gris, Blanc and Noir, the Muscat, the Gewürztraminer or, to a decreasing extent, the Sylvaner.

Talk to the Alsatians about their German neighbours' recent conversion to dry wines and again they will smile; round here, dry Riesling is no novelty and, as they will point out, in Alsace's warm climate the grapes actually ripen much more easily than they do on the other side of the Rhine.

The History

The Alsatians have a way with knowing, if wry, smiles, and when you consider their history, it's hard to blame them. Over the years their region has been a territorial ping-pong ball; they've seen it all. As early as the fourteenth and fifteenth centuries, Strasbourg was at the heart of a thriving wine-producing area that included vineyards on both sides of the Rhine, exporting 100 million litres a year from its river docks.

But this early prosperity did not last. When the French took control in 1648 at the end of the Thirty Years' War, Alsace was no prize acquisition. The war had so devastated the region that immigrants from neighbouring lands were offered free land to encourage them to cultivate it once more.

However hard these times were, they did not deter some from starting wine businesses; among the family firms that are still in operation today, Hugel, Dopff, Trimbach, Zind-Humbrecht and Kuen had all opened their doors by 1700. Over the following century, they learned to work with another immigrant – the Riesling grape, from the Rheingau on the other side of the river. The end of the Franco-Prussian War in 1871 brought a return to German rule. Less than 50 years later, at the end of the First World War, Alsace became French again

– only to fall back into German hands in 1940. The Second World War brought some of the worst times Alsace has ever known; villages were fought for house by house. In Bennwihr, precious wine literally boiled in the cellars as the buildings were burned to the ground.

Today, some of the people speak French; others retain a Germanic dialect – but, whatever the language, they are all quick to stress that they are, above all, Alsatian. And perhaps that's the best image for Alsace wines, too: German spoken with a French accent. Or *vice versa*.

The Best of Both Worlds

This dual nationality is just as apparent in the villages; both in their names and their appearance. This is one of the few parts of the world in which holiday brochure expressions like "fairy tale" and "picturesque" actually do ring true; the narrow streets, the crooked, half-timbered houses, often painted pink, yellow or blue, with their gilded signs are straight out of an illustrated volume of stories by the Brothers Grimm. And overlooking all of the villages, there are vineyards, basking in the sun that, thanks to the shelter of the Vosges mountains, gives the vines one of the driest, warmest environments they could want.

In the autumn, these vineyards are packed with families sharing the task of picking. The slopes are too steep for mechanical harvesters; besides, most of the plots are too small for their owners to afford a machine. Although the soils of particular villages can suit particular varieties (for example, the Muscat does particularly well in both Mittelwihr and Gueberschwihr), most growers produce wines from several different grapes.

But here, there is another contrast with Germany. Whereas the liberal German wine laws have allowed wine-growers in even the best parts of the Rhine and Mosel to replace their Riesling with a range of new, easy-to-grow varieties, in Alsace, the trend has been toward the Pinot Blanc and the region's four traditionally best white grapes, the Riesling, Pinot Gris, Muscat and Gewürztraminer.

There are no new varieties here, and indeed even traditional ones such as the dull Sylvaner and Chasselas

Konigsbourg in Alsace. Vines get the best land here: forest grows in places that are unsuitable for wine-growing

are now treated as second-class citizens; neither can be used to make Alsace's recently established *Grands Crus*.

With these *Grand Cru* vineyards, first introduced in 1983 and fast growing in number, the Alsatians have characteristically put together an *Appellation* system that's half-French, half-German too. Although it is often imagined that each of the region's grape varieties has an *Appellation* of its own, in fact it is the region of Alsace as a whole to which the *Appellation* applies. The names of individual villages, thus, have no legal significance, but those of the 50 *Grand Cru* vineyards (see box) around those villages do – provided that the wines made there are produced from one of the four permitted varieties.

So much for the French-style part of the rules; the Germanic part is all to do with the ripeness of the grapes – in other words, their natural sweetness. Although Alsace is almost exclusively a dry wine

region, the Alsatians love to prove that they can make sweet wine that's every bit as luscious as the stuff produced across the Rhine.

Sweet Alsace

These sweet Alsace wines have two designations, Vendange Tardive – literally "late-harvest", the equivalent of Germany's Spätlese; and Sélection de Grains Nobles – "selection of nobly rotten grapes", similar in style to a German Beerenauslese or Trockenbeerenauslese. Beyond just two more terms – the increasingly rare Edelzwicker (used for a basic blend of various varieties) and Crémant d'Alsace (the region's often excellent *méthode champenoise* sparkling wine) – there is almost nothing else to learn. Expressions such as the commonly seen Réserve Personelle and Cuvée Speciale have no legal significance, but they should indicate that the producer believes the wine to be a cut above the rest of his production.

Comparing Alsace's dry and sweet white wines with their German counterparts is a fascinating experience, and one that sends writers scurrying in search of similes. One somewhat pretentious analogy that nevertheless makes sense likens the wines of the Mosel and Rhine to Mozart quartets, and those of Alsace to Beethoven symphonies.

The difference is all to do with volume and richness. The peculiar warm, dry micro-climate created by the Vosges mountains allows the grapes to develop those few extra grammes of sugar almost every year and that, in turn, makes for a higher level of alcohol and a richness rarely attained in northern Germany; if a wine seems Germanic, yet exotically spicy and tangibly oily in texture, there's a strong chance that it comes from Alsace. And if you are looking for a wine to go with food, you've come to the right place.

The Grapes

Riesling

Is this the greatest of Alsace's varieties – or should that honour go to the Pinot Gris? The answer is not certain, but it is pretty clear what the Riesling would say. Tasted young, Alsace Rieslings can be forbidding, hiding their richness behind their acidity. Leave them to sulk for a few years and you'll be rewarded with an extraordinary appley, spicy glassful that can smell – not unpleasantly – just like petrol. Weinbach, Blanck, Sick-Dreyer, Trimbach and Kientzler make good examples.

Tokay-Pinot Gris/Tokay d'Alsace

Until recently confusingly known as the Tokay, this is no relation of the Hungarian wine of that name (which is made from the Furmint, another variety altogether). Some stories say that the Pinot Gris was imported from Hungary to Alsace; others that the reverse is true. Whichever is correct (and it is grown in Hungary – where it is called the "Greyfriar"), this pale-pink-skinned grape produces some of the spiciest, smokiest wine in Alsace. Like the Riesling, it's worth waiting for, but far easier to drink when young. Ostertag, Kreydenweiss, Schlumberger and Muré make good examples.

Gewürztraminer

A Burgundian who had never encountered Gewürztraminer before was caught unawares. "Bizarre!" he said. "Is this wine or is it perfume?" One can see why a fair number of people are put off by the sweet-yet-dry, pungent smell and taste of wines made from this dark-pink-skinned grape. It is over-the-top, but unashamedly so. The words that often appear on tasters' notes are "grapey", "lychees", "Parma violets", "rose water" and, above all, "spice". And that's how it's supposed to taste; the word "Gewürz" in German means "spice", and thus one can deduce that this is the spicy version of the Traminer grape. If it didn't taste this way, it simply wouldn't be living up to its name. For a taste of Gewürztraminer at its best, try it made by Schlumberger, Zind-Humbrecht, Schleret, Trimbach or Faller.

Muscat

The Muscat has all the Gewürztraminer's grapiness – and then some – but far, far less of its spice. Tasting Alsatian Muscat alongside a Muscat de Beaumes de Venise is like seeing a great actor in two very different roles. Here, unless it is late-picked, the style will be dry and wonderfully refreshing. But there is not a lot made, so you may have to search a little to find a bottle. Names to look for include Kuentz-Bas, Dopff & Irion and Zind-Humbrecht.

Pinot Blanc

The least characterful, and thus the most immediately approachable of Alsace grapes, this cousin of the Pinot Noir is the same variety that the Italians often misleadingly label as Chardonnay (here, confusingly, producers can legally do the reverse). Alsace Pinot Blanc is reminiscent of the fatty, hard-to-define flavour of Brazil nuts and offers an affordable introduction to Alsace for people who are deterred by the spice and perfume of some of the region's more characterful varieties. Among tasters' favourites are examples from the Cave de Turckheim, Hugel and Kreydenweiss.

Sylvaner

This rather earthy-flavoured grape used to be one of the most widely grown here, but is rapidly going out of favour. Good examples can have a rich style of their

What to look for Rich, spicy, dry whites and sweet late-harvest wines, plus occasional good fizz and more occasional light Pinot Noir reds.
Location North-eastern France, on the border with Germany, along lower slopes of the Vosges mountains.
Official quality AOC Alsace, usually followed by the name of the wine's grape variety. Crémant d'Alsace is the region's sparkling AOC. Around 50 vineyard sites are currently entitled to use an additional Grand Cru Appellation, adding their name to that of the grape variety. Although the growers of Alsace would like this designation extended to cover yet more sites, outside observers feel that even the current figure is too high, thus devaluing the Appellation. There is nothing to prevent wine-makers printing their vineyard name on a wine's label, be it Grand Cru or not, and, in view of the fact that cru status has in some cases been granted somewhat arbitrarily, this seems excusable. However, it does confuse matters for the average wine-drinker, who might in turn be forgiven for not committing to memory all 50 (and rising) Grand Cru names.

In similar vein, Réserve or Cuvée Personelle/Spéciale/Particulière are commonly seen, indicating the producer's favourite wines but having no official significance. Ironically, while these anomalies would be cause for concern almost anywhere else, Alsace as a region has one of the best reputations for honest and reliable wine-making in France, although yields from one vineyard can be on the high side.
Style Rich, spicy, dry still whites, usually from a single grape variety (Edelzwicker, a blend, is losing favour); usually sweet Vendange Tardive; always sweet Sélection de Grains Nobles. Light-bodied Pinot Noir reds. Crémant d'Alsace is a méthode champenoise sparkling wine, dry and often quite full-bodied. Though little seen, it can be good value.
Climate Continental: sheltered by the Vosges mountains, this area is warmer and drier than the surrounding countryside.
Cultivation Middle and lower hillside vineyards, usually south or south-easterly in aspect. Soils are diverse and complex.
Grape varieties Predominantly white: Riesling, Gewürztraminer, Muscat, Pinot Blanc, Tokay-Pinot Gris (Tokay d'Alsace), Auxerrois, Knipperlé, Sylvaner, Chasselas and a little Chardonnay; Red: Pinot Noir.
Production/maturation Traditionalists prefer old oak for fermentation and maturation while modernists use stainless steel. The jury is still out over which is better. Crémant d'Alsace fizz can be good. Some new oak is being used for Pinot Noir.
Longevity Riesling: 5–20 years; Gewürztraminer: 3–5 years; Pinot Gris: 5–10 years. Most Muscat, Sylvaner and Pinot Blanc are best drunk young, though the last can keep for up to 4 or 5 years, as can the reds.
Vintage guide 79, 81, 83, 85, 88, 89, 90, 92, 94, 97.
Top 23 Adam, Deiss, Albrecht, Blanck, Cattin, Zind-Humbrecht, Ostertag, Josmeyer, Hugel, Trimbach, Faller, Muré, Rolly Gassmann, Kreidenweiss, Schaller, Schlumberger, Dopff & Irion, Weinbach, Sick-Dreyer, Kientzler. The co-operatives at Turckheim, Eguisheim and Pfaffenheim produce reliable, sometimes excellent, wine.

own, particularly if they are made from old vines (look for the words *vieilles vignes* on the label) but they are rarely exciting. Rolly Gassmann makes a good one, as does Domaine Ostertag.

Chasselas
Another, and rather duller, traditional resident that has been chased out by more attractive newcomers. Chasselas is grown in some places as a table grape, and seems often better suited to that role.

Pinot Noir
The one style that seems to unite Germany and France in Alsace is red wine; on both sides of the Rhine, the Pinot Noir produces wines that, in warm years and when yields are kept low, can be very raspberryish and attractive like a light-to-middleweight Burgundy.

Good examples benefit from being matured in new oak too – provided that they have enough guts to carry the woody flavour. Many wines, however, are light in colour, hardly more than dark rosés, and are best drunk slightly chilled. Look out for examples from Hugel, Rolly Gassmann and the Turckheim co-operative.

Other Wines of the Region
Crémant d'Alsace sparkling wine is often underrated. There are two VDQS regions close to Alsace. Côtes de Toul, in what was once the huge wine-growing region of Lorraine, can produce pleasant light red and rosé (known as *vin gris*). And in Lorraine the Mosel crosses the border into France to become the Moselle – but the wine of this name, made on the banks of the river, is very dull. It is seldom seen outside the region.

CHAMPAGNE

Everybody has their own image of Champagne. The word itself, with its connotations of luxury, the sound of the cork popping out of the bottle, the stream of foam fired at the crowds by victorious racing drivers, the glass raised to toast a bride and groom... All of these take Champagne out of the wine rack and turn it into something that really is rather magical.

What's more, however hard they have tried, however often they have turned out wine that outclasses poor-quality Champagne, none of the world's would-be sparkling wine-makers – including overseas subsidiaries of the Champenois themselves – has yet produced anything that quite compares with Champagne at its best.

So what is it that gives Champagne its edge? Well, the one thing it is most emphatically not is the way in which the wine is made. The Champagne method – what used to be called the *méthode champenoise* and is now more often known as *méthode classique* or *traditionnelle* – is used all over the place, often by those subsidiaries. No, the answer lies in a peculiar combination of climate, soil and grape varieties which is particular to the region of Champagne itself.

The climate in this northern part of France is ideal for making fizz, simply because it's not much good for any other kind of wine; it's just too cold and damp for the grapes to ripen properly. But acidic grapes that have partially ripened in a cool climate are just what you want for sparkling wine – far better than the juicier sweet ones grown in warmer climes.

Then there is the soil – the deep chalk that gives the wines their lightness and delicacy – and lastly, there are the grape varieties: Burgundy's Pinot Noir and Chardonnay, and the Pinot Noir's paler-skinned cousin, the Pinot Meunier.

Put all, or even some, of these elements together somewhere else and you might begin to make a wine that is a little like Champagne. But you'd still have to learn one of the Champenois' other tricks: the art of blending that they call *assemblage*. The closest parallel to this is to be found in Bordeaux, where wine-makers marry together varying proportions of Cabernet Sauvignon, Cabernet Franc, Merlot and Petit Verdot from a number of vineyards within the same commune. The difference in Champagne is that here the blend is often of wines from villages scores of miles apart and, in the case of non-vintage Champagne (the vast majority of the region's production), from different years. The wine-makers of Champagne share with the port producers of the Douro a peculiar habit of not making vintage wine every year, but of only "declaring" a vintage when they think its wine is good enough.

Of course, every Champagne producer is delighted to be able to declare a vintage and to bottle a batch of wine from a single harvest, but the greatest compliment you can pay him is to say that the most recent glass of his non-vintage wine tastes exactly the same as the one you had a year ago.

What every Champagne house is selling is a combination of a recognizable style and consistency. (The Krug brothers, who run one of the greatest Champagne houses of all, believe this so strongly that they price their non-vintage wine nearly as highly – and it *is* highly – as their vintage.) Most producers believe that the best way to achieve that consistency is to blend wines made from two or three of the region's grape varieties, produced in several vintages, and in vineyards throughout the region.

The Regions

If you were to ask the Champenois producers where they go for the wines to blend, for white grapes, they might well look to the Côte des Blancs, the Chardonnay-covered slopes south of Epernay where, in villages like Cramant and Le Mesnil-sur-Oger, the best *blanc de blancs* – white wine made from white grapes – is made.

For the Pinot Noir, they'd probably head north to the Montagne de Reims where, in villages like Bouzy, Verzenay and Mailly, this hard-to-ripen grape can surprisingly – though only occasionally – produce red wines with almost as much depth as some Burgundy. Most of the Pinot Noir goes into blends, but occasionally

Opposite: *vineyards near Epernay, planted at different angles to catch the sun*

you can find a *blanc de noirs* or a rosé that will give you a taste of what the grape can do here.

West of Epernay, following the Marne river toward Château-Thierry, there is the essential, but unsung, region of the Valle de la Marne, where huge quantities of Pinot Meunier are grown. The Champenois rarely say much about the Pinot Meunier, a grape grown in England as the "Dusty Miller" because of the fine white powder that covers its skin (*meunier* means "miller" too), and they certainly don't mention the fact that it is the most widely planted grape in Champagne.

The advantage of the Pinot Meunier is that it ripens well in clayey soil that the Chardonnay and Pinot Noir disdain. It can give a soft fullness to any blend; its disadvantage is that, in itself, it doesn't have much to offer in the way of fruity flavour. Most cheap Champagnes contain a fair whack of Pinot Meunier; but only Rémy Krug acknowledges the essential role it plays in his wine.

If most of Rémy Krug's fellow producers refrain from mentioning the Pinot Meunier, they are just as reticent about the Aube region, way to the south of Epernay. If pressed, they might mumble something about the vineyards there being quite good for the Pinot Noir (because they are a little warmer) but imply in the same breath that Aube wines lack delicacy. A glance at some of their annual shopping lists will reveal, however, that most of them are very happy to put Aube Pinot Noir in their blend. The proportion may vary from year to year, but few Champagne houses own enough land to supply the grapes for more than a fraction of their production; most

A typical range of Champagnes. Champagne corks start out cylindrical: they only take on the familiar shape once they are in the bottle

like to buy the same varieties from the same regions every year.

The quality of each vineyard and the price of its grapes is officially designated on a percentage scale, known as the *échelle*. Those of Champagne's 18,500 growers lucky enough to own a vineyard in one of the 17 villages, including Bouzy, Cramant, Le Mesnil-sur-Oger and Ay, that are rated as *Grands Crus* receive 100 per cent of the annually agreed price per kilo of grapes. Their neighbours in the 140 *Premier Cru* villages, whose land is rated at 90–99 per cent, get proportionately less money per kilo while those unfortunates in the rest of Champagne's vineyards, including most in the Aube, are rated at 80–89 per cent.

The Styles

Brut

This is the most common dry Champagne style but, however dry they may taste to some people (and there are examples that can scrape your teeth cleaner than any dentist), all Brut Champagnes are slightly sweetened.

Extra Dry, Brut Zéro, Brut Sauvage

They sound similar, but for a taste of bone-dry Champagne, don't try Extra Dry – which is, in fact, slightly sweeter than Brut. Look instead for Brut Zéro or Brut Sauvage. These wines are sugar-free and are thus sometimes recommended to diabetics; for most people, however, they are considered to be too dry to be enjoyable.

Demi-Sec, Doux, Rich

For the sweeter-toothed, *Demi-Sec* is, as its name suggests, semi-sweet while the rarer *Doux* and *Rich* are really very sweet indeed. Good examples of these styles are rare.

THE ESSENTIALS
CHAMPAGNE

What to look for Creamy, ideally biscuity, fizz which is at once rich and fresh.
Location Centred on Epernay and Reims, 90 miles north-east of Paris.
Quality Within the Champagne AOC, villages may be further classified as Grands or Premiers Crus. Practically, this is less important than elsewhere because of the blending of wines from different areas. AOCs for still wines are Coteaux Champenois, Bouzy Rouge and Rosé de Riceys.
Style Champagne varies from the very dry Brut Zéro, which has no dosage, through Brut – the most common – to the dessert styles Demi-Sec and Doux. It varies greatly in quality but, from the better non-vintage Champagnes upward, should be biscuity with soft, ripe fruit (particularly if from the Chardonnay grape) and clean, balancing acidity. Coteaux Champenois is white, bone-dry and fiercely acidic; Rosé de Riceys and Bouzy Rouge can be fair to good examples of Pinot Noir, but are usually wildly overpriced.

Climate Similar to that of southern England with long, often cool summers and cold, wet winters. Frost may be a problem at times.
Cultivation Because of the inhospitable climate, vines need careful placing and vineyards are normally on south- or south-east-facing slopes. Soil is mainly of chalk with occasionally sandy topsoil. To combat the effects of frost, growers now employ sprinklers. AOC Champagne regulations forbid mechanical harvesting.
Grape varieties Chardonnay, Pinot Noir and Pinot Meunier.
Production/maturation Champagne production is an exact science. The grapes are quickly and carefully pressed. Fermentation is mainly in stainless steel and lasts approximately 10 days. The still wines are then blended to make a particular style of cuvée. A sugar, yeast and wine solution, the liqueur de tirage, is then added to make the bottled wine undergo a second fermentation. The bottles are stacked on special racks in the cellars during which time remuage takes place. This involves turning and tapping

each bottle of wine, while gradually inverting it so the sludge containing the dead yeast cells from the second fermentation falls on to the cap. Traditionally this was done by hand; now machines called giropalettes are more common. Then the bottle neck is placed in freezing brine to freeze the sludge; the bottle is turned upright and the cap, and with it the sludge plug, is removed. This is called dégorgement. Finally, the dosage is added to the wine.
Longevity The better the base wine, the longer the finished Champagne will last. Most Champagne, including non-vintage, will benefit from up to 3 years' ageing before drinking.
Vintage guide 75, 76, 79, 81, 82, 83, 85, 88, 89, 90, 95, 96, 97.
Top 22 Krug, Bollinger, Henriot, Louis Roederer, Gosset, Jacquesson, Pol Roger, Ayala, Laurent Perrier, Alfred Gratien, Boizel, Deutz, Billecart-Salmon, Jacquesson, Jacques Selosses, Ruinart, Salon, Moët & Chandon, Taittinger, Comtes de Champagne, Veuve Clicquot-Ponsardin, Charles Heidsieck, Pommery & Greno.

Blanc de Blancs and Blanc de Noirs

The words *blanc de blancs* feature on so many white wines nowadays that it is worth remembering that the expression is only relevant to sparkling white wines – for the simple reason that these are almost the only ones that can ever be made from anything other than white grapes.

A *blanc de blancs* Champagne will be made exclusively from the Chardonnay, while the rarer *blanc de noirs* can be made from a blend of Pinot Noir and Pinot Meunier.

Prestige Cuvée

The first "Prestige Cuvée", or super-Champagne, was Dom Pérignon, the 1921 vintage of which was launched, after much hesitation, by Moët & Chandon in 1937. After the Second World War, Roederer entered the competition with its Cristal, a wine originally created for the Tsar of Russia and, over the last 50 years, almost every Champagne house has felt constrained to have a vintage or non-vintage prestige cuvée.

Some of these wines can be sublime: Dom Pérignon, despite its image of being every newly famous pop star's first choice, *is* a great Champagne, as are Taittinger's Comtes de Champagne, Roederer's Cristal and Bollinger's Grande Année Rare.

Rosé

While other pink wines – or at least the ones that haven't renamed themselves "blush" – have gone out of style, rosé Champagne has caught the public fancy in a way that has surprised even the Champenois, who don't really approve of the style, possibly because of the effort they take to keep the pink colour out of their wine.

Rosé Champagne can be made in two ways. You either crush the grapes as if you were going to make white Champagne, but leave the skins in the juice for just long enough to tint the wine, thus producing what the Champenois call Rosé de Noir; alternatively you simply blend a little of the region's red wine into the white fizz.

Purists prefer the first of these methods; unfortunately, their preference is not supported by blind tastings in which skilled judges are often unable to differentiate between the best wines of both styles.

Vintage

Vintage Champagne can be made by any producer in any year reckoned to be up to the mark. Small domaines tend to produce a vintage fizz every year simply because they lack the old stock with which to blend a good non-vintage. Thus there is no guarantee that a vintage Champagne will be better than a good non-vintage, but it should have been made from the best available grapes harvested in a ripe year. Just as crucially, it must have been aged on its lees – or yeasts – for at least 36 months, which should give it a richer, yeastier, nuttier flavour than non-vintage, which enjoys a legal minimum of just 12 months' yeast contact (though good Champagne houses will aim to give their non-vintage fizz three years or so too).

The non-sparkling wines of Champagne

Coteaux Champenois Blanc

At its best, Coteaux Champenois Blanc can be a little like Chablis, but rarely like top-class Chablis. In cooler vintages, a glass could save you from having to visit the dentist; do-it-yourself teeth-scaler. Laurent Perrier's version comes in a pretty bottle; Saran and Ruinart are usually better.

Coteaux Champenois Rouge

If the white grapes find it hard to ripen, the Pinot Noir and Pinot Meunier have very little chance of doing so. In some ripe years, however, Coteaux Champenois Rouge can be made, which has some of the character of basic red Burgundy – but at a much higher price. Bouzy Rouge is the one to look for, if only because of its delicious name, but several other villages – for example, Ay and Ambonnay – proudly put their name to their own reds.

Rosé de Riceys

Rosé de Riceys is a more interesting wine, if only because Pinot Noir rosé is quite rare. It is produced in the Aube, a region which is not generally thought to make the best Champagne. Like its still red and white neighbours, it can be lean stuff – and expensive – but good examples are juicily raspberryish.

Opposite: *The underground cellars of Champagne Veuve Clicquot, cut into the chalk rock of the region*

EASTERN FRANCE

The Jura is caught in a time warp, making eccentric, old-fashioned wine in precisely the same way it has done for centuries. But the Jura has a place in wine history because it was in this region of vineyards and dairy cattle that Louis Pasteur was born, and it was here that he carried out his first experiments on ways to prevent milk from going bad, and wine from oxidizing.

The wines that fascinated Pasteur were the dry, but curranty-raisiny *vins de paille* still produced (though rarely nowadays), like some of Italy's most traditional wines, from grapes laid out to dry on straw mats beneath the autumn sun and, more particularly, *vin jaune* which, like *fino* sherry, is allowed to oxidize in its barrels beneath a film of scum-like yeasts that the Spanish call *flor*.

Vin jaune is an exception that proves a pretty reliable rule. Leave almost any other red or white wine in a cask that hasn't been topped up properly and you will end up with vinegar; *vin jaune* is protected from harmful bacteria by its blanket of yeast during the 18 months it can take to ferment and the six years that it has to be matured. The flavour of *vin jaune* is inevitably more like that of sherry than any other white wine, but it's lighter in alcohol (not having been fortified) and packed with more of a punch of flavour because, unlike the neutral Palomino used for *fino* sherry, the French wine is made from the assertive Savagnin grape. Some people hate it; others revel in its extraordinary nutty, salty, woody, flower-and-leaf flavours.

The best *vin jaune* is made (in tiny quantities) at Château-Chalon and l'Etoile, but examples from the small market town of Arbois and the regional Côtes du Jura are slightly less rare. Despite efforts at standardization by the authorities in Brussels, all *vin jaune* comes in the eccentric 62 cl clavelin bottle, because, the Juraçiens claim, six years' evaporation from the barrels "costs" them 13 cl a time.

Of the Jura's other wines, the whites, even when they are made from the Chardonnay, seem to have unwanted *vin jaune* character – and get sent back in restaurants for being oxidized. L'Etoile is, again, the one *Appellation* that gets it richly right, often by blending

A Savoie farmhouse with its rows of vines up in the hills

the Savagnin with Chardonnay and even a little of the red-wine Poulsard grape.

There is no red l'Etoile, but Arbois makes red and rosé wines from the Pinot Noir, sometimes blended with the Pinot Gris, both of which taste a little like middle-weight Pinot Noir from Alsace and rarely repay ageing. Arbois reds made from the Trousseau and Poulsard vary in style, depending on the blend; the former makes heavy, tannic wines with little discernible flavour, while the latter can be delicate and floral, but with a hint of woodsmoke; a marriage of the two is decidedly characterful. The Pupillin Co-operative makes a good example.

Savoie

Far less bizarre, but even less well known beyond this region, are the wines of Savoie. Of course, every year, there are a whole lot of people who discover these wines for the first time – because this is winter sports country, and if you ask for a bottle of something white as an *après-ski* refresher in Val d'Isère, this tangy, floral and often slightly sparkling wine is what you'll probably be given.

It would be easier for the Savoyards if those vineyards were all in a single area, but instead they're scattered around the valleys and on the slopes like patches of melting snow left over from what was once a far larger area; in the eighteenth century, there were around 22,500 acres (9,000 ha) of vines; today the figure is just over 2,500 acres (1,000 ha).

The local grapes are a curious bunch too: the Jacquère, Roussanne, Roussette, Cacabboué, Gringet, Mondeuse and Persan and the Petite-Sainte-Marie. This last may sound like the most obscure of them all, but actually the Little-Saint-Mary is one of the only two that are grown anywhere else; it's the local name for the Chardonnay.

There's something about the cool climate of Savoie, as in nearby Switzerland, that lets this variety shine. Here, it's used as an ingredient in a wide range of tangily floral whites; but it's not the one that gives them their distinctive spicy character; that comes from the obscure Roussette (also known as the Altesse) and Jacquère, and in some cases, the Pinot Gris. The blanket regional *Appellation* of Vin de Savoie includes some good, lightweight but emphatically refreshing *méthode champenoise pétillant* and *mousseux* whites made from blends of local grapes; and reds and rosés that combine the Gamay and Pinot Noir with local red and even (up to 20 per cent) white varieties. There are a number of individual villages whose names can appear on labels. Of these, the best are Ayze (which makes good sparkling wine) Apremont, Abymes and Chignin-Bergeron (whose white offers a rare chance to experience pure Roussanne).

Best-known of Savoie's other *Appellations* is Crépy, which, like Muscadet, is bottled *sur lie* and is thus very slightly sparkling. But it's got bags more flowery freshness than most Muscadet. For the flavour of pure Roussette, try the dry, flowery Seyssel; the *mousseux* made here can be good but slightly less distinctive, probably because of its high Chasselas content. Roussette de Savoie and Roussette de Bugey can both (with the exception of a few specified villages) include Chardonnay, which tends to make for a creamier, less tangy flavour. The Vins du Bugey are often single-varietals, including some first-class pure Chardonnay, but the label also appears on some refreshingly fruity Gamay/Pinot Noir /Poulsard/Mondeuse blends.

THE ESSENTIALS

EASTERN FRANCE

What to look for Fresh, light, if overpriced, young Savoie white and reds, and pleasant Pinot Noir, rich fizz and nutty, sherry-like whites from Arbois.

Location To the east of, and running parallel to, Burgundy: Savoie comprises a series of small wine-producing areas from Lac Léman (Lake Geneva) south to Grenoble; Arbois lies within the Côtes du Jura to the north of Savoie, on the slopes of the Jura mountain range.

Official quality AOCs: Arbois and Arbois Mousseux; Arbois Pupillin; Côtes du Jura and Côtes du Jura Mousseux; L'Etoile; Château-Chalon (vin jaune); Crépy; Roussette de Savoie (and cru); Seyssel; Seyssel Mousseux; Vin de Savoie (of which the most widely seen cru is Apremont) and Vin de Savoie Mousseux. The best-known VDQS is Bugey (and cru); Bugey Mousseux is also made.

Style Still and sparkling white wines are very fresh, floral and light, reminiscent of the wines of nearby Switzerland; more traditional wood-aged Jura whites are slightly fuller. Jura reds and rosés are light and vaguely Burgundian, while Savoie reds can sometimes be quite robust. Vin jaune and vin de paille are the Jura's speciality styles; the former, though unfortified, has been called France's answer to fino sherry, while the latter is extremely sweet with an appealing nuttiness. Arbois Pupillin reds can be characterful, if rustic.

Climate The area is affected by the proximity of the Alps and, while the summers are warm, it can be very damp, cold and frosty during the winter and spring.

Cultivation The vineyards are found on gentle lower slopes. The soil is predominantly clay, with some limestone and marl.

Grape varieties Cacabboué, Chardonnay, Chasselas, Gringet, Jacquère, Molette, Mondeuse, Mondeuse Blanche, Pinot Blanc, Pinot Noir, Poulsard, Roussanne, Roussette (Altesse), Savagnin, Tressot, Trousseau.

Production/maturation Stainless steel and, in the Jura, large wood is used for fermentation. Sparkling wines are made by the méthode champenoise. Côtes du Jura Mousseux is the best sparkling wine Appellation here. Vin jaune must be matured for at least six years in oak with no topping up, and a yeast flor develops, as in fino sherry; vin de paille is made from bunches of grapes that have been laid out to dry for up to six months while the sugar concentration intensifies. Vin jaune is made entirely from the Savagnin grape, while vin de paille is generally made from a blend of grapes, but always including the Savagnin. Labour-intensive to produce, these are fairly rare, expensive wines.

Longevity All Savoie whites should be drunk as young as possible, as should rosés. Red wines will last for between 3 and 6 years, while vin jaune and vin de paille appear to last almost indefinitely.

Vintage guide 95, 97.

Top 10 Arbois: Château d'Arlay, Jean Bourdy, Château de l'Etoile, Henri Maire, Aubin Co-operative, Pupillin Co-operative, Domaine de Montbourgeau;

Savoie: Pierre Boniface, Goy, Mercier.

PROVENCE
AND CORSICA

PROVENCE

Somewhere, close to the village of Cassis, so the locals say, there's a staircase to Heaven built by God to facilitate deliveries of His favourite wine. Sitting at a café on the seafront here, watching the fishing boats bobbing away, with a plateful of olives on the table and a glass of chilled, fresh peppery Côtes de Provence pink in your hand, it's extremely easy to imagine that they are right.

For most people, thoughts of Provence's wines are all too often wrapped up in memories or conjured-up images of sun-baked holidays. When they actually taste the same wines on a chilly day in London, New York or Paris, doubts begin to creep in. Is it the wine that's changed, or is it me? It's probably a bit of both – but no matter which, the wines never taste as good without the accompaniment of olives and sunshine.

This is far too easy a region in which to be lazy. And then, there are all the traditional ways that no-one wants to cast off – such as allowing dull, local, white grapes to ferment at high temperatures, of leaving the reds for too long in old casks and allowing the rosés to become bronze-coloured and stale.

The Provençaux are at last beginning to get their act together, making consistently better, fruitier wines from fruitier grapes. Côtes de Provence is not all rosé; a fifth of the wine made here is red and a tenth, white. Too much of the red and pink is still made from the Carignan, but growers are busily planting Cabernet Sauvignon, Syrah and Mourvèdre, and taking more care of their Grenache. Cool fermentation and a little Sémillon and Sauvignon have arrived for the whites too, to help the workhorses, Ugni Blanc and Clairette.

Much the same could be said for two recent AOC promotions, Coteaux d'Aix-en-Provence and its enclave, Les Baux de Provence. Both already made adequate-to-good whites and rosés, but the focus now is on fruity, spicy, modern reds, made from blends of Grenache, Syrah, Mourvèdre, Cinsault and lots – up to 60 per cent in Coteaux d'Aix-en-Provence – of Cabernet Sauvignon. The flagship estate here, Château Vignelaure, is back on form after a dull patch and other investment is moving in fast.

The marriage of Syrah and Cabernet, once acceptable for Bordeaux such as Château Cos d'Estournel and now familiar in Australia, is given its most dramatic French showcase in Les Baux de Provence at the Domaine de Trévallon, a wine which can fetch a higher price than many a claret.

Palette is curious stuff, and very characterful. Its best wine is the rosé which, like the white, is exclusively made and aged in oak by Château Simone. Both these wines are very herby in flavour, but pleasantly so; the red is simply herby and dry.

Bandol proudly claims the best climate of the Côte d'Azur. Californian wine-makers hasten from one cellar to another. What brings them here is the chance to sample a grape that they've heard a lot about in the Rhône.

Red Bandol has to include at least 50 per cent Mourvèdre (the rest is made up by Grenache, Cinsault and Syrah) and should reveal that variety's spicy, herby flavour and, in good examples, its ability to age. The rosé, made from the same grapes, is similarly good (but expensive).

On the maps of wine regions, Bellet looks huge, covering 17,500 acres (700 ha) of steep slopes around Nice. And there's the rub; the land here is worth too much as gardens for millionaires' villas. A mere two dozen producers farm just 125 acres (50 ha) to make these crisp whites and rosés, using the local Rolle, Roussanne, Pignerol and Mayorquin for the former, and Braquet and Folle Noire for the latter. Prices, like those for almost everything else in Nice, are very high.

Lastly, there are the country wines here at the mouth of the Rhône and heading eastwards and westwards along the coast: the variable *vins de pays* des Bouches du Rhône, excellent de Mont Caume and *vins de pays*

PROVENCE AND CORSICA

What to look for Fresh Provence rosés, traditional Rhône-style reds and modern blends. New-wave efforts at traditional Corsican grape varieties.

Location The south-east corner of France, bounded by the Rhône and the Italian border. The Mediterranean island of Corsica lies 110 km off the coast, south-east of Provence.

Official quality Provence AOCs: Bandol; Bellet; Cassis; Côtes de Provence, Coteaux d'Aix-en-Provence; Les Baux de Provence; Palette. The best-known VDQSs are Coteaux de Pierrevert and Coteaux Varois. Vins de pays include: Bouches-du-Rhône, Mont Caume, Oc, Var and Maures. Corsica AOCs: Vin de Corse (with a number of suffixes) – Aiaccio and Patrimonio are the best-known; the vins de pays de l'Ile de Beauté and of Pieves, however, include some of Corsica's more interesting wines, from Cabernet Sauvignon, Syrah, Chardonnay and Sauvignon Blanc. Vins doux naturels are from Patrimonio and Cap Corse.

Style The red wines of Corsica and Provence are generally deep, dense and ripe, varying in style from Bandol, which must contain at least 50 per cent Mourvèdre, to the excellent Château Vignelaure, made from Cabernet Sauvignon. Provence rosés tend to be dry, often with an evocative herby character, while the white wines, although rarely exciting, are pleasantly aromatic.

Climate The Mediterranean influence ensures mild winters and springs and long, hot summers and autumns. The vines are planted on both hillside and plain sites. The soil is mainly composed of sand and granite, plus some limestone.

Grape varieties Aramon, Aramon Gris, Barbarossa, Barbaroux, Barbaroux Rosa, Bourboulenc, Braquet, Brun-Fourcat, Cabernet Sauvignon, Calitor, Carignan, Chardonnay, Cinsault, Clairette, Clairette à Gros Grains, Clairette à Petits Grains, Clairette de Trans, Colombard, Counoise, Doucillon, Durif, Folle Noir, Fuella, Grenache, Grenache Blanc, Marsanne, Mayorquin, Mourvèdre, Muscat d'Aubagne, Muscat Blanc à Petits Grains, Muscat de Frontignan, Muscat de Die, Muscat de Hamburg, Muscat de Marseille, Muscat Noir de Provence, Muscat Rosé à Petits Grains, Nielluccio, Panse Muscado, Pascal Blanc, Petit Brun, Picardan, Picpoul, Pignol, Rolle (Vermentino), Roussanne, Sauvignon Blanc, Sémillon, Sciacarello, Syrah, Teoulier, Terret Blanc, Terret Gris, Terret Noir, Tener Ramenée, Tibouren, Ugni Blanc, Ugni Rosé.

Production/maturation New-tech applied to traditional grapes and styles is producing some exciting reds. Provence rosés are benefiting from the introduction of cool-vinification methods, although large old wood is still widely used for fermentation and maturation of other wines. Red Bandol must be matured in cask for a minimum of 18 months.

Longevity White and rosé wines should be drunk within 3 years; red wines generally within 5, although Bandol and the wines of the producers starred (*) below will last a decade.

Vintage guide 92, 94, 95, 97, 98.

Top 14 Provence: Domaine Ott*, Château Simone, Domaine de Trévallon*, Château Vignelaure*, Domaine Tempier*, Terres Blanches, Mas de Gourgonnier, Mas de la Dame, de Beapré, Fonscolombe, du Seuil.

Corsica: Domaine Comte Peraldi, Skalli-Fortant de France, UVAL.

---

des Sables du Golfe du Lion, in which is situated the large Listel winery, near the tourist-trap walled town of Aigues Mortes.

CORSICA

Corsica is part of Italy. They may not believe that in Paris, and the Corsicans may probably (just) prefer to be French than Italian, but the wine-makers of this glorious island have far more in common with their neighbours in Campania than their counterparts on the French mainland.

The names of the producers, Torraccia, Peraldi, Gentile – and of the grape varieties, Nielluccio, Sciacarello, Vermentino – and the styles of most of the traditional wines – dull, oxidized whites and rosés·and big, alcoholic reds – all support Corsica's case as a long-lost cousin of Sardinia and Sicily.

And so does the extraordinary generosity with which the *Appellation Contrôlée* authorities have dished out no fewer than eight inadequate *Appellations*, deftly avoiding giving one to the only style that actually deserves it, the raisiny Muscat produced in various parts of the island.

What Corsica has needed is modern-ization. Unfortunately, until quite recently, neither Corsicans nor the North African immigrant wine-makers have been keen on ideas like that.

The wines are improving fast, though. For the best examples, and the best value, apart from the Muscat, go for the offerings of Skalli-Fortant de France, the wonderfully named *vins de pays* de l'Ile de Beauté, made by the UVAL co-operatives, and now featuring Chardonnay, Syrah and Cabernet alongside the local varieties.

And if you're there and want a Corsican classic with your dinner, try the good but overpriced, very old-fashioned reds and even a carefully oaked white from the Domaine Comte Peraldi.

SOUTHERN FRANCE

One of the sadder figures in the wine world is the Burgundy or Bordeaux producer with an obsession about the competition his region is now facing from New-World countries such as the Americas, the Antipodes and South Africa. It is a little like a jealous husband who's worried about being cuckolded by a rival from another country when the true challenge lives in the house next door.

It is easy to sympathize with the Burgundians and Bordelais for underestimating Languedoc-Roussillon: a few years ago, it may have been the world's biggest single vineyard region, but it was also a major tributary of the wine lake. Every year wine-makers, whose French accent was almost as impenetrable to a Parisian as it would be to any foreigner, got on with the business of producing huge quantities of wine, most of which might just as well have been turned directly into industrial alcohol.

The plug began to be removed from the lake in the 1980s, as an increasing number of farmers switched their attention from growing unwanted wine-grapes to planting orchards. And, while the bulk-wine producers reduced their production, their younger, keener neighbours began, with a bit of help from a growing number of newcomers, to think quality. They studied modern wine-making at the nearby University of Montpellier, tasted wines grown in other warm parts of the world like California and Australia, compared their region to the Barossa and Napa Valleys and thought, "Why not us?"

Hidden Strengths

But before considering the new wines the new-wave producers are now making, let's look at the wines which were never at risk of ending up in any lake. First of these were the *vins doux naturels*. Ironically, while the sweet, fortified Muscat for which France is best known comes from Beaumes de Venise in the Rhône, the far wider range of sometimes richer Muscats here goes almost unnoticed.

The Muscat de Frontignan was once well enough known to have given its name to the finer kind of Muscat, the Muscat à Petits Grains. As in Beaumes de Venise, the co-operative makes almost all of the wine, but an independent jury tastes each year's production to ensure regularity of quality which is generally good, but not quite as zingy as the wine from the Rhône. The rather bigger, richer, Muscat de Mireval owes its style to the way in which it is matured at often very warm outdoor temperatures for two years before bottling. Like the far more delicate Muscat de St Jean de Minervois, however, it is produced in very small quantities.

There are two other Muscats, both of which claim to be the best in France: the light Muscat de Lunel and the beefier Muscat de Rivesaltes. They come in white and pink styles and are usually of at least good quality – and often rather better than wine that is just labelled Rivesaltes which is made in red, white, pink and tawny styles from a rag-bag of local varieties, and accounts for half of France's *vins doux naturels*. The mixture of Grenache and Muscat used for the red and pink tends to make for emphatically old-fashioned flavours that seem reminiscent of stewed fruits, though the Maccabeo white can taste fascinatingly like currants and spice. Rivesaltes is also a good place to discover the style the French call "rancio", produced by ageing *vin doux naturel* in barrel and intentionally allowing it to oxidize. This sweet sherry-like stuff is an acquired taste, but good examples can have lots of spicy, plummy flavour.

Banyuls, the *Appellation* that's usually described as France's answer to port, also comes in a *rancio* style. The interesting wine here, though, is the red which, made primarily from the Grenache, tastes the way cheap ruby port would if that wine were better made. Sadly, really good examples are rare, but look for the words "*Grand Cru*" on the label; they indicate that there's at least 75 per cent Grenache and 30 months' ageing in wood. The Grenache is used to make the fortified red and rosé at Maury too – and some *rancio*. All three are curiously spicy – but they have their fans.

From Dull to Divine

Grapes for Banyuls are picked late; earlier-harvested fruit from the same vineyards can be sold as Collioure, taking its name from the tiniest and least-spoiled fishing village of this region. There's very little made, but what is produced is wonderfully intense red wine. Clairette du Languedoc is made from the Clairette grape in three styles: dull table wine, dull fortified and dull *rancio*. All are, however, more impressive than the even duller unfortified wine made from the same grape at Clairette de Bellegarde.

The Clairette was once used in the sparkling wines of Blanquette de Limoux which are now made mostly from the local Mauzac. The banning of the Clairette in 1978 led to an instant improvement in what claims to be the oldest sparkling wine of all, though styles and quality vary depending on how much Chenin Blanc or (increasingly) Chardonnay feature in the blend. The efforts made to improve quality, and the modernization of the highly impressive Limoux co-operative, have been rewarded by the award of a separate *Appellation* to the Chardonnay which previously was merely a *vin de pays*. The coolish climate and the limestone both suit the variety well and make for wines that often have little difficulty in outclassing basic Chablis.

Back toward the coast, in the mountainous region around Perpignan, you know you're close to the Spanish border. Some of the villagers speak Catalan, some speak heavily accented French, but it makes little difference – both are almost equally unintelligible even to a Frenchman from a few hundred miles away. The Côtes du Roussillon is the place to find some fast-improving, good-value, juicy-fruity reds and rosés – and some aniseedy whites that need drinking straight from the co-operative vat before they lose their freshness. The Côtes du Roussillon Villages, especially from the communes of Caramany and Latour de France, produce the *Appellation*'s best wines but these too need drinking young.

Fitou has a reputation for flavour and value, too, which seems slightly surprising, given the fact that this *Appellation*'s reds have to be made from 70 per cent of the usually derided Carignan and aged for 18 months in (usually old) wood. Fitou isn't specifically fruity, but it is big-bodied and rich, and everyone's holiday-driven idea of how good, southern red should taste.

Corbières got its *Appellation* after Fitou, but the wines made in this savage region are also Carignan-dominated and have a similar style, except that here, lighter, fruitier wines are being made. For real class, though, go to the Château de Lastours, a home for the mentally handicapped whose residents helped to produce a red wine good enough to beat the world at the 1989 *Wine Magazine* International Challenge.

Minervois is improving, too, thanks to a number of innovative producers, including the Châteaux de Gourgazaud, de Blomac and Ste Eulalie, which are producing reds with all kinds of rich flavours. For far finer fare, though, head for the hills, to Faugères and St Chinian, two villages that compete in making fruity, plum-'n'-cherry reds, using traditional blends of Carignan and Rhône varieties. Faugères, in particular, is a beautiful, made-for-vines region, where you would certainly spend a windfall on buying an estate. The berryish wines produced so far are only scraping the surface of what could be achieved. Watch this space.

On the coast, the Coteaux de Languedoc is a region – and a collection of villages including the commune of La Clape – which, in the Middle Ages, was actually an island, connected to the mainland by a bridge. Malvasia and Terret Blanc are used to make distinctively grapey whites that can last. The reds and rosés lean heavily on the Carignan but include Cinsault and Grenache. La Clape is the region's only white wine; of the other villages, the best are St Saturnin which makes a good, light *vin d'une nuit* rosé by leaving the juice with the skins overnight, St Drézéry, with a 24-hour rosé, St-Christol (a favourite, for what it's worth, of Tsar Nicholas II of Russia) Quatourze, Coteaux de Verargues and Cabrières, famous in the fourteenth century for its "bronze" rosé, and still the place to sample the local Oeillade grape.

Of the region's VDQSs, the best are the Costières du Gard which can be perfectly pleasant, if sometimes dull, reds, whites and pinks from mixed assortments of local grapes. The wines of the Côtes de la Malepère can be more impressive – and in the case of the red, a bit more Bordeaux-like – as can the Rhône-like Cabardès.

Brave New World

So much for the improved and improving classics of the regions. Now let's get back to those revolutionaries. Professor Emile Peynaud, the genius behind the modernization of Bordeaux, once elegantly defined tradition as "an experiment that has worked". Mahler had an alternative view: for him, tradition was laziness. Until the 1960s, the vineyards of southern France proved both men right. An experiment in making wine lazily had succeeded quite well. For as long as people were prepared to buy flavourless, often quite vinegary, stuff, the men and women of Languedoc-Roussillon could provide it without too much difficulty. Things became trickier when customers at home and abroad began to demand flavour and freshness – qualities their particular tradition of shoddy wine-making simply could not provide.

Fortunately, examples of those traditional wines are becoming rarer with every year, but it would be nice to collect up a set of them and force a glass past the lips of every critic you hear complain about modernists who are making everything taste the same. There are probably people who feel nostalgic for the sort of cars Skoda made in the good old days of Communism when taking a bend at over 40 mph often involved defying death. To most people, though, the way they are made today is pereferable.

Several people deserve credit for introducing southern France to the modern world of wine. Aimé Guibert, the foxy creator of Mas de Daumas Gassac, the self-termed "*Grand Cru*" Vin de Pays de l'Hérault, which sells for the price you might expect to pay for a classy Bordeaux or Burgundy, proved that one did not have to go to the classic wine regions to find "special" soil – and that you didn't have to follow the classic recipes of which grapes could go into which blends. If

---

THE ESSENTIALS
SOUTHERN FRANCE

What to look for Traditional reds, fresh modern styles, especially varietals, rich fortified Muscats and fast-improving fizz.

Official quality AOCs: Banyuls (VDN – vin doux naturel); Blanquette de Limoux; Clairette de Bellegarde; Clairette du Languedoc; Collioure; Corbières; Costières de Nîmes; Coteaux du Languedoc; Côtes du Roussillon; Côtes du Roussillon-Villages; Faugères; Fitou; Limoux; Maury (VDN); Minervois; Muscat de Frontignan (VDN); Muscat de Lunel (VDN); Muscat de Mireval (VDN); Muscat de St-Jean-de-Minervois (VDN); Muscat de Rivesaltes (VDN); St Chinian; Vin Noble du Minervois. VDQSs include: Costières du Gard; Côtes de la Malepère; Cabardès. Vins de pays include: Gard; Coteaux Flaviens; Hérault; Coteaux de Murviel; Côtes de Thongue; Aude; Vallée de Paradis; Oc; Pyrenées Orientales; des Sables du Golfe de Lion.

Style The majority of wines produced are red. At their best, Corbières or Côtes du Roussillon-Villages, for example; they are firm, rounded, deeply coloured and packed full of spicy, peppery fruit. White and rosé wines may be dry or medium-dry and are improving fast. Sparkling Blanquette de Limoux is produced using a local (and ancient) variation on the méthode champenoise; appley-lemony, sometimes quite full and earthy, it can more resemble Spanish Cava than more northerly French sparkling wines. Some of the region's most interesting wines are its vins doux naturels from Banyuls, Maury and Rivesaltes; deep, dark and raisiny-sweet. Muscat de Frontignan is lighter but just as intensely sweet. Bordeaux grapes – especially Merlot – are increasingly being planted in the Midi and more modern vinification techniques are being incorporated into the wineries. The resulting wines are cleaner, fresher and decidedly fruitier. These southern French wines are some of the best value-for-money wines to be found anywhere.

Climate Influenced by the Mediterranean and also the savage marine and mistral winds.

Cultivation Vineyards are found on the alluvial soils of the plains and on slopes above valleys such as the Aude.

Grape varieties Alicante-Bouschet, Aspiran Gris, Aspiran Noir, Auban, Bourboulenc, Cabernet Franc, Cabernet Sauvignon, Carignan, Carignan Blanc, Cinsault, Clairette, Couderc, Grenache Blanc, Grenache Rosé, Fer, Lladoner Pelut, Malbec, Malvoisie, Maccabeo, Marsanne, Mauzac Blanc, Merlot, Mourvèdre, Muscat d'Alexandre, Muscat Blanc à Petits Grains, Muscat de Frontignan, Muscat Rosé à Petits Grains, Négrette, Oeillade, Palomino, Picpoul, Picpoul Noir, Roussanne, Syrah, Terret, Terret Noir, Tourbat, Ugni Blanc, Villard Blanc.

Production/maturation While (old) wooden vats are still sometimes used for fermentation, stainless steel and new oak are now common. Vins doux naturels (VDN) are half-fermented, then a very strong spirit is added to stun the yeasts and raise the alcohol level.

Longevity Most wines are made to drink within 3 years, although some of the better reds may last beyond 5. If a VDN is non-vintage it should be ready to drink, but vintage VDNs can continue to develop in bottle for decades.

Vintage guide 94, 95, 98.

Top 12 Languedoc: Pech-Redon, Abbaye de Valmagne; Roussillon: Cazes Frères, Château de Jau, Corneilla, Dom Gauby; Vin de Pays de l'Hérault: Mas de Daumas Gassac; Minervois: Château de Gourgazaud; Corbières: Château de Lastours; Vin de Pays d'Oc: Skalli-Fortant de France, Domaine de la Baume, Domaine Virginie.

his red tastes better because he's included Pinot Noir and Cabernet, well, why not do it?

Guibert's influence has been enormous, and helped to inspire the giant Australian firm Penfold's when it came to make its own, large-production versions of Guibert's blends in partnership with Val d'Orbieu, one of the biggest, most dynamic firms in the south.

The collection of co-operatives brought together by Val d'Orbieu is today highly successful, using New-World techniques to make modern varietals and more traditional local styles. What it has so far failed to do is create an international brand for its wines – unlike Skalli-Fortant de France which, under the leadership of Robert Skalli, a canny, Corsican, marketing genius, has introduced wine-drinkers in Europe, the Far East, the USA and, most significantly, France, to the idea of buying a reliable, smartly packaged, fairly priced bottle of Vin de Pays d'Oc Chardonnay, Merlot or Viognier rather than a potentially unreliable *Appellation* wine from a supposedly "better" region.

Finally, but just as crucially, there have been the foreigners, mostly Australians, who have brought their money, skills and enthusiasm to the region. If James Herrick had not planted one of the world's biggest Chardonnay vineyards, if BRL Hardy had not bought its Domaine de la Baume, if Antipodean wine-making had not been introduced at Domaines Virginie, and if countless Flying Wine-makers had never been deployed throughout the region on behalf of British and Dutch buyers, by men like Hugh Ryman, Kym Milne and Jacques Lurton, it is unlikely we would be seeing half the exciting wines that are now emerging from Languedoc-Roussillon, nor the creation of a wholly new set of traditions and exciting experiments.

Up from the Country

The one thing the revolutionaries all have in common is that they have been working outside the straitlaced *Appellation Contrôlée* system which has, until now, been the sole focus of attention for France's wine experts and critics. The new wines are, among some 125 *vins de pays*, the "country wines" of France.

Some of these regions encompass huge swathes of land that seem to stretch from one end of France to the other, while others are tucked away in small, obscure corners

you only ever find your way to by accident. Whatever the relative sizes of the *vin de pays* areas, however, their rules all allow far greater experimentation with grape types than those governing *Appellation Contrôlée* wines – and, unlike *Appellation* wines, they permit reference to two grape varieties on the label.

The larger regions, such as the prettily named Vin du Pays du Jardin de la France in the Loire, tend to offer something of a lucky dip: some of their Sauvignon Blancs and Chardonnays can be good examples of these varieties, while others – most of the Chenin Blanc, for example – can be either dull or downright poor. The most interesting *vin de pays* regions, however, are down here in Languedoc-Roussillon in the warmer, southern part of France where the grapes ripen far more reliably than the ones in most of the more marginal *Appellations* further north. The quality of these wines depends less on vintages than on the attitude of the producers.

Ironically, while the motor that is supposed to drive the *vins de pays* to improve the standard of their wines is the knowledge that they might one day, like Limoux, climb the ladder to become a fully-fledged *Appellation Contrôlée*, many now relish the New-World freedom allowed to the humbler designation.

Although there are *vins de pays* throughout France, the most reliable are the ones from Catalan, Coteaux du Quercy (in its tough, "old-fashioned" way), Côtes de Gascogne (from Yves Grassa's various domaines, and from the Plaimont co-operative), Côtes de Thongue, Ile de Beauté, Drôme, Gard, Hérault, Principauté d'Orange, Vaucluse, Collines Rhodaniennes, Uzège, Mont Caume (especially the Cabernet Sauvignon from the Bunan estate), Sables du Golfe du Lion, Mont Bouquet, Coteaux de Peyriac, and Vallée du Paradis. The common Vin de Pays d'Oc covers far too large a region to offer much in the way of reliability; best buys here come from the names of reliable producers like Skalli-Fortant de France, Val d'Orbieu, Dom de la Baume and Dom Virginie.

To the east and north-east, there are some first-class, spicy, Rhône-like wines from the Coteaux de l'Ardêche and Bouches du Rhône that easily compete with good Côtes du Rhône, but neither region could be described as reliable. Further north, the whites of the Loire- Atlantique, Charentais, Loire-et-Cher and Maine-et-Loire can be good – if acidic – alternatives to Muscadet.

THE SOUTH-WEST

The South-West of France is rather like one of those disaster movies in which as disparate a group of people as might ever be found in the same ship, aeroplane or skyscraper are all gathered together in order to add interest to the plot.

Apart from finding themselves within this area of France, wines like Cahors, Vin de Pays des Côtes de Gascogne and Monbazillac have almost nothing in common except that, like the people in the movie, they all have readily defined characters of their own. Until now, few of the wines have been known outside their own patch but, as the prices of good Bordeaux have continued to rise and the quality of wine-making in the South-West has improved, this has quietly become one of France's most interesting up-and-coming regions – and one that will certainly repay a little study.

Perhaps the easiest way of dealing with the South-West is to separate its wines into two groups: ancient and modern. Among the "ancient", one would include the *Appellations* with names like Pacherenc du Vic-Bilh, made from local grapes such as the Gros Manseng and the Petit Manseng. The "modern" group principally includes wines made from Bordeaux-style varieties and/or by up-to-date methods.

Cahors was until recently one of the most ancient styles of all. The "great black" wine, drunk by the Romans, was once either sold as Bordeaux or used to beef up Bordeaux. Made from the Tannat and the Malbec (Bordeaux's unwanted red variety), Cahors has always had the reputation of being extremely old-fashioned: tannic, tough, and sweetly tobacco-spicy – more Italian in style than French. In fact, however, this old-timer has had a partial face-lift; some of its wines taste the way they used to and some taste light, fruity and very agreeable. They're more approachable – and less interesting.

For light, fruity reds, iti is better to go to Gaillac, another ancient *Appellation* whose name means "fertile place" in Gallic. All sorts of odd grapes are used, from the wonderfully named, tangy L'En de l'Elh ("far from the eye"), to the rather dull Mauzac. Of white Gaillacs, the best are probably the slightly sparkling Perlé, the semi-sweet *méthode rurale* fizz (made by allowing the wine to finish fermenting in the bottle), and some good attempts at wines with low alcohol. The sweeter versions are rarely exciting. Of the reds, the best are the Beaujolais-style *macération carbonique* wines, made from the local Duras, the Gamay, Syrah and Cabernets.

Sweet Pacherenc du Vic-Bilh sounds more like Normandy cider than wine. Its name refers to the fact that this was one of the first places to plant vines in rows ("piquets en rangs") and is rather more memorable than "Madiran Blanc" which is what it really is. It is made from the Gros and Petit Manseng and the local Arrufiat, often *"sur lie"* and, when young, has attractive soft, peachy, peary flavours.

Côtes de St Mont is mostly (and well) made by the large Plaimont co-operative, according to the same rules as Pacherenc, but makes more use of less outlandish grape varieties such as the Sémillon and Sauvignon. The red, which can be similarly good, is made from a blend of the local Tannat and Fer grapes softened considerably by the Bordeaux varieties.

Madiran is now making a comeback after almost disappearing in the late 1940s. Today, it's still resolutely tough stuff, thanks to the presence of the Tannat and Fer grapes, but the Cabernet Franc is making inroads, rounding off the style and adding a touch of blackcurrant fruit. The star turn here is unquestionably Alain Brumont whose Château Montus has the sophisticated country appeal of Gérard Depardieu in a well-cut suit. Mind you, the Plaimont co-operative doesn't do a bad job. As for Béarn reds, they contain more Tannat, are lighter in weight, but even tougher. The rosés are pleasant though, as are the Gros and Petit Manseng whites. Tursan is similar.

Finally, like the unexpected hero in the disaster movie, there has been the unpredictable commercial success story of Vin de Pays des Côtes de Gascogne, which was probably the first significant example in France of New-World wine-making techniques being

Opposite: *Château de Montbazillac, home of sweet whites*

applied to pretty basic grapes. Until the Plaimont co-operative and Yves Grassa separately began to exercise their skills on them, the Ugni Blanc grapes were thought best suited for distillation into Armagnac – or for sale at rock-bottom prices as an ingredient of very basic sparkling wine.

For several years in the 1980s, these clean, fruity, slightly off-dry white wines made instant friends for themselves, especially in countries like Britain where wine-drinkers were often graduating from far sweeter German efforts. Today, their future is slightly less certain, now that they have to compete with a new wave of similarly priced Chardonnays from the warmer regions of Languedoc-Roussillon. All of which is not to say that this hero is likely to expire before the final reel, but it'll take a lot more heroics for it to survive.

Jurançon

Jurançon is Manseng country too, and an *Appellation* that has survived by swapping the emphasis from sweet to dry. Good examples of both can be oddly spicy with flavours of tropical fruits and a refreshing whack of acidity that allows the sweet versions to last for aeons. But beware; it is easy to buy sweet Jurançon when you want the (less interesting) dry. Unless the label says "sec", the wine isn't. Up in the Pyrenées, Irouléguy makes interesting, earthy-but-spicy reds and rosés and dull whites. Côtes du Frontonnais reds are much more fun; lovely juicy, rich wine, made from the unusual Négrette.

There are four VDQSs here, the basic Vin d'Entraygues et du Fel, Vin d'Estaing, and Vin de Marcillac, and the rather better Négrette-dominated Vin de Lavilledieu.

The Shadow of Bordeaux

The town of Bergerac has, like Cyrano himself, always been kept out of the limelight in which Bordeaux, made on the other side of the Dordogne from the same grape varieties, has so happily basked. Edward III, an English king who ruled this part of France during the Middle Ages, banned the passage

---

of wine, fruit, men, women and children across the river. In the seventeenth century, in a similar mood, the local authorities sneakily obliged Bergerac's winemakers to use smaller casks than the Bordelais; at the time, tax was levied per barrel, irrespective of size.

Despite these handicaps, Bergerac, which now grows one in six of France's strawberries and a fair amount of tobacco (it even has a tobacco museum!), made a market for its wines in the Netherlands, where the sweet wines we now know as Monbazillac first became popular. In post-war years it fell out of favour and its unimpressive dry successor made little impact and few new friends.

Ironically, Bergerac owes its current renaissance to the enthusiasm of an Englishman, Nick Ryman, his son Hugh, and a visiting young wine-maker from Australia who, between them, proved that Ryman's Château de la Jaubertie Bergerac Blanc could compete with all but the best Graves, and that his juicy, blackcurrant red – though less impressive – could beat many a bottle labelled Haut Médoc. Others are following Ryman's lead with Bergerac Sec, which explains why the local, slightly sweeter alternative *Appellation* of Saussignac is fast disappearing. Still surviving near here though, is Pécharmant, which really can be of Médoc *petit château* standard.

Thanks to the growing popularity – and sadly the rising price – of Sauternes, the wine-makers of Monbazillac have finally found the patience necessary to wait for *botrytis* to develop and the skills required to make better, cleaner wines. Good examples easily outclass many shamelessly poor efforts in that illustrious Bordeaux *Appellation*. Nearby Rosette makes tiny (and shrinking) quantities of pleasant, delicate, Cadillac-like *demi-sec* rather more success-fully than the various sweet and dry

wines made at Montravel which, when compared to most modern white Bordeaux, taste quaintly old-fashioned. And generally dull.

Côtes de Duras can be good basic red and white Bordeaux-by-any-other-name, produced from the same kinds of grapes grown in the same kind of soil; only the fact that it's just over the border in the next *département* denies it the *Appellation*. Buy some and try to tell the difference between a red made here and a cheap basic claret. If you can't, let the Bordeaux *Appellation Contrôlée* authorities know; they'd love to hear from you. The same applies to the generally excellent Côtes du Marmandais, and the Côtes de Buzet, produced within the region of Armagnac (but only for the Buzet reds and rosés; the whites are dull). The Côtes du Brulhois makes no white, but its rosé is pleasantly light and Cabernet-ish and rather better than the rustic red made here from the same varieties.

Of the South-West *vins de pays*, there are the region-wide Vin de Pays du Comte Tolosan and the Vin de Pays des Côtes de Gascogne which, as mentioned above, have revolutionized their region. Vin de Pays d'Agenais can be either Bordeaux-style or old-fashioned, depending on the grapes that are used. Vin de Pays de Dordogne is similar in style to Bergerac; Coteaux de Quercy and tiny Coteaux de Glanes are good Gamay- and Merlot-influenced reds; Bigorre is like mini-Madiran; Côtes Condomois are old-fashioned Tannat reds and dull Ugni Blanc whites, and Côtes de Montestruc include unusual, beefy reds made partly from the dark-fleshed Alicanté Bouschet. Close to Toulouse, the Côtes du Tarn combines local and Bordeaux varieties with, for some reason, the Portugais Bleu, and Saint-Sardos produces traditional reds, whites and rosés from local varieties.

ITALY

Italy is the most gloriously confusing country on earth – except that, like Germany, as would-be national leaders have increasingly discovered in recent years, it is not so much a country as a collection of disparate regions, seemingly stuck together with experimental glue. What realistic link could there be between the German-speaking, *lederhosen*-clad producers of Lagrein Dunkel in the mountains of the South Tyrol on the Austrian border, the Franco-Italian wine-makers of Valle d'Aosta who give their wines French names like Enfer d'Arvier, the Sardinians who use the Spanish Garnacha grape for their Cannonau, and the peasants of Sicily, who farm grape varieties such as the Frappato and Perricone, that have never been seen on the mainland of Italy?

It would be tempting to file Italy in the "too hard" basket and switch to the easier subject of California or Australia, if it weren't for all those fascinating flavours and styles which, like Italy's myriad dishes, are found nowhere else.

Latin Labyrinth

The more closely you look at Italy's wines and wine regions, the more confusing it all becomes. You could, of course, start as you would in other countries, by learning the names of the regions – but, unlike France, for example, the ones listed in the atlases rarely feature on labels. Bordeaux comes from Bordeaux, Champagne from Champagne and Rioja from Rioja; Barolo, on the other hand, comes from Piedmont and Chianti from Tuscany.

Of course, you could bone up on Italy's 1,000 or so different grapes, but you'd still end up banging your head against the wall in frustration. The Montepulciano grape is used to make Montepulciano d'Abruzzo, but not for Vino Nobile di Montepulciano which is made from another variety altogether. The same grape can be called the Nebbiolo in one Piedmont vineyard and Spanna in the one next door.

Holes in the DOC Net

In 1415, long before Christopher Columbus sailed for America, Chianti became the first wine region in the world whose boundaries and production were controlled by law. Five centuries later, in 1924, Italy began to lay the ground rules for regional designations that finally led to the allocation in 1966 of the first DOC – Denominazione di Origine Controllata – to the Tuscan white wine of Vernaccia di San Gimignano.

If the DOC had achieved its objective of fulfilling the same role as France's *Appellation Contrôlée*, it would today provide at least some kind of indication of where one ought to look to find Italy's better wines. The list of DOCs, however, included so many wines – good, bad and indifferent – that a "super-DOC" called DOCG (*Denominazione di Origine Controllata e Garantita*) had to be created. This, too, was soon allocated over-generously, for political reasons, to entire regions and to generally dull wines like Albana di Romagna.

Worse still, even when the DOCs and DOCGs made geographical sense – as in the case of Chianti and Bardolino, for example – they included all sorts of rules and regulations requiring producers to make their wines in ways that had everything to do with politics – again! – and the worst aspects of tradition. So, to earn the term "*superiore*", Bardolino has to spend at least a year in barrel, despite the fact that, ideally, this fruit-packed wine's true role in life is to compete with Beaujolais; like that wine, most of it should be in the bottle and on the streets as young as possible. With few exceptions, for "*superiore*" read "*inferiore*". The same idiocy has been apparent in the requirement for Chianti

Harvested grapes in Coltibuono Abbey, Italy

producers to include flavourless white grapes in the recipe for their red wine.

Perhaps unsurprisingly, given the Italian attitude to authority, the meaninglessness of the legal designations and frequently the downright silliness of the wine-making rules associated with them, the makers of many of Italy's best, most innovative and often priciest wines have preferred to sidestep the system completely by labelling their bottles as *vino da tavola* – "table wine" – ludicrously setting them alongside the cheapest plonk on the market.

What these pioneers are fighting against is the steady trend away from wine quality of the last 50 years. For them, as recently as the early 1980s, their country's wines were still suffering from the mistakes made during the years after the Second World War

when, almost throughout the land, the call was for productivity; for vines and vine varieties that would yield plenty of bottles.

In some regions – Soave, for example – wine-growers took over areas previously used to grow maize; in others, such as Chianti, anaemic red wines were beefed up with heady stuff from the southern parts of the country. The more wine people made, the more problems they had; space was short, and so was the money to pay for the bottles, so a single vintage would often be bottled in several sessions spread over two, three and even four years – during which time the quality of the wine in the barrels could and would change and deteriorate. So, three bottles of identically labelled Chianti, of the same vintage and producer, could taste completely different.

The Renaissance

The renaissance of Italian wine brought cooling equipment which helped to make fresh, clean white wines rather than fat, flabby ones. It brought a new understanding of the texture of red wines – and the knowledge that tough-and-tannic is not a description that has to apply to high-quality, young, red wine. Highly skilled oenologists were employed to advise on every stage of production: today a winery owner sometimes seems to be prouder of his consultant than of his house, his vineyard or even his wife. Under the watchful eyes of these experts, old barrels were thrown out and replaced by clean new ones. Throughout Italy, wine-makers planted Chardonnay and Cabernet Sauvignon and started to make wines that competed with white Burgundy, red Bordeaux and the best varietals of California.

Traditionalists began to complain that this sudden rush to make "international"-style wine was undermining Italy's own vinous heritage. Almost as if anticipating this, pioneers like Paolo di Marchi in Tuscany fixed their attention on the indigenous grapes that had for so long been under-exploited – and revealed some extraordinary unsuspected potential. The uninspiring flavour of most pre-1980 Chianti could, it

was discovered, be attributed to the fact that a large proportion of the wine was not made from the flavoursome clones of the Sangiovese today's wine-makers' grandparents would have grown, but from more productive, lower-quality efforts created by clever nurserymen.

New-wave Chiantis and "Super-Tuscan" reds – *vino da tavola* wines made from the old clones of Sangiovese and nothing else (and consequently barred by the silly DOC laws from carrying an official designation) – did not just impress open-minded Italians; they dazzled critics overseas. Suddenly, Californians who had been obsessively planting Merlot and Cabernet Sauvignon in their attempts to mimic Bordeaux cleared space in their Napa Valley vineyards for Sangiovese.

Elsewhere, almost throughout the country, individualists experimented with the potential of Italy's indigenous grapes. In Piedmont, for example, Angelo Gaja startled his neighbours by producing a range of stunning single-vineyard wines which sold internationally at prices higher than those paid for top-flight claret. Packed with glorious berry fruit and sweet new oak, these had nothing whatsoever to do with the tough, dried-out husks traditionally associated with the region. If Gaja had achieved this feat in Barolo,

Casks of wine ageing before the bottling process begins

traditional emperor of the region's red wines, it would have been impressive but unsurprising; in fact, though, he had made these world-beaters in Barbaresco, traditionally Barolo's humbler neighbour.

Gaja's influence on the entire region – and on Italy as a whole – cannot be under-estimated. With Antinori, the leading mould-breaker of Tuscany, he proved that Italy's wines could break free of the bargain shelf and local pizzeria and stake a claim on the most serious wine lists and dining tables in the world. This self-confidence was soon exhibited in other ways by countless Italian producers who discovered that a smart new label and bottle could do as much for their wines as a new wardrobe from Armani could do for them. Visitors to the annual Vinitaly fair in Verona return with their heads reeling.

Spurred on – or should we say shamed? – by the success of these wines, in the mid-1990s, the authorities took another look at the system, proposing to reallocate DOCG far more precisely and to bring in another new designation – IGT or *Indicazione Geografica Tipica* – to cover those "super *vino da tavola*" wines.

On paper, the new proposals had much to be said for them and might indeed be worth considering by would-be reformers in France and Germany. However, one must never forget that this is Italy where any new measures will have to be introduced region by region by more or (frequently) less willing and efficient local organizations who are hardly likely to run them with any great rigour.

The Burden of Tradition

Over the last few years, Italy has seen the most extraordinary three-way battle between a new wave of wine-makers whose obsession has been the flavour of their regions' indigenous grape varieties, neighbours who have been seduced by the Californian notion of recreating Burgundy and Bordeaux, and the old guard who'd like wine to taste the way it did in the old days when you could taste the (old) wood of the barrel rather than the fruit of the grape – whatever its variety.

Unlike those of Germany and France, Italy's wine laws have not officially acknowledged the identity of specific vineyard sites. The closest they have come to recognizing that some parts of a DOC make better wines than others is the set of Classico sub-regions –

such as Chianti Classico, Soave Classico and Valpolicella Classico – whose French equivalent is the "Villages" (Beaujolais Villages, Côtes du Rhône Villages) Appellation.

What there is not, however, is the system of prestigious *Grand Cru* and *Premier Cru* vineyards on which the French have built their vinous reputation. Burgundy's vineyards are divided into good, better and best; those of Barolo have – so far – all been considered equal. By everyone, that is, except the wine-makers who, as elsewhere, have just gone right ahead and printed the names of their particular bits of land on their labels. Unfortunately, and inevitably, this has allowed all sorts of fudging to go on, and all sorts of meaningless and misleading references to non-existent or no-better-than-ordinary pieces of land. So while one Barolo Cannubi, from a good part of the Cannubi hill, could be the equivalent of a *Grand Cru* Burgundy, another, from a less well-exposed section of the same hill, might be no better than an ordinary Barolo.

As it happens, the wine-growers of Barolo and nearby Barbaresco have tidied this up by establishing their own list of top-class vineyards – but that's not to say that there aren't going to be heated battles between producers on the right and wrong side of the newly laid tracks. So, there's every reason to welcome the creation of the new DOCGs which are intended to give recognition to particularly good vineyards.

The Unofficial Elite

In response to the often lax regulations, growers in some regions have formed *consorzii* – associations – that are supposedly devoted both to improving quality and to promoting their local wines. The best-known of these is the Chianti Classico Gallo Nero Consorzio, membership of which is proclaimed by the presence of a collar depicting a black cockerel around the neck of the bottle. Unfortunately, even the best *consorzii* rarely include all the producers of their region (Antinori, probably the biggest name in Chianti Classico, is not a member) and some seem to be all promotion and little quality. One much more reliable national alternative to the *consorzii* is the VIDE association, the wines of whose 30 members have to be tasted and analysed before they are allowed to carry the VIDE symbol on their labels.

THE NORTH-EAST

The north-eastern corner of Italy is a crazy, mixed-up part of the world, full of people who refuse to speak Italian, call their wines by all sorts of confusing names and, in the Veneto at least, have for a long time seemed actively to have sought to ensure that the wines anyone is likely to have heard of, such as Valpolicella and Soave, are often the ones that taste worst.

To complicate matters further, this is also a region of false starts where sparks of promise often seem to go unfulfilled. And yet this is a great region for vinous explorers – for people who are ready to brave the labyrinth of language for the sake of excitingly different flavours.

Alto Adige

In deference to the official maps, we shall call this former Austrian region the Alto Adige, but the majority of its inhabitants prefer it to be known as the Sud Tirol, and many of the wines they make bear such un-Italian names as Vernatsch, Müller-Thurgau and Lagrein Dunkel. Thankfully, those labelled Pinot Grigio, Chardonnay, Cabernet Sauvignon and Franc, Traminer and Sauvignon are reasonably straightforward. But then there is the oddly and deliciously smoke-and-cherry-flavoured Schiava, or Vernatsch, grape which makes wine most outsiders would describe as deep rosé but the locals insist is red. Some of the best examples come from St Magdalener (or Santa Maddalena), and from the region around the Kalterersee (Lago di Caldaro).

The wild-berry-flavoured Lagrein makes light, raspberryish rosé (Kretzer or Rosato) and beefy reds (Dunkel or Scuro) and can do wonders for Schiava. It might also be beneficial blended with some of the region's Cabernet Sauvignons and Cabernet Francs, some of which can taste a little raw. A few of these can be impressive though – as, in their light, raspberryish way, can the Pinot Noirs.

Betwixt red and white there is an extraordinary wine that is made almost nowhere else. Rosenmuskateller is the nearest thing to a liquid rose garden. Recommended are the dry example made by Tiefenbrunner and Graf Kuenbeg's sweeter versions, which can last for a decade or more developing all kinds of fascinating rose-petal flavours (yes, flavours) and smells.

Of Alto Adige whites, the ones that have received the greatest media attention have been the oaked and unoaked Chardonnays, though not everyone is convinced; the unwooded versions taste light and pineappley, and are hard to distinguish from the Pinot Biancos made by the same producers in the same region. A few of the better examples, such as those from Tiefenbrunner and Lageder, can handle ageing in oak, but most seem to be overpowered by the experience. The more exciting wines are those made from more aromatic varieties such as the Muscat, the Pinot Gris, the Gewürztraminer (the grape that is supposed to have its origins here in the town of Tramin), the Riesling and, believe it or not, the Müller-Thurgau. Anyone who doubts that this variety can make special wine should try the one made by Herbert Tiefenbrunner from grapes grown in his mountain-top Feldmarshall vineyard.

Unfortunately, despite the excitement the region created in the early 1980s, fine, concentrated wines such as this are not as common in the Alto Adige as the region's apologists like to claim; far too many show the signs of vines that have been allowed to produce far too much juice. There are signs of improvement, however, particularly among the co-operatives.

Trentino

South of the Alto Adige, Trentino is a warm, productive area where huge amounts of anonymous fizz are made, usually from a blend of Chardonnay, Pinot Bianco and Pinot Grigio. The climate and the terrain make Trentino an easy place to grow grapes; unfortunately, most of the farmers here prefer to grow as many as they can per hectare and leave the wine-making to co-operatives such as Càvit which processes over half the region's crop. There is very little wrong with any of the wines Càvit makes, but most have the typical over-cropped Trentino characteristic of tasting pleasantly bland. The Lavis co-operative, by contrast, is trying to raise quality by limiting yields. So far, the growers' reaction has been to take their flavourless grapes elsewhere, but, in a wine-glutted world, the young team at Lavis may well have the last laugh.

Trentino's reds have more to offer, provided that you generally sidestep such "French" varieties as the Cabernets, Merlot and Pinot Noir and turn to the characterful local grapes. The Teroldego, used to make Teroldego Rotaliano, and grown almost nowhere else, is one of Italy's underrated varieties. Its wines are rich and fairly spicy, as are those from the almost mentholly Marzemino.

The Wine of Meditation

The term *recioto* is used to describe the strong and naturally sweet wines produced from grapes taken from the ears ("*recie*" comes from "*orecchie*") of the bunches. These upper parts of the bunch receive the most sun, and have much higher sugar levels than the others. When picked, the grapes are hung indoors in lofts or barns to allow them to dry partially and to concentrate the sugars. The semi-dried grapes – the *passito* – are then pressed and fermented very slowly to produce the strongest natural wine possible (up to 17 per cent alcohol).

Recioto is a speciality of the Veneto region and can be made from either red or white grapes. Classic, creamy, honeyed, Recioto de Soave dei Capitelli is made by Anselmi, while Maculan produces the rather finer Torcolato. The red Recioto della Valpolicella from producers such as Quintarelli, Masi and Tedeschi ranks among the greatest and most unusual wines of Italy. If all the sugar is fermented out of the wine, it is known as *amarone* and combines the fascinating smells and flavours of bitter chocolate, plums, raisins, cherries and smoky charcoal. Wines that do not undergo a second fermentation remain sweet and are termed *amabile*.

Valpolicella *ripasso* is produced by pumping young Valpolicella over the lees of a *recioto* to precipitate a second fermentation. Such wines have a higher alcohol content and take on some *recioto* character, but can only be sold as *vino da tavola*.

Veneto

The greatest red wine of the Veneto has one of the most abused wine names in Italy. If your only experience of Valpolicella is of dull, flavourless stuff from a two-litre bottle, you'd be forgiven for finding it hard to believe that this wine is capable of any kind of real drinkability, let alone greatness.

Back in the 1960s, the authorities generously extended the name Valpolicella to a huge area of undistinguished

---

What to look for Light cherryish reds, rich, raisiny reds and whites with the character of the dried grapes from which they were made.

Location North-east Italy, bordered by the Adriatic, Trentino-Alto Adige, Friuli, Austria and the river Po in the south.

Quality Soave is Italy's largest white DOC which, together with red Valpolicella and Bardolino, accounts for well over half of the region's output. Other DOCs: Breganze, Colli Berici, Gambellara, Piave Raboso, Recioto di Soave/della Valpolicella/della Valpolicella Amarone.

Style Soave, Valpolicella and Bardolino are, because of the size of their output, often cheap, dull, commercial, even rather nasty, wines but one can get much higher quality at only a slightly higher price. Soave at its best is dry and nutty with a pleasant creamy texture, and Recioto di Soave can be lusciously delicious. Bardolino is soft and light with some cherry-stone bitterness – it needs to be drunk young. Valpolicella is a richer, heavier version of Bardolino, and single-vineyard wines reveal a much greater depth of plummy fruit. The rich, alcoholic, port-like Recioto della Valpolicella can be dry (amarone) or sweet (amabile). Fine Cabernet Sauvignons are made by Maculan (Breganze) and Conte Loredan-Gasparini (Venegazzù della Casa), and some excellent-value wines with soft, plummy fruit are made from the indigenous Raboso grape. The Prosecco grape is capable of producing some decent sparkling wines at Conegliano.

Climate Hot summers and warm autumns. Winters are cold and can be foggy.

Cultivation Alluvial plains in the coastal region provide very fertile soil for vine-growing.

Grape varieties Red: Cabernet Sauvignon, Cabernet Franc, Merlot, Corvina, Rondinella, Molinara, Negrara, Raboso, Pinot Nero. White: Garganega, Trebbiano, Prosecco, Pinot Grigio, Pinot Bianco, Tocai, Riesling, Verduzzo.

Production/maturation Veneto is dominated by co-operatives and industrial concerns which mass-produce cheap commercial wines. A Bordeaux influence can be detected in the production of some of the Cabernets and Merlots. Recioto is produced from passito grapes, slowly fermented to give their characteristic alcoholic strength and richness.

Longevity Reds: Most basic reds should be drunk within 5 years; Recioto can be left for some 15 years; good Cabernets for 10 years; Whites: Basic whites – within 1 year; good Soave Classico 2–4 years; Recioto di Soave, Torcolato up to 10 years.

Vintage guide Reds: 85, 86, 88, 90, 91, 93, 94, 95.

Top 10 Quintarelli, Masi, Tedeschi, Santa Sofia, Allegrini, Boscaini, Guerrieri-Rizzardi, Anselmi, Maculan, Conte Loredan Gasparini.

---

land, effectively undermining the reputation of the good producers with individual vine-yards within the original Valpolicella Classico zone. Today, those producers, such as Masi, Allegrini and Boscaini, are still making serious Valpolicella with lots of plummy, cherryish flavour and a fascinating bitter, almondy twist, but they sensibly focus wine-drinkers' attention on the names of their vineyards rather than that of the region; some labels barely seem to mention Valpolicella at all.

For really great Valpolicella, seek out the rather rarer Recioto della Valpolicella, made from grapes dried in barns and slowly fermented. Wines bearing this label are sweet and raisiny; those also labelled *amarone* are dry. Both can be as alcoholic and intense as some fortified wines, amply deserving their local name of *vini da meditazione*; wines to sip at thoughtfully.

Bardolino – and pink *Chiaretto* – is a lighter-weight red cousin of Valpolicella, made from the same grape varieties a few miles to the west of that region. Good examples can be packed with cherry fruit and compete easily with Beaujolais, though without ever quite losing the characteristic bitter twist of the region. Buy young vintages labelled *Classico*, but as a rule avoid *Superiore* wines, which legally have had to spend a year in barrel losing their flavour.

If Valpolicella is a debased name, Soave has been dragged through the dirt. Today a few other producers have come to Soave's rescue, producing rich-yet-fresh wines with lovely lemony flavours. Look for the rare, honeyed, curranty Recioto di Soave, the white version of Recioto della Valpolicella.

One producer – Maculan – has almost single-handedly put the region of Breganze on the map. A favourite of the range of wines made here is the gorgeous, raisiny-honeyed Torcolato, made from a blend of this region's native Vespaiola and Tocai grapes that have been left to dry before fermentation and maturation in new oak. But the Maculan Cabernet reds are just as impressive, and the oak-aged white Prato di Canzio shows what the Tocai can do in a blend if it is given the chance.

Piave's interesting grape is the Raboso, which can pack a real punch of rustic fruity flavour. The white Verduzzo is locally just as well thought of, but its naturally low acidity tends to make for soft, dull wine; if you want a white from Piave, stick to the Pinot Bianco or Grigio, or the Tocai.

Friuli-Venezia Giulia

If the Alto Adige is overtly Austrian in style, parts of this easterly region – usually referred to simply as Friuli – are Slovenian in all but name. But who cares about nationalities when there's a glassful of flavour to be drunk? While wine-writers have taken a growing interest in this region's wines, its unwieldy name has yet to make its mark with most wine-drinkers. All you really have to remember is the name of the grape variety you enjoy drinking, and take your pick. No one quite knows precisely how large a number you can choose from, but it's certainly over 70. Unlike the Alto Adige, though, Friuli doesn't complicate matters by swapping around the names of its grapes, but it does confuse newcomers with its major white variety, the Tocai, which isn't the Tokay of Hungary, the Tokay-Pinot Gris of Alsace, or the Liqueur Tokay-Muscadelle of Australia. It can make dull wine, but it can also produce unusual, rich, figgy, pear-flavoured stuff.

Of Friuli's seven regional zones, the one to start with is the large, flattish area of Grave del Friuli, where the red varieties of Bordeaux produce refreshing, unpretentious wines with plenty of crunchy berry fruit; there's some pleasant, similarly undemanding Chardonnay here, too, that can be every bit as good as, and rather cheaper than, examples from the Alto Adige.

The black grape the locals would prefer you to concentrate on, though, is the tough, spicy Refosco dal Peduncolo Rosso (its friends just call it Refosco) which is indigenous to the region. There are some good examples of this variety produced in Grave de Friuli, but, like all of the region's best wines, the ones to write home about are the intensely fruity examples made up in the hills of Collio and the Colli Orientali (the eastern hills) on the Slovenian border.

There are all sorts of familiar flavours to be found here, ranging from crunchy blackcurranty Cabernets and plummy Merlots to creamy Pinot Bianco and spicy Pinot Grigio. But the unfamiliar ones are worth looking at too. Try the Refosco, the tangy white Ribolla, the spicy-berryish Schioppettino and the limey-lemony sweet or dry Verduzzo di Ramandolo.

Finally, a word or two about Silvio Jermann and Francesco Gravner, two of Italy's best, and least-vaunted, producers, who have arguably made their greatest wines by blending various grapes together. Jermann's unoaked Vintage Tunina and Gravner's Vino Gradberg are among the most deliciously intriguing white wines in the world.

THE ESSENTIALS

FRIULI–VENEZIA GIULIA

What to look for Exciting, tangy and richer, fuller-bodied whites, good reds from "French" varieties and spicy reds from indigenous grapes.
Location North-east Italy, on the Slovenian border.
Quality One-third of production is from seven DOC areas – Grave del Friuli, Carso, Collio, Colli Orientali, Latisana, Isonzo and Aquilea.
Style Whites are crisp and dry at best, with tangy lemon fruit. There is also a fine pair of new-wave vino da tavola whites: Ronco delle Acacie, which combines this appealing fresh fruit with understated new oak, and Vintage Tunina, which has the added weight and richness of Chardonnay. Some dessert wines, notably the very pricy Picolit and Verduzzo di Ramandolo, are also produced. Reds are generally light,

refreshing and slightly grassy, but the local Schioppettino produces a big, spicy wine with rich fruit flavours which can mature extremely well. Friuli produces some of Italy's best varietal Cabernets and Merlots.
Climate Cool European climate with warm summers and cold winters. Extremes are moderated by the Adriatic. Lack of sun may be a problem for reds in some years.
Cultivation Flat, alluvial plains with the better vineyards in the hills.
Grape varieties Red: Merlot, Cabernet Franc, Cabernet Sauvignon, Pinot Noir, Refosco, Schioppettino; White: Chardonnay, Sauvignon, Tocai, Pinot Grigio, Malvasia, Pinot Bianco, Picolit, Ribolla, Traminer, Müller-Thurgau, Verduzzo.

Production/maturation Stainless steel and cold-fermentation have been widely adopted to the detriment, in some cases, of the personalities of the grape varieties. More recently there has been some experimentation with oak in order to add complexity to the fruit flavours.
Longevity Reds may last for 8 years – Schioppettino can be kept for 5–15 years – although most are best drunk within 3–5 years. Whites are at their best within 1–3 years of the vintage. The "super-deluxe" vino da tavola whites can benefit from up to 8 years' ageing.
Vintage guide Reds: 85, 86, 88, 90, 91, 93, 94, 95, 98.
Top 7 Jermann, Schioppetto, Marco Felluga, Collavini, Gravner, Dri, Puiatti.

THE NORTH-WEST

The North-West is by far the most exciting part of Italy. And in the Nebbiolo grape is one of the most exciting – yet frustrating – varieties of them all, to be found in the communes around Barolo.

You are reminded of Burgundy, where the similarly pernickety Pinot Noir is just as difficult to grow, just as easy to get wrong, just as influenced by the precise character of the piece of soil in which it is planted and, when everything goes right, just as fascinating in the variety of its flavours.

Despite the differences in flavour, the links between Barolo and red Burgundy are actually remarkably close. Both are wines made from a single grape and both have long suffered by being adulterated with beefier wines from further south. Like Burgundy, Barolo used to be a far lighter wine – indeed until the early twentieth century the wines bearing this name would have been sweet and slightly fizzy. Then in the 1930s Barolo slid into the phase of trying to be too big for its boots. The grapes were over-pressed to extract every possible ounce of tannin and the wines were left to age for far too long in barrel. That was the way people liked them – until Professor Emile Peynaud arrived from Bordeaux and shocked his hosts by declaring some of the most illustrious wines to be oxidized.

Since the French guru's visit, there have been all manner of discussions about the way Barolo ought to be made. Should it be fermented for a long time with the grape skins to extract as much tannin as possible, and aged for several years in large *botti* casks to be softened by oxidation? Or should it be handled in much the same way as Bordeaux, and matured less lengthily in small (new) oak barrels? The local jury is still out on all these questions, but outsiders are rapidly coming to their verdict; what they like is wines with personality and fruit that age well, but can be enjoyed in their youth. In practice many of these are usually from single vineyards, and made by producers like Mascarello, Clerico, Roberto Voerzio, Aldo Conterno and Elio Altare who fight to prevent their wine from oxidizing as it matures, bending the rules if necessary by allowing it to spend less than the regulation two years in cask.

Under present law all Barolos are equal. Until, that is, you begin to read the labels and find yourself immersed in such names as Cannubi and La Morra. But hold on, say some of the traditionalists, "real" Barolo shouldn't come from a single vineyard; it ought, like Champagne, to be a blend of wines grown in various plots. That argument is still raging; as always, both sides can make a convincing case for themselves, the blenders claiming that some of the vineyard names appearing on labels are far from special, while the plotters talk keenly about the way the new DOCG rules will finally help ennoble the best pieces of land.

The Kid Brother

The traditional view of Barbaresco is that it is a more approachable, lighter-weight version of Barolo. But if good examples of Barolo have been hard to come by, good Barbaresco has been rarer still. One man who has done more than any to stake a claim for Barbaresco is Angelo Gaja, who makes a range of extraordinarily pricy single-vineyard wines here. At their best, these are excitingly spicy, intense wines that benefit from legislation allowing them to go into bottle after one year rather than Barolo's two.

Those who question Barbaresco's potential for greatness cheekily point out that Gaja has committed the sacrilege of planting Chardonnay here, and that he has "disloyally" begun to make Barolo. Gaja's supporters

Vineyards at Alba, Piemonte, in the north-west of Italy

PIEMONTE

What to look for Rich, tannic reds; lighter, juicy reds from Dolcetto; crisp, dry whites; aromatic, grapey fizz.

Location North-west Italy, in the foothills of the Alps around Turin.

Official quality Barolo and Barbaresco are two of only five Italian reds with the top level DOCG designation. Around 25 per cent of production is DOC, notably Asti Spumante, Barbera, Gavi, Gattinara, Ghemme, Moscato d'Asti, Dolcetto, Arneis and Freisa.

Style Some dry, lemony whites are produced at Gavi, while a rich and full-flavoured wine is made from the Arneis, an ancient grape variety grown in the foothills of the Alps, north of Alba. The region around Asti is renowned for its light, refreshing, grapey spumante wines. Equally famous are the massive, chewy reds of Barolo and Barbaresco, wines that can take many years to reveal all of their complexities. Rich in tannins and high in acidity, both have a variety of fruit flavours – raisins, plums, prunes, blackberries – together with liquorice, chocolate and a whiff of smoke. Also from the Nebbiolo grape, but more readily

approachable, are Gattinara, Ghemme, Nebbiolo d'Alba and Spanna, the local name for Nebbiolo. Barbera from Alba, Asti and Monferrato can produce a rich, raisiny wine with good underlying acidity. The Dolcetto makes soft, juicy wines which at their best combine succulent cherry fruit with bitter chocolate.

Climate Severe winters with plenty of fog – the "nebbia" of Nebbiolo – relatively hot summers and long autumns, although lack of sunshine can cause problems.

Cultivation The best vineyards, in Barolo, are situated on free-draining, south-facing hillsides. Around Asti the hills are much gentler. Soils are varied, but calcareous marl mixed with sand and clay predominates.

Grape varieties Red: Nebbiolo, Barbera, Dolcetto, Bonarda, Vespolina. White: Moscato, Arneis, Cortese, Chardonnay, Pinot Bianco.

Production/maturation Traditionally, Barolo spent a long ageing period in wooden vats; today, ordinary Barolo is released at 3 years old, riserva at 4 years old and riserva speciale at 5 years old, and there has been a move away from oak to

bottle age. Barbaresco must be aged for a minimum of 2 years, one of which must be in oak. Asti is made by the cuve close method.

Longevity Reds: drink Dolcetto within 3 years, but most other reds (Barbera, Ghemme, Gattinara, good Spanna) require 4–12 years. Barbaresco can be kept 5–20 years while Barolos are capable of ageing for between 8 and 25 years. Whites: Asti and Moscato d'Asti should be drunk within a year. Gavi requires 2–3 years.

Vintage guide Reds: 78, 82, 83, 85, 86, 88, 89, 90, 96, 97. Whites: 94, 95, 97.

Top 36 Barolo: Giacosa, Ceretto, Ratti, Fontanafredda, Pio Cesare, Pira, Roberto Voerzio, Borgogno, Altare, Clerico, Scavino, Poggio, G Mascarello, B Mascarello, Vajra, Vietti, Aldo Conterno, G Conterno, Conterno Fantino, Sandrone, Prunotto, Gaja, Elio Grasso; Barbaresco: Gaja, Moccagatta, di Gresy, Ceretto, Giacosa, Castello di Neive, Pio Cesare; Other reds: Vallana, Brugo, Dessilani, Bava, Bricco dell'Uccellone, Vigna Arborina, Darmagi; Dry whites: Gaja, Bava; Asti/Moscato: Fontanafredda, Duca d'Asti, Cantina Sociale Canelli, Bava.

fairly reply that it is traditional for producers in Piedmont to make several styles of wine and that his Chardonnay is one of Italy's most successful whites.

If Barolo and Barbaresco are the potentially daunting Everest and K2 of wine here, there are some wonderfully individual, far less demanding, smaller peaks among the region's reds that are just as worth exploring. You can find various versions of less-matured wines sold with a DOC as Nebbiolo d'Alba, or as *vino da tavola* as Nebbiolo delle Langhe.

Up in the north of the region, Carema, Gattinara, Ghemme, Bramaterra and Fara all make floral, delicate wines based on the Nebbiolo, but that also include Bonarda and, in a few instances, Vespolina. *Vino da tavola* wines made here from this kind of blend (with a fair dollop of the Aglianico) tend to be sold as Spanna and can be of very variable quality.

Even the lightest Nebbiolo can be a bit of a mouthful,

though, which makes the Barbera such a very welcome alternative. But Barberas vary too, depending on where and how they are made. Some versions are best classified as basic table wine to be drunk by the jugful; some are really quite serious. Look out for Barbera d'Asti, Barbera d'Alba and Barbera del Monferrato from producers such as Bava.

Five other varieties make wine for easy drinking. The Dolcetto sounds as though its wines ought to be sweet. They're not, but when well made, they are so perfumed and so packed with plummy, chocolatey, raspberryish flavours that they taste as though they can't be 100 per cent dry. Look for Dolcetto d'Alba, Dolcetto di Dogliani and Dolcetto delle Langhe Monregalesi.

The Freisa, for its part, sounds as though it ought to taste of strawberries; actually, raspberries or mulberries are probably closer to the mark – but, whichever fruit it is, Freisa wines are more tightly packed with it than many a pot of jam. Like many of the wines in this region, Freisa used to be sweet and fizzy; sadly, few producers make it that way now but, whatever the style, good Freisa should have a lovely, refreshing acid bite of not-quite-ripe fruit. Try examples from Bava, Voerzio and Vajra.

Ruche is a variety that very few of the books, ever bothered to mention, for the simple reason that it was so rarely grown. According to some local producers, it was brought to the region from Burgundy, which is quite believable; Bava's example tastes like one of the best, most creamy and floral Beaujolais.

Grignolino has always been a name that seemed to promise juicy-fruity flavours, but many seem disappointingly unripe. Try one from Vietti, though, with a plate of antipasto prepared with good olive oil, and you might just develop a taste for it. There is also Brachetto, both in its dry and wonderfully grapey-floral sweet styles. Blended with the black Muscat, this is one of the best arguments for sweet red wine. Low-alcohol (5.5 per cent) versions compete on level terms with Moscato d'Asti and Asti.

Both these wines provide a wonderful means of testing for wine snobbery; the moment you see the nose begin to lift at the mention of sweet fizz, you know that you are in the presence of a label drinker. Great Asti is quite simply one of the most unpretentious, fun drinks there is; served chilled on a warm summer's afternoon it's the nearest thing to drinking ripe grapes. And that's hardly surprising because the Muscat grape from which both wines are made is quite simply the grapiest grape of them all.

Apart from Asti and Moscato d'Asti, Piemonte is not usually thought of as white-wine country. There are, however, two characterful whites that are worth looking out for. Gavi's gain – and most wine-drinkers' loss – was to be likened to white Burgundy. This meant that this perfectly pleasant, dry, creamy, appley wine made from the local Cortese grape rapidly became a "smart", over-priced, pleasant, dry, creamy, appley wine. Some bottles are labelled Gavi, some as Gavi di Gavi, which is a sort of Chianti Classico-style designation for wines from the village itself. The latter are rarely worth their extra price.

A better bet is the far more distinctive Arneis di Roero made in small quantities from the Arneis grape, whose name in local dialect actually means "little difficult one". It may be difficult to grow, but it is remarkably easy to drink – and one of the freshest, most spicy mouthfuls in the world. Try the ones from Gianni Voerzio or Deltetto.

THE ESSENTIALS

LOMBARDY/LIGURIA/VALLE D'AOSTA

What to look for Light, crisp whites; reds from light and fresh to richer, more tannic; the occasional dessert wine; some fizz.

Location North-west Italy. Lombardy is in the foothills of the Alps around Turin while Valle d'Aosta is very much in the Alps. Liguria is in the Appennine country of the coastal strip around Genoa.

Official quality Mostly vino da tavola with a few DOCs in each region, notably Lombardy with Franciacorta, Lugana, Oltrepò Pavese and Valtellina. Liguria has 3 DOCs, Cinque Terre, Riviera Ligure di Ponente and Dolceacqua.

Style Valle d'Aosta makes fresh, tart white wines and light, fruity reds for local consumption. Donnaz, from Nebbiolo grapes, is sturdier stuff and is one of only two DOCs in this region, the other being the softer Enfer d'Arvier. Some good dessert wines are made. Liguria, again, produces a lot of wine for local consumption from over 100 grape varieties. Lombardy produces some very good méthode champenoise wines at Franciacorta, dry with a fine biscuity character. Franciacorta also produces some rich, bitter-sweet reds and smooth, fruity whites. Oltrepò Pavese produces many styles of red and white, the best being red Barberas. Valtellina produces rich reds from the Nebbiolo. Some pleasant whites are made at Lugana.

Climate Winters are severe, but the growing season is hot and long.

Cultivation A wide range of soils, with calcareous marl being common. Relief ranges from the Alpine scenery of Valle d'Aosta to the alluvial plains of the river Po.

Grape varieties Red: Nebbiolo, Barbera, Cabernet Sauvignon, Merlot, Bonarda, Cabernet Franc, Rossola, Brugnola, Pinot Nero. White: Trebbiano, Pinot Bianco, Pinot Grigio, Uva, Chardonnay, Riesling.

Production/maturation Sparkling wines are generally made by the méthode champenoise.

Longevity Most whites are for early drinking. The sparkling wines may be fruitfully kept for 2 to 3 years. The reds of Valle d'Aosta are best drunk young. Oltrepò Pavese: 2–5 years; Franciacorta: 3–8 years, Valtellina: 5–15 years; other reds: 2–8 years.

Vintage guide Reds: 82, 83, 85, 86, 90, 94, 97, 98.

Top 4 Sparkling wine: Berlucchi, Ca' del Bosco; Lombardy: Ca' del Bosco, Longhi de Carli; Lugana: Ca' dei Frati.

Lombardy

Lombardy is to Milan what Chianti is to Florence and Barolo is to Turin: the city's vinous backyard. Surprisingly, given the thirst of the Milanese, their historic mercantile fortune, and the tourist attraction of the lakes, none of the region's wines have achieved as much fame as their counterparts in other parts of the country. The problem is perhaps one of definition; too many of the wines of Lombardy are often too like – if frequently better than – more famous stuff produced elsewhere.

So Lugana, in the east, is fairly described as up-market Soave (good Trebbiano in other words); in the Oltrepò Pavese hills there is a mass of varietals – Riesling, Pinot Grigio, Moscato *et al.* – producing pleasant wines that could be made almost anywhere in Italy. In Valtellina, up in the mountains, close to Switzerland, a quartet of villages called Grumello, Inferno, Sassella and Valgella produce wine that is at once delicate, floral and fruity – like a water-colour version of Barolo. Bottles labelled Valtellina Sfursat can command a higher price because of their beefier flavour and alcohol, characteristics that, to my mind, rather diminish the appeal.

Lombardy does have some very characterful wines of its own, though even here they often owe their individuality to the fact that they are blends of grapes that elsewhere rarely share a blending vat. The reds made in Oltrepò Pavese, for example, are produced from blends of the Barbera and the Bonarda, a variety normally only found in the Veneto. And then there is the fact that many of these wines are slightly sparkling. Judged on their own terms, like real Lambrusco, they can be refreshingly fruity wines with just enough of an acid bite to balance their juicy, plummy fruit. The whites often fizz here too; indeed Franciacorta is one of Italy's best-known sparklers. For a good example, try Maurizio Zanella's Ca' del Bosco, then take a deep breath, forget your bank manager and buy one of his brilliant Pinot Noir, Chardonnay or Cabernet table wines.

Liguria

The crescent-shaped region of the coast around Genoa is arguably the least well-known of all the wine-making areas of northern Italy. The most characterful wines here are the fragrant, floral red Rossese (reputedly the wine Napoleon drank when he wasn't sipping at his watered-down Chambertin) and two whites: the light, lemony Vermentino (no relation of the Sardinian grape of the same name) and the rather heavier Pigato. All three need to be drunk with rich Genovese cooking and are, in any case, rarely seen outside the region.

Valle d'Aosta

This is such a tiny region, with less than 2,500 acres (1,000 hectares) of steeply sloping vineyards, that it is hardly surprising that a single DOC bearing its name is used for all of the various wines produced here. Unfortunately, the range is so wide that the DOC is really rather meaningless. Linguistically this is tricky country too; Valle d'Aosta is as French as it's Italian.

Unfortunately, too, this is another of those regions where vine-growing is an endangered occupation. Tucked away among the eminently skiable mountains, Valle d'Aosta is a far from easy place in which to grow grapes. Trained monkeys might be happy working these terraces and slopes that overlook the Dora Baltea river, and they might even enjoy leaping between the pergolas on which the vines are trained; the young men of the 1990s tend to prefer a monthly pay-packet from Fiat.

There is, we have said, no such thing as a typical Valle d'Aosta wine, but you could start your exploration of the region by trying the Donnaz or an Arnad-Montjovet, both of which give a different accent to the Nebbiolo, allowing it to display a pungently distinctive, violetty perfume. From those semi-familiar flavours you could progress to Chambave Rosso, Torrette and Enfer d'Arvier (all of which are made from the local Petit Rouge), the Nus Rosso (made from the Vien de Nus) and thence to such obscure whites as Blanc de Morgeux (from the grape of the same name) and Nus, which will bring you back to the familiar territory of the Pinot Grigio. (See what we mean about it being varied?) And then, of course, there's the Pinot Nero (used to make red, pink and white – yes, white), the Gamay and even the Müller-Thurgau.

CENTRAL ITALY

Shut your eyes and imagine Italy; then think of this part of the country – the part that includes the regions of Emilia-Romagna, Latium and Tuscany – and the two visions are sure to overlap almost perfectly. There are Roman-tiled villas, dramatic landscapes and that extraordinary Italian co-existence of style and scruffiness to be found in every town. And such traditionally famous (and in some cases infamous) wines as Chianti, Frascati and Lambrusco, plus some of Italy's most exciting new wines, the "Super-Tuscans".

Tuscany

Tuscany is Renaissance country – in every way. The towns, the villages, the terracotta-roofed houses and the absurdly hummocky hills have changed little since the days when Leonardo da Vinci painted them, but this is also the heart of the renaissance of Italian wine. During the years when Italy seemed to be sliding down the same slope of mediocrity as Germany, fans of the classics of France lamented the paucity of Italian wines that could be realistically compared to the best of Bordeaux and Burgundy. And the region that attracted most of the flak was Tuscany.

Chianti's shortcomings had been less evident in the old days when most of the wine was sold cheaply in straw-covered *fiasco* bottles. But when the region's producers became pretentious enough to introduce Bordeaux-style bottles and to spend money promoting the black cockerel emblem of the supposedly quality-oriented Chianti Classico consortium, the general reaction among outsiders was that they were simply dressing their mutton as lamb.

The late 1970s saw a reassessment of what Chianti could and should be. The definition of where Chianti might legally be produced had been more or less established for nearly 700 years; the region had, however, grown in that time and split into segments including the central Chianti Classico and the Chianti Rufina zones. What remained questionable was the grape varieties from which this region's wines ought to be made. The principal and traditional variety, the Sangiovese, seemed unwilling to provide much in the way of flavour, which explains

why some of the producers began to think about adding Cabernet Sauvignon to their vats. The only problem was that to do so in any bottle labelled as Chianti would have involved breaking the law.

But the Cabernet campaigners maintained that even if their wines could only be sold as *vini da tavola*, they could still gain a reputation of their own and sell for a higher price than most Chianti. Thus were born the Super-Tuscans, that have catapulted Italy's wines back onto the world stage and are still giving the law-makers headaches.

During the 1970s, among the long list of wine-makers who turned to making Bordeaux-style *vini da tavola*, the most famous was Piero Antinori, whose ancestor had used Cabernet in his Chianti at the beginning of the century. Antinori's Sangiovese-Cabernet Sauvignon blend, Tignanello, was instantly acknowledged to be one of Italy's finest reds – and proof that you could sell a *vino da tavola* at a higher price than a DOC. The authorities belatedly read the writing on the wall, granting a DOC to the Chianti Montabano region of Carmignano for wines made from a blend of Sangiovese and Cabernet.

Just as it began to seem as though Chianti would become Cabernet country, in which all the best wines would owe at least some of their flavour to the Bordeaux

The Castello di Brolio, central Italy

THE ESSENTIALS

TUSCANY

What to look for Good traditional and excitingly made modern reds. Pleasant whites.

Official quality Possesses 3 of the 6 DOCGs in Brunello di Montalcino, Chianti Classico and Vino Nobile di Montepulciano. Notable DOCs are Carmignano, Pomino and Vernaccia di San Gimignano. There are also some red vini da tavola ("Super-Tuscans") such as Solaia and Tignanello which, like Sassicaia, should soon get their own DOCs.

Style Vernaccia di San Gimignano is the most famous local white. Smooth and nutty, with lots of fresh fruit and a hint of honey, it should be drunk within 2 to 3 years. Galestro and Pomino, a blend of Trebbiano, Pinot Bianco and Chardonnay, are both good. Chianti is by far the most important Italian red but, as a consequence of its large production, quality varies considerably. However, single-estate and riserva wines show good depth of raspberry and cherry fruit, gentle oak and a whiff of tobacco. Produced nearby, Carmignano gains chocolatey richness from around 10 per cent Cabernet Sauvignon, while Vino Nobile di Montepulciano has a richer, generous fruit character in its finest wines. Mature Brunello di Montalcino, at its best, is rich, heady and complex, full of concentrated dried fruit, plum and tobacco flavours. Some of the best wines of Tuscany, though, are the new-wave, barrique-aged wines from a handful of producers using Sangiovese, Cabernet Sauvignon or a blend of the two. The sherry-like Vin Santo, a red or white passito wine, can be dry, semi-sweet or sweet and, at its best, has a fine concentrated richness.

Climate Summers are long and fairly dry. Winters are cold.

Cultivation The best vineyards are on free-draining exposed hillsides where altitude moderates the long, hot growing season. Soils are complex; galestro, a crystalline rocky soil, dominates the best vineyards.

Grape varieties Red: Sangiovese, Cabernet Sauvignon, Brunello, Canaiolo Nero, Colorino, Mammolo; White: Trebbiano, Malvasia, Vernaccia, Grechetto, Chardonnay, Pinot Grigio, Pinot Bianco, Sauvignon Blanc.

Production/maturation Barrique-ageing has become much more common. Vin Santo is still very traditional, with grapes being dried indoors and the wine being aged for up to 6 years in sealed casks.

Longevity Reds: Chianti: 3–6 years for ordinary Chianti, but up to 20 for the best; Brunello di Montalcino: 10–25 years; Vino Nobile 6–25 years; barrique-aged reds: 5–25 years; other reds: 3–10 years; Whites: up to 5 years, although Vin Santo can last far longer.

Vintage guide 85, 87, 88, 90, 91, 94, 95, 97, 98.

Top 23 Antinori, Avignonesi, Castello di Volpaia, Marchese Incisa della Rochetta, Isole e Olena, Villa di Capezzana, Il Poggio, Vinattieri, Altesino, Badia a Coltibuono, Ruffino, Fontodi, Castelli di Ama, Castell'in Villa, Castellare, Felsina Berardenga, Monte Vertine, Argiano, Fattoria dei Barbi, Val di Suga, Talenti.

---

variety, Antinori and a number of his fellow producers began to experiment with different clones, including old Sangioveto (Sangiovese Toscano) vines, and to make pure Sangioveto wines, which they aged in small, new oak barrels. These managed to blend regional typicity with the ultra-fashionable flavour of new oak.

Tuscany is now an anarchic mess. Chianti Classico has been promoted to a DOCG, producers are now allowed to add 10 per cent of Cabernet to their vats, and a blind eye is turned to those who neglect to put in the obligatory white grapes. These developments have finally encouraged a move toward higher-quality Chianti – both in the Chianti Classico region and in other parts of the area – but they haven't deterred anyone from making at least one *vino da tavola* that, until new rules are sorted out to allow it a *denominazione* of its own, stands outside the DOC system. In fact, today Tuscan wineries have Bordeaux-style or pure Sangioveto wines like newly fledged republics have airlines. At their best, these wines are some of the tastiest reds in the world with a distinctly "Italian" flavour of blackcurrants, and fresh herbs. At their worst, they are impeccably packaged, shamelessly overpriced imposters.

Ask most well-read wine-drinkers to name Italy's greatest wine and some, at least, are sure to come up with the estate of Biondi-Santi in Brunello di Montalcino. Then ask them when they last tasted a bottle of its wine. Biondi-Santi and Brunello (as the DOCG is known) have lived on their reputations for a very long time, relying on the sheer muscle of their wines and the requirement that they be aged for four years in wood to convince people that they were the best in the region. What used to make Brunello special was the fine character of the grape, the brown-skinned clone of the Sangiovese.

Today, as other Tuscans pay greater heed to their clones, Brunello's producers have had to work hard to compete. Some of the old-fashioned, long-aged wines can shed their tannic husks to develop glorious herby, spicy, dried-fruit flavours; some never make it. If you are impatient, or not much of a gambler, try more modern examples from producers like Altesino or Tenuta Caparzo – or the less woody, more immediately approachable Rosso di Montalcino. Old Biondi-Santi wines are worth tasting if you are offered the chance, if only because they provide an insight into the way wines used to taste here.

Until quite recently, the least noble thing about the wonderful hilltop town of Montepulciano was its Vino Nobile di Montepulciano. In blind tastings, few people could tell the difference between Vino Nobile and fairly basic Chianti; both were dull, over-aged and often oxidized. Becoming a DOCG (the first in Italy) has changed things here, too, just as it did in Chianti. Spurred on by the quality of Avignonesi's wines, Montepulciano's producers have begun to make finer, spicier, more intense wines. Some are still left for too long in barrel, but a new DOC – Rosso di Montepulciano – now gives an incentive for all but the very best wine to be bottled earlier.

There is no longer any such wine as white Chianti, but that's what Galestro is in all but name. Light, slightly Muscadet-like (though with even less character than the best examples of that wine), Galestro is the commercial brainchild of a group of Chianti producers who sought a way to dispose of a surplus of white grapes.

For the moment it has no DOC, but is controlled by an association of its makers. Its quality rarely rises above, nor descends below, a basic level of adequacy. Vernaccia di San Gimignano (from the extraordinary town of that name whose medieval towers dominate the landscape like so many ancient skyscrapers), on the other hand, is a white wine that has both a DOC and the delicious, tangy flavour of the Vernaccia grape.

Before leaving Tuscany, don't miss the chance to taste the local examples of the sweet or (less impressive) dry Vin Santo. These wines' sherry-like flavour comes partly from intentional slight oxidation, and partly from the fact that good producers use a type of *solera* system, adding a little "*madre*" (mother) of the previous year's wine to the new cask. Dunk a *cantuccini* almond biscuit in a top-quality Vin Santo (Avignonesi makes an especially good one) and you will wonder why this wine is so little known. Taste the cheap, syrupy versions served in most restaurants and you'll wonder why anyone drinks it at all.

THE ESSENTIALS

UMBRIA/LATIUM

What to look for Characterful whites and – from Lungarotti – tasty modern reds.

Official quality Approximately 10 per cent of production is DOC, the best-known of which are Orvieto, Torgiano, Est!Est!!Est!!! and Frascati.

Style Frascati is the most significant white of Latium. Often very dull, it can have soft, refreshing citrus fruit. Est! Est!! Est!!! is the most memorable name – but the same cannot be said of this often disappointing dry or semi-sweet wine itself. Orvieto, sadly, is rarely seen at its best, when it has a lovely fat richness to it, combining honey and peaches with nutty overtones. It can be dry or semi-sweet (abboccato/amabile), the latter style often including botrytized grapes. Two good oaked Chardonnays are produced by Antinori and Lungarotti. Torgiano, the Umbrian DOC created and virtually wholly owned by Dr Lungarotti, produces well-structured reds that are packed with soft, plummy fruit coupled with a good portion of oak. Lungarotti also makes a fine Cabernet Sauvignon, rich, perfumed and well-balanced. Torre Ercolana and Fiorano are good Cabernet-Merlot blends produced in Latium. Falerno, by contrast, is rich and rustic.

Climate Hot, dry summers and warm autumns. Winters are fairly mild.

Cultivation Soils vary greatly but outcrops of limestone, clay and gravel are frequent. Most vineyards are located on hillsides for drainage and exposure to the sun while altitude is used to moderate the heat.

Grape varieties Red: Sangiovese, Canaiolo, Cabernet Sauvignon, Merlot, Cesanese, Montepulciano, Barbera, Aglianico, Aliegiolo; White: Trebbiano, Malvasia, Grechetto, Chardonnay, Pinot Bianco.

Production/maturation Modern vinification techniques are resulting in a general improvement in the quality of wines. Experimental blending of foreign grapes with indigenous varieties has shown what potential can be realized by wine-makers in Italy and has given added impetus to similar experimentation elsewhere.

Longevity Most whites should be drunk young, within 1 to 3 years. Some Orvieto abboccato can be aged for up to 10 years while the few examples of oak-aged Chardonnay can be matured for 3 to 8 years. The majority of basic reds can be drunk within 5 years though Torgiano can be kept for 3 to 8 years, the riserva for 5 to 12 and Torre Ercolana and Fiorano require some 5 years to show their class and can last for 12 to 15 years.

Vintage guide Reds: 90, 91, 93, 94, 95, 97.

Top 8 Colli di Catone (Colle Gaio), Fontana Candida (Santa Teresa), Lungarotti, Antinori, Bigi, Decugnano del Barbi, Cantina Colacicchi, Boncompagni Ludovisi.

Umbria

Umbria has never quite had the magic of Tuscany; Perugia has yet to gain the cachet of Siena and Florence. But, as the more northerly region increasingly deserves John Mortimer's witty description of it as "Chiantishire", the focus of attention is bound to shift downward. And when it does, hopefully Orvieto, one of Italy's most ancient wines, will be taken more seriously. Sadly, most modern Orvieto lacks the honeyed, nutty character that earned this town's wines their reputation. The occasional sweet, nobly rotten examples can be good, but the more usual medium-dry *abboccato* or dry examples are unmemorable. Antinori's is pleasant but uninspiring; for a more special experience, try the Terre Vinati from Palazone.

But it isn't Orvieto that is attracting the attention these days, it is Torgiano, a region that owes its reputation almost exclusively to the efforts of Dr Giorgio Lungarotti, whose extraordinarily successful wines – notably the Rubesco reds – have become so established that he has single-handedly won Torgiano its own DOCG.

Latium

Rome's backyard is a surprisingly barren source of good wine. The one DOC almost everyone has heard of, Frascati, has, like Soave, sadly become "just one of those cheap Italian whites", produced and drunk in bulk by people who care little about quality. Actually, Frascati is, if anything, often an even worse buy than Soave, because, while the latter wine is rarely worse than dull, the former can be just the other side of likeable because of its odd sour-cream character. And don't imagine that paying a little extra for Frascati Superiore will buy you anything better; it won't – just a wine that's a little more alcoholic.

The problem, as so often in Italy, is silly local laws; if you make wine in this region exclusively from the local Malvasia del Lazio, it can be terrific – but it's illegal as Frascati, because the rules limit its proportion to 30 per cent. To produce a wine that can call itself Frascati, you have to use the lesser quality Malvasia di Candia or, worse still, the Trebbiano. In other words, the less palatable it tastes, the more likely it is to be genuine.

Fortunately, there are Frascati-makers who get their Malvasias mixed up and sidestep the law by using the good Malvasia del Lazio instead of the di Candia. And, as in Soave, there is a move toward wines from individual vineyards, such as Fontana Candida's Santa Teresa. Even so, it does not bode well for Frascati's image that Colle Gaio, the best wine to come out of the region recently, makes almost no mention of Frascati on its label.

Marino and Montecompatri can both be better buys – provided that they are caught young. Traditional writers like to pretend that Est! Est!! Est!!! di Montefiascone is one of the region's finest wines, recounting the old story that it owes its name to the enthusiasm of a visitor who shouted, with growing enthusiasm, "It is! It is!! It is!!!". For most of the examples on offer today, the words "Boring! Boring!! Boring!!!" would be rather more appropriate.

There is so little Aleatico di Gradoli produced that it is hardly worth mentioning, but for the fact that this is one of Italy's more unusual grapes, and the fortified and unfortified sweet whites it produces close to Rome boast a perfumey, grapey character.

Up in the Castelli Romani hills, Velletri's is a name that deserves to be better-known. The Wine Research Institute of Latium has experimental vineyards here and makes tasty reds from a blend of Cesanese, Sangiovese and Montepulciano, and a rich white from the Malvasia and Trebbiano that is immeasurably better than all but the very best Frascati. The Cesanese is also used to make a number of other reds, such as Cesanese di Olevano Romano, Cesanese di Affile, Cesanese del Piglio and, with a little help from the Montepulciano and the Nero Buono di Cori, Cori Rosso.

Emilia-Romagna

Think of Parma ham, of Parmesan, of Spaghetti Bolognese... Emilia-Romagna is the home of all of these, and of the barrel-aged, intense balsamic vinegar of Modena, and of one of the world's most commercially successful wines: Lambrusco, the sweet, frothy red, white or pink stuff drunk directly from its screwtop bottle by countless thirsty drunks in Britain and the USA. But the stuff those drunks enjoy would be unrecognizable to an Italian; his version of Lambrusco has a DOC, comes in a bottle with a cork and is bone-dry, with an unripe-plum acidity that takes a lot of getting used to. The best comes from Cavicchioli.

Beyond Lambrusco, Emilia-Romagna – a hot, flat swathe of land – has some worthwhile wines to offer. The place not to look for good wine is, paradoxically, Italy's first white DOCG, Albana di Romagna, which is rarely other than pleasantly boring. Much the same (though without the "pleasantly") could be said for Trebbiano di Romagna. The red Sangiovese di Romagna is better, but don't go expecting it to taste like Chianti; the clone is different and the style lighter. Fattoria Paradiso makes one of the few decent ones.

Down in the south-west of the region, Bianco di Scandiano proves that the Sauvignon can make good wine in the warmer parts of Italy, but it is up in the Colli (the hills) that most of the region's tastiest wines are to be found. Close to Umbria, Colli Piacenti produces dry and *amabile*, slighty fizzy whites, in which the aromatic qualities of grapes such as the Malvasia and Moscato are sometimes smothered by the ubiquitous Trebbiano. The reds – particularly Gutturnio, a tobaccoey-fruity blend of the Bonarda and local varieties – are more interesting.

There is some first-class red, too, made by Terre Rosse and Tenuta Bissera from the Cabernet Sauvignon in Bologna's hills – the Colli Bolognesi, a DOC that confusingly encompasses the DOCs of Monte San Pietro

and Castelli Medioevali. Other varieties, including the Malvasia and (unofficially, because it is not allowed by the DOC) Chardonnay, are similarly well handled, but it is the Sauvignon that is the real star, both here and in nearby Colli di Parma, provided you aren't looking for wines with the bite of good Sancerre.

Marche

For some reason Verdicchio has achieved greater fame and popularity in the USA than it has in Britain or even in Italy itself. Outsiders imagine that the shape of the recognizable bottle is traditional, and based on that of ancient *amphorae*. Older Italians wink knowingly; they refer to it as the "Gina Lollobrigida", after the spectacularly proportioned Italian actress, and recall its introduction back in the 1950s.

There are actually several kinds of Verdicchio, all made in this hilly region from the Verdicchio grape, a high-acid variety that needs careful handling. Used carelessly, its wines taste the way they sound – green, or "verde". The fact that a wine comes from the castles of Jesus – Castelli di Jesi – or from the lesser-

---

THE ESSENTIALS
EMILIA-ROMAGNA

What to look for Light, tangy reds (including "real" Lambrusco) and tasty Sauvignon whites.

Location The region surrounding Bologna in central-east Italy.

Official quality Contains the first white DOCG, Albana di Romagna, and a number of DOCs but the bulk of the production is vino da tavola. DOCs you may come across are Colli Bolognesi and Sangiovese di Romagna.

Style Straightforward commercial wines of all types, including sparkling and semi-sparkling. The generally dull Albana di Romagna typifies much of the white-wine production. It comes in either a dry or semi-sweet version that may be spumante. Fortunately there are a few outstanding wines, such as the buttery Terre Rosse Chardonnay or Baldi's rich, balanced Sangiovese reds. Lambrusco is by far the most well-known wine

produced in the region and may be dry, semi-sweet or sweet, red, white or rosato, barely frizzantino or virtually sparkling. Traditional red Lambrusco is low in alcohol, off-dry and full of ripe, cherry-flavoured fruit. "Commercial" Lambrusco, recognizable by its screwcap, is more like fizzy pop.

Climate Hot, dry Mediterranean summers, the effects of which are alleviated by altitude and aspect. Winters are cool.

Cultivation Flat plains of rich alluvial soil, notably in the valley of the river Po, result in abundant yields. The best vineyards are, however, located in the well-drained foothills of the Appennines.

Grape varieties Red: Sangiovese, Barbera, Bonarda, Cabernet Sauvignon, Pinot Nero, Cabernet Franc; White: Trebbiano, Lambrusco,

Albana, Malvasia, Chardonnay, Sauvignon, Pinot Bianco, Pinot Grigio, Müller-Thurgau.

Production/maturation Viticultural practices and vinification techniques are as varied as the quality of the reds. Bulk-blending is used for the commercial wines but elsewhere traditional practices are maintained with the adoption of modern methods where necessary.

Longevity Most wines – red, white or rosato – are best drunk young, although the quality reds of producers like Baldi, Vallania and Vallunga may need up to 15 years to be at their best. Terre Rosse Chardonnay requires 2–5 years.

Vintage guide Vintages have little effect on the majority of commercial or blended wines from this fertile area.

Top 6 Fattoria Paradiso, Baldi, Vallania, Vallunga, Il Moro, Cavicchioli.

THE ESSENTIALS

MARCHE/ABRUZZI-MOLISE

What to look for Rich, traditional reds to drink with game and light appley whites.

Location Central-east Italy.

Official quality The majority of wines are vini da tavola but around 12 per cent are DOC, notably Montepulciano d'Abruzzo, Rosso Conero, Rosso Piceno, Verdicchio dei Castelli di Jesi and Biferno.

Style Verdicchio del Castelli di Jesi is the most famous wine of Marche which, at its best, has a full appley flavour with hints of honey and nut. Rosso Piceno produces firm, fruity, sometimes herby reds with good acidity. Those from Rosso Conero are richer, more complex, combining under-ripe plums, dried fruit and herbs with a pinch of spice. Montepulciano d'Abruzzo ought to be the only wine of real quality from the Abruzzi region; at its best it can be full of ripe, plummy fruit with a velvety texture and fine balancing acidity. The rosato is called Cerasuolo. Molise produces tannic reds and dry rosatos that as yet have proved unexciting.

Climate Typical Mediterranean climate with dry, hot summers and cool winters. Cooler micro-climates occur at higher altitudes.

Cultivation Limestone and granite outcrops occur often in these hilly regions, although alluvial soils dominate in the coastal plains.

Grape varieties Red: Montepulciano, Sangiovese, Ciliegiolo, Merlot; White: Trebbiano, Malvasia, Verdicchio, Pinot Grigio, Riesling Italico.

Production/maturation Still a traditional area, although modern methods are beginning to creep in. Barrique-ageing is employed for Rosso Conero, Rosso Piceno and for some whites. Molise in particular requires considerable investment to improve its poorly equipped wine industry.

Longevity Reds: Rosso Conero and Rosso Piceno: 5–15 years; Montepulciano d'Abruzzo: 4–20 years, depending on the style and the producer; other reds: up to 8 years; Whites: Verdicchio: 2–3 years; other whites: within 4 years of the vintage, though most are best drunk young.

Vintage guide Reds: 90, 91, 93, 94, 95, 97.

Top 11 Mecvini, Umani Ronchi, Marchetti, Tatta, Tenuta S. Agnese, Valentini, Pepe, Illuminati, Masseria di Majo Norante, Barone Cornacchia, Villa Pigna.

known DOC of Verdicchio di Matelica means little too. Everything depends on the producer; Umani Ronchi has proved that Verdicchio from a good single vineyard, such as his Casal di Serra, can handle new oak and can even age quite well; others are taking advantage of the variety's acidity to use it for sparkling wine. Another local grape, the Bianchello, also produces pleasant, if unexciting, light white wines that are labelled as Bianchello del Metauro.

Marche reds are blends of the Montepulciano and the Sangiovese, and vary depending on which of the two grape varieties has been allowed to take charge. Rosso Conero has bags of rich depth, thanks to the 85 per cent of Montepulciano that it has to contain; Rosso Piceno is more common, lighter and less emphatically fruity because of its higher Sangiovese content.

It is also worth looking out for Cumaro, Umani Ronchi's answer to the Super-Tuscans, and the pure Montepulciano Vellutato from Villa Pigna. This last winery is also breaking new ground in a very Tuscan style with a Cabernet/Sangiovese/Montepulciano blend called Tenuta di Pongelli. Watch these two wineries; they may be the forerunners of a wave of interesting Marche wines.

Abruzzi

One day soon – when it catches up with the last decade of wine-making progress in Tuscany and Piemonte – this empty, mountainous region on the Adriatic coast is going to be worth knowing about. There are two main grape varieties grown here, the red Montepulciano, used for Montepulciano d'Abruzzo, and the local clone of the Trebbiano, from which the white Trebbiano d'Abruzzo is made. The former wine can be rich, peppery and chocolatey (from producers such as Valentini and Barone Cornacchia), but the latter is rarely better than dull.

Molise

This tiny region is better known for its pasta and honey than for the two DOCs – Pentro and Biferno – that it received years after every other part of Italy had been allotted its quota. Pentro deserved to remain unknown, but Biferno is of greater interest, partly because of the proximity of its vines to the sea and partly because one estate, Masseria di Majo Norante, is using Montepulciano and Sangiovese to make a first-class red called Ramitello. The spicy white made here from Trebbiano, Malvasia and Falanghina, is good too, but has no DOC because of the presence of the Falanghina. Such are the rules.

THE SOUTH

The probable birthplace of California's Zinfandel, this poor, sun-baked region was, until recently, handicapped by a lack of equipment and modern wine-making know-how and, most crucially, an absence of the will to produce better wine. And why should the wine-growers here bother? For far too long, they had a ready market for the thick, alcoholic soup with which the northerners repaired the defects in their own cooler-climate reds. Fortunately, however, as some more enterprising producers have recently rediscovered, they also had characteristic grape varieties grown nowhere else.

Campania

The region overlooked by Mount Vesuvius is one of the cradles of Italian wine-making and the home of the ancient Falerno del Massico, whose three styles provide the opportunity to taste the local grape varieties. The old-fashioned, woody reds and rosés are made from the Aglianico, the Piedirosso and the Primitivo; the dull white is 100 per cent Falanghina. Far more interesting than these, though, is the pure Aglianico Taurasi, which can display all sorts of plummy, spicy flavours. Mastroberardino, who makes most of the Taurasi, also produces the white Fiano di Avellino and the spicily attractive Greco di Tufo.

Calabria

This poor, windy and mountainous region deserves to be better known for its success with one grape, the Greco. With the help of equipment to cool the fermentation tanks, producers are now using this variety to make creamy-peachy dry wines in the shape of Melissa and the rather more intense Ciro Bianco, and gloriously sweet and fairly alcoholic bianco in Greco di Bianco (look for examples from Umberto Ceratti). Calabria's reds are mostly made from the local Gaglioppo grape. Best of these potentially chocolatey wines are Ciro Rosso and Savuto.

Basilicata

If Calabria appears poor, this scrubby region seems positively poverty-stricken. It's not a good place to farm anything really; some areas are parched by the sun and drought; others, on the hills, are astonishingly cool. But it is on the extinct volcano of Mount Vulture here that the Aglianico can make its most impressive wine. Donato d'Angelo makes long-lived, deep spicy, chocolatey Aglianico del Vulture here and a *vino da tavola* called Cannetto, which is one of the south's most exciting "modern" wines.

Puglia

The heel of the Italian boot has long been considered the source of blending wine for the north, but modern wine-making techniques are beginning to pay off. Castel del Monte is a good DOC for red (mostly Montepulciano), rosé (made from the Uva di Troia) and, to a lesser extent, white. Look for the Il Falcone made by Rivera, this region's best producer. Brindisi is very characterful stuff, largely made from the Negroamaro. The best example is probably Taurino's Patriglione in which the bitterness is toned down with a little Malvasia Nera. The Gravina co-operative is proving that a little disrespect for the official rules – they leave out a couple of dull grape varieties – makes for characterful white, aromatic yet dry Greco di Tufo. Look out too for the fresh inexpensive wines, including a delicious rosé made here by Australian-born Flying Wine-maker Kym Milne.

Sicily

Sicily is trying to improve its image by funding one of Italy's most go-ahead wine-research stations, with a brief to find the most modern methods to bring out the best in indigenous grapes such as the Nero Mascalese, the Frappato and the Perricone.

These are all varieties you'll have encountered in wines from Corvo – as the Casa Vinicola Duca di Salaparuta prefers to be known. This range of *vini da tavola* wines has been so well marketed internationally that the company name is widely thought to be a DOC. None of the wines is bad – but they're pricy. The red and white *vini da tavola* of Regaleali are cheaper and worth trying, as are the more modern Terre de Ginestra and the increasingly attractive offerings of the Settesoli co-operative.

The best-known Sicilian wine, though, is of course, Marsala. A potentially great fortified wine, Marsala's name has been debased by the limited aspirations of its producers and consumers and by wrapping itself up in silly and lax laws (you can use almost any grape variety, make almost any style and bottle it at almost any age). For a taste of the real stuff, look out for Marco de Bartoli's great fortified Moscato Passito called Bukkuram.

For similarly fine sweet wines go to the volcanic Lipari islands where Carlo Hauner's Malvasia delle Lipari is one of the prettiest raisiny wines I've tasted. Florio's Erba di Luce runs it a close race, though.

Sardinia

Until recently this was a better place for a holiday than for wine. Today thankfully, as in Sicily, there's a busy wine-research station helping a growing number of producers to discover new ways of using the island's grapes. Arguably the best wines being made in Sardinia today are from Sella e Mosca, whose Anghelu Ruju, an extraordinary port-like wine made from the Cannonau (the Spanish Garnacha and the French Grenache), has now been joined by a dry red called Marchese di Villamagna, good enough to beat many a Super-Tuscan. Nuragus di Cagliari, the best-known of Sardinia's whites, is cleaner and fresher than in the past, but is still pretty anonymous; Vermentino can be better. For something a little different, try the sherry-like Vernaccia di Oristano and the Malvasia and Moscati.

THE ESSENTIALS
SOUTHERN ITALY

What to look for Hefty reds, a few traditional, characterful Greco whites, sweet and fortified wines and, most excitingly, the impact of modern wine-making on unusual indigenous grape varieties.

Official quality The vast majority is vino da tavola with small quantities of DOC wine. DOCs include: Castel del Monte, Primitivo di Manduria, Salice Salentino, and Squinzano in Apulia; Aglianico del Vulture, Cirò and Greco di Bianco in Basilicata; Greco di Tufo, Taurasi and Vesuvio in Campania; Marsala, Malvasia di Lipori and Etna in Sicily; and Cannonau di Sardegna in Sardinia.

Style Most whites are dull and flabby while the reds are rich, heady concoctions. Nevertheless, there are a growing number of crisper, more characterful wines. Apulia produces a great deal of ordinary wine but Il Falcone, Castel del Monte Riserva and Favorio are good, fruity exceptions. Full-bodied, robust reds of good quality can also be found from Squinzano, Salice Salentino and Manduria. A light, well-balanced and fragrantly fruity rosato is produced by Calo as Rosa del Golfo. Famous for Lacrima Christi del Vesuvio, which is produced in all styles, Campania's best wines are the robust and rustic Falerno and the vigorous Taurasi with its rich chocolate, liquorice and herby flavours. Greco di Tufo and Fiano di Avellano are good, dry, fruity whites. The rich, bitter-sweet, chocolate-cherry Aglianico del Vulture from d'Angelo is Basilicata's only wine of real quality while the same can be said of Calabria's luscious and vibrantly sweet Greco di Bianco. Sicily is famous for its fortified Marsalas but produces full, smooth and fruity reds – Corvo and Regaleali – and the nearby island of Lipari makes some great, grapey Malvasia and some well-made crisp, dry whites. Sardinia produces a full range of styles: best are the improving, Beaujolais-style Cannonau, the aromatic Moscato, the dry, slightly bitter Vernaccia, and Sella e Mosca's port-like Anghelu Ruju.

Climate The hottest and driest part of Italy, though altitude and sea-breezes have an effect.

Cultivation Apulia has fertile plains and gentle slopes but much of the rest of this area is composed of volcanic hills and outcrops of granite. The best vineyard sites are located on the cooler, higher north-facing slopes. New grape varieties and earlier harvesting, which preserves what acidity the grapes can muster in this hot climate, have been employed to good effect.

Grape varieties Red: Aglianico, Barbera, Negroamaro, Primitivo, Malvasia Nera, Cannonau, Cabernet Franc, Malbec, Pinot Nero, Carignan, Montepulciano, Monica; White: Pinot Bianco, Chardonnay Trebbiano, Greco, Vernaccia, Vermentino, Torbato, Sauvignon, Moscato, Malvasia, Fiano, Inzolia, Grillo, Catarratto.

Production/maturation Poverty, together with unrelenting heat, results in a large amount of ordinary wine. But considerable modernization of equipment has been undertaken in some areas, notably in Sicily and Sardinia, with evident improvements in quality. Temperature-controlled fermentation and early bottling are beginning to show improved results.

Longevity Reds: Most should be drunk within 5 years. The following are exceptions – Il Falcone, Aglianico del Vulture, Taurasi: 8 to 20 years; Favorito: 3 to 10 years. Whites: Most are for drinking within 1 to 3 years, though Greco di Bianco requires 3–5 years.

Vintage guide 81, 82, 83, 85, 86, 88, 90, 92, 94, 98.

Top 12 Sicily: Terre di Ginestra, Regaleali, de Bartoli, Hauner, Florio; Sardinia: Sella e Mosca; Taurasi: Mastroberardino; Aglianico del Vulture: Fratelli d'Angelo; Greco di Bianco: Ceratti; Puglia: Rivera, Taurino, the Gravina co-operative.

GERMANY

"Made in Germany". Three words which, when applied to a car, a washing machine or a piece of hi-fi equipment, are synonymous with the highest quality – albeit at some of the highest prices. But high quality and high prices are hardly the words that spring to mind when most non-Germans think of the wines of the Rhine and Mosel.

Sadly, over the last 50 years, the vast mass of Germany's wine sold outside its borders has increasingly and shamefully lived down to a basic image of cheap, sugary plonk which has helped to edge finer examples off the pages of smart wine lists.

Ironically, the style of wine for which Germany has become best-known is not the stuff the Germans like to drink themselves, nor the style their northern European vineyards are best suited to produce. It's as though Robert de Niro had developed a reputation as a performer in tacky musicals.

The Quality Compromise

Some years, trying to ripen grapes in Germany can be a little like trying to grill a steak over a candle. Which might seem to be a pretty good reason for not making wine here at all – except that, like the Loire and Burgundy, Germany enjoys the benefits of a "marginal" climate. Like a racing driver whose skills come to the fore when his car is closest to its top speed, grapes tend to produce their most impressive feats of flavour in the testing conditions provided by regions where they cannot ripen too easily.

Vines are grown on the steep slopes either side of the river Mosel

Before the Second World War, Germany used to produce two kinds of wine: dry and often rather raw-tasting stuff in the frequent cool years, and sweeter, sometimes gloriously sweet, wines in the rare years when the sun shone sufficiently to ripen the grapes and, more especially, when noble rot (here called *Edelfäule*) appeared in the autumn to give the wines their characteristic, rich intensity of flavour.

Unfortunately, those rare years came far too rarely to guarantee grape-growers a decent livelihood and, after the war, the rest of the world was not overly eager to buy German wines of any description. It was hardly surprising, therefore, that the growers embraced any new idea that promised to make their lives easier. First came the simple but radical decision to begin replacing the Riesling, which had made Germany's reputation, with a range of easier-to-grow, easier-to-ripen varieties such as the Müller-Thurgau, Optima and Reichensteiner, all of which were especially developed to be reliable producers of large quantities of fruit even in the least hospitable climates. None of these new grapes were used to make wine that was remotely as good as Riesling – even when they were capable of doing so.

Then, the wine-makers developed ways of countering the quality problem. Following Mary Poppins' advice, they added a spoonful of sugar – or, to be more precise, two spoonfuls. The first was of granulated sugar, to raise the alcohol level (the same legitimate process of chaptalization that has long been used in such northern French regions as Burgundy), while the second was in the form of sweet grape juice, or *süssreserve* which, "backblended" with the wine, gave it an appealing grapiness that would either make a good but not-quite-ripe wine taste better, or turn a dull, unripe dry wine into an equally dull sweet one. It was this combination of the new grape varieties with the widespread adoption of backblending, and thus sweeter flavours, that revolutionized the style of German wine.

The German Wine Laws

None of this would, however, have been possible without the rather eccentric set of wine laws drawn up in 1971 and vainly amended as recently as 1989. The best way to understand these laws is to compare them with those of Germany's neighbour on the other side of the Rhine. France's vinous legislation is unashamedly class-conscious; if you are Château Latour, or a slice of a Burgundy *Grand Cru* vineyard such as Le Corton or Le Montrachet, your wine will be classed among the French wine nobility because, for hundreds of years, these particular vineyards have consistently made the best wine. But if you are a parcel of land on the other, the middle-class, side of the tracks, then, however well your vines are tended and your wine is made, it will never earn you the respect paid to a true aristocrat.

In Germany, almost all vineyards are created equal. Although, as in France, there are inevitably slopes and parts of slopes that have a centuries-old reputation for making the best wines in their regions, German legislation, unlike French law, recognizes no such inherent superiority. In other words, a piece of poorly situated, flat land could theoretically produce a wine of the same legally designated "quality" as one on the finest hillside in the country.

Ripeness is All

Why? Because the only criterion is ripeness. The more natural sugar the grapes contain, the higher the quality designation the wine can claim. So, a wine labelled as *Auslese*, for example, will have been made from riper, sweeter grapes than one labelled as *Spätlese*, which would, in turn, have been produced from riper ones than a *Kabinett*.

All three of these designations, along with the still riper *Beerenauslese*, *Trocken-beerenauslese* and *Eiswein*, fall into Germany's top category of QmP – *Qualitätswein mit Prädikat* (literally, "quality wine with distinction") – and are subject to (somewhat) stricter regulation than wines that are simply labelled QbA – *Qualitätswein bestimmter Anbaugebiete* ("quality wine from a given area").

A Lack of Definition

"Quality wine from a given area"? Isn't that the equivalent of France's AOC? No – for the simple reason that the "given area" in question encompasses all of Germany's recognized vine-growing land. It is the "quality" (ripeness) factor that earns the wine its designation. In all but the very best or very worst vintages, around 80 per cent of Germany's wine – including every drop of Liebfraumilch – is legally sold as QbA, with the finer QmP wines and the two most basic, least ripe categories, *Landwein* and *Tafelwein*, making up the remaining 20 per cent. In a great, warm year like 1990 or 1993, for instance, around half of Germany's production could be sold as QmP and nary a drop had to languish as *Landwein* or *Tafelwein*. In France, by comparison, much less than a third of the national annual harvest can ever be sold as *Appellation Contrôlée*, and there is in France no national "super-AOC" equivalent of QmP.

Supporters of the way the German laws have been drawn up claim, quite reasonably, that the ripeness rules themselves help to sort out the good, well-sited, hillside vineyards (which get a lot of sun) from those on poor, flat land (which don't). This may well be true for the Riesling, but it conveniently ignores the readiness of those newer varieties to ripen in cooler places.

For the egalitarianism of German wine law also extends to the kinds of grapes that are grown. In the regions of France, there exists what could be called viticultural apartheid. If you want to make Gevrey-Chambertin, you have to use the Pinot Noir; if your label says Sauternes, there are only four grape varieties you can legally grow. In Germany it's almost a free-for-all. All of which makes buying German wine pretty complicated, as anyone who has wondered what on earth all those words on the label mean will testify.

Gothic Horror

Apart from the vintage and producer, there is the region (one of a possible 13), the district and/or village and/or vineyard (of which there are over 2,500, most of which have dauntingly long and complicated names by themselves, let alone in combination), the grape variety, the quality level (in other words, the ripeness) and, quite possibly, an indication of the wine's sweetness or dryness in the form of such terms as *Kabinett*, *Spätlese* and *Auslese*, *Trocken* and *Halbtrocken*.

And this is where it all gets more complicated still. Most wine books equate the ripeness "quality ladder" with an ascending order of sweetness – hence an *Auslese* will be sweeter than a *Spätlese*, which will, in turn, be sweeter than a *Kabinett*. Except that the amount of

natural sugar in the grape may not have any bearing on the sweetness of the finished wine; the super-ripe grapes of the sunny Rhône, after all, make wines that are more alcoholic – not "sweeter" – than those of cooler Burgundy. And, in recent years, the Germans have increasingly turned to making "*Trocken*" (dry) and "*Halbtrocken*" (off-dry) wines to compete with white Burgundy and Sancerre. So an *Auslese Trocken* will be a bone-dry wine made from (much) riper grapes than a decidedly sweet traditional *Kabinett*.

Is it any wonder that the average wine-drinker just feels too confused to dare to buy a bottle of finer German wine? (If it's to accompany a meal, knowing how sweet a wine is in advance can be crucial.) The German authorities have handicapped their producers still further by interpreting EC wine laws so literally that they forbid a German wine-maker (or his British or other European importer) to describe his wines in the same way as, say, the Australians or Californians do.

So a producer in the Mosel cannot even print a back-label telling potential customers that his wine is "dry and appley" – because, the authorities claim, he might possibly mislead consumers into thinking that it was made from apples rather than grapes.

In this bedlam, it sometimes seemed as though the only people who were doing well out of the German wine industry were the companies who specialized in holding tastings in the homes of unsuspecting people, who were persuaded to pay way over the odds for wines often made from decidedly ordinary grapes in decidedly ordinary vineyards. Meanwhile, some of Germany's finest estates, by contrast, annually fought off financial disaster.

Producers Take the Lead

Rescue for these estates came, in at least one case, in the form of investment from Japan. Meanwhile a growing number of producers have begun to take matters into their own hands to dissociate themselves from the Liebfraumilch lobby, to create new styles and revive traditional ones, to devise clearer labels and, above all, to rehabilitate Germany's reputation as a producer of some of the most uniquely exciting wines in the world.

Thanks to demand for new styles from German wine-drinkers themselves, to the enthusiasm of

Harvesting grapes can be back-breaking working especially on the steep slopes of the rivers Mosel and Rhine

importers in other countries – particularly Britain – and to a series of good and very good vintages, the range and quality of German wines is improving by the year. Today, wine-drinkers can find dry German whites that compete for quality and price with Muscadet, Chardonnays and, more particularly, Pinot Noirs, to worry quite a few producers in Burgundy; juicy reds made from such varieties as the Dornfelder and Lemberger; and versions of the Pinot Gris and Gewürztraminer that are excitingly different from the Alsatian examples most people have encountered.

The New Wines

And then, of course, there are the Rieslings, the wines that still set Germany apart and that now come in almost any style you could desire: dry (*Trocken*), off-dry (*Halbtrocken*), with or without the vanilla of new oak barrels... You name it, somebody is probably trying to make it from the Riesling somewhere in Germany, extracting all the nuances of flavour they can find in what, in the right hands, can be the most aristocratic white grape of them all.

The good guys who are making these wines get precious little help from their government – which is anxious to keep the votes of the rather more numerous and vociferous bulk-wine brigade – so they have set up their own self-help, self-regulating associations.

One of these, the Charta association of the Rheingau, is responsible for what could be a most constructive initiative: an attempt to introduce a French-style system of vineyard classification – probably limited initially at least to *Grands Crus* – which would recognize the best sites, the kinds of grapes grown in them, and the quantity of wine they can produce every year.

The day on which these efforts are granted official recognition will be a red-letter one for those people dismayed at the prospect of a world in which there are only two kinds of white wine – Liebfraumilch and Chardonnay.

THE MOSEL

If the Rhine is the most famous wine river in Germany, it is the Mosel that is the most exciting, and the most dramatic. Rivers all over the world are so often said to curve like snakes that the description has become a cliché, which is a pity, because the Mosel genuinely is just about the nearest thing to a liquid boa constrictor you would ever want to see. From Perl, the meeting point of Luxembourg, France and Germany, it carves its way sinuously for 145 miles (233 km) north-eastwards to meet the Rhine at Koblenz. On its way it passes forests, castles, tiny precariously perched villages, and sheer slopes covered with vineyards facing in every direction.

These slopes, and the Riesling grape grown on them, are the Mosel's greatest gifts and its greatest curse. Even when it is planted on flattish, easy land, the Riesling is not the easiest of grapes to grow, and far from the most productive; when it is grown on slopes that rise almost vertically from the river, the challenge is well-nigh impossible.

At its very best, Mosel is precisely what the Riesling is all about: a glorious mixture of crisp apples, of flowers and honey, coupled with the "slatey" character derived from the soil. And it is here that many of Germany's most impressive wines are now being made.

The essence of these wines is their acidity; the Mosel is not the region to go looking for rich, fleshily ripe wines, or for Germany's best dry or red wines; most of these come from the warmer vineyards further south. No, the words most applicable to the Mosel's wines are "racy", "elegant" and "finesse" – terms that I normally struggle to avoid. Another word that springs to mind is "perfume", because of their floral style. Interestingly, when perfumiers talk about the precious liquids in their bottles, they traditionally divide them between daytime perfumes, such as Nina Ricci's *l'Air du Temps*, most of which they call "green", and evening scents, such as *Chanel No. 5* or *Poison*, which they generally term "brown". If you apply the perfumiers' rules to wine, it seems highly appropriate that the riper, more spicy wines of the Rhine are bottled in brown glass and those of the Mosel always come in green bottles. These are the "daytime" wines – perfectly suited to warm summer afternoons.

All of these descriptive terms are worth remembering when you are tasting Mosel wines, because all too often they won't apply, for the simple reason that far too many wines from the Mosel are pale shadows of what they ought to be. In many cases they are handicapped by being made from the Müller-Thurgau rather than the Riesling; all too often the vines will have been so overburdened with flavourless fruit that they taste like dilute apple juice.

The slopes of the Mosel should be covered with Riesling vines that are physically incapable of this kind of over-production, but in the "good old days", when the growers here did tend Riesling vines on their hillsides, they got precious little thanks for doing so. Most years the wretched grapes never ripened sufficiently to make wine of even *Kabinett* level and, even when the climate did allow good, naturally sweet wines to be produced, no one was rushing to pay a price for them that repaid the work, struggle and risk their production had entailed. So when it was suggested (by Professor Helmut Becker at the Geisenheim Wine School) that the growers replace their old Riesling with some new Müller-Thurgau, who could blame them for saying yes?

The change in the make-up of the region was dramatic. The Riesling used to cover so much of the Mosel that producers didn't even bother to mention its presence on their labels, any more than a grower in

Harvesting grapes on the slopes above the Mosel can be challenging

Burgundy might tell people that his Nuits-St-Georges is made from the Pinot Noir. Today less than half of the Mosel's vineyards, and far less than half of its wines, are Riesling. Any label that doesn't name a grape variety today is almost certainly hiding the fact that the wine is at least partly made from the Müller-Thurgau.

So the first lesson when buying Mosel is "look for the Riesling". This is not to say that good wines are not being made from other varieties – some Müller-Thurgau can be refreshingly drinkable if it has been treated with care – but they won't give you the peculiar Mosel cocktail of apple, flowers, honey and slate.

Fortunately, the chances of your finding it are slightly brighter than they appeared a few years ago, when the onward march of the Müller-Thurgau seemed almost unstoppable. Today, the advent of *Trocken* and *Halbtrocken* wines has made producers stop and think; these dry styles suit the Riesling far better than the

newcomer. The decision to replant with Riesling has been made easier, too, by the development of new, easier-to-work and more productive vineyards that run vertically rather than horizontally – and by generous local government grants toward the costs of replanting.

Well over three-quarters of the region's vineyards have been transformed in this way, and the success of the scheme has been great enough to ensure that terraced vineyards will disappear from all but the very steepest slopes. This modernization of the way vines are grown was the first dramatic change in the vineyards since wine-growing was introduced to the Mosel by the Romans 2,000 years ago. It was the Romans who invented the system of using individual stakes to support the vines that is still used here – and almost nowhere else in the world.

Among the other aspects of life in the Mosel that have barely changed over the centuries has been the ownership of the vineyards. There are co-operatives here, but they are less

THE ESSENTIALS
MOSEL-SAAR-RUWER

What to look for Delicate, floral, off-dry and lusciously sweet Riesling.
Location Western Germany, from Koblenz south to the French border.
Quality Mostly QbA, although there are some exceptional QmP wines in the best years.
Style White wine only: Rieslings from the northerly vineyards of the Mosel-Saar-Ruwer are pale and light-bodied, with racy acidity and surprisingly intense flavours of crisp apples, steel and slate with a hint of honey. In hotter years some superb wines of Auslese quality or above are produced which retain vitality and freshness amidst the luscious, honeyed flavour of the overripe grapes. Mosel-Saar-Ruwer wines, never fat and overblown, age extremely well and can be superb. The Doctor vineyard in Bernkastel produces Germany's most famous and most expensive wine. Müller-Thurgau, only introduced in the nineteenth century, is now almost as widespread as the Riesling, but its rather angular mixture of thick grapiness, flowery overtones and an unnerving sharpness does not produce very

exciting wines.
Climate Temperate, with modest rainfall. The steep valley sides provide protection for the vines and also allow rapid warming during the day.
Cultivation Soils are varied, with sandstone, limestone and marl in the upper Mosel giving way to slate and clay soils in the lower reaches. There are, in addition, alluvial and gravel soils. The best sites for Riesling are the slatey slopes of the Saar-Ruwer and Bernkastel Bereiche. The valley has very steep sides (at Bernkastel rising 700 ft above the river as a virtually sheer face), giving altitudes of 100–350 m (330–1,150 ft) and making cultivation laborious; in some places, tractors have to be winched up the vineyards.
Grape varieties Riesling, Müller-Thurgau, Bacchus, Kerner, Optima, Elbling, Auxerrois, Ortega.
Production/maturation Cool fermentation results naturally from the early onset of winter. Individual growers – most with long family traditions of wine-making – predominate, although co-operatives flourish and play an important role.

There are some important merchants with the best, like Deinhard, amongst the leading producers.
Longevity Mosel-Saar-Ruwer wines generally age better than their counterparts in the Rhine because of their higher acidity. Deutscher Tafelwein and Landwein should be drunk immediately; QbA wines: within 1–3 years; Kabinetts: 2–10 years; Spätlesen: 3–15 years; Auslesen: 5–20 years; Beerenauslesen: 10–35 years; Trockenbeerenauslesen, Eiswein: 10–50 years.
Vintage guide 71, 76, 79, 83, 85, 86, 88, 89, 90, 93, 94, 95, 97.
Top 22 Wegeler-Deinhard, Pauly-Bergweiler, Dr H Thanisch, J J Prum, S A Prum, Friedrich-Wilhelm Gymnasium, Von Schubert/Maximin Grünhaus, Dr Loosen, Bischöfliches Priesterseminar, Lauerburg, Max Ferd Richter, Bert Simon, Selbach-Oster, Schloss Saarstein, Von Kesselstatt, Peter Nicolay, Grans-Fassian, Egon Müller-Scharzhof, J Lauerberg, Mönchhof, Bischöfliches Konvikt Trier, Eitelsbacher Karthäuserhof.

powerful than they are elsewhere and account for just one bottle in every five that are produced. Wine-making here remains in the hands of the church, the state, old families (some of which can prove ownership over 12 generations) and merchants, including, most notably, the innovative and quality-conscious Wegeler-Deinhard in Koblenz. Between them, this disparate band produces one of the most diverse collections of wines of any of Europe's wine regions.

Moseltor and Obermosel

These two *Bereiche* in the southernmost part of the Mosel both produce basic, light, acidic wine, most of which, thankfully, ends up having bubbles put into it by the producers of Sekt. The only interest here lies in the continued presence in the Obermosel of the Elbling, the grape variety the Romans grew here; if you ever wonder what Roman wine may have tasted like, try a modern example from this region – it'll make you believe in progress.

Saar-Ruwer

This *Bereich* is the one part of the region that involves rivers other than the Mosel. Both the Saar and the Ruwer deserve to stand alongside the Mosel as part of a great region because they produce some of the best, least-well-known wines here.

The Ruwer would be worth visiting, if only to spend an hour or so in the Roman town of Trier. There are vines around the town itself, but these produce fairly run-of-the-mill wine; for the good stuff you have to head down to the water. The Ruwer has one *Grosslage* – Romerlay – within which are situated the Maximin Grünhaus, Karthaushofberg (notable for its bottles that wear nothing but a neck label) and Marienholtz vineyards, all of which can, in the right hands, make sublime, steely wines. The "right hands" here, as elsewhere in Germany, are generally the state domaines, the old family estates and the church. Names to look out for include Von Schubert, Bert Simon, Bischöfliches Konvikt Trier and Eitelsbacher Karthauserhof.

Very few producers market their wine under the *Grosslage* name – as they do in Bernkastel for example – because they make so little; by the same token, they have no need to sell much to merchants, and the co-operatives have little role to play here. For all these reasons, the odds

on getting a good wine from the Ruwer are among the best in Germany.

The same cannot quite be said of the Saar, partly because producers do off-load fair quantities of unimpressive wine under the *Grosslage* name of Wiltingen Scharzberg, and partly because the climate tends to be cooler, so, in all but the ripest years, the wines can taste a bit raw. But when the sun hangs around for long enough at the end of the year, the Saar can produce some of Germany's most intense, longest-lived wines.

As elsewhere, the best vines are grown on the slopes, a fact that is emphasized by the vineyards that are named Kupp after the round-topped hillsides. Among these, the best are Ayler Kupp, Wiltingen Scharzhofberger, Wiltingen Braune Kupp, Filzener Herrenberg, Serriger Herrenberg and Schloss Saarfelser, Saarburger Rausch and Ockfener Bockstein. Look for wines made by Egon Müller, Hohe Domkirche-Trier, Reichsgraf von Kesselstatt and Staatl, Weinbaudomäne.

Bernkastel

This name, which must be the most famous *Bereich* in the Mosel, covers the whole region of the Mittelmosel, the central stretch of the river's course from the frontier to Koblenz. In the confusing jungle of German wine, few words are more misunderstood than the name of this small town. On the one hand there is the great Bernkasteler Doctor vineyard that overlooks the town and river and makes one of Germany's finest wines, and on the other, there are the oceans of dull wine legally labelled as Bereich Bernkastel produced in vineyards nowhere near the town of Bernkastel at all – which ought to bear the regional name of Mittelmosel they were allowed in the 1960s.

There are two *Grosslagen* here: Kurfürstlay and Badstube. The former contains the least interesting of Bernkasteler's vineyards and the best of those of Brauneberg; the great Doctor vineyard and Bernkasteler Lay are both in the *Grosslage* Badstube. Named after the supposedly healing qualities of its wine, this sheer, slate-soiled, 3.5-acre (1.4-ha) vineyard is the German equivalent of Burgundy's Romanée-Conti. In ripe years its wines are everything that the Mosel should be: rich, honeyed and as "slatey" as the roofs the vines overlook, but with a balancing acidity that makes this a wine to keep for decades. The Bernkasteler Doctor should long ago, like the Romanée-Conti, have been recognized as some kind of *Grand Cru* or First Growth to distinguish it from its neighbours. Instead, it found itself at the centre of a ludicrous court case begun because the German authorities decreed in 1971 that no vineyard could be smaller than 12.5 acres (5 ha).

Instead of changing the rules to fit the tiny size of this particular plot, the authorities then sought to justify expanding it. Hardly surprisingly, they were supported in this by the 13 owners of the neighbouring vines, who were keen to sell their wine as Bernkasteler Doctor. Ultimately – it took 13 years and considerable effort on the part of the three original owners of the Doctor vineyard – a compromise was agreed, whereby the size of the plot was increased to 8 acres (3.24 ha). The story says a great deal about everything that has been wrong with the German wine industry since the war. The official prestige of a piece of vine-growing soil should be judged by the quality of the wine it produces, not by its ability to fit legal criteria drawn up by those for whom numbers and neatness are all-important.

There is a very similar problem at Piesport, another wine-producing village within the *Bereich* of Bernkastel. Look at the bottles on the shelf: on the left, there's Piesporter Michelsberg, on the right there's Piesporter Goldtropfchen. Both seem to come from Piesport, so which should you buy? The answer is that the Goldtropfchen ("golden droplets") is a single, hillside vineyard that produces wine that should taste distinctive and wonderful, while the Michelsberg is a huge, flat *Grosslage*, most of whose wines are produced in enormous quantities and rarely have much more flavour than tap water. Unfortunately the international fame of Piesporter Michelsberg has not only debased the wine of that name; bottles of Piesporter Goldtropfchen don't always come up to scratch either.

Brauneberg is less well known than either Bernkastel or Piesport and consequently often a better buy. The best vineyard here is the Juffer, which overlooks the village of Brauneberg itself from the other side of the river and produces delicate wines that once sold for higher prices than those of the Bernkasteler Doctor. It still competes at the equivalent of First Growth level with that vineyard, but at a (relatively) lower price.

The *Grosslage* of Munzlay boasts some of the region's best estates and three riverside villages – Graach, Wehlen and Zeltingen – all of which can produce some of the finest, ripest, wines in the Mosel. Graach's best vineyards are the Domprobst, the Josephshofer and the Himmelreich. Zeltinger Himmelreich is worth looking out for too, as is Wehlener Sonnenuhr, named after the vineyard clock that ensures the pickers are never late for lunch. Best producers include Max Ferd Richter and Dr Loosen.

Collectors of bizarre wine labels will appreciate the *Grosslage* Nacktarsch, which, literally translated, means "naked arse" and whose label depicts a small boy having that particular part of his anatomy spanked. Unfortunately, the wine made here is far less exceptional than either the name or the label.

Zell

The village of Zell used to be better known outside Germany than it is today, thanks to the success of one of its wines, the Zeller Schwarze Katz. Recognizable by the black cat on its label, this wine is supposed to owe its name to an occasion when three merchants could not make up their minds over which of three barrels to buy. As they asked for another sample from one of the casks, the grower's cat sprang onto it, hissed, arched its back and generally treated the merchants as though they were Dobermanns intent on stealing a kitten. This, the men decided, must be the best wine in the cellar.

Until quite recently, the producers of Zell adopted a slightly more scientific method of selecting the wine that could call itself Schwarze Katz – by holding a blind tasting. The region of Zell has now been expanded by the addition of the villages of Merl and Kaimt and, sadly, the tasting is no longer held. The cat can now grace the labels of any wine from this *Grosslage* and today you would be far better advised to opt for a bottle of Zeller Domherrenberg. Elsewhere within the *Bereich* of Zell, the best wine probably comes from the village of Neef, whose Neefer Frauenberg can be great Riesling.

A Liebfraumilch-equivalent called Moselblumchen can be found throughout the Mosel. It should be treated with the same suspicion as Liebfraumilch. However, bottles bearing this label will probably be no worse, and cheaper, than many that abuse the name of Bereich Bernkastel and Piesporter Michelsberg.

THE RHINE

Forget Liebfraumilch and basic bottles of hock. OK, so they're all made here, but to associate the wines for which the vineyards of the Rhine are best known outside Germany with the kind of glorious, unique wines produced by the regions of the Rheingau, Rheinpfalz and Rheinhessen is like imagining there to be some kind of link between a bottle of "French dry red" and top-class Bordeaux or Burgundy.

In a sense, though, the success of these wines has probably done less damage to the image of the rest of the Rhine's wines than the generally mediocre quality of the contents of bottles bearing such apparently "classier" names as Niersteiner Gütes Domtal and Bereich Johannisberg, and the less than entirely successful attempt by some of the most quality-conscious producers during the 1980s and early 1990s to compete with the rest of the world by switching from their characteristic sweet and off-sweet wines to ones that were bone-dry – often teeth-scouringly so.

Let's set the plonk-purveyors and the dry-brigade largely to one side, however, and focus our attention on the main regions of the Rhine, each of which should produce identifiably different styles of wine of a quality and flavour found nowhere else in the world.

The Rheingau

This ought to be the "best bit" of the Rhine – if not of the whole of Germany. In the eighth century the Emperor Charlemagne recognized the potential of the slopes and decreed that they should be planted with the vines that have been there ever since. The emperor was quite a visionary; how did he come to appreciate the way in which the mountains shielded the vineyards from the wind and the river reflected the sunlight? How could he have known that the rocky – often slatey – subsoil was so perfect for the Riesling? Or that the tricky set of fragmented hillsides might include vineyards with unique qualities of their own – some of which might be helped by the mist to attract noble rot? Maybe he just struck lucky – like he did in that other area to which he took a liking, the Côte d'Or in Burgundy.

The Rheingau distinguishes itself from other parts of the Rhine in several ways. It is far smaller than its neighbours, with only a little over 10 per cent of the vineyard area of either the Rheinhessen or Rheinpfalz; and the Riesling is still the major grape variety, producing yields of around 350 cases per acre (140 per hectare), compared to around 430 and 500 (174 and 200) respectively for the other Rhine regions. Thanks to these factors, and to the individualism of the Rheingau's 500 estates and 2,500 growers, the co-operatives have not achieved the stranglehold on production and marketing here that they have elsewhere, so quality has every reason to be higher than almost anywhere else in Germany. And so, occasionally, it is. The mark of a typical Rheingau will be the same appley-grapey flavour that the Riesling produces in the Mosel, but with more honeyed richness, and less of that region's acid bite.

Unfortunately, sales of such wines are less than brisk – which helps to explain why a group of Rheingau producers decided to switch their emphasis from sweet to dry, announcing their decision to the world with the establishment in 1983 of the Association of Charta Estates, whose recognizable seal appears on members' *Trocken* and *Halbtrocken* wines.

The first thing to be said about Charta wines is that, apart from being dry, they will always be produced from the Riesling (this is obligatory), and are likely to be more carefully made than many of the Rhine's other wines. The second thing to be said about them, though, is that their dryness has all too often made them far less enjoyable to

The Assmanshausen vineyards in the Rhine region of Germany

drink when they are young than slightly sweeter wines made from similar grapes – or than dry French wines that achieve a higher natural level of ripeness.

Dry wines of equal or greater than *Spätlese* ripeness can compete with their counterparts from Alsace, and genuinely do achieve their object of being a good accompaniment to food. As QbAs, too, they can be softened up sufficiently to make them drinkable.

Charta members counter any such comments from visitors with the argument that these wines need time to soften and that, in any case, they are being ordered by the cellarful by German restaurants, whose customers seem ready to pay high prices, patriotically drinking them instead of a French import. Today the dry Rheingaus are indeed selling so well that most of the people making them have cut their production of sweeter wine to just 30 or 40 per cent of the total. The Rheingau is now, quite literally, going dry; tragically, its producers seem resolute in their desire to rewrite history by claiming that their region's wines were traditionally made without any remaining sweetness. Maybe in cool, unripe, years this was the case; in warmer ones, however, as anyone who has been lucky enough to pull the cork on a glorious, petrolly, 30- or 40-year-old *Auslese* or *Spätlese* knows, they were still producing the kind of sweet, part-fermented wines that had so enchanted the Romans 2,000 years earlier. When buying Rheingau wines, beware of wines labelled as Bereich Johannisberg; although some are good, they could come from literally anywhere in the region – this is the Rheingau's only *Bereich*.

Assmanshausen has a local reputation for the quality of its Pinot Noir reds, few of which stand comparison with good examples from the Rheinpfalz, let alone those from across the French border. As you round the elbow of the river, however, you come to the tourist town of Rüdesheim, with its street of wine bars and its steep Berg vineyard, source of some of the biggest-tasting wines of the region.

Next stop on the river is Geisenheim, site of Germany's top wine school and research institute, and the place where vine experts labour to create new kinds of easy-to-grow grapes that are ideally adapted to these northerly conditions. The best vineyard here is probably the Mauerchen. Beyond Geisenheim, you arrive at Winkel and its Hasensprung vineyard, and two German oddities:

Schloss Johannisberg and Schloss Vollrads, old-established estates that are allowed to print their own names rather than that of an individual vineyard on their labels. Both are in the forefront of the dry-wine movement. Today the Steinberg vineyard planted by the monks houses the German Wine School and a wine museum, but it still produces full-flavoured, honeyed wine with a dash of slate and flowery acidity that is sold as Steinberger.

The nearby riverside villages of Oestrich and Hattenheim make similar, if less intense, wines. Hattenheim is also the place to come in June for its annual Erdbeerfest – strawberry and wine fair. The Nussbrunnen and Wisselbrunnen are the top vineyards here. The little hillside villages of Hallgarten and Kiedrich make great, if slightly more spicy and floral, less honeyed Riesling, especially good examples of which come from the Sandgrub and Grafenberg vineyards, while Erbach has the Rheingau's greatest plot of vines, the Marcobrunn, as well as Schloss Rheinhausen, one of its oldest (eighth-century) and best estates. The Rieslings and dry Chardonnays here are impressive.

Eltville is the place to find one of Germany's best state-owned estates, the Staatsweinguter, which makes a wide range of top-class wines – including, when possible, extraordinary Eiswein. Back in the hills, Rauenthal makes small quantities of intensely flavoured wines that need longer to soften than those made closer to the river – but they're worth the wait. Nearby, Walluf boasts two of the oldest vineyards in the region, while Martinsthal has the impressive Wildsau vineyard. Finally, on the River Main close to Wiesbaden, is Hochheim, the town that gave the English "hock" – their easy-to-remember term for the wines of the Rhine. Like all the vineyards on the Main, Hochheim makes "earthier" wine than the rest of the Rheingau, but the flavours can be rich and tangily refreshing.

Rheinhessen

The biggest wine region in Germany – with some 165 vine-growing villages, 11,000 growers and around a quarter of the annual production – this is also one of the oldest. Historically, at least, the Rheinhessen could be called the heartland of the Rhine. Fifty per cent of all Liebfraumilch is made here, and millions more bottles of undistinguished wine are labelled Bereich Nierstein or Niersteiner Gütes Domtal.

The weather here is comparatively mild, with neither the frosts suffered in the Mosel, nor the greater warmth enjoyed by the Pfalz. The Riesling can fare well; unfortunately, this is lazy wine-making country in which bulk-oriented merchants and co-operatives hold sway and the Müller-Thurgau and its recently developed fellow varieties have taken over in the largely flat, featureless vineyards. Just one vine in 20 is now a Riesling and most of these are grouped around a set of nine riverside towns and villages called the Rhein Terrasse including Auflangen Bodenheim, Nackenheim, Oppenheim and Nierstein.

Pfalz

The most exciting region in Germany today, the Pfalz, is benefiting both from its climate, and from the presence of some of Germany's most go-ahead wine-makers. Just across the southern border from Alsace, and in the same rain shadow provided by the range the French call the Vosges and the Germans know as the Haardt mountains, the Pfalz is warmer country. Grapes ripen better here, taking on the richer, spicier character often found in Alsace. And the more spice and perfume you find, the greater the likelihood that it was made by a maverick like Müller-Catoir, Kimich, Koehler-Ruprecht or Kurt Darting, quite possibly from some new-fangled grape variety like the Rieslaner or Scheurebe, both of which can make exceptional wines here.

Beyond those rising superstars, though, you have to pick and choose. That ripeness can mean a lack of fresh acidity; much of the wine here is soft, dull Müller-Thurgau

THE ESSENTIALS
THE RHINE

What to look for Rieslings with a wonderfully taut balance between fruit and acidity. They are richer in the Pfalz, softer in the Rheinhessen and majestic in the Rheingau.
Location Western Germany, bordering Switzerland.
Official quality Plenty of Deutscher Tafelwein and QbA but also the full range of QmP styles.
Style As elsewhere in Germany, apart from the Ahr which produces pale, light, cherryish reds, almost all wine produced is white. The Mittelrhein and Nahe make good, slatey, refreshing Riesling. The Pfalz and Rheinhessen produce virtually all of Germany's Liebfraumilch, whose dull sweetness or, if they are more fortunate, mild, flowery grapiness is the first introduction to wine-drinking for many people. From the Rheinhessen, too, comes Niersteiner Gütes Domtal, produced in dull and dubiously large quantities, a wine that has debased the good name of the Nierstein vineyards as bulk Liebfraumilch has the original Liebfrauenstift wines. Further up the quality scale, around 16 per cent of production is Riesling of Kabinett and Spätlese standard, full of soft, honeyed, floral fruit in Rheinhessen, riper and spicier in the Pfalz, more delicate in the

Rheingau, with underlying acidity and steeliness to balance the richness of the fruit. Intensely rich, honeyed and unctuous wines of Auslese quality and above are produced in small quantities (around 5 per cent of total production and only in the very best years) in the Rhine from famous vineyards such as Schloss Vollrads and Schloss Johannisberg in the Rheingau, and Forster Jesuitengarten in the Pfalz. A tiny quantity of light red wine is produced, and an increasing amount of Trocken and Halbtrocken (dry and semi-dry) white is made, with a steelier, mineral character to it.
Climate Temperate, due to the moderating effects of the river, the protection of the Taunus mountains to the north and local forests.
Cultivation Soils are varied, with quartzite and slate at higher levels and loams, clay bess and sandy gravel below. Vineyards are located on the flat hinterlands and gentle slopes of the Rhine, the best sites being the south-facing river banks. New crosses of grapes such as Kerner and Scheurebe have been introduced since the 1960s.
Grape varieties White: Riesling, Müller-Thurgau, Silvaner, Kerner, Bacchus, Huxelrebe, Morio-Muskat, Scheurebe, Muskateller, Gewürztraminer;

Reds are from the Spätburgunder and Portugieser; Ahr: Riesling, Müller-Thurgau, Kerner, Silvaner, Scheurebe, Rulander, Blauer Portugieser, Spätburgunder, Ahr Domina, Dornfelder.
Production/maturation The finest-quality wines are produced in minute quantities, allowing for great attention to detail. Many of the independent producers market their own wines as well. At the other extreme, a great deal of bulk-blended generic wine, such as Liebfraumilch and Niersteiner, is produced.
Longevity Deutscher Tafelwein and Landwein: drink immediately; QbA: 1–3 years; Kabinetts: 2–8 years; Spätlesen: 3–12 years; Auslesen: 5–18 years; Beerenauslesen: 10–30 years; Trockenbeerenauslesen, Eiswein: 10–50 years.
Vintage guide 85, 86, 88, 89, 90, 92, 93, 94, 95, 97.
My Top 17 Ahr: Winzergenossenschaft Heimersheim; Mittelrhein: Heinrich Weiler, Toni Jost; Nahe: Staatliche Weinbaudomäne/Graf Von Plettenberg, Diel, Kruger-Rumpf; Rheingau: von Bretano, Künstler, Deinhard, von Simmern; Rheinhessen: Carl Sittman, Bruder Dr Becker; Pfalz: Lingenfelder, Kurt Darting, Müller-Catoir, Neckerauer, Bürklin-Wolf.

– basic Liebfraumilch in name or nature. This is not only Germany's second largest wine region, but also, on occasion, its most pro-ductive, thanks to the combination of the sun and those generous Müller-Thurgau vines. It is also co-operative country – as you might expect from any region whose 25,000 wine-growers have less than two and a half acres (one hectare) of vines each, where the wine-makers know that their grapes are likely to ripen most years, in a climatically privileged part of Germany, and whose pre-eminence, they would argue, was recognized 2,000 years ago by the Romans and, more recently, by Napoleon.

Just as the Mosel has its best part in the Mittelmosel, the Pfalz's finest vineyards are to be found around a set of half a dozen villages in the *Bereich* Mittelhaardt-Deutsche Weinstrasse to the north of Neustadt. Inevitably, however, the allocation of *Bereichen* was as mishandled here as it was elsewhere, and this one takes in the whole of the northern half of the Pfalz, leaving the south to the *Bereich* Südliche Weinstrasse. The most northerly vineyards of the *Bereich* Mittelhaardt-Deutsche Weinstrasse are an undistinguished bunch, and the first village of any interest is Kallstadt, whose Annaberg vineyard produces great Riesling. Unusually, the labels of the wines made in the Annaberg, like those of a Burgundian *Grand Cru* such as the Corton, do not need to include the name of a village. Which is just as well because, while most of the rest of Kallstadt's vineyards are in the *Grosslage* Kobnert, the Annaberg confusingly falls into the *Grosslage* Freurberg, along with Bad Durckheim, another source of potentially great wine.

It is in the next most southern *Grosslage*, the Mariengarten (Forst an der Weinstrasse), and in Wachenheim, Forst and Deidesheim, most specifically, that the wine-making fireworks really begin. Other wines produced in the Rheinpfalz may equal the best made here; none beats them. The secret of these vineyards lies in their exposure to the sun, to the black basalt of Forst's vineyards – especially in the Forster Jesuitengarten – that helps to give the grapes a little extra ripeness, and to the quality of the producers. The names of the estates with vines here – Basserman-Jordan, Reichsrat von Buhl, Bürklin-Wolf – read like a roll-call of Germany's vinous aristocracy, though not necessarily of Germany's present-day best.

Nahe

The wines of the Nahe don't really have a style of their own. In fact, the region is a meeting point of the Mosel and the Rhine; some wines taste like basic Rheinhessen, while others combine the depth of fruit of the Rheingau with the acid bite of the Mosel. The Riesling is a newcomer here, but at its best – in villages such as Bad Münster and Münster Sarmsheim – it can be richly intense. Another speciality of the region is its grapefruity Scheurebe.

Good wine is, however, the exception to the Nahe rule. Look for Rieslings from the cellars of Hans Crusius (especially from the Traiser Rotenfels and Traiser Bastei vineyards) and von Plettenberg (from Schlossböckelheimer Kupfergrube and Bad Kreuznacher Narrenkappe).

Mittelrhein

From its name, one might expect this region to be as important a part of the Rhine as the Mittelmosel is of the Mosel. But in fact, the Mittelrhein is best described as tourist country, the Germany on which Hollywood based its version of Grimms' fairy tales. Its riverside villages are almost too well kept, but so, thankfully, are the sheer, sloping vineyards in which the Riesling still holds sway. Unfortunately, the wines produced here are rather less spectacular. The best – from villages such as Braubach, Bacharach, Boppard and Oberwesel – can be quite intensely, if often rather acidically, reminiscent of the Mosel, but very little is made, and very few bottles escape the grasp of the region's landlords, who have no difficulty in selling them. For the moment, the region's one international star remains Toni Jost.

Ahr

The wines from this area rarely leave German soil either, partly because Ahr is so tiny – under 1,000 acres (400 ha) of vines are divided among nearly 1,000 growers – and partly because over two-thirds of its wine is red (pink) Weissherbst, made either from the Portugieser or Spätburgunder (Pinot Noir).

Making red wines this far north, even in the favourable micro-climate provided by the valley slopes of the river after which the region is named, is impracticable.

THE OTHER WINES OF GERMANY

If the wine-makers of the Rhine and Mosel went on strike, would-be German wine-drinkers would still have a surprisingly wide range of bottles from which to choose – a far wider range, in fact, than either of those regions could ever begin to offer.

Franken

Poor old Franken. Very, very few people know its wines and at least some of those who do imagine that this region stole its Bocksbeutel bottle design from Mateus Rosé rather than *vice versa*. The earthy Silvaner grape still occupies much of the land, producing often similarly earthy wine; but, like the Chasselas in Switzerland, the Silvaner does its very best here, producing dry wines that go well with the region's heavy Bavarian dishes.

Wurttemberg

When German wine-drinkers want a red wine produced by their countrymen, this is the region to which they look. The only problem, to an outside observer, is that, while the locals accept the stuff they are given as red, most non-Germans would call it sweet and pink. The handicaps here are the heavy-handed influence of the co-operatives (half the growers have vineyards of less than half an acre) and the range of grapes that is used.

The main varieties are the Trollinger, the Pinot Meunier (here known as the Schwarzriesling) and the Lemberger, all of which make better rosé than red. Some decent Pinot Noir is made, and some better Riesling – particularly in the *Grosslage* of Heuchelberg and in the Stuttgart suburb *Einzellagen* of Berg, Goldberg, Hinterer Berg, Steinhalde, Wetzstein and Zuckerle – but these wines are rarely seen outside the region.

Hessische Bergstrasse

"The spring garden of Germany", this is orchard country where the 1,000 acres (400 ha) of grapes have to compete with a wide range of fruits and vegetables. The Riesling can ripen well enough, but its wines (most of which are made by two co-operatives) are rarely better than middle-of-the-road Rhines.

Baden

For decades now, under the guidance of its huge Badische Winzerkeller co-operative, Baden has gone its own way. While other regions were busily planting Müller-Thurgau with which to make semi-sweet plonk, Baden has been increasing its acreage of Riesling, and concentrating its attention on making dry and off-dry wines, including some increasingly impressive Pinot Noir. Today, of course, growers throughout the rest of Germany have followed Baden's example; unfortunately for them, few enjoy the warm climate of this region.

Few, too, enjoy seeing their countrymen sending their wine overseas in Burgundy-shaped bottles whose labels seem to go out of their way to hide their Germanic origins. To a Rhine or Mosel traditionalist, these Baden bottles are turncoats; to many a casual overseas wine-drinker, they are a far more attractive prospect than the more classic German bottle whose value has been undermined by too many unhappy experiences with cheap-and-nasty Liebfraumilch. It would be wrong to paint too rosy a picture of Baden's wines, however – many of the co-operatives' 500 different wines are neutral, dry, Müller-Thurgau, Gutedel, or unexciting red or pink Weissherbst – but both the Riesling and Rülander can make really tasty wine here. Look out for slightly sparkling *spritzig* examples.

Sachsen

If the name is unfamiliar, don't worry; it wouldn't ring loud bells with most German wine-drinkers either – certainly not the ones living in what used to be known as West Germany, on the other side of the old Iron Curtain. Once upon a time, this was one of the more significant wine regions, with vineyards covering some four times as much land as Sancerre does today. Sachsen had already shrunk before Communism did its inefficient worst, but today, there are just 300 acres, one-twentieth of what it had in its prime. There's Riesling here along with Gutedel and Traminer but, despite low yields, wines are unexciting and unmemorable. Still, the tourists following the new Wine Route will probably lap them up.

Saale-Unstrut

Another wine region that came from the cold of East Germany, Saale-Unstrut is slightly larger, but suffers from the effects of the same 50 years of neglect. Apart from the Riesling and Müller-Thurgau, there's also a bit of Silvaner which might prove to be the region's strongest suit.

Sekt

This is not a region, but a peculiarly ignoble style of wine which confirms everything the most cynical critic has ever said about the German wine industry. Before going any further, we should point out that the banning of the harmless words *méthode champenoise* from the labels of classically made fizz was originally instigated, not by the Champenois as one might have expected, but by German fizz-makers who were desperate to protect their (non-Champagne-method) wines from competition (Champagne-method) wines such as Cava from Spain.

What those Sekt producers hated to admit was that the very worst Cava is a million times more drinkable than most German sparkling wine. At its finest, *flaschengarung* – champagne-method – Riesling can be both delicious and refreshingly different but, unfortunately, such examples are very, very rare; most Sekt is made by the *cuve close* method from dull, unripe Müller-Thurgau or Elbling. And, unless the label says *Deutscher Sekt*, the mass of the wine in the bottle won't even be German. Try the ones made by Deinhard and Schloss Rheinhartshausen or stick to Cava.

SPAIN

Something strange and wonderful is happening to Spain. If you watched the flamboyant finale to the 1992 Olympics in Barcelona, or have relished the culinary wit of the cooking at restaurants like the Michelin-bestarred El Bulli, not far from that city, or wandered through the new architecture of Seville, you'd have to be blind to have missed sensing a new mood. As you would if you'd spent any time talking to the sophisticated young Spaniards who throng the colourfully tiled bars in the heart of Madrid. It seems fanciful, but it is almost as though an entire country is slowly shrugging off its heavy shroud of melancholy, and somehow swapping the heavy dark oils of El Greco for the gaiety of Joan Miró.

Now taste a glass of the Marques de Riscal's white wine from Rueda; of Berberana's various fruitily young unoaked Tempranillos; of Martinez Bujanda's unofficial Cabernet Sauvignon Rioja; of Chivite's new-wave Chardonnay from Navarra or Lagar de Cervera's

Laguardia, one of the principal towns in the Rioja region

Albariño from Galicia. These are all fresh, fruit-packed wines that have nothing to do with the dull, woody efforts of which Spain's wine-makers were often so proud. And just the stuff to take over from some of the increasingly tired players that were slowing down the Spanish team and preventing it from being fully competitive with both the Old and New World.

The new wines arrived in the nick of time – at the moment when the European authorities were demanding the uprooting of large sections of the vineyards of La Mancha, and when increasing numbers of wine-drinkers were switching allegiance to Australia, California and southern France. Mind you, Spain's more old-fashioned wines had performed well enough for a very long time. The reds were for decades the easy-going seducers of the wine world, the wines that gently led countless white-wine-drinkers down the path toward more "sophisticated" claret and Chianti. The point was that while, to many novice drinkers, those French and Italian wines were dauntingly tannic, Spain's reds were soft and, to use a term cherished by the hacks who write the descriptive labels on the backs of bottles, "mellow". They were, above all, very, very approachable. The trouble was that once those novice drinkers had been introduced to red wine, where did they go next? Straight to claret.

So what was wrong? Well, if an independent analyst had been called in to define the problem, he or she would undoubtedly have initially focused on the raw materials – Spain's indigenous grape varieties, of which there are over 600. This may sound like a wealth of choice, until you go on to discover that just 20 of these cover 80 per cent of the vineyards. And these 20 produce wine as monotonous and undemanding as the contents of an average Top Twenty pop chart. The Airén, for example, the most widely planted grape in the world, covers nearly a third of the country's vineyards – and makes dreadfully dull white wine.

The second most widespread variety, the Garnacha – the grape the growers of the Rhône know as the Grenache – covers around 10 per cent of the vineyards and is rarely encouraged to make wine of any great distinction. And none, apart from Priorato, built to last. The only red grape of note, the Tempranillo, accounts for around a fifth as much land as the Garnacha, and only achieves real recognition for its essential contribution to the flavour of Rioja and Ribera del Duero, despite the fact that, under one alias or another, it is grown almost throughout Spain's vineyards. Italy and Portugal's widely planted grape varieties are a far more interesting lot. Spain does have top-class grapes, to be sure – varieties like the Graciano, Loureira, Verdejo and Albariño – but it has done far too little to exploit them.

So, while the rest of the world lapped up Cabernets, Merlots, Chardonnays and Sauvignons made almost anywhere, and highly priced designer Italian reds in designer bottles, Spain's wines remained, if not in the bargain basement, at least among the cheaper wines on the shelf, vulnerable to competition from more flavoursome, fashionable fare. Cava, Spain's sparkling wine made by the Champagne method but from dull indigenous grapes, did sell well internationally, but usually at lower prices than many New-World offerings that were made in the same way, but from Champagne grape varieties.

There were, thankfully, a few pioneering wine-makers who took a broader view. Miguel Torres, for example, proved what could be done with Gewürztraminer, Riesling, Cabernet Sauvignon, Sauvignon, Pinot Noir and Chardonnay, and his lead was followed by Jean León, by Carlos Falco at his Marques de Griñon estate and by Raimat, a sizeable subsidiary of the huge sparkling wine producer Codorníu, which broke ranks by introducing a pure Chardonnay fizz. Despite a strong reactionary backlash – in 1996 there was a major public row between Codorníu and its main rival Freixenet over the legitimacy of using Chardonnay in Cava – the international success of these wines encouraged experimentation.

The region in which this bore the most impressive fruit was Navarra, whose high-tech Evena research station helped growers to convert the DO from one that was associated with cheap rosé to one in which firms like Chivite made world-class Cabernet Sauvignon and Chardonnay. Across the regional boundary in Rioja, there was a grudging acknowledgement that the Cabernet Sauvignon that had been a major component of the prize-winning Riojas of the nineteenth century might just possibly be legally used to make their twentieth-century counterparts.

Encouragingly, though, the "international" varieties were not the only beneficiaries of this wind of change. In the best parts of Rioja, the easy-to-grow Garnacha, which had largely supplanted the finer Graciano and Mazuela, was pushed back to allow those varieties to return – and to give more emphasis to the Tempranillo. Elsewhere, there were successful efforts to exploit the often underrated potential of the Verdejo and Viura grapes.

If the grape varieties were a handicap, so too were the ways in which the wine was produced and matured. To most older Spaniards, an old wine is, by definition, better than a young wine. And a wine that has been matured for a long time in oak barrels is best of all. Spain's recently updated *Denominación de Origen* system – its equivalent of France's *Appellation Contrôlée* – has traditionally had age as one of its central tenets, officially designating wines that have undergone the required period of maturation with the words *Con Crianza, Reserva* or *Gran Reserva*.

All three terms may indicate higher-than-usual quality – based on the assumption that the *bodegas* only produce *Reservas* and *Gran Reservas* in the best vintages. All too often, however, the same terms and rules are applied to wines made from grapes that have no natural propensity for ageing. Visitors from other countries often left the tasting rooms of *bodegas* – wineries – shaking their heads in dismay that the wine-makers insisted on keeping ready-to-drink young wine to flatten out and lose its fruit in cask. But it's hard to blame the wine-makers; the oak-aged wine not only sold for a higher price, but did so very easily on the local market.

In the past, this Hispanic keenness on ageing was catered for by displaying on the labels of wine bottles not a vintage, but that the wine was a "2nd", "3rd" or "4th" *Año*, or "year", meaning that it had been matured for two, three or four years. When vintages did appear, they were often used in what one might call a rather "relaxed" fashion, with a single batch of labels being used on wines from a succession of harvests. But what did it matter? After all, the wines were almost always ready to drink when they were sold and all but the best producers liked to promote the erroneous idea that there was little variation in wines of different vintages. Indeed, one quite go-ahead wine-maker freely admitted having blended together wines of two or three years so as to maintain a commercially successful flavour. As he said, people liked the 1982, so he made the 1983 taste as similar to it as he could.

There was work to be done too in the *bodegas*. Some lacked the equipment needed to make good wine; others lacked the know-how or will. As recently as 1995, it was possible to see a modern conveyor-belt system, of which any Californian winery would be proud, carry to the press a mixture of rotten and healthy grapes no Californian would countenance for an instant. Elsewhere, trucks full of grapes stood cooking in the sun while the wine-makers enjoyed a long, leisurely lunch. Pipes that should have been washed through thoroughly every day were cleaned only at the beginning and end of the harvest.

A Pride of Wine-makers

This easy-going attitude began to change, however, when overseas customers unintentionally bruised the most sensitive part of any male Spaniard – his pride. Foreigners openly suggested that Spanish wine-makers did not know how to do their job properly. In one famous joint venture, a French co-operative so distrusted its partners across the border that, having supervised the crushing of the grapes and the fermentation in Spain, it shipped the wine back home to take care of it until bottling. Elsewhere, wines intended for sale in Britain and the Netherlands were fully produced and bottled on Spanish soil – but, under the supervision of young Australian and French "Flying Wine-makers". In Australia, wineries do not shut for an instant during the vintage; in Spain, they traditionally close at lunch, for the weekend and for saint's day fiestas, whatever is going on in the vats. When one young Antipodean was denied access to his fermenting wine on a Sunday, he simply smashed a window, climbed inside – and telephoned the boss of the *bodega* to warn him to hand over a key, or expect a lot more break-ins.

In Eastern Europe when visiting foreigners made such efforts beyond the call of local wine-making duty, the response was usually an apathetic shrug. In Spain, they had a more direct impact. As did the international success of wines like the Rueda whites made by Jacques Lurton and by Hugh Ryman for the Marques de Riscal. The huge Bodegas y Bebidas group, for example, swiftly decided that anything the foreigners could do, they could do just as well – if not better – and proved it with a fresh new-wave Rioja called Albor and a set of pure varietals made from local grapes which would have been inconceivable a few years earlier.

Taking a more traditional route, Telmo Rodriguez of the great family-owned Remelluri estate undertook research into the tannins in the Tempranillo grape and the effect various systems of fermentation had on a wine's ultimate toughness or softness. Where his neighbours were throwing out old wooden vats to install stainless steel, Rodriguez was doing the opposite – except that his vats were clean, well-kept and their contents overseen as though they were a new-born baby in an incubator.

Tiny Production

Quality-conscious Spanish wine-makers following in Rodriguez's footsteps faced two other barriers, however: one connived at, and one wholly created by the DO system. The authorities not only favour large *bodegas*, but make life very difficult for small ones. Ageing *bodegas* in Rioja, for example, are legally obliged to stock a minimum of 2,250 hectolitres – or around 1,000 225-litre barrels. Even spread over several vintages, 1,000 barrels could hold the production of four or five estates in Burgundy or St Emilion. And without a legally recognized ageing *bodega*, you can't use those magic *Con Crianza*, *Reserva* and *Gran Reserva* labels that guarantee a valuable extra few pesetas per bottle. The inevitable consequence of this is that Spain still has had far too few maverick wineries to pioneer new developments; compared with Italy, for example, it has a pitifully small band – less than a dozen strong – of internationally recognized superstars.

Then there are the vineyards. Yields in Spain are very low – on average only 25 hl/ha or half those of Burgundy, for example. It is these low yields that explain why, although Spain has more vineyards than any other country in Europe and nearly half as many again as France, its annual production is far smaller than it ought to be. This limited production is directly attributable to the lack of rain. But even when available, irrigation was, until 1996, against the law in the denominated regions. This might seem reasonable enough, were it not for the international success of wines made at Raimat whose huge swathes of vineyards would have a hard time supporting cactus if it weren't for the "experimental" irrigation system. In other words, some vine-growers could water their vines while others could not.

In the early 1990s, however, the bubble burst. Wine-makers in Rioja and elsewhere introduced their own equally "experimental" irrigation schemes so successfully that the authorities conceded that the ban on adding water might have to be reconsidered. Newly planted Cabernet Sauvignon vines made their contribution to new-wave Riojas (even if their presence too was deemed "experimental"); smaller estates like José Puig's Augustus in the Penedés joined Torres's Milmanda in producing world-class Chardonnays; and, in Rueda, a whole new white-wine region was born.

It will take time for these revolutionary tendencies to make an impact throughout Spain, and courage for more *bodegas* to flout custom by offering better wines with less oak-ageing. The first regions to escape from the shadow of Rioja have been Ribera del Duero and Navarra, but Rueda is on track with its whites and

Grape-treading at the harvest festival in Jerez

could soon prove to be just as good a place to make reds. Galicia will gain an international reputation for its white wines, as will previously unknown areas like Conca de Barberá (where Torres makes his Milmanda Chardonnay) and Somontano. Who knows? Valencia's sweet Muscats may finally get the recognition they deserve as lighter alternatives to France's Beaumes de Venise.

Spain has recently followed Italy's (questionable) lead by upgrading Rioja from plain DO – *Denominación de Origen* – to the first DOC – *Denominación de Origen Calificada* – and tightened the controls on the way it is made. All that's needed now is a version of the newer Italian rules that shift the emphasis toward the intrinsic quality of particular pieces of land and away from the way a wine has been made and matured.

RIOJA AND NAVARRA

After a certain point, good old wines all begin to look alike. Judging solely by its appearance, a wine from as far back as 1871 can actually look like one from the 1960s or the 1940s.

The difference in quality and character of the wines of such different ages has little to do with *when* or indeed where they were made, but everything to do with the grape varieties from which they have been produced. Under modern law, both wines would have been illegal – at least, they would if anyone were to reveal the amount of Cabernet Sauvignon the Tempranillo-dominant wines contained because, despite the part played by the French grape in the award-winning Riojas of the nineteenth century, today it may not be used other than on an "experimental" basis.

Rioja's history could be separated into four phases. There was the period during the last century when the region produced simple wine, most of which was for early drinking by the jugful. Then, in the 1860s, expertise – and grape varieties – were imported from Bordeaux, just across the Pyrenées. The newcomers, many of whom came to Spain when their own vineyards first fell prey to the *phylloxera* louse, introduced novel ideas such as the prolonged ageing of the wine in small (50-gallon/225-litre) casks and the practice of crushing the grapes rather than the Beaujolais-style method of fermenting them whole. Rioja became a wine worth keeping.

The third phase – from the early part of this century until quite recently – was often one of chauvinism and laziness: it saw the expulsion of the Cabernet Sauvignon, the relegation of the (characterful) Graciano to the sidelines, and the promotion of the easy-to-grow, but often featureless, Garnacha. By the early 1970s, Rioja was an internationally acknowledged, softly attractive wine with a sweet oaky flavour – but little justifiable claim to stand among the great wines of the world.

Today, faced with competition from regions elsewhere in Spain, and from overseas, the Riojanos have finally begun to raise their game. Despite the big-is-beautiful rule which obliges any *bodega* that is going to mature wine that will sell as *Crianza*, *Reserva* or *Gran Reserva* to hold at least 1,000 barrels of wine in stock at any given time, smaller individual estates have been established (generally by the big companies which used to run the region). The Garnacha's horns have been trimmed, the Graciano encouraged and there has even – though this is rarely acknowledged openly – been a return of the Cabernet Sauvignon. Just as important has been the acknowledgement that, alongside its traditional oak-aged *Crianza*, *Reserva* or *Gran Reserva* wines, the region should exploit the lovely strawberry flavour of young, unoaked – "*sin crianza*" – Tempranillo.

There are now four Riojas: the autonomous region which does not precisely match the DOC, the overall wine area of the same name which in parts stretches beyond it – and elsewhere stops short; and the three component parts, the Rioja Alta, the lower Rioja Baja and the Rioja Alavesa.

Most Riojanos traditionally used to maintain that the best Rioja is a blend of wines from two or three of the regions. The Rioja Alta's calcium-rich soil is well suited to the Tempranillo and produces fine, long-lived red wines, while the Alavesa, shaded by mountains, has fewer extremes of temperature and makes the plummiest, best early-drinking wines. That leaves the Baja, which some unfairly say lives down to its "low" name by making the region's most basic wine.

The oaky flavour associated with red Rioja was once also the mark of the region's whites. For these, the ageing requirements are slightly less stringent; sadly only a handful of *bodegas* now make good oaky, traditional wine that conforms to these rules, but firms like Berberana are spear-heading a renaissance of white Rioja.

Navarra

Every now and then, when right-wing politicians rant about the evils of "intervention", it would be fascinating to lead them to the old kingdom of

Navarra, birthplace of Spanish wine-making, next-door neighbour to Rioja and, until the 1980s, one of the most run-down wine regions in the country. Left to the devices of the free market, this varied region devoted itself to the production of dull rosés and duller reds.

Then the local government became involved and sank substantial sums into a world-class research station called EVENA where men and women in white coats were employed to discover why Navarra's wines always tasted so recognizably different from – and less impressive than – the wines of Rioja. It didn't take long to discover the answer; 80 per cent of the region's growers farmed less than one hectare (2.5 acres) and delivered mostly Garnacha grapes. Then, 90 per cent of its wine was made by ill-equipped and old-fashioned co-operatives.

Having defined the problem, EVENA had a solution: further planting of the Garnacha was to be banned and growers were to be given financial incentives to plant better varieties, principally the Tempranillo, but also newcomers such as the Cabernet Sauvignon and Chardonnay and undervalued local varieties like the Graciano.

EVENA would advise on what would grow best, and where and how the wine should be made, and – *pour encourager les autres* – the government would invest its own money in Cenalsa, a new showcase blending and bottling *bodega* that sells 20 per cent of all the Navarra wine sold in Spain.

And what did all this intervention achieve? Well, just taste some of Navarra's fruity and emphatically "modern" whites and rosés which have often leapfrogged over their more famous counterparts from Rioja. Try the young, unoaked reds that are among the most plummily refreshing in Spain. Some of the big *bodegas* of Rioja should look to their laurels. Navarra is quietly regaining Spain's vinous crown.

THE ESSENTIALS
RIOJA AND NAVARRA

What to look for Rich, soft, oaky, and juicy "joven" unoaked Riojas, and increasingly impressive "new-wave" Navarra reds and whites.

Official quality Navarra is classified as Denominación de Origen (DO) while Rioja is now a Denominacion de Origen Califica (DOC). Rioja is divided into three sub-regions: the Rioja Baja, Alavesa and Alta, in ascending order of quality.

Style Red Rioja should have soft strawberry and raspberry fruit with rich vanilla overtones from ageing in American oak barriques. There are two very different styles of white Rioja. One is the very clean, cool-fermented, anonymous new-wave style exemplified by Marqués de Cacerés. The other is the traditional reserva style with a very deep golden colour and intense vanilla flavour imparted by oak. Some wines, such as CVNE'S Monopole, successfully combine the two styles, producing fruity wines that have an attractive creamy vanilla character. The wines of Navarra tend to be more overtly modern, reflecting the flavours of the (diverse set of) grape varieties grown here.

Climate The Pyrenées and the Cantabrian mountains moderate the climate, offering protection from the Atlantic winds and the excessive heat of the Mediterranean. The climate becomes hotter and drier as one moves toward the coast.

Cultivation Topography in the region ranges widely, from the foothills of the Pyrenées to the flatter, hotter Rioja Baja. The best vineyards are in the central hill country of Rioja Alta and Alavesa. Limestone is the dominant component of the soils with additional sand and clays in Alta and Alavesa and silty alluvium deposits in Baja and Navarra.

Grape varieties Red: Tempranillo, Garnacha Tinta, Graciano, Mazuelo, Cabernet Sauvignon; White: Viura, Malvasia, Garnacha Blanca, Muscat Blanc à Petits Grains.

Production/maturation Ageing in Bordeaux-style barriques imparts the characteristic vanilla flavour to the wines of Rioja, where the new-style whites are cold-fermented. A lowering of minimum ageing periods in cask and bottle has, some say, resulted in a lessening of quality and character in red Riojas, many of which are now sold much younger than previously.

Longevity Red Rioja Crianza: 3–8 years; Reserva: 5–30 years; Gran Reserva: 8–30 years. New-wave white Rioja is for drinking young (within 3 years); the traditional white can be kept for 15 years but good examples are rare; Navarra reds: 3–10 years; whites: 1–3 years.

Vintage guide 82, 83, 85, 86, 87, 89, 90, 91, 94.

Top 22 Rioja: Lopez de Heredia, La Rioja Alta, CVNE, Remelluri, Contino, Campillo, Marqués de Cacerés, Marqués de Riscal, Riojanas, Martinez Bujanda, Marqués de Villamagna, Amézola de la Mora, Campillo, Navajas, Baron de Ley; Navarra: Chivite, Senorio de Sarria, Ochoa, Guelbenzu, Palacio de la Vega, Agramont.

CATALONIA

First things first. According to the Madrid government, Catalonia may appear to be part of Spain – but that's not the way the Catalans see it. They have their own capital in Barcelona, their own language and, from the way it looked to many observers, they had their own Olympic Games. A decade or so ago, though, before autonomy was on the menu, wine pundits were predicting that the Penedés, Catalonia's most famous wine area, would soon become one of the world's most exciting wine regions. In fact, after a promising start, the Penedés has had to watch some of its neighbours catch up and even overtake it, almost from a standing start.

There are nine Catalonian DOs, ranging from the huge Penedés to tiny Costers del Segre and Conca de Barberá, both of which owed their DO to the presence of a single large producer. Only one bottle in 10 leaves the winery without a regional *denominación* to its name. but ask most Spaniards to name as many as three of these regions and you'll be lucky to get much of a reply.

Penedés

This is the most successful part of Catalonia, thanks almost exclusively to the efforts of its Cava – sparkling wine – producers and to the dynamic Miguel Torres, the man who persuaded his neighbours of the benefits of clean, temperature-controlled fermentation; who proved, by winning international tastings against the best of Bordeaux with his Gran Coronas Black Label (now called Mas La Plana), that the Cabernet Sauvignon could make top-class wine in the Penedés; and who, following a spell in France, took a fresh look at the local varieties.

A few small estates, such as Puig i Roca, have followed in Torres' footsteps toward the Cabernet Sauvignon and Chardonnay, but none of the big *bodegas* – with the exception of Codorníu's Raimat winery – has even begun to compete on any kind of major scale. And yet there are few regions in the Old World in which an adventurous wine-maker would have greater scope to experiment; between them, the Upper, Middle and Lower Penedés really do offer an extraordinarily broad range of climates. Down near the coast in the Lower Penedés, it's hot, ripe country – ideal for Muscat, but less suited to even medium-bodied reds and whites. For better examples of either of these styles, you have to cross the hills to the white-wine country where the grapes for Cava are grown, and where Torres has produced his prize-winning Cabernet Sauvignon. Even here the temperature is still a bit high for really fine whites; these are to be found in the Upper Penedés at 2,000–2,600 ft (600–800 m).

Surprisingly, the one style Torres has never marketed has been Cava, the Penedés *méthode champenoise* sparkling wine. Cava's early success merely served to confirm to a few cynical critics, who maintained that these wines tasted earthy, dull and unrefreshing, how easy it is to sell bubbles. Old-fashioned wineries (including co-operatives) do little to maintain the wine's freshness and flavour and the climate where the grapes are grown is less than ideal, but the main problem is the grape varieties – the Parellada, the Macabeo and the dull, alcoholic Xarel-lo.

When the Raimat winery introduced its Chardonnay Brut Nature, few who tasted it blind recognized it as a Cava and non-Spaniards, used to Champagne, declared it a winner. Today, despite howls of anguish from conservatives like Freixenet, Chardonnay is rapidly appearing in all sorts of Cavas, and efforts are being made by newcomers like Moët & Chandon to improve the quality of wine made from the traditional varieties. Even so, too many producers are still promoting old-fashioned vintage *cavas* and "special reserves". Save money and stick to young non-vintage examples from Raimat, Codorníu, Freixenet and Segura Viudas.

Conca de Barberá

Some day, the name of this almond-growing region ought to be as well known as that of the Penedés. This is the cool area from which Torres gets the grapes to make Milmanda, its top-of-the-range Chardonnay, and in which Flying Wine-maker Hugh Ryman has made some successful commercial whites.

Costers del Segre

This one-estate *denominación* to the west of the Penedés owes its reputation to the success of the wines made at Raimat. The Raventos family of Codorníu, who own this ultra-modern *bodega*, today have over 5,000 acres (2,000 ha) of vineyards, where they make good reds (from Cabernet Sauvignon and Tempranillo), pure still and sparkling Chardonnay. Interestingly, it would be quite impossible to grow anything very much here without the benefit of – theoretically illegal – irrigation. Raimat was highly fortunate in being allowed the "experimental" status which permitted it to install its sophisticated irrigation system.

Tarragona and Terra Alta

Despite their dusty, hot summers, two of Tarragona's three regions specialize in white wine. Little of it is worth going out of your way to find, however, and much the same can be said for the Cariñena- and Garnacha-based reds. Look for the dry, grapey Moscatel Seco from De Muller and Viña Montalt Blanco Seco from Pedro Rovira. Though technically within Tarragona, the hot dry region of Terra Alta has its own DO for the fairly hefty whites and dullish reds it produces. The *denominación* is more deserved by its organically produced, sweet, lightly fortified altar wines.

Priorato

Primitive wine from a primitive region, in which olive trees, men and vines struggle to survive on steep, rocky slopes. Lack of rainfall, an intensely hot climate and slatey soil mean tiny yields, mostly of Garnacha and Cariñena, which are used to make wines that are highly alcoholic – often up to 18 per cent.

Alella and Ampurdán-Costa Brava

Alella has become a doomed wine region; over the last 25 years over half of its vineyards have been stolen to extend Barcelona. True, the world can live without the sort of dull, wood-aged, semi-sweet wine made by the Alella co-operative, but the Marqués de Alella makes a range of dry whites, including promising Chardonnay, and good Cava from its sister company Parxet.

THE ESSENTIALS

CATALONIA

What to look for Varied and possibly quite innovative red and white wines whose character and quality can depend on altitude as much as grape variety and wine-making.

Official quality Penedés, Alella, Terra Alta and Priorato are notable areas with DO status.

Style Both red and white wines are varied, ranging from light and fruity to full, oak-matured to oak-free, dry to juicy-sweet. Although Catalonia is renowned as being Spain's most go-ahead wine-making region, most wines tend to be little more than sound and commercial. A significant difference can be seen in those wines from producers such as Torres and Jean León who use foreign grape varieties, oak-ageing and the latest techniques. Cava is the largest source of sparkling wine outside Champagne. Most are dry although there are sweet and rosado versions. Once recognizable by a characteristic earthy flavour, Cava has improved remarkably in recent years. The area around Tarragona is the source for much of the world's sacramental wine.

Similarly rich and dark reds are produced at Terra Alta and Priorato.

Climate A relatively mild Mediterranean climate on the coast, becoming more continental further inland, with frost an increasing hazard. High-altitude vineyards are cool enough for Riesling.

Cultivation A wide variety of soils ranging from the granite of Alella to the limestone chalk and clay of Penedés and Tarragona, where there are, in addition, alluvial deposits. There is a similar variety of relief, ranging from the highest vineyards of Alto Penedés, which benefit from cooler temperatures, to the flat plains of Campo de Tarragona.

Grape varieties Red: Cabernet Sauvignon, Merlot, Tempranillo, Garnacha, Monastrell, Pinot Noir, Cabernet Franc; White: the Parellada predominates, with some Chardonnay, Sauvignon, Gewürztraminer, Muscat, Riesling, Garnacha Blanca, Macabeo, Malvasia and Xarel-lo.

Production/maturation With the exception of the very traditional Priorato, techniques are modern. Torres introduced cool-fermentation to Spain while the Cava companies have invented their own apparatus and methods besides adopting some – for example, the méthode champenoise – from outside. The Raimat estate at Lerida exemplifies the good use of ultra-modern vinification techniques.

Longevity Reds: up to 5 years for most, but top-class Penedés wines can last for 15; Whites: best drunk early, but between 3 and 8 years for fine whites such as Jean León's Chardonnay; Cava: within 1 to 3 years for non-vintage. Old vintage Cava is generally earthy and dull and unrecommendable to anyone who enjoys fizz with freshness and fruit or the kind of rich biscuitiness to be found in mature Champagne.

Vintage guide Penedés: Reds 82, 85, 87, 91, 94, 95, 96, 97; Whites: 91, 94, 95, 96, 97.

Top producers Penedés: Torres, Jean León, Marqués de Monistrol, Puig Roca; Alella: Raimat;Cava: Torre de Gall (a.k.a. Cava Chandon), Masia Bach, Codorníu, Freixenet, Castellblanch, Juve i Camps, Rovellats.

THE OTHER WINES OF SPAIN

Travelling through the rest of Spain's wine regions can be as frustrating as it is fascinating. Every region seems to have its own official denomination, irrespective of the quality of wines being produced – and despite the fact that a *vino de tierra* might well be a better buy. But the trip is worthwhile, if only to watch how the wine revolution is gradually taking hold of the country as a whole.

The North-West

Rias Baixas

Up in Galicia far too many of this cool, damp region's wines have traditionally been made from European hybrid grapes left over from the days following the ravages of the *phylloxera*. For a taste of what Galicia can produce, seek out the spicy Albariño made by Bodegas Cardallal and the "Martin Codax" from Bodegas de Vilariño-Cambados.

Ribeiro

This warm, dry region has high aspirations. The reds – made from the Brencellão, Caino and Souson – can be light and herby, but the trend is toward white wines. Those made from the Albariño, Godello, Treixadura and Torrentés are promising, but the Palominos are as dull as almost every other non-fortified example of this variety.

Valdeorras

The Palomino is as prevalent in the mountainous vineyards here, along with the dark-fleshed Garnacha Tintorera. Sadly, while the growers of Ribeiro are experimenting with new varieties and more modern wine-making techniques, the producers up here are handicapped by low yields, low prices and land that's almost too difficult to tend.

El Bierzo

The Bodegas Palacio de Arganza, the best *bodega* here, is most widely respected for its skills at blending, ageing and bottling wines from various other regions. The red wines produced from the local Mencia grapes are pleasantly light and grassy but hardly distinguished enough to justify El Bierzo's promotion from *vino de tierra* to *Denominación de Origen*.

Toro

This is another "new" region (it received its DO in 1987) that hopes to benefit from the success of its eastern neighbour Ribera del Duero. The grape here, known as the Tinto de Toro, is that region's Tinto Fino – and indeed the Tempranillo of just about everywhere else. The lower altitude and rainfall, and the use of up to 25 per cent Garnacha, tend to give Toro's wines a softer, more beefily alcoholic style. Wines made by Bodegas Fariña, including the oaky Gran Colegiata, show this is a region to watch.

León

The unhappy acronym VILE – for Vinos de León – appears on every bottle from this region's modern co-operative. The reds, mostly made from the Prieto Picudo, are soft, woody and comparable to some mid-range Rioja.

Rueda

Once exclusively the source for unimpressive sherry-like fortified wine, Rueda has, partly thanks to the encouragement of the Bordeaux guru Emile Peynaud, pinned its colours to the mast of modern white wine-making. In this, the region's producers have a great advantage over their neighbours in the Penedés; their Verdejo grape (not to be confused with Portugal's Verdelho) has far more character than the latter region's Parellada and Xarel-lo.

Cigales

A recent DO, it's close to Ribera del Duero, grows the same grape varieties (reds have to contain at least 75 per cent Tempranillo), and can produce high-quality pink rosados – which, for the moment at least, are still its strongest suit.

Ribera del Duero

Historically almost unknown to many Rioja drinkers, Ribera del Duero has long been famous among Spanish wine buffs as the region that produces Spain's most historically illustrious and expensive wine, Vega Sicilia.

The traditional grape variety here is the Tempranillo (locally known as the Tinto Fino) and that's what's used, for example, in Protos, the over-praised wine made by the Bodega Ribera Duero. Vega Sicilia's position as the region's top *bodega* has been challenged by the sudden stardom of Pesquera, a wine made by another *bodega* from local varieties, but with much less ageing in oak. Today, led by these two and a growing number of other increasingly impressive wines, the region is rapidly developing a reputation for red wines that ought to worry the Riojanos.

The North-East

Campo de Borja

Alcohol levels of the dull Garnacha-based red and pink wines here have traditionally been too high. There are hopes that good wine-making – especially Beaujolais-style fermentation – will make for lighter, fresher styles.

Cariñena

This hot, dry region was where the Carignan grape apparently got its name. The red wine varieties used here are – inevitably – the Cariñena, the Tempranillo and, more particularly, the Garnacha, though the Cabernet is making (welcome) inroads. Few wines are better than basic, hefty, table fare, though the softly fruity Don Mendo red and pink from Bodegas San Valero show what can be done.

Somontano

Cool, green Somontano is Aragón's most exciting region, though its potential is only beginning to become apparent. Wine-making techniques are still pretty old-fashioned, and too much of the production remains in the hands of the co-operative. Even so, the local co-operative producies decent reds from Tempranillo, Moristel and Macabeo while the go-ahead COVISA is proving what can be done with foreign grapes such as the Chenin Blanc, Gewürztraminer and Chardonnay. Look for the Viñas del Vero label.

The Centre

Madrid

Despite their DO status, the wines produced to the south and east of the capital have more in common with the most backward village in the country than with the restless modernity of Madrid, but there are a few improving exceptions to a dull, rustic rule. Look out for Ricardo Benito's light young reds.

Mentrida

It is hard to imagine many people getting too ecstatic about pink wine that, at a strength of 18–24 per cent, packs more of a punch than some vermouth, but the wine-drinkers here seem keen enough on the style. The region also makes a similarly strong red, often adding tannic bite to the alcohol by drawing off half the juice at the beginning of fermentation and thus doubling the proportion of skins to juice.

La Mancha

La Mancha's indigenous Airén grape is, incredibly, the world's most widely planted variety and the region itself is the largest appellation in Europe. But it's far from the most productive; the lack of water, the high summer and low winter temperatures make for tiny yields. In addition, the authorities have until recently decided that – even when available – irrigation is forbidden.

The area as a whole is sadly underexploited. Only one in 10 of the bottles made in La Mancha can carry the distinctive Don Quixote logo of the *Consejo Regulador de la Denominación de Origen*, simply because most of the wine is still made in apparently medieval *bodegas*, where the juice of over-ripe, intrinsically flavourless Airén grapes is fermented in *tinajas* (*amphorae*), with only the most rudimentary attempts at cooling.

These methods of wine-making can, when carefully employed, produce creditable reds, but are less well suited to the production of dry white wine. If you like young wine with the colour of ochre, the flavour of nuts that have been left to mature for a few years in a dusty loft and the alcoholic kick of a lethargic mule, traditional La Mancha whites are for you. But not for long. Today, a fight is on between the region's wine-producers and the European bureaucrats who want to see a large proportion of the vines uprooted. While sympathizing with the growers who'll have a hard time finding a replacement crop, it has to be said that they've stubbornly gone on making bad white wine, much of which has been taken straight to the distillery, while they could have turned their attention to

CENTRAL SPAIN

What to look for Young reds and whites, usually as young as possible.

Quality La Mancha, Valdepeñas, Galicia, Valencia, Tierra de Barros, Utiel-Requena, Alicante, Yecla and Jumilla have their own DOs, although La Mancha produces a large quantity of non-DO wine of mostly fairly basic quality.

Style Reds, whites and rosados are generally dull and flabby with a lack of balancing acidity. However, Valdepeñas can, with the help of oak-ageing, produce well-balanced wines that can be good value. Valencia is now producing light-bodied, fruity wines that can give immediate pleasure, besides the richer Moscatels for which it is more famous. Similarly, Utiel-Requena is producing some lighter wines but Alicante still makes old-style Spanish reds, full-bodied and high in alcohol and of very little interest.

Climate Very hot and arid in most regions, though there are some cooler, damper micro-climates in areas such as Rias Baixas.

Cultivation Efforts are being made to counter the effects of the climate on the grapes – harvesting earlier to retain acidity and freshness, for example. There has also been investment in replanting, particularly in Valencia.

Grape varieties Red: Garnacha Tinta, Bobal, Monastrell, Cencibel, Macabeo; White: Airén, Garnacha Blanco, Jaén, Muscatel, Malvasia, Cirial.

Top producers Valdepeñas: Señorio de los Llanos; La Mancha: Felix Solis, Castillo de Alhambra.

Longevity As a rule, drink young. Whites: 1-2 years; Reds: top Valdepeñas: 1-5 years; others: 1-3 years.

Vintage guide 90, 91, 94, 95, 96, 97.

---

the red wine varieties for which the region is better suited – and for which there is more demand.

Valdepeñas

The "Valley of Stones" is white, Airén, country too, but its reputation was won by the red and pink wines made from the Cencibel grape. The Bodegas Félix Solis and Los Llanos provide the best chance to try this variety's red wines in their *Reserva* and *Gran Reserva* form, but most Valdepeñas reds should be caught as young as possible, and bought with care, too, because the use of Airén white grapes in their production makes many of them taste flat and earthy. It's a good idea to avoid the *clarete* pink wine too; it's often only Airén dyed with a little Cencibel.

The South-West

Condado de Huelva

Interesting sherry-like versions of *fino* and *oloroso* are produced here, as well as some promising whites that display a triumph of modern wine-making over dull local grapes and hot summers. Ignore the Extramedura, close to the Portuguese border; its wines are boring bruisers.

The South-East

Valencia

This is the region into which Swiss investors have pumped enormous amounts of money, and the one in which they and Spanish exporters have combined forces to discover the kinds of wine they should be selling to the USA. Unfortunately, with the exception of the Moscatel which can be every wine-drinker's ideal Sunday afternoon drink, Valencia is handicapped by a surplus of dull local grapes.

Utiel-Requena

The wines of this neighbouring region have often been sold under the better-known name of Valencia, despite its right to bear its own DO. But a combination of a high altitude that is ideal for crisp wine-making, the Bobal, one of Spain's few underrated grapes, and reasonably plentiful Tempranillo are helping Utiel-Requena to develop a growing reputation for its reds and rosados. The whites are – so far – less worthwhile.

Almansa

This is the place to go for a real taste of the Garnacha Tintorera; this variety is widely planted here and used, along with the Monastrell and Cencibel, to make mostly beefy, unsubtle red wines.

Jumilla

Jumilla was originally by-passed by the *phylloxera* louse when it munched its way through the rest of the continent, but whole vineyards have been wiped out. New vines are being grafted onto the same kinds of resistant rootstock that are used elsewhere, and the opportunity has been taken to introduce experimental plantings of foreign grape varieties to supplement the traditional Monastrell which has conspired with "traditional" wine-making methods to make tough, often unlovable, stuff.

Yecla

Another recent DO, Yecla is, nevertheless, still at risk of extinction. The altitude is high (at 2,000 ft/650 m above sea level) and the soil stony, so yields are uneconomical. The hope for the area lies in the modern Bodegas Ochoa, which makes and exports large quantities of soft reds, and the huge Co-operative La Purisima.

Alicante

This is not only the name of a region, but also that of a grape that was traditionally prized by wine-makers in Burgundy and Bordeaux. The variety, which is also known as the Garnacha Tintorera, is still grown here, though it is the Monastrell that is more frequently used to make the region's big, dark, alcoholic reds. The most interesting drink made from grapes in Alicante, though, is Fundillon, a cask-aged liqueur.

The Islands

Majorca

What most tourists miss is a range of ripe reds and fresh, young *vino joven* wines, produced in the hot, windmill-bestrewn land around Binissalem on a plateau nearly 500 ft (150 m) above sea level. Most are made from the good-quality, local Manto Negro and Callet grapes and the dull Fogoneu, though both the Jaume Mesquida and José Ferrer wineries have been quite successful with Cabernet Sauvignon, while the Swedish-owned Santa Catalina winery has made some reasonable Chardonnay. Other wine grapes are Moll, Xarel-lo and Parellada.

Canary Isles

Some of the most interesting-looking vineyards are to be found here – because of the black volcanic soil in which Lanzarote's vines are planted – but they produce some of the least interesting-tasting wines. The problem in the Tacoronte-Acentejo region to the north-east of Tenerife is partly the grapes – Listan Blanco and Negro and Negramoll – and partly the way they are vinified.

THE ESSENTIALS
OTHER SPANISH DOs

Official quality Ribera del Duero, Toro, Rueda, Ribeiro and Rias Baixas are the notable DO areas.
Style Some of these areas are producing good-quality, even exciting, wines. Good Ribera del Duero reds are packed with rich plummy fruit and have a velvety texture which, when combined with generous oaking, has resulted in a wine – Pesquera – which has been compared to Pétrus by Robert Parker. Toro is capable of producing similarly generous wines, which are often oak-aged, while neighbouring Rueda makes good-quality whites from classic and local grape varieties. Ribeiro and Valdeorras are both located in Galicia, producing fresh, aromatic and slightly sparkling whites, resembling the vinhos verdes of Portugal, and attractively fresh and fruity reds. Few of these wines are exported but as boredom

and dissatisfaction grow with Rioja, hopefully, they will attract greater attention.
Climate Ribera del Duero, Toro and Rueda have typical continental climates – hot summers and cold winters. Ribeiro and Rias Baixas in the far north-western tip of Spain, influenced by the Atlantic, have a warm wet climate.
Cultivation Ribera del Duero and Rueda compare favourably to Penedés in terms of innovative use of foreign grape varieties.
Grape varieties Ribera del Duero: Albillo, Cabernet Sauvignon, Garnacha, Malbec, Merlot, Tinto del Pais; Toro: Albillo, Garnacha, Malvasia, Palomino, Tinto de Toro (Tempranillo), Verdejo; Rueda: Cabernet Sauvignon, Chardonnay, Palomino, Sauvignon, Verdejo, Viura; Galicia: Albariño, Albilla, Caiño, Garnacha, Godello, Mencia, Merenzão, Palomino,

Sousão, Tempranillo, Treixadura, Valenciano.
Production/maturation These areas show what can be achieved in Spain by the adoption of modern vinification methods and the use of the latest knowledge, combined, in some cases, with the best of local wine-making tradition. The wines of Bodegas Alejandro Fernandez, sold as Tinto Pesquera, are the result of both old and new techniques; Vega Sicilia Unico is produced combining an age-old formula requiring 10 years' oak-ageing with the local Tinto Fino and French grape varieties.
Longevity Reds: Ribera del Duero: 3–25 years; Toro: 3–8 years; Whites: Rueda: 1–3 years; Galicia: within 2 years.
Vintage guide Reds: Ribera del Duero 85, 87, 90, 91, 94, 95, 96, 97.

145

SHERRY

Let's play a word-association game: we'll start with "sherry", and you reply with the first word that comes into your head. If you're British, it's almost even odds that you would say "vicar", "maiden aunt", "Bristol Cream" or "trifle". If, on the other hand, you were brought up on the other side of the Atlantic, your mind is almost sure to shoot straight to Bowery bums drinking locally produced headache-juice hidden in a brown paper bag. And if you were French, you'd more than likely be thinking of an ingredient to use in the kitchen.

The word that probably wouldn't have occurred to you, unless you happen to be Spanish, is "wine". It's precisely the one most Spaniards – but no-one else – would come up with; they not only think of sherry as wine, they drink it that way – bone-dry, with food, and out of glasses that hold a proper mouthful of liquid.

So put all those Anglo-American prejudices out of your mind and try to look at sherry through Spanish eyes. Which means accepting right away that, just as one small corner of north-eastern France is the only place in the world that makes genuine Champagne, the only source of real sherry is a similarly small area around Cadiz, near the southernmost point of Spain. And, like Champagne, the best sherries (particularly *fino*, the region's main style) have traditionally been dry.

Nor does either region make table wine of any great quality; while Champagne's grape varieties produce thin, acidic stuff in their cold-climate region, sherry's dull Palomino makes even duller wine in the near-drought conditions of vineyards where there are only 10 weeks of the year when the sun doesn't shine. Both wines owe their natural lightness of touch to the fact that they are made from grapes that have been grown on some of the chalkiest soils in the world – in sherry's case, on the brilliantly white *albariza* that covers much of the vineyards. Both are made in a peculiar way that depends on prolonged contact with yeast, and both are essentially non-vintage wines that call for great expertise in blending different vintages – usually by merchants with huge stocks of wine. And if you agree that not only is Champagne a wine, but a great and historic one, then you're half-way to being convinced that so, too, is sherry.

The History

Sherry is one of the oldest wines of all. The town of Cadiz had been founded by the Phoenicians before 1200 BC, and a thousand years later a wine called Ceretanum which almost certainly came from Ceret – Jerez – was being exported to Rome to be praised by the Roman poet Martial.

In the fourteenth century, the naturally high alcohol levels of wine from this hot region made it travel well, and sherry had become a firm favourite in Britain. Chaucer wrote of the wine of Lepe (a village near Jerez) "*of which there riseth such fumositee*" that three draughts were enough to confuse a drinker as to whether he was in La Rochelle, Bordeaux or home in bed.

In 1587, a short-term supply was assured when Sir Francis Drake took Cadiz and captured 2,900 butts of what was by then known as "sherris" or "sack" after the Spanish word for export, "*saca*". Ten years later, it was given its first testimonial under its new name when

Sherry grapes spread out on mats to dry in the sun

Shakespeare's Sir John Falstaff declared, in *Henry IV, Part 2*: "*If I had a thousand sons, the first humane principle I would teach them would be to foreswear thin potations and addict themselves to sack.*" In Shakespeare's day, this naturally dry wine was already being sweetened for the English palate; at the Boar's Head Tavern in Eastcheap, where Falstaff supposedly lived, sugar was sometimes added, as were pieces of toast and even egg (vividly described by Sir John as "*pullet-sperm*").

During the eighteenth century, the English and Irish moved into Jerez in much the same way as they moved into Bordeaux; soon, the *bodegas* of Thomas Osborne, William Garvey, Sir James Duff and James Gordon were shipping wine to England where, in the port of Bristol, firms like Harvey's and Avery's had established their own blending and ageing cellars.

Styles

It was in these cellars in both countries that the styles of sherry we know today gradually evolved. Some barrels developed an unpleasant-looking white scum on their surface – it was later discovered to be a kind of yeast which, unlike the other kinds of bacteria that attack wine, actually kept it fresh and fragrant.

In honour of this quality, the Jerezanos dubbed the scum *flor*; or "flower". The wine it made was thought the finest in the cellars, and so, quite naturally, was called *fino*, though the slightly lighter version made and aged a little further up the coast, at Sanlúcar, became known for some reason as "the little apple", *manzanilla*, a word still used elsewhere in Spain for camomile tea. These wines were said to be saltier because of the sea air; this character and the lightness may, however, be attributable to the fact that the yeast grows more thickly here.

Usually, the inhabitants of Jerez drank the wine soon after it was made; when they left it in its barrel for a few years, the wine darkened and took on a nutty flavour. By topping up last year's *fino* barrels with this year's *flor*-affected wine, however, they found that the freshness could be maintained. Soon, they developed the *solera* system, keeping back a number of casks every year from which to refresh the wine of the preceding vintage, and from there to the vintage before that, and so on.

The art of pouring sherry with a long-handled venencia

Today, the oldest barrels are never emptied – indeed, no more than a third is ever removed from them – and the transfer is always made from one year's casks to that of the year before. Somehow – and no one is quite certain precisely why – provided the quality of the initial wines is carefully chosen and the chain of ever-older barrels – the *solera* – is well maintained, this relay-race gives the oldest casks the vinous equivalent of immortality, allowing *bodegas* to sell a consistent style every year.

The blending of *flor*-affected wines of different ages remains the basis of *fino* sherry production today, but a great many of the barrels did – and do – not develop *flor*; these are fortified by the addition of brandy. These stronger, darker, wines were called *oloroso*, or "fragrant", but they were never as well-considered by the Jerezanos as their *fino* and *manzanilla*. A third style, a cross between *fino* and *oloroso*, was invented too. *Amontillado*, literally "in the fashion of Montilla"*(see below)*, was made by leaving *fino* unrefreshed by younger wine to develop a deeper colour and a rich, nutty flavour.

Neither *fino* nor *manzanilla*, with a natural strength of around 15 per cent alcohol, was sturdy enough to ship overseas; without the protection of their *flor*, they oxidized very quickly. So, the Jerezanos developed a tradition of fortifying them and of sweetening them up with cooked grape juice. This not only created a number of new styles, but had the useful side-effect of masking any defects in taste or style.

Today, too many non-Spaniards still expect sherry to be sweet, and many firms in Jerez and England still obligingly sweeten all of their styles for the British palate. It can be infuriating, when one expects the bone-dry, nutty tang of a good *fino*, to find a sweetened or an over-alcoholic version. Thankfully, today, while sweet and over-fortified dry sherry can still be found, real, lower-strength examples are increasingly available throughout the world.

But don't dismiss all sweet sherries out of hand. Gonzalez Byass's Matusalem and Noë and Osborne's Pedro Ximénez, for example, are packed to the brim with the sweetness of the best fruit cake and molasses; these are among the world's most delicious, indulgent yet demanding drinks. Or, to be more accurate, "wines".

The Business of Sherry

Most sherry is produced by big sherry houses, some of which have *soleras* that were begun in the last century.

The size of the companies is partly dictated by rules that require any *bodega* to store a minimum of 100,000 litres of wine. There are, however, around 50 smaller *Almacenistas*, small maturers that buy wine from co-operatives or small producers and age it, selling most for blending by the bigger *bodegas*, but bottling a little themselves. These *Almacenista* wines, because of their small-scale production, can be some of the most exciting sherries on the market.

Montilla-Moriles

Montilla-Moriles – or plain Montilla, as it is more generally known – is the region and the style that gave its name to *amontillado*. The wines produced here are often quite reasonably considered to be "poor man's sherry", because they tend to be low-priced and of fairly basic quality.

They can be not only good, but indeed better and more delicate than poorly made sherry. Montilla's

---

THE ESSENTIALS

SOUTHERN SPAIN

What to look for Fresh zingy pale fino and manzanilla; rich, nutty, raisiny oloroso and amontillado and Christmas puddingy Pedro Ximénez.

Location Spain's south-west corner, from Condado de Huelva near the Portuguese border south-west to Málaga and inland to Montilla-Moriles.

Official quality DOs are Jerez, Manzanilla, Condado de Huelva, Málaga, Montilla-Moriles.

Style Sherry is one of the world's greatest and, in England at least, most misunderstood fortified wines. Its style varies enormously; in general, dry manzanilla sherries are thought to be lighter and more delicate than their Jerezano counterparts. Montilla-Moriles, to the north-east of Jerez, produces a similar range of wines, but they are generally softer and lower in alcohol – they may or may not be fortified. Málaga makes wonderful sweet wines with a strong raisiny flavour which are still underrated.

Climate The Mediterranean climate makes southern Spain the hottest wine region in the

country, although the climate is moderated by the Atlantic toward Portugal. The Atlantic poñete wind is wet and encourages the flor yeast that produces fino sherry to grow on the surface of the wines. The easterly levante wind is hotter and drier and partially dries the grapes on the vines while they ripen, concentrating their sugars.

Cultivation The land of southern Spain is generally flat, but ranges in altitude from the low-lying coastal plains near Sanlúcar de Barrameda to the plateau of Málaga at some 1,650 feet. The unique albariza soil of Andalusia is a lime-rich marl that is able to soak up and retain moisture, while its brilliant white colour reflects the sun on to the lower parts of the vines, helping the grapes to ripen.

Grape varieties Principally the white Palomino (Listan), plus Moscatel Fino, Pedro Ximénez, Baladi, Garrido Fino, Lairén, Mantuo, Torrontés, Zalerna.

Production/maturation Sherry-making involves

the art of mastering wine and naturally occurring yeast. The solera system, coupled with skilful blending, ensures that a consistent style of sherry is produced over a number of years, though Almacenista wines, from a single unblended solera, are worth seeking out for their characterful individuality, particularly if shipped by Lustau. Sweetening and colouring agents – usually thick, concentrated wines from grapes such as Pedro Ximénez or Moscatel – may also be added.

Longevity Fino sherries should ideally be drunk soon after they are bottled. An opened bottle should be consumed within a very few days. Sweeter, more alcoholic, traditionally made styles can be kept indefinitely but will not normally improve in the bottle.

Top 13 Sherry: Lustau, Diez-Merito, Osborne, Harvey's, Hidalgo, Garvey, Gonzalez Byass, Valdespino, Diez Merito, Domecq, Caballero, Barbadillo;

Montilla-Moriles: Gracia Hermanos.

producers use grapes grown in chalky soil to make a range of styles that are just like those of Jerez – from *flor*-affected *fino* to rich dry *oloroso*.

There are, though, two differences. First, the Pedro Ximénez grape, used almost exclusively here, ripens so well that Montilla can often achieve the same strengths as sherry without fortification. And second, there's the continuing tradition of fermenting Montilla in large terracotta *tinajas*, which are nothing more nor less than the same kind of *amphorae* the Greeks and Romans would have used to ferment their wine, over 2,000 years ago. But despite this evidence of tradition, the Jerezanos until quite recently managed to prevent the Montilla producers from using the term "*amontillado*", which was a little like the *parfumiers* of France barring their counterparts in Cologne from selling eau de Cologne.

What Montilla needs most urgently is to be taken seriously. Sales of the most illustrious wines of Jerez and Sanlúcar are far from brisk, and the need for cheap alternatives reduces every year. Watch out for wines labelled Moriles. Produced in the village of that name and rarely seen elsewhere, they can be more delicate than those from the town of Montilla – and lighter and more evidently wine-like than many sherries.

Málaga

Málaga was being shipped from the port of the same name as early as 1500 and was first sold in Britain as "sack", then as "Mountain". In the eighteenth century, when sherry fell out of favour and the British turned to port, the harbour town of Málaga lowered its export duties and effectively stole the London "sack" market from Jerez. But everything went wrong late in the following century, when the *phylloxera* louse made Málaga its first Spanish port of call. The vineyards were never properly replanted; today, they cover just 3,000 hectares, compared with 112,000 before the arrival of the louse.

The wine has gone out of fashion too, and standards of wine-making have often dropped to accommodate a small, undemanding market. Unlike their counterparts in Jerez, the Málaga *bodegas* have mostly turned their backs on tradition, and make little effort to attract the attention of tourists. But when

Whitewash and dappled sunshine: a bodega *in Jerez*

Málaga is good – as it was from the now sadly defunct Scholtz Hermanos – it can be wonderful, molasses-rich wine. The *solera* system is used here, on wine that is often a mixture of dry wine and grape juice, part of which has been boiled until it has turned into sweet treacle (*arrope*), and part (the *vino maestro*) fortified in a very similar way to sherry.

Málaga can vary enormously both in colour, which ranges from white (*blanco*) to black (*negro*), rough golden (*dorado*), tawny (*rojo-dorado*) and dark (*oscuro*), and sweetness (from *seco* to *dulce*). Bottles labelled *dulce color* are pretty simple in their syrupy style; ones that describe themselves as *lágrima* ought to be of far higher quality, and are made without recourse to a press, from free-run juice. The difference in flavour between a good example of *lágrima* and a basic Málaga is as great as that between a top-class Bordeaux and a house claret. The finest Málagas have an intensity of flavour and a balancing acidity which combine to prevent the sweetness being in any way cloying.

"*Solera*" wines are common too; examples like the excellent Scholtz Hermanos Solera 1855 proudly proclaimed the year in which their particular *solera* was founded. Unfortunately, none of the other Solera Málagas is of anything like as high a quality as the Scholtz Hermanos.

PORTUGAL

"You see, Señor, we are a calm, conservative people. Even when we have a revolution we avoid making too much fuss and noise." The Portuguese wine-maker raised the subject of the almost violence-free political upheaval of 1974 to illustrate the fundamental quality of his countrymen's character: they are people who aren't terribly fond of change. Wine-makers in other countries may have been importing tons of cooling equipment and thousands of new oak barrels for decades; the Portuguese have, until recently, preferred to go on drinking the kind of wine they've always drunk. And doing so in some quantity; this is the seventh largest wine-producing country in the world and its small population has always done a pretty good job of making sure that none of its produce goes to waste.

The Portuguese divide their wine into two very different styles: the stuff they sell to foreigners, and the stuff they drink themselves. The off-dry, slightly sparkling rosé and white wines that most people associate with Portugal are treated very sniffily by the Portuguese themselves. The wine they enjoy most is still either the mouth-scouringly dry, red Vinho Verde (traditionally made in far greater quantities than the white, but unsaleable anywhere outside Portugal and its former colonies), or tough, inky dark, venerable reds from Dão, Bairrada or the Douro.

To understand the Portuguese taste for these wines, you have to have experienced Portuguese cooking. Until you have ploughed your way through a deep bowl or

Cork oak after bark harvesting at Santana do Mato, near Coruche, Portugal

three of *caldo verde* vegetable soup, a platter piled high with *bacalhão* (the national dish of salt-cod), half a suckling pig and a pudding that can best be described as half-cooked cream caramel, you can never imagine the essential role those tannic, high-acid reds manfully perform.

Of course, few people outside Portugal live on a diet of salt-cod and suckling pig, which explains why, in the middle of the twentieth century, a few Portuguese producers cleverly created the export styles of light, sweetish pink and white wine with which most foreigners have become familiar.

Today, as wine-drinkers around the world increasingly turn away from off-dry pink and white wine, and as the increasingly health-conscious Portuguese themselves cut back on the suckling pig, Portugal's wine-makers are beginning to take a fresh look at the kind of stuff they are making. They know that they have one tremendous advantage over their Spanish neighbours; theirs is a far more interesting arsenal of grape varieties.

To exploit these varieties, however, the Portuguese have had to launch another "calm revolution" – in the vineyards and wineries. First, they have had to sort out the system of regional appellations, the *regiãos demarcadas*. Portugal more or less invented the idea of *Appellation Contrôlée* years before the French got around to it. Until the beginning of the 1990s, however, the whole country had just 11 such regions, of which four – Bucelas, Carcavelos, Colares and Moscatel de Setúbal – produced tiny amounts of wine, while another – the Algarve – made appalling wine and owed its legal recognition solely to its importance as a tourist region. Not surprisingly, many of Portugal's best wines have carried no regional denomination at all, and the label of Barca Velha, Portugal's top red, doesn't trouble to mention that it comes from the demarcated region of the Douro. For most Portuguese, the word "*garrafeira*", indicating a mature, special-reserve wine, curried more favour than any mention of a particular area.

The second problem is the way in which the industry has been held in a virtual stranglehold by a small number of giant co-operatives that bought in most of the grapes and made most of the wine, selling it to an even smaller number of merchants, whose creative input

has often been restricted to the way in which they have aged and bottled it. Inevitably, this has encouraged the Iberian tradition of keeping wine for a long time before bottling. Quite often this is far more appropriate here than in Spain, because a lengthy period in tank will generally allow a tough red to shed some of its impenetrable tannic husk. In some cases the final result is a wine with fascinating, mature, tobaccoey flavours. Far too often, though, it makes for dull wines that lose their fruit along with the tannin. Portugal is a great place to buy inexpensive old wine; some of it tastes attractively old, but some tastes of almost nothing at all.

In recent years a growing number of small producers and innovative merchants have begun to wrest back control from the co-operatives and to take a more careful look at their grapes and the best ways to extract as much fruit as possible from them, however long the wine is going to be aged.

For the first time, too, the Portuguese are looking overseas for inspiration. For the moment at least, they are not falling into the trap of copying everybody else with lookalike Chardonnays and Cabernets, but they *are* discovering the methods of modern wine-making from people such as Peter Bright and David Baverstock, who learned to make wine in their native Australia and are now independently producing some of the most exciting wines in Portugal.

The tough, old-fashioned reds and the semi-sweet pinks and whites are finally making way for fruity young wines that can compete with Beaujolais, for clean, dry whites that have nothing to do with Vinho Verde, and for deep, richly flavoured red wines that stand comparison with the best from Italy. Of course, as you'd expect in a "calm, conservative" country, the wine revolution is a leisurely, undramatic affair. Given time and encouragement, though, Portugal is steadily becoming one of the most exciting wine countries of all, with one of the broadest ranges of different flavours. Companies such as Sogrape, JM da Fonseca, JP Vinhos (the winery at which Peter Bright makes his wines) and the huge Herdade do Esperão estate (where David Baverstock produces some of his) are already proving what can be done – and at prices that are low enough to encourage even the most timid wine-drinker to risk buying a bottle.

THE NORTH

Vinho Verde

Among the first of Portugal's less commercial wines to be shipped overseas in any quantity was the "real" Vinho Verde on which Guedes had based Mateus. Surprisingly to foreigners, who rarely encounter it, most Vinho Verde is red (the "verde" part of its name refers to "green" youth, not colour), though the proportion of white has increased dramatically in recent years. Made in the (relatively) cool Minho region in the north of the country, from grapes grown on high trellises and among the trees so as to allow the farmers to plant cabbages and other vegetables at ground level, these wines give an insight into the way wine might have tasted a thousand or so years ago.

All sorts of local grapes were – and still are – used and, if asked, few of the growers (most of whom farm garden-sized plots) could name any of them. The traditional wine-making techniques were pretty basic too, but their peculiarity was the fact that the wine was bottled during, rather than after, the malolactic fermentation, which transforms the natural appley malic into creamier lactic acid.

The flavour, the fizz and the unpredictability from one bottle to the next were often as reminiscent of home-made cider as of wine. Unfortunately, the flavour of unripe apples and plum skins (of the red) and of unripe apple and lime (of the white) took more getting used to than most non-Portuguese drinkers were prepared to allow. Hence the switch to more modern wine-making techniques, the use of CO_2 canisters to provide the bubbles, and the generous dollops of sugar that go into the whites that are to be sent overseas (little of the red is exported).

Vinho Verde seemed destined to become another commercial drink. Fortunately, under the leadership of estates such as the Palacio da Brejoeira and the Solar das Bouças, and of Peter Bright, the Australian wine-maker at JP Vinhos, a small band of producers have begun to take Vinho Verde seriously, growing the vines more conventionally and concentrating on the best varieties – the Alvarinho and Loureiro.

Whichever colour you buy, though, try to ensure that it is of the most recent harvest, which is not always an easy task, given the producers' tendency to print the vintage in tiny figures on the back label or, more frequently, nowhere at all.

Douro

Portugal's top red wine is made here, but you'd never know it from the bottle. The only hint that Barca Velha comes from the same part of Portugal as Taylor's and Dow's port lies in the presence on the label of the producer's name Ferreira and its address in the port-shipping centre of Vila Nova da Gaia; otherwise it might come from anywhere in Portugal. The precedent of a port producer making a first-class red has, however, been followed by a number of other companies, all of whom have, to one extent or another, produced wines that are packed with berry flavours and, when young, taste like a cross between ruby port without the sweetness, and freshly made Bordeaux. First off the stocks was the Quinta da Cotto whose table wine is rather better than its somewhat rustic port. Next, and with far more balanced quality, was the Quinta de la Rosa which, like the even more successful Quinta do Crasto, is made by David Baverstock, one of those two Australians. These are wines to watch: Europe's answer to some of Australia's bigger reds.

Tras os Montes

Baking summers and freezing winters in this, one of Portugal's northernmost regions, situated just "behind the mountains" and the Spanish frontier, make for impoverished agriculture. Vines survive here and their fruit is used to produce Valpaços, Planalto-Mirandês and Chaves, none of which is much seen outside the region. Neither the wines nor the region are worth a hedonistic detour.

Bairrada

When Bairrada finally joins the ranks of the world's internationally recognized wine regions, three producers will share the credit for dragging the region into the twenty-first century. The wine-makers at Caves Alianca and Caves São João have been unusually quality-conscious and Luis Pato has seen the wines made at his estate thrown out of local tastings – because the overly conservative judges, many of whose own Bairradas tasted of nothing at all, could not come to terms with the blend of new oak and plummy-herby fruit they found in them. Hopefully, Bairrada's characterful Baga grape will soon be given rather more opportunities to show off these flavours. In the meantime, stick to the reds from these three producers, and explore their lemony whites and often impressive *méthode champenoise* fizz.

Dão

Until Portugal joined the EC, local protectionist rules more or less restricted the production of Dão to the region's co-operatives. Almost incredibly, given Dão's reputation as one of Portugal's best appellations, there

was only one individual estate, the Conde de Santar; its wines rarely did the region much credit. The rest of the wine was made by the co-operatives who then sold it to the merchants; they, in their turn, matured, bottled and sold it. Blind tastings of Dão were so monotonous.

Sogrape, the company behind Mateus, tried to improve the quality of the wine it was buying by supervising the wine-making at the Tazem co-operative, where its Grão Vasco is made, and managed to transform the region's flabby nutty whites into fresher, more lemony versions. Finally, in the late 1980s, Portugal's entry into the Common Market, and the banning of that restrictive monopoly, has allowed Sogrape and others to concentrate on buying the best grape varieties – including two that are used to make port, the Touriga Nacional and the Tinta Roriz which is thought to be Spain's Tempranillo – and to make their own wine. At last, Dão has the chance to show what it can do.

THE ESSENTIALS

NORTHERN PORTUGAL

What to look for Improving, modern rich reds; light, lemony whites.

Official quality Denominação de Origem Controlada (DOC).

Style Both DOCs, for red and white, still produce a great deal of disappointing wine; however, good white Dão has an appealing nuttiness and is crisp and dry, while white Bairrada can have an attractive fresh, lemony tang as can real Vinho Verde. There is also some sparkling white Bairrada produced. The better red Dãos, although quite fiery in youth, soften out into deep, rich, easy-drinking wine. Red Bairrada again benefits from bottle-ageing and is characterized, at its best, by lovely deep blackcurrant fruit. Red Douro could be the best of all, however: rich, concentrated, berryish stuff.

Climate Summers are dry but short, and the temperature then falls sharply in the autumn. The area also has relatively high rainfall. Despite its higher altitude, inland Dão is hotter than Bairrada.

Cultivation Clay soil characterizes the low-lying

coastal vineyards of Bairrada, while vines in the Dão area are scattered across an uncompromising landscape of granite outcrops. Vinho Verde vines are traditionally grown high on pergolas, though new plantings are more conventional.

Grape varieties Red Vinho Verde: Azal Tinto, Borraçal, Brancelhão, Espadeira, Rabode Ovelha, Vinhão; White Vinho Verde: Alvarinho, Avesso, Azal Branco, Loureiro, Perdena, Trajadura; Red Dão: Touriga Nacional (20 per cent minimum), Alfrocheiro Preto, Bastardo, Jaen, Tinta Pinheira, Tinta Roriz, Alvarelhão, Tinta Amarela, Tinta Cão; White Dão: Encruzado (20 per cent minimum), Assario Branco, Barcelo, Borrado das Moscas, Cercial, Verdelho, Rabu de Ovelha, Terrantez, Uva Cão; Red Bairrada: Baga (50 per cent minimum), Alfrocheiro Preto, Agua Santa, Bastardo, Jaen, Preto de Mortagua, Trincadeira; White Bairrada: Arinto, Bical, Cerceal, Cercealinho, Chardonnay, Maria Gomez, Rabo de Ovelha; Douro: Touriga Nacional, Tinta Roriz, Touriga Francesa, Tinta Cão, Tinta Barroca.

Production/maturation Throughout, there is a combination of old-style production by small growers, larger co-operatives using modern techniques and, more recently, even more modern larger companies. Modernity has paid off, particularly in Bairrada and the Douro where there has been a move away from the traditional coarseness caused by leaving the fermenting juice on the skins and stalks. New oak is occasionally showing its worth too.

Longevity Whites and red Vinhos Verdes should be drunk young. Other red wines begin to show their potential after about 5 years. Thereafter their lifespan is dependent on quality, the best being capable of lasting for over 20 years.

Vintage guide 75, 80, 83, 85, 91, 92, 94, 95.

Top 15 Bairrada: São João, Alianca, Sogrape, Luis Pato, Cava da Insua; Dão: São João, Sogrape, Santar, Quinta do Serrado Douro, Barca Velha, Quinta da Cotto, Quinta de la Rosa, Quinta do Crasto, Quinta de Gaivosa; Vinho Verde: Palacio da Brejoeira, Quinta da Aveleda, Solar das Bouças.

THE CENTRE AND SOUTH

Ribatejo

The temperate climate region of the banks of the Tagus – the Ribatejo – is gradually earning the recognition it deserves for making fruity, easier-going wines than most other parts of the country. For the moment, there are just three names to look out for: the huge co-operative at Almeirim, Caves Velhas (producers of the reliable Romeira red and some good *garrafeiras*) and the Heredeiros de Dom Luis de Margaride estate, where the local João de Santarem and Fernão Pires grapes are successfully used alongside such imports as the Cabernet Franc and Merlot.

Arruda and Torres, which like so many other Portuguese regions were given their original demarcation because the largest co-operative asked for it, both make pleasant, light, "modern" wines of a style that goes down better abroad than locally.

Colares

Colares's immunity to the *phylloxera* is explained by the desert sand in which the vines are grown, but these conditions can make it pretty difficult for people too; the sand is up to 16 ft (5 m) deep and every time an old vine has to be replaced a hole has to be dug down to the clay beneath. The reds they make are tough and tannic and need at least a decade to soften enough for their intense, plummy fruit to become (vaguely) apparent.

Bucelas

Twenty miles (32 km) from Lisbon, this tiny region produces just half a million bottles of exclusively white wine, from around 420 acres (170 ha) of vines. Confusingly, the young wine made here by Caves Velhas, the region's biggest producer, is labelled as Bucellas Velho, combining an archaic spelling of the region's name with a misleading implication that the wine is old. At its best, Bucelas can marry a fatty, almost Chardonnay-like, texture to some fairly biting, lemony acidity. Even so, it takes some imagination to understand how, a century ago, British gentlemen drank it as an alternative to hock. Neighbouring Carcavelos is of only passing interest – as the source of generally unimpressive fortified wine which may soon cease to exist if eager local urban developers get their way.

Setubal/Terras do Sado

Made from vines grown almost in Lisbon's backyard, the Moscatel here is one of Portugal's – and the world's – most famous fortified wines, competing directly against Muscat de Beaumes de Venise, but with far greater age on its side. Almost all of the production is in the hands of a single firm: José Maria da Fonseca, whose go-ahead winery also produces a range of table wines from this region, most notably the Periquita, and Camarate reds (and the TE and CO *garrafeira* reserve versions), as well as Pasmados and Quinta de Camarate, both of which are worth looking out for in red and white versions. Also nearby is JP Vinhos, the winery at which Peter Bright makes the excellent Bordeaux-like Quinta da Bacalhôa, the João Pires unfortified white Muscat, the good Ma Partilha Merlot and some impressive attempts at Chardonnay.

Alentejo

JM da Fonseca's ultra-traditional JS Rosado Fernandes estate is typical of the kind of *adega* with which this warm southern region is associated. The grapes are still trodden by foot and fermented in terracotta *amphorae* precisely like the ones the Romans would have used. The only concession to modernity is the careful way in which the *amphorae* are hosed down to cool the temperature of the fermentation, and a concentration on red rather than the white that was more usually produced here. When they are under the control of the Californian-trained wine-maker at JM da Fonseca, the old ways clearly work; the high-strength Tinto Velho is, given five years or so in the cellar, one of Portugal's more impressive reds. Elsewhere, however, wines made in these ways live down to the regional reputation of "country of bad bread and bad wine".

Fortunately, better wine is being made by more modern methods – such as Peter Bright's Tinto da Anfora and Santa Marta, and his countryman David Baverstock's efforts at the huge Esporão estate where he

CENTRAL AND SOUTHERN PORTUGAL

What to look for Some of Portugal's most modern – and most old-fashioned wines.

Official quality Denominação de Origem Controlada (DOC).

Style Almost as many styles of wine as there are wineries – or, indeed, wines.

Cultivation The Atlantic coast has a cooling influence on the vineyards of the Estremadura regions, the Ribatejo is highly fertile, while the Alentejo is a hot, broad plain.

Grape varieties A wide range of varieties is grown, including Aragonez, Trincadeira, Muscat, Fernão Pires, Castelão Frances/Periquita, Cabernet Sauvignon, Merlot, Chardonnay, Esgana Cão, Arinto, Jampal, Vital, João de Santarem, Tinta Miúda, Verdelho, Chardonnay, Maria Gomez, Rabo de Ovelha.

Production/maturation Some of the most old-fashioned wine-making in the world goes on in the Alentejo – almost alongside bright new stainless steel. Modern wines are bottled early and, in the case of Esperão, are made to be enjoyed young.

Longevity Other red wines such as Periquita and Quinta da Bacalhôa are probably at their best 5–10 years after the harvest.

Vintage guide 75, 80, 83, 85, 90, 92, 94, 95, 98.

Top 14 Setúbal: JM da Fonseca, JP Vinhos, Alentejo Esperão, Cartuxa, Quinta do Carmo, co-operatives of Borba, Redondo and Reguengos; Ribatejo: co-operative of Almeirim, Caves Velhas, Carvalho, Ribeiro & Ferreira, Margaride; Bucelas: Caves Velhas.

---

has some 40 varieties of grapes to play with. For lovers of wines with aristocratic connections, there's the Quinta do Carmo in which Château Lafite Rothschild is involved and, for democrats, there are the improving co-operatives of Borba, Reguengos and Redondo.

Bucaco

Lovers of grand hotels, over-the-top architecture and good wine can indulge themselves in all three at the extraordinary Buçaco Palace Hotel, tucked away in the Buçaco forest. The rich red and white wines are made – very traditionally – by the hotel general manager, José Santos, and they last for ever, taking on an increasingly piney flavour from the mixture of beeswax and resin with which the bottles are sealed. But don't go looking for these wines in the shops; they are only available at this and three other Portuguese hotels.

Algarve

The kindest way to deal with the wines of the Algarve would be to say nothing about them at all. They owe their demarcation to local politics, are (poorly) made from the Tinta Negra Mole, and are among the least impressive of the entire country.

PORT

To understand port you have to take the slow train up alongside the Douro River to the farms or quintas where it is made. Before you do so, however, wangle your way into the Oporto Lawn Tennis and Cricket Club down on the coast. Previously known as the British Club, this is a good place to watch the Portuguese play the British at tennis, and to watch the British play each other at cricket. The nuance translates directly to port. The Portuguese drink copious amounts of wine; little of it is port and even less is remotely comparable to the kind of vintage port most British wine-drinkers would recognize and enjoy. Port is a drink invented by and for Anglo-Saxons.

The History of Port

Although Portuguese wines from various regions had been shipped to Britain since the days of Chaucer, the first Anglo-Saxons to discover the wines of the Douro were sixteenth-century merchants – or "factors" – visiting the market town of Viana do Castelo in search of olive oil and fruit. By 1666 there were sufficient of these factors to start a club, called the Factory House, at which their successors still meet every week for lunch and a decanter or three of port.

When the first shipments of "pipes" – the region's rugby-ball-shaped, 115-gallon (522-litre) casks – arrived on British soil, the wine was called *Vinho do Porto*, after Porto, the harbour town from which it was shipped. It would have had some of the plummy, damsony flavour of the port we know today, but none of the sweetness or the strength it now gets from its fortification with brandy.

There are several stories to explain how brandy was first added to the Douro wine. According to one explanation, two British merchants chanced upon a monastery at Pinhão that was making particularly delectable wine. To satisfy the abbot's sweet tooth, some of the sugar and the grapes had been preserved during fermentation by adding spirit before it had all been fermented out. Another more prosaic, but probably more credible, explanation was that the naturally sweet wine continued to ferment while being transported in barrels across the Atlantic to Newfoundland, where the ships used to stock up on cod, the fish that the Portuguese needed for their national dish of *bacalhão*. The addition of brandy before the wine left Portugal was intended to stop the fermentation and thus to prevent the casks exploding in mid-ocean.

We know that the sweet strong wine had already begun to create a small market for itself in Britain by 1677, when French wines were banned in what could fairly be described as a seventeenth-century cold war between Britain and France. The 10 years of hostilities that followed meant a heyday for the Portuguese wine-makers, who, in 1683, despite the poor quality of most of their wine, apparently managed to sell the British some eleven and a half million bottles of the stuff.

The signing of the Methuen Treaty in 1686 more or less gave the Portuguese a monopoly of wine sales to Britain, in return for which the British received a similar concession for the export of woollen textiles to Portugal. (The tax on French wines was set at a hefty £55 per tun while importers of Portuguese wines had to pay only £7.) The British (and a few Dutch) merchants were not slow to take advantage of this privilege. During the early years of the eighteenth century, they established offices and warehouses – "lodges" (*loja* in Portuguese means storehouse) – for themselves in the village of Vila Nova de Gaia on the south bank of the Douro opposite the harbour town.

During the 1750s the market for port grew too quickly and, perhaps inevitably, the lack of scruples of the growers (who adulterated their wine with elderberries) and of the merchants (who paid little attention to the quality of what they bought) led to a slump. The growers blamed the merchants, the merchants blamed the growers, and the already questionable quality of the wine deteriorated still further. The man who rescued port was the Portuguese Chief Minister, the Marqués de Pombal. In 1756 he started the Douro Wine Company and effectively wrested back control of the region's wines from the foreigners, who were allowed to buy and ship port only once it had been tasted by officials of the company.

The late eighteenth century was a heyday for the port trade, with 50,000 pipes (nearly 36 million bottles) being shipped to Britain each year – three times as much as is exported today. Port's popularity owed much to the development in 1775 of a new way of bottle-blowing. Until then, bottles were squat containers that could only be stored standing up, and for a limited period of time. That year, the first port bottle – purpose-designed for laying down – was made and, with it, the first vintage port.

How Port is Made

Every bottle of wine legally labelled as port comes from grapes grown in vineyards planted along a 45-mile (72 km) stretch of the River Douro as it ambles its way from Spain. On the western, Oporto, side of the town of Regua, the region is known as the Lower Douro; it is this part of the river that produces the more basic styles of ruby and tawny port. To the east of Regua is the Upper Douro, where grapes used for vintage, crusted and top-quality tawny port are grown.

The Upper Douro is extraordinary, savagely beautiful country, good for nothing but grape-growing and goats. The steep banks that were once fought over by the armies of Napoleon and Wellington are now covered with terraces of vines, but the lot of the vineyard worker is scarcely more enviable than that of the eighteenth-century soldier. There could actually be 10 times as much vineyard land, but the dry-stone walls are crumbling, allowing the vertical steps to erode under the elements. The terraces cannot be worked by machines, and there are few Portuguese men who fancy the work.

The salvation of the region, as in the steeply sloping vineyards of the Rhine, has been the reorganization of the slopes to enable the vineyards to be planted the other way – up and down, rather than along the hills. All this work in the vineyards has inevitably redirected attention to the kinds of grapes that are planted.

No fewer than 88 different varieties are permitted for the production of port; in older vineyards perhaps a dozen or more different types will be planted side by side on the same hillside, and all will be vinified together. Top-class port, like most top-class claret, will never be made from a single variety. Now, though, the port shippers increasingly concentrate on isolating which – probably the Touriga Nacional, the Roriz, the Mourisco, and the Tinta Francesa, which is rather dubiously said to be related to the Pinot Noir – make the best wine.

The grapes are grown on quite small *quintas* or farms, which belong either to the port houses themselves or to the 28,000 peasant-farmers. Each shipper carefully oversees the yearly cycle and knows precisely when the harvest will begin (generally about September 20th) in each vineyard. Bands of pickers called *rogas*, headed by a *rogador*, bring the grapes into the farm for crushing.

Until 1960, all crushing took place by foot in low, open, concrete or wooden troughs called *lagares*. About 14 men per *lagare* would trample back and forth to the accompaniment of an accordion, four hours on, four hours off, until the grapes were crushed and the juice floated on top of the solids. When a sufficiently high alcohol level had been achieved, still leaving a good deal of sugar in the must, the wine would be run off into wooden vats and blended with neutral *aguardente* – grape brandy – at 77 per cent strength. The spirit stops the fermentation process, leaving the strong sweet liquid that is port.

Today, most of the annual harvest is crushed and fermented mechanically and the *lagares* are paradoxically only used by the most primitive farms and by the best port shippers for the grapes from their best vineyards.

Following the harvest, the port shippers travel around the *quintas* to gain an overall impression of the tannic new wines. In the spring following the harvest, most of the wine is shipped down the Douro to the lodges in Vila Nova de Gaia. Originally, the trip would have been made on *Barco Rabelo* sailboats, but since the building of roads and railway track these picturesque boats have been relegated to use as mobile advertising hoardings for the producers.

Once in the port lodge, the wine of each "pipe" is tasted again to decide on its future. Top-quality wines are separated from the others, blended only among themselves, held for 18 months, and re-tasted to establish whether they are potentially good enough to be sold as vintage port, late-bottled vintage, or whether they will be kept in wood for long enough to become tawny.

Types of Port

In 1877 a visiting English writer called Henry Vizetelly complained that there were "almost as many styles of port as shades of ribbon in a haberdasher's shop". Today, thankfully, the range is narrower, but it still offers ample scope for confusion.

Theoretically, port can be divided into two fundamentally different styles: wood-aged – wine that has been matured in barrel – and bottle-aged – wine that has been bottled young, with a significant amount of the solid matter that will eventually drop out in the form of a deposit.

Unfortunately, nothing is that simple. There are several types of bottle-aged, and several types of wood-aged, wine and their producers have traditionally made little effort to make it clear to prospective customers which is which. Until recently, the producers used to defend their ways with the explanation that "most port drinkers know what they are buying". So saying, they shrugged off any criticism of their indiscriminate labelling as tawny of both old, wood-aged wine and young blends of white and ruby, and any complaint that terms such as "fine old" really ought to mean something.

Today labelling is a little clearer, but it's still far from precise. So a bottle of Taylor's (and just about everybody else's) Late-Bottled Port will have been filtered to ensure that it needs no decanting, while one bearing the same words from Warre's or Smith Woodhouse will have as much of a deposit as any vintage port – and taste twice as delicious as most other shipped LBVs.

Ruby port

Ruby is yesterday's basic port style – the stuff people used to drink in British pubs as half of that memorable cocktail, the "port 'n' lemon". The snootier members of the port trade would naturally never have dreamed of drinking their wine in this way – but it didn't stop them from making vast amounts of a raw, spirity drink that needed a good dose of lemon to help disguise what would otherwise be fairly awful.

THE ESSENTIALS

THE DOURO

What to look for Rich, deep plummy vintage styles and nutty, tangy tawny.

Location The Douro valley traverses northern Portugal.

Quality Região demarcado (RD) for port, which is further classified, in descending order of quality, from A to F. Unfortified table wines are vinhos de mesa only, but can be good.

Style Red port comes in a variety of styles (see above). In most of its forms, it is classic after-dinner drinking, full of rich, spicy sweetness. The best old tawnies have faded in wood to a dry yet mellow smoothness. White port can be sweet or dry and is commonly drunk chilled as an aperitif, often mixed with tonic water. A few unfortified Douro reds are of very high quality and all are characterized by weighty berry fruit. The white wines are dry and again can have good fruit.

Climate High summer temperatures and rainfall. Winters can be surprisingly cold.

Cultivation The steeper and more inaccessible vineyards higher up the valley have better-quality schist soils which produce the finest ports. Thus production of Douro table wines is concentrated on the granite soil of the lower valley.

Grape varieties Port: of the over 40 permitted red port grapes the best are Tinta Amarela, Tinta Barroca, Tinto Cão, Tinta Roriz, Touriga Francesa, Touriga Nacional. White port is made from a ragbag of varieties. Little selection is practised. Red table wines: as for red port plus Tinta Francesa, Bastardo, Mourisco Tinto, Alvarelhão, Comifesto, Donzelinho, Donzelinho Tinto, Malvasia, Malvasia Preta, Mourisca de Semente, Periquita, Rufete, Sousão, Tinta Barca, Tinta Carvalha, Touriga Brasileira. White table wines: Arinto, Boal, Cercial, Codega, Donzelinho Branco, Esgana Cão, Folgosão, Fernão Pires, Malvasia Corada, Malvasia Fina, Malvasia Parda, Moscatel Galego, Rabigato, Rabo de Ovelha, Verdelho, Viosinho.

Production/maturation Port grapes are brought back to the central quinta where they are in many cases still trodden by foot in stone troughs, or lagares. Fermentation takes place at temperatures up to 32°C until the alcohol content reaches 6 per cent. It is at this stage that the wine is fortified with clear grape spirit (aguardente). The port is then matured and bottled at Vila Nova de Gaia, a suburb of Oporto.

Longevity The best vintage ports will last at least 20 years and often double that. White port should be drunk young; the unfortified white wines should be drunk within 3 years and the red wines between 2 and 10 years.

Vintage guide The best of recently declared port vintages are 63, 66, 77, 85, 91, 94. Red table wine: 80, 83, 84, 85, 91, 92, 94, 95.

Top 14 Port: Taylor, Warre, Graham, Dow, Fonseca, Noval, Ramos Pinto, Fonseca-Guimaraens, Niepoort, Quinta do Crasto, Quinta do Vesuvio, Quinta do Bomfim, Quinta da Vargelas, Quinta de la Rosa; Table wine: Quinta do Crasto, Quinta de la Rosa.

White port

White port is supposed to be a "smart" drink, to be sipped at by elegant folk at the right kind of cocktail party. If only it were. Revealingly, its makers routinely serve it with a handful of ice cubes and a generous dollop of tonic or soda. In other words, white port is a very pricy alternative to vermouth – and one that has the added disadvantage of coming in unpredictable levels of sweetness and freshness.

Tawny port

Port labelled as "Tawny", "Fine Old Tawny", "Superior Old Tawny" and so on, is another of the port men's little jokes. Unlike real tawny, which owes its name, its colour and its tangy, nutty flavour to its prolonged sojourn in barrel, this stuff is simply a blend of young white and ruby ports, mixed to look and taste vaguely like the genuine article. A specific age of 10 or 20 years old will ensure that you are getting the real thing. Real tawny is a delicious alternative to vintage, but in the heat of the Douro the shippers often surprise visitors by serving it chilled.

There is another style of tawny less frequently encountered overseas: *Colheita* ports, or tawny port with a vintage date. To the traditionalists, the very idea makes no sense because, in theory at least, the best tawny is always a blend of ports of different ages (according to the rules, it only has to have the character of the age it claims) and, in fact, younger tawnies are often tastier than older ones. But that doesn't stop those same traditionalists from selling their own *Colheita* ports in countries such as France and Portugal.

Vintage port

Even in a very good year, no shipper will declare a vintage as soon as the wine is made. Instead he wants to see how the juvenile protégé develops after 18 months, and then, if both he and the Instituto do Vinho do Porto agree that the wine of a given year is exceptional enough, a vintage is declared, and the wine of that single year is bottled during the following year. For some reason, although British port houses often disagree over which vintage to declare, none will ever declare in two consecutive years. Vintage ports take considerably longer to mature than wood-aged ports, though their longevity does vary from one vintage to another. All vintage ports throw a sediment in the bottle and need decanting anything up to a day before drinking.

Late-bottled vintage port

This is wine from a single vintage, matured in wood for between four and six years. The result is usually a wine that has been filtered and consequently has less character and weight than vintage port and lacks the fine nuttiness of good tawny. Look out, though, for traditional, earlier-bottled, unfiltered examples made by Warre's and Smith Woodhouse.

Crusted port

Crusted port is a blend of good wines from different vintages. Bottled young, it retains a lot of body and should be decanted. It offers one of the best alternatives to real vintage port.

Single-quinta port

Vintage port produced at a single *quinta* or farm (as opposed to blends of wines from several different farms). Until quite recently, most single-quinta ports were produced and sold by well-known port houses in years when they had chosen not to declare a vintage.

Now, however, these ports are facing strong competition from a growing number of privately owned, single-estate *quintas* whose wines are never sold off for blending. Among these, the best are Quinta de la Rosa, Quinta do Crasto and Quinta do Vesuvio (which belongs to the Symington family, owners of Dow's, Graham's and Warre's).

Of the "off-year" single-*quintas*, Taylor's Vargellas, Warre's Cavadinha and Dow's Bomfim all offer real vintage style for a lower price.

MADEIRA

Once the favourite tipple of American and English gentlemen, Madeira would have been the staple of every self-respecting dinner table of the late eighteenth and nineteenth centuries. George Washington, for example, a man described by his friend Samuel Stearns as "very regular, temperate and industrious", used to dine every day at three, drinking "half a pint to a pint of Madeira wine, this with a small glass of punch, a draught of beer, and two dishes of tea".

But what would Washington's "Madeira wine" have tasted like? According to one Edward Vernon Harcourt, whose A *Sketch of Madeira* was published in 1851, it would have been made from a mixture of three grapes: the Verdelho (for "body"), the Tinta, and the Bual (both for "flavour"). This use of several different grape varieties in a single blend may come as a surprise to anyone who has learned that each of the four principal types of Madeira – Sercial, Verdelho, Bual and Malmsey – is named after, and made from, its own grape. But our ancestors would have known about wines with those names, *as well as* one known simply as "Madeira"; such names were fairly loosely applied.

In the late nineteenth century there was also a Madeira Burgundy, made from the Tinta Negra Mole, a grape supposedly grown originally in France as the Pinot Noir. Always less well thought of than the quartet of better-known "Castas Nobles", the Tinta wine was said by one contemporary author to have "the astringent property of port", losing some of its fine aroma and delicate flavour "after its first or second year". Even further down the quality scale were the colourfully named Bastardo and Moscatel. Wine simply called "Madeira" would have been made from a mixture of any or all of these. Casks that had had the benefit of the warm voyage through the tropics were sold as either "East" or "West India Madeira"; Madeira that had not taken either trip was simply styled "London Particular".

As the years passed, and as producers discovered that the wine could be "cooked", Madeira passed from being the preserve of the Anglo-Saxon gentleman to that of the Gallic or German cook. The quality of the wine inevitably fell, and the four difficult-to-grow fine varieties – the "Castas Nobles" – were gradually

THE ESSENTIALS
MADEIRA

What to look for Rich, concentrated wine with a marmaladey tang – whatever the level of sweetness.

Location This Atlantic island under Portuguese jurisdiction lies 370 miles off the coast of Morocco.

Quality Denominação de Origen Controlada (DOC).

Style Table wines rarely leave the island, which is chiefly famous for its classic fortified wines. These vary in style (see box opposite) from dry Sercial and Verdelho, for drinking chilled as an aperitif, through to lusciously sweet, after-dinner Bual and Malmsey. All have extraordinary ageing potential and good balancing acidity.

Climate Hot summers and mild winters. High rainfall.

Cultivation Terraced vineyards hug the island's cliffs, the best sites being in the south of the island. The soil is fertile, due in part to its volcanic origins and the fire-raising of the island's first settlers. Vines are trained on trellises to allow other crops to be grown underneath.

Grape varieties The four quality grapes are Sercial, Bual, Verdelho and Malmsey. Should a bottle not specify any of these, it will probably be produced from the Tinta Negra Mole, either on its own or blended.

Production/maturation The grapes are fermented and then placed in a heated storeroom – an estufa – heated gradually to 45°C and then cooled. Fortification takes place before this estufagem "baking" for dry Madeira, and

afterward for the sweeter styles. The wine enters a solera system, similar to that used in Jerez, 18 months after cooling.

Longevity Madeira, vintage or otherwise, is ready to drink when it is bottled. After this time it will keep almost indefinitely; it is also one of the rare wines that still tastes good – sometimes better – even weeks after the bottle has been opened, since air contact is such a crucial and desirable factor in its style.

Vintage guide Most Madeiras are a product of the solera system, although there are still a few old single-vintage wines available.

Top Producers Henriques & Henriques, Rutherford & Miles, Cossart Gordon, Blandy, Artur Barros e Souza, d'Oliveira.

MADEIRA STYLES

Sercial Made from a grape thought to be related to the Riesling, this is the driest, palest and most perfumed style of Madeira. Ideal as an alternative aperitif to fino sherry – or as an accompaniment to consommé.
Verdelho Also drinkable as an aperitif, this is slightly sweeter, with a hint of the lime flavour that is the mark of this variety.
Bual/Boal The second-sweetest type of Madeira, smoky and complex, with a typical marmaladey tang of acidity that sets it distinctly apart from sherries of similar levels of sweetness.

Malmsey The original and sweetest Madeira style, made from the Malvasia grape. Rich, dark and brown-sugary but, like the Bual, with a tangy vein of balancing acidity that makes it a far easier drink than vintage port.
Rainwater US name for a dryish blend of Sercial and Verdelho, so named because the casks were stood outside in the rain.
Reserve At least 5 years old.
Special Reserve At least 10 years old. **Exceptional** Reserve At least 15 years old.
Vintage At least 20 years in cask and 2 in bottle.

replaced by the easier Tinta Negra Mole. After all, so the producers often thought, the wine it produces can be pretty similar and, once it's in the soup, who is going to notice?

For the true Madeira-lover, the more serious wine-lodges continued to produce Madeira of a remarkable quality, using the "noble" grapes and a *solera* system, and wines bearing specified vintages were made in good years. Even so, it was not until the late 1970s that the island's wine-makers finally decided to take a firm grip on the situation and concentrate on quality – or rather on reminding the rest of the world about the quality they had never really stopped producing. Suddenly, wines such as Blandy's 10-year-old Malmsey began to appear: beautifully packaged, fairly highly priced, but, most essentially of all, with the depth of flavour that Madeira shares with no other fortified wine. Where sherry has its own kind of identifiable savoury woodiness, and port its stemmy, tannic acidity, Madeira has a unique quality – a nutty, old-English marmaladey "tang" that can be quite addictive.

This concentration on reinstating Madeira in the public mind as a quality product stems partly from the fact that the costs of production of even the most mediocre wine on the island are so high that it can never be sold as cheaply as port or sherry, and partly from the accession of Portugal into the EEC. Among the more meddlesome of European laws, there is one that states that a product must conform to the description that appears on its label. So Sercial, for instance, has to be made 85 per cent from the Sercial grape. (Traditionally, the amount of pure Sercial in an average bottle bearing that name might well have been as low as 10 per cent or even less.) Equally, the Eurosnoops have not been as lenient as the Portuguese authorities toward some of the "vintaged" Madeira that used to fill the shops on the island. Rows of bottles, each proclaiming its vintage as 1884, inevitably inspired suspicion.

The island's future success or failure lies in well-tested hands. The Madeira Wine Company – which embraces no fewer than 26 brands, including such well-known names as Blandy, Cossart Gordon and Rutherford & Miles – was recently sold by Richard Blandy, a descendant of the subaltern who founded it, to the dynamic Symington family who own the Dow's, Graham's and Warre's port houses on the mainland.

Among Portuguese Madeira houses, the best – and best-known – is Henriques & Henriques where visitors can compare run-of-the-mill Madeira, sold on price, with 30- and 40-year-old examples of Bual and Malmsey that fill both mouth and memories with their richness and orangey tang. Some people on the island say that such *solera* wines are a thing of the past, that from here onward the best commercial wines will be like tawny port and fine whisky in declaring an age (10 years old for instance) rather than a specific *solera* year. It would be a great pity if they were to disappear because, like some of the real vintage wines, they offer delicious proof that, thanks to the way that it is made, Madeira can be the longest-lived drink of them all.

The taste of cheap, "cooking" Madeira hints at a wine that is capable of better things – but only hints. Tasting the real stuff is something else again, an experience like sampling the finest table wines in the world. Cooking wine will always have its place – in the saucepan rather than the glass – but fine Madeira has a far more important role to play. Try a bottle of the finest 10-year-old or older and you may be converted for life.

THE UNITED KINGDOM

The British are a strange race. Given a choice when buying anything – a car, a cheese, a beer, a computer – they all too frequently opt for an import; foreign is best. In no instance is this more marked than that of wine. A growing number of English and Welsh men and women have thrown themselves body, soul and savings account into wine-making over the last few years, only to be rewarded with the almost total indifference of their countrymen.

Of course, Britain's characteristically grey skies and chilly temperatures do little to dispel prejudice; surely the climate cannot be warm enough to ripen grapes? But the people who hold this view clearly have not spent much time in such classic cool wine regions as Champagne, Chablis and northern Germany, where producers regularly manage to use what seem to be inhospitable conditions to make fine wine.

No, the problem facing England's wine industry has been a deadly blend of the cottage-industry mentality of many of the growers themselves and the unwillingness of British governments to help them. Wine-makers in other parts of Europe are feather-bedded in all sorts of ways; in Britain, they are told to stand on their own two feet – and, just for good measure, given a few hefty blows to the ankles by the revenue-gathering arms of the state.

Supporters of English (which confusingly also means Welsh) wine never tire of proudly reminding those who scoff that the Roman and Norman invaders made wine here, that Henry VIII probably drank it – until he dissolved the monasteries and put a stop to its production – and that Vine Street, the City of London thoroughfare familiar to generations of English Monopoly players, was once a place in which were grown good, ripe grapes.

The modern British wine industry dates firmly from the late 1960s and early 1970s – at around the time when wine suddenly began to interest a broader range of Britons who previously thought of it as something exotic and "foreign".

In those early days, farmers all too often simply expelled a pony from its paddock and planted a few vines without applying any real thought – let alone expertise – to the question of whether the grape variety and the plot of land were remotely suited to each other. Hardly auspicious

beginnings. But luckily, more sensible would-be wine-growers did seek advice, perhaps inevitably looking to Germany, a country they rightly saw as having similar climatic conditions and whose viticultural tradition seemed entirely appropriate to English conditions.

It was immediately clear that Germany's greatest grape, the Riesling, would not ripen in England, but the experts at the Geisenheim Wine School on the Rhine saw no reason why newer varieties developed for Germany's cold climate should not succeed. In particular, they set great store by the Müller-Thurgau, the variety which was rapidly supplanting the Riesling almost throughout Germany. The combination of Germanic grapes and advice meant, inevitably, that most of the early efforts were semi-sweet versions of wines that were already being imported from the Rhine and Mosel. Like the producers of many of those wines, the English could only make their wines sweet by "backblending", adding *süssreserve* – sweet grape juice – which they generally imported from Germany. While the quality of these wines was often comparable to that of the German examples they were mimicking, the price was almost invariably higher than that, for example, of a mass-produced Piesporter. Why then, English wine-drinkers asked with a degree of logic, should we buy a local product instead of the cheaper import?

During the second half of the 1980s, however, the business of making English wine became more businesslike. Hobbyists tired of what no longer seemed such a romantic occupation; the vines grew older and, like all mature vines, began to produce richer wine; and, most important of all, many of the English wine-growers, who were growing in confidence, decided to stop copying the Germans. And when they did their own thing, hey presto!

Their Germanic grapes began to produce dry and off-dry wines that seemed a whole lot closer in style to the Loire than to the Rhine. At their best – and that's an increasing proportion – these new styles are packed with the flavour of (ripe) grapefruit and gooseberries. The acidity – which was always their hallmark – is now balanced by a smokiness and a fatty richness that you'd never expect from cold-climate vineyards.

Most growers still add *süssreserve*, but some most emphatically don't; both groups, thanks partly to (in German terms) tiny yields, partly to increasingly skilful wine-making and partly, ironically, to the cool climate, seem consistently to produce intensely flavoured, good-quality wine with a capacity to age that surprises even their makers. Late-harvest wines are succeeding, as are – perhaps predictably, given the chalky soil southern England shares with Champagne – sparkling wines. The only cul-de-sac is presented by the eccentric reds, produced at high cost and effort from grapes grown, like tomatoes, in plastic tunnels.

Today there are 2,500 acres of British vines – well over 200 times as many as there were when a dozen pioneers gathered, in 1967, to launch the English Vineyards Association, the body that still oversees the quality of English, Welsh and Channel Island wines through the allocation of its gold seals of approval.

If the future for English wine looks bright, it is thanks to the growing professionalism of the wine-makers. John Worontschak, an ambitious young Australian, has proven both at Thames Valley Vineyards and with the dozen wineries which form the Harvest Wine Group that skilled wine-making can transform the quality of English wine. Elsewhere, after a bumpy start, the heavy investment began to pay off at the Denbies winery-cum-vinous-theme-park in Surrey and, for the first time, a number of the biggest producers actually agreed to co-operate in trying to market their wines to a surprisingly receptive market on the European mainland. All that's needed now is for the Britons themselves to take their country's wines as seriously as some of those Europeans do.

THE UNITED KINGDOM

What to look for Fresh, floral dry and off-dry wines possibly with a flavour of grapefruit and/or gooseberry.

Location The majority of English vineyards lie south of Birmingham, all the way down to the Isle of Wight. Many of the areas now cultivating vines are the same areas used for wine-making in the Middle Ages. Fertile Kent and Sussex are particularly well-populated with English wine-makers. The handful of Welsh vineyards, particularly those around the Monnow Valley – and usually lumped together with the English – should not be overlooked by any means.

Official quality A Quality Wine Scheme was introduced in 1992, the year England's production broke through the European Union's 25,000 hectolitre threshold. However, several producers have opted out of the Scheme and it remains largely irrelevant to English wine production as a whole. The English Vineyards Association awards seals of approval and various trophies to par-ticularly good wines. Accept only "English" wine:

"British wine" is made from foreign grape juice diluted with British water, and should be avoided.

Style Whites range from dry, even austere, through clean, fruity Loire-style to Germanic, medium-sweet wines. Many are made from a single grape, though blends can be very successful. Süssreserve is used by some producers to soften the high acidity, and chaptalization is essential to raise the alcohol level in grapes which can never produce enough sugar by themselves. There is proven potential for sparkling and, in warm years, dessert styles. A little light red is made.

Climate Maritime, at – cynics say beyond – the northerly extreme of table-wine production. Even some warmer areas of south-west England can get 100 in/254 cm of rain a year.

Cultivation Wide range of soils, including chalk, limestone, gravel and granite. Slopes play an important role as suntraps and windbreaks.

Grape varieties Principally white and Germanic, though there is some experimentation with

French varieties. Kerner, Müller-Thurgau, Scheurebe, Reichensteiner, Schönburger, Huxelrebe and Madeleine Angevine are most commonly seen. Despite the opposition of the EU to hybrids, the Seyval Blanc is still successfully grown. Reds including Pinot Noir, Gamay, Merlot and Cabernet Sauvignon are grown – mostly beneath plastic sheeting.

Production/maturation Stainless steel predominates. Occasional efforts with new oak are surprisingly promising.

Longevity Surprisingly high – 1 to 8 years, thanks to the wines' high acidity.

Vintage guide 88, 89, 90, 92, 93, 94, 95, 97.

Top 29 Astley, Carr Taylor, Hambledon, Breaky Bottom, Lamberhurst, Three Choirs, Thames Valley, Ditchling, Pulham, Wootton, Penshurst, Adgestone, Bruisyard, Berwick Glebe, Pilton Manor, Staple, Nutbourne Manor, Chiltern Valley, Wickham, Bodenham, Biddenden, Headcorn, Shawsgate, Tenterden, Chilsdown, Wraxall, Elmham Park, Bruisyard St Peter, English Vineyard.

AUSTRIA, SWITZERLAND AND LUXEMBOURG

AUSTRIA

"It's either Burgundy or a really top-class Australian or North American Pinot Noir, but I'm damned if I can place it precisely." One of the most distinguished palates in Britain was clearly flummoxed by the stuff in his glass, but he and his fellow tasters were sufficiently impressed to make it share the Pinot Noir Trophy for the 1995 International Wine Challenge with a *Grand Cru* Burgundy. The look of consternation on his and his fellow tasters' faces was a picture when they learned that the wine that had beaten an impressive field of Old- and New-World Pinots was not even a Pinot Noir – it was made from the little-known St Laurent – and came from a winery called Umathum in Austria, of all places. A decade or so after the so-called anti-freeze scandal Austria, as Mr Schwarzenegger might put it, was decidedly back.

The exciting thing about the manner of its return, though, is the way Austria has cast off its old role as purveyor of cheap, sweetish, German taste-alikes and the illegal means to beef up inadequate offerings from the Rhine. Using grapes little-known in western Europe, like the St Laurent, and taking full advantage of the far easier climate enjoyed here than across the frontier in Germany, a new wave of producers is determinedly aiming high.

Visitors may still enjoy Austrian wine the way the Austrians do, as young and as cool and dry as possible and by the jugful in Heurigen ("*nouveau*") taverns, but for the really interesting stuff, the first place to go is to the wineries of the north-east – Niederösterreich – where they'll find all sorts of examples of the spicy, dry Grüner Veltliner, Austria's true white wine speciality. Steiermark – Styria – is the place to look for good Sauvignon and a white called Morillon that tastes rather familiar – for the simple reason that it is a local alias for the Chardonnay. While there, they could try a glass (one will probably suffice) of bone-dry Schilcher rosé made from the local Blauer Wildbach grape.

Then there's the Wachau and Krems which offer dry Rieslings richer than most of those of Germany but less aromatic than versions from Alsace. There are reds made in the Weinviertel, but for Austria's best efforts at these, the key region is the warm southern area of Burgenland where the local berryish red Blaufrankisch is now competing with imports such as the Cabernet Sauvignon.

Finally, of course, there's the jewel in Austria's crown: the Neusiedler See, a lakeside area whose foggy conditions are made for producing late-harvest wines to match the best of France and Germany – but far more reliably. Some of the wines made here are simple and lusciously delectable; others, like those of Willi Opitz, Lang and Kracher, offer explosive taste experiences that do for the taste buds what pricier and less legal substances do for the brain.

SWITZERLAND

It is easy to see why the Swiss like holding referenda – and hard to imagine how they work. Theirs is, after all, a country that has three names for just about everything, depending on the region and its language. So, the German-speakers call the Pinot Noir the Klevner or the Blauburgunder and have Rauschling as an alternative name for the Elbling, while the widely grown Chasselas is known as the Fendant, the Gutedel (in Bern), the Perlan (in the regions of Geneva and Neuchâtel) and the Dorin (in the Vaud). Another popular Swiss style, the red blend of Pinot Noir and Gamay, is variously called Dôle, Goron and Savagnin (allowing further confusion with Sauvignon, which isn't grown here).

The wines produced from all these grapes are less confusing. In fact, they are precisely what you'd expect them to be: impeccably made, meticulously clean – and expensive, given their lightness of body and lack of longevity, both of which have been exacerbated by a tendency to over-produce. Following a glut of such wines in the 1980s, however, (somewhat) tighter rules were introduced and the flavour (somewhat) intensified.

AUSTRIA, SWITZERLAND & LUXEMBOURG

What to look for From Switzerland, light, pricey, early-drinking reds and whites; from Austria, crisp, dry and luscious late-harvest whites and increasingly impressive reds.

Official quality Luxembourg and Switzerland have "Appellation d'Origine" systems used to protect certain names. In Switzerland these include Dôle, Dorin, Fendant, Goron, Malvoisie, Perlan, Savagnin. In the Valais, there is a higher quality level of "Appellation d'Origine", while other regions have Grands and Premiers Crus, Winzer Wy and VITI. Austria uses the German classifications, the only different category being Ausbruch, which falls between Beerenauslese and Trockenbeerenauslese.

Style In Switzerland, the Chasselas grape can produce dry, fragrant whites. White wines from Luxembourg and Austria are generally Germanic in style, those from Luxembourg being dry or off-dry and those from Austria covering the full range of sweetness levels. Luxembourg also produces dry to off-dry, quite full méthode champenoise sparkling wines. Austrian wines tend to have less acidity than their German counterparts but the best sweet wines, luscious yet elegant, do have ageing potential. Austria's fuller-flavoured white wines include the peppery Grüner Veltliner. Swiss red wines tend to have more weight in the southerly Italian-speaking cantons. All Swiss wines are soft and approachable in youth with good fruit. Austrian reds vary greatly between regions and draw from both their eastern and western neighbours. The fragrant Pinot Noir-like St Laurent is an Austrian speciality.

Climate In Switzerland, continental Alpine conditions mean early sun but late frosts. The Austrian climate is generally warm and quite dry. Burgenland, in the south-east, is the hottest area and here, in the autumn, botrytis often affects the vines.

Cultivation Vines are found mainly on the slopes above lakes and rivers – for example, the Danube in Austria and the Mosel in Luxembourg.

Grape varieties Switzerland: Chasselas (here often called the Fendant), Gamay, Pinot Noir, Cabernet Sauvignon; Luxembourg: Riesling, Gewürztraminer, Elbling, Müller-Thurgau, Pinot Gris, Auxerrois; Austria: Blauer Portugieser, Bouvier, Cabernet Sauvignon, Furmint, Gewürztraminer, Grüner Veltliner, Merlot, Müller-Thurgau, Muskateller, Muskat Ottonel, Neuberger, Pinot Blanc, Pinot Gris, Riesling, Rotgipfler, St Laurent, Welschriesling, Zierfandler.

Production/maturation Almost all wines are naturally cool-fermented and bottled young. New oak is very rare.

Longevity All whites, apart from the sweeter Austrians, should be drunk within 4 years. Red wines are also for early drinking, although there is the occasional exception from Austria.

Vintage guide Austria: 81, 83, 85, 86, 87, 88, 90, 92, 94, 95, 97 (dry only).

Top 18 Switzerland: Château de Vaumarcus, Château d'Auvernier, Porret, André Ruedin, Domaine du Mont d'Or, Testuz, Dubois; Luxembourg: Bernard Massard; Austria: Siegendorf, Nittnaus, Schlumberger, Unger, Igler, Umathum, Kracher, Opitz, Hopler.

Although they find it hard to compete on pure price with wines made in neighbouring France, Germany and Austria, Switzerland's wines can at least offer a range of styles and flavours not often found in those countries.

The real success story has to be the Chasselas. French versions of the Chasselas are generally dull but, in the hands of the meticulous Swiss, this grape can sometimes produce surprisingly refreshing and long-lived wines. Look out for the slightly sparkling examples that have been bottled *sur lie* – on their yeast. Of Switzerland's other whites, try the Malvoisie (the local name in the Valais for sweet wines made from the Pinot Gris), the (quite rare) Riesling and the Riesling-Sylvaner known elsewhere as Müller-Thurgau, produced around Thurgau, the home of Dr Müller, its inventor.

In Geneva and Neuchâtel the Chardonnay is also producing some tasty, pineappley wines not unlike the best examples from north-east Italy. If you like Beaujolais and don't mind paying classy Burgundy prices, you should enjoy some of the Dôle blends of Pinot Noir and Gamay.

LUXEMBOURG

Luxembourg is another of the more quietly efficient wine-producing countries: nearly three-quarters of the annual production is drunk within the Duchy and most of the rest is exported to Belgium. The key grapes are the Elbling, Riesling-Sylvaner (here often called Rivaner), the Auxerrois, Pinot Blanc and Pinot Gris (also known as Rülander), Traminer and Riesling. Of these, the most successful are probably the Riesling and the Pinot Gris, both of whose wines have more substance than the rather neutral ones made from the Elbling and Auxerrois.

Even so, Luxembourg is not the place to come looking for full-flavoured wines. The key style, whatever the grape, is lightweight. Also beware of "Luxembourg" sparkling wines, which, like "British" wine, can be made from imported juices.

EASTERN EUROPE

At the beginning of the 1990s, pundits throughout the wine world rushed to book flights to Budapest, Sofia, Sarajevo and Prague, following the return of capitalism to Eastern Europe, and eagerly began to predict the imminent arrival of a wave of wonderful new wines. All that was needed, they chorused, was a bit of free-market encouragement and the right kind of investment.

Heading for a decade later, the wave is still a long way offshore; indeed, while some areas have benefited enormously from an inflow of money and expertise, others seem, if anything, to be making worse wine than ever.

Among the first post-Cold-War initiatives were the unashamedly opportunistic attempts by Western firms to buy up complete regions including – incredible as it may seem – such internationally celebrated ones as Tokaj in Hungary. (Just imagine every bottle from Sauternes being made by the same firm!) That deal foundered; others progressed somewhat further, including a short-lived agreement by a Dutchman with a minister in Moldova to take responsibility for all of that newly (semi-) independent country's wines.

In theory, little could be worse than the old collectivist system under which Soviet-Bloc states routinely swapped wine for petrol on a gallon-for-gallon basis. Vineyards were often appallingly managed and planted with varieties whose primary quality was their ease of farming.

Do not, however, imagine that no one cared about the quality of the wines they were making. Not a bit of it. Every year, wineries throughout the region submitted their best efforts to a so-called "international" wine competition in Ljubljana in former Yugoslavia where, if they were liquid and reasonably transparent, they stood a good chance of picking up at least some kind of award. Unfortunately, the certificates of which the wine-makers were so touchingly proud cut little ice with foreign buyers. Wines rarely had to compete seriously with overseas efforts on any basis apart from price.

Even when good wines were produced, one of the major problems – as in other Communist-run industries – was the relaxed attitude toward quality control.

Wines were often as reliable as the timetables of the railway sstems that ran through their regions. Travellers who remember some of the stuff they bought in Eastern Europe in the 1980s may be interested to know about the birds which used to fly around the bottling hall of at least one winery, occasionally leaving their mark on – and in – the unprotected bottles on the conveyor belts below. Fortunately, few such establishments managed to sell their wines overseas. Today, the battle is to raise the standards overall, and few people have done more to achieve that than the teams of young Australians and New Zealanders who are annually sent in by – principally British – customers to supervise the wine-making in wineries throughout the region.

THE BALKAN STATES

Before Yugoslavia fell to pieces, it was collectively best-known to foreigners for white wines whose dubious role was to undercut the cheapest Liebfraumilch. Tiger Milk, Laski, Lutomer or Olascz Riesling, as these wines were known before EC officials sensibly insisted on a change to "Rizling", not only helped to besmirch the reputation of wines made from the real Riesling (to which they are no more related than paraffin), they also gave a totally false impression of the kind of wine the inhabitants of these states like to make and drink.

This is not light, sugar-watery, white-wine country; it's a land of big, hefty reds that are about as approachable as some of the political leaders were under the old regime. Among the most typical of these heavyweights are the wines made from the local Plavac Mali in Dalmatia, from such regions as Pitovske Plaze, Bol, Vis, Brela, Postup, Dingac, Lastovo and Sveta. Another popular local variety is the Prokupac (once known as the "national vine of Serbia"), but this too is now rapidly giving way to the Cabernet Sauvignon, Merlot, Gamay and Pinot Noir.

In Croatia, apart from the Plavac Mali and a raft of apparently obscure local varieties, some of which might be related to ones we know elsewhere, the most familiar grapes are the Cabernet Sauvignon, Merlot and Pinot Noir. Success stories are rare – so far. In Serbia, the province of Kosmet on the Albanian border makes full-bodied Cabernet Sauvignons and Merlots, and Montenegro's Vranac is one of the region's best fuller-bodied reds.

RUSSIA

Ironically, one of the regions whose wine industry suffered most in the first stages of the transition from hard-line Communism was the old Soviet Union. Under Mikhail Gorbachev, Moscow imposed a set of draconian measures to combat Russia's endemic alcoholism. Huge areas of vines were ripped up and wineries mothballed.

Despite the internationally acknowledged leniency of President Yeltsin's attitude toward alcohol, the industry has yet to recover. The stuff most visitors to the old Soviet Union remember – Krim "Champagnski" fizz, from Crimea – is as unpredictable and indeed "grim", as it was more familiarly known by foreign correspondents, as ever. Modern Crimean wine-makers have yet to recreate the great sweet and dry, fortified and unfortified wines of the past.

Georgia, the supposed birthplace of wine-making, is still proudly treating white grapes as though they were red, fermenting them with their skins to make strange, golden wine that, 12 months after the harvest, looks like century-old Château d'Yquem. And – to non-Georgians – is only just on the drinkable side of the line that separates interesting from disgusting. Reds are better but still far from suited to Western tastes for fresh fruit or subtle richness of flavour. Kazakhstan, Azerbaijan and Uzbekistan are similarly caught in the time warp of trying to produce wines with as much modern appeal as some of the lard-and-gizzard offerings served up with pride by the cooks of earlier centuries.

Despite the efforts of the aforementioned Dutchman to control the market, an influx of Australian and German investment into Moldova has helped the Hincesti winery to modernize its equipment and to create a successful, if unambitious, brand of its own, while using an Anglo-Saxon name for the bottles it sends to the US where buyers of cheap Chardonnay rarely trouble to read the small print at the foot of the label. So far, no one has managed to produce current wines as impressive as some of the 30-year-old Moldovan reds that reappeared in the early 1990s, but conditions here are perfect and one day the vast areas of vine-covered hillside – over a tenth of the countryside – will once again produce world-class wine.

HUNGARY

The first Eastern European country to sell its wines successfully in the West was Hungary which, trading on the prestige achieved by what used to be known as Tokay – the "king of wines and wine of kings" in the days of the Austro-Hungarian empire – exported huge quantities of a red called Bull's Blood. This internationally familiar wine, from Transdanubia in the north of the country, is made from a blend of Kadarka, Kékfrankos, Cabernet Franc and Merlot (known here as "Médoc Noir") and owes its name to the strength it was supposed to have given the defenders of a besieged town to beat off their attackers.

Under Communism, Bull's Blood – or to give it its full name, "Egri Bikaver" or "Bull's Blood of Eger" – was anaemic stuff, but privatization is bringing progress here as it is with Hungary's other reds, particularly the Merlot and the local Kadarka and Kékfrankos from the pre-Roman vineyards of Villanyi-Siklos. Another grape grown here with some success is the Pinot Noir.

Small quantities of this variety have also been produced successfully with Antipodean help at the Gyöngyös winery by Hugh Ryman, the young Australian- and French-trained Englishman behind the rejuvenated Hincesti winery in Moldova. The most successful Gyöngyös wines so far, however, have been the Sauvignons and Chardonnays, both of which have been among the best, most consistent, dry whites to come out of Eastern Europe.

None of these wines is of top international class, however. Tokay – or, as it is now more commonly known, Tokaji – should be, though this could rarely be said of examples made by the all-powerful co-operative under the old collective system. Quite

THE ESSENTIALS
EASTERN EUROPE

What to look for A bewildering array of indigenous grape varieties – and examples of familiar Western styles – all at affordable prices.

Official quality Under Communism, quality control tended to be non-existent in what were almost always directly or indirectly state-run industries. Capitalism has brought greater awareness of the importance of this aspect, but it is taking time to change hardened attitudes – which is why so much of the best wine has thus far been produced by or under the supervision of foreigners. However, Bulgaria, in line with its success in Western markets, had already established a quality system under the old regime: "Country Wine" is table wine from a particular area; DGO or Declared Geographical Origin indicates a specified village appellation; and Controliran is wine from a designated grape from a specific DGO. A time-honoured hierarchy exists for Tokaji: the higher the puttonyo number on the bottle, the sweeter the wine.

Style White wines are generally "international" or Germanic in style, from off-dry and medium with basic fresh fruit through to lusciously sweet wines, such as the Romanian edelbeerenauslese. Bulgaria produces some passable but dull Chardonnay; Hungary's efforts with Sauvignon, Chardonnay and Riesling have been more successful. There are also several sparkling wines produced in these countries, particularly in the former Czechoslovakia and USSR, the latter producing sweet, red sparkling wine called "Champagnski" and "Krim". Hungarian Tokaji is made from aszu – semi-dried (somewhat) botrytis-affected grapes mixed, in varying quantities, with a dry base wine to make a number of styles. Szamorodni is made in the Tokaj region from the same grapes but is rarely botrytized. Eastern European red wines are generally full-bodied and approachable with lots of ripe, rich fruit though they are traditionally spoiled by sweetness and oxidation. Bulgarian red wines owe not a little to Bordeaux, in terms of both style and grape varieties: putting up spirited competition to these is the local Mavrud grape. Modern examples of the famous Bull's Blood from Eger in Hungary are improving.

Climate The wine-growing areas of Romania, Hungary, Bulgaria, the Czech and Slovak republics, southern Yugoslavia and Russia have a warm continental climate. Hungary's climate is particularly affected by Lake Balaton, which is the largest in Europe.

Grape varieties Too many to list in full, but including: Aligoté, Cabernet Sauvignon, Chardonnay, Dingac, Furmint, Gamza, Gewürztraminer, Grüner Veltliner, Kratosija, Laski Rizling, Lenyka, Mavrud, Melnik, Merlot, Misket, Muskat Ottonel, Pinot Blanc, Pinot Gris, Pinot Noir, Plavac Mali, Plovdina, Prokupac, Riesling, Saperavi, Sauvignon Blanc, St Laurent, Ugni Blanc, Vranac, Zilavka.

Production/maturation Varies from medieval to ultra-modern.

Longevity Drink dry and medium whites within 3 years. Good-quality sweet wines and Tokaji will age for at least 5 years. Red wines are often non-vintage and are released when ready to drink. Most will keep at least 2 years in bottle.

Top 9 Tokaj: Disznókó, Royal Tokaji Wine Co, Oremus; Other Hungarian: Gyöngyös Estate; Bulgaria: Russe, Suhindol, Svichtov; Moldova: Hincesti; Slovakia: Nitra.

---

unrelated to the Tokays produced in Alsace and Australia, Hungarian Tokaji is produced in the region of Tokaj close to the River Bodrog, from a blend of the local Furmint, Hárslevelú and Yellow Muscat, all of which are regularly attacked by noble rot, thanks to the mist that rolls off the water. Unlike Sauternes and other top-quality sweet wines, Tokaji is made by turning the nobly rotted grapes into a paste – *aszu* – which is then blended by the 35-litre hodful – *puttonyo* – in varying proportions into 140-litre containers of dry – *szarnorodni* – wine. The sweetness of the Tokaj is measured in *puttonyos*, the most intense being a "six *puttonyo*". Aszu Essencia is a kind of "super-Tokaji" made in the best years, while Tokaji Essencia is a phenomenally pricy syrup made exclusively from nobly rotted grapes which is supposed to work wonders on the (presumably wealthy) male libido.

Everything changed for Tokaj with the arrival of an army of investors, principally from Britain, Spain and France where wine-makers were eager to lay their hands on the equivalent of *Grand Cru* vineyards. From the outset, the foreigners, including Jean-Michel Cazes of Château Lynch Bages, raised fundamental stylistic questions. The old guard of the co-operative believed that Tokaji was supposed to taste oxidized – like sherry – and made their wine accordingly. The newcomers disagreed – and used old papers and old bottles to prove that, in its heyday, Tokaji would have been no more sherry-like than Sauternes.

The battle is far from over, but the first releases – Tokaj takes a long time to mature – certainly support the Western Europeans' views. More immediately, the introduction of modern methods has led to the renaissance of a forgotten style of light dry wine, made from the pleasantly aromatic Furmint.

ROMANIA

At first sight, the slowcoach of Eastern Europe – watching peasants collecting water from roadside wells reminds one of a Breugel painting – Romania has, despite the handicaps of outdated and inefficient equipment, quietly begun to show signs of becoming one of the most dynamic as well as the largest wine-producing countries of the region. Much of the progress here can be attributed to the state research centres of Murfatlar and Valea Calugareasca which have introduced Romania's wine-makers to such Western varietals as the Cabernet Sauvignon, Merlot and Pinot Noir. Previously, the vineyards, which were first planted even before the arrival of the Greeks in the seventh century BC, tended to be filled with local grape varieties like the Babeasca de Nicoresti, Negru Virtos, Frincusa, Tamiioaca Romaesca, Feteasca Negra and Kadarka.

The climate, though northerly, is well suited to the production of both red and white wines, but the best regions for reds are Murfatlar, close to the Black Sea where both Pinot Noir and Cabernet Sauvignon have been good; Banat, which makes Cabernet Sauvignon and the locally famous Kadarka de Banat; Vrancea where the Pinot Noir and Cabernet Sauvignon are grown as well as the Babeasca de Nicoresti and Feteasca Negra; and Dealut-Mare on the lower slopes of the Carpathians where the biggest, richest Cabernet Sauvignons and Pinot Noirs tend to be produced. Until recently, this last grape in particular was generally used to make sugary, jammy stuff which was popular among Germans and sweet-toothed Eastern Europeans. Today, more modern versions are dry and better than some less successful, but far pricier, New-World efforts.

BULGARIA

Bulgaria, the success story of the Eastern Bloc, thanks to the provision (by Pepsi Cola of all people) of Californian wine-making know-how, had a surprisingly bumpy return to capitalism. At the root of the problem was land restitution – and the way in which the Communist monopoly of distribution somehow became a post-Communist duopoly.

Let's hope these are short-term problems, because the potential here is enormous. Conditions are fundamentally ideal for wine-making. The Black Sea is a crucial influencing factor on the land to the east of the Balkans, while the region to the west of the mountains is more affected by the Atlantic. Throughout the country, however, while conditions are typical of a continental climate, with warm summers and cool winters, local micro-climates are produced by hilly and mountainous regions.

The two most widely planted black grape varieties are the Gamza which is used to make daily-drinking, lightweight reds, and the more serious Mavrud which produces long-lasting, hefty wines. Further south, the Pamid and Saperavi are both good for simple fare, but the key red grapes for quality wines are now the Merlot and, more particularly, the Cabernet Sauvignon. The best wines from these varieties can be rich and almost Bordeaux-like. And very good value. Whites – even when made from internationally vaunted varieties like Chardonnay and Sauvignon by visiting Australians – so far remain resolutely unrecommendable. Until smaller estates are recreated, the best way to find a worthwhile red is to look for the names of the best wineries: Russe, Suhindol and Svichtov are recommended.

THE CZECH REPUBLIC AND SLOVAKIA

The two parts of the former Czechoslovakia are regions to watch as their vineyards begin to develop their modern potential, and to exploit a micro-climate not unlike those of Austria and Alsace. At present, the greatest successes have been in Slovakia in the Nitra region where light, characterful Grüner Veltliner, Pinot Gris, Pinot Blanc and Pinot Noir are all grown, as well as good examples of the grapey Irsay Oliver. St Laurent is another berryish red to look out for.

ALBANIA

Albania's isolation from the rest of the world has denied outsiders the opportunity to sample its wines, of which there were reportedly once quite large quantities. But living and working under the longest-lasting, hardest-line Communist regime has not made for the most quality-conscious, co-operative of attitudes amongst wine-makers. An Australian wine-maker did produce one vintage there in the mid-1990s. The wine never left the country and the experiment was not, so far as anyone knows, repeated.

THE EASTERN MEDITERRANEAN

This, of course, is where it all started – where man first got involved in the business of turning grapes into wine. The trouble is that, having begun there, wine-making never really developed beyond its infancy. For hundreds of years, the general impoverishment of the region following the Mongol invasions of the thirteenth century and the lack of enthusiasm for wine of the Turkish Empire more or less put a stop to the development of wine-making.

GREECE

After centuries of arrested development, Greek wine-making finally encountered international modernity when John Carras converted some of the money he had made out of shipping into an ambitious vineyard planned by the great Professor Emile Peynaud and using the Bordeaux grapes with which the Frenchman was most familiar. A quarter of a century after the first vintage of the now famous Château Carras, it is interesting to see that a new wave of pioneering producers have – thank goodness – mostly preferred to concentrate on indigenous varieties, some of which are probably as old as any in the world. Throughout Greece and the islands, exciting wines are beginning to appear from bigger producers like Kourtakis (with its Kouros brand), Boutari, Tsantalis and Achaia Clauss, and more especially from smaller estates like Gentilini, Hatzimichali and Papaioannou, most of whom are exploring the benefits of higher altitude and wind-cooled vineyards.

Over the next few years, there will be a lot more where these came from. Who knows? We might even find some enthusiastic Californian marketeer declaring the Assyritiko or Tsaoussi grape to be flavour of the month and planting it in the Napa Valley. In the meantime, seek out the recommendations in the *Essentials* box, and don't forget the great traditional Samos Muscats, the sweet dark Mavrodaphnes and, dare we say it, fresh examples of well-made Retsina.

CYPRUS

Forget Cyprus "sherry" and "British" wines. Head straight for the Commandaria, a potentially delicious fortified wine made from Xynistyeri and Mavron grapes that have been allowed to dry in the sun. It tastes the way you wish Bristol Cream did. For something lighter, look out for the youngest available bottles of table wines from Keo and Etko whose efforts at modernizing their styles are beginning to pay off.

MALTA

Maltese wines used to be famous for the minimal use of grapes grown on the island. Now, there are signs of local vinous pride – especially the efforts of the Delicata winery.

TURKEY

Tourism is guilty of all manner of cultural vandalism throughout the world, but if the recent rise in popularity of Turkey among young Northern Europeans has helped to encourage a few go-ahead producers there to make crisp, modern white wine, we can raise a glass to Thomas Cook and American Express. None is memorable as yet, but all are preferable to the dull, yellow stuff they have begun to supplant.

LEBANON

As Beirut tries to regain its role as the hedonistic capital of the Middle East, the world should see more of the wines of Lebanon's three best wineries, Château Musar, Kefraya and Ksara. Of these, it is Château Musar which has the strongest and longest claim to international fame, thanks to Serge Hochar's bravery in making wine in the Bekaa Valley despite tanks and bullets – and his bravery in doing so in his own highly individual Bordeaux-meets-Rhône style. Lebanese whites still lag behind the reds, making it hard to judge the validity of local claims that the Obaideh is the ancestor of the Chardonnay.

ISRAEL

There is a lot to be said for playing to a captive audience – such as the global community of strictly orthodox Jews who cannot drink any wine that has not been produced by kosher methods and under the control of a rabbi. But for far too long, despite high-profile investment by the Rothschilds and characteristically ingenious irrigation schemes, Israel's (mostly) kosher wine producers got away with producing wine of dismal quality.

The change came in the mid-1980s when the Golan Heights winery showed what Californian know-how could achieve. Since then, the high-altitude vineyards have turned out a consistently respectable set of wines under the Yarden and Gamla labels including a Yarden Cabernet good enough to compete with the best of the New and Old Worlds. The huge Carmel winery, which is responsible for nearly three out of every four bottles of Israeli wines, has also learned to make wine of at least adequate quality, though Askalon and Baron Wine Cellars are both better bets.

SYRIA, JORDAN, EGYPT & IRAN

There is some wine made in Syria – from Muscat grapes left over from this country's fairly sizeable table-grape industry – and in Jordan. But far less than in the past.

One day, a kind soul may remind the present generation of Egyptian wine-makers of the care which their ancestors devoted to wine-making. For the moment, at least, modern Egyptian wines are best avoided – especially when, as in the case of a Cabernet Sauvignon which killed a Briton in 1996, they turn out to be laced with poisonous methanol.

In 1948, wine writer André Simon wrote of the then Persia, "Once upon a time the country was famous for its wines; today the making and sale of wine is not allowed to Persians, but there are a few Armenians who make and Jews who sell wine". Today, any wine is produced in secret, which is a pity because there are at least a few lovers of Australian wine who would like to visit the hillside town of Shiraz, purported birthplace of the grape of that name.

THE ESSENTIALS

EASTERN MEDITERRANEAN AND THE LEVANT

What to look for Wines made using modern methods which bring out the flavour of indigenous grapes.

Official quality Greece alone has a broad Appellation of Origin system; the term Traditional Appellation is specific to Retsina.

Style Most Greek wines, whether white or red, are flabby, alcoholic and frequently oxidized, suiting local tastes. Greek Muscats can have an attractive raisiny character. Some full-bodied, richly flavoured reds, notably from Macedonia, are made, while Mavrodaphne can resemble Recioto della Valpolicella and Château Carras has made progress with Cabernet Sauvignon. Most traditional Turkish wines are flabby and alcoholic but Trakya, a dry white Sémillon, and the reds, Buzbag and Hozbag, are better, as is the Gamay from Villa Doluca. Cyprus is starting to produce clean, fruity whites and reds as well as the traditional strong wines, such as Commandaria, and Cyprus "sherry". Good-quality Israeli Sauvignons, Cabernets and Grenaches are now

being made, while in Lebanon, though Domaine des Tourelles and Domaine de Kefraya reds are improving, quality wine-making is restricted to Château Musar.

Climate Very hot and dry, although moderated by the Mediterranean and by the mountain slopes of these countries.

Cultivation A variety of soils – volcanic, alluvial and gravelly – and vines grown at all altitudes, from flat coastal plains to mountain slopes. The more innovative wine-makers have grasped that sites enjoying cooler micro-climates produce better wine.

Grape varieties Greece: Xynomavro, Agiorgitiko, Mavrodaphne, Cabernet Franc, Cabernet Sauvignon, Cinsault, Grenache, Vertzami, Mandilaria, Savatiano, Rhoditis, Assyritiko, Moschophilero, Muscat, Robola; Turkey: Papazkarasi, Hasandede, Gamay, Sémillon, Karalhana, Altintas, Cinsault, Carignan, Cabernet Sauvignon; Cyprus: Mavron, Maratheftikon, Xynisteri, Cabernet Sauvignon, Cabernet Franc,

Grenache, Muscat, Ugni Blanc, Palomino, Mataro; Lebanon: Cabernet Sauvignon, Carignan, Cinsault, Pinot Noir, Muscat, Chasselas, Chardonnay, Sauvignon, Ugni Blanc, Aramon; Israel: Cabernet Sauvignon, Sauvignon, Grenache, Clairette, Muscat.

Production/maturation Temperature-controlled fermentation and earlier bottling are being employed to produce lighter, fresher wines.

Longevity Most wines lack the acidity to be long-lasting, although Musar and the best Greek reds can last for some 8 to 20 years.

Vintage guide Vintages have less effect than wine-making on quality.

Top 24 Greece: Château Carras, the co-operatives of Samos, Naoussa and Zitsa, Korinthiaki, Kourtakis (Kouros), Boutari, Laziridis, Tsantalis, Achaia Clauss, Strofilia, Château Vatis, Gentilini, Hatzimichali and Papaioannou; Turkey: Kavaklidere, Diren, Villa Doluca; Lebanon: Château Musar, Kefraya; Israel: Yarden, Gamla, Baron; Malta: Delicata.

NORTH AMERICA

Once upon a time (in the late 1930s), two young brothers decided to start a winery. Their sense of time and place was impeccable; they were in California, the grape-growing heart of a nation that had just been freed from 14 years of Prohibition. If they could make the right kind of wine, there was a huge and very thirsty market, including plenty of immigrants, who were ready to buy it by the gallon.

Today one of those same brothers still owns and personally controls the world's largest winery. And the second largest. And the third. Every year his company makes more wine than the entire region of Champagne; the annual production of New Zealand would barely fill one of its larger vats.

A short drive from those giant wineries, there's a small estate whose owner lovingly produces just 1,500 bottles of wine per year – around half the annual output of Château Pétrus, the fabled Pomerol property whose scarcity value is beyond peer among the larger, Bordeaux estates.

The big wineries belong to E & J Gallo; the tiny one

to the Lambourne family. And it's a fair bet that, until Ernest Gallo decided to start exporting overseas in the late 1980s, unless you lived or spent time in North America, you'd almost certainly have heard of neither their wines nor the Lambourne's. That's the first crucial thing to remember about the wine industry of North America; it's huge, varied and as challenging to would-be explorers as the continent itself. And, as with so many other industries in that country, it is remarkably self-sufficient.

The second thing to bear in mind is that, while the Gallo and the Lambourne operations are as different as they could possibly be, they share, with every other US

Vines in the Stags Leap district of California's Napa Valley. Wines from here are among California's finest

winery from the smallest to the most humungous, that peculiarly American spirit of pioneering possibility, the belief in the key words: "can-do".

In some states this kind of confidence is entirely justified; in California, where almost any kind of farmer can grow almost any kind of crop, there is little excuse for not making good wine. Elsewhere, however, the climatic handicaps are often so severe that "can-do" seems rather reminiscent of the sickly child who stubbornly believes that he is going to grow up to be a champion heavyweight boxer.

But climate has not been the only handicap would-be wine-makers have had to overcome. Throughout North America there is a deeply puritanical resistance to alcohol that has, of course, led to its total ban in the past. In more recent years, though, this has been immeasurably strengthened by healthy-living and road-safety campaigners who, for the best of motives, have endeavoured to ensure that wine is never treated as casually as it is in the Old World.

North America is riddled with a confusing mass of restrictions that vary from state to state and even from county to county. Some counties have remained "dry" since Prohibition finally ended in 1933; elsewhere, wine sales are controlled by state monopolies; shops that sell wine are forbidden to sell peanuts or glasses (or *vice versa*); importers are barred from trading as wholesalers and retailers (and *vice versa*); and there is almost nowhere that a young man or woman can buy a bottle or glass of wine until they are 21 years old.

With hurdles like these to be cleared, most European producers and merchants might be forgiven for thanking their lucky stars that they are still allowed to ply their trade in the relative freedom of the Old World.

But the North Americans have their own advantages. Selling wine may sometimes be less than straightforward, but there's very little to stop would-be producers from making the stuff in any way they choose. A Bordeaux château would encounter all kinds of problems if it wanted to plant a few acres of Chardonnay, and it certainly couldn't label the wine made from that grape as "Bordeaux". A wine-maker in North America can take his – or her – pick from all of the varieties on offer in the nursery, and (unless they're

in the state of Oregon) call the wine more or less anything they like. So, if it's got bubbles, label it "Champagne", if it's sweet and pink, dub it "Blush Chablis".

And then there's the Madison Avenue factor. Wine-makers in the Old World are often still far more firmly rooted in the era of feudalism than that of twentieth-century marketing. If your father, grandfather and great-grandfather made Barolo in a particular way from the Nebbiolo grape, and sold it to a local merchant for whatever he was prepared to pay, that's what you would most probably go on doing. And if one of those forebears had taken the brave step of deciding to bottle his wine himself, then you'd more than likely go on using the label he chose from the local printer. The words "promotional budget" almost certainly wouldn't feature in your vocabulary; your entire marketing effort might well consist of a hand-painted roadside sign to tell passers-by that you have wine to sell, and a few printed cards bearing the name of your estate.

In North America, there is a far greater appreciation of the fact that while wine-making is part of an agricultural tradition, it also inhabits the same, hard-selling business world as the motor, computer or even entertainment industries. So the 1995 vintage Cabernet Sauvignon from the Mondavi winery will be described and marketed as that producer's latest "release" – just as though it were a pop record or a movie.

And if the success of a feature film can lie in the hands of the critics, so can that of a wine. If Robert Parker, author and publisher of an enormously influential newsletter called *The Wine Advocate*, and leading Internet pundit, or the contributors to the glossy *Wine Spectator* magazine give a new wine a top mark, it can sell out before the first case reaches the shops. And if they decide that a wine isn't up to scratch, woe betide the unfortunate salesman who's trying to persuade a wine-retailer to stock it.

This critical spotlight, coupled with the US enthusiasm for all things fresh and new, has not only led to a wine industry in which scarcely a week goes by without another new winery opening its doors, but one in which wine-makers are constantly aware of the style of wine the public wants to buy at any given moment.

While his Italian cousin in Barolo remains wedded to the Nebbiolo vines he inherited from his father, the US producer can decide, almost from one vintage to the next, to switch production from Zinfandel to Chardonnay, or from Chenin Blanc to Cabernet Sauvignon. In Europe, even if legal, such an upheaval would not only be unlikely; it would also be time-consuming, as the land is normally left to rest for three or four years between the pulling-up of the old vines and the planting of new ones which, in their turn, would take another three or four years to begin producing good wine.

In California, particularly, where the vineyards are almost all much younger, the switch is sometimes made far more simply, by a process known as "T-budding" which involves grafting a new variety on to the old one, possibly even for one vintage, producing two kinds of grape on the same rootstock.

This expertise at grafting vines might seem shockingly new-fangled to a European traditionalist but, ironically, harks right back to a historical link between European and US vine-growing – a link which was perhaps the most significant development in vinous world history.

Vines were growing on North American soil before the earliest European settlers arrived. These were of the *vitis labrusca* species – producing table grapes, rather than the wine-making *vitis vinifera* traditionally grown in Europe – hardy plants that were tough enough to survive cold winters and sweltering summers. In particular, they were resistant to various kinds of disease and pest, most notably the locally prevalent and voracious *phylloxera vastatrix*, a louse that simply loves to kill vines by chomping away at their roots.

Until the late nineteenth century, thanks to the ocean separating the two continents, the vineyards of Europe were as untroubled by the *phylloxera* as British kennels are by rabies. Then disaster struck: the louse was carried over the water and, in the space of a few decades, lived up to the *vastatrix* part of its name by devastating almost all of Europe's traditional vine-growing regions.

All kinds of remedies were tried; ultimately the only avenues left open to the Europeans led back to the source of the problem. If the louse didn't kill the vines in America, why not plant these American vines and use them to make wine in Europe?

The answer to this was simple. Although the American vines were easy to grow and their grapes pleasant to eat, the wine produced from their grapes tasted rather awful. But it wasn't the grapes the Europeans were interested in; what they wanted was the rootstock on to which – and this was the clever part – they grafted their good *vinifera* vines. This combination of resistant American rootstock and quality *vinifera* vine was soon adopted by wine-makers everywhere. Today, almost every top-quality vineyard in the world (with the exception of areas of South America and the Antipodes and tiny pockets of Europe that escaped the attentions of the louse) is planted in this way.

Initially, this was thought to be a two-way solution, engendering visions among US planters of an America gushing forth quality *vinifera* wine wherever the hardy *labrusca* flourished. Unfortunately, however, there are regions of North America where *vinifera* grapes simply will not grow. In parts of Canada and the northern states of the USA, the winters can be so cold that the plants freeze to death. Elsewhere, perversely, the weather can be too good for them. One of the main reasons why Florida has become such a popular holiday destination also explains why that state has never been able to attract top-quality wine-makers. The virtual absence of winter denies the vines the essential period of dormancy that protects them against disease. Only one type of vine can survive in this tender trap, and this, a native variety with the wonderful name of Scuppernong, produces less than wonderful wine.

Earlier this century, the USA was broadly divided between those regions that could produce good wine from *vinifera* grapes, and those that could make poor-to-mediocre stuff from *labrusca*. Expertise in the nursery improved matters considerably by creating hybrid vines with one *labrusca* and one *vinifera* parent whose wines tasted better than those made from the former, but less good than those of the latter.

Similarly, increased knowledge of vine-growing and of cloning, and improved pesticides and fungicides, permitted producers to plant *vinifera* vines in some regions where it had previously been impossible.

Today, there are vineyards in no fewer than 43 US

Spraying herbicide for weed control in Sonoma County

to ensure Hollywood's continued success.

The Napa and Sonoma Valleys are the Hollywood of California's wine world, the magnets that have not only attracted wine-makers from other parts of the USA, but also such illustrious overseas investors as Baron Philippe de Rothschild of Château Mouton-Rothschild and a clutch of some of the best-known producers in Champagne. And, with every new release from every new winery, the "can-do" confidence grows; it's a foolhardy man who'll tell a top Napa Valley wine-maker that he'll never make a wine to compete with Château Pétrus or Le Montrachet. Quite often he's half-convinced that he's already made it – and has a quote from a well-known wine critic to prove it.

Over the last few years, however, Californians have begun to find themselves facing increasingly stiff domestic competition from other states. Further north, Véronique Drouhin, one of the biggest names in Burgundy, is helping to prove how well Oregon's cool climate and red soil suit the Pinot Noir. Also on the western coast, Washington state's wine-makers are taking advantage of a completely different set of climatic conditions to make classy Chardonnays, Sauvignons, Rieslings, Cabernet Sauvignons and varieties (especially Merlots) that also seem to flourish on the eastern seaboard, in the micro-climate the Gulf Stream annually creates on Long Island.

Throughout North America, this growing understanding of the varying climatic requirements of different types of grapes and the readiness of producers to explore new regions has led to the creation of *Appellation Contrôlée*-style districts called AVAs – Approved Viticultural Areas – each of which is supposed to have its own identifiable characteristics.

In some cases, as in Long Island and Carneros in California, both of which genuinely do have micro-climates of their own, the existence of their AVA designation makes perfect sense. Elsewhere, there are all sorts of curious boundary definitions that seem horribly reminiscent of the political way in which DOCs and DOCGs have been doled out in Italy.

In general, though, the scheme has been well-received. All the same, the prosaic "Approved Viticultural Area" does not have the same ring to it as, say, "*Premier Grand Cru*".

states and in three regions of Canada. Of these, though, California remains far and away the most important in terms of both quality and quantity. It not only produces around 95 per cent of all the wine made in North America, but it is also the area in which two of the world's best oenological colleges have been established and where the country's greatest wines have all been made.

The supremacy of California is easily explained. Quite apart from the quality (and the useful diversity) of its climate, wine-making here has benefited from what might be called the Hollywood effect. The fact that Hollywood has a thriving film industry has encouraged thousands of talented and ambitious actors and directors to flock there – which has, in turn, helped

CALIFORNIA

According to atlases of North America, California is neither more nor less than one of the 50 states of the union. In reality, as anyone who has come into even the slightest contact with this uniquely privileged part of North America will have discovered, California is far more like a nation within a nation. And a highly successful one at that.

Apart from movies, computers and oranges, its 250,000 square kilometres (160,000 square miles) produce sufficient grapes to keep hospital bedsides amply supplied in several countries, while still allowing California's wineries to make this the sixth-biggest wine-producing nation on earth, with an annual production approaching some three billion bottles of wine.

As any Californian will readily tell you, this state has all of the attributes a farmer could ask for: an ideal climate – or rather a range of different ideal climates – relatively inexpensive Mexican immigrant labour, two of the world's most advanced training colleges and plentiful local investment. Perhaps most valuably,

though, California has the extraordinary self-confidence that comes from being the choicest segment of the chosen land that is the USA.

It was the brilliant Californian wines made by pioneering wineries like Mondavi, Stag's Leap, Heitz and Ridge in the 1970s that, more than anything else, helped to launch wine-making in the rest of the New World, and to revolutionize methods and attitudes in some of Europe's most traditional wineries and estates.

If California's wine industry is an undeniable success story, it unfortunately sometimes seems to have more in common with Hollywood than with Silicon Valley. Far too many wines have been made according to a formula that has worked elsewhere – like sequels to box-office hits or, very often, like the US remakes of French movies.

Ask almost any Californian wine-maker with aspirations to quality what styles he sells most easily, and it's a dollar to a dime that top of his list will be Chardonnay and Cabernet Sauvignon. Then wander out and look at what's being planted and grafted in the vineyards – that's right, more Cabernet and more Chardonnay.

Ask him about his ambitions and, all too often, you'll find that they are focused on making wines that will successfully compete with the best of Burgundy or Bordeaux – or more recently, the Rhône and Tuscany. Apart from the Zinfandel – California's "own" grape variety – there are far too few reds and whites that do not either closely conform to models already established in Europe – or represent "commercial" (for which, with white wines, you might often read "sweet") versions of those wines.

When the Australian wine-maker at Geyser Peak, reprising a formula that had worked at home in the Antipodes, introduced Semchard, a Bordeaux-meets-Burgundy blend of Sémillon and Chardonnay, the general reaction among his peers was that the public would never catch on to it; they'd be too busy wondering where to find Sémillon on the map. Even today, few competitors have so far had the courage to launch similarly offbeat blends.

Vines belonging to Beringer Vineyards, in Knights Valley

If Chardonnay and Cabernet have been the object of too obsessive a focus, so has Napa, a politically defined county which is treated as though its every corner was somehow predestined to make better wine than that produced elsewhere in the state.

Fortunately for those of us who dread the idea of living in a world where wines all taste the same – even if that sole flavour were that of the finest Meursault or Pauillac – in the late 1980s and early 1990s, California in general and Napa in particular were given an unexpected opportunity to take a fresh look at the styles and wines they were making. The catastrophic reappear-ance of the *Phylloxera vastatrix* louse in vines which, according to the experts at the University of California, were supposed to resist it has led to the replanting of well over three-quarters of the Napa Valley.

It remains to be seen whether, when they come to choose what they are going to plant and where, the vine-growers and wine-makers find the courage required to explore new varieties, styles and blends, and to create wines that owe nothing to Bordeaux, Burgundy, or anywhere else.

The History

Wine-making began in California in the late eighteenth century, following – or so it is generally believed – the arrival of Franciscan missionaries from Mexico. Initially, the grapes planted were the same, basic, Criolla variety that was grown in Mexico (though here it soon became known as the Mission) but, in the early 1800s, higher-quality French varieties were introduced from the east coast by an appropriately named Bordelais wine-maker called Jean-Louis Vignes, and an eccentric Hungarian who liked to be known as "Colonel" or "Count" Agoston Haraszthy and reputedly ended his days as a meal for alligators in Nicaragua.

However he died, Haraszthy's legacy to California's infant wine industry was a 160-hectare (400-acre) nursery, stocked with some 300 different types of grape brought back from a three-month expedition to Europe, and the still-functioning Buena Vista Winery in Sonoma County. Surprisingly, though, the one grape the Hungarian probably did not introduce to California was the Zinfandel, a variety which is thought to have originated in Italy as the Primitivo.

The mid-nineteenth century was the first heyday of Californian wine-making. Using Haraszthy's cuttings and the widely planted Mission grape, a large number of such familiar names as Paul Masson, Wente and Almaden dug the foundations of the industry we know today. In the 1870s, however, their progress was halted by the devastation of the vineyards by the *phylloxera vastatrix* louse which had already begun to put a halt to wine-making in Europe. Half a century later, the louse's work was completed by the introduction of full-scale Prohibition in 1920.

The Prohibition years were a time of keen amateur wine-making, and of similarly keen overnight conversion to almost any religion that used sacramental wine. It was wryly said that there was scarcely an apartment block in Manhattan that didn't have a resident rabbi or priest, and scarcely a household that wasn't experimenting with do-it-yourself kits that included a block of dried grapes and some powdered yeast, along with the strict injunction not to allow the two to come into contact with each other, lest they ferment.

After Repeal in 1933, although a few of the old-established wineries, such as Inglenook and Beaulieu, continued to produce wine from high-quality varieties, most preferred the more versatile table grapes that could be turned into poor-quality wine, juice or jelly depending on what the market demanded.

It was not until the 1960s and 1970s that a new generation of wine-makers began to explore the potential that Vignes and Haraszthy had revealed over a century earlier. The region that attracted most of their interest during those years was the Napa Valley, despite the fact that some of the most successful pioneering producers, including Haraszthy, had made their wine in neighbouring Sonoma County.

Over the following couple of decades, the Napa Valley consolidated its reputation, attracting big-money investors whose architectural follies sometimes seemed to attract far more reverence than the wines produced in them deserved – and far too much public attention. By the mid-1990s, however, the return of

THE ESSENTIALS

NAPA, SONOMA, LAKE & MENDOCINO COUNTIES

What to look for Top-class Cabernets, Chardonnays and Pinot Noirs.

Official quality Principal Napa AVAs and sub-AVAs are: Carneros (Napa and Sonoma); Rutherford; Oakville; Mount Veeder; Spring Mountain; Howell Mountain; Napa Valley; Stag's Leap District; Atlas Peak; McDowell Valley; Potter Valley; Sonoma Alexander Valley; Chalk Hill; Dry Creek Valley; Knight's Valley; Los Carneros; Northern Sonoma; Russian River Valley; Sonoma Coast; Sonoma County Green Valley; Sonoma Mountain; Sonoma Valley; Mendocino and Lake; Cole Ranch; Clear Lake; Guenoc Valley; Anderson Valley.

Style Dry whites and reds, with small quantities of botrytized whites. Some sparkling blush rosé or white wines are also made. Wines tend to be rich and powerful with maximum varietal expression. Chardonnays have good fruit character and the best, particularly from the cool Carneros region, have good acidity and balance. At their best, the Sauvignons are fresh and grassy with an attractive softness. Some rich, intense, botrytized Johannisberg Rieslings can also be found. Napa County produces some of the finest North American reds, particularly good Cabernet Sauvignons. Good Pinots are made in the cool Carneros region which is shared by Sonoma. Wines from Sonoma are generally softer and more approachable than their Napa counterparts. Chardonnays are well structured with good fruit and acidity, and, at their best, are stunning. Quite good "Fumé-style" Sauvignons are also made. Cabernet Sauvignons tend to be soft and juicy,

although denser and more austere styles are made. Excellent Zinfandels with rich, spicy varietal character, and seductively soft Merlots are produced by several wineries. Pinot Noirs can be spectacularly good, too.

Cultivation Vines tend to be grown at altitudes ranging from sea level near the bay to 125 m (409 ft) at Calistoga. Soils consist of gravel loams in the north and more fertile silt loams in the south. Most vines in Sonoma are grown on the floors or the gentle lower slopes of the Sonoma and Russian River Valleys. Soils vary considerably from loams to alluvial deposits; there are also local varieties such as Dry Creek Conglomerate.

Grape varieties Red: Cabernet Sauvignon, Merlot, Pinot Noir, Zinfandel, Syrah, Petite Sirah, Grenache, Barbera, Sangiovese, Alicante Bouschet, Cabernet Granc, Carignan, Gamay Beaujolais, Malbec; White: Chardonnay, Sauvignon Blanc, Chenin Blanc, Johannisberg Riesling, Gewürztraminer, Muscat, Sémillon, Pinot Blanc, French Colombard, Viognier.

Production/maturation Methods, like the size of wineries, vary widely, although small "boutique" wineries increasingly tend to employ "European" methods (including natural yeasts, barrel-fermentation etc.) where possible, while large firms use the latest, high-tech methods.

Longevity Red: many are approachable when young, but the best are capable of ageing for up to 20 years, though some tannic reds have proved to be surprisingly short-lived. White: At their best (Simi, Kistler, Sonoma Cutrer, Saintsbury, Mondavi,

Beringer, Clos du Val Chardonnays, some Trefethens) they can last for 10 or more years. Others have died early.

Vintage guide Red: 74, 76, 84, 85, 87, 88, 89, 90, 93, 95, 98; White: 89, 91, 92, 94, 95, 98.

Top 86 Napa: Caymus, Cuvaison, Beringer, Dominus (post-1990), Dunn, Flora Springs, Heitz, Long, Mayacamas, Mount Veeder, Château Potells, Robert Mondavi, Joseph Phelps, Silver Oak, Stag's Leap Wine Cellars, Sterling (Reserve wines), Newton, Saintsbury, Fetzer, Château Montelena, Crichton Hall, Niebaum Coppola, Peter Michael, Schramsberg, Grgich Hills, Hills, Forman, Cain 5, Franciscan, Beringer, Clos du Val, Shafer, La Jota, Acacia, Duckhorn (post-1990), Far Niente, Lamborne Family Vineyards, Frog's Leap, Opus One, Villa Mount Eden, Chappellet, Mumm Domaine Napa (good value), Domaine Chandon (recent wines), Atlas Peak, Spottswoode, Kent Rasmussen, Swanson; Sonoma: Alexander Valley Vineyards, Buena Vista (Chardonnay), de Loach, Chalk Hill, Gundlach Bundschu, Carmenet, Arrowood, Benziger, Voss, Château St Jean, Nalle, Clos du Bois, Dry Creek, Laurel Glen, Mark West, Matanzas Creek, Ravenswood, Sonoma Cutrer, Kistler, Preston, Iron Horse, Kenwood, Quivira, Simi, Rochioli, Joseph Swan, Seghesio (Zinfandel), Duxoup, Gallo Sonoma (single-vineyard wines), Jordan ("J" sparkling and Cabernet), Rafanelli (Zinfandel), Geyser Peak, Williams Selyem (Pinot Noir), Marimar Torres; Other: Monteviña, Madrona, Scharffenberger, Domaine Roederer, Calera, Jekel.

the *phylloxera* louse to Napa's vineyards (other regions had planted more resistant rootstock) had helped to redress the balance. Today, sensible wine-buyers choose good wines produced throughout a wide variety of Californian regions.

The Regions

If far too many of California's wines taste alike, the regions where they are made could hardly be more varied. Visitors who drive up from San Francisco to the Napa Valley wander around the one or two well-known wineries – and imagine that they have "seen" vinous California. In fact, there are vineyards and producers throughout the state, and even the big names in the Napa buy grapes from other regions to broaden their range.

The climate varies enormously, too. There are vineyards that are as cool as those of northern

Germany, vineyards with growing periods similar to Bordeaux, and others which have everything in common with the oven-like conditions of north Africa. Elsewhere in the northern hemisphere, you might reasonably expect the temperature to rise as you head south. In California, latitude has far less of a role to play than the situation of the vineyard in relationship to the coast and to the range of mountains that runs parallel to it. Almost all of the best vineyards of the Napa Valley and Sonoma County benefit from the cooling effect of fogs. Without them, the viability of most of the state of California as a quality wine region would be very questionable.

Until recently, the majority of wine-makers tended to believe that the difference between any two wines lay in the grapes from which they were made, the style of wine-making and the climate. Today, acknowledging that maybe the Europeans who talked about such things had a point, they are giving greater recognition to the effect of the soil.

So, within each of California's wine-making regions, the authorities have allocated AVAs – "Approved Viticultural Areas" – in a manner that recalls a mediaeval monarch creating dukes and earls. The legitimacy of some AVAs, like Stag's Leap in the Napa Valley, for example, is unquestionable; that of some others, like Lodi in the bulk-wine region of the Central Valley, smacks of local politics.

Napa Valley

Napa is about the same size as the Médoc, but that is only one of several parallels between the two regions: both are uninspiringly flat, though Napa has the advantage of being surrounded by picturesque hills; both have large numbers of impressive buildings associated with their wines; and both regularly produce a limited number of stunning red wines – and far larger amounts of frankly ordinary fare.

There are, however, some equally crucial differences. The climate in the Médoc is relatively constant from one end to the other, while Napa includes regions as warm as North Africa and as cool as Germany. In the Médoc, prices are based on a well-established hierarchy; in the Napa, they often have rather more to do with the skills of the winery's

Rustic architecture in Sonoma County, California

architect, label designer and marketing team.

So, it is probably better to forget about Napa as an appellation – or treat it with no more respect than you would the Médoc – and concentrate instead on the sub-regions and producers that have proved their worth over time. There are some really special vineyards here, both on the valley floor, such as those around Oakville, Rutherford and Yountville, and in Stag's Leap, as well as the extraordinary Martha's Vineyard where Heitz produced a 1974 Cabernet Sauvignon which was one of the finest red wines many connoisseurs have ever tasted. Other wineries to follow include Caymus, Swanson and the Mondavi-Rothschild Opus One.

Elsewhere on the flatter land, however, the soil is often too productive and grapes often simply fail to mature properly, developing plenty of alcohol, while never losing the stringy character of unripe skins. Until quite recently, these unbalanced wines were treated over-charitably by local critics who believed that they

Mustard growing between the vines in Napa Valley

impressively with this variety. Even so, for consistency, few would argue that the one part of the Napa Valley which bears comparison with the greatest white-wine regions on earth is Carneros. Here the mists that roll in reliably from the bay keep the temperatures low enough to suit both the Chardonnay and Pinot Noir – and, for most producers, to deter even the notion of growing Cabernet, though Cuvaison has made some fine Merlot to set alongside its Chardonnay.

To Carneros's credit, too, this is a region whose producers take a collective attitude towards quality, jointly producing, for example, a prototypical Pinot Noir to serve as a benchmark for any winery attempting to make wine from this trickiest of red varieties. For a taste of what Carneros can do, head straight for Saintsbury's matchless Pinots and Chardonnays, and for the wines of Acacia, Kent Rasmussen, Etude, Carneros Creek (Fleur de Carneros) and the excellent Domaine Carneros fizz.

Sonoma

If Napa has happily taken the credit for Carneros, few non-Californian wine-buffs are aware that this region actually – like the Montrachet vineyard in Burgundy – straddles two counties: Napa and the lesser-known Sonoma, where Agoston Haraszthy made wine at the Buena Vista winery.

True lovers of Californian wines have, however, long known about Sonoma. Their cellars probably included bottles of Chardonnay from wineries such as Simi, Clos du Bois, Kistler, Hanzell and Sonoma Cutrer, Sauvignon from Dry Creek and Adler Fels, Zinfandel from Ravenswood, Joseph Swan, Nalle, Quivira and Rafanelli, Merlot from Matanzas Creek, Cabernet from Simi and Kenwood, Bordeaux blends from Carmenet and Laurel Glen, Pinot Noir from wineries like Rochioli and Duxoup and sparkling wine from Iron Horse and Jordan.

If some or most of these names are unfamiliar to you, it is not particularly surprising; that is what the Sonoma region is all about. If Napa does its best to be, like the Médoc, a couple of parallel roads punctuated by big-name wineries, Sonoma prefers to be far more like St Emilion and Sauternes: a fragmented region that is full of often small-scale

would soften after a few years in the cellar. Unfortunately, time told a different story and, while California's great reds from producers like Mondavi and Beaulieu's Georges de Latour Reserve wines stayed the course magnificently, the tough youngsters merely turned directly into embittered pensioners before their time.

Today, while acknowledging the potential of the best parts of the valley floor, producers here, as in other parts of the New World, have increasingly begun to head for the hills – to regions like Mount Veeder where Mayacamas, Mount Veeder, Château Potelle and the Hess Collection wines are made, and to Howell Mountain where La Jota is a name to watch. Given time, it is very likely that it will be from these hillsides that some of Napa's best and most sought-after wines will be made, long after the lustre has worn off some of today's less well-sited superstars.

For other top producers, see the Essentials box.

Carneros

White wines are made throughout Napa with widely varying success: Frog's Leap and Franciscan both, for example, show how brilliantly Chardonnay can perform without the addition of cultured yeasts, and Swanson and Beringer have both hit the target discoveries, some of which produce top-class wine albeit in tiny quantities.

In the mid-1990s, however, Sonoma was yanked from Napa's shadow by the arrival of a giant, in the shape of a huge vineyard physically remodelled and planted by E & J Gallo who are now marketing the region's name for all it is worth. Gallo's first efforts in Sonoma are already impressive – light-years away from the dull fare from its base in Modesto.

Sub-regions to look out for are Russian River (a cool region for Chardonnay, Pinot Noir and fizz), Dry Creek (Sauvignon Blanc and Zinfandel), Alexander Valley (Chardonnay, Cabernet and Merlot – especially from Clos du Bois, Simi and Geyser Peak), Sonoma Mountain (Cabernet from Laurel Glen), Sonoma Valley (Cabernet and Zinfandel from Kenwood) and Knight's Valley (Cabernet from Beringer).

Lake County

Taking its name – and a welcoming cooling effect – from the biggest lake in the state, this is one of the most quietly interesting regions of California. The actress Lillie Langtry started wine-making here around a century ago, and a label depicting her face still helps to sell bottles of Cabernet Sauvignon and Chardonnay made at the Guenoc Winery. The Kendall Jackson winery needs no such help to sell its wines; it relies instead on making "dry" white wines that strike Europeans as tasting positively sweet. Today, another up-and-coming winery to watch is Konocti, whose lesser-priced wines can be among the best value anywhere in the state.

Mendocino

One of the frequently quoted "facts" about this

French-owned Domaine Carneros, imitating a château

schizophrenic region which, through a fluke of geology, can produce rich reds and lean whites, is that marijuana actually features in official records as one of the county's most widely grown crops. Well, it sounds believable – given the laid-back, 1970s atmosphere that still prevails throughout the region. Just take a look at those *Easy Rider* chopper bikes parked outside the (excellent) micro-brewery in Hopland – and look at the Woodstock hairstyles sported by their owners. But the 1970s ethos runs deeper than that: this is where some of the early ecological ideals have survived – in the form of California's first major organic vineyard which was started here by the dynamic Fetzer family.

Fetzer hits the mark with Chardonnays and red blends, while Parducci produces a textbook, spicy Petite Sirah; for many, though, the region's most impressive wines come with bubbles. This is where the Champagne house of Roederer set up shop, and it is the place to find Scharffenberger, maker of another of California's best fizzes.

The coastal range protects red-wine districts from the cooling fog, while a gap in the hills allows it to have its beneficial effect on the heat-sensitive white grapes in the Anderson Valley. So, when the obsession for Chardonnay eases up, this may be the place to look for Alsace-style Gewürztraminer (try the ones from Husch and Navarro), Riesling (Hidden Cellars) and Pinot Gris.

Sierra Foothills

A large region to the east of the Napa Valley, this is old gold-mining country where, if you hurry, in El Dorado, Fiddletown and the Shenandoah Valley of Amador County, you can still find thick, port-like Zinfandels made the way they liked them in the days when real men panned for gold and never did the washing-up. Sutter Home atones for the crime of inventing so-called "white Zinfandel" (most examples of which taste nothing like that grape) by using the variety to make top-class red. Monteviña and Madrona are other names to look for, as is Karly and, for Italian varieties, Noceto.

The Bay Area

Some of the roots of California's wine-making are to be found here, in Livermore, in wineries like Wente and Concannon, both of which were founded in the 1880s. Today, Concannon still produces some really fine, full-flavoured Cabernet and brilliant Petite Sirah. Wente preferred for a while to concentrate its efforts on more commercial fare, though more recent efforts have included some classier reds.

For the jewel in the region's crown, though, get a good map or directions (you will need them), head for Santa Clara County, and drive up the mountain track to the Ridge winery. It's grown a bit grander in recent years, but visitors are still surprised to find the wooden shed that serves as headquarters for one of California's best-known wineries – and vineyards situated almost precisely on the San Andreas fault. Some spectacular Zinfandel, Cabernet and Merlot is made here and in vineyards elsewhere in the state. If you had to choose a wine from just one Californian producer, it would be a Ridge Zinfandel.

North Central Coast

Once written off as too cold and dry and the source of "vegetal" wines, the region of Monterey to the south of San Francisco actually has conditions that vary from those of Champagne to those of the Rhône; the trick has been to sort out precisely which grapes to grow where, and how to train the vines to grow best. Jekel was the pioneer here and, after a sticky period, it's a name to look for again for juicy Cabernets and clean, fruity Rieslings produced in Arroyo Seco. Another trailblazer close by was Chalone whose founders planted Pinot Noir and Chardonnay on one of California's rare bits of limestone and at a cool 600-m (2,000-ft) altitude.

For another version of limestone Pinot Noir, head for the AVA of San Benito County where Joseph Jensen of Calera makes individual-vineyard examples of Burgundy standard, as well as a fine Viognier. And don't miss out on Bonny Doon, in mountainous Santa Cruz County, where Randall Grahm is producing wittily labelled Rhône- and Italian-style reds that have helped to spawn a movement unofficially known as ABC – "Anything But Chardonnay".

South Central Coast

Santa Barbara

Santa Barbara is an old region that has recently come into its own. Once dismissed as being too cool for quality wine, it has two AVAs, Santa Maria and Santa Ynez, which have become a focus of attention for would-be Pinot Noir- and Chardonnay-makers, following the success of Au Bon Climat in Santa Maria and Sanford in Santa Ynez. In fact, while the Pinot can thrive in similar conditions in the two regions, they actually enjoy quite different climates. Where Santa Maria is generally mild, as Firestone has proved, parts of Santa Ynez can be warm enough to make ripe, Bordeaux-style reds, too. Other names to watch out for include Carey, Qupé (source of pioneering Rhône-style reds), Meridian (Pinot Noir), Robert Mondavi's Byron winery and Kendall Jackson's Cambria, Foxen and Rancho Sisquoc.

Paso Robles, San Luis Obispo

Dick Graff, founder of Chalone and a Burgundiphile to his fingertips, found a bit more Burgundy-style limestone at Edna Valley and produced one of California's biggest, butteriest Chardonnays. Today, the butter is a little less rich, but this is still a terrific wine, as is the Maison Deutz fizz made in Arroyo Grande, directly to the south west, which takes advantage of chalky soil conditions far closer than most in California to those its parent company is familiar with in Champagne.

Parts of Arroyo Grande are warm enough to ripen Zinfandel but, for reds like this, Paso Robles is a far better choice, which helps to explain why the owners of Château de Beaucastel in Châteauneuf-du-Pape have picked this region to plant their Rhône varieties. Elsewhere the accent is on rich reds, especially Cabernets, Zinfandels, Syrahs (good value from Meridian), and Italian varieties such as Barbera, Nebbiolo and Sangiovese. Names to follow include Wild Horse, Eberle and Martin Brothers, who make good Sauvignon Blanc and Nebbiolo.

Central Valley and Southern California

The warm, fertile, "jug-wine" region of the Central Valley produces around two-thirds of California's wines, almost none of it worthy of note. It is hard to say quite why the Central Valley wines should be so much poorer than those produced in the apparently similar conditions of Australia's irrigated riverland regions, though it might be that quality could be improved by a little more work in the vineyard, and by less heavy-handed, industrial wine-making by the major wineries. Unfortunately, tasting the wines, it is hard to believe that most of the producers are even trying to make anything of better than very basic quality. Robert Mondavi's white Woodbridge wines, for example, though pleasant, bear far less family resemblance to the Reserve wines produced in Napa than do the cheapest Penfold's or BRL Hardy reds to the top-of-the-range wines from those Australian firms.

It may teach some of these bigger companies a lesson to learn that when an Australian wine-maker was commissioned to make a set of wines at the Arciero winery, under the "King's Canyon" label, the resulting efforts were good enough to beat pricier wines from starrier regions to pick up medals at the 1996 International Wine Challenge in London.

The only other name worth remembering is that of Quady, the winery that makes spectacular, sweet Essensia Orange Muscat. Southern California is mostly hot and dry, too, but the Temecula Valley has a cooler micro-climate, allowing Callaway to make good, crisp wines.

PACIFIC NORTH-WEST

If anyone ever tries to convince you that all Americans are the same, send them on a journey north from Los Angeles to Boise, Idaho. Along the way, they will drive through the northern European climate of Oregon and western Washington State and across the mountains to what looks like desert land where the only successful agriculture happens beneath huge circular irrigators. The people your friend will have met will be nothing like southern Californians. Oregon is the kind of country where a fashion statement is the purchase of a pair of sandals and an annual trim for the beard. In Washington State there will have been successful wine-makers with a winery that's a converted garage and a home-made basket-press cobbled together from scrap bits of stainless steel.

Oregon

Oregon is Pinot Noir country, and the red soil of the Dundee hills in this part of the Willamette Valley has produced Pinots that have held their own in tastings against top-class Burgundies. But until the early 1960s, the only grape thought suited to these cold, damp conditions was the Riesling, and the potential of even this relatively hardy variety was disputed by the experts at the University of California, who more or less discounted Oregon's chances to make it in the big time of quality wine-making.

In 1965, however, a California-trained wine-maker called David Lett, recognizing similarities between the Oregon climate and that of Burgundy, resolved to prove those experts wrong by establishing the Willamette Valley's first vineyards – and planting them with Pinot Noir vines. Over the following two decades Lett was joined by a succession of fellow pioneers, almost all of whom shared his passion for the elusive wild raspberry flavour. Almost from the beginning, these producers proved successful in replicating Burgundy in a remarkable number of ways. Their estates were small, their vintages were varied (though astonishingly similar to those of Burgundy itself), their prices were high, and they often had little idea of why one wine had turned out to be so much better than the next.

Partly as an attempt to expand their knowledge, and partly as a piece of public relations, the Oregonians launched an annual Pinot Noir celebration in the small town of McMinville and invited wine-makers from around the world to participate in seminars covering every aspect of wine-making. It was a brilliant coup, which brought instant credibility for the region – and helped to encourage Robert Drouhin and his daughter to come and make what has become the state's top Pinot Noir in their own winery.

Despite the attention Oregon received from US pundits (Robert Parker has an interest in a winery here), and despite the competition success of a number of wines, for a long time the state promised far more than it could deliver. Its hand-crafted, high-price Pinots often tasted too similar to basic rather than top-class Burgundy; wine-lovers seeking value for money often found it more easily in the increasingly successful efforts from California.

But Oregonians are stubborn experimenters. Techniques were sharpened, new clones tried and, sure enough, a growing number of wineries began to prove that what frequent visitor James Halliday said of the Yarra Valley was just as true here: this is one of the rare places in which the Pinot Noir has found a natural home.

Other grapes are looking better too, especially now that the Chardonnay clone mistakenly proposed by the experts from UC Davis in California is being replaced by one that ripens properly in Oregon (Shafer's and Bethel Heights make good ones). The Pinot Gris (especially from Adelsheim and Eyrie) is worth watching, as are fizzes from producers like Australia's Brian Croser at Argyll and Laurent Perrier.

Washington

Washington State is the place to bring anyone who ever fell asleep during their geography classes. You remember the teacher saying something about rain forests? Well, Seattle's got one. And you recall a reference to "rain shadows"? Well, there's a king-sized one of those too – on the east side of the Cascade Mountains.

The Cascade Mountains provide the key to Washington State. On the west, the conditions are cool, damp and attractive only to a small group of masochists led by Joan Wolverton of Salishan Vineyards, who, like her counterparts in Oregon, believes that this kind of "marginal" weather does wonders for grape varieties such as Pinot Noir and Chardonnay.

It is the area east of the Cascades, however, that produces most of the wines. At first glance this looks like land in which nothing thirstier than a cactus could ever be farmed. But there's sophisticated irrigation from the nearby river; half-mile long sprinklers pivot on the centre of the vineyards, feeding them a steady mist of life-preserving moisture. Mind you, no good wine was made here until 1969 – partly because the farmers had not planted high-quality grape varieties, and partly because local laws effectively prevented producers from selling their wine anywhere other than in bars. These rules more or less obliged would-be wine-drinkers to make their own.

From the beginning, one of Washington's greatest successes has been the Riesling, with some wonderful late-harvest versions being made by Kiona. But Washington's wine-makers are having just as much success with buttery Chardonnay (try the one from Hogue Cellars), green, gooseberryish Sauvignon Blanc (from Columbia Crest) and, perhaps most particularly, Merlot (from Gordon Brothers, Stewart, Quilceda Creek and Leonetti), Sémillon and Gewürztraminer. At their best these wines are packed with fruit, but with a bite of fresh acidity often lacking in California. And don't underestimate the seriousness of these producers: wines like those of Woodward Canyon and Leonetti have world-class complexity.

Idaho

Idaho's wines come mostly from the savagely barren Snake Valley in the east of the state, from vineyards planted at an altitude of 2,300 ft (700 m). According to the Winkler scale of heat units, which acknowledges only the average amount of heat received by the grapes, this oughtn't to matter. In practice, however, the grapes produce wine that tastes as though it comes from somewhere far cooler.

Grapes have been shipped in from Washington and Oregon – which one producer famously forgot to mention on its label. Today Ste Chapelle – the winery responsible for that lapse of memory – uses local fruit to make good sparkling wine and Riesling, and "Washington Cabernet" now openly and unashamedly graces the labels of its deep, rich reds. The Rose Creek winery has also enjoyed spectacular success with Cabernet, and Hell's Canyon is doing well with a light Chardonnay many a Californian would be proud to have made.

THE PACIFIC NORTH-WEST

What to look for Northern European-style wines from the west of the mountains and rich, ripe, fruity stuff from the east. Good fizz.

Official quality AVAs: Columbia Valley, Umpqua Valley, Walla Walla Valley, Willamette Valley, Yakima Valley.

Style Washington produces soft, ripe Chardonnays, fragrant Rieslings and tasty Sémillons and Sauvignons. The Merlots are particularly impressive. Oregon is best-known for its high-quality Pinot Noirs. Idaho makes crisp yet alcoholic Chardonnays and Rieslings. Reds are generally less successful.

Climate Oregon is the coolest Pacific state as a result of sea breezes; otherwise its climate is generally continental. Washington is very variable: over 100 inches of rain falls on the coast, but vineyards inland rely heavily on irrigation; the Cascade Mountains shield eastern Washington from the rain and sea breezes. Idaho enjoys typical continental climatic conditions with a high altitude and widely varying temperatures. The vintage variations in Washington are far less significant than in Oregon.

Cultivation Vines are mainly located in valleys or on low-lying slopes to escape frosts. Soils are silty, sandy or clay loams.

Grape varieties Reds: Pinot Noir, Merlot, Cabernet Sauvignon, Zinfandel, Pinot Gris. Whites: Chardonnay, Riesling, Sauvignon Blanc, Chenin Blanc, Gewürztraminer, Sémillon, Muscat.

Production/maturation

Stainless steel is widely used for fermentation and oak for maturation, although the wine-makers are open to experimentation. Washington vines are ungrafted.

Longevity Most wines are bottled ready to drink but whites can develop for up to 5 years; Washington reds and good Oregon Pinot Noir reds for up to 8 years.

Vintage guide (Oregon) Reds: 85, 87, 88, 92, 93, 95, 97, 98.

Top 27 Oregon: Amity, Domaine Drouhin, Argyle, Adelsheim, Eyrie, Knusden Erath, Cameron, Bethel Heights, Rex Hills, Veritas, Ponzi; Washington: Leonetti, Arbor Crest, Hogue, Columbia, Château Ste Michelle, Covey Run, Gordon, Woodward Canyon, Kiona, Stewart, Quilceda Creek, Chinook, Salishan; Idaho: Ste Chapelle, Hell's Canyon, Rose Creek.

THE OTHER WINES OF NORTH AMERICA

Compared to Australia where five out of seven states lay justifiable claim to making world-class wine, in the USA the focus is pretty tightly on just three: California, which produces 95 per cent of the nation's wine, Washington State and Oregon. So it may come as a surprise to learn that there are wine-makers in some 43 other US states all doing their best to compete.

The North-East

There are two main wine-making regions of New York State: the Finger Lakes in the far north of the state and Long Island just over the bridge from Manhattan. The former area can be very chilly, but it produces good Germanic-style whites and, at the Wagner winery, some wonderfully fruit-salady Chardonnay. The Gulf Stream gives Long Island a Bordeaux-like micro-climate that allows wine-makers such as Alex Hargrave to make top-class Merlot and Chardonnay.

Elsewhere on the north-east coast, Connecticut has lots of hybrids and *labrusca* and the Crosswoods winery, which makes good Chardonnay, Pinot Noir and Gamay. Massachusetts is the region where, in 1602, Bartholomew found a vine-covered island he called Martha's Vineyard. Today various *vinifera* are grown and made into wine here by the Chicama winery; their Chardonnay is particularly good.

New Hampshire has little to offer the wine-lover, but several wineries in New Jersey are trying hard with *vinifera*. The best of these are probably Tewksbury, Renault and Alba. Good Pennsylvania Rieslings are made on Lake Erie, while less hardy varieties do better in the south-east of the state. Names to look out for here are Chadds Ford, Allegro, Naylor and Presque Isle.

The South-East

Despite the curious allocation of the first AVA on the east coast to Mississippi, a state where all of the wine is made from the low-quality local Muscadine, there are few friendly places for quality grapes in the south-east. In Virginia, however, there is still a vineyard and winery at Monticello, the old home of the wine-loving President Jefferson. This state is gearing itself up to compete with Oregon and New York State as a good cool-climate region. Whites are generally better than reds, but wineries such as Meredyth have been successful with Cabernet Sauvignon.

The Mid-West

Few of the states here have proved successful with *vinifera*, but cool Michigan has wineries such as Boskydel, Fenn Valley and Tabor Hill making good Riesling, while Ohio, once the biggest wine-making state of the Union, has Firelands, Grand River and Markko, all of which are making impressive Chardonnay and are progressing with other quality varieties.

The South-West

The wines of Texas and Arizona stand as tributes to the self-belief of the residents of these states; it's a brave man who'll tell a Texan that he can't make anything bigger and better than a Californian. So, despite the hot climate of both states, cool, high-altitude sites have been found where decent, if not great, wines can be made. In Arizona, look for Cabernet Sauvignon made near Tucson by Sonoita Vineyard and Riesling produced in the Four Corners region by RW Webb. In Texas, a joint venture between the Bordeaux firm of Cordier and the State University has made successful Sauvignon Blanc, and Pheasant Ridge and Llano Estacado have produced good reds.

Canada

The readiness of Canadians to drink "Canadian" wine made from imported grape concentrate for a long time offered little incentive to quality-oriented producers to test their skills against winter temperatures cold enough to kill vines. Fortunately, a few wineries in Ontario and British Columbia have persevered with vineyards situated in warmer micro-climates – and been rewarded with prize-winning sparkling wines, Rieslings and Chardonnays, and even some promising reds. The best wines – so far – are white, late-harvested and – a speciality this – ice wine. Seek out a bottle of Summerhill's British Columbian fizz or of Reif Estate 1993 Ice Wine which, despite being made from the Vidal, a hybrid variety despised by Eurocrats, managed to beat a number of classic Europeans to win one of a small number of gold medals at the 1995 International Wine Challenge in London.

THE REST OF THE UNITED STATES AND CANADA

Official quality North-east AVAs: Catoctin, Cayuga Lake, Central Delaware Valley, Cumberland Valley, Fennville, Finger Lakes, Grand River Valley, Hudson River Region, Isle St George, Kanawha River Valley, Lake Erie, Lake Michigan Shore, Lancaster Valley, Leelanau Peninsula, Linganore, Loramie Creek, Martha's Vineyard, Monticello, Northern Neck, George Washington Birthplace, North Fork of Long Island, Ohio River Valley. Other AVAs: Arizona: Sonoita; Arkansas: Altus, Arkansas Mountain, Ozark Mountain; Mississippi: Mississippi Delta; Missouri: Augusta, Hermann, Old Mission Peninsula, Ozark Highlands; New Mexico: Middle Rio Grande Valley, Mimbres Valley; Texas: Bell Mountain, Fredericksburg, Mesilla Valley; Canada, despite a laudable voluntary Vintners' Quality Alliance created by the wineries, is hampered by having archaic liquor legislation instead of quality-control laws. The main wine-producing areas are: Niagara Peninsula, Ontario; Okanagan Valley, British Columbia; Alberta and Nova Scotia.

Style The white wines produced in the states of the Atlantic seaboard tend to be crisp and light, although the Hudson River area produces richer, toasty Chardonnays. Reds are similarly light and acidic. The best wines come from Long Island, notably some lovely grassy Sauvignons and crisp, intense and oaky Chardonnays. Cabernet Sauvignons and Pinot Noirs tend to be rather green. Sound sparkling wines are produced along with tiny quantities of sweet Riesling or Gewürztraminer. Elsewhere, most wines are made from classic grape varieties with some creamy Chardonnays coming from Texas and decent Cabernet Sauvignons from Arkansas and Texas. Both these states show good potential for the future. In Canada, plenty of labrusca wine is produced although some good dry whites and light fruity reds are made in the Niagara region.

Canadian Chardonnays often show good fruit character with a restrained oaky richness. Rieslings can be made dry or rich and honeyed if harvested late as "ice wines". Some good-quality sparkling wines are produced from Chardonnay. Light, fruity reds are made from Pinot Noir, Gamay and Cabernet Sauvignon. Imported grape concentrate is also used. Labrusca varieties are used for sparkling and sweet wines.

Climate Obviously, varies considerably. In the north-east, it is continental, with severe winters moderated by the tempering effects of the Atlantic Ocean and the large areas of inland waters, such as the Finger Lakes and Lake Michigan, to produce suitable vine-growing micro-climates. Elsewhere, Texas and New Mexico are hot and fairly dry, the other states of the south-east being wetter. In Canada, near-European conditions may prevail: despite cold winters, parts of Ontario can enjoy a surprisingly temperate climate similar to that of Tuscany, with the Niagara Escarpment acting as a wind-break. Similarly, the Okanagan Valley of British Columbia has hot days and cold nights.

Cultivation In the north-east, vines are mainly grown on the flat shores of lakes or the lower slopes of mountain ranges. Soils vary considerably with limestone-based soils in Pennsylvania, Ohio and Virginia, glacial scree in Michigan and a mixture of shale, slate and limestone in New York. Silty loams and gravel are also found, mainly in Virginia. Elsewhere, vines are grown on a variety of soils. Canadian vines tend to grow on lakeside slopes, where the main soil types are sandy loams and gravel.

Grape varieties North-east, vinifera: Chardonnay, Cabernet Sauvignon, Gewürztraminer, Merlot, Pinot Noir, Riesling; Labrusca: Concord, Catawba, Delaware, Ives; Hybrids: Vidal Blanc, Aurore, Seyval Blanc, Baco Noir, Marechal Foch and Chelois.

Elsewhere, Red: Cabernet Sauvignon, Carignan, Grenache, Merlot, Zinfandel; White: Chardonnay, Chenin Blanc, Gewürztraminer, Moscato, Riesling, Sauvignon Blanc. Canada also grows the vinifera Aligoté, Cabernet Franc, Chasselas, Gamay, Petite Sirah, Pinot Gris and Pinot Noir, as well as the labrusca Agawama, Alden, Buffalo, Catawba, Concord, Delaware, Elvira, Niagara, Patricia and President.

Production/maturation

Most wineries have modern equipment with stainless steel fermentation and wood maturation in common use. In the cool, damp north-east the vines sometimes have to be buried under several feet of earth in order to survive the harsh winters.

Longevity Varied.

Vintage Guide This is a huge area and few wines are made to last long. Drink the youngest available.

Top producers Maryland: Catoctin, Elk Run, Boordy; Michigan: Lakeside Vineyard, Tabor Hill; Hudson/New York Finger Lakes: Rivandell, Millbrook, Gold Seal, Knapp, Treleaven, Wagner, Swedish Hill, and Hermann Wiemer; New York Long Island: Hargrave, Bridgehampton, Gristina, Palmer, Pindar, Lenz, Glenora, Bedell, Bidwell; Arizona: RW Webb; Ohio: Firelands, Debonné; Pennsylvania: Allegro, Chaddsford; Arkansas: Wiederkehr Wine Cellars; Mississippi: Almarla Vineyards, Clairbone; Missouri: Mt Pleasant Vineyards, Stone Hill, Hermannhof; New Mexico: Anderson Valley Vineyards, La Vina; Texas: Pheasant Ridge, Sanchez Creek, Llano Estacado, Fall Creek, Cordier Estates/Ste Genevieve. **Canada**: British Columbia: Gray Monk, Gehringer Bros, Summerhill, Calona Wines, Mission Hill; Ontario: Brights Wines, Château des Charmes, Hillebrand, Inniskillin, Sumac Ridge, Cave Spring, Pillitteri, Vineland Estates, Konzelmann, Henry of Pelham, Reif Estate.

SOUTH AND CENTRAL AMERICA

One of the things that most upsets some of the more precious wine-makers of California is to be included among the wine regions of the "New World"; they resent anything that sets them apart from their role models in Bordeaux and Burgundy. Tinkering with previously acceptable names is perhaps unsurprising at a time when short people are unsmilingly described as vertically challenged.

Even so, until the Californians get round to dropping the more popular description of Dvorak's Ninth Symphony, the New World will continue to be an apt description for a state which is, after all, the most avowedly experimental and high-tech wine region on earth.

The wine-producing countries of South and Central America, on the other hand, have a far stronger case for inclusion in the Old World. After all, vines were being planted in Venezuela in 1523, long before most of the châteaux of Bordeaux were dreamed of.

Venezuelan wine has not, it has to be admitted, enjoyed quite as starry a reputation over the last four and a half centuries as Bordeaux or, in more recent times, California, but other countries in South and Central America are increasingly beginning to make wine that is worth taking seriously. Chile, in particular, is rapidly building a name as one of the world's most serious wine-making countries and has attracted the efforts and investment of an impressive array of big names from France and California. Argentina, historically – if surprisingly – one of the planet's five biggest wine-producers, is also, with outside help and investment, developing an internationally competitive wine industry, while producers in both Uruguay and Brazil have now entered the international arena with wines that certainly bear comparison with some of the less lustrous efforts of supposedly "classic" regions of the Old World.

CHILE

Chile's reputation as anything more than a source of inexpensive, old-fashioned, Spanish-style reds and whites has, until recently, relied not so much on its wines as on its vineyards. A combination of mountain ranges and ocean provides a *cordon sanitaire* against the *phylloxera* beetle and other pests, making this a living horticultural museum. Visitors from France were surprised to see vines growing on their own roots as they were in Bordeaux a century ago, and internationally respected critics like Hugh Johnson declared Chile's vineyards to be a national treasure worthy of preservation. Conveniently, though, in their enthusiasm, Mr Johnson and others overlooked the fact that, *phylloxera* or no *phylloxera*, most of the wines that were being produced by the grapes grown in those vineyards were downright ordinary.

A palm tree next to vines in Chile's Maipo Valley

Part of the problem, ironically, lay in the fact that quite apart from the absent menace of *phylloxera* and a host of other pests, Chile is simply too easy a place to grow grapes. The clement climate of the best regions of the Central Valley might have been made to measure for the growing of Bordeaux and Burgundy-style wines. As Bruno Prats of Château Cos d'Estournel in St-Estèphe explains, the weather in an average Chilean vintage is like that of a top-class year in the Médoc. And those "average" Chilean vintages come along nine years in 10 – about thrice as often as good years in Bordeaux.

Throughout the Old World and even in New-World regions like Marlborough in New Zealand and the Hunter Valley in Australia, grape-growers are at the mercy of untimely rainstorms late in the growing season and during the harvest. In Chile there is almost no rainfall. Unlike other dry regions, however, there is no risk of drought: as the snow melts on the Andes, it provides an unlimited source of the irrigation water which flows through the vineyards in an elaborate network of trenches.

So far, so good. Unfortunately, just as there might be a surfeit of milk and honey in Paradise, all this water has frequently proved to be too much of a good thing. Grape-growers with no interest in the quality of the wine produced from their fruit tend to pour water into the ground to increase yields.

To be fair to those grape-growers, until the outside world began to take a serious interest in buying Chilean wines in the mid-1980s, a major part of every year's harvest was sold in the same kind of cartons most of us associate with milk and orange juice. There was supposedly finer fare, but a lack of temperature control in the vats and cellars, and the European tradition of prolonged ageing in old casks made from the local raule wood, ensured that most of that more ambitious wine lost whatever fruit it may ever have had.

This Hispanic attitude – that an older wine is by definition a better wine – was coupled with another belief familiar in Spain and Portugal: that, when it came to wine-producers, big was decidedly beautiful. So, almost the entire industry remained in the hands of fewer than a dozen key producers who concentrated very nearly all their efforts on selling wine to their countrymen. As recently as 1982, less than 1.5 per cent

of Chile's wines were drunk beyond its frontiers.

The French – and Spanish – connection

There is a dangerous – not to say condescending – tendency to attribute almost all of the credit for the modernization of the Chilean wine industry to the wealth of foreign expertise and investment the country has attracted in recent years; even so, there is little question that it was the arrival in 1978 of Miguel Torres from Spain that first helped to change local attitudes – and to stimulate a taste for exports.

Torres brought with him techniques learned in Montpellier in France, a genuinely international outlook, stainless steel tanks, cooling equipment and small oak barrels – all of which were then still novelties to the Chileans.

Soon after the launch of Miguel Torres's South American winery, Agustin Huneeus, the similarly open-minded Chilean-born head of the Franciscan winery in California, became involved as a joint-venture partner with the local firm of Errazuriz in the Caliterra winery. Next, in 1988, in a highly publicized deal, Eric de Rothschild of Château Lafite bought 50 per cent, and took over the running, of Los Vascos, one of Chile's few smaller estates.

Mistakenly likened by some observers to the Opus One collaboration between Eric's cousin Philippe and Robert Mondavi in California, this was in fact a very different operation from that quality-at-all-costs effort. Only a few insiders knew that the Franco-Chilean marriage was not entirely unconnected to a debt the owners of Los Vascos had to the Rothschild Bank – and to Eric de Rothschild's desire for a relatively low-price, high-volume, cash-cow wine brand he could sell internationally with a Lafite-style label.

Since Rothschild's arrival, and despite much scurrying around by wine-makers from Bordeaux, Los Vascos has produced uninspiring reds, and whites of which even a less illustrious name ought to have been thoroughly ashamed.

While other Frenchmen and Californians began to take a serious look at Chile, a number of younger Chilean wine-makers were already showing that they needed little help or instruction to make top-class wine.

Most famous of these is the charismatic Ignacio Recabarren who, after a spell at Santa Rita, has gone on to make wines or advise on wine-making at a wide range of wineries, while taking full responsibility for the Casablanca operation.

It was Recabarren who first proved what Chile could achieve with its white wines. Cousiño Macul had long made fine traditional reds and Paul Draper of Ridge Vineyards in California recalls, as a young man, producing a top-class Cabernet while he was in Chile. International-quality whites, however, for a long time remained stubbornly beyond the Chileans' grasp. Part of the problem lay in the vineyard: the wrong grapes were often planted in the right places – as in the case of the Sauvignonasse, a lesser variety erroneously identified as Sauvignon Blanc – or *vice versa*. In the wineries, there was either a lack of cooling equipment or a tendency to over-filter and to remove flavour.

Recabarren and progressive vineyard managers, like Pablo Morande of Concha y Toro, addressed the first problem by seeking out – and planting – the right grapes in the right places (such as real Sauvignon in the cool Casablanca Valley) and, with equally progressive wine-makers like Alvaro Espinoza at Carmen, solved the second by using New Zealand and Australian techniques to preserve as much as possible of the wine's natural fruit. To understand the difference in philosophy this has required, all you have to do is taste a dull, traditional Chilean white alongside one of Recabarren's perfumed new Casablanca Gewürztraminers.

While recognizing the skills of Chile's best wine-makers, it would be wrong to underestimate the part played by visitors like Hugh Ryman (who helped to add zing to Montes's Sauvignon); Kym Milne and Brian Bicknell who separately brought New Zealand techniques to Errazuriz; Gaetane Carron, the Frenchwoman who did much at Concha y Toro; Michel Rolland, the Bordeaux superstar consultant at Casa Lapostolle; Jacques Lurton, his neighbour, who has been sweeping a new broom through the once hide-bound San Pedro winery; and Paul Pontallier of Château Margaux and Bruno Prats of Château Cos d'Estournel whose Paul Bruno/Aquitania winery looks set to achieve everything one might have hoped for from Los Vascos.

No other wine-making country has attracted so much global expertise in such a short time – even without taking into account the investment of such high-profile Californians as Robert Mondavi, William Hill and Agustin Huneeus of Franciscan (now in his own right). Unfortunately, so far at least, some of the efforts of these Chilean and non-Chilean wine-makers have been undermined by the demands of Chile's thirstiest customers.

While Americans Paul Hobbs and Ed Flaherty were respectively helping to make and making high-quality wine at Valdivieso and Cono Sur, most of their compatriot wine-merchants were concentrating on obtaining the cheapest possible commercial reds and whites they could find. So vines which might have produced delicious, blackcurranty wine were over-irrigated to increase production and the grapes were then squeezed tightly to extract as much juice as possible. Whites sent north to the USA were light, off-dry and simple.

By 1996, US critic Robert Parker was dismissing Chile almost out of hand. Revealingly, Parker's shortlist of recommended producers included the disappointing Los Vascos and excluded some of Chile's most exciting newer-wave wineries. However, his judgement, or misjudgement maybe, was based on what he had tasted in the USA. If he had travelled to Chile or sampled some of the wines on offer in London, for example, his impressions might well have been rather different and more positive.

In 1995, spurred on by the desire for international recognition and by the success enjoyed by recently created AVAs – appellations – in California, the Chilean authorities introduced a system of designated wine regions. In part, this move was a laudable step toward regularizing an industry which had historically often blended wines from different grapes, regions and vintages with impunity. However, for some observers, the legislation may have been as premature here as it has been elsewhere in the New World.

Aconcagua

One hundred miles north of Santiago, this is great Cabernet country, with old vines that can produce blackcurranty flavours unrivalled elsewhere.

SOUTH AND CENTRAL AMERICA

What to look for Improving reds and whites, especially from Chile and Argentina.

Official quality Only Chile has a form of quality control – and a recently launched programme of controlled appellations.

Style Chile is best known for its slightly earthy, soft, fruity reds made from Cabernet Sauvignon, Merlot and Malbec. Clean but dull Sauvignons and some Chardonnay and Gewürztraminer are also made. Argentina produces a large amount of inexpensive and generally well-made wine. The whites are soft and rounded and may lack acidity: the reds are better, medium-weight with good fruit. Mexico has a long history of wine-production but much of it is distilled into brandy or Tequila. Recent investment by European companies has produced red and white wines of decent quality. Brazil and Uruguay produce large amounts of wine; the whites tend to be rather dull but the reds show more promise.

Climate Widely varying in most countries with extreme fluctuations of temperature and either too much or too little rain causing great problems. Chile is particularly variable. The north is hot and arid while the south receives a great deal of rain. Around Santiago it is dry, frost-free and sunny. Argentina's Mendoza district has a semi-desert climate, with lower rain levels than Chile, although it is spread over the growing season.

Cultivation Vines are generally cultivated on flatter lands, notably coastal and valley plains, but some hillside sites are used in Chile. Soils vary considerably, although sand, clay and alluvial soils are common. Chile has good limestone-based soils.

Grape varieties Red: Barbera, Bonarda, Cabernet Franc, Cabernet Sauvignon, Carignan, Grenache, Malbec, Merlot, Nebbiolo, Pais, Petite Sirah, Pinot Gris, Pinot Noir, Syrah, Tempranillo, Zinfandel; White: Chardonnay, Chenin Blanc, Riesling, Lambrusco, Sauvignon Blanc, Pinot Blanc, Sémillon, Ugni Blanc, Palomino.

Production/maturation Recent interest in wine-production in these regions means that modern equipment and methods are fairly widespread, but Chile and Argentina still use traditional methods as well. Irrigation is widely used, as is cold fermentation, resulting in fresher, fruitier wines.

Longevity Whites are best drunk within 2 to 3 years and reds within 4 to 5 years, though some can develop for 10 years or more.

Top producers Chile: Casablanca, Caliterra, Cono Sur, Valdivieso, Concha y Toro, Cousiño Macul, Paul Bruno, Santa Rita, Miguel Torres, San Pedro, Errazuriz, Nogales/Montes, Santa Carolina, La Fortuna, Canepa, Carmen, Viña Porta; Argentina: Esmeralda/Catena, Navarro Correas, Finca Flichman, San Telmo, Norton, Chandon, Weinert, Etchart (Torrontes), Goyenechea (Aberdeen Angus Cabernet), Luigi Bosca, Trapiche/Peñaflor, Leoncio Arizu, San Telmo; Uruguay: Santa Rosa; Mexico: L.A. Cetto; Brazil: Forestier.

Casablanca

Chile's answer to Carneros in California: a cool, foggy, frost-prone region whose climate is heavily influenced by the ocean. Sauvignon and Chardonnay work brilliantly here, as will Riesling and Gewürztraminer. Merlot and Cabernet have yet to prove themselves here, though those who favour cross-regional blends may use Casablanca reds as components with grapes grown in warmer areas.

Maipo

Macul, the region on the edge of the Chilean capital, Santiago, just above the smog-line, has long proved its worth with the Cousiño Macul reds made here. Now the Paul Bruno estate and a new enterprise launched by Ignacio Recabarren are set to establish definitively that this is still one of Chile's premier sites for red wine.

But will that be enough to keep the house-builders at bay? Elsewhere in Maipo, wineries like Santa Rita and Carmen make some of the country's best reds.

Rapel

Rapel is the place to find some of Chile's most intense, slightly cooler-climate reds: crunchy Burgundian Pinot Noirs, blackcurrant Cabernets and plummy Merlots.

Curico

Curico's cool nights make for tangy whites – from companies like Caliterra – but reds can be made too.

Maule

Even more firmly established as good white-wine territory, thanks to cool breezes at the end of the day which slow the ripening process, this can be the source of impressive – if potentially slightly herbaceous – Cabernet.

Mulchen

The new kid on the block, way down to the south, beyond the basic region of Bio Bio, this cool region may well prove to be the natural counterpart to Casablanca up north.

ARGENTINA

The fact that this is the fifth largest wine-producing country in the world comes as a surprise to most people. And you can't blame them for their ignorance – after all, until very recently, little Argentinian wine ever left the country. Or not as wine anyway; plenty was shipped in the form of grape concentrate to be diluted, fermented and sold as Japanese or Canadian or even, illegally, European wine.

Conditions are similar to those in Chile, though Argentina lacks the natural protection against the *phylloxera* which is slowly making its way through the vineyards. Most of the vineyards are planted around the small and surprisingly racy city of Mendoza where conditions are as warm as in some of the hottest parts of the Central Valley on the other side of the Andes.

The best wines produced here and in the similarly warm region of San Rafael a little further south are red, but increasingly decent whites are now being made nearby in the neighbouring, but higher-altitude, towns of Maipú, Tupungato and Luján.

The technology employed by Argentina's thousand or so producers is often decidedly old-fashioned; most have had little commercial need to modernize their operations, especially since much of the vineyard land is still planted in the basic Criolla grape.

But, thanks to the thirst of North America for inexpensive varietal wines, and an economy that has been restored to good health, Argentina's wine industry is evolving very quickly. At the Catena/Esmeralda *bodega* close to Mendoza, for example, the combined efforts of Paul Hobbs, one of California's best wine-makers, and Pedro Luis Marchevsky, the vineyard manager, have led to good Chardonnay and some impressive Cabernet, Merlot and Syrah being made.

Peñaflor, the other biggest wine-producer – it boasts the world's largest storage vat – has done similarly well in commercial terms, with its Trapiche wines which are probably Argentina's best-known vinous exports to the USA.

The Trapiche Chardonnays were among the first to benefit from the careful use of new oak in the late 1980s, and today the company boasts some appealingly woody reds to match.

New plantings are in full swing, though the grape that may be among the most interesting in Argentina could be Bordeaux's reject, the Malbec. Not ideally suited to being used by itself, it can when blended with a dash of Cabernet or Merlot produce some wonderfully spicy flavours. Another Argentinian speciality is the Torrontes, a Muscat-like grape grown in the high-altitude, northern region of Salta. Its wines smell as though they are going to taste as sweet as Asti but are, in fact, drier than many a Californian Chardonnay.

MEXICO

Despite the efforts begun in the sixteenth century by the conquistadors and sustained ever since, this, the country from which the first vines to be planted in California were imported, is not an ideal place to make wine. Half of Mexico is within the tropics and wholly unsuitable for grape-growing; the rest is divided between areas that are too hot or too dry. To compound the problem, wine-making skills traditionally imported from Spain have also been less than impressive.

Until 1982, these handicaps were less onerous than they might have been because wine-lovers had little alternative to the local product whatever its quality; the importation of non-Mexican wine was effectively forbidden. Perhaps unsurprisingly, most Mexicans turned their back on fermented grape juice and took their alcohol in the form of Tequila or beer. In the late 1980s, they drank little more than a tenth as much as their neighbours in the USA.

Today, apart from the improving Los Reyes and Château Domecq wines of Casa Pedro Domecq, a subsidiary of the Spanish sherry and brandy producer, made from vines grown on some 60,000 hectares (150,000 acres) of semi-desert area in the Guadaloupe Valley, the best Mexican wines come from the north of Baja California, just south of the US border. Of the producers here, the best is undoubtedly L.A. Cetto, whose Petite Sirah was named Wine of the Year in the International Wine Challenge.

BRAZIL

The notion of Brazilian wine ought to be familiar to cheapskate US consumers who drink some 12 million bottles of wine bearing the Marcus James label; unfortunately, most of the people who enjoy that undistinguished sweet stuff probably assume that it comes from California. Most of the rest of Brazil's annual production is consumed by Brazilians in the warm conditions of their own country where it is most appreciated in the form of a long, cool, refreshing drink.

Most of the wine-producers are based close to Porto Alegre around the towns of Bento Goncalves and Garibaldi, the latter of which is entered through an arch in the form of a giant concrete barrel. Despite the fact that the climate is far too wet to be ideal for vine-growing, this is where you'll find the Aurora co-operative, Brazil's biggest producer, and the maker of all that Marcus James wine. For quality wine, though, the names to look for are Forestier, de Lantier (a subsidiary of Bacardi-Martini) and Chandon, all of which are making surprisingly good wine. Only the most wickedly mischievous would ask why the latter company and its fellow Champagne house subsidiaries have continued to sell their Brazilian fizz as "Champanha", while their parent companies in France were so resolute in their efforts to protect the name of their region that even the tiniest European or American soap- or chocolate-maker was threatened with legal action if they made even a passing mention of Champagne when referring to their products.

A far more sensible place to grow grapes is at Palomas on the southern border with Uruguay. Here, in a California-style, high-tech winery, grapes grown in immaculately laid-out, California-style vineyards are regularly and efficiently turned into unmemorable, light, fruity stuff to be drunk in Rio night clubs.

OTHER COUNTRIES OF SOUTH AND CENTRAL AMERICA

Over the years, a number of distinguished visitors, including Professor Denis Boubals, France's leading vineyard expert, have recognized the potential of Uruguay's wine industry and its 20,000 hectares of vines. Until recently, however, that potential remained entirely unrealized. This tiny country's wine equipment was as outdated as the 1940s and 1950s cars which are commonplace on Uruguay's often half-surfaced roads.

In the mid-1990s, the industry was taken sufficiently seriously for the OIV – the foremost international organization of wine-producers – to hold its annual assembly here.

The Santa Rosa winery is the first to produce international-quality wines, but Calvinor, Juan Carrau/Castel Pujol (who also make wine in Brazil) and Los Cerros San Juan are worth looking out for in Uruguay. Try particularly to get hold of examples of the Tannat that is widely grown here – and compare them with the wines this variety is used to make in south-west France.

Peru's Tacama winery makes much of the encouragement it claims to have received from visiting French experts – Professor Emile Peynaud apparently described its "Gran Tinto" Cabernet-Malbec as "civilized and full of tenderness" – but the only examples I have tasted seemed "dull and full of oxidation".

The days here are warm and dry and the nights are cool; with a little care, decent wine ought to be achievable, especially given the range of French varietals subsequently planted on the advice of some of those Gallic visitors.

Venezuela, like India, can make two vintages per year, using a range of French and Italian varieties. The company that performs this feat most successfully is Bodegas Pomar whose French-born wine-maker learned his craft in the somewhat less tropical conditions of Bordeaux.

Despite those tropical conditions, Bodegas Verecianas in Colombia makes all sorts of wines, including the hybrid Isabella, the Pinot Noir and Riesling, while Paraguay, Bolivia and Ecuador all try to make wine from labrusca. True wine-lovers in all these countries rapidly learn to develop a taste for beer or pisco.

AUSTRALIA

Of all the world's vinous ugly ducklings, few can have achieved a more dramatic metamorphosis than Australia. Back in the 1970s, which of us shouted "Unfair!" when the Monty Python team described Australia's wines as stuff "to lay down ... and avoid"? Probably none of us; we were far too busy laughing along with everyone else. A decade later, the laughter had died in a few countries – principally Canada, Scandinavia and the UK – where millions of wine-drinkers had been won over by Australian Chardonnays, Sémillons, Cabernets and, especially, Shirazes, the Aussies' version of the great Syrahs of the Rhône.

Elsewhere, people have been slower to notice the transformation. Robert Parker, the US wine guru, dismisses most of Australia's wines almost out of hand, as does his French counterpart, Michel Bettane. Despite the regular successes of Australian wines in international competitions and the efforts of the 100 or so Aussie "Flying Wine-makers" who annually show producers throughout Europe, South Africa and South America how to do their jobs, it is a rare French or Californian wine-maker who would acknowledge them to represent any kind of serious challenge. In some ways, it's quite an understandable point of view.

For starters, by comparison with those wine industries, Australia produces a laughably small amount of wine. And then there's the fact that the Aussies have been relatively slow to promote their wines. While the world was growing familiar with names such as Mondavi, Stag's Leap and Heitz, few people outside of Australia had so much as even heard of Penfolds, Lindemans or Henschke.

To most outsiders, the Australians were far busier extolling the qualities of their beers. One of the most surprising things about the ever-surprising continent of Australia is the way in which a nation of beer-drinkers has fallen in love with wine. Today the Australians are some of the keenest wine-drinkers in the world, with an annual *per capita* intake of over 20 litres per person – around twice the figure for Britain or the USA. And they don't just drink a lot of the stuff – they take an enormous interest in what it tastes like, how it is made and where it comes from. Books on what most non-Antipodeans would consider to be such obscure Aussie wine regions as the Clare Valley can sell as many copies to a market of 16 million Australians as one on Chablis might to 270 million Americans.

So what was it that turned the Australians on to wine? Travel must have played a part; this is a remarkably well-travelled nation. Europe is liberally scattered with Volkswagen-loads of young Antipodeans eagerly working, eating and drinking their way from one part of the continent to the other, before heading back home with a taste for the good

Long shadows on the vines at Wynn's, Coonawarra

life. Then, of course, there have been the immigrants who have brought with them all kinds of "foreign" flavours that would have been quite unfamiliar to the Anglo-Saxon colonists.

A more mischievous explanation was provided by a cynical journalist who gave the credit to the sexual revolution, which led to young Australian males growing bored with the men-only, beer-swilling ethos of the bars and "hotels" in which they used to do their drinking. Wine was a social drink that you could enjoy with the "barbie" or take down to the beach (in a special, custom-designed cooler pack), or, in the case of two out of every three glasses drunk, pour at home from a four-litre box with a tap on the side.

None of this would have been possible, however, without the fundamental change that took place in the way wine was made. Even as recently as the early 1980s, Jack Mann, one of the veterans of the Western Australian wine industry, unblushingly told wine writer James Halliday that "unless a wine can be diluted with an equal volume of water, it wasn't worth making in the first place..." Mann's ideal of big, thickly alcoholic red and white wine was shared by most of his contemporaries, and by a great many wine-drinkers overseas. In the days when doctors took a rather different attitude to alcohol, they used to prescribe Guinness to pregnant women and Australian "Burgundy" to anyone who was suffering from anaemia.

As Adam Wynn, one of the modern wine-makers, says: "Thirty years ago, 80 per cent of consumption and production in Australia was of fortified wine. With the exception of Coonawarra, every wine region now existing was then geared to fortified wine. This meant they were in warmer areas, with rich soil, and produced from very, very ripe grapes." In real terms this made for wines that often tasted as though they were fortified even when they weren't. Today, production of those "ports" and "sherries" has dropped to around 10 per cent of the annual production as wine-growers have switched to making lighter wines in the existing regions and steadily gone looking for new, cooler ones.

This is another factor that sets Australia apart. Where the Californians have placed the Napa and Sonoma Valleys on a pretty unassailable pedestal, the

Australians are continually discovering wholly new regions in which they hope to produce some of their finest wines. Today's top areas such as Coonawarra, the Piccadilly Hills and Margaret River could, for example, soon face tough competition from recently developed locations with unfamiliar names like Robe, Orange and Tumbarumba.

That word "competition" is crucial to the way the industry has evolved; this is one of the most innately competitive nations in the world, and nowhere is this more true than in wine-making. Every region has an annual show at which hundreds of wines slug it out against each other for medals and trophies. Tastings such as these are held in every wine-making country, but it is the Australians who have elevated wine competitions to a level unknown elsewhere. Interestingly, France, which makes much more wine, has far fewer such events than Australia and none with the national recognition of, say, the Canberra Show. Trophies are worth real money to their winners; a winery whose young red has been awarded the Jimmy Watson Trophy can expect to sell at least a million dollars' worth more wine than it might have done otherwise.

Unlike their counterparts elsewhere, Australia's producers enter almost every wine they make into these competitions, including their most basic bag-in-box reds and whites. And then they allow their top wine-makers to devote as much as six or more weeks per year to vinous jury service. Being asked to judge these competitions, though, is an honour. Almost any French producer can be invited to taste at the major competitions in Paris and Mâcon; in Australia, wine "judges" have to undergo a testing apprenticeship that can last several years.

Lastly, there has been a welcome Aussie resistance, so far at least, to hype. Of course, there is a growing number of superstar wineries and one or two "gurus" whose advice on what to buy is taken seriously. But, by and large, Australians are as unimpressed by heavily promoted, highly priced "big name" wines as they are by old school ties. What they want is flavour and value for money – which is exactly what most Antipodean wine-makers have provided in increasing quantities, both at home and abroad.

NEW SOUTH WALES

If the climate is less than ideal, it's a lot better than the humid weather the first settlers encountered when they planted their vines at Farm Cove soon after dropping anchor in Sydney harbour in 1788.

Almost from the beginning, Australian wine was seen by the authorities as a preferable alternative to rum. Unfortunately, the humidity caused the Sydney vines to succumb to pests and disease, so the shipment to Britain in 1823 was Sydney's vinous swansong. The following year, a 2,000-acre (800-hectare) plot of land in the Hunter Valley was granted to an immigrant engineer called John Busby whose 23-year-old son James had briefly studied vine-growing and wine-making in France. It was James Busby who would not only found the wine industry of Australia, but also, a few years later, that of New Zealand.

The Lower Hunter

Today visitors can hardly imagine the Hunter Valley of as recently as the 1950s and 1960s. Much of what they produced was pretty basic fare. But, as anyone who has had the chance to taste wines produced in the 1950s by Maurice O'Shea at McWilliams will confirm, they were made to last.

The switch to more "modern" wine-making began with the introduction of Chardonnay and Pinot Noir by the iconoclastic John Wayne-like Murray Tyrrell, and was accelerated by the arrival in the 1960s of young "weekend wine-makers" from Sydney who had discovered wine in Europe and saw no reason why they shouldn't produce some for themselves. Despite the success of Murray Tyrrell's Pinot Noir in a blind tasting against a set of Burgundies, this is not really Pinot country. And although Lake's Folly and Brokenwood have both produced good Cabernet Sauvignons, these are exceptions to an uninspiring regional rule.

No, the three grapes to look for are the classic Sémillon and Shiraz, and Chardonnay, the comfortably installed newcomer. There is a big difference in the way

THE ESSENTIALS
NEW SOUTH WALES

Official quality A Geographical Indications system is being worked out; the Mudgee region established its own appellation in 1979, and the Hunter Valley is creating an appellation system of its own. Other notable production areas are Upper Hunter Valley, Lower Hunter Valley, Griffith, Canberra, Cowra, Orange, Tumbarumba, Corowa and the Murrumbidgee Irrigation Area (MIA).
Style Generally warm, soft, ripe wines in all styles, with plenty of richness. The classic Hunter Valley Sémillon is rich and honeyed and frequently tastes oak-aged even when it has had no contact with wood at all. Rieslings and Gewürztraminers are aromatic and show good varietal flavour. Chardonnays are packed full of ripe tropical fruit, often with a good dose of sweet vanilla from ageing in new oak. The Hunter Valley Shiraz has a distinctive earthy, peppery character. Cabernet Sauvignon is often blended

with the Shiraz to produce soft, jammy reds, but on its own the Shiraz produces some of Australia's best wines. Some interesting Verdelhos are made.
Climate The climate is sub-tropical, becoming progressively drier as one heads inland.
Cultivation Sand and clay loams of varying fertility are widespread, with alluvial soils on the valley floors. Vines are grown on low-lying or flat valley sites; the slopes of the Brokenback range and the Great Dividing Range in Mudgee (both up to 500 m) are used.
Grape varieties Red: Cabernet Sauvignon, Grenache, Pinot Noir, Shiraz, Pedro Ximénez; White: Chardonnay, Chasselas, Colombard, Marsanne, Muscat, Palomino, Riesling, Sauvignon Blanc, Sémillon, Muscadelle, Gewürztraminer, Verdelho.
Production/maturation Modern methods are

employed with machine-harvesting, temperature-controlled fermentation in stainless steel and judicious use of new oak for finishing. A number of Chardonnays are barrel-fermented.
Longevity White: most are at their best between 2 and 4 years, but top examples will develop for up to 15 years; Red: most are best drunk when 3 to 5 years old, but top examples will quite possibly improve over 8 to 12 years.
Vintage guide Red: 79, 80, 83, 85, 86, 87, 91, 92, 93, 94, 95, 96, 98; White: 86, 87, 91, 92, 93, 94, 95, 96, 98.
Top 16 Hunter: Brokenwood, Simon Whitlam, Lake's Folly, Lindemans, Rosemount, Rothbury, Tyrrells, McWilliams, Mount Arrow, Reynolds, Evans Family, Petersons; Orange: Rosemount, Reynolds; Barwang: McWilliams; MIA de Bortoli, Kingston Estate, Lindemans; Mudgee: Huntingdon Estate, Botobolar.

the varieties behave here, though. The Chardonnay is rich and tastily enjoyable, especially with a bit of toasty oak. The Sémillon and Shiraz need time to shake off the hard edgy character of their youth. Give them a decade or so, however, and they develop all sorts of complex flavours – and, particularly in the case of the Sémillon, do so best without the benefit of new oak.

The Upper Hunter

In wine terms, the Upper Hunter Valley is a comeback-kid. Wine was made successfully in this hotter, drier region in the late nineteenth century, but there was a dry spell until Penfold's opened a winery in 1960, moving north from the Lower Hunter, made wine for 17 years and gave up. They assumed, not unreasonably, that the Shiraz would fare as well here as further south.

The man who proved that assumption wrong was a wealthy businessman called Bob Oatley who bought the Penfold's winery, renamed it Rosemount and, with the help of his wine-maker John Ellis, introduced the world to the unashamedly easy-to-drink white wines that were to make Rosemount's, and ultimately the entire Hunter Valley's, name famous internationally.

Those first 1975 whites were made from the Traminer grape; Rosemount's real crowd-pleasers, the heavily oaked "Show Reserve" and less wooded basic (now Diamond Label) Chardonnays, did not come along until five years later, followed by the more ambitious Roxburgh Vineyard Chardonnay in 1983. Today, the Rosemount engine is driven by two men: Philip Shaw, one of the greatest wine-makers in Australia, even if we have yet to see him make a truly great wine, and Chris Hancock, a rare blend of wine-maker and brilliant marketeer who revels in declaring the Rosemount philosophy: "We want people to *enjoy* our wines. If they don't take them seriously, so be it…".

Unsurprisingly, this success has led other producers including Len Evans to revise their sceptical views of the Upper Hunter. Among Rosemount's more recent neighbours are Rothbury's Denman Estate and Tyrrells.

Mudgee

Up in the hills, to the north-west of Sydney, Mudgee takes itself seriously enough to have created its own appellation – Australia's first. There are some good producers here, and some rich reds including the organic Botobolar, but quality and distinctive character both need to improve before most non-Australian wine-drinkers are going to go out of their way to buy a bottle.

Cowra and Corowa

Corowa is fortified wine country where Lindemans once made traditional "port" and "sherry" just across the river and the state boundary from Rutherglen in Victoria. Cowra, by contrast, is a "new" region that is fast gaining a reputation for its cool-climate Chardonnay, thanks in no small measure to the lead taken by Len Evans of Rothbury Winery.

Orange, Hilltops, Barwang, Hastings Valley, Tumbarumba

As the focus shifts away from the Hunter Valley, new regions are being developed in several parts of the state. Cassegrain is the sole supporter of the hot, wet region of the Hastings Valley – where it makes impressive reds and whites. Greater attention though is being devoted to Orange, a source of grapes that traditionally ended up in bottles with Hunter Valley labels. More recently, Reynolds and Rosemount have shown that, despite spring frosts, this is a great place to grow Chardonnay and Cabernet at an altitude of some 900 metres. Hilltops is another cool region to watch (some producers call it Young after the nearest town), and McWilliams' Barwang with deep-red soils and an altitude of 600 metres is yielding top-class Cabernet.

For real cool-climate wine-making, though, the name to remember is Tumbarumba. Ian Mackenzie, chief wine-maker of Seppelts, enthuses about the potential of these vineyards for fizz – and then quietly pulls the cork on a stunning experimental non-sparkling Pinot Noir he's made there.

Riverina/Murrumbidgee Irrigation Area (MIA)/Griffith

Hot and isolated, this is great raisin country and, thanks to excellent irrigation from the Murrumbidgee River, a very easy place to produce huge quantities of wine. Recently, Cranswick Smith has done well with inexpensive varietal table wines, while De Bortoli has helped to create a new Australian style with its prizewinning *botrytis*-affected "Noble One" Sémillon.

VICTORIA

Victoria is like a vinous exhibition park, with examples of familiar but unex-pected wine styles such as Italy's Barbera and the Rhône's Marsanne, and of frankly eccentric fare such as the sparkling Shirazes of Great Western and the fortified "Tokay" Muscadelles of Rutherglen. South Australia is Big Company country; Victoria's raggle-taggle army of small wineries makes far less wine, but sets off far more fireworks.

The North-East

Rutherglen, Glenrowan and Milawa

Rutherglen has range of extraordinary "sticky" Liqueur Muscats and Tokays (made from Bordeaux's Muscadelle). Both are – or should be – brilliant, long-aged wines, full of Christmas pudding intensity. The best are made by Mick Morris, but Campbell's and Stanton and Killeen's are good too.

Glenrowan is still a one-winery town, but what a winery! Baileys is, like Morris's, a living museum of Australian vinous tradition. Try the Liqueur Muscats; then move on to the Shiraz. It's less beefy than it was, but it would still support a teaspoon.

Good Cabernet Sauvignon grapes are also grown in the Koombalah vineyard here. Follow them to the winery and you'll arrive at the Brown Brothers' winery in Milawa. John Brown Sr (a doyen of the industry whose experience rivals that of Robert Mondavi) and his wife head a team of Browns who between them divide the responsibilities of growing, making and selling.

Brown Brothers produce a wide range of wines, from Liqueur Muscat to lean, dry whites from new, cooler-climate vineyards in the King River Valley and new experimental wines from the frankly chilly Whitlands high in the hills. They have yet to make a really stunning dry red or white, but they produce nothing that is less than good, and wines like the unusual marmaladey Late-Harvest Orange Muscat and Flora have developed a cult following worldwide.

Central Victoria

Great Western, Pyrenees, Goulburn Valley, Bendigo, Giaconda and Delatite

Say "Great Western" to any Australian and he'll think bubbles. Seppelt created an enviable reputation for their commercial sparkling wines here, including the some-what variable Salinger. The star of Seppelt's Great Western show, though, is a style made nowhere else in the world: fizzy, slightly off-dry Shiraz that goes by the name of Sparkling Red Burgundy. If the idea appalls you, seek out a 20-year-old bottle and taste it. The reds here are good too – especially the Shirazes from Mount Langhi-Giran and Best's – while up in the cool foothills of the Pyrenees, Dominique Portet, the son of the former cellarmaster at Château Lafite, makes impressive European-style, long-lived Shiraz, Cabernet Sauvignon and lean fizz from grapes picked over a two-month period in one of the most beautiful vineyards on the planet.

In the warm region of the Goulbourn Valley, Château Tahbilk, the oldest in the state (it was founded in 1860), uses traditional methods to make big, old-fashioned reds which, like the lemony Tahbilk Marsannes, demand patient cellaring. Bendigo, to the west of Goulburn, is, like Rutherglen, good old gold-rush territory, but today the nuggets to look for are concentrated, often minty, long-lived reds from wineries like Jasper Hill, Passing Clouds and Balgownie. Finally, there are two more individualists who fit into no specific region. Rick Kinzbrunner's tiny Giaconda winery stands alone, high in the hills near Beechworth. The key wines here are stunning Burgundy-style Chardonnay and Pinot and a Bordeaux-style red. At Delatite, close to Mount Buller, on the other hand, the focus is on concentrated, long-lived wines including a Gewürztraminer with no competitor in Australia or anywhere else.

Murray River/ Sunraysia/Mildura

The river water here permits growers to harvest copious amounts of grapes. The Mildura winery never produces table wines that are remotely as good as the ones from its Coonawarra vineyards, or as impressive as the "sherry" and "port" made from ripe Mildura fruit, but they can be undemandingly appealing.

The South

Yarra Valley/Mornington Peninsula

If the traditional Victorian rivalry is between the fortified wines of Rutherglen and Glenrowan, modern Pinot Noir-lovers have the choice of supporting the cool-climate regions of the Yarra Valley or the Mornington Peninsula. Dr Bailey Carrodus's Yarra Yering Dry Red No. 1 is a great Bordeaux-style blend, beaten only by the Shiraz Dry Red No. 2. A growing plethora of star wineries here includes St Hubert's, Yarra Burn Mount Mary (famous for its Pinot Noir), Domaine Chandon (who make some of Australia's best fizz), Tarrawarra (producers of some very complex Chardonnays) and Seville Estate (source of glorious late-harvest sweeties). Don't underestimate the Merlots and Cabernets (especially from Yeringberg).

The Yarra Valley has tripled its production in recent years and looks set to go on growing, despite the high cost of land. The Mornington Peninsula stands no chance of that kind of expansion – it is far too close to the city of Melbourne. Among the professionals, Stoniers, Dromana (very commercially) and Hickinbotham have proved that this, too, is great Pinot and Chardonnay country, while T'Gallant has shown what Pinot Gris can do here.

Geelong, Macedon and Gippsland

Stay on the Pinot trail and head west from Melbourne to Geelong where Prince Albert, Bannockburn and Scotchman's Hill make some of Australia's best. Idyll's reds can be good, too. Then head along the coast to the new region of Gippsland to taste Bass Philip's stunning, plummy Pinot and Nicholson River's rich, biscuity Chardonnay. End your tour in the little-known region of Macedon where the Pinot is used for sparkling wines by producers like Hanging Rock and Cope-Williams.

THE ESSENTIALS
VICTORIA

What to look for Variety, variety, variety.
Official quality Important Victorian areas of production are: Rutherglen; Glenrowan; Milawa; Goulbourn Valley; Central Victoria; Pyrenees; Yarra Valley; Geelong and Mornington Peninsula; Great Western; Murray River; Macedon, Gippsland.
Style Good-quality whites and reds, some sparkling wines and stunning dessert and fortified wines. Chardonnays are creamy with rich depth of flavour yet also have good acidity and balance. Rieslings show fine varietal character, and there are good examples of Sauvignon Blanc, Sémillon, Gewürztraminer, Chenin Blanc and Marsanne. Cabernet Sauvignons from the more temperate southerly regions exhibit classic blackcurrant and cedar flavours and have great balance. Elsewhere the style is slightly richer. Fine, spicy Shiraz, which generally requires some ageing, is produced, together with small quantities of improving Pinot Noir and Merlot. Glenrowan and Rutherglen produce some luscious and rich fortified Liqueur Muscat and Tokay. These traditional "stickies" are of outstanding quality.
Climate Inland, conditions are hot and continental, but toward the coast the climate is tempered by the maritime influence.
Cultivation The better-quality wines are produced at the cooler, high-altitude sites around 500 m – 1,600 feet – above sea level. Wines of lesser quality are made from vines grown on all types of land. Soils vary widely, from the rich alluvial soils of the Murray Basin to the gravelly soils of the Pyrenees. North-east Victoria has red loams.
Grape varieties Red: Cabernet Franc, Cabernet Sauvignon, Cinsault, Dolcetto, Malbec, Merlot, Pinot Meunier, Pinot Noir, Shiraz; White: Chardonnay, Chasselas, Chenin Blanc, Gewürztraminer, Marsanne, Müller-Thurgau, Muscat, Pinot Gris, Riesling, Sauvignon Blanc, Sémillon, Tokay, Viognier.
Production/maturation Modern, high-quality production methods are used, with mechanical harvesting, temperature-controlled fermentation in stainless steel and early bottling common in most districts. The top wines, particularly the reds, are oak-aged. The fortified wines of the North-East are produced using a solera-type system.
Longevity Reds: The best can age for some 10 to 15 years; Whites: Most are excellent upon release but can develop in bottle for up to 8 years.
Vintage guide Reds: 85, 86, 88, 90, 91, 92, 96, 97, 98; Whites: 90, 91, 92, 93, 94, 96, 97, 98.
Top producers The North-East: Bailey's, Brown Brothers, Morris, Chambers, Campbell's, Stanton and Killeen, Pfeiffer, All Saints; Central and Southern: Delatite, Giaconda; Goulburn: Château Tahbilk, Mitchelton; Pyrenees: Taltarni, Dalwhinnie; Yarra: Coldstream Hills, Yarra Yering, Tarrawarra, Mount Mary, St Hubert's, Domaine Chandon, Yeringberg, de Bortoli; Mornington: Stoniers, T'Gallant, Merrick's; Bendigo: Jasper Hill, Passing Clouds, Heathcote, Balgownie; Great Western: Best's, Seppelt, Mount Langi Ghiran; Geelong: Idyll, Scotchman's Hill, Prince Albert; Gippsland: Nicholson River; Macedon: Cope-Williams, Hanging Rock, Craiglee.

SOUTH AUSTRALIA

If Australia had to choose just one wine-making state, this would have to be it, for both quality and quantity. That is not to say that the other parts of the country don't make great wines too (the competitive spirit between states is so fierce that you could not suggest any such thing even if it were true), but nowhere else can combine the capacity to produce around two-thirds of Australia's annual harvest with the ability to make huge quantities of good basic wine, as well as the Antipodes' greatest reds and some of their most impressive whites.

The potential of this state was appreciated as early as 1849, the year in which a horticulturist called George McEwin predicted that "Wine rivalling the most famous growths of the old world will be produced in South Australia as soon as we gain the requisite knowledge and the practical experience necessary to success…" It took just over a century for the wine-makers of South Australia to justify what must have appeared to be an absurdly high-flown prediction.

No one knows who began it all. Walter Duffield, Richard Hamilton and John Reynell are all said to have planted vines near Adelaide in the 1830s, using, in Reynell's case, cuttings from Tasmania, but it was a doctor from Sussex, Christopher Rawson Penfold, who was to found the company which would grow to become the largest in Australia and gain the reputation for consistently making the finest red wines in the continent.

Ironically, given the current medical touchiness

about alcohol, Penfold's initial reason for making wine was as a tonic for his patients. South Australia's early success owes much to the efforts of men like Penfold, but it has also to thank the *phylloxera vastatrix* which, though devastating most of the rest of Australia's vines, left this state alone. Which also explains why visitors today have to pass through an anti-*phylloxera* Checkpoint-Charlie when crossing its borders.

The Regions

The Barossa Valley

Although the first vineyards were planted around Adelaide by (non-convict) Britons, the region that would become the most important in the state was more or less founded by 28 families of – to judge by contemporary photographs – spectacularly miserable-looking Lutherans from Silesia in Germany. Today, the Barossa Valley, in which they settled in the 1840s, is still a curious mixture of Australian, British and Germanic, where coachloads of wine-thirsty tourists pour out of the Kaiser Stuhl winery and into the "Olde Englishe Tea Shoppe".

Initially, as elsewhere, the first wines to be made were "sherries" and "ports"; it did not take long, however, for the Germans to use the Riesling to make classy, dry unfortified wine. Despite a few good examples of unfortified reds, the man who taught the region and the rest of Australia a lesson in how to make and, more importantly, blend, red wine was another German, a pint-sized, bow-tied showman known as Wolf Blass. Before Blass, Australia's reds, though often big and tasty, needed to be left to soften before drinking. He it was who, after a spell in Champagne, developed a skill at blending wines from different regions which enabled him to make well-balanced (not too big, not too light) wine that was ready to drink the day it was sold.

Wolf Blass's unashamed preparedness to mix wines from several regions was – and is – completely at odds with the European tradition of making wines in individual vineyards and villages. But he was far from alone. Grange, Australia's most famous – and priciest – red, like most of the other wines made by Penfold's, is

Picking grapes by machine in the Barossa Valley

also the result of careful blending.

Another man with German roots whose name will long be remembered in the Barossa is Peter Lehmann, a keen gambler who staked everything to save the Shiraz from being uprooted at a time when no one seemed to want it. Lehmann's guarantee to the growers helped to keep the vines in the ground until the world began to appreciate the special spicy, berryish flavours of Barossa Shiraz.

Today, a Shiraz vineyard is in as much danger of being pulled out as the Eiffel Tower has of being demolished. Indeed, the trend today, led by men like Rocky O'Callaghan of Rockford and Bob McLean of St Hallett, is to seek out and buy the fruit from 100-year-old vineyards. As McLean says, the wines these make are rarely subtle, but they are among the most seductively generous in the world.

Adelaide/Adelaide Plains

Penfold's original Magill vineyard is now surrounded by metropolitan Adelaide, but the winery still makes wine from the fruit grown here as well as from vineyards elsewhere in South Australia. In the plains, heading up the highway north, the fields are full of fruit of almost every kind. Joe Grilli, however, concentrates on grapes, sometimes partially drying them to make wines in the style of traditional Italian *amarones*. His sparkling red is good, too, and his Colombard probably the world's best example of a generally abused variety.

Heading for the Hills

Eden Valley, Pewsey Vale, Lenswood

A number of producers have done the same as their counterparts in that other warm wine valley, the Napa in California: they have headed for the hills. In the Eden Valley, Henschke makes what is possibly Australia's finest red, the Hill of Grace Shiraz, which owes its depth and complexity of flavour to vines that are 130 years old, and a climate that is not quite so warm as that of the Barossa floor. Climb up to the High Eden Ridge, though, at over 500 metres above sea level, and you'll move right out of Shiraz territory. It was up here that the late David Wynn, the man who planted South Australia's first Chardonnay at Wynn's winery in Coonawarra, founded the Mountadam winery with his

son, Adam. The wines – especially the Chardonnay – are among the most stylish whites in Australia. Up in Pewsey Vale, Hill Smith and its Yalumba sister company, which make some of Australia's most reliable fizz, are producing similarly stylish Rhine Riesling, particularly from the grapes grown in its Heggies Vineyard, high up in the hills.

At an even higher altitude, however, in one of the buzziest of Australia's "buzz" regions, the Adelaide Hills is the source of a growing range of cool-climate wines. The leader of the pack is Brian Croser, whose Piccadilly Chardonnays have, with those of Leeuwin Estate in Western Australia, become known as the most consistently classy in the continent.

Another name to watch is Lenswood, where Henschke, Geoff Weaver and Tim Knappstein have all planted vines. At first, this seemed set to be great Sauvignon and Riesling territory, but Knappstein's Lenswood Pinot Noir and Henschke's Abbott's Prayer Merlot show that what can be good for the white goose can be just as good for the red gander.

Coonawarra

There is not a lot to Coonawarra: a couple of "hotels", as pubs are known here, a few shops and a strip of very special, terra rossa soil that runs like a one-mile-wide red carpet for about 10 miles. Australian wine-buffs wax as lyrical about the qualities of this soil as Bordeaux fans do when talking about gravel, and there certainly is something magical about the richness of the blackcurranty-minty fruit that is packed into the Coonawarra Cabernet Sauvignons and Shirazes. But the climate plays a role too; judged by the Californian Winkler system of Heat Units, it is actually comparable to Champagne and Burgundy. Arguments rage over where the boundaries of Coonawarra should be drawn – there are numerous outcrops of Coonawarra-style red soil between here and Padthaway which rightly or wrongly escape the appellation.

Apart from the soil and the climate, Coonawarra benefits from top-quality wine-making, both from local wineries such as Rouge Homme and Wynn's (both of which belong to Penfold's) and by "outsiders" such as BRL Hardy, Mildura and Lindemans (another Penfold's subsidiary).

SOUTH AUSTRALIA

What to look for Australia's biggest, richest reds – and a growing range of impressive, high-altitude, cool-climate whites.

Official quality Significant areas: Clare/Watervale; Southern Vales; Riverland; Adelaide Hills; Barossa Valley; Eden Valley; Langhorne Creek; Keppoch/Padthaway; Coonawarra; McLaren Vale; Adelaide; Lenswood.

Style Sauvignons and Sémillons are richly flavoured and Muscats are packed full of grapey fruit. Chardonnays have tended to be rich and buttery but are increasingly being made in a more elegant, balanced style combining rich fruit and good acidity. Of the reds, the best-known are the intensely flavoured, plummy Shirazes and the herbaceous Cabernet Sauvignons which have soft, juicy blackcurrant and stewed-plum fruit flavours. Some top-quality dessert, fortified and sparkling wines are also made, including honeyed – and occasionally botrytized – Rhine Rieslings, together with "ports" and "sherries".

Climate Temperatures range from the very hot continental conditions of the Riverland to the cooler areas of Coonawarra and the Adelaide plains.

Cultivation Soils are varied, but tend to be sand, loam or limestone topsoils over red earth and limestone subsoils.

Grape varieties Red: Cabernet Sauvignon, Grenache, Malbec, Merlot, Pinot Noir, Shiraz, Pedro Ximénez; White: Chardonnay, Muscat, Rhine Riesling, Sémillon, Sauvignon Blanc, Gewürztraminer, Ugni Blanc.

Production/maturation Mass-production methods are used to produce cheap and well-made basic wines. The producers of premium wines use traditional vinification methods. Oak-ageing is common for these wines.

Longevity Most quality whites will develop for 2 to 5 years, and selected examples for up to 20 years; Reds improve for 5 to 15 years.

Vintage guide Reds: 82, 84, 85, 86, 87, 88, 89, 90, 91, 93, 94, 96, 97, 98; Whites: 86, 87, 88, 90, 91, 93, 94, 96, 97, 98.

Top producers Barossa: Wolf Blass, Penfold's, Peter Lehmann, Basedows, St Hallett, Rockford, Charles Melton, Krondorf; Coonawarra: Katnook, Petaluma, Hill Smith/Yalumba, Wynn's, Rouge Homme, Ravenswood, Hollick, Penley Estate, BRL Hardy; Adelaide Hills: Mountadam, Orlando, Shaw and Smith, Henschke, Heggies, Pewsey Vale, Gramps, Jim Barry (the Armagh) Clare, Tim Adams, Petaluma, Leasingham, Pikes, Tim Knappstein, Wakefield/Taylors, Penfold's, BRL Hardy; Southern Vales: Hardy's/Château Reynella, Geoff Merrill; Riverland: Berri-Renmano.

Padthaway

So far, although some good Coonawarra whites have been made, like the Médoc, with which it likes to be compared, Coonawarra does best with its reds. For classy Chardonnay and Sauvignon Blanc, it is worth heading 40 miles north to Padthaway. Dubbed "poor man's Coonawarra" because it was partly developed in reaction to the rising cost of land and grapes in that area, this region has a small patch of red soil of its own, on which have been grown some very tasty red wine grapes.

Clare/Watervale

If the name puts you in mind of lush, green Irish meadows, think again. The country here is warm, dry and very woody – and about as far removed from the Emerald Isle as it could be. Reds are making a comeback – especially Shiraz – but the famous wines here are Rieslings which seem to thrive as readily on the slatey subsoil here as they do in the rather cooler climate of Germany.

Southern Vales

McLaren Vale, the most famous regional name here, has no shortage of supporters for what is said to be the "European" character of its wines. There is no question that the reds from producers like Château Reynella and Geoff Merrill are leaner than those from, say, the Barossa, but conditions vary enormously from one part of the region to the next. Despite the success of these wines and plentiful local pride, Southern Vales' greatest contribution may be as a top-quality blending component in wines labelled "South Australian".

Riverland

Around a third of Australia's grapes are harvested in this irrigated region. Much of the juice is distilled, but big companies such as Berri-Renmano – now part of BRL Hardy – use high-tech methods to make good, easy-drinking wines.

Opposite: Controlling weeds by hand in the Clare Valley

WESTERN AUSTRALIA, TASMANIA AND OTHER REGIONS

"I know about Australia ... I was there a few years ago... The conditions are far too warm to make fine wine." The dismissive Bordeaux château-owner whose experience of Australia consisted of a single mid-summer visit to the Hunter Valley ought to ask his countryman Jean-Claude Rouzaud of Roederer to describe his experiences of making Champagne-style fizz in the windy conditions of Tasmania. Or he could ask Gérard Potel of the Domaine de la Pousse d'Or in Burgundy to tell him about the Pinot Noir he has seen growing at Moss Wood, the winery with which he has been associated in the Margaret River in Western Australia. Both of these regions are, in their very different ways, arguably far closer to Europe in the conditions they offer wine-makers than most of their better-known counterparts in the rest of Australia.

WESTERN AUSTRALIA

"Don't forget to take your passport..." Such might be the wry response of a South Australian when you tell him you are off to visit his compatriots in Western Australia. If the whole continent seems isolated, this state sometimes appears to have wilfully chosen to cut itself off from the rest of the nation. While Australia as a whole ponders the pros and cons of republicanism, the populace here half-seriously murmurs about secession.

Wine-making began in Western Australia in 1829 at around the same time as it did in Tasmania, a few years before the first vineyards were planted in South Australia or Victoria. For nearly 150 years, although there were vineyards in the late nineteenth century at Mount Barker and Margaret River, almost all of the attention was paid to the wineries of the Swan Valley, where huge amounts of full-bodied red and white were made by men like Jack Mann of Houghton. He firmly believed that all wine should be intense enough to stand diluting with water.

Swan Valley

This is the kind of hot, arid country that the Frenchman imagined he'd find throughout the continent; a vast oven, ideally suited to the making of "sherry" and "port" but rather less appropriate for subtler, "modern" table wines. Companies like Evans & Tate and Houghton have managed to produce good wine here, including Australia's best-selling white, a blend known as HWB but more familiar to its fans under its old name of "Houghton's White Burgundy". Even so, most quality-conscious wineries have shifted their focus southward to the cooler areas of Margaret River and Great Southern.

There is one exception that proves the warm Swan rule: a quirky micro-climate called Moondah Brook where a spring provides almost limitless amounts of irrigation water, and a cool breeze is funnelled from the sea through a break in the hills. A range of reds and whites is made here, but none comes close to competing with the gloriously refreshing, lime-flavoured Verdelho. Otherwise, the Swan wines to look for are Evans & Tate's Gnagara reds and old-fashioned fortifieds like Sandalford's Sandalera.

Margaret River

This cattle-and-sheep-farming, and now world-famous surfing, region saw its first vineyard planted in the late nineteenth century. For around 75 years, however, its potential went largely unexplored; in those days, its (relatively) cooler climate and its wet winters seemed less suitable for winemaking than the well-established Swan Valley. But, in the 1970s, a number of doctors independently followed the advice of an encouraging report published in 1965 and planted vines. Soon, Doctors Cullen, Cullity, Lagan, Pannel, Peterkin and Sheridan had all established their vinous practices and were making wine to rival the best in Australia.

Even today, Margaret River is often mistakenly

thought to be cool; in fact its proximity to the sea gives the region what its wine-makers like to call a "Mediterranean" climate: warm enough to ripen the Cabernet Sauvignon with no difficulty whatsoever, but gentle enough to make for some of the classiest, longest-lived Chardonnay and Sauvignon in the country.

The only problems encountered by wine-growers are occasional shortages of rain, vine disease and the unwelcome attention of parrots and kangaroos. In 1978 the region became Australia's first appellation and it still is far more deserving of official recognition than some other regions currently debating the question. Leeuwin Estate's claim to fame – apart from its Californian-style winery, the big-name orchestral concerts held on its lawns, and the fact that its vineyards were originally selected by Robert Mondavi when he was thinking of making wine in Australia – lies in the quality of its Chardonnay. Vasse Felix's success has been with its rich, blackcurrant Cabernet Sauvignon, while Moss Wood, despite its owners' links with Burgundy associates and some early successes with Pinot Noir, now seems to hit the bull's-eye most often with its whites.

Leeuwin's Chardonnay has to fight hard to beat the ones made by Pierro and by Vanya Cullen, one of Australia's most gifted wine-makers who also produces first-class, Bordeaux-blend reds and whites. Cape Mentelle shares its founder, the charismatic David Hoehnen – and now its French owners – with the Cloudy Bay winery in New Zealand. The wines here are as exemplary as they are in Marlborough and include a spice-packed Zinfandel good enough to take on all comers from California. Also worth looking out for are Château Xanadu (for its Sémillon) and, from a little further north, Capel Vale.

THE ESSENTIALS

WESTERN AUSTRALIA, TASMANIA, QUEENSLAND AND THE NORTHERN TERRITORIES

What to look for Cool(er)-climate wines from Margaret River and the southern regions of Western Australia, and decidedly cool-climate wines from Tasmania.

Official quality Margaret River of Western Australia and (heaven knows why) Queensland's Granite Belt have controlled appellations. The Swan Valley, the Southwest Coastal Plain, the Great Southern Area and Mount Barker are important areas in Western Australia. Ballandean is significant while Alice Springs is the only notable region in the Northern Territory.

Style Western Australia, particularly Margaret River, produces some of Australia's finest wines, notably some vibrantly fruity, yet extremely elegant Chardonnay, Sauvignon, Sémillon, Shiraz and Pinot Noir. Queensland produces a wide range of styles from the fruity and delicate "Ballandean Nouveau", a Beaujolais-style wine, to some rich Cabernets and Shirazes and traditional fortified wines. The Northern Territory has very few wineries but those that exist produce Shiraz-Cabernet blends of decent quality.

Climate The climate of Western Australia is very varied. Queensland is hot with moderate rainfall which can cause problems at vintage time. The Northern Territory has a very hot and dry continental climate. Tasmania, with its cooler, windier conditions, produces some rich, elegant Chardonnays and vibrantly fruity Cabernet Sauvignons.

Cultivation Most vineyards in Western Australia are on flat, coastal plains or river valley basins, although higher-altitude sites are being used in the hotter areas. Soils are rich, free-draining alluvial and clay loams. Queensland and Northern Territory vines are grown at an altitude of 1600–1900 m (5,240–6,222 ft) to temper the heat. Granite is common in Queensland.

Grape varieties Red: Cabernet Franc, Cabernet Sauvignon, Malbec, Merlot, Pinot Noir, Shiraz, Zinfandel; White: Chardonnay, Chenin Blanc, Muscat, Riesling, Sémillon, Sauvignon, Verdelho, Traminer.

Production/maturation Modern viticultural and vinification techniques are necessary in most of Western Australia, and in Queensland and the Northern Territory, to combat the problems of heat.

Longevity In Queensland and the Northern Territory most wines are for immediate consumption. Whites of Western Australia can develop for 2 to 4 years, the best for 6-7; Reds benefit from 3 to 6 years' bottle ageing, with selected examples requiring up to 15 years.

Vintage guide Red: 86, 87, 88, 89, 91, 92, 93, 95, 96, 97, 98.

White: 87, 89, 90, 94, 95, 96, 97, 98.

Top producers Western Australia: Alkoomi, Capel Vale, Moss Wood (whites), Evans & Tate, Cape Clairault, Cape Mentelle, Cullens, Houghton, Leeuwin Estate (Art Series Chardonnay), Plantagenet, Goundrey, Wignalls, Pierro, Vasse Felix; Tasmania: Pipers Brook, Freycinet, Rochecombe; Queensland: Robinsons Family; Northern Territory: Château Hornsby.

Lower Great Southern Area/ Mount Barker/ Frankland/Pemberton

A broad and ill-defined area which is still being developed, Lower Great Southern offers a rare chance to buy good wine made in Denmark – a small town almost on the southern tip of the state. Mount Barker is also the region to look for impressive, coolish-climate Rieslings, Pinot Noirs and Chardonnays (the last styles especially from Wignall's). Local superstar wine-maker John Wade led the way at Plantagenet with some very Rhône-like Shirazes, and is still making impressive wine at Howard Park. Goundrey is the other big-name success story.

TASMANIA

Yes, despite the occasional tendency of Australian cartographers to forget the fact, Tasmania is part of Australia, but it's a very different part. This is either Australia's Oregon, or its Siberia. According to the island's supporters, it has the cool-climate conditions that are essential for lean, long-lived, Champagne-like sparkling wine and Burgundy-style Pinot Noir; for a large number of other Australian wine-makers, it's a chilly wasteland where no one would ever voluntarily choose to grow grapes.

In fact, though, wine-making is no novelty here; vines were growing in Tasmania in the 1830s, some years before they were introduced to South Australia or Victoria. But the first flourish of Tasmanian wine-making did not last long and it was the 1950s before serious attempts were made to try again.

The man credited with introducing Tasmania to the world of modern wine-making is Dr Andrew Pirie, one of the Antipodes' first academically trained wine-makers, and a man who disarmingly explains his presence in Tasmania by saying that he was looking for a cheap place to make the kind of expensive wine he had enjoyed in France. In fact, as he discovered, while land is inexpensive here, low yields make wine-making significantly costlier than it might be on the mainland. But he is not complaining – and nor are the people who have bought his wonderful, long-lived Chardonnay (including a Chablis-like unoaked version) and

promising Pinot. Jantz, the sparkling wine which was originally produced by a joint venture between Louis Roederer and the Heemskirk winery, Pirie's next-door neighbour, Taltarni's Clover Hill, and the recent investment by Domaine Chandon all indicate Tasmania's potential for fizz.

Despite the success of his wines, Dr Pirie would readily admit that since he and Heemskirk set up shop at Pipers Brook, newer regions have been developed in micro-climates in the south-east and south that are already showing equal and possibly greater potential – especially for red wines.

Look out for the excellent, raspberryish Pinot Noir from the tiny Freycinet whose wines sadly rarely leave Australia because of petty opposition by the huge Freixenet sparkling wine producer in Spain, who appear to believe that customers are likely to confuse still, red Pinot from Tasmania with sparkling Cava from Spain.

OTHER WINE-MAKING REGIONS OF AUSTRALIA

Canberra District

Australia's top wine writer James Halliday evocatively described the wine-making of this region as being carried out "on a doll's house scale" at weekends by off-duty civil servants. It's an appealing image; presumably every task is performed slowly and in triplicate.

However they make their wine, though, there's no shortage of customers. In Australia, the inhabitants of big towns like to drink locally produced wine and Canberra is no exception (actually, apart from visiting the excellent National Art Gallery and watching Australian politicians use unparliamentary language, there's precious little else to do).

Until quite recently, though, this area was thought to be too cool to ripen grapes. Now, it has come to be appreciated that the climate is as warm as that of Bordeaux but that there is insufficient rainfall for the needs of the vines. None of the wines is easily obtainable outside the district, nor are they of particularly high quality; the best efforts so far have been achieved by Doonkuna Estate and with red wines made from Bordeaux varieties and late-harvest whites. The vineyards themselves are usually outside the Australian Capital Territory in New South Wales – the reason being that you cannot buy freehold land within the ACT.

Queensland

The Granite Belt, as it is known because of its acidic, decomposed granite soil, is cool, high-altitude, apple-growing country. The grapes that are grown here do not readily lend themselves to the production of stunning wine, though the Robinsons Family tries its best with Shiraz and Chardonnay. Roma, the region that used to be the centre of winemaking here, has shrunk drastically. It is very, very hot.

Northern Territories

The very idea of a wine being made in Alice Springs ought to be the stuff of satire. This is not the kind of country any wine-growing manual would recommend: vines don't really like being asked to perform in the equivalent of a furnace. Denis Hornsby has, however, cleverly overcome the climatic impediments by building an underground winery and a highly sophisticated system of year-round drip irrigation. The grapes – which include Cabernet Sauvignon, Shiraz, Riesling and Sémillon – ripen long before those in most other parts of the country; indeed Hornsby was able to produce the world's first wine of the new century and millennium, from grapes picked within moments of the old one ending. None of the wines is bad, but the light, Beaujolais-style red is the best buy.

NEW ZEALAND

If there were a prize to be won for late developer of the New World, the wine-makers of New Zealand would carry it off without losing a drop of sweat. That award would end up sharing the mantleshelf with the trophy for fastest learner, too.

A Star is Born

Just look back over the last few decades. At the beginning of the 1980s, a patriotic Kiwi wine-bar owner in London frankly answered a query about the quality of his country's wines: "They're okay, I suppose – just don't get any on your hands." Needless to say, his patriotism stopped short of offering them to his customers. Within five years, however, Montana Sauvignon Blanc from Marlborough in the South Island had been named White Wine of the Year by *Wine Magazine* and had developed such a cult following that warehouses were emptied throughout the world.

The commercial success of that affordably priced Montana wine was swiftly followed by the critical plaudits given to the classier, pricier Cloudy Bay Sauvignon produced in the same region. Reckoned by many to be among the finest Sauvignons in the world, this elegantly and evocatively labelled wine soon shared the distinction, along with such illustrious wines as Burgundy's Romanée-Conti, of having to be rationed on its release.

Today, New Zealand – and especially Marlborough – Sauvignon is so well known that it is worth pausing to reflect that the first commercial example of the grape was put on the market as recently as 1981, and Cloudy Bay in 1985, the wine-maker Kevin Judd was still impatiently waiting for the builders to finish constructing his winery.

The influence of what the fans describe as the tangily fresh flavour of these Sauvignons has been felt in countries as diverse as France, Spain, Hungary and Chile. Even so, some wine-drinkers remain largely immune to their appeal. In North America, for example, where the innately "herbaceous", "leafy" flavours of the variety are unpopular and thus commonly masked in Californian examples by sweetness and/or new oak, New Zealand's wines have been slow to win respect. Robert Parker, a critic who has yet to visit the Antipodes and is similarly dismissive of most Australian wines, attributed New Zealand's reputation almost exclusively to the free trips he believed to have been offered to British critics. Conveniently forgetting the similar number of visits offered by such regions as California, Champagne and Bordeaux, Parker grudgingly conceded that "this country does produce some very fine Sauvignons", but described all except six wineries' efforts to be "often ferociously vegetal and dried out".

French tasters, whose palates are formed by often flavourless, "green" Bordeaux, are not bothered by the "vegetal" character that troubles Parker and his compatriots. What they dislike is the intensity of fruit flavour to be found in these wines. It is true that, compared to a really fine, subtle Sancerre or Pouilly-Fumé, most fruit-salady New Zealand Sauvignons do come across like less than intellectual beach-blondes; on the other hand, really fine, subtle examples of these Loire wines are rare. Far too many are aggressive, over-cropped, over-sulphured – so it is hardly surprising that Sauvignon lovers outside France and the US have taken to the newcomers.

The significant point raised by these differences of tasting opinion is that, in a world that is increasingly full of lookalike wines, New Zealand makes some of the most immediately identifiable reds and whites of all. Some of the character comes from the climate which is generally – but not exclusively – cooler than that of, say, the Napa or Barossa valleys. Some comes from fertile soils, and some comes from a young generation of wine-makers who, though often trained in Australia, have increasingly learned that the techniques they use successfully in the warmer regions of that continent often have no place here.

Despite Robert Parker's scepticism, New Zealand has already proved what it can achieve with all sorts of dry and late-harvest white wine. Reds are taking longer to master, but give them a few years and it's a fair bet that we'll be including a raft of them in the line-up of the best in the world.

The Background

Even 25 years ago, though, it is doubtful whether anyone in or outside New Zealand could have imagined that its wine-making would attract the international spotlight. In 1946 a Royal Commission on Licensing stated that: "More than 60% of the wine made by the smaller wine-makers is infected with bacterial disorders... A considerable quantity of the wine made in New Zealand would be classified as unfit for human consumption in other wine-producing countries."

Wine-making had begun in New Zealand 150 years earlier when the "Father of Australian viticulture", James Busby, was made the "British Resident" in New Zealand, planted vines "between the house and the flagstaff" and made a white wine that in 1840 impressed the visiting French explorer Eumont d'Urville as "light ... very sparkling, and delicious to taste".

Busby's career as a wine-maker was, however, curtailed by the ravaging of his vineyards by horses, sheep, cattle and pigs, and by soldiers during local clashes. Although settlers followed his example, it was not long before they realized that they would need to import wine-making expertise. While small groups of French and German wine-growers were persuaded to stay for a while, two shiploads of German vintners who had, as New Zealand author Michael Cooper narrates, "been promised perfect conditions for viticulture by the New Zealand Company, arrived on our shores, contemplated the steep bush-clad hills surrounding Nelson and left for South Australia".

Over the following years several New Zealanders attempted to make a living from wine-making, but only a handful succeeded. Furthermore, in the late nineteenth century, any who might have been tempted to take up vine-growing were deterred by the arrival of powdery mildew in the vineyards, which prevented wine from being made – and a virulent set of temperance societies, which sought to prevent it being drunk.

The man who saved New Zealand from full-scale prohibition went by the wonderful name of Romeo Bragato, an Italian-trained wine-maker born in Dalmatian Yugoslavia. Thanks to Bragato, New Zealand's wine industry survived. Thanks to his countrymen, it began to flourish. Because, despite their efforts, it wasn't the early British settlers who really set New Zealand wine-making on its feet, but a group of Dalmatians who had come to tap gum from trees in the far north of the North Island. These men, isolated by racial prejudice, settled, planted vines and opened wine shops for their countrymen.

The peevish Anglo-Saxons, galled by this modest success, opened up yet another avenue of prejudice. As the 1916 Aliens Commission complained, "A great deal of feeling against these men ... is due to many of them being wine-growers, and the belief that Maori women are able to get, through them, intoxicating liquors... Where young and vigorous men, attractive young women free from conventional social restraints, and abundance of intoxicating liquors are found together, debauchery will very certainly result ...."

The Dalmatians, following the exhaustion of the gum trees, began to concentrate on wine-growing, using expertise learned in Yugoslavia and from Romeo Bragato's book *Viticulture in New Zealand*, and with the assistance of a government research station at Te Kauwhata in the North Island.

During the first two decades of the twentieth century, despite the arrival of *phylloxera* (correctly identified by Bragato, whose initial warnings and advice were, needless to say, ignored by the authorities), both the wine-makers and the prohibition lobby strengthened their position. In 1919 the temperance societies appeared to have won a conclusive victory when a national referendum voted for prohibition. Had it not been for a contingency of servicemen returning from the war just in time to swing the ballot, wine-making here might have undergone the same period of hibernation as it did in the USA.

By 1960 there were still fewer than 1,000 acres of vines planted. But, within a few years, a rapid influx of money from outside New Zealand, partly fuelled by the beginnings of the Australian wine boom, encouraged heavy plantation.

Unfortunately, at the time, there was little reason for outsiders to argue with the image of this distant ex-colony as a shared annexe to Australia and Britain with a climate somewhere between the two.

One visitor who was evidently taken with the idea of New Zealand as a cool place with moderate potential was the German wine and vine expert, Professor Helmut Becker, who advised the New Zealanders to plant a variety he was recommending for such European countries as Germany and England. This grape – the Müller-Thurgau – had the advantage, Becker explained, of ripening early and yielding generous crops of grapes which, with a little "back-blending" (the addition of a little sweet juice), could produce an alternative to cheap German wine.

The New Zealand wine-makers of the 1960s and 1970s saw little reason to argue. After all, the world was not exactly clamouring at the door to buy bottles of New Zealand "port" or "sherry". So, within a decade, the Müller-Thurgau took over the industry.

To say that this was under-exploiting New Zealand's vinous potential is something of an understatement. The arrival of the Müller-Thurgau set New Zealand's wine-making back a decade.

Between 1965 and 1970 the acreage under vines tripled; by 1983 it had risen to 15,000 acres; two years later the country found itself awash with mock-German wine for which there was something less than a brisk international demand. The glut was solved by a

THE ESSENTIALS
NEW ZEALAND

What to look for Fresh vibrant whites and improving reds.

Official quality Designated regions are: North Island: Bay of Plenty, Fast Cape, Gisborne, Esk Valley, Hawke's Bay, Henderson, Huapa Valley, Ihumatao, Kumeu, Manawatu, Marigatawhiri Valley, Poverty Bay, Riverhead, Te Kauwhata, Tolaga Bay, Tikitiki,Waiheke, Waihou, Waikanae, Waikato, Waimauku, Wairarapa, Wellington; South Island: Canterbury, Marlborough, Nelson, Renwick.

Style Wines have crisp, varietal character with plenty of fruit but less heaviness than their Australian counterparts. Chardonnays are rich yet have an elegant freshness too. Sémillons can be rich and tart, or crisp with piercing fruit. Gewürztraminers, when made dry, have excellent spicy character but can also be lusciously sweet when late-picked, as can Rieslings. However, the most famous New Zealand wines are world-beating Sauvignon Blancs, packed full of green flavours – gooseberries, grass, asparagus and nettles – and occasionally oak-aged. Red wines have, until recently, enjoyed less acclaim but as vines grow older the Cabernets and – particularly – Merlots are showing greater depth of clean blackcurrant and plummy fruit, while some Pinot Noirs are showing greater varietal expression. These wines have potential.

Climate In general, a relatively cool maritime climate prevails, although the North Island has more tropical conditions, with higher temperatures and higher rainfall producing greater humidity. This, together with the heavy rains, can cause problems of rot and grape damage during harvest time.

Cultivation Vineyards are planted on a variety of clay and alluvial loams over volcanic subsoils. Drainage is often a problem, so some north-facing slopes have been cultivated on the North Island, although flatter land is used elsewhere.

Grape varieties Red: Cabernet Sauvignon, Merlot, Pinot Noir, Pinotage, Pinot Gris; White: Chardonnay, Chenin Blanc, Gewürztraminer, Müller-Thurgau, Muscat, Pinot Blanc, Riesling, Sauvignon Blanc, Sylvaner, Sémillon.

Production/maturation Very modern viticultural techniques are used for premium varieties; mechanical harvesting and temperature-controlled fermentation in stainless steel are widely employed. Barrel-fermentation is used to produce top-grade Chardonnays, while new oak is frequently used for maturation.

Longevity While all wines can be drunk immediately, the better-quality whites can benefit from 1 to 5 years' ageing. Reds can benefit from 3 to 8 years' ageing, although they may last longer in future as the vines become older.

Vintage guide Red: 89, 91, 93, 96, 98;White: 91, 93, 96, 98 (note that vintage conditions vary widely).

Top 37 Auckland/HastingsWaihiki Island: Kumeu River, Collards, Babich, Cloudy Bay, Cooks, Corbans, Delegats, Hunters, Matua Valley, Villa Maria, Coopers Creek, de Redcliffe, Goldwater Estate; Gisborne: Millton; Hawke's Bay: Te Mata, Vidal, Montana Church Road, Mission, Cooks, Ngatarawa, CJ Pask; Martinborough: Martinborough, Dry River, Ata Rangi, Palliser; Marlborough/Awatere: Montana, Deutz Marlborough Cuvée sparkling, Daniel le Brun, Nautilus, Rothbury Estate, Hunters, Cloudy Bay, Jackson Estate, Allan Scott, Cooks Stoneleigh, Vavasour, Corbans, Merlen; Nelson: Weingut Seifried, Neudorf; Canterbury: Giesen.
(Note that most medium-to-large producers now make wine in several regions.)

government-funded "vine-pull" scheme which encouraged growers to uproot uneconomical vineyards. Some turned to other forms of farming; others simply replanted the land, using more classic French grape varieties. Today, as an increasing number of sophisticated wine-drinkers have discovered, New Zealand has been transformed from backwater into mainstream.

THE REGIONS

Unlike Australia, where producers routinely blend wines from different areas, New Zealand's producers generally prefer to concentrate on single regions: most notably Hawke's Bay, Marlborough, Martinborough, Kumeu and Gisborne. That is not to say, however, that the larger wineries are loyal to the part of the country in which they are based: most offer ranges of wines representing the way particular grape varieties perform in particular regions.

Given the often uncertain nature of the climate – and the tendency of the North Island and South Island to enjoy quite different conditions – there is a clear argument that a more Australian attitude might sometimes not go amiss. A skilful blend of lean Chardonnay from Marlborough in the South Island and a richer example of this grape from Gisborne in the North Island could produce a stunning wine. So far, of the bigger wineries, Villa Maria remains the only forthright supporter of this kind of wine-making, but others may follow in its wake.

North Island

Professor Becker's impression of New Zealand as a cool-climate, southern hemisphere version of Germany makes little sense to anyone who has spent even a few days on the North Island. Ireland with the volume turned up would be an accurate description of this warm, damp, green, ultra-fertile land.

This is the part of the country where the most successful reds have been made – and, until recently, some of the less successful whites. The problem lay partly in that fertile soil: it was too easy to grow large amounts of grapes which never really ripened and were often subject to rot.

The answer lay either in finding regions with meaner soil, or in persuading the vines to be less fruitful by a combination of training and pruning that is now known by progressive grape-growers internationally as "canopy management". The father of this technique is Professor Richard Smart, a visionary who developed it after studying the way vines grow in the best parts of Bordeaux, and now travels the vineyards of the world applying the lessons he learned in New Zealand.

Northland

Northland, the region where wine-making really began in New Zealand, has been largely abandoned, although for two or three years it appeared as though this region might be the source of New Zealand's top red wine. Two lawyer brothers created a California-style mini-estate, grandly called it "The Antipodean", planted Bordeaux-style grape varieties, and presented their first wine "blind" to an audience of London wine experts, who were invited to compare it to a range of Bordeaux first-growths. The experts all spotted the New Zealand wine, but generally acknowledged the potential quality of the challenger.

The lawyers hyped the wine for all they were worth, sold every bottle they made for a very high price, had an argument and closed the winery. Today, the winery has been renamed Heron's Flight, but the Cabernet sold under this label is not from the vineyards originally used for The Antipodean.

Auckland

Until about 30 or so years ago the North Island had only two main wine regions: Auckland itself and Hawke's Bay. That number has now risen to five, plus the increasingly successful Waiheke Island, where the Goldwater Estate winery has produced some very impressive Cabernet-Merlot.

While Auckland still boasts an impressive set of wineries such as Matua Valley, Coopers Creek, Selaks and Nobilos, all of which are variously hitting the mark with white wines produced in various parts of the country, the wine-growing region of Kumeu near the city has recently been somewhat overlooked in the rush to areas with starrier reputations. But just taste the white and red wines Michael Brajkovich is making at

Kumeu River and the Chardonnay Collards are producing in their Rothesay vineyard, and you'll know that this is once again a region to watch.

At Henderson, 12 miles (20 km) to the west of Auckland, Babich and Delegats are the names to look out for while, to the south of the city, Villa Maria, the country's third-largest winery, regularly produces high-quality wines.

Further south still, Te Kauwhata, site of New Zealand's wine-research station, was once thought of as good red-wine country – particularly by the giant Cooks (now Cooks-Corbans) who made Cabernet Sauvignon here. Today, as the wine-making potential of other, less rainy, parts of New Zealand has been discovered, the black grapes have mostly been replaced by white ones. Three wineries that show what can be produced are Morton Estate, de Redcliffe and Rongopai.

Gisborne

Gisborne, out on the east coast, is one of those places whose name rings loud bells with any well-informed wine-drinker. Finding even a well-travelled wine expert who has actually been there, however, is another matter. For starters, while lots of big companies buy Gisborne Chardonnay, often using the name on their labels, only a handful of small estates are actually based in this region. The best-known names are Matawhero, makers of New Zealand's finest Gewürztraminer, and Millton Estate where James Millton has quietly built a reputation for some of the world's most reliable organic white wines, from both the Chardonnay and Chenin Blanc.

Gisborne's creamy Chardonnays deserve their growing reputation, but one cannot help wondering whether this region's greatest contribution to New Zealand wine might not be in blends with some of the more fruit-salady efforts produced in Marlborough.

Hawke's Bay

There are relatively few well-known thoroughfares in the wine world, but two to remember are Gimblett and Church Roads, on which are found some of the best vineyards of the sunny, holiday-resort region of Hawke's Bay.

The secret of this region's long-predicted success lies beneath your feet. Look at the gravel of the old river bed, and think claret. Then taste some of the Hawke's Bay Cabernets and Merlots made by wineries like CJ Pask, Brookfields and Ngatarawa. The whites can be top-class too – Montana's Church Road Chardonnay is one of the most reliable in the country, while Te Mata's Elston has long been a benchmark for this style.

It was John Buck of Te Mata who also first demonstrated what could be done with red wine in New Zealand with his Coleraine and Awatea Bordeaux-blends. While others have produced showier wines, these remain fine models for any wine-maker seeking to compete with the best of France.

Wairarapa/Martinborough

Known until recently as Martinborough after the town here, but now more commonly referred to by the regional name of Wairarapa, this wide, flat region has earned an instant reputation for its Burgundy-style reds and whites, but that's not all it can do. The superstar is Larry McKenna of Martinborough Vineyards, whose Pinot Noir and Chardonnay are among the best in the Antipodes. Palliser is good at these styles, too, but has also done well with Riesling, while Dry River is equally successful with Pinot Gris. Reds, apart from Pinot Noir, have been less impressive, though Ata Rangi has done the seemingly impossible, by making raspberryish Pinot Noir and richly spicy Shiraz, thus producing Burgundy and Rhône-style wine from grapes grown in almost the same vineyard. If only the Burgundians themselves had mastered this trick – just think how much effort they could have saved by not having to ship Syrah for blending up to Beaune in the good old days.

South Island

Marlborough

Blenheim airport makes no bones about its isolation in the north of the South Island: a signpost reveals just how many thousands of miles new arrivals are from most of the rest of the planet. But those arrivals have included some of the most distinguished wine-makers and experts in the world, all of whom have been attracted by what seems to be the made-in-heaven marriage of Sauvignon grape, Marlborough gravel and climate. The union between region and grape was first consummated in 1973 when the large Montana winery bought a dozen or so farms for a ludicrously low price and bravely planted around 400 hectares (1,000 acres) of vines. At the time, the variety chosen was, almost inevitably, the Müller-Thurgau. Fortunately, though, they experimentally filled a 25-hectare corner with Sauvignon, a grape that was then almost unknown in New Zealand.

The rest, as they say, is history. The vineyard area now covers nearly 20 times Montana's original plantation and land prices are ludicrously high: everyone, from Australians like Rothbury, Hill Smith and Mildara Blass to French Champagne houses like Laurent Perrier and Moët & Chandon, wants a slice of this gooseberry pie.

The only question hanging over the region is what styles of wine it should make. The Sauvignons and fizzes are acknowledged world-class success stories. There have been good Chardonnays – especially from Cloudy Bay – but few with the class of, say, Te Mata's Elston. Marlborough Gewürztraminer and Riesling are both delicious, but generally overlooked by a Chardonnay-obsessed world. As for reds, the jury is still out. Hunters have made some impressive Pinot Noir, and Corbans astonished New Zealand tasters with a Cabernet Merlot; even so, it is questionable whether Marlborough's marginal climate will allow these and other producers to hit the bull's-eye as often as they do with their whites.

Close to Marlborough, though, there is another valley where slightly different conditions seem better-suited to red wine. Awatere is the Châteauneuf-du-Pape of New Zealand – not because of the temperature, which is cooler than that of the southern Rhône, but because of the round stones on the terraces that store and reflect the heat of the day. For a taste of what South Island Cabernet can be like at its best, try the ones Vavasour is making here.

Nelson

One of the greatest country-bus rides in the world takes you from Marlborough westward through the folds of the hills to the almost unknown wine region of Nelson.

There are five wineries here, but only two that are producing good wine in any quantity. Tim and Judy Finn of Neudorf Vineyards and Hermann and Agnes Seifried of Weingut Seifried and Redwood Valley used ruefully to admit to having something of an inferiority complex. Years of being told by "experts" that their region was too cool, and less ideally suited to wine-growing than Marlborough or Hawke's Bay, for example, had their effect; wines from Nelson tended to cost less than those of other regions. But talent will out. Neudorf's Pinot Noir and Sémillon (one of the few New Zealand successes with this variety) are among the best in the Antipodes, while Seifried's late-harvest Redwood Valley Rieslings are good enough to teach many a big-name German estate a lesson.

Canterbury

Further south, Canterbury became famous as the cool, dry region in which was situated St Helena, the winery at which, in 1982, a Burgundy-mad wine-maker called Danny Schuster made New Zealand's first world-class Pinot Noir. Less successful subsequent vintages and hotter competition from wineries in other parts of the country have shifted the spotlight of attention away from this southern region, but Canterbury remains a name to watch. Its future may lie less with the Pinot Noir than with the Riesling, a variety in which the German-born Giesen family, who own the region's largest estate, fervently believe. But the Giesens are realists: some of their best wines are made from grapes grown further north in Marlborough.

Central Otago

If Canterbury is cool, Central Otago, the world's southernmost wine region, ought to be positively glacial. But geography is far more complicated than that: where other areas are cooled by sea breezes, this is an area surrounded by land. And, like other such places – Burgundy and the Northern Rhône (its latitudinal counterpart in the northern hemisphere) spring to mind – it enjoys warm summers and cool winters. Pinot Noir has been quite successful in Central Otago, but it is probable the cool nights, which temper the ripening effect of the hot days, will always make this a place to make white wine. And why not?

SOUTH AFRICA

The election of Nelson Mandela as head of state was almost certainly the best thing that could ever have happened to the wine-makers of the Cape – though I doubt that many of them saw it that way at the time. After all, the ruling National Party had, for decades, repaid their votes by featherbedding their industry with a system of quotas and minimum prices. It was thanks to the government that South Africa's annual surplus of grapes – around half the harvest – enjoyed a guaranteed price and found just as guaranteed a home in distilleries where it was converted into industrial alcohol or brandy for export to liqueur producers in countries like France.

Since South Africa's re-admission into world markets, the picture has changed completely. Today, the surplus has virtually disappeared as wine-drinkers in the Netherlands, Britain, Scandinavia and North America, who once fastidiously avoided Cape reds and whites, now queue to sample the efforts of one of the latest passengers on the New-World bandwagon.

Ironically, though, South Africa first climbed on to that wagon long before most of the other New-World countries. In fact, as the proud Boers readily remind outsiders, this is a place where wine has been produced for over 300 years. During the 1960s, before Robert Mondavi had opened the doors of his Napa Valley winery and in the days when most red Australian table wine was indistinguishable from port, South Africa was internationally recognized for the quality of its reds, fortified wines and late-harvest whites.

From the outset, the achingly beautiful region close to Capetown looked an ideal place to grow grapes, with a naturally warm climate tempered by the proximity of the coast, and hills whose slopes cried out to be dressed in vineyards. But, as any wine-maker will tell you, climate and site are only two of a number of essential components that go to make up a wine. Without good soil, grape-growing and wine-making, you might as well have cool, non-stop, wet weather from one end of the season to the other – and South Africa had problems on all three fronts.

The years of isolation did the Cape no good. As the rest of the world's wine industry developed new techniques, South Africa's remained stuck in a conservative groove, brushing fundamental problems under the carpet, and using ordinary grape varieties to make similarly ordinary, old-fashioned wines. Acid soils in much of the flatter land, and vine diseases, said to affect up to 90 per cent of the vineyards, prevented the grapes from ripening fully, and made for harsh, "green" flavours reminiscent of Bordeaux in a cold year. These were, supposedly, softened by ageing in big old casks, but the warmth of the cellars and the state of the wood in those barrels often gave the finished wine a smoky, stewy, cooked character that made South Africa's reds some of the easiest to spot in blind tastings.

Even when attempts were made to join the modern wine-making world, they often went sadly awry. One of the Cape's first shipments of Chardonnay vines proved, for example, to be another, lesser variety. New oak barrels, bought at great expense from cynical French coopers, turned out to have been insufficiently dried and, instead of imparting an attractive, sweet vanilla flavour, merely amplified the green nature of wines made from those unripe grapes.

White wine-making, though generally far more successful, suffered from the influence of the German wine school in Geisenheim, an establishment with which the Cape producers generally had far more contact than they did with its counterparts in California and Australia. The Germans encouraged the South Africans to follow their European quantity-at-the-expense-of-quality lead by increasing production in the vineyards and stripping flavour out of the juice and wines by heavy-handed filtration.

If South Africa's wine-makers were handicapped by their isolation, they also hobbled themselves by setting up an extraordinary set of constraints. A monolithic organization called the KWV, originally formed for the best of reasons at a time of chronic wine surplus, was allowed to control the entire industry in a way unknown elsewhere in the capitalist world. For example, quotas were established that deterred adventurous wine-makers from exploring new regions and styles. When Tim Hamilton-Russell first began to make what was to become South Africa's first successful Pinot Noir in the now-vaunted region of Walker Bay, he had to sell it under a code name which merely hinted at the identity of the grape from which it was made.

Inevitably, there was a political angle too. The National party relied on the grape-farmers for their votes, so had every reason to allow them, and the co-operatives to which they belonged, to continue to use second-rate grape varieties like the Welsch Riesling to make second-rate wine.

Efforts to promote quality wine were generally misconceived. Large appellation districts such as Stellenbosch and Paarl were established and promoted and a system initiated vaguely mimicking that of France's *Appellation Contrôlée*. On paper, this, like the paper seals introduced to mark quality wines, seemed quite sensible. In practical terms, however, the rules were unnecessarily stricter than those operating in France. In Bordeaux, grapes may legally move around with impunity within the region and within communes; a top-flight château can buy in Cabernet Sauvignon harvested by any of its neighbours, provided that the land on which they were grown falls within the same *appellation* as its vines. In the Cape, estates were forbidden to bring in wine or grapes from outside their own land. Compare this with the Australian model where such famous estates as Rosemount produce wine across states, and Rothbury's Estate appears to extend beneath the sea to reappear in New Zealand. The South African rules – which were finally changed in 1995 – may satisfy the purists; but it is the wine-drinkers who benefit from the more relaxed Antipodean legislations.

Another Gallic tradition that was followed too slavishly in the Cape was the division of labour between wine-making, maturing and bottling. Until very recently, like British upper-class parents despatching their offspring to boarding school, most of the Cape's most prestigious wineries happily handed over responsibility for the ageing and bottling of their wines to the huge Bergkelder. In doing so, they were behaving as the châteaux of Bordeaux used to with their local merchants. Except, that, following the lead of Philippe de Rothschild who decided 50 years ago to bottle every drop of Mouton Rothschild at the château himself, even the humblest Bordeaux producer has since insisted on maturing his own wine.

This review of the background to the industry is essential if one is to appreciate just how traumatic an experience South Africa's wine-makers have undergone in recent years – and the challenge many of them have faced in adapting to the modern world of wine-making.

Today, the spirit of peaceful revolution is becoming as apparent in the vineyards and wineries as in every other facet of South African life. An army of wine-buyers and investors from other countries has poured through the gates of Cape Town airport while Cape wine-makers have travelled the world learning how things are now being done elsewhere.

The infected vines have been largely cleared from the vineyards and replaced in what has to be the most sophisticated programme of plant husbandry in the world. Previously little-grown varieties – principally Chardonnay and Merlot – have been planted and modern European, Californian and Antipodean wine-making methods introduced.

The first evidence of change came with the improvement in the quality of the Cape's fresh, inexpensive, light, dry and off-dry white wines: Sauvignons, Chardonnays and the Cape's local success story, Chenin Blancs or Steens. Hard on their heels, and even more impressive, were sparkling wines – known here as Méthode Cap Classique – good enough to see off all but the best examples of Champagne, let alone most efforts from other parts of the New World.

The reds, however, and the more serious whites have taken longer to get right. Too many producers – and their local customers – are so used to unripe-tasting wines that they distrust the richer, more accessible styles produced by some of their more go-ahead neighbours, even when these have been supported by such highly qualified visitors as Paul Pontallier of Château Margaux who is involved with making the wine at the impressive new Plaisir de Merle winery. How, the traditionalists want to know, will the new-wave, ripe-tasting wines age? Like a 1982 claret, comes the confident reply, from foreign critics and from local producers, basking in the unfamiliar sensation of international approval. And not, they might have added, in the mean way of 1975 Bordeaux which sometimes seems to have been the Cape producers' preferred model.

The move toward more sensitive wine-making encouraged by Pontallier has brought some surprises. Until recently, foreigners tended to be polite about the wines made from the Pinotage, an odd South African grape with the characteristics of its joint Burgundian and Rhône parentage. Usually, though, they switched their attention from these often muddy-tasting wines to the more conventional appeal of the Cabernet Sauvignon.

Today, however, the newer-wave wine-makers are discovering unsuspected potential in the Pinotage which reveals it to be as ideal a grape for fresh, Beaujolais-style wines as for rich, spicy reds to set against the Shirazes of Australia and the wines of the Rhône in France. New styles have been developed too, for the Merlot and Pinot Noir – grape varieties almost unknown in the Cape a decade or so ago.

There is still a fair degree of confusion over the direction the wines of the Cape ought to be taking. Some producers reasonably wonder whether the overseas market is not pushing them toward making "big", Australian-style wines, but a growing number are proving that South Africa doesn't have to copy anywhere else – and that they can produce reds and whites with a unique combination of New-World fruit and Old-World subtlety.

THE REGIONS

The future of South Africa's finest wines depends – as in California – on producers shaking off the reverence they have had for over-large and actually quite disparate regions such as Stellenbosch and Paarl, and the realization of the need to promote far smaller areas, the character of which are only now becoming clear. So far, only Walker Bay has been demarcated according to the sort of wines it produced; all the others, including old warhorses like Stellenbosch, were marked out according to already existing administrative boundaries.

THE ESSENTIALS

AFRICA

What to look for Evolving styles in South Africa.
Official quality South Africa has long had a Wine of Origin system. The regions and sub-regions are: Coastal region: Swartland, Tulbagh, Paarl, Stellenbosch, Constantia, Durbanville, Boberg; Breede River Valley region: Worcester, Robertson, Swellendam; Klein Karoo region; Olijantsriver Region; Overberg; Piketberg; Northern Cape: Lower Orange River, Douglas.
Style North Africa produces all styles of wine, not all attractive to European palates; best are Algerian and Moroccan reds, full-bodied and rustic with a slightly coarse flavour, and Tunisian Muscats which range from the sweet Vin de Muscat de Tunisie to the dry, fragrant Muscat de Kelibia. Grenache-based Moroccan rosé can be pleasant. South Africa's best-sited

vineyards should produce great wine, but top-class examples are still rare. Zimbabwe's attempts to produce wine are hindered by heavy rains during harvest.
Climate North Africa is, of course, hot and dry, as is most of South Africa, though the coast is cooler and wetter.
Cultivation Rich alluvial soils predominate in the flat coastal plains of North Africa, while the cooler hill sites inland have limestone, sand and volcanic soils. South Africa's often acidic soils vary from the sandy gravels of the coastal area to the lime-rich soils inland.
Grape varieties North Africa: Alicante Bouschet, Cabernet Franc, Cabernet Sauvignon, Carignan, Cinsault, Clairette, Grenache, Merseguera, Mourvèdre, Morastel, Syrah, Pinot Noir, Ugni

Blanc; South Africa: Cabernet Sauvignon, Pinotage, Syrah, Sauvignon Blanc, Chenin Blanc, Chardonnay, Muscat d'Alexandre.
Production/maturation In North Africa, a strong French influence persists, notably in grape varieties and appellations. The African climate necessitates strict harvesting control and cool fermentation.

Top 20 Algeria: Cuvée du Président; South Africa: Meerlust, Hamilton-Russell, Thelema, Fairview, Plaisir de Merle, Vergelegen, Boschendal, Kanonkop, Simonsig (sparkling), Nederburg (late-harvest), Allesverloren, Mulderbosch, Vriesenhof, Rustenberg, Klein Constantia, Buitenverwachting, Blaauwklippen, Nederburg Auction Wines, Clos Cabrière.

Coastal Region

Stellenbosch and Paarl

The best-known regions, the first of which owes its name to the quaint Cape Dutch university town, are quite disparate. Temperatures can vary significantly, from North African to Burgundian, depending on the effects of the sea breezes and of the altitude of the vineyards. The soils are far from homogenous too: some are acidic, others sandy. The best wines will come from hillside vineyards, especially those around the Helderberg mountain, and from valleys like Franschoek where producers like Boschendal, Dieu Donné, l'Ormarins and Clos Cabrière are to be found.

Constantia

For a decent drink in this region, you would be advised to head for Klein Constantia where a delicious replica of the sweet Muscat wine for which this region was once as famous as Sauternes and Tokaj, called Vin de Constance, is now being made. Today Constantia is enjoying a renaissance, thanks to its sea-cooled climate. Buitenverwachting is recommended here as is the recently opened Steenberg.

Olifants River

A hot, productive northerly region where the huge Vredendal co-operative is now proving that it can produce classily labelled, world-class, light, easy-drinking whites with the memorable Goiya Kgeisje.

Walker Bay/Elgin

The apple-growing region of Elgin has rapidly become one of the most exciting in South Africa – for the whites made by Neil Ellis and by Newald Marais of Nederburg for Paul Cluver, a brain surgeon. Walker Bay, the southernmost vineyard region of the Cape, was pioneered by Tim Hamilton-Russell with Pinot Noir and Chardonnay. His lead was followed by Bouchard Finlayson, a joint venture between Burgundian merchant Paul Bouchard and local wine-maker Peter Finlayson.

Robertson

This is a warm region where lime soil makes for better-balanced wines, and a dynamic co-operative makes highly successful commercial white wines. Look out, too, for Chardonnays made here at de Wetshof.

Swartland/Tulbagh

Warm temperatures and yields kept low by a lack of irrigation make this region ideal for intense, long-lived Pinotage and Shiraz. Allesverloren is also worth watching.

ZIMBABWE AND KENYA

The economic sanctions of the 1960s forced Zimbabwe into wine-making. The stuff they have made has been a triumph of optimism, effort and ingenuity over climatic adversity. Every year, it rains at almost precisely the time when the grapes are ready to be picked, so rot and dilution are major problems. Nor have the producers been helped by the poor quality of many of the types of grapes and of the soil in which they have been grown. For outsiders, the wines remain curiosities – as do the small quantities of wine produced by Kenya in its two annual harvests.

NORTH AFRICA

In 1995 an opinion poll was held in France which asked 1,000 consumers to name as many brands of wine as they could recall: most were unable to name a single brand. The ones who could, came up with an interesting top four: Château Margaux, Mouton Rothschild, Kriter (an undistinguished French fizz) and … Sidi Brahim. The familiarity of this Algerian brand is a handy reminder of the relationship which existed between France and North Africa in the 1950s and 1960s.

Given the growing influence in Algeria of Islamic fundamentalists, however, and their less-than-sympathetic attitude toward wine, there is little chance of this country modernizing its vineyards. Indeed, as vines die of old age, they are not being replanted and production will continue to dwindle from the once-huge figures of the nineteenth century.

Morocco's vineyards are rapidly shrinking, but wineries like the Domaine de Sahari are bucking the trend by making good Bordeaux-style reds. The wine to drink with the greatest confidence in Tunisia is Muscat which, at its best, can be of world standard.

THE OTHER WINES
OF THE WORLD

INDIA

One of the very nastiest tastings experienced was of an impromptu line-up of Indian wines bought from a busy retailer in the heart of Bombay. The contents of the screwtop bottles were so bad, and so far removed from even the feeblest efforts at wine-making elsewhere, that the best way to treat them was as a kind of satire. However, as a small step toward redeeming India's vinous reputation, it is possible to find one or two gems hidden away, such as a sparkling wine produced in high-altitude vineyards a day's drive from the city with the help of expertise imported from Champagne.

Variously labelled as Omar Khayyam and Marquise de Pompadour, it was initially made largely from the basic Emerald Riesling, though subsequent bottlings have included Chardonnay. It is perfectly drinkable stuff, provided you catch it young, and the same Indage winery's red and white Riviera wines offer an alternative to poorly cellared European imports. Even so, given the choice, a bottle of locally brewed Elephant beer would be preferable.

JAPAN

The vineyards of Bordeaux and Burgundy have featured surprisingly rarely in movies – and none has provided as dramatic a setting as one of Japan's did in the final scenes of the Michael Douglas thriller *Black Rain*. Unfortunately, despite the growing Japanese enthusiasm for buying fine wine at international auctions and more basic wine from vending machines, and despite heavy investment, high-tech equipment and expertise and vineyards dotted around all but one of Japan's 47 provinces, the stuff in the bottle is certainly rather less memorable.

Wine is no novelty for the Japanese; they have known about it since the twelfth century when the Muscat-like Koshu grape was apparently grown with some success.

The problems for Japan's would-be wine-makers are a lack of space and a climate – monsoons, earthquakes, typhoons and worst of all, general humidity – that waterlogs the often over-acidic soil, encourages all kinds of bugs and diseases and dilutes the juice in the grapes.

These conditions are best suited to local grapes, few of which would pass international muster, and hybrids such as the unspectacular Delaware, grown because of their early ripening and resistance to all those diseases. All of which helps to explain why the Japanese import such huge quantities of concentrated grape juice from other countries which they blend with a little local juice, labelling the result as Japanese.

Apart from offering examples of these pseudo-Japanese wines (is there anyone in Tokyo pulling the same stunt with European hi-fi or cameras?), whisky

Protecting grapes with paper bags in Japan

THE ESSENTIALS

ASIA

What to look for Memorably off-beat drinking experiences. (Keep a pot of tea or a can or two of lager in reserve, however.)

Official quality You have to be joking.

Style In the Far East plenty of thick, sweet, very unpleasant wine is still produced, but reasonable dry whites are made with French grape varieties under French or Australian supervision in China. The technically well-made Indian Omar Khayyam (méthode champenoise) can be a pleasant alternative to Spanish Cava.

Climate Conditions in India are, of course, extremely hot and dry. China's wine-producing areas are generally cool, tempered by the Pacific and Indian oceans. Japan's wine production is at the whim of a climate of extremes with summer typhoons, spring and autumn monsoons and freezing winters, hence the readiness to use imported concentrate.

Cultivation In both China and Japan, the best vineyard sites are on south-facing slopes. China has good alluvial soils; those of Japan are more acidic.

Grape varieties Cabernet Sauvignon, Chardonnay, Ugni Blanc, Pinot Noir, Muscat and Merlot are being introduced. Otherwise India: Ariab-e-Shahi, Arka Kanchan and Arka Shyam; China: Beichun, Dragon's Eye, Cow's Nipple and Cock's Heart; Japan: mostly labrusca vines such as Campbell's Early and Delaware and hybrids, together with the native Koshu vinifera. Suntory uses Bordeaux varieties.

Production/maturation Increasing use of modern techniques throughout the regions.

Longevity None, though some late-harvest Japanese efforts can last.

Vintages (see above)

Top 5 India: Indage (Omar Khayyam/ Marquise de Pompadour); China: Great Wall, Dynasty; Japan: Suntory (Château Lion), Château Lumiere.

giant Suntory tries hard to make French-style wines using traditional French varieties grown in genuinely Japanese soil. Their best wine is probably the Yquem lookalike Château Lion Noble Sémillon, produced from grapes whose bunches are protected from the elements by little paper hats. It costs Yquem-like prices, too and would certainly be a welcome gift to Japanese hosts. Most Japanese wine-lovers would, however, prefer something from overseas – such as a bottle from the (Japanese-owned) Ridge Vineyards in California, Château Lagrange in Bordeaux or Robert Weil in Germany.

CHINA

The sleeping – or more properly waking – giant of the industrial world may well be about to rise from its vinous slumbers. As in Japan, wine once featured as strongly on the cultural agenda as it did in many parts of Europe.

Wine was being imported as early as 128 BC and, in the thirteenth century, Marco Polo described the Shangsi province as growing "many excellent vines". Sadly, over the succeeding years, the lines between distilled drink (the Chinese may have invented the process), grape wine and rice wine became quite blurred. When Rémy Martin announced the launch of its Great Wall co-production of wine and rice wine in the 1980, it was the first modern effort at Chinese wine-making to reach the rest of the world.

By 1993, however, China was producing some 500 million bottles: 10 times as much wine as New Zealand and more than other high-profile countries such as Chile, Greece, Austria and Bulgaria. More dramatically, it has a larger area of vineyards than Germany, South Africa and Australia.

If you haven't yet managed to come across one of those bottles, don't worry; until now, with the exception of occasional sightings of Dynasty and Great Wall offered as curiosities by wine merchants and Chinese restaurants, most of the wine is light, white and off-dry and – like Chinese computers, cars and washing machines – intended for sale to an increasingly enthusiastic local market. And, like those cars and washing machines, their production involves a great deal of foreign expertise – in this instance French and Australian.

But, just like the Japanese, the Chinese are rapidly (re-)developing their taste for European-style wine. It is chastening to think that, when the 1995 vintage of Bordeaux came onto the market in 1996, large numbers of cases which might once have gone to London or New York were sold to keen wine-drinkers in Hong Kong. When we get to the 2005 vintage, those Hong Kong claret enthusiasts may well have to compete with buyers in Beijing. All of which should help to encourage a new breed of quality Chinese wine-makers.

BEER

Ask many people to impart their entire knowledge of beer, and it's likely they will run out of inspiration after telling you that there are two types – lager and bitter – and that one is cold, fizzy and golden, while the other is warm, flat and dark. But, as we'll see in this section, that doesn't even scratch the surface of the subject of the world's oldest alcoholic drink.

From its origins in Egypt and Babylon several thousand years BC, beer has travelled a circuitous – and often perilous – route. Roman historians report that ale was drunk by the Saxons and Celts among others, and many of the terms used in brewing even have their origin in the Anglo-Saxon language.

Thanks to the enterprise and creativity of monastic orders and the church in general, brewing skills were preserved and refined – during the somewhat dissolute period of the Middle Ages – and the beer market almost completely sewn up into the bargain.

The Industrial Revolution in the eighteenth and nineteenth centuries transformed the brewing industry, introducing large-scale mechanization and better temperature control, and allowing for a more reliable end product. The work of the French chemist, Louis Pasteur, in the 1860s also revolutionized brewing with advances in microbiology that are still in widespread use today.

Increasing globalization looked as if it would sound the death-knell of specialist brewers in the latter half of the twentieth century, as the multinational brewing concerns swallowed up many of the minnows. But, thankfully, a backlash against rationalization and perceived mediocrity – led by the likes of the Campaign for Real Ale (CAMRA) in the UK – has revitalized specialist brewing and preserved breadth of choice for the beer drinker. At the beginning of the twenty-first century, beer is undoubtedly on a high.

So next time you take a trip to your local off-licence or supermarket, walk past the cans and bottles of mass-produced bitter and lager, and seek out the more unusual brews on offer today. And for really esoteric beers, don't forget the Internet – a number of specialist importers out there are eagerly waiting to introduce you to the delights of ultra-strong Belgian Trappist brews, the golden beers of the Czech Republic, or Californian steam beer.

Opposite: *Inside the Winter Bierhaus in Vienna (detail from a 1901 watercolour by Wilhelm Gause, 1853–1916)*

THE HISTORY OF BEER

"I feel wonderful, drinking beer in a blissful mood, with joy in my heart and a happy liver." These words were not written by someone in the corner of a pub one Friday night, but by a Sumerian poet around the year 3,000 BC. For beer is as old as history. Glasses of modern ale, lager or stout have their roots deep in ancient civilizations stretching back to the dawn of time.

The words of that Sumerian poet are revealing. He knew that beer not only made him feel cheerful, but was also good for his health. For most of recorded time, water was insanitary and unsafe. People could refresh themselves, however, by drinking alcohol, which contains antiseptic qualities, and in which water has been boiled. Fruit quickly perished in the ancient world, while grain could be stored for long periods. So beer, more than wine, became the drink of the people. Since it was made from a vitamin-rich porridge, beer made them content, flushed out their livers and kidneys, and kept both heart and skin diseases at bay. Along with bread, beer was a vital part of a staple diet.

ANCIENT ORIGINS

Beer, according to some anthropologists, helped create civilized society. When people of the ancient world realized they could make bread and beer from grain, they stopped roaming and settled down to cultivate cereals in recognizable communities. The American anthropologist Alan Eames says: "Ten thousand years ago... barley was domesticated and worshipped as a god in the highlands of the southern Levant. Thus was beer the driving force that led nomadic mankind into village life." At that time, the world was a warmer place than today by two to three degrees Celsius. North Africa and the Middle East enjoyed a much heavier rainfall than they do today and the warm, moist climate encouraged the growth of cereals. It has been suggested by some experts that beer came before bread, that ancient people learned to make a pleasant, relaxing drink from soaked grain. It is more likely, however, that the reverse was the case: wet dough was left to rise in the open, starches turned to sugar by natural enzymic activity, and then wild yeasts in the air turned the sugars into alcohol.

Brewing became a major industry in the ancient world. Clay tablets with cuneiform writing discovered in Nineveh in the 1840s showed that beer was paid as a form of currency to stonemasons working on the great buildings of the pharoahs. The role of the brewer was sufficiently important for him or her – many women were brewers – to have their own hieroglyph: "fty". A drawing made with a stylus on wet clay shows a person bent over a vessel straining a cereal mash through a sieve. Spices and plants were added to primitive beer as flavourings and to prolong the life of the drink. In Egypt, beer was drunk by the upper classes through reeds to prevent the husks of the grain being swallowed.

The early beers

The two main cereals used by ancient people in brewing were barley and a type of wheat called "emmer". The first beers were made from raw grain and would have been thin in alcohol, using the small amount of natural sugar present in the ears of wheat and barley. A giant step forward came in the second and third millennia, when brewers in Mesopotamia learned to turn barley into malt. Malting may have been accidental at first. Raw grain was left to soak and then dried in the sun. Magically, the grain had yielded up its starches and sugar caused a violent fermentation, resulting in a drink that was rich in alcohol. Malting rapidly became sophisticated and the Mesopotamians were able to produce dark, as well as light, beer by scorching the malt over fire.

The first brewers had no understanding of yeast. They knew only that when they made beer, the deposits from previous brews left in their clay vessels spontaneously turned the liquid into alcohol. Lactic acid bacteria in the vessels would also have attacked the sugary solution, giving a sour but quenching character to the beer, while wild airborne yeasts would also have had a role to play. No hops were used, as the plant was not known at the time. A major study of brewing in Babylon and Egypt, published in Germany in 1926, described the Babylonians as using unmalted emmer wheat and malted barley. It seems that from very early in the history of brewing, brewers discovered that barley malt produced the best extract of sugars, while wheat gave a fine tart and fruity character to beer. The brewers first made "beer bread", which was baked either light or dark brown, depending on the colour of beer required. A mash was then made by pouring heated water over the bread. It was filtered and left to ferment spontaneously. When fermentation finished, the rough beer was transferred to smaller vessels which were stored in cool cellars where a secondary fermentation occurred.

Beer-making in Egypt

The Egyptians, on the other hand, used all malted grain and produced only dark-coloured beer. Plants, such as mandrake, and salt were added. The plants were used to balance the sweetness of the malt, while salt is a flavour-enhancer (it was still used in brewing until the nineteenth century AD). Brewing in the ancient world was not, like modern home-brewing, a sideline, but a major industry. The Pharaoh Rameses gave 10,000 hectolitres a year of free beer to his temple administrators – and that amount was just the tip of the pyramid!

A matter of taste

All the knowledge of brewing in the ancient world unearthed by anthropologists and Egyptologists left one tantalizing question unanswered, however: what did beer of the period taste like? The answer came thanks to the remarkable work of Fritz Maytag, owner of the Anchor Brewery in San Francisco. In the 1980s, Maytag contacted scholars throughout the world, who gave him detailed descriptions of how beer had been brewed in ancient civilizations.

Maytag used recipes found on tablets from Sumeria in 3,000 BC and began by making 5,000 loaves of "bappir" bread from barley, roasted barley and barley malt. The loaves were baked twice to ensure they were dry in the centre, and were then cut into strips. The finished bread looked remarkably like Weetabix breakfast cereal.

The loaves were placed in the brewery's mash tun, along with some additional barley malt. Maytag had discovered – in a song dedicated to the goddess of brewing, Ninkasi – that sweetness was added twice to Sumerian beer. So he added honey to the mash and dates (for a touch of spiciness) to the beer. No hops were used. Ninkasi beer, as it was called, was not sold commercially but it was drunk at a banquet in the USA. Guests were invited to drink it through straws in the approved manner of the ancient world. It was five per cent alcohol and had an orange-red colour. As the sweetness from the honey and dates had fermented, the beer was remarkably dry and refreshing. It was not bitter but, made from an ancient recipe almost lost in the dust of time, it was clearly and definably *beer*.

Islamic invasion

The art of brewing in Egypt and the surrounding lands was ended abruptly in the eighth century AD by the invasion of the Muslims and a Koran that banned the use of alcohol. But the secret was out. The Phoenicians, great sea-going traders, had taken cereals to other countries, and brewing developed in Bavaria and Bohemia, as well as spreading north to the Baltic and across the sea to the British Isles. As the world's climate changed yet again, wine-making was confined to the hot Mediterranean countries as grapes struggled to flourish in the cooler north. But from northern Spain to the Arctic Circle hardy cereals grew in abundance, and the peoples of that vast territory brewed with vigour, not only to refresh themselves, but also to keep healthy with the aid of a drink that was rich in vitamin B.

The skill of brewers exceeded that of wine-makers. Cooperage – fashioning casks from heated and hooped staves of wood – allowed brewers to store their beers in large, air-tight containers. The Romans and the Greeks, by comparison, were still using the older technology of clay pots in which to store wine. In 21 AD, Strabo noted seeing wooden "pithoi" in Northern Europe. "The Celts are fine coopers," he wrote, "for their casks are larger than houses." As the Romans marched across Europe, they saw that from Spain northwards, the tribes made beer. "The nations of the west have their own intoxicant from grain soaked in water," wrote Pliny; "there are many ways of making it in Gaul or Spain and under different names, though the principle is the same. The Spanish have taught us that these liquors keep well." In Britain, the Celtic tribes made a beer they called "curmi". They also made cider from apples and mead from honey. In the Scottish Highlands, the tradition was to use heather, both as a flavouring and also to aid the fermentation of barley malt in brewing. The Romans, however, were unimpressed by beer and preferred to drink wine. But when supplies of wine ran out, they turned to brewing in order to keep their troops happy and healthy. Recent excavations of Roman sites in England have discovered large maltings, which suggests that brewing was carried out on a regular and organized basis.

There was no Roman diffidence about drinking beer when northern Europe was overrun by the Danes and Saxons, since they already had a great beer-drinking culture based on feasts – and every day seemed to offer the excuse for a feast of some type. From this period comes the expression "wassail" for a boozy celebration. Even Valhalla (paradise), according to Norse myth, was a great hall where the dead passed their time drinking beer, while in the living world, beer or malt were used to pay fines, tolls, rents and debts.

The first pub

Brewing was confined to the home and it was the responsibility of the woman of the house – the ale wife – to ensure the men were kept well supplied. A good ale wife was held in great esteem: Alreck, King of Hordoland, chose Geirhild to be his queen not because of her looks or her dowry, but because she brewed good ale. It was natural to make beer at the same time as bread, as key ingredients were common to both. Gradually, the best ale wives or brewsters became so celebrated in their communities that people would go to their houses to drink and, eventually, to buy ale. When a brew was ready, the ale wife would put a long pole covered in evergreens through a window. This "ale stake" was the first rudimentary ale-house sign. In England, pubs called the Bush or Hollybush commemorate the ale stake, and when a new pub is opened, a garland of evergreens is hung over the door for luck. But the Romans can lay claim to the first inn sign. A chequer board would be hung outside a building that both sold wine or beer and also changed money. There are still many English pubs called the Chequers.

The Nordic people called their beer öl or ealu, from which came the term "ale". Another Saxon term for beer was woet, which survives today as "wort", the sweet liquid made by mashing malt and water. For centuries, ale meant a drink made from the fermented sugars of malt and flavoured by plants, herbs and spices – but not hops. Beer, from the German bier, came later and was ale with the addition of hops. Today, both words are used in ale-drinking countries, but all modern beer – including mild ale, pale ale and winter ale – is made with hops. Ironically, the British could have used hops in their early ales, as the plant was eaten as a delicacy by the Romans. But the British, in common with brewers in mainland Europe, preferred to use other plants, such as bog myrtle, rosemary and yarrow.

The Germans and Scandinavians added a mixture of herbs called gruit. In Scandinavia, juniper was a common addition to beer. This use of spices and berries in brewing almost certainly influenced the first distillers of spirits from grain, such as gin and vodka.

THE EARLY HISTORY OF BEER

Throughout Europe, a small commercial brewing movement started to spread, almost always based on inns and taverns where the owners brewed ale. When the Normans invaded England, they brought with them a powerful love of wine and cider. But the locals went on doggedly brewing ale. The Norman Domesday Book in 1086, a remarkable survey of the lives of the English, recorded 43 cervisiarii, or commercial ale brewers, who could be fined four shillings or ducked in the village pond if they made malam cerevisiam faciens (bad ale).

Commercial brewers, however, soon found a major competitor – in the form of the Christian church. Archbishops, abbots and clerics had stepped in to cure the excesses of the Anglo-Saxons and to corner the market in ale. Ale was brewed for monks as a staple

A medieval brewer takes beer samples from his barrels

part of their diet and it was also offered to the hordes of pilgrims who visited monasteries and sought food and drink. The Benedictines were the most enthusiastic brewers, though other orders were quick to emulate them. In medieval Germany there were 400–500 monastic breweries.

Ecclesiastical Heritage

Monastic brewhouses were enormous. The Abbey of St Gaull in Switzerland in the ninth century had a

malthouse, kiln, and millroom for grinding the malt, as well as three brewhouses and storage cellars. The malthouse was big enough to allow four different "couches" of grain to be laid out for germination. To make beer, the monks used barley, oats and wheat. The partially germinated green malt was heated in a kiln, which had a central chimney round which were placed wickerwork platforms covered with material. The grain was spread out on the material and heated from below by wood fire. After kilning, the malt was ground by

In Elizabethan times, beer was commonly drunk by the whole family

hand and then mixed with water in an open copper vessel that was heated by fire.

Monastic brewhouses were built near rivers. Clairvaux Abbey in France used water power to grind the grain, provide liquor for the mash, and wash away the detritus after brewing. Smaller abbeys that didn't have malthouses would leave the grain on grassy ground overnight and the dew would start germination. When the grain sprouted, it was moved to a rudimentary kiln and heated by laying it on a hair cloth above a hearth. The malt was chewed to test it for softness and friability. The holy brewers preferred soft water and added soap to get the required effect. The mash was stirred with a wooden fork and when the wort simmered round the handle, it was estimated that saccharification (changing starch into sugar) had taken place. After this the wort was allowed to cool and then ladled into wooden casks which were known as "rounds". This was then mixed with yeast. When fermentation was complete, the tuns were sealed to allow the *cervoise* (from the Latin for ale, *cerevisia*) to mature and undergo a secondary fermentation.

The best record of medieval brewing came from the Queen's College brewhouse at Oxford University. It was built in 1340 and had changed little by the time it was destroyed by bombs in the Second World War. The mash tun was made of memel oak and had two outlet pipes covered with strainers to keep back the grain. The sugary extract – wort – flowed to an underback, or collecting vessel, below the mash tun and was then pumped manually to an open copper boiled by heat from a furnace.

Hops were not used when the brewery was first built, although boiling the wort was essential to kill bacteria. After boiling, the wort was cooled in large open wooden pans called cool ships, then ladled into a large wooden round where yeast was pitched. Once fermentation had started, the wort was taken in a vessel called a tun dish to casks in the cellar, where fermentation continued. Troughs were arranged below the casks to collect the yeast that frothed out of the bung holes – a modified version of the system survives in Marston's Brewery in Burton-on-Trent. When fermentation was finished, the casks were sealed and left to condition. The strength of this College Ale was around seven per cent alcohol by volume. A Chancellor's Ale of twice the strength was also brewed occasionally.

Elizabethan Times

Ale brewing was different from modern practice in one key way: beers of different strength would be made from just one mash of malt. A strong beer would be made first, then the malt would be mixed with liquor for a second and third time to produce ales of declining strength. Monks called the strongest ale *prima melior* and kept it for the abbot and his distinguished guests. The second brew, *secunda*, was given to lay workers in the monasteries, while the brothers and poor pilgrims had to make do with a weak *tertia*. In Elizabethan times, Shakespeare immortalized *tertia* as "small beer". It was drunk by nursing mothers and children, as milk was unsafe. In 1512, the household records of the noble Percy family of Northumberland showed they consumed for breakfast each day during Lent a quart of ale for "my lord and lady", two pints for "my lady's gentlewoman" and one and a half gallons for the gentlemen of the chapel and the children. Small beer would have been around three per cent alcohol or less. In seventeenth-century Amsterdam, children in the civic orphanage were given a pint of small beer a day, as milk was thought to be infected with tuberculosis.

It should not, however, be thought that people in earlier times were in a state of perpetual drunkenness. Most of them were engaged in heavy manual labour and so would have quickly sweated off the alcohol. Moreover, houses were poorly heated and ale provided an easy form of internal warmth. Also, the overwhelming majority of the population lived lives of abject poverty. They had to sell cattle, poultry and eggs to the towns to survive and had a repetitive diet of thin vegetable soup and bread. So ale played a vital part in keeping them healthy.

The malthouse at Fountains Abbey in Yorkshire measured 60 square feet and the monks produced 60 barrels of strong ale every 10 days, the equivalent of almost 17,000 pints. The Domesday Book recorded that the monks of St Paul's Cathedral in London brewed 67,814 gallons of ale a year, or 542,512 pints. English ale was considered to be of high quality. Thomas à Becket, who became Archbishop of Canterbury and was murdered in his cathedral, brewed ale as a young priest for the Benedictine monks of St Albans Abbey in Hertfordshire. In 1158, he took two chariot-loads of ale on a diplomatic mission to France. The ale was "decocted from choice fat grain as a gift for the French who wondered at such an invention – a drink most wholesome, clear of all dregs, rivalling wine in colour and surpassing it in flavour".

Commercial Brewing

At different periods of European history, the dissolution of monasteries broke the church's power over brewing. This was seen most dramatically in England when Henry VIII sacked the monasteries as part of his long-running dispute with Rome. Centuries later, monks forced out of France at the time of the revolution moved north into the Low Countries, started to brew and began the tradition of Trappist ales that survives to this day. In general, though, the decline of monastic brewing paved the way for the rise of a commercial brewing industry.

Commercial brewing was aided by the arrival of the hop plant. Hops were first noted as being grown in Babylon in 200 AD. The plant was taken to the Caucasus and then into parts of Germany by the Slavs following the migration of peoples after the fall of the Roman empire. Hop gardens were recorded in the Hallertau region of Bavaria in 736 AD. It is likely that at first hops were used as just another plant to balance the sweetness of malt, but brewers quickly grasped that they not only added a pleasing citric bitterness to ale, but also had antiseptic qualities that helped fight infections. Hopped beer had better keeping qualities, as was noted by Reynold Scott in his best-selling *A Perfitte Platforme for a Hoppe Garden* in 1574. As well as instructing growers in England on how to plant hops in the best soil and train them to climb up poles, he added: "Whereas you cannot make above eight to nine gallons of indifferent ale from one bushel of malt, you may draw 18–20 gallons of very good beer. If your ale may endure a fortnight, your beer through the benefit of the hop, shall continue a month, and what grace it yieldeth to the taste, all men may judge that have sense in their mouths." At a royal banquet in Windsor Park in 1528, 15 gallons of ale and 15 gallons of beer were ordered for the guests. The beer cost 20 pence, the ale two shillings and sixpence. The reason for the price difference was that less malt was needed to make hopped beer owing to its better keeping qualities. But ale did not disappear overnight and the hop was not universally welcomed.

Waging war against the hop

The *gruit* market – the plants and spices added to ale before hops arrived – was a powerful one, often controlled by the church, and they saw that market threatened by the hop. The archbishop of Cologne, who controlled the sale of *gruit* through a decree known as the *Grutrecht*, attempted to outlaw the use of hops. In Russia, Archduke Vasili II banned the plant, as did Henry VIII in England. But consumer preference won the day. In fourteenth-century Holland, Amsterdamers demanded hopped beer from Hamburg and Bremen in preference to the local unhopped brews. Eventually, the controllers of *gruit* were bought out with substantial cash inducements.

The use of other plants did not immediately stop. In 1588, Jacob Theodor von Bergzabern, writing about brewing practice in Europe, said that while hops were used in the copper boil, "The English sometimes add to the brewed beer, to make it more pleasant, sugar, cinnamon, cloves and other good spices in a small bag. The Flemings mix it with honey or sugar and precious spices and so make a drink like claret or hippocras. Others mix in honey, sugar and syrup, which not only makes the beer pleasant to drink, but gives it a fine brown colour." He added that brewers had learned from "the Flemings and the Netherlanders" that adding laurel, ivy or Dutch myrtle to beer strengthens it, preserves it and prevents it going sour. London brewers were still using bog myrtle as late as the 1750s, and Belgian wheat beers are spiced today with coriander and orange peel.

The hop arrived late in England when Flemish traders brought the plant to the south-east corner of the country. A century later, encouraged by the policy of land enclosure that created rich yeoman farmers, Kent became a major hop-growing region. The plant still met with lingering resistance, though. In an astonishing diatribe in his *Compendyous Regyment or Dyetary of Health* of 1542, Andrew Boorde almost burst with xenophobic rage: "Beer is made of malte, hoppes and water; it is the natural drynke for a Dutcheman, and nowe of lete dayes it is much used in England to the detryment of many Englysshe people; specyally it kylleth them the which be troubled with the colyke; and the stone and the strangulion; for the drynke is a colde drynke, yet it doth make a man fat, and doth inflate the bely, as it doth appere by the Dutche men's faces and belyes. If the bere be well served and fyned and not new, it doth qualify heat of the lyver." Ale, on the other hand, "is made of malte and water; and they the which do put any other thynge to ale than is rehersed, except yest, barme or godesgood, doth sofyticat theyr ale. Ale for an Englysche man is a naturell drinke. Ale must have these propertyes: it must be fresshe and clear, it muste not be ropy or smoky, nor it must have no weft or tayle. Ale should not be dronke under V [five] days olde". But the times were out of joint with Mr Boorde. Most

"Englyschemen" preferred the cleaner, refreshing taste of hopped beer. By the middle of the sixteenth century, a few years after Andrew Boorde had railed against the hop, there were 26 "common" or commercial brewers in London. They were undoubtedly brewing hopped beer, since most of them were based in Southwark, close to the major hop market.

A question of taste

How did ale and beer taste in those times? We can get an idea from the far north of Norway, the old Norseland, where farmers still brew in the medieval manner. Juniper branches, rich with berries, are used as a filter in the mashing vessel and in the copper after the boil, though today hops are added alongside the juniper berries. Yeast is collected on a "totem stick" from one brew and then dipped in the fermenting vessel for the next one. The finished beer is around 10 per cent alcohol and has a rich, malty fruitiness with a distinct juniper character. In the north of Finland, a handful of brewers still produce the medieval beer style known as *sahti*. It is made from a mash of barley malt and rye, which is filtered over juniper. Hops are also added to the boil. The beer has a herbal, winey aroma, with a pronounced fruitiness in the mouth and a spicy finish.

The tiny Sint Martinus Brewery in Groningen in the far north of The Netherlands brews a beer called *Cluyn*, pronounced "clown", based on a 1340s' recipe for a strong wedding ale. The grist is a complex blend of malted barley, oats and wheat with unmalted versions of the three grains and some crystal malt for colour. As the beer is sold commercially, the brewery is forced by Dutch law to use hops; none was in the original recipe, which used *gruit* instead. The beer is 8.8 per cent alcohol and is naturally conditioned in the bottle. It has a hazy copper colour and a fruity and herbal aroma. There is sour fruit in the mouth with hop bitterness, and more ripe fruit in the finish.

The first hop beers

A recreation of an ale from 1503, based on a recipe in a book by Richard Arnold called *Customs of London*, is the earliest example of a beer that genuinely used hops. The original ingredients were listed as 10 quarters of malt, two quarters of wheat, two quarters of oats and 40 pounds of hops to make 60 barrels of beer. Home-brewing expert Graham Wheeler, who recreated the beer, smoked the malt over a wood fire in a garden barbeque. (At the time, all malt was kilned over wood fires.) Wheeler used Goldings hops, which did not exist at the time but there are no sixteenth-century varieties available today. The beer had an original starting gravity of 1065 degrees and finished with 6.7 per cent alcohol. As a result of the use of wheat, the beer had a hazy bronze colour and a pronounced smoky and herbal aroma. There was more smoked malt character on the palate, with a resiny underpinning from the hops, while the finish was intensely dry and bitter with dark fruit notes.

The Industrial Revolution

Most beer drinkers today would find the smoky character of Arnold's ale unacceptable. But it is likely that the beer is typical of its period. It was not until the Industrial Revolution of the late eighteenth and nineteenth centuries that coke became available as a source of fuel. Kilning malt by coal fire created noxious gases that tainted the grain, and coal fires were banned in many major cities because of the pollution they caused. Wood, on the other hand, was in plentiful supply in countries still largely covered by forests. In Britain, hornbeam was the preferred type of wood used in malt kilning. But wood fires were hard to control. They could flare suddenly and scorch the grain. As a result, all malt up until the turn of the nineteenth century was brown rather than pale. It produced a low level of sugary extract (10 per cent less than pale malt) and would, as Arnold's ale has shown, have had a pronounced smoky character.

THE EARLY DEVELOPMENT OF LAGER

But while all beer was brown, significant changes were taking place in brewing practice that were to fashion the future development of the industry. From the fifteenth century, attempts were made in central Europe to store beer at low temperatures so that it could survive the hot, torrid summers. In Germany, brewers started to keep their brews in ice-filled caves and discovered that at low temperatures the yeast would behave in a quite different manner. Instead of creating a deep, fluffy head on top of the wort and producing alcohol in a few days, it produced only a thin head and settled to the bottom of the vessel.

Fermentation was also much slower and took several weeks. But, protected by both the cold and alcohol, the yeast was free from attack by wild, airborne strains. "Cold fermented beer" was mentioned in a report of Munich town council in Bavaria in 1420. A report from the city of Nabburg said: "One brews the warm or top fermentation; but first in 1474 one attempted to brew by the cold bottom fermentation and so preserve part of the brew for the summer."

It was not until the late nineteenth century that it was possible to culture a pure lager yeast strain, but the development of cold fermentation was of profound importance to brewers who had tussled with the problem of being unable to brew and thereby earn a living during the summer months. But it would be a mistake to over-emphasize the spread of lager brewing in the medieval period. As late as 1831 there were 16,000 breweries in Prussia producing top-fermenting beer. It was only from this date that cold fermentation began to dominate. By 1839, the number of Prussian brewers using top-fermentation had fallen to 12,000, and to 7,400 by 1865. Nor did every area of Germany accept lager brewing. In 1603, the city authorities of Cologne, in agreement with the brewers, banned cold fermentation. The people preferred top-fermenting beer and considered lager beer too intoxicating. Cologne has a mild climate and the brewers considered lagering unnecessary. Today, Cologne and neighbouring Düsseldorf still produce Kölsch and Alt beers by warm fermentation.

Bavaria was also to have a second impact on the future of brewing in the whole of Germany with the decision in 1516 by the Dukes Wilhelm IV and Ludwig X to introduce the Purity Pledge – known as the *Reinheitsgebot* – in the Assembly of the Estates of the Realm meeting in Ingolstadt. This stipulated that only barley malt, hops, yeast and water could be used to make beer. Similar decisions had been made for Munich in 1487 by Duke

Albrecht IV and for the Landsheit area in 1493. These decisions were not entirely altruistic. The Bavarian royal family monopolized the growing and distribution of barley and they did not want that monopoly challenged by the use of other cereals or sugars.

It is significant that wheat was excluded from the terms of the *Reinheitsgebot* (though it was added later). Wheat beer, like white bread, was considered to be a delicacy fit only for the aristocracy. The *Reinheitsgebot* declared that the masses should drink pure beer, but it could only be barley-based beer – their rulers alone could enjoy the pleasures of wheat beer. The royal family, however, allowed commercial wheat beer brewing to develop on a limited scale in the nineteenth century and the family lost any power over brewing when it vacated the throne as a result of the First World War. The *Reinheitsgebot* covered the whole of Germany when the various principalities were united in 1871. In the 1980s the European Parliament, urged on by French brewers in the Strasbourg area who were anxious to sell their beers across the border, declared the *Reinheitsgebot* a "restraint of trade". But a flood of what the Germans call *chemi-bier* did not pour into the country. Consumers supported brewers who declared their allegiance to the Purity Pledge.

The twin Bavarian developments of lagering and "pure beer" did not coalesce into a powerful force on the world stage until the nineteenth century. Before that, the shaping of a modern brewing industry came in England with the arrival of a beer style called "porter".

PORTER

A major book on brewing techniques, *The London and Country Brewer*, published in 1754, contains no reference to porter. Yet four years later, H. Jackson, in his *Essay on Bread*, described porter as "the universal cordial of the populace". Porter came from nowhere to dominate first London, then British, brewing as the result of a number of changes in the drinks industry.

Mothers' ruin

At the turn of the eighteenth century, the government had to act to combat the appalling deprivations caused by gin-drinking which was literally killing thousands of people. The tax on distilling corn increased the price of gin three times, with the result that beer consumption increased dramatically.

The demand for beer also coincided with improvements in its production. Although coal fires were banned in London and coal itself was taxed, specialist country brewers were making pale ale that was carefully kilned over coal fires. When the tax on malt was increased to help pay for England's wars with France, brewers started to use less malt in their beers and more hops. But London drinkers missed their sweeter ales and started to mix the hoppier beers on sale with beer brought to London from the country by specialist wholesalers known as "ale drapers".

The country brewers had also cornered the market in the supply of "stale" beer. This was a beer that was matured for a year or more in large oak vats. During its long conditioning, lactic acid bacteria gave the beer a slightly sour character, a flavour that was much appreciated at the time. London brewers were mainly publicans who had neither the capital nor the space in their cellars to store beer for a long period. So, in order to blend beer to suit the taste of Londoners, they offered a mixture in their pubs known as "Three Threads" of pale, brown and stale. The name Three Threads comes from the fact that the beer was mixed from three casks into which spigots or taps had been threaded. The blended beer became enormously popular, but the publicans realized they were losing money by having to buy pale and stale beers from the rich country brewers. The Londoners were determined to cut out the country brewers and corner the market for themselves.

"Entire Butt"

The breakthrough came in 1722, when Ralph Harwood, owner of the Bell Brewhouse in Shoreditch, produced a beer he called Entire Butt; this attempted to replicate the flavour of Three Threads. It is not known whether Harwood brewed three beers and then blended them in one cask or butt, or whether he brewed just the one ale, though the former theory is the more likely. He could even have advanced the ageing of the stale beer by innoculating it with a portion of genuine stale beer bought for the purpose. Whatever the method, Entire Butt became a sensation and was soon known as "porter" as a result of its popularity among street

market workers, who were a sizeable force in London at the time.

A retired brewer who used the pen name of Obadiah Poundage, writing in 1760, recorded that: "On this footing stood the trade until about the year 1722 when the Brewers conceived there was a method to be found preferable to any of these extremes [of buying beer for blending]; that beer be well brewed, kept its proper time, became racy and mellow, that is, neither new nor stale, such as would recommend itself to the public. This they ventured to sell for one pound three shillings per barrel that the victualling might retail at threepence per quart. The labouring people, porters etc, experienced its wholesomeness and utility, they assumed to themselves the use thereof, from whence it was called Porter or Entire Butt."

The early porters were blended beers, a mix of pale and brown, or pale, brown and stale. It was not until the nineteenth century that all porter was made from just one beer, and that only occurred when new technology made it possible to roast grain to a dark colour. The porters of the previous century would have been dark brown in colour. Different strengths of porter existed and the strongest versions were known as "porter stout" or "stout butt" beer. The term "stout" had been used for some time to denote the strongest (i.e. the stoutest) beer in a brewery, but gradually stout came to mean a strong version of porter.

Social change

The popularity of porter coincided with a major social upheaval in Britain, as the growth of land enclosure drove an army of people from the country into the towns. London's population grew at twice the rate of the rest of England and Wales and it soon became the most populous city in the world. A vast population of impoverished people, living in often squalid conditions, needed the solace of good beer in pleasant pubs. The success of porter and the Industrial Revolution, however, sent pub-brewing into terminal decline. By Victorian times, only four per cent of beer in London came from brewpubs. The insatiable demand for porter – rich, fruity and heavily hopped – outstripped the ability of publicans to supply enough of it. So commercial brewers sprang up to meet the demand.

Samuel Whitbread, for example, had a small ale brewery in Old Street in 1742, but he moved to new premises in Chiswell Street in the north perimeter of the City about six years later to concentrate on porter. He was able to invest in all the new technologies becoming available: steam engines, mechanical pumps, powered rakes for stirring the mash, and hydrometers for measuring the sugars in the wort and thermometers for registering temperatures – all beyond the means of publican brewers.

By 1760, Whitbread had built a Porter Tun Room at Chiswell Street, "the unsupported roof span of which is exceeded in its majestic size only by that of Westminster Hall". Before the tun room was opened, Whitbread had rented 54 different buildings throughout London to store porter. In Chiswell Street, porter could be stored in vast underground cisterns, the largest one containing the equivalent of 3,800 barrels of beer. The cisterns were cooled by internal pipes through which cold water was pumped, keeping the maturing beer in good condition in hot weather.

Brewing and storing beer in great bulk slashed the costs of production. Within less than a century, porter had moved from being an expensive beer made by blending to a cheap one produced in bulk, and in so doing it made the fortunes of the brewers. The likes of Whitbread would deliberately acetify a portion of their beer to give it a stale flavour and would then supply both young and stale, in different casks, to pubs. Publicans would then blend the beers to achieve the desired character demanded by their customers. Such a system still exists in Belgium today, where lambic and gueuze beers are blended for individual bars.

By 1812, Chiswell Street was producing 122,000 barrels of porter and stout a year. Barclay Perkins brewed 270,000, Meux Reid 188,000 and Truman Hanbury 150,000. These were mighty, modern, capital-intensive breweries, using great cast-iron vessels. They were the wonder of the rest of the world which, even in Germany, was a century behind Britain in brewing techniques.

Roasted malts

The character of porter and stout changed dramatically in the early years of the nineteenth century with the invention of a roasting machine to produce roasted malts. With the ending of coal tax and the use of coke, brewers now had access to pale malt, with its higher level of sugary extract. But drinkers wanted a dark beer, which they believed to be stronger than a light one, and Daniel Wheeler's patent roasting machine, introduced in 1817, enabled the brewers to use black and chocolate malts for flavour and colour with the extract supplied by pale malt. In this way, the brewers were able to use less malt to make a greater volume of beer, with a resulting boost in profits.

Today, it is the porters and stouts of the nineteenth century that survive or are being recreated. There were so many variants on the theme in the previous century that even if a modern brewer took one recipe and reproduced it, it would be impossible to claim that it was a "typical" porter or entire butt of its day. And it must be remembered that a key constituent of the early porters was the use of a stale beer that had been matured for many months in oak vats.

The spread of porter

The influence of porter was enormous. It spread from London to other towns and cities in Britain. Ireland, then under British control, was a ready market for porter and brewers there decided to make their own. Beamish & Crawford were brewing porter in Cork by 1792, while a young ale brewer named Arthur Guinness switched entirely to porter by the turn of the century. David Carnegie, a Scottish brewer, emigrated to Sweden to brew porter and it still survives today, made by top fermentation by the giant Pripps brewing group. Across the Baltic, the Sinebrychoff Brewery in Helsinki also brews a genuine porter.

Porter was also understandably popular with the settlers of North America. It was George Washington's favourite tipple and it was specially imported for him until the War of Independence. Strong "stout porters" were in great demand in Russia, including the court of Catherine the Great. This spawned a version of stout known as Russian Imperial. The Courage group still produces a bottle-conditioned Russian Imperial Stout. It is brewed by its Yorkshire subsidiary John Smiths in Tadcaster where, just down the road, a distant relation, Samuel Smith, also brews an Imperial Stout as well as a Taddy Porter.

PALE ALE REVOLUTION

Porter and stout brewing went into sharp decline at the turn of the twentieth century. Drinkers were already showing a preference for both the new pale ales and the sweeter mild ales. But the death knell was sounded by government legislation during the First World War that stopped brewers using roasted malts because of the additional energy that was used. The government did not dare impose the same restrictions on Ireland, though, where the battle for Home Rule was reaching fever pitch. And so porter and stout became Irish specialities, and stout remains so to this day.

Porter's domination was already under attack in the previous century from the move to lighter-coloured beers. In Britain this was marked by the rise of pale ale. In central Europe, lager beer soared to success. Both were made possible by the new technologies of the Industrial Revolution and more should be made of the similarities of pale ale and lager rather than their differences. Both were made possible by the ability to produce pale malt, to culture pure yeast strains, to use better quality hops, and to control fermentation temperatures with the aid of ice machines and refrigerators. The difference between them lay in the fact that British brewers remained faithful to warm fermentation – there was an undoubted jingoism and anti-Germanism about this – while the Europeans and Scandinavians embraced cold fermentation.

The pale-ale revolution began in Burton-on-Trent. The small Staffordshire town had been a renowned brewing centre since the twelfth century. Once the Trent Navigation Act of 1699 made the Midlands river navigable as far as Hull on the north-east coast, the Burton brewers began to export their sweet brown ales far and wide, and especially to the Baltic countries. But the lucrative Baltic trade was closed to the British during the Napoleonic Wars. Most of the Burton breweries closed and the handful of survivors searched desperately for new markets.

Colonial trade

Salvation came in the form of the colonial trade. Britain had first colonized India in 1772 and brewers had diligently exported ales to slake the thirsts of soldiers and civil servants. But mild ale and porter were not best suited to that climate. The word from India was simple: "We need light, well-hopped and refreshing beer." It had to be a special beer, though, to survive the three-month journey in the hold of a ship with the violent motion of the sea and sudden and severe fluctuations in temperature.

The first attempt at brewing a special beer for the India trade came, surprisingly, from London – surprising because London's soft waters were not ideal for making a light and hoppy beer. But George Hodgson, of Abbot & Hodgson's Bow Brewery, was based close to the East and West India Docks and Hodgson learnt that ships left for India virtually empty in order to pick up spices and silks for the return journey. Cargoes, therefore, were cheap on the outward run and Hodgson determined to fashion a beer that would make his fortune. No records remain of the brewery and no one can be certain what Hodgson's "India Ale" was like, save for the fact that the Burton brewers bought supplies in secret in an attempt to imitate it.

As their India Pale Ales were extremely light in colour, using just pale malt – in some cases lager malt – and brewing sugar, it is safe to assume that Hodgson's beer was similar. It was probably around 6 per cent alcohol, with twice the hop rate of other beers. The hops not only gave a tart and refreshing bitterness to the ale, but they also acted as a preservative on the long sea journey. Primed with brewing sugar in the casks, the beer would also have undergone a second fermentation, which would have increased the level of alcohol. Hodgson's ale was successful and for years the Bow Brewery cornered the India trade. But the powerful East India Company, which handled Hodgson's beer, approached the Burton brewer Samuel Allsopp in 1821 and suggested he should provide choice and competition. Allsopp began to experiment with pale ale and was quickly followed by other Burton brewers, including William Bass.

The benefits of calcium

Within a decade, Allsopp and Bass were supplying more than half the beer shipped to India. Hodgson's fortunes

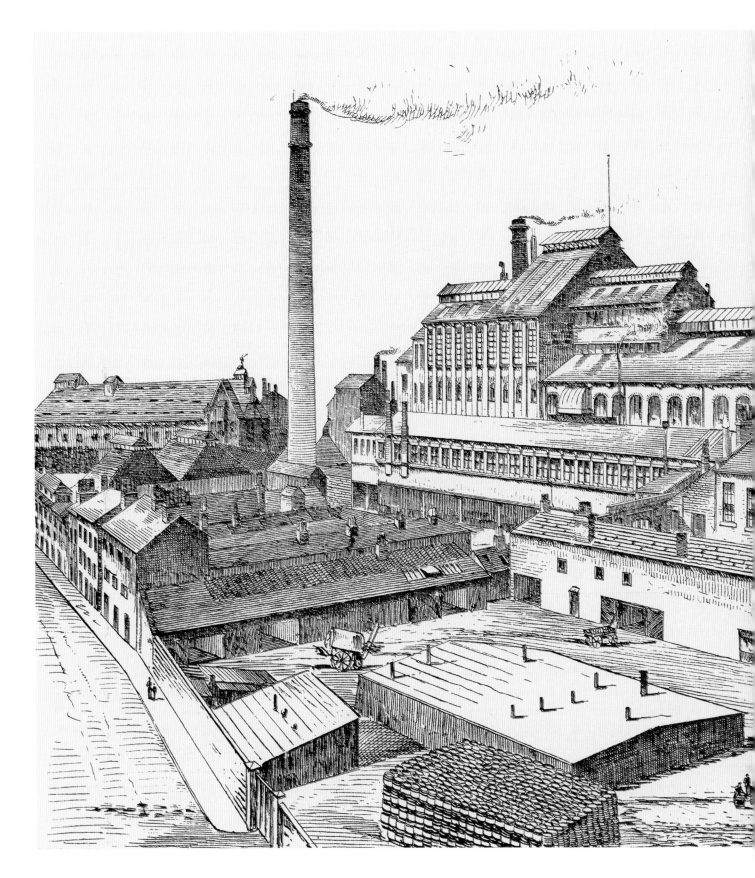

The Ind Coope brewery, Burton-on-Trent, in the nineteenth century

duly waned and the company closed in 1885. The success of the Burton brewers lay in the remarkable mineral-rich waters of the town, with calcium keeping yeast active in the cask and improving hop character. (Sulphate, on the other hand, increases bitterness.) The yeast strain developed by the Burton union system of fermentation also had a crucial role to play. It attacks malt and brewing sugars voraciously, producing a dry beer. It created a powerful second fermentation in the cask, producing more alcohol that helped fight off bacterial infection during the long sea journeys. India Pale Ales were also massively hopped, with three to four pounds in the copper and dry hopped in cask at around six ounces per barrel. The hops also acted as a preservative, prolonging the life of the beer. Units of bitterness would have been extremely high, around 70 to 80, but the beer would have softened during the long voyage.

The success of the Burton brewers encouraged competitors from London and other cities to open plants in the East Midlands town and avail themselves of the fine waters there. But India Pale Ales were a short-lived phenomenon, lasting from the 1830s until the 1880s. With the lager revolution sweeping Europe, it was natural that its proponents should seek markets overseas. The light, chilled and quenching beers suited the colonial climates better than pale ale, especially as lager beers were conditioned in the brewery, did not have to settle on arrival and did not have a sediment.

Railways and class

The Burton brewers switched to an internal market. With the arrival of the railway system, they could send their beers all over Britain. Pale ales became a sensation, particularly with the rising and aspiring new middle class who appreciated a beer that was too expensive for the working class.

Pale ale was the beer of the railway age, but the manner of its production began to change fundamentally. At the turn of the century, brewers started to buy pubs and create a "tied house" system. They could sell their beers direct to their outlets, but they could not wait several weeks or months for those beers to come into condition. As a result, India Pale Ales were replaced by "running beers". New strains of yeast were developed that settled out quickly and crystal malt, in which the starches had been turned to sugar in the maltings, started to be used to give flavour, colour and body to beer in an attempt to speed up maturity. These running beers are what we know today as "bitter". They developed out of the pale ale revolution, they are cask-conditioned in the pub cellar, but they are different in many ways from the amazing nineteenth-century style that spawned them.

THE ADVANCE OF LAGER BREWING

Outside of the British Isles, lager brewing was growing apace. A system tinkered with since the fifteenth century as a way of keeping beer free from infection became possible on a vast commercial scale with the development of ice-making machines.

The pace-setters in lagering were the great Munich brewers, especially Gabriel Sedlmayr II at Spaten. He had worked and studied in breweries throughout Europe, but returned to his family's company in 1834 to attempt to put his new theories into practice. Ice-making machines developed by Carl von Linde made it possible for brewers to store beer within their breweries, rather than transporting it to icy caves in the mountains. These machines were quickly followed by refrigerators, and the technology was now in place to enable lager brewing to develop on a massive scale.

The advantages of lagering were three-fold: it gave brewers far greater control over fermentation, avoiding bacterial infection; it produced beers with a cleaner, less fruity character; and, because the beers were filtered and conditioned in the brewery, they were less prone to being affected by poor and unskilful service in cafés and bars. Lagering was capital-intensive, with major investment needed in conditioning tanks and cooling equipment, and with the beer tied up for months in brewery cellars before it could be released for sale. Spaten, Paulaner, Löwenbräu and the other Munich brewers aided the lagering technique by using hops predominantly for aroma rather than bitterness and varieties of barley that produced clean, malty aromas and flavours. They were also restrained by the *Reinheitsgebot* and could use only malt in their beers, with no sugars or roasted grain.

It comes as something of a shock, then, to realize that the first commercial lagers were dark in colour. Coal was expensive in Bavaria and brewers had continued to kiln their malt over wood fires. The beers were rounded, clean-tasting with hints of spice, chocolate and coffee: the style is still brewed in considerable quantities in the Franconia region of Bavaria, centred on the town of Kulmbach. A dark beer is known in Bavaria as a *dunkel* or a *dunkles*, and beers of this style continued to dominate the market there – rather as English mild ale did – until the 1950s.

A gift from Bohemia

The first golden lager came not from Bavaria, but from neighbouring Bohemia. Pilsen had been an important brewing centre since the foundation of the town in 1295, when King Wenceslas II gave 260 citizens the right to brew. In the sixteenth century, a treatise on scientific brewing was written in Latin by Tadeas Hajek, while the research of Frantisek Ondrej Poupé in the late eighteenth century spurred the use of modern methods of malting and control of the mash with the use of a hydrometer. Professor Karel Balling, whose name was later used to measure the strength of beer, began to lecture on brewing chemistry in Prague in 1833. A Czech brewing school was opened in 1869 and a maltsters' school followed in 1897. For all its bucolic charms, Bohemia was not a brewing backwater.

The variable nature of Bohemian beer, in a country with severe winters but blazing summers, had long been a problem. When an entire batch of beer was poured down the Pilsen drains in 1838 after it had been declared unfit for consumption, a group of citizens who still held the seal of Wenceslas decided to take emergency action. They set up a "citizen's brewery" and invited a Bavarian brewer named Josef Groll to work for them.

Groll brought with him the knowledge of cold fermentation, but he decided to use only the finest Bohemian malt, local Zatec hops and the soft water of Pilsen. Groll's golden beer may have been an error – according to legend, he had intended to make a *dunkel* but the maltsters made a mistake with the kilning temperature – but it was an immediate sensation and has since been copied throughout the world.

At the end of the century, the beer was renamed Pilsner Urquell in German (*Plzensky Prazdroj* in Czech), meaning "original source Pilsner beer". But it was a classic case of locking the stable door after the dray horse had bolted. Pilsner – often spelt Pilsener or shortened to Pils – is the most abused beer style in the world and too often stands for a pale, thin, undistinguished beer lagered for a short period of a few weeks. The only two beers that deserve the name Pilsner are Pilsner Urquell and Gambrinus, both brewed in Pilsen.

Lager's inexorable rise

Lager brewing spread like a forest fire throughout the world. In Scandinavia, where the first pure lager yeast culture was isolated at the Carlsberg Brewery in Copenhagen, wheat beers and such medieval styles as *sahti* were dumped in favour of the new style. The Germans, with their colonial foothold in Africa, busily introduced lagering to that vast continent, and also to China.

In Japan, meanwhile, there was no brewing tradition at all until the Americans and the Germans helped set up breweries there. The Germans also introduced lagering to South America, though the major influence in Mexico was Austrian: the country was briefly part of the Austrian Empire. The Viennese style of brewing was to use well-kilned "red" malt, and the style survives today in Mexico in such beers as Dos Equis and Negra Modelo.

The beers that reputedly made Milwaukee famous

Lager reached the United States with the second wave of immigrants from central Europe. Germans who settled in Milwaukee found a plentiful supply of ice from a nearby lake and were able to start brewing. The Americans grasped new technology with enthusiasm and, with the aid of refrigeration, lager brewing spread rapidly.

The particular type of six-row barley that grows in the USA is rich in enzymes and allowed brewers to use large amounts of unmalted cereals, such as rice and corn, in their beers to reduce production costs. The result has been the rise of bland, refreshing but uninteresting interpretations of the lager style. This development was aided by Prohibition, the total ban on the manufacture and sale of alcohol in the USA that lasted from 1920 to 1933.

The effect, though, was quite the opposite to the one wanted by the legislators. Alcohol was still freely available in illegal drinking places and was of a low and often dangerous quality. Increasingly, "bootleg" liquor came under the control of the Mafia, who even set up their own breweries and distilleries. Most commercial breweries went out of business. Only the biggest survived by producing soft drinks and legal "near beer" constituted of less than three per cent alcohol.

When Prohibition ended, a handful of giant brewers had the market to themselves and started to fashion a new industry based on bland lagers. This move intensified during the Second World War: with a vast number of men abroad on active service, the brewers set out to woo women with even lighter concoctions.

Modern developments

Since the 1980s, brewers in North America and Japan have tinkered with such new versions of light lager as "dry beer" and "ice beer". The former – developed in Japan – is filtered to remove most of the "beery" taste, especially hop bitterness, while the latter – a Canadian invention – is produced by a complex system, similar to distillation, in which the beer is frozen to form ice crystals and then slowly warmed up until it liquefies. These are likely to be transitory brews, however, aimed essentially at people who do not like the taste of beer.

Dry beer and ice beer seem to deny the fact that the last decade of the twentieth century saw a remarkable revival of older beer styles and a greater appreciation of quality by consumers. In Britain, cask-conditioned "real ale" is the beer of the moment, while porters and stouts are once more in demand.

The ales of Belgium are reaching an ever-growing audience, the *bières de garde* of Northern France have emerged from the long shadow cast by wine, and even in Germany top-fermenting wheat beers are challenging the hegemony of lager.

It has been a long journey for beer from the ancient world of the Pharaohs, but it has survived the voyage and looks set to find even greater appreciation in the twenty-first century.

THE ART AND SCIENCE OF BEER MAKING

Beer is as old as civilization. The methods that produce some types of ale have scarcely changed for centuries. Modern lager brewing has introduced new technologies aided by yeast cultivation and refrigeration. But the essentials of making beer – turning barley into malt, extracting the sugars, boiling with hops and fermenting with yeast – remain today fundamentally the same as when early man first discovered the joys and mystery of brewing.

When water was turned into wine, it was described as a miracle. But making beer from barley is rather more difficult, since a harvest of golden grain produces beer only as a result of profound and natural chemical reactions, and enormous skill from maltsters and brewers. Along the way other cereals may be blended in, while the remarkable hop plant imparts quenching bitterness and tempting aromas.

In Germany, the biggest beer-drinking nation in the world, they do their best to keep it simple. The ingredients that can be used in brewing are controlled by a sixteenth-century law called the Reinheitsgebot, or "Purity Pledge", so German beer drinkers can be certain that only malted barley or wheat, along with hops, water and yeast, go into their favourite tipple. In the rest of the world, however, unravelling the contents of a glass of beer is more complicated.

Many brewers use "adjuncts", either because they are cheaper, or because they help to produce the right balance of flavours. Germans turn their noses up at "impure" beers from abroad, but English pale ales and milds, as well as Belgian Trappist beers and Irish stouts, would change character noticeably if brewers were not able to use special sugars and unmalted cereals to give their creations their own unique colours and tastes.

In a few regions of the world, where it is difficult to grow barley, brewers are forced to use the raw ingredients available – such as rice in the Far East, or sorghum in Africa. Barley, though, is the preferred grain for brewing. In the Ancient World of Egypt, Mesopotamia and Sumeria, the first brewers found that, while wheat made excellent bread, it caused problems if it was the only grain used in the beer-making process.

Barley, on the other hand, makes relatively poor bread, but was found to be the ideal grain for brewing. Even today, with the dramatic revival of interest in wheat beers, wheat makes up only one per cent of the total grain used in brewing world-wide. All modern "wheat beers" use between 30 and 50 per cent malted barley in their composition.

Cereals such as barley and wheat developed from tall grass. Barley, though, is unusual because it has a husk. The early brewers soon found that this husk acted as a natural filter in the first stage of brewing. This is known as "mashing", when the natural sugars are extracted from the malt. Other cereals, such as wheat, have no husk and so can clog up pipes and machinery in brewing vessels.

The other important advantages of barley are that it has the highest "extract" of fermentable sugars, and also produces a cleaner-tasting beer. Wheat, on the other hand, has a distinctive, fruity tartness that does not blend well with the bitterness of hops, while oats and rye have to be used in small proportions or they will impart to the beer a flavour that is either too creamy or too grainy. Some specialist ale brewers in Britain, however, have rediscovered oats and are using small amounts in stouts that are radically different in flavour from the dry Irish style.

Opposite: *Barley is the ideal grain for brewing*

MAKING MALT

Many people make the mistake of assuming that brewing is a simple process – unlike wine-making, which needs enormous skill. The opposite is the case. If you crush grapes, the natural yeasts on their skins will ferment the sugary liquid.

But nothing happens if you crush an ear of barley. It needs the gentle craft of the maltster to take the raw grain and turn it into malt. During the malting process, natural chemical reactions begin to turn the starches in the barley into fermentable sugars.

The barley of choice

Brewers choose malt with great care, preferring to stick to a tried and trusted variety that they know yeast will work with in harmony. Change the barley, and the yeast will react badly or even refuse to ferment and produce alcohol.

Brewers, if they can possibly acquire it, prefer two-row barley. The name refers to the number of rows of grain within each ear. The finest two-row barley grows close to the sea on rich, dark soil and is known as "maritime barley" as a result. The East Anglia region of England, the Scottish Lowlands and Belgium produce some of the finest varieties of two-row maritime. In warmer climates – the Mediterranean countries and the USA – six-row barley is more common. As well as having six rows of grain in each ear, the barley has a thicker husk; this contains tannins known as polyphenols. Both the husk and the tannins can cause a haze in finished beer, and brewers who use six-row barley tend to blend in substantial amounts of adjuncts, such as corn and rice, to counter this haze. Six-row barley is also particularly rich in enzymes that will convert the starches in corn and rice, as well as the malt, into sugar. American "lite" lagers are often made from six-row with large amounts of adjuncts. But master brewers in Germany and the Czech Republic, the birthplaces of modern lager brewing, will only use two-row barley. Pale ale brewers agree with them. They feel that six-row gives an astringent and harsh character to beer.

But whether it is two-row or six-row, only a small proportion of barley is suitable for brewing. It must be low in nitrogen to avoid hazy beer, and with the widespread use of pesticides and fertilizers, nitrogen is a growing problem. Ale brewers tend to prefer winter barleys – sown in the autumn and able to withstand frosts and snow – for their robust character, while lager brewers use spring varieties which possess softer, lighter qualities.

Under pressure from farmers and big brewers, seed merchants have developed new varieties of barley that have a high "yield". This means that they produce more grain per acre than some of the more famous barleys, such as Maris Otter in England and Golden Promise in Scotland, though traditional brewers are willing to pay a premium price for low-yield varieties of barley, since they produce the best flavours and ferment in harmony with yeast. Changing the barley variety can result in a "stuck" fermentation.

The maltings

When the brewer and the maltster are satisfied with the quality of the barley, it goes to a maltings to start the long journey that will end with beer. At the maltings, the grain is washed thoroughly to remove dirt, agro-chemicals and other impurities. This is done by "steeping", or soaking, the grain with water in a deep trough or, in modern maltings, in large metal tanks. During this process, a primitive type of fermentation occurs as bacteria attack wild yeasts on the grain and the water bubbles and froths alarmingly. The water is changed frequently to flush away both bacteria and any wild yeasts that could interfere with the natural development of the grain. At the same time, the grain is absorbing moisture – vital if germination is to start – and the moisture level of the grain will increase from 14 to 40 per cent.

At the end of steeping, the water is drained and the grain is left to stand for several hours. In a traditional floor maltings, the grain is spread on a floor to form a "couch". In a modern maltings, the grain goes into large revolving drums. In either system, the grain will begin to germinate, and it must be turned or raked frequently to allow it to breathe. Germination and the biochemical changes that take place within the grain lead to a build-up of heat that must be carefully controlled, or the grain will suffocate.

Modification

What happens to the grain is known as "modification". The embryo of the grain, the acrospire, starts to grow while tiny roots break through the husk. The grain is composed of two parts, the starchy endosperm and a tough, outer, aleurone layer that protects the endosperm and also contains proteins. The growth of the acrospire causes natural chemical reactions to transform the proteins into enzymes and so make the starches soluble. While the acrospire becomes soft, the rootlets grow at great speed. The maltster tests the degree of modification by a simple test: he puts some grain in his mouth and chews it. If it is soft and "friable", then modification has gone far enough and the barley has become what is known as "green malt".

An ale brewer will want a fully modified malt with as much of its protein as possible turned to enzymes. This enables him to use a simple infusion mashing system that turns starches into brewing sugar. Lager brewers traditionally have used less modified malt with a lower rate of protein conversion, while a more complex decoction mashing system is needed to convert the sugar and avoid beer haze. The reason for the differences lies in the fact that lager brewers in central Europe didn't have access to maritime barley and so had to make do with inferior varieties. Today, all two-row barleys are of high quality, but many lager brewers – and German wheat beer brewers – prefer to stick with decoction mashing.

Drying the malt

The green malt has to be heated to dry it and preserve the vital enzymes. In a modern maltings, this is done inside a drum that is heated externally. A kiln in a traditional maltings is like a large chimney. A coke, gas or electric fire at the bottom heats the malt, which is spread out above on a mesh floor. The temperature is carefully controlled to produce the type and colour of malt needed by the brewer. The first temperature stage, around 60°C (150°F), stops the process of germination. To produce white malt for lager brewing, the heat is increased slightly and held for 24 hours, while a marginally higher temperature is used for pale malt, the classic type for ale brewing. Malt destined for darker beers, such as English mild, will be kilned at an even higher temperature. The important factor is that the heat must be maintained at a level that will not kill the enzymes which will turn starch into sugar in the brewery. Heavily kilned malts will have no fermentable sugars and so are used solely for producing colour and flavour.

Dark malts

Dark malts – amber, chocolate and black – are produced in machines similar to coffee roasters. Unmalted roasted barley, used principally in dry Irish stouts, is also made in this way. Green malt is loaded into the roasters where temperatures range from 200°C (430°F) to 210°C (450°F), depending on the colour required. Roasted malts have an intense, bitter flavour.

Special types of dark malt are made in a different way. Carapils and caramalt used in lager brewing, and crystal malt used for ale, are produced by loading green malt into a sealed kiln. The moisture cannot escape and, as the temperature is raised to 45°C (113°F), the enzymes convert starches into sugar. The husks of grain contain soft balls of malt sugar. As the vents of the kiln are opened and the heat is increased, the sugar crystallizes and the colour deepens. Not all the starches are converted, however, and much of the sugar produced is dextrin rather than maltose. As dextrin cannot be fermented by brewer's yeast, it gives not only flavour and colour to the beer, but also "body", a roundness of fullness and flavour.

Brewers specify the colour of the malts they need by quoting a scale agreed by the European Brewing Convention. The scale applies either to the malt or to the colour of the finished beer. A classic pale-gold Pilsner will have around six to eight units EBC, an English pale ale using crystal malt will register between 20 to 40 units, while dark beers in the porter and stout category will be as high as 300 units on the scale. In the USA, brewers use a system known as Degrees Lovibond to measure colour. Under this system, pale lager will have 1.6 degrees, a pale ale three degrees, and a stout 500 degrees.

Pale or dark, the maltster has now taken raw grain and turned it into an ingredient rich in soluble starches. The first and staple ingredient in making beer is now ready to go to the brewery.

HOPS

Wine makers are fortunate. Everything they need to make wine is contained within the grape, including natural preservatives that single the grape out from other fruits. Brewers, however, have to balance malt, with its biscuity sweetness, with plants or herbs that not only add aroma and bitterness, but also prevent bacterial infections during the brewing process. For centuries brewers tackled the problem of how to offset both the poor keeping qualities of ale and its cloying sweetness by adding a variety of herbs and plants. These included yarrow, rosemary and bog myrtle. But from around the eighth century AD, hops started to be used in brewing in central Europe. In Britain, the hop, *humulus lupulus*, was eaten as a delicacy by the Romans, but was not used in brewing at the time.

The essential ingredients of beer – barley, hops and yeast – remain the same as in the early days of brewing

Knowledge of the hop and hop cultivation was taken into the Caucasus and Germany as part of the great migration of people that followed the collapse of the Roman Empire. By the early ninth century, hops were being grown in the Hallertau region of Bavaria. Brewers who used other plants, or a mixture of herbs, plants and spices known as *gruit*, fiercely resisted the hop, while in many countries the church controlled the *gruit* market and could rail against the demon hop from the pulpit.

The hop arrived late in England in the fifteenth century and was banned by such luminaries as Henry VIII and the aldermen of Norwich and Shrewsbury. But eventually the superiority of hopped beer put paid to ale and *gruit*. Though the term "ale" is still widely used in the British Isles and the USA to define a warm-fermenting style, today all ales are brewed with hops.

Pity the poor male

Left to itself, the hop will trail across the ground and grow wild in hedgerows. Hop farmers train it to climb up poles, its thick stalk or bine wrapping round the pole. This gives the plant maximum exposure to sun and light. The hop plant is dioecious: the male and female plants grow separately. Except in the British Isles, the male hop has a short and miserable existence. Lager brewers want unfertilized hops that will give aroma to their beers, but they avoid too much bitterness and shy away from any suggestion of astringency. In most countries the male hop is ruthlessly persecuted to stop it mating with female hops. Classic ale producers, on the other hand, want an earthy, peppery aroma and flavour in their beers and a deep and intense bitterness. As a result they use fertilized female plants and encourage the male to enjoy a healthy sex life.

The flower of the hop – the cone – contains resins known as alpha acids (or humulones) and beta acids (or lupulones), as well as oils. Alpha acids give bitterness to beer, while the oils impart flavour. The beta acids and tannins in the cone help to stabilize the beer and also have vital disinfectant qualities to ward off infections. The hops grown in such famous European regions as the Hallertau in Bavaria and Zatec (Saaz in German) in the Czech Republic are known as "noble hops" because of their superb aroma but comparatively gentle

Hops growing in the Löwenbräu region of Bavaria in Germany

bitterness. Modern varieties, known as "high alphas", have been developed to give twice the level of bitterness to beer compared to noble varieties. Many brewers are wary of high alphas as they feel they give a harsh and astringent character to their brews. They prefer to blend in different varieties to achieve the right balance of aroma and bitterness. English ale brewers, for example, use the Fuggle for bitterness and the Golding for aroma. Both are named after their original growers.

Hops around the world

The major hop-growing areas of the world are the USA and British Columbia in North America, Kent and Worcestershire in England, Bavaria in Germany, Zatec in the Czech Republic, and Styria in the former Yugoslavia. Hops are also grown in Poland and China, while the Pride of Ringwood variety from Tasmania is highly regarded and is much in demand from brewers of organic beer.

Recently, leading growing areas, such as the German Hallertau and the English counties, have seen their hops attacked by pests and diseases, so new strains (including "dwarf hops" that grow to half the height of conventional varieties), resistant to attacks from the likes of downy mildew and red spider mite, have been developed. The USA is expected to dominate world hop-growing within a few decades as a result of the ideal climates in Idaho, Oregon and Washington State which produce such varieties as Cascade, Chinook, Cluster and Willamette. All hops give an appealing citric character to beer, and this is most apparent in American varieties – the Chinook in particular imparts a powerful aroma and flavour of grapefruit.

Picking the hops

Hops are picked in the early autumn. (Before mechanization, hop picking provided a short paid holiday for working-class families who lived close to the hop fields. In England, special trains were used to take London Cockneys and "Brummies" from Birmingham to pick hops in Kent and Worcestershire respectively.) Hops have a high water content and they must be dried and packed quickly to stop them going mouldy. Drying is usually carried out close to the hop fields – in England it is done in attractive oast houses topped by cowls that keep a steady draught of warm air circulating over the hops. When they are dry, the hops are compressed into sacks and stored in dark, cool areas in breweries to avoid oxidation and photosynthesis.

Brewers with traditional equipment prefer whole hops, while breweries with modern hop whirlpools use pelletized hops that have been milled to a powder and reduced under pressure into pellets. Hop oils and hop extracts, produced by boiling hops with hydrocarbons or in an alkaline solution, are not popular with craft brewers, since they feel they give an unpleasant harshness and bite to the beer.

IBUs

The bitterness of beer is measured by an internationally-agreed scale, International Bitterness Units, or IBUs. They are sometimes known as EBUs (from European Bitterness Units), but the scale is now used in North America as well. The measurement is based on the level of hop acids and the quantity of hops used in a beer. IBUs do not give an indication of hop aroma or flavour, since they have to be balanced against the alcoholic strength of a beer and the amount of malt used. A "lite" American lager may have around 10 IBUs, whereas a genuine Czech Pilsner will have 40. An English mild ale will have 20 units, an India Pale Ale 40 or higher, an Irish stout 55 to 60 and a barley wine 65.

WATER

Even the strongest beer is made up of 90 per cent water. Yet, brewers apart, we tend to ignore the role of water in brewing, except when we accuse brewers of "watering" their beer. In fact, every brewer in the world has to water the beer, otherwise there would be nothing to drink. In a brewery, water is treated with a care bordering on religious fervour. For a start, it is never called water but "liquor": water is the stuff used for washing floors and equipment.

Hard versus soft

The quality of the brewing liquor is essential to the clarity and taste of the beer. It encourages malt and hops to give up their sugars, aromas and flavours, and it also stimulates yeast to turn sugars vigorously into alcohol. The purity of water destined for brewing helps to produce a beer that is free from infections, while its hardness or softness will help determine the "mouthfeel" of finished beer. Brewers who want to produce a genuine Pilsner beer will need a soft water, while a pale ale brewer will want a water that is hard and rich in mineral salts. The level of salts in the water of Pilsen in the Czech Republic, home of Pilsner beer, is 30.8 parts per million.

Before the Industrial Revolution and the ability to make chemical changes to water, London's water, high in calcium carbonate, was ideal for brewing milds, porters and stouts. In Burton-on-Trent, where the classic flinty English pale ales were born, water is hard and salts add up to 1,226 parts per million. Centuries ago, when public water was unsafe to drink, breweries would be set up next to natural springs or wells, or water diviners would be paid to find a supply of fresh water that would not only provide clean brewing liquor, but could also be used to germinate barley.

All water, whether it comes from wells, rivers or ponds, is the result of rain falling on to the earth. As it falls, it picks up gases that acidify it. Carbonic acid is the main acid in rain water. When it hits the ground, rain water drains through the top soil and finds its way through porous rocks and mineral layers until it settles on a water table of impervious rock. During that long, slow passage, the water will absorb mineral salts. The type and quantity of salts will depend on the rock formation in a given area. Soft water collects on insoluble rock, such as slate or granite, and is virtually free of minerals as a result. Water returns to the surface by forcing its way as a spring or flowing into a river, or bores will be sunk to pump it to the surface.

Likes and dislikes

Calcium bicarbonate is the most common cause of temporary hardness in water. It comes from chalk and is a nuisance in a brewery because the salts impede fermentation and reduce the effectiveness of other minerals. As those who live in a hard-water district will know, calcium bicarbonate leads to a heavy build-up of deposits in kettles. Brewers remove as much of it as possible by boiling or filtration.

On the other hand, calcium sulphate – or gypsum – is as welcome in a brewery as free beer in a pub, since it encourages enzymes to turn starch into sugar during the mashing stage of brewing, maintains the correct level of acidity – the pH or "power of hydrogen" – in the unfermented beer, and ensures that the yeast works in a lively manner. The high levels of gypsum in the water of Burton-on-Trent enable brewers there to produce sparkling and clean-tasting pale ales of dazzling quality. The sulphury aroma on a true Burton beer is known locally as the "Burton snatch".

Yeast loves magnesium sulphate (Epsom Salts) and attacks the sweet sugars in the fermenters with enormous vigour thanks to the presence of magnesium. The salts also help to stabilize the sugar extract when it is boiled with hops. Edinburgh, which also became a leading pale ale centre, has water rich in mineral salts.

Burtonization

At the other end of the brewing scale, great brewing centres, such as České Budějovice and Pilsen in the Czech Republic, and Munich in Bavaria, have soft waters with a negligible mineral content. This enables them to produce lager beers with a satiny, rounded smoothness. When London was a great centre for dark beers, the chlorine in the water accentuated the sweetness of the malt. But London is now, on a much reduced scale, a pale-ale centre, and brewers there "Burtonize" their liquor to match the hardness of Burton-on-Trent. The expression "Burtonization" is now used worldwide to describe the addition of mineral salts. Even brewers in Bavaria, speaking in German, use the term, though the amounts of gypsum and Epsom Salts added to Munich brewing liquor must be small as the lager beers of the city are noticeably soft in texture. But it is a sign of the importance that brewers attach to the quality of water that they have universally adopted a method to replicate the liquor of a small town in the English Midlands.

With the aid of modern technology, almost any water can be used in brewing. While it is pure Irish folk lore that Guinness in Dublin uses water from the River Liffey, there is nothing to stop the company from doing so. Brewers are meticulous in filtering liquor several times to remove any impurities. Many use double osmosis systems. It is a sad reflection on modern life that brewers in the East Midlands of England, home of pale ale, can no longer use some of the natural wells due to their high levels of nitrates. They have turned instead to the public water supply, and as a result have to add back calcium and magnesium to achieve the right levels of hardness.

YEAST

For centuries they called it "God-is-Good". Brewers didn't understand yeast, but they knew that if they saved the foam from one brew, it would magically turn sweet liquid into beer when used again. The earliest brewers probably did not even save the foam, but instead allowed deposits of yeast in their brewing vessels to ferment subsequent brews. Wild yeasts in the air would also attack the sugary liquid, while micro-organisms in storage containers added a lactic sourness. The production of lambic and gueuze beers by spontaneous fermentation in Belgium is a link with brewing's past.

It was not until the eighteenth century, with the pioneering work of the Dutch scientist Anton van Leeuwenhoek, followed by Louis Pasteur with his microscope in the following century, that the mystery of yeast was revealed. Today we know that yeast is a single-cell micro-organism – a fungus – that can turn a sugary liquid into equal amounts of alcohol and carbon dioxide by multiplying and reproducing itself. Pasteur's book *Etudes sur la Bière* changed brewing practice throughout the world.

Prompted by the French scientist's work, brewers realized that yeast had to be cultivated and stored to remain pure and uncontaminated. They also had to keep their breweries scrupulously clean to avoid bacteria and wild yeasts infecting beer and turning it sour. With the aid of the microscope, brewers discovered that yeast was made up of several different, competing strains which fought each other and so impeded a successful fermentation.

Gradually, yeasts were cultured, both to remove unnecessary strains and also to retain one or two that would attack brewing sugars with the most success. For example, Guinness in Dublin still uses Arthur Guinness's original yeast from the eighteenth century, though it has now been cultured down from five strains to one.

Banking on success

Today, nothing is left to chance. Brewers realize how vital yeast is, not just to a clean fermentation, but also to the flavour and character of their beers. After each brew, the yeast is collected, pressed to remove any liquid, then stored in refrigerators.

Yeast is not neutral. It picks up and retains flavour from one brew to the next. So if a brewer wishes to produce a classic Pilsner or Pale Ale, he will need not just the right malt, hops and water, but also the correct yeast strain. He can take a bucket to the brewery of his choice and ask for a supply, but he is more likely to go to a special yeast bank and buy a culture. All brewers keep samples of their yeasts in special banks.

A yeast infection is like a death in the family. If a brewery does get an infection, then it immediately orders a sample from a yeast bank. In Britain, the National Collection of Yeast Cultures, located in Norwich, has a vast range of cultures, as does Weihenstephan near Munich, VLB in Berlin and Jorgensen in Copenhagen. Craft brewers in the USA, anxious to produce ales and lagers in the true style, order their yeasts from these banks.

Ale and lager yeasts

There are two basic styles of brewer's yeast – ale and lager. Ale yeast, known by its Latin name of *Saccharomyces cerevisiae* – meaning literally "sugar fungus ale" – is a development of the type of brewing yeast that has been used since the dawn of time. It works at a warm temperature in the brewery, creating a vast blanket on top of the liquid. The temperature will start at around 15°C (59°F), but the heat created by fermentation will increase it to 25°C (77°F). Ale yeasts are used in the production of wheat beer and such German specialities as the Alt beers of Düsseldorf and the Kölsch beers of Cologne, as well as conventional British ales and Irish stouts.

Although they are carefully cultured and scientifically analysed, these beers remain a throwback to the age before the Industrial Revolution. Unlike a pure, isolated, single-strain lager yeast, an ale yeast may be a two-strain variety with sugars turned into alcohol at different stages. Ale yeasts give a rich fruitiness to finished beer.

Ale yeast is often used in open fermenters. The heavy blanket it creates on top of the liquid keeps oxygen at bay, and it is this tendency to rise to the top of the fermenting beer that has given ale yeasts the name of "top fermenters", while lager yeasts fall to the bottom of the vessel and are known as "bottom fermenters". The terms, however, are seriously misleading, because any brewer's yeast must work at all levels of the liquid

After each brew, yeast is collected, pressed to remove any remaining liquid, and then stored in refrigerators to be re-used

if it is to convert sugars into alcohol. Better terms are "warm fermentation" for ale yeast and "cold fermentation" for lager strains.

In some modern ale breweries, fermentation takes place in enclosed conical fermenters. The yeast gradually falls to the bottom of the vessel as though it were a lager strain. Brewers will replace such yeasts with a pure culture after just a few brews, otherwise it would not produce the correct ale characteristics.

Lager yeast is classified as *Saccharomyces carlsbergensis*, as the first pure culture was isolated at the Carlsberg brewery in Copenhagen. Today it is more commonly called *Saccharomyces uvarum*. Lager brewing began in central Europe in the fifteenth century, when brewers in Bavaria stored – lagered in German – their beers in deep, icy caves to keep them in drinkable condition during the long, hot summers. The cold stopped wild yeasts attacking and infecting the brews, and also forced the brewer's yeast to work more slowly and precipitate to the bottom of the vessels.

Golden Pilsner

In the nineteenth century, with the aid of ice-making machines and refrigerators, a brewer named Gabriel Sedlmayr II, working at the Spaten brewery in Munich, developed lager brewing on a commercial scale. These first commercial lagers, however, were dark. It was when a golden lager was produced in Pilsen, in neighbouring Bohemia, that the new method of brewing became an international craze and Pilsner a much-imitated – and ultimately, much-abused – style. Lagering became popular because the beer was more stable, with fewer flavour fluctuations from brew to brew. As a result of lower temperatures, brewers had better control over fermentation. The yeast turns more sugar into alcohol, producing a dryer beer with little or no fruitiness. Fermentation is in two stages: primary fermentation starts at around 5–9°C (41–48°F) and lasts for as long as two weeks, twice the time ale fermentation takes. The beer is then stored – lagered – at 0°C (32°F). During lagering, a secondary

A mash tun at Marston's brewery in Staffordshire

fermentation takes place, with the yeast slowly turning the remaining sugars into alcohol and carbon dioxide.

Today, there is a trend towards shorter lagering periods. Some "international" brands enjoy a brief honeymoon of just a couple of weeks in the lagering tanks. But classic lagers, such as the Czech Budweiser Budvar, enjoy three months' lagering and emerge with clean, quenching palates, delicate aromas and a complex balance of malt and hops.

Wild fermentation

There is a further type of fermentation in the world of brewing. It is confined to the Senne Valley area of Belgium, based in Brussels, where a handful of specialist brewers produce beers by wild, or spontaneous, fermentation. These lambic and gueuze beers are left to cool under the roofs of the brewhouses; during the night, airborne yeasts enter through open windows and attack the sugars in the solution. The two main yeast strains have been identified as members of the *Brettanomyces* family and are labelled *lambicus* and *bruxellensis*, though more than 100 wild strains have been identified in lambic breweries. The resulting beers, some fermented with fruit, are vinous and cidery, and break down the boundaries between wine and beer.

THE STRENGTH OF BEER

Alcoholic strength used to be expressed in many different and confusing ways. In Britain, beer was taxed on its "original gravity" before fermentation, while other European countries used degrees Balling or Plato. Fortunately, most countries have now adopted the system of Alcohol by Volume (ABV), which is, as the name suggests, a measure of the amount of alcohol in the finished beer. The only major exception is the USA, which prefers to use Alcohol by Weight (ABW). As alcohol is lighter than water, ABW figures are approximately 25 per cent lower than for ABV, so a 4 per cent ABV beer would be 3.2 per cent in the USA. Not that you will find any indication of strength on most American labels, though a Supreme Court ruling in spring 1995 allowed breweries to state alcohol ratings if they wish. Some American craft breweries are now using ABV in preference to ABW.

In Canada, strength is shown as Alcohol by Volume (ABV).

IN THE BREWERY

No two breweries are alike, and many modern breweries blur the distinction between ale and lager. Some breweries use the same equipment for both types of beer, though ale and lager yeasts are kept strictly apart to avoid cross-fertilization. (The brewing processes for ale and lager described below are the classic methods for both styles.)

Both start in the same way, with the arrival of malt in the brewhouse. The malt is first screened to remove any small stones or other impurities that may have survived the malting process. It is then "cracked" in a malt mill to produce a rough powder called "grist", which gives us the expression "all grist to the mill".

Most of the malt is ground to a fine flour, but it is also blended with coarser grits and the rough husks of the grain, which act as a natural filter during the mashing stage. The grist is then ready to start the brewing process.

Classic ale brewing

The first stage of ale brewing is an infusion mash. Grist and brewing liquor are mixed in a large circular vessel known as a mash tun, which may be made of copper, cast iron or stainless steel, and is covered by a lid that can be raised by pulleys. Balanced above the tun is a large tube, a nineteenth-century device called a Steel's Masher, after the Mr Steel who invented it. Exact proportions of grist and hot liquor are mixed by an Archimedes screw inside the masher, and the mixture then flows into the mash tun.

Temperature is crucial at this stage. If it is too high, the enzymes will be destroyed; too low, and the enzymes will work sluggishly and fail to convert some starches

into sugar. The liquor, which has been stored in special tanks in the roof of the brewery, is heated to 75ºC (180ºF). This is known as "strike heat". It is higher than mashing temperature – 65ºC (150ºF) – but the coolness of the grist will quickly reduce the temperature of the liquor to the desired level. If the temperature falls too low, more hot liquor can be pumped into the mash tun through its slotted base. The brewer has to avoid "cold spots" in the mash where the grist would turn into a paste, refuse to release its sugars and block every pipe and outlet.

Adjuncts

At this stage, the brewer may blend in other cereals with the malt. These are known as adjuncts, and are used to help clarify the beer, reduce nitrogen haze and give the right flavour balance the brewer seeks. The usual adjuncts in ale brewing are torrefied wheat or barley, which are similar to popcorn. The grain is scorched – torrefied – and the heat pops the endosperm and gelatinizes the starch. Flaked maize, another popular adjunct, is made by steaming or milling the grain to gelatinize the starch. Wheat flour is also widely used and gives a fine flavour to beer, but it can only be used in tiny amounts or it will clog up the brewing equipment. Adjuncts do not contain enzymes. It is up to the enzymes in the malt to convert the adjuncts' starches into sugar. All adjuncts have to be used in small amounts: add too much popcorn to beer and it will taste like breakfast cereal.

Starches to sugar

The thick, porridge-like mixture is now left to stand in the mash tun for one or two hours as saccharification takes place. This means that starches turn to sugar as a result of enzymic activity. Enzymes are biological catalysts. The two most important ones in brewing are alpha-amylase, which converts starches into maltose and dextrins, and beta-amylase, which produces only maltose. Maltose is highly fermentable, while dextrin cannot be fermented by brewer's yeast and is important for giving "body" to beer. If all the sugars turned to alcohol, the beer would be high in alcohol, but thin in flavour.

The sugars dissolve into the liquor, producing a sweet liquid called wort, pronounced "wurt". The mash

"Real ale", unique to Britain, in "racked" into casks – final conditioning takes place in the pub cellar

tun has taps fitted to the side and the brewer can run off a sample of the wort to check that saccharification is under way. He can usually tell just from the bready smell and taste of the liquid, but if necessary he can carry out a simple chemical test by mixing some wort with a few drops of iodine. If the iodine stays clear, sugar has been produced. If it turns blue-black, then starch is still present. It is important to stop the mashing process once saccharification has taken place, otherwise tannins in the wort will produce an unpleasant flavour, rather like stewed tea. Mashing is terminated by pumping more hot liquor into the tun to kill the enzymes.

The slotted base of the vessel is now opened and the sweet wort starts to filter through the thick cake of spent grain. Perforated tubes in the roof of the tun start to revolve and "sparge" the grains with more hot liquor to flush out any stubborn sugars that remain behind. Sparging was a Scottish invention and the word stresses the Old Alliance between Scotland and France, for sparge comes from the French word *esparger*, meaning "to sprinkle".

Waste not, want not

Next, the hot sweet wort flows from the mash tun into a receiving vessel known as the "underback". Several vessels in a brewery have "back" in their name, an old word that is derived from the same root as bucket. In medieval breweries, wort would have been ladled from the mash vessel into a series of metal or wooden buckets. The spent grains left behind are not wasted and are sold to farmers as protein-rich cattle feed. In the brewing industry, nothing is wasted. Used hops are in great demand as garden fertilizer, while excess yeast is sold to companies that make yeast extract.

Run-off from the mash tun takes two hours. The wort is then pumped from the underback to the coppers. Many modern "coppers" are made of stainless steel, but a genuine copper copper is a delight, a domed and burnished vessel, like a cross between a diving bell and a lunar module. In the days before hops were used in brewing, the wort had to be boiled in order to kill any bacteria. Today, boiling has a dual purpose: to ensure absolute purity of the wort, and to add the essential acids, oils and tannins of the hops. If an ale mash tun is like a giant tea pot, infusing malt and hot water, then the copper is akin to a coffee percolator. It has a central tube – the calandria – topped by a dome called a "Chinese hat". As the wort starts to boil, it gushes up the tube into the main body of the copper and begins what is known to brewers as a "good rolling boil".

Hops are then added through a porthole in the domed roof of the copper. They are not, however, added in one batch. Instead, the brewer will add them at stages, usually twice or three times. The almost magical qualities of the hop will kill any bacteria in the wort, destroy the enzymes to stop any further saccharification and force proteins in the wort to come out of suspension and coagulate at the bottom of the copper. If all the hops were added in one batch, many of the vital bittering and aroma qualities would be lost in the boil. So the brewer will add bittering hops in one or two stages and then will "late hop" just a few minutes before the end of the boil with aroma hops.

Invert sugar

Some brewers will add sugar during the copper boil. Sugar is often considered to be an adjunct, but it has no starches that need to be attacked by enzymes, which is why it is added in the copper, not the mash tun. It is totally fermentable and the problem with brewing sugar is that if too much is used, then the finished beer will be high in alcohol but thin in body. Brewing sugar is called "invert sugar", as it has been inverted into its component parts of glucose and fructose. It comes in different colours, depending on the brewer's requirements, and is simply labelled Number One Invert, Number Two Invert and so on up the colour scale. Some of the sugars from both the malt and the invert will be caramelized during the boil, adding colour to the finished beer.

At the end of the boil, a powdered seaweed called Irish moss is added to the copper to clarify the wort by encouraging any remaining proteins and other detritus to settle at the bottom of the vessel. The spent hops act as a filter as the wort flows out through the slotted base of the copper into a hop back, where it is left to cool. The residue left behind is known as "trub". Mixed with the spent hops, it makes a rich compost for gardeners.

Some brewers will add further hops in the hop back to give additional aroma to the wort. Three famous ales from England – Adnams Extra and Greene King Abbot Ale, both from Suffolk, and Timothy Taylor's Landlord, from Yorkshire – circulate over a deep bed of hops in the hop back and have a pungent "hop nose" as a result. If pelletized hops rather than whole flowers are used, the hopped wort is pumped from the copper to a whirlpool, where the spent hops are removed by centrifugal force.

Cooling the wort

Before fermentation can begin, the temperature of the boiling hopped wort has to be lowered to 18°C (64°F). In a few breweries, the wort is left to cool in an open shallow vessel called a "cool ship", but there is always the danger that it can be attacked by wild, airborne yeasts as it cools. The vast majority of breweries use heat-exchange units known as paraflows. The wort is pumped through a series of plates that look like old-fashioned school radiators. Each plate containing wort is next to one filled with cold water. As the wort flows along the plates, it will get progressively cooler, until it is finally ready to be turned into alcohol.

Pitching the yeast

The cooled wort is pumped into fermenting vessels and liquid yeast is then mixed or "pitched" into it. Before it is pitched, however, a sample of the yeast will have been checked under a microscope in the brewery laboratory. Yeast cells are invisible to the naked eye, but under the microscope they can be seen darting and diving around. What the brewery is looking for are white yeast cells. Blue cells are dead and would impede fermentation, while black rods among the cells indicate a yeast infection, which would require the entire batch to be poured down the nearest drain.

Fermenting vessels vary from one ale brewery to the next. (Specialist fermenters unique to certain areas, such as Burton union and Yorkshire squares, will be covered in the England section pp318–30) Most conventional ale breweries use open vessels, though nowadays there is a trend towards covering them in order to stop CO_2 escaping into the atmosphere. Depending on their age, fermenters may be built from wood, stone or various metals. Stainless steel is used to build modern vessels. Older ones are normally lined with polypropylene to avoid a build-up of bacteria and old yeast in cracks and other rough surfaces.

The role of oxygen

Brewer's yeast respires in two ways: aerobically (with oxygen), and anaerobically (without oxygen). Pasteur described the ability of yeast to breathe without oxygen as *la vie sans air* – "life without air". Yeast works with oxygen at the start of fermentation. In fact, brewers agitate and aerate the wort to make sure there is plenty of dissolved oxygen present. The yeast works rapidly, with bubbles rising to the surface of the wort. Within a few hours, a brown slick covers the surface and within 24 hours this has grown to a dense, rocky head that rises to peaks known as "cauliflowers". The yeast head is streaked with brown and black from proteins in the wort. The yeast head will be removed, or "skimmed off", from time to time to stop dead cells and detritus from impeding the work of the yeast in solution.

Enzymes in the yeast – maltase and invertase – turn sugar into alcohol and carbon dioxide. The converted sugars are assimilated by the yeast cells which at the same time are growing by dividing and fusing into fresh cells. Maltase enzymes produce glucose, while invertase turns sucrose into glucose and fructose. Dextrins cannot be fermented, neither can lactose – "milk sugar" – which is sometimes added to sweeten stouts. They remain to give body and sweetness to beer.

Fermentation causes the temperature of the wort to rise. Yeast is pitched at around 15°C (60°F), but during fermentation this will rise to 25°C (80°F). Fermentation also creates chemical compounds, known as "esters", which are present in the atmosphere above the vessels in the form of fruity aromas. Depending on the strength of the beer and the balance of malts, adjuncts and sugars, the aromas may be reminiscent of apples, oranges, banana, pineapple, pear drops, liquorice or molasses. In some very strong beers, the esters can be reminiscent of fresh leather.

Eventually, the yeast will be overcome by the alcohol. After about seven days, the yeast cells will start to clump together and rise to the surface. This is known as flocculation. If it happens too early in the process, the brewer will have to aerate the wort again. When almost all the yeast has risen out of suspension, fermentation is at an end. Throughout the entire process, the brewer will check the transformation of sugar into alcohol by measuring the sweetness of the liquid with a hydrometer or saccharometer. Before the yeast is pitched, the wort may have a "gravity" of 1,040 degrees. Water has a gravity of 1,000 degrees, which means that 40 degrees of fermentable sugar is present in the wort. Since maltose, unlike brewing sugar, is not totally fermentable, the final gravity will be around 1,006 degrees, though stronger beers may have more sugar remaining.

Green beer

Brewers, being fundamentalists as well as traditionalists, like to give the beer seven days or "two Sabbaths" in the fermenters. When fermentation is at an end, the wort has been turned into beer, but it is not yet ready to drink. It is known as "green beer" and has to spend several days in conditioning tanks to mature. Some of the rougher alcohols and fruity esters will be purged, producing a cleaner and drinkable beer. When it is ready to leave the brewery, the beer may go in two different directions. Packaged beer, either for bottle, can

The beer is checked for impurities as well as its colour and clarity

or keg, will be filtered to remove any remaining yeast and then pasteurized. Carbon dioxide is pumped into the container as the beer is packaged to give it both sparkle and a lively head when poured.

Real ale

The beer style unique to Britain, "real ale", does not go through any one these processes. Instead, it is racked from the conditioning tanks straight into casks, though

253

additional hops for aroma and sugar for a secondary fermentation may also be added. The beer leaves the brewery in an unfinished state because final conditioning takes place in the pub cellar, where the yeast in the cask continues to turn the remaining sugars into alcohol. As the beer matures, it gains not only a small amount of additional strength, but also rounded and fruity flavours. A glutinous substance known as "finings", made from isinglass, is added to attract yeast cells and other detritus to the bottom of the cask, leaving a clear beer above. Casks are vented by porous pegs hammered through a hole in the top of the cask to allow carbon dioxide to escape, though the cask has to be sealed when secondary fermentation is finished in order to keep sufficient gas in the beer to give it sparkle.

Classic lager brewing

The aim of a lager brewer is identical to that of an ale brewer: to extract the sugars from the malt, boil the wort with hops, ferment the hopped wort and produce beer. But the methods used are a variation on the theme, a variation that extends beyond the use of bottom-fermenting yeast, since it is based upon lower temperatures at almost every stage of production.

As lager malt is often less modified than ale malt, a decoction mashing system is used in which the grist is mixed with hot brewing liquor in a mash kettle at a starting temperature of around 38°C (100°F). Part of the mash will be pumped to a cooker, where it is heated to a higher temperature – between 43–56°C (120–130°F) – and then returned to the kettle. Another portion of the mash will be pumped to the cooker and the temperature will rise to 65°C (150°F) before being returned to the kettle. Returning the portions of heated mash to the kettle raises the temperature to around 50°C (120°F).

Rest period

The central feature of the decoction system is that the main body of the mash has a "protein rest" at around 45–55°C (113–130°F) for periods of an hour of more. This rest period allows excessive protein, contained in malt that is high in nitrogen, to be degraded by a process known as "proteolysis". The heating of portions of the mash at higher temperatures gelatinizes the starch present in poorly modified malt, so allowing it to be attacked by enzymes. Both protein and starch would cause haze in the finished beer if they were not tackled during mashing.

When double or triple decoction has taken place, the temperature of the kettle is raised to 75°C (167°F) – the same as the mashing temperature in an ale brewery. At this heat, the mash is pumped to a third vessel, called a "lauter tun", which has a false bottom and clarifies the wort as it is run off. It also sparges the spent grain. Unlike an ale mash tun, though, this cannot be done in the mash kettle (which does not have a false bottom) because of the pumping required to the cooker and back.

Different coloured malts can be used during mashing but, if the beer is being produced in Germany, the Czech Republic or other countries that adhere to the German Pure Beer Pledge, no cereal adjuncts will be used. Similarly, no brewing sugars are added during the boil in a wort kettle. These days, most lager brewers use pelletized hops and they are added in two or three stages during the boil. The hopped wort is then pumped to a whirlpool and centrifuged to remove the mushy pellets and other detritus.

Fermentation

Next, the hopped wort is cooled and pumped to fermentation vessels. Lager fermentation is in two stages. The first stage – primary fermentation – may take place in either a tall, conical, stainless steel vessel, or in a more traditional, horizontal one. Temperature ranges between 5–9°C (41–48°F). At such temperatures, the yeast will work much more slowly than an ale strain as it converts sugars to alcohol and CO_2. As a result, there is much less build-up of yeast head and the purity of the single-strain variety creates few fruity esters.

Primary fermentation lasts for around two weeks. The green beer is then pumped to lagering tanks, where it is held at 0°C/32°F or just above. During this period of cold conditioning, which may last for several weeks or months, the yeast continues to turn sugars into alcohol as it precipitates at the bottom of the tank.

The finished beer will be clean and quenching, but it will deliberately lack the rounded, fruity quality of an ale, unless it is an exceptionally strong "bock" beer that has been lagered for as long as a year. The cool temperatures and slow conditioning enable the brewer to remove most of the flavour characteristics that an ale brewer seeks, leaving a lighter, malt-accented beer with a delicate hop character. Neither dry hopping nor the use of isinglass finings are permitted under the Reinheitsgebot.

Pasteurization

When lagering is complete, the finished beer will be filtered and often pasteurized. Louis Pasteur was a mixed blessing to the brewing industry. He solved the problems of infection in breweries and unravelled the mysteries of yeast. But he also introduced a heating method that can unbalance the subtle aromas and flavours of beer and give it hints of burnt toffee and cardboard. As the head brewer of the Brand brewery in the Netherlands once stated: "Pasteurization is for the cow shed, not the brew house." Grolsch, another leading Dutch lager brewery, does not pasteurize its beers. And what is good enough for them should be good enough for the rest of the world.

Cherries are sometimes blended with Belgian wheat beers to give a tart and quenching character and the increase the alcohol level

THE FAMILIES OF BEER

Ale is the world's oldest style of beer, and modern ales are descendants of the beers brewed in around 3,000 years BC in Ancient Egypt and other parts of North Africa and the Middle East. The British Isles remains the major centre of ale brewing. Though lager has made considerable incursions into Britain and Ireland, around half the beer produced in those islands is still in ale form. England is best known for bitter, a well-hopped beer that is best drunk in unpasteurized draught form in pubs. Bitter evolved from the India Pale Ales and other forms of pale ale introduced in the nineteenth century and brewed primarily in Burton-on-Trent, a town famous for its brewing since the twelfth century.

Porter and stout

Before the arrival of pale ale, the British Isles, like all other countries, produced brown and dark beers. Before the development of pale ale and lager, England's singular contribution to the history of beer was porter, a dark brown or black beer first brewed at the turn of the eighteenth century. In fact, the craze for porter created the modern commercial brewing industry. The strongest – stoutest – version of porter was called "stout". Although support for porter and stout declined in Britain as pale ale grew, it took deep root in Ireland and has never diminished. Irish ale and lager are both brewed in the Irish Republic, but dry stout remains the dominant beer. In Britain, mild ale, a dark brown and lightly hopped beer, which was once blended into porter, has kept some support, especially in areas of heavy industry where workers need to refresh themselves with light and slightly sweet beer. Britain also enjoys a growing range of seasonal beers. Rich and fruity old and winter ales have been joined in recent years by spring, summer and autumn beers.

Belgian varieties

In Belgium, ales are only a small proportion of a market dominated by such famous lager brands as Stella Artois and Jupiler. But the ale market is growing as both Belgians and the outside world have come to marvel at the enormous variety available in such a small country. Trappist monks, for example, brew ales of enormous complexity in their monasteries, while wheat beers, often flavoured with herbs and spices, have become cult drinks with the young. Pale ales and golden ales have enormous hop character, while in French-speaking Wallonia, seasonal or *saison* beers recall an earlier, bucolic time, when ale was brewed by farmers for their families and workers. In parts of Flanders, russet-coloured ales are stored in oak vats and have a sour and lactic taste. The most remarkable of all the Belgian ales are the wild beers of the Senne Valley, where lambic and gueuze beers are produced by spontaneous fermentation. When fruit – usually cherries or raspberries – is blended with these beers, they have a wonderful tart and quenching character. The success and interest in Belgian ales is creating a smaller revival in ale in the neighbouring Netherlands, dominated by the giant Heineken lager group.

German varieties

Germany is the world's leading lager-brewing nation, producing beers of awesome quality, a long way removed from the light, bland, international interpretations in other countries. There are also powerful variations in the style, with malty versions in Bavaria, rounded but hoppier ones in Dortmunder, and intensely bitter beers in the north. Not all lagers are pale. In the Munich region in particular, dark lagers – dunkel – are still popular. The Germans also brew seasonal beers and strong beers. "Bock" means strong and the name is a corruption of the name of the town of Einbeck, where the style was first brewed many centuries ago. Bock also means "goat" in German and many bock beer labels depict the animal. In the Munich area, exceptionally strong lagers have names ending in -ator, as in Celebrator or Triumphator. Seasonal beers are recalled in the Märzen (March) beers, brewed at the end of winter and stored until the autumn. Traditionally, it was Märzen beers that were served at the world-famous Oktoberfest in Munich. Other German specialities include the smoked beers of Bamberg, using wood-smoked malt, and beers in which the malt sugars are caramelized in the mash kettle by plunging in red-hot stones.

Germany also has some distinctive ales. Cologne has golden-coloured Kölsch beers, so treasured that they have the equivalent of an *appellation côntrolée* from the government, while nearby Düsseldorf has amber-coloured Alt – "old" – beers. Wheat beers have become vogue drinks, the spicy, fruity Bavarian style growing in recent years to 30 per cent of the beer market. In Berlin, the wheat beers are injected with a lactic culture to give them a mouth-puckering sourness.

The golden Pilsner

Bohemia, now part of the Czech Republic, was the home of the first golden Pilsner lagers. The name comes from the great industrial city of Pilsen, also famous for the Škoda motor car. While Munich developed commercial lagering, the first pale beer of the style came from Pilsen at the height of the Industrial Revolution. Today, only two breweries brew genuine Pilsners, Pilsner Urquell – meaning "Original Source Pilsner" – and Gambrinus. Beers made in Prague or České Budějovice (Budweis in German) are termed respectively "Prague" beers or "Budweiser" beers. Outside the Czech Republic, though, brewers are not so punctilious. Any light lager is termed Pilsner or Pils, even though it has little in common with the rich complexity of the genuine article.

In both Scandinavia and the Far East, lagers ranging from the bland to the complex are the norm, but there are small pockets of dark beer. The Japanese, for example, brew some flavourful dark beers, while Sweden and Finland brew porters produced by proper warm fermentation.

Brewed in the USA

The history of American brewing has been dominated by both immigration and politics. The first settlers from England took an ale culture with them across the Atlantic, but ale took second place to lager when the second wave of immigrants from central Europe arrived. During the long years of Prohibition in the 1920s, quality ales and lagers largely disappeared, and the breweries that survived dominated the market with increasingly bland light or "lite" lagers.

Today, however, there are more than 1,000 small craft breweries producing ales and lagers of enormous quality, while the one true American beer style – steam beer, a hybrid lager-cum-ale – has been rescued and resuscitated by the Anchor Brewery in San Francisco.

In Australasia, ale was supplanted by lager early in the twentieth century. Today, famous brands such as Foster's and Castlemaine XXXX dominate the market, but the success of one traditional ale brewery in Adelaide, Cooper's, has prompted a small ale revival in other parts of the country. There are now several brewpubs in Australia and New Zealand that are concentrating on ale brewing. As the twentieth century drew to a close, ale, against all the odds, was the world's most sought-after revivalist beer style.

THE BEER FAMILY

Ale (warm fermenting) types and styles

Belgium Ales. Golden ales. Lambic and gueuze spontaneous fermentation/kriek and frambozen. Brown ales/brown kriek. Flemish red ales. Trappist ales. Abbey ales. Saison. Wheat beers.

The Caribbean Stout.

England Mild (pale and dark). Sweet/"Milk" stout. Stout and porter. Bitter. Northern brown ales. Special bitter/India Pale Ale. Strong bitter. Summer ale. Harvest ale. Old ale/Winter ale. Barley wine.

France Bière de garde. Bière de Mars. Bière de Printemps.

Germany Alt. Kölsch. Wheat beer (Berlin/Bavaria). Stone beer.

Ireland Irish ale. Irish red ale. Dry stout.

The Netherlands Aajt. Amber. Bock. Oud Bruin. Trappist ale. Wheat beer.

Scandinavia Porter. Sahti/Juniper beer.

Scotland Light/60 shilling. Heavy/70 shilling. Export/80 shilling. 90 shilling/Wee Heavy.

Sri Lanka Stout.

United States Amber ale. Cream ale. Steam beer*. India Pale Ale. Porter/Stout. Wheat beer.

Lager (cold fermenting) types and styles

Czech Republic Budweiser. Pilsner. Prague beer. Black lager.

Germany Munich Dunkel, Munich Helles.

Dortmunder/Export. Bock/Double Bock. Märzen/Oktoberfest. Rauchbier. Black beer. German Pilsner.

Japan Dry beer. Black beer. American/German-style lager.

United States Lite lagers. Malt liquor. Pilsner. Oktoberfest/märzen. Steam beer*. Bock/Double bock. Ice beer.

Canada Ice beer.

Mexico Vienna-style dark lager. Light lager.

Note *Steam beer is a hybrid, made with a lager yeast but fermented at an ale temperature. Most other countries brew international-style lagers, based loosely on the Pilsner style.

THE WORLD A-Z OF BEER

Fancy a beer? It is one of the oldest invitations in the world and one that sets the tastebuds tingling. Beer, more than any other drink, means conviviality, a pleasure shared. But simply to ask for "a beer" in a bar or a pub is to risk missing out on the diversity and the complexity of styles available on the world stage. If you ask for "a beer" in an English pub you may be handed the stock bitter or, if you're unlucky, the standard lager. An interested barperson, on the other hand, may ask you to specify. Perhaps a mild ale, or a pale ale, or a special bitter, a porter, a stout, an old ale, a barley wine or a winter warmer? You begin to see that beer is not such a simple thing; that not all brown liquids are the same.

In Germany it would be absurd and mildly irritating to call for "ein bier, bitte" or, even worse, "a lager", which to the Germans is a brewing term and certainly not a definition of a style. Again, you would be asked to be specific: a Helles (light), or a Dunkel (dark), a strong Bock, an export, a Pils, a Weizen (wheat) beer or the two proud and idiosyncratic warm fermenting styles of Cologne and Düsseldorf, a Kölsch or an Alt.

Belgium packs within its small territory such a manifold range of beers that a waiter confronted by the demand for just "a beer" would respond by handing you a drinks menu conveniently divided into pale ales, Trappist, Abbey beers, red beers, white beers and fruit beers – and that is just scratching the surface of the choice available.

Even in the USA, where for generations the call for "a beer" was synonymous with asking for a standardized bland, mass-marketed lager, the explosion of small craft breweries – close to 1,000 by the turn of the century – the beer world has been turned on its head. A bar specializing in craft beers may offer you an India Pale Ale, an amber ale, a red ale, a "London" porter or an "Irish" stout. If lager beers are the specialities, they will be far removed from a Bud or a Coors. You may get a genuine Märzen, a Bock, a Celebrator, an Oktoberfestbier, a Dunkel, a Pilsner, or a Dortmunder.

In Australia, where for decades beer drinking was epitomized by the "six o'clock swill" – as many schooners as possible knocked back before the shutters came down – more liberal opening hours have encouraged greater emphasis on quality and a willingness to experiment. Craft breweries and brewpubs may not challenge the hegemony of such mass market brands as Castlemaine and Foster's, but choice is beginning to seep across the continent. The revival of ale, personified by the doughty Adelaide firm of Cooper's, founded by an emigrant from Yorkshire, has created interest in a beer style that pre-dates the lager revolution and proves that warm-fermented beer can be enjoyed in hot climates.

In countries considered to be quintessentially within the lager fold, there are surprises. In Japan you will find black beers and stouts that offer welcome choice in a country where pale lagers dominate. And in pockets of Scandinavia warm-fermented porters and stouts stick their heads above the ice floes.

The world of beer is not noted for its conformity. As beer makes inroads even into great wine-making countries such as France and Italy, drinkers are discovering a multiplicity of flavours and aromas.

In Northern France – or "French Flanders", as the locals prefer to call it – the ancient style of *bière de garde* has been resurrected with considerable success.

Similar to the *saisons* of Belgium, these French "keeping beers" were originally made by farmers for consumption during the summer and the harvest. They are members of the ale family and their critical acclaim has stimulated a number of small craft breweries to start production and introduce other interpretations of the style, such as March, autumn and winter beers. They have become a fashion beer in Lille, capital of French Flanders, where specialist cafés offer an abundance of choice and even brew on the premises. Jenlain, leading city of the revivalists, has its own café. Not to be outdone, Italians who used to dismiss beer as a light summer refresher are taking a greater interest. The big commercial breweries have added some beers of distinction to their portfolios, while several new craft breweries in the north of the country are producing ales, wheat beers and German-style lagers with great dedication to style.

The term "beer" covers a host of drinks, from mild ale to barley wine

THE BEERS OF EUROPE

Europe is the cradle of modern brewing. The lagering or storing of beer – usually in icy caves – developed empirically in Central Europe from medieval times and then spread like a bush fire when ice-making machines were invented during the Industrial Revolution. The first commercial lagers in Munich were dark in colour. It was Pilsen in Bohemia – today's Czech Republic – that produced the first golden lager and gave the world a style known as Pilsner or Pils. Britain and Ireland remained faithful to ale: pale ale or bitter in Britain and dark, roasty dry stouts in Ireland while Belgium offers a remarkable choice of ales, including some brewed by Trappist monks.

AUSTRIA

Austria lost not only a great empire but a beer style as well. Today brewers will argue there was no such thing as a Vienna style based on "red" malt, but history tends to prove them wrong. In far away Mexico, briefly and incongruously ruled by Austria, red-brown lagers such as Dos Equis and Negro Modela pay homage to a style that marked Vienna out from such all-conquering neighbours as Munich and Pilsner.

Anton Dreher was one of the great brewing innovators. He worked closely with Sedlmayr in Munich to develop commercial lager brewing in the nineteenth century. While the first Munich lagers were dark brown – Dunkel – Dreher's were amber-red. No information exists about Dreher's recipe, but he was known in Vienna as the "English maltstar" and he may have brought from England a coke-fired kiln that enabled him to produce a paler malt than the wood-cured ones in Munich. The water in Vienna is harder than in Pilsen, which would give the finished beer an amber colour not dissimilar to the pale ales of Burton-on-Trent. In the 1840s Dreher would not have had access to stewed malts such as caramalt and crystal, which did not appear until the turn of the century.

Vienna lager beers were first produced by Dreher around 1841 from his brewery in Schwechat in the Vienna suburbs. The brewery still exists, a remarkable group of buildings, both bucolic and baronial, parts dating back to a hunting lodge built in 1750 for Archduchess Maria Theresa, ruler of most of Europe,

who is thought to have used the lodge for less than courtly purposes.

In Dreher's day, Schwechat was a vast enterprise challenging Pilsner Urquell in size. He built other breweries in Bohemia (at Michelob, a name still in use as Anheuser-Busch's premium beer in the USA), in Budapest and in Trieste. The Italian brewery still bears Dreher's name though it is now owned by Heineken. In his heyday of the 1870s, with the Industrial Revolution going full bore and the world of beer turned upside down as a result of new technologies, Dreher was exporting beer far and wide. But his Vienna company went out of business in the 1930s and the style of beer he had created became just a fading memory for elderly Viennese. Today Austrian beers tend to ape the Bavarian style across the border, though they do not adhere to the Reinheitsgebot. Corn, wheat and rice are used as adjuncts, and hop rates in general are not high. The result is pale, golden lagers that tend to be malty with a sweetish edge and only light bitterness.

The Schwechat Brewery is now part of Austria's biggest group, Bräu AG, short for Osterreichische Bräu-Aktiengesellschaft – the Austrian Brewing Corporation, with head offices in Linz. Schwechat Lager (5.2 per cent ABV) is malty and rounded while the premium Hopfenperle (5.3 per cent ABV) has more hop character and a dry finish. It has no connection with the Swiss beer of the same name. Bräu AG also brews under the Kaiser and Zipfer labels. Zipfer Urtyp – Original – (5.4 per cent ABV) has a fine perfumy hop aroma and finish with good balancing malt.

The second biggest Austrian group is Steirische Bräuindustrie of Graz. The name means Styrian Breweries and it is based in the hop-growing region of Styria, though most hops today that carry the name come from a province of the same name situated over the border in Slovenia. The most assertive and characterful beers from the group are brewed under the Gösser label. Gösser Export is 5.0 per cent ABV, brewed with pale malt, caramalt, maize and rice, with Hallertau, Spalt, Styrian and Goldings hops (20 IBUs). With just gentle hop bitterness, the beer has a rich malt and vanilla aroma and palate with some hop notes in the bitter-sweet finish.

Stiegl in Salzburg was founded in 1492, the year Columbus landed in the Americas. The connection is celebrated by Columbus (5.3 per cent ABV) a rich, malty but well-hopped lager.

Ottakringer in Vienna dates from 1837 and is still family-owned. Its beers are among the most characterful in the country due to the generous use of Saaz hops. Its Helles (5.1 per cent ABV) is tart, quenching and aromatic while its Gold Fassl Spezial (5.6 per cent ABV) has a more pronounced maltiness balanced by perfumy hops.

The small Eggenburg Brewery in the town of the same name has a beer that panders to Scotch whisky drinkers while offering a colour akin to a genuine Vienna Red. MacQueens Nessie Whisky Malt Red Beer is a powerful 7.5 per cent ABV with 26.7 IBUs from Hallertau hops. The malt is imported from Scotland and imparts a delicious smoky, peaty character. The colour of the beer is amber and the finish is long and smoky with hop undercurrents. "It's like a whisky and soda," according to the brewer. He also makes an Urbock 23°, the number referring to its strength on the Plato scale

which translates into 9.3 per cent ABV. It is lagered for an impressive nine months, has a rich fruity aroma, rounded malt and hops in the mouth and a big vinous and hoppy finish. It is made from Pilsner and Munich malts and Saaz and Hallertau hops (40 IBUs).

The Josef Sigl Brewery in Obertrum keeps the wheat beer tradition alive with a warm-fermenting Weizen Gold (5.2 per cent ABV). It is hopped with Hallertau and has a spicy cloves aroma, a tart and refreshing palate and a lingering bitter-sweet finish.

The Kapsreiter brewey in Schärding brews a pale Landbier Hell (5.3 per cent ABV) with a superb orange fruit aroma, a fruity palate and a bitter-sweet finish with a good hop character.

The new, family-owned St Georgs brewery specializes in traditional, cloudy, unfiltered "Vollbiers", both pale and dark, as well as a pale wheat beer.

Two brewpubs of note are the Fischer Gasthof at Billroth Strasse 17, Döbling in Vienna, which offers a Helles and a Bock. In Nüssdorf, Baron Hendrik Bachofen von Echte has a fine brewery and restaurant in the cellars of his castle. He makes warm-fermenting beers, including a Helles brewed with 30 per cent wheat malt, a malty Altbier and a chocolatey and dry Irish-style stout called Sir Henry's.

AUSTRIAN BREWERS

Braueuerei Eggenberg, Eggenberg 1, 4655 Vorchdorf.
Braueuerei Kapsreiter, A-4780 Schärding.
Josef Sigl Brauerei, A-5162 Obertrum SLBG.
Steirische Bräuindustrie, Reininghausstrasse 1-7, A-802 Graz STMK.
St Georgs-Bräu, A-8861 St Georgen o Murau.

BELGIUM

Belgians are passionate about beer. If you show an interest in the subject, waiters or bar owners tend to dive into cellars and return with dusty bottles they have been saving for "a special occasion". Often the bottles are wrapped in coloured tissue paper and have Champagne-style cradles and corks. Without any hesitation or fear of being derided, they will call such offerings "Grand Cru" or the Bourgogne (Burgundy) of the beer world. Unlike the British – whose collective stiff upper lip refuses to acknowledge that they also make some amazing ales – the Belgians have no qualms about proclaiming their beers to be as good as fine wine.

Belgian Pils

The choice in this small country is astonishing. But the recent revival of interest in Belgian ales – pale, golden, red, Trappist, Abbey, wheat and lambic – cannot disguise the fact that for everyday drinking the people consume vast amounts of Pilsner-style lagers. Purists may argue that only lagers from Pilsen in the Czech Republic should carry the appellation, but it cannot be said that the

Stella Artois, one of the two leading Pils brands, traces its origins to the fourteenth century

Belgian interpretations of the style are anything less than good. The two leading Pils brands, Stella Artois and Jupiler, come from the giant Interbrew group, the result of a 1980s merger between Stella Artois of Leuven and Piedboeuf of Jupille-sur-Meuse near Liège. The merger not only brought two leading breweries under one roof but also, as their places of origin suggest, managed to bridge the linguistic divide. Leuven – Louvain in French – is a university city. In the sixteenth century there were 42 breweries in the city and not surprisingly the university developed a brewing faculty – the Academy of Brewing – that today offers laboratory and yeast cultivation facilities for Belgium's 150 breweries.

Stella Artois traces its origins to the Den Horen (the Horn) tavern that brewed beer from 1366 and began to supply the university from 1537. Sebastien Artois was an apprentice brewer at Den Horen, graduated as a master brewer and bought the brewery in 1717. His grandson Léonard busily expanded the business and bought two rival companies in Leuven. Den Horen Artois became one of the major commercial breweries in Europe and switched with enthusiasm to the new lagering methods in the late nineteenth century. Its first golden, cold-fermented beer was called Bock but unlike German Bocks, which are high in alcohol, this was weaker than a genuine Pilsner. The company achieved greater fame and fortune in 1926 when it brewed a stronger 5.0 per cent Pils-style beer, Stella Artois, that is now Belgium's best-known – though not best-selling – Pils. It is exported widely and brewed under licence in several countries. Stella Artois is made with great dedication to traditional methods. The brewery has a six-storey maltings in Leuven, using the floor method rather than modern tanks. Brewers believe that malt

spread out on warm floors and regularly turned and aerated produces a cleaner, sweeter beer. In the brewhouses – Artois once had a dozen but is consolidating them – the wort is boiled with Czech Saaz hops along with some German Northern Brewer and Tettnanger, as well as Styrians. The Saaz dominate, giving the finished beer (30 IBUs) an aromatic, slightly spicy aroma. Stella is lagered for around two months and is clean and quenching in the mouth with a finish that becomes dry as the hops emphasize their character. The Artois side of Interbrew also produces a stronger (5.7 per cent ABV) lager beer called Loburg, designed to counteract Danish "super premium" imports.

Jupiler (5.0 per cent ABV, around 25 IBUs) is the biggest-selling Pils in Belgium. The Piedboeuf family founded its brewery in 1853 in Jupille, believed to be the birthplace of Charlemagne and with a history of brewing that dates back to 1256. Jupiler's rise to popularity is impressive as it was launched as recently as 1966. It is an easy-drinking, soft, malt-accented beer lacking the hop character of Stella. Interbrew also owns the Lamot Pils brand, though the Lamot Brewery in Mechelen closed at the end of 1994.

Four-fifths of all Belgian Pils are accounted for by Interbrew and the second biggest brewing group, Alken-Maes, half-owned by Kronenbourg of France. Cristal Alken is the Pils favoured by connoisseurs. It was formulated in 1928 to suit the tastes of miners in the Limburg region. As a result it is more aggressively hoppy than other leading Belgian Pils. Alken is close to the German border and it could be the German Pils brewing tradition that has prompted Alken to make its beer a shade dryer and more positively bitter, though the brewers who formulated the beer claimed they were attempting to recreate a genuine Czech Pilsner.

Alken's partner, Maes (pronounced "Marse"), is based in Flemish-speaking Waarloos near Antwerp. In common with Limburg, this was once a heavy industrial area and there were some mighty thirsts to quench. Maes Pils first appeared in 1946 with some help from a German brewer. The company survived a period of ownership by the British Watney group and retains a magnificent copper brewhouse. Brewing is firmly traditional, with a double decoction mash using mainly Czech malt, more Czech influence in the Saaz

SELECTED PILS BREWERS

Alken, Alken-Maes, Stationstraat 2, 3820 Alken.

Maes, Alken-Maes, Waarloosveld 10, 2571 Kontich-Waarloos.

Haacht Brouwerij, Provinciesteenweg 28, 2890 Boortmeerbeek.

Brasserie Jupiler, Interbrew, rue de Vise 243, 4500 Jupille-sur-Meuse.

Stella Artois, Interbrew, Vaartstraat 94, 3000 Leuven.

hops in the copper, and a slow, cool, two-to-three months' lagering.

There are around 100 Pils brands in Belgium. Even some specialist ale brewers also produce a Pils in order to have a small slice of the substantial market. The most highly regarded Pils from a smaller brewer comes from Haacht near a village of the same name that is roughly equidistant from Brussels, Leuven and Mechelen. The Pils is called Primus and is a complex beer with a sweetish start leading to a refreshing palate and a dry finish with good hop influence. French and Dutch malts are joined by the ubiquitous Saaz and German varieties of hops.

Lambic

Lambic, a beer produced by spontaneous fermentation as a result of action by air-borne yeasts, is a potent link with brewing's past. Before brewers understood the mysteries of yeast, they allowed wild strains either in the air or in brewing vessels to attack malt sugars and turn them into alcohol. With the aid of science and technology, ale brewers and later lager producers turned their back on such antiquated methods and produced their beers with the aid of carefully cultured yeast strains.

In the Payottenland area of Belgium centred on the Senne valley (Zenne in Flemish) a handful of dedicated brewers has remained faithful to a tradition that produces beers which, with their tart, vinous and even cidery characteristics, seem to break down all the barriers between cereal-based and fruit-based alcoholic drinks. They hark back to a period when all alcoholic drinks were bucolic, peasant ones, made from the raw ingredients to hand in the surrounding fields.

Lambic (sometimes spelt "lambik") is the world's oldest beer style still made on a regular commercial basis. It has existed for some 400 years and it is fitting that its area of production almost exactly matches that part of Belgium dubbed by the tourist board "the Breugel Route". For the paintings of the Breugels, Pieter the Elder in particular, personify a rural idyll in which the consumption of a rough ale called lambic was at the heart of family and communal life. The recent revival of interest in lambic and its off-shoots – gueuze, faro, mars, kriek and frambozen – has prompted both the

Belgian government and the European Union to protect the style and to lay down strict rules for its production.

Lambic is a country beer style. It declined as industry sprang up and the great city of Brussels expanded into the Senne valley. City dwellers switched first to strong ales brewed in the conventional manner and then to the new Pilsner beers.

Although two of the remaining lambic brewers are based in Brussels – Belle-Vue, owned by Interbrew, and the smaller craft brewery of Cantillon – it remains a rustic beer in its methods of production. As with farm brewers of earlier times, brewing does not take place during the summer months because of the impossibility of controlling the temperature of a spontaneously fermenting ale.

In order to qualify as a genuine lambic, the beer must be brewed with at least 30 per cent wheat in the mash. Unlike a classic Bavarian wheat beer, the wheat in a lambic is unmalted. Busy farmers understood that barley malt provided sufficient enzymes to convert starch to sugar without the need to malt their wheat as well. The barley malt is as pale as Pilsner malt. With the addition of wheat, the resulting mash is cloudy and milky white. The starting gravity is around 1050 degrees with a finished ABV of 4.5 to 5.0 per cent.

The hop rate is high but the hops used are four years old. They have lost their aromatic quality and have a deliberate "cheesy" smell. The varieties are used primarily for their antiseptic qualities. Lambic brewers discovered, along with wheat beer producers in other regions, that the tart nature of fresh hops does not blend well with the spicy, fruity and slightly lactic character of wheat beer.

When the copper boil is over, brewing is left to nature. The hopped wort is pumped to a shallow, open fermenting vessel known as a "cool ship". The ship is always high in the roof of the brewery. Louvred windows are left open and a few tiles are even removed from the roof. During the night yeasts come in on the breeze and attack the inviting malt sugars in the ship.

After spontaneous fermentation, the green beer is transferred to oak casks where it is attacked by microflora. In the cellars, cobwebs and spiders abound, as nothing must be done to alter the eco-structure. Spiders are important as they attack fruit flies which would otherwise feast on the beers, especially those to which fruit is added. The casks, made mainly from wood with a few of chestnut, are bought from port producers in Portugal. Belle-Vue, the biggest producer of lambic, has 15,000 casks on five floors, ranging in size from 250 litres to 30 hectolitres.

Wild *Brettanomyces* yeasts give what brewers call a "horse-blanket" aroma to ale, a grainy, slightly musty character. But it takes some time for *Brettanomyces* to dominate other microflora active in lambic. The beer will stay and mature in cask for a few months, in some cases for as long as six years. A young lambic is yeasty and immature, and even after a year the beer will still have some "cheesiness" from the hops. At 18 months the beer takes on a sherry colour and *Brettanomyces* has started to dominate the aroma. An aged lambic of six years will have a pronounced vinous aroma, a deep sherry character in the mouth, and a sour and lactic finish.

Gueuze

Lambic is usually served on draught while its most widely available bottled form is known as gueuze. To counteract the green flavours of young lambic, gueuze is a blend of mature and young brews. The mature lambic gives gloss, depth and a tart vinous character to the beer while the young, which contains unfermented malt sugars, causes a second fermentation in the bottle. The blend is usually 60 per cent young to 40 per cent mature. The bottles are stoppered with Champagne corks and laid down horizontally in cellars for between six and 18 months. When a bottle is opened, the ale rushes, foaming into the glass: it is truly the Champagne of the beer world. As more alcohol has been produced during the bottle-conditioning, a gueuze will have around 5.5 per cent ABV. It is tart, cidery and refreshing.

Some gueuze makers have tended to sweeten their beers in order to reach a wider audience, but the resurgence of interest in the style has concentrated brewers' minds. In 1993, Belle-Vue responded to its critics by launching a Séléction Lambic, a bottle-conditioned gueuze of 5.2 per cent ABV with an intriguing aroma of roast chestnuts, sour and quenching in the mouth, and with a dry and fruity finish. It was

---

LAMBIC PRODUCERS AND GUEUZE BLENDERS

Belgor Brouwerij, Kerkstraat 17, 1881 Brussegem.

Belle-Vue, Rue Delaunoy 58, 1080 Brussels. Owned by Interbrew: lambic, gueuze, kriek and frambozen.

Frank Boon BV, Fonteinstraat 65, 1520 Lembeek: lambic, gueuze, kriek, frambozen and faro.

Cantillon Brouwerij, Gheudestraat 56, 1070 Brussels: lambic, gueuze, kriek, frambozen and faro.

De Keersmaeker Brouwerij, Brusselstraat 1, 1703 Kobbegem (owned by Alken-Maes, brews under the Morte Subite and Eylenbosch names): lambic, gueuze, kriek, frambozen and faro.

De Koninck Gueuzestekerij, Kerstraat 57, 1512 Dworp (not related to De Konick of Antwerp): gueuze and kriek.

De Troch Brouwerij, Langestraat 20, 1741 Ternat-Wambeck: lambic, gueuze and faro.

De Neve Brouwerij, Isabellastraat 52, 1750 Schepdaal. Owned by Interbrew and linked to Belle-Vue; similar range of products.

Drie Fonteinen, H. Teirlinckplein 3, 1650 Beersel: lambic, gueuze, kriek and frambozen.

Girardin Brouwerij, Lindenberg 10, 1744 Sint-Ulriks-Kapelle: lambic, gueuze and kriek.

Hanssens Gueuzetekerij, Vroenenbosstraat 8, 1512 Dworp: gueuze and kriek.

Lindemans Brouwerij, Lenniksebaan 257, 1712 Vlezenbeek: lambic, gueuze, kriek and frambozen.

Moriau Gueuzestekerij, Hoogstraat 1, 1600 Sint Pieters-Leeuw: lambic, gueuze and kriek.

Timmermans NV, Kerkstraat 11, 1711 Itterbeek: lambic, gueuze, kriek and frambozen.

Vander Linden Brouwerij, Brouwerijstraat 2, 1500 Halle: lambic, gueuze, kriek, frambozen and faro.

Vandervelden Brouwerij, Laarheidestraat 230, 1650 Beersel: lambic, gueuze and kriek.

Van Honsebrouck Brouwerij, Oostrozebekestraat 43, 8770 Ingelmunster (produces lambic and fruit beers under the St Louis name: uses mainly syrups, not whole fruit.)

Wets Gueuzestekerij, Steenweg op Halle 203, 1640 Sint Genesius Rode: gueuze, kriek and faro.

---

immediately awarded an *appellation contrôlée* by the European Beer Consumers' Union. As Belle-Vue, which also produces lambic under the De Neve label, dominates the market, its refound enthusiasm for traditional gueuze has helped to give credibility and longevity to the style, though, disappointingly, Séléction Lambic is available only in a handful of outlets.

Kriek and frambozen

In a world where there is a sharp but wholly absurd dividing line between beer and wine, a "fruit beer" sounds bizarre, but the origins of the style are functional and sensible. Before the hop was adopted both to make beer bitter and to act as a preservative, country brewers used all manner of herbs and spices to balance the malty sweetness of their brews. Brewers in the Low Countries found that cherries, which grow in abundance, added a further fermentation to their brews, increasing the level of alcohol and imparting a pleasing tartness. Fruit marries especially well with wheat beers, with their fruity flavours in which apple and banana predominate.

Kriek is the Flemish word for cherry. Raspberry beers are called both *framboise* in French and *frambozen* in Flemish. The preferred cherry is the small, hard Schaarbeek that grows around Brussels. Rather like "noble rot" grapes, the cherries are picked late so that the fermentable sugars are well developed. The cherries are not crushed but the skins are lightly broken

and added at the rate of one kilo of cherries to five kilos of beer in the lambic cellars. Some young lambic is also added. The fruit sugars and the young beer encourage a new fermentation and the skins of the cherries add dryness to the beer. As fermentation proceeds, the yeasts even attack the pips which impart an almost almond-like quality. You can tell which casks in the cellar contain cherries as the brewers place some twigs in the open bung hole. These stop the cherries floating to the top of the beer, blocking the bung and preventing attack by fruit flies.

Fruit beers improve and deepen with age. A young kriek, with its luscious pink colour, will offer an aroma and palate of fruit whereas a year-old version will have developed a sour palate and a long, dry finish. At 18 months, a kriek will have taken on earthy, vinous characteristics. A frambozen of around one year will have a delicate perfumy aroma, bitter-sweet fruit in the mouth with a spritzy, refreshing finish.

The small craft lambic brewery of Cantillon in

KRIEK · LAMBIC
CANTILLON

BR. CANTILLON 1070 BRUXELLES
BIERE BELGE · BELGISCH BIER L 3.94   ALC. 5 % VOL.   ℮75 cl.

The small craft brewery of Cantillon in Brussels makes a lambic that uses grapes as well as cereals

Brussels produces a magnificent range of beers. Its classic is considered to be Rosé de Gambrinus, a blend of kriek and frambozen. The brewery has further blurred the distinction between beer and wine by making a lambic that uses grapes as well as cereals. Cantillon has regular open days where visitors can taste the beers and see the brewing vessels. Cantillon and some of the other lambic brewers also occasionally make faro, a lambic produced by remashing the grains of the first brew and adding candy sugar to encourage fermentation. Faro is drunk on draught at around 4.0 per cent ABV as a good refreshing beer. The even lower-alcohol mars is no longer made.

Brown ale

The historic waterside Flemish city of Oudenaarde and the surrounding area are the home of brown ales. The best known of the Old Brown (Oud Bruin) ales come from Liefman's, a brewery dating from 1679. The fame of Liefman's spread in the 1970s when the owner died and the company was taken over by his former secretary, Rose Blancquaert-Merckx, known as "Madame Rose". With her son Olav she expanded the business and won worldwide acclaim for her brews. Madame Rose has now retired and Liefman's was bought by the Riva group in the early 1990s.

The brewing water of the region adds a special character to local beers. It is low in calcium and high in sodium bicarbonate, which suggests beers using the liquor are good for the digestion and may help explain their appeal to chefs. The basic Old Brown is brewed from a blend of Pilsner, Munich and Vienna malts and a little roasted barley. Hops are English Goldings, with some Czech and German varieties. The slow copper boil lasts for 12 hours. The 5.0 per cent ABV beer is fermented for seven days in open vessels and is then matured for four months. A stronger, 6.0 per cent ABV, version called Goudenband (Gold Riband) is a blend of the basic beer with one that has matured for six to eight months. The blend is primed with sugar, re-seeded with yeast and stored for three months. Goudenband can be laid down and will improve for several years, taking on a dark, sherry-like wineyness.

Once a year Liefman's makes both a kriek and a frambozen from fresh cherries and raspberries, with the

---

OLD BROWN BREWERS

Clarysse Brouwerij, Krekelput 16-18, 9700 Oudenaarde.

Cnudde Brouwerij, Fabriekstraat 8, 9700 Eine.

Het Anker Brouwerij, Guido Gezellaan 49, 2800 Mechelen.

Liefman's Brouwerij, Aalstraat 200, 9700 Oudenaarde.

Roman Brouwerij, Hauwaert 61, 9700 Mater.

---

basic Oud Bruin. The beers are stored and refermented for up to two months. The 7.1 per cent ABV Liefman's kriek has a delectable dry and tart fruitiness while the 5.1 per cent ABV frambozen has a lilting aroma of fresh fruit and is bitter-sweet on the palate. All the Liefman's beers come in tissue-wrapped bottles.

As a result of being incorporated into the Riva group, the Liefman's beers are mashed and boiled at Riva's main brewery at Dentergem. The wort is trunked to Oudenaarde for fermentation and maturation. Riva also brews brown ales at its Het Anker brewery in Mechelen, a dry 5.5 per cent ABV Bruynen and the rich, chocolatey Gouden Carolus, a bottle-conditioned 7.8 per cent ABV dark ale full of spicy and fruity character. Among other brown ale brewers, the splendidly artisanal Roman, which dates from 1545, has a chocolatey 5.0 per cent ABV Oudenaards and an 8.0 per cent ABV Dobbelen Bruinen (double brown) packed with dark malt and hop flavours.

Red ale

If the brown ales of East Flanders are a rare style, the sour red beers of West Flanders are even more esoteric. They are beers that are matured for long periods in unlined oak vats where micro-organisms attack the malt sugars and add a lactic sourness. Such beers are yet another fascinating link with brewing's past, when beers were deliberately "staled" and were then blended with younger ales. The major producer of sour red ale is Rodenbach of Roeselare. The Rodenbachs came from Koblenz in Germany. Alexander Rodenbach bought a small brewery in Roeselare in 1820.

The St George's Brewery in Roeselare is supplied with brewing water from underground springs beneath a lake in the grounds of the brewer's stately home. The brewery site is dominated by an old malt kiln now used as a museum. Beer is made from a blend of pale malts, both spring and winter varieties, and darker Vienna malt. Vienna malt is similar to English crystal and adds both the red/copper hue and body to the beer. Malt accounts for 80 per cent of the grist, the rest made up of corn grits. The hops are Brewers' Gold and East Kent Goldings, used primarily for their aroma. Too much bitterness would not marry well with the tartness of the beer. Primary fermentation takes seven days and is followed by a second fermentation in metal tanks. The "regular" Rodenbach, 4.6 per cent ABV, is bottled after six weeks and is a blend of young and mature beers. Beer destined for ageing is stored in tall oak tuns for a minimum of 18 months and as long as two years.

As the beer matures in the wood, *lactobacilli* and acetobacters add a sour and lactic flavour to the beer. The blended beer has a sour, vinous aroma, and is tart in the mouth with more sour fruit in the finish. Grand Cru, bottled straight from the tuns, is 5.2 per cent ABV and has 14 to 18 units of bitterness. It is bigger in body and flavour than the blended beer: woody, tannic, sour and fruity. Both beers have some sugar added to take the edge off the sourness and they are pasteurized. Devotees plead with Rodenbach to produce an unsweetened, bottle-conditioned Grand Cru. There is also a version of Grand Cru known as Alexander Rodenbach to which cherry essence is added.

Among smaller West Flanders breweries, Bavik Petrus Oud Bruin, 5.5 per cent ABV, is fermented in oak casks for 20 months and then blended with young beer. The brewery also produces a 7.5 per cent ABV Triple Petrus.

White beer

When Pierre Celis brewed a "white beer" in the 1960s he had no idea he would spark a small revolution in Belgium. Today white beers (bière blanche/witbier) are cult drinks. Celis revived a beer style that was once very important in the Low Countries, and to do so he chose the small town of Hoegaarden near Leuven, where 30 white beer producers operated in the nineteenth century. All had succumbed to the onslaught of lager brewing. The rich soil of Brabant, that produces barley, oats and wheat in abundance, encouraged farmers, peasants and monks to brew: monks were brewing in Brabant from the fifteenth century. Herbs and spices were added to the brews to balance the sweetness of the grains.

White beer is wheat beer, a member of the ale family, brewed by top or warm fermentation: centuries ago it was fermented spontaneously. The grist is a 50:50 blend of barley malt and unmalted wheat. Pierre Celis used oats as well in his early days but they are no longer used. The units of bitterness in Hoegaarden are around 20: the brewer is not looking for excessive bitterness. The varieties are East Kent Goldings for aroma and Czech Saaz for gentle bitterness. Coriander seeds and orange peel are milled to coarse powders and added with the hops to the copper boil. After fermentation the green beer is conditioned for a month, primed with sugar, re-seeded with yeast and then bottled or kegged. Hoegaarden is 4.2 per cent ABV and has a rich, appetizing spicy nose with a clear hint of orange. It is tart and refreshing in the mouth followed by a clean, bitter-sweet finish. It will improve with age for around six months and takes on a smooth, honey-like character. Hoegaarden is served in a heavy, chunky glass and is cloudy from the yeast and protein left in suspension. The beer is a pale lemon colour with a dense white head of foam. Hoegaarden is now owned by Interbrew. Pierre Celis moved to Texas and now brews white beer in association with the Miller group.

Among other wheat beer producers, the Riva group gives prominence to its Dentergems Witbier (5.0 per cent ABV), made without spices but with a pleasing apple-fruitiness. The Wallonian brewers have not been slow to spot a large niche in the market. Du Bocq's Blanche de Namur (4.5 per cent ABV) is named after a princess from the region (Snow White?) who became queen of Sweden. The beer has a herbal aroma and palate, while the small Silly Brewery's Titje (5.0 per cent ABV) is uncompromisingly spicy, tart and quenching.

Trappist ales

When Trappist monks were hounded from France during the French Revolution they stoically headed north into the Low Countries to establish new centres of religious devotion. Their simple life included eating the produce from the surrounding fields and making their own alcohol to sustain them during Lent and to help keep them healthy. In France they had made wine liqueurs. In the Low Countries the absence of grapes forced them to make beer from cereals. Thus was born one of the world's great beer styles.

The encroaching secular life has closed many of the abbeys in the Low Countries. Today just six abbeys in Belgium and one in the Netherlands still make beer and they need help from lay brewers to sustain production. Unless sufficient numbers of young people can be attracted to the austere way of life, there is a real fear that true Trappist beers could cease to exist.

Chimay is by far the most famous of the Belgian Trappist breweries. Its ales are sold worldwide. The

The Abaye de Notre Dame de Saint=Rémy in the Ardennes produces Rocherfort beers

success of Chimay is a fascinating example of God and Mammon pooling their resources: the monks are in charge of brewing but a few miles from their abbey in a complex of utilitarian buildings a large secular staff skilfully markets their beers.

Chimay once had a fine, traditional copper brewhouse but expansion and demand led to a new functional modern plant being installed. Most of the vessels are behind tiled walls. The monks, following a dispensation from the Vatican, are now allowed to talk but are disappointingly close-mouthed about the ingredients they use. The local water is soft and acidic and is not treated for brewing. It is thought that malts are a blend of Pils and caramalt, with candy sugar used in the copper. German hops, possibly Hallertau, are blended, surprisingly, with some American Yakima. All the beers are primed with sugar for bottling. The three beers produced are known by the colour of their caps. Chimay Red is the original beer, 7.0 per cent ABV. It is

TRAPPIST BREWERS

Abbaye de Notre-Dame d'Orval, 6823 Villers-devant-Orval.

Abbaye de Notre-Dame de St Rémy, rue de l'Abbaye 8, 5430 Rochefort.

Abbaye de Notre-Dame de Scourmont, rue de la Trappe 294, 6438 Forges-les-Chimay.

Achel, Achel, near Eindhoven.

Abdij Trappisten van Westmalle, Antwerpsesteenweg 496, 2140 Malle.

Abdij Sint Sixtus, Donkerstraat 12, 8983 Westvleteren.

copper-coloured with a fruity nose – blackcurrant is the dominant aroma – and great peppery and citric hop bitterness. Red is also known as Première when it is in large, Bordeaux-style bottles. Chimay Blue is 9.0 per cent ABV and is called Grande Réserve in large bottles. It has great depth of complex flavours, with spice and fruit from the hops and yeast. Dark malts give it a vinous character. Chimay White (8.0 per cent ABV) is sharply different from red and blue. It was first brewed in 1968 and, although the monks deny it, it is widely believed that white was introduced as a competitor to the beer from the nearby abbey of Orval. In common with all the true Trappist ales, Chimay's are bottle-conditioned. They will improve with age, red and blue taking on a port-wine character. They should be served at room temperature.

The Abbaye de Notre-Dame d'Orval is in the Belgian province of Luxembourg and is unusual in producing just one beer. The first abbey was built by Benedictines in 1070, but it was sacked and rebuilt several times: the present buildings date from the 1920s and 1930s. Orval Trappist ale is made from pale malt and caramalt, with candy sugar in the copper. German Hallertau and East Kent Goldings are the hop varieties: the brother brewers prize the earthy/peppery aromas of Goldings. The 5.2 per cent ABV beer in a club-shaped bottle has 40 units of bitterness. Following primary fermentation with an ale yeast, the beer has a second one lasting from six to seven weeks using several strains of yeast, including a wild one similar to lambic's *Brettanomyces*, circulating over a bed of Goldings. The beer is then bottled and seeded with the original ale yeast, which creates a third ferment. Not surprisingly, it is a highly complex ale, spicy with tart and quenching fruit, the finish becoming dry and dominated by hops.

Rochefort ales come from the Abbaye de Notre-Dame de Saint-Rémy in the Ardennes. There are three beers brewed from pale Pils and darker Munich malts, with dark candy sugar in the copper. Hop varieties are German Hallertau and Styrian Goldings. The beers are labelled Six, Eight and Ten from a now-defunct method of measuring alcohol. Rochefort Six is 7.5 per cent ABV, pale brown in colour and with a soft, fruity and slightly herbal palate. Rochefort Eight (9.2 per cent ABV) is a rich and rounded ale, copper-coloured with a

dark fruit character that recalls dates and raisins. Rochefort Ten is a mighty 11.3 per cent ABV. Hops meld with dark fruit, nuts and chocolate. The brothers point out that the strength of their beers and their malty/fruity character developed from their use as "liquid bread" during fasting.

There are two Trappist breweries in Flemish-speaking areas. Westmalle ale comes from the Abdij der Trappisten north of Antwerp. The 9.0 per cent ABV Tripel is extremely pale, with just 13 units of colour, with 35 to 38 IBUs. The monks use French and Bavarian pale malts with Czech, German and Styrian hops. Candy sugar is also added to the copper. The beer has a secondary fermentation in tanks lasting from one to three months and is then primed with sugar and yeast for bottle conditioning.

The Abdij Sint Sixtus in the hamlet of Westvleteren near Ypres (Ieper) is the smallest of the Trappist breweries and the least accessible. Visits are difficult but the full range of beers can be enjoyed in the Café De Vrede across the road. There is a malty/spicy Green corked Dubbel (4.0 per cent ABV), a Red (6.2 per cent ABV), fruity and hop-peppery, and the Blue Extra (8.4 per cent ABV) with great warming fruit and alcohol. The 10.6 Abbot is an explosion of raspberry and strawberry fruits (from the yeast, not from actual fruit) with a deceptively smooth drinkability.

A new Trappist brewery opened in 1999. Achel, in a village of the same name, brews only for consumption on the premises at present. The beers are Achelse Blond (4.0 per cent ABV), Extra (also 4.0 per cent), a 6.0 per cent Blond and a 5.0 per cent Bruine.

Abbey beers

Abbey beers are modelled on Trappist ones. The original idea was a reasonable, even noble one: monks who no longer had the resources – money as well as manpower – licensed a commercial brewer to produce beer for them. But the success of genuine Trappist ales has encouraged scores of breweries to produce abbey beers, diluting the style as well as the intention.

The Norbertine abbey of Leffe has not brewed since the Napoleonic wars – the brothers struck a deal with the local brewer to make beers for them. In the way of the modern secular world, the brewery was taken over

The Abbaye de Notre Dame d'Orval is in the Luxembourg province of Belgium, not the Grand Duchy; it brews only Orval Trappist ale

and Leffe beers finally ended up controlled by Interbrew. The abbey of Grimbergen, once in the country and now in the northern suburbs of Brussels, has followed a similar fate: its beers are now brewed by Maes, a subsidiary of Kronenbourg of France. The beers from the Benedictine abbey of Maredsous south of Namur are produced by the Moortgat Brewery in Breendonk.

The best of the Leffe beers is the bottle-conditioned Triple (8.4 per cent ABV) which was brewed for a time by De Kluis of Hooegaarden. It is golden in colour with an appealing citric lemon from the hops on the nose and palate and an aromatic finish. Vieille Cuvée (7.8 per cent ABV) is a one-dimensional darker ale while the 8.5 per cent ABV Radieuse has a strong hop presence.

Grimbergen beers, perhaps unintentionally mimicking the style of Benedictine liqueurs, are sweet in the mouth. The 10.0 per cent ABV Optimo Bruno is a deep amber colour with a pear-drop character on the palate. The 6.1 per cent ABV Tripel is darker and its aroma and palate are dominated by sweet fruits. The 6.2 per cent ABV Dubbel is copper-coloured with toffee and vanilla on the palate.

The Corsendonk range of abbey ales is brewed for the priory at Turnhout by Bios and Du Bocq. The 8.1 per cent ABV Agnus Dei has good citric lemon notes from the hops and more hop perfume in the finish. The 7.0 per cent ABV Pater Noster has a pleasant chocolate-and-raisins character.

Ales

The most famous of Belgium's pale ales is Duvel. It looks like a lager and many think it is pronounced, in the French manner, "Duvelle". But it is warm-fermented and is pronounced Doovul in the Flemish manner. The golden beer dates only from the 1970s, but the Moortgat (Moorgate) Brewery was founded in 1871 as a specialist ale producer. When sales of Pilsner beers started to take off in Belgium, Moortgat remained true to ales but introduced Duvel alongside its darker brews to expand and protect its market. Two-row Belgian and French barleys are specially malted for Duvel, which has

271

a colour rating of seven to eight, only a fraction more than for a Pilsner. The brewing process is complex and intriguing. The ale is infusion-mashed in the traditional manner. Saaz and Golding hops are added to the copper boil in three stages to produce between 29 and 31 units of bitterness. Dextrose is added before primary fermentation to give body to the beer. Two strains of yeast are used in the first stage of fermentation: the hopped wort is split into two batches, which are fermented by two different yeast strains. A second fermentation takes place during cold conditioning,

which lasts for a month. It is then primed with dextrose and re-seeded with yeast to encourage a third fermentation in the bottle. The end result is a beer of 8.5 per cent ABV. It throws such a dense, fluffy head that it has to be poured into a large tulip-shaped glass to contain both foam and liquid. Duvel is such an enormous success that several rivals have been launched with similar names, including Judas from Alken-Maes, Joker from Roman and Rascal from du Bocq.

Belgium's biggest selling pale ale is Palm (5.2 per cent ABV), brewed by a family-run brewery in Steenhuffel. Spéciale Palm has a citric aroma from the hops, is bitter and quenching in the mouth and has a fruity/hoppy finish. Antwerp is home to a superb ale rightly called De Koninck – "the king" (5.0 per cent ABV). The brewery began life in 1833 as a brewpub and its owners have resisted any suggestion that they should move from ale to lager. The copper colour of De Koninck comes from pale and Vienna malts. No sugars are used in the brewing process. Saaz hops are added three times during the copper boil. Following fermentation the beer has two weeks' cold conditioning.

Wallonia

Brewers in the French-speaking region of Belgium complain that, with the exception of the Trappist ales, their contributions are overshadowed by those from the Flemish areas. But the *saison* or seasonal ales of Wallonia are worthy of respect, a beer style in their own right. They date from the time when farmer-brewers produced strong beers in the winter and spring that would survive the long, hot summer months.

Saisons are warm fermenting, dark malts are often used and they are generously hopped. The classic of the style comes from Dupont at Tourpes. The brewery was founded on a farm with its own natural spring in the 1850s. The small brewhouse uses pale and caramalts with East Kent Goldings and Styrian hops. Vieille Provision (Old Provision) is 6.5 per cent ABV and has a peppery hop aroma and palate. Dupont also brews beers under the Moinette (Little Monk) label, a blonde and a brune, both at 8.5 per cent ABV. The blonde is hoppy and perfumy, the brune sweet and fruity.

There is nothing Monty Python-ish about the Silly Brewery. It is based in the village of Silly, on the river Sil.

La Chouffe is brewed in the eponymous town – literally "the gnome"

SELECTED SAISON BREWERS

Brasserie Dupont, rue Basse 5, 7911 Tourpes-Leuze.

Brasserie de Silly, Ville Basse A141, 7830 Silly.

Brasserie à Vapeur, rue de Marechal 1, 7904 Pipaix.

Brasserie Voisin, rue Aulnois 15, 7880 Flobecq.

Like Dupont, it is a farm-brewery that once ground its own grain. The 5.4 per cent ABV Saison Silly is brewed from French and Belgian malts with English Goldings hops. In common with several smaller *saison* brewers, the mash tun doubles as a hop back: after the copper boil, the hopped wort is pumped back to the mash tun for filtration. The beer is warm fermented for a fortnight, then matured in tanks for a further two weeks. The finished beer is copper coloured with a pronounced earthy hop aroma and dark vinous fruit in the mouth. Silly also brews an "artisanal" Double Enghien – the name comes from the neighbouring village which had its own brewery – and a hoppy, perfumy and fruity Divine (9.5 per cent ABV).

Speciality beers

The strongest beer in Belgium is brewed by a small company in Wallonia called Dubuisson. In the style of the region, Dubuisson is a former farm in Pipaix. Dubuisson means "bush" in French and the name of the 12 per cent ABV beer, Bush, was Anglicised in the

1930s to cash in on the popularity of strong British ales in Belgium. The amber-coloured Bush is made from pale and cara malts, with Styrian and East Kent Goldings. It is sold in the USA as Scaldis, the Latin name for the major Belgian river, the Scheldt, to avoid confusion with Busch beer brewed by Budweiser giant Anheuser-Busch.

"Mad beer" can surely not be a style, yet it vies to become one as a result of the success of the Mad Brewers – De Dolle Brouwers – in Esen. The small brewery was on the point of closing in 1980 when some keen home-brewing brothers bought the site. Architect Kris Herteleer runs the enterprise with a rag-bag of equipment: a pre-First World War mash tun, a copper fired by direct flame, and an open wort cooler or cool ship. The main beer, Oerbier (Original Beer) is 7.5 per cent ABV and is brewed from six malts, including caramalt and black malt, with Belgian hops from Poperinge and English Goldings. It has a sour plums aroma – the yeast came originally from Rodenbach – and is bitter-sweet in the mouth with a fruity finish. An 8.0 per cent ABV Arabier is bronze-coloured, with a fruity and spicy aroma and more ripe fruit on the palate and finish. Boskeun (Easter Bunny) is an 8.0 per cent ABV season ale sweetened with honey, while the 9.0 per cent ABV Christmas ale, Stille Nacht, is packed with fruit and a hint of sourness.

La Chouffe, in the Belgian province of Luxembourg, takes its name from the village of Chouffe which in turn is named after a legendary local gnome. The brewery was opened in the 1980s. As well as using Pils and pale malts, Kent Goldings and Styrian hops, the beers are spiced in the medieval fashion with coriander, honey and bog myrtle. La Chouffe, 8.5 per cent ABV, has a sweetish start but a dry and spicy finish. McChouffe, inspired by Scottish ales, is 8.8 per cent ABV, bottle-conditioned with a big spicy aroma and palate.

SELECTED SPECIALITY BREWERS

Brasserie d'Achouffe, Route de Village 32, 6666 Achouffe-Houffalize.

Brasserie Dubuisson, Chaussée de Mons 28, 7904 Pipaix.

De Dolle Brouwers, Roeselarestraat 12b, 8160 Esen-Diksmuide.

CZECH REPUBLIC AND SLOVAKIA

It is one of the great unsolved mysteries of the world of brewing: why did Pilsen in Bohemia brew the first golden beer by the method of cold or bottom fermentation? It seems remarkable that this small country, locked at the time into the Austro-Hungarian Empire and, before that, part of the German Empire, was the first to break out of the dark beer straitjacket before such mighty cities as Vienna and Munich.

The true answer is complex and rooted in history. Bohemia – which now with Moravia makes up the Czech Republic – has a long brewing tradition. A brewery was recorded in Cerhenice in 1118 and both Pilsen and Budweis had breweries from the thirteenth century. As in other European countries, monasteries dominated beer production for centuries until the power of the church waned. From the thirteenth century many towns and cities had "citizens' breweries" – essentially co-operatives – while the aristocracy supplied beer from their castles. The Moravian capital, Brno, had been granted rights to brew beer from the twelfth century and King Wenceslas I (Václav I in Czech) decreed in 1243 that no one could brew within a mile of the Blue Lion inn in the city. Similar brewing rights were given to Pilsen in 1295.

Hops had been grown in the region from as early as 859 AD. While the first Bohemian beers were spiced and flavoured with berries and leaves, the superiority of the local hops encouraged their early use in brewing. From the twelfth century there are records of hops from the region being shipped to the hop market in Hamburg. Meanwhile Moravia had established a reputation for the quality of its malting barley, though for centuries wheat beer appears to have been the dominant style in what is now the Czech Republic.

For all its "Bohemian" associations with an unconventional lifestyle dominated by writers and artists living in Ruritanian surroundings, the real Bohemia was never a bucolic backwater. Tadeas Hájek wrote one of the first books on brewing technology in

1585, Professor C.J.N. Balling studied the role of enzymes in the mashing and fermentation processes while the Jecmen brothers developed the Czech method of cold fermentation.

The history of Bohemian brewing fused with the present in 1842 when the new "Burghers' brewery" of Pilsen employed a German brewer to make beer for them. Josef Groll or Grolle was employed because he was an expert in the new method of cold fermentation and came from the old brewing town of Vilshofen in Bavaria. The reputation of Pilsen beer was poor at the time and the brewery, a co-operative of tavern keepers, needed good beer because they faced stiff competition from the new brown lagers from neighbouring Bavaria. While no records survive, it is possible that Groll was supplied with an English coke-fired malt kiln that enabled him to produce a pale malt. The exceptionally soft waters of Pilsen would have helped produce a pale-coloured beer.

The golden Pilsner beer was a sensation. Its clarity in the glass was immediately appealing while its complexity of aromas and flavours, at once rich and malty yet enticingly hoppy and bitter, entranced all who drank it. Its reputation spread at great speed, aided by canals and a new railway system that carried supplies to all the great cities of the Austrian Empire, across into Bavaria and up the Elbe to Hamburg and beyond. A Pilsen Beer Train left every morning for Vienna. It became a cult drink in Paris and by 1874 it had reached the USA.

The success of the first Pilsen lager brewery prompted a second to be built in 1869. The Gambrinus Brewery, funded among others by Škoda the car manufacturer, was named after Jan Primus, the thirteenth-century toping Duke of Brabant, and built on land adjacent to the other brewery. In the German fashion, the beers from the town of Pilsen were known as "Pilsners", just as the rival brews from Budweis were

Opposite: *The Regent brewery in Trebon is reckoned to have one of the finest brewhouses in the Czech Republic*

called "Budweisers". In 1898, the first Pilsen lager brewer registered "Pilsner Urquell" as its official name. It is the German for "Original Source Pilsner" (Plzensky Prazdroj in Czech). The document referred to the "absurdity and illogicality of using the word 'Pilsner' for beers brewed in towns outside of Pilsen".

It was too late. With the exception of the British Isles, brewers throughout Europe rushed to emulate, replicate and too often denigrate the original with their versions of pale lagers. Germans and Czechs emigrated in large numbers to the USA, taking with them the technology to brew cold-fermenting beers.

The preponderance of German Pilsners tended to hide the originals. Drinkers could be forgiven for thinking the beer was a German style. The misunderstanding was heightened by the Cold War when Czechoslovakia disappeared from Western eyes. When it surfaced briefly during the "Prague Spring" of 1968 visitors from the West returned with the news that Czech beer was one of the wonders of the world. Beer had such deep roots in the Czech way of life that the Communist regime did not tamper with it.

The breweries were state owned but a surprisingly large number were allowed to operate, providing a wide choice, albeit within one general style. Even the fact that most of the breweries were starved of funds for modernization had its positive side as managements were forced to remain true to methods of production considered old fashioned, conservative and quaint in other countries.

While other Eastern bloc regimes forced breweries to use inferior ingredients so that the best barley and hops could be exported for hard currency, the Czech government stayed true to the German Reinheitsgebot for its premium beers. The Purity Law had been imposed on Bohemia and the other Czech regions when they were under German domination.

Now the walls are down and the West can marvel at Czech brewing. But the move to a market economy and the double-edged sword of modernization pose threats to the finest Czech traditions. There are around 70 breweries there but the number is falling as market forces take effect. Under the old regime the price of beer was kept low, but prices are rising and consumption is falling.

Ingredients

The quality of Czech beer is based on the ingredients used and the balance between them. The barley from the plains of Moravia and the Elbe produces a luscious sweet malt. Brewing liquor is soft and low in salts, allowing the sweetness of the malt and the aroma of the hops to best express themselves. The hop-growing area around the town of Žatec is in the north-west of Bohemia between Karlovy Vary (Carlsbad) and the capital, Prague. There is a smaller region north of Prague in Mustek. Žatec is known as Saaz in German and most Western brewers who buy the hops use the German name. Žatec hops grow in areas protected by mountains from high winds and rains. The soil is limestone and red clay. The hops are renowned for their fragrance, their softness, their ripe yet delicate aroma. They are not high in bittering acids but are rich in the tannins that give a distinctive piney, resiny aroma to beer. As a result of their aroma, Pilsner and other Czech beers have a late addition of hops towards the end of the copper boil.

Strength

The strength of Czech beers is expressed in degrees Balling, devised by Professor Balling. Most exported beer is 12 degrees, which is equivalent to 4.5–5.0 per cent ABV. But for everyday drinking, Czechs choose 10-degree beers, around 4.0 to 4.2 per cent ABV. Eight-degree beers are consumed in large quantities in industrial areas, and they are low in alcohol, around 3.2 per cent ABV. Some speciality beers are stronger, with 13-, 14-, 16- and even 19-degree ratings. Twelve-degree beers are all-malt but adjuncts are permitted in 8- and 10- degree beers, usually unmalted barley, wheat and sugar. The proportion of adjuncts does not usually exceed 10 per cent of the total grist. Premium beers are lagered for long periods – three months for Budweiser Budvar – but 21 days is normal for the lower strength beers.

Pilsner

The Pilsner Urquell Brewery is a temple of brewing. At night its neon-lit name blazes out over the city. By day visitors enter through a great triumphal arch to be confronted by tall chimneys, an almost Moorish water tower, and a warehouse complex that looks

The legendary King Vaclav, or Good King Wenceslas, asleep with his warriors beneath the Berge Blanik, until such time as his countrymen need him – or so the myth goes

remarkably like London's King's Cross railway station. A meeting room in the grounds, with polished oak and stained glass windows, is like a chapel. In the 1980s the brewery yard was filled by giant oak casks, brought up from deep sandstone cellars to be re-pitched, the air rich with the smoky, autumnal aroma of fresh pitch. Both primary and secondary fermentation took place in pitch-lined oak vessels. Was it just the water, or did the oak vessels help impart a comforting softness to the beer?

In the two brightly-lit, tiled brewhouses the mash is a thorough triple decoction system. Žatec hop flowers are added three times in direct-flame coppers. Until changes were introduced, the hopped wort went first to a vast, cool dimly-lit room packed with small oak tubs each set at a slight angle as though the vessels were about to raise imaginary hats. The angle was designed to allow brewers to clamber up and check the progress of fermentation. When primary fermentation was complete, the green beer was pumped to six miles of sandstone cellars where the beer was lagered for 70 days at a natural temperature of 0–3.5 degrees C/32–38F. The oak lagering vessels were barrel-shaped and arranged horizontally.

The beer has 40 units of bitterness. Under the old lagering system, the original gravity was 1048 degrees with a finished alcohol of 4.4 per cent. This meant the beer was not fully attenuated – not all the malt sugars turned to alcohol.

The use of the past tense in describing fermentation and flavour profile is deliberate. For fundamental changes have taken place at the brewery since the fall of the old regime and the arrival of the market economy. Mashing and boiling remain the same but fermentation now takes place in modern stainless steel conical fermenters. The brewery claims that change had been under way since the 1970s but there had been no sight of conical vessels during the 1980s when Western journalists visited the brewery. It is more likely that the 10-degree version of the beer was brewed in modern vessels not open to inspection, and the 12-degree beer was switched to them in the early 1990s following privatization.

In spite of claims to the contrary, the character of the beer has changed. The reason lies in the nature of conical fermenters. Unlike a horizontal lagering tank, where the yeast works slowly, almost lazily, turning remaining sugars into alcohol, a conical causes yeast to work more voraciously, hungrily attacking the sugars. The result is a more fully attenuated beer. Pilsner Urquell now has more in common with a German version of Pilsner: it is drier and more assertively bitter. It will be a tragedy if the inexorable demands of the market economy lead to any further blurring of its distinctiveness.

The Gambrinus Brewery next door is now part of the same privatized company as Pilsner Urquell. The brewery has also switched to fermentation in stainless steel conicals. Oak vessels were not used at Gambrinus: stainless steel replaced cast-iron. It is 4.5 per cent ABV and has 33 IBUs with a fresh-mown grass aroma, a

SELECTED CZECH BREWERS

Bernard, 5 Kvetna 1, 396 01 Humpolec.

Branik, Udolni 212/1, 101 00 Prague 4.

Breznice, 262 72 Breznice.

Budějovicky Budvar, Kar. Svetlé 4, 370 21 České Budějovice.

Černá Hora, 679 21 Černá Hora.

Gambrinus, U Prazdroje 7, 304 97 Pilsen.

Krušovice, 270 53 Krušovice.

Kutná Hora, U Lorce 11, 284 1t Kutná Hora.

Nová Paka, Marantova 400, 509 01 Nová Paka.

Ostravar, Hornoplni 57, 728 25 Ostrava.

Pardubice, Palackého 250, 530 33 Pardubice.

Platan, Pivovarská 856, 393 01 Pelhrimov.

Plzeňské Prazdroj (Pilsner Urquell), U Prazdroje 7, 304 97 Pilsen.

Regent, Trocnovské nám. 379 14 Trebon.

Samson, Lidická 51, 370 54 České Budějovice.

Starobrno, Hlinky 12, 661 47 Brno.

Staropramen, Nádrazni 84, 150 54 Prague 5-Smichov.

Trutnov, Krizikova 486, 541 01 Trutnov.

Velké Popovice, Ringhofferova 1, 251 69 Velké Popovice.

Žatec, Zizkovo nám. 78, 438 33 Žatec.

Note: In Czech, Prague is Praha, Pilsen is Plzen.

CZECH BREWERS

Martin, Hrdinov SNP 12, 036 42 Martin.

Urpin, Sládkovicova 37, 975 90 Banská Bystrica.

more delicate bitterness than Urquell and a malty/hoppy finish that becomes dry. The 10-degree version, made with a proportion of sucrose, is the most popular beer of that strength in the Czech Republic. In late 1999, the Pilsner Urquell-Gambrinus group was bought by South African Breweries.

Budweisers

Deep in the south of Bohemia and close to the Austrian border, the town of České Budějovice, with its magnificent central square and a fountain topped by a statue of Samson, vies with Pilsen as the great brewing centre of the Czech Republic. Its two breweries are smaller but Budweis, to use the old German name, had 44 breweries in the fifteenth century and was home to the Royal Court brewery of Bohemia. The royal connection allowed beers from the court brewery to be known as the "Beer of Kings" while all the town's brews became famous under the generic title of "Budweisers".

The standing of Budweiser beers can be seen in the decision of the American Anheuser-Busch company to give the name to its main product when it was launched in 1875 in St Louis, Missouri. Further confusion was added by the American sub-title "the King of Beers".

Twenty years later, in 1895, the Budejovicky Pivovar company started to brew. The name means the Budejovice Brewery, and its beer is always known simply by the contraction "Budvar" at home. But it is exported as Budweiser Budvar and the clash of names has led to endless law suits and wrangles over copyright. Anheuser-Busch can claim that it has precedent over Budvar for the use of the name but this ignores the fact that the older surviving brewery in České Budějovice, now called Samson, exported beer under the Budweiser name long before the American company took up the title. The Czech Budvar brewery cannot export to the USA using Budweiser on its labels while the American giant has to call its beer simply "Bud" in such countries as Germany and Spain where the Czechs registered the title first.

Since the arrival of the market economy, Anheuser-Busch has lobbied hard to win a stake in its smaller Czech rival. It has offered to buy 34 per cent of the shares, to inject capital to allow Budvar to expand, and to help Budvar market its beer worldwide. A-B has opened a St Louis Center in České Budějovice, donated to Prague University and taken full-page advertisements in newspapers to tell the Czech people that its intentions are honourable towards Budvar. So far the Czechs are unimpressed and the brewery remains in state hands, though it is due to be privatized.

The Budvar Brewery is one of the most modern in the country. The old regime invested money in new plant to enable Budvar to export. Ironically, the beer had for years been hard to find in the Czech Republic as so much of it went for export. The brewhouse is magnificent, with large copper mash and brew kettles on tiled floors. A double decoction mash is used. Primary fermentation is in open vessels, lagering in horizontal ones. Lagering lasts for three months for the 12-degree beer, one of the longest periods in the world. It is an all-malt beer, using Moravian malt and Žatec hops. The original gravity is 1049 with a finished alcohol of 5.0 per cent ABV. The beer is well attenuated and has 20 units of bitterness. The balance of a Budweiser beer is therefore demonstrably different from that of a Pilsner. Budvar has a rich malt and vanilla aroma, it is quenching and gently hoppy in the mouth, while the finish has a balance of malt, hops and a delicate hint of apple fruit from the yeast.

The Samson Brewery was the result of a merger in 1795 of two breweries, Velky (Great) and Maly (Small). It became the Citizens' Brewery and moved to a new site in the town in 1847. It changed its name to Samson but exported for some time under the Budweiser name until the arrival of the Budvar Brewery. Samson's management felt it received a bad deal under the old regime as all the investment available went to Budvar. Today Samson is independent and plans to stop sharing yeast with Budvar. It is a classic Czech lager brewery, with cast-iron mashing and boiling vessels, open squares for primary fermentation and horizontal ones for lagering. The management plans to install conicals but will continue to ferment its 12-degree beer in the old vessels to avoid any changes to the flavour profile. The premium product (4.3 per cent ABV) has a creamy note from the malt, some citric fruit from the hops and a well-balanced finish. An uprated version is exported to Britain under the name of Zámek (Castle) at 4.5 per cent ABV.

Prague beers

Three of the Czech capital's four breweries merged in 1992 to form Prague Breweries. The biggest of the three in the group is the Staropramen (Old Spring) Brewery in the Smichov district, which started to brew in 1871. Its beer was praised by Emperor Franz Josef I and production soared. It is one of the biggest breweries in the Czech Republic, producing more than a million hectolitres a year. It is a classic lager brewery with secondary fermentation in horizontal tanks. In 1994 the British Bass group took a 34 per cent stake in Prague Breweries and said it would not change the brewing method as horizontal tanks were crucial to the flavour of the beer. The 12-degree Staropramen is 5.0 per cent ABV. It has superb hop aroma, is well-balanced in the mouth between malt and hops and the finish is dry and bitter.

The second partner in the group is the Holesovice Brewery which brews under the Méstan name. Méstan comes from the original title of the brewery when it was founded in 1895 as První Prazsky Méstanský Pivovar – First Prague Burghers' Brewery. Its 12-degree beer is aromatic, soft, malty and bitter in the finish. The third member of Prague Breweries, Braník, started production in 1900. Its 12-degree beer is notably fresh, clean and well-hopped. Since privatization the brewery has undergone substantial modernization. Fermentation now takes place in conical vessels and beer is canned for export.

The most celebrated beer in Prague comes from the world-famous beer hall, brewpub and beer garden known as U Fleků at 11 Kremencova in the New Town, the entrance marked by a large hanging clock. Beer has been brewed on the site since at least 1499: isotopic measurements of the remains of paintings on the wooden ceiling of the brewhouse have dated them back to 1360. The present name of the establishment stems from 1762 when Jakub Flekovský and his wife bought it. In the Czech fashion, the tavern was known as U Flekovskych, which over time was shortened to U U Fleků. In Czech "U" serves the same purpose as the French "chez" – "at the house of". The tiny brewhouse, with a capacity of 6,000 hectolitres, is the smallest in the republic. With its open "cool ship" fermenter, it is reminiscent of a Belgian lambic brewery, but no wild fermentation is allowed here. New brewing vessels are made of copper and date from 1980. The one beer is a dark lager, Flekovaky, 13 degrees (4.5 per cent ABV). It is made from four malts: Pilsner pale (50 per cent), Munich (30 per cent), caramalt (15 per cent) and roasted malt (5 per cent). A double decoction mash is used and Žatec hops are added in three stages.

Brno

The capital of Moravia has a long history of brewing, dating back to monastic times. The Starobrno (Old Brno) Brewery dates from 1872 when the family firm of Mandel and Hayek built the plant. Expansion was rapid, with exports moving from horse-drawn wagons to the railway in 1894. In the economically turbulent decades of the 1920s and 1930s, Starobrno bought several smaller breweries in the area. The plant was severely damaged by an air raid in 1944. It was nationalized in 1945 and during the course of re-building was considerably modernized. It now produces some 700,000 hectolitres of beer a year. Its 12-degree Lezak Export (Export Lager) is rounded and soft in the mouth, with a delicate hop aroma, and a gentle, bitter-sweet finish.

Country breweries

"Baker, priest, farmer, butcher, all drink beer from Breznice" an old slogan says. Brewing in the town dates back to 1506 and the town brewery was in the hands of the aristocratic Kolowrat Krakowsky family for 150 years. The coats of arms of the family with the emblem of an eagle adorns the labels of today's Herold beer. The Breznice brewery produces 10- and 12- degree Herold pale lagers but its main claim to fame is the first wheat beer seen in the Czech lands for at least a century. Pivo Herold Hefe-Weizen is a cloudy wheat beer in the Bavarian style, 12 degrees, unpasteurized and bottle-conditioned with a spicy, fruity aroma, a rich palate with apple fruit, and a long quenching finish. The brewery also makes kits for home-brewing: the new Czech Republic is learning an early lesson in basic capitalism – when commercial beer becomes expensive, drinkers turn to home-brewing.

The entrance to the Krušovice Brewery is guarded by an old wooden lagering tank bearing the company symbol of a cavalier. Krusovice malts its own barley

U Fleků, the world-famous beer hall, brewpub and beer garden in Prague New Town; beer has been brewed here since at least 1499

With the fall of Communism in the Czech Republic, the West can enjoy some of the best beers in Europe

using a traditional floor maltings where the grains are turned by hand. The 12-degree beer is one of the most highly prized beers in the Czech Republic, a fine blend of sweet malt and aromatic Žatec hops, a quenching palate and a long, delicate finish with good hop notes.

The Platan Brewery in Protivin is one of the finest in the country. Platan means plane tree, and an avenue of the trees leads down to a complex of brewing buildings surrounded by woodland. There has been brewing on the site since the late sixteenth century. The feudal Schwarzenberg family built a new brewery between 1873 and 1876 and adopted all the new methods for producing lager beer. The first cultivation plant for Bohemian yeast was set up in the brewery and the beer was so highly prized that it was sold not only in Prague and Pilsen but also in Vienna, Trieste, Zagreb, Berlin, Leipzig, Geneva and as far afield as New York and

Chicago. The brewery was nationalized in 1947 but has now been restored to its original owners. The 12-degree beer is closer to a Budweiser than a Pilsner in style, due to Protivín's proximity to České Budějovice. It is soft and malty in the mouth, with a rounded, well-balanced malt and hops finish.

Closer to Prague, the beer from Velké Popovice would be declared a world classic if it were better known. The original brewery was built by monks in 1727, using the master of Czech baroque architecture, Kilian Dienzenhoffer. The plant was extensively expanded in 1871 and brewing capacity has been extended further in recent years. It is planned to build capacity to more than one million hectolitres, making it one of the biggest Czech breweries. The brewery has always been able to draw on natural water supplies from surrounding woodland and today takes its supply from 12 wells. The 12-degree beer has an enticing citric aroma of oranges and lemons, which dominate the palate and the finish, balanced by a sweet maltiness. The beer can be sampled in U Cernéha Vola, the Black Ox, in Prague, opposite the Loretto church at 1 Loretanské námesti, Hradcany, Prague 1.

The Žatec Brewery is in the heart of the great hop-growing region north of Prague and enjoys the pick of the crop. The brewery was built in 1801 as a citizens' brewery on the site of a former castle. The ancient castle cellars are used to lager the beers. It is a small brewery producing 120,000 hectolitres a year, concentrating on quality and supplying surrounding towns.

Dark lager

Bohemia did not turn its back on dark beers as a result of the success of golden Pilsners. Many breweries still produce dark beer (tmavé), all cold fermented today though there have been occasional spottings of beers called "porter", an indication that in its day London porter had an impact as great as those of Pilsner.

The Regent Brewery in Trebon has one of the finest brewhouses in the country. The brewery was founded in 1379 and came to be owned by the Schwarzenbergs, who moved the plant into their castle armoury and had it rebuilt, complete with its own maltings, by the Italian master builders, the brothers De Maggi, the Viennese Martinelli and the Prague architect Bayer. It has been privatized since the "Velvet Revolution" and recent investment has restored the brewhouse to its former glory.

The brewing process is meticulous: mashing and boiling takes twelve hours, followed by primary fermentation for up to 12 days and lagering, for the 12-degree beers, for 90 days. Although Regent makes splendid pale lagers – closer to Budweiser than Pilsen in style – its classic beer is Dark Regent (12 degrees: 4.8 per cent ABV). Brewed from pale, caramalt and dark malts, it is ruby red in colour, with an appealing aroma of hops and bitter chocolate, dark malt in the mouth, and a hoppy/malty finish reminiscent of cappuccino coffee.

The Breclav Brewery has a 12-degree dark Breclav Speciál, sweet with a burnt sugar, caramel character. As the Czechs are a little late in learning about Political Correctness, this sweet style of dark lager is often referred to as "women's beer". Černà Horà's 12-degree Granát is highly complex, with a sweet aroma but a dry finish and a smooth palate. The name means "garnet", a reference to the beer's appealing red-black colour. The Bernard Brewery in Humpolec also has a Granát (11 degrees) made from pale and caramalt. Nová Paka Granát is 12 degrees and has a bitter coffee finish after a malty start and palate. Velké Popovice has a dark version of its Kozel billy-goat lager, malty and chocolatey.

The Ostravar Brewery is in the mining town of the same name. It was founded by Czechs in 1897 to rival another brewery that was controlled by Germans. The present brewery's 10-degree Vranik has a delicate bitterness and dark maltiness and seems to avoid the sweetness of other brands. Gambrinus markets Purkmistr (4.7 per cent ABV) brewed for it by the Domazlice Brewery.

The most memorable dark beer comes from the Pardubice Brewery in eastern Bohemia close to the Slovakian border. The 19-degree Pardubice Porter (7.0 per cent ABV) has a fine roasted malt aroma with powerful hop notes, a big palate of dark fruit and bitter hops, and a long finish bursting with coffee, chocolate and hop notes.

SLOVAKIA

Slovakia is a wine-making country with only a handful of breweries. The Urpin Brewery in Banská Bystrica produces a fine interpretation of the Pilsner style using Pilsner malt and Žatec hops. The 12-degree beer has a marked hop aroma, a firm malty body, and a long finish, hoppy and becoming dry.

The Martin Brewery in the town of that name was formed in 1893 with Jan Mattus, former head brewer at the Pilsen Brewery, in charge. As well as 12- and 14-degree pale beers, both delicately hopped, the brewery also produces the strongest known beer in both republics, Martin Porter. The 20-degree beer, around 8.0 per cent ABV, has a complex bitter-sweet palate after a hefty start of dark malt and bitter hops. The finish is long and deep with a charred malt character. It is only brewed occasionally.

EASTERN EUROPE

With the exception of the former Czechoslovakia, the beers of the old Eastern bloc were hidden from Western eyes. All the breweries were state owned and the switch to market economies will lead to fundamental changes. Western brewers are hurrying to establish bridgeheads and to brew their strongly-branded products locally.

HUNGARY

The great Austrian brewmaster Anton Dreher stamped his mark on Budapest. When Buda's twin city, Pest, was being constructed, large caves were dug in the rocky foundations and Dreher seized on them to lager his beer after he set up a company there in the middle of the nineteenth century, when Hungary was linked to Austria politically and economically. His Köbànya Brewery has survived and among its beers **Rocky Cellar** pays oblique homage to the founder. The 12-degree beer – approximately 5.5 per cent ABV – uses a substantial amount of adjuncts and is lightly hopped with 20 IBUs.

More interesting brews are all-malt – a hangover perhaps from the days when the Bavarian *Reinheitsgebot* held sway – and include a 5.0 per cent **Köbànyai** with delicate hop bitterness and a dark and sweet beer with some sultana fruitiness called **Bak** (7.5 per cent ABV), a local interpretation of the German Bock, and a pale lager of 5.5 per cent called simply Budapest.

The Kanizsa Brewery in Nagy-kanizsa was founded in 1892 in an important barley and malting region. Production stopped during the Second World War and did not begin again until 1957. In 1984 the brewery went into partnership with Holsten of Hamburg and now brews the German group's beer under licence. Its own main brand is a malty lager called **Sirály** – Seagull – a rounded Export style called **Korona** and a Dunkel-type known as **Göcseji Barna**.

Belgium's multi-national Interbrew has a majority stake in the Borsodi group while Heineken has bought Komaromi near Budapest and will brew Amstel there.

POLAND

Poland is a major brewing country with a sizeable hop-growing industry in the Lublin region and a well-developed barley and malting industry. As a result its lager beers have both good malt character and a strikingly perfumy and resiny hoppiness.

The Zywiec Brewery in Cracow takes its name from the old Polish name for the city. Its brewing liquor comes from the Tatra Mountains and is close to the hop fields of Krasnystaw. **Zywiec Beer** is called Full Light and the inspiration is as much a Munich Hell as a Bohemian Pilsner. It has a soft malt and powerful, peppery hops aroma, is tart and quenching in the mouth, with a finish that becomes dry and bitter.

Okocim Brewery has a goat on its label, though this comes from the heraldic sign for the city of Okocim and is not a reference to a Bock beer. **Okocim Pils** is 5.1 per cent ABV, has a rounded malty aroma, with rich vanilla and hops in the mouth, and a big bitter-sweet finish. The biggest-selling Pils in Poland is EB Specjal (5.4 per cent ABV), a rich, malty/hoppy beer from the Elb Brewery, now owned by Heineken. The brewery makes much of the fact that EB is triple filtered for purity.

The Warsaw Brewery (Browar Warszawksi) in the Polish capital produces two full-bodied lagers in the Pilsner and Export styles, **Stoteczne** and **Krolewskie**. Of most interest is a beer called Porter, a cold-fermenting dark beer with plenty of dark malt and coffee character, a reminder that porter and stout were once exported in vast amounts from Britain to the Baltic states. When the Napoleonic Wars closed the trade to Britain, local brewers responded to demand with their own versions but preferred to use lagering techniques.

A fascinating top-fermenting beer comes from the Grodzisk Wiekopolski Brewery near Poznan. Called **Grodzisk**, the beer is a blend of malted barley cured over an oak fire, with some wheat and help from wild yeasts in fermentation. The result is a beer with a tart, refreshing sourness, some spice from the wheat and a smoky, oaky tang.

FORMER YUGOSLAVIA

With the regions and new states of the former Yugoslavia in turmoil, the brewing picture is complicated. Except in Muslim areas, the region has powerful brewing traditions dating back to the thirteenth century. Slovenia has been a major hop-growing area for centuries and the quality of the hops from the Žatec region has stamped its mark on beers that are broadly in the German and Austrian moulds, though cold-fermented dark beers and porters have been spotted occasionally. Austrian practices, from the time when the Austro-Hungarian empire included the Slav regions, is evident in the use of the Plato scale to indicate strength. The Apatin Brewery was built in 1756 with financial support from the Imperial Chamber of Commerce in Vienna.

In Belgrade, Bip was founded in 1850. Its **Belgrade Gold** is a full-bodied malty lager of around 5.0 per cent ABV with a tart and citric hop character. Serbia's oldest brewery was built in Pancevo in 1722 and brews a **Standard** lager of around 4.5 per cent ABV and a stronger, malty/vanilla **Weifert** of 5.5 per cent.

The Trebjesa Brewery at Niksic was founded in 1896 and takes its brewing liquor from the natural spring waters of the surrounding mountains. Its main product is **Big Nik Gold Beer** – the name suggests it's a steal at the price.

ESTONIA

The Tartu Olletehas brewery launched a German-style Bock beer in 1995. Called **Rüütli Olu**, the 7.5 per cent alcohol beer is dark brown in colour and is lagered for 70 days. It is the strongest beer brewed in Estonia. It has a dark fruit and spicy hops character, is rich and warming and is promoted as the ideal beer for festivals.

RUSSIA AND THE UKRAINE

Russia is a major producer of beer but that is due to the sheer size of the country. Consumption is low and the favourite tipple is vodka. Just as the English attempted to stamp out the evils of gin-drinking by promoting beer, the Soviet regime encouraged brewing until Mikhail Gorbachev clamped down on all forms of alcohol. Beer is now reviving and the country is open to imports,

Empress Catherine the Great, a devotee of beer who porposed it should be given to the sick

to such an extent that England's Newcastle Brown Ale has become something of a cult drink among the young.

For centuries the Russian people, especially in the countryside, drank a home-made porridge beer called *kvass*, and it survives as a cheap and nourishing drink. It is made from rye. Barley and wheat are sometimes added and the drink is sweetened with unfermented hedgerow fruits such as bilberries. It has never been made successfully on a commercial scale.

Commercial breweries were established early in the twentieth century and were nationalized following the Bolshevik Revolution. The industry was damaged severely during the Second World War and was re-built mainly with Czech expertise in the 1950s and 1960s. The Czechs were called in again to build additional plants in the 1980s but these were mothballed when Gorbachev called for a crackdown against drunkenness. It is estimated that there are some 16 brand-new and unused brewing plants dotted around the countries that made up the USSR.

The most popular beer in Russia comes from the Ukraine, its popularity underscored by its own beer garden in the Russian capital, the Zhiguli Cellar off Kalinin Prospekt. The Obolov Brewery in Kiev that makes **Zhiguli** (4.4 per cent) uses pale malt, brewing sugar and around 5.0 per cent rice with Klon hops. Bitterness units are low, around 17. The beer is conditioned for 45 days and has a light malt aroma and palate, with some delicate hops in the finish.

The Moscow Brewery, established in 1863, makes a 4.6 per cent **Moskovkoye Lager** broadly in the Pilsner style, and a fuller-bodied, almost amber **Radonej**. It has added **August** (4.5 per cent ABV), an all-malt beer named after the failed August coup that brought Boris Yeltsin to power. It is bronze coloured with a rich toffee/vanilla aroma, hops on the palate and a light but fruity and hoppy finish.

"Russian stout"

In the nineteenth and early twentieth centuries the Baltic states had a love affair with the dark porters and stouts brewed in Britain. The strongest versions became known as Imperial Stout as a result of their popularity with the Russian court. The Empress Catherine was a devotée and encouraged the beer to be given to the sick. Imperial stouts were brewed in London by several companies based along the Thames. They were black and viscous, and heavily hopped in order to withstand long sea journeys to the Baltic. The sole surviving example, **Imperial Russian Stout**, came from the Courage group, which began life as Henry Thrale's brewery in London, founded in the seventeenth century. It was bought by a Scottish-American called Barclay, and became Barclay-Perkins before joining the Courage group founded by John Courage, a Scot of French Huguenot origins. There is a further convoluted ethnic twist to the story, for Imperial Russian Stout was exported to the Baltic for Barclay Perkins by a Belgian named Le Coq. Monsieur Le Coq produced a booklet in Russian extolling the healthy attributes of the beer. He boosted the popularity of Russian Stout by giving away cases of the beer to Russian soldiers injured in the Crimean War. At the turn of the century Le Coq bought a brewery in Tartu in what is now Estonia to brew both porter and stout for the Baltic market. His success was short-lived for the brewery was nationalized by the Bolsheviks in 1917. Records show that the brewery last brewed a cold-fermenting porter in 1969.

Back in Britain, Courage continued to produce Imperial Russian Stout in small batches every other year. When it closed its London brewery, it moved production to its John Smith's subsidiary in Tadcaster in Yorkshire. In London the beer used to be conditioned in the brewery for 18 months before being released. The bottle-conditioned beer had a starting gravity of 1104 degrees and was declared 10 per cent ABV, though 11 has been reached. Its complex grist included some Pilsner malt as well as pale, amber and black malts with some brewing sugar: perhaps the habit of using Pilsner malt stems from boats that had been full of stout returning to England with cargoes of European barley. It was hopped with the Target variety in the region of 24 pounds per barrel – four times the normal rate. Bitterness units were in the region of 50. Tragically, when Courage merged with Scottish and Newcastle Breweries in the 1990s, Imperial Russian Stout was discontinued.

Next door to John Smith's Brewery, the distantly related but independent firm of Samuel Smith introduced an **Imperial Stout** (7.0 per cent ABV) in the 1980s, a superb bottled beer with great dark malt, winey fruit and hops character, more quenching than the Courage version.

IMPORTANT ADDRESS

Kiev Obolon Brewery, Bogatyrskaya Street 3, Kiev 212.

Elbrewery Company, 82–300 Elblag Browarnu 71, Elblag.

FRANCE

The French make beer. The French drink beer. If that sounds trite, it is because the international image of France is inextricably linked to wine; beer needs to be dragged from the giant shadow cast by the vine. Beer is drunk throughout the country, often in bars and cafés called brasseries – breweries. Beer was once brewed all over France, too. The Gauls were famous for their *cervoise*, from the Latin *cerevisia* – ale. At the turn of the twentieth century there were still 3,000 French breweries, many of them tiny and run from farms, operating in Nice, Limoges and Toulouse as well as in beer's northern heartlands.

Today there are just 33 breweries left, plus a handful of microbreweries. That marks a fall from 76 breweries in 1976. The decline of beer is remarkable in a country that is still largely rural and with a powerful agricultural lobby. But, outside the far North, beer was never treated as seriously as wine, was never so much part of the tapestry of life. It was a refresher, not a drink to savour or ponder. As a result, it became prey to industrialization. Today brewing is dominated to an astonishing degree by just two companies: Kronenbourg, part of the giant food and drinks group BSN, and Heineken. Kronenbourg controls 50 per cent of the market, Heineken 25 per cent. The Belgian Interbrew group also busily sells beer in France, though it no longer brews there. Most of this production takes place in the North, mainly in Alsace-Lorraine, an area under German rule from 1871 to 1919 and also during the Second World War, experiences that stamped their mark on the language, the cuisine and the beer. And even within the region, brewing is concentrated in Alsace and its capital, Strasbourg. The last independent brewery in Lorraine (Amos of Metz) closed in 1992. The last regional brewery of any size or note outside the North, Schneider of Puyoô, closed in 1990 and even here there was an obvious German influence. Heineken has a plant in Marseilles but it scarcely ranks as a French brewery.

Change is taking place, though. Consumption is increasing and there is a flowering of brewing of a quite different kind from the German-influenced lagers of Alsace. In the Nord-Pas de Calais region, strung out along the border with Belgium, ales are flourishing, albeit on a small scale. The brewers of the region, many of them new, small micros, concentrate in the main on the style known as *bière de garde*, a warm-fermenting beer that has powerful links with the farmhouse *saison* and *vieille* provision ales of Wallonia. The sudden interest in French ales has not gone unnoticed and even the giants of French brewing are reviving such long-lost styles as Christmas and March beers.

Alsace-Lorraine

This is lager-brewing territory. The German influence is obvious in the names of breweries, cities, towns and villages as well as in the cuisine, in which pork dishes abound. But the beer is a long way removed from the influence of the German *Reinheitsgebot*. Twenty to 30 per cent of cereal adjuncts are not uncommon in the lagers of the region. Hopping rates are not high, with bitterness units in the low to middle 20s. The results are beers of between 5.0 and 6.0 per cent ABV that are pleasant, refreshing but in general unremarkable.

Kronenbourg is based in Strasbourg. It has a second brewery in nearby Obernai and its subsidiary Kanterbräu brews at Champigneulles in Lorraine, and Rennes in Britanny. The history of Kronenbourg is

Christmas beer is one of the long-lost styles being revived in Alsace

stamped on the label of one of its best-known brands, 1664, for that was the year when Jérôme Hatt started to make beer in a tavern called Au Canon (Zur Karthaune in German) on the Place de Corbeau (the Raven) in Strasbourg, close by the Customs House on the banks of the Rhine (Le Rhin). Hatt had qualified as a master brewer and cooper and he quickly won acclaim for the quality of his beer, which would have been warm-fermenting in those days. His tavern became the top meeting place for the Strasbourgeois (the tavern has survived but now sells beer from the Schützenberger Brewery).

In 1850 Frédéric-Guillaume Hatt moved the brewery to a new site in the suburb of Cronenbourg, meaning the crown or brow of the hill. In the Germanic fashion, the brewery took on the name of its place of domicile and the spelling was subsequently changed to Kronenbourg. It achieved national status in the 1920s with a bilingual beer called Tigre Bock which frustratingly no longer exists. In the 1950s Kronenbourg began to expand aggressively. It pioneered beer in 25-centilitre bottles and made a big play for supermarket sales with disposable containers. Kronenbourg 1664 was launched in 1962, two years short of the brewery's double centenary, and a second brewery known as "K2" was opened at Obernai in 1969. A year later Kronenbourg became part of the BSN group, which also acquired Kanterbräu. The brewing groups were merged in 1986.

The main brand is simply called **Kronenbourg**, with medieval lettering on a quartered red and white label that is supposed to emulate a shield but looks more like a rugby shirt. The beer is 5.2 per cent ABV, with 23 IBUs. The aroma is light, delicate, unobtrusive, with a clean palate and finish, and some hop and malt notes. The 5.9 per cent ABV 1664 has a more pronounced aroma but is disappointingly light for a beer of the strength. The version brewed under licence in Britain by Courage is 5.0 per cent ABV. A brown version, **1664 Brune**, is a percentage point stronger and has a pleasant chewy, dark caramel character. A 4.7 per cent ABV **Bière de l'Eté** is a light summer refresher while a Christmas beer, **Bière de Noël**, has a fuller golden colour with a hint of red – perhaps a dash of Munich or caramalt – and more body.

The Kanterbräu subsidiary came about as a result of series of mergers and takeovers. Its origins are as Les Grandes Brasseries de Champigneulles, founded in 1897 by Victor Hinzelin and Victor Trampitsch. Victor Trampitsch was a Slovenian who had learned his brewing skills in Pilsen, an impressive pedigree. Following the Second World War the company swallowed many other breweries in the region, becoming Société Européene de Brasseries (SEB) before being bought up by BSN in 1970 and renamed Kanterbräu. At one stage SEB had 11 breweries but now only two operate. The main brand, Kanterbräu, takes its name from a German brewmaster, Maître Kanter, who came to France from Germany. A romantic interpretation of him, in broad-brimmed hat and holding a foaming jug of beer, adorns the beer labels. **Kanterbräu** (4.5 per cent ABV) is light in aroma and body. A stronger **Kanterbräu Gold** is in similar vein to 1664 while a recent revival of **Bière de Mars** (March Beer) is disappointingly thin. The group has had considerable success with **Tourtel**. It is a low-alcohol beer named after another closed brewery: surely the ultimate indignity.

The small town of Schiltigheim – "Schillick" to the locals – is called "ville des brasseurs" (brewers' town). It is home to four brewing companies that provide jobs for around 2,000 people. The Grande Brasserie Alsacienne d'Adelshoffen was founded in 1864 by the Ehrhardt brothers. It was renamed Strassburger Münsterbräu during the years of German control and was bought by the Fischer/Pêcheur group in 1922, though it has always been given a considerable degree of independence to run its own affairs. It has an everyday light lager in the Alsatian style but a more characterful **Adelshoffen Export** (4.5 per cent ABV). It is brewed from pale malt and maize (corn) with Hallertau and Styrian hops (20 IBUs). It has a clean malt aroma with some citric notes from the hops, a malty palate and a bitter-sweet finish that becomes dry. The company created enormous interest in 1982 with **Adelscott**, a beer made with some peated whisky malt. It cashed in on the French fascination with Scotch malt whisky. The beer is 6.6 per cent ABV, made from pale malt, whisky malt and maize. It is hopped with Alsace Brewers' Gold, Hallertau and Styrian varieties and has 16 to 20 IBUs.

Three beers from Maison La Choulette; they are sealed like champagne with a twist-off cage and cork stopper

It is lagered for two months and has an appealing aroma of smoked malt, rich malt in the mouth and a light smoky finish.

Fischer/Pêcheur is the largest independent brewery in France. It hedges its bets with its name, having used both at various times when under French and German control but today is known simply as Fischer. It was founded in 1821 in Strasbourg by Jean Fischer, who moved to Schiltigheim in 1854. Its ebullient chairman, Michel Debus, caused a storm of controversy in 1988 when he instigated the court case against the German *Reinheitsgebot* (see German section). He is a great innovator, constantly creating new brands that have considerable public relations impact but are a dubious contribution to the greater appreciation of beer. He has produced an aphrodisiac beer **36.15 – La Bière Amoureuse**, flavoured with ginseng, a rum-flavoured beer, and non-alcoholic beers for dogs and cats called **Mon Titi** and **Mon Toutou**. A 6.5 per cent ABV kriek is an attempt to replicate a Belgian cherry beer, using a fruit concentrate rather than whole cherries.

Among the standard brews, **Fischer Gold** (6.4 per cent ABV) in a Grolsch-style swing-top bottle, has a perfumy aroma and good hop character, and a soft, malty, smooth *bière de mars* is brewed for the spring.

The brewery that became Schützenberger was founded in Strasbourg in 1740 but may be older. It was bought by Jean-Daniel Schützenberger in 1768. It was called the Brasserie Royale until the revolution of 1789 when it was hastily renamed Brasserie de la Patrie, which translated into Brauerei zum Vaterland – the Fatherland Brewery – under German rule. It moved to Schiltigheim in 1866. It is run today by Rina Müller-Walter, who succeeded her father. She is believed to be the only woman running a major brewing company in Europe. The company brews some rich and beautifully-crafted beers, a long way removed from the general Alsatian style. Its **Jubilator** and **Patriator** brews (7.0 per cent ABV) are pale and dark German-style double Bocks, with great hop character. The pale is smooth and perfumy, the brown rich and fruity. **Schutz 2000** was brewed to mark the two-thousandth anniversary of the founding of Strasbourg. It is an unfiltered, bottle-conditioned beer (6.5 per cent ABV) bursting with rich, tart fruit and resiny hops. Another celebration beer, **Cuivrée** (house brew) marked the brewery's own 250 years. This is a luscious, 8.0 per cent Vienna-style strong lager, gold-red, malty and fruity, underscored by perfumy hops. There are seasonal March (5.2 per cent ABV) and Christmas (6.0 per cent ABV) brews.

The cuckoo in the Schillick nest is Heineken, which went on the rampage in Alsace in the 1970s and 1980s. It is based on the site of the old Brasserie de l'Espérance (ironically, the Great Expectations Brewery) which was founded in Strasbourg in 1746 and moved to Schiltigheim in 1860. It merged with four other breweries, including Mützig, to form Alsatian Breweries, Alba for short. In 1972 Alba was bought by Heineken, which then staged a mammoth three-way merger in 1984 with Union de Brasseries, famous in Africa and South-east Asia for its 33 brand, and Pelforth of Mons-en-Baroeul, whose pelican trade mark is recognized throughout France. The new group, with a quarter of French beer sales, went through several changes of name until the dominant partner exerted its influence. It is now Brasseries Heineken. As well as the Schillick plant, it has the Pelforth Brewery near Lille and one in Marseille. The major emphasis goes into promoting the ubiquitous Dutch Heineken. The fate of other brands is less clear. It is likely that the Pelforth beers will continue because of their popularity in the Lille area. **Pelforth Blonde** and **Pélican** (4.8 per cent ABV) are standard French lagers but **Pelforth Brune**

(6.5 per cent ABV) has plenty of rich dark chocolatey malt character. It is to be hoped that the characterful Mützig brands, **Mützig** (4.8 per cent ABV) and **Old Lager** (7.3 per cent ABV), both with rich malt and dry, hoppy finishes, will survive. The Pelforth plant produces **George Killian's Bière Rousse**, based on Killian's Irish Ale. It is sold in The Netherlands under the name of Kilyan.

Météor is in the Alsatian village of Hochfelden. Brewing dates back to 1640 and beyond: beer was supplied to a local abbey and to farms in the area. The present brewery was bought by the Metzger family of Strasbourg in 1844 and is now owned by their relations through marriage, the Haags. The name **Météor** was adopted in 1925 and the company launched a Pilsner-style beer under the name two years later. It signed an agreement with Pilsner Urquell to use the term "Pils", the only such agreement in the French brewing industry. The beer is 4.9 per cent ABV and is brewed with pale malt and corn grits. Hops used are Czech Saaz (Žatec) and Alsatian varieties. The beer, by local standards, is well-hopped, achieving 35 IBUs. A single decoction mash is used and the beer is lagered for one month. It has a toasty malt and hops aroma, with sweet malt and bitter hops in the mouth, and a long dry finish with more hops and some honey/vanilla notes. It lacks the depth and finesse of a true Pilsner but is a well-made and attractive beer. **Ackerland Blonde** (5.9 per cent ABV) is a rich and malty pale lager. A brown version, **Ackerland Brune** (6.3 per cent ABV), is packed with dark malt and hops character. The brewery has cashed in on the Scotch malt whisky craze with **Mortimer** (8.0 per cent ABV), an amber-coloured beer, fruity and lightly hopped.

Nord-Pas de Calais

If Alsace is a triumph of modernization, of state-of-the-art brewing, then Nord-Pas de Calais is a time-warp where beer is made by ancient, hand-crafted methods. This is the region of "artisanal beer". Some lagers are produced, but in general the beers of border country recall a more ruminative and rural period when beer was made on farms and in homes as naturally as bread would be baked and the land tilled and harvested. It is a region of flat land, lowering skies and distant horizons where political borders do not impinge on the reality of everyday life, a region rich in Flemish as well as French traditions. The locals speak of "French Flanders" and cock a snook at history.

On the coat-tails of the Belgian revival, beer lovers have disovered the ales of French Flanders, Artois and Picardy once just a footnote in the brewing books, now a recognizable style in their own right. Between Calais and Lille there is a tradition known as "bière de garde". These were beers brewed on farms, usually in the winter, to provide important sustenance for farmers and all those who worked the land.

Many of the breweries are still small and are based on farms, though farming is no longer the major preoccupation as the interest in beer from Flanders grows. The beers are often pale as well as brown, but the

Schützenberger Brewery in Strasbourg, probably the only brewery in Europe run by a woman, brews some beautifully-crafted beers

original versions would have been dark. Wherever possible brewers use barley and hops from the region, which allows them to carry the appellation "Pas de Calais/Région du Nord" on their labels. From Ypres – across the border in Belgium – down into French Flanders, stretches a small and very ancient hop-growing area, while Flanders, the Champagne region and Burgundy produce malting barley of the highest quality.

The classic style is a strong beer of between 6.0 and 8.0 per cent ABV, malty and spicy from the use of well-cured malts. Mashing is often long to achieve some caramelization of the brewing sugars. Hop rates are not high, with IBUs in the 20s: the brewer is seeking roundness, fullness, a certain alcoholic warmth rather than a hard bitterness. Finished beers now are stored for a month: centuries ago this would have been a far longer period.

Commercial success has brought problems in its wake. Some brewers have switched from the use of traditional top-working yeasts to lager cultures. They say this gives them greater control over fermentation, and the beers are more stable once out in the trade. But

at the same time they are still fermenting at ale temperatures in order to achieve a fruity ale character. Nevertheless, it would be a tragedy if the true concept of a warm-fermenting *bière de garde* is lost in the rush to embrace all the demands of the modern market with its insatiable belief in "shelf life".

The beer that breathed life back into the style is Jenlain. It became a cult drink with students in Lille in the 1980s and features prominently in festivals and celebrations in the city. Jenlain comes from the Brasserie Duyck in the village of Jenlain south-east of Valenciennes. Brewing started on a farm and in 1922 Félix Duyck, of Flemish stock, started brewing on the farm. The business is now run by his son Robert and grandson Raymond. Production has grown to 90,000 hectolitres a year but brewing has remained traditional in copper vessels. Malts from Flanders, Champagne and Burgundy are used along with four hop varieties from Belgium, France, Germany and Slovenia. **Jenlain**, 6.5 per cent ABV, is russet-coloured, spicy and malty. It is a highly complex beer with great depth (25 IBUs). The Duycks did experiment with a bottom-fermenting yeast but latest information is that they have returned to proper ale brewing. They also brew a Christmas beer and a pale spring (Printemps) beer.

Beer was brewed in the region for coal miners as well as farm workers – Lille was once at the heart of the mining industry of northern France. The Castelain Brewery at Bénifontaine near Lens once made a special 2.0 per cent alcohol beer for miners, but all the pits have gone and the only reminder of the industry is the ghostly figure of a coal miner with his lamp on the label of the brewery's main brand Ch'ti. The name comes from Picardy dialect and means "c'est toi" – "it suits you". The brewery, part of a farm, was built in 1926 and was bought by the Castelain family in 1966. The handsome brewhouse with gleaming copper kettles produces 28,000 hectolitres a year. Yves Castelain uses Flemish and French barley and hops for pale and brown versions of Ch'ti as well as for an organic beer called Jade, Christmas and March beers, and an abbey-style beer called Sint Arnoldus. Yves Castelain has switched to lager yeast but ferments at 15 degrees C/59F. The beers are fermented for 10 to 12 days and then conditioned for up to two months. **Ch'ti Blonde** is made

SELECTED FRENCH BREWERS

Grande Brasserie Alsacienne d'Adelshoffen, 87 route de Bischwiller, 67300 Schiltigheim.

Brasserie d'Annoeullin, 4 Place du Général de Gaulle, 59112 Annoeullin.

Brasserie Bailleux, Café-Restaurant Au Baron, Place du Fond des Rocs, Gussignies, 59570 Bavay.

Brasserie Castelain, 13 rue Pasteur, Bénifontaine, 62410 Wingles.

Brasserie Duyck, 113 rue Nationale, 59144 Jenlain.

Brasserie des Enfants de Gayant, 63 Fauborg de Paris, 59502 Douai.

Brasserie Fischer, 7 route de Bischwiller, 67300 Schiltigheim.

Brasseries Heineken SA, 19 rue des Deux-Gares, 92565 Rueil-Malmaison.

Kanterbräu SA, Tour Chenonceaux, 92100 Boulogne.

Brasserie Kronenbourg SA, 86 route d'Oberhausbergen, 67067 Strasbourg.

Brasserie Météor Haag-Metzger & Cie, 6 rue du Général-Lebocq, 67270 Hochfelden.

Brasserie Saint Sylvestre, 1 rue de la Chappelle, 59114 Saint-Sylvestre-Cappel.

from four malts, the **Ch'ti Brune** from eight, including Munich, cara-Munich and torrefied varieties. The 6.5 per cent ABV beers are rich and fruity, with the Brune in particular having a strong hint of raisins in the mouth. The 4.6 per cent ABV **Ch'ti Jade** has more hop character, pungent and perfumy, with sweet malt in the mouth and a fruity finish that becomes dry.

In the hills of French Hainaut, close to the Belgian border, the Bailleux family runs the Café Restaurant au Baron in Gussignies and also brews on the premises. All the products are true warm-fermenting, bottle-conditioned *bières de garde*, though one is called a *saison* in the Belgian fashion. The **Cuvée des Jonquilles** does not, in spite of the name, use daffodils in the brewing process but it has an entrancing golden colour and flowery-fruity aroma and palate. The 7.0 per cent ABV beer is brewed in the spring, which explains the daffodil associations. Four malts and four hop varieties are used. The **Saison Saint Médard**, also 7.0 per cent ABV, has a fine cherry colour and a fruity aroma similar to a Belgian kriek but without the lambic sourness. There is also a chocolatey and spicy Christmas beer.

The Brasserie d'Annoeullin is in the small town of the same name between Lens and Lille. The brewery was once a farm and Bertrand Lepers' wife, Yvonne, comes from farmer-brewers at Flers. When they married they merged the two breweries. The mash tun doubles as a copper after the wort has been clarified. The beer ferments in horizontal tanks in cellars that were once cattle byres. Primary fermentation lasts for a week, followed by two weeks' conditioning. The *bière de garde* is called, tongue-in-cheek, **Pastor Ale** with the sub-title "C'est une symphonie". It is 6.5 per cent ABV and is made from pale malt only. It has a rich gold colour, pronounced orange fruit and earthy hops on the aroma, more tart fruit in the mouth and a dry and fruity finish. A 7.3 per cent ABV **Angelus** is a wheat beer, using 30 per cent buck wheat in flour form. It is bronze coloured and has a powerful citric tangerine aroma backed by spicy hops, with more tart fruit in the mouth and a long, bitter-sweet finish: a magnificent beer.

The St Sylvestre Brewery at Steenvoorde, in the heart of the hop country, produces a gold *bière de garde* called **3 Monts** (8.5 per cent ABV). It is named after three local hills, worthy of celebration in such flat country. The beer is dry and winey with good hop character from local Brewers' Gold and German Tettnang.

The depth of support for beer in the region can be seen in the annual summer festival in Douai where ale is the main lubricant. The two legendary giants that lead the parade are known as Monsieur and Madame Gayant and the local brewery calls itself Les Enfants de Gayant.

The enterprising brewery has a large portfolio of beers, including an Abbey beer and a 12 per cent ABV perfumy lager, **Bière de Démon**. Its interpretation of the *bière de garde* style is called Lutèce Bière de Paris – Lutèce comes from the Roman name for Paris, Lutetia. Brewers in Roman Paris were based in an area known as La Glacière, fed by the waters of the river Bièvre, named after beavers that bred there. Beer was stored in icy caves – an early form of lager brewing. The beer style was called **Brune de Paris**. The Lutèce Brewery was founded in Paris in 1920 on the site of an old Brasserie de Glacière and, although brewing has been switched to Douai, the style of the original beer is meticulously maintained. It is 6.4 per cent ABV and is made from pale, Munich, crystal and caramel-amber malts. Spalt and Saaz hops achieve 23 IBUs. The beer is conditioned for 60 days. It has a rich malt and fruit aroma, with malt and raisins in the mouth and a deep finish with hints of chocolate and liquorice.

Visitors to Lille can find instant refreshment when they leave the railway station in Les 3 Brasseurs at 22 Place de la Gare. It is a large, beautifully-appointed brewpub, the first in a small chain owned by Patrick Bonduel in Northern France (other pubs are in Angers, Mulhouse, Paris and Strasbourg). The beers are all-malt and unpasteurized, brewed in a tiny brewhouse. Customers can order La Palette du Barman, four taster glasses of each beer. The Blonde has a malty, perfumy aroma with a bitter-sweet palate; the Ambré has a dark toasty character; the Brune has hints of sweet nuts and bitter chocolate; while the cloudy wheat beer – Blanche – has a tangy apples-and-cloves aroma, citric fruit in the mouth and a dry finish with a powerful hint of apples. There are also March and Christmas seasonal beers.

GERMANY

Germany is the world's greatest beer nation. Beer is rooted in the lifestyle and culture of the people. It underscores every celebration. And in the Catholic south, the Bavarians seem to find good reason to celebrate all year round. Their Munich Oktoberfest is the world's most famous beer festival but it is not sufficient to satiate the Bavarians. They have winter beers, March beers, May beers and strong Lent beers they call "liquid bread".

It is not just "lager" that Germans drink. Ask for a lager in a German bar and you will get a puzzled look. You may be shown the storage area or the refrigerator instead of being served a cool, pale beer. Lager, from *lagerung* meaning "to store", is a stage in the brewing process. The term lager is mainly confined to exports to the British Isles where it is used to distinguish beers brewed by cold fermentation from warm-fermented ales. In Germany drinkers need to be more specific.

Bavarians will call for a Hell or a Dunkel or, depending on the season of the year, they might demand a Märzen or a Bock. In the North, the call may be for an Export. And everywhere the shout for "a Pils" will bring forth a dry and bitter interpretation of the Bohemian Pilsner.

And Germans do not only drink beers made by cold fermentation. Members of the ale family of beer are growing in favour. Bavarian wheat beers are enormously popular and have grown to around 30 per cent of the total beer market. Berlin has its own idiosyncratic version of wheat beer while Cologne and Düsseldorf proudly brew golden Kölsch and copper-coloured Alt beers.

Reinheitsgebot

The history of the *Reinheitsgebot*, the sixteenth-century Bavarian "Pure Beer Pledge", is covered in the history section. It is still in force throughout Germany. It

Hops growing tall in Germany; in the background, left, the stakes stand ready for another planting

stipulates that beer can only be brewed with malted barley and wheat, hops, yeast and water: sugars and "adjuncts" – cheap unmalted cereals – are outlawed. The pledge is adhered to with fierce pride by brewers who were angered by a decision of the European Court in 1987 to declare the pledge "a restraint of trade". The case was taken to court by French brewers based ironically in the former German region around Strasbourg. French and other European brewers were irritated that they could not export beer to Germany as they did not brew according to the *Reinheitsgebot*. But, despite a court ruling in favour of non-German brewers, imported beer has made little headway in Germany. The German brewers launched a campaign against what they call "chemi-beer", an attempt to suggest that beers from other countries are grossly inferior to their own and brewed using chemicals. While some poor quality packaged beers are sometimes brewed with the help of small amounts of chemicals to speed up fermentation and to create a thick head on beer, the use of chemicals or natural compounds is in the main confined to water treatment to enable brewers to harden or soften their brewing liquor. And nothing in the *Reinheitsgebot* stops German brewers treating their water.

Every brewery in Germany, and many bars, too, display plaques announcing that the beers produced or on sale adhere to the *Reinheitsgebot*. Consumers are intensely loyal to their local breweries and the German brewing industry has been largely untouched by imports, though Czech beers, which are brewed to the Purity Pledge, are popular. It should be noted, however, that with the exception of Bavaria, German beers brewed for export do not have to meet the requirements of the *Reinheitsgebot*.

Bavaria

Germany has around 1,400 breweries. The country has so far not been overtaken by the merger mania of the rest of the world. Some 750 of the total are located in Bavaria. Every town and just about every village has a brewery, sometimes more than one, brewing to traditional recipes, producing seasonal specialities, ignoring the outside world and pressures to produce beers by faster and less perfect methods. Monasteries and even convents brew beer, often for just their own

and visitors' consumption. Bavaria remains a largely rural region and brewing is a time-honoured, bucolic ritual, as natural as baking bread, using the barley and the hops from the surrounding fields and pure, icy water from the Alps. The choice is literally staggering, around 5,000 different beers, in a wide variety of styles and strengths. By avoiding mergers, only a handful of brewers, mainly in Munich, are large, producing more than half a million hectolitres a year. Five hundred Bavarian breweries make no more than 10,000 hectolitres a year and some of those produce as little as 2,000 hectolitres.

The only major change in brewing practice in Bavaria has been the switch from warm to cold fermentation. The earliest empirical attempts to store or lager beer came in the great Bavarian capital of Munich. The city was founded in 1158 when a Bavarian duke built a bridge across the River Isar, and Munich became a major trading town on the salt route from Austria to the north German ports. Munich – München in German, from Mönchen, "the monks' place" – is close to the foothills of the Alps and brewers stored their beers in deep caves to withstand the rigours of hot summers. The low temperatures encouraged yeast to settle at the bottom of the fermenting vessels and to turn malt sugars into alcohol much more slowly than conventional warm fermentation. The result was a cleaner-tasting, less fruity and more stable beer.

As massive industrial innovation swept across Europe in the late eighteenth and nineteenth centuries, brewers rushed to embrace all the new technologies available to them. Steam power, temperature control, yeast propagation, better hop utilization, kilning of malt over coke fires and, above all, refrigeration led to fundamental changes in the way beer was brewed. Gabriel Sedlmayr the Younger, a member of the great Munich brewing dynasty that owns the Spaten group, travelled widely in Europe to learn his brewing skills. He returned to Munich in 1834 to put his knowledge into operation and to use new technology to develop lager brewing. From the late 1830s Sedlmayr became famous throughout the world of brewing as the man behind the new cold-fermenting beer. He collaborated with Anton Dreher, another innovative brewer in Vienna, and the two worked with Carl von Linde, builder of ice machines, to develop a commercial refrigerator that would enable beer to be stored not in caves but in brewery cellars at near-freezing temperatures.

Dark lagers

The first Munich lagers were dark. Malting techniques must have been behind those in England, where pale ales appeared early in the nineteenth century. Coal was notoriously expensive in Bavaria and coke, made from coal, was vital to produce pale malt on a large scale. And continental varieties of barley, high in protein, were more difficult to work with, needing a triple-decoction mashing regime. So the revolutionary new beer that emerged from Sedlmayr's Spaten brewery was a dark copper-to-mahogany colour. The style survives and is called Dunkel, sometimes rendered as Dunkles, which means dark. Today the malt grist for the beer will be a careful blend of pale and darker malt. The latter is known world-wide as Munich malt, which has been kilned in the maltings to a high temperature but avoids the bitter, roasty character of a much darker English black or chocolate malt. A Munich brewer looks for sweetness from his malt which he can balance with aromatic Bavarian hops.

Spaten's **Ludwig Thoma Dunkel** is the classic Munich dark beer. It is 5.5 per cent ABV, with 47 colour units and a gentle 20 IBUs. It has a malty, slighty spicy aroma, a malt-and-coffee palate and a finish that begins bitter-sweet and becomes dry. Among the other Munich brewers, Augustiner's Dunkel is 5.0 per cent ABV, exceptionally dark with russet tints, a malty nose, a nutty palate and a dry finish. Hacker-Pschorr's **Dunkel** (5.2 per cent ABV) is rich, malty and chocolatey with a dry finish. The Hofbräuhaus, the world-famous "royal court brewhouse", with oompah bands and a large beer garden, has a distinctive 5.2 per cent ABV **Dunkel** with a complex malt and vanilla aroma, tart dark fruit in the mouth and a long finish with hints of hops, dark fruit and chocolate. Paulaner's 5.2 per cent ABV **Dunkel** is both extremely dark and well-hopped for the style, with an aromatic malt and hops aroma, dark fruit in the mouth and a dry and bitter finish.

Outside Munich, the Kaltenberg Brewery has turned its dark lager into a speciality. The brewery is based in a splendid neo-Gothic castle and is owned by an aristocratic brewer, Prince Luitpold of Bavaria. He is a member of the German royal family that lost power at the end of the First World War. When he took over the family castle and brewery in 1976, he decided to beef up the Dunkel and make it his leading brand.

The 5.6 per cent ABV **König Ludwig Dunkel** – named after a royal ancestor, King Ludwig – is well-attenuated, with most of the brewing sugars turned to alcohol. The mashing is an exhaustive triple decoction one and hops – Hersbruck and Tettnang – are added three times during the copper boil. The British practice of dry-hopping – adding a handful of hops to the beer in cask – is used for additional aroma: this is frowned on by most German brewers. The finished beer has 24 to 26 IBUs. The beer is kräusened during lagering, which means that some partially-fermented wort is added to the beer to encourage a powerful second fermentation. Lagering takes place in the castle cellars in small stainless steel conical vessels. The beer has a pronounced bitter-hoppy character from aroma to finish, balanced by dark malt, coffee and bitter fruit. It is a splendidly refreshing beer.

Franconia, the northern region of Bavaria (Franken in German), is packed with breweries. The main towns of Amberg, Bamberg and Nuremberg have 18 breweries between them, nine of them in the half-timbered, medieval splendour of Bamberg. The relative isolation of Franconia, heightened by its proximity to East Germany and Czechoslovakia during the years of the Cold War, has made it a conservative region with a great belief in traditional values, including a devotion to dark lagers. Many of the breweries are tiny, no more than brewpubs. A classic is the Hausbrauerei Altstadthof in Nuremberg, which means "the house brewery in the old town courtyard". Based in sixteenth-century buildings, the brewhouse has copper mashing and boiling vessels and wooden fermenters and lagering tanks. Using organically-grown barley and hops, the 4.8 per cent ABV dark beer is red-brown in colour, has a yeasty and malty aroma, a creamy palate and a malty finish with some hints of dark fruit.

In Kulmbach, the Kulmbacher Mönchshof was once a monastic brewery, secularized at the end of the eighteenth century. Its speciality is Kloster Schwarz Bier – cloister black beer – a 4.7 per cent ABV brew known

Spaten's brewery produces the famous Ludwig Thomas Dunkel; the GS stands for Gabriel Sedlmay the Younger

locally as "the black Pils" because of its unusual hoppiness for the style. It begins malty and yeasty on the nose but picks up hop character on the palate and finishes dry and bitter.

Also in Kulmbach, EKU, the brewery famous for its 13.5 per cent ABV Doppelbock, one of the strongest beers in the world, also makes a 4.8 per cent ABV **Rubin Dunkel**, rich and malty with a hint of tart fruit and a dry finish.

The Klosterbräu Bamberg is another brewery with monastic origins. It dates from the sixteenth century when it was owned by the local bishop and monks carried out the brewing. The dark beer, available in the tavern next door, has a tongue-twisting name: **Achd Bambärcha Schwärzla** (5.3 per cent ABV), Franconian dialect for "real Bamberg black". It is a dark brown, almost black beer, hoppy on the nose, with coffee and dark fruit on the palate and a bitter-sweet finish.

In Bayreuth, with its Wagner associations, Maisel

brews a 5.1 per cent ABV **Dunkel** with a pleasant nutty palate, dry finish and delicate hop bitterness.

Pale lagers

To call the pale lagers of Munich and Bavaria "everyday beers" is to diminish the quality and the respectable strengths of brews of between 4.5 and 5.0 per cent ABV. They are known as Helles or Hell for short, meaning pale. (The only exception is Franconia where the style is often referred to as *Vollbier*.) Helles beers sit just below Pilsners, which are slightly stronger and a shade dryer and more hoppy. Helles is the drink of the beer garden and the keller, refreshing, spritzy, malty and delicately hopped.

The first pale lager appeared from the Spaten Brewery in 1894. Paulaner, which now includes Hacker-Pschorr, busily promoted the style in the 1920s and 1930s. But Helles did not overtake Dunkel in popularity until the 1950s, rather as pale ale replaced mild in

British beer drinkers' affections. Helles beers tend to be extremely pale while a Pilsner is golden. Spaten's **Hell** is 4.8 per cent ABV, and its **Pilsener** – note the variation in spelling – is 5.0 per cent ABV. But the Pilsner has 38 IBUs, the Hell just 22. The Hell is a Bavarian classic, with an entrancing bitter-sweet, malt-and-hops aroma, malty in the mouth and finish that becomes dry but not bitter.

Augustiner's **Hell** (5.2 per cent ABV) is the most popular among Munich's beer lovers, perhaps as a result of its more robust strength, with a malty-creamy aroma, malt in the mouth and on the finish. Hacker-Pschorr's 4.9 per cent ABV **Hell** is darker with a fruity aroma and palate, and a dry finish (20 IBUs). Löwenbräu's **Hell** (5.3 per cent ABV) is soft and malty from aroma to finish. In sharp distinction, Paulaner's **Original Münchner Hell** (4.9 per cent ABV) has a dry edge to the finish and is much more generously hopped.

The oddest beer comes from Forschung at Perlach,

an outer suburb of Munich. As well as brewing, the Jakob family also carries out research work for other breweries. The name of the 5.4 per cent ABV **Pilsissimus** suggests it is a junior version of a Pilsner but the strength belies this. It is copper coloured with a big floral hop aroma, soft malt in the mouth and a finish packed with great hop character.

Another brewery close to Munich, Bachmayer of Dorfen near Erding, brews a 4.7 per cent ABV **Hell** that is exceptionally pale with a fruity aroma and palate and a dry finish. The 4.8 per cent ABV **Hell** from Dimpfl in Fürth im Wald is golden in colour, sharp and tangy on the aroma, with a rounded maltiness offset by good hop character: the character of the beer is clearly influenced by its proximity to the Czech border.

Examples of Franconian **Vollbier** include Bärenbräu's 4.8 per cent ABV in Staffelstein, hoppy and dry, Brauhaus's crisp and quenching 4.6 per cent ABV offering in Amberg, the bitter-sweet 5.1 per cent ABV

A sign outside one of the Oktoberfest venues; the date on the JW badge suggests it has been brewing since the early fourteenth century

from Eichorn of Forcheim, and the apple-fruity 4.8 per cent ABV from Falkenloch of Neuhaus.

Pilsner

In spite of the geographical closeness of Bavaria and Bohemia, the brewing of golden lagers was slow to spread from their town of origin, Pilsen, to Munich. But now "Pils" is such a widespread style that most beer drinkers think of it as German rather than Czech beer. Unlike the more austere Pils of Northern Germany, with their flinty dryness, Bavarian versions have much in common with the genuine article from Pilsen: a rich maltiness offset by generous bitterness, using hops from the Hallertau that have a similar aromatic quality to Bohemian Žatec or Saaz varieties. Most Bavarian breweries include a Pilsener – the German interpretation of the spelling – in their portfolios. Drinkers invariably shorten the word to demand "ein Pils".

In Munich, Löwenbräu's **Pilsener** (5.4 per cent ABV) is the hoppiest of the city's contributions to the style. With bitterness units in the high 30s from Hallertau and Saaz hop varieties, it has a superb citric aroma, a fine balance of malt and hops in the mouth and a shatteringly long finish packed with hop bitterness. Löwenbräu buys malt from Bavaria and also from the Champagne region of France. Paulaner's 4.8 per cent ABV **Pilsener** has a floral, aromatic hop nose, a big malty body underpinned by hops and a long, dry finish. In the manner of German winemakers, Paulaner describes the beer as "Extra Trocken" – Extra Dry. The world-famous brewing university of Weihenstephan ("Holy Stephen") at Freising on the Munich outskirts and close to the new airport is connected to a brewery of the same name. Its **Edelpils** (4.9 per cent ABV) is extremely dry with a fine perfumy hop aroma, a malty body and a dry and bitter finish.

Elsewhere in Bavaria, Aukofer of Kelheim brews a 4.8 per cent ABV **Pilsener** with a complex hoppy aroma, bitter-sweet malt and hops in the mouth and long, lingeringly hoppy finish. In Franconia, Becher of Beyreuth produces a 4.7 per cent ABV **Pilsener** that, in the Franken fashion, is unfiltered, with a yeasty aroma balanced by good bitter hops. In Amberg, the Brauhaus 4.7 per cent ABV Pilsener has a big hop attack on the aroma and palate, with some malt in the mouth and big

bitter finish. At Zapfendorf near Bamberg, the Drei Kronen – Three Crowns – brewery has a superb 4.8 per cent ABV **Pilsener** with a dense head, firm body, malty palate and long dry finish. EKU's Pilsener (4.9 per cent ABV) from Kulmbach has a rich, floral hop bouquet, bitter hops in the mouth backed by sweet malt and a bitter-sweet, malt and hops finish. In Bamberg, Mahrs's **Pilsener** (4.7 per cent ABV) is rich and malty balanced by aromatic hops, with a dry and bitter finish. In the heart of the great Hallertau hop-growing area, the Schlossbräu (Castle Brew) **Pilsener** is 4.9 per cent ABV and, fittingly, has a nostril-expanding hop aroma, more hops with balancing malt on the palate and a bitter finish.

March beer

In spite of the enormous interest in Bavarian beers both within and without the region, one style is under threat. Märzenbier means March beer, an ancient style from the days before refrigeration. March was the last month when it was safe to brew before the hot summer weather arrived. So in that month beers strong in alcohol and high in hops were made and stored for drinking during the summer, with any left over consumed in September and October. The Märzenbiers of Bavaria took on a special significance in the nineteenth century with the arrival of the Munich Oktoberfest in 1810, followed by the moves towards commercial lagering of beer in the 1830s. March beers became an Oktoberfest treat, a special beer to mark a special occasion. The beers at first were dark brown but when Gabriel Sedlmayr at Spaten began his work on cold fermentation he worked closely with Anton Dreher in Vienna where beers had a reddish tinge as a result of using a well-kilned amber malt. Spaten's Märzenbier became the benchmark for other brewers to copy, a reddish-brown brew developed by Gabriel Sedlmayr's brother Josef at his own Franziskaner Brewery in Munich (the two breweries were to merge in 1920). The 5.6 per cent ABV beer today, called Ur-Märzen (Ur being short for Urtyp, or Original) is lagered for three months, has 32.5 colour units and 21.5 IBUs. It is a malty beer but the maltiness is clean, quenching and slightly spicy, not cloying, underpinned by a delicate but firm hoppiness, with a bitter-sweet finish.

Sales of Märzenbier are declining – down to less than 10 per cent of the total Bavarian beer market – as a result of the changing nature of the Oktoberfest. The festival is now so renowned that it attracts a vast number of visitors from abroad, mainly from the English-speaking world: it is packed with Americans, Australians and New Zealanders. Most of them are unaware of the history of Märzenbier and come to Munich expecting to drink pale lagers. The brewers oblige and some Oktoberfestbiers, though of good quality, are in every way a pale shadow of the brews originally proudly stored for the occasion. Even Spaten, with its classic Märzen, also produces a separate Oktoberfestbier today.

Fortunately the Hofbräuhaus sticks to tradition. Its 5.7 per cent ABV **Märzen** is another classic brew, red-brown in colour, with a rich malty aroma, a light and quenching palate and a gently dry finish. Outside Munich, the Bräuhaus at Fussen close to the Austrian border has a suitably dark red **Märzen**, with a honey aroma, a rich and fruity palate and malty finish that becomes dry. The Eichorn Brewery at Forcheim has a much paler **Märzen** (5.7 per cent ABV) with an apple-fruit nose, malt and hops in the mouth and big bitter-sweet, well-balanced and complex finish. Fässla of Bamberg has a 5.3 per cent ABV **Märzen**, also known as **Zwergla**, that has a dark amber colour, a nutty palate, and firm hops in the mouth and the finish. Goss's interpretation of the style in Deuerling is a 5.5 per cent ABV pale amber brew, more hoppy than most, with malt and light fruit on the palate and a clean, quenching finish. The St Georghen Brewery in Buttenheim in Franconia produces a magnificent **Gold Märzen** (5.6 per cent ABV) which, despite the name, is a true amber colour with great hop attack on the aroma and palate, a rich and rounded maltiness with a dry finish and a hint of apple fruit. Wagner in Eschenbach plays all the right tunes with its 5.3 per cent ABV **Märzen**: rich malt arpeggio, spicy and fruity notes with a good hop glissando.

Bock

Outside Bavaria the most popular theory for the origin of the term Bock is that it comes from the town of Einbeck in Lower Saxony. For centuries Einbeck has been associated with brewing strong beers, known as Einbecker beers and corrupted to just Beck (which has nothing to do with Beck's Brewery in Bremen). In the Bavarian dialect Beck became further corrupted to Bock. The style of beer had spread to the south as a result of a marriage in the seventeenth century between a duke of Brunswick in Lower Saxony and the daughter of an aristocrat from Bavaria. They were married in Munich and a century later there were records of an "Oanbock" beer being brewed in the Hofbräuhaus, the royal court brewery, in the Bavarian capital.

The Bavarians will have none of these airy Northern theories. For them Bock is a local style, a strong seasonal beer associated with Lent and brewed by monks as "liquid bread" to help them sustain themselves during the fasting period.

The early Bocks would have been dark and warm-fermented. Today there are pale Bocks, amber Bocks and copper Bocks as well, and they are cold-fermented. They are strong in alcohol, ranging from 6.0 to 8.0 per cent by volume. There are several seasonal versions: winter Bocks, Maibocks for the early summer and even stronger Double Bocks for Lent. The Double Bocks are also known as Starkbier (Strong Beer) and are drunk on draught for Starkbierzeit, "Strong Beer Time", in Munich.

The classic Maibock comes from the Hofbräuhaus in Munich, where the first casks are tapped on May Day by the Mayor and Prime Minister of Bavaria who, like a bibulous double act, perform the same ceremony at the Oktoberfest. Although the beer is described as "Helles Bock" (pale Bock) it is a burnished amber colour with 7.2 per cent alcohol. It has a dense head of foam through which springs the punch of alcohol balanced by a rich nutty maltiness and floral hop background leading to a deep malty palate and a finish that becomes dry with malt, fruit and hops.

Hacker-Pschorr's 6.8 per cent ABV **Hubertusbock** is a copper-coloured Maibock with hops and rich, dark fruit on the aroma, a massive malt and hops palate and a long bitter-sweet finish that becomes dry. The Union brewpub in Munich, owned by Löwenbräu, produces a 6.3 per cent unfiltered **Maibock** with a pronounced hoppy aroma, nutty in the mouth from the malt, and a bitter-sweet finish. South of Munich, the Ayinger

Brewery in Aying brews a delicious 7.2 per cent **Maibock**, straw-coloured, with a rich, perfumy hop aroma, apple and apricot fruit in the mouth and a dry, superbly balanced finish.

Franconian interpretations of Bock include the Malteser Brewery's **Rittertrunk** Bock (6.5 per cent ABV) in Amberg, reddish-brown, malt and hops aroma and a fruity palate and finish, and Mönchshof of Kulmbach's **Klosterbock** (6.3 per cent ABV), amber-coloured, with a malty start and a long, bitter and dry finish.

Double Bock (Doppelbock in German) is not double the strength of a Bock but is an indication that the beer is stronger than an "ordinary" Bock. They are Lent beers and are meant to be sustaining, a meal in a glass and a blanket round the shoulders. They are usually dark, warming, rich, glowing, more heavily malty and less hoppy than a Bock. The benchmark Double Bock comes from the Paulaner Brewery in Munich. So famous is the beer that the company is officially named Paulaner Salvator in order to incorporate the name of the beer in the title. The brewery was founded by monks of the order of St Francis of Paula in 1634, who naturally made a Lent beer. (This Saint Francis came from Calabria in Italy and must not be confused with the founder of the Franciscan order, St Francis of Assisi.) Beer from the monks' brewery was sold commercially from the late eighteenth century, and early in the nineteenth a brewer named Franz-Xaver Zacherl began to develop the Salvator brand. Salvator means "Holy Father Beer". The impact of the Double Bock that honours him led to all other God-fearing brewers adding the letters "-or" to their versions of the style.

Paulaner Salvator Doppelbock is 7.5 per cent ABV and is brewed from three malts and Hallertau hop varieties. It is a deep, dark brown in colour, has a big malty-fruity aroma with a good underpinning of hops, a malty, yeasty, fruit-bread palate and an intense finish packed with dark fruit, malt and hops. The beer is lagered for around three months. Löwenbräu's **Triumphator** is 7.0 per cent ABV and has an intriguing and complex aroma and palate of roasted malt, nutmeg and spices, hints of chocolate, and a big, fruity, bready finish. Hofbräu offers a rich, warming, malty-hoppy Delicator (7.4 per cent ABV).

Ayinger brews a **Fortunator** (7.5 per cent ABV) with a Dundee-cake aroma and palate, warming and rich, with a dry finish. Eck in Böbrach brews a 7.0 per cent **Magistrator**, a slightly sinister name that suggests those who over-indulge will appear before the bench next morning. It is dark brown verging on black, with a deep malt and hops aroma, bitter chocolate in the mouth and a long bitter-sweet finish. With his determination to boost dark lagers, Prince Luitpold of Kaltenberg's **Dunkel Ritterbock** (6.8 per cent ABV) has a pronounced coffee aroma, a good balance of malt and hops in the mouth, and a dry, smooth finish. The monastic Klosterbräu Brewery in Ettal produces a 7.3 per cent Curator, reddish-brown, with a big malt aroma, a winey palate and a late burst of hops in the finish. The Klosterbräu at Irsee, south-west of Munich, uses the alternative **Starkbier** name for its strong Bock (6.8 per cent ABV). It is unfiltered with a yeasty, malty aroma, hops and fruit in the mouth and a dry, quenching finish.

The most famous Double Bock beers to drinkers outside Germany come from the EKU Brewery in Kulmbach. The letters stand for Erste Kulmbacher Unionbrauerei: Erste means first and Union indicates a merger of two former breweries in 1872. Using local barley, Hallertau hops (Perle, Hersbruck and Tettnang) and mountain water, EKU brews a 7.5 per cent **Kulminator** with an appealing claret colour, big malt on the aroma and palate, and hops and dark fruit in the finish. Not satisfied with this rich brew, the brewery then packs even more malt into its mash kettles to produce **Kulminator 28**, known abroad as **EKU 28**. For many years the beer vied with **Samichlaus** of Switzerland as the strongest lager in the world, though the Swiss beer is now the acknowledged leader. But 13.5 per cent alcohol by volume at EKU tests to the limits the ability of conventional brewer's yeast to ferment malt sugars before being overcome by the sheer weight of alcohol it has produced.

The beer is brewed from only pale malt but the amount of malt and some caramelization of the malt sugars gives the beer an amber glow. The alcohol gives a glow as well, backed by rich malt on the aroma, some citric fruitiness on the palate and a long, deep, intense, rich and warming finish with more fruit, malt and hops (30 IBUs). The beer is lagered for nine months and towards the end of the storage period ice forms in the lager tanks. But the brewery does not claim this makes it an "Eisbock" in which the creation of ice crystals concentrates the beer: there is quite enough alcohol in EKU 28 without any additional help. Some afiçionados claim the beer is a cure for the common cold. It would certainly take your mind off it.

Close by, the Kulmbacher Reichelbräu brews a definably ice beer in the Bock style, known both as **Eisbock** and **Bayrisch G'frorns** ("Bavarian frozen"). The beer is 10.0 per cent alcohol and is made from five malts, including a dark variety and one that is deliberately slightly sour and lactic to avoid any cloying sweetness in the finished beer. It has 27 units of bitterness from Brewers' Gold, Perle, Hersbruck and Tettnang varieties. After primary fermentation, the beer is frozen for two weeks. Water freezes at a higher temperature than alcohol, forming ice crystals in the brew. The ice is removed, concentrating the alcohol. The beer is then kräusened with partially-fermented wort to start a strong second fermentation. The finished beer is warming, aromatic from both malt and hops, rich and fruity in the mouth, and with a long, rich finish with coffee from the dark malt and an alcoholic kick. Eisbock may have been the inspiration for the heavily-hyped Ice Beers developed in Canada. The Franconian version has the advantage of strength and a long lagering to give it great depth of character. The beer is brewed every year in August and September and stored until the last Saturday in March when a frozen cask is ceremonially broached at the Eisbock Festival in Kulbach's Rathaus – town hall.

Franconian specialities

The smoked beers of Bamberg are a powerful link with brewing's past and a more tenuous link with Scotch malt whisky where the grain is cured over peat fires. In the Bamberg area, the beers get their smoky character from barley malt kilned over beechwood fires. Until the Industrial Revolution and the switch from wood to coke, it is likely that all beers had a slightly smoky note from the kilning of the malt.

Bamberg, with its impressive blend of Romanesque, Gothic and Baroque buildings, is a malting centre as well as being rich in breweries. Beechwood is gathered from the surrounding forests to supply fuel for the malting kilns. The classic smoked or Rauchbier comes from the Heller-Trum Brewery which started in the Schlenkerla tavern in the town in 1678, when the beer was lagered in caves in the nearby hill of Stephansberg. The need for more space in the tavern and a growing demand for the beer forced the brewers to move to new premises. The brewery yard is packed with beechwood logs. Inside, there is a smokehouse where the barley lies on a mesh above a beechwood fire that throws up marvellous aromas reminiscent of autumnal garden fires. The copper brewhouse uses a double decoction mashing regime with primary fermentation in open vessels followed by two months' lagering. The main beer produced is **Aecht Schlenkerla Rauchbier** (5.0 per cent ABV; 29–32 IBUs), dark brown in colour and with an intense smoked malt aroma and palate, with dry malt in the mouth and a deep smoked malt finish. The brewery also makes an autumn smoky Bock and a Helles, which also has a hint of smoked malt.

The Christian Merz family's Spezial Brewery in Bamberg is a brewpub dating from 1536 that produces only smoked beers. Malt is made in a courtyard at the back of the pub. The Rauchbier is called, simply, **Lagerbier**. It is 4.9 per cent ABV with a light brown colour, with a malty-smoky aroma and palate, and a dry and fruity finish with a hint of burnt toffee. The Bürgerbräu-Kaiserdom Brewery has a full range of beers; its speciality is a 4.8 per cent **Rauchbier**, amber-coloured, with a malty/smoky aroma and palate leading to a dry finish.

Steinbier is a Franconian speciality even though the brewery using the method has moved from Neustadt, near Coburg, to Altenmünster in Southern Bavaria. Before metal kettles were widely used in brewing, it was dangerous to build fires under wooden vessels and it was a widespread custom in Northern Europe to lower hot stones into the mash. In 1982 Gerd Borges bought the brewery in Neustadt and decided to revive the fashion. Stones are brought from a nearby quarry and heated to white-hot temperature in an oven fired by beechwood logs. The stones are then lowered by the jaws of a small crane into a copper kettle. The mash boils, foams and steams while some of the malt sugars are caramelized and stick to the stones. When the stones have cooled they are placed in the maturation tanks where the caramelized sugar acts as a priming agent for a second fermentation. A top-fermenting yeast strain is used. Steinbier is 4.9 per cent alcohol, brown in colour, with a smoky aroma, toffee-like palate and a long, well-balanced malt, hops and dark fruit finish. The mash is a 50:50 blend of barley and wheat malts. Hersbruck and Tettnang hops are used and create 27 IBUs.

A version of the beer, using 60 per cent wheat malt, is called Steinweizen and is bottle conditioned.

Bavarian wheat beers

The beer world has turned upside down in Bavaria. A warm-fermenting type of ale that was doomed to extinction with the development of lager brewing in the nineteenth century is undergoing a revival of Biblical proportions. Wheat beer, derided for decades as a beer for pensioners, enjoyed spectacular growth in the 1980s and achieved cult status among the young. As a result of bottle-conditioning, which leaves a sediment rich in yeast and proteins, it is perceived by the "green generation" as being a healthier drink than lager beers.

In the fifteenth century the barons of Degenberg appropriated the right to brew wheat beer and passed the right on to the Wittelsbachs, the Bavarian royal family. Their Royal Court Brewery – the Hofbräuhaus – in Munich was opened in 1589 and by the early part of the next century was producing large quantities of wheat beer. At one stage there were around 30 royal brewhouses in Bavaria producing the style. The ordinary people had no choice in beer, for the royal family controlled the grain market and refused to release wheat for brewing. Wheat beer only became available commercially in 1850 when the royal family licensed a Munich brewer named Georg Schneider to brew it in their Munich Hofbräuhaus. Perhaps the royals were losing interest in wheat beer and were casting envious eyes on Sedlmayr's new lager beers. Georg Schneider later moved a short distance to a brewery in Im Tal (the Dale), just off the Marienplatz with its stunning Gothic town hall, the Rathaus. Even though lager beer was being developed in the same city, Schneider's wheat beer was a sensation and he had to buy a second brewery in Kelheim in the heart of the Hallertau hop-growing area to keep up with demand.

The Munich brewery was destroyed by the British Royal Air Force in the Second World War. It has been rebuilt as a beer hall but no beer is brewed there now.

Many Bavarian brewers followed in Schneider's footsteps and brewed wheat beer as a sideline, something to have in their portfolio alongside mainstream dark and pale lagers. But now wheat beer accounts for 30 per cent of the vast Bavarian beer market and, along with low alcohol (Alcoholfrei) beers, is the only growth sector. Although some brewers have introduced draught versions of wheat beer, they are usually bottled. A secondary fermentation in bottle gives the beers a high level of natural carbonation, creating a dense and foaming head and adding to the refreshing character. Wheat beers are made from a blend of wheat and barley malts: wheat malt by law must make up at least half of the grist. Barley malt is essential as it has a greater number of enzymes that turn starch into sugar and it also has a husk that acts as a filter during mashing. Wheat is a huskless grain and used on its own would clog up brewing vessels. The main contribution wheat malt makes to the beer is an appealing pale and hazy yellow colour and a characteristic aroma and flavour of spices and fruit: cloves are the dominant spice while apple and banana are typical fruit aromas.

The surge in popularity of wheat beer has encouraged some brewers to cut corners in its production. Ale yeasts for the second fermentation in bottle are being replaced by lager yeasts because of their greater stability and ability to give beer longer "shelf life". The use of lager yeasts removes some of the fruity and spicy flavours that only an ale yeast can impart. Some brewers even pasteurize the beer after primary fermentation before re-seeding with lager yeast and adding sediment to give a false impression of natural cloudiness. Most wheat beer producers make two versions: Hefe Weisse or Hefe Weizen, which means wheat beer with yeast, and a filtered version called Kristall or Ohne Hefe, without yeast. The unfiltered versions are by far the most popular and flavourful. Connoisseurs like to pour the beer slowly until the glass is almost full then twirl the bottle and deposit the sediment of yeast into the glass. The habit of placing a slice of lemon in the glass is declining. The reasons for

The Schneider brewery in Erding, on the outskirts of Munich

doing this are lost in time but it may have played a similar role to the addition of fruit or herb syrup to Berlin wheat beers to reduce some of the acidity.

Schneider – the name means Taylor in English – is the wheat beer brewer by whom all others are judged. The Kelheim Brewery produces nothing but wheat beer, though the family owns a smaller plant near Regensberg where it brews lagers. The Kelheim Brewery, an odd but fetching blend of Spanish and Gothic architecture, was built in 1607 and is thought to be the oldest continuous wheat beer brewery in the world. It is run today by Georg Schneider V and his son, Georg VI, who will take over when his father retires. The brewery has open fermenters, a rare sight in Germany where brewers

prefer to keep their beers locked away from possible air-borne infections. But the Schneiders will do nothing to interfere with the workings of the single-strain yeast culture, which has been used for as long as anyone can remember. Nothing is altered in the fermentation hall. Rather like whisky distillers who will replace one vessel with a slight kink with a new one with an identical kink built in to it, the Schneiders will replace one fermenter with another of exactly the same dimensions. They will not change the specification of their malts in case it upsets the temperamental yeast.

Schneider makes 300,000 hectolitres a year, 90 per cent of which is a 5.4 per cent **Weisse**. The rest is made up of an 8.0 per cent wheat Bock named **Aventinus** and

stainless steel mashing and boiling kettles standing on marble floors. A double decoction mash is used: portions of the mash are pumped from one vessel to another, heated to a higher temperature and then returned to the first vessel, raising the temperature of the entire mash. As modern continental European malts are "well modified", with the cell walls of the grain easily broken to enable the starches to be attacked by enzymes, double decoction mashing is probably not necessary but the Schneiders will not tamper with tradition. Mashing starts at 38 degrees C/100F, a lower temperature than a typical English infusion mash.

As the wort is pumped from one vessel to another the temperature rises by stages to 43, 48 and 56 degrees, reaching a final 65 degrees. The spent grains are sparged at 75 degrees. Hops are added in two stages during the copper boil, then the hopped wort is cooled and pumped to the fermentation hall. Sixteen stainless steel vessels hold 350 hectolitres each. The hall is heady with tempting aromas of fruit, with banana dominating, underscored by delicious hints of apple. Fermentation lasts between three and five days at 20 degrees C/68F. Twice a day the yeast is skimmed from the top of the wort, cleaned and then pitched back into the vessels. At the end of primary fermentation the green beer is not filtered and is bottled with a blend of the same top-fermenting yeast and some sugar-rich wort to encourage a second fermentation. The bottles are warm conditioned at 20 degrees for a week, which causes a lively carbonation as fermentation gets under way. The beer is then cold conditioned at 8°C (46°F) for a fortnight to stabilize it.

Schneider Weisse has a complex bouquet of banana, cloves and nutmeg, tart fruit in the mouth and a creamy, fruity finish with hints of bubblegum. Aventinus is bronze-red in colour due to the addition of caramalt. It has a rich spices and chocolate aroma and palate, with more spices, vinous fruit and cloves in the finish. It makes a splendid nightcap or winter warmer.

Schneider may be the flagship wheat beer producer but the biggest brewer of the style is Erdinger. The company in the town of Erding, on the far outskirts of Munich, is based in a modern brewery built in the early 1980s. The original site in the town centre brewed from the mid-1850s and is now a tavern. Erdinger has

a lighter beer called **Weizen Hell**. The brewery uses half a million tonnes of Bavarian barley and wheat. In the Weisse they are blended in the proportion of 60 per cent wheat to 40 per cent barley. Some Vienna and darker malts are added to give the beer its attractive bronze colour. Hersbrucker hops from the surrounding Hallertau are used in pellet form with a small amount of hop extract. The Weisse has 14 to 15 units of bitterness: hops in wheat beer are used primarily for their antiseptic and preservative qualities, as too much bitterness will not blend with the spicy, fruity character of the beer. The local well water is softened by osmosis to remove some of the natural salts.

The modern brewhouse was built in 1988 with

specialized in wheat beer since the 1930s and now produces two million hectolitres a year.

All the wheat and most of the barley is grown locally by farmers who work to specifications drawn up by the brewery. The wheat is low in protein, producing a soft-tasting beer. Water comes from an underground lake believed to be two million years old.

A double decoction mash is used and Perle and Tettnang hops are added three times, achieving 18 IBUs. Primary fermentation is unusual, taking place in horizontal tanks just 2.8 metres high – the brewers think this produces a cleaner-tasting beer. Breaking with tradition, Erdinger uses a lager yeast for bottle conditioning and the bottles are warm conditioned for a month.

Hefe-Weissbier is 5.3 per cent ABV. It has a relatively restrained aroma for the style, with hints of apples and cloves, more fruit in the mouth, and a gently fruity finish. A filtered version is sold as Kristallklar. A dark Dunkel Weissbier (5.6 per cent ABV) has pleasant chocolate and liquorice notes while Pikantus Bock (7.3 per cent ABV) has spices and chocolate on the aroma and palate.

The most remarkable revival of wheat beer is seen at the Spaten Brewery in Munich. Even though the brewery is the cradle of lager brewing, it now devotes 50 per cent of its capacity to wheat beer production. The wheat beers are sold under the Franziskaner name, the bottle labels showing a cheerful monk holding a mug of beer. The original wheat beer brewery, bought by Josef Sedlmayr and merged with his brother Gabriel's plant, was the oldest in Munich and was next to a Franciscan monastery. The main Spaten wheat beer, **Franziskaner Weissbier** (5.0 per cent ABV) has an ususually high wheat malt content of 75 per cent. The brewer admits this occasionally causes problems during mashing but feels it gives a better flavour to the finished beer. The other brands, Hell, Dunkel, Kristall and Bock, are made more conventionally from a 50:50 blend of German and French barley and wheat malts. A complex hops recipe is made up of Hallertau, Tettnang, Spalt, Perle and Orion varieties. Fermentation takes place in conical fermenters where a "top" yeast sediments to the bottom of the vessels. The beer is then centrifuged to remove the ale yeast and is re-seeded with a lager

culture for bottle conditioning. The main wheat beer has a gentle fruity aroma, tart fruit and spices in the mouth and a light but quenching finish. The **Dunkel** (also 5.0 per cent ABV) is bitter for the style with dark fruit on the palate and finish.

Elsewhere in Munich, Löwenbräu's 5.0 per cent **Löwenweisse** has a strong apples and cloves aroma, hints of banana in the mouth, and a dry and spicy finish. Augustiner's **Weissbier** is 5.2 per cent has a malty aroma and palate and tart, lingering finish. Hacker-Pschorr's **Weisse** (5.5 per cent ABV) is light and undemanding. Höfbräuhaus honours its royal tradition with a crisp, lemon-fruity, tart and marvellously refreshing 5.1 per cent beer.

Outside Munich, Prince Luitpold brews a Hell and a Dunkel wheat beer, both 5.5 per cent ABV, in Fürstenfeldbruck. The dark is a delight, packed with malt-loaf fruitiness with a slightly sour and quenching finish. In an idyllic setting in the Obberbayern mountains, the Hopf Brewery of Miesbach brews only wheat beer. As the German for hop is Hopfen, the owner, Hans Hopf, has a head start over his competitors in the brand image stakes. The small brewery has had to be substantially extended to cope with demand. Old copper vessels nestle against modern stainless steel ones in the brewhouse, which produces 50,000 hectolitres a year. The brewing liquor is Alpine water. German and French malts are used, with wheat malt making up 65 per cent of the mash. Hops are Hallertau and Spalt varieties. After primary fermentation the beer is kräusened with brewhouse wort and mixed with a blend of top and bottom yeasts for a second fermentation. The main beer, **Hopf Export** (5.3 per cent ABV; 12 IBUs) has a nostril-widening spicy and peppery aroma underpinned by banana and bubblegum.

In Passau, the Andorfer Brewery's 5.3 per cent **Weissbier** is amber coloured and balances a malty palate with a tart, fruity finish. South-west of Munich, Karg in Murnau has a coppery, yeasty, fruity and tartly uncompromising 5.0 per cent **Weissbier**. In Bayreuth, the Maisel Brewery's 5.2 per cent **Hefe-Weissbier** is a deep reddy-brown, with a delightful apple aroma and palate and a tart, dry finish.

Throughout Bavaria most breweries now have wheat beers in their portfolios. The success and revival of the style, like the cask-conditioned ales of Britain, mark another victory for consumer preference over marketing zeal.

Baden-Württemberg

The adjacent state to Bavaria is known by a variety of names: Schwaben, Schwabian-Bavaria or, to the outside world, the Black Forest. Swaben was an independent duchy from the tenth to the fourteenth centuries: Schwabia today in Germany means an area famous for its distinctive cuisine and spectacular countryside. It tends to be overshadowed by its better-known Bavarian neighbour but hits back with its own beer festival held at the same time at the Munich Oktoberfest. The Cannstatter Volkfest (the "People's Fest" in the suburb of Cannstatt in Stuttgart) begins at the end of September and runs for two weeks.

Stuttgart's three breweries, Dinkelacker, Stuttgarter Hofbräu and Schwaben Bräu, produce Volkfestbiers broadly in the Munich Märzen style. Local custom determines that these beers are lower in strength – around 4.5 per cent ABV – than the Munich versions but, like their Bavarian cousins, they are amber in colour, rich, malty and satisfying with a good hop character. Almost identical beers are produced for Christmas and the New Year under the name of Weihnachtsbier.

The Stuttgart breweries concentrate on Pilsners – soft, malt-accented, with gentle hop character – all in the classic 4.8 to 5.0 per cent alcohol range. Dinkelacker is the major brewery in the region and its biggest brand is the oddly-named **CD-Pils**. The CD tag has nothing to do with either Compact Discs or the Corps Diplomatique, but comes from the initials of the founder of the brewery, Carl Dinkelacker. The Dinkelacker family has been brewing since the late eighteenth century, built the present city-centre plant in 1888 and still controls the company at a time when most larger breweries are owned by banks or other financial institutions. CD-Pils is mashed and hopped in fine, traditional copper kettles and kräusened during the secondary fermentation. It is hopped four times, the final addition being with Brewers' Gold for aroma as the hopped wort is pumped from the kettle. The finished beer has a malty nose and palate with delicate hop notes in the mouth and a soft

finish. Dinkelacker owns the Cluss Brewery in Heilbronn which produces a 5.0 per cent **Cluss Pilsner** and a dark, creamy **Bock Dunkel**.

Schwaben Bräu, in the district of Vaihingen, has an impressive copper brewhouse and vast cellars where the comparatively dry **Meister Pils** is lagered. The Hofbräu, once a royal court brewery but now a public company, is on the edge of Stuttgart and produces malty-sweet beers, the main brand being **Herren Pils**, which translates as Pils for Men, surely Politically Incorrect today.

Fürstenberg from the Black Forest is the best-known of the region's beers as it is widely exported. The beer has noble connections: the Fürstenberg family are aristocrats who have been involved in brewing for more than 500 years. They are renowned patrons of the arts and have a fine collection of paintings in their museum at Donaueschingen, which is also the site of the brewery. **Fürstenberg Pilsener** (5.0 per cent ABV) is decidedly hoppy for the regional style, with an aromatic and malty aroma, a full palate and a dry and bitter finish. **Export** (5.2 per cent ABV) is a deep gold colour with hints of fruit in a big malty body and crisp, dry finish.

In the north of the region, Eichbaum of Mannheim dates from 1697 when Jean de Chaîne founded a brewery called Zum Aichbaum in the Stammhaus tavern: the brewery moved to its present site in 1850 but the tavern has survived as a main outlet for the brewery. At one stage Mannheim had 40 or more breweries but only Eichbaum has survived. It brews both a cloudy and filtered wheat beer (5.3 per cent ABV) with a spicy and fruity palate and an **Apostulator Doppelbock** (7.5 per cent ABV), using caramalt and dark malt. The main product is a 4.6 per cent **Ureich Pils**: Ur means Original and Eich means Oak, the oak tree, Eichbaum, being the brewery's symbol. It is hopped with Hallertau and Tettnang varieties. The beer has malt and citric fruit from the hops on the aroma, a malty-hoppy palate and a dry finish with delicate hop notes. A 5.3 per cent **Export**, in the Dortmund style, has a more rounded and malty character.

Dortmunder Export

Dortmund, the great steel and mining city on the Ruhr, is a brewing conundrum. It produces more beer than any other city in Germany or Europe yet it is absurdly shy about its main style of beer, Export, and prefers today to emphasize its Pilsners. The reasons are to do with the decline of heavy industry and its attendant blue-collar working class who were the main consumers of the rounded and malty Exports.

Dortmund has had a brewing tradition since the thirteenth century. It specialized in dark wheat beers until the oldest brewery in the city, Kronen (Crown) switched to cold-fermentation. When the large Dortmunder Union Brewery began to make lager beers in the 1870s they achieved such renown that they were sold to all parts of Germany and Europe, acquiring the name of Export as a result. Belgian and Dutch brewers were sufficiently impressed by the Dortmund beers to produce specialities they call simply "Dort".

The two giants of Dortmunder brewing are Dortmunder Union and Dortmunder Actien. The giant letter "U" – 17 metres or 55 feet high – blazes out at night from the 1920s functional building that would remind Londoners forcibly of the Thames-side Battersea Power Station. Union in Germany has nothing to do with labour unions or the fermentation system of far-off Burton-on-Trent but refers to a merger, in this case the spectacular bringing together of a dozen breweries under one roof in 1873. Actien indicates a company going public and making its shares available on the stock exchange. Dortmunder Actien, founded by the Fischer family in 1868, went public in 1872, which may have been the springboard for the mergers that formed the rival Union group.

Dortmunder Actien's **DAB Export** is 5.0 per cent ABV with a sweet malt aroma, a full malty body and bitter-sweet finish with a late flourish of hops. It also makes a **Meister Pils**, a full-bodied 5.0 per cent **Original Premium** and, with a nod in the direction of Bavaria, a **Maibock** and a **Termanator Doppelbock**.

The rival **DUB Export** – malty, light-bodied, delicately hopped – is now difficult to find and the brewery concentrates on its 5.0 per cent **Siegel Pils**, hopped with Hallertau varieties (30 IBUs) and lagered for six to eight weeks.

The smaller, family-owned Dortmunder Kronen claims to be the oldest brewery in the region of Westphalia. It traces its roots to a brewery-cum-tavern called the Krone in 1430. It was bought by Johann Wenker in 1729 and it passed to his sons-in-law, whose family name was Brand.

The Brand family still runs the business now based, fittingly, in a district of Dortmund called Kronenburg – the brow or crown of a hill. The brewery was bombed in the Second World War and has been extensively rebuilt and modernized. Its **Export** is the most malt-accented of the city's beers, with a rich body and a big, bitter-sweet finish.

Sadly, Kronen is so shy about Export that it releases no information about it, preferring to concentrate on its 5.0 per cent **Pils**, hopped with Hallertau (32 IBUs) with a delicate malt and hops aroma, light palate and a lingering bitter-sweet finish, and its 5.3 per cent **Classic** (26 IBUs) with a rich malt nose, rounded malt and a hop balance on the palate and long bitter-sweet finish. Only Classic is available in the brewery museum. Export, the great Dortmunder style, proud beer of a power-house of a city, is no longer considered worthy of being even an artefact.

Münster

In Münster, the delightful old university city of Westphalia, Pinkus Müller produces a fascinating variety of highly individualistic beers using organic malt and hops. Pinkus Müller is well-known throughout Germany even though it is no more than a beer tavern, making around 10,000 hectolitres a year. The tavern has four dining rooms, specializing in local cuisine. Founder Pinkus Müller started in business producing beer, bread and chocolate and the company has been on the same site since 1816.

The best-known brand today is **Pinkus Münster Alt**. Alt means "old" and is a major beer style in Düsseldorf. The Pinkus brand is not a true Alt in the Düsseldorf style as 40 per cent of the grist is composed of wheat malt, the remainder being Bioland organic Pilsner. Organic hops come from the Hallertau, the mash is single-decoction and the brew is kräusened during secondary fermentation, which lasts for four months. A top-fermenting yeast is used and a lactic culture is allowed to breed in the lagering tanks, imparting a deliberate hint of sourness to the finished beer. It is 5.1 per cent ABV, with a rich, slightly vinous aroma, malt

Henninger, Frankfurt's second brewery to Binding

area of the country produces the least interesting beers. Certainly Frankfurt and its environs has no distinctive beer style and Binding, which also owns DAB in Dortmund and the Berlin Kindl Brewery and makes in total 2.5 million hectolitres a year, is best known abroad for its Clausthaler low-alcohol lager. Its main brand for the Frankfurt market is broadly in the style of a Dortmunder Export. **Export Privat** has some hops on the nose, a firm, malty body and some delicate fruit in the dry finish.

The second Frankfurt brewery, Henninger, is no slouch in the production stakes, making around 1.75 million hectolitres a year. Its main products are a smooth and undemanding **Kaiser Pilsner**, brewed principally for the international export market, and a slightly stronger and marginally hoppier **Christian Henninger Pilsener**.

Cologne and Kölsch

The golden, top-fermenting ales of Cologne (Köln in German) are so highly regarded that the style is protected by federal law. Brewing has been rooted in the culture and way of life of Cologne, capital of the Rhineland, since Roman times. The name Cologne stems from "colonial" and it was an important city of the Roman Empire. Monasteries dominated the production of beer for centuries and gave way to commercial brewers and tavern owners. The modern Kölsch beers are pale but would have been darker in previous centuries when all malt was brown. But they remain warm-fermenting, a member of the ale family. The determination of brewers in Cologne, along with their kin in nearby Düsseldorf, to stick to the old tradition may be the result of temperature as well as temperament – cool summers do not demand a chilled beer – and the city's proximity to the Low Countries. The region has long had close links with what is now Belgium and was influenced by the beers enjoyed by such bibulous luminaries as Duke Jan Primus (Gambrinus). Cologne's Guild of Brewers dates from 1396 and has been in the van of protecting the city's beer culture. Today the city and its surroundings have some 20 or so breweries dedicated to brewing Kölsch. Cologne has more breweries than any other major city in Germany or the world. Kölsch came under great

and tart fruit in the mouth, and a long and fruity finish with slight acidity.

The brewery does not claim the beer is a wheat one and could not legally do so, as less than 50 per cent of the mash comes from wheat. It underscores the point by producing a **Hefe Weizen** (5.2 per cent ABV) with 60 per cent wheat malt. It is conditioned for one month and has a light fruit aroma, delicate malt and fruit in the mouth, and a dry and fruity finish. Pinkus Müller makes two cold-fermenting beers, a hoppy and dry **Pils** and a stunning **Special** (5.2 per cent ABV), lagered for three months and producing a full malty aroma and palate with hops developing in the dry, quenching finish.

One of the specialities of the tavern is a syrup made from fresh fruit – strawberries or peaches in summer, oranges in winter – which is added to the Alt to cut the beer's acidity.

Frankfurt and Hesse

A cynic might say that it is because Germany's biggest brewing group, Binding, is based in Frankfurt that this pressure at the turn of the century to switch to lager brewing but the offer was refused: one brewer has even removed Pilsner from his portfolio.

The language of the style can be confusing. Kölsch beers look like lagers. They are often called "Wiess", a local spelling of white, but they are not wheat beers even though some brewers use a proportion of wheat malt in the mash. A typical Kölsch is around 5.0 per cent ABV with a malty aroma and some gentle fruitiness. It will be soft due to the local water and there will a delicate, perfumy hop character. Bittering units will be in the high 20s but extreme bitterness is avoided. Hallertau and Tettnang hop varieties are preferred. The Kölsch yeast is a greedy strain, busily turning most of the malt sugars into alcohol, with a dry beer as the result.

The biggest producer of Kölsch today is the Küppers Brewery, founded just 20 years ago. It has built market share through clever promotions that have not pleased some traditionalists. **Küppers Kölsch** is soft, easy-drinking and undemanding. An unfiltered version called **Wiess** is more fruity, yeasty and distinctive.

The best-known and most highly-regarded of the Cologne brewers is P. J. Fruh's **Cölner Hofbräu**. The beer used to be brewed in a tavern on the Am Hof in the city centre but the house brewery became too small to meet demand and a new plant has been built a short distance away. **Früh Echt Kölsch**, all malt without wheat, is wonderfully drinkable, with delicate fruit on the aroma, and hops from Hallertau and Tettnang in the finish. Gaffel in the Old Town district has been brewing since 1302 and produces a beer of considerable pedigree: intriguingly nutty for a pale beer and a dry finish. The Heller brewpub in Roon Strasse offers a malty-sweet **Kölsch** and an unfiltered, fruitier and slightly tart version called **Ur-Wiess**. The Malzmühle (malt mill) brewpub on Heumarkt – Haymarket – uses some wheat malt in the mash and produces a rounded, malt-accented beer with a hint of spice and some delicate hop character from Hallertau. Päffgen in Frisen Strasse has a distinctive floral hop bouquet and a hoppy finish: by far the hoppiest of the style. Sion in the Old Town has a floral hop bouquet from the use of the Hersbrucker variety.

It is part of the delight of drinking Kölsch beers that most of the producers are small and many operate from taverns. Discovering the beer makes for a splendid pub crawl.

Düsseldorf Alt

Alt means old but the young have taken it to their hearts. Düsseldorf is another great industrial city that was once at the heart of the mining industry. The copper-coloured, warm-fermenting beers of the region again have a link with the malty, refreshing milds of industrial England, brewed to refresh people after a shift at the coal-face or the furnace. But unlike English mild or Dortmunder Export, the Alts of Düsseldorf have not declined in step with heavy industry but have found a new audience among white-collar employees, the young in particular. As with Cologne, there is a Low Countries connection: Düsseldorf is close to the Low Countries, in particular the tongue of the Netherlands that includes Maastricht, and the influence of Dutch brewers has seeped across the border.

Alt beers superficially are the closest to English ale, but the similarities should not be over-stressed. Decoction mashing is used by some brewers and all the beers are cold-conditioned for several weeks, though at higher temperatures than for lager beers, around 8°C (46°F). Hop bitterness will range from the mid-30s IBU to 50. Open fermenters for primary fermentation are used by some of the smaller producers, many of them based in characterful city brewpubs where the beer accompanies vast platefuls of local cuisine. Typically, an Alt will be around 4.5 per cent alcohol by volume.

The fortunes of Alt brewing have waxed and waned. Two of the biggest producers, Hannen and Schlösser, lost market share as a result of mergers: Hannen is owned by Carlsberg of Denmark, Schlösser by DUB of Dortmund. The major brewer is now the family-owned independent Diebels in the hamlet of Issum a few miles from the city. The brewery was founded in 1878 by Josef Diebels and has been in the family for four generations. It produces more than one and a half million hectolitres a year, and doubled production between 1990 and 1991.

Diebels **Alt** has a gravity of 1045 degrees and is 4.8 per cent ABV, which means it is well attenuated. The beer has an appealing burnished copper colour with a peppery hop aroma balanced by rich malt. It is bitter in the mouth with a dry and nutty finish and a hint of orange fruit. Ninety eight per cent of the grist is pale Pils malt. The remaining two per cent is provided by roasted malt, more a Scottish practice than a German one. (Other Alt brewers prefer to use Vienna or black malt for colour and flavour.) Hops are Northern Brewer for bitterness and Perle for aroma, producing 32 to 33 IBUs.

Diebels' modern Steinecker brewhouse has tiled walls decorated by a mosaic showing the old brewery at the turn of the century. Four mash kettles feed four wort kettles, where the hops are put in in one addition. A decoction mashing regime is used. The 50-year-old yeast culture is a top-fermenting strain but is cropped from the foot of conical vessels. As with Guinness in Dublin, primary fermentation is rapid and lasts for just two days. The green beer then has a short "diactyl rest", which purges toffee-like flavours, and is stored in tanks for between 10 days in summer and three weeks in winter.

The best way to taste Altbier is to visit the taverns of the Alt Stadt, the cobbled and gas-lit Old Town of Düsseldorf. Im Füchschen, the Little Fox, at 28 Ratinger Strasse, is a cavernous building with tiled walls, red-tiled floors and wooden bench seats. The house beer is tapped from casks on the bar and is served by its own natural pressure, free from applied gas. The beer is maltier than Diebels with a toasty flavour and a sweet, fruity finish that becomes dry. In common with all Altbiers it is served in a short, stubby glass that is immediately replaced by another as the drinker downs it. Alts are a good companion for local dishes. Im Füchschen's speciality is a huge pickled knuckle of pork.

Zum Uerige offers salted pig's trotter with its Alt. The tavern is at 1 Berger Strasse and the name means the Place of the Cranky Fellow, though the present-day staff are helpful, attentive and friendly, and happy to discuss their beer in English as well as German. The beer is brewed in copper kettles and fermenters viewed from the main bar, part of a warren of rooms. The Alt, dry hopped and made with a dash of roasted malt, is fruity, aromatic and hoppy. Zum Schlüssel, the Key, at 43–47 Bolker Strasse, birthplace of the poet Heinrich Heine, also has its brewhouse on display at the back of the bar. The Alt has a delightful aromatic hop perfume, it is bitter-sweet in the mouth and has a dry finish.

Inside the Bitburg brewery in the Eifel Lake district of Germany

Rhineland Pilsners

The Rhineland's love-affair with Pilsner beers shows the impact that the Bohemian style had in the nineteenth century. For this vast and remote region of Germany is a considerable distance from Pilsen and, before the arrival of the railway, beer and its raw materials moved slowly by water transport. Yet the brewers of the Rhineland switched to cold-fermenting Pils with a fervour matched only in the far north around Hamburg. Several of the leading companies brew just one beer. Their dedication to the style and rigorous attention to the quality of materials and uniformity of production baulks at the notion of such Bavarian largesse as Dunkels, Bocks and Weizens.

Bitburger is a good case in point. It is brewed in the small town of Bitburg in the Eifel Lake district, close to the historic city of Trier, birthplace of Karl Marx. The company was established in 1817 as a humble farmhouse brewery and made warm-fermenting beers. But by 1884 it was producing Pilsner, using ice from the lakes to lager the beer. Its fortunes were boosted when a rail line was built to supply the Prussian army with cannon from the steelworks of Saarbrücken. The Simon

family, which still owns the company, began to export its "Pils" to Northern Germany. Today it is one of the most widely exported German beers.

Bitburger's offices, original brewery and "brewery tap" tavern are in the centre of the small town. The superb copper brewhouse is still used but the main production has been switched to a state-of-the-art 1980s plant on a greenfield site on the edge of town. Wort is pumped by underground pipes between the two brewhouses. Enormous care is given to the selection of the finest raw materials: spring barleys – Alexis, Arena and Steiner – and Hersbrucker, Hüller, Perle and Tettnang hops. The beer has three hop additions in the kettle, and is 4.6 per cent ABV with 37 to 38 IBUs. It is lagered for three months and is not pasteurized, which helps the delicate balance of malt and hops flavours. Beer for export is sterile filtered.

The Rhineland Pilsners are hoppier than those from the south but less dry and bitter than the interpretation of the style in the far north. Bitburger has a rich malt aroma underscored by floral hops, soft malt in the mouth and a long, complex finish with both bitterness and light citric fruit from the hops, balanced by sweet malt.

The biggest-selling Pilsner in Germany comes from the Warsteiner Brewery. The town of Warstein is in an area of woods and lakes to the east of the Rhine and the Ruhr. The ultra-modern brewery is coy about its ingredients, saying nothing more than "barley malt and Hallertau hops". **Warsteiner Premium** is 4.8 per cent ABV and is lagered for two months. It has a light malt and hops bouquet, rounded and bitter-sweet in the mouth, and a delicate dry finish with some citric notes from the hops, finally becoming dry.

Krombacher Pils from Kreuztal-Krombach uses Hallertau and Tettnang hops. The beer is 4.8 per cent with 24 to 26 IBUs. It has a comparatively brief lagering of just one month. The aroma is soft and malty, with delicate malt and hops in the mouth, and a dry finish with good hop notes. Brauerei Felsenkeller Herford produces yet another fine example of the style, well-attenuated (1046 degrees original gravity but brewed out to 4.8 or 4.9 per cent ABV). It is brewed from premium Pilsner pale malt and 60 per cent Hallertau

Opposite: *A collection of biersteins – traditional German beer jugs*

Northern Brewer hops for bitterness and 40 per cent Perle and Tettnang for aroma. The hops produce 32 units of bitterness. The beer has a rich honeyed malt aroma, rounded malt and hops in the mouth, and a long, dry, delicate malty finish balanced by some citric fruit from the hops. Herford also brews a malty Export, a pale Maibock and a dark and fruity Doppelbock.

Hamburg and the North

Hamburg and Bremen have had a major influence on German beer and its impact abroad. They are major ports and for centuries have exported German beer to other countries. In common with all ports, they are cosmopolitan, polyglot places, open to many influences. They were at the heart of the great fifteenth-century trading group of cities known as the Hanseatic League. Other countries' beers came into their ports and had an impact on local styles. In particular, hops from Bavaria and Bohemia came up the Elbe, encouraging the Prussians to use the plant in their own brews.

The love affair with the hop married well with a later infatuation with the beers from Pilsen. Pilsner Urquell from Pilsen was given an award in a brewers' competition in Hamburg in 1863. The Prussian interpretation of the style is dry and intensely bitter, almost austere, a reflection of the time when beers were heavily hopped to help them withstand long sea journeys.

The best-known of the region's brewers is Holsten of Hamburg, a major exporter, some of whose beers in other countries are brewed under licence.

In its home market, Holsten and its subsidiaries produce more than one million hectolitres of beer a year. Its biggest brand is **Edel**, a 5.0 per cent beer with a good malty/hoppy palate and bitter finish: the name means "noble". The 4.8 per cent **Pilsener** is dry in the finish after a hop-accented start and firm palate. A 5.6 per cent **Export**, with a nod in the direction of Dortmund, has a rounded malty character underscored by rich hops. There is also a seasonal Bock called **Ur-Bock** (7.0 per cent ABV). Its brewery in Lüneburg produces a hoppy and dry **Moravia Pils** (38 IBUs), stressing the influence of beers and malt from the Czech lands.

The name of Hamburg's other leading brewer, Bavaria St Pauli, also emphasizes the deep admiration the Prussians feel for the brewers of the south. It was common in the nineteenth century for northern brewers to append either Bavarian or Bohemian imagery to their company name as lager-brewing developed in those regions. The present company is the result of a merger in 1922 of two separate companies, Bavaria and St Pauli: St Pauli is a district of Hamburg. To confuse the issue further, its products are produced under the label of Astra. They include **Astra Urtyp**, lightly hopped, and **Astra Pilsener** with a splendidly aromatic hop bouquet and palate. It also brews a seasonal **Urbock**.

Its most remarkable beer comes from its Jever subsidiary in the resort town of the same name in German Friesland. Friesland or Frisia, the setting for Erskine Childers' famous spy novel *The Riddle of the Sands*, was once a tiny independent state, a buffer between Germany, the Netherlands and Denmark. The Frisians like bitter drinks and the Jever Brewery, founded in the 1840s, meets the demand with **Jever Pils** which registers 44 IBUs. It is 4.9 per cent ABV, brewed from two-row barley with Hallertau and Tettnang hops. It is lagered for an impressive 90 days. The brewery uses an infusion rather than a decoction mash. The beer has a massive hop bouquet from Tettnang hops, a malty, hoppy and yeasty palate, and a stunningly dry, bitter and hoppy finish with some honey notes from the malt. Jever Pils is exported widely. The brewery also makes for the local market a rounded, malty **Export** and a **Maibock**.

Bremen also has a brewery named in honour of St Paul. It has the full and curious title of St Pauli Girl. The company claims it doesn't know where the Girl came from but uses the image of a young woman carrying foaming jugs of beer. The harbour town formed the first brewers' guild in Germany in 1489 and once had a substantial number of brewing companies. Today the three main breweries share a modern brewing factory and are linked through a complex financial structure. The best-known, as a result of its vigorous export policy, is **Beck's**. The 5.0 per cent beer belongs to no clearly defined style, has a light, malty aroma, a bland palate with some hints of hop from Hallertau varieties, and a short finish. As television commercials testify, Beck's has an impressive, traditional copper brewhouse where anchors in stained-glass windows stress the importance of exporting to the company. **St Pauli Girl** is crisp and clean but hard to distinguish from Beck's. Haake-Beck, in the same complex, makes far more distinguished and hop-accented **Edel-Pils** and **Pils**. An unfiltered version of the Pils is sold as **Kräusen-Pils** in Bremen taverns. The brewery also produces a Berlin-type wheat beer called **Bremer Weisse** (2.75 per cent ABV), quenching and refreshing, fermented with the aid of a lactic culture to give a deliberate sourness. It has a tart and fruity aroma and palate. Locals underscore the fruitiness by adding a dash of raspberry syrup.

Lower Saxony and Bock

Whatever the Bavarians may think, the origins of strong Bock beers almost certainly lie in the town of Einbeck. Beer has been brewed in the small town near Brunswick and Hanover since at least 1351. It calls itself "Beer City" and marks the fact with three beer casks on its boundary, even though only one brewery survives there today.

Einbeck's beers were sold as far afield as Amsterdam and Stockholm and were brewed strong to help them withstand long journeys by road and water. The early brews would have been dark and top-fermenting, probably made from a blend of barley and wheat malts. Such was their fame that they were referred to by the truncated "Beck", which became "Bock" in the Bavarian accent.

At a time when most brewing was undertaken in monasteries or castles, the burghers of Einbeck permitted the production of beer for commercial sale. It was done on a contract basis: citizens would buy malt and hops, which they dried in their lofts. A licensed brewmaster, with a publicly-owned brew kettle, would visit their homes and help them make beer which they then sold. Einbeck, despite its small population, became a powerhouse of modern brewing during the life of the Hanseatic League between the thirteenth and fourteenth centuries.

A commercial brewery was built in Einbeck in 1794 and has been rebuilt on several occasions. The present modern brewery, Einbecker Brauhaus, carries the legend: "Ohne Einbeck gäb's kein Bockbier" – Without Einbeck there would be no Bock beer. Three versions of Bock are produced, all with alcoholic strengths of 6.9 per cent ABV and all quite reasonably labelled **Ur-Bock** – Original Bock. Soft water comes from deep springs,

The façade of the Löwen brewery; Germans may not understand the "lowenbrow" ordered in England; they call it "Lurvenbroy"

malt from the Brunswick area and hops – Northern Brewer, Perle and Hersbruck – from Bavaria. The beers are hoppier and drier than a Bavarian Bock on the sound historic grounds that the original Einbeck beers would have been heavily hopped to help them withstand long journeys. But the main characteristic of the beers is a rich, rounded maltiness that avoids an overbearing, cloying sweetness. The pale **Hell**, with 38 IBUs, has an appealing malt aroma and palate and a late burst of hops in the finish. The **Dunkel** or dark beer has the same bitterness rating. The aroma and palate are dominated by rich malt with hints of dark fruit and coffee, and again the hops make a late entrance in the dry and complex (malt, fruit, hops) finish. A **Maibock**, on sale between March and mid-May, has 36 IBUs, is crisp, quenching and refreshing, an ideal way to celebrate the arrival of spring. It is lagered for six weeks. The Hell and Dunkel have eight to 10 weeks' maturation.

In Brunswick the Feldschlössen Brewery brews a 4.9 per cent **Pilsner** (and spells the word in the correct Czech manner). It also produces two warm-fermenting beers, a **Brunswick Alt** and the Disney-sounding **Duckstein**, a tawny, fruity ale matured over beechwood chips, with a bitter and tart finish. In the days when there were two Germanys divided by a wall, the East also had a Feldschlössen Brewery. Today both plants are owned by Holsten.

The origins of Hanover's 114-year-old Lindener Aktien Bräuerei lie in a civic brewery run by a brewers' guild: the beers are labelled Gilde to record the historic detail. The founder of the guild was called Cord Broyhan or Broyan and the brewery produces a **Broyan Alt** in his honour. This warm-fermenting ale is 5.25 per cent ABV and has a copper colour, rich malt aroma and delicate hop finish. It has several cold-fermenting beers including a **Pilsner** and a stronger **Edel-Pils**.

Berlin wheat beers

When Napoleon's troops reached Berlin they described the local wheat beers as the "Champagne of the North". It was a fitting and perceptive description, for the Pinot and Chardonnay grapes of the Champagne region produce such a tart wine that it only becomes drinkable after a long, slow process in which a secondary fermentation in the bottle involves some lactic activity and finally becomes spritzy and sparkling. Berliner Weisse beers are so tart and lactic that drinkers add a dash of woodruff or other syrups to the beer to cut the acidity. The style is traditionally low in alcohol, around 3.0 per cent ABV, is extremely pale in colour, has a light fruitiness and little hop aroma. The origins of the style are unknown but one theory is that the fleeing Huguenots picked up the skill of brewing sour beer as they migrated north from France through Flanders. At its height Berliner Weisse beer was brewed by no fewer than 700 producers in the Berlin area. Now there are just two.

The lactic cultures that work with a conventional top-fermenting yeast to produce Berliner Weisse were isolated early in the twentieth century by scientists who founded Berlin's renowned university research and brewing school, the Versuchs und Lehranstadt für Brauerei or VLB for short. The culture is named *lactobacillus delbrücki* after Professor Max Delbrück, the leading research scientist. The Berliner Kindl Brauerei is the bigger of the two remaining producers. Its well water is softened. The proportion of wheat malt is around 30 per cent and the finished alcohol is 2.5 per cent. Bitterness units register a modest 10 from the use of Northern Brewer. After mashing and boiling, the *lactobacillus* is added first to start acidification, followed by a top-fermenting brewer's yeast. Fermentation lasts for a week followed by several days of cold conditioning. The beer is then filtered, bottled with a top yeast and kräusened with partially fermented wort.

The Schultheis Brewery blends equal amounts of wheat and barley malts in the mash to produce a 3.0 per cent beer. Hallertau hops produce four to eight IBUs. Top-fermenting yeast and *lactobacilli* are blended together with wort that is between three and six months old to encourage a lively fermentation, which lasts for three to four days. The beer is warm conditioned for three to six months. It is then kräusened and *lactobacillus* added for bottling. The finished beer is complex, fruity, sour and quenching, more assertive than the Kindl version. Unlike Bavarian wheat beers, the Berliner Weisse style is not enjoying a revival and is in serious decline.

Black Beer of Thuringia

When the wall between East and West Germany came down, West German companies rushed to buy up breweries in the East, many of them run down and in urgent need of an injection of capital. Many old East German beers were lacking distinction, mainly because the old regime did not adhere to the *Reinheitsgebot*. They exported malt and hops for "hard currency" and were prepared to allow all manner of cheap adjuncts to be used in brewing.

Many breweries have closed. Others have been swallowed by such giants as Holsten. Bitburger alone was motivated by affection as much as commercial enthusiasm.

The present chairman of Bitburger, Dr Axel Simon, a descendant of the founder, remembered **Köstritzer Schwarzbier** from his youth and thinks he may have drunk it even before the family's Pilsner. Bad Köstritz was a spa town (Bad means bath) near the great cities of Weimar and Erfurt in Thuringia but had disappeared into obscurity along with its beer behind the wall.

But Black Beer from the region is a style in its own right and may even have inspired the black beers of Japan. It is a style different from the dark but not quite black Dunkel beers of Munich and Franconia, and it is likely that the beers were warm-fermented much later than in Bavaria. Certainly under the old Communist regime, Köstritzer Schwarzbier varied between being warm- and cold-fermented and was even exported to the West at one stage as "stout".

When Dr Simon arrived he found a superb red-brick Victorian brewery built in 1907 covered in scaffolding. It had fallen into disuse. Brewing was carried out in an ugly modern brewhouse with East European vessels that looked fittingly like army tanks. A weird tangle of pipework led to wort and yeast being trapped in joins, creating yeast infections. Bitburger could have closed the place and moved production to the Rhineland but Dr Simon was determined to make the black beer of Köstritz a Thuringian speciality again.

Black beer, rather like stout in Britain and Ireland, was recommended for nursing mothers: Dr Simon's mother drank it when she was breast-feeding him. It eased rheumatism though, unlike Mackeson, did not claim to stop drinkers farting. Older drinkers still like to beat sugar and egg into the beer: the brewery used to make a sweetened version of the beer but this is now prohibited by the *Reinheitsgebot*, which has been restored to the Eastern lands.

Bitburger has pumped millions of marks into the brewery to restore it. When the sweet version of **Köstritzer Schwarzbier** was dropped, the brewery concentrated on a 3.5 per cent ABV beer brewed with 50 per cent pale malt from the Erfurt area, 43 per cent Munich and the rest roasted malt, the last two from Franconia. Hüller hops for bitterness and Hallertau

Mittelfrüh for aroma created 35 units of bitterness. Local spring water is softened for brewing liquor.

Since then Bitburger has dramatically upped the alcohol level to 4.6 per cent. The beer is bigger and dryer but still has an aroma of dark fruit/malt loaf and bitter chocolate, a creamy palate and a long, complex finish with more dark, bitter roasted malt, coffee and chocolate, underpinned by hops. It is a minor classic but perhaps, in the rush to make an acceptable beer for the whole of a united Germany, some of the traditional if quaint Thuringian originality has been lost.

SELECTED GERMAN BREWERS

Altstadthof, 18 Berg Strasse, 8500 Nürnberg (Nuremberg).

Augustiner Brauerei, Neuhauserstrasse 16, 8000 Munich 1.

Bavaria-St Pauli Brauerei AG, Hopfenstrasse 15, Hamburg 4.

Bayerische Staatsbrauerei Weihenstephan, Postfach 1155, Freising, Munich.

Berliner Kindl Brauerei AG, Rollbergstr. 26-80, Berlin 44.

Bitburger Brauerei Theo Simon, Postfach 189, 5520 Bitburg/Eifel.

Brauerei Inselkammer Aying, 1 Zornedinger Strasse, 8011 Aying.

Brauerei Beck GMBH & Haake-Beck/St Pauli Girl, Am Deich 18/19, Bremen 1.

Brauerei Binding AG, Darmstädster Landstrasse 185, Frankfurt 70.

Brauerei Felsenkeller Herford, Postfach 1351, Herford.

Diebels, Privatbrauerei Diebels GMBH, Brauerei-Diebels Strasse 1, Issum 1, Düsseldorf.

Dinkelacker Brauerei AG, Tübinger Strasse 46, Postfach 101152, Stuttgart 1.

Dortmunder Actien Brauerei, Steigerstrasse 20, Postfach 105012, Dortmund 1.

Dortmunder Kronen GMBH, Märkische Strasse 85, Dortmund 1.

Dortmunder Union Brauerei, Brau und Brunnen, 2 Rheinische Strasse, 4600 Dortmund 1.

Eichbaum-Brauereien AG, Käfertaler Strasse 170, Mannheim 1.

Einbecker Brauhaus, 4-7 Papen Strasse, 3352 Einbeck.

EKU Erste Kulmbacher Actien Brauerei AG, EKU-strasse 1, Kulmbach.

Erdinger Weissbräu, 1-20 Franz Brombach Strasse, 8058 Erding.

Fürstlich Fürstenbergische Brauerei KG, Postfach 1249, Donaueschingen.

Gaffel, Privat Brauerei Gaffel-Becker, 41 Eigelstein, 5000 Köln (Cologne).

Gilde Brauerei AG, Hildesheimer Strasse 132, Hanover 1.

Hacker-Pschorr Bräu GMBH, Schwanthalerstrasse 113, 8000 Munich 2.

Heller-Trum Schlenkerla, 6 Dominikaner Strasse, 8600 Bamberg.

Heller, Brauhaus Heller, 33 Roon Strasse, 5000 Köln (Cologne).

Henninger-Bräu, Hainer Weg 37-53, Frankfurt/Main 70.

Holsten Brauerei AG, Holstenstrasse 224, 22765 Hamburg.

Jever, Friesisches Bräuhaus zu Jever, 17 Elisabethufer, 2942 Jever.

Kaisderdom Privatbrauerei, Breitäckertasse 9, Bamberg 14.

Köstritzer Schwarzbierbrauerei, Heinrich Schütz Strasse, Bad Köstritz, 6514 Thüringen.

Krombacher Brauerei, Hagener Strasse 261, Kreuztal-Krombach.

Kulmbacher Mönchshof-Bräu GMBH, Hofer Strasse 20, Kulmbach.

Küppers Kölsch Brauerei, 145-155 Alteburger Strasse, 5000 Köln (Cologne).

Löwenbräu AG, Nymphenburger Strasse 4, Munich 2.

Maisel, Hindenburger Strasse 9, Bayreuth.

Malzmühle, Brauerei Schwarz, 6 Heumarkt, 5000 Köln (Cologne).

P. J. Früh Cölner Hofbräu, 12-14 Am Hof, 5000 Köln (Cologne).

Päffgen, Gebrüder Päffgen, Obergarige Hausbrauerei, 64-66 Friesen Strasse, 5000 Köln (Cologne).

Paulaner-Salvator-Thomasbräu, Hochstrasse 75, Munich 95.

Pinkus Müller, 4-10 Kreuz Strasse, 4400 Münster.

Reichelbräu AG, Lichtenfelser Strasse 9, Postfach 1860, Kulmbach.

Schlossbrauerei Kaltenberg, Augsburger Strasse 41, Fürstenfeldbruck, Bayern.

G. Schneider & Sohn, 1-5 Emil Ott Strasse, 8420 Kelheim.

Schultheiss-Brauerei, 28-48 Methfessel Strasse, Kreuzberg, 1000 Berlin 61.

Schwaben Bräu, Hauptstrasse 26, Stuttgart 80.

Gabriel Sedlmayr Spaten-Franziskaner-Bräu KGA, Marsstrasse 46-48, Munich 2.

Staatliches Hofbräuhaus in München, Hofbräuallee 1, Munich 82.

Warsteiner Brauerei, Wilhelmstrasse 5, Warstein 1.

Zum Eurige Obergarige Hausbrauerei, 1 Berger Strasse, Düsseldorf.

ENGLAND

Most visitors to England know three things about the country before they arrive: the natives are transported in red buses and black taxis, they are ruled by the Queen, and they drink a warm beer called bitter. Buses and taxis come in a multitude of colours these days, the monarchy has its problems, while there is often more to tempt visitors to pubs than bitter ale. Bitter is a twentieth-century development and many brewers and discriminating drinkers are rediscovering ales from earlier times.

Nevertheless, bitter is the dominant type of beer, drunk usually in large pint glasses filled by decorative handpumps on pub bars. Statistics will show that a poor copy of European cold-fermenting beer, always called "lager" in Britain, commands around half of total beer sales. But statistics can be misleading. Packaged lagers dominate the take-home trade. But the British, uniquely, prefer to drink most of their beer in the cheerful surroundings of the public house. More than 70 per cent of British beer is drunk in draught form. Ale of all types – mild, bitter, porter, stout, strong and seasonal beers – is the preferred tipple of pubgoers.

The English are returning to their ale-drinking roots. With Ireland included, the British Isles is the only major centre of population in the world where the people have stayed loyal to beers brewed by warm fermentation. In England in particular, many drinkers show a preference for cask-conditioned ale, a style much admired in other countries but rarely copied. Cask-conditioning is to beer what the champagne method is to wine: just as real champagne is allowed to ripen naturally in its bottle, so too does a beer that leaves the brewery while still in an unfinished form and matures in its cask in the pub cellar.

It may seem quaint, part of the pageantry of a country that lays great stress on its history and traditions, but cask-conditioning is rooted not in soft-headed folksiness but in good business practice. In the nineteenth century, when Britain's imperial grandeur had reached its zenith, British brewers had vast markets to supply at home and abroad and saw no need to switch to the new methods of lagering beer. At the turn of that century brewers began to build substantial "tied estates" of pubs which they supplied directly with their products. As they owned the premises, the brewers were able to train bar staff in the arcane rituals of tapping and venting casks of ale maturing in pub cellars whose contents had been neither filtered nor pasteurized in the brewery.

Mild

You will often find more than bitter served by handpump in pubs throughout the country. Mild ale – usually a dark copper, russet or tawny red colour – survives in a few areas of England and is worth seeking out as one of the oldest enduring beer styles in the world. Until the Industrial Revolution of the eighteenth and nineteenth centuries and the use of coke in kilning malt, all beer was brown in colour as malt was cured over wood fires. Brown beer was the type of beer drunk in every country until the arrival of pale malts. Mild or brown beer was an important constituent of the first porters and stouts in the eighteenth century in England. They were made by blending two or three different beers, one of which was brown. Until the twentieth century, most beers were stored and matured for long periods in wooden vats. But in the nineteenth century, brewers started to produce a special version of brown beer called mild. To avoid the harsh tastes of immature beer, mild was brewed using a blend of pale, brown and black or chocolate malts as well as brewing sugar. The hop rate was also reduced: the term mild has nothing to do with alcoholic strength but with the fact that fewer

MILD ALE BREWERS

Banks's (Wolverhampton & Dudley Breweries), Bath Road, Wolverhampton WV1 4NY.

Bass Highgate Brewery, Sandymount Road, Walsall WS1 3AP.

Daniel Batham & Son, Delph Brewery, Delph Road, Brierley Hill DY5 2TN.

Holden's Brewery, George Street, Woodsetton, Dudley DY1 4LN.

hops are used than in pale ales and porters.

Mild became popular with drinkers who preferred the malty flavour of the ale to the more bitter and sometimes astringent and even acidic character of well-matured beers. Mild appealed to workers engaged in heavy manual labour and, as it was cheaper than other beers, to those on low incomes.

Mild – called brown ale when it is bottled – remained the most popular beer in England until after the Second World War. But the decline of heavy industry and changing tastes that saw a switch to pale-coloured alcoholic drinks of all types, sent mild into an almost terminal spin. It survives today in a few areas of heavy industry. The greatest mild-drinking region is the Black Country based on the great Midlands city of Wolverhampton, though the name Black Country comes not from the beer but from the factory chimneys and mines that once dominated the area.

The grip of mild can best be seen at Banks's, England's biggest regional brewer, part of Wolverhampton and Dudley Breweries, which produces half a million barrels a year. **Banks's Original** accounts for 60 per cent of production, outselling bitter. In a superb brewhouse of burnished copper vessels, mild ale

Inside the Marston's brewery in Burton-on-Trent, Staffordshire, probably the town most associated with the English brewing industry

(3.5 per cent ABV) is made from Maris Otter malt, caramel for colour, and with whole Worcester Fuggles and East Kent Goldings hops. The ale has 40 units of colour and 25 bitterness units. The tawny-red beer is wonderfully drinkable with a pronounced port-wine character from the caramel, a gentle but persistent hop presence and light fruit in the finish. It's what they call "empty glass ale" in the Black Country: as soon as one pint is finished you feel the need for a refill.

There are some fine milds to be found in and around the Black Country town of Dudley. Batham's Brewery stands alongside the Vine pub in Brierley Hill, its façade carrying a quotation from Shakespeare's *Two Gentlemen of Verona*: "Blessings of Your Heart, You Brew Good Ale." Daniel Batham started to brew in 1881 when he lost his job as a miner and today Tim and Matthew Batham are the fifth generation to run the brewery and the handful of pubs. Bathams produces 6,000 barrels a year. Most of that is now bitter but sales of mild are picking up again. The 3.6 per cent mild is made from Maris Otter barley, caramel for colour, and Herefordshire Northdown and East Kent Goldings hops. More Goldings are added in the cask, giving the ale considerable bitterness for the style.

A couple of miles away, Holden's Brewery in Woodsetton also began life as a brewpub. Edwin Holden, grandson of the founders, brews 9,000 barrels a year for his small estate of pubs. Like Bathams, Holdens began as a dark mild brewer but also produces bitter today. **Black Country Mild** (3.6 per cent ABV) is made from Maris Otter malt with a complex blend of amber, crystal and black malts for colour. Hops are Fuggles specially grown in Worcestershire.

Bass, Britain's biggest brewing group, sold the Highgate Brewery in Walsall to its management. It's a Victorian plant dedicated to the production of **Highgate Dark**, a chocolatey and liquorice 3.25 per cent mild brewed from pale, crystal and black malts with Fuggles and Goldings hops and some maltose syrup and caramel.

Pale ale and bitter

While there are a few pockets of mild in other parts of England – Manchester has a good choice with **Holt's Mild** (3.2 per cent ABV), **Hyde's Anvil Mild** (3.5 per cent ABV) and **Lees' GB Mild** (3.5 per cent ABV) – bitter leads the field. Bitter is a twentieth-century development of the pale ales brewed primarily for the colonial trade in the previous century. Those pale ales, India Pale Ale in particular, were brewed to both a high alcohol content and hopping rate in order to withstand long sea voyages of three months or more. At the turn of the century, as brewers began to buy their own outlets, they wanted beers that would be ready to be served within days of arriving in the pub instead of having to mature for months.

"Running beers" were the result, made possible by carefully-cultured yeast strains that enabled beers to "drop bright" quickly in cask. New varieties of hops were high in acids and tannins, which meant that fewer had to be used to create the required level of bitterness. Whereas the original pale ales were light in colour, the new running beers tended to be copper-hued due to the use of crystal malt. During the kilning process, the starches in the malt are caramelized. Although crystal malt is added to pale malt in the mash tun, it is not necessary to have its starches converted during the mashing process.

"Running beers" was brewers' terminology. They were dubbed "bitter" as a result of their tangy hoppiness by drinkers who in so doing invented a name for a style. The term is applied only to draught beers – bottled versions are known as light ale or pale ale. The most remarkable aspect of running beers or bitter was that they continued to be conditioned in the cask. English brewers remained faithful to a form of technology rejected by the rest of the world as lager-brewing took hold. The running beers of the early twentieth century were the forerunners of the "real ales" of the 1990s.

With the exception of a handful of specialist breweries, every brewery in England produces at least one bitter. Usually there are two, a lower-strength "supping" bitter of around 3.6 per cent ABV, and a stronger best bitter of 4.0 per cent or more. Some produce three or four. Crouch Vale, a well-regarded micro in Essex, brews an **IPA** (3.5 per cent ABV), **Best Bitter** (4.0 per cent), **Millennium Gold** (4.2 per cent ABV), and **Strong Anglian Special** (5.0 per cent). The giant of the region, Greene King, produces **IPA** (3.6 per

PALE ALE AND BITTER BREWERS

Adnams & Co, Sole Bay Brewery, East Green, Southwold, Suffolk IP18 6JW.

Bass Brewers, 137 High Street, Burton-on-Trent, Staffordshire DE14 1JZ.

Bass Mitchells and Butlers, Cape Hill Brewery, PO Box 27, Birmingham B16 0PQ.

Black Sheep Brewery, Wellgarth, Masham, nr Ripon, N Yorkshire HG4 4EN.

Boddington, Whitbread Beer Co, PO Box 23, Strangeways, Manchester M60 3WB.

Burton Bridge Brewery, 24 Bridge Street, Burton-on-Trent, Staffordshire DE14 1SY.

W. H. Brakspear & Sons, The Brewery, New Street, Henley-on-Thames, Oxfordshire RG9 2BU.

Crouch Vale Brewery, 12 Redhills Road, South Woodham Ferrers, Essex CM3 5UP.

Thomas Hardy, Dorchester Brewery, Weymouth Avenue, Dorchester, Dorset DT1 1QT.

Fuller, Smith & Turner, Griffin Brewery, Chiswick Lane South, London W4 2QB.

Greene King, Westgate Brewery, Bury St Edmunds, Suffolk IP33 1QT.

Joseph Holt, Derby Brewery, Empire Street, Cheetham, Manchester M3 1JD.

Hook Norton Brewery Co, Brewery Lane, Hook Norton, Banbury, Oxfordshire OX15 5NY.

Hydes Anvil Brewery, 46 Moss Lane West, Manchester M15 5PH.

Ind Coope Burton Brewery, 107 Station Road, Burton-on-Trent, Staffordshire DE14 1BZ.

King & Barnes, 18 Bishopric, Horsham, Sussex RH12 1QP.

J. W. Lees & Co, Greengate Brewery, Middleton Junction, Manchester M24 2AX.

Lloyds Country Beers, John Thompson Inn, Ingleby, Derbyshire DE7 1NW.

Marston, Thompson & Evershed, PO Box 26, Shobnall Road, Burton-on-Trent, Staffordshire DE14 2BW.

McMullen & Sons, The Hertford Brewery, 26 Old Cross, Hertford, Hertfordshire SG14 1RD.

Frederic Robinson, Unicorn Brewery, Stockport, Cheshire SK1 1JJ.

St Austell Brewery Co, 63 Trevarthian Road, St Austell, Cornwall PL25 4BY.

Shepherd Neame, 17 Court Street, Faversham, Kent ME13 7AX.

Samuel Smith, The Old Brewery, High Street, Tadcaster, W Yorkshire LS24 9SB.

Timothy Taylor & Co, Knowle Spring Brewery, Keighley, W Yorkshire BD21 1AW.

Joshua Tetley & Son, PO Box 142, The Brewery, Hunslet Road, Leeds, W Yorkshire LS1 1QG.

T. & R. Theakston, The Brewery, Masham, nr Ripon, N Yorkshire HG4 4DX.

Tolly Cobbold, Cliff Road, Ipswich, Suffolk IP3 0AZ.

Wadworth & Co, Northgate Brewery, Devizes, Wiltshire SN10 1JW.

Young & Co, Ram Brewery, High Street, Wandsworth, London SW18 4JD.

---

cent ABV) and **Abbot Ale** (5.0 per cent ABV). In neither case does the low-strength "IPA" reflect the true style. In London the revered independent Fuller's brews **Chiswick Bitter** (3.5 per cent ABV), **London Pride** (4.1 per cent ABV), and a redoubtable 5.5 per cent **Extra Special Bitter**, as fruity as a street market.

Is there a true descendant of the nineteenth-century pale ales that spawned modern bitter? Fittingly you have to go to Burton-on-Trent in the Midlands, where pale ale was fashioned, to find it. Marston, Thompson and Evershed started brewing in Burton in 1834 and moved to the present site, the Albion Brewery, in 1898. Although Marston's is classified as a regional brewer, its **Pedigree Bitter** (4.5 per cent ABV) has national distribution and is second only to **Draught Bass** in "premium" (strong) bitter sales. Pedigree uses no dark malts. In common with the first pale ales, it is brewed from only pale malt (83 per cent) and glucose sugar (17 per cent). It is hopped with Fuggles and Goldings which create 26 units of bitterness, on the low side for the style.

The character of Pedigree – at once subtle yet robust, aromatic as well as malty and lightly fruity – is due to the singular fashion in which it is fermented. Marston's is the last brewer in England, and the only one of Burton's much-reduced clutch of breweries, to use the "union room" method of fermentation. The system was developed in Burton in the nineteenth century and rapidly spread to the rest of the country in order to cleanse fermenting beer of yeast. Pale ale production coincided with the arrival of mass-produced glass – now drinkers could see their beer and they clamoured for clarity. The union system removed yeast from beer efficiently and effectively. It was based on the medieval method of brewing where the ale fermented in large wooden casks and frothed up and ran into buckets beneath the casks, allowing the yeast to be collected and re-used, but the union system turned the medieval method on its head. Troughs are placed above large oak casks, each one holding 144 gallons, with pipes fitted into the bung holes of the casks. The fermenting wort rises up the pipes and drips into the troughs, which are slightly inclined. The liquid runs back into the casks while the yeast settles in the troughs. The end result is a well-attenuated and crystal clear beer.

The Joshua Tetley brewery in Leeds produces some of the most popular brands, not just in Yorkshire but in all of England

The Marston's yeast voraciously turns malt and glucose sugars into alcohol. As a result of the high levels of gypsum in the local well water, Pedigree has a renowned sulphury aroma, known locally as the "Burton snatch". Only Pedigree is brewed in the union sets although the same yeast strain is used for the company's other brands of ale.

Union sets are expensive to run and maintain. Brewers abandoned them as new and simpler methods of yeast cleansing were developed. Marston's remained faithful to them to such an extent that an additional fermenting hall with brand-new unions was built at enormous cost in the early 1990s. The company believes that the taste and character of its beers would change for the worse if the yeast was asked to work in conventional vessels. In 1999, after a protracted battle, Marston's was bought by Wolverhampton & Dudley Breweries, which has confirmed that Pedigree will continue to be brewed in Burton.

There are other fine examples of bitter ales brewed in Burton. Britain's biggest brewer, Bass, produces the biggest-selling premium cask ale in the country: **Draught Bass** (4.4 per cent ABV). Until the early 1980s, Draught Bass was also brewed in union room fermenters. The group thought the system was too capital and labour intensive and the beer is now fermented in conventional open vessels. It has lost some of its subtle balance of flavours and aromas as a result. But it is still a superb beer with a malt and creamy toffee aroma, a hint of sulphur from the water, pronounced malt in the mouth balanced by gentle hop bitterness from Challenger and Northdown varieties (26 IBUs) and a long finish in which malt dominates but with some light hop and a delectable hint of apple fruit. Apple is also present in Marston's Pedigree and is a hallmark of the Burton style.

Bass used to brew the bottle-conditioned **Worthington White Shield**, another ale that can claim to be a direct descendant of the original India Pale Ales. William Worthington was a member of the great Burton brewing breed whose company merged with Bass in the 1920s. The beer was brewed at Burton until the 1990s when, as a result of declining sales, Bass licensed the brand to King & Barnes of Horsham in Sussex. White Shield (5.6 per cent ABV, 40 IBUs) has an enticing aroma of spices, peppery hops (Challenger and Northdown), light fruit and sulphur. There are malt, hops and spices in the mouth, with a deep nutty finish, plenty of hop character and a hint of apple fruit. It is brewed from a blend of Halcyon and Pipkin pale malt with a touch of black malt for colour. At the end of the brewing process the beer is filtered and then primed with sugar to encourage a second fermentation in the bottle and re-seeded with a special yeast strain. Although it is an ale culture, the yeast sinks to the bottom of the bottle as though it were a lager strain, and slowly turns the remaining sugars into alcohol. The beer is warm-conditioned for three weeks before it leaves the brewery. It can then be drunk, but true White Shield devotees prefer to keep the beer for a longer time. After a year to 18 months the beer takes on a more rounded and fruity character. It is a difficult beer to pour: glass and bottle have to be held almost horizontal and then the pourer slowly raises the elbow of the arm holding the bottle to allow the beer to enter the glass. As soon as the sediment begins to move towards the neck of the bottle, pouring must stop to ensure a clear glass of ale, though the sediment will do no harm.

Ind Coope Burton Ale, a draught version of the renowned **Double Diamond** bottled pale ale, is owned by Carlsberg-Tetley, which closed its Burton brewery and has switched production to Marston's. Burton Ale undergoes such a volcanic second fermentation in cask that while it is declared at 4.8 per cent ABV it can reach 5.1 or 5.2 per cent by the time it reaches the drinker's glass. It is brewed from pale and chocolate malts with liquid brewing sugar, English hop pellets with Styrian Goldings added for aroma in the cask.

The Burton Bridge microbrewery, based behind the Bridge Inn, produces a fruity/hoppy **Bridge Bitter** (4.2 per cent ABV), using Pipkin pale malt and 5.0 per cent crystal, with Challenger and Target whole hops in the copper and Styrian Goldings for dry hopping in cask. It

also brews a magnificent bottle-fermented Empire Pale Ale (7.5 per cent ABV) that is matured in casks for three months to match the sea journey of a nineteenth-century IPA *en route* from England to India.

The importance of yeast in brewing can be seen in the ales brewed by Lloyds Country Beers at the John Thompson Inn in Ingleby, Derbyshire. The brewer uses yeast bought from Burton every week, giving his ales a hint of Burton sulphuriness. The main brew is **Derby Bitter** (4.1 per cent ABV), with a hoppy and fruity aroma, rich malt in the mouth, and well-balanced finish packed with hops and fruit.

Two other fermentation systems that date back to the eighteenth and nineteenth centuries are the Yorkshire square and the dropping system. The Yorkshire square method is still widely used in both that region and adjacent counties. The only truly traditional stone squares are found in Samuel Smith's Brewery in Tadcaster, North Yorkshire, a company founded in 1758 and the oldest in the region. The square was invented to cope with the particular problems of the yeast strains used in Yorkshire. Yorkshire yeasts are highly "flocculent". This means the cells clump together, separate from the wort and refuse to turn sugars into alcohol unless they are regularly roused by agitating and aerating the wort. A simple answer would be to use a different, less flocculent strain of yeast, but Yorkshire brewers are jealous of the rounded, malty character of their beers. In order to encourage the yeast to work effectively, the two-storey square fermenter was developed. The top chamber is known as the "barm deck", barm being a dialect word for yeast. The bottom chamber is filled with wort and yeast. Fermentation forces liquid and yeast through a manhole, where the yeast is trapped by a raised flange while the wort runs back into the bottom chamber via pipes. Every couple of hours wort is pumped to the top chamber to aerate it and mix yeast back into the liquid. When fermentation is complete the manhole is closed, the green beer is left to condition in the bottom storey while the yeast is collected from the top.

Yorkshire beers are not only full bodied as a result of unfermented sugars but also have the famous "thick, creamy head", the result of high levels of carbonation created during fermentation. Samuel Smith's beer – **Old**

Brewery Bitter (3.8 per cent ABV) – is a classic of the style: rich, malty and nutty but underpinned by good Fuggles and Goldings hop character.

The top-selling standard bitter in the country, **Tetley Bitter** (3.6 per cent ABV), is brewed in modern stainless steel Yorkshire squares in Leeds. It is a highly complex beer with an aromatic, citric lemon aroma from Northdown hops – the beer is dry hopped in cask – a malty, creamy palate, and a long, dry finish packed with more fine hop flavour.

Yorkshire, the largest region of England, has many fine breweries, and great stress is placed on tradition. When Paul Theakston opened his brewery in Masham in 1992 he was insistent that he would ferment in Yorkshire squares and managed to buy some, ironically from a brewery in Nottinghamshire. His **Black Sheep Bitter** (3.8 per cent ABV) has a powerful Fuggles hop aroma, with more peppery hops in the mouth and a long bitter finish. **Special Strong Bitter** (4.4 per cent ABV) is highly complex, with malt, hops, cobnuts and orange fruit on the aroma, a bitter-sweet palate and big hoppy and fruity finish.

Paul Theakston left his family company when it was taken over by the giant Scottish and Newcastle group in the 1980s. Theakston's Brewery and Black Sheep brew cheek-by-jowl in Masham, the former famous for its pale **Best Bitter** (3.8 per cent ABV; 24 IBUs) with a delicate fruit and hops aroma and palate and the famous strong ale, **Old Peculier** (see Special Ales).

In Keighley, Timothy Taylor's brewery has won a cupboardful of prizes from the Campaign for Real Ale for its magnificent **Landlord Bitter**. The 4.3 per cent ABV beer is brewed only from Golden Promise malt, with Worcestershire Fuggles for bitterness and Kent Goldings and Styrians for aroma.

A rudimentary but highly effective method of cleansing beer of yeast is the dropping system. This is still in operation at Brakspear's Brewery in Henley-on-Thames. When fermentation is under way in open vessels, the wort is dropped one floor to a second bank of vessels, leaving behind spent hops and dead yeast cells as well as yeast in suspension. The wort is roused and aerated and a fresh head quickly forms on the wort. **Bitter** (3.6 per cent ABV) and **Special** (4.0 per cent) are brewed with Maris Otter pale and crystal malts with a touch of black malt for colour. Hops are Fuggles and Goldings. The Bitter, with 38 units of bitterness, has a pronounced citric aroma from the hops, a full malt and floral hop flavour, and a delicate dry finish with continuing firm hop presence.

Also in the Thames Valley, Hook Norton Brewery in the Oxfordshire village of the same name, is a fine example of a traditional Victorian "tower" brewery in which all the stages of the brewing process flow logically from floor to floor: mashing at the top, boiling in the middle, fermentation and racking at the bottom. **Hook Norton Best Bitter** (3.3 per cent ABV), despite its modest strength, has a fine hop character from Challenger, Fuggles and Goldings varieties, balanced by rich malt and some fruit in the finish. **Old Hooky** (4.3 per cent ABV) is richly fruity with hints of raisins in the finish.

Most bitters are produced in conventional fermenting vessels where the yeast is skimmed off by vacuums, which suck the yeast head from the wort, or by "parachutes", metal funnels placed apex-down on top of the wort so that yeast can collect inside the funnel. Traditional brewers prefer open fermenters, made from wood, iron, stainless steel or lined with polypropylene, so they can rouse the wort by hand. But good beer can equally be made in modern brewhouses. Charles Wells of Bedford, for example, uses all the trappings of high tech, including mash kettles, lauter tuns and closed conical fermenters, but its bitters are highly regarded. **Bombardier** (4.2 per cent ABV), made from pale and crystal malts with Challenger and Goldings hops – 34 units of bitterness – has a complex malt, hops and fruit character that makes it popular in Germany, Italy and Spain as well as in Wells' own pubs.

Further east, in the grain basket of East Anglia, Adnams of Southwold in Suffolk, Greene King in historic Bury St Edmunds, and Tolly Cobbold in Ipswich, brew bitters rich in malt but balanced by generous hopping. Both **Adnams Bitter** (3.8 per cent ABV) and **Tolly Bitter** (3.6 per cent ABV) are pungent with Goldings hops and orange fruit while Greene King's **Abbot Ale** (5.0 per cent ABV) is packed with marmalade fruit in the mouth balanced by an intense

Opposite: *Adnams brews a special winter ale called Adnams Old Ale*

hop bitterness (36 units). McMullen of Hertford has a superb brewhouse with wooden, high-sided fermenters. Its two bitters, **AK** and **Country**, are well-attenuated ales in which most of the brewing sugars turn to alcohol. AK (3.8 per cent ABV; 22 IBUs) is hoppy and fruity with hints of orange peel on the aroma, while Country (4.6 per cent ABV; 30 IBUs) has a massive hops and fruit appeal.

In London, Young's of Wandsworth produces a standard bitter – always known by its Cockney nickname of "Ordinary" – and a Special Bitter that are uncompromising in their tart hoppiness. **Ordinary Bitter** (3.7 per cent ABV) is extremely pale (14 units of colour), brewed only from Maris Otter barley with a little torrefied barley and brewing sugar. Hops are Fuggles and Goldings, which create 32 to 34 IBUs. **Special Bitter** (4.8 per cent ABV; 32 IBUs) has a peppery hop aroma balanced by rich citric fruit, ripe malt in the mouth and a big finish packed with fruit and hops. Target hops are added to Fuggles and Goldings and the beer is dry hopped in cask.

South of London in the heart of the Kent hop fields, Shepherd Neame of Faversham is the oldest surviving brewery in England, dating from 1698. It brews two bitters and a strong ale, all bursting with a complex blend of Omega, Goldings, Target and Zenith hops. **Master Brew Bitter** (3.8 per cent ABV) and **Master Brew Best Bitter** (4.0 per cent ABV) have tangy, hoppy and citric-fruit aromas, bitter-sweet palates and massive hop finishes. **Spitfire Ale** (4.7 per cent ABV) is ripe and fruity, balanced by great depth of hop bitterness.

The family-owned King and Barnes Brewery in Horsham, Sussex, brews a range of highly distinctive ales with an appealing new-mown grass aroma from the house yeast. **Sussex Bitter** (3.5 per cent ABV; 31.5 IBUs) has a complex grist of pale, crystal and chocolate malts, with flaked maize and invert sugar. The hops are Challenger and Goldings. The copper-coloured **Broadwood** (4.0 per cent ABV; 37 IBUs) has a more malty note to the aroma and palate and rich fruit in the finish. The darker **Festive**, which is bottle as well as cask-conditioned, is 4.8 per cent ABV with 41.5 IBUs.

In the West Country, the superb red-brick Victorian brewery of Thomas Hardy of Dorchester produces four bitters: a 3.3 per cent **Dorchester Bitter**, a 3.8 per cent

Best Bitter, **Thomas Hardy Country Bitter** (4.2 per cent ABV, bottle-conditioned as well as draught) and the renowned **Royal Oak** (5.0 per cent ABV). The beers have great depth, with floral hops from Challenger and Northdown varieties, rich malt from Pipkin pale and crystal, and a delicate hint of banana fruit from the yeast.

In Devizes, Wadworth's imposing red-brick brewery produces a clutch of bitters of which the best-known is the 4.3 per cent **6X**, an ale that takes its name from the medieval habit of branding casks with Xs to indicate strength. 6X is brewed from Pipkin pale malt, crystal malt and brewing sugar, and hopped with Fuggles and Goldings (22 IBUs).

In the far west, St Austell Brewery in the town of the same name brews a 3.8 per cent **Tinners Bitter** with a delicate aroma of hops and buttercups, with light fruit and hops on the palate and the finish. The powerful five per cent **HSD** is nicknamed "High Speed Diesel" by locals, though officially it stands for Hicks Special Draught, named in honour of the brewery's founder.

In the north-west of England, a vast region that takes in the beauty of the Lake District to such great cities as Liverpool and Manchester, there are many fine bitters to enjoy. Manchester is a Mecca for ale lovers. From Boddingtons, with its tart and quenching pale **Bitter** (3.8 per cent ABV), to Hydes' malty/fruity **Bitter** (3.8 per cent ABV; 28 IBUs) and Lees' 4.0 per cent **Bitter** (27 IBUs) and strong **Moonraker** (7.5 per cent ABV; 30 IBUs) with a pronounced orange ester, there is a splendid choice. But the finest pale ale in the city is the uncompromisingly and shockingly hoppy **Holt's Bitter** (4.0 per cent; 40 IBUs). Holts is an old-fashioned, traditionalist family firm that refuses to advertise or even to provide its beers outside a small radius around the brewery. It still supplies its beers in 54-gallon hogsheads to some of its larger pubs. The complex bitter is brewed from Halcyon, Pipkin and Triumph pale malts, with a touch of black malt, flaked maize and invert sugar. Hops are Goldings and Northdown.

Down the road from Manchester, Frederic Robinson in Stockport brews a 4.2 per cent **Best Bitter** that strikes a brilliant balance between malt and hops, with pungent Goldings and tart fruit on the aroma, malt, hops and citric fruit in the mouth, and a long, dry and bitter finish.

Lees Brewery in Manchester produces the Beaujolais Nouveau of the beer world

Old Tom (8.5 per cent ABV) boasts a picture of a tom cat on the label but the feline does not affect the taste of this powerful vinous, darkly fruity and deeply bitter beer.

Special ales

Brewers are adding to the pleasures of ale drinking in England with a surge of new beers, many of them seasonal. Summer ales, light but well-hopped and refreshing, have been launched in recent years. Several are now producing harvest ales made from the first malt and hops of the new season, making them the Beaujolais Nouveaux of the beer world. John Willy Lees of Manchester was the first in the field with its **Harvest Ale** (11.5 per cent ABV; 34 IBUs), brewed from 100 per cent Maris Otter pale malt and East Kent Goldings whole hops.

The winter months are enlivened by a growing number of old ales and barley wines. Old ale in previous centuries was a beer aged for up to a year in oak vats. It is now brewed conventionally but there is a wide range of aromas and flavours to enjoy. Some old ales are now brewed all the year round. Classics of the style include the world-famous Theakston's **Old Peculier**, with a relatively modest 5.6 per cent ABV but a massive winey bouquet, roast malt on the palate and a bitter-sweet, delicately hopped finish, to George Gale's bottle-conditioned **Prize Old Ale** from Horndean in Hampshire (9.0 per cent ABV; 47.5 IBUs), with great hop attack and complex fruitiness with hints of apple and raisin, to the stunning **Thomas Hardy's Ale** from Dorchester. Hardy's Ale is bottle-conditioned and reaches 12 per cent alcohol. It is brewed from 100 per cent Pipkin pale malt and its tawny colour comes from three months' maturation and some caramelization of the sugars during the copper boil. It is a rich, winey yet intensely bitter ale with 75 units of bitterness. It will improve with age and some older vintages have remarkable flavours of liquorice, old leather and fresh tobacco. It is brewed in honour of West Country author Thomas Hardy who praised the ales of "Casterbridge" (Dorchester) in his novels.

Barley wine traditionally was the strongest ale in a brewery. There are two superb examples of the style in London. Fuller's **Golden Pride** (9.0 per cent ABV) is matured for three months in untreated wooden hogsheads in the approved eighteenth- and nineteenth-century fashion. It has an appealing sherry colour, a smooth, rich, Cognac-tinted palate with noticeable hop attack in the finish. Young's **Old Nick** is darker (75–80 colour units; 50–55 IBUs) with nutty crystal malt notes, bitter-sweet fruit and a typically powerful Young's hop presence.

SELECTED BREWER

George Gale & Co, The Brewery, Horndean, Portsmouth PO8 0DA.

PORTER BREWERS

Burton Bridge Brewery, 23 Bridge Street, Burton-on-Trent DE14 1SY.
Castle Eden Brewery, PO Box 13, Castle Eden, Hartlepool TS27 4SX.
Harvey & Son, Bridge Wharf Brewery, 6 Cliffe High Street,
Lewes BN7 2AH.
Larkins Brewery, Larkins Farm, Chiddingstone, Edenbridge TN8 7BB.

Porter

The revival of cask-conditioned ale encouraged brewers to widen their portfolios and dig deep into history and recipe books. Porter, the style that created the modern commercial brewing industry, is back in fashion, along with several interpretations of its strongest version, stout. Among the fascinating examples available are two in bottle-conditioned as well as draught versions: **Harvey's of Lewes** (4.8 per cent ABV) and **Burton Bridge** (4.5 per cent ABV). The latter is dark brown with tawny hints, probably close to the colour of an early porter before roasted malts were used. Whitbread, a towering presence in the history of porter brewing, invited three of its breweries in Castle Eden (near Durham), Cheltenham and Sheffield to brew porters to an 1850s' recipe from its London plant. A panel of beer writers tasted them blindfold and unanimously chose the Castle Eden version. Brewed from pale, brown, chocolate and black malts, with English Goldings in the copper and dry hopped with Styrian Goldings, **Castle Eden Porter** (4.5 per cent ABV) has 290 units of colour and 36 units of bitterness. Castle Eden, now an independent company, continues to brew porter. The tiny Larkins Brewery of Chiddingstone is based on a Kent hop farm and its **Porter** (5.5 per cent ABV), with 59 bitterness units, is packed with piny, resiny Fuggles and Goldings character and a bitter-sweet palate and finish dominated by dark fruit and hops. The strength, bitterness and residual sweetness make it as close to the original style as it is possible to get.

Brown ales

Most brown ales are bottled versions of mild. The 3.0 per cent **Manns Brown Ale** is one of the last reminders

The Tyne Bridge provides a backdrop for the famous Newcastle Brown Ale from the Scottish & Newcastle Group

of a malty-sweet London mild, even though it is now brewed by Ushers of Trowbridge in Wiltshire. Manns was a large brewing company in East London that became part of the Grand Metropolitan-Watney group. Manns Brown is a lightly-hopped and gently fruity beer, available only in bottle.

In the north-east of England brown ale has deep roots in a region once famous for its shipbuilding and mining industries. Brown ales there are far more robust than southern mild. They tend to be reddish in colour, more in keeping with the red beers of Flanders than a darker mild. The best-known version is **Newcastle Brown Ale** from Newcastle Breweries, the Geordie end of the Scottish and Newcastle group. Brown ales were developed as the north-east's rival to the pale ales of the East Midlands, and Newcastle Brown Ale was the result of the pioneering work of the splendidly named Colonel Porter in the 1920s. The beer is complex, a blend of two beers: a dark brown beer that is not sold commercially and a 3.0 per cent Newcastle Amber. The blended beer is 4.7 per cent ABV with 24 IBUs. The recipe is made up of pale ale and crystal malts, brewing sugar and syrup and a touch of caramel. A complex blend of Hallertau, Northdown, Northern Brewer and Target hops is used, primarily for bitterness. Newcastle Brown Ale is the biggest-selling bottled ale in Britain and is exported to 40 countries. It is sold in draught form in the USA and has become a cult beer in Russia.

"Milk" stout

Milk stout was a late Victorian speciality, a beer designed to be sweeter, lower in alcohol, less gassy and with claimed food value. The best-known example of the breed is **Mackeson Stout**, brewed by a company in Hythe in Kent that had produced ales since the reign of Charles II. The "milk" came from lactose or milk sugar, a by-product of cheese making. Lactose cannot be fermented by brewer's yeast and it is this that gives the finished stout body and sweetness.

MILK STOUT BREWER

Whitbread Beer Co, Salmesbury, Nr Preston, Lancashire.

BROWN ALE BREWERS

Newcastle Breweries, Tyne Brewery, Gallowgate, Newcastle upon Tyne NE99 1RA.

Ushers of Trowbridge, Directors House, 68 Fore Street, Trowbridge BA14 8JF.

Milk stouts achieved massive sales and were popular with people who disliked the roasty, astringent and heavily hopped nature of a dry Irish stout. Mackeson's label claimed that "each pint contains the energizing carbohydrates of 10 ounces of pure dairy milk" and a promotional pamphlet said the stout was ideal for invalids, nursing mothers and even helped those who suffered from stomach disorders, including flatulence. In the aftermath of the Second World War, with severe shortages of food in Britain, the government instructed all sweet stout producers to remove the word "milk" from labels and advertising on the grounds that it was misleading and gave the impression that such beers actually contained milk. Mackeson even had to stop using the image of a milk churn on its label, though it has since been restored.

In spite of these restrictions, Mackeson's sales soared to such an extent that in the 1960s it accounted for an astonishing 60 per cent of the sales of Whitbread, which had bought the Kent brewery. It is now a minority beer but is still a sizeable brand for Whitbread. Although it begins with an original gravity of 1042, the finished alcohol is just 3.0 per cent as the lactose, which accounts for around 9.0 per cent of the grist, does not ferment. The rest of the recipe is made up of pale and chocolate malts and caramel.

"Sweet stout" is a misnomer and does the beer little credit, as it has a respectable 26 IBUs. It has a rich aroma of dark, chocolatey malt and delicate hops, with a hint in the mouth of those old-fashioned sweets known as "milk drops". The finish starts sweet but becomes dry. An export version with 5.0 per cent alcohol and 34 IBUs is firmer, fruitier and more rounded. It is possible that Whitbread may introduce it to the home market.

SCOTLAND

The history, the culture and even the climate have determined the course of Scottish brewing. The end result is a style radically different from that of the bigger country to the south.

Commercial brewing was slower to develop north of the border. Ale production was confined to the home and the farm, and it faced competition from home-grown whisky and imported French wine. The Napoleonic Wars cut off the supplies of wine from Bordeaux and from around 1730 commercial brewers sprang up to meet both local supply and a demand from Scots who had emigrated to the West Indies and North America. The term "export" for a strong and malty brew developed into a generic style and even today one of the major brands in Scotland is **McEwan's Export**.

The new entrepreneurial Scots brewers grew at astonishing speed. Companies such as Younger and McEwan not only became powerful forces in Scotland but exported considerable quantities of ale to North America, India and Australasia while Scotch Ale sent to north-east England via the new railway system out-sold local brews.

The brewing industry was mainly confined to the Lowlands, where the finest malting barley grows, and Alloa, Edinburgh and Glasgow became major brewing centres. Although pale malt provides the bulk of the grist in Scottish brewing, amber, brown, black and chocolate versions are widely used even in what are nominally called "pale" ales, while roasted barley and oats add further distinctive tart and creamy flavours.

The cold climate determined the particular nature of Scottish beer. Hops cannot grow in Scotland and as they are expensive to import they are used more sparingly, with a short time in the copper to avoid boiling off the aroma and bitterness. And before temperature control was introduced, fermentation was naturally cooler than in England, around 10°C (50°F). The yeast works more slowly and fermentation lasts for around three weeks, followed by a long conditioning period. Slow, cool fermentation, allied to the large number of Scots who worked abroad and acquired a

taste for lager, help explain the enthusiasm to embrace the new style of brewing in Scotland. Tennent's Wellpark Brewery in Glasgow started to brew lager as early as 1885. The rush to merge in the 1960s and 1970s, creating the Scottish duopoly of Scottish and Newcastle, and Tennent-Caledonian (a subsidiary of Bass), was driven by the demands of the lager market and the heavy costs of investing in new brewing plant.

Far more than in England, Scottish ale seemed destined for the scrapheap. But due to a long rearguard action by CAMRA and the enthusiasm of a small but growing number of specialist ale brewers, cask beer is starting to revive to such an extent that the busiest bars in Aberdeen, Edinburgh and Glasgow are those that offer real ale.

The revival has also seen a welcome reappearance of the names given to Scottish styles, such as "light", meaning a lightly-hopped ale, "heavy" for a standard bitter ale, "export" for a stronger ale, and "wee heavy" for a powerful beer akin to an old ale. Many revivalist ales are also branded with the term shilling, as in 60, 70, 80 and 90 shilling ales, based on a nineteenth-century method of invoicing based on strength. This means that a light may be called Sixty Shilling and so on up the strength table to Ninety Shilling for a wee heavy.

The pacesetter in the Scottish ale revival has been the Caledonian Brewery in Edinburgh. Bought by a handful of enthusiasts in 1987 when its previous owners closed the plant, Caledonian struggled to survive but won through on the sheer quality of its ales and its commitment to traditional methods and ingredients. The brewery uses open-fired coppers that encourage a good rolling boil, according to the brewer, who says his ales are properly boiled with hops and not stewed.

While the bitterness units of most Scottish ales rarely exceed 30, Caledonian's are noticeably hoppy due to the generous use of Fuggles and Goldings that give the ales a delectable aroma and palate of citric fruit. The 4.9 per cent ABV **Merman XXX**, a recreation of a genuine Scottish nineteenth-century "export", has

The most northerly brewery in Britain is on Orkney, run by an Englishman in what was once an old schoolhouse

between 48 and 50 bitterness units. With pale, crystal, amber, chocolate and black malts, it is a highly complex beer with hops, fruit and chocolate on the aroma, and a biscuity, fruity and hoppy palate and finish. Other Caledonian ales include a malty/hoppy **Caledonian Eighty Shilling** (4.1 per cent ABV), an organic **Golden Promise** (4.9 per cent ABV; 50–52 IBUs), and a magnificent **R&D Deuchar's IPA**, a loving recreation of the Scottish interpretation of the India Pale Ale style. Deuchar's IPA, 3.9 per cent ABV; 34–36 IBUs, is brewed from Golden Promise pale and crystal malts with Fuggles and Goldings whole hops.

Another Scottish brewer that ploughed a lonely ale furrow for years before breaking through to plaudits

and success is Belhaven in Dunbar. The brewery, based in old maltings buildings, is in a superb setting on the coast, close to the English border. It brews the whole gamut of traditional Scottish ales, from 60 to 90 shilling. Its **Belhaven Eighty Shilling** (4.1 per cent ABV; 33 units of colour; 29 of bitterness) is the Scots classic, with a pronounced gooseberry character on the aroma and palate underscored by peppery, resiny Fuggles and Goldings.

Two other breweries in Border country offer fascinating examples of the art. Broughton Brewery is in the town of the same name where novelist John Buchan was born – it names its major product, **Greenmantle Ale**, after one of his Richard Hannay adventures. It also brews a strong **Old Jock** (6.7 per

finish with a hint of chocolate from dark malt. Maclays has a wide portfolio, including 60, 70 and 80 shilling ales, a porter and a superbly quenching **Maclays Summer Ale** (3.6 per cent ABV) with great hop character (50 IBUs). Maclay's beers are all far more hoppy than the Scottish norm.

The most northerly brewery in the British Isles is run by an Englishman, Roger White, on Orkney. The Orkney Brewery, based in an old school house, produces **Raven Ale** (3.8 per cent ABV), **Dragonhead Stout** (4.1 per cent ABV), **Dark Island** (4.7 per cent ABV) and **Skullsplitter** (8.5 per cent ABV). The beers are rich and complex, fruity with good hop balance.

The origins of Scottish – or rather Pictish – brewing have been captured in the remarkable **Fraoch**, an ale that uses heather as well as barley malt in its make-up. Heather was widely used centuries ago to augment the poor quality of the barley grown in the Highlands.

Bruce Williams, who runs a home-brew shop in Glasgow, discovered a woman living on the Western Isles who was able to translate a recipe for heather ale from Gaelic. Fraoch is brewed for him at Maclays and uses ale malt, carapils, wheat malt, ginger root and 12 litres of heather. Hops are used primarily for their preservative quality and did not feature in the original recipe. Part of the heather is added to the copper, the remainder in the hop back, where it acts as a filter for the hopped wort. Fraoch comes in two versions, a 4.0 per cent ABV draught and a 5.0 per cent ABV bottled. It has a crisp heather aroma with a hint of liquorice, a dry herbal palate, and a fruity and minty finish.

cent ABV; 32 IBUs) and a traditional **Broughton Oatmeal Stout** (3.8 per cent ABV; 28 IBUs) in which the oats give a pleasing creamy sweetness to balance the slight astringency of roasted barley.

Traquair House near Peebles is a restored medieval brewery, based in the oldest inhabited stately home in Scotland. **Traquair House Ale** (7.0 per cent ABV; 35 IBUs) is brewed from pale malt and a touch of black, with East Kent Goldings specially grown for the house.

The old independent company of Maclays is based in the famous brewing town of Alloa. In common with Broughton, it has brought back a traditional stout using oats. **Maclays Oatmalt Stout** (4.5 per cent ABV; 35 IBUs) has hops and dark grain on the aroma, subtle malty sweetness in the mouth, and a long bitter-sweet

SCOTTISH BREWERS

Belhaven Brewery Co, Dunbar, East Lothian EH42 1RS.
Broughton Brewery, Broughton, Biggar, Lanarkshire ML12 6HQ.
Caledonian Brewing Co, Slateford Road, Edinburgh EH11 1PH.
Maclay & Co, Thistle Brewery, Clackmannanshire FK10 1ED.
McEwan and Younger, Scottish & Newcastle Breweries, Fountain Brewery, Edinburgh EH3 9YY.
Orkney Brewery, Quoyloo, Sandwick, Orkney KW16 3LT.
Traquair House Brewery, Traquair House, Innerleithen, Peebles-shire EH44 6PW.

WALES

The course of brewing in Wales has been determined by the power of the Nonconformist church and the temperance movement. The influence of both has waned but Welsh beers remain remarkably low in alcohol, a reflection of the time when brewers and their products kept a low profile.

Low-gravity beers, pale ales and dark milds, of around 3.0 per cent ABV, suited the tastes of industrial workers when South Wales was a powerhouse of mines and steelworks. In spite of the decline of heavy industry, the two biggest-selling beers in the principality, both filtered and pasteurized, are **Allbright** (3.3 per cent ABV) from Bass and Whitbread's **Welsh Bitter** (3.2 per cent ABV).

The cask-conditioned flag has been waved most vigorously by Brains of Cardiff. Its **Red Dragon Dark** (3.5 per cent ABV) is a classic mild ale with a fine chocolate aroma, malty in the mouth, and a light and refreshing finish. In Llanelli, Felinfoel also produces a dark mild of 3.4 per cent ABV. Both breweries produce light bitters but drinkers' preferences are switching to stronger ales. **Brain's SA** – nicknamed "Skull Attack" –

is 4.2 per cent ABV, malty and fruity. Felinfoel's **Double Dragon** is 5.0 per cent ABV, fruity, slightly vinous and lightly hopped with 25 IBUs. In Llandeilo, the new but vigorously expanding Tomas Watkin Brewery produces a clutch of rich, malty ales including Whoosh (3.7 per cent ABV), OSB (4.5 per cent) and Merlin's Stout (4.2 per cent).

Brewing in North Wales, long dominated by the **Wrexham Lager Company** (due to close in 2000), is now seeing a small flowering of micros, with the Plassey Brewery near Wrexham producing hoppy and distinctive ales.

WELSH BREWERS

S. A. Brain & Co, The Old Brewery, St Mary Street, PO Box 53, Cardiff CF1 1SP.

Felinfoel Brewery Co, Farmer's Row, Felinfoel, Llanelli SA14 8LB.

Plassey Brewery, Eyton, Wrexham LL1 0SP.

Welsh Brewers, Crawshay Street, Cardiff CF1 1TR,

IRELAND

Ireland vies with the Czech Republic for the honour of being the world's smallest nation to impose a major beer style on the consciousness of drinkers everywhere. Bohemia produced Pilsner but few of the beers outside of Pilsen have more than a passing resemblance to the original. But ask for "a Guinness" and you will get the real thing. In Ireland itself there is no need even to mention the brand name: "a glass of stout" will suffice. The only exception to the rule occurs in the city of Cork and its environs where two other brewers, Beamish and Murphy, also brew stout and where drinkers have to be more explicit.

Stout is rooted in the Irish way of life to such a degree that Guinness uses the harp, the national

symbol, as the company logo. Just like the people, you cannot hurry a glass of stout. Pouring a pint is an art form. Drinkers must wait patiently as the barperson allows it to settle into black body and white head and then tops it up to ensure that you receive a full measure.

Ale is also brewed in Ireland but it commands a relatively small share of the market. Lager has made some inroads but consumption of stout increased in the late 1980s and 1990s, with clever advertising and presentation winning young people to the joys of the black stuff.

Dry Irish Stout – the dryness a result of the use of roasted barley and generous hopping – is a style in its own right. But the origins of porter and stout lie in

London, not Dublin. Before porter became a major style in the early eighteenth century and found its way across the Irish Sea, Ireland produced sweet and unhopped ales in the Celtic tradition, a tradition that goes back 5,000 years. St Patrick, the monk who brought Christianity to the island, employed a brewer and for centuries the production of ale was controlled by the church. As a result of the damp climate, it is difficult to grow hops in Ireland and the English found to their astonishment that as late as the eighteenth century Irish ales were unhopped. There is even a suggestion that the first ale brewed by the young Arthur Guinness contained no hops.

The English had become used to heavily hopped, intensely bitter ales. Irish ale did not suit them. English brewers – and Scottish brewers in the north – exported ale to Ireland in vast quantities. As Ireland was ruled from London, it suited both British politicians and brewers to inhibit the growth of an indigenous Irish brewing industry.

Guinness

The history of Irish brewing is inextricably linked to Arthur Guinness. He used £100 left to him by a benefactor to open a small brewery in County Kildare in 1756. Three years later he moved to Dublin and took a lease on a disused brewery in St James's Gate at an annual rent of £45. He brewed ale but in 1799 he decided to challenge the English brewers' domination of the Irish market by switching production to porter with the aid of a brewer hired from London. His business expanded rapidly and he used canals and the new railway system to sell porter nationally. Guinness produced two beers, **X** and **XX**. The XX was later renamed **Extra Porter Stout** while a third beer, **Foreign Extra Porter Stout**, was developed for export to the British colonies. Eventually the term "porter" was dropped and the beers became known simply as stout.

Arthur Guinness's son, also called Arthur, not only expanded the business rapidly at home and abroad but was responsible for developing the generic style of dry stout. Until the 1880s, British and Irish brewers paid tax not on the strength of their beers but on malt. In order

to avoid paying any unnecessary imposts to the London government, Arthur Guinness II experimented with using some unmalted – and therefore untaxed – roasted barley in his grist. The barley added colour and a roasted, slightly charred character to the stout, making it far more bitter and dry than a London porter. Arthur II also produced the recipe for Foreign Export Stout, which, in common with English Pale Ales, was high in alcohol and massively hopped to withstand long sea journeys. When Arthur II handed over control of the company to Benjamin Guinness, Benjamin built up substantial sales in Belgium – where a taste for strong stout remains undiminished today – and North America. A third of Ireland's population had already emigrated to America following the famine of the 1840s.

By the turn of the century Guinness was the biggest brewer in Europe and by the end of the First World War was the biggest in the world, a remarkable achievement for a company based on an island with a population of five million. Its fortunes were boosted by a decision of the British government in the First World War to ban the use of dark, highly-kilned malts in order to save energy. As a result, porter and stout brewing went into steep decline in Britain, leaving the market clear for the Irish.

There are now 19 different versions of Guinness brewed in both draught and packaged versions. The classic Dublin brews use malt, unmalted roasted barley, flaked barley and a blend of English and American hops. Water comes from the Wicklow Mountains and is treated with gypsum to harden it. Arthur Guinness's original yeast is still used though it has been cultured down from some five strains to one. It is a remarkable type of yeast, highly flocculent, and working at a warm temperature of 25 degrees C/77F. Fermentation is rapid, lasting just two days, with the yeast remaining in suspension. It is removed by centrifuge. The magnificent bottle-conditioned **Guinness Original** (4.1 per cent ABV; 43 to 47 IBUs), available only in the Dublin area, is produced by blending wort with the fermented beer to create a second fermentation in the bottle. **Irish Draught Guinness** has the same strength and IBUs as the bottled beer. **Export Draught** for Europe is 5.0 per cent ABV, 45

Overleaf: *Guinness sign at Dan Foley's pub, Anascaul, Dingle Peninsula, Co Kerry*

GUINNESS
IS GOOD
FOR YOU
GUINNESS'S EXTRA STOUT
JAMES'S GATE DUBLIN

Beamish is one of the two main breweries in Cork

time of the first Arthur Guinness. Fresh stout is blended with beer that has been stored for between one and three months in unlined oak vats where it is attacked by wild *Brettanomyces* yeast – a beer known as "stale" in the eighteenth century. As a result, the finished beer (7.5 per cent ABV; 60+ IBUs), brewed from pale malt, 25 per cent flaked barley and 10 per cent roasted barley, has a magnificent unmistakable hint of sour fruit on the aroma that comes from the wild yeast fermentation.

Cork

The stout tradition is also carried on with great fervour by the two Cork breweries of Beamish and Murphy. Beamish and Crawford were Scottish Protestants who came south, bought an ale brewery on the banks of the River Lee and were brewing porter by 1792. The company's single X porter disappeared in the 1960s and it concentrates on just one version of stout. **Beamish Stout** (4.3 per cent ABV; 38–44 IBUs) is brewed from pale and dark malts, malted wheat, roasted barley and wheat syrup, and is hopped with Irish, German and Styrian varieties.

Murphy's Lady's Well Brewery across town from Beamish is on the site of a religious shrine that once supplied water for the brewery. James, William, Jerome and Frances Murphy, devout Catholics, built their brewery in 1856 and, in common with their rivals, produced porter as well as stout. Murphy's is now part of Heineken, which gives the stout a presence in Europe, in Britain through the Whitbread group – which brews it under licence – and in the USA. **Murphy's Stout** is 4.3 per cent ABV with 35–36 IBUs, and is brewed from pale and chocolate malts and roasted barley, with Target hops.

Irish ales and lagers

Stout accounts for 55 per cent of the Irish beer market. Ale has a 19 per cent share and the rest is lager. **Harp** (3.6 per cent ABV) is the dominant lager brand, owned by Guinness and brewed in Dundalk. It was one of the first major lager brands to build a large market share throughout the British Isles and is typical of the bland and heavily-carbonated lager beers developed in the 1960s and 1970s. Guinness also brews Harp in London and it is produced under licence by several other British

to 53 IBUs, has a pronounced hop aroma, dark and bitter malt in the mouth and a dry finish. Guinness exported to North America has the same IBUs as the European version but is higher in alcohol and has some fruit on the aroma and a characteristic hoppy finish.

Bottled Guinness brewed in Dublin for Belgium is 8.0 per cent ABV, IBUs around 50 and has ripe dark fruit on the aroma, great depth of hop, burnt raisins in the mouth and a long, bitter-sweet finish. But bottled **Foreign Extra Stout** puts even this remarkable beer in the shade. **FES**, as it is called, is a powerful link to the breweries. **Harp Export** (4.5 per cent ABV) is claimed to meet the demands of the German Purity Law, which means no cereal adjuncts or sugars can be used in the brewing process. The Dublin giant also owns the country's three ale brewers, Cherry's of Waterford, Macardle's of Dundalk and Smithwick's of Kilkenny. Smithwick's is the major ale producer, based on a site built by John Smithwick in 1710 in the ruins of a Franciscan abbey. The tower and nave of the abbey survive, surrounded by the modern brewery. **Smithwick's Draught** – sold as **Kilkenny Ale** outside Ireland – is firmly in the Celtic tradition, with roasted barley alongside pale malt and maltose syrup. A complex blend of Challenger, Golding, Northdown and Target is used and is added in three stages during the copper boil. It is 3.5 per cent ABV with 22 IBUs and has a creamy, malty, lightly fruity aroma with some dark fruit in the mouth and a bitter-sweet finish. Stronger versions are brewed for export, including a 5.2 per cent ABV for Germany. A fruity 5.0 per cent **Smithwick's Barley Wine** is brewed by **Macardle's**. The **Cherry's** and **Macardle's** draught ales are almost identical to Smithwick's.

NORTHERN IRELAND

In Northern Ireland stout from the republic is the main brand. Bass has a brewery in Belfast producing keg bitters including the highly successful "smooth" ale called Caffrey's. The only cask-conditioned ale on the island comes from Hilden, near Belfast, which produces a malty/fruity 3.8 per cent ABV **Hilden Ale**, a 3.9 per cent ABV porter and a 4.0 per cent ABV hoppy **Special** while Whitewater in Kilkeel, Co. Down, brews six beers, including a 3.9 per cent ABV **Best Bitter** and a 4.3 per cent **Wheat Stout**.

IRISH BREWERS

Beamish & Crawford, South Main Street, Cork.

Arthur Guinness & Son, St James's Gate, Dublin 8.

Hilden Brewery, Hilden House, Grand Street, Hilden, Lisburn, Co Antrim.

Murphy, Lady's Well Brewery, Leitrim Street, Cork.

E. Smithwick & Sons, St Francis Abbey Brewery, Kilkenny.

Whitewater Brewing Company, 40 Tullyframe Road, Kilkeel, Co. Down.

Smithwick's brewery in Kilkenny is one of Ireland's three ale brewers

LUXEMBOURG

The Grand Duchy of Luxembourg, with its small population of 350,000, is wedged between Belgium, France and Germany. Its influence is Germanic, and it brews mainly Pilsner type beers, but the country does not adhere to the *Reinheitsgebot*. There is often a high proportion of cereal adjuncts in its beers.

In Luxembourg city, Brasserie Réunies de Luxembourg brews under the names of Mousel, Clausen and Henri Funck. **Mousel Premium Pils** is 4.8 per cent ABV, brewed from 90 per cent pale malt and 10 per cent rice, and hopped with Hallertau and Saaz varieties (28.5 IBUs). It is lagered for five weeks, has a rich malt aroma with some delicate hops, is light and quenching in the mouth, and has some hop character in the finish. **Henri Funck Lager Beer** is brewed with an identical specification to the Mousel Pils. A 5.5 per cent ABV **Altmunster** is in the Dortmunder Export style, with a firm body and a good malty characteristic.

The Brasserie Nationale in Bascharage brews **Bofferding** (4.8 per cent ABV) from pale malt and corn (maize), with Hallertau Northern Brewer and selected aroma hops (25 IBUs). It is lagered for a month. It is a refreshing but rather thin beer with some light hops and malt on the aroma, a medium body, and a short, bitter-sweet finish. Diekirch, from the town of the same name, has an all-malt **Pils** with slightly more character than its rivals. Two tiny breweries, Simon at Wiltz, and Battin in Esch-sur-Alzette, produce occasional **Bocks** along with their **Pils**.

LUXEMBOURG BREWERS

Brasserie Nationale SA (Bofferding),
2 Boulevard John F. Kennedy, L-4930 Bascharage.
Brasserie Réunies de Luxembourg Mousel et Clausen SA,
BP 371, L-2013 Luxembourg-Clausen.

THE NETHERLANDS

Holland, as most of the world insists on calling the Netherlands, is so closely identified with Heineken that casual observers could be forgiven for thinking the Dutch drink nothing else. But prompted by the cross-border interest in Belgian speciality beers, the Dutch market is beginning to change. A number of microbrewers have appeared, producing Pilsners with rather more character than the brand leaders. Some micros are also brewing fascinating versions of ales, some based on old and long-forgotten Dutch styles. They have prompted the beer giants to widen their portfolios to brew brown, dark and Bock beers.

But the speciality beers are pebbles on the Dutch beach, and most of the beach is owned and controlled by Heineken. It not only accounts for well over half of the beer brewed and sold in the Netherlands but is a giant on the world market. As the Netherlands has a small population of around 14 million, all the leading brewers have turned to other markets to boost production and sales. Heineken produces more than 40 million hectolitres of beer a year from both its Dutch breweries and some 100 plants world-wide.

This powerful position is a long way removed from the origins of the Dutch company, though the origins were far from humble. In 1863 Gerard Adriaan Heineken bought De Hooiberg (the Haystack), the largest brewery in Amsterdam, with records going back to 1592. Such was his success that within a few years he built a second brewery and opened a third plant in Rotterdam in 1873.

In the Netherlands, Heineken had a curious on-off love affair for years with its great rival Amstel. In 1941 the two companies took over another leading Dutch brewery, Van Vollenhoven, and jointly managed it. But it was not until 1968 that Heineken and Amstel formerly merged. Amstel was founded in 1870 by C.A. de Peters and J. H. van Marwijk Kooy. The awe in which brewers held Munich beer can be seen in the original title of their company: "Beiersch Bierbrouwerij de Amstel" – the Bavarian Beer Brewery of the Amstel. Amstel is the name of the river that flows through Amsterdam.

The merger in 1968 was prompted by the incursion into the Netherlands the previous year by the large British group Allied Breweries, which had bought the second biggest Dutch brewery, Oranjeboom in Rotterdam. Heineken and Amstel were worried that Allied and other overseas brewers would snap up other Dutch companies and sought strength through merger. The view was heightened when Allied later acquired the Drie Hoefijzers (Three Horseshoes) brewery in Breda. But Allied had mixed fortunes in the Netherlands. It attempted to foist its undistinguished Skol lager brand on a largely unimpressed Dutch audience.

Dutch Pilsner

Heineken today has its headquarters in Amsterdam but no longer brews there. The old Haystack site is now a restaurant and hotel. The second brewery built by the founding Heineken near Museum Square is a visitors' centre with views of superb copper vessels and video shows depicting the history of the company.

Heineken Pilsner is 5.0 per cent ABV and, in keeping with all its pale lagers, has between 20 and 25 bitterness units. This enormously successful beer is something of a hybrid, a half-way house between a true Pilsner and the light-bodied international style. It has a delicate hop and malt aroma, a clean palate and a refreshing finish with some hop notes. **Amstel Bier** is also 5.0 per cent ABV, has a deeper golden colour and a fraction more hop character. These two beers are the ones by which the group is best known internationally. For its home market, Heineken also produces beers of considerably greater character. Amstel 1870 is also 5.0 per cent ABV but has a decidedly more hoppy edge while **Amstel Gold** (7.0 per cent ABV) is rich and fruity, balanced by great hop character.

The best Pilsners within the Heineken group come from the Brand Brewery, bought in 1989. It is the oldest brewery in the Netherlands, dating from the early fourteenth century, in the village of Wijlre, close to Maastricht – the present brewing site dates from 1743. In the 1970s Brand became the official supplier of beer to the Queen of the Netherlands and now calls itself the

The Amstel river, which flows through the heart of the Amsterdam, gives its name to a number brands

An advertisement for Heineken dating from the early 1950s

Royal Brand Brewery. Its **Brand Pils** is sold in North America in a white ceramic bottle and is called "Royal Brand Beer". It is the standard 5.0 per cent ABV and is brewed from 90 per cent pale malt made from two-row summer barley and 10 per cent maize grits. Hops are German Northern Brewer, Perle and Hersbrucker, achieving 26 to 28 IBUs. The beer is lagered for 42 days. It has a perfumy hop aroma, is malty and hoppy in the mouth followed by a firm, hoppy finish. **Brand-UP** is a premium 5.5 per cent Pilsner, not a soft drink despite the title (UP stands for "Urtyp Pilsner" – Original Pilsner). It is all-malt, uses Hersbrucker, Spalt and Tettnang hops and has an impressive 36 to 38 IBUs. It is lagered for up to 56 days.

The Brand beers are distinguished by their long lagering periods and the company's refusal to pasteurize them. The head brewer declares: "Pasteurization serves to lengthen the shelf-life of a beer but only marginally and at enormous costs to the taste and aroma of the beer".

The most characterful Pilsner in the Netherlands comes from the small St Christoffel Brewery in Roermond in Dutch Limburg. It is owned by Leo Brand, a member of the Brand family. He built his brewery in 1986 after studying brewing at Weihenstephan in Munich and then working in the German brewing industry. His brewery is named after the patron saint of Roermond, once a major coal-mining area, and is distinguished by a fine domed and brick-clad copper kettle which he found in a barn. Leo Brand's main product is **Christoffel Bier**, 5.1 per cent ABV, made only from barley malt, with Hallertau and Hersbrucker hops. It has 45 IBUs, a massive hop-resin aroma, a tingle of hops on the tongue and a big dry and bitter finish. The beer is not pasteurized and Mr Brand tells critics who claim his beer is too bitter with the riposte: "I am not brewing to please everyone!" The beer is also known as Blond and sub-titled Dubbel Hop to underscore the hoppy intent. He has introduced a "double malt" **Robertus** (6.0 per cent ABV) with a tinge of red in the colour from darker, Munich-type malt: the name comes from Robyn, the Dutch for Robin Redbreast. It is rich and malty with a dry finish.

The name of the company is Grolsche, the name of the beer is Grolsch and both derive from the ancient town of Grolle, now named Groenlo. Grolsche has a second brewery in nearby Enschede and both are in the region of Gelderland. Grolsche is a major Dutch brewer – the country's largest independent – with considerable overseas presence, sold in 40 countries and now brewed under licence in Britain by Bass. It is famous for the old-fashioned "swing-top" stoppered bottle that has become its international symbol.

Grolsch is called **Grolsch Pilsener** at home and **Grolsch Premium Lager** abroad. It is 5.0 per cent ABV, brewed from a complex blend of spring barley malts from Belgium, England, France, Germany and the Netherlands with a small proportion of maize (corn). Hops are Hallertau and Saaz, with aroma hops added at the end of the copper boil. The beer is lagered for 10 weeks and has 27 IBUs. It is not pasteurized, even for export.

Alfa is a small independent brewery in Limburg dating from 1870. Its **Edel (Noble) Pils** is 5.0 per cent ABV, an all-malt brew made from French and Dutch malts, with Hallertau, Saaz and Tettnang hops. It is lagered for two months but with just 19 IBUs it has only a light hop character.

Oranjeboom of Breda, now in the hands of Interbrew of Belgium, has a light interpretation of the Pilsner style (5.0 per cent ABV) and a drier version called **Oranjeboom Klassiek**. The range of beers is liable to change under new ownership but any improvement in beer character is less likely, given Interbrew's **Dommelsch Pilsener** (5.0 per cent ABV), another light beer from a plant in Dommelen.

The village of Gulpen near Maastricht is home to a highly-regarded independent, Gulpener, established in 1825. Its regular 5.0 per cent ABV **Gulpener Pilsener** is pleasant but unexciting. But the **Gulpener X-pert** premium Pils of the same strength is superb, an all-malt

brew bursting with Tettnang hop aroma and flavour with 35 IBUs.

Brown & dark beers

A few breweries produce dark lagers that bear some resemblance to the Dunkel beers of Munich and Bavaria. They are usually called Oud Bruin – Old Brown – and are around 3.5 per cent ABV, lightly hopped, smooth and easy drinking. Heineken has an everyday brown lager and a stronger, 4.9 per cent ABV **Heineken Special Dark** in some export markets. A new micro, Zeeuwse-Vlaamse in Flemish Zeeland, has a strong 6.0 per cent ABV **Zeeuwse-Vlaamse Bruine** while Gulpen and Grolsche have Oud Bruins in their ranges.

The Düsseldorf influence can be seen in a handful of Alt or Old ales. Arcense has a 5.0 per cent ABV **Altforster Alt**, amber-coloured, with a malty, slightly roasty aroma, thin palate and dry finish. (The same brewery has a warm-fermenting Kölsch-type beer called Stoom – Steam – Beer, also 5.0 per cent ABV, using a blend of barley and wheat malts, Northern Brewer and Hersbruck hops – 22 IBUs – with fruity and peppery hop aromas and flavours.) Grolsche introduced an Alt in the late 1980s called **Amber** (5.0 per cent ABV) with a malty

Heineken has one of the most recognizable logos in the beer world

aroma but growing hop character in the big palate and long dry finish. De Leeuw – the Lion – Brewery in Valkenberg, near Maastricht, has **Venloosch Alt** (4.5 per cent ABV) with plenty of dark and roasted malt character. The Us Heit – "Our Father" – micro in Dutch Friesland, founded in a cow shed in 1985, has a 6.0 per cent ABV **Buorren Bier**, copper-coloured, fruity and dry: not strictly an Alt but it fits most easily into the category. The energetic Budels Brewery has a 5.5 per cent ABV **Budels Alt** with massive peppery hops on the aroma, dark chocolate and malt in the mouth, and a deep, dry and intensely bitter finish with some fruit and toffee.

Dutch "Dorts"

The proximity of Dortmund to the Netherlands created great interest in the rounded, malty beers of the great German city. The style has been shortened to the simple expostulatory "Dort" in the Netherlands. Gulpener has a 6.5 per cent ABV **Gulpener Dort**, brewed from pale malt, maize and caramel – hardly *Reinheitsgebot!* – with Hallertau hops. It has 20 IBUs and is lagered for 10 weeks.

Alfa's **Super-Dortmunder** has a redoubtable 7.0 per cent ABV. The beer is ripe and fruity with a clean but sweet finish. De Ridder in Maastricht is owned by Heineken but is given considerable independence. With Dortmund close at hand, this handsome brewery overlooking the river Maas – the Meuse in France and the Mosel in Germany – makes a Dort called **Maltezer** (6.5 per cent ABV) a name that for British drinkers conjures up the image of small chocolate-covered sweets but which is a fruity lager, smooth from the malt and with good hop character in the long finish. De Leeuw produces Super Leeuw (5.9 per cent ABV), rich and malty, becoming dry in the finish.

Bocks

The major revivalist beer style in the Netherlands is Bock or Bok. As in Germany, the word means billy-goat and the potent animal features on several labels. For years Bok meant a dark and sweet beer which had little connection with the well-crafted German versions. From the late 1980s Bok has undergone a transformation. Bok beers come in many colours; some are warm-fermented, others are lagered. Strengths vary to accommodate Dubbel Boks and Meiboks.

Brand has an impressive **Imperator**, which should be a double with such a name but is brewed all year round and is a single Bock of great quality. It is all-malt, using pale, chocolate and Munich malts with Hallertau, Hersbrucker and Perle hops (6.5 per cent ABV; 22 IBUs). A 7.5 per cent ABV **Brand Dubbelbock** is a winter beer with a tempting port-wine colour, fruity and malty. The spring **Brand Meibock** (7.0 per cent ABV) has a spicy aroma, a citric fruit palate and more spice in the finish.

The Drie Ringen Brewery in Amersfoort makes a 6.6 per cent ABV warm-fermenting **Drie Ringen Bokbier**, amber-coloured, packed with ripe fruit and gentle hops and a 6.5 per cent ABV **Drie Ringen Meibok**. Interbrew's Dommelsch subsidiary produces a 6.5 per cent ABV **Dommelsch Bokbier**, dry with light fruit. Its Dominator suggests it should be a double but is lower in alcohol (6.0 per cent ABV) than the Bok and is fruity in the mouth. Drie Horne in Kaatsheuvel brews a 7.0 per cent ABV **Drie Horne Bokbier** that is warm fermenting and conditioned in the bottle with a dry, fruity and peppery hop character.

A taste of an old-fashioned Dutch Bok comes from arch-traditionalist Grolsche. It is 6.5 per cent ABV, dark, sweet and potable. Its **Grolsche Mei Bok** (6.0 per cent ABV) is amber coloured and much drier, with a good balance of fruit and hops. Heineken has an **Amstel Bock** (7.0 per cent ABV), dark, malty and chewy. Its **Heineken Tarewebok**, also 7.0 per cent ABV, has 17 per cent wheat in its grist and is smooth and fruity with chocolate notes from dark malt. The Lindeboom (Linden Tree) independent in Neer, Limburg, has two Boks: a 6.5 per cent ABV **Lindeboom Bockbier**, dark, dry and bitter, and **Lindeboom Meibock** (7.0 per cent ABV), amber-coloured, bitter-sweet and fruity. Maasland, a micro in Oss, brews warm-fermenting, bottle-conditioned beers of great character and integrity. Its 7.5 per cent ABV **Maasland MeiBockbier** bursts with dark fruit, malt and resiny hops. A 6.5 per cent **Maasland SummerBock** is amber coloured, hopped with Hallertau and German Brewers' Gold, rich, spicy and chocolatey.

Ales

Dutch ale was once as rare as a lofty hill in the Netherlands. But brewers are losing their fear of warm-fermentation and are re-creating ales of quality and character.

For decades the ale flag was flown by the country's single surviving Trappist brewery near Tilburg. The abbey is called Koningshoeven, a name meaning "King's Garden" – the land was a gift to the monks from royalty.

The brewery has had a chequered history since the end of the Second World War. It was bought by Stella Artois but the monks then raised the money to buy the brewery back from Stella. They had, with great prescience, held on to their brewing equipment and their top-fermenting yeast strain.

Today their beers, all labelled La Trappe, are made from pale, Munich and other coloured malts, with Hallertau and English Goldings hops. **La Trappe Dubbel** (6.5 per cent ABV) has a tawny appearance with a superb Muscat aroma and palate underscored by peppery hops. The 8.0 per cent ABV bronze-coloured **La Trappe Tripel** has a big Goldings aroma and a spicy palate and finish. **La Trappe Quadrupel** (10.0 per cent ABV) is an annual autumn vintage, reddish in colour with a smooth palate that belies the rich alcohol. In 1995 the abbey launched a new pale **La Trappe Enkel** (Single), at 5.5 per cent ABV, dry, quenching and hoppy.

In Amsterdam ale brewing has been put firmly on the map by the 't IJ brewpub. It was opened in 1984 by songwriter Kaspar Peterson in an old bath house beneath a windmill. The name of the brew-pub is an elaborate pun. The IJ is the name of the waterway that fronts Amsterdam harbour. The pronunciation of IJ – "ay" – is virtually identical to the Dutch for egg, which explains the ostrich and an egg on the pub sign. In the sign's background, a windmill standing in a desert suggests that Amsterdam was a beer desert until Kaspar Peterson started to brew.

't IJ brews 10 beers but they are not all available at the same time. **Natte**, meaning "wet", is a 6.5 per cent ABV brown ale in the style of a Belgian dubbel. Zatte (8.0 per cent ABV) means "drunk" and is in the tripel style, pale, with a spicy, hoppy character. **Columbus's Egg** (9.0 per cent ABV), is cloudy bronze in colour with a deep winey aroma, citric fruit in the mouth and more fruit in the finish. **Struis**, also 9.0 per cent ABV, is the Dutch for ostrich and is spicy, fruity and dry. The

brewery also produces an autumn Bok, beers for New Year and the spring, an English-style bitter and Vlo, "flea beer".

A second enterprising brewpub in Amsterdam was opened in 1992 by two brothers, Albert and Casper Hoffman. While 't IJ is a plain and utilitarian bar, the Brouwhuis Maximiliaan is smart and comfortable, based in a former convent near the city's infamous Red Light district. The beers, unfiltered and unpasteurized, include a Belgian-style Abbey ale, **Kloosterbier** (7.5 per cent ABV), a Cologne-style Kölsch, a 7.5 per cent ABV Tripel, a Winter Warmer and a spring Märzen. The Hoffmans have worked with a Canadian, Derek Walsh, now based in the Netherlands, to brew a recreation of a London porter (4.5 per cent ABV), ruby red in colour with a dark malt, hops and spices aroma, a spicy and bitter palate, and bitter chocolate on the finish.

Drie Ringen's Hopfenbier (5.0 per cent ABV) has, as the name suggests, a powerful hop character to offset rich and fruity maltiness. 't Kuipertje (the Little Kettle) in Herwijnen brews a similarly fruity/hoppy pale ale called **Lingewal Vriendenbier** and a strong and ripely fruity **Nicks** (7.0 per cent ABV). Maasland's **D'n Schele Os** means the Dizzy Bull (7.5 per cent ABV) with a label showing a cross-eyed bull suffering over-consumption of this strong pale ale made from barley malt, rye, wheat, spices and hops with a marvellously rich, complex spicy, hoppy and fruity palate and finish. An Easter Bunny beer, **Paasbier** (6.5 per cent ABV) is also spicy, spritzy from hops and with delicious chocolate notes from the use of dark malt.

Budels produces Parel (6.0 per cent ABV) a golden ale with great hop character, malt and vanilla in the mouth and a bitter-sweet finish. Its **Capucijn** (6.5 per cent ABV) is an Abbey-style beer, deep brown, with a nutty aroma and some resiny hops, sultana fruit in the mouth and bitter-sweet finish.

Even Heineken is experimenting with an ale. It refuses to allow top-fermenting yeasts to come anywhere near its Dutch breweries and is test-marketing **Kylian** (6.5 per cent ABV), brewed by its French subsidiary Pelforth, in Lille. It is the same beer as George Killian's Irish Red Ale, sold on the French market, and is smooth but tart with a gentle hop character. (Killian's brewery was in Enniscorthy but closed in 1956.)

Wheat beers

De Ridder (the Knight) in Maastricht has a wheat beer as its main product. **Wieckse Witte** (5.0 per cent ABV) is packed with tart, lemon and spices characteristics and is deliciously refreshing. Wiecske comes from the same Saxon root as the English wick and means a settlement. The brewery is in an area of Maastricht known as the Wieckse.

The Raaf Bierbrouwerij (Raven Brewery) started life as a farmhouse, brewery and maltings at Heumen near Nijmegen in the 1700s, closed in the 1920s and re-opened in 1984. It was bought by Allied Breweries' Oranjeboom subsidiary, which busily promoted its spicy and tart **Raaf Witbier** (5.0 per cent ABV). Raaf also brewed a dubbel, a tripel and a Bok but Allied closed the brewery and the future of the beers is now in the hands of Interbrew. Whether Witbier survives will depend on whether Interbrew sees it as a threat to its heavily-marketed Hoegaarden wheat beer. Arcen has **Arcener Tarwe** (5.0 per cent ABV), brewed from a 50:50 blend of barley and wheat malts, and Hallertau Northern Brewer and Hersbruck hops. It has 17 IBUs and uses a Bavarian wheat beer yeast culture. There is a delicious aroma of cidery apples, with more tart fruit in the mouth and a bitter-sweet finish. De Drie Horne has a powerful 7.0 per cent ABV **De Drie Horne** Wit, darker than is usual, sweet and fruity. **De Leeuw's Witbier** (4.8 per cent ABV) is packed with spices and tart fruit.

Old ale

Gulpener has recreated a long-lost speciality of the Limburg area with its **Mestreechs Aajt** (old dialect for Maastricht Old). It is fermented by wild yeasts, based on a style last seen in the 1930s. The wort (made from pale malt and brewing sugar, hopped with Hallertau: 10 IBUs) is exposed to the atmosphere until it is attacked by *Brettanomyces* yeast and *lactobacilli*. The wort is then stored in unlined wooden casks for a year or more while a secondary fermentation takes place. It is then blended with the brewery's dark lager. This complex and fascinating beer (3.5 per cent ABV) has a sweet and sour aroma with hints of cherry fruit, sour in the mouth with a dry and bitter finish.

Stout

Arcener Stout (6.5 per cent ABV) is genuinely warm-fermenting, brewed from pale, chocolate, Munich and coloured malts, with Hallertau Northern Brewer and Hersbruck hops (27 IBUs). It has rich malt and chocolate aromas, coffee and chocolate in the mouth and a dry and bitter finish. **Heineken's Van Vollenhoven Stout** (6.0 per cent ABV) is cold-fermented. The name comes from the Amsterdam brewery founded in 1733 and closed after it was bought by Heineken and Amstel. Its complexity and fruitiness would increase if Heineken took the plunge and converted it to a true ale, fermented with a top-working yeast.

DUTCH BREWERS

Adbij Koningshoeven, Trappistenbierbrouwerij de Schaapskooi, Eindhovensweg 3, 5056 RP Berkel-Eschot.

Alfa Bierbrouwerij, Thull 15-19, 6365 AC Schinnen.

Amersfoort De Drie Ringen Bierbrouwerij, Kleine Spui 18, 3811 BE Amersfoort.

Arcense Bierbrouwerij BV, Kruisweg 44, 5944 EN Arcen.

Koninklijke Brand Bierbrouwerij BV, Brouwerijstraat 2, Postbus 1, 6300 AA Wijlre.

Brouwhuis Maximiliaan, Kloveniersburgwal 6-8, Amsterdam.

Budelse Brouwerij, Nieuwstraat 9, 6021 HP Budel.

Dommelsche Bierbrouwerij, Brouwerijplein 84, 5551 AE Dommelen.

De Drie Horne Bierbrouwerij, Berndijksestraat 63, 5171 BB Kaatsheuvel.

Grolsche Bierbrouwerij, Eibergseweg 10, 7141 CE Groenlo/Fazanstraat 2, 7523 EA Enschede.

Gulpener Bierbrouwerij, Rijksweg 16, 6271 AE Gulpen.

Heineken Nederland NV, Postbus 28, 1000 Amsterdam.

't IJ Brouwerij, Funenkade 7, 1018 AL Amsterdam.

't Kuipertje, Waaldijk 127, 4171 CC Herwijnen.

De Leeuw Bierbrouwerij, Pater Beatrixsingel 2, 6301 VL Valkenberg an den Geul.

De Lindeboom Bierbrouwerij BV, Engelmanstraat 52-54, 6086 BD Neer.

Maaslandbrouwerij, Kantsingel 14, 5349 AJ Oss.

Oranjeboom Verenigde Bierbrouwerij Breda-Rotterdam, Ceresstraat 13, 4811 CA Breda.

De Ridder Brouwerij BV Oeverwal 3-9, 6221 EN Maastricht.

St Christoffel Bierbrouwerij, Bredeweg 14, 6042 GG Roermond.

US Heit Bierbrouwerij, Buorren 25, 8624 TL Uitwellingerga.

SCANDINAVIA

History is hard to hide. While the Scandinavians attempt to control drinking by heavy taxation, and restrictions on strength and availability, the image of roistering Vikings downing foaming tankards of beer contains a germ of truth. Beer has a long, deep-rooted history in these lands of the far north. Home-brewing and distilling are major craft industries in rural communities while the Finns still make sahti, a rye, oats and barley beer flavoured with juniper. Sahti and similar home-brewed beers go back for around a thousand years. The Vikings brewed a barley-based beer they called aul and handed down, via the Finnish olut, the Swedish öl and the Danish ol, the universal term ale for a warm-fermenting beer. Today there are a few dark beers, both warm and cold fermenting, but Scandinavia is firmly in the lager camp where its mainstream beers are concerned.

DENMARK

Denmark is a country with a population of five million. In common with Heineken of The Netherlands and Stella Artois of Belgium, the largest Danish brewing group has had to turn itself into an international giant to achieve success. For many beer drinkers, Carlsberg is as quintessentially Danish as Hans Christian Andersen and his Little Mermaid.

The great brewing dynasty was founded by Christian Jacobsen, a farmer with brewing skills who arrived in Copenhagen from Jutland in 1801. Within 10 years he had saved sufficient money to rent his own brewery where he made wheat beers. He quickly decided that science and technology had to become the allies of modern brewing. When his son, Jacob Christian Jacobsen, heard of the experiments in lager brewing going on in Bavaria, he made the long and arduous coach journey to Munich and went to work with Gabriel Sedlmayr at the Spaten Brewery.

Jacobsen was fired with enthusiasm for the new beer and determined to brew it in Denmark. When he reached home he made a beer in his mother's wash-tub using the Munich yeast and then turned to making lager beer commercially.

His first lager beers were, like those in Munich, dark brown in colour and were well received. He inherited money on his mother's death and built a new brewery outside Copenhagen. It was on a hill – berg in Danish – and Jacobsen named it after his son, Carl. From that simple conjunction of words a legend was born.

The first beers from the new brewery appeared in 1847. They were a great success. Within a decade or two, Jacobsen built a second brewery alongside the old one. It was dubbed "New Carlsberg" and was run by his son, Carl. It was not so much a brewery as an architect's dream, gleaming copper vessels set amid cool tiling and bronze sculptures, all fronted by the world-famous elephant gates modelled on the Minerva Square obelisk in Rome.

In 1875 Jacobsen created the Carlsberg Laboratories that carried out research in brewing technique. He hired a young scientist, Emil Hansen, who isolated the first pure single-cell yeast culture, one of the major breakthroughs in brewing practice. Both the Old Carlsberg brewery and the rival Tuborg plant had been experiencing problems with their beers. Hansen proved that the cause in both cases was multi-strain yeasts which contained bad strains as well as good. By isolating the good strains he was able to allow them to produce beers of consistent quality.

Carlsberg and Tuborg merged in 1970 to form United Breweries, although the Tuborg brewery closed in the mid-1990s.

Overseas Carlsberg and Tuborg are both identified by pale, clean, quenching but undemanding versions of the Pilsner style. At home they have a wider portfolio. The main Carlsberg brand is a 4.7 per cent **Carlsberg Pilsner** that is often referred to as Hof from the Danish for "Court". It is a well-balanced and refreshing beer with a malty edge, but lacking great hop character. Let – "Light" – **Pilsner** is a mere 2.8 per cent ABV and is typical of the thin lagers produced throughout Scandinavia to deter over-consumption of strong alcohol. At the other end of the scale, the 5.8 per cent **Carlsberg Black Gold** is a big, buttery-malty beer of considerable character.

The entrance to the famous Carlsberg Brewery, on a hill – literally Carl's berg – just outside Copenhagen

Tuborg was founded in 1873. The brewery launched a pale lager in 1875, the result of research in Germany by head brewer Hans Bekkevold. Its main pale beers today are in the same strength range as Carlsberg's. The best-selling beer is **Tuborg Green**, which takes its name from the colour of the label, similar to Carlsberg Hof but with a shade more hop character. **Tuborg Gold Label**, at the top of the range, has a good balance of malt and hops. **Tuborg Classic**, 4.8 per cent ABV, was brewed to commemorate 100 years of brewing, and has a deep golden colour.

Both companies produce characterful dark beers. Carlsberg has a cold-fermenting beer called **Gammel** ("old"), **Porter and Imperial Stout** – all on one label. It is not a mistake, for the early stouts were called porter stouts and one constituent element of them was a well-aged old or "stale" beer. It is an impressive 7.7 per cent ABV with rich dark fruit, bitter coffee and scorched vanilla notes. Tuborg's porter is similar with a creamy palate and dry finish, dominated by burnt malt and dark fruit. Carlsberg recalls its origins with **Gamle**, a Munich-style dark lager (4.2 per cent ABV), smooth and chocolatey, and Tuborg has a similar beer called **Tuborg Red Label**. Seasonal beers include two for Easter, Carlsberg and Tuborg **Paskebryg** (7.8 per cent ABV), red-gold in colour, and similarly coloured Christmas beers, **Julebryg** (5.5 per cent ABV).

Several Danish brewers produce beers they call Bock in the German style. Carlsberg makes no such claim for its **Elephant** but this rich, malty-sweet, dangerously drinkable beer falls into the category. Named after the brewery's elephant gates, it is 7.5 per cent ABV and is made from pale malt and brewing sugar, with Hallertau hops (38 IBUs). Carlsberg does not declare the lagering period for the beer but its smoothness implies considerably more time than that given to its **Carlsberg Special Brew** (8.9 per cent ABV), brewed by its English subsidiary in Northampton. Like an ageing boxer, the beer punches its weight, but is short on style and easily falls flat on its face. It is heavy and syrupy.

United Breweries controls around 80 per cent of the Danish beer market and owns two subsidiaries, **Wiibroe** and **Neptun**. Wiibroe was founded in 1840 at Elsinor, scene of Shakespeare's *Hamlet*, and even brewed a beer under the Hamlet name. It now makes a light lager (3.6 per cent ABV) but concentrates on low-alcohol products. Its one beer of note is an **Imperial Stout** (6.5 per cent ABV), similar to Carlsberg's. Neptun does not brew in the conventional sense: Carlsberg supplies it with wort which it turns into beer.

The second biggest Danish group is Ceres, in the old university town of Aarhus in Jutland. Its brands include those from another Jutland brewery, Thor. United Breweries also has a small stake in the company. Ceres has a splendid, cold-fermenting dark beer called **Ceres Porter** and **"Stowt"** – a phonetic spelling to help Danish consumers – with the subsidiary tag of **Gammel Jysk**, which means "old Jutland". It is 7.7 per cent ABV, brewed with Munich as well as pale malt, and is delightfully spicy, slightly oily and darkly fruity with hints of liquorice. Ceres also brews a golden lager called **Red Eric,** in honour of the Viking who discovered Greenland and brewed beer there to celebrate. The group has a strong lager of 7.7 per cent ABV, **Dansk Dortmunder**, with a strong nod across the border to the

home of German Export, which is also sold as **Ceres Special Brew Export Lager** and has a malt and pear drops aroma, a creamy/malty palate and a long, bitter-sweet finish. It makes a rich, sweetish Ceres **Christmas Beer** (5.8 per cent ABV). With a name like Thor, Ceres's partner has to brew a strong lager – it is called **Buur**, an old Danish dialect word for beer (7.6 per cent ABV).

Albani, based on the island of Odense, has cashed in on the success of Carlsberg's Elephant with a 6.9 per cent **Giraf**, sweet and yeasty. The strongly independent Faxe achieved cult status in the 1970s with its **Faxe Fad**, a "draught" beer in a bottle, meaning the beer was not pasteurized. It too has a strong lager in the Export style which it sold in Britain in cans under the risible title of **The Great Dane**. Its 5.0 per cent mainstream Pils has a delicate malt, hops and vanilla aroma, a firm-bodied, malty palate and a gently hoppy finish.

NORWAY

Taxation on beer is steep in Norway. In a blinkered approach to drinking problems, the government increased taxes on beer in the 1980s more steeply than on wine and spirits. It is impossible to find beers of more than around 4.5 per cent ABV, which tends to reinforce the production of Pilsner-style lagers. Stronger beers are made mainly for export.

The country's brewers persevere, despite the prohibitionist attitudes of politicians and bureaucrats. As well as pale lagers, there are some Bocks, summer beers, Christmas beers and Munich Dunkels, rendered respectively in Norwegian as Bokkol, Summerol, Jule Ol, and Bayerol. Beers in the Dortmunder Export style are known as "Gold Beer". The country has its own version of the German Purity Law, which means the beers are all-malt, clean, rounded and quenching. Brewers tend to fully attenuate their beers, leaving them dry and crisp.

In Oslo, the major brewing group of Ringnes brews some dry, rounded, malt-accented beers. **Frydenlund** has tart, hoppy offerings. Close to Oslo, the Aass Brewery in Drammen dates from 1834 and is still independent and family-owned. Aass means a summit and is pronounced "orss". The brewery produces a conventional but high quality **Aass Pilsner**, a 6.0 per cent Christmas beer and a rich, malty, firm-bodied **Amber** of the same strength. Its 6.1 per cent **Aass**

Bokkol is dark, rich and creamy, with a slightly tart finish, and is matured for between five and six months.

Mack of Tromsø is 300 kilometres inside the Arctic Circle and is the most northerly brewery in the world. Its **Artic Lager** (4.5 per cent ABV) is pale gold with a pronounced vanilla/toffee aroma, hoppy in the mouth and with a tart, refreshing finish. It also brews a stronger (6.0 per cent ABV) **Gold**, a dark and tasty **Bayer** and a rich **Bokkol**.

SWEDEN

The Swedes are troubled more than their neighbours by anxieties over the pleasures and problems of consuming alcohol. As a result beer is taxed to the hilt, to such an extent that scores of smaller breweries have been driven out of business. Beer sold in pubs and bars cannot exceed 3.6 per cent ABV. Stronger beers can only be bought in state shops and restaurants at daunting prices. Confusingly for the consumer, and especially for visitors, beers of the same name are produced in both Class II and Class III strengths, 3.6 and 5–5.6. As in all countries that have attempted to suppress alcohol, production has been concentrated into fewer and fewer hands until there are only three breweries of size left.

The biggest by far is Pripps, founded in Gothenburg in 1828 by Albrecht Pripps. It merged with Stockholm Breweries in 1964 but retained the old family name. Its mainstream lager is called **Pripps' Bla**, which is not a critical noise but means blue. It is a sweetish, malt-accented beer with a buttery palate and some light citric fruit in the finish. It is called **Pripps' Fatöl** when sold in draught form. Pripps brews several light lagers under different labels. The most characterful is **Royal**, an all-malt Pilsner bursting with Hallertau hops on the aroma and finish. Pripps' most interesting beers are the darker ones: a malty Munich dark called **Black & Brown**, a warm, rounded, nutty Christmas beer **Julöl**, and a coppery, hoppy **Dart**. But the stand-out beer is **Carnegie Porter**. This intriguing beer dates back to 1836 when a young Scottish brewer named David Carnegie opened a brewery in Gothenburg, one of many Scots who sought work in Scandinavia and the Baltic states. Although interest in the beer has waned over the years, Pripps, to its credit, never turned its collective back on the brand. Even though the group

has closed the specialist brewery that produced it, it is still properly warm-fermented in the main brewery near Stockholm. Interest has risen in recent years and Pripps is giving it some promotion. It has launched a vintage-dated version every year that has six months' maturation in the brewery and is then bottle-matured for the same period. Although the beer is then filtered and pasteurized, it does improve slightly over time, developing what the brewers call a "port-like" note. The 3.5 per cent version is pleasant but the 5.6 one, restored in 1985 after years of abandonment, is superb with a dark malt aroma reminiscent of Dundee cake – appropriate given the origins of the founder – a cappuccino coffee palate and a finish that becomes dry with more dark malt and hops developing. It won a gold medal at Brewex, the international brewing exhibition held in 1992 in England's Burton-on-Trent, for the best foreign stout in the show: the award was given by British judges – quite an accolade.

Spendrup in the Stockholm suburbs, with splendid views over a tree-fringed lake, is the result of a merger between several old-established companies in an attempt to survive both the prohibitionist tendencies of the government and the might of Pripps. From a handsome and traditional brewhouse it produces a malty, flavoursome **Spendrup Premium** and a **Spendrup Old Gold** of quite outstanding quality. Old Gold, in its 5.0 per cent form, has a rich malt and vanilla aroma, a quenching citric fruit palate and an intensely dry and bitter finish. It is a world-class lager beer.

Falken Breweries of Falkenberg is owned by the world giant agribusiness Unilever. The brewery was founded in 1896 by a spring of natural pure water and has never moved from the spot. It uses the Anglicized spelling of Falcon for its beers which include a **Bayerskt Munich Dark** and a sweetish Julöl Christmas beer. Warby, which has fine breweries with burnished copper vessels at Varby and Solleftea, is a co-operative owned by Swedish retail shops. Its beers are rounded and full-bodied. The small Till company is famous for a pale lager with good hops and fruit notes called Sailor.

FINLAND

The Finns are a fiercely independent people who have, to their chagrin, been ruled at various times by the

SCANDINAVIAN BREWERS

Carlsberg Brewery, 100 Vesterfaelledvej DK 1799, Copenhagen.

P. Lauritz Aass, PO Box 1107, Drammen, Norway 3001.

Oy Hartwall AB, PO Box 31, SF-00391 Helsinki.

Swedes and the Russians. In spite of a long period of prohibition that lasted from the turn of the century until 1932, the country has a proud brewing record that labours under the same restrictions as its Scandinavian neighbours. Beers are available in four classes and only the weakest Class I versions can be advertised.

The oldest brewery in Finland was built by a Russian, Nikolai Sinebrychoff, in 1819 to produce porter and other warm-fermenting beers. By 1853 it had switched to cold-fermentation.

After the Second World War Koff Porter, one of the brewery's original beers, was reintroduced. The brewers were keen to make it in the true warm-fermenting fashion but they didn't possess an ale yeast. They claim they saved the yeast from a bottle of Dublin-brewed Guinness and made a culture which is still going strong today. **Koff Porter** is made only in the strongest Finnish bracket at 7.2 per cent and is the most powerful beer produced in the country. It is made from four malts and is hopped with German Northern Brewer and Hersbruck varieties (50 IBUs). It is conditioned in the brewery for six weeks and is then pasteurized. In common with Pripps of Sweden's Carnegie Porter, the brewery is now producing a vintage version in a fine club-shaped bottle.

Sinebrychoff – the Finns shorten it to Koff for convenience and to mark a long-nurtured distrust of the Russians – brews a strong lager named in honour of the founder Nikolai, a reddish **Jouloulot Christmas beer** of around 5.0 per cent ABV and a copper-coloured ale type beer called **Cheers**, which is cold-fermented. A 6.8 per cent **Extra Strong Export Lager** – perfumy, sweetly malty – is sold only for export and on ferries to Sweden. It is aimed at the Carlsberg Elephant market.

Hartwall has three breweries, including one in the major city of Turku and another in remote Lapland. **Lapin Kulta** is 5.3 per cent ABV, is brewed from pale malt and some unmalted cereals and hopped with Hallertau and Saaz varieties. Brewing liquor comes from a fjord.

The beer is lagered for an impressive six months and has a smooth malty aroma, bitter-sweet malt and hops in the mouth and some light citric fruit in the finish. Hartwall produces other lagers under the Aura and Karjala labels. Its most interesting brew is a **Weizen Fest** wheat beer, the only one in Finland, made to a recipe devised by Sigl of Austria and using an Austrian yeast.

The small Olvi Brewery produces a Bavarian Märzen style beer called **Vaakuna** (5.5 per cent ABV) with a big malty aroma and palate.

Great interest has been aroused in recent years by the revival of sahti, the traditional rustic beer style of Finland. The basic cereal used in sahti is rye, which gives the finished drink a tart and spicy character. Oats are also used, as is barley malt for its enzymes and husk. Hops are used sparingly, and then mainly for their antiseptic qualities: the main seasoning comes from juniper berries. **Sahti** was made for centuries as part of the natural way of rural life, using saunas to kiln the grains. The mash is filtered through juniper twigs and then fermented, often using the household's bread yeast.

Perhaps as part of the worldwide revival of traditional brews, several small commercial breweries in Finland are now making sahti, though they tend to use more barley malt and less rye as a result of problems of mashing with the dark, huskless grain. The Lammin Sahti Brewery is the best known and sells the beer in a container like a wine box. It is around 8.0 per cent alcohol, has a hazy copper colour and a winey, spicy, aromatic "nose" and palate.

ICELAND

Iceland has just one brewery for its small population of 200,000. Tongue in cheek, the company is called **Polar Beer** and brews a good Pilsner-style of the same name (5.3 per cent ABV) and a low-gravity brew rather oddly called Märzen.

SOUTHERN EUROPE

ITALY

The Italians have discovered beer. Or rather young Italians, concerned with "la bella figura" – life style – have decided that beer is the drink of the moment. They leave wine to their fuddy-duddy parents. In Milan and Rome there are bars and even replicas of English pubs specializing in beer. British brewers have responded by exporting enthusiastically to Italy. Other overseas brewers have moved into the Italian market by acquisition as well as exports. Kronenbourg-BSN of France has a stake in the biggest Italian brewing group, Peroni. Heineken owns Peroni's main rival, Moretti. Wünster, founded in the nineteenth century by a Bavarian aristocrat, Heinrich von Wünster, is also part of the Belgian Interbrew group, while Poretti belongs to Carlsberg.

Anton Dreher, the great Viennese brewer, opened a brewery in Northern Italy in the 1860s. Today a brewery bearing his name is owned by the omnipresent Heineken. While the ghost of Dreher would be less than impressed by the thinnish lagers brewed in his name he might be amused by McFarland, an attempt at a Celtic "Red Ale", which attempts to cash in on Italian interest in Scotland and its malt whiskies but which unintentionally pays homage to Dreher's "Vienna red" style. **McFarland** (5.5 per cent ABV) is cold-fermented and lacks the rounded and fruity character it seeks to emulate, but the company deserves some praise for effort.

Poretti of Varese, to the north of Milan, has also brought some much-needed variety and innovation to the Italian beer market with its **Splügen Fumée**, a multi-lingual beer using smoked malt from Franconia in Bavaria – Splügen is the name of a mountain pass. The beer has a light but evident hint of smokiness on aroma and palate. Poretti also brews a rich, slightly fruity and vinous strong lager called **Splügen Red** (7.0 per cent ABV) and a German-style Bock of 6.0 per cent.

The most characterful beers are brewed by Moretti, due as much to the labels of the beers as to the contents of the glass. The brewery is famous for its image of a man in a fedora hat and large drooping moustache sipping a glass of beer. Moretti was founded in Udine to the north of Venice in 1859 when the region of Friuli was still annexed to the Austro-Hungarian empire. The Austrian connection lingers on in **La Rossa** – the Red – an all-malt beer of 7.5 per cent and 24 IBUs, made from pale malt and 10 per cent darker Munich malt. **La Bruna** (6.25 per cent ABV) is in the style of a Munich Dunkel, malty, smooth, with hints of roasted grain and chocolate. Moretti also has in **Sans Souci** (4.5 per cent ABV) an interpretation of the German Export style, with a firm malty body and a perfumy hop aroma. The company's main brand, **Birra Friulana**, is marketed as an "Italian Pilsner" – at least the spelling is correct – made from pale malt and 30 per cent maize (corn). A restaurant next to the brewery's offices sells in the winter an unfiltered and more aggressively hopped version of the beer called **Integrale** – whole.

Market leader Peroni's main brand is **Nastro Azzuro** – Blue Riband. Brewed from Alexis and Prisma pale malts, with 20 per cent maize, and hopped with Saaz, it is 5.3 per cent ABV and is lagered for 10 weeks. Peroni also brews a similar beer called **Raffo**, named after one of many breweries it has acquired. The company was founded in 1846 in Vigevano and soon moved to Rome. It has plants strategically placed throughout the country and in the 1960s it opened three state-of-the-art breweries in Bari, Rome and Padua. Its **Gran Riserva** (6.6 per cent ABV) is a pale bock style beer with a rich malt and hops character.

In the Italian region of South Tyrol and close to the Austrian border, the Forst (Forest) Brewery has not only labels but even its address – Lagundo/Algund – in both Italian and German. **Forst Pils** (4.8 per cent ABV) is brewed from pale malt and maize and hopped with Hallertau (30 IBUs). Forst also produces a 5.0 per cent

---

ITALIAN BREWERS

Birra Forst SPA/Brauerei Forst AG, Via val Venosata 8, 1-39022 Lagundo.
Birra Moretti SPA, Viale Venezia 9, 33100 Udine.
Birra Peroni Industriale SPA, GA Guattini 6/A, 00161 Rome.

Forst Kronen in the Export style and a 6.5 per cent **Forst Sixtus** made from pale, chocolate and crystal malts that – as the name implies – is in the Trappist/Abbey tradition.

Choice for Italian drinkers improved in the late 1990s with the emergence of a number of brewpubs and micro breweries in the north of the country in such towns and cities as Cremona, Milan and Udine. Several produce ales as well as lagers and several are influenced by Belgian and British styles. Half a dozen are grouped together under the title of Union Birra. More information is available from Guido Taraschi on 0335 426246 or 0372 33267.

SPAIN

Spain has a long association with beer. When the Romans marched through the Iberian peninsula, they were impressed by local intoxicants made from soaked grain. Flemish and German members of the court of Charles V set up the first commercial Spanish breweries. The Spanish beer market was closed to outside influence during the long Franco dictatorship but now brewing groups from other countries have arrived in force to exploit the growing interest in beer among both Spaniards and the vast number of tourists.

The only major independent is Damm of Barcelona. It was founded in 1876 by Augusto R. Damm, who had learned his brewing skills in Alsace. It panders to the hordes of Germans who pour into Spain every summer with Voll-Damm, a 5.5 per cent lager more in the Dortmunder Export style despite the Franconian term "Voll", which is similar to a Munich Helles. Most of the Spanish brewers make an Extra or an Especial of around 5.0 per cent with a malty rounded character similar to a Dortmunder. Coruña's **Especial Rivera** and **Estrella Extra** are good examples, as are **Ambar Export** from Zaragoza and **Keler 18** from San Sebastian. Damm's other main claim to fame is a low-alcohol beer brewed for the 1992 Barcelona Olympics with the intriguing name of **Sin**.

El Aguila – the Eagle – has had its seven breweries whittled down to four by Heineken. Its **Aguila Reserva Extra** is a powerful 6.5 per cent ABV with 28 IBUs. **Adlerbrau** is an interpretation of a Munich Dunkel, brewed from pale and caramalts with some corn grits. Northern Brewer and Brewers' Gold produce 28 IBUs. It has an estery, fruity aroma, quenching malt in the mouth and a smooth finish with hints of dark chocolate.

Aguila's everyday beer is **Aguila Pilsener** (4.5 per cent ABV), brewed from pale malt and corn grits with Northern Brewer and Brewers' Gold hops, which are Spanish varieties of German hops. The beer has 23 IBUs and is conditioned for three weeks.

San Miguel's Premium Lager (5.4 per cent ABV, 24 IBUs) is made from pale malt, with Hallertau Northern Brewer and Perle varieties plus Styrian Goldings. Selecta XV, also 5.4 per cent, has a fruity and hoppy aroma, with rich malt and hops in the mouth, and a long finish with good hop character.

Mahou Lager, with its Kronenbourg influence, is 4.7 per cent ABV and has a pronounced malt and toffee aroma, sweet malt in the mouth and a full finish that becomes dry with some late hops developing.

In general Spanish beers suffer from short conditioning periods, which means they lack the finesse of a Northern European lager and often have yeasty, estery and grainy textures.

PORTUGAL

Two major brewing groups dominate Portugal and, while the influence is yet again Northern European, the quality is high. Brewing records go back to the seventeenth century and there have been French, German and Danish influences since the eighteenth. But, in common with its Iberian neighbour, Portugal was shut off from the outside world during the long years of the Salazar dictatorship.

Central de Cerjevas of Lisbon brews under the Sagres label. **Sagres pale lager** is rich and malty with good hop character on the palate and finish while a brown version in the Munich Dunkel style is smooth and chocolatey. The company has also launched a warm-fermenting beer known incongruously as **Bohemia**, which with its fruity and hoppy character is more akin to Belgium than the home of golden Pilsners. When Portugal joined the European Union, Sagres launched **Sagres Europa**, a firm-bodied, malt-accented, 5.4 per cent Dortmunder-style lager.

Unicer in Oporto was nationalized until 1991, since when it has gone into partnership with Carlsberg of Denmark. Its everyday lager, broadly in the international Pils style, is malty and quenching. A 5.8 per cent **Unicer Superbock** is yet another curious interpretation of practices further north.

GREECE

The Greek brewing industry has been virtually wiped out as a result of opening its door to foreign groups. The only Greek brewery of any size or influence, Fix, went out of business in 1984. It was owned by the Greek Minister of Defence, and when his political fortunes waned his brewery followed him into extinction.

The market is now dominated by Heineken, which brews both Heineken and Amstel locally. Henninger Hellas was created by the German Henninger group but has been bought by Kronenbourg-BSN, which plans to concentrate on Kronenbourg. Löwenbräu has built a brewery under the name of Löwenbräu Hellas to promote a Greek version of the Munich beers.

In the north of the country, **Aegean** produces a 5.0 per cent lager with a sweet malty aroma, pronounced toffee on the palate and a bitter-sweet finish.

The country had its own Purity Law, which meant the beers were all malt, but this has been abandoned under pressure from foreign brewers. It is a pity there is so little ethnic interest.

MALTA

Malta has long been independent but a benign British influence hovers over the beers of the George Cross island. The Farson's Brewery produces lagers under the Cisk name but is best known for its ales. These include a well-hopped **Hop Leaf** pale ale (1040 degrees – the brewery still endearingly declares strength by original gravity), a stronger **Brewer's Choice** (1050), fruity and hoppy, a mild **Blue Label** (1039) and a genuine **Milk Stout** (1045; 3.4 ABV), brewed with lactose (milk sugar) to give a rounded, creamy, slightly sweet palate and a surprisingly dry finish with hints of dark fruit and chocolate. The stout is called **Lacto** and carries the claim "Milk Stout with Vitamin B for Extra Energy" – the island has yet to meet Environmental Health Officers.

IMPORTANT ADDRESS

Simonds, Farsons Cisk The Brewery, Mriehel, Malta GC.

Harvesting maize – which is sometimes used in Italy to make beer – at Civitella d'Agliano

SWITZERLAND

Not surprisingly, it is the German region or canton of Switzerland that has the best beer traditions. It was in this canton that an Irish Benedictine monk called St Gall built an abbey in the seventh century, which over time developed several brewhouses. St Gall, who brought learning and Christianity from Ireland to Europe, is considered to be the founder of Swiss brewing and the town where his abbey stood is named St Gallen in his honour.

In modern times the Swiss government has attempted to stop monopolies in brewing appearing by restricting breweries to their cantons of origin. But the system fell apart in the early 1990s when the leading Swiss brewer Feldschlössen signed a trading agreement with Kronenbourg-BSN of France and then merged with the Cardinal group. The Swiss market is now wide open and the result is likely to be a rapid fall in the number of 30 breweries.

Feldschlössen

The most remarkable aspect of the Feldschlössen beers is the brewery, whose name means "Castle in the Field". It is a former chemicals factory near Basel, set in rolling and verdant grounds, designed, as the name indicates, like a castle. The magnificent interior has a stained glass window that incorporates a picture of the founder, Théophil Roninger, who had worked in German breweries before launching his own in 1874. The brewhouse is a symphony of burnished copper set on marble floors, the plaster ceiling supported by marble pillars. After all this inspirational architecture, the beers are rather less than dramatic. The 5.2 per cent **Hopfenperle** has some light fruitiness on the aroma along with a delicate hop presence, is lightly malty in the mouth, and with a finish that becomes dry with tart hoppiness. A version of the beer using darker malts is called **Dunkleperle** while the castellated brewery is commemorated by a stronger, maltier Castello.

Hürlimann

Hürlimann of Zürich was the country's most energetic exporter and was best-known for the world's strongest beer, **Samichlaus** – Santa Claus. The 14.0 per cent beer was made possible by the brewery's long association with the cultivation of pure yeast strains. Hürlimann was founded in 1865 by Albert Hürlimann – his father had started a brewery in the family's name in 1836 but had gone out of business. The move to cold fermentation for lager beers demanded a more scientific knowledge of the workings of yeast and Hürlimann became a world leader in developing specific strains that would work at the fermenting and conditioning temperatures required for different types of beer. The major problem with producing strong beers is that the yeast is eventually overwhelmed by the alcohol it produces: the yeast "goes to sleep", brewers say. Hürlimann tackled this problem and produced a strain of yeast that could ferment beer to a high level of alcohol. In 1979 it used the yeast to brew a strong Christmas beer as an experiment. The interest created by the beer encouraged the brewery to make it every year and in 1982 it was given the accolade of the strongest beer in the world by *The Guinness Book of Records*, much to the chagrin, no doubt, of EKU in Germany.

Sadly, this rich tradition disappeared in the late 1990s when Hürlimann was bought by Feldschlössen, which announced it planned to discontinue Samichlaus. The last batch appeared for Christmas 1998 and frantic efforts by European beer lovers to get other brewers to take on the brand were unsuccessful.

The Swiss are punctilious about brand names and no beer can be called a Pilsner for fear of upsetting the Czechs. Hürlimann's main beer is simply called **Hürlimann Lager** and is 4.7 per cent ABV. It has a hoppy aroma, a medium body and a short finish. Its subsidiary company Löwenbräu (no relation to the Munich brewery of the same name) also has a bluntly named **Löwenbräu Lager** of 4.8 per cent ABV, brewed only from pale malt and with Hallertau and Hersbrucker hops (21 IBUs). It has a malty nose and body, with some light hops in the finish. **Sternbräu** at 5.5 per cent ABV and 28 IBUs is a richer and more distinctive beer in the Export style, firm bodied, malty

The German canton of Switzerland has the best beer traditions

and with a good Saaz hop character. A 5.4 per cent Dunkel is called **Hexenbräu** – Witches' Brew – and is rich and chocolatey while **Drei-Königs Bier** is a 6.5 per cent strong pale beer with great malt character. It is named after the coat of arms of a district of Zürich. The future of all these brands is in doubt following the takeover by Feldschlössen.

Cardinal in Fribourg has a 4.9 per cent Helles or pale lager that carries the brewery name and **Anker**, a dark and top-fermenting beer in the German Alt tradition (5.8 per cent ABV). Cardinal was founded in 1788 and was substantially rebuilt in 1877 when it was bought by the renowned watchmaker Paul-Alcide Blancpain, who may have some connection with the French Blancpain who settled in England and became Whitebread or Whitbread. The brewery's strong **Rheingold** (6.3 per cent ABV) is malty and perfumy, firm bodied and with a big and complex malt-and-hops finish.

Calanda of Chur, Frauenfeld in the town of the same name, and the Ueli Brewery in Basel all produce wheat beers in the Bavarian style. Ueli is a micro based in the Fischerstübe beer restaurant at Rheingasse 4, founded in 1974 by Hans Nidecker with the help of a member of the German Binding brewing family. Ueli means jester but the beers are serious without being pompous: a delicate, clean, refreshing lager, a 3.5 per cent **Dunkel** with heavy malt and toffee notes, a tart, aromatic, spicy 4.0 per cent **Weizenbier** and a pale **Reverenz**, also 4.0 per cent. The restaurant specializes in dishes cooked with beer.

BEERS FROM THE AMERICAS

The first beers in both North and Latin America were native brews using the cereals from the fields and plants from the ground or the jungles. In North America, English settlers brought an ale culture with them while the second wave of immigrants from Central Europe rapidly spread the lager message. As a result of Prohibition and the Great Depression, a handful of American brewers dominated the market with thin versions of the lager style but now a beer renaissance led by small craft brewers is producing ales and lagers of great quality. In Latin America, Spanish, German and even Austrian influences have developed some good examples of the Pilsner and Vienna styles, as well as some bland international brands. The Caribbean's beers range from thin lagers to high-quality, Pils-style and – as a legacy from colonial times – some fine dry and sweet stouts.

The red writing says it all – Budweiser is the world's largest selling beer

USA

The USA is a conundrum. It is a brewing colossus, the world's biggest producer. But that statistic reflects only the size of the country, for the Americans are moderate consumers, well down the list of drinking nations and not even in the top ten. It is also a country where marketing zeal has triumphed over tradition, where craftsmanship plays second fiddle to the need to flood bars and taverns with mass volume beers made to identikit recipes from the Canadian to the Mexican borders.

The beer styles of the USA.

In a country that lauds the free market, brewing has been concentrated to an astonishing degree, with more than 90 per cent of all beer sales controlled by just a handful of producers, the biggest of which accounts for nearly half the beer brewed.

Yet the conundrum is a deeply complex one. Most beer lovers who inhabit or have occasion to visit the USA complain that the mainstream lagers found there are bland and watery. But the dedication to quality of the producers of these beers cannot be gainsaid. The beers are often produced in breathtakingly beautiful plants, using the finest ingredients, which are then used so sparingly that the end products are almost devoid of malt or hop character. It may be the awesome size of the country that dictates to the people who run the breweries that beers cannot be too memorable in order to appeal to the lowest common denominator. There is little room for diversification when, in the case of Anheuser-Busch, biggest of the giants, you are making more than 90 million barrels of beer a year, most of it in the shape of just one brand, Budweiser.

American beer is locked into a culture and economy that had to grow, compress, rush and cut corners in order to catch up with the rest of the industrialized world. And now, as the world's single super-power, it can build only on what it knows. Nowhere is that more true than in the brewing industry. Other great brewing nations – Britain at first, then Ireland, Germany, Bohemia and the Netherlands – brought their styles and the ability to make them to the New World. But

Americans applauded when Henry Ford declared history to be "bunk" and those pioneering styles have been ignored, denied and subsumed by mass-produced and massively promoted pale lagers that were once from the Bavarian and Bohemian moulds but have long lost any authenticity or credibility. There is a cynical saying in the brewing industry that "people drink the advertising". It is as true of the perpetrators as it is of the recipients. If you call your main product "the King of Beers", you had better believe it or the whole corporate structure falls apart like castles built of sand.

Yet a counter-culture is developing. It has to be searched for, teased out, but it is worth the effort. For alongside the everyday beers, there is now a remarkable surge of small breweries dedicated to the consumer, not the production chart. Beers rich in choice and heritage are available, some based on long-forgotten but indigenous styles, others that look to Europe for their inspiration. There is a pleasing irony in the fact that while many European brewers now ape the American giants by neutering their beers of flavour, the new wave of American craft brewers is rediscovering the joys of the barley corn and the hop flower. If you fancy a rich Märzen, a ripe Bock, a roasty stout, a chocolatey porter, or an India Pale Ale so hoppy your eyeballs pop, then the USA is now the place to drink. It is a counter-culture that points to a country at ease with itself. Conformity in beer drinking was a by-product of an immigrant nation in which people did not wish to over-stress their Dutch, German or Italian roots and ate and drank "all-American" products. Now that pasta and Pilsner are no longer seen as a threat to the American way of life, a thousand beers can flourish.

The beer produced by all the small companies amounts to between 1 and 2 per cent of the total. The percentage will double but will not threaten the hegemony of the giants. That is not the aim of the operation. Unlike Britain, where more than 70 per cent of all beer is sold on draught in pubs, the American craft brewers are not attempting to muscle in on the big producers' markets. In a country where packaged beer for home consumption is the dominant type, the small producers are offering a specialist product unashamedly aimed at those prepared to pay a dollar more for a beer than those who pack the supermarket trolleys high with **Bud** or **Miller Lite**.

Prohibition is another facet of the American beer conundrum. Although the right to manufacture and sell alcohol was restored in 1933 after 13 years of illegality, the shadow of that frightening period – in which bootleg liquor was in the hands of the Mob – hung over the brewing industry for many decades. Only the biggest brewers survived Prohibition, able to make a living from soft drinks, yeast production and ice cream. Thousands gave up the ghost and more followed during the Depression of the 1930s. Brooklyn, once the greatest brewing borough in the whole country thanks to its Dutch settlers, lost all its producers. With a mass market to themselves, the giants went for the hard sell and the soft option of national brands. The country lost much of its regional diversity and traditional beer styles. In particular, it lost its ales.

Brewing existed in North America before the first settlers. The Indians and Mexicans made porridge-type beers, quickly made and spiced with herbs and plants. When the British arrived on the East Coast they began to brew in order to keep their communities healthy as well as happy. Brewers from the old country were cajoled into joining the settlers in the New World. They brought with them ale yeasts while farmers grew barley and other cereals and began to nurture a hop industry. As in Europe, beer-making moved out of the home and the hearth and into specialist factories. The first commercial brewery was set up in New Amsterdam (now New York City) in 1623. Ale, porter and stock ale – a strong, long-matured beer similar to old or stale in England – were the staple products of the first brewers. George Washington brewed his own ale at Mount Vernon. Thomas Jefferson was a brewer and his recipe at Monticello has been preserved. Another of the great American revolutionaries, Samuel Adams in Boston, was a significant brewer. He is now immortalized by a modern craft brewery bearing his name.

From 1840 the beer scene changed dramatically and fundamentally. The second wave of immigrants, a vast army of central Europeans forsaking despotism, unemployment and the drudgery of semi-feudal rural life, brought with them the skills and the thirst to make the new cold-fermented beers perfected in Munich, Pilsen and Vienna. Lager-brewing established itself rapidly and the Germanic influence can be seen in such famous names as Anheuser-Busch, Pabst, Heileman, Schlitz and Stroh. Samuel Adams in Boston may commemorate a great American patriot but the owner is Jim Koch, descendant of German immigrant brewers, though to avoid bringing a blush to American cheeks he delicately pronounces it "Cook".

The original British settlers were no match for the Central Europeans. Determined to stamp their mark on the New World, they grasped all the technologies made possible by the Industrial Revolution to produce beer in enormous quantities. They used the railroad to speed their products outside their home bases and they made a Faustian pact with the new service industries of marketing and advertising to tell the American people that their beers were the best, the greatest, the kings. By the turn of the twentieth century, there were 4,000 American breweries. Before the marketing men took over with their mission to turn beer into a commodity, those breweries served cities, towns and neighbourhoods with a vast range of styles.

The twin attacks of Prohibition and the mass-market mentality caused such havoc that by the 1980s there were just six national giants and 20 independent regional brewers left. It has been the enthusiasm of the craft brewers that has restored choice and style – in every sense of the word – to the American beer scene. As Charles Finkel, founder of the Pike Place Brewery in Seattle, says: "It is not a beer revolution, it is a renaissance. We're going back beyond Prohibition and the second wave of immigrants with their lager culture to the Founding Fathers. Americans are going back to their roots."

The giants

No study of world beer is complete without looking at the remarkable Anheuser-Busch empire that brews the biggest beer brand ever known. Its origins lie in St Louis, Missouri, literally and physically Middle America. With the birth of the railroad, a far-sighted brewer in St Louis could send beer across the Rockies to the West Coast, down the Mississippi to the South, up to the Great Lakes and Chicago in the North, and to the burgeoning cities of the East. It was the genius of Adolphus Busch to seize these opportunities. On a vaster scale, he followed in Arthur Guinness's and William Bass's footsteps by building national brands while others were content to stay loyal to their localities.

The first brewery to bear the name of Anheuser-Busch was bought from George Schneider who had built a "hole in the ground" plant called the Bavarian Brewery in 1852. The South German influence was obvious and extended as far as Schneider bearing the same Christian and surname as the founder of the famous wheat beer brewery in Kelheim south of Munich. But the German-American Schneider was a business failure, and his small neighbourhood concern was bought and sold three times before being acquired in 1860 by Eberhard Anheuser.

Anheuser was born in 1805 in Kreuznach in the German Rhineland. He emigrated to the United States in 1843 and settled first in Cincinnati and then in St Louis. He had trained as a soap manufacturer and became first general manager and then partner in a soap business called Schaffer, Anheuser & Co. When he died in 1880 at the age of 75 his brewing business had become one of the biggest in the country. Among the many tributes to him was a lengthy obituary in a German language paper produced for German-Americans, *Anzeiger des Westens*.

In 1861 Adolphus Busch married Lilly Anheuser, daughter of Eberhard. Three years later he joined his father-in-law at the Anheuser Bavarian Brewery. Busch was born in 1839 in Kastel near Mainz in the Hesse region of Germany, the son of an innkeeper and landowner. He arrived in the USA in 1857 and reached St Louis via New Orleans and the Mississippi. He worked on the riverfront as a clerk and gradually worked his way in business until he owned a successful wholesaling company. Five years after joining Anheuser, Busch bought out the half-share in the brewery owned by William D'Oench – who retired back to Stuttgart – and became a full partner in the company. In 1879 the "Bavarian" tag was dropped from the company's name, which became Anheuser-Busch Brewing. When Anheuser died, Busch became president and the

company has remained in the family ever since. The current president is August Busch III. In common with many dynastic American corporate giants, Anheuser-Busch has had its share of family squabbles and scandals but they have not inhibited growth. Today A-B has plants in Newark, New Jersey; Los Angeles; Tampa, Florida; Houston, Texas; Columbus, Ohio; Jacksonville, Florida; Merrimack, New Hampshire; Williamsburg, Virginia; Fairfield, California; Baldwinsville, New York State; Fort Collins, Colorado; and Cartersville, Georgia.

Busch had a flair for marketing. He grasped the opportunities for selling beer outside its city of origin, using the new means of transport at his disposal. Ice-making and refrigerators not only made cold-fermentation possible on a commercial scale but enabled beer to be transported in refrigerated trucks on rail and road. Busch also recognized that commercial success would come from producing a type of beer acceptable to the great bulk of Americans, not just those of German origin used to the dark and heavy Bavarian style. Encouraged by Anheuser, Busch travelled widely in Europe in the late 1860s and early 1870s, concentrating on Bavaria and Bohemia. He studied the brewing process in Pilsen closely but knew that Pilsen-style beers were already being brewed extensively elsewhere in Europe and in parts of the United States, especially in Michigan and Wisconsin. He wanted something different and he found it in Budweis. This small town in Southern Bohemia (České Budějovice today) was a brewing legend. For centuries the quality of its beers – called generically, in the German style, Budweisers – had made them popular among the Bohemian court to the extent that they were known as the "beer of kings". The marketing appeal of such a fine title was not lost on Busch. He enjoyed, too, the style of beer, maltier and less aggressively hopped than Pilsners, and with a delicate hint of apple fruit. While he was in Europe, Busch became acquainted with the work of Louis Pasteur on yeast propagation and the heat-treatment called "pasteurization" that prevented beer from being attacked by bacteria, giving it longer shelf life. Busch's experiences coalesced into a determination to make a pale, golden lager with a soft and appealing palate, pasteurized to withstand long journeys

Miller will follow Busch and Coors in sponsoring the local baseball team's stadium – aptly the Milwaukee Brewers – when it opens in 2001

throughout the United States. It is not known whether he took any Budweis yeast back with him but he did introduce European two-row barley to his adopted country, a variety that produces a sweeter beer than the native six-row. He also picked up – probably in Franconia, northern Bavaria – the German habit of maturing and clarifying beer over a bed of beechwood chips. Adopted by Busch, the method was to become an important (though largely irrelevant) element of the Budweiser myth.

Back in St Louis, Busch put his plans into action. He called in Carl Conrad, a St Louis wine merchant and restaurateur, to help him develop a beer that, in his own words "would be acceptable to all tastes – a beer lighter in colour and with a more delicate taste than Pilsner beer". After, it is claimed, much thought Busch chose Budweiser as the name for his new "national beer" because it had a slightly Germanic sound yet was easily pronounceable by native Americans. Busch also claimed that, as no other American brewer was using the title, he could not be accused of passing-off or copying an existing brand. Budweiser was launched in 1876. It was not an overnight success. Until the turn of the century, A-B's leading beer was called simply **St Louis Lager Beer**. It also had a second beer with the extravagant name of **Anheuser-Busch St Louis White Label Pilsener Exquisite**. If the company's own description is anything to go by ("It combines all the virtues of the European Pilsener – the excellent aroma of hops; the strengthening, pure taste of malt; the clear Rhine Wine color; the small-beaded, creamy, white-as-snow foam which covers the last drop left in the glass") it must have been quite a beer.

But gradually sales of Budweiser climbed in step with the growth of the company. In 1870 A-B was brewing a modest 18,000 barrels a year. By 1901 it had passed the million mark. Budweiser was now the flagship and had been joined in 1896 – at first only on draught – by a "super premium" lager called **Michelob**, which also took its name from a Bohemian town (it is pronounced with a hard "ch": Mikelob). A-B had gone national and such local and regional specialities as a Munchener, an Erlanger (Märzen), a Bock and an Old Burgundy barley wine fell by the wayside.

By the 1890s Budweiser was being promoted as the "King of Beers" and the "Original Budweiser". The first claim is effective but, on closer examination, devoid of meaning: who crowned it? And by no stretch of the imagination could it claim to be original, for the beers beloved of the Bohemian court were called Budweiser and the old Samson Brewery in Če-ské Budějovice had also used the term. When the Budweiser Budvar brewery was formed in České Budějovice in 1896 and attempted to enter the American market early in the twentieth century, A-B blocked the move with a law suit, the first of many between the two companies.

The A-B catalogue for 1889, with a charming naivety, described Budweiser as a "pale and innocuous beverage". The company claims the recipe has never changed in the beer's long history. That is remarkable, for few beers have never been "tweaked", to use a brewer's expression. New varieties of malt and hops appear in every generation and brewers are always experimenting to improve the aroma, flavour and colour of their beers. If the A-B claim is true, this means that from the outset the company used substantial amounts of rice as an adjunct to barley malt. Rice is listed before barley on the label and it is thought to constitute around 40 per cent of the grist. All the large American brewers use substantial amounts of unmalted adjuncts, usually corn (maize) rather than rice. This is because the high level of enzymes in native six-row barley can convert the starches in unmalted grains – which have no "diastatic power" – as well as in the malt. In the case of rice, it is cooked to break down the cell walls and then added to the mash, where the malt enzymes add its sugars to the wort. Rice is a useful adjunct if the aim is an exceptionally pale beer with a light flavour.

Budweiser is brewed from a blend of two-row and six-row pale malts and rice. The hops are both US and European varieties in the form of whole flowers. A single decoction mash is used and the beer is lagered for a maximum of a month – 21 days is usual. The beer has a starting gravity of 1044 degrees and a finished alcohol by volume of 4.8 per cent: it is well attenuated. In spite of the careful choice of hops and their skilful blending, the units of bitterness are just 12 (it is thought this figure may have been lowered to around 10 IBUs since the data was revealed). With such a low malt content, too high a hop rate would overpower the flavour. During maturation strips of beechwood, about a foot long and a couple of inches wide, are placed in the conditioning tanks where they attract yeast particles. During lagering, the beer is kräusened by adding a portion of partially-fermented wort to encourage a second fermentation. The finished beer has no discernible aroma, a light, clean, quenching palate and a short finish. The brewery calls the finish "fast", which says it all. Even these characteristics are masked by the house rule that the beer must be served at 42 degrees Fahrenheit (6 Celsius). When the beer warms up there is the faintest of hints of apple fruit, suggesting that old man Busch may have emulated Jacobsen of Carlsberg by bringing some yeast back from Budweis under his hat.

The premium **Michelob** (4.8 per cent ABV; 10 IBUs) has a similar specification to Budweiser's but a lower rice ratio. As a result it has a pleasant malt aroma and palate and a smooth finish with a hint of hop. Both beers are also brewed in Light (low calorie) and Dry versions to fit the fashionable sector of the market. Dry beers are attenuated fully to ensure that as little flavour as possible remains. Do the people who make them go home in the evening and declare: "I had a swell day at the brewery: I made a totally tasteless beer"? **Michelob Dry** has a starting gravity of 1041 degrees but is brewed out to 4.8 per cent ABV. As the company's own tasting charts state, the beer has "no aftertaste". On the credit side, A-B introduced in the 1980s **Michelob Classic Dark** (4.7 per cent ABV; 10 IBUs), with some roasted malt added to the pale malts and rice. It has some pleasant malty character with hints of dark fruit in the finish. **King Cobra Malt Liquor**, another 1980s launch, belongs to the style of American beers that are high in alcohol and aimed at the urban poor in search of a cheap buzz. They are often brewed with substantial amounts of brewing sugar to cut production costs and help boost the alcohol. A-B's contribution is 5.9 per cent ABV, with 11 IBUs. It is brewed from pale and crystal malts and maize with US hop varieties and is malty and syrupy with a full-bodied palate and a sticky finish. **Busch** (4.7 per cent ABV; 10 IBUs) is a survivor from the early days of the company but is now a disappointingly thin brew, with a slight sweetness of palate and a grainy aroma.

At the quality end of the production line, A-B experimented with both a Märzen and a Pilsner (the latter with just 9 IBUs) but they have been discontinued. The group has entered the fast-growing, but probably short-lived, "ice beer" market. Of greater interest is the introduction of **Elk Mountain Amber**, an ale that takes its name from the group's own hop fields. It may well be the first ale ever brewed in the history of the company and is an attempt to guard its flank from the growing power of the craft brewers and their "specialty" beers.

The second biggest brewing group in the USA, Miller of Milwaukee, had a far slower rise to fortune than Anheuser-Busch. It was founded in 1855 as Charles Best's Plank Road Brewery and was bought by Frederic Miller, who built it into one of the region's biggest breweries. In 1965 it was in eleventh place in the pecking order. In 1969 it became part of the giant Philip Morris cigarette group, which began aggressively to

build the brewing division's market share. For years the brewery's flagship brand had been **Miller High Life** (4.67 per cent ABV; 3.65 per cent by weight), a pale lager that pre-dated Prohibition. Under Morris's tutelage, Miller launched **Miller Lite** (4.18 per cent ABV; 3.30 per cent by weight), one of the first low-calorie beers. Fully brewed out to turn the maximum amount of sugar into alcohol, light beers appealed to Americans concerned with health and expanding waistbands. Miller Lite was an enormous success, though this "fine Pilsner beer brewed from the finest ingredients" had to undergo some rapid changes in the 1980s when Miller was charged by the Center for Science in the Public Interest of using a foam enhancer, propylene glycol alginate, chill-proofing the beer with papain, using amyloglucosidase to speed up starch conversion and preserving the finished beer with potassium metabisulphite. Miller said it had stopped using all chemical aids in the beer. The shock waves caused other large brewers to take greater care in the ingredients they used.

Miller improved its image in the late 1980s with **Miller Genuine Draft** (4.67 per cent ABV; 3.65 per cent by weight), a dark golden beer that, despite the name, came only in bottled form. It used the new Japanese system of cold filtering, rather than pasteurizing beer, to enhance aroma and flavour.

Miller, which now brews some 40 million barrels a year, has bought the old Jacbob Leinenkugel Brewery of Chippewa Falls, Wisconsin. It was created in 1867 by Leinenkugel and his partner John Miller, no relation to the Milwaukee Millers. It has added some new products, including a **Red Lager** and a **Genuine Bock** to its standard brews.

Adolph Coors of Golden, Colorado, is the third biggest US brewer. As a result of its isolated base high in the Rockies it is often dismissed as the Mr Nobody of American brewing, but it runs the single biggest brewing plant in the country, producing some 20 million barrels a year. The site was chosen by Adolph Coors in 1873 because of its easy access to the fine spring waters from the Rockies: the company makes great play of the quality of its water. Locked in its mountain fastness, Coors is as famous for its corporate and political conservatism – it fought long and hard against labour union recognition – as it is for its beer.

The Golden Brewery is superb, packed with burnished copper vessels. As with Anheuser-Busch, enormous care is taken in choosing the finest ingredients. Coors owns its own barley fields and hop gardens. Its beers are a blend of pale malted barley and cereal adjuncts (refined starch) and whole hops. The finished results have the minimum of taste and character. Drinkers could be forgiven for thinking the Rocky Mountain spring water was the most memorable flavour. For years the brewery produced just one brand called **Coors** (5.0 per cent ABV) with the tag line "banquet beer". It has now branched out with a low-calorie **Coors Light** (4.2 per cent ABV) – nicknamed the "Silver Bullet" as a result of the aluminium can in which it comes – and a super premium **Coors Gold. Herman Joseph's Original Draft** has a fraction more body; a Winterfest beer brewed for Thanksgiving has a slight spicy aroma and palate from dark malt and is broadly in the old Vienna Red tradition; while George Killian's is yet another version of the long-dead Irish ale from Wexford now reincarnated in France and the Netherlands as well as in the USA. In 1987 Coors opened a second brewery in the Shenandoah Valley near Elton, Virginia. The group makes much of the fact that, in the wake of the Miller Lite furore, it brews without preservatives or additives. It does not pasteurize its beers, preferring to sterile-filter them. Coors survived Prohibition by making **Coors Golden Malted Milk**, which may have had a shade more barley character than its modern beers.

Stroh of Detroit became the fourth biggest American brewing group by taking over one of the most famous names in beer – Schlitz. The fall of Schlitz, once America's biggest brewing concern with the slogan "the beer that made Milwaukee famous", is testimony to the fact that you can fool some of the drinkers some of the time but not all the drinkers all of the time. Schlitz was founded in 1849 by August Krug who sold the Milwaukee plant in 1858 to his son-in-law Joseph Schlitz. Schlitz died the following year during a boating holiday in his native Germany but his name lived on, and his brewery grew until it rivalled Anheuser-Busch in size. Disaster struck Schlitz in the 1970s. The national brewers launched a price war to gain market share and

Schlitz attempted to undercut its rivals by reducing the barley and hop content of its brews, saving 50 cents on each barrel brewed. In order to give the beers shelf-life and a foaming head, Schlitz replaced a silica-gel containing enzymes with a stabilizer called Chillgarde. Unfortunately for Schlitz, Chillgarde reacted with another ingredient called Kelcoloid (propylene glycol alginate) causing tiny flakes of protein to coagulate in the beer. When drinkers complained about Schlitz's "flaky beer", the company removed the Kelcoloid, a foam stabilizer. As a result the beers, lacking natural malt proteins to give a good natural head, went, according to one wholesaler, "as flat as apple cider". Schlitz's sales nose-dived and in 1982 the company was only saved from extinction when it was bought by Stroh. The Schlitz brands linger on but Stroh concentrates on its own brews.

Stroh was founded in 1850 by Bernard Stroh whose family came from Kirn in the German Rhineland and included at least one innkeeper. Bernard started to brew "Bohemian" beer in the Pilsner style and adopted the European fashion of heating the brew kettles in America by direct flame. This method encourages what brewers call "a good rolling boil" to extract the best aromas and flavours from the hops. It also causes a slight caramelization of the malt sugars which leaves a slight but distinctive port-wine note to the beer, evident in the "super premium" **Signature** (4.84 per cent ABV; 3.78 per cent by weight). Stroh has moved in recent years into more characterful beers that recall its roots. Using the Augsburger title, it produces **Augsburger Golden** (4.93 per cent ABV; 3.85 per cent by weight), with some hop notes on the aroma and finish, and **Weiss**, a wheat beer with some fruitiness but lacking the true Bavarian spiciness. Under the Schlitz name, **Erlanger** is a firm-bodied beer that promises the flavour of a Bavarian Märzen but fails to deliver.

Pabst, another Germanic giant of Milwaukee, was the biggest brewery in the United States at the turn of the century but its fortunes have declined, though it remains one of the six national giants. It was founded in 1844 by Jacob Best from Rheinhessen who joined forces with Captain Frederick Pabst from Leipzig. (Best also founded the Plank Road Brewery which subsequently became Miller.) Pabst's fortune was made by its **Blue**

Ribbon beer (4.56 per cent ABV; 3.65 per cent by weight), which became the mass drink of the industrial working class – fortuitously known as "blue collar" workers. The decline of industry was matched by the falling sales of Blue Ribbon. Pabst became entangled in mergers and takeovers. It bought Olympia Brewing of Tumwater, with a pale lager called **Olympia** (4.56 per cent ABV; 3.65 per cent by weight) and known as "Oly", which itself had acquired Hamm's Brewery in St Paul, Minnesota. Finally, and in the way of those that go down the takeover trail, Pabst itself was bought by the California millionaire Paul Kalmanovitz, who already owned the Falstaff, General and Pearl Breweries.

The last of the national giants, Heileman, was founded in 1858 by Gottlieb Heileman and John Gund in La Crosse, Wisconsin. It remained a sizeable regional company until it bought other breweries in the 1960s. It now owns Blitz of Oregon, Henry Weinhard, Rainier of Seattle, and Lone Star, the famous beer of Texas. The mainstream beers are typical of the light lager style. The flagship **Old Style** (4.84 per cent ABV; 3.80 per cent by weight) is more post- than pre-Prohibition, with a strong corn syrup character. Even the ales in its portfolio are now thin and disappointing. Rainier's was nicknamed the Green Death (5.50 per cent by weight) from its emerald-coloured label and reputed alcoholic kick, but its hops and malt attributes are now muted. On the credit side, Heileman has brought back the old Blatz name in Milwaukee, building a new small plant under the name of a company that was one of the national giants until the post-war years. Among the interesting beers brewed by Blatz are a **Kulmbacher Imperial** (4.33 per cent ABV; 3.40 per cent by weight) and **Milwaukee Weiss**, a Bavarian-style wheat beer.

The revivalists

Good beer, unlike a good man, is no longer so hard to find. In San Francisco it may be a struggle to get a Budweiser but the local beer, **Anchor Steam**, is on tap in dozens of bars. The impact of the micros is now considerable. They have set up their own distribution networks and as a result their beers are now widely available. Their presence and their availability have been enhanced by the work of the American Homebrewers'

Association which fostered an interest in good beer and encouraged a generation of keen homebrewers to turn their skills into commercial ventures. The AHA's related organization, the Association of Brewers, organizes the annual Great American Beer Festival, a showcase for the work of the micros. Some of the leading American craft brewers are now sufficiently big to shrug off the "micro" tag. They brew more beer than many British and German companies and are major producers by any standard.

Two men have played a pivotal role in the revival of craft brewing in the United States. They come from different stock. One was the scion of a rich family of German origin, an amiable man who used his wealth to save a brewery and revive the country's only indigenous beer style. The other is a gruff, bluff man of Scottish-Canadian stock who brews ales with a devotion to style in a remote town in the hop fields of Washington State. Their impact has been nationwide, encouraging a generation of beer lovers to invest in mash tuns, brew kettles and fermenters, and produce ales and lagers of often startling quality.

The first man is Fritz Maytag, a member of the powerful washing-machine dynasty. He was a student at Stanford University and enjoyed a local speciality called Steam Beer. One day in 1965 he went into his favourite bar, asked for a glass of Steam and was told it would be his last as the Anchor Steam Brewery was about to close. So Maytag cashed in his chips in the family firm and bought the brewery. There are some cynics who scoff at any suggestion that Maytag was playing out a part in the American Dream, but he stood to lose every penny of his fortune by taking over a failed business which produced a beer that only a handful of people wanted to drink.

Steam Beer is a San Francisco speciality that dates from the California Gold Rush of the 1890s. When the gold diggers poured into the small town with a largely Mexican, wine-drinking population, they demanded beer – and they wanted the cold, refreshing lager beers they had enjoyed on the East Coast. The few ale brewers in San Francisco had neither ice nor mountainous caves in which to store beers. The one ingredient they could get was lager yeast and they used it to brew a beer but still using ale temperatures. They developed special shallow vessels, a cross between a fermenter and a cool ship, that exposed more of the beer to the atmosphere, causing it to cool quickly. The high level of natural carbonation created by the system caused casks to "hiss like escaping steam" when opened in bars.

Fritz Maytag inherited a clapped-out brewery with just one employee – it was so broke it was using baker's yeast to ferment its beer. It took 10 years for Maytag to turn Anchor Steam into a profitable concern. He has now moved from its former run-down site under a freeway to an Art Deco building in Mariposa Street that was once the headquarters of a coffee-roasting company. As well as turning Anchor into a successful brewery, Maytag has toured the world in order to immerse himself in the history and practice of brewing. In particular, a visit to some of Britain's finest producers of cask-conditioned ales encouraged him to branch out from his flagship beer into ale brewing where he has adopted with fervour the English habit of "dry hopping" – adding hops to the finished casks to give beer improved aroma. His new brewery is magnificent, packed with gleaming copper vessels built to his specification by a German firm.

After mashing and boiling, **Anchor Steam Beer** is fermented separately from the ales to avoid any cross-fertilization of yeast strains. Fermentation takes place in open vessels just 2 feet deep, using lager yeast but at a warm temperature of 16–21°C/60–70°F. The beer has a finished strength of 5.0 per cent ABV, 4.0 per cent by weight using the American system. The grist is a blend of pale and crystal malts and no brewing sugars are used. Hops are Northern Brewer, added three times in the kettle. Following fermentation, the green beer is warm-conditioned for three weeks and is then kräusened by adding some partially-fermented wort to encourage a second fermentation. The beer is bronze-coloured and highly complex, with a rich malty-nutty aroma, malt and light fruit in the mouth, and a finish in which the hops slowly dominate. It has 30 to 35 units of bitterness. While it is clean and quenching like a lager, it also has a decidedly ale-like fruitiness.

The other beers are fermented in conventional vessels that are 6 feet deep. **Liberty Ale**, launched in 1975, was inspired by Maytag's tour of British brewers even though it commemorates the ride by Paul Revere from Boston to Lexington to warn the American revolutionaries that the British army was marching to arrest them. His ride signalled the beginning of the American Revolution. Liberty Ale is a world classic, 6.0 per cent ABV, 4.8 by weight, brewed from pale malt and hopped with American Cascades. American hop varieties, like the grapes of California, are big, bold and assertive, adding a citric fruitiness to beer that often borders on a grapefruit note. In the case of Liberty Ale, Cascades are added to the kettle and the maturation tank, giving the beer an intense lemon-citric aroma and palate and a dry and hoppy finish.

The remaining Anchor beers include **Porter** (5.0 per cent by weight, 6.0 by volume) with a smooth coffee character, a refreshing **Wheat Beer** with delicate apple notes, made with 70 per cent wheat, **Old Foghorn** barley wine (7.0 per cent by weight, 8.75 per cent ABV), winey and intensely bitter with 85 IBUs, and **Our Special Ale**, brewed every year for the Thanksgiving and Christmas periods. It is brewed with a different specification each year and always includes a secret spice, which in the past has included cloves, coriander, cinnamon and nutmeg.

Some of Fritz Maytag's disciples are now criticizing his conservatism which causes him to pasteurize both his bottled and draught beers. A handful of craft brewers are now offering draught beer in cask-conditioned form and are producing bottle-conditioned packaged versions. Maytag counters these arguments by saying bluntly that he does not trust retailers to stock and serve his beers sufficiently well to allow him to make them in a naturally-conditioned form. Fritz Maytag is not a man to be either left behind or overtaken, and it is likely that he will adapt to the changing demands of American beer lovers. Whatever the outcome, nothing should detract from his enormous contribution to the revival of American beer.

From his redoubt in the Yakima Valley, surrounded by the Cascade Mountains, Bert Grant makes clear his allegiance. His Oldsmobile carries a registration plate with the words REAL ALE. He is a tough and committed practitioner of the brewers' art in a region that still has a powerful feel of the old frontier about it and where visitors are asked to hand in their guns before entering hotels. Bert Grant was born in Scotland but left for Canada at the age of two. He became an

Bert Grant (pictured here with wife Sherry) is a real-ale devotee whose specialist beers are sold in 27 states across the USA

analytical chemist for Canadian Breweries, which became Carling O'Keefe. When the company started a headlong slide towards oblivion, he crossed the border and worked for Stroh in Detroit for four years before moving to Yakima to rebuild a hop-processing plant in the heart of the American hop fields. He started to brew at home and his efforts were appreciated by friends. When production reached 500 barrels a year, he decided to go commercial. His first brewpub was in the former Yakima Opera House. He has moved to a greenfield site on the edge of town where he has the capacity to make 25,000 barrels a year. He also has a brewpub in the old railroad station where his ales are cask-conditioned, though the bulk of his production is filtered as bars do not understand the concept of sedimented beers.

Bert Grant is a stickler for style. His **Scottish Ale**, which he describes as "the best beer in the world", has an amber colour and nutty roastiness from dark crystal malt but is perhaps a shade too hoppy to be genuinely Scottish. The hoppiness is accounted for by Cascades in the kettle and Willamettes (a Fuggle derivative) used for dry hopping. The 5.6 ABV (4.5 by weight) beer has 45 IBUs. It has a rich sultana fruitiness balanced by a pungent hoppiness, with more dark fruit in the mouth and a fruity and bitter finish. Grant's **Celtic Ale** is also too generously hopped to emulate a soft Irish beer. Grant's **India Pale Ale**, complete with a label showing British soldiers in front of the Taj Mahal, is closer to style. It bursts with hop character, has 50 IBUs and is 4.5 per cent ABV. Other Grant beers include a wheat beer, pungent with lemon and bubblegum, a chocolatey **Porter** with a pronounced hint of peat smoke from imported Scottish malt, and a 7.0 per cent ABV **Imperial Stout** with a resounding 100 IBUs. It is packed with aromas and flavours of liquorice, fresh leather, coffee and apple fruit. Bert Grant's ales are sold in 27 states of the USA, as far south as Florida. He sold the company in the mid-1990s but remains as a consultant.

West Coast breweries

The Sierra Nevada Brewing Company in the university town of Chico, northern California, was one of the first of the new wave of specialist craft breweries. It was founded in 1981 by Ken Grossman and Paul Camusi. Grossman made the leap from home-brewing to commercial production and concentrated at first on ales for the simple reason that he lacked conditioning tanks for lager. A new brewhouse was installed in 1987 and in 1993 production exceeded 70,000 barrels. Sierra Nevada is growing by 50 per cent a year. The flagship beer is bottled **Pale Ale** (4.2 per cent by weight, 5.3 per cent ABV); in draught form it is called **Sierra Nevada** and is a shade darker and a fraction less strong. It has won four gold medals at the Great American Beer Festival. It has a spicy, citric Cascade hop aroma, malty on the palate and with a dry and hoppy finish. Sierra Nevada also brews a coffeeish **Porter**, a 6.0 per cent ABV **Stout** with a roasted malt character, and the renowned **Big Foot Barley Wine**, at 12.5 per cent ABV one of the strongest beers brewed in the United States. It has a vast aroma of hops and dark malt, massive alcohol and hops in the mouth and a shatteringly rich and warming finish. The hops are Nugget for bitterness, with a late addition of Cascade for aroma, and Cascade and Centennial for more aroma during conditioning. Sierra Nevada does not filter in bottle or keg. All the bottled beers are naturally conditioned, the ales filtered, re-seeded with yeast, primed with sugar and matured for several weeks before leaving the brewery. The brewery also produces lagers of exceptional quality.

Pete Slosberg is another Californian home-brewer who went the whole hog. His beers – **Pete's Wicked Ale** and **Wicked Lager** – have upset some traditionalists on the grounds that they don't sound serious beers, but Slosberg is now one of the most successful small brewers in the USA. Wicked Ale (5.0 per cent ABV) has won the Great American Beer Festival's gold medal in the brown ale category. It is copper coloured with a distinctive chocolate and slightly winey palate. It is brewed from pale, crystal and black malts and is hopped with Cascades. Slosberg introduced a range of excellent seasonal beers including summer and winter beers and a **Maple Porter**. In the late 1990s he sold the company but remains as a consultant.

Mendocino Brewing has the ideal address: Hopland, about 90 miles north of San Francisco. It is based in an old saloon in Mendocino County and was founded by Michael Laybourn, Norman Franks and John Scahill in 1982 who planted hops amid the vines of the area. It was California's first brewpub since Prohibition. The beers are named after birds of the area and include **Peregrine Pale Ale**, hoppy and fruity, **Blue Heron Pale Ale**, full-bodied and with great hop character, a copper-coloured **Red Tail Ale** (4.4 per cent by weight, 5.5 ABV) with nutty, crystal malt character and a superb hop aroma and finish from Cascade and Cluster varieties, and the stand-out **Black Hawk Stout**, as smooth and dangerously drinkable as a chocolate liqueur.

San Andreas is based in Hollister near the famous San Andreas Fault. The brewery survived the 1989 earthquake but now tempts fate with beers named **Earthquake Pale Ale** (dry and hoppy), **Earthquake Porter, Survivor Stout** and **Seismic Ale**.

Across the bay from San Francisco in Oakland, Pacific Coast offers a fine range of English-style ales: a dark **Mariners' Mild**, a hoppy **Gray Whale Ale**, a rich, firm-bodied and malty **Blue Whale Ale**, and a dry and tart **Killer Whale Stout**.

There are powerful German influences on the West Coast. The name of the Gordon Biersch Brewing Company in San Francisco is an amalgam of the names of the two founders, Dean Biersch and Dan Gordon. Restaurateur Biersch's antecedents are obvious while Gordon studied brewing skills in Germany. The company, which also has brewpubs in Honolulu, Pasadena, San José and Palo Alto, concentrates on a wide portfolio of German styles, including an Export, heavily influenced by the renowned Dortmund beers, a Märzen, a Dunkel, a Maibock, and an unfiltered Weizen wheat beer (4.5 per cent ABV).

In Modesto, St Stan's Brewing has established a reputation for its Alt beers, modelled on the warm-fermenting style of Düsseldorf. The main brand is **Amber** (5.8 per cent ABV) which, as the name implies, uses some darker, roasty malt alongside the pale for colour and flavour. Owner Garith Helm and his German-born wife Romy Graf also brew a Dark Alt, rich with chocolate malt character, a Winterfest Alt, and two English-style pale ales, **Red Sky Ale** and **Whistle Stop Pale Ale**. The label of the Alt shows a monk with a foaming tankard of beer and the slogan "Conceived in heaven, brewed in California".

The Sudwerk Privatbrauerei Hübsch is quite a mouthful, as are its beers. Founder Ron Broward took his mother's German maiden name for his brewpub in Davis, bought authentic Steinecker equipment from Germany, and employed a trained German brewmaster. The success of his venture has enabled him to open a second brewpub in Sacramento. His Pilsner (5 per cent ABV) uses Hallertau and Tettnang hops that give a floral lilt to the beer. Other beers include a 5.3 per cent Märzen, a Dunkel and a Hefeweizen.

The North-west

Portland, Oregon, is one of the major revivalist brewing centres in the United States. The success of the Portland Brewing Company moved it from its delightful, Irish-style bar with attached brewhouse in the city centre to a greenfield site in 1995 in a custom-built, Germanic-style brewery. The new plant has a capacity of 100,000 barrels a year and vessels that match Anchor in San Francisco for beauty. One of the founders, Fred Bowman, was a keen home-brewer who recreated an English strong ale called Bishop's Tipple from Salisbury, fell in love with brewing and found partners to go commercial. **Portland Ale** (5.0 per cent ABV) is made from pale malt only and has a big citric fruit aroma from Cascade hops, tart fruit in the mouth and a quenching finish. **McTarnahan's Ale** is a degree stronger and is named after a major shareholder in the brewery. It is made from pale and crystal malts and is hopped with Cascades. It has a rich, nutty aroma, dark sultana fruit on the palate and a bitter-sweet finish. Portland has added a distinctive Bavarian-style **Weizen**, a **Haystack Black Porter, Oregon Honey Beer** and **Wheat Berry Brew** flavoured with a local variety of blackberries.

The BridgePort Brewing Company is based in Portland's oldest warehouse, brick-built and smothered in climbing ivy. The brewery was opened in the early 1980s by the Italian-American wine-making Ponzi family who sold out to Gambrinus of Texas in 1995. The stainless-steel brewhouse produces a cask-conditioned ale in the English style called **Coho**, 4.4 per cent ABV. The hops are English Goldings and Nugget and the beer is dry-hopped in cask. It has a lilting citric aroma from the hops, more bitter hops in the mouth and a dry and bitter finish. Other beers include a peppery-hoppy **Bridgeport Ale**, a **Blue Heron Ale** named after Portland's emblem, made from pale, crystal, black and chocolate malts with a hoppy aroma, soft malt in the

The Pacific North-west has a burgeoning brewing industry with Harts Brewery in Seattle being one of the newest kids on the block

mouth and a tart and quenching finish. **India Pale Ale** and **Porter** have been added to the portfolio.

In Seattle the Redhook Brewery is the major craft brewery in the north-west. It was launched in 1982 by Gordon Bowker and Paul Shipman. Their success led to a move in 1988 to a converted "trolley barn" (tramshed) in the old Swedish Fremont district of the city. In 1994 it built a new brewery on the edge of the city. Before the move, Redhook produced 90,000 barrels a year. Its range includes a spicy **Wheat Hook**, a piny and orange-fruity **Extra Special Bitter** hopped with Tettnang and Willamettes, and a **Blachook Porter** made from black malt and roasted barley, and three hop varieties. It has a bitter chocolate and coffee aroma and a dark fruit finish, more of a stout than a porter.

In 1994 Redhook rocked the brewing industry when it agreed to sell 15 per cent of its shares to Anheuser-Busch. A-B said it would use its know-how and marketing muscle to sell Redhook beers nationally. By 1995 the A-B stake had grown to 25 per cent and Redhook announced it planned to build a new, 30-

million-dollar plant in Portsmouth, New Hampshire, opening up the East Coast to its products. The arrival of A-B is seen by some microbrewers as a sinister threat, by others as a boost for the image of craft brewing. Writing in the New Jersey-based *Ale Street News* in April 1995, industry analyst Mort Hochstein observed: "When elephants march, ants get trampled."

The Seattle-based Pike Place Brewery was founded by Charles Finkel, a man as dedicated to beer style as Bert Grant. As well as the tiny brewery, Finkel launched a brewery museum and a store selling both beer books and home-brew supplies. His ales include **Pale Ale**, **East India Pale Ale** and **Porter**. The Pale Ale (4.5 per cent by weight, 5.5 ABV) uses imported Maris Otter malt from Norfolk, England, 20 per cent crystal malt and is hopped with East Kent Goldings. It is a rich amber colour, has a peppery hop aroma, a biscuity palate and hops and dark fruit in the finish. East India Pale Ale (6.0 per cent by weight, 7.0 ABV) is brewed with pale, carapils and Munich malts and is hopped with Chinook, British Columbian and Goldings hops. It is

The Redhook Brewery is the major craft brewery of the north-western USA

tawny gold in colour, has a massive grapefruit aroma from the Chinooks, more tart fruit in the mouth and a powerful hoppy finish. **Porter** (5.0 per cent by weight, 6.0 ABV) has a rich coffee and chocolate aroma and palate from pale, crystal, chocolate and black malts, and dark winey fruit in a bitter finish.

Charles Finkel has now retired but Pike Place forges ahead and has boosted capacity to 250,000 barrels a year since moving to new premises.

Full Sail Brewing in Hood River, Oregon, enjoys one of the finest settings of any brewery in the world, overlooking the Columbia River Gorge at its confluence with the Hood River. The company has added a small brewpub in Portland. Full Sail's main plant has a capacity of 250,000 barrels a year and produces a full-bodied, malty **Amber** (5.8 per cent ABV), a German-style **Oktoberfest** (5.7 per cent), **Golden and Nut Brown Ales**, and a superb **Equinox ESB** (5.6 per cent) tingling with great hop character from English Target and Czech Saaz varieties. ESB, short for Extra Special Bitter, is now a recognized style in the USA, due to the success and fame of Fuller's ESB in far-away London, England. Full Sail, with a nice touch of humour, also brews a strong winter beer called **WasSail**.

In Seattle, Pyramid Ales and Thomas Kemper Lagers are two jointly owned companies, one concentrating, as its name implies, on warm-fermenting ales, the other on genuine German-style beers. Pyramid, with the enthusiastic support of American beer writer Benjamin Myers, has researched deeply into traditional styles to produce such richly malty and hop-tingling delights as **Pale Ale** (4.9 per cent ABV), **Espresso Stout** (5.6 per cent) and **Snow Cap Ale** (6.9 per cent). The success of its products enabled it to open a second brewery in Berkeley, California in 1997. Thomas Kemper uses an imported Bavarian yeast strain to ferment a wide range of lagers that includes a pale **Mai-bock** (6.6 per cent ABV), rich in tart fruit and hops, a robust, rounded **WinterBräu** (6.6 per cent), an **Amber** lager, a **WeizenBerry** wheat beer brewed with raspberry wheat, plus a **Belgian White** (4.4 per cent).

John Maier, head brewer at Rogue Ales in Newport, Oregon, is what Americans call a "hop head". He loves hops and the subtle and not-so-subtle aromas and flavours the small green herbs add to beers. Based in the Pacific north-west, Maier is able to buy some of the choicest hops from both Oregon and Washington State and he adopts the British practice of dry-hopping his finished ales in kegs. The bottled versions come in distinctive 22 fluid ounce (650 ml) bottles with embossed labels and welcome information about ingredients. **Shakespeare Stout** (6.1 per cent ABV), for example, is brewed from Harrington, Klages, and crystal malts, with imported English Beeston chocolate malt, plus rolled oats and roasted barley, with Cascade hops. **Mogul Ale** (6.5 per cent) bursts with hop character balanced by rich pale and darker malts. Maier and founder Jack Joyce produce two beers of stunning strength as well as flavour: an 11 per cent **Imperial Stout**, roasty and creamy, and **Old Crustacean** barley wine, bursting with fruit and hops (11.3 per cent). Tongue-in-cheek, Maier's own face appears on the label of the 6 per cent **Maierbock**, a warming, flavourful beer fermented with an ale yeast.

Alaskan Brewing of Juneau is famous for its **Smoked Porter**, which has won many awards. Founded by Geoff and Marcy Larson, the 5.5 per cent beer is made from pale, black, chocolate and crystal malts, with Chinook and Willamette hops. A local smokehouse takes the dark malts, spreads them on racks and smokes them over alder wood for three days. The finished beer, brewed once a year in winter and then vintage dated, has an intensely smoky aroma and palate, overlain by spicy hops and dark malt and chocolate. The smoked dark malts, allied to an intense bitterness, mean that beer brewed close to the Arctic Circle is the closest we may ever come to the aroma and flavour of an eighteenth-century London porter. The Larsons also brew an Alt-style beer called **Frontier Amber** (4.2 per cent), made from pale and caramel malts with American cascade and Czech Saaz hops. It has a big malt and light fruit bouquet and palate, with hops dominating the smooth finish.

East Coast

The Brooklyn brewing tradition has been revived by former journalist and keen home-brewer Steve Hindy and banker Tom Potter. When they planned their production they sought the advice of veteran brewer Bill Moeller, who was keen to recreate a pre-Prohibition

Brooklyn recipe. **Brooklyn Lager** (4.5 per cent by weight, 5.5 ABV) is a revelation, an indication of how rich and full-bodied American lager beers must have been before Prohibition, the Depression and the rise of the national giants suppressed aroma and flavour. It is almost ale-like in character, is brewed with crystal as well as pale malt and is dry-hopped. It has a rich malt, hops and cobnuts aroma, ripe malt in the mouth and a long finish full of malt and hops character. **Brooklyn Brown** is a warm-fermenting ale (4.8 per cent by weight, 6.0 ABV) made from pale, crystal, chocolate and black malts and hopped with Cascade and Northern Brewer. It is dry-hopped. Chocolate and coffee dominate the aroma and palate and the finish is dry, hoppy and chocolatey. Both beers have won awards from the Great American Beer Festival. They have been contract-brewed by F. X. Matt of Utica, but Hindy and Potter opened their own brewery in Brooklyn in 1996. Garrett Oliver, former brewmaster at the Manhattan Brewery, joined them in 1994 and has added a chocolate stout and an India Pale Ale.

A superb pale ale is brewed by the Geary Brewing Company in Portland, Maine. Peter Austin was again involved in designing the equipment for David Geary, who produced his first ale in 1986. Geary learnt his brewing skills in England, which explains the character of his Pale Ale, made from pale, crystal and chocolate malts imported from Britain. The hops are American varieties. **Pale Ale** is 3.6 per cent by weight, 4.5 ABV, and has a fine hop aroma and palate with a rich but restrained fruitiness in the finish. Geary also produces a stronger winter beer, **Hampshire Special Ale**, its label showing boats frozen in Maine. It is 5.6 per cent by weight, 7.0 ABV, and is rich, warming, spicy, fruity and hoppy.

David Geary worked for a while with Alan Pugsley, an English brewer who learned his skills with the renowned Peter Austin, founder of Ringwood Brewery in "Old" Hampshire and credited as the founding father of the British micro-brewing revolution. Pugsley, a devotee of good ale and Manchester United soccer club, moved from Geary to co-found with Fred Forsley the Shipyard Brewing Co., also in Portland, whose portfolio includes Ringwood's **Old Thumper** (5.6 per cent ABV), one-time winner of CAMRA's Champion Beer of Britain award, and produced under licence. All the Shipyard

brews have the characteristic Ringwood yeasty fruitiness, as Pugsley brought supplies with him. Other beers include an **IPA**, and **Longfellow Winter Ale** (5.5 per cent ABV). Brewing giant Miller has taken a half share in Shipyard: the plan (as with Anheuser-Busch and Redhook) is for Miller to market the beers, leaving Forsley and Pugsley to brew to their own recipes. Only time will tell whether Miller will be happy with the distinctiveness of Shipyard beers and their forceful malt and hop characters.

Catamount Brewing has the distinction of being the first commercial brewery to open in Vermont since 1893. It takes its name from New England's mountain lion. In common with many New England brewers, owner Steve Mason is heavily influenced by the Old Country, producing a **Pale Ale** with imported Fuggles and Goldings hops, an **Extra Special Bitter**, and a 5.3 per cent **Porter** rich in chocolate malt character.

Jeff Biegert at Atlantic Coast Brewing in Boston is also heavily influenced by English brewing practice, down to using Ringwood yeast. His flagship **Tremont Ale** (4.8 per cent ABV) is tart and hoppy, even has a hint of Burton-on-Trent sulphuriness and is sold cask-conditioned on draught. He also brews a tart, citric **IPA** (6.4 per cent) and an intensely fruity and hoppy **Old Scratch Barley Wine** (9 per cent).

One day Carol Stoudt may brew a stout when she grows tired of the jokes about her name. She trained in Germany and the brewery/restaurant/beer garden she runs in Adamstown, Pennsylvania with her husband Ed concentrates on brilliant, fastidious interpretations of German cold-fermented beers that have won more than 20 medals at the annual Great American Beer Festival. There is a powerful following for all things German in an area known, perversely, as "Pennsylvania Dutch", Dutch being a corruption of "Deutsch". Mrs Stoudt brews a **Pils** (4.5 per cent ABV) that, in her own words, is "assertively hopped with Saaz", a rich, malty **Gold** (5 per cent) in the Dortmunder Export style, and a smooth, full-bodied **Honey Double Mai Bock** (7.5 per cent).

There's yet more German influence behind the Penn Brewery in Pittsburgh where owner Tom Pastorius is a descendant of the Germans who first settled the city's "Germanstown". Pastorius worked as a brewer in the

Steve Hindy and Tom Potter, founders of the Brooklyn Brewery that producers beers which have the properties of the pre-Prohibition era

375

homeland and has installed German brewing equipment to produce a range that includes a **Dark** (Dunkel) at 5 per cent ABV, packed with roasty, chocolatey malt character, a wonderfully rich, nutty and spicy **Oktoberfest** (5.8 per cent), and a big-bodied **St Nikolaus Bock** (8.4 per cent). The expanding range at Penn includes a **Munich Helles**, a **Maibock**, several wheat beers, and a warm-fermented **Alt**.

The Yuengling Brewery in Pottsville, Pennsylvania, is the oldest surviving commercial brewery in the USA. It was founded by a German immigrant, David Yuengling, to supply thirsty workers when Pottsville was a mining town. The current brewery, built in the 1830s, was constructed, in the European and Scandinavian style, on a hill so that deep cellars could be dug underneath to lager or store the beer. Yuengling's beers were so prized that the company opened further breweries towards the end of the nineteenth century, but it almost went out of business during Prohibition. It survived and revived and now produces a wide range of beers, all cold-fermented lagers despite having an "ale" or two in the portfolio.

The company has joined the craze for Black & Tan beers, which in the USA means a blend of stout and lager, unlike Britain and Ireland where it indicates a mix of stout and bitter or mild. But Yuengling's stand-out beer is a 4.7 per cent **Porter**, full of rich, dark, chocolate malt character that, despite the name, is more in the style of a Bavarian Dunkel. Yuengling's success can be measured by the fact that brewing giant Anheuser-Busch has attempted unsuccessfully to strip the smaller brewery of its logo of the American eagle, which A-B also uses.

In Philadelphia, the Dock Street brewpub panders to the city's roots with some stunning beers in the Central European tradition: two Pils, Bohemian and German, a malty Dunkel, a vinous Bock, and a spicy Hefe-Weisse. Appealing to a wider audience, Dock Street also brews an English-style bitter and IPA, an Irish Red Ale and a smooth, chocolatey stout. It is renowned for its winter **Barley Wine** (9.5 per cent by weight, 11.8 ABV) which is fermented with an English ale yeast and finished with a Champagne culture. Hops in the kettle are English Fuggles and German Perle and Tettnang and dry-hopping uses Fuggles and Northern Brewer. The beer has 60 IBUs, a spicy aroma, smooth and creamy on the palate, and a lively, fruity/spicy/hoppy finish.

The Midwest

The powerful influence of German immigrants underscores the beers from August Schell Brewing in Minnesota. This is an "old German" brewery, complete with a large beer garden, not a new-wave micro. It survived Prohibition, introduced some bland lagers to compete with the giants, but kept tradition going with an acclaimed Bock. In recent years, Schell has added a hoppy/malty **Pils** (5.6 per cent ABV), that uses imported Hallertau hops, a Weizen wheat beer, and a rich, full-bodied **Maifest Bock** (6.9 per cent).

Goose Island Beer Company in Chicago started life as a brewpub and is named after an island in the Chicago River. It has expanded into a new stand-alone brewery in the city but the brewpub still produces a wide range of tasty ales, served in a spacious lounge that is a cross between American bar and English pub, with hearty food to boot. Depending on the time of year, you may find a range that stretches from a **Blonde Ale**, through a **Red Ale**, to a Cologne-style **Kölsch** (4.5 per cent ABV), a wheat Bock, and even a Finnish Sahti. The main beer is **Honker's Ale** (because geese honk), a 3.8 per cent ABV beer with an orange-gold colour and a tart hop character from the use of Styrian Goldings and some delicious fruit on the palate and finish. **Demolition Ale** (8 per cent) is a rich and potent Belgian-style ale in the style of Duvel, while the remarkable **Bourbon County Stout** (11.5 per cent) is aged for at least one hundred days in oak casks previously used to store Jim Beam whiskey. The casks impart a delicious hint of Bourbon to the beer alongside the impact of roasted malt and bitter hops.

Great Lakes has restored Cleveland's once vibrant brewing tradition with some of the most highly regarded beers in the Midwest and further south. The brewery has added a restaurant and beer garden. The **Eliot Ness** (5.6 per cent ABV) is a Vienna "red" lager that makes a deep bow in the direction of the pioneering work of Dreher. It is full-bodied, malty and spicy from the use of Hallertau and Tettnang hops. It is named after Eliot Ness, the Director of Public Safety (a title that seems to step from the pages of the French Revolution), who took on the mobsters when Cleveland was a tougher and rougher city between the two world wars. **Burning River Pale Ale** (6 per cent) is deliciously hoppy and packed with citric fruit: the name comes from the time when the heavily polluted local river caught fire (it has been cleaned up since then). **Conway's Irish Ale** (6.8 per cent) is malty and delicately hopped in the manner of the style. The **Edmund Fitzgerald Porter** (5.4 per cent) takes its name from a freighter that sank with all hands in the Great Lakes in 1975. Hopped with Cascade, Northern Brewer and Willamette varieties, producing a massive 60 units of bitterness, the porter has floral hops on the aroma, dark grain and chocolate in the mouth, and a gentle, fruity finish. There are several seasonal beers, including an IPA and a Christmas ale. The brewery is based in buildings once used by industrialist John D. Rockefeller and, with a nice touch of humour, he is honoured by a beer called **Rockefeller Bock**, which carries the slogan "as rich as its name".

Lakefront Brewery in Milwaukee is based in a former bakery and has restored flavour to beer in a city once synonymous with the bland offerings of national brewers. Its flagship beer is **Riverwest Stein Beer** (5.9 per cent ABV), yet another interpretation of Vienna Red, malty and spicy, and hopped with American Cascade and Mount Hood varieties. Other beers from Lakefront include a **Dunkel**, a **Pilsner**, **Pumpkin** beer and a **Spring Bock**.

The South-west and the South

Celis Brewery in Austin, Texas, is run by the much-travelled Pierre Celis, the man who revived the fortunes of Belgian "white" wheat beers with Hoegaarden in Belgium. When Interbrew bought Hoegaarden, Celis moved to the USA to bring the joys of Belgian beers to the Americas. He launched a new company in Austin with his daughter Christine, the first new brewery in the city since 1907. They imported hand-hammered copper brewing vessels made in Belgium in the 1930s that had once brewed Pilsner and pale ale. The brewing liquor comes from limestone wells, while Texas winter wheat is grown in Luckenback and is blended with barley malt imported from Belgium. **Celis White** (4.8 per cent ABV) is hopped with American-grown Cascade and Willamette varieties and spiced with coriander and Curaçao orange peel. It is a highly complex, soft, mellow, spicy and quenching beer. Celis has added **Grand Cru** (8.8 per cent), a golden ale also spiced with coriander and orange peel, and rich in floral hops and delicious fruit and spice notes. **Golden** (4.9 per cent) is a hoppy Pilsner using Saaz hops, lagered for six weeks, and other brews include a pale bock and a fruit wheat beer. In 1994, Celis sold a controlling interest in the company to Miller, but Pierre and Christine have been left in charge of brewing and development while the giant sells the beers more widely.

Denver, high in the Colorado Rockies, used to be a city dominated by Coors of nearby Boulder. There is now such choice in Denver that Coors has had to respond with a brewpub in the local baseball stadium it sponsors that offers ales and stouts. The pacesetter in the Denver revival has been the Wynkoop brewpub close to the railroad station. Launched by John Hickenlooper, who also runs a major book store in Denver, Wynkoop is the biggest brewpub in America and, by definition, the world. Some of the beers are sold in cask-conditioned form in the pub. The main brand is **Railyard Ale**, a cross, says Hickenlooper, between an English pale ale and a Bavarian Oktoberfest. The proliferating range includes an **IPA** (5.3 per cent ABV), and smooth and creamy **Sagebrush Stout** (5 per cent). Hickenlooper has joined forces with David Bruce from England, founder of the Firkin chain of brewpubs. They are now busily opening Wynkoop-style operations in other parts of the country. A massive operation opened in Jersey City in 1997 while a planned brewpub at Niagara Falls will allow Canadians as well as Americans to sample the tasty beers.

Tabernash of Denver offers a different drinking experience. Brewmaster Eric Warner trained at Weihenstephan in Munich and has written the definitive book on German wheat beers. His **Weisse** (5.5 per cent ABV) is considered the best American interpretation of the style, with spicy, fruity, banana and bubblegum flavours. All Warner's other beers are lagers, including a malt-loaf tasting **Munich** (4.9 per cent), and a rich and toasted malt **Oktoberfest** (6 per cent). The name Tabernash comes from a town of that name in Colorado, which in turn comes from the name of a Native American Chief of the Ute tribe.

In North Carolina there is a powerful English brewing tradition at Top of the Hill in Chapel Hill, near Durham. Owner Daniel Bradford is descended from the Pilgrims who made the legendary trip to the Americas on the *Mayflower*. Bradford, former publisher of the USA's most influential beer magazine, *All About Beer*, employs English brewer John Withey, formerly of Shepherd Neame in Kent, to fashion an **IPA**, **Golden Ale**, **Porter**, stout and now obligatory **Extra Special Bitter**.

In Texas, Yellow Rose of San Antonio is also, surprisingly, mainly influenced by English traditions, with gritty frontier images grafted on. **Vigilante Porter** (4.4 per cent ABV) is a fine example of a quenching dark beer that should be quite distinct from a heavier stout. It is delightfully chocolatey, with dark fruit and tart hops. **Pale Ale** (5.1 per cent) is well-hopped with a good balance of malt, while **Honcho Grande** (5.1 per cent) is a big-bodied and full-tasting brown ale.

Oldenberg Brewing of Fort Mitchell, Kentucky, offers a wide range of beers, including pale ale, brown ale, stout and Hefe-Weiss, but its flagship beer stresses its German origins, **Bock** (5 per cent) is a smooth, creamy version of the style and has helped to revive interest in quality beers in a region of the USA where the heat, early Prohibition, God-fearin' folk, and the dominance of large producers have combined to offer bland brews and weaken choice.

Opposite: The Celis Brewery in Austin, Texas, was founded by Piere Celis to introduce the delights of Belgian-style beers to the USA

UNITED STATES BREWERS

Alaskan Brewing, 5429 Shaune Drive, Juneau, AK 99801.

Anchor Brewing Co, 1705 Mariposa Street, San Francisco, CA 94107.

Anheuser-Busch Inc, 1 Busch Place, St Louis, MO 63118-1852.

Atlantic Coast Brewing, 50 Terminal Street, Boston, MA 02129.

Boston Beer Company, 30 Germania Street, Boston, MA 02130.

Brooklyn Brewery, 118 North 11th Street, Brooklyn, NY 11211.

Catamount Brewing, 58 South Main Street, White River Junction, VT 05001.

Celis Brewery, 2431 Forbes Drive, Austin, TX 78754.

Adolph Coors Company, East of Town, Golden, CO 80401.

Dock Street Brewery and Restaurant, 2 Logan Square, Philadelphia, PA 19103.

Full Sail Brewing, 506 Columbia, Hood River, OR 97031.

D. L. Geary Brewing Company, 38 Evergreen Drive, Portland, ME 04103.

Goose Island Beer Co., 1800 West Fulton, Chicago, IL 60612.

Gordon Biersch, 2 Harrison Street, San Francisco, CA 94105.

Grant's Yakima Brewing and Malting Company, 1803 Presson Place, Yakima, WA 98902.

Great Lakes Brewing, 2516 Market Street, Cleveland, OH 44113.

G. Heileman Brewing Co Inc, 100 Harborview Plaza, PO Box 459, La Crosse, WI 54601-4051.

Lakefront Brewery, 818 East Chambers Street, Milwaukee, WI 53212.

Mendocino Brewing Company, 13351 Highway 101, Hopland, CA 95449.

Miller Brewing Company, 3939 W Highland Blvd, Milwaukee, WI 53208-2816.

Oldenberg Brewing, 400 Buttermilk Pike, Fort Mitchell, KY 41017.

Pabst Brewing Company, 917 W Jumeau Ave, PO Box 766, Milwaukee, WI 53233-1428.

Pacific Coast Brewery, 906 Washington Street, Oakland, CA 94607.

Penn Brewery, 800 Vinial Street, Pittsburgh, PA 15212.

Pete's Wicked Brewing Company, 514 High Street, Palo Alto, CA 94301.

Pike Place Brewery, 1432 Western Avenue, Seattle, WA 622-1880.

Portland Brewing Company, 1339 Northwest Flanders Street, Portland, OR 97209.

Pyramid Ales/Thomas Kemper Lagers, 915 Royal Brougham Way, Seattle, WA 98134.

Redhook Brewery, 3400 Phinney Avenue North, Seattle, WA 98103.

Rogue Ales, 2320 OSU Drive, Newport, OR 97365.

St Stan's Brewing, 821 L Street, Modesto, CA 95354.

August Schell Brewing, PO Box 128, New Ulm, MN 56073.

Shipyard Brewing Co, 86 Newbury Street, Portland, ME 04101.

Sierra Nevada Brewing Company, 1075 East 20th Street, Chico, CA 95928.

Stoudt's Brewing, PO Box 880, Adamston, PA 19501.

Stroh Brewery Company, 100 River Place, Detroit, MI 48207-4224.

Sudwerk Privatbrauerei Hübsch, 2001 Second Street, Davis, CA 95616.

Tabernash Brewing, 205 Denargo Market, Denver, CO 80216.

Top of the Hill, 100 East Franklin Street, Chapel Hill, NC 27514.

Wynkoop Brewing, 1634 Eighteenth Street, Denver, CO 80202.

Yellow Rose Brewing, 17201 San Pedro Avenue, San Antonio, TX 78232.

Yuengling Brewery, 5th & Manhantongo Streets, Pottsville, PA 17901.

CANADA

Canadians understandably bridle when Europeans think of their country as an appendage to the United States. But there are striking similarities in the development of the beer market, with substantial cross-border trading and link-ups. Labatt, for example, now owns the major US brand Rolling Rock, and the introduction in the 1990s of "ice beer" was spearheaded by Canadian brewers and taken up by the giants in the United States.

The shape of Canadian brewing, in common with its neighbour, was determined in large measure by Prohibition, which ran for longer, throughout the First World War and until 1932. The result was an industry dominated by a few giants. The big three all started as ale brewers but, encouraged by what they saw in the USA, have concentrated on lagers in the 5.0 per cent ABV bracket. Six-row barley enables them to use substantial levels of adjuncts, usually corn. With low bitterness rates of around 10 IBUs, mainstream lagers tend to be sweet, creamy, undemanding and underhopped. The domination of the giants was intensified in 1989 when Molson and Carling merged, giving the new group around 50 per cent of the market. Foster's of Australia, the previous owner of Carling, now has a substantial stake in Molson and Miller of Milwaukee also has a minority shareholding.

The beer scene is changing slowly, but for the better. Micros are emerging and there are now some characterful ales. But brewpubs are illegal in many provinces and the new generation of entrepreneurial brewers has had to fight a guerrilla war to establish their outlets.

Molson is the oldest brewery in Canada and the whole of North America. Its origins date from the nineteenth century when John Molson emigrated from Lincolnshire in England, clutching a copy of John Richardson's *Theoretical Hints on the Improved Practice of Brewing*. In 1786 he opened a brewery in Montreal and the company he founded is still controlled by his descendants. Carling O'Keefe dates from a merger in the nineteenth century between the breweries founded by Sir Thomas Carling in 1840 and

Eugene O'Keefe in 1862. Today Molson brews in Ontario, Vancouver, Edmonton, Winnipeg, Prince Albert, Regina, and St John's, Newfoundland. Its main brands are 5.0 per cent light-tasting beers, **Golden** and **Export**, plus the ubiquitous **Carling Black Label**, also 5.0 per cent and firmer-bodied. It produces specialist beers for some regional markets, including a 6.25 top-fermenting **Brador**, rich and fruity, and **Royal** and **Imperial Stouts**. In 1993 Molson declared it was no longer using preservatives in its products and launched "Molson Signature", specialist all-malt beers, including a smooth, fruity **Cream Ale** with a hint of hop, and a malty/nutty **Amber Lager**. **Molson's Ice**, also introduced in 1993 to counter the pioneering Labatt's version, has a slightly skunky, perfumy aroma but no discernible palate or finish.

Labatt dates back to a small brewery built in 1828 in London, Ontario by an innkeeper named George Balkwill. He sold the business to William and George Snell in 1828 who in turn sold it to Samuel Eccles and John Labatt in 1847. Labatt became the sole owner in 1853.

In June 1995 Labatt was bought by Interbrew of Belgium. As well as Rolling Rock in the USA, Labatt also controls Moretti in Italy. Its Canadian beers are thin, with some perfumy aroma from malt and adjuncts. The flagship brand is the bland **Labatt's Blue** (5.0 per cent ABV), which is also produced in a Light version. **Labatt's Classic** is all-malt but light in flavour while **Labatt's 50 Canadian Ale** has some faint malt and hop character. Its **IPA** has nothing in common with the style, while its **Porter** is thin and caramel-tinted. **Ice Beer**, launched with a crescendo of hype in 1993, started the craze for the style. During the brewing process the temperature of the beer is lowered until ice crystals form. These are removed, according to the brewery, to take out proteins and other undesirables. Although the finished beer is high in alcohol, 5.8 per cent ABV in the case of Labatt, most of the flavour has also been removed. Beers brewed in this fashion can only have rounded and pleasing flavours if they are lagered for lengthy periods. In the case of the Canadian and American ice beers, the rapid brewing method adopted leaves behind some rough esters that give a perfumy, nail-polish aroma and finish.

Moosehead is the largest and longest-surviving independent in Canada. Its remote plants in New Brunswick and Nova Scotia have had a turbulent history. Its story began with John and Susannah Oland brewing in their backyard in Dartmouth, Nova Scotia, in 1867, using old family recipes brought from Britain. Their ales were sufficiently popular for the Olands to win a contract to supply the armed forces. Renamed the Army & Navy Brewery, the company moved to new premises on the waterfront at Dartmouth. Three years later John Oland was killed in a horse-riding accident and his widow was forced to sell a controlling interest in the brewery. With the help of an inheritance, she bought back her stake in 1877 and renamed the company S. Oland, Sons & Co. When Susannah died, her youngest son George took over control of the brewery, but again they faced tragedy. When two ships collided in Halifax Harbour in 1917 brewmaster Conrad Oland was killed and his brother John injured. The family soldiered on. With the help of the insurance money, George Oland and his son moved to a new site in St John, New Brunswick. Even though Prohibition was still in operation and beer was restricted to 2.0 per cent ABV, the Olands prospered and returned to Halifax. Their fortunes soared in 1931 when George Oland rechristened his main ale brand with the charismatic name of Moosehead. Such was the success of the brand that the company name was changed in 1947 from New Brunswick to Moosehead. Today Moosehead has breweries in St John, New Brunswick and Dartmouth, Nova Scotia.

Moosehead has had enormous success in the United States but the brewery's beers have paid the price. **Moosehead Pale Ale** has some light hop aroma from the use of Czech Saaz and is dry in the finish but has little ale character, while **Canadian Lager** (5.0 per cent ABV) is in the inoffensive but unexciting mainstream.

It is scarcely surprising that ale brewing has taken root in Victoria on Vancouver Island, British Columbia, for this is the most English of Canadian regions, its population packed with ex-patriates. Spinnakers, on the outskirts of the town, was the dream of Paul Hadfield and John Mitchell, both from Vancouver town on the mainland. Mitchell returned home in 1982 from a trip to Britain with samples of 14 English ales. When the two men and their friends tasted them they were fired with enthusiasm to build a small brewery to produce beers along similar lines. They faced major legal obstacles. The city of Victoria refused to grant a licence for a brewpub but later said it would give planning permission as long as local people supported the idea in a referendum. Ninety-five per cent voted yes. Permission to brew and retail beer needed an amendment to Federal law; it came just two months before the brewpub was due to open. Spinnakers, with superb views out over the sea, was packed from opening day in May 1984.

The small attached brewhouse, built by an English firm in Manchester, has been expanded twice to meet demand. Paul Hadfield's main brew is **Spinnaker Ale** (4.2 per cent ABV). It is made from pale malt with a dash of crystal and is hopped with Cascades from Yakima and Centennial from Oregon. It has an apple fruit aroma, more tart fruit in the mouth and a light dry finish. **Mount Tolmie**, also 4.2 per cent, uses caramalt, chocolate and crystal blended with pale malt. Mount Hood hops are added in the copper and the beer is dry hopped with Cascade. It has a citric fruit aroma, dark, tart fruit in the mouth and a dry and bitter finish. **Doc Hadfield's Pale Ale** (4.2 per cent ABV) uses Mount Hood for aroma and bitterness. The ale has a piny aroma with citric fruit in the mouth and a light, dry finish with fruit notes. **Mitchell's ESB**, named in honour of the other founding partner, is 4.6 per cent, copper-coloured, with a grapefruit aroma and palate from Chinook hops and a citric finish, with hints of sultana fruit from crystal and chocolate malts. There is a late addition of Cascade hops.

A 4.9 per cent **India Pale Ale** is hopped with Centennials and is mashed with pale malt only. It has a resiny hop aroma, tart fruit and hops in the mouth and a citric fruit finish. A complex **Porter** (4.9 per cent ABV) uses pale, crystal, chocolate and roasted malt and malted wheat, with Centennial and Hallertau hops. It has a herbal, slightly lactic aroma, and is tart

The Toronto based Upper Canada Brewing Company is named after the early settlers' name for the province now called Ontario

Michael Williams from Shropshire in England. He emigrated to Canada and became a sheep farmer. He moved into property, bought an old warehouse in Victoria and turned it into Swans. The brewhouse is run by Chris Johnson, a home-brewer who worked in the hotel kitchen and graduated to head brewer. Malt, including pale, crystal, chocolate and roast plus oatmeal, all come from the major English malting company, Bairds. He brews a 5.0 per cent **Bitter** with a nutty, malty aroma with piny hops, dark raisin fruit in the mouth and a dry, bitter finish. The 4.5 per cent **Pandora Pale Gold** has light citric fruit on the aroma, quenching hops in the mouth and a bitter-sweet finish. An impressive 8.0 per cent **Scotch Ale** has big winey fruit and hops on the aroma, raisin and sultana fruit in the mouth and a complex finish with malt, nuts and late hop. **Appleton Brown Ale** (5.0 per cent ABV) is named after the designer of the brewhouse, Frank Appleton. It has pronounced apple fruit and cinnamon aromas, dark fruit in the mouth, and a creamy, bitter-sweet finish. **Rye Weizen** has a four-hour run-off from the mash tun because of the sticky rye grain. It is 5.7 per cent, has a dark biscuity aroma, a bready, spicy palate and a dry finish with a late burst of fruit. **Oatmeal Stout** (5.4 per cent ABV) has a rich, dark coffee and hops aroma, bitter-sweet malt, chocolate and hops in the mouth, and a tart and bitter finish.

German brewer Hermann Hoerterer helped to develop the beers at Vancouver Island Brewery, one of Canada's earliest micro producers. **Hermann's Dark Lager** (5.5 per cent), rich in chocolate malt character, pays homage to him, as does the tongue-in-cheek name of a winter Bock called **Hermanntor** (the strength varies from year to year but usually classifies as a double bock). The brewery also produces a splendid **Weizen**, rich in banana aroma and flavour, and a pale ale.

Okanagan Spring Brewery in Vernon, British Columbia, also has strong Germanic influences. It was founded by German immigrants and is now the biggest micro-brewery in the province. Starting with a fine **Premium Lager**, it has spread to a more eclectic range that includes a pale ale, brown ale, porter, stout and wheat beer. The **Old English Porter** (8.5 per cent ABV) is especially highly regarded. It is bottle-fermented and

in the mouth. **Empress Stout** is the same strength, with bitter chocolate and hops in the mouth. As a sight for sore British eyes, the beers are served by beer engine and handpump. Paul Hadfield has now branched out with a Hefe-Weizen and a lambic.

There are more handpumps on view in Swan's Hotel in the centre of Victoria. The hotel, restaurant and attached Buckerfields Brewery are owned by

C A N A D I A N B R E W E R S

Labatt Brewing Co Ltd, 150 Simcoe Street, PO Box 5050, London, ON N6A 4M3.

La Cervoise, 4457 Blvd St Laurent, Montreal, PQ H2W 1Z8.

Le Cheval Blanc, 809 Ontario Street, Montreal, PQ H2L 1P1.

Creemore Springs Brewery, 139 Mill Street, Creemore, ON L0M 1G0.

Molson Breweries of Canada Ltd, 3300 Bloor Street W, Suite 3500, Toronto, ON M8X 2X7.

Moosehead Breweries Ltd, 89 Main Street, PO Box 3100, Station B, St John, NB E2M 3H2.

Okanagan Spring Brewery, 2801-27A Avenue, Vernon, BC V1T 1T5.

Spinnakers, 309 Catherine Street, Victoria BC V9A 3S8.

Swans Hotel/Buckerfields, 506 Pandora Street, Victoria BC, V8W 1N6.

Unibroue, 80 Des Carrieres, Chambly, PQ J3L 2H6.

Upper Canada Brewing Company, 2 Atlantic Avenue, Toronto, ON M6K 1X8.

Wellington County Brewery Ltd, 9500 Woodlawn Road W, Guelph, ON N1K 1B8.

has a delicious chocolate malt character balanced by bitter hops and dark fruit.

Upper Canada Brewing Company in Toronto uses the early settlers' name for the province of Ontario. The sizeable micro was founded in 1985 by Frank Heaps. The 5.0 per cent **Dark Ale** is a cross between a strong English mild with a dash of Belgian red ale sourness. It has an intensely fruity aroma and palate with more tart dark fruit and bitter hops in the finish. A 6.0 per cent **Rebellion Malt Liquor** is fruity and spicy, while **Upper Canada Lager** is malty and firm bodied. A 4.3 per cent **Wheat Beer** has more than 35 per cent wheat malt blended with pale barley malt. Hops are Northern Brewer (18 to 20 IBUs). The beer is filtered and has a tart and fruity aroma and palate with some light spiciness in the finish. **True Bock** is rich, malty and fruity. All the beers are brewed without additives and are not pasteurized.

In the old brewing town of Guelph, the Wellington County Brewery produces an **Arkell Best Bitter** to mark a family connection with the Swindon brewing family of Arkell in Wiltshire, England. The 4.0 per cent cask-conditioned ale has a peppery Goldings hops aroma, malt and fruit in the mouth and a long,

hoppy-fruity finish. The brewery also produces a fruity **Wellington SPA** (4.5 per cent ABV), a hoppy **County Ale** (5.0 per cent ABV), a rich and fruity strong ale called **Iron Duke** (6.5 per cent ABV), and a roasty and chocolatey **Imperial Stout** (8.0 per cent ABV).

The Francophone areas of Canada are also joining the beer revival. Many of the first French settlers came from Normandy and Flanders and have an ale-brewing tradition. Les Brasseurs du Nord in St Jerôme, north of Montreal, brews a dry **Blonde**, a fruity **Rousse** and a smooth, dark **Noire**. La Cervoise in the heart of Montreal has **La Main**, a sweetish amber ale, a golden **Good Dog** ale, and a dry stout called **Obelix**.

Le Cheval Blanc, also in Montreal, has a chocolatey **Ambrée**, an espresso-like **Brune** and a tart **Weissbier**.

Unibroue in Chambly, Quebec, is now the leading small brewery in the French-speaking area. One of the founders was Canadian rock singer Robert Charlebois, and the company was initially helped by the Belgian Riva group, producers of Dentergems Witbier. The main brand, **Blanche de Chambly** (5 per cent ABV) is delicious, with tart orange and lemon fruit flavours. **Maudite**, meaning "damned", is 8 per cent, styled in the fashion of a Belgian strong ale, and packed with fruit and spice character. A fetching label shows a flying canoe with the devil waiting below: it is taken from a legend concerning a party of trappers who sold their souls to the devil to get home in time for a party. The alarmingly named **La Fin du Monde** (End of the World) is 9 per cent and is in the style of a Belgian Trippel. **Quelque Chose** (8 per cent) is a spiced cherry beer that includes some whisky malt that imparts a smoky texture. All the Unibroue beers are bottle fermented.

Creemore Springs, in a small town of the same name in Ontario, is based in a converted hardware store in a ski resort. It concentrates on just one beer, **Premium Lager** (5 per cent), brewed from spring water, malt, hops and, as the bucolic label says, "all the good stuff and lots of tender loving care". Placed between a Pilsner and a Czech Budweiser, it has a rich malt, vanilla and floral hops character.

LATIN AMERICA AND THE CARIBBEAN

Latin America has a fascinating and long brewing tradition and it is tragic that the tradition has largely been submerged and suborned in recent years by modish thin lagers from Mexico that are neither typical of that country nor the continent as a whole. Yuppies in Manhattan, London and Berlin who drink Corona and Sol straight from the bottle with a wedge of lime stuck in the neck may be making a statement about their lifestyle – raspberry would be a better fruit – but are denying the quality and the heritage of good Latin American beer.

LATIN AMERICA

Long before Europeans arrived in Latin America the natives were making a variety of beers from the ingredients to hand. The Mayans of Central America brewed from fermented corn stalks while the Aztecs of northern Mexico produced a more advanced beer made from maize that had been allowed to sprout. According to legend, it was the task of specially chosen maidens of the Inca tribe living around Lake Titicaca to chew the cooked maize pulp used in brewing. Only their beauty and the purity of their saliva would start fermentation, it was believed. Even when the Spanish had conquered vast areas of the continent, peasants continued to make *pulque* from the juice of the algave plant. The name comes from a Spanish word meaning "decomposed", as the drink will keep for only a day before going off.

Pulque and other native drinks survive in Latin America. In the remote areas of the Upper Amazon a black beer has been made since at least the fifteenth century. The colour comes from the use of roasted barley and grain that are dark brown in colour. It is flavoured with lupin plants. The American beer writer and anthropologist Alan Eames – nicknamed the "Indiana Jones of Beer" – searched and found the beer in remote areas and encouraged a Brazilian brewery, Cervejaria Cacador in Brazil, to make it commercially. It is called **Xingu** (5.0 per cent ABV), pronounced shin-gu, the name of a tributary of the Amazon River. It is a modern, conventionally-brewed interpretation of the style, using hops for both flavouring and as a preservative.

Small Spanish breweries – *cervecería* – were established from the sixteenth century, but distilled spirits such as mescal and tequila were more popular than beer until the arrival of ice-making machines in the nineteenth century. The first lager beers were known as *sencilla* or *corriente* and were matured for short periods.

Some earlier breweries achieved remarkable success, however. In December 1543 Don Alonso de Herrera from Seville, known as a citizen of "New Spain" (Mexico), built a brewery in Mexico City and launched a beer called **Zerbeza**. It means Desire, the sort of name that modern marketing departments of breweries would pay a lot of money for. Such was the local desire for Zerbeza that Don Alonso had to add 100 additional vats to keep up with demand.

The modern influences in Mexican brewing are Germanic. Some of the first lager breweries were established by Bavarians, Swiss and Alsatians. The country was briefly and incongruously a colony of the Austrian empire, with Archduke Maximilian doubling as Emperor of Mexico. One of the few benefits of the association was the influence of the great Viennese brewer Anton Dreher, who invented the style of amber beers. The style has virtually vanished from Austria but is alive and well in the former colony.

Today two giants dominate Mexican brewing. In Mexico City, Modelo runs the biggest brewing plant in the country, which rivals all but the top five American groups in size. It is best-known today for **Corona**, the beer that spawned the Mexican lager-and-lime craze. Like its competitor, **Sol**, **Corona Extra** (4.6 per cent ABV) has been around for decades and was a bottom-of-the-range product made cheaply for poor peasants and industrial workers. It comes in a utilitarian plain glass bottle with an embossed label. It has around 40 per cent rice in its recipe and a low hop rate that creates

Modelo brews the famous Corona dark beer in Mexico City

around 10 to 12 IBUs. Served extremely cold, it is a refreshing drink for those engaged in hard manual labour, which is more than can be said for the well-heeled young Americans on surfing holidays. They took up the beer with enthusiasm and extolled its peasant-cum-worker attributes when they returned to California and Manhattan – a middle-class attitude known as being "prolier than thou". It was the Americans who added lime to the beer, which caused amusement and consternation in Mexico, though sad to say the habit has now been taken up there as well.

A beer with not only pedigree but taste is Modelo's **Negra Modelo** – Black Modelo. It is dark brown rather than black, a cross between a Vienna Red and a Munich

Dunkel, 5.3 per cent ABV, 19 IBUs, with a chocolatey aroma with some hop character, sweet dark malt in the mouth and a long finish with a hint of spice, more chocolate and hops, ending with a dry roastiness. Modelo also owns the Yucatán Brewery which produces a similar dark beer called **Negra Leon**. The dark colour of these beers owes only part of its inspiration to Vienna. Before modern malting developed, Latin American brewers dried their grain in the sun, giving beers a russet hue as a result.

Modelo has the single largest brewing plant but the group has been overtaken in size by the merger of Moctezuma and Cuauhtémoc. They both belong to a holding company called Valores, which runs seven

From Monterrey in Mexico, thousands of bottles filled with beer are ready to be packed and despatched to all parts of the world

breweries in Mexico. Moctezuma dates from 1894 when it was built by Henry Manthey, William Hasse, C. von Alten and Adolph Burhard in Orizaba, Veracruz. Cuauhtémoc, named after an Aztec emperor, took on the name in 1890 when the Casa Calderón Brewery in Monterrey was extended. Moctezuma is best known today for **Sol** (4.6 per cent ABV), a Corona lookalike also produced in a clear glass bottle. It is believed to have an even higher level of adjuncts than Corona. Of far greater interest is **Dos Equis** – Two Crosses – dark

lager (4.8 per cent ABV), widely available in foreign markets. It is in the Vienna style, a fraction paler than Negra Modelo, and with a rich dark fruit and chocolate aroma and palate, with more chocolate and light hops in the finish. **Superior** (4.5 per cent ABV) is a far more interesting pale lager than Sol, with some hop bite.

Cuauhtémoc also has a thin quencher in the Corona/Sol style with the risible name – to outsiders – of **Chihuahua**, which is a Mexican state as well as a small dog. Tecate – once advertised as "the Gulp of

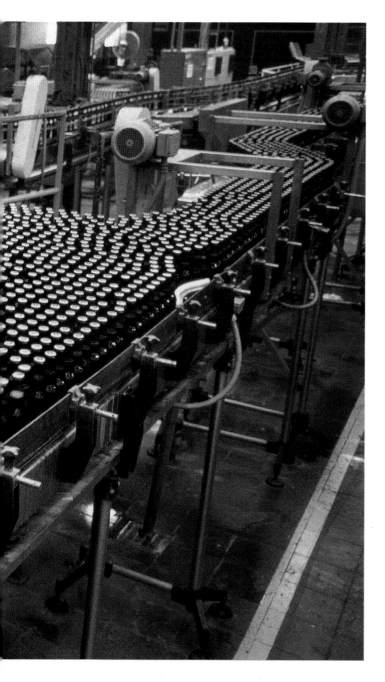

Schuehle who also built the original Moctezuma Brewery. **Pacifico Clara** is a light lager while **Pacifico Oscura** is a thin amber beer.

Brazil was invaded by the Portuguese rather than the Spanish but the modern brewing tradition is Germanic. **Brahma**, brewed by Companhia Cervejaria in Rio de Janeiro, is a fine Pilsner-style beer (5.0 per cent ABV) with a rich malt and vanilla aroma, a malty palate and a bitter-sweet finish with late developing hops. The group produces more than 31 million hectolitres a year and, surprisingly, its brands include a warm-fermenting, 8.0 per cent ABV **Porter**. Some zealous porter sniffers suggest another possible origin of the beer style's enigmatic name: they say it comes not from London street porters but from Portugal!

In Peru, the similarly-named Compañia Cervecera brews **Peru Gold** with a striking native face mask on the label. The beer is 5.0 per cent ABV, has a rich corn and vanilla aroma, is tart and quenching in the mouth, and has a dry finish with some citric fruit notes from the hops. It also produces **Cuzco Peruvian Beer**. In Venezuela, the Polar brewing company's **Polar Lager** (5.0 per cent ABV) is so remarkably thin that it makes Corona and Sol seem malty and hoppy by comparison. It is nevertheless a major brand, responsible for more than 12 million hectolitres a year. The Cardenal group in the same country has a more distinctive range, including **Nacional "Cerveza Tipo Pilsen"** – Beer Type Pilsen, which indicates the astonishing impact of Pilsen beer and deserves marks for honesty of promotion. A German influence can be seen in the brewery's **Tipo Munich** beer, a malty, burnished gold lager, while **Andes** is more typical of the light beers of the continent.

Cervecería Bieckert in Buenos Aires, Argentina, despite being a former Spanish colony, is also heavily influenced by German and Czech styles. **Cerveza Pilsen** (4.8 per cent ABV) is brewed from pale malt, rice and maize and is hopped with American Cascades. It has 13 IBUs. Pilsen is more of an illusion than an allusion, for the lightly hopped and heavily adjuncted beer is low on aroma, body and flavour. **Especial** (5.0 per cent ABV) has 14 IBUs and the same grist recipe and has a shade more character. The most interesting product is **Africana** (5.5 per cent ABV), a cold-fermenting beer that is a hybrid Munich Dunkel and Vienna Red. It is

Mexico" – is another pale ("clara") beer useful for quenching the thirst, as is **Carta Blanca** ("white label") launched in 1890 in the Pilsner style but now another thin mainstream beer. **Bohemia** is in a different league, an indication of what Mexican brewers can achieve when they turn their gaze away from their neighbour to the north. At 5.4 per cent ABV it has some clout and good hop character – Saaz are used – that complements the rich malt and vanilla aroma and firm malty body.

Mazatlán in Sinaloa state is now owned by Modelo. It opened in 1900 and was established by Jacob

Carib, from the island of Trinidad, is not brewed under licence in the UK unlike Red Stripe, the Caribbean's best-known beer

LATIN AMERICAN BREWERS

Cervecería Bieckert SA, Ponsato 121 Llavallol (1836) Pcia, Buenos Aires, Argentina.

Cervecería Moctezuma, Avenida Alfonso Reyes 2202, Nte, Monterrey NL 64442, Mexico.

Cervecería Modelo, 156 Lago Alberto, Mexico City 11320, Mexico.

brewed from pale, crystal and chocolate malts with rice and maize and is hopped with Cascades (14 IBUs). It has a tempting roasted malt aroma, a smooth chocolate palate and a dry finish with hints of dark fruit, more chocolate and a tart Cascade note.

THE CARIBBEAN

The islands of the Caribbean have brewed beer for centuries. The quickly made native porridge beers, known by a welter of names in the different islands – *tesguino, chicha, izquiate, sendecho, zeydetha* and *zeyrecha*, the last two sounding like derivatives of the Spanish *cerveza* – succumbed to both the imported beers of the British, Spanish and French and to the comfort of locally-made rum. Guinness's **West Indies Porter** had a profound impact in the early nineteenth century. Known today as **Foreign Extra Stout** (7.3 per cent ABV), it is brewed in Spanish Town, the former capital of Jamaica, and by the Carib company in Trinidad.

The main beers today are light lagers but several Caribbean brewers keep a stout in their lockers. There is even a **Prestige Stout** from the unlikely location of Haiti where there is a morbid joke that under the old Duvalier regime all beers were lagered or stored for very long periods. Cuba's main brewery was founded in the last century by two brewers of German extraction, Obermeyer and Liebmann, who went to Havana from Brooklyn. The Nacional Dominicana Brewery in Santo Domingo, Dominican Republic, produces more than two million barrels/2.4 million hectolitres a year and is the biggest brewery in the region. **Bohemia** is the main

product, a 5.0 per cent lager that is a rather thin interpretation of the Pilsner style.

The major brewery in the former British West Indies is Desnoes & Geddes of Kingston, Jamaica. It was founded in 1918 as a soft drinks business by Eugene Desnoes and Thomas Geddes. The families are still in control, with Peter Desnoes and Paul Geddes running the company, though Heineken now has a small shareholding. The flagship brand is **Red Stripe** (4.7 per cent ABV; 14 IBUs), a malty, sweetish rather perfumy beer, the product of a short lagering regime. Its grist is made up of 70 per cent barley malt and 30 per cent corn. In common with many Australian beers, Red Stripe began life as an ale but switched to cold fermentation in the 1930s. Red Stripe is brewed under licence in Britain by Charles Wells and is popular in the West Indian community. The company's **Dragon Stout** (7.0 per cent ABV) is also a lager, with a sweet malt character overlain by chocolate and dark fruit with some hop character. The Jamaicans do not shy away from stressing the alleged aphrodisiac qualities of the beer. Its most famous promotion declared that "Dragon Puts It Back".

On Barbados, the Banks Brewery produces **Banks Beer**, a 4.5 per cent lager made from two-row pale malt and brewing sugar. It is hopped with Yakima Clusters and Styrian Goldings and has 16 IBUs. The beer has a delicate, citric hop aroma, smooth malt in the mouth and a finish that becomes dry with good hop notes. It is lagered for a month. **Carib Lager** from Trinidad is a fully brewed-out beer, dry and quenching in the finish with some hops on the aroma and a firm, malty body.

IMPORTANT ADDRESSES

Banks (Barbados) Breweries Ltd, PO Box 507C, Wildey, St Michael, Barbados.

Desnoes & Geddes Ltd, 214 Spanish Town Road, PO Box 190, Kingston 11, Jamaica.

BEERS FROM THE REST OF THE WORLD

Modern brewing methods – for both ale and lager – were part of the baggage of imperialism in the eighteenth and nineteenth centuries. British, French, Dutch and German settlers brewed for themselves and their troops but the taste for beer remained and spread when the troops and sometimes the settlers returned home. Lager is now the dominant beer style in Africa, India and Asia and often of the highest quality. But there are residual pockets of ale brewing, including the post-imperial stouts of Sri Lanka and a warm-fermenting beer or two in Japan.

AFRICA AND THE MIDDLE EAST

Africa was the birthplace of brewing. Although no records exist, it is likely that beers similar to those in Ancient Egypt were widespread throughout the vast continent. They exist today in the traditional "porridge beers" in which a mash made of millet, sorghum, cassava flour, palm sap, maize and even banana is allowed to ferment spontaneously with wild yeasts in the atmosphere and in the brewing pots and is then spiced with bitter herbs. In countries still struggling to throw off the last vestiges of colonialism and create modern societies, porridge beers are an important part of the diet of poor people, containing vitamin C and several important B vitamins. The beers have many different names such as *chibuku* in Central Africa and *dolo* in West Africa.

The survival of these traditional beers is important, for conventional modern brewing is expensive, as barley and hops do not grow in most parts of Africa and have to be imported. The Kenyan government is attempting to create barley and hop industries in the cooler altitudes: so far the barley grown can only be used as an unmalted adjunct in brewing as its quality is not sufficiently high for malting. Hops are also grown in South Africa. European brewing groups with interests in Africa have been reluctant to experiment with beers made from local cereals, though the Nigerian government decided in the mid-1980s that 25 per cent of local grain should be used in brewing. Nigeria has the largest number of breweries in Africa, around 30. The main brewing group, Nigerian Breweries, is jointly owned by Heineken and the United Africa Company and they made it plain to the government that if it pressed ahead with plans to make all breweries use only local cereals then some beers would be withdrawn from the market. They consider that cereals such as sorghum do not contain sufficient starch to convert into fermentable sugar.

SOUTHERN AFRICA

Modern brewing in Africa came as part of the baggage of colonialism. British, French, Dutch and Germans needed to refresh themselves and they set up rudimentary breweries, often on farms, that blossomed into substantial commercial plants once the newcomers had set down firm roots. Southern Africa, in particular, became a melting pot of brewers. In 1820 the Mariendahl Brewery was set up at Newlands; the Germans arrived in Natal in the 1840s and began brewing; the British opened a brewery in Durban; and in 1862 a Norwegian named Anders Ohlsson bought the Mariendahl Brewery. Ohlsson opened a second brewery and rapidly became a brewing giant on the Cape, eliminating most of the competition and establishing his Lion Beer as the principal brand.

The gold rush in the Transvaal created an enormous demand for beer. Ohlsson now faced serious competition from the British. The leading British-owned brewery was Castle and Castle Beer soon vied with Lion as the main brand in the region. Castle, owned by Frederick Mead, merged with smaller companies to form South African Breweries. SAB expanded from the traditional heartland of beer-drinking in Johannesburg, Durban and Cape Town to Port Elizabeth and Salisbury, Rhodesia (now Harare, the capital of Zimbabwe). After many years of talks and stand-offs, SAB and Ohlsson finally merged in 1956, making the enlarged SAB the biggest brewing group in the whole of Africa.

SAB experimented with lager-brewing as early as 1896. Today **Lion Lager** and **Castle Lager** (5.0 per cent ABV) dominate the market from the Zambezi to the Cape. Anders Ohlsson's memory is recalled in **Ohlsson's Lager**, also 5.0 per cent. In the 1980s a microbrewery started to produce an all-malt lager at Kynsa in Cape Province and tested occasional cask-conditioned ales and stouts. A second micro called Our Brewery opened in Johannesburg, brewing an unpasteurized ale.

During the years of apartheid, blacks were not encouraged to drink conventional beer. They were confined to insultingly-named "kaffir bars" where the only beer was a porridge-type called "kaffir beer". The end of race discrimination and rising expectations among the black population are likely to cause a demand for modern beer. The demise of porridge beer in South Africa and Zimbabwe will be a mixed blessing, marking the end of years of oppression but also the loss of a link with brewing's past.

KENYA

The most characterful Pilsner-style beer in the whole of Africa comes ironically from a brewery in Kenya founded by British settlers, including a gold prospector. East African Breweries – now Kenya Breweries – imported both equipment and a brewer from the old country: the brewer came from the famous brewing town of Burtonwood, near Warrington. Hops were imported from Kent and the main products were ale and stout. Lager brewing was developed in the 1930s. White Cap and Tusker rapidly became admired lager beers, not only winning prizes at international competitions – including two gold medals and one silver at the World Beer Competition in 1968 – but gaining even more chutzpah from the fact that Ernest Hemingway pronounced them his favourite beers when he was hunting in Kenya.

Tusker Premium Lager is a well-attenuated beer, with a starting gravity of 1044 degrees but reaching 4.8 per cent ABV. It is brewed from 90 per cent barley malt and 10 per cent cane sugar and is hopped with imported Hallertau and Styrian hops. A regular,

everyday version of **Tusker** and the more fruity **White Cap** are around 4.0 per cent ABV. Pilsner Lager is almost identical to Tusker Premium. Kenya Breweries has subsidiaries in Uganda and Tanzania and supplies the Zimbabwe market.

NIGERIA

Nigerian Breweries built its reputation on the quality of **Star Lager**, brewed to mark the opening of the first of the group's plants in Lagos in 1949. Additional breweries were built in Aba, Kaduna and Ibadan to quench the thirst of the Nigerians, the greatest beer drinkers in Africa. The influence of Heineken is clear to see in **Gulder**, also 5.0 per cent but with a shade more hop character than Star. Gulder has become the flagship brand, with a gentle malt and citric hops aroma, tart and refreshing in the mouth and a finish that starts malty and becomes dry with good hop character. The company also produces a 7.0 per cent **Legend Stout**, roasty and chocolatey, brewed to meet the enormous demand for stout in Nigeria and to counter the challenge of Guinness.

Guinness has three breweries in Nigeria producing an 8.0 per cent version of the stout. These breweries make a beer using conventional pale malt. Guinness sends out from Dublin a concentrate made by making dark stout and removing the water. The concentrate (the recipe of which is a closely-guarded secret) is blended with the pale beer to make **Nigerian Guinness**.

Golden Guinea Breweries in Umuahia is another leading Nigerian company. It started life as the Independence Brewery in 1962 and came under state control. It receives support today from Holsten of Hamburg, which advises on raw materials and technical processes. **Golden Guinea Lager** is 5.0 per cent with a good balance of malt and hops on the aroma and palate. The brewery also produces **Eagle Stout**.

FRANCOPHONE AFRICA

The biggest non-African brewery group operating on the continent is the French BGI – Brasseries et Glacières Internationales. Founded in Tonkin, Indochina, in the nineteenth century, BGI has been active in all the countries that were French colonies in Africa and Asia. It is best known for its **33 Export** lager but also brews for the African market such brands as Beaufort, Castel, Flag, Gazelle and Regag. It has a powerful presence in Benin (main brand **La Béninoise**), Cameroon, Central African Republic (**Mocaf** and **Mocaf Blonde**), Gabon, Niger (**Bière Niger**), Ivory Coast, Mali, Tunisia and Zaire. The main producer in Zaire, formerly the Belgian Congo, is the Belgian giant Interbrew, best known for Stella Artois. It brews under the name of Brasimba and produces two lager beers, **Simba** and **Tembo**. In the finest Belgian tradition, the first brewery in the Belgian Congo was founded by Jesuits in 1902 at Ki-Santu.

In the Republic of the Congo, the SCBK Brewery at Pointe Noire near Brazzaville brews **Ngok**, local dialect for Le Choc – crocodile. One of the most highly-regarded lagers in Francophone Africa, **Mamba**, is brewed in Abidjan, capital of the Ivory Coast by Solibra, owned by Interbrew. The brewery also produces a strong Bock lager and a tawny Brune, the latter with a faint hint of an Abbey-style beer from Belgium.

The island of Madagascar's Star Brewery has three plants devoted to just one lager brand called **Three Horses Beer**. The smaller island of Réunion has a lager with the enticing name of **Bourbon**, which takes its name from the town where the brewery is based and has no whisky connections. Mauritius, for a small island, has had impressive success with the lager beers produced by the Mauritius Brewery. **Phoenix** (4.5 per cent ABV) won a gold medal at the International Brewers Exhibition (Brewex) in 1983 and a gold at Monde Sélection in 1989. Stella Lager – no connection with Stella Artois – has also won two golds. **Blue Marlin** (5.6 per cent ABV) was introduced in 1989 and won a Monde Sélection gold three years later.

NORTH AFRICA AND THE MIDDLE EAST

The surge of Islamic fundamentalism in North Africa and the Middle East makes the future of brewing in the region uncertain. All the Iranian breweries have closed since the ayatollahs came to power. The fate of Iraq's state-controlled breweries, producing **Ferida**, **Golden Lager** and **Jawhara** beers, is unknown. Egypt has a state-controlled brewery in Cairo producing **Pyramid** lager. Arab Breweries in Amman, Jordan, brews **Petra** lager.

Tempo Beer Industries in Israel dominates the market through five brewing plants. Its flagship brand is **Maccabee** (4.9 per cent ABV) with a pronounced malt aroma, bitter-sweet malt and hops in the mouth, and a dry finish with some hops and vanilla notes. Tempo also produces **Gold Star** and **Malt Star** lagers.

The major brewing group in Turkey, Anadolu Industri, brews **Efes Pilsen** (5.0 per cent ABV) with a tangy malt and hops aroma, rich malt in the mouth, and a long bitter-sweet finish that becomes dry and hoppy. The beer is exported widely throughout the Middle East, Africa and Europe. A smaller company, Türk Tuborg, is a subsidiary of the Danish Carlsberg/Tuborg group and brews Tuborg under licence. The island of Cyprus has **Keo Beer**, a 4.5 per cent lager, with a good balance of malt and hops on the aroma, some vanilla notes and hops on the palate, and a bitter-sweet finish.

AFRICA AND MIDDLE EASTERN BREWERS

Anadolu Industri, Ankara, Turkey.

Arab Breweries, Prince Muhammad Street, Amman, Jordan.

Brasimba, Avenue du Flambeau 912, Kinshasa, Zaire.

Brasseries et Glacières Internationales, Algiers, Algeria.

Golden Guinea Breweries, 5 Route de Coyah, Conakry, Guinea.

Kenya Breweries, Thika Road, Ruaraka, Nairobi, Kenya.

Mauritius Brewery, Phoenix, Mauritius.

Nigerian Breweries, PO Box 496, Aba, Nigeria.

SCBK Brewery, Kronenberg, Point Noire, Brazzaville, Republic of Congo.

Solibra, Abidjan, Ivory Coast.

South African Breweries, Sandton 2146, South Africa.

Star Brewery, Antananarivo, Madagascar.

Tempo Beer Industries, Tel Aviv, Israel.

Opposite: *Heineken has a strong influence on the Nigerian beer market; Nigerians are the greatest beer-drinkers in Africa*

AUSTRALIA

Foster's Lager is one of the world's biggest beer brands, yet it takes its name from two New York brothers who lived in Australia for little more than a year. They changed Australian brewing due not to a devotion to good beer but as a result of owning a refrigeration plant. The brothers set up the Foster Brewing Company in Melbourne in 1887, sold it the following year and returned to total obscurity in the United States.

But the Foster brothers determined the future of

Despite being a lager beer, Castlemaine XXXX is called Bitter Ale in its home country

Australian brewing. The first settlers from Britain took with them an ale culture, but ale was not best suited to the searing heat of the vast continent. The reality was that, before refrigeration, the high temperatures made it difficult to brew a consistent beer of any type. Today lager beers dominate the country but, confusingly, many of them are still called "bitter", perhaps to pander to older Australians who still think of Britain as "home". Even the ubiquitous **Castlemaine XXXX** is called Bitter Ale in its country of origin.

In common with other countries, Australia has been the victim of a spate of takeovers, mergers and closures. To the intense annoyance of proud Australians, half of their brewing industry is now in the hands of the New Zealand Lion Nathan group. The collapse of the Bond Corporation allowed Lion Nathan to buy up Castlemaine, Toohey's and Swan. It then moved on to acquire Hahn of Sydney and South Australian of Adelaide.

The other half of Australian brewing is in the hands of Foster's, formerly Carlton and United Breweries. The worldwide fame of Foster's can be seen by its owner's decision to subsume both CUB and even the overall holding company, Elders IXL, into the name of the beer brand. Aided by the international success of the film *Crocodile Dundee*, whose star Paul Hogan had also advertised Foster's Lager, the brand is now one of the world's leaders.

Foster's and Lion Nathan have encouraged a wide choice of brands to remain, no doubt to appease those drinkers who have always been loyal to the likes of Tooth, Toohey, Emu and Swan. But there is little to choose between any of the mainstream lagers. They are all served ice cold and, when the temperature in the glass rises, tend to be sweet and lightly hopped: cane sugar is widely used as an adjunct in Australian lager brewing, usually in the ration of 70 per cent malt to 30 per cent sugar. Units of bitterness range from 14 to 22 while lagering is extremely brief, lasting between one and two weeks. British drinkers, used to the versions of Foster's and XXXX brewed in their country, would be surprised to find that the originals are more robust, both being around 5.0 per cent ABV, the standard strength for everyday Australian beers.

Both Castlemaine Perkins and Foster's became truly national groups in the 1980s when they muscled in to the biggest Australian beer market in New South Wales. By this time, Castlemaine Perkins had merged with Swan of Western Australia. Continuing the Irish link, Castlemaine bought Toohey's of Sydney, a brewery that had once primarily served the Catholic community, while the rival Tooth brewery, of English Anglican stock, served the Protestant one.

Western Australia

Two birds dominate brewing in this enormous but sparsely-populated state: the black swan, the state symbol, and the emu, indigenous to Western Australia. The Swan Brewery started brewing in Perth in 1857. The rival Emu Brewery began life as the Stanley Brewing Company, run by a William Mumme, a name similar to both a French Champagne and a type of beer once brewed centuries ago in the Brunswick area of Germany. In 1908 Stanley became Emu. After decades of tough and raucous competition, the two birds merged in 1928. Swan, now based in a new brewery in Canning Vale and part of the Lion Nathan group, has on paper a wide range of products but with scarcely perceptible differences between them. The Emu name is kept alive with **Emu Export** (4.9 per cent ABV), almost identical to Swan Lager. **Emu Bitter** (4.6 per cent ABV, with 26 IBUs) is the most bitter of the brewery's products, with hop varieties from Victoria and Tasmania. **Emu Draft** is not draught at all but a 3.7 per cent packaged beer, lightly hopped but with more body from the use of crystal malt.

Among the main Swan brands, **Export Lager** (4.8 per cent ABV) has marginally more body and hop character than the 4.9 per cent **Swan Lager**. **Swan Gold** sounds like a premium product but is a modest 3.5 per cent ABV aimed at the low-calorie market. The roasty/chocolatey and well-hopped **Swan Stout** (6.8 per cent ABV) is brewed for Swan by Cooper's of Adelaide and is a rare warm-fermented genuine ale.

The Matilda Bay Brewing Company was set up by a former Swan brewer, Philip Sexton. He built a pub brewery in the Sail and Anchor hotel in Fremantle in 1984 and then added a micro-brewery in Nedlands called Matilda Bay. In 1988, with four million dollars of investment from Foster's, a new custom-built brewery was set up in Perth, using a redundant all-copper brewhouse from de Clerck in Northern France.

Sexton's main beer is RedBack, named after a local spider, and is the first-known wheat beer to be brewed in Australia. **RedBack** is made from 65 per cent malted wheat, grown in the Avon Valley. The rest of the grist is two-row barley malt and the hops are Saaz and Hersbrucker. The 4.8 per cent ABV beer is available in both bottle-conditioned and filtered draught versions. It has a lightly spicy and fruity aroma and palate. **Dogbolter** started life as a strong ale but is now fermented with a lager yeast culture. A Pils has, by Australian standards, a robust 40 IBUs.

The Sail and Anchor brewpub specializes in handpumped, top-fermenting beers. Matilda Bay has added a brewpub called RedBack in Melbourne which brews a spicy, fruity **Hefe-Weizen** in the Bavarian fashion, and a **Pils** with a Munich-style rounded maltiness.

South Australia

The South Australian Brewing Company in Thebarton, Adelaide, was a major independent until it was bought by Lion Nathan. The modern brewery is high-tech and produces only cold-fermenting beers, even though they include a stout. The company grew by a succession of mergers, dating from 1888 when the Kent Town Brewery, the West End Brewery and a wine and spirits merchant joined forces. Later acquisitions included the Broken Hill Brewery – whose beers were popular with the tough breed of miners in the area – Waverley, Port Augusta and, in 1938, the biggest coup in the shape of a merger with the larger Southwark Brewery. The new Thebarton plant is called the Southwark Brewery as a mark of respect for the dear-departed.

South Australian brands also pay homage to former breweries. **West End Premium** (5.0 per cent ABV), named after the company's old site, is dry in the finish; Pride of Ringwood and Hersbrucker Hallertau hops create 25 IBUs. **Southwark Premium** (5.5 per cent ABV) has a good balance of malt and perfumy hop, with 22 IBUs. **Old Australia Stout** (7.4 per cent ABV) is a dark

The Swan Brewery began brewing in Perth, Western Australia, in 1857; the city is two times zones west of Australia's other main cities

lager but with an abundance of roast and chocolate character. It is brewed from pale malt, roasted barley and cane sugar, with Pride of Ringwood hops. IBUs are 37. **Broken Hill Lager** (4.8 per cent ABV, 22 IBUs) also has some roasted barley in its make-up. It is one of the most characterful of the mainstream Australian lagers, with a good hop aroma (Ringwood), a rounded palate and a quenching, bitter-sweet finish.

Port Dock is a brewpub in Port Adelaide producing a golden **Lighthouse Ale**, a malty **Black Diamond Bitter** and a fruity 6.0 per cent **Old Preacher**.

Cooper's of Adelaide

The swing to lager brewing threatened the total eclipse of ale in Australia. One company went on producing ales, to the derision of the rest of the industry, but today Cooper's ales of Adelaide are now not only cult beers throughout Australia but are recognized as classics of the style worldwide.

Thomas Cooper emigrated from Yorkshire in 1852. His wife was the daughter of an innkeeper and she used the skills of brewing she had picked up from her father to make beer at home. Thomas worked first as a shoemaker and then as a dairyman in their new country before setting up as a commercial brewer. When his first wife died Thomas remarried and produced an impressive 16 children.

The Cooper family still runs the company. Against all the advice of marketing experts, they have remained faithful to ale and didn't add a lager to their portfolio until 1969. The 5.8 per cent bottle-conditioned and draught **Sparkling Ale** throws a heavy sediment after six weeks' conditioning in the brewery. The title "sparkling" causes some amusement as the beer tends to be cloudy in the glass. It is brewed from pale and crystal malts with cane sugar making up around 18 per cent of the recipe. Hops are Pride of Ringwood pellets, with 26 bitterness units. Primary fermentation used to be in open wooden vessels made of local jarrah hardwood. The beer was cleansed of yeast by dropping it from the fermenters into 108-gallon "puncheons". Cooper's has now switched to primary fermentation in conical vessels. The beer is centrifuged and given a dosage of fermenting wort and sugar to encourage a second fermentation in bottle and keg. Sparkling Ale is intensely fruity, with apple and banana dominating, a peppery hop aroma, citric fruit from the hops in the mouth, and a quenching finish with more hops and fruit.

Cooper's Stout (6.8 per cent ABV) is also a sedimented beer. Roasted malt is added to pale and crystal. It has an oily, coffeeish aroma and palate. A lower strength version of Sparkling Ale has been introduced (4.5 per cent ABV, 26 IBUs) with delectable apple fruit on the aroma and palate, and good hop character. Cooper's Dark (4.5 per cent ABV) is made from pale, crystal and roast malt and has a fruity and chocolate character. It is based on a famous Welsh beer, Brain's Dark from Cardiff, discovered by a member of the Cooper family when he was visiting Britain.

The success of Cooper's has prompted others to emulate the sparkling ale style, which is believed to have been developed early in the twentieth century to counter the threat of lager. The Lion Brewing micro in Adelaide opened in 1992 to make a 5.0 per cent Sparkling Bitter Ale, packed with hop aroma and with a bitter finish.

New South Wales

The biggest beer-drinking state is home to Tooth's and Toohey's of Sydney, now in the hands of Foster's and Castlemaine/Lion Nathan. The Tooth plant is known as the Kent Brewery in honour of founder John Tooth's home in Kent in South East England, the principal hop-growing region of the old country. The symbol is no longer used, but Tooth's used to inscribe its products with the White Horse of Kent, which can still be seen on the hop "pockets" or sacks used back in England. The white horse is derived from the battle flag of two legendary Saxon chiefs who invaded England, Hengist and Horsa, whose names mean Stallion and Horse.

Both Tooth's and Toohey's pay homage to a dark or amber style of beer known in the state as Old Ale. Tooth's version is best known as Old or XXX but it has been renamed Kent Old Brown after the brewery. It has a sweetish palate and a lightly fruity aroma, and is warm-fermenting. Sheaf Stout (5.7 per cent ABV, 35 IBUs) is also a genuine ale with a woody, earthy aroma,

coffee on the palate and a dry finish. Resch's Draught is a well-balanced lager, more aggressively malty and hoppy than the norm, and is named after a brewery bought by Tooth's in 1929.

Toohey's has continued the legacy of old ales with the exotically-named Tall Ships, a higher strength version of the long-running Hunter Old (4.7 per cent ABV), a warm-fermenting brown ale with some fruity and roasted barley character. Conventional lagers include Toohey's Red, with some late hop in the finish, and Toohey's Light Bitter which, despite the British ale connotations, is cold-fermenting.

Hahn was set up as a microbrewery in 1988 in Sydney but has been bought by the all-conquering Lion Nathan, which descended on Australia like the All Blacks pack in full cry. Hahn Premium Lager is an all-malt beer with plenty of hop aroma and bitterness.

Victoria

Melbourne is the home of Foster's/CUB, which also has a second plant at Ballarat. As well as Foster's Lager (5.0 per cent ABV), sweetish and with a hint of fruit – the result of a short lagering – the group produces Carlton Crown Lager, almost identical to Foster's. Carlton Draught is a shade more rounded in flavour and slightly darker in colour. Victoria Bitter is a lager with malty dryness in the finish while Melbourne Bitter has some hop bitterness. Abbots Lager and Abbots Stout take their name from the Abbotsford Brewery, the main Melbourne site. The stout is roasty with hints of coffee and chocolate and is cold-fermenting. With the exception of the Abbot brews, the hallmark of Foster's is the remarkable similarity of all the beers.

Queensland

If Elder's dominates Victoria, Queensland is the undisputed home of Castlemaine XXXX. What was once a simple cask marking handed down from medieval monks has become, in the hands of modern marketing gurus, a secular synonym for "Stuff you, Jack". Queensland drinkers couldn't give a XXXX for any other beer, according to the advertising, and at night the four letters blaze out from the Castlemaine Brewery like a neon-lit, two-fingered salute.

The Brisbane version of XXXX, still sold as Bitter

Ale, uses whole hops rather than pellets, an unusual practice in modern Australia. The 4.8 per cent lager does have a hint more hoppiness than its main rivals but, like them, is malty sweet. **Gold Lager** is 3.5 per cent and even more malt-accented. **Malt 75** (4.8 per cent ABV) is an additive-free lager, drier than XXXX. The most characterful beer from the brewery is **Carbine Stout**, named after a famous racehorse. It is the last surviving stout from a brewery that once made several. At 5.1 per cent ABV, it is now cold-fermenting with a roasty palate and a dry finish.

Powers was set up near Brisbane in 1987 to bring some much-needed choice to the region. Busily promoted, especially at major sports events, Power's success annoyed the giants and it succumbed to the blandishments of Foster's. Whether **Power's Big Red**, a more flavourful lager than most, will keep its distinctive character under new ownership remains to be seen.

Tasmania

The island of Tasmania is one of the major barley-growing areas of Australia and, with Victoria, supplies most of the continent's hops – Pride of Ringwood is the leading hop variety grown. With a famous English independent brewery called Ringwood based in

Hampshire it would be pleasing, if fanciful, to believe that the hop strain first came from the old country. As Hampshire is not known as a hop-growing area there is little to support the notion, though Tasmanians claim that cuttings from Hampshire were smuggled on to the island in breach of the quarantine laws. If the story is true, the hop has found its way home again, for the organic version – free from pesticides and fertilizers – is used by a handful of British brewers producing organic beers.

With the pick of the barley and hop crops to hand, it is not surprising that Tasmania's two breweries produce some of the tastiest beers in the country.

The Cascade Brewery in Hobart is the oldest continuously working Australian brewery. The superb plant, looking like a cross between a traditional English brewery and a Yorkshire woollen mill, started to produce ale and porter in 1832. It drew both its brewing liquor and its inspiration from the pure waters flooding down from the Cascade Mountains. In 1922 it merged with Tasmania's other brewery, Boag's of Launceston – both breweries still operate – and in 1927 switched to lager brewing when it installed a new plant from Switzerland.

Cascade Premium Lager is a well-attenuated beer (original gravity 1044–1048 but with 5.2 per cent ABV) and is noticeably full-bodied with a crisp finish and some citric hop notes. In spite of their names, **Cascade Draught**, **Cascade Bitter** and **Cascade Stout** are all cold-fermenting. The stout has plenty of roasted malt and chocolate character.

Boag's, at the other end of the island, traces its origins to 1927 but there have been some interruptions in brewing over the years. Cascade has left it to brew in the fashion the managers prefer: Boag's uses the traditional European double-decoction mashing system that uses several mash kettles, while Cascade has a hybrid ale-and-lager step-infusion system in which the temperature of the mash is raised within one vessel. **Boag's Draught** is a lager, again well attenuated, from a gravity of 1040 degrees to 4.7 per cent ABV. It has a perfumy hop aroma and a dry finish. **Boag's Lager** (5.4 per cent ABV) has 27 IBUs, hoppy by Australian standards. **Boag's Stout** is less characterful than Cascade's, though.

AUSTRALIAN BREWERS

Cascade Brewery Co, 156 Collins Street, Hobart TAS 7000.

Castlemaine Perkins (Lion Nathan), 11 Finchley Street, Milton QLD 4064.

Cooper's Brewery Ltd, 9 Statenborough Street, Leabrook, Adelaide SA 5068.

Foster's/Carlton and United Breweries Ltd, 1 Bouverie Street, Carlton VIC 3053.

Matilda Bay Brewing Co Ltd, 130 Stirling Highway, North Fremantle WA 6161.

Power Brewing Co Ltd (Foster's), Pacific Highway, Yatala QLD 4207.

South Australian Brewing Co Ltd (Lion Nathan), 107 Port Road, Thebarton SA 5031.

Swan Brewery Co Ltd (Lion Nathan), 25 Baile Road, Canning Vale WA 6155.

NEW ZEALAND

Modernization has been a recurrent theme in New Zealand brewing since the turn of the twentieth century. The Captain Cook Brewery in Auckland made much of the fact that as early as 1907 its ales and stouts were filtered, pasteurized and artificially carbonated. Today the two groups that dominate Kiwi brewing, Lion Nathan (formerly New Zealand Breweries) and Dominion, produce sweet, malty, lightly hopped and undemanding lagers.

As New Zealand is a more conservative society than Australia and is less ambivalent about its links with Britain, it might be expected that a revival of traditional brewing would have taken root in the islands, but even the micros that sprang up in the 1980s and 1990s have had to bow to prevailing attitudes. When former All Blacks rugby player Terry McCashin opened his Mac's micro in Nelson in 1982 he was encouraged by a visit to Britain and the success there of the Campaign for Real Ale. But today, under the screw from consumers, he concentrates on lager. Mac's Lager is generously hopped by local standards, his Real Ale uses a lager yeast and is pasteurized in the bottle while his best-selling product is an everyday sweetish lager.

Lion Nathan has had great success at home and abroad with its **Steinlager**, a 4.8 per cent beer with 22 IBUs. It has the greatest hop character of any of the mainstream New Zealand beers. **Rheineck** (3.8 per cent ABV) is sweet and undemanding, **Leopard DeLuxe** has some light fruit but little hop, while **Lion Red** (3.7 per cent ABV) is malty and amber coloured. **Lion Brown** is easily the most interesting of the group's beers. Although it is fermented with a lager yeast, the temperature is kept high, leaving considerable estery fruitiness in the finished beer.

Hop farm in Sunrise Valley, in the Nelson region of South Island

Dominion Breweries has a **Double Brown** in the same style. Its mainstream lagers, **DB Draught** and **DB Export**, are malty but **Kiwi Lager** has some good hop aroma.

Harrington's is a new micro based in Victorian brewing buildings in Christchurch. It produces – bravely for New Zealand – a sweetish **Harrington's Wheat Beer** and a **Harrington's Dark** with coffee notes. Another wheat beer, WeissBier, can be found in the Loaded Hog brewpub in Christchurch. The pub also offers an interpretation of an English brown ale called **Hog's Head Dark**. In Auckland the pioneering Shakespeare brewpub has a lager with good hop bitterness, a malty Red Ale and an English-style bitter called **Falstaff**.

NEW ZEALAND BREWERS

Dominion Breweries, 80 Greys Avenue, Auckland.

Lion Nathan, 54–65 Shortland Street, Auckland.

Mac's Micro, Stoke, Nr Nelson.

JAPAN AND THE FAR EAST

Japan has come a long way in a short time in brewing terms. Beer was introduced, almost by accident, by the Americans in 1853. The United States was keen to develop trade with Japan but placed a knuckleduster inside the velvet glove by sending the US Navy under Commodore Matthew Perry to negotiate a treaty. A Japanese who went on board one of Perry's ships was offered a beer. Intrigued, he found a handbook on brewing – written in Dutch – and managed to make beer for home consumption.

Following the Meiji reforms of 1868, when Emperor Mutsuhito encouraged Westernization and industrialization, efforts were made to establish commercial breweries. The Americans gave a hand and a brewery was established in Yokohama by Wiegand and Copeland. Eventually the brewery became wholly owned by Japanese and was named Kirin after a mythical creature, half dragon and half horse.

Black Beer

The black beer influence may come from the Franconia region of Bavaria but the dark lagers there are brown rather than black. Schwarzbier is now confined to Saxony and the opaque, cold-fermenting beer from Köstritz may be the historic link with Japan's black beers.

Kirin and Sapporo, the oldest of Japan's breweries, produce the most interesting versions of the style. **Sapporo Black Beer** is the classic. At 5.0 per cent ABV, it is brewed from pale, crystal, Munich and chocolate malts with a small amount of rice.

Kirin Black Beer, also 5.0 per cent, has a pronounced roasted coffee and liquorice palate after a gentle, grainy start. The finish is light and quenching with some gentle hop character. **Asahi Black** (5.0 per cent ABV) is less dark, with a hint of red/brown in the colour. It is by far the sweetest of the Japanese black beers and many drinkers blend it with lager to balance the caramel character. **Suntory's Black Beer** (5.0 per cent ABV, 23 IBUs) is jet black and opaque. All the black beers are minority brands, sold on draught or packaged for specialist bars or restaurants. The brewers deserve credit for maintaining a style that in most modern brewing climates would have been consigned to the grave decades ago.

Pilsners and lagers

Kirin Lager is the most distinctive of the Japanese mainstream Pilsners, lagered, it is claimed, for an impressive two months. At 4.9 per cent ABV and 27.5 IBUs from Hallertau and Saaz hops, it is full-bodied and rich-tasting and is firmly in the Pilsner mould. A stronger lager (6.5 per cent ABV) stresses the German influence with the remarkable name of **Mein Bräu** – My Brew. More recent beers include a hoppy **Spring Valley**, an all-malt **Heartland**, **Ichiba** made from the first malt of the season, and the confusingly named **Golden Bitter**, which is cold-fermenting and has a fine, resiny hop character.

Sapporo's most impressive brand is **Yebisu**, a fragrant malty/hoppy beer broadly in the Dortmunder Export style and hopped with Hallertau Mittelfruh and Hersbruck. It is 5.0 per cent ABV and has an enticing golden colour. It takes its name from a Shinto god. Other lagers include 4.5 per cent **Sapporo Draft Beer** (which comes in bottles and cans) and has a grainy aroma, malt in the mouth and a dry finish with some hop notes; and a German-influenced **Edel-Pils** with a delightful hop aroma.

Suntory's state of the art breweries can be programmed to produce almost any type of beer. In general Suntory's range is mild and light-tasting, dry in the finish but with only delicate hoppiness. **Suntory's Malt's**, as the name suggests, is on the malty side while **Suntory's Light's** (4.5 per cent ABV), aimed at the calorie-conscious, may be "a healthy delight" but has little else to recommend it. **Dynamic Draft** is fermented with a Canadian yeast.

JAPANESE BREWERS

Asahi Breweries, 23-1 Azumabashi 1-chome, Sumida-ku, Tokyo 130.

Kirin Brewery Co, 26-1 Jingumae 6-chome, Shibuya-ku, Tokyo 150.

Sapporo Breweries, 7-10-1 Ginza, Chuo-ku, Tokyo 104.

Suntory Brewery, 1-2-3 Motoakasaka, Minato-ku, Tokyo 107.

Chojugura, Chuo 3-4-5, Itami.

You can buy almost anything from a vending machine in Japan, including a selection of beers from Suntory's Asahi range

Asahi's Super Dry is brewed out or fully-attenuated to turn all the malt sugars to alcohol. It launched a brief craze for dry beers in several countries, the United States in particular, but the decline was almost as rapid as the rise: it seems that beer drinkers, contrary to the views of marketing departments, do like taste and flavour. Asahi also produces **Asahi Z**, another well-attenuated beer, and a more flavoursome **Asahi Gold**.

Japanese specialities

Kirin brews a superb 8.0 per cent ABV **Kirin Stout**, a complex bitter-sweet, cold-fermenting beer with delicious dark toffee notes. A microbrewery set up in Kyoto produces a German-style, warm-fermenting **Kyoto Alt**, copper coloured and with a delectable nuttiness from crystal malt. Sapporo brew **Yebisu Stout**, soft and mellow, while **Asahi's Stout** is big-bodied, full of dark bitter-sweet fruits. Suntory has experimented with a Bavarian **Weizen** wheat beer, beautifully made and with a delicious apple-and-clove quenching palate.

A change in the law in the early 1990s made obtaining a brewing licence easier. As a result, several brewpubs and micro breweries have opened. The best-known is Chojugura in Itami, which produces a hoppy **Blond** (5.0 per cent ABV) and a fruity/malty **Dark** (5.5 per cent ABV).

CHINA

The most populous nations on earth remains an enigma, not least where brewing is concerned. For centuries an alcoholic drink was made from rice but it is not clear whether this was beer or wine. Today there are thought to be 100 breweries in the country, but the number could be far higher as China slowly opens up to Western influence and technology while living standards rise. But only one beer is well known outside China and it comes from a brewery set up with the aid of German technology in the late nineteenth century.

When the Germans leased the port of Tsingtao on the Shantung peninsula close to Japan and Korea they naturally built a brewery which survives and thrives. The name of the port is now Qingdao in Shandong province but Tsingtao is still used as the name of the extremely pale Pilsner-style lager brewed there and exported widely: it is something of a cult beer in the United States among afiçionados of Chinese cuisine.

China now has its own barley and hop industries, though supplies and quality are erratic. The 5.2 per cent **Tsingtao**, when it is on form, has a good Pilsner malt and hop attack with some vanilla notes in the finish.

A malty, lightly hopped beer from Shanghai known either as **Shanghai Lager** or **Swan Lager** from the emblem on the neck label has occasionally been seen in the West. It has no connection to the Swan subsidiary of Lion Nathan in Australia. Shanghai also produces a dark lager called **Guangminpai**. The capital, Beijing, has a lager called **Mon-Lei** with a reddish hue as though influenced by Austrian "red" lagers. A similar beer, **Wei Mei**, comes from Guilin. The Hong Kong Brewery has a 5.0 per cent **Sun Lik Beer** with a traditional Chinese dragon adorning the label.

Beer consumption is rising fast in China, especially among the young. This vast and largely untapped market is being fed by new breweries, many of them with support from the West. The British Bass group has invested $40 million in the Ginsber brewing company and is marketing Tennents Lager there. Anheuser-Busch, Heineken and Foster's of Australia, also major investors in China, are linking up with existing Chinese breweries. The problem for the Chinese is that they are being force-fed mainstream, bland Western lagers. Let us hope they can use their own determination and flair to introduce more tasteful brews.

Across the border in South Korea, the OB Brewery in Seoul produces two lagers, **OB** and **Crown**.

THE REST OF ASIA

German technology built the Boon Rawd Brewery in Thailand and the German influence continues today in the production of the superb **Singha Lager**. The Singha is a mythical lion-like creature and the beer named in its honour is suitably powerful. The rival **Amarit**, in contrast, is a much milder and malty-sweet brew that contains some ale-like fruitiness.

One of the best-known Asian beers, Tiger of Singapore and Kuala Lumpur, refreshed the British during the colonial period and the Second World War. It was immortalized by the British writer Anthony Burgess in his novel *Time for a Tiger*, a marketing slogan used by the brewery since the late 1940s. **Tiger** (5.1 per cent ABV) and **Anchor** of the same strength are both clean-tasting, quenching light lagers. Tiger has the greater hop character and is now much influenced by the Heineken style. APB also brews a roasty/creamy, cold fermenting **ABC Stout** with a powerful 8.1 per cent ABV rating. APB introduced a **Tiger Classic** seasonal beer for the New Year festivities as well as **Raffles Light**, named after Raffles Hotel in Singapore, a legendary watering-hole in colonial times.

APB has joined with the Vietnamese to build a brewery in Ho Chi Minh City (Saigon). The French BGI group was called in by the Vietnamese at the end of the war with the USA to build a brewery at My Tho to revive the 33 brand, which had refreshed the French during the colonial period.

The Bintang Brewery in Indonesia produces beer with a Dutch influence, down to the familiar stubby

Dutch bottle. **Bintang** is 5.0 per cent ABV with a grainy aroma, a malty/perfumy palate, and a finish that becomes dry with some light hop notes.

One of the most famous beers in Asia and the Pacific is **San Miguel** of the Philippines. The company is a giant concern with several breweries as well as interests in food and agriculture. **San Miguel Pale Pilsen** is 5.0 per cent ABV with around 20 IBUs. It is made with 80 per cent malt and is lagered for a month. **Gold Eagle** is similar to San Miguel, a fraction lower in alcohol and a shade darker in colour. **Cerveza Negra** (Black Beer) is 5.2 per cent ABV with a pleasing roasted malt character. **Red Horse** (6.8 per cent ABV) is a full-bodied, malty lager in the Bock style.

INDIAN SUB-CONTINENT

The British stamped their mark on India with India Pale Ales brewed in Burton-on-Trent for export to the sub-continent. By the 1880s German lagers had replaced ales as they were more suited to both brewing and consumption in the torrid climate. Even today some lagers have a fruity, ale-like character caused by problems of temperature control. Burma's **Mandalay Beer**, for example, is a notably fruity brew even though it is cold-fermenting. Napal's **Star Beer** is more in the lager mould with a hoppy intensity.

While some Indian states are strictly prohibitionist, breweries range from the far north in the Simla Hills to Bangalore and Hyderabad in the south. The main brewing groups are Mohan Meakin and United Breweries. Lager beers tend to be malty and sweetish with only light hop character. The best-known brands are **Cobra** and **Kingfisher**, both widely exported; Kingfisher is brewed under licence in Britain by Shepherd Neame in Kent. Mohan Meakin, founded in 1855, brews a large portfolio of lagers for the home market, including **Baller, Gymkhana, Lion, Krown** and

Golden Eagle, ranging from 4.0 per cent to 5.0 per cent ABV. In Hyderabad, Vinedale Breweries produces two premium lagers called **Flying Horse** and **Jubilee**, both around 5.0 per cent ABV, and two stouts called **Kingfisher** and **London**.

Stout is a hangover – a pleasant one – from British colonial times, the finest examples of which are found in Sri Lanka. McCallum's Three Coins Brewery in Colombo has a rich, fruity, chocolatey **Sando Stout** (6.0 per cent ABV), named after a Hungarian circus strongman who toured the country. It is cold-fermenting, along with the all-malt **Three Coins Pilsener**.

A remarkable stout is found at the Ceylon Brewery in Nuwara Eliya in the tea-planting area and close to the Holy City of Kandy. **Lion Stout** (7.5 per cent) is warm-fermenting, using Czech, British and Danish malts, Styrian hops and an English yeast strain, all transported up precarious roads to the brewery 3,500 feet above sea level. It is served in cask-conditioned form by handpump in the Beer Shop in the brewery's home town and in UKD Silva, Kandy.

ASIAN BREWERS

Asia Pacific Breweries, 459 Jalan Ahmad Ibrahim, Singapore.
Bintang Brewery, Jakarta, Indonesia.
Boon Rawd Brewery, Bangkok, Thailand.
Ceylon Brewery, Nuwara Eliya, Kandy, Sri Lanka.
Hong Kong Brewery, 13 Miles Castle Peak Road, Shan Tseng NT, Hong Kong.
McCallum's Brewery, 299 Union Place, Colombo, Sri Lanka.
Mohan Meakin, Solan Brewery, Himacar, Tredesh, India.
OB Brewery, Seoul, South Korea.
San Miguel, 40 San Miguel Avenue, Mandaluyong, Manila, Philippines.
United Breweries, 24 Grant Road, Bangalore, India.
Vinedale Breweries, Hyderabad, Pakistan.

SOUTH PACIFIC

Papua New Guinea

The South Pacific Brewery of Port Moresby, Papua New Guinea, was the inspiration of Australians who had gone to the territory to work in the gold fields. Imports of beer were erratic and the quality variable – Allsopp's beer from England was dubbed "Allslopps".

In the late 1940s Joe Bourke, a gold prospector, applied for a licence to build a hotel in the town of Wau. Annoyed by the lack of beer from Australia and other countries, he planned a brewery. With other Australians he founded a syndicate which raised £150,000 to launch South Pacific Brewery in Port Moresby, the capital of the islands. They were fortunate to discover Rudolf Meier, a Hungarian who had trained and brewed in Germany.

Production started in 1952 on a small basis. In spite of problems getting supplies of ingredients and often running short of water – the brewery uses rain water collected in tanks – the company prospered. Sales soared in the 1960s when Prohibition was ended for the islanders – until then only settlers had been allowed access to alcohol. Today the company is run largely by Papuans, though Australians are still involved.

The brewery made headlines in 1980 when its **Export Lager** won the gold medal in the Brewex international beer competition. It has also won awards in the Monde Sélection competition.

Although it faces competition from a San Miguel brewery built by the Filipino giant, South Pacific is the brand leader with a modern plant. In the 1990s it added a stout to its range, a reflection perhaps of the residual support for the style in Australia.

SP Lager (4.5 per cent ABV) has a perfumy aroma, a malt and vanilla palate and a cornflour finish that becomes dry. The estery character of the beer suggests a brief lagering,

SP Export Lager (5.5 per cent ABV) has a delicate aroma with a faint malt note, a light malt palate and short finish that becomes dry with faint hop notes. It doesn't drink its strength.

Niugini Gold Extra Stout (8.0 per cent ABV) is a deep brown-black in colour and has a rich chocolate and cappuccino coffee aroma, with dark fruit in the mouth and a big finish packed with hops and tart fruit.

Hawaii

In the spring of 1995, Hawaii got its first microbrewery, the Kona Brewing Company. It was the dream of Spoon and Pops Khalsa, who both grew up in Oregon, USA, and became lovers of good beer. When they planned their brewery they called in Ron Gansberg, John Kittredge and John Forbes from the BridgePort micro in Portland, Oregon. Together they planned two ales for the 25-barrel brewery. Brewing liquor is water naturally filtered through the volcanic aquifer. Barley and hops are imported from the USA along with BridgePort's top-fermenting yeast strain.

The two beers are **Pacific Golden Ale** (3.5 per cent by weight; 22 IBUs), using a blend of pale and honey malts and hopped with Bullion and Willamette, and **Fire Rock Ale** (4.1 per cent by weight; 40 IBUs), a darker, amber beer using pale and Munich malts and hopped with Cascade, Galena and Mount Hood varieties.

The beers should appeal not only to Hawaiians and Americans but also to the British, for a half acre of the main island is still British territory and the site of an obelisk commemorates the site of the death of Captain Cook. Ships of the Royal Navy regularly visit Hawaii and the crew will now have some good ale to enjoy.

IMPORTANT ADDRESS

Kona Brewing Company, PO Box 181, Kealakekua, HI 96750.

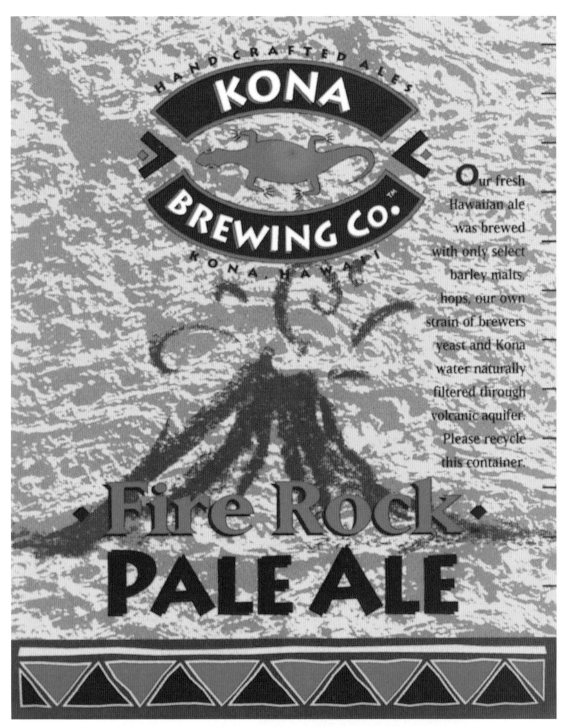

Fire Rock Ale, from the Hawaiian brewing company Kona, holds appeal for US and British tastes

SPIRITS

The earliest distillers distilled from ingredients that were to hand – grapes, sugar cane, barley or agave – but in time these spirits took on a human element, became rooted in the physical environment and more abstract national identity. The greatest spirits have always drawn their character from this melding of the environmental and cultural landscape.

In the recent past this element has been missing. As technology and communications improved, so there was nothing to stop the same spirits being made everywhere in the world. As this happened, so the whole category was in danger of becoming homogenized. The sense of belonging was in danger of disappearing.

At one time, spirits were thought to be quintessential in the truest sense – the mysterious fifth essence, the physical manifestation of the stuff of life itself. These days many people see them as interchangeable own-label brands on the supermarket shelf.

But on closer investigation there are people for whom the magic is still there. The distillers with a passion for their product, who don't see it as a commodity, but as a palpable mystery; the people for whom there is still mystery – and a human element. Thankfully, these are the spirits that are growing in popularity.

Why has it happened? Maybe it's part of a millennarian desire to try and rediscover naturalness. Maybe it's thanks to a change in attitude by drinkers who have rediscovered the joy of flavour. People have realized that they don't need to accept mediocrity any more; they have the chance to revel in diversity.

Malt whisky, tequila and rum are different, but the greatest examples of each contain a spark that transcends the category and allows the imbiber to compare their similarities and delight in the contrasts. The greatest spirits act like Proust's Madeleine – a taste that inspires a flood of memories and associations.

AN AGE-OLD ELIXIR

Distillation fuses the practical and the philosophical. It's been used by the alchemist trying to reveal the mysteries of existence, the doctor attempting to find medicines, the perfumer creating scents for his master and mistress – and the producer of alcohol. Because distillation has had so many uses, it's impossible to say who the first distiller was.

THE EARLIEST DAYS

All we can say is that alcohol has always been used by man. It was probably discovered by chance – someone ate some fermenting fallen fruit, and discovered the strangely pleasurable effect. All ancient peoples drank some form of fermented drink – grape beer and palm wine were being produced in 4000 BC in Mesopotamia and Egypt, and by 1000 BC the Greeks and Phoenicians were trading in wines throughout the Mediterranean.

All of them used whatever crop was native to their region. In time, distillers would do the same, thereby establishing the main differences between the major styles of spirits. But where does distillation come in? From a twentieth-first-century perspective, it doesn't seem to be a huge jump in logic from fermenting to distilling, yet it's widely believed that distillation didn't start in Western Europe until the Middle Ages.

There are tantalizing snippets of information that encourage you to put two and two together ... and end up just making five. By 800 BC, most Eastern and Caucasian cultures used two terms to differentiate between their fermented and stronger drinks. In China, rice beer was called *tehoo*, and the "distillate" was *suatchoo*; in India "toddy" palm wine became *arrack* when processed a second time, and the fermented mare's milk drink of the Tartars, *kumiss*, was given the second name *arika* or *skhou*. It seems plausible that distillation may have taken place. The trouble is, there's no evidence that it did.

The evidence

To find the first possible written evidence of distillation of spirits, you have to go to fourth-century China, where the alchemist Ko Hung wrote about the transformation of cinnabar in mercury as being: "like wine that has been fermented once. It cannot be compared with the pure clear wine that has been fermented nine times". Is he talking about distillation? It seems possible. How do you ferment a wine nine times unless you distil it?

By that time, the Alexandrian Greeks had already discovered that by boiling you could transform one object into another. Pliny writes about distillation being used to extract turpentine from resin, while Aristotle recounts how sea water could be turned into drinking water in about 350 BC, but at no point is wine mentioned – despite the fact it was being made. Perhaps they never made the leap. There again, they might have, but in 290 AD the emperor Diocletian ordered that all the records of the Alexandrian School should be destroyed, and any possible record of spirits production vanished with them.

So who were first: the Chinese, the Egyptians or the Greeks? Alchemy historian Anthony M. House takes a sensible middle ground. "It's entirely possible that these cultures were simultaneously experimenting with distillation in roughly the same period, unknown to each other."

SECRET ALCHEMY

You see, alchemy lies at the root of it all. These days, the most common image of an alchemist is some bearded madman lurking in a laboratory trying to turn base metal into gold. That's a misunderstanding. Alchemy is a school of thought that tries, through a variety of disciplines, to capture the mysteries of life itself. It tries to make sense of the world by, among other things, working with the elements to transform matter and attempt to strip away the extraneous and capture its purest essence.

Alchemy was much more than the "magic" of turning base metal into gold

Pu-Qua, Canton, Delin.

Dadley.

Evidence from fourth-century China indicates that distillation was already employed at that time

Alchemists came from every religion, and all approached this quest in slightly different ways, but they were all trying to comprehend the mysteries of the world by somehow making the substance of existence visible. Out of their investigations came perfume, make-up, medicine, the ability to gild metal, mummification and, in time, alcoholic spirits. When alcoholic spirits were "discovered" by Raymond Lull (*see* page 412), they were seen as a powerful elemental creation – a possible answer to this abiding mystery.

As Denis Nicholl points out in his paper on the history of distillation, alchemy's founding father was the Egyptian god Thoth (in Greek, Hermes). Both are symbols of mystical knowledge, rebirth and transformation – Hermes' staff could turn base material to gold, but both gods could also turn death into life.

Alchemy appears to have started in Ancient Egypt (*al-khem* means the art of Egypt in Arabic) but in time, after being influenced by the Alexandrian Greeks, it became central to the philosophical and scientific investigations of the early Islamic scientists. In this way, Arab scholars became the guardians of the secret of distillation. Because Islam banned alcohol, scientists used distillation in *al-ambiqs* (our alembics) for different ends – making perfume, make-up (*al-kohl*, our alcohol) and medicine.

The most notable of these scholars was the eighth-century scientist Rhazes, the founder of modern medicine, who is credited with being the first to use alcohol for medicinal purposes, while his compatriot Avicenne invented the condensing serpent. If you are looking for a name, Rhazes' is as good as any.

The art of alchemy travelled with Islam as it spread across Northern Africa and into mainland Europe with the Moorish invasion of Andalucia. There are records showing that stills were being used in Andalucia in the tenth century.

That said, you can't put your finger on any one location as being the birthplace of spirits. The reality is that it probably sprang up in a number of places at around the same time. While stills were being used in Moorish Spain, the Benedictine monks of Salerno were beginning to translate Arabic and Greek texts. Inevitably, they came across the secret and started their own experiments.

There is also evidence that distillation was being practised in the far north-west of Europe at the same time. As Islamic scholars were starting modern-day medicine, the Celts were distilling, rather than just fermenting, honey into mead. In his "Mead Song", the Welsh bard Taliessin refers to "mead, distilled, sparkling", while Skene's *Four Ancient Books of Wales* refer to the Celts of this time as being: "distillers, furnace distillers or kiln distillers".

So how did it get all the way up there? There are hints that the Celts knew not just of making beer, but distilled spirits as well – though, sadly, there's no concrete evidence. It is far from impossible, though, given the evidence that knowledge of distillation had started in China and spread through India and the Caucasus, that the Celts – who were originally a tribe from this area – had carried the art with them as they wandered through Europe, finally reaching the rugged shores of the West.

Monkish habit

From these three centres of knowledge – Andalucia, Salerno and Ireland – a web of information began to be established, with monks taking over from alchemists as the guardians of the art. Monasteries were the great centres of learning of this time, and during the Dark Ages, Ireland was a key centre of knowledge. It was Irish monks – wandering the roads of Europe, along with their brethren in Salerno – and the Moors who spread knowledge of the art across Europe.

We now reach a time when written descriptions of distillation begin to appear. The Salernan school was distilling by the eleventh century, and when Henry II invaded Ireland in 1174 he found the natives making *aqua vitae* – unknown in England at the time.

Although drinks like mead would have been drunk for celebratory reasons, at this point spirits were still being used as medicines. Alcohol was used not just as a marvellous new remedy in itself but, as Rhazes had discovered, it was the perfect medium for medicinal herbs.

The monks, therefore, were dispensing cordials and elixirs – one is still made by the monks of Chartreuse – produced from spirit made from whatever grew around them. Those in the south used grapes; in the middle, fruit was more common; while in the cold north, grains and honey were the bases for spirits. These broad divisions still remain.

Spirits only started becoming the property of the people when the tight control of the monasteries was loosened. As the knowledge of spirits spread, so the art split into three camps. Monks and early medical scientists like Thaddeus Florentus (1223–1303), a medical lecturer at Bologna, made remedies; alchemists were still trying to capture the essence of existence; while the people – Highland crofters, Polish landowners and the European peasantry – were beginning to take an interest in spirits as a social pleasure.

The father of European distillation is, for some reason, still given as the thirteenth-century Moorish scholar and alchemist Arnold de Villanova, who taught the art at Avignon and Montpellier. His pupil Raymond Lull (or Lully) is credited with producing the first true alcoholic spirit – a distillation of wine using double distillation and a cold-water condenser. He was so astounded by the potency of the spirit, that he believed it could bring about the end of the world. Lull was looking for ether, the elusive fifth element (quintessence) regarded by alchemists as being the element that was latent in all things. It must have seemed as if he had succeeded. Lull is credited with bringing the art to England when John Cremer invited him to visit the court of Edward I.

Drinking For Pleasure

Spirits were now firmly established. In 1483, Schrick of Augsburg published the first printed book on alcohol, while 12 years later Friar John Cor bought his famous eight bolls of malt and, allegedly, started off whisky production in Scotland.

Although gins and liqueurs were becoming identifiable as similar to the spirits we now know, many of the spirits of this time were a long way removed from the pure distillates we know today. Virtually all whiskies and vodkas at this time would have been flavoured with herbs and spices to mask the off-flavours produced by poor-quality distillation.

Spirits by now had escaped from the cloisters and arrived in the homes of the people. As they did, so their usage began to change dramatically. While they were still used as a beneficial medicine – *aqua vitae* made from *genever* (the precursor of gin) was used as a cure for the Plague in the fourteenth century – there's little doubt, when you look at who was making them, and what was going into them, that they were also being drunk for pleasure.

The art of distillation was vital to gracious living. "From medieval times (until the eighteenth century at least) the rich had a still-room, run by the still-room maid, where she would prepare potions. She managed the herb garden and orchard and made sure they were harvested at the right time, in tune with the phases of the moon", writes Rosamund Richardson in *Country Wisdom*.

Alcohol therefore easily slipped off the shackles of medicine and became part of daily life and celebration. As Terence McKenna points out in his *Food of the Gods*, alcohol was nothing less than the first synthesized drug, predating heroin, cocaine and mescalin by hundreds of years.

A major international expansion in spirits production took place in Renaissance times for two main reasons. Firstly, the marriage of Catherine de Medici to Henri II brought the Italian mastery of liqueur production to France. Meanwhile contact with Italian monks had brought the hitherto arcane techniques of pot-still distillation into both Poland and Russia.

COMMERCIAL ENTERPRISE

By the end of the sixteenth century, commercial distilleries began to appear (immediately followed by taxation). Many were no more than a still in a great house, but some distillers, such as Amsterdam's Lucas Bols, were already involved in large-scale commercial production of genever and liqueurs, while vodka distillers in Poznan had begun to export their new vodkas.

Distillation equipment was becoming more advanced. Hieronymus Braunsweig's 1519 manual, *Das Buch zu Distilliern*, has illustrations showing stills with up to four retorts. In Scotland triple distillation was common practice, while in Poland and Russia quadruple distillation was used as part of those countries' never-ending quests for the purest spirit possible.

Every country was beginning to sow the seeds that would eventually flower into the great spirits we know today. The expansion of the "industry" allowed greater experimentation and the development of national and regional styles. As ever, this was predominantly a matter of developing and perfecting the spirit made from local ingredients, but each country (and region) had a slightly different idea as to how to do it. In the East, the goal was a pure spirit base that could then be flavoured with various exotic ingredients ranging from grass to gold. In the West, in Scotland and France, distillers were beginning to use distillation itself (rather than botanicals) to produce powerfully flavoured spirits.

Impact of empire

Although export was beginning, with the exception of the Dutch and English trade in brandy, spirits remained local specialities which were becoming increasingly popular with the growing population – and with governments, who were delighted at this easy target for raising revenue for wars.

The world was becoming smaller, and the spread of the European empires provided the next spur to spirits' development. The Spanish and Portuguese had established their colonies in Brazil and the Caribbean in the fifteenth century, and started sugar production almost immediately. The new settlers wanted a spirit to drink – it took too long for brandy to reach them from Europe – and so they did what all distillers have done throughout history: they used the local crop, in this case sugar cane. Rum started off as a drink for slaves but soon became an important profit-making industry, particularly when the British, French and Dutch began colonizing the other islands and started their own sugar industries.

By the end of the sixteenth century this fermented sugar beer was known as "kill-devil", and within 100 years it was being produced commercially across the Caribbean, and England was trading in sugar and rum.

In the American Colonies, the early settlers started out by drinking Caribbean rum, but soon realized that they could make it more cheaply at home, and so began importing molasses, distilling rum and, following England's example, using it to buy slaves.

In Mexico, the Spanish settlers who were spreading inland from the cane plantations on the coast had started experimenting with distilling the local fermented drink, *pulque*, that was drunk throughout the country. In time, *mezcal* joined the other fast-growing spirits of the world.

In Peru, Chile and Argentina, meanwhile, settlers brought grape cuttings with them (*vitis vinifera* is not indigenous to South America) and began producing brandy (*Pisco*). Every wave of immigrants brought new knowledge and new spirits. The Scots and Irish, arriving in America and Canada, started replicating what they had done at home – making whisky from grain (although in this case it was rye rather than barley). Within a short period of time the world of spirits had become increasingly diverse.

One of the main catalysts for this development was the influence of the Dutch mercantile empire. Not only were their ships bringing back flavouring spices from around the world, affording gin and liqueur producers an ever-growing range of flavourings to play with, but they kicked brandy production into life. The Dutch needed spirit to keep the water on ships drinkable during long sea voyages. In the seventeenth century they therefore started to buy wine from the region close to the French port of La Rochelle, and then started to make brandy *in situ*. In this way, Cognac was born.

Drinking to forget

By the eighteenth century spirits were being consumed in vast quantities across the world. It was a time of excess, and it was the beginning of the exodus from the country to the city. The new urban poor needed something to take their minds off their wretched existence and mass-produced, cheap alcohol was the drug of choice. Suddenly it was a long way from the mystical aims of the alchemists.

By the beginning of the nineteenth century drinking spirits was a serious business that was enjoyed by all classes in virtually every country. The next development was to increase this mass-appeal still further. For years, distillers had been faced with the fact that to make their drinks they had to use pot stills. That meant distilling once, collecting the spirit, recharging the still and redistilling a second or third time. It was time-consuming, it was expensive and the return was small into the bargain. If only a way could be found to produce large quantities of good-quality spirit at low cost.

Aeneas Coffey is credited with being the inventor of the answer to their prayers, the continuous still, although it seems likely that different scientists were all coming up with similar ideas across Europe. These stills solved the problem, and continuous production of high-strength, clean, light-flavoured alcohol had arrived. It was to change the face of spirit production. Over the next 150 years pot stills became rarer and spirits became lighter. As huge volumes of this new spirit were produced, so many of the small distillers found they could no longer compete. The industry began to shrink in numbers as it increased in volume. The age of the global spirit loomed.

MASS PRODUCTION

At that point, though, pot-still brandy was the world's best-known spirit. Then, in the 1870s the *phylloxera* louse infested and killed off the European vineyards. The sudden cessation of supplies forced drinkers to look elsewhere – and there were the new blended Scotches that could be produced in huge quantities, thanks to the continuous still. The Scots (and Irish) stepped into the gap left by brandy, and within a few years whisky was the world's top-selling spirit, with gin – the essential base for the new cocktails – following hard on its heels.

The world shrank that little bit more when America embarked on the lunacy of Prohibition. By effectively killing off its whiskey industry, it allowed British firms to flood the market, first after Repeal and once again after the Second World War. By then, though, a subtle change had taken place. The post-war consumer – particularly in America – was looking for a lighter spirit to drink long and mixed. It was the start of vodka's rise from the obscurity of Eastern Europe to overtake whisky as the world's favourite spirit.

The global market

It wasn't long before the larger distillers thought, "What's the point of shipping our spirit from A to B; why don't we just establish distilleries in other countries?" Smirnoff, Gordon's and Bacardi ceased to be regional or national spirits, and became international brands. Some of the ancient ties between country and spirit had been severed. The continuous still meant that neutral base spirit could be made in any country – allowing gin and, more commonly, vodka to be produced by anyone with the requisite equipment. No longer was it necessary to make a distillate purely from local ingredients and expect it to taste of them. Stateless neutrality was fast becoming the theme.

Scotch was holding its own, however. The affluent USA and Britain of the 1960s were happy to drink a whole range of spirits. Everyone was happy – especially the major distillers who, by taking the next logical step into a truly global market, began to treat their brands as commodities.

Their marketing and distribution had been so effective that soon everyone in the world was drinking more or less the same thing. National and regional differences existed, but they were significantly less pronounced than they had been 50 years previously. This meant, from the distillers' way of looking at things, that all spirits could be treated in the same way in every country. The market was buoyant. In the eyes of the multinationals, if their whisky brands were declining, then as long as their vodka was growing at the same rate, what was the problem?

As the 1970s and 1980s wore on, that shift from whisky to vodka was beginning to accelerate. In general, since the late 1970s "brown spirits" have fallen – most significantly, in their oldest markets. To be strictly accurate, it's "old spirits" that have fallen, as gin and rum (with the exception of Bacardi) have also hit the slide. Part of this was down to the fact that the new generation of drinkers that was emerging didn't want to drink the same spirits as their parents – in the 1980s, many of them didn't want to drink spirits at all!

The arrival of multinational drinks firms opened up the market and made what used to be national specialities into international brands. As this has happened, however, so many have simply become commodities – their specialness, their history and strangeness being lost to the strict framework that uninspired marketing theory applies to everything, whether it's baked beans, nappies or malt whisky. In spirits it meant that Cognac was sold in the same way as vodka, rum, whisky and gin. So we ended up with greater choice but less understanding than ever before. Never have spirits been so far removed from their spiritual homes.

Prohibition killed off the US whiskey industry and allowed imports to flood the market on Repeal

Craft revival

Of course there were exceptions. The small industries of Cognac and Armagnac managed to retain their individuality, while some far-sighted malt distillers in Scotland also realized that people might just be interested in old-fashioned tradition and hand-crafted quality after all.

This return to "authenticity" has underpinned the major shift in spirits since the end of the 1980s. It started with malt, but soon moved to small-batch bourbon, premium imported vodka and top-aged rums, and now tequila, mezcal and even gin are in on the act.

Today's younger drinkers are looking for spirits with flavour and with a story to tell; spirits that speak of their place. Spirits are being looked at in the same way as wine. Drinkers don't only want to know where they come from and what they taste like, but why they taste the way they do and who made it. Distillers are now more important than marketing managers. At long last the human element in distillation is being given the attention it deserves.

Today's consumer is able to choose from the largest range of high-quality spirits the world has ever seen. Along the way spirits may have lost their mystical quality, but in recent times they have managed to regain something equally important – their sense of place.

MAKING SPIRITS

Distilling is the means of concentrating the alcohol in a fermented liquid. The theory is simple: alcohol and water boil at different temperatures – water at 100°C and alcohol at 78.3°C. Therefore, when a fermented liquid is heated, the vapour that contains the alcohol is released first. This vapour can then be trapped, cooled and condensed into a spirit at a higher strength.

Heating is not the only way to achieve this result. Early "distillers" in eighth-century Poland (and later in Canada) used freezing to separate water from alcohol. This is known as fractional crystallization, although they didn't know that at the time.

A fruit wine, or cider, would be left outside to freeze and the (brutally strong) liquor would be removed. This works because water freezes at a higher temperature (0°C) than alcohol. It's an inexact science, however, as it first requires the temperature to hover around –15°C, and still doesn't remove any potentially harmful alcoholic compounds.

The early distillers therefore used small glass flasks, which were soon to be replaced with copper pots. These were filled with the fermented liquid, heated and the vapour would rise along a thin tube, which ended immersed in a vat of cold water.

"It is to be understood that distilling is nothing else but a purifying of the gross from the subtle, the subtle from the gross each separately from the other to the intent that the corruptible shall be made incorruptible and to make the material immaterial." So begins the first great treatise on distillation written in 1500 by Brunschwig, a physician of Strasbourg. That principle remains true today.

Alcohol contains a huge range of chemical compounds, the main one being ethyl alcohol. However, there is also a wide range of by-products such as aldehydes, amyl alcohols (fusel oils), esters, acids and methanol, all produced by a combination of the raw material and fermentation.

Some of these are harmful, others are what gives a spirit its taste and smell – the congeners. The question facing distillers is how many of them they want to retain.

In simple terms, the distillers of those spirits that use pot stills – such as malt whisky, Cognac and some top rums – will be aiming to produce a more flavoursome spirit with a higher percentage of flavours of the raw material than those which are distilled in continuous stills.

The pot still

In today's terms, a pot still isn't an efficient method of distilling. The base (wine for brandy, or a crude beer for the grain spirits) has to be distilled twice – sometimes three times – in order to remove the harmful elements.

At the end of the day, though, the distillate will still contain relatively high amounts of congeners. The downside is that these heavy alcohols are a major contributory factor in producing hangovers; their advantage is that they are the elements that give the spirit its complex flavour.

Normally two, sometimes three, distillations take place in batch distillation. The first distillation gives a light concentration of the fermented liquid resulting in a spirit of around 20 per cent ABV. The second distillation is where the distiller concentrates the spirit further and discards or captures the congeners.

The distillation is divided into three different parts: heads, heart and tails. The first alcohols to be condensed (known as the heads) are highly volatile and are retained and redistilled with the next batch. But then, usually at around 72 per cent ABV, the heart begins to reveal itself. This is what has to be captured by the distiller.

This starting point of the heart of the spirit run is

vital to the final flavour of the spirit. Make it too early and you'll end up with heads in the spirit; too late and you'll miss the most delicate, floral and fruity esters, which arrive just after the volatile elements have disappeared.

As the spirit flows, not only does the strength drop, but the aromas begin to change from being light to heavy. Logically enough, the last alcohols to come across (known as the tails) contain the heaviest alcoholic compounds with the richest and most powerful aromas.

Some of these are desirable – they contribute palate weight and bass notes to the final spirit – but capture too many and you'll end up with a rank spirit. The tails are also retained and added to the next batch.

Knowing when to start and stop collecting the heart is an art, for while there are undesirable elements in heads and tails, they also contain flavours that the distiller wants to retain. The secret is to capture just enough of the last of the heads and the first of the tails to give each spirit its identity.

Needless to say, this will vary between distillers. Those who want to produce a light and delicate spirit will, by and large, collect the spirit at a higher strength. Those who want something with weight and guts will allow more of the latter part of the distillation to be collected. There again, the less you collect the more expensive the operation is, so economics often have their part to play in the decision.

The size and shape of the still and the speed of distillation all have a hugely important role to play. The effect of the shape of the still is seen most clearly in malt whisky distillation. No two distilleries have the same shaped stills, and every distillery manager will have his or her own theory on how they impact on the vapour to help produce the distillery's signature flavour.

In general, the smaller the still the heavier the spirit; the taller the still, the lighter the spirit. This is because only the lightest, most delicate aromas can rise to the top of a tall neck; the other, heavier elements fall back and are vaporized again, a process known as reflux. Some stills have large goitre-like balls that encourage this process.

Of course in reality it's not quite as simple as that. The speed of distillation (which corresponds to the temperature of the heat applied to the still) will also have a significant impact on flavour and quality. The slower and gentler it is, the more effectively the congeners are separated. As one distiller says: "It's like stewing fruit. The lower the flame on the stove, the more intense the aromas released." You don't want a hot, fast distillation where all the aromatic elements come rushing across like children at the end of the school day; you want a slow, even procession. This is how a distillery with small stills can still manage to produce a complex and delicately flavoured spirit.

The continuous still

Until the beginning of the nineteenth century, all spirits were produced in pot stills, but distillers were already searching for a more cost-effective method of producing larger volumes.

This was particularly important in Scotland, where the distillers in the Lowlands wanted to produce huge volumes of cheap whisky for the growing urban population, and in Eastern Europe where vodka producers, always searching for ways to make their spirit as pure as possible, had to distil three or four times in pot stills to obtain the required result.

The solution was the continuous still. This is usually credited to whisky distillers Robert Stein and Aeneas Coffey, but similar apparatus was popping up at the same time in Armagnac and Poland. All of these stills worked to the same principle. As long as you put a fermented liquid in one end, you'd get high-strength spirit out of the other.

Most continuous stills consist of two linked columns called the analyser and the rectifier, each of which is divided with perforated horizontal plates. The cool fermented wash enters the top of the rectifier and runs down inside a pipe to the bottom of the column and up to the top of the analyser, where it sprays out and starts to descend through divisions in the horizontal plates.

At the same time, hot steam is being constantly fed

into the bottom of the analyser. This rises through the perforations in the plate and meets the descending wash, then strips the alcohol vapour off. As the wash travels down the analyser, therefore, it becomes progressively weaker.

The steam and alcohol vapour rise to the top of the analyser and pass along a pipe to the bottom of the rectifier, where they are released and start to rise once more. At this point they come into contact with the pipe containing the wash with which they perform a sort of heat exchange. The steam and vapour warm the pipe up, while the pipe begins to cool the vapour down, and this causes it to start to condense.

Continuous distillation works on the principle that not only do water and alcohol boil at different temperatures, but the different congeners also boil (or, to be more precise, vaporize) at different temperatures as well. Therefore as they rise up the column, so the different components begin to separate (fractionate).

The column is therefore a far more efficient way of separating almost everything except the higher alcohols, which are collected on a solid plate. This can be placed at any point in the column, allowing the distiller to collect spirit at whatever strength he wants.

The end result is a spirit of, on average, 90 per cent ABV or more with most of its congeners stripped out. Here speed is important as well. Just as in pot-still distillation, the best-quality spirit will come from those stills that are run slow and steady, achieved by varying the flow rate of the wash and the pressure of the steam. Too fast, and you'll end up with burnt aromas.

There are various types of continuous still. In vodka, gin, most white rums and grain whisky – where the aim is to have a low-flavour, high-strength spirit – linked columns will be used. In the case of some vodka and all gin, the spirit will be rectified once more to produce what is known as neutral alcohol. Some rum and vodka distilleries have three, four or five linked columns, giving the distiller a huge range of possibilities, from neutral spirit to flavoursome.

Charcoal is often used for filtering whisky to give it a special character; here charcoal is being made

It's often thought that continuous distillation gives a uniformly bland spirit. Not true. Although the vast majority of vodka distillers will distil to the same strength, a tasting of a cross-section of brands will reveal totally different flavours. Part of this comes from the raw material used (and proves that they aren't neutral), but also is the result of the skill of the distiller in capturing the style and personality of the spirit that he wants.

In Kentucky and Tennessee, the spirit isn't rectified but comes off a single column still and into a basic pot-still apparatus called a doubler, which concentrates the alcohol to around the same as a malt whisky or Cognac. In Armagnac and some islands in the Antilles, meanwhile, they use tiny single-column stills which, although working on the same principle, produce a spirit of lower strength than one from a pot.

To age, or not to age

In general, white spirits (vodka, gin, white rum, silver tequila and mezcal) are reduced in strength, given time in a vat to mellow and are then bottled. Brown spirits (whisk(e)y, brandy, aged rum, reposado and anejo tequila) are given some time in oak barrels.

Each country and region will have its own specifics when it comes to what type of oak to use, what size of barrel, whether it is new or not – and, if not, what it has previously held. Oak and oak maturation is probably the area that is receiving the greatest attention in Cognac, Scotland, Ireland and Kentucky. A popular statistic that's being bandied about at the moment is that up to 60 per cent of a malt whisky's flavour will come from the wood it is kept in. Good reason to pay close attention to the barrels.

The aim of maturation is to give the spirit a period of controlled oxidation, and also to allow it to mingle and extract the flavour and colouring compounds that are contained in the barrel. Oak contains a huge range of phenolic compounds, which are easily broken down by high-strength alcohol.

These include tannins (giving fragrance and grip), lignins (which give spiciness) and cellulose (light sweetness), all of which build complexity in the spirit as they break down.

As the spirit matures, it moves in and out of the layers of wood, sucking up the wood compounds and colour and absorbing them into itself.

Each spirit has a different approach to wood and maturation. By law, bourbon can only use new, heavily charred American oak. New wood is brimful of flavouring such as vanillins, which American oak is particularly high in, and colour extracts. Cognac and Armagnac producers usually only give their brandies a couple of years in new wood in order to extract some of these compounds, before transferring the brandy to older barrels, where the level of extract is lower. They can then start slowly oxidizing and breaking down the remaining flavouring compounds in the wood.

The thrifty Scots only use second-hand wood – either ex-bourbon barrels or sherry butts, both of which impart their own distinct character on the spirit (*see* the chapter on Whisky from P422).

It's already evident that there's no one correct way in which to make a spirit; what's important is knowing which technique is the most appropriate, given the local conditions, ingredients and environment.

You couldn't copy bourbon techniques in Scotland or Ireland and expect to produce the same spirit, just as you couldn't replicate Scottish or Irish techniques in America – that has already been proved, because it is what the early American distillers attempted to do. Raw materials are different, as are ferments, distillation techniques and maturation. Diversity is the welcome result.

At their root, the greatest spirits are human creations that are inextricably linked to their place of birth. They distil human experience and the physical environment – and amplify them both.

Opposite: *Water purity is essential for distilling top-quality whisky; this mountain stream in the USA is untainted by industrial waste*

WHISKY

The wild coasts of north-western Europe have long sheltered people for whom spirits are part of the national psyche. Scotland and Ireland have given the world many things – but whisk(e)y remains their greatest gift. It was emigrants from these Celtic nations who took the art of distilling to North America and helped make the drink the world's favourite spirit. Whisky's story encompasses legend, internal strife, the pain of forced emigration and the triumph of Victorian capitalism.

That said, whisky is the same as every other category when it comes to trying to get tabs on who first made it. In all of the major categories there will be plenty of conjecture, a smattering of rumour, some hypotheses, a touch of speculation and numerous leaps of logic. Bloody-minded national pride will rear its head occasionally, but at no point will we be able to say that a certain type of spirit was first distilled on this date, in this year, by this person.

Scotch whisky is typical of this state of affairs. It's true that in 1994 the whisky industry celebrated the 500th anniversary of Scotch, but to be strictly accurate the cause of this worldwide rejoicing was actually the 500th anniversary of the first documentation of distilling taking place in Scotland. This was a record in the Exchequer Roll of 1494 that said: "To Friar John Cor, by order of the King, to make *aqua vitae*, VIII bolls of malt." There you have it; the first distiller was a man of the cloth domiciled in Lindores Abbey, near Newburgh, Fife.

But hang on a minute. A boll of malt is 140 lb. Eight bolls are enough to make 400 bottles of whisky. This suggests that Friar Cor wasn't just conducting an experiment, but had already mastered the art and was making commercial quantities. He was a distiller, of that there is little doubt, but the first? Unlikely. It's more probable that he was continuing a practice that had already been refined and perfected.

We still can't say who it was that first distilled whisky in Scotland, but Friar Cor provides two clues. The first is that he was a monk. Monasteries in this period were the universities of their time – places not just of prayer, but laboratories, hospitals, centres of philosophy, writing and art. As we have seen, the secret alchemy of distillation is most likely to have spread along a network of learning, being passed from its origins in Arabia to the wandering monks of the early Church.

One conjecture about Scotch is that distilling was brought to the country by the monks of the Celtic Church who sailed from Ireland to the Western Isles, making their first landfall on Islay in the sixth century. From there they sailed north, establishing their first religious base on Iona, before spreading the word of the Gospel (and the other holy spirit?) into the Highlands and Central Scotland.

This theory implies that distillation was already being practised in Ireland – legend says that it was taken there by St Patrick when he arrived from France in the fifth century, although this seems unlikely. What's possible is that Irish monks, roving across Europe, were taught the art and brought it back with them. You could even speculate that information about distillation could have arrived in Ireland via the trade with the Phoenicians, who brought viticulture to Europe. If distillation was being practised in the Middle East at this time, then why shouldn't that science be shared as well?

The second theory, most famously proposed by Scots author Neil M. Gunn, is that whisky-making was known to the Celts as they trekked from their Indo-European homeland to the fringes of the utter west. There's a logical argument here as well. If distillation was known to the Chinese, the Huns, the

Indians and the Scythians, then why not to the Celts as well?

Julian the Apostate (Roman Emperor, 361–363 AD) taunted the northern "barbarians" when, on trying a "barley brew", he said: "For lack of grapes, from ears of grain your countrymen, the Celts, made you." Some scholars have seized on this as meaning spirits, but it could be beer.

There's a more intriguing mention by the early Welsh bard Taliessen who wrote in his "Mead Song": "Mead distilled sparkling, its praise is everywhere." Given that Taliessen also wrote at length about brewing and didn't use the term "distil" in that treatise, it is possible that the art of making spirits was known in sixth-century Celtic Britain.

Whoever was first, by Friar Cor's time spirits were being distilled in considerable quantities in monasteries. Significantly, he distilled in the reign of James IV – a true Renaissance king, fuelled by a lust for life, loved by his people, a patron of the arts. He was the king at whose court Scots poetry first flowered, and who financed investigations into alchemy. He spoke Gaelic, as well as French and Scots, and visited Islay to try to quell a rebellion by the Lords of the Isles. The strands come together. Islay, monks, a lost art, and an alchemist king whose mind was on higher learning.

Perhaps it's best that the birth of Scotch remains obscure. There's nothing better than debating the possible truth over a few drams in a Scottish bar. You can be guaranteed that everyone will have their own pet theory – not surprisingly, as this spirit is everyone's drink. It is inextricably bound up with the development of Scotland as a nation, it has dictated the national psyche, and echoes the land from which it springs.

All early distillers made their original compounds from readily available ingredients. Malt whisky came into existence because Scotland's climate produced a hardy grain (barley) and plenty of water, which, thanks to the country's geological structure, was virtually pure.

There was also a plentiful supply of fuel (in particular, peat) to fire the stills and dry the barley. Malt came about when these natural ingredients,

peculiar to Scotland, were manipulated by man.

Don't think for a minute, though, that the early whiskies would be anything like the malts we enjoy today. The stills, although they had developed from crude alembics to something equating to today's models, were small. Malted barley – from the archaic, indigenous strain of the plant called bere – was used, but so were other cereal crops, while plants and flavourings would also have been added. These early whiskies were not only used for celebrations, but also as medicines.

It was only after the dissolution of the monasteries that whisky-making became a people's art. Initially it was practised by ex-monks who became apothecaries, barbers and surgeons, but it was soon taken into the crofts and great houses of the Highlands. By the sixteenth century, not only was triple distillation common practice in the Western Isles, but exports had started to Ireland and France.

By then, *uisge beatha* (the Gaelic translation of *aqua vitae*, from which is derived today's whisky) was a central part of the rhythm of Highland life. Crofters would make it with surplus grain, and the by-products were fed to the cattle wintering indoors. It was a spirit that fuelled dancing and celebrations, drowned sorrows, numbed the hard life and helped to pay the rent. It became part and parcel of life itself.

Although the bulk of Highland whisky was distilled in small batches for personal use, either on the croft or in the larger houses, distilleries were beginning to appear. The first notable example was Ferintosh in the Black Isle, which, thanks to the political allegiance of its owner, Duncan Forbes of Culloden, was granted duty-free status in 1715. The capital generated by this allowed Forbes to build three more distilleries and sell this first "brand" across Scotland. He had a ready market. Whisky consumption was booming and, for the first time, Lowland distillers had begun to produce spirit in significant amounts. Whisky was Scotland's drink.

Then disaster struck. The failure of the 1745 Rebellion ushered in a new era for the Highland distiller. After Culloden, every aspect of Highland life and culture was systematically and ruthlessly crushed. It wasn't as simple as English versus Scots; it was aristocracy against peasant, Protestant against Catholic, Lowlander against Gael. This process of ethnic cleansing culminated in the Clearances of the nineteenth century, when a people who had made their life on the land were either herded into new towns on the coast and forced to learn new trades, or shipped to Nova Scotia, America and Australia – leaving the glens where they had farmed and distilled for centuries silent, apart from the bleating of sheep.

The post-Culloden repression took place on many fronts and directly affected how whisky developed. Crofter-distillers on islands like Tiree or Pabbay, who had exported whisky to the mainland, found themselves caught in a pincer movement of increased governmental legislation and a culture of depopulating rural areas. They were given no option but to shut down their stills, thereby losing a significant percentage of their income, and to move.

The taxman cometh

Almost inevitably, tax played its part. The saying is that "Freedom and Whisky go together", but to be strictly accurate it's taxation and whisky that have been inseparably linked since 1644. Tax had been used to fund wars and curb drinking; now it was being used to help eradicate Highland culture.

To be fair, the taxation measures affected Lowland producers as well, and the effect of a law in 1774 banning stills smaller than 200 gallons effectively drove distilling underground (often literally). This ridiculous ban made the small Highland stills illegal overnight, so smuggling increased. The Wash Act of 1784 made matters worse for the Highland distiller, for although duty was cut and smaller stills could be used in the North, it was on the proviso that only local grain be used, while the whisky produced couldn't be sold below the Highland Line.

Not surprisingly, the smuggling war intensified, mainly because by this time Highland whisky (by now similar to today's malt whisky) was considered to be better quality than the rough firewater produced by the large distillers in the Lowlands.

Distilling in the sixteenth century; detail of a blockbook of the period

Then, in 1816, the Highland Line was scrapped, restrictions on still size and shape were dropped and duty was cut. By the time a further act was passed in 1823, legal distilling was not only an option but a desirable one.

Whisky-making had become the preserve of the rich, often the very landowners who had forced the crofters from their land. It had ceased to be a cottage craft, but had been moulded (some would say deliberately) into an industry that could be effectively legislated by the government and controlled by relatively few men of capital.

The death-knell for single malt came with the invention of the continuous still and the rise of the blenders. Some distilleries managed to hang on to their markets – most notably producers in Campbeltown and Port Ellen on Islay, who had built up trade with America – but they were the exception. Malt was considered too heavy, too much of an acquired taste, for the world markets.

As the Victorian capitalists took control of a fast-expanding industry, malt was relegated to providing the fillings for the new-fangled blends that were to make Scotch the world's favourite spirit category. Malt would remain virtually forgotten until the 1970s.

The blenders

Lowland producers were always working to a different agenda from that of the Highlanders. Whisky played less of a central role in the cultural life of the cities, where the bottom line for distillers was to supply as much alcohol as possible as a palliative for Scotland's growing urban proletariat.

The Lowland distillers had always thought "larger" than their counterparts in the Highlands. The latter preferred to use small stills and malted barley, while the Lowland producers (richer, and therefore able to comply with the legal requirement to produce only from large stills) used rapid distillation and any cereal that came to hand. The grain spirit that cascaded out of their stills was undoubtedly a deeply unpleasant creation, but so what? It wasn't a drink for the refined bourgeois palate – they still drank wine and brandy (or illegal malt).

Then, in 1827, Robert Stein invented a still that not only made distilling less labour-intensive, but improved the quality of the grain spirit and allowed this more palatable drink to be mass-produced. His invention, adapted in 1831 by Aeneas Coffey, was the invention for which the Lowland producers were crying out. The continuous still had arrived, and with it the grain whisky we know today.

Much of this new drink was exported to England to be turned into gin, but it was only a matter of time before someone with a bit of imagination worked out that if they added some flavoursome malt to the light grain, they might come up with the best of all worlds – a drink that would be ideal for everyday drinking across Scotland, maybe even in England, perhaps across the world.

Crude blends would undoubtedly have been made in pubs, but after the launch of Usher's Old Vatted Glenlivet in 1853, it was grocers and wine merchants who first refined the art – men like Johnnie Walker in Kilmarnock, George Ballantine in Edinburgh, James Chivas in Aberdeen and William Teacher in Glasgow – while in Perth, Arthur Bell, John Dewar and Matthew Gloag made the town the blending capital of Scotland. Whisky was ready to be sold to the world – ironically, initially to the expatriate communities founded by the same Highlanders who had been turfed off their land.

Today's market

It needed a further stroke of fortune, in the shape of a louse, to turn blended whisky from a national into an international drink.

In the 1880s, just as the blenders were perfecting their first brands, the root-eating parasite *phylloxera vastatrix* was happily munching its way through the vineyards of Europe. When the louse destroyed the entire Cognac vineyard (the international spirit of choice at the time), blended whisky stepped into the breach and never looked back. By the time the brandy-producing regions were up and running again, blends had taken an unassailable lead.

The blended boom initiated a frenzy of distillery-building in the best locations in the Highlands – but these new whisky palaces weren't built to produce bottled single malt; they were filling stations for the new blends.

While malt distilling had become a profitable business, it was the blenders who called the shots and, despite a rearguard action by the malt distillers to define "whisky" as being a spirit produced only from pot stills, in 1909 Scotch whisky was defined as being malt, grain and blended whisky. The road was clear for blends to take over the world.

Even the onset of Prohibition in the USA (1920–1933) ended up helping blended whisky, as the best-quality brands were considered to be Scotch. Prohibition may have crippled domestic production in the USA and devastated the fortunes of Irish whiskey, but blended Scotch simply shrugged off another inconvenience and just carried on growing.

Partly this was due to the distillers' canny strategy of establishing their brands in a number of international markets, rather than just relying on sales at home and in one export market in order to survive.

The combination of the Depression and the Second World War severely restricted production and most malt distilleries closed – but in the post-war world (despite high taxation in the UK) blended whisky took advantage of a more optimistic outlook and growing consumerism. New distilleries were built, while old ones reopened and increased in size. Tied to a boom in consumer spending and the development of multi-media communication, blended whisky grew rapidly throughout the 1960s and early 1970s, but a slump was not far off.

An air of complacency descended on the distillers in the late 1970s. They thought that they only had to say "drink whisky" and people would, but before they knew it the young generation in the old markets like the USA, Australia and the UK had turned away from the drink – seeing it as old-fashioned and out of touch, the drink their parents enjoyed. A combination of high oil prices, world recession and a downturn in the biggest markets saw distilleries closing again.

Thankfully, as old markets have struggled, so new ones have opened up. Europe has proved a fertile selling ground where young people have been turned on to the "new" taste of blended Scotch by the very marketing strategies that could well have turned around the decline in the old markets. The Far East, too, has clasped whisky to its bosom – particularly at the *de luxe* end of the market – while South America is also booming. The industry, although growing, is approaching life cautiously.

Intriguingly, as blends have declined in the old markets, new drinkers have switched their allegiance to malt. Single malts have always been available, thanks to the work of independent bottlers like Gordon & MacPhail and Cadenheads, while some distillers always bottled their own product. But until the early 1970s malt was unknown on the mass market.

Then, in 1971, William Grant & Sons decided to actively market its single malt Glenfiddich by advertising, promotions and opening the distillery to the public... It's all old hat now, but 30 years ago Glenfiddich was hugely innovative – it caught the rest of the industry on the hop, and encouraged the development of single malt.

Malt may still only account for around five per cent of Scotch's sales, but as far as image is concerned it's leading the way forward. Increasing numbers of new whisky drinkers of both sexes aren't starting their whisky education with blends and then "graduating" to the malts, but are going straight into them.

It's become a full-time occupation to try to keep tabs on the new brands and variants that are appearing. Each week brings new malts, not only from established players, but from distilleries that were forgotten by their owners.

There are malts from long-closed plants, malts that have been "finished" in different types of wood, cask-strength malts, special bottlings – the list is endless. Blends may remain all-powerful, but malt, after a century of languishing in the shadows, is now showing its true colours and may yet prove to be Scotch's saviour – not in volume, but in image.

MAKING WHISKY

Malt whisky is produced from three ingredients: malted barley, water and yeast. The barley is germinated, dried over a fire, ground, mixed with hot water, fermented and then distilled twice in pot stills. The spirit is then aged in oak casks for a minimum of three years. Simple.

How it's made

If it were just a matter of following a recipe, then all malt whiskies would taste pretty much the same. The fact that they don't have exactly the same flavour as one another is a fundamental part of malt's magic, and every distillery manager will have his or her own theory as to why each one is different. Every aspect of production is subtly different in each distillery. The same process is happening, but each site will have its own unique take on proceedings – from the type of grain used to the shape of the stills.

Take barley. There is a rumbling debate about which strain is the best. The days of bere are long gone. These days, malt is made from super-strains. Since whisky-making is an industrial-scale process, distillers are looking

The kiln at the Balvenie maltings, one of the numerous distilleries in the Dufftown, Banffshire, region of Speyside in Scotland

for a type of barley that not only gives consistent quality, but which can deliver a minimum of 400 litres of alcohol per ton.

That requires the barley to be ripe, dry, high in starch, but low in protein and nitrogen, and able to break dormancy easily. Despite the large number of strains available, a distillery will use only one or two at a time, as each type has to be processed slightly differently. There are even some romantics, most notably Macallan and Glengoyne, who insist that barley contributes to the final flavour of the spirit. Both insist on using the "old-fashioned" (and expensive) Golden Promise.

Each grain has a genetic memory of a plant within it. Malting fools the grain that it's time to start growing, and then stops that growth when the starches are suitable for whisky-making. This is done by first steeping it in water and getting it to start germinating – when two of its three enzymes are triggered, converting the starches into soluble sugar (maltose).

The sight of a traditional malt barn is a glorious one – the stone floor covered in a sea of gold, rucked up into waves, the barley softening, bursting out of its shell, the whisky itself starting to come alive – but these days you'll find floor maltings only at Bowmore, Laphroaig, Springbank, Benriach, Balvenie, Glen Garioch and Highland Park – although there's a chance that Ardbeg will start up again.

The rest use malt from the commercial maltsters (with the single exception of Tamdhu, which uses a system called a Saladin Box) who can process the malt in one machine. Commercial maltsters may not be as romantic, but they are highly skilled operators – vital for an industry that has to keep pace with demand.

Whatever the method, the germination has then to be stopped. Traditionally, this took place in the kiln, and even though few distilleries malt their own barley, most of them have retained the kiln's pagoda-shaped roofs. In floor malting, a fire is lit below the floor of the kiln, which is perforated to allow hot air and smoke to rise. Traditionally the fire would have been lit with peat whose smoke, on entering the barley, permanently locks in its fragrant reek.

These days the majority of distilleries start drying with either hot air or coke, and then add a specific amount of peat for a set number of hours. The length of time the malt is under the blanket of peat smoke dictates how many phenolic parts per million (ppm) will be in a malt. Heavily peated malts like Ardbeg, Lagavulin or Laphroaig have between 40 and 50 ppm; medium-peated examples, like Bowmore or Highland Park, have 20 ppm; while lightly-peated Speysides, like Aberlour, Glenfarclas or Cragganmore, are all around 2 ppm. There are malts such as Glengoyne and Deanston that have no peat at all.

The malted barley, crisp and fragrant, then goes to the mill – where it's crushed to a specific grind. Too fine a grind, and you get a thick porridge that won't drain; too coarse, and you won't have exposed sufficient sugars. A percentage of husks is also needed to act as a natural filter in the mash tun. Once in the mash tun, hot water is poured over the grist, completing the final conversion. Since Scotch is only allowed to use the natural enzyme in the barley, the water has to be at a temperature that can do this without killing the enzyme.

This sweet water (worts) is drained off, and a second

PEAT

Peat, technically, is decomposed vegetation that has been carbonized by water. It's the fuel that's widely used in the Highlands and Islands, and the black incense that gives many whiskies a flavour that immediately whisks you back to their place of birth.

There are also different types of peat, giving different aromas. Islay's contains seaweed and moss and gives a denser, more aromatic nose; that on the mainland has more wood and heather, and is lighter; while on Orkney – where they even have different names for the different layers – heather is the main constituent.

The days of distilleries using nothing but hand-cut peat are long gone. Bowmore uses 150 tons of peat a year in its own kiln, but the maltings at Port Ellen, which malts most of Islay's barley, needs 2,500 tons of peat each year. To get that, it has to rip the peat up with industrial tractors.

The question of (ab)using a non-renewable natural resource arises. In fact, the whisky industry uses just 0.1 per cent of the peat cut every year. A nagging doubt still remains though. The old peat banks allow the heather and grasses to regrow which, in turn, protects a fragile ecosystem. The slash-and-rip technology leaves nothing behind. Surely another method needs to be found?

Native Irish barley which is used in the distillation of Jamesons Irish Whiskey

WATER

This, the first element in the creation of a malt whisky, is also the most mysterious. Why does water affect how a whisky tastes? It comes down to purity. What you want in good 'whisky water' is an absence of elements such as iron, but beneficial minerals such as calcium and zinc. Scottish water also has a low pH level – often because it contains traces of acidic peat – which will help with fermentation. What the water flows over on its way to the distillery will also have an impact on flavour. The three peaty monsters on Islay's south coast – Ardbeg, Lagavulin and Laphroaig – all use water that has run for miles over peat and picked up phenolic elements. Every little thing makes a difference.

and third waters are poured on. The first of these gets rid of those stubborn starches that cling to the husk. This, too, is drained off and kept with the first water. The third water is kept as the first water of the next mash. The worts are then cooled and pumped into fermenting vessels (washbacks) made either from steel or Oregon pine. Yeast is then added, and here's another area that's open to debate. The wine industry accepts that yeast imparts flavours, as do bourbon producers. Most Scotch distillers reject this and use whatever yeast gives the best yield. But if the flavour of the water, the aroma of peat and, perhaps, the flavour of the barley impart tiny elements of flavour, then why can't yeast?

The washbacks seethe as the ferment starts. Huge, puffy bubbles form on the scummy surface and pop in nose-tingling explosions. This goes on for between 48 and 60 hours, by which time the worts have been transformed into a strong wash. Now comes the final transformation: distillation in large, copper pot stills. The first distillation gives a spirit called low wines, of around 21 per cent ABV. This is collected and, once the distillation is finished, is pumped into the spirit still for a second distillation.

WOOD

The whisky industry has always used second-hand casks to age its product. In the early days these would have been wine, rum or sherry barrels that had been shipped to Scottish wine merchants. The Celtic nations are known for their thriftiness, so it made sense to re-use the casks. The industry now uses two main types of cask: ex-Bourbon barrels, and butts that have previously held sherry. Good casks will then be refilled once, or maybe twice, and some may be recharred to give them a new lease of life after the second fill. Components for blends, by and large, are filled into second- or third-fill barrels, while malts will go into a combination of first- and second-fill. Some malts, like Glenmorangie, use only first- and second-fill ex-bourbon barrels, while Macallan will use only sherry wood – although most distilleries use a combination of the two.

In the old days, choosing the percentages of bourbon and sherry was about as far as it went.

These days, distillers are looking at how the two different woods behave and what qualities they give. It's been estimated that between 50 and 60 per cent of a whisky's flavour comes from the wood, and Glenmorangie has taken the radical step of designing its own casks – the logic being that if you know which wood works best, you'll be more likely to get consistent whisky.

The conclusion was that they wanted air-dried, 100-year-old, white US oak from north-facing slopes of the Ozarks. Why? Air-drying eliminates the acrid astringent notes that kiln-drying can produce, while trees from north-facing slopes have a slower rate of growth, giving the right pore size and structure.

Macallan is equally obsessive. Its research showed that it got greater colour extraction and a more even maturation from Spanish, rather than American, oak. Now Highland Distillers (Macallan's parent) gets casks built to order. Macallan,

Highland Park and Glengoyne all use Spanish oak, as does Bowmore.

Where the whisky is matured makes a difference as well. It is generally agreed that the old, low slung "dunnage" warehouses with their earth floors perform the best – retaining humidity and giving good air circulation. Trouble is, there isn't enough space to build this style, and many distillers now age in rack warehouses. Macallan invested heavily to ensure its new racked sheds performed as its old-style warehouses, but others are suffering from the short-cuts they took.

Where the whisky matures is the final element in its building a sense of place. It has received its personality from the water, the peat, the barley and the shape of the still, and now wood. As a spirit sits in a cask, it is slowly drawn in and out of the wood, not only taking in the colours and flavouring compounds of the cask, but the air as well. A little bit of the microclimate is captured.

Like all forms of batch distillation, this process is concerned with separating the heads and tails (known as foreshots and feints here) from the heart of the spirit – or "making the cut", as it is known. Once the cut has started, the speed of the distillation is slowed down, and the heart is allowed to flow into a receiving tank until the distiller decides the true character of his malt has been captured.

The key is knowing when to stop – a rule of thumb is that the lightest, most fragrant whiskies tend to be cut at a higher strength than the phenolic, almost oily malts, which are cut significantly lower. Each distillery will do it differently. Macallan is notoriously tight with its cut, while the unctuous Laphroaig lets it run for longer than most. Once the heart is collected, the feints are run into the low-wines receiver to join the foreshots, ready for the next charge of the spirit still. Then the new spirit is poured into casks – made either from ex-bourbon or sherry butts – for its long, slow maturation. [See box on P431.]

While distilleries may now be equipped with computers that can calculate quicker than the human brain, whisky-making is a human activity. For, despite all the research and increased technology, no one knows quite what makes each malt special. For Mike Winchester at Aberlour, it's quite simple: "As understanding increases, so we'll realize why we are here, but the fact is we're here already! There's still a lot of witchcraft and magic to it all."

You need spend only a short time with the men in a distillery to realize that this isn't an industrial process – it's a labour of love; producing whisky taps into living folk wisdom. It's about guys who care about their product: the maltmen, who know that the malt is ready to be kilned when they can write their name on the wall with the soft grain; the stillmen, who can tell when to make the cut just by the look of the swirl the spirit makes in the hydrometer; the coopers, obsessively caring for each cask. That isn't industry, it's love – generations of knowledge being passed down from father to son. At the end of the day malt whisky, like all great spirits, is still about people.

The giant whisky stills at the Macallan Distillery; the distiller has a reputation for "making the cut" very early

Because the water used in distillation has different, unique properties, it follows that the whisky produced from it will also be unique

THE SENSE OF PLACE

The issue of whether malt whisky regions actually exist is another topic best discussed over a few drams with a fire blazing in the grate. The "antis" argue (rightly) that since each malt uses different water, has a slightly different malting specification, distils in a unique set of stills and matures in its own selection of casks, it's impossible to quantify what effect the environment has on the final product. There are too many variables – and it's too easy to manipulate.

Ah, but while it's difficult to bind together distilleries from a disparate region, there are some parts of Scotland where the "regional" argument holds up.

For example, the reason that the majority of Islay's malts are peaty and have a bracing iodine aroma is because on Islay there was no option but to use the local fuel, which was (and is) peat. The composition of the water will also have a minuscule, but significant, effect. Phenolic water will impart a different flavour to the purer water on the mainland.

There's also little doubt that you find a saltiness in malts that are matured by the sea – no great surprise there. Casks that have been matured in a salt-laden atmosphere will have sucked in some of that air to mingle with the spirit as the wood inhales.

In other words, there are regions where you can say the physical environment has dictated some of the malt's final flavour. The rest? Well, perhaps it's just romantic nonsense to claim that there's a pasture-like quality to the malts from the gentle Lowlands, a softness in those from the rolling hills of Perthshire, and a dry heatheriness to the ones from the harder lands in the north – but somehow, once you have visited the distillery, the landscape becomes inextricably linked with it.

THE LOWLANDS

The Lowlands aren't immediately associated with malt. Surely whisky comes from the Highlands? Aren't the Lowlands Scotland's overpopulated, industrialised heartland? Well, most of the heavy industry has long gone and the urban sprawl has always been surrounded by gentle hills, moors and farmland. Yes, Lowland malts are a perfect place to start.

The Springbank distillery is the only one in Campbeltown to remain open; 100 years ago there were two dozen more in the town

LOWLANDS AND CAMPBELTOWN – THE CLASSIC MALTS

The whiskies from the Lowlands are a perfect introduction to malt. Peating levels are kept to a minimum and triple distillation is common – techniques which produce whiskies that have a delicate, charming surface. That doesn't mean they have missed out on complexity though. Campbeltown should be considered a region in its own right and one which fuses all of malt whisky's greatest characteristics in the glass.

Auchentoshan 10-year-old (40% ABV)
Turfy, light and slightly sweet nose without water. Fresh, mealy and refreshing. A crisply attractive malt that's as fresh as a daisy with a long, clean finish.

Auchentoshan 21-year-old (43% ABV)
A nose of freshly cut turf. Good, nutty fruit with toasty aromas. Sweet, with a rich weight that rolls around the tongue before a rich, sweet finish. A revelation.

Bladnoch 10-year-old (40% ABV)
Fresh, almost minty, nose with a hint of caramelized orange and hay. A delicate, slightly sweet start, before drying out a little mid-palate. Decent weight.

Glenkinchie 10-year-old (40% ABV)
A typical Lowland nose: grassy, crisp and invigorating. A touch of lemon on the palate intensifies the overall impression of freshness.

Glenkinchie 1986 Amontillado Finish (43% ABV)
Delicate walnut aromas mingling with malt loaf and the signature grassiness. Rounder and sweeter than the 10-year-old with fruity tingle on the finish.

Rosebank 12-year-old (43% ABV)
Tremendous, complex nose with green grass, apple and an undercurrent of hay-accented fruit. Wonderfully balanced, with some smoke on the palate before a huge lift of sweet fruit that lasts forever. A classic.

Springbank 12-year-old (46% ABV)
An astounding, powerful, perfumed nose that is delicate and lightly smoky with positive, malty, lightly sherried notes. A sweet, hugely ripe start before dried spices and smoke peek out.

Springbank 1966 Local Barley (54.4% ABV)
Intense, powerful nose. This is a crunchy, mouth-watering mix of smooth, elegant wood, butter, lemon peel and peaches. Layer upon layer of flavours that grow in the mouth and stay there for eons.

That said, the bulk of the spirits produced in this part of the country is grain whisky for blends, but there are other factors which make Lowland malt subtly different from its northern neighbours.

The distinctive Lowland style

There has always been a wide variety of cereal crops grown in these fertile lands, and in the past many distillers used a mix of different grains rather than just barley. There wasn't much peat here to dry the barley, but there was coal, and distillers also often triple-distilled. The Lowland style therefore emerged as one that was soft, dry and relatively light in character.

This isn't being dismissive. Good malt whisky has always been produced here, often in distilleries within grain plants, such as Grant's Ladyburn, or Inverleven and Lomond from the innards of Allied's Dumbarton plant.

These days, though, there's the merest smattering of malt distilleries. Auchentoshan, situated next to the Clyde on the outskirts of Glasgow, still produces a fine triple-distilled malt. UDV's Glenkinchie is one of the firm's Classic Malts and is a pleasant, hay-like dram. In fact, Glenkinchie was the lucky one out of UDV's Lowland plants. A slump in demand meant it had to close Bladnoch, Scotland's most southerly distillery, and Rosebank, which produced the finest of all Lowland malts. The good news is that both look likely to re-open (in a limited way) soon, enabling us to enjoy more examples of a style that's as charming as this part of the country.

The Campbeltown saga

Technically speaking, Campbeltown is a separate region, although these days it has only one distillery in operation. It wasn't always like this. At one time Campbeltown was Scotland's whisky capital. At the end of the last century there were 25 distilleries cluttering up this small fishing port at the foot of Kintyre. Campbeltown's speedy decline was down to a combination of greed and Al Capone and his buddies. The town had supplied America with whisky for years, and when Prohibition struck the orders increased. Trouble was, as production was upped, so quality fell. The bootleggers also realized they could get more money for any old hooch by slapping Campbeltown on the label. The town's reputation plummeted, and by 1930 there were only three distilleries left.

Somehow Springbank, the only Campbeltown distillery still open, has managed to remain a magnificent dram. It still malts its own barley, uses coal-fired stills, a form of triple-distillation, and even bottles, unfiltered, on the premises. If only Campbeltown Loch were full of this stuff! Truly magnificent.

ISLAY

This, the most southerly of the Scottish islands, is home to the country's most distinctive group of malts. If finding a regional style for parts of the mainland sometimes involves making rather creative connections, then there's no doubt that the majority of Islay's mighty brood are from the same family.

Whisky's cradle

Opinion is moving toward the conclusion that this friendly island could have been the first part of Scotland to make whisky. The southern tip of Islay is only 30 miles from the north of Ireland, and in the fifth century it was the site for the first landing of Christian missionaries from Ireland. Given it is believed that these monks held the knowledge of distilling, there's every possibility that once they had established their monastic strongholds on the island they continued with their experiments in making medicinal spirits.

In the confusing world of early Scotland, Islay was part of a separate Norse kingdom. Even after the Vikings had relinquished control it was the seat of power for the Lords of the Isles who, though they swore fealty to the Scottish crown, ruled the Western Isles as their own domain.

Much has been made of an apparent visit by King James IV to the island in the 1490s, just before he gave permission for Friar John Cor to make whisky. Might he have picked up the secret on Islay? It seems unlikely. Firstly, the King never visited Islay; in fact in the 1490s he was in the process of stripping the last Lord of the Isles of his title and installing his own man. He might have tasted whisky, but as far as being taught the secrets...?

Also, Friar Cor was making a huge amount of whisky, implying that the secret had long been known on the mainland. Islay may be the birthplace, but it is highly unlikely that it managed jealously to guard the secret for centuries.

Whatever the origins of distilling on Islay, the fact remains that it is particularly blessed for whisky making, one reason for it being able to still have seven distilleries when every other one of the Western Isle islands has, at most, one.

A benevolent climate

Islay is low-lying, fertile, the recipient of copious quantities of rain from the westerlies which strafe across it, but it also enjoys plenty of sunshine. Crofters on other islands may have had to struggle with raising barley, but on Islay there was little problem. To make matters even better for the whisky-maker, half of the island is smothered in peat. Until recently, Islay was self-sufficient in whisky-making ingredients. During the smuggling era – though it's due west of Glasgow, Islay is in the Highlands – stills could be hidden in its shoreline caves and the whisky quickly transported out. When legal distilling arrived, the old farmer distillers banded together (as at Lagavulin) and continued to make their whisky on the coast. This meant that barley could be imported easily (when commercial distilling started, Islay could no longer provide sufficient barley to supply the distilleries) and barrels of whisky could be taken off the island by boat. Bunnahabhain, the remotest distillery on the island, got all of its supplies by boat until the 1970s.

Another important reason for the high survival rate of Islay's distilleries was the fact that the island was less badly affected by the Clearances. While the population of neighbouring Jura was decimated to make way for sheep and estates, Islay was reorganized, with crofts being absorbed into larger farms. Though people were forced to leave their land, virtually all found employment elsewhere on the island. It therefore had a relatively large, stable population – and one that appears to have had a fearsome thirst!

As the whisky industry began to realign itself as a mighty commercial machine, many of Islay's farm distilleries – like the one at Bridgend which now houses the Post Office and general store – fell by the wayside.

ISLAY – THE CLASSIC MALTS

Islay remains home to Scotland's greatest collection of peated malts. The island's very soul seems to be encapsulated in the glass – the sea-laden air, the reek of the local peat, the combination of ruggedly robust flavours and gentle fruit. That said, there are two which have little peat – the best for the Islay virgin, while the rest, though rich and smoky have a graceful power. Once tried, these are malts that are never forgotten.

Ardbeg 17-year-old (40% ABV)
Orange and lemon marmalade nose. Chewy, with rich, integrated peatiness and balanced wood. Rich, with vanilla mingling with the fragrant smoke. Opulently flavoured, laced with lapsang souchong tea and ripe fruit.

Ardbeg 1978 (43% ABV)
Big, grumbly unreduced nose before the peat reek gracefully unfolds. A light touch of peat oil on the palate along with rich, smoky fruits and toffee, heather and salt. Glorious.

Bowmore 17-year-old (43% ABV)
Intense, elegant nose that mingles peat smoke, Jaffa cakes and a malty lift. On the palate are cigar box, peat smoke and chocolate. Elegant, soft and very long.

Bowmore Darkest (43% ABV) Glowing colour. Subtle and rounded nose of walnuts, chocolate and smoky fruit. Very well balanced.

Bruichladdich 10-year-old (40% ABV)
Rounded, slightly salty nose with a light smokiness. With water, beachy aromas appear with a little bergamot. On the palate some smoke and then attractive, almondy fruit. Charming.

Bunnahabhain 12-year-old (40% ABV)
Toffee-ish nose with a manzanilla-like salty tang. A bracing start, well rounded and gentle on the palate with a sudden ping of ginger on the finish.

Caol Ila 15-year-old (43% ABV) A mix of medicinal, rooty notes with lanolin and soft peatiness. Full on the palate with tobacco leaf and peat smoke. Crisp finish, with a touch of salt.

Lagavulin 16-year-old (43% ABV)
A great waft of fragrant smoke with some elegant woodiness, nutty fruit and tanned leather. Rich and plummy start before the peat surges back on the finish.

Laphroaig 10-year-old Cask Strength (57% ABV)
Hugely peaty nose with some fishy oiliness, a rich and powerful mix of seaweed and ozone. Very fresh malt on the palate, powerful and weighty. A classy dram.

Laphroaig 10-year-old (40% ABV)
Peat-sodden nose, medicinal with a light biscuity crunch. Great banks of peat, seaweed and trawler decks waft out. Oily, rich, salty, with some coconut on the finish.

That said, of the distilleries that Alfred Barnard visited in the 1880s only one, Lochindaal, no longer exists. Two, Bruichladdich and Port Ellen, are mothballed but there's every chance that the former will reopen soon, while Port Ellen now supplies virtually all of the island's malted barley. That's an amazing survival rate when you compare what happened in Campbeltown only 30 miles away. The reason is down to the singular flavour and high quality of Islay's malts.

The island falls quite neatly into two halves both geologically and stylistically. The younger southern part – home to Ardbeg, Lagavulin, Laphroaig and Port Ellen – contains the largest deposits of peat and, surprise surprise, the peatiest malts. The older northern half – home to Caol Ila, Bunnahabhain and Bruichladdich – is rockier and the style, generally speaking, is firmer and less heavily peated. Bowmore, the island's capital, sits half-way between – its water source is from the old north, and its peaty character nods to the south.

The influence of water

Water is a particularly important element in the flavour of Islay's malts. The southern group all take their water from burns which rise and flow over the peat bogs. The water that comes out of taps here is brown and with the faintest touch of a peaty, mossy flavour. In the north the water comes from springs or burns which have had little or no contact with peat.

Needless to say, the actual peating level given to the malted barley also makes a huge difference. Nowhere is malt given such a lengthy time with peat. Ardbeg's peating level is an astounding 50–56ppm, Laphroaig, Lagavulin and Caol Ila are around 35ppm, Bowmore is 20ppm while Bruichladdich and Bunnahabhain are at the industry average of 1–2ppm.

Significantly, all the distilleries use Islay peat either malted to their specifications at Port Ellen or, in Bowmore's and Laphroaig's case, malted in traditional floor maltings. You may think all peat is the same, but you'd be wrong. On the mainland it's made up of wood, moss and heather, but Islay's peat has layers of carbonized seaweed intertwined with the moss and heather. The wind also means that trees are an endangered species so wood-fired stills were never an option. Because the island is regularly lashed with sea spray, the peat has a slight iodine, salty tang.

Stir all these components together and add in the fact that all the distilleries age their whisky in warehouses on the seashore – again increasing the interplay between whisky and salt-laden air – and you can begin to see why Islay remains so special.

The distiller's art

That's not to say that its malts are all identical. Far from it. This is where the art of the distiller comes into play. Take the threesome from the whitewashed citadels on the bleak, eerie south coast. Peaty to the core, each shows a subtle variation on the theme. Laphroaig is the oiliest and heaviest – filled with tarred ropes, seaweed, oilskins and not so much a peat reek as a damp fire smouldering in the glass. The standard 10-year-old is good, but the cask-strength is magnificent – like Talisker, this is whisky whose flavours need a high-strength foundation to express themselves fully.

Lagavulin is equally peaty and muscular, but has greater elegance, partly down to the use of sherry wood (Laphroaig uses only ex-bourbon barrels); a deep and contemplative malt. Ardbeg, which you'd expect to be brutally, almost one-dimensionally peaty is instead superbly complex. The distillery was saved from an ignominious fate in 1997 when Glenmorangie snapped it up for a bargain price. Its future as a producer of magnificent malts looks assured. Port Ellen, which sadly looks unlikely ever to reopen, produced the most uncompromising of all Islay malts – one exclusively for the peat freak.

Variety in the north

The situation is more varied in the north of the island. Caol Ila shares the same peating regime as Lagavulin, but its malt is a considerably different beast. For years this massive plant was used by owner UDV to provide all manner of shadings of whisky – from hugely peaty to virtually unpeated. This was good for the blenders as it meant that they could use fewer components in a blend, but was pretty confusing for the malt aficionado. You were never quite sure what you'd be getting – one bottling would smell of fish heads on the beach, the next would be rather thin and greasy. These days it seems to be on a more even keel, providing a single malt that shows good phenolic character, but allied to the

firm style you get from the northern part of Islay.

Further up the same north-east coast is Bunnahabhain. Here, a combination of pure water, low peating and tall stills gives a malt which is miles away from what people consider to be a true Islay character. But while the reek may not be there, the malt has a delicious seashore freshness, a quality it shares with Bruichladdich. This marvellous old distillery, complete with ancient cast-iron mash tub, produced the malt that is most widely drunk on the island, and you can see why. There's some of the smoke that hangs in the Islay

The Bowmore distillery, on the island of Islay; one of its warehouses has been turned into the community swimming pool

air on the nose, even a whiff of sea-shells drying in the sun at the high-water mark. It's not peaty, but somehow it could only come from this island.

Bruichladdich sits on the shores of Lochindaal, directly opposite the island's capital, Bowmore. This town is the axis around which the rest of the island spins, and its malt is a superb fusion of all of Islay's unique characteristics. A complex mix of woods, good peating levels and high-quality distilling, it's difficult to surpass.

Islay, like all of the islands, remains a place apart, an island with its own rules, its own character, its own way of approaching life. The concentration of distilleries has given whisky a central part in the island's economy – the whole community depends on it, not just the men who work in the distillery, but their wives and daughters who guide tourists round. It provides employment for local transport firms, while the farmers rely on the spent grains for cattle feed. Bowmore has even converted one of its old warehouses into the community swimming pool, whose water is heated by waste heat from the distillery. You'll not find anywhere else in Scotland where whisky plays such a central role.

WESTERN ISLES AND ORKNEY

The islands that lie scattered in the sea off Scotland's western and northern coasts are home to some of the country's most individual whiskies. The islands bore much of the brunt of the Clearances, which started after the failure of the 1745 Rebellion and reached their peak in the middle of the nineteenth century. People were driven off the land and either forced to learn new trades in custom-built settlements or were herded on to boats sailing to America, Canada and Australia.

It's easy to think that the islands were always the bleak, lonely, beautiful places they are today. But only 100 years ago they were filled with small communities, tending their crops and animals and making whisky. The production may not have been huge, but it helped to pay the rent. At one time whisky was made on Lewis, Pabbay and Tiree, while Skye alone could boast seven distilleries. Now, outside Islay, only five island distilleries remain.

The island distilleries remain places of pilgrimage. You don't chance upon them as you can on the mainland; you make a conscious decision to take the ferry and the often long drive to reach your destination. It's well worth the effort.

Jura

The largest building in the only settlement on the island, Jura's distillery has clung on while the population of the island has declined. If it's isolation you want, head here.

Given its proximity to Islay, you might expect Jura's malt to be a big, peat-filled bruiser – the island's rugged landscape would imply that this should be a great hairy malt to sustain you over the last few miles of a hike. Instead, it's a little charmer, with only a wisp of peat and the lightest of salty tangs on the finish. The 10-year-old is an easy-drinking malt, pretty and commercial. Sadly its owner hasn't yet seen fit to release some of the remarkable older stuff that lurks in the warehouses. Here, given age and a bit of sherry wood, Jura comes into its own. There again, everyone forgets about Jura.

Mull

It's much the same with Mull. Although it's the second largest island in the Inner Hebrides, hardly anyone bothers to spend time here, other than using it as a stopping-off point for Iona, which lies off its western coast. Given it's likely that it was the monks of the early Celtic church who brought the art of distillation to Scotland, it's entirely possible that Mull was an early centre of distilling. By the late eighteenth century, up to a third of the island's barley harvest was turned into whisky and now-abandoned settlements, self-sufficient in barley, were important centres for whisky-making. By the time Barnard arrived, the sole distillery left was importing its grain from the mainland.

That distillery has had a chequered career. It's been closed for long periods, changed its name with baffling frequency from Tobermory to Ledaig (and back again) and had a series of absentee owners. Thankfully, it has been saved by Burn Stewart and now two malts – unpeated Tobermory and peated Ledaig – are on offer. There are some good examples from independent bottlers – but given the ups and downs of Tobermory's recent past there are some shockers as well. Tread carefully.

Skye

This island, the largest in the Hebrides, has a humbling effect on the visitor. It doesn't throw its arms open to you, but forces you to love it on its own terms. The mountains, rarely free from straggling clouds, loom around you, making you feel very insignificant indeed. It's uncompromising land – and there's little surprise that Skye's only malt, Talisker, shares some of these qualities.

Filling whisky casks at the Talisker Distillery, Isle of Skye; the uncompromising Hebrides island produces an uncompromising dram

The distillery on Jura is the largest building on the tiny island; its produce is unlike that which comes from the neighbouring isle of Islay

WESTERN ISLES AND ORKNEY
– THE CLASSIC MALTS

Every one of Scotland's many islands has its own distinctive feel. The same can be said for the relatively few malts which hail from this "region". The two camps – peated (traditional) and unpeated (modern) – give the island-hopping connoisseur plenty of scope for exploration. Here you'll encounter malts which seethe with almost volcanic power, others which are like a stroll along the sea-shore and on Orkney, a distillery which makes one of the most gorgeous malts of all.

Highland Park 12-year-old (40% ABV)
Softly succulent nose of heather honey, ripe orangey fruit, hazelnuts, smoke and a light medicinal air. Rich, complex palate with heather, silky, fudgy fruit and a smoky finish.

Highland Park 18-year-old (43% ABV)
An elegant, concentrated, rich nose with positive peat smoke. Gorgeous, supple palate with orange peel, sweet honeyed tones and a fragrant herbal lift. Superbly balanced with a long, smoky finish.

Isle of Jura 10-year-old (40% ABV)
Tight and a little woody on the nose, but clean with a nodule of sweetness on the palate. Fresh, decently balanced and a tingle of salt on the finish.

Scapa 12-year-old (40% ABV)
A pleasant mix of sweet fruit and lightly toasted wood on the nose. Dry and clean with a tickle of peat smoke. A firm, nutty palate with good drive.

Talisker 10-year-old (45.8% ABV)
A powerful, pungent nose with massive peatiness, charred heather, ozone and rich fruit. It explodes on to the palate, balancing sweet fruit with spicy, salty flavours before a black pepper kick on the finish.

Talisker 1986 Amoroso Finish (45.8% ABV)
Rich and smoky, but the elemental force of the 10-year-old is toned down. Rich sweetness, with dark, raisined fruit and peat reek.

Tobermory (40% ABV)
A nose reminiscent of damp earth and nuts that carries through on to the palate, along with positive fruitiness and a little honey. Pretty simple, with a clean, firm finish.

It's a peaty dram, but in a different way from that of Islay. The water flows over peat, and the barley is peated, but probably only to around 25ppm, about half that of Lagavulin. Why then does Talisker remain one of Scotland's most uncompromising malts? One reason may be the shape of the wash stills. They have high necks, a long lye pipe with a U-shaped kink in it and a purifier pipe that takes the heavier alcohols back into the still to be redistilled. This strange configuration increases reflux and also helps to give a long, slow condensation – as do the worm tubs situated outside the distillery.

You'll find it a peaty, smoky dram with touches of burnt heather root and black pepper, but also sweet fruit. There's some ozone freshness on the nose, but no iodine. The standard 10-year-old is matured in refill casks: there's no overt bourbon or sherry wood here. It isn't fazed by high alcohol, in fact it needs it. It's an enigmatic dram, as craggily individual as its island birthplace.

Orkney

If Skye is the most elemental of Scotland's islands, then Orkney is the most other-worldly. The feeling on these islands is one of timelessness; it's a part of Scotland where the old ways have been absorbed and warped into the regular fabric of life.

Inevitably the church plays a central role in Orcadian life – and in the birth of its finest malt, Highland Park. During the smuggling era, the distillery was operated by one Magnus Eunsen, a preacher who used to hide casks of whisky from the excise men beneath the pulpit.

Its top distillery, Highland Park, still malts some of its own barley using Orkney's heathery peat – an aroma which is carried through to the glass. Bundles of dried flowering heather are still added to the peat to impart an aroma to the malt. There's a judicious amount of (Spanish) sherry wood used, seen most noticeably in the 18- and 25-year-old versions. But even at 12 years of age, Highland Park is a superbly rounded malt. There's honeyed sweetness, smokiness, a little heather and a long, dry finish. It's a malt that can be drunk at any time of the day.

Orkney's other distillery, Scapa, has always been in the shadow of its famous neighbour on the hill. For long used as a filling station for blended whisky, its single malt is light and pretty, but not hugely memorable.

At the end of the day this is a disparate grouping of malts, whose only real connection is that they all come from islands. Yet it's not too fanciful to believe that the best of them have managed to weave the special qualities of their place of birth into the whisky.

SPEYSIDE

Speyside contains the greatest concentration of malt whisky distilleries – and many of the best. Roughly triangular in shape, it unfolds to the north along the watershed of the River Spey, starting at the edge of the Grampian mountains and running down to the flat, fertile coastal plain. The isolated, wild and beautiful southern part is as remote as any other part of the Highlands, while the bulk of the distilleries in the centre and north are clustered around solid, reserved grey stone towns. The whole area is ribboned by fast-running rivers, burns and springs that flow from the peat-capped granite mountains. All in all, it's perfect whisky-making country.

Distilleries at every turn

The southern part of Speyside contains a smattering of distilleries, like Tomintoul and Braeval, before you reach The Glenlivet, the distillery that kick-started the region as one famed for high-quality malt. If you then follow the river Avon to its meeting with the Spey, you'll pass by neat and tidy Cragganmore and, further on, Glenfarclas. Then, distilleries begin to come thick and fast, every small road and glen bringing you face to face with well-known names like Tamdhu, Knockando and Cardhu. Heading into Dufftown, you'll pass by Dailuaine, Benrinnes and the great Aberlour – and up on the hill on the other side of the river catch a glimpse of the manor house that serves as Macallan's head office.

You can either then follow the course of the Dullan Water into Dufftown or travel north to Rothes. In Dufftown you can take your pick from seven distilleries – three of which, Glenfiddich, Balvenie and Kininvie, are on one site (which also includes a cooperage). Less obvious is Mortlach, the distillery that established Dufftown as Speyside's capital.

The good folk of Rothes would say that their town has a rightful claim to that title, as five distilleries are tucked away behind its rather dour façade (there's something very Scottish about that). Only the imposing Victorian buildings and elegant gardens of Glen Grant indicate that this is a whisky town. You'll have to search to find Caperdonich – not that it's worth the search: better to winkle out the underrated Glen Rothes and, hidden away up a tiny valley, Speyburn.

The last main whisky town is Keith, which lies roughly 10 miles to the east of Rothes. By now the heather-clad moors and hills have given way to fertile agricultural land. To get to Keith you pass Auchroisk, which looks more like a modern hotel than a distillery, before arriving at the first of Keith's distilleries, the wonderful Aultmore, a distillery whose top-notch whisky is so loved by blenders that very little is allowed to slip out as a single malt.

Although Strathmill and Glen Keith make pleasant enough drams, Keith's glory is the ludicrously picturesque Strathisla which produces one of Speyside's most charming and complex malts.

From there the long, flat Elgin road takes you north-west towards the coast, passing by two other overlooked classics, Longmorn and Linkwood. While Elgin has only one distillery, Glen Moray, the forgotten member of the Glenmorangie group, it is home to whisky's greatest retailer, Gordon & MacPhail, a Highland grocer and whisky specialist whose shelves groan under the weight of a mind-boggling range of malts.

Fame and fortune

That quick tour demonstrates what a concentration of top-notch distilleries is in Speyside. So why has this region become so famous? Whisky has flowed from Speyside's stills for centuries, although no matter how

Opposite: *The Glenlivet Distillery in Southern Speyside produced a favourite tipple of King George IV; it brought about a change in the laws allowing Highland whisky to be sold in the Lowlands*

SPEYSIDE – THE CLASSIC MALTS

Speyside has been called the "Golden Triangle" of malt. Certainly no other region has such a concentration of high-quality malts. Complexity and marvellous balance is the order of the day here. Though they share a certain high-toned sophistication, you'll find infinite variations being played on this theme. There are some which revel in the lavish, rich notes given by sherry wood, others which remain clean, "airy" and always utterly elegant.

Aberlour 10-year-old (40% ABV)
Clean nose with toffee and vanilla notes. Rich and smooth with a clean drive.

Aberlour 15-year-old Sherry Finish (40% ABV)
Creamily sweet nose with some butterscotch. Rich and luscious with a raisin/sultana fruit centre and a wheat-cracker finish.

Aberlour 18-year-old Sherry Matured (43% ABV)
Elegant nose with plummy fruit. Sweet, rich and chewy with a very long rounded finish.

Balvenie 10-year-old (40% ABV)
A slightly shy aroma with citrus, herbs and a little smoke. Sultry, sweet and elegantly balanced.

Balvenie Double Wood 12-year-old (43% ABV)
A similar herbiness, but with richer consistency. Tangerine, butter and nuts on the palate. Great poise.

Cragganmore 12-year-old (40% ABV)
A complex, perfumed nose that melds incense, plums and smoke. The palate starts in a malty fashion that leads to a sweet centre with sloe berries and smoke. Rich and superbly balanced. Quintessential Speyside.

Glenfarclas 105 (60% ABV)
The alcohol is a little too aggressive, but there's a juicily sweet core lurking behind.

Glenfarclas 30-year-old (43% ABV)
Sweet, almost raisined/pruney nose with a touch of rancio – sweet fruits, nuts and cheese. Roast almonds, walnuts and Seville orange-accented fruitiness on the palate. Powerful, everlasting finish. A malt to kill for.

Glenfiddich 40% ABV
Very pale with a very light, sweet nose. Simple.

Glenfiddich 18-year-old
Pale colour with a light, brackeny nose and a sweet, clean palate.

Glenlivet 12-year-old (40% ABV)
A clean nose with plenty of creamy, floral fruitiness and a wisp of smoke. Light and heathery on the palate. Fruity and crisp all the way.

Glenlivet 18-year-old (43% ABV)
Rich, lightly smoky nose with notes of peel, nutmeg, honeyed fruit and some hickory notes. It eases into the mouth with smooth, elegant sherry nuttiness, cream and a kick of peat. Long and smooth.

Glen Grant 10-year-old (40% ABV)
Mealy and floral with some crisp apple aromas. With water, strawberries and cream emerge. Mid-weight and crisp, but with surprising substance.

Knockando 1980 (43% ABV)
Light, airy nose with gentle blossom aromas. Flowery and with hints of Greek yoghurt and honey behind the crisp palate. A gracious lunchtime dram.

Linkwood 12-year-old (43% ABV)
Zingy nose with lemon, sandalwood and some alcohol. A lightly herbaceous start, clean and crisp.

Longmorn 15-year-old (45% ABV)
Hugely ripe fruit with some treacle, toffee and honeycomb. On the palate there are molasses, dried herbs and nuts. Unctuous, elegant and dense.

Macallan 18-year-old (43% ABV)
Rich and well-sherried nose reminiscent of Dundee cake, walnuts and ripe, plummy fruit. A rich, complex nose with tablet and chocolate. A crisp, floral mid-palate stops it being cloying. In a different class.

Macallan Gran Reserva (40% ABV)
Complex nose of pink grapefruit, butterscotch, honey, walnut and a hint of clove. Surprisingly delicate given its dark colour. Fresh with deep fruit. Elegant and long.

Mortlach 16-year-old (43% ABV)
Firm and rich nose with a rugged earthiness and pent-up potential. Ripe and concentrated exotic aromas of incense, caramelized fruit. A massive, powerful dram that's rich but not sweet.

Strathisla 12-year-old (43% ABV)
Rich with good depth. Soft, bracken aromas with complex layers of toffee and toasted hazelnuts. Elegant palate with subtle smoke and creamily layered plum and date fruit.

Tamdhu 40% ABV
Crisp, crunchy nose with some grass and freesias. A hint of smoke and mint on the palate. Floral with a clean finish.

---

hard you search, you won't discover when it was first made here. It's entirely possible that the large monasteries that were established in and around the area would have contained stills, but there's no hard evidence of this.

Alan Winchester, the distillery manager at Aberlour and a man who combines Scottish pragmatism with the heart of a poet, likes to believe that the Celtic monk, St Drostan – who, handily enough, is buried under the Abelour still house – may have been the man who brought whisky to this part of Scotland. It is as good a theory as any other.

By the beginning of the nineteenth century, it must have seemed as if there was as much whisky coming out of Speyside as there was water in its rivers. This was the height of the smuggling era, and the region's woods and hidden valleys were perfect for hiding illegal stills. There were around 200 stills in Glenlivet alone at this time.

The end of smuggling

It was a Speyside aristocrat, Alexander Gordon, fourth Duke of Gordon, who initiated the change in law which brought the smuggling era to an end and ushered in the modern era of malt. He argued that if distillers were allowed to take out licences and sell their whisky on the open market, then he and the other landowners would help to put a stop to illicit distilling.

The first person to make this shift from moonshiner to legal distiller was George Smith, who had previously been making whisky on his farm in Upper Drumin. His change of status didn't exactly endear him to his neighbours, who threatened to burn down his Glenlivet distillery, and for years Smith always wore two loaded pistols to protect himself from the vengeful smugglers. By then the government, aided by landowners, had put paid to the illegal distillers' resistance. By 1836 the majority of smugglers were either legal whisky-makers, or had returned to farming.

Royal patronage

Glenlivet had already built a considerable reputation for itself prior to the change in law. It was a favourite of King George IV, who asked for it when he visited Edinburgh in 1822. This was slightly embarrassing as, under the laws of the time, it wasn't legal to sell whisky made above the Highland Line in the Lowlands. But George got his way (as kings always do) and Speyside began to build on this patronage.

Above: *Cragganmore produces a single malt that typifies the Speyside region* **Next page:** *Macallan's still is tiny and heated with flame*

George Smith was soon joined by other gentlemen distillers and Speyside's first blossoming was underway, with many of the new distillers trying to pass their whisky off as Glenlivet. In time, there were so many Glenlivets on the market that it became known as the longest glen in Scotland. In 1880, Smith's son took action to protect the appellation. The compromise that was reached gave Smith the sole right to use the title The Glenlivet, but other Speyside distilleries were allowed to affix the designation after their name. Until recently, up to 20 distilleries, including Macallan, Glenfarclas and Balvenie, continued to do this.

This was still a remote region in the nintheenth century. There were no roads: you had to use packhorses to get the whisky to the sea ports. It was only once James Grant (of Glen Grant fame) brought the first railway line into Rothes that Speyside became properly linked with the south of Scotland. This not only allowed distillers to get their malts to the blending centres in Perth, Glasgow and Leith, but enabled coal from the Lowlands to be brought up to fuel the maltings and stills – and therefore increase production.

That said, Speyside still clung to the old ways. Sir Robert Bruce Lockhart's marvellous book *Scotch* contains an evocative recollection of his boyhood in the region at the beginning of the century. In those days it was a quiet area where fishing was free, landlords were benign and Gaelic was still widely spoken. These days, it's full to the brim with whisky tourists and you're more likely to hear Japanese or German than Scotland's native tongue.

By the end of the nineteenth century, blended whisky was the world's favourite spirit. That meant the blenders needed increasingly large amounts of malt. Speyside was perfectly positioned to take advantage – not only could the whisky get to the blending centres quickly, but the first master blenders recognized that it produced hugely impressive malt which gave complexity and added sophistication to a blend. Even today there are few top blends that do not have a clutch of Speysides as their core malts.

There's no real surprise, then, that when malt whisky was finally taken out of the hands of a few aficionados and placed onto the world stage, it was a Speyside malt that led the way – Glenfiddich.

The ideal ingredients

Speyside was (and is) blessed with the perfect components for whisky making. It's adjacent to Scotland's main barley-producing region – the Laich O'Moray – there was peat from the Faemussach Moss, abundant water, years of expertise and transport links.

The water is ideal for making whisky. It has picked up some acidity from the layer of peat that blankets the granite hills, it's iron-free and contains trace elements such as calcium and copper. Virtually every distillery has its own water source and the tiny variations between them are a fundamental difference to each malt.

There's little peat used here these days – although the situation was different at the end of last century. That said, Seagram experimented by giving one of its malts, Glen Keith, a heavy peating. The resulting whisky, Glenisla (pun no doubt intended), is a tremendous dram which, when it was shown at a recent nosing, had everyone in attendance clamouring for the firm to start making it on a commercial basis. Although that, sadly, is unlikely to happen, the Glenisla experiment does demonstrate how some malts bloom in the presence of peat. In normal circumstances, Glen Keith is a pretty bland dram; with peat it is multi-dimensioned.

There again, trying to get hold of just what it is that makes each whisky unique is as easy as trying to catch a Spey salmon with your fingers. Every distillery manager will have his (or her) own opinion on what the magic ingredient is. Some place the emphasis on the water, others talk up the strain of barley, some insist it's the stills that make the real difference, while others point to the type of wood used.

Stills in all shapes and sizes

Take the stills, for example. You've never seen such a weird collection of shapes in your life. They are enormous (Glenfarclas) and minuscule (Macallan and Glenfiddich), there are some that are heated with steam, with gas or with flame (like Macallan, Glen Grant, Glenfarclas and Glenfiddich), some have got reflux bulbs, others have purifiers (Glen Grant has both). The lye pipes go up, down and sideways, at Cragganmore you've even got a flat-topped still, while each still in Mortlach is a different shape and size. Is there any surprise, then, that we're dealing with a host of different flavours here?

Wood, and in particular ex-sherry casks, also has its part to play in the unique character of Speyside's malts. There aren't many malts that can cope with sherry – it tends to swamp light, estery flavours – but there are some rich, complex spirits flowing out of Speyside's stills that revel in its rich, ripe fruit flavours. Macallan only ages in Spanish sherry wood, Glenfarclas is almost all sherry these days, while the recent upping of the sherry component in Aberlour has elevated this good dram into a great one.

The Speyside divide

So is there such a thing as an identifiable Speyside style? It may be logical to group malts into regions, but it's often the case that they bear little resemblance to each other. Regionality becomes more of a topic in Speyside simply because of the large number of distilleries. Surely there must be similarities between them? The trouble is that there are so many it's difficult to find any sort of overall pattern.

There have been some novel ways of trying to get to grips with this dilemma. Tim Fiddler, in the Scotch Malt Whisky Society Newsletter, proposed eight clusters of distilleries that can be compared and contrasted. He divides Speyside into the Banffshire Bank, the Morayshire Bank, then the distilleries in each of the following towns: Rothes, Dufftown, Elgin, and Keith. The remaining two groupings take in the distilleries on the coast and the eastern hills.

If this seems a little excessive, then try the compromise approach taken by Chivas Brothers, which is to split Speyside into north and south. The coast, Elgin, Keith and Rothes are in the north, and Dufftown, the Banffshire and Morayshire Banks and the upland distilleries are in the south. This gives you two roughly equal groups. While each malt has its own personality, you can generalize and say that the Northern Speyside group has greater complexity and sweetness than the drier more malty band from the south.

That said, one of the joys of Speyside is having the opportunity to walk from one distillery to another and compare and contrast the two malts. Tamdhu and Knockando, for example, are opposite each other but make completely different whiskies. Glen Grant and Caperdonich have the same water source, but you'd never confuse one with the other. They may have a family resemblance – the elusive Speyside signature – but they are not copies of each other.

Top Speyside malts

Right enough, maybe we shouldn't be that surprised about the number of top-drawer Speysides. If you've got close on 60 distilleries, you'd rightly expect that a number would be at the top of the tree. The rewarding thing is how many of them are truly world-class. Choosing the distilleries that make up the Speyside Classics (see page 445) was a very tough assignment.

They range from the big, boisterous, richly-flavoured examples like the supremely elegant, rich Macallan to the magnificent selection from Glenfarclas, which gain in weight and style the older they get. Light and slightly grassy as a 10-year-old, Glenfarclas picks up flavours of mint, fruit and nuts after a further five years in sherry wood. By the time it's reached 30 years of age it has turned into one of the greatest malts in Scotland – and one of the finest spirits in the world.

Then there's also creamy, elegant Aberlour which, after being hidden from most people's view for years, now seems to be releasing a new version every week. There's a cracking cask strength, a sherry finish and a 100 per cent sherry wood to choose from. Cragganmore, despite being one of UDV's Classic Malts, is little talked about – a baffling state of affairs since it represents Speyside's complexity at its best. Rich, slightly smoky, with a lick of sweetness in the middle of the palate, this is a malt you can roll around the mouth for ages and never quite capture all of the flavours. Equally subtle is the range from Glenfiddich's sister distillery Balvenie, or the fresh and delicate Knockando or the beautifully balanced Tamdhu.

There are also malts that are often dismissed without a second thought. Glenlivet is one that's well worth re-examining, as is Glen Grant, which is often castigated for being light and inconsequential – mainly because it's sold as a five-year-old in Italy. Give it some time in wood, though, and astonishing things happen. Glen Grant is one of those malts that benefits from long ageing – in fact, it continues to develop when other malts are holding up their hands in submission. On first tasting you think it's a pretty, easy-drinking drop, but under that attractive facade is a surprisingly tough, complex core.

Brand or malt?

Then there's Glenfiddich. These days the biggest-selling malt in the world has outgrown the category it established back in the 1970s. It's less of a malt now, more a brand. In fact its owner handles it more as a premium whisky that competes with the likes of Johnnie Walker Black Label or Chivas Regal. That is no bad thing, because the standard bottling does not have much in common with the glorious malts that Speyside can produce.

It may make sense commercially, but the end result has been that malt aficionados dismiss the distillery out of hand. It's a pity, because when Glenfiddich is aged for a decent time – say 18 years – it reveals its true colours as an elegant balanced dram, though the current vatting leaves much to be desired.

That still leaves four other distilleries that are criminally passed over: Mortlach, Strathisla, Longmorn and Linkwood. Mortlach, like so much of the UDV stable, has remained lurking in the shadows. Rarely seen, talked about in reverent tones by those fortunate enough to have discovered its charms, it's not so much big as massive. A powerfully-built, broody, intense malt, it shares some characteristics with the weighty, rich Longmorn. Both are as solid and enigmatic as the bulk of Ben Rinnes, the gloomy mountain that dominates the Speyside landscape. Strathisla and Linkwood, meanwhile, are as elusive as the Spey itself, charming, peaceful but with surprising hidden depths.

Unrivalled quality

At the end of the day, the reason that Speyside has endured while other regions have fallen by the wayside is because its whiskies, on the whole, have a quality that no other region can rival.

While other areas rely on one or two dominant characteristics to give them their identity – sweetness in Perthshire, heathery aromas in the north, peat smoke and ozone from the islands – Speyside has a vast range of balanced flavours to its name. It remains malt's glorious, golden heart.

The Strathisla Distillery produces whisky that is one of Speyside's best-kept secrets, a rich dram with good depth

THE HIGHLANDS

Geographically, the Highlands of Scotland lie above a fault line that runs diagonally from Girvan in the west to Stonehaven on the east coast. For a time, this was also the boundary of the infamous Highland Line. In an attempt to eradicate small-scale distilling post-Culloden, the British Government decreed that although whisky could be made in the Highlands (in a designated size of still and with local ingredients), from 1784 to 1816 it couldn't be sold below the Line. Needless to say it was. In fact, the smaller still and the exclusive use of barley made Highland whisky a highly desirable drink, although it wasn't until the licensing of distilleries and the column still that commercial quantities of Highland whisky were made, most of which ended up in blends.

For simplicity's sake, the Highlands have traditionally been divided into four: South and Perthshire; West; East and Aberdeenshire; and North. It makes assessing easier – and also provides the malt lover with some intriguing comparisons.

Scotland is a collection of mini-lands banded together by river, mountain ridge and loch. First-time visitors will not only be surprised at often finding four seasons in one day, but in the 170-mile drive from Glasgow to Inverness you'll pass from flat, alluvial plains through soft hills and moors and then into wild areas with no sign of habitation.

If walking is easy in the southern hills, by the time you reach Dalwhinnie distillery, the 3,000 foot summits of the Monadhliath and Cairngorm mountains are lowering around you – wild and beautiful tundra country, lit gold and blue by the sun. The malts themselves offer a parallel journey.

South and Perthshire

Most of the distilleries in this grouping owe their existence to the emergence in the nineteenth century of blended Scotch. Although a huge number of new sites were built, there were also many which were upgraded farm distilleries.

Transport to the blending centres of Perth, Glasgow and Leith was easy, peat was only used lightly (after all, coal was plentiful) and a lighter style soon evolved.

Although few of these nineteenth-century plants have survived, this refreshing, slightly sweet style can be seen in malts such as Glengoyne, which markets itself as Scotland's unpeated malt. This charming old farm distillery is within sight of Glasgow's north-western suburbs, but lies at the foot of the first band of low hills that straggle along the Highlands' southern border.

In fact, Glengoyne's warehouses, although just across the road from the distillery, are technically in the Lowlands! Deanston, another of the malts from this area, shares this discreet, soft, unpeated style.

Once north of Perth the hills become higher, and though the valleys are still broad and lush, there is a feeling that you are now in the ante-chamber of the Highlands. Traditionally, the emphasis has been on supplying malt (fillings) for the blends – no surprise that Aberfeldy and Blair Atholl were built by Dewar's and Bell's respectively. You can find single malt bottlings of both – if a choice is to be made, go for the Aberfeldy.

Glenturret – a beautifully situated distillery – hardly needs to sell on the open market. Up to

Opposite: *Situated on the Highlands' southern border, the Deanston distillery produces a soft, unpeated style of whisky*

SPIRIT VAT
CONTENT 33050 LTRS
DEANSTON
1991
DOUNE
DEANSTON
1991
122
DOUNE
LTD.

250,000 visitors parade through its doors every year, the bulk of them buying one or more bottles. The amazing success of Glenturret as a tourist attraction has made its owners a little too keen to sell it at every age and strength known to man – and even as the base for a liqueur.

All these malts share a common Perthshire character of soft, slightly honeyed aromas combined with smidgens of smoke and a dry finish. Pleasant enough, but not a patch on the malt that comes from Edradour, Scotland's smallest distillery. This is distilling as it used to be. Hidden up a glen, out of sight of the road, next to a fast-running burn, using minuscule stills, the end result is the quintessential Perthshire dram, flowery, spicy, layered with honey and cream.

The last of these southern malts is Dalwhinnie which lies, splendidly isolated, close to the top of the Drumochter Pass. The scenery has changed from expansive vistas of mountain and glen to a feeling of being crushed between the massive bulwarks of peaks that loom on either side of the road. It's a crossroads – between two types of landscape and between the soft malts of the south and the more heathery, peat-accented drams that thrive in the north. A middle ground, perhaps, but not a compromise.

West

If the southern malts form an easily-followed trail, then you have to be prepared to travel large distances to take in the distilleries on Scotland's west coast. The small distilleries that thrived among the crofting communities of this, the most spectacularly beautiful part of Scotland, have long disappeared; as have those which sprang up on the shores of Loch Fyne and the Clyde estuary, whose whisky would have been taken by boat or by train to the blenders in Glasgow. Now there are only two left.

Oban looks out to the town's pier, filled with the ferries sailing to and from the Western Isles, and its malt has more of an island character. Some 50 miles north, in the depressing town of Fort William, is Ben Nevis. Owned by the Japanese firm Nikka, most of its production finishes in Japanese brands, which is a

shame, for the single malt is a bruiser, filled with rich, concentrated flavours. In many ways it's like the mountain from which it takes its name, massive, apparently impenetrable, but worth exploring.

East

Perhaps it's just the power of suggestion, but Ben Nevis shares this rich character with another mountain malt, although this comes from the

Glenmorangie, despite producing Scotland's best-selling malts, experiments with different types of casks for finishing; others now copy them

eastern extremity of the Grampians – Royal Lochnagar. It's a fine representative of what is now an endangered species, malts from the eastern Highlands.

At one time these could have quite easily formed two exclusive groups – those from the valley of Strathmore and the Mearns, the pasture land that runs inland from the coast to the eastern limits of the Grampians – and the rest, from the hills and fertile valleys in central and northern Aberdeenshire.

Now, sadly, there are only four distilleries in operation: Glencadam in Strathmore; Old Fettercairn in the Mearns; Glen Garioch in the Aberdeenshire town of Oldmeldrum; and Royal Lochnagar in the heart of Deeside.

The first two are eminently forgettable, but Royal

THE HIGHLANDS – THE CLASSIC MALTS

It's unfair to lump every mainland malt not in Speyside or the Lowlands into this catch-all category. The southern Highland and Perthshire malts have a honeyed charm, while those from the east coast show a distinctive malty, succulent exoticism. The west coast is virtually distillery-free, but one of its top malts shows a distinct seaside air – a quality that dominates the aromas of the malts from the far north, a region whose range of complex, multi-faceted malts is often overlooked.

Clynelish (North) 14-year-old (43% ABV)
Filled with seashore aromas: rugged, with a hint of kelp at the high water mark. Smoky start with an iodine tingle, before a sweet mid-palate with some sultana fruitiness and a dry finish.

Dalwhinnie (Central) 15-year-old (43% ABV)
Light, slightly malty nose. The palate balances honey and pepper well.

Dalmore (North) 12-year-old (40% ABV)
A big, bracing, slightly salty aroma with blackcurrant sweetness behind. Rich, oily start then the complex flavours atomize across the palate, with black fruit dominating.

Edradour (Central) (40% ABV)
Rich, evocative nose with hints of silage, waxed raincoats, sawdust, herbs and wild flowers. Ripe, luscious palate with silky-smooth fruit and a lick of heather honey on the finish.

Glen Garioch (East) 15-year-old (43% ABV)
Highly intense, perfumed lemon/ginger nose with some floor polish and peat. The smoke is more pronounced on the palate.

Glengoyne (South) 17-year-old (43% ABV)
Some almond, lightly-sherried fruitiness on the nose along with calf leather, hazelnut and clover. Well rounded palate. A perfect lunchtime dram.

Glenmorangie (North) 10-year-old (40% ABV)
Delicate, pear-drop nose. Fresh and grassy.

Smooth, creamy, gentle and approachable.

Glen Ord (North) 12-year-old (40% ABV)
Excitingly fresh, malty nose where the sweetness is checked by a lime leaf tingle. An ever-changing palate with a hint of smoke, citrus fruits, sweet fruit and a dry, roasted nutty finish.

Oban (West) 14-year-old (43% ABV)
Clean, tingly nose filled with dried herbs and sea breezes. A softly spicy, slightly smoky palate balanced with refreshing saltiness.

Pulteney (North) 12-year-old (40% ABV)
An ozone-fresh nose that also has attractive cakey notes. Starts sweet, with some sugared almond, then menthol and cigar-box flavours. A complex beauty.

Royal Lochnagar (East) 23-year-old (59.7% ABV)
Sherry sweet on the nose. A hugely muscular, sturdy number with good spicy notes. Rounded, rich and mellow, it copes with its high strength easily.

Lochnagar is a stunner – while Glen Garioch is an oft-overlooked charmer. Hailing from the eastern end of the Garioch valley, it's part of the Morrison Bowmore stable, so little surprise that it has floor maltings and also uses a fair whack of peat. Herbal and highly aromatic, it shows that this part of the country can produce characterful drams which are more than capable of coping with the influence of sherry wood.

It has only recently reopened, unlike two other distilleries from further west in the Garioch – Glendronach, from Huntly, and Ardmore, whose single malt (often at a similar peating level to Glen Garioch) is a rarity.

Most of the other eastern distilleries have either been bulldozed or converted. You may be able to find the occasional bottling of brands like North Port (from Glencadam's home town of Brechin) and Glenurie Royal (from the seaside town of Stonehaven), but stocks are running out.

There could be better news for another coastal distillery, Montrose's Lochside, but apart from that, there's little hope that the east will rise once more.

North

What of the north then? Well, there are currently seven distilleries operating in the coastal fringe to the north and east of Inverness – although sadly there's nothing in the capital of the Highlands to show that it, too, used to produce a fair amount of whisky. The Black Isle, which lies between the Moray and Cromarty firths, was home to Scotland's first whisky brand, Ferintosh, a drink which was granted duty-free status thanks to the political allegiance of its owner after the first Jacobite uprising. Ferintosh is long gone; the only distillery close to it is Glen Ord, home not only to a massive maltings – which produces malt for most of UDV's Highland and island distilleries – but a medium-bodied, slightly smoky, sherried malt that's gathering a considerable following.

The rest of the northern distilleries are situated on the coast, a location which lends most of them some maritime character, a whiff of ozone on the part of Glenmorangie; salty notes in Pulteney and Balblair; to the kelpy, drying sea-shell aromas of Clynelish. Although the group contains malts that range from

Towser, the late, celebrated mouser at the Glenturret Distillery; the distillery attracts up to a quarter of a million visitors every year

the delicate, aromatic Glenmorangie to the ruggedly handsome Clynelish and Balblair, they can be linked with a thread of heathery, sometimes earthy, aromas and flavours that often contain notes of wild herbs. The honey and cream of the southern Highlands has given way to something harder.

They can stand up to high peating levels – the old Brora distillery was used to produce a (very fine) Talisker-style malt when the Skye distillery was gutted by fire – but tend to shy away from heavy use of sherry wood.

That latter quality hasn't prevented Glenmorangie, which remains Scotland's top-selling malt, from undertaking an in-depth analysis of wood management to see which type suits its malt the best.

While extended sherry maturation is out of the question, there's nothing to stop the distiller from ageing the malt first in ex-Bourbon casks and then giving it a short period of finishing in other types of cask. The fascinating, complex range of Glenmorangie "Finishes" has prompted other distillers to try similar experiments – and a new mini-category has been born.

This region was the scene of the most brutal clearances on the Scottish mainland. In a final bitterly ironic twist, the landowners who perpetrated this ethnic cleansing, most notably the Duke of Sutherland, then started distilling with the crops grown on their tenants' old land. This wild, often lonely, country sits in mute memory to them.

BLENDED SCOTCH

Blended whiskies have, in recent times, been seen as the also-rans of the Scotch. The fact remains that 95 per cent of the Scotch whisky sold in the world is blended. All these dedicated drinkers can't be wrong, but we are now in a world that apparently believes that the individual is of greater worth than the collective. Blends are suffering. Their share of the international whisky market is slipping, no one writes about them with any seriousness, and they are an anachronism in today's single malt world.

Don't write off blends

Well, before they finally disappear from consideration, let's have a look at how blends put Scotch whisky on the world stage, and how their assembly is every bit as creative an exercise as the making of a malt.

Scotland in the early part of the nineteenth century was a country in flux. The Highlands were being brutally cleared to make way for large tracts of land for sheep, initiating a mass exodus from country to town – and to America, Canada and Australia. The population became concentrated around the new centres of heavy industry in the coal-rich Lowland belt.

The arrival of heavy industry put central Scotland at the forefront of the Industrial Revolution, with Glasgow as its engine room, the furnace that fuelled the growing power of the British Empire. But Glasgow's fires ran not only on coal, but on people's sweat, and they needed something to slake their thirst.

The Lowlands had long made whisky, but by and large it was pretty poor stuff. While Highlanders concentrated on making small batches of malt to sell or drink in their own communities, Lowland distillers had always to serve a much larger market – and that meant building bigger stills, running them as fast as they could and using whatever grain which came to hand.

A trade in alcohol had long been established with England in which Lowland whisky would be sent south to be rectified (redistilled) and turned into gin. We are already therefore talking about industrial-sized volumes. The influx in population meant that production had to be increased once more, but the whisky that came off the stills was pretty foul stuff.

Clearly something needed to be done to satisfy the thirst of the growing urban masses.

The Coffey still

In 1826, Robert Stein, cousin of John Haig, a member of the family which dominated Lowland distilling at that time, appeared with a revolutionary new still which Haig promptly installed in his Cameronbridge distillery.

The theory behind this was that as long as you put wash in one end you could get high-strength spirit out of the other, with no need for a second distillation. It worked, but needed some tweaking, which was done in 1830 by the former Excise General of Ireland, Aeneas Coffey.

Coffey's patent still was a godsend to the Lowland distillers, all of whom soon had one working in their distillery. The whisky it produced was high-strength and light in flavour, which suited the English gin distillers, but it wasn't quite to the taste of the Lowland Scots.

Then fate took charge. The Wash Act of 1823 had created a rash of newly legal malt distilleries, which had expanded their production. Though malt was highly regarded by the *cognoscenti*, it was too heavily flavoured for most people in the Lowlands and in England.

The birth of blends

Then some bright spark had the idea that if they combined a small amount of the richly-flavoured malts with the lighter grain, they'd come up with a commercially acceptable middle ground. Officially,

BLENDED SCOTCH – THE CLASSICS

In these times when malt whisky is receiving all the attention, it's easy to forget the sheer quality of the greatest blended Scotches. These whiskies, after all, were the brands which helped Scotch become the world's favourite spirit and the best of them deserve the same attention and respect as single malts. "Approachable", "easy-drinking" and "versatile" are too often thought of as negative terms. Give blends another chance – you'll be surprised.

Ballantine's gold seal 12-year-old (43% ABV)
A gentle, sweet, chewy nose with a touch of heather, and a lovely, pure, grainy centre. A lush, plush dram.

Ballantine's 18-year-old (43% ABV)
Despite its age, this has retained a clean, grassy nose with well-balanced wood. On the palate it's round with chewy, creamy weight and a hint of pulpy fruit. A gentle, smooth finish. Elegant.

Bell's 8-year-old (40% ABV)
A clean nose with light toasty wood in evidence. A light grassy aroma then yields to good maltiness with a hint of peat. On the palate it's fairly sweet and round with good balance.

Black Bottle 10-year-old (40% ABV) Richly coloured. Pungent peatiness mixed with fresh turf and some coconut matting. The palate is pure and sweet with a refreshing peppery needle and is very well balanced. The finish is long, rich and smoky. One for Islay fanatics.

Chivas Regal 12-year-old (40% ABV)
Light and estery nose with sweet hay and a seductive smokiness in the distance. Clean US wood on the palate and a little touch of sugared almonds mingling with soft, bouncy grass. A gentle and graceful blend.

Chivas Regal 18-year-old (40% ABV) Big, rich, complex nose with notes of wild herbs, mint, pruney fruit and a light, medicinal character. Robust palate with weighty, almost chocolatey flavours. On the finish there's a touch of heather and lime.

The Famous Grouse 40% ABV
A subtle, smooth and gently smoky nose with hints of sweet sherry wood and mild peatiness. The same character shows on the palate alongside ripe red fruits. A crisp, refreshing finish. Well balanced. Still the finest standard blend on the market.

J&B 40% ABV
Very pale in colour. The crisp nose is of cut straw mixed with some light nuttiness. A creamy note emerges when water is added. A soft, light dram with excellent balance between sweet fruit and a crisp, dry finish.

Johnnie Walker Red Label 40% ABV
Hugely popular – and you can see why. There's a distinct island influence on the nose, along with clean, medium-bodied fruitiness. Clean and easy-drinking.

Johnnie Walker Black Label 40% ABV
The nose is instantly seductive, showing the signature touches of peat smoke and rich, sherried fruit character. Big with a malty richness, giving extra texture to the palate. A beautifully complex finish rounds off the benchmark blend. Better than many malts.

---

blends were born in 1853 when Usher's Old Vatted Glenlivet appeared in Edinburgh. The floodgates were opened.

The majority of the early blenders were high-class grocers and wine merchants based in the growing centres of population. John Dewar, Arthur Bell and Matthew Gloag were all in Perth; James Chivas in Aberdeen; William Teacher in Glasgow; George Ballantine in Edinburgh; John Walker in Kilmarnock. All were well versed in blending teas. The principle of blending whiskies was much the same.

That, of course, didn't guarantee success. For that it needed business skills previously unseen in the British drinks trade. The sons and grandsons of the whisky blenders weren't just concerned about selling to their existing clientele, they wanted to sell whisky to the world.

Their story is worthy of a book in its own right. What they did, briefly, was to cajole, bully and charm their way into the bars, hotels and restaurants of the world through a succession of stunts and slightly dodgy business practices. By the end of the century they were shipping millions of bottles worldwide.

This entrepreneurial zeal was undoubtedly helped by the effects of the vine louse *phylloxera* which halted brandy production in its tracks, by the reluctance of the Irish to use the patent still, and by the distribution network of the British Empire which took the blends to the Highland diaspora.

The blenders started building distilleries in Speyside, the Perthshire glens and on Islay to satisfy the growing demand. From then on, the function of the majority of malt distilleries was to provide fillings for blends. The situation remains virtually unchanged today.

The art of blending has remained much the same as well, even though the constituent parts of the blend will also have changed. Many of the malt distilleries that supplied fillings for the early blends no longer exist. The blenders therefore have to find alternatives.

But how, if, as legend would have it, every malt has its own taste, is this possible? Welcome to the world of the blender.

What is a blend?

In its simplest sense, a blend is a *mélange* of grain and malt whiskies assembled to produce a consistent, identifiable brand. But things are never as simple as they seem in the world of whisky. Take malt, for example. Each day's distillate is slightly different, each cask is a distinct individual. The palette changes continually.

Grain whiskies, contrary to popular belief, behave in the same way. Each distillery has its own signature – from clean and light, to round, buttery and fat. Some are more suitable to long ageing than others – and they, too, will vary in aroma from day to day.

When you add in the fact that distilleries close down rather too regularly for comfort – meaning there's a finite supply of some whiskies – you can begin to understand that the blender, rather than working with unchanging blocks of flavour, is dealing with ever-shifting aromas and possibilities.

At the heart of each blend are a number of core malts, usually from Speyside. These give the signature flavour(s) to the final product – at the heart of Johnnie Walker, for example, are Cardhu and Talisker, while Chivas relies on Strathisla. Although vitally important, these core malts should never dominate the blend; in other words, although you may be able to detect a smoky element in Johnnie Walker, you shouldn't be able to say that it smells and tastes of Talisker.

This unchanging core is then buttressed by a layer of supporting malts, each of which adds some other shading of aroma or flavour; and then finally by a larger amount of packers. The function of these is to give the blend body and texture, rather than flavour. This is the interchangeable part of blending. The packers can come from a large number of distilleries, and the blender can switch from one packing distillery to another without affecting the overall character or flavour of his blend.

At the end of the day there are some malts that are more highly prized as blending whiskies than others. Malts like Aultmore, Mortlach and Cragganmore are in the top league – one reason why the first two are rarely seen as single malt bottlings. All share a complexity of flavour and a richness of texture that melds well with other malts and grains. There are other fine single malts – Glen Grant, for example – which are awkward customers in a blend. What the master blender is looking for is a nucleus of malts that complement each other and bring out different aspects of each other's personality.

Some blenders use malts from each of the regions, others rely on one – Bell's is a country-wide blend, Chivas and J&B are exclusively from Speyside, Black Bottle is predominantly from Islay. Much, to be honest, depends on how many distilleries the blender controls. It's often thought, therefore, that the higher the number of malts in a blend the better it is. That isn't necessarily true. It's the quality of the whiskies and the nature of their interplay that matters.

Wood flavouring

The final element in building flavour and character is the type of wood that the malt has been aged in. A light blend like Cutty Sark will use predominantly refill, while the richer Famous Grouse will very possibly have malts that have been aged in ex-sherry butts made from Spanish oak.

Age is important as well. Different malts (and grains) will be used at different times. A single malt bottling will ideally show the malt at its peak; a blender, however, may want to show a slightly different aspect. This means a mass of possibilities exists for the blender.

Then there's grain. It, too, undergoes the same process as malt – a central grain at the heart, supported by others, each of which brings its own personality to the party. Finally all the components are brought together, but before blending they are nosed one final time and adjustments are made – some malts may be upped, others dropped, substitutes brought on. The final bottle may taste the same as ever, but the components may be slightly different.

Today's whisky market may be finally allowing malts to shine, but don't ignore the great blends. Take some time and look at the hugely impressive Chivas range, reacquaint yourself with brands such as Ballantine's, J&B, Johnnie Walker and Grouse. You will find that the best can rival many malts for complexity and subtlety.

The high-tech stills of William Grant's Girvan distillery; for many drinkers a fine blended scotch is at least the equal of some single malts

IRISH WHISKEY

For a country that can claim to be the birthplace of whiskey, distilleries are few and far between in Ireland. In fact, there are only three in the whole of the country. Yet at the turn of the century, Ireland was seemingly set fair to rival Scotch as a major international player. How could a country that produces such delicious, ludicrously drinkable whiskies become a bit-part player in whiskey's epic picture?

Whiskey (*sic*) is inextricably bound up in Ireland's history. It was likely to have been first produced (for medicinal purposes only) by the scholar-monks of the early Celtic Church, the very men who spread the Gospel and learning from Ireland into Scotland and Western Europe at the end of the Dark Ages.

By the twelfth century, *uisce beatha* was no longer just a medicine but a powerful stimulant – used by warlords to give their troops a jolt of courage before going into battle.

Ireland has always had a rural economy and the people, eking out their living on its green fields, supplemented their income with making and selling whiskey. It had a practical as well as a social function – helping to pay the rent, as well as making the fiddler's elbow go that little bit faster. That said, there has always been a split between country (also known as poitin) and town whiskey. Up until the beginning of the nineteenth century much of the town whiskey – the commercial brands – was flavoured with herbs and roots. The spirit enjoyed as fine a reputation as Cognac, and in the eighteenth century Ireland boasted 2,000 distilleries.

This flavoured whiskey was sipped in salons in Dublin, London and Paris, while the poor people of Ireland supped on the poitin that ran out of their small, peat-fired stills – until they were clobbered by the same legislation that fuelled the smuggling wars in the Scottish Highlands.

Actually, the farmer-distillers didn't disappear, they just went underground. Even today if you ask in the right places for poitin you'll find it without too much trouble. Right enough, whether you'll get a good drop or not is a matter of luck and how good your connections are. There's some wild and frightening stuff out there, but there are also decent (if highly potent) examples. After all, Ireland is all about the craic, and the often farcical trip needed to root out poitin is one that is well worth taking.

Back in the nineteenth century though, the major effect of the legislation was to consolidate whiskey-making in the hands of a few town distillers like John Jameson and John Power, whose pot-still whiskies, now no longer flavoured, had a reputation that outstripped that of Scotch. When the Irishman Aeneas Coffey came up with his patent still they saw the whiskey it produced as a crude imitation and refused to use the new technique.

The distillers in the Lowlands of Scotland (among them Jameson's brother-in-law, John Haig) had no such reservations and soon the international markets were being flooded by their new blends. Ireland was caught napping. Then America, the single biggest market for Irish whiskey, declared Prohibition. At the same time, Ireland won its struggle for independence but was immediately hit by a trade embargo that banned sales of Irish goods in Britain and the Empire. In the space of 20 years Irish whiskey was ruined.

Bizarrely, the Irish Government decided to kick the industry when it was already down and stopped distilling during the Second World War. By 1952, Irish whiskey exports amounted to £500,000. Scotch was worth £32.5 million.

By the mid-1960s, it made sense for three of the last four distilleries in Ireland to join forces and make all their whiskey in one plant in Midelton, Co. Cork.

Emptying a whiskey cask ready for filtering, draining into a vat and bottling; each cask produces 250 bottles of whiskey

The Jameson Heritage Centre is on the site of the old Cork Distillers plant is more pictureque than the functional Midleton distillery

IRISH WHISKEY – THE CLASSICS

Irish whiskey is undergoing a renaissance. The country may only be able to boast three distilleries, but what Ireland lacks in stills it makes up for in high-quality brands. The best are some of the most drinkable drams you'll ever come across. They combine a fresh drive with ripe, sweet tropical fruitiness. They can cope with sherry wood, while (most of) the single malts have a creamy, clover-like charm. Be prepared to be seduced.

Black Bush (Irish Distillers) 40% ABV
A full, sweet nose brimming with nutty butter toffee and a hint of sherry wood. A complex, elegant whiskey.

Bushmills (Irish Distillers) 40% ABV
Very soft and fruity nose that mixes white pepper and orange. A delicate, slightly toasty palate.

Bushmills (Irish Distillers) 10-year-old malt (40% ABV)
A gorgeous mix of vanilla ice cream, clover and liquorice on the nose. A malty bite on the palate before a soft, dry finish.

Connemara Malt (Cooley) 40% ABV
A similar level of peatiness to Lagavulin, but altogether more aggressive. The rather damp peatiness dominates an assertive citric palate.

Crested Ten (Irish Distillers) 40% ABV
A weighty mix of freshly turned earth, malt and fruit on the nose. Broad and almost tarry on the palate, it coats the whole of the mouth.

Jameson (Irish Distillers) 40% ABV
Soft, full and slightly malty nose. Fresh with a green unmalted barley edge combined with light sweetness. Medium intensity, but still a creamy, smooth experience.

Jameson (Irish Distillers) 1780 (40% ABV)
A heady mix of ripe fruit and dog-rose aromas leap out of the glass. Creamy, long and soft with a creamy, crisply nutty palate and a magnificently long finish.

Kilbeggan (Cooley) 40% ABV
A mix of camphor and grass on the nose. A middle-weight whiskey that starts sweetly then finishes with a chilli pepper bite.

Locke's (Cooley) 40% ABV
Soft, clean and quite malty with some nutty sherry wood on show. This sweet component carries through the palate to the peppery finish.

Power's (Irish Distillers) 40% ABV
A noseful of super-ripe, pulp, apricot, peachy fruit. Softly weighted on the palate, but with a refreshingly edgy backbone. A true classic.

When Bushmills, the sole distiller left in Northern Ireland, joined the new Irish Distillers Group in 1973, all Irish whiskey was made by one firm.

In recent times a newcomer, Cooley, has joined the fray and proved to be the spark the industry needed. Now the two firms are vying with each other to show the wide range of styles that Ireland can produce. Irish Distillers insists on triple distillation and unpeated malt, Cooley uses peat in some brands and has no reservations about double distillation. The added choice has led people back to the gentle Irish style.

The white-walled buildings at Bushmills wouldn't look out of place in Scotland. Indeed, from the nearby Giant's Causeway you can make out the blue fuzz of Islay and Kintyre.

The whiskey itself is a spirituous link that replicates the basalt strip that surfaces at the Causeway and Fingal's Cave in Staffa. Midleton is the polar opposite of the classic lines of Bushmills. That said, the public are not allowed to see this miraculous ultra-modern distillery; that would ruin the illusion. Instead they are shown round the much more picturesque old Cork Distillers plant, now rather confusingly called the Jameson Heritage Centre. Midleton isn't romantic, but, like Cooley's highly functional plant in Dundalk, it produces some great whiskies.

Bushmills remains rooted in the paradoxical landscape of the Antrim coast, rugged yet soft, gentle yet bracing. What of the rest of Ireland's brands? Has technology replaced the notion that whiskies reflect their place of birth? Maybe. But each brand still uses its own recipe of malted and unmalted Irish barley, its own combination of pot and column still, and its own choice of casks.

At the end of the day, Power's is still the juiciest, peachiest, dreamiest dram you could ask for, Crested 10 and Redbreast are as rich and weighty as ever, and Jameson 1780 still hits the mark. The magic has been retained.

Overleaf: *Locke's Whiskey from the Cooley Distillery is a relative newcomer to the Irish market*

BOURBON

A central character in Native American mythology is Coyote. He represents the maverick, the creative individual, the free spirit. Anarchic and mischievous, he is regularly killed, but always manages to put his body back together again. American whiskey has that Coyote spirit.

The history

Spirits across the world have been intertwined with the rise and fall of societies. They have helped form nations, becoming part and parcel of the living history of a country. Behind virtually every step in America's progress, from colony to nationhood, is whiskey.

Spirits were distilled in the new American colonies from the word go, but to find the birth of American whiskey you have to wait for the second wave of immigrants who hit its shores. These were Scots and Irish fleeing clearances and famine, who carried with them the knowledge of grain distillation.

They distilled from the raw ingredients around them, and although barley proved difficult to grow in Maryland, Pennsylvania and the Carolinas, rye thrived on their hard soils, so rye it was. Good rye is a wonderfully bitter, lemon-accented spirit, but can have an astringency if not handled with care. You can just picture the early settlers sucking their teeth as the first slug of Pennsylvania rye hit their mouths.

Whiskey, just as with any spirit of that time, became a vital source of income. Transport was difficult, and grain was too heavy to lug by mule to the markets. However, if the grain could be distilled, not only was it easier to carry, it was actually more valuable. So, while the east continued to drink rum, as the colonists slowly moved west, whiskey went with them.

So vital a contribution did whiskey make to the settlers' income, that when George Washington decided to tax distilling, the producers rose up in the three-year Whiskey Rebellion. There is a deep irony in this, as not only was Washington a distiller of note – he made a handsome $1,032 from spirits in 1789 – but it was the taxes applied to rum that had been a contributory factor in the Colonies rising up against

the British. Washington's bottom line, though, was that the fledgling USA needed cash fast. Spirits (as ever) were the softest target.

So aggrieved were the distillers that they tarred and feathered the tax collectors and marched on Pittsburgh, threatening to burn it down. Washington decided on a show of brinkmanship and mustered 15,000 men to march on the rebellious distillers, who backed down.

Some distillers gave up entirely, but more decided to flee west to Kentucky and Tennessee, which had not yet achieved statehood. This is the start of the whiskeys that remain America's national spirit.

The first settlers had arrived in Kentucky in the 1770s, taking advantage of the incentive of 400 acres for free if they could clear the land and plant corn. What they found was an environment that is almost unsurpassed in the world for the production of high-quality spirits. There was clear, limestone-rich water, there were massive stands of oak for barrels, there was a river for easy transportation and, vitally, there was a native crop, Indian corn (maize), which made a smooth, soft spirit. Kentucky whiskey (bourbon) was born.

These early distillers didn't hang around and soon began producing in commercial quantities. Evan Williams was producing good volumes in Louisville in 1783; Jacob Beam arrived in Kentucky in 1788 and founded his distillery in 1795; Robert Samuels arrived in 1780. Then there were Elijah Pepper, Daniel Weller and Basil Hayden, names that still appear on bottles today.

The invention of the "bourbon" style is generally credited to the semi-legendary Rev. Elijah Craig, who combined hell-fire Baptist preaching with whiskey-making. Craig may have acquired the same mantle for bourbon as Friar John Cor has for Scotch, but he wasn't the first distiller in Kentucky. It's also unlikely that he invented the charred barrel that gives bourbon some of its most distinctive characteristics.

Quite where the charred barrel originated is a mystery. It could have been an accident – a cooper toasting a barrel may have nipped off to the toilet and left the barrel over the fire for too long. It could also have been good, old-fashioned Celtic prudence, recharring a barrel that had previously held some other goods; or it could have been deliberate, with a distiller realizing that the charcoal on the inside of the barrel would help to leach impurities out of the young spirit. Waymack & Harris, in their *Book of Bourbon*, argue plausibly that, since charring was used for other goods to stop them going off, the technique was likely to be used for whiskey as well.

What's significant is that bourbon was known as an aged spirit from its birth, simply thanks to Kentucky's geographical situation. It would have been distilled in the fall, barrelled and left to wait until the rivers were navigable before it set out on the three-month river journey to New Orleans. That means a whiskey could have been up to a year old when it reached its final destination. Given that new spirit greedily sucks the colour and flavour out of a barrel as soon as it hits the wood, by the time the merchants in the south got their consignment of Bourbon County whiskey it would have acquired a reddish hue and lost some of the rough edges. Enter Red Eye.

It would still have been pretty rough stuff. Distillation remained an inexact science until the arrival of a Scottish chemist and physicist, James (Jim) Crow, who began working at the Oscar Pepper distillery in 1823. (The site is now Labrot & Graham's distillery.) What Crow did was to apply scientific rigour to whiskey production. He brought the first hydrometer, and he experimented with and perfected sour mashing, distilling, charring barrels and ageing. His breakthroughs tamed what had been a pretty archaic process, and gave consistency to the product.

The frontier was moving inexorably west and whiskey went with it, its progress speeded up by the building of railroads. It no doubt caused more than

its fair share of gunfights, but then it helped to numb the wounded bodies. Whiskey helped build the West (and also made it wilder than it might otherwise have been). It also played a significant part in the genocidal annihilation of the Native American tribes.

After the Civil War, Lincoln needed money fast – so a further tax was imposed, forcing many of the smaller distilleries into the arms of the larger concerns, starting the steady consolidation of the industry that continues today. Another significant change happened at this time, with the arrival of the first continuous stills. A lighter style of whiskey emerged – and there was also more of it. Despite the best efforts of the taxman, brands grew in strength. But bubbling below the surface was a greater threat than the excise man: the Temperance Movement.

Temperance had started as an attempt to moderate people's drinking habits. The same thing was happening in Ireland, England and Russia – with some justification. People simply drank more in those days. In America, though, the two camps became polarized and, by the turn of the century, Temperance had given way to Total Abstinence. The industry didn't take the threat seriously or attempt to curb its more excessive stunts aimed at getting people to drink more and more, and somewhere down the line compromise was forgotten.

By 1910, Prohibition was common in every state – in fact, by 1915 Tennessee and Kentucky were dry. Even today, it's pretty damned hard to get a drink in certain counties in these whiskey-making states.

Full Prohibition came into force in 1919, and the industry has only just recovered from the blows it, the Depression and the Second World War dealt it. The twentieth century may have been "the American Century", but it as sure as hell won't be known as the American Whiskey Century. These days you have to search hard to find good rye whiskey, and you'll be hard pressed to find any (legal) corn whiskey at all. There are now just over a double-handful of distilleries producing all of the American whiskey in the world. Prior to Prohibition there were 2,000.

Draconian measures have a habit of producing the opposite reaction to the one they intended. America actually drank more during Prohibition than it had before. The amazing thing is that the bean counters in the Department of the Treasury forgot just how much money whiskey taxes contributed to the economy – it has been estimated that $500 million per year was lost during Prohibition, a vast sum in those days, even for an affluent nation.

When you add in the jobs lost in distilling and its infrastructure, it's fair to conclude that Prohibition managed to establish organized crime in America, and was a contributory factor in precipitating the Great Depression.

The industry emerged blinking in the sunny uplands of Repeal in a sorry state. Many producers simply couldn't afford to restart operations. Some brave individuals, like 70-year-old Jim Beam, started up again from scratch. Others pooled their resources. Heaven Hill was formed in 1935, when a group of former distillers approached the Shapira brothers. "It was doggone scary," says current president Max Shapira. "This was an industry that hadn't existed for 16 years; it was full of bootleggers, its product wasn't respected and there wasn't any of it anyway."

This consolidation picked up pace after Repeal. More seriously, the quality of the whiskey wasn't great. The bulk of the stock had been held in barrels for 19 years, and there wasn't sufficient young spirit distilled on the brief distilling holidays to get the category up and running again.

Booker Noe of Beam and Gerard White of UDV both have samples of whiskeys distilled before Prohibition and bottled on Repeal, but the surviving samples show the scale of problems the whole industry faced. Woody, oily and pungent, these whiskies hit the mouth with a rasping, sour quality. No one would drink that. Imported whiskies, which had been producing all through Prohibition, had no such problem and walked straight in.

Things may have been different had Roosevelt not decided to shut down production during the war and make distillers produce industrial alcohol to help the war effort. In Britain, Churchill had realized that sales of Scotch would generate much-needed revenue, and kept production going.

The result was that in 1945 the American whiskey industry had to start up yet again. The result was

more consolidation and a drive for the fighting end of the market. Once again, the distillers saw Scotch ride roughshod over "their" market. "This industry has had the worst record on being beat up of any I know," says Max Shapira. "We ended the War with no inventory – and then we made the mistake of not looking globally."

Initially this concentration on the domestic market was moderately successful, but, with some notable exceptions, much of the spirit produced was bottom-end stuff. Sales began to slide, but distillers just kept churning the stuff out. When the "brown spirits" crash came in the late 1970s, American whiskey went into freefall. If you drive down Distillers Row in Louisville today, behind the tatty strip joints are elegant, empty brick warehouses, the mausoleums of a once-prosperous industry.

Then, something miraculous happened. The Japanese, having already discovered malt whisky, woke up to the fact that aged bourbon was also a high-quality premium spirit. The same thing happened in Australia, Germany and, to a lesser extent, the United Kingdom. Much of the credit for this must go to Maker's Mark who, by word-of-mouth promotion – and paying attention to high-quality standards – had woken up the export markets to the top end.

Only once the export markets had begun demanding premium brands did the American public wake up to their heritage. This shift upmarket coincided with the emergence of Generation X – younger drinkers who wanted, well, flavour in their lives. Fine cigars, flavoursome beers, quality food and premium spirits have all boomed in the past few years. "It all came good when the last yuppie died," said Bill Samuels at Maker's Mark. "But it's been 40 years of struggle. Jeez, it was tough."

There's a new confidence in the industry, and American whiskey is finally being allowed to show what it can produce, but the booming top end can't bail out the industry. Things may be getting better, but the industry isn't out of the woods yet.

Opposite: *Labrot & Graham's Distillery in Kentucky, the only one in the USA to use the pot-still distillation method*

HOW IT'S MADE

Why does bourbon taste the way it does? Like all of the great spirits of the world, it draws from its immediate environment. The reason settlers began to produce whiskey in Kentucky was because they had plentiful crops to distil with; they took advantage of a supply of pure, iron-free, calcium-rich water; oak trees to make barrels from; as well as a climate capable of producing a specific style of maturation; and a river system to get the product down-river to market.

The water is as good a place to start as any. Kentucky sits on a bed of limestone, which filters out any minerals (most importantly, iron), but produces a water that's rich in calcium. This plays a vital role at different stages in the process.

Regulations state that Straight Bourbon must be made from a minimum of 51 per cent corn and a collection of "small grains" – usually rye and malted barley, but Maker's Mark and W. L. Weller both replace rye with wheat. Rye or wheat give flavour, while malted barley provides the enzymes that turn starches into fermentable sugars. When a whiskey contains more than 80 per cent corn, it becomes corn whiskey. Rye whiskey has a minimum of 51 per cent rye, while blended whiskey is 20 per cent straight whiskey blended with neutral spirit.

The exact combination of grains (the mash bill) will be different in each distillery – and, sometimes, different mash bills are used for each brand. UDV's Weller, for example, has 16 per cent wheat and 76 per cent corn, while its Old Charter has six per cent of rye and no wheat. Wild Turkey uses the highest percentage of small grains (mainly rye), while Heaven Hill has the highest percentage of corn.

The grains are checked for moisture content, mould and cracked kernels, and the corn is also nosed to see if it has the right sweet aroma. The grains, still kept separate, are ground into a roughish flour. The corn then gets cooked in scalding water to release its starches, next it's cooled and the rye (or wheat) is added. Wheat needs to be cooked at a lower temperature to preserve its aroma, while if you put rye in at too high a temperature you run the risk of rye balls

forming, which can cause bacterial infection.

The mixture is then cooled before the malted barley is added. At Four Roses, some malt is added with the corn – not for enzyme activity, but to help liquefy the slurry.

The sweet mash is transferred to fermenters (made either of steel or cypress) where yeast is added. No other spirit holds yeast in such high regard. Each distillery jealously guards its own strain – and, for safety's sake, often has stashes in different sites. These yeasts are strains that have been developed and passed down through the generations. Booker Noe – Beam's master distiller *emeritus* – remembers his grandfather, Jim Beam, stinking out the house as he developed one of the yeasts that's now used in the Jim Beam brands. Some distilleries use one strain while others, like Beam, use different strains to suit different mash bills. What the old distillers knew intuitively was that yeast is a living organism that not only turns sugar into alcohol (and carbon dioxide), but imparts its own flavour.

The ferment, on average, lasts between three and four days, but this period can be extended to fit in with working weeks, or types of mash. Most distilleries now have a form of temperature control built into their fermenters to stop the heat rising above 90°F, when it would kill the yeast.

A third thing is then added to the fermenter – backset. This is the liquid part of the yeast and grain residue that is collected from the bottom of the beer still. This "sour mash" must make up a minimum of 25 per cent of the volume of the mash, but again each distillery will have its own recipe. Wild Turkey uses 33 per cent backset, while some – like Barton, Four Roses and Heaven Hill – add a percentage of backset at the cooking stage.

The tart, acidic backset does a number of things, most importantly killing harmful bacteria and lowering the pH of the ferment. Because Kentucky's water is calcium-rich, the mash has a tendency to become alkaline – which can lead to infection and off notes. Backset therefore provides an environment in which the yeast can propagate correctly, and give flavour and consistency from one mash to another. This could explain why, although Scotland uses soft water and Kentucky uses hard water, they both produce such consistently fine spirits. Scottish water is naturally low in pH, so the mash doesn't need any backset; Kentucky's is higher, so it does.

The resulting 'beer' is distilled in a column still several storeys high called, logically enough, a beer still. The beer passes down the column, meeting steam, which is being pumped in under pressure from the bottom (although Beam pumps the mash in under pressure at the bottom).

As the steam rises, it strips the alcohol off the descending beer, so that by the time it reaches the foot of the still it is a non-alcoholic mix of water, dead yeast and spent grains – which is then used as backset.

The vapours are then condensed and passed through a second still called a doubler. Once again, each firm will have its own variation on this process. Maker's Mark condenses all of the charge from its beer still before redistilling it in the doubler. Others keep the flow going continuously, while some use a contraption called a thumper, which involves passing the vapour through water. The heaviest alcohols cannot break through because of the surface tension, and are retained – effectively giving a second distillation.

Only one distillery uses pot-still distillation – Labrot & Graham. The whiskey they produce is currently sitting in barrel – watch this space.

The rate of flow, and the strength at which the spirit comes off the still, can be regulated by adjusting the pressure and the temperature of the steam. This strength is vitally important to the spirit's final character, and while legally it can be no stronger than 160° proof, everyone takes it off considerably lower. Four Roses comes off the highest – and produces a light, flavoursome spirit. Maker's Mark takes it off lower to preserve the delicacy of the wheat, while Wild Turkey is the lowest of them all – and the fullest flavoured. "It's like cooking a steak," says Jimmy Russell at Wild Turkey. "If you want a tasty one you have it rare, if you have it well done you won't get any flavour."

The 'white dog', as the new make is known, is diluted (again this varies between distilleries) and placed in new, charred American white-oak barrels. The level of char will also vary between distilleries. Ancient Age, for example, has recently moved to a heavier char after finding it gave greater consistency.

Increasingly, barrels are being made from kiln-dried timber, which is cheaper and quicker to produce, but some distillers, such as Wild Turkey, Labrot & Graham and Maker's Mark, all continue to use air-dried staves, as they feel the barrels have none of the acrid notes that poorly kiln-dried timber can give. Even producers who use kiln-dried wood will admit in private that they prefer the other option.

The majority of distilleries age their spirit in huge rick warehouses up to nine floors high, with three barrels on each floor. It's at this point that Kentucky's climate once again enters the equation. Not only has it given ideal conditions for growing cereal crops and sufficient water for distilling, its temperature range has a huge impact on the way in which the whiskey matures. In other words, Kentucky's distillers harness their climatic conditions to produce their style of whiskey.

The state has cold winters and hot summers, which means that the whiskey will mature in a different way from that in Scotland. The physical shape of the rick warehouses also plays an important role. Think of it this way. Heat rises; therefore, in a hot and steamy Kentucky summer, when you should be sitting in a shady porch, Mint Julep in hand, the top of a warehouse will be as hot as hell, while the bottom will remain cool. In winter the top will be warm, the bottom cold.

The rate of passage in and out of the wood is therefore greater in the hot upper floors than at the bottom, so the same whiskey aged for, say, four years will look, smell and taste different on each floor. Distillers will also manipulate the temperature by opening and closing windows on each floor to cool or heat as required. Ancient Age and Labrot & Graham also centrally heat their warehouses in winter.

There are two ways to work with this style of maturation. One is to rotate the barrels, taking them from the top and putting them on the bottom – and *vice versa*. It's a laborious option, but Wild Turkey and Maker's Mark insist it does have a beneficial effect. The other way is to leave the barrels positioned where they are and blend from a cross-section of floors. The barrels are therefore usually spread out on all floors and across warehouses.

This also means that not all your eggs are in one basket – an important consideration, given Kentucky's occasionally violent climate. One of Beam's warehouses was ripped apart by a tornado, while Heaven Hill lost five warehouses and its distillery in a fire.

The small-batch and single-barrel brands are nearly always taken from the middle floors, where the temperature fluctuations are less extreme. Ancient Age's Blanton always comes from the mid-section of its H warehouse.

Until recently, the word was that bourbon didn't improve much after eight years in barrel, but it's no coincidence that, at that time, most players were trying to sell young whiskey. Now that small batch and single barrels have been promoted – surprise, surprise – it's been shown that by careful wood management bourbon can age as long and as gracefully as any great spirit.

When you get down to it, the secret of the way bourbon tastes is contained in the souls of the master distillers – men like Jimmy Russell of Wild Turkey, Booker Noe of Jim Beam or Maker's Mark's Bill Samuels – and the young distillers who are taking over the reins, like Carl Beam at Heaven Hill or Jim Rutledge at Four Roses.

You know that a great whiskey is going to be produced at a distillery like Wild Turkey when you see the love that Jimmy Russell lavishes on his product. For him the distillery is a living thing – and at times, with steam billowing out of chimneys, making strange whooshing noises, the whole plant seems to behave like a weird, antediluvian beast.

Russell can recognize the stage a ferment has reached simply by the appearance of the surface and the speed at which the liquid swirls around the tub. The control room in the stillhouse may contain charts and controls and dials, but here, too, it's the personal touch that counts.

"In the old days, you'd be sitting here with one hand on the flow handle and the other on steam," he says. "People would think you were asleep. But do you hear that noise, hear how the still's whistling? Well, you'd be listening to that whistle, and if it changed you'd adjust either the flow or the pressure. We'd do it by sight and by sound – and we still do it all by nose and taste."

The great bourbons are all produced by people who have this deep love. The final element is the heart.

TENNESSEE WHISKEY

Ironically, most non-Americans' favourite "bourbon" isn't one at all; it's from Tennessee – and Tennessee whiskeys are made in a significantly different manner from those of its neighbour.

In Tennessee's early days, whiskey-making evolved in much the same way as in Kentucky. The state was colonized by Scots and Irish, who were fleeing the imposition of Washington's first taxation on spirits. When they arrived they used the local corn, rye and barley, drew their water from the limestone bedrock and shipped their wares down-river.

The split between the Kentucky (bourbon) and Tennessee styles came in the early 1820s when the Lincoln County Process appeared. Its invention is credited to Alfred Eaton who, in 1825, was reported as filtering his whiskey through several feet of maple charcoal, but there is evidence that the principle was already in use prior to Eaton's "discovery". Whoever

was first, it became the signature Tennessee technique by the middle of the nineteenth century.

There's still some mystery as to why this practice should spring up in Tennessee, and nowhere else. Although there is no concrete evidence, it's entirely possible that a Polish or Russian distiller had arrived in the state by that time.

Water was charcoal filtered in sixteenth-century Poland before it was used for vodka production; and by the eighteenth century, most Polish vodka was being filtered through charcoal before being bottled or flavoured. This pre-dates any record of it being used in Tennessee.

It can't be proved, but given that the history of distilling is about producers adapting and adopting techniques from across the world, it's entirely possible that this could provide the answer to how charcoal mellowing suddenly appeared in Lincoln County.

Jack Daniel, who was running his own distillery by the tender age of 13, is immortalized by this statue at the distillery that bears his name

One of the first distillers to use the technique was the young Jack Daniel. He had started distilling at the tender age of seven, and by 1859 (aged 13) was running his own distillery, finally moving to the limestone water of Cave Spring Hollow in Lynchburg in 1866.

Eleven years later, George Dickel, a whiskey merchant and distributor, bought the Cascade distillery near Tullahoma (another town blessed with limestone water) – enough to supply eight other distilleries. By the turn of the century Dickel's Cascade distillery was the largest and most modern in the state.

It was a tricky time to be involved in the whiskey business. The Temperance movement was showing its teeth, and in 1910 it bit, turning Tennessee dry. Jack Daniel's, by then run by Jack's nephew Lem Motlow (after Jack had died from septicaemia, caused when he kicked a safe door), was forced to move to St Louis for the nine years before Prohibition shut down the rest of America. It managed to return to Lynchburg in 1936 only after a mighty struggle over the rights to the name.

George Dickel was faced with similar problems, and when Tennessee went dry it shifted production to Louisville – although it was still produced with the charcoal mellowing. It took a long time before Dickel could go home.

After Prohibition it was made in Frankfort, only returning to Cascade Hollow in 1958. It and Jack Daniel remain the only two distilleries in a state that once boasted in excess of 700.

By definition, a Tennessee whiskey must be made from a minimum of 51 per cent of one grain. Technically, it could be rye or wheat, although in practice both Jack Daniel and Dickel use corn – it makes up 80 per cent of Jack Daniel's mash bill.

While mashing, fermenting and distillation are the same as in Kentucky, Tennessee whiskey acquires its special character when the white dog is slowly filtered through 10–12 feet of ground-up maple charcoal. This is a double process – removing impurities from the new spirit, but also giving back a mellow sweetness, some say "sootiness", since sugars are retained in the maple when it is burnt, and are leached out when the spirit passes down the vat.

At Jack Daniel's, it takes fives days to filter out of the woollen blanket that's at the bottom of the vat. The firm also uses a double mellowing process for its premium Gentleman Jack.

Dickel has a subtly different approach, as its mellowing vats have wool blankets at the top and bottom. Certainly, the style is considerably more delicate than the rich, liquoricey Jack.

This, however, may have something to do with the radically different ways in which the two distilleries age their whiskeys. While Jack Daniel's uses rick warehouses and rotates the barrels, Dickel ages in single-storey buildings that are heated in winter. This, in combination with the extra mellowing, means you get a considerably more delicate whiskey.

If there is one brand that has turned the world on to American whiskey, it's Jack Daniel's. It has somehow managed to cultivate a rock-and-roll image without ever advertising itself as a rebellious drink. It's a marketing success story without parallel in brown spirits – and one that no one has yet been able to replicate.

But there's more to American whiskey than one brand; perhaps now is the time to start exploring.

Old Whiskey jars from the George Dickel Distillery, Cascade Hollow, Tennessee; Dickel only returned to Tennessee in 1958

KENTUCKY WHISKEY

Kentucky is home not only to America's indigenous spirit, but to America's first native musical instrument, the five-string banjo, the key instrument in Kentucky's own roots music – bluegrass. Just as bluegrass has its roots in Celtic music, but is a 100 per cent American creation, so whiskey is a fusion between Irish and Scottish knowledge, with an American twist.

Spirits evolve, and bourbon is no different. "Whiskey was the lubrication that allowed the West to be won," says Bill Samuels, President of Maker's Mark. "They didn't want any fancy frou-frou drinks in those days." Right enough; you can't imagine Wyatt Earp and Doc Holliday discussing the finer points of a single-barrel, small-batch bourbon in Tombstone. Red Eye was hard liquor for hard men, and most whiskey remained in that style until Prohibition.

Even after Repeal, the style of bourbon remained in the abrasive camp. You can understand why. The industry needed to build up its stock levels in ultra-quick time, so stills were run hot, hard and long to collect as much alcohol as possible. "I remember Dad sitting at the table before the end of the Second World War saying how he wanted to reinvent bourbon as a softer style of spirit," Samuels now recalls. "Someone at the table, I forget who, said: 'the last thing we need in this country is sissy whiskey'." Only when you see photos of some of the small, registered, pre-Prohibition distilleries does this all make sense. There's a photo of the Hadan distillery in Kentucky, which is nothing more than a wooden shack with moonshining equipment inside it. The proud owners are standing outside, guns at the ready. You can bet your bottom dollar they wouldn't have been making no sissy stuff.

There again, why should they have been? The majority of people who were drinking the stuff weren't high-flying executives, but the proletariat – scrabbling for jobs, working in heavy industry, digging for coal in the Appalachians – men who had been moonshining all the way through Prohibition.

But things were changing. Post-war, blended Scotch took the high ground in America, while vodka, gin and Bacardi all boomed. As drinking spirits long became the norm, so whiskey producers released their product young. The top end of the market – with the exception of the small-scale Maker's Mark –

TASTING NOTES

BARTON

Ten High A strange mix of lemon cordial and young wood. Light and dry with dried herbs and a peppery bite.

Kentucky Gentleman Soft, juicy, though strangely mealy, fruit. Crisp, concentrated and simple.

Kentucky Tavern Creamy wood on the nose, some floral, orangey notes. Good feel and a zip of spice at the end.

Col. Lee Dry wood with some hazelnut and cream. Soft and oily to start, then a crunch of small grains behind with a rye freshness on finish.

Tom Moore Muted with Juicy Fruit chewing gum aromas. Little feinty.

Very Old Barton Certainly old in the wooded stakes and certainly rich. Long and fresh, with crisp zippy acid/lemon finish.

HEAVEN HILL

Evan Williams 90° Balanced wood aromas of spice, cinnamon, caramel and a little smoke. A good, rounded feel with a mid-palate bite. Soft but lean.

Elijah Craig 12-year-old 94° Rich woodiness with spice, smoke and a hint of nutmeg. Firm in the mouth but enough soft fruit to carry it to great lengths.

Elijah Craig 18 year-old Almost heathery nose with touches of saddle soap and nuts. Soft and fruity in the mouth with great spicy, peppery length. Excellent.

FOUR ROSES

Yellow Label Gentle, slightly wooded, and lightly citric on nose. Clean, light, fragrant with a gentle zippiness.

Black Label Firm on the nose with hickory wood smoke. On palate, light and clean. A sweet start, then a firm rye grip.

Super Premium In the house style, but with a richer undertow. Solid in the mouth and a fine tingle of zesty rye. Smoky and smooth. Good.

Apart from whiskey, Kentucky is probably most famous for the Derby, the USA's premier 3-year-old horse race, run at Churchill Downs

remained untouched, and the category undersold itself. Then, in the face of the worst slump this century, people's palates changed again. They began drinking less, but drinking better. "It's fascinating to chart," says Gerard White at UDV. "There was a change in style after Prohibition, then it changes post-war when young whiskey appeared. Then from the mid-80s on there's this switch upmarket and we're back to the old style again. Now bourbon is a fundamentally American spirit again."

What hasn't happened, however, is a return to the fusel oil, over-wooded overload of the old days; the new premium bourbons take the best qualities of the old style, but add elegance, style and finesse to it – as long as they control the alcohol levels. They aren't sissy whiskeys, but Bill Samuels Sr's belief in quality has finally been proved to be correct.

These days, you are spoilt for choice – from the spice and nutmeg of Heaven Hills' Elijah Craig 12-year-old, and the saddle soap and heather of its 18-year-old version; the small-batch range from Beam that shifts from the zippy, crisp Basil Hayden; to

Knob Creek's generosity and the all-out multi-faceted attack of Booker's. From UDV comes the beautifully balanced, intense Old Charter, and the rum and raisin, chocolatey W.L. Weller. Then there's Ancient Age's sweet single-barrel Blanton's; Maker's Mark's honeyed, buttery elegance; the orange peel and mint on Labrot & Graham's Woodford Reserve and, at the top of the tree, Wild Turkey's opulent, unctuous, flavoursome Rare Breed.

The two enforced shutdowns of the twentieth century killed two other truly American whiskeys – rye and corn. Rye, however, is a great style. The grain gives a bite to some of the best bourbons, but on its own it develops into a marvellously spicy, zesty drink, filled with the scents of cumin seed and citrus fruits, exploding in your mouth with mouth-watering acidity. These days, only Wild Turkey and Jim Beam make straight ryes, although Gerard White – trawling through UDV's massive inventory looking for possible limited-edition releases – discovered a stash of 16-year-old rye from the George T. Stagg distillery. Powerful, spicy and lemony on the nose, it sets off a

TASTING NOTES

JIM BEAM

Basil Hayden 8 year-old 80° Powerful and rich. A zesty drive with chewy, tingly rye finish. Very good.

Knob Creek 9 year-old 100° Rich caramel/treacle nose. Fruity, elegant, ripe, rich.

Baker's 7 year-old 107° Firm, and heavy with some liquorice on the palate. An oily texture with a tingle on the finish.

Booker's 7 year-old 126/7° Rich, complex but alcohol-dominant nose with caramel, tobacco boxes, hickory and whiffs of lapsang souchong tea and bitter orange peel. Powerful with an elegant orange/oak character.

Jim Beam Rye Zesty lemon lift with cumin powder spiciness. Tight and crisp that belts your tastebuds back into shape.

ANCIENT AGE

Ancient Age 4 year-old A quite delicate, almost nutty nose. Smooth with a touch of vanilla and a clean, corny middle.

Blanton Single Barrel Nutty, cereal nose, light perfume and high alcohol.

Ancient Ancient Age 10 year-old Rich, elegant, plump with cinnamon, treacle and grassiness. Soft with good length.

LABROT & GRAHAM

Woodford Reserve Bitter orange, smoky wood and some sweetness on the nose. Fine grip on the palate with a melding of mint and honey.

WILD TURKEY

Wild Turkey 4 year-old Creamy, rich, vanilla notes with a cakey touch. Rich, clean and spicy with a fresh finish.

Wild Turkey 101 8 year-old Ripe, rich with menthol and mint, rich vanilla, toffee and concentrated fruits. Mixes freshness with weight, instant appeal with ripe raisin and baked apple fruit.

Wild Turkey Rare Breed The wood shows on the nose, but the palate is all opulent, unctuous layered fruits. Rich and chocolately.

UDV MAKER'S MARK

Old Charter 13 year-old 96° Menthol, lemon thyme nose. On palate, very clean and zesty.

Balances wood and floral fruit with a mouthful of spices that give a piquant, acidic attack. Brilliant.

W.L.Weller 10 year-old 100° Rich mix of spice, butter, molasses and some rum and raisin. Rich and sweet start that mixes chocolatey fruit and spice.

George T. Stagg 16 year-old 110° Pungent and powerful. Lemon balm/lime zest leaning to aftershave. Clean, bitter chocolate spiciness that hits the mouth and then explodes and expands. Stunning, but not for the faint-hearted.

Taylor & Williams 15 year-old 115° Rich smoky wood with some plump fruitiness behind. Very smooth to start, then it builds into a powerful mouth-filling mix of fruit, treacle, orange and chocolate.

Old Quaker 21 year-old 130° (Indiana corn whiskey). Pale yellow. Fragrant and gentle with cream and clover aromas. Gentle and smooth to start, then an astringent bite which yields to mellow sweetness on the finish.

Medley 18 year-old barrel proof wood-dominant with pungent whiffs of creosote and prunes. Dense and sweet on the palate with coffee bean, acid and chewy toffee wood on the finish.

---

chain-reaction in the mouth, building up to an incredible intensity of bitter chocolate and lime zest. It might not be the prettiest drink in the world, but it reinforces the evidence that America makes classic, world-class whiskeys.

Corn whiskey labours under the image of being nothing more than moonshine, a whiskey without any finesse. Certainly, when you hear blues singers like Dock Boggs singing: "Give me corn bread when I'm hungry good people/Corn whiskey when I'm dry," you know he's not talking about top-end stuff. You'll be hard pressed to find (legal) corn whiskey these days, but UDV (again) has unearthed a small batch from the Old Quaker distillery in Indiana. Pale gold, it's fragrant, creamy and gentle on the nose, and lulls you into a sense of false security with its dreamy start. Then it bites, before yielding again to a sweet, almost-malty finish. You wonder what Dock Boggs would have made of it – he'd probably have approved of the 130° proof.

The sad thing is that, as this is being written, it's unclear what will happen with this fascinating initiative. UD's merger with IDV leads you to fear that small batches won't feature in the corporate plans. Let's hope and pray that they do.

You can't help but wonder what might have happened to American whiskey if Prohibition and the Second World War hadn't closed the industry for such long periods. For Booker Noe, small batch is like going back to the future. "Years ago it was aged for longer and distilled lower in proof, and you got a more concentrated whiskey. Booker's is what whiskey was 200 years ago. It's kosher whiskey." We should all drink to that.

Opposite: *Four Roses (with the Yellow Label, left, probably the best known) is one of the premier brands of Kentucky whiskey*

CANADIAN WHISKY

Although fruit brandies, applejack and rum were the early drinks of Canadian settlers, it was inevitable that whisky would become the nation's native spirit. Canada, after all, was the destination for the majority of the Scots fleeing the Highlands in the aftermath of the suppression of the second Jacobite Rebellion in 1745. In fact, an Orcadian explorer had established a Scottish settlement in Nova Scotia in 1394! Even today, Gaelic is spoken in Cape Breton.

The whisky they made, however, was always destined to be different from the malts of their homeland. The earliest distillers, farming on the hard lands of Nova Scotia, would have used rye – still a vitally important ingredient in today's whiskies – but as the settlers began to spread out along the St Lawrence river to the Great Lakes, so they came to farmland where all sorts of cereal crops could thrive.

Whisky provided a handy extra income for these small farmers who were putting down roots across this vast country, but like every other country the world over, the government soon got wise to the fact and

Above: *Canadian Mist pots produce a clean-tasting whisky;* **Opposite:** *Hiram Walker's distillery is on the Canadian side of the Detroit river*

The Great Lakes were filled with vessels carrying whisky to the USA during Prohibition

slapped a prohibitively high tax on whisky. The effect was to kill off the small farmer-distiller and concentrate whisky-making in the hands of a few cash-rich producers.

This tax hike came at the same time as continuous stills were being installed – giving these large distillers an extra incentive to produce from the more efficient, high-volume columns rather than the less efficient pots.

The Canadian government has kept a pretty close watch on the whisky industry. On the positive side, by the end of the nineteenth century, Canadian whisky (it has retained the Scottish spelling) was the most tightly controlled in the world. It could only be made from cereal grains, it had to be distilled in a continuous still and had to spend a minimum of three years in oak.

On the negative side, Canada flirted for a year with Prohibition and then came to its senses, by coincidence at the very same time as the lights were going out on the American whiskey industry. The Great Lakes were filled with boats carrying Canadian (and Scotch) to the thirsty American markets and the industry was saved. It prospered until relatively recently when the downturn in whisky sales forced closures of massive plants across the country.

We have already seen how the whiskies differ from all others. Canadian whisky is the triumph of the blender, just as Irish is the triumph of distillation. For starters there's the huge range of grains that can be used: corn, rye, malted and unmalted barley, and wheat. These can either be distilled individually or in different mash bills, often with their own yeasts. They are all distilled in a column still, but different types of still will be used – linked columns, single columns and doublers as in America, and Coffey stills. The stills can be manipulated to give spirits of different strengths.

These building blocks will then be aged for differing lengths of time, often in different types of wood. Canadian distillers can draw on new, charred and uncharred wood, ex-whisky, ex-sherry, ex-bourbon and ex-rum casks. Sometimes different distillates are aged separately, then blended and aged again, this time in different wood. There's a mass of possibilities.

The whiskies are smooth and soft, but never boring. Instead they are gentle, intriguing and elegant. In today's market, where all the talk is of malt and bourbon, good Canadian whisky remains overlooked. Be bold, try some.

CANADIAN WHISKY – THE CLASSICS

A combination of a country where all manner of grains can prosper and government legislation has given Canada a style of whisky unlike any other. Here, the blender is king, cunningly weaving together distillates from different grains aged in different woods into brands which have a discreet, reassuring quality. Canadian whisky has long been looked down on internationally – it's time for a reappraisal of what it has to offer.

Black Velvet 40% ABV
Typically soft and smooth. An attractive, rounded feel with the merest hint of rye to pep up the mid-palate.

Canadian Club 40% ABV
A very delicate nose with a hint of smoke. Quite crisp on the nose. Clean, with a little lemony bite from the rye. A clean, easy-drinking (if slightly woody) whisky.

Canadian Club Classic 12 year-old 40% ABV
Rich and elegant with sweet, well rounded, fruity notes. Ripe and smooth on the palate with a tingle of rye, toasty/sawdust wood and long, clean, slightly herbal fruitiness.

Canadian Mist 40% ABV
Light nose, but a fairly plump palate that gives way to a dry finish. Clean and gentle.

Crown Royal 40% ABV
A rich, succulent nose, brimful of spicy oak and sweet, almost toffee, fruit. Excellently balanced and elegant, it's a rich, unctuous, mouthfilling whisky.

Seagram V.O. 40% ABV
An appealing, delicately aromatic nose. The palate is complex, with zesty rye and smooth, mature fruit all on show.

THE OTHER WHISKIES OF THE WORLD

JAPAN

The existence of Japanese whisky is down to one man, Masataka Taketsuru, who arrived in Scotland in 1918 to learn the art of distilling. On his return to Japan in 1920, complete with Scottish wife in tow, he was employed by Shinjiro Torii, the founder of Suntory, at that firm's Yamazaki distillery, selling his first whisky four years later. In 1940 (in retrospect, not, perhaps, the ideal time to start a new business venture) he started up on his own at his Yoichi distillery deep into the snowfields of Hokkaido.

On paper, Japan could produce great whisky (in fact, Yoichi does). It has pure water, there's peat in the hills, the country is fertile and the climate is suitable for even maturation. The Yamakazi and Yoichi distilleries both have the ability to peat their malt to different levels, distil in a wide range of stills and age in a vast range of wood types. The trouble is that there seems to be a fear that they won't be able to do it as well as the Scots, so malt whisky is brought over in bulk and blended in, resulting in the Japanese character being drowned out. With the Japanese public these days preferring single-malt and small-batch bourbon, it's going to be tough to change that mentality.

Other whisky-producing countries

In almost every country you come across you'll find someone making a drink that they call whisky. Some are the genuine article – DYC in Spain, for example, is a perfectly decent blend, while Tesetice in the Czech Republic has long enjoyed a good reputation.

Indian whisky, however, has not been so well received. Scottish distillers, including Glenmorangie and Whyte & Mackay, are entering into joint ventures, but you get the feeling it's more to get their brands a foothold in what could become a huge market for Scotch. That may be unfair, but Indian whiskies are rarely anything other than cheap spirits to be drunk quickly, then forgotten. Much the same can be said for the "whiskies" that come out of Thailand and China. Admire the labels, by all means, then buy something else.

Barrels at the Yamazaki Distillery, Suntory, Japan

JAPANESE WHISKY – THE CLASSICS

JAPAN

Nikka All Malt Decent malty weight on the nose, but not overly heavy on the palate, which has a clean crunch and a nudge of peat.

Suntory Hibiki Proof that complexity can exist in Japanese whisky. More fruit dominant than most on the nose, there's some smoke, perhaps from the wood which gives the palate a decent grip.

Suntory Reserve Substantial nose, with fruity, nutty character showing well. Rich and elegant.

"Traditional" whisky is distilled in a variety of countries, including Thailand – experts might recommend going elsewhere for real quality

BRANDY

It was the Phoeneicians and the Romans who took it upon themselves to spread the art of winemaking throughout the whole of Southern Europe. Much later, in the sixteenth century, learned Italian monks and Moorish scholars introduced the remarkable process of distillation – and, lo and behold, a new spirit was born – its name was brandy

COGNAC

Cognac, like any major spirit-producing region, is living proof of man's interaction with a beneficial environment. The Romans brought viticulture to this area around the Charente river (the Gaulish provinces of Angoumois, Saintonge and Aunis) in the third century, as they did across France. What made this particular area important was that it had access to the Bay of Biscay at what is now La Rochelle, thereby linking it to the trade routes with the Celtic nations and Northern Europe. In those days rivers were arteries that not only carried goods but ideas as well – a nervous system of intellect.

By late medieval times, coastal trade had become increasingly important and La Rochelle had been elevated to the status of a major port. Initially trade revolved around the salt that was produced there – salt, at that time, being as valuable as gold, and prized in Northern European states. As the salt trade developed, the region's wines also began to be exported to Scotland (Macbeth drank Charentais wines), Ireland, England, Scandinavia, the Baltic States and, most significantly, Holland.

Importantly, La Rochelle – unlike Bordeaux – never silted up, which allowed merchants easy access to the interior and easy transport away – a fact that was to count against Armagnac (see below), and in time the Charente prospered. It wasn't to last.

In the thirteenth century, when the English and the French were battling for ascendancy in France, the Charente found itself stuck between the (French-held) Loire and (English-held) Bordeaux. It allied itself with France which, as Axel Behrendt says in his book *Cognac*, was a "fateful" decision as the region became a battleground, the vineyards for ever being destroyed by the marauding English troops. Farmers gave up viticulture as a bad job and planted wheat in the chalky soil, and trees elsewhere.

Then fate smiled on the area. In the sixteenth century, La Rochelle aligned itself with the Protestant Huguenots, a move which, although isolating it from much of the rest of France, brought it close once more to the Protestant north of Europe. Trade (initially in salt rather than wine) grew, but in time the vines went back into the ground – then distilling arrived.

It's ironic that the world's premier brandy-producing region was such a late starter. The first record of brandy being made in the region was in 1638, when Lewis Roberts wrote about "a small wine that is called Rotchell, or more precisely cogniake".

Although it's entirely possible that small-scale distilling was happening before this – after all, by then Armagnac and Jerez had been making brandy for two centuries – Cognac didn't produce brandy in commercial quantities until the middle of the seventeenth century.

But why, then, did this late starter find itself elevated rapidly to the finest brandy region of them all? It was down to the Dutch. The sixteenth century had seen Holland becoming the most powerful trading nation in the world, controlling spices (see Gin), wine, rum and brandy, and the Dutch had been trading in salt and wine with the merchants of La Rochelle since the time of the Hanseatic League.

Now, with the Dutch mercantile empire encompassing Sumatra, the Caribbean and Northern Europe, they needed *brandewijn* (burnt wine) to make the drinking water on ships drinkable, and to fortify

La Rochelle in France was a major European port in medieval times; its harbour is quieter nowadays

Château de Chanteloupe, the ancestral home of the Martell family – Martell began ageing and blending Cognac in 1715

TASTING NOTES – COGNAC

COURVOISIER

Courvoisier VS Light and rather hard. A sweet start, but fairly hot and average.

Courvoisier VSOP Round and sweet, almost fat. Touch of cedar wood and good fruit.

HINE

Hine Antique On the nose there's roasted spices: coriander, garam masala, cumin along with boot-polish and dried thyme. Stylish.

Hine Rare & Delicate Clean with some elegant high notes – clover, apple blossom, lemon, honey, but then you sink into walnuts, tobacco, cedar and roasted spices. A Cognac that demands you take your time.

Hine Triomphe Delicate, crisp nose. Clean and gentle on the palate with delicate fruit all the way through. Light and clean.

Hine Triomphe An autumnal nose with leaf mulch, nuts and mushrooms but also a hint of peaches in syrup. Filled with a complex interplay between fruit and nut.

MARTELL

Martell VS Fairly waxy, spicy fruit. Clean but tough. Well made and the great starter Cognac.

Martell VSOP Thick and well wooded. Some smoke, ripe fruits but a little one-dimensional.

RÉMY

Rémy 1738 Fruit interlaced with mint, lemon balm and slightly hard wood. Great energy and drive.

Rémy XO Tangerine peel and bergamot on the nose. Gentle, but with substance on the palate.

Rémy VSOP Lightly herbal with some citric notes. Clean and appetising with fine weight. Well

poised with a touch of quince. Benchmark.

MISCELLANEOUS

Ch. de Beaulon VSOP Ethereal nose. Fruit-dominant, refined and clean.

Delamain Pale & Dry Oranges and cashews with a hint of dates on the nose. High-toned and discreet.

Duboigalant VSOP Complex nose, mixing nuts, honey, raisins, cinnamon and ginger. Full and ripe.

Gourmel Age des Fleurs Clean and complex array of vanilla, fruit and the merest hint of nut on nose. Complex and elegant with a very gentle core that has great concentration and grip.

Peyrat VSOP Light and very fine on the nose. Soft and floral.

Ragnaud-Sabourin VSOP Great depth. Long and stylish.

---

table wines in order to stabilize them. This led to the creation of Pineau de Charentes.

Although the Dutch initially imported the Charentais wine and distilled it at home, it soon made economic sense to make the brandy *in situ* and then ship it – after all, you can fit more barrels of brandy than barrels of wine on board a ship. Ever resourceful, they invented a pot still and switched production to the region around the towns of Cognac and Jarnac.

The quality of Cognac was apparent from the word go. English wine merchants were asking high prices for the new "cogniacke" almost as soon as it appeared on the market – and with some justification. Once again fate had looked on the region kindly.

Economic and social pressures had "discovered" a region that was perfectly situated for the making of high-quality brandy. The wood to fire the stills and make the barrels was in the area's forests, there was easy access to the sea and long-established foreign trading links.

What made the difference, though, was the climate and the soil (particularly the chalky part around Cognac) which gave ideal conditions for viticulture, while the microclimate next to the river was perfect

for slow, steady maturing. In 1669, when Louis XIV gave the inspired decree to establish oak forests in the nearby regions of Limousin and Troncais, all the elements were in place for a glorious future.

Cognac soon became established as the preferred drink of the Northern European bourgeoisie, especially in England. Even when boycotts were applied, it was smuggled in to England – either via Holland, or via Jersey, where one Jean Martell was a merchant. Martell moved to Cognac in 1715 to start ageing and blending his own Cognacs. The industry was fast becoming as recognizable as it is today.

The demands of a growing export market soon led to the development of the three tiers of trade which are still in place today. Growers cultivated grapes, made wine and occasionally distilled and shipped; others stopped growing grapes and became distillers; while the merchants bought *eaux-de-vie*, blended, aged and shipped.

As the merchants grew in importance (and size) in the nineteenth century, so they needed to control ever greater supplies, and in time built up considerable inventories of older Cognacs. Major houses, including Courvoisier, Delamain and Hine were founded at around this time.

The outlook was rosy. In a relatively short time, Cognac had become the world's premium spirit. Unlike most other major categories, it didn't have to fight against prejudice and wait to gain the approval of the middle classes; it had that from the start. It was recognized as being of high quality, and there was a massive vineyard to support growing demand.

Then, disaster. In 1871, a vine pest called *phylloxera vastatrix* began gnawing away at the roots of the vines. Within a few years the entire vineyard had been destroyed. It took time to recover. Vines aren't like grain crops, or sugar cane. You don't just plant a new vine and harvest it a year later.

First, a way had to be found to make the vines resistant to *phylloxera* – which didn't happen until the mid-1880s, when it was discovered that grafting vines onto American rootstock had the desired effect. However, not all rootstocks could cope with French conditions; the rootstocks and the vines had to be paired up. While this research was scientifically done, it was still needed trial and error – and it was expensive.

As the whole of the French vineyard was slowly obliterated, the demand for rootstocks was high – and many growers simply could not afford to (a) buy the new plants and (b) wait for them to bear fruit. Given that it takes between three and five years for a vine to bear its first crop suitable for winemaking (and distilling), you can see why it took close on 20 years for Cognac to be replanted – and many growers didn't bother. By the time commercial quantities of Cognac were back on the market, Scotch and gin had become more popular.

Cognac, successfully, set its sights on regaining the top end of the market. While the effect of two world wars and an economic depression served to consolidate the industry, it also allowed the major shippers to tighten their control and, by developing major brands, they helped to rebuild Cognac's image as the luxury spirit.

This was augmented by the fact that Cognac has always been stronger in its export markets than at home. Even today 95 per cent of Cognac is exported, and the industry has always looked to sell into as many markets as possible. Therefore when the 1970s slump hit the European and US markets, the Cognac houses were already selling large quantities of deluxe brands to the Far East.

Even though the decline in the European markets necessitated a vine pull, the merchants thought that nothing could harm them, that the Far East would save them, and that Europe and the USA would, eventually, regain their senses and return to the fold. But they had grown complacent.

Now the Far East is in trouble and sales have fallen again. Although the major firms have sufficient stocks to ride out the storm, this latest slump is seriously affecting the growers. Traditionally, they have sat on high-quality older stock and sold it to the major houses as and when it was needed. When the Far East was booming it was a nice regular earner. The recent fall in demand has driven grape prices down and removed this demand for old stock. It may result in a welcome rise in small producer houses, but few of them can afford to make a significant impact on the market – or have the necessary stock to build long-term brands. The solution to Cognac's problems lies with the major houses.

There are a number of possibilities. Firms could emphasize the quality of the individual regions, they could promote VS (3-Star) Cognac as a mixable drink, or they could start releasing more vintage Cognac. The widespread introduction of age statements on the bottle is long overdue (indeed it is already being done by firms such as Prunier), and would bring Cognac into line with every other premium spirits category. All approaches, thankfully, are being tried, but with varying degrees of conviction. The question remains as to whether people will buy it. No matter which way you look at the problems facing the region, you end up with the same conclusion. To prosper once again, Cognac must rid itself of its stuffy, elitist image.

It also needs to justify its price. Cognac has higher fixed costs than, say, malt whisky, which means that a VS (3-Star) Cognac is priced around the same as a malt – but it can't compete in quality terms. "Ah!," the houses say, "but if you pay a little more you'll find the finest brandies in the world." That's undoubtedly true, but the houses are not giving consumers a reason to do this.

Cognac vineyards; climate, altitude and exposure to the sun are just as important as the soil

The image of the most sublime brandies in the world is out of step with the new spirit drinker who is willing to lay out that little bit extra. The Cognacs are there; whether they can be sold is another question.

HOW IT'S MADE

To try to understand what makes Cognac such an inspirational spirit, you have to start digging in the soil that makes up the six sub-regions (*crus*) of this tranquil, gently expansive region. The French have a word for it – *terroir*. To be accurate, it's more than just the soil. *Terroir* is about climate, altitude, exposure to the sun and how they impact on the vine – and then how man uses the fruit.

Without the different *terroirs* of Cognac, the master-blenders of the region wouldn't be able to draw on such a diverse richness of *eaux-de-vie*. Certainly, different approaches to distillation will have an effect, but the fundamental difference between the *crus* lies in their differing *terroirs*.

It's all to do with the bands of chalk that run across the region. The two main quality regions, Grande and Petite Champagne, have the highest percentage of chalk – in fact, some claim that "Champagne" comes from the Latin *campania* (light, chalky soil), although others argue that it's from the old French *campagne* (open land). The *crus* radiate out from the town of Cognac, the epicentre of the region, rather like rings on a target. To get to the heart of the region, therefore, you must start in the two Champagnes. As Alain Braastad-Delamain argues, their physical location and the resulting influence of climate are vitally important. His point is that, since Cognac is located between the Atlantic Ocean and the Massif Central, it's on the cusp of maritime and continental climates and also between northern and southern climatic conditions. This

Courvoisier proudly proclaims its association with the Emperor Napoleon on the label

results in a mass of different microclimates.

Grande Champagne, lying to the south of the Charente, is at the axis of these different climatic conditions and this equable climate – combined with the highest percentage of chalk in the soil – results in *eaux-de-vie* which are the most delicate, subtle, elegant and refined in the region, but which need time before they reveal their full glory.

Petite Champagne is a semi-circular curve that encloses the southern part of Grand Champagne. Although twice as large, it only produces the same volume of *eaux-de-vie* as its prestigious neighbour. There is less chalk here and slightly greater variance between east and west. The *eaux-de-vie* are correspondingly less intense and more floral and fruity. If a Cognac is made exclusively from these two *crus* – and a minimum of 50 per cent is made up by the Grande Champagne portion – it can be called Fine Champagne.

The small region of Borderies lies on the north bank of the Charente opposite the western part of Petite and Grande Champagne. Here the maritime climate has more of an influence, as does the higher percentage of flint and clay in the soil. The resulting distillates are highly distinctive, being rich, full-bodied and almost waxy, but with a flowery elegance. They are used by blenders to give roundness, guts and vigour to a blend. They are an important component for many of the major houses – in particular, Martell (*see* below).

These three central regions are encircled by the Fins Bois (so named, as the *cru* was forested when the vines for brandy were planted). Fins Bois supplies the bulk of Cognac, and is often unfairly dismissed as a result. Once again, situation is all-important. There are chalky strips running through the clay, which makes up most of the area, and the vineyards produce delicate, refined *eaux-de-vie*. Since this is the largest area, there are huge differences in climate between the eastern and western sections, as well as from north to south. In other words, it's dangerous to generalize.

Most firms use the robust, quick-maturing style for their higher-volume blends but the exceptions, such as Gourmel, show that Fins Bois can produce light, floral, graceful Cognacs, which can hold their own against the more prestigious *crus*.

Fins Bois itself is surrounded by the Bons Bois, and here quality begins to decrease, although again there are exceptions to this rule if chalk is involved. Most of the *eaux-de-vie* from here is used to give punch and drive to a blend.

The final *cru* is Bois Ordinaires, where the chalk has given way to sand, and the sea plays an important role. It's not the ideal combination for quality.

The proof of the influence of *terroir* is demonstrated by the fact that this vast range of spirits is produced by the same form of distillation, and by and large from the same grape variety – Ugni Blanc. The main pre-*phylloxera* variety, Folle Blanche, can still be found, but it proved to be difficult to graft on to American rootstocks and is prone to rot, so Ugni Blanc took over. It's not a particularly exciting variety as far as wine goes, but it has the advantage of being a late ripener, and therefore retains its acidity when it is being harvested.

High (though not excessive) acidity is essential for distillation for two reasons. Acidity acts as a natural preservative, making it more difficult for the wine to oxidize. Given that no sulphur (the normal protection against oxidation) can be added to a wine that's going to be distilled, the distiller must rely on acidity to guarantee that the wine is as fresh as possible. Acidity also has an impact on the aromas and flavours produced by distillation which, after all, is about concentrating the flavours and aromas in a fermented wash.

High levels of acidity mean that the wine is low in sugar (and therefore in alcohol), and a distiller wants a low-alcohol wine, as it is easier to concentrate. An alcoholic wine will give a flabby brandy. As Nicholas Faith points out in *Cognac*: "A wine of 12 per cent distilled to 70 per cent ABV is only concentrated six times, while a wine of 9 percent ABV is concentrated nearly 8 times." Cognac, on average, is made from a wine of around 8 per cent ABV.

A few producers distil on their own property, but most of the wine is taken to the professional distiller. Although the regulations allow distillation to be done until 31 March of the year after vintage, ideally you want to get the wine distilled as quickly as possible after the ferment.

All Cognac is distilled in the *alembic charentais*. This elegant, rather exotic-looking still consists of a boiler (*chaudière*), with an onion-shaped head (the *chapiteau*, which reminds you of the domes on Brighton Pavilion) and a long, thin neck (*col de cygne*) that swoops into the condenser. Some stills have a preheater, which sits in between the boiler and the condenser.

The vapour from the boiler passes through this preheater, which contains wine waiting to be distilled. The hot vapour gently heats the wine, while the cool wine acts as the start of a slow condensation. Not all distilleries like to use them. Martell, for one, has no preheaters, Bisquit uses one only for the first distillation, while Camus uses one for both. As ever, each producer puts a slightly different spin on proceedings.

This also applies to whether the wine is distilled on its lees or not. Some firms will distil some of their *eaux-de-vie* without lees, some with a little and others with the full lees. It all depends on the style of the distillate that's required. A wine with heavy lees will give an *eau-de-vie* with higher congeners which, in turn, take longer to break down in cask. If you are making an *eau-de-vie* destined for a young Cognac, you'll tend to cut down (or eliminate) the lees.

"A clear wine may give too lean a spirit," says Bernard Hine, master-blender at Hine. "Fine lees in the wine give fruity aromas, but too much may make the distillate too heavy. A proper balance between the average strength of the *eau-de-vie* and a reasonable quality of fine lees in the wine will give the aromatic Cognac, which contributes to the Hine style."

The first distillation yields a slightly cloudy spirit known as *brouillis*. Then comes the all-important second distillation (*bonne chauffe*), which must be done in stills that contain no more than 25hl of *brouillis*. As with any batch distillation, the aim here is to remove the heart (*coeur*) from the heads and the tails (*secondes*).

Each house will have its own specifications, and run the stills at different speeds and to different strengths, although on average the spirit comes off the still at 70 per cent ABV. The *secondes* are then added either to the wine or to the *brouillis* and, once more, the percentage added will vary between houses and distillates and give different results.

Normally, the spirit is placed in new, toasted, 350-litre Limousin oak barrels (although Martell prefers Troncais). Limousin is a medium-grained oak (good for a long, steady oxidation), which is rich in tannin – again making it beneficial for long ageing.

In general the young spirit will spend only one year in new wood – any longer, and you run the risk of it extracting too much from the barrel. It's then decanted into older barrels. Again, this will depend on the house. Frapin is unusual in giving its young spirit two years in new wood, while Delamain only uses used casks (*futs roux*) in its maturing, as the house feels that new wood gives excessive tannin.

Ageing

The process of ageing is a complex one (see Making Spirits, P416). The spirit is extracting tannins, colour and flavouring from the wood, while also being slowly oxidized. A young Cognac will therefore be filled with the spicy vanillin character that comes from new oak, but in time the barrel begins to endow the spirit with its other components, making it richer, sweeter and more complex. After around 20 years in barrel the famed rich, raisined, fruit and nut (some think Roquefort cheese) rancio character begins to emerge.

Some barrels can continue to give this slow, steady exchange for 40 years, but they are the exception – and any longer than that will give too much wood character. These ancient Cognacs are decanted into glass demijohns and stored in an inner sanctum, the appropriately named Paradis.

Where the barrels are placed is important as well. The warehouse, too, has a microclimate. Relatively humid conditions are needed, which allow a steady, gentle maturation. Over-dry conditions mean that the spirit evaporates too quickly and becomes dry and hard. Too damp, and it absorbs too much water and becomes flabby. The siting of these ageing cellars is therefore a major contributory factor to the final quality of the Cognac – and the old ones by the river are demonstrably the best.

While old Cognacs acquire their colour and complexity from the exchange between spirit, wood and air, the law allows young Cognacs to be adulterated with caramel and a substance known as *boise* – made from wood shavings and brandy. This allegedly gives the Cognac the impression of being older than it is, but it doesn't. All *boise* and caramel does is to distance the Cognac from the *terroir*.

The Cognac also has to be reduced in strength before it is bottled, a process that some shippers feel is one of the most important elements of all. Reduction is a carefully executed technique, which can take years to complete. Methods vary and, although distilled water can be used, most of the top houses use a mix of Cognac and water (*faibles*) to bring it down to bottling strength. Delamain takes two years to complete the reduction, while Gourmel's Age des Fruits is slowly reduced over a period of three years, and its top brand Quintessence is brought down to bottling strength over seven years. "The quality of the Cognac depends on the quality of the reduction," says Pierre Voisin at Gourmel. "This long reduction creates a significant formation of fatty acids, essential oils and natural sugars."

It's often thought that Cognac is blended at this point. In fact, most Cognacs are blended from the word go. The master-blender will start making up his blend immediately after distillation, either mixing different distillates from the same region, or blending between regions. This process will continue throughout the ageing process, when it's decanted from new to old wood, and after reduction and prior to bottling. The art of blending Cognac is the use of nose and memory to meld the different distillates from the various *terroirs* into a consistent house style – reflecting the gentle, unhurried beauty of the region.

The taste

Cognac has long been seen as the pinnacle of spirits. When bourbon or rum producers want to demonstrate how elegant and sophisticated their top brands are, they invariably say that they are "comparable to a fine Cognac". You'll never find a Cognac producer saying that its wares are like a fine rum! However, if you ask the major Cognac houses why their region produces such magnificent spirits, invariably they'll start by defining the legal requirements of the *appellation*. It's a strange response, as AOC rules – which govern the boundaries of the *crus*, varieties, distillation and ageing – are there to guarantee typicity, and not to define quality.

Even the grading designations are there to set minimum requirements; it's entirely up to the individual house how it wants to make its brands. In theory a Cognac can be sold when it is 30 months old, but the youngest element of 3-Star/VS is usually between three and five years old (although there are indications that this has dropped in recent times). VSOP can be four-and-a-half years old, although most brands are between seven and 10 years. Brands carrying terms like XO, Napoleon, etc., can be as young as six years old, but are usually between 15 and 20. Then, at the top of the tree, that tiny group of astronomically priced Extra, Grand Reserve, etc., is likely to have as its youngest component a Cognac which is 40 years old or more. As you can see, it's vague, it's open to interpretation, and once you get past VSOP there are so many names that the only indication that you are getting something really old is from the expensive price tag.

In Cognac, as in any spirits-producing area/category, there are stunning, good and less-than-good examples. The joy is that there are so many extraordinary brandies produced in a huge range of styles. The question is, how do you choose?

THE HOUSE STYLE

The simple answer is to find a house style you like – whether it's the richness of Courvoisier or the delicacy of Hine or Delamain – and then start to find other smaller brands that align themselves with these. In time, you'll find that there's a Cognac for every occasion.

Not all the houses own their own distilleries. Some, like Martell, contract distillation out to distillers in each of the *crus*, while others, like Delamain, select mature *eaux-de-vie* before buying. For a professional distiller it's a good income.

A producer such as Duboigalant, although making a magnificent range under its own name, actually distils the bulk of its annual production to the specifications of one or more of the major houses.

Each firm has its own preference as to the *cru* and also the method of distillation. It will also specify how the wine is to be distilled – an *eau-de-vie* destined for a short ageing will be made in a different fashion from one that's going to sit in the barrel for 40 years. The amount of lees used and the percentage of *secondes* will not only vary between houses, but between the distillates in each of the houses. This will also depend on sales projections. A major house such as Martell will have estimated how much VS it can sell in three years' time, so it can deduce how much quick-maturing *eau-de-vie* it needs from each vintage.

Of the major houses, Courvoisier is the heaviest (due to its running a high percentage of *secondes* through the stills), then Martell, followed by Hennessy, Rémy-Martin, Hine and the smaller Delamain. As well as this style being dictated by small differences in distillation, each of the houses will have its own preferences in *crus*.

Martell, for example, while sourcing from the four main *crus*, uses a significantly higher percentage of *eaux-de-vie* from Borderies in the blend. The firm reserves 60 per cent of the *cru*'s production each year, and the Borderies' distinctive fat quality is immediately apparent in all of its brands, giving a waxy roundness to a brand like Cordon Bleu.

Courvoisier will vary the percentage of *crus* depending on the brand. *Eaux-de-vie* from Fins Bois tend to be used for VS; the VSOP and the powerful, deep Napoleon are both Fine Champagne, while the top brands (the richly complex XO & Initiale) are Fine Champagne & Borderies. Rémy-Martin and Hine, on the other hand, specialize in Fine Champagne *eaux-de-vie*, giving their Cognacs a distinct delicacy. In Rémy's case this is accentuated by the use of small stills and high lees content, which provides a signature citric element in all its brands, from the benchmark VSOP to the fruity, floral drive of the XO. Hine's range demonstrates the superb balance given by Fine Champagne Cognac, as refined a selection as you could wish for – with VSOP and Antique personifying the house's discreet charm.

Delamain chooses to use *eaux-de-vie* only from Grande Champagne – and has to age them for considerably longer before it can release them. Its youngest brand, Pale & Dry, is an average of 25 years old and personifies Delamain's signature of graceful poise. There are few better at crystallizing Cognac's elegance.

And that's just the start. There are close to 150 Cognac houses, each of which offers an extensive range. They range from the big-hitting, fruity Bisquit, the robust, cigar-smoke-accented Cognacs from the Polignac co-op, to the drier elegance of Camus and the spicy drive of Otard. This firm also now owns Exshaw, one of the great Grande Champagne producers, noted for its complex, expansive style. Exshaw, along with Hine, is a specialist in Early Landed Cognac – light, dry, gentle vintage Cognacs, which have been shipped and matured in Britain.

Among the smaller producers is A. de Fussigny, whose range (which includes single-barrel bottlings) all share a sweet mouth-feel, tinged with the wild aromas of the countryside.

While Fussigny sources Cognacs from the two Champagnes and Fins Bois, Leopold Gourmel specializes in Cognacs from the best sites in Fins Bois. Owner Pierre Voisin's abiding obsession is with examining how Cognacs evolve and develop flavours during maturation – to the extent that he has abandoned the standard VS, VSOP, XO designations and named his brands after the dominant aromas that emerge with extended ageing. The youngest is Age du Fruit, then Age des Fleurs and Age d'Epices. There may be an element of auto-suggestion, but these are the aromas of these balanced Cognacs.

What Gourmel does for Fins Bois, Ragnaud-Sabourin and Duboigalant do for Grande Champagne. The former produces a superbly poised range – one of which is le Paradis, whose blend includes some pre-*phylloxera* Cognac. Duboigalant, meanwhile, is profound and elegant.

The tranquil, winding Charente is mirrored in the slow swirl of an amber-coloured Cognac in the glass. The region's calm and measured approach to life is reflected in the finest of its brandies. The greatest of them retain the purity of the distillate, the *terroir* and the wood. No single element is dominant; they are the personification of harmony.

ARMAGNAC

France's lesser-known brandy hails from Gascony – an unspoilt region, off the tourist track. Winding through the narrow lanes of its fourteenth-century villages is like stepping back in time – it's hardly surprising then that Armagnac claims to be France's oldest brandy.

The history

Armagnac takes its name from Hermann, an ancient feudal lord whose name was Latinized to Arminius when the Romans arrived bearing vines. Just like Cognac, it's a product of self-sufficiency – the grapes for distillation are grown locally, and the wood for the barrels originally came from the local forests. Its best brandies retain this deep sense of identity.

The first recorded instance of spirits production was in 1411, and it's logical to assume that the secret of distillation was transported over the Pyrénées from Moorish Spain – though woe betide you suggest to a Gascon that distillation is anything but a French invention!

After a period producing medicinal potions, Armagnac's fame began to spread, so that by the seventeenth century the Dutch were buying the pot-still brandy. So, if Armagnac had this head start on Cognac,

TASTING NOTES – ARMAGNAC

Vintage

Ch. Laubade 1975 Some rancio and a gorgeous mix of butter and crème anglaise among the prunes.

Ch. Laubade 1967 Exotically perfumed – violets, prunes, wild herbs and spice. Powerful and elegant, it expands in the mouth exposing a creamy heart. Extraordinary and complex.

Dom. de Boigneres 1984 Floor polish, saddle soap and earth. Massive concentration of multi-layered, dark fruit on the palate. Awesome.

Janneau 1976 Refined, with earth, nut and a dark undertow of beechwood mulch. On the palate the fruit is soft and plummily rounded with a grip of chilli on the finish.

Janneau 1966 Pulpy fruit, with a whiff of musk. Smoky and subtle. High-toned with gorgeous length.

Janneau 1958 Great colour. The wood shows slightly on the cigar-box, rancio nose. Full and powerful with the high-toned elegance that's typical of the house style.

Laressingle 1942 Extraordinary dark colour. A truffley, fungal nose with beechwood mulch. Subtle and soft, then beeswax. Amazing length.

Tariquet 1982 Buttery on the nose, with some vanilla and light plum. In the mouth the plum/prune fruit is almost honeyed before a hazelnut crunch finish.

Tariquet 1985 Earthy and rich. Heavy in the mouth with some nuts and flowers and really weighty fruit. Great structure.

Tariquet 1972 Touch of rancio – burnt matches, then treacle and beeswax. Well-balanced wood. Soft and elegant with walnut veneer and plums. Superb.

Tariquet 1975 Some rancio, but deeper fruit on the nose. Rich, rounded, soft and plump. Smoky, spicy with great length of plummy fruits. A solid citizen.

VSOP

Baron de Sigognac VSOP Spent matches on nose. Fine, pruney weight. Plump, elegant and profound.

Ch. Laubade VSOP Lightly wooded. Powerful fruits on the palate, good feel and fine weight. Mature, plummy depth.

Janneau VSOP Clean, light earthy tones with a touch of sandalwood. Easy.

Laressingle VSOP Well-balanced. Soft and round on the palate. Fairly simple.

M. de Caussade Big, fat and soft. Lightly honeyed with decent length.

Age Statement/Varietal

Janneau 8 year-old Soft and rich on the nose with some spicy wood. Walnut veneer and earth on the palate.

Janneau 15 year-old A haunting aroma filled with dried roses, apples, cinnamon, butterscotch and nuts. Weighty.

Tariquet Folle Blanche 8 year-old Gold. Picking up light mushroom notes and herbal tobacco leaf. Very soft and gentle with a precise lift.

Tariquet folle Blanche 12 year-old Graceful, deep, almost toffee-like nose. On the palate, it's attractive with chewy, nutty fruits and really fresh finish.

M. de Caussade 30 year-old Some rancio character on a fairly elegant, well-rounded nose. Clean.

XO/Reserve/Region

Ch. Laubade Hors d'Age Nicely rounded with a touch of crème brûlée. Soft in mouth with a fair bite.

Janneau XO Woodsmoke and earth with a hint of plum and light perfume. Good weight on the palate. Chewy, long, full and fat.

Janneau Reserve Complex aromas. Rich with a touch of rancio and a clear bell of fruit.

Laressingle 20ans Bas-Armagnac Soft, clean and long. A little woody, but good fruit and earth.

Laressingle Tenareze Rich, heavy and fruit-driven. Complex silky power.

Tariquet Hors d'Age Hints of sultana, vanilla and butterscotch. Supple in mouth. Clean, fresh finish.

why isn't it more famous? One reason is its geographical situation. Cognac came into being because it had direct access to the sea. Take one look at a map, and you can see that Armagnac isn't anywhere near a port. Originally the brandies would have had to be transported by land to Mont-de-Marsan and then by river either to Bayonne or Bordeaux. The latter had a tendency to silt up, so supplies were irregular for the export markets, while Cognac could always guarantee getting supplies out of La Rochelle. Because of this geographical disadvantage, Armagnac had to wait until the arrival of the railways and the building of canals before it could hit the affluent markets of the north. By the middle of the nineteenth century, production was booming, the vineyard area was growing and the bulk of the major houses was founded.

A significant development occurred at this time, which was to have immense repercussions on Armagnac's style – the arrival of the continuous still, credited to a M. Verdier, a chemist from Montpellier. The new invention was an immediate hit with the producers, so much so that by 1936 it was the only type of still allowed to be used – although now pot stills are once again permitted. By the 1930s, though, Armagnac was once again a forgotten area. Although it enjoyed a brief period of success when the Cognac vineyards were obliterated by *phylloxera*, the bug eventually decimated Armagnac as well. What with two world wars and a depression, it wasn't until the end of the Second World War that Armagnac started exporting in seriousness once more.

Even so, it remains a tiny producer when compared with Cognac but, while it can't compete in volume terms, it can offer a quality alternative. Armagnac isn't a poor man's Cognac; neither is it, as some seem to think, a more rustic version. It's a product of distinctive *terroir*, produced in a fundamentally different fashion, and is capable of reaching great heights.

At the moment, though, the region is burdened with a massive stock surplus. Convinced that the Far East was going to be a huge market, firms increased production – but then demand slumped. The BNIA, the region's controlling body, is currently trying to find ways of coping with the problem, but it seems obvious that the only way Armagnac will get itself out of its current crisis is to promote itself as a quality region.

HOW IT'S MADE

Once again you are faced with that indefinable term *terroir* – the physical (and philosophical) interaction between soil, exposure, climate, vine and man. In clinical terms, Armagnac is divided into three regions: Bas-Armagnac, Tenareze and Haut-Armagnac, with the best-quality *eaux-de-vie* coming from the first two.

Bas-Armagnac is covered in forest and rolling hills, dotted with vineyards on the higher slopes. The sand and clay soil, stuck with large pebbles, produces a supple, relatively quickly maturing style of *eau-de-vie*.

Armagnac, France's lesser-known brandy, comes from Gascony, a region which has a more moderate climate than the Cognac area

Tenareze, which arcs around Bas-Armagnac's eastern border, is higher and with a higher amount of chalk in its soil. Its *eau-de-vie* is significantly different – a more rounded, aromatic, fruit-driven style capable of long ageing.

Producers are allowed to make Armagnac from 12 varieties, but the majority make their *eaux-de-vie* from Folle Blanche, Ugni Blanc, Colombard and a hybrid variety Baco 22A, which has the advantage of being resistant to the mould that can hit the region in the autumn months. However, hybrids have now been banned by the EU, and while the Armagnac producers are fighting their corner, most are looking into alternatives – Ch. de Laubade has had success with the little-used Plant de Graisse.

Harvest normally takes place in October, and because Armagnac enjoys a slightly more moderate climate than Cognac, the grapes are higher in potential alcohol when they are picked, at around nine per cent ABV. There is, however, still good acidity. Ideally

Janneau is the only brandy house to release a pot-still Armagnac

distillation should take place as soon as the wines have finished fermenting, in order to preserve the light estery aromas, but until recently distillation could take place up until 30 April. In an attempt to curb excess production, this date has now been brought back to 31 January, which conceivably could have a positive effect on quality. The danger with letting wine sit around until

the distiller – who is not always the grower or producer – is ready means that you run the risk of the wine oxidizing. Stale wine produces stale brandy.

However, it's the stills that produce the most significant difference between Armagnac and Cognac. The vast majority of distillers continue to use the "traditional" *Alambic Armagnaçais* or column still.

On paper, this is no different from any other column still, but there is a significant difference between an Armagnac column still and most others. They are tiny. Because of this, the distillate is significantly lower than you would normally expect from a column still – it can be as low as 52 per cent ABV, but on average distillers collect the spirit at between 55 and 63 per cent ABV. Here is where many of Armagnac's rich, earthy characteristics come from. The problem is being able to control the quality of the distillate at this low strength. "It's true that single distillation can produce poor quality if it is distilled either too fast or at too low a strength," says Patrick Heron, *maître de chais* at Janneau. "But if you are looking for an Armagnac that you can sell in 15 years' time you'll distil to 55–60 per cent. If you want one to age for longer, you'll drop to 55 per cent, but no lower." It takes a master craftsman to be able to produce flavoursome, elegant spirit at this strength without collecting any pungent fusel oils.

Pot stills (or *double chauffe*) remain mildly controversial. They are permitted, but in practice only five or six producers use them. Janneau is the only house to release a pot-still Armagnac, although other firms, such as Laressingle, use pot-still *eau-de-vie* as a blending component. The type of still used is the same as that for Cognac, but because of the low-strength spirit that's obtained from the column stills, for once a pot still actually gives a lighter, higher-strength distillate which is better suited to a short period of ageing. But pot stills are mostly dismissed by other producers. Yves Grassa at Tariquet, for example, makes some of the finest Armagnacs in the region from an ancient wood-fired column still. "*Double chauffe* can eliminate the fruit esters, which can be the most interesting part of the distillate," he says. "And because you can separate the tastes at the beginning and end, you can get a more neutral result. I'd argue that if you use good wine you can get the finesse of pot still plus the richness of alembic from the continuous still – but then you have to age it for longer!"

The debate as to whether column is better than pot rather misses the point. The bottom line should be whether it is of good quality and whether it has typicity. Good pot-still Armagnac, most notably from Janneau, just gives a different spin on that typicity.

This consists of two chambers, one containing a preheating chamber and the serpentine condenser, and the other a boiler (or boilers) and perforated plates. The wine is gently heated and flows into the distilling column, where it passes down through gaps between the plates, getting the alcohol stripped away by the rising heat. The vapour then passes back into the serpentine where it is cooled, condensed and collected.

Virtually every producer will distil wines from the different regions and varieties separately, and won't blend the *eaux-de-vie* until the Armagnac is ready to be bottled. Traditionally, Armagnac was aged in the local Monlezun oak, which allegedly gave its own particular richness to the spirit but, due to expansion, most producers now use either Limousin or Troncais wood.

The new spirit will first be put in new wood, then after an initial period of ageing (which varies between producers) each batch will be decanted, mixed and then placed in older barrels.

As the Armagnac ages, so the spirit will regularly be decanted into progressively older (and often larger) barrels in order to cut down the impact of the oak, but still to allow slow and steady oxidation. The very top casks will be good for up to 40 years, but after that the Armagnac is removed and put into large glass jars and stored in the holy of holies – known as "Paradis".

The quality of the wood is central to the production of high-quality Armagnac. Yves Grassa, for example, insists on only using barrels made with air-dried staves, often sourced from different regions, and made by different coopers, with barrels being given different toasts.

Sadly, though, you get the feeling that the industrial-sized producers are more concerned with keeping costs down, so the prevailing ethos is: get it made, get it in cask for a short time and get it sold. That means that not only is wood often only of secondary importance, but the spirit is given insufficient time to mellow and age. The fact that Armagnac is made from a low-strength distillate means it takes time to evolve in barrel. It is a spirit that is meant to be aged for a long time. *Boise* is permitted, and is widely used to give the impression of oak ageing, but it doesn't even do that. The consensus among top producers is that Armagnac only begins to give an indication of its true potential after a minimum of seven years.

The quality designations are assessed in the same way as Cognac, with VS being allowed to be bottled after 18 months, although in practice most producers hold it for around three years. The youngest brandy in a VSOP is on average seven years old, or 10 years for an Hors d'Age/XO. In private, most quality-oriented firms will tell you that they would love to see VSOP as the starting point, but that's extremely unlikely.

Armagnac, however, has another trick up its sleeve. Since the *eaux-de vie* are kept separate until they are ready to be blended, it's possible to release Vintage Armagnacs. Most firms will have a regular range of vintages, but some small producers like Marcel Trepout have decided to specialize in this field. Walk into Trepout's "Paradis", and you are faced with a sea of raffia-covered jars with neck labels that date back to 1865. Paradis indeed for the Armagnac lover, although it has to be said that most producers, while seeing Vintage as a handy selling point (the market in Vintage has grown significantly in recent years) personally prefer their blends.

That said, tasting a great vintage Armagnac is an unforgettable experience. The extraordinarily complex Ch. Laubade 1967, with its rancio nose filled with violets, prunes and cinnamon and creamy, elegant palate; or the 1972 Ch. du Tariquet, with its nose of pine honey/beeswax and rich, plummy, walnut palate – are both proof of the region's ability to produce magnificent Vintage spirits.

It would be wrong to think that Armagnac is sitting back and waiting for people to (re)discover it. Go-ahead firms are trying to find new ways of generating interest in the region. Janneau has, controversially, launched a three-strong, 100 per cent pot-still range – a soft and gentle five-year-old; an oily, earthy, rich eight-year-old and a hauntingly complex 15-year-old (from Tenareze) which mixes dried roses, apples and cinnamon with a nutty, pruney palate.

Grassa, meanwhile, has released a range of single-varietal Folle Blanche – a charming, toasty/smoky four-year-old; a gentle grapey/plummy eight-year-old that also has hints of tobacco leaf and mushroom, and a 12-year-old that has typical Armagnac richness mixed with beech nuts and an amazing fresh finish. Not to be outdone, Laressingle has gone down the regional route with its silkily powerful 20-year-old Tenareze.

The bottom line is that these (and other) producers are all driven by a passion for their region. They all want to produce brandies that speak of their place, and when you get your nose into a glass of old Armagnac and breathe in the aromas of violets, prunes, figs, plums, truffle and the beech wood mulch – you are instantly transported back to the woods of Gascony – The *terroir* is retained in the glass.

BRANDY DE JEREZ

When you think of the ancient centres of distilling spirits in Europe, you tend to consider Ireland, Italy and France; Spain doesn't get a second thought. But if you are looking for the origins of brandy-making, then you have to go to Moorish Andalucia and the city of Jerez.

It was the Phoenicians who brought vines to Southern Spain, but it was the Moors who brought their *al-ambiqs* (stills) and started distilling – initially for cosmetics, perfumes and medicines. Given that the Moors were benign rulers, it is inevitable that this art was practised by the non-Muslim occupants of Spain at that time. Certainly, there is evidence that stills have been used in Jerez since 900AD – long before anyone in Cognac had even heard of a still.

This early brandy was originally low-quality wine that was used solely for fortifying the local wine (now known as sherry), a process which stabilized it when it was transported. It wasn't until the arrival in the seventeenth century of those indefatigable traders and brandy drinkers, the Dutch, that exports of brandy from Jerez started. In fact, so much brandy was shipped in sherry casks to the Netherlands that the best *eaux de vie* used in Brandy de Jerez is still known as *holandas* while, in a direct link with its Moorish origins, the pot stills used are called *alquitaras*.

Jerez remained a supplier of bulk spirit until the nineteenth century, when a number of sherry firms decided to copy what was happening in Cognac and began ageing the brandy *in situ*. Domecq likes to tell the story of butts of brandy being sent back to Jerez after the *bodega* and its Dutch customer had fallen out. The casks mouldered in the back of a warehouse until they were chanced upon. They were tasted and the first Brandy de Jerez brand, Fundador (the founder), was born.

These days, though, times are tough. Never rivalling Cognac in the export markets, Brandy de Jerez has relied on Spain's insatiable thirst for large glasses of brandy to be drunk after their meal. Brandy is inextricably bound up in Spanish culture. Keen

Look to Jerez for the origins of brandy-making

filmgoers will recall how the action in the cult flick *Jamon Jamon* took place under the *cojones* of one of the black bulls advertising Osborne brandy that dot the hills across Spain. It's an image that, quite simply, sums up Spain.

But, in a repetition of what has happened to all the "old" spirits, in recent years young drinkers have decided that the time was right to look for something else. The ending of the Franco era brought a wave of liberalization to Spain, and a newly affluent, young population was suddenly able to buy imported brands. Brandy was the main victim as the young turned to blended Scotch as their drink of choice. Spend some time at a bar in Spain (even in Jerez itself) and you'll find that almost everyone will be drinking Scotch and cola.

The domestic brandy market has fallen by 50 per cent in the past 20 years as young drinkers turn their backs on a drink they see as old, boring and representative of the Old Spain. To its credit, Brandy de Jerez's controlling body has started a promotional campaign to promote the style, while some top brands have been repackaged and promoted not just in Spain, but internationally. Only time will tell if it's too late.

HOW IT'S MADE

The wine for today's Brandy de Jerez doesn't actually come from the chalky, dusty hills of Jerez, but the flat, hot plains of La Mancha. The reason is simple. Jerez is a demarcated region – *bodegas* (producers) can't just keep planting vines and calling their wine sherry, so, when international sales grew for both sherry and brandy, it was impossible for the region to cope with the demand for both styles. The Jerez vineyards (and the Palomino variety) had to be kept for sherry production, but grapes for distilling could be found elsewhere. Now brandy producers either own, or have shares in, distilleries in the town of Tomellosa.

Although Brandy de Jerez is a distilled wine, it bears very little resemblance to any of Europe's other top brandies. For a start, the hot climate of La Mancha produces grapes – mainly from Airen, although Bobadilla and Gonzalez Byass (G-B) also use Palomino – which are considerably higher in alcohol and lower in acidity than those used in Cognac and Armagnac.

This base wine can be distilled in two ways – either using a pot still (*alquitaras*) or column (*continuous*) still. This gives three types of distillate – *holandas*, which must be distilled in an *alquitaras* still to between 60 and 70 per cent ABV; and two types of *aguardiente* from the column – the first of which can be no more than 85 per cent ABV, the other between 86 and 94.5 per cent ABV.

Needless to say, the stronger the spirit, the lower the number of flavour compounds. To ensure that the final brandy is full of flavour, by law more than 50 per cent of the final blend must comprise spirits that are below 86 per cent ABV. The result of these regulations is that bodegas can then play with different percentages of thethree distillates for their brands – some might be pure *holandas*, some a blend of the three, some a blend of the two *aguardientes*. A rule of thumb is that Solera brands (like Domecq's Fundador or G-B's Soberano) will be column-still *aguardiente*, while the top Gran Reserva brands (Domecq's Carlos I and G-B's Lepanto) are 100 per cent *holandas*.

The first blending takes place immediately after distillation, when the spirits are taken to Jerez to start their unique ageing process. The new spirit is blended according to the criteria for each brand. The young Solera brandies can be aged for as little as six months, but on average spend a year in *solera*; Solera Reserva can be bottled after more than one year, although most producers keep them in the *solera* for two-and-a-half years; the top designation of Solera Gran Reserva can be released after a minimum of three years, but the average is eight years, and the best brands are aged for considerably longer. Conde de Osborne Cristal, for example, is an average of 10 years old, while the same firm's Dali is on average at least 20 years old.

But what is this *solera* system? It's another great Jerez invention that can best be described as fractional blending. Rather than ageing brandy in one barrel – or decanting it totally from young to old barrels – in Jerez the casks are never completely emptied, and no more than one third of the brandy can be removed from the cask at any one time. Once again, it gets a bit technical. Each *solera* comprises a series of collections of butts, each horizontal tier (or scale) of which holds brandies of the same approximate age. The *solera* scale itself is traditionally on the floor and contains the oldest brandy. This is where the brandy comes from when it is ready to be bottled. After brandy is taken from each barrel in the *solera* scale, it is refreshed with the same amount of brandy from all the barrels in the next oldest scale – the first *criadera* – and so on back down the system to the newest brandy being poured into the top scale.

The principle is fiendishly simple. The young brandy, rather than dominating the flavours in the cask, gets absorbed into the character of the old. Also, because the casks are never emptied, there will always be some of the original brandy in the cask – this becomes increasingly important as you move up the quality scale. The regular decanting also increases

TASTING NOTES – BRANDY DE JEREZ

Solera Reserva

Lustau Burnt, more than a touch of PX, some complexity and crispness from young spirit.

Magno Smooth, but not complex. Rich with a hint of plummy fruit. Soft in the mouth. Simple but attractive.

Fundador Young, nutty. Clean and simple.

Solera Gran Reserva

(1=Dry 5=Sweet)

Lepanto Clean, nutty and dry, but gently subtle. Fresh finish. (1)

Cardenal Mendoza PX and coffee beans on the nose. Rich and deep with chewy complexity and a fresh dry finish. (5)

Osborne Dali Quite complex on the nose. Clean wood on show. Smooth, sweet as a nut. Very long and rich. (3)

Carlos I Imperial Soft, rich plummy/figgy fruit. Very soft to start, followed by lifted, delicate top notes. Long and clean. (3)

Carlos I Rounded, with walnut/Dundee cake notes on the nose. Chewy and clean with good range of flavours and soft, vanilla fruit. (3)

Senor Lustau Subtle, soft and elegant on nose with hint of burnt Madeira-like fruit. Very soft on the palate, but with decent grip. (4)

Conde de Osborne Medium intensity on the nose. A full, sweet, raisined impact with clean grip. (3/4)

Gran Duque d'Alba Full and sweet, little more than raisins steeped in alcohol. (5)

---

oxidation and changes the nature of the ageing process – but it doesn't, as many people think, speed the process up. Rather, the regular addition of newer spirit affects the interaction between wood and spirit.

Equally, it's also thought that the best brandies come from the *soleras* with the highest number of scales. Not true. It's the number of times the brandy is moved that affects quality. Osborne's Solera Reserva brand Magno is moved fairly speedily through its *solera*, while the top brand, Gran Reserva Cristal, is moved very little. Inevitably, each bodega approaches brandy production differently. The initial distillate will be different, as will the blend between *holandas* and *aguardiente*. Each will manage the *solera* in its own way, and the kind of wood used will also differ.

The majority of bodegas use butts that have held oloroso sherry, but Gonzalez Byass prefers fino for its top brand Lepanto, while Sanchez-Romate goes to the other extreme and uses the sweetest sherry style of all, Pedro Ximenez (PX), for its Cardenal Mendoza. Osborne's Cristal *solera* comprises 25-year-old butts that have had PX maturing in them for at least five years.

Tasting through different *soleras*, you can see not only how the brandy evolves, but how the wood has an impact on the maturing spirit. In Domecq's Carlos I *Solera*, the rich, walnut/sultana oloroso shows when the spirit is on average five years old. By the third *criadera*, the wood begins to appear, while on the first *criadera* and *solera* level, the three components – wood, sherry and spirit – have fused to give plummy, figgy aromas.

At Gonzalez Byass, the youngest scale of the Lepanto *solera* has vivacious fruit and aromas of grilled hazelnut. As it passes down the *solera* it begins to shed the crisp nuttiness and pick up a mellow fruitiness combined with the elegance you can only get from extended ageing in good-quality casks.

At Sanchez-Romate they put a slightly different spin on things. The young spirit is first aged statically for two years in PX casks before entering the *solera*. Now PX isn't exactly a subtle form of sherry, and it makes an immediate impact on the spirit, so that by the time it hits the first scale of the *solera* it's already filled with rich, raisiny flavours. Then it seems to quieten down, slowly extracting the unctuous sherry flavours out of the wood. By the third *criadera* it's sexy, silky, with a mix of walnut whip and raisin. By *solera*, the wood has done its work, giving a clean bite to the brandy, while not masking its huge flavour.

These Gran Reservas then get a final addition of a brandy from an even older "mother" *solera*. Not only will this *solera* have gained in richness and intensity over the years, it too will work its magic on the younger brandies. For Cristal, this is a tiny *solera* of 28 butts from which a minuscule drop is taken and blended in. At Sanchez-Romate, the firm's top brand Non Plus Ultra, is part of a *solera* that was laid down 150 years ago. The brandy is as dark as a Goya etching, and smells of liquorice and treacle, but although dominated by PX, it has an astoundingly long, fresh, tangy finish. One drop is all that's needed. The flavour stays in the mouth for hours.

Each house has its own approach, and it's little surprise that Brandy de Jerez is a totally different beast from Cognac or Armagnac. But are the brandies any good? Well, it's much the same as any category. The firms who take great care with their distillation and use the top-quality spirits get the best results. To be honest, if you are working with young spirit and you only give it six months in wood, then you'll end up with a young spirit no matter what – even in a *solera* system.

Sadly, there's an awful lot of Brandy de Jerez at the bottom end of the market that is nothing more than raw alcohol, a touch of wood and a splash of sweetening agent. Even at the top end there are firms who appear to take short-cuts in the ageing process and believe that "old" simply means "sweet", and don't concern themselves with producing aged brandies with the grip and structure that defines a high-quality style.

In order to prosper, Brandy de Jerez must turn its domestic problems around, and become a force on the international market. At home young brandies are now being promoted as the perfect mixer for cola, which is fine as they do mix well. They are also an essential part of the traditional Spanish breakfast – the *caragillo* (an espresso coffee with a shot of brandy). The top end contains some classy brandies that deserve more attention; brandies which are, quite simply, easier to drink than the Cognacs and Armagnacs of similar age – and of similar complexity.

The important thing during the process is to maintain tradition. Brandy de Jerez is a unique style, almost more akin to wine than spirits. It's not Cognac, but the best examples are easy-drinking, surprisingly complex spirits, which deserve to be better known.

The rest of Spain

It is not only Jerez that produces brandy. Catalonia is home to two producers, Mascaro and Torres – both with a high reputation. Catalonia shares several techniques with France in brandy terms, but neither firm slavishly copies what is done across the Pyrénées.

The Poli distillery is at the forefront of the grappa turnaround; grappa has become popular with non-Italians and Italians alike

Torres has a six-strong range of brandies, two of which are made in continuous stills, the other four being made in Charentais stills. Torres 10 is the more obviously "Spanish", being a column distillate aged in *solera* in heavily toasted US oak, and can be seen as a halfway house between a Brandy de Jerez and an Armagnac. Miguel Torres Imperial, however, is double-distilled in pot stills, then aged statically in Limousin oak.

Mascaro, which distils entirely from its own wine, is proud to align itself with Cognac. Like the Torres brands, it is a Parellada distillate, the grapes picked at low alcohol, double distilled in a Charentais still, followed by static ageing in a mix of Limousin and Alliers oak.

GRAPPA

For years grappa was one of those spirits that non-Italians tried to avoid. In fact, to be honest the majority of Italians tried to avoid it as well. It wasn't an issue of image or a lack of trendiness; it was, quite simply, that it didn't taste any good.

We have all tried to sip it at the end of a meal, but few of us have enjoyed the experience. Grappa, like its French equivalent, marc, had the astonishing effect of inducing a hideous hangover before you even got drunk. But that was then, this is now. Grappa, like some spirituous ugly duckling, has cast off its dull, unattractive past and emerged as a pure, elegant drink that deserves to take its place among some of the world's best spirits. The story of this fairy-tale transformation is a distillation of what has happened in Italian winemaking over the past decade.

HOW IT'S MADE

Italy has an ancient history of spirits production that dates back to monks in Salerno in the ninth century. Even today, it's a country where you'll find the widest (and most bizarre) range of spirits, from brandies to bitters, liqueurs to rustic concoctions that hark back to the earliest spirits of all. Then there's grappa. As ever, we can't be sure when the first grappa was produced, but it appears always to have been a speciality of the regions in the north of the country, from Piemonte in the west to Friuli and Trentino in the east. Grappa is certainly produced elsewhere, but this is its spiritual heartland.

Many spirits have started life as products of excess or surplus raw materials – barley, rye, potatoes, poor-quality wine. Grappa is similar, up to a point. In fact, it's closer to the rums of the British West Indies, as it too is made from the waste material produced by another process. In rum it's molasses that are left after sugar is made; in grappa's case, it's the pressings that are left at the end of winemaking.

Strictly speaking, therefore, grappa isn't a brandy as it isn't made from distilled wine. It's the runt of the litter, the afterthought. You can imagine how it first came into being. A winemaker was looking at the pile of skins (*vinaccia*) left over after his wine had been pressed. He could either throw them out, put them on the fields as fertilizer – or distil them. This has been grappa's greatest problem. Producers would only think of making their grappa after the important business of winemaking was finished, or when the mobile still came into their village. But *vinaccia*, like wine itself, oxidizes if left for too long. The result was that distillers were ending up working with poor-quality raw material and, contrary to popular belief, distilling can't improve inferior base material. That didn't stop industrial-sized producers springing up and handling vast quantities of *vinaccia* which was sent to them from all over the country. Rural winemakers and farmers would quite happily sit back and knock down a few glasses of their own grappa, people would pour one into an espresso and drink this *coretto* as a heart-starter in the morning. But it wasn't pleasant stuff.

Quite what happened to turn grappa production around is a chicken-and-egg question. From the mid-1970s, Italian wine underwent a renaissance in quality. Great wines had been made for centuries before, but this was the dawning of a new era. Stainless steel and temperature control started being used in wineries, vineyards were better managed – the intention was to produce the highest possible quality. Importantly, grapes going into red wine production didn't have the life pressed out of them.

At the same time a Friulian distiller, Nonino, decided to make a grappa that reflected this new Italian stylishness. His grappas, packaged in clear, hand-blown bottles, were the catalyst for a revolution in grappa production. Nonino's example was soon followed by Jacopo Poli who, by the late 1970s, was sneaking into his father's distillery late at night to experiment with these new-style grappas. The trend spread. In Trentino, Bertagnolli took up the cause, as did Maschio in Veneto.

All of a sudden the options were endless. The next step to take was logical enough. Since winemakers were beginning to separate each grape variety, there was a ready supply of different *vinaccia*. Nonino once again started single varietal off, with a grappa made from the rare Picolit variety. Winemakers then began producing single vineyard wines – the very same thing happened with grappa. The industry had changed from industrial production to something infinitely more sophisticated.

The starting point of this new grappa lies in ensuring that the *vinaccia* is fresh and moist, which means getting it from the winery to the distillery quickly. If the *vinaccia* isn't distilled within 24 hours of being pressed, then the aromatics disappear and the process of oxidation speeds up. It also means ensuring that there are no stalks or stems in the *vinaccia*, as they produce methanol. Since Poli's stills, for example, only hold 15kg, he will only buy enough *vinaccia* to supply one day's distillation. "It means we are only buying 10,000kg every day," he says, "And we're going against our own interests by doing this as we can't satisfy demand, but we are making the best quality we can."

Getting this quality inevitably means paying more for the *vinaccia*, but it's a price they are happy to accept. "The quality is defined by the grapes," says Antonio Moser at Bertagnolli. "It depends on how hard they have been pressed and how healthy they are – we can't use any grapes that have had mould. It's only when the wines improved that grappa could as well." The *vinaccia* from red varieties, such as Cabernet, Merlot, Nebbiolo and Teroldego, can be distilled immediately, but the *vinaccia* from white grapes usually has to be fermented first. This is because it's normal practice not to ferment the white wines with their skins when making new-style Italian white wine.

The top producers continue to distil in small pot stills (Nonino has 42 of them) or, in the case of Bertagnolli, a cunning combination of pot and column. This has a *bain marie* in the pot which allows the *vinaccia* to sit in an inner chamber surrounded by another wall that contains the steam. It allows a slow, even heating and avoids the problem of the *vinaccia* sticking to the sides of the still and producing off notes. Each variety will also be handled slightly differently, as the aromatics appear at different strengths. It may seem far-fetched to a newcomer to grappa, but there are marked differences between all the different single-varietal grappas.

The majority are reduced in strength and then bottled, but there's a growing trend to barrel-age certain varieties. In Trentino, Zeni has recently made a stunningly delicate example, while in Piemonte, Barolo producer Rocche dei Manzoni has a superb, hugely aromatic range of barrique-aged grappas. Nonino is even experimenting with ageing in ex-sherry wood!

The most recent step has been to start distilling whole grapes. The grapes are fermented in vacuum-sealed stainless-steel tanks and then placed in the pot still. Nonino has Ue (and has established a vineyard planted to Picolit, Ribolla Gialla and Fragolino specifically for Ue production); Maschio has Prime Uve, while Bertagnolli makes a Grappino. These *eaux-de-vie* have a purity of fruit and lightness of character in contrast to grappa's firm grip, although to be fair we are talking degrees of delicacy here.

The innovations are endless. If you ask for a grappa these days in any Italian restaurant, a shuddering trolley will be dragged out laden with bottles. There will be grappas from well-known varieties like Chardonnay, Cabernet, Merlot, Riesling, Muller-Thurgau and Nebbiolo, but then there will be a raft of some of Italy's myriad other grape varieties – Prosecco, Teroldego, Torcolato, Picolit, Schiopettino, Pignolo, Ribolla Gialla, some of which have been saved from extinction by grappa producers.

The best grappas personify what a great spirit should be, the capturing of the essence of the raw material. The heart of the grape variety is revealed in the finest examples. They are not big spirits; rather they are fragile, contemplative drinks. But, as Philip Contini, of Edinburgh's shrine to Italian food and drink Valvona & Crolla points out, they remain an acquired taste.

"These days you don't need to drink stinking rotgut, but grappa's a taste you either love or hate. There's no middle ground; it's the spirit world's equivalent of truffles."

Some superb Italian-style grappas are being produced in the United States – most notably by Clear Creek and the Bonny Doon winery. Elsewhere, the production of pomace brandies remains relatively small-scale and often resolutely rustic.

Most wine-producing regions have a speciality spirit made from the pressings of the year's vintage. However, most of Europe has yet to catch up with Italy when it comes to producing high-quality pomace brandy. There's nothing preventing them, though – they have the technology and the techniques. All that is needed is time and patience.

TASTING NOTES – GRAPPA

Whole Grape

Jacopo Poli Uva Viva Fragrant with citric aromas. Soft, balanced with perfumed finish.
Bertagnolli Grappino di Uva Fragrant and gentle in mouth with some pepperiness.
Maschio Prosecco/Riesling Uve Clean, peachy, light earth. Juicy and delicate.

Varietal

Endrizzi Chardonnay Restrained, quite aromatic. Good palate weight. Elegant.
Maschio Chardonnay Depth of fruit, some apricot. Juicy mid-palate. Clean finish.

Giovanni Poli Nosiola Earthy nose with plums and some nut. Fresh and well balanced on palate with light walnut on finish.
Bertagnolli Nosiola Light, almost like a grain spirit. Strong start gives way to lingering marzipan/violet flavours.
Zeni Muller-Thurgau Autumn leaves, wood bark and aromatic yellow fruits on nose. Sweet start before dry finish.
Jacopo Poli Torcolato Honeycomb and fragrant herbs on the nose. Pure, sweet fruit on palate with tremendous feel.
Casa Girelli Moscato Lemon tending to aftershave, but with good richness.

RUM

The merest mention of rum conjures up images of the lush calm of the Caribbean. A sweet, exotic spirit that insists you take it easy, it's the essence of relaxation. But beneath this benign image lurk tales of revolution, war, piracy, colonialism and slavery. Few other drinks have such a blood-soaked past or have wallowed in such misery.

Rum's hidden history starts 10,000 years ago when the sugar cane plant (*sacchorum officinarium*) began its migration from its home in the East Indies into China and India, acquiring a mythic power similar to the agave in Mexico. There are some commentators who believe that soma, the intoxicating, hallucinogenic drink of early Indo-European civilization, was the fermented juice of the sugar cane. "Like impetuous winds, like swift horses bolting with a chariot, the drink has lifted me up," it says in the Rig Veda, talking of a drink produced by crushing the stems of a long, leafless plant. Was it describing shamanic ecstasy brought on by drinking fermented cane juice? Certainly, Indian civilization knew of two other fermented sugar drinks, Sidhu and Gaudi.

As the plant spread west into Arabia, then North Africa, so it began to be cultivated for sugar production. The Spanish and Portuguese, who were cultivating it on the Canaries and Madeira in the early part of the fifteenth century, then took it with them as they sailed across the Atlantic to newly "discovered" Brazil and the Caribbean islands. Columbus himself planted cane in Hispaniola and Cuba on his second voyage across the Atlantic. Sugar and the colonization of the Caribbean have been inextricably linked ever since.

Early days

Sugar cane became the main Caribbean/South American crop as soon as the early Spanish settlers realized that, contrary to their wishes, there wasn't any gold to be mined. When rum (or its early equivalent) first appeared is less clear, but since molasses will ferment naturally if left to its own devices, it seems quite probable that the first people to discover the new alcoholic beverage were the slaves working on the plantations.

A distilled sugar cane brandy (*chiringuito*) made from molasses was made and drunk by slaves on Spanish settlements in Mexico, and in the Portuguese ones in Bahia almost as soon as they were established. It's probable, therefore, that the first Mexican spirit was rum, rather than mezcal. The same happened throughout the Caribbean islands.

By the end of the sixteenth century, this distilled sugar drink was building itself a fearsome reputation – one that led to it rejoicing in the name "kill-devil", a title that was also given to gin in West Africa.

By the seventeenth century, the French, English and Dutch had joined in the rush to colonize the small islands of the Caribbean. They, too, planted cane for sugar production, and where cane went distillation followed. It made perfect economic sense – by making rum from molasses, you'd get more money from one crop.

When Richard Ligon arrived in Barbados in 1647 and wrote his history of the island, he described the workings of a distillery and the taste of kill-devil, which he claims was a strong, unpleasant beverage, only consumed by the poor and "laying them asleep on the ground" almost immediately.

At this stage, the planters were still drinking imported brandy. Kill-devil was given to their slaves as a field medicine and as "payment" for their toil – a practice that was used by some employers in the South African wine industry during the years of apartheid. Another account of Barbados in the 1660s that is mentioned in *The Barbados Rum Book*, describes: "The chiefe fudling they make in the Island is Rumbulion, alias Kill Divill and this is made of suggar canes distilled, a hot hellish and terrible liquor."

Around the same time in French-owned Martinique, sugar cane was being used to make spirits such as Veson

Cutting sugar cane in the French West Indies, from an anonymous eighteenth-century watercolour

Guildive/Guildire and Tafia, again purely for consumption by slaves.

"It's all that savages, Negroes and modest inhabitants look for," said Père Labat, the father of rhum distillation, on his arrival on the island in 1694. "It is enough for them that this liquor should be strong and violent. It matters little to them that it is harsh and unpleasant."

By this stage, distillation was providing sugar planters a nice little extra income from kill-devil – Ligon claimed that a Barbadian distiller could make the vast sum of £30 a week from the spirit, which seems an unbelievable amount – and it was also starting to be sold to the crews of the ships which patrolled the Caribbean. By now the drink had begun to be known as rum, although there's a continuing debate over where the term came from.

Some believe it's a derivation of the Mala *brum*, meaning a sugar cane drink, a word that could have arrived via the Dutch traders. The Dutch at that time also drank from glasses called roemers or rummers.

Others think it comes from rumbullion which, according to who you consult, either means "an uproar" or is a Creole word which conflates the Andalucian *rheu* (stems) with the French *bouillon* (stew).

Whatever the correct derivation, by the late 1660s the drink was known as rum on the British islands and rhum on the French. [This is a spelling we shall use here to differentiate between these two very different styles.]

THE SLAVE TRADE

By this time, rum had not only begun to be drunk by the Navy (*see* page 517) but was being exported to the American Colonies. Trade soon sprang up between New England and the important distilling islands of Barbados and Jamaica whereby supplies (including lumber for barrels) were shipped from New England in exchange, at first, for sugar and rum. In time molasses, rather than rum, was destined for the distilleries which had begun to be established in Boston, Rhode Island and along the eastern seaboard.

At this point rum entered the darkest phase of its evolution. Eighteenth-century European society was seized with sugar addiction. As Terence McKenna writes in his *Food of the Gods*: "Sugar is unnecessary to the human diet; it is a kick, nothing more. Yet for this kick, Europe was willing to betray the ideals of the Enlightenment by its collusion with slave traders."

The result was an evil triangle of "trade". Since the market demanded sugar, more people were needed to produce sugar cane, which by then was planted on every island in the Caribbean. Slave ships would leave New England loaded with rum and sail to West Africa, where they would trade the liquor for slaves and gold. (English-based vessels would do the same with gin.) The boats would then sail back across the Atlantic with their human cargo and the slaves would be sold in the Caribbean in exchange for molasses and rum, which was then taken to New England for distillation, and so on. Alcohol has long been used as a tool of barter, but never in such an obscene fashion.

Rum 'n' revolution

The molasses/slave trade was a main pillar of the American colonies' economy – so much so, that it was the curbs the British put on the molasses trade that caused the spark which was to explode into the War of Independence. The New England distillers needed a regular supply of cheap molasses to make sufficient rum to satisfy domestic demand and buy slaves. At that time the cheapest source for molasses came from either the French-controlled islands, since France banned the import of rhum to protect its domestic brandy industry, or those eternal middle-men, the Dutch.

The British wanted to force the New England distillers to buy (expensive) molasses from the British islands, and in 1733 and 1765 passed two Molasses Acts, imposing heavy duties on "non-British" molasses. When they then did the same with tea, the colonists had had enough. Tea may have been the final straw, but it was rum that was the catalyst.

Rum continued to play a significant role in the newly emerging America. George Washington allegedly swayed voters in Virginia by giving them free rum punch in exchange for votes, and he ordered a barrel of rum for his inauguration dinner.

Equally, Paul Revere's famous ride was notably silent until he arrived at Isaac Hall's house. Hall was the owner of the Medford rum distillery, and it was only after he gave Revere a few tots of a rum "which would have made a rabbit bite a bulldog" that the rider began to shout his warning that, "The British are coming!" Who knows what would have happened without rum?

In the navy

The American colonists were not the only enthusiastic drinkers of rum. From the earliest days of distillation it had been given (or sold) to the crews of ships that guarded the Caribbean with quasi-legal authority. The French and British navies in those days were quite likely to be supplemented by boats stuffed with pirates, privateers and buccaneers. One side's guardian angel was the other's bloodthirsty pirate. What was clear was that supplying a ship with a few barrels of rum guaranteed that it would protect your waters.

If this slightly dodgy trade protected the colonists in what was a volatile region, the legitimate navy also enjoyed its rum – indeed Nelson asked for his body to be preserved in rum should he die at Trafalgar.

Rum's popularity with the navy was partly for health reasons. Beer soon went off in the tropical heat, as did wine. The Dutch had been early to realize that fortifying wine allowed it to be kept stable (*see* Cognac, pages 490–500), and in 1687 the English Navy had decreed that ratings be given the ration of half a pint of rum a day instead of the usual gallon of beer. Needless to say, it was a great success. The only trouble was that rum was also used as a reward for a particularly dangerous task – such as splicing the mainbrace. This meant that while ships may have had a happy crew, they also had a drunken one. The number of fatalities with sailors falling off the rigging made the Admiralty reconsider the practice.

In 1740 Admiral Vernon ordered rum to be diluted with two parts water (although he also increased the ration to a pint a day – and half a pint for boys). Later lime juice was added to help offset scurvy, giving the Navy their nickname of Limeys.

This daily rum ration – called grog after Admiral Vernon's grogham cloak – continued until 1970, although by then it had been reduced to one eighth of a pint a day. The tradition lives on in the Pussers brand, a dark, intense, tannic rum produced in the British Virgin Islands.

Meanwhile in Britain

With the Navy supping at its rum ration and the Americans knocking it back with gusto, it wasn't long before English society became enamoured with the new drink, and rum became an integral constituent of the spiced drinks which were so popular at the turn of the eighteenth century. Elizabeth David, in her *Spices, Salt and Aromatics In The English Kitchen*, quotes Congreve's *The Way of the World* (1700) in which the playwright jokes about "all auxiliaries to the tea-table such as orange brandy, all aniseed, cinnamon, citron and Barbadoes (*sic*) water [a spiced rum cordial]".

Rum arrived at the start of the gin boom which had gripped England's urban poor and, as a result, rum became the acceptable spirit among the middle classes. Rum houses became fashionable watering holes for the literati, and rum punch – rum mixed with wines, other spirits and beers – was the fashionable "cocktail" of its day, drunk by such luminaries as Boswell, Garrick, Fox and Sheridan.

Not surprisingly, rum merchants like the interestingly named Lemon Hart became significant men of capital. Hart's grandfather had been a rum merchant in Cornwall, but Lemon moved the firm to London's West India Docks in 1804, as did fellow merchant Alfred Lamb. The two firms were to join forces along with the sugar refiner Booker McConnell after the Second World War to form United Rum Merchants (URM).

THE INDUSTRY TODAY

The mention of Booker McConnell underlines the fact that rum and sugar have always been linked. Indeed without a sugar industry there would be no rum distilling. Both businesses were badly hit in the nineteenth century when Europeans managed to produce sugar from sugar beet, and therefore no longer needed to rely on the Caribbean for their supplies. Planters had borrowed heavily to invest in sugar cane plantations (which always had a distillery attached), and when the market collapsed many distilleries failed.

Although the sugar industry received a boost after the First World War (when the European beet fields were blown up), by then most of the Caribbean islands were producing under strict quotas. Consolidation of the sugar/rum industry was the inevitable result, a process that accelerated after the "double whammy" of the Depression and the Second World War. These days, the rum industry is like any other spirits sector, with a few large players and a clutch of smaller producers who have somehow managed to hold on.

The decline in sugar cane production hit the smaller islands particularly badly and some, such as Antigua, now have to import molasses for rum-making. On many islands, farmers simply switched from sugar to bananas. Now, these independent Caribbean banana producers are being crippled by multinational firms, forcing farmers to pull up their plantations and turn once more to rum as an important money-earning industry.

Even a major sugar/rum producer like Jamaica was economically crippled by the emergence of the European sugar-beet industry and the starting of the massive Florida cane fields. With the post-war exodus of much of its workforce, Jamaican sugar's decline in profitability was inevitably very severe – it was only

An aerial view of the Bacardi distillery in San Juan, Puerto Rica, an ideal location for importing to USA

saved when the industry was nationalized in the 1960s.

As distilleries have closed and molasses production has been nationalized, so distilling has become centralized, and much of today's rum is made in hi-tech distilleries that are among the most complex in the world. There are two each on Jamaica, Trinidad and Barbados, and one in Guyana. On Martinique, distilleries produce rhum for their neighbours, simply because it is more economical to centralize production. This is common practice these days, although it does make things pretty confusing, since you can find rums that seem to hail from an island which hasn't any distilleries, or from a producer who has no distillery.

All the way through this process of consolidation, one firm had taken on the world – and won. Don Facunado Bacardi had seen the potential for a light-style rum in 1878 when he brought the first Coffey still to Cuba and revolutionized the way the island's rum was made – and tasted. No longer did people have to drink heavy, rich pot-still rums; now there was a light, mixable alternative.

The fact that Bacardi rum was claimed to have cured King Alfonso XIII of Spain of a nasty bout of flu only helped its sales in Spain – and the extended Spanish Empire. The firm built a distillery in Mexico in 1931 and one in Puerto Rico a few years later. This latter facility allowed it to escape American import duty, and also enabled it to stay open during the Second World War, giving it access to an American market starved of any other domestic spirits. When Fidel Castro nationalized production in Cuba, Bacardi had already registered itself in Nassau and simply switched production to its other facilities.

It was Bacardi and Smirnoff who ushered in the era of the light, mixable drink which was virtually to kill off brown spirits from the late 1970s on, but Bacardi has achieved something that Smirnoff can only dream of – it has become a category in its own right. People ask for Bacardi and Coke, not white rum and Coke. In fact, to most people Bacardi isn't even rum: it's simply Bacardi.

In Britain, rum still meant (and still means) a dark, almost black, sweet spirit. URM and Seagram have long been shipping rums from Barbados, Guyana, Jamaica and Trinidad to Scotland, where they are aged and blended into brands like Lamb's, Captain Morgan, Lemon Hart, OVD and Black Heart. Even today on the rural west coast of Scotland, you'll more likely find people drinking Trawler rum than Scotch. Whisky specialists like Cadenheads also import rum and their bottlings, though little known, are among some of the finest on the market today. The firm, which is part of Springbank Whisky, then sends its rum barrels to the Campbeltown distillery for re-use.

The main UK brands, though, have been caught in the "old spirit" slump, and have yet to find out how to get out of the hole. The big dark warming style which was invented to suit the British palate (and climate) has been rejected in favour of something lighter.

Rum's future success may lie back in the Caribbean. Today's drinker is looking for authenticity, quality and flavour, and rum has all of that in bucketloads. White rums are hugely versatile – as Bacardi drinkers have long known – but it's the aged rums that may hold the key to growth. Firms like Mount Gay, Cockspur and Wray & Nephew have premium brands that are ideally suited to the new market. There's also growing interest in the aged and vintage rhums from Martinique and Guadeloupe. Only time will tell if this ancient, underrated spirit will get another lease of life.

HOW IT'S MADE

Rum is one of the few spirits that came into being as the by-product of another industry. In the past, sugar refining was the main business, while rum was made from the left-overs. These days, however, it has usurped sugar as the main income on a number of islands.

Caning it

To get to rum's starting point, you have to journey into the luxuriant plantations of the Caribbean and get to grips with sugar cane. The plant is a giant grass that grows quickly and vigorously – on average, young plants are ready for harvesting a year after they have been planted, although some new, quick-maturing varieties can be ripe in as little as six months.

Each island will have a selection of strains best suited for its soil and climate – there's *terroir* in rum as well as Cognac! It's claimed, for example, that Antigua's dry conditions give a sweeter cane, while on Barbados cane research has been developed into an agricultural

A fermentation tank at a rum distillery on the French-speaking island of Guadeloupe

science, with new disease-resistant varieties that give higher sugar levels in harsh conditions being developed. In Cuba, the producer of Havana Club claims that the climate in Oriente in the south of the island produces a particularly high-quality cane suitable for rum making, while the volcanic soil on Martinique is credited with producing particularly high yields.

Harvesting starts in February and continues (depending on the location) until June, when the canes are taken to the refinery to be turned into sugar. Or not, if you are in one of the French islands that produce rhum agricole from cane juice, rather than from molasses (*see* page 524).

The canes are cut and shredded to allow their sweet juices to flow. They are then crushed by a series of rollers, after which the juice is sent one way and the spent fibres (*bagasse*) go another. This is then used as fuel to run boilers and stills.

At this stage the cane juice is still dirty and has to be cleaned – traditionally by using lime and allowing the mud to precipitate to the bottom of a settling tank. This mud is then used as fertilizer on the fields. Once again, here's proof that spirits production is ecologically sound.

While technology has come to the assistance of the major refineries, in principle the next process remains the same as the one you'll find on the old estates. To produce sugar you need to boil the cane juice or syrup until it crystallizes. Traditionally this is performed in a series of progressively smaller pans. The cane juice is boiled, crystallized, then the crystals are extracted and the liquid is transferred to the next pan. Hi-tech refineries use centrifuges and vacuum boilers, but the aim is the same – to extract as much of the sugar solids as possible from the sweet syrup.

Eventually there isn't any more sugar to be crystallized, and you are left with a thick, black, sweet, gooey gunk – molasses. Now rum-making can start.

In the early days of sugar-refining, this waste product would have been left in pits until one day someone, somewhere, noticed that since it still contained the wild yeasts that grow on the joints of the cane, it had started to ferment. It was probably in a Spanish colony, as molasses comes from the Spanish *melazas*, from *miel* meaning honey.

It wasn't a huge jump of logic to realize that if they used the same techniques as they had done to make brandy back home, they could make a stronger liquor.

Ferment and yeasts

All distillers will dilute the molasses to a sugar level of around 17° Brix and then pump the mash into fermenting vats where, usually, yeast is added. In the old days some acid (lime or vegetable ash) would have also been tipped in to lower the pH. These days, distillers wanting to produce a heavy, full-flavoured rum will add some of the acidic lees from the previous ferment – similar to the backset used in Kentucky and Tennessee. As this practice pre-dates bourbon distilling, it's entirely possible that the technique was taken from the Caribbean to Kentucky.

It's not essential to add yeast to molasses, and some small distillers, such as Callwood on the British Virgin Islands, or River Antoine and Dunfermline on Grenada, still prefer to use the old technique of letting nature take its course. The result, needless to say, is a long ferment that can be difficult to control and can give variable yields of alcohol, but it's a style they prefer to use. Other firms, like Mount Gay and Wray & Nephew, have isolated their own yeast strains that they will use, while other distillers use industrial cultured yeast. It's horses for courses.

As with any other spirit, the length and temperature of ferment (and the type of yeast) will have a direct effect on the flavour compounds produced, and this is a main difference between each island's rum. You can find ferments that last for as little as two days, while others rumble and grumble on for over a fortnight.

These days, the light rums that are distilled in column stills will be innoculated with yeasts that give a short ferment, and therefore lighter flavours. The heavier rums to be distilled in pot stills are given a longer ferment in order to build in richer flavours at an early stage.

The end result, wherever you are, is a wash of around 5 to 9 per cent ABV that is ready to be distilled.

Distilling

As ever, the distiller is faced with two choices: whether to use a pot or a column still. In general terms, light rums will be made from a short-ferment wash that's been distilled in column stills, while the big-flavoured "traditional" rums are from a long ferment, and are distilled in pots. "Traditional" because originally all rums would have been made in pot stills – and some of them still use that ancient alchemical device, the retort.

The principle of pot-still rum distillation is the same as anywhere else in the world – to distil batches of a fermented wash and separate the heart (here called seconds) from the heads and tails (high and low wines). The retort is a way of doing the process in one batch, rather than redistilling.

A Jamaican pot still with two retorts works along the following lines. The fermented wash is heated in the still but the hot vapour, rather than being condensed as usual, passes into a chamber (similar to the doubler used in Kentucky), which is quarter-filled with the low wines from the previous distillation. The vapour heats the low wines, lifts off the alcohol and then passes into another retort, this time filled with the high wines. The process is repeated and further concentrates the flavours. Only then does the alcohol vapour pass into the condenser. The

TASTING NOTES – WHITE

Appleton White Clean and a little green on nose. Coconut flavours on palate. Soft and mellow. Good.

Bacardi White Rounded and smooth but virtually neutral. A real needle on the palate. Crisp finish.

Wray & Nephew Overproof Rotten banana, heavy, oily and pungent. Oily in mouth, full and flavoursome. In time, a citric edge unveils itself. Clean and a weighty base for cocktails.

heads are then kept aside to fill the retort for the next run. There are variations of this basic rectifying technique across the Caribbean. Some use one retort, some three.

In Jamaica, pot stills are also used to produce a range of styles. As well as the "standard", rich, flavourful spirit, they can also give a high-ester distillate from a complex process which involves a long-ferment wash and concentrated spirit from the high wines retort being redistilled to give a high concentration of esters. This type of rum is predominantly used as a flavouring agent for rums in Germany, Holland and Austria, where they are mixed with local neutral spirit to produce *rum verschnitt*, or inlander rum. This style is also a significant part of the blend in URM's South African brand, Red Heart.

Column distillation is a far more complex process than it is believed to be. Every rum distillery, inevitably, will have its own recipe to work to. Each one will also have its own type of column, ranging from stills that wouldn't look out of place in Armagnac to the wooden Coffey still (the only one left in the world) used in Guyana to produce a smooth, light and balanced spirit. Then there are the technological marvels in place in Guyana, Trinidad and in Bacardi's various plants.

There you can find four or even five interlinked columns which the distillers can play like an instrument, taking off spirit at different strengths (and therefore capturing different flavours) then redistilling it, rectifying it or perhaps retaining it at low strength. One plant can therefore produce a seemingly infinite variety of flavouring spirits. They aren't just factories that churn out some flavourless whistle-clean product, but are set up to produce a range of styles in order to give the blenders as wide a range of basic ingredients as possible.

Ageing

Most white and overproof rums are kept in tank for a short period before being bottled. The other rums are normally aged in ex-bourbon casks (although Cognac, whisky and wine barrels are also used), with light rums being in wood for no longer than one or two years (and then often charcoal-filtered to remove any colour). The heavier rums will spend from three to four years in wood, although some firms keep rums for 10 or more years in barrel.

The rate of maturation is affected by the climate. The Caribbean is a hot, humid area of the world, which means that the spirit extracts the tannins, colouring and flavouring agents from the wood quickly. Much of rum's character is derived from this rapid extraction.

The hot, humid conditions mean that the spirit fairly flies out of the barrel and into the waiting glasses of the angels (or duppies) hovering above the warehouses – producers in Martinique estimate that they lose eight per cent a year, meaning that they regularly have to top up the barrels with rhum from the same year. The standard British brands avoid this expensive option by taking their rums off the islands and into bonded warehouses in the far less romantic (but cooler) settings of Dumbarton or Leith.

TASTING NOTES – GOLD

Havana Club 3 anos Lifted aromatic nose, spearmint and spices. Soft, initially crisp finish. Freshness personified.

Appleton Special Coffee and crème brûlée with a touch of banana. Good weight. Rich and smooth with a wooded fruity finish.

Bacardi Black Neutral.

Mount Gay Lifted and sweet nose with some banana/toffee notes and a hint of smoke. Very clean, elegant and long.

Mount Gay Extra Old Rich toasted wood, some coconut, orange and banana. Positive wood on palate, but balanced by sweet, complex layers of fruit flavours.

Cockspur Light and fragrant with touches of brown sugar and banana. Delicate and pleasant.

Cockspur VSOR Some walnuts and dates on the nose with some well-balanced fruity sugar. Rich on the palate and a good, lingering finish.

Appleton V/X Slightly vegetal with banana esteriness before a raspberry compote fills the nose. Good grip mid-palate before rounding out for a long, pleasant finish.

Appleton 12 year-old Immediate vanilla/toasted coconut wood on the nose. On the palate, it's smokily complex and mellow. Very good.

Some companies keep rums in barrels for ten or more years; Appletons have an excellent 12 year-old

Blending

The rums are then blended – each to its own recipe. It's rare these days that you can find a rum which is bottled as it comes off the still – although Iron Jack (distilled in Trinidad) or River Antoine's Royale Grenadian are once-tasted, never-forgotten exceptions to that rule.

Blenders in the UK can use rums from different stills, distilleries, countries, ages and barrel types to make up their blends. Brands like Captain Morgan and Lamb's blend rums from Jamaica (for richness), Guyana (finesse and spice), Barbados (balance) and Trinidad that have been distilled in both column and pot stills, meaning that a typical "British" blend may contain 15 to 20 different types of rum. That said, each brand also gives emphasis to a certain core style – Lemon Hart, for example, is a light, golden "Jamaican" style; Black Heart is a dark Guyanan.

A blender like Mount Gay's Jerry Edwards uses different ages of rums from pot and column stills. For him, the column distillates give aromatics of oak and vanillin, while the pot-still rums are richer and more complex. The rule of thumb is: the richer the aromatics and body, the higher the percentage of pot still in the blend. Other distillers, such as Trinidad Distillers, can use different rums from the same still. Caramel can then be added, to the blender's specifications. Some argue that the heavy caramel addition given to some rums is only appropriate, as caramel is burnt sugar. That may be the case, but caramel is too often used as a masking agent rather than a flavouring one.

Rum need not hide behind artificial sweeteners and colourings. At its best it is a glorious and complex drink which can compare with any of the world's finest spirits. For some reason, however, it is often dismissed as a simple drink – useful for its kick, but not its flavour. Nothing could be further from the truth.

EASY IN THE ISLANDS

Rum is the kind of subject you could quite happily spend the rest of your life getting to know. There's a mind-boggling variety of rums available in three broad styles: Light (white/overproof); Heavy (gold and aged); and Dark (the British brands).

There are also three main regional production techniques – the sugar cane distillate produced on the French islands; the molasses-based spirit from the rest of the Caribbean; and the UK-aged blends.

The French colonies

The story of rhum begins in 1694, when the Dominican priest, Père Labat, finally arrived on Martinique after a long voyage during which his ship was attacked by the English. Labat not only brought religion, but also knowledge of the very latest distillation techniques from France.

Prior to Labat's arrival, distillation in Martinique (like distillation everywhere else in the Caribbean) had been a pretty hit-and-miss affair, producing a strong rhum known as *tafia* – the French equivalent to the kill-devil coming off the stills in Barbados. Labat, quite simply, was the Jim Crow (*see* Bourbon, page 470) of rhum, bringing science to bear on an agricultural way of processing waste material.

In the early days, French rhum-makers would have used molasses like everyone else – in the 1750s they were supplying molasses to the New England distilleries and playing their part in the ending of British rule in the American Colonies. It was only after the discovery of sucrose extraction from sugar beet that there was a wholesale switch from molasses to cane juice. At that point, the French stopped seeing sugar as a commodity, while the British still continued to view it as the main crop.

The French are also very good (some would say obsessional) about regulating every agricultural product. Cheese, chickens, wine and brandy all have their own appellation controls, ostensibly to guarantee a minimum quality and (less clearly) ensure typicity.

Rhum, therefore, is produced under restrictions similar to those that regulate Cognac or Armagnac. The raw material, the method of production and the manner of ageing are all defined in law.

Only cane juice is used for Rhum Agricole, the stills must be pot, single or linked column, and the wood must be less than 650 litres in capacity (smaller than the large vats used elsewhere). Most commonly, rhum distillers use 250-litre barrels that have previously held Cognac, wine, bourbon or, occasionally, whisky. Rhums are themselves divided into two classes: Rhum Agricole, which is produced by sugar cane (or *vesou*) for roughly six months after the harvest (i.e. when the cane is fresh); and the less evocatively named Rhum Industriel, which is made from molasses during the rest of the year. Check the label when buying rhum; it's an important difference, and Rhum Industriel often tastes the same as its name suggests.

Within Agricole, there are two broad categories – the high-strength (overproof) white rhums that have been kept in tank for a minimum of three months, and which are usually used as the base for punches; and the aged rhums, which are lower in strength and have been barrel-aged.

There is also a rhum that has been aged for a shorter time (a bit like *reposado* in mezcal/tequila) which is called *paille*, after the straw colour it acquires as a result of this short period in wood, while there are also Vieux and Hors d'Age rhums which have been aged (often for considerably longer).

At the top end of the market there's Millessime, or vintage rhum. These are rhums that have been transferred from small to large barrels to allow a slower maturation to take place – the vintage indicates the start of this secondary maturation, rather than the year in which it was distilled.

Rhum production remains, in essence, an agricultural creation with clear ties to the past; there's a timeless quality to be found in many of the distilleries. The products speak of this different way of doing things, having a finer, more floral and less pungent aroma than molasses rums, and a more delicate drive on the palate. Little known in the English-speaking world, they deserve a wider audience.

The regions

At one time, each island could be said to have its own identifiable style, but with inter-island blending now commonplace and more complex distillation practices in place, this is less clearly defined than it used to be. Still, there is a clear difference between rums from, say, Barbados, Jamaica and Trinidad. "It's always been thought that rums from different countries had their own peculiar characteristics," says Jerry Edwards at Mount Gay. "Today, though, because most countries make rum in continuous stills, the difference in taste between rums from different countries is small. When they are blended with heavier rums, though, the difference between countries is detectable. I don't know why, but climate, soil, water and the preparation of the molasses wash and the ferment must all play their part."

Barbados

Barbados can claim to be the home of commercial rum; certainly it was producing kill-devil by the mid-seventeenth century, only two decades after the Dutch planter Pietr Blower brought cane from Brazil. It soon became one of the most famous rum-producing islands, whose spirits were requested by name, implying that the Barbados style was in place virtually from the beginning. By the end of the last century every plantation on the island possessed its own distillery.

Traditionally this is the home of elegant, fruity rums, although these days you can find anything from light white to the classic aged rums. This is despite the fact that there are only two distilleries on the island, both of which buy their molasses from the nationalized Barbados Sugar Industry.

Barbados is home to Mount Gay, a justifiably famous name in the premium rum market, and an estate that has been producing rums since 1663 at least. This allows it to claim to be the oldest rum brand in the world – although Calwood in the British Virgin Islands can put forward an equally strong case. When William Gay bought the plantation, he purchased "Two stone windmills, one boiling house with seven coppers, one curing house and one still house", so it seems likely that rum was already being produced when he arrived.

Although pot stills make up the heart of the Mount Gay brands, the firm also has a column still which can be used either to rectify the pot-still distillate or to produce a lighter style on its own, allowing Jerry Edwards three blending blocks. Compare the ever-popular Eclipse with the succulent, mellow Extra Old, and discover Barbados in a glass.

The other Bajan distiller is the less evocatively named West Indies Rum Refinery, which produces rum (and Gilbey's gin) under contract to the specifics of the other Barbadian bottlers – the best-known being Cockspur (whose VSOR is one of the best aged rums on the market), and Doorly's.

Jamaica

The Jamaican rum industry was built on the back of the trade with the Navy and the privateers who guarded the island in the early days of the colony. After years of sugar being the dominant industry, these days – in common with many islands – it's rum that appears to offer a greater opportunity for profit. As in Barbados there are only two distilleries, including the excellent Wray & Nephew, which was founded in 1825 by John Wray. He owned three estates – among them the justifiably revered 250-year-old Appleton estate, a brand that proves that rum isn't just a white drink, but can age gracefully into a superbly balanced spirit. Its pot-still V/X, 12-year-old and 21-year-old are three of the finest aged rums in the Caribbean, building up layers of nutmeg, spice and

TASTING NOTES

Flor de Cana Mild and well-balanced with soft and lightly floral aromas. Good gentle character.
Dillon Tres Vieux Spicy and aromatic nose with touches of ginger and white pepper. Attractive depth and weight. A world class rhum.
Captain Morgan Dry curry spice on the nose. Sweet start, but with a good solid, firm grip.

Commercial but very sound.
Bally 1986 Rose petals, anise and sugar on the nose. The palate is crisp and very clean with a lovely feel. Fruit-filled with tremendous drive.
El Dorado 15 year-old Deep, ripe and resonant. The aromas tend towards those of brandy. Highly complex with touches of

Demerara sugar and some balancing wood.
OVD Sweet caramel and burnt sugar on the nose. Chewy, soft and young with a roasted coffee-bean palate. Rich, soft and undemanding.
Lamb's Navy Neutral, clean, young and hard. Hint of coffee, but green.

GISTERED STILLS
No 75 - 76
NO SMOKING
ALLOWED
EX-STILL
LITRES.
STR.
L/ALC.

luscious, mellow sweet ripe fruit as they age.

Though Jamaica remains most famous for its rich, pungent pot-still rums, like any other island it can produce rums to any style – Wray & Nephew's White Overproof and Sangster's Conquering Lion Overproof (from the National Rums of Jamaica distillery) are classics of their style, but be wary!

Trinidad & Tobago

Although late being colonized, Trinidad was still managing to produce half a million gallons of rum by the end of the eighteenth century. These days, however, it is best known as the home of Angostura Bitters (*see* Bitters, pages 585–6), the flavouring ingredient that is used in every drink and dish made here.

If Jamaica and Barbados have retained their evocative estates and links with the past, on Trinidad you come face to face with the future. The two distilleries here (Trinidad Distillers, owned by Angostura, and Caroni) operate plants whose linked columns give a seemingly endless range of blending spirits from virtually neutral spirit to heavy, low-strength distillates. It may not be romantic, but for the spirit hunter this is a triumph of the distiller's art akin to Midleton in Ireland or Lancut in Poland.

Much of the production is destined for blending, but Trinidad's bottled brands range from the brutally strong Puncheon (Trinidad Distillers) and Stallion (Caroni) to fine, blended aged rums like Caroni's Old Cask or Trinidad Distillers' Ferdi's. Trinidad Distillers also produces Iron Jack, a barrel-strength rum which deserves to be treated with considerable caution.

Bacardi

Bacardi isn't a national style; it's an international one – you could say stateless. The biggest spirit brand in the world, Bacardi has distilleries in Puerto Rico, Mexico, Spain and other places, all produced to the formula invented by Don Facunado Bacardi when he brought the first Coffey still to his original distillery in Santiago de Cuba in 1878.

What Bacardi (the man and the brand are inseparable) did was to revolutionize rum production – quite appropriate in Cuba – creating the first light, easy-drinking brand. When the firm moved to Puerto Rico in 1960 it had already started out on its aim of world domination. Tightly controlled – woe betide anyone who crosses swords with the Bacardi lawyers – it jealously guards its production methods.

All you can say is that Bacardi produces a hell of a lot of rum, it uses wood judiciously and it tends not to like caramel. You have to sit back in open-mouthed amazement that it has maintained such high quality control over such a vast empire.

In Puerto Rico, Bacardi supplies the spirit for the little-seen, but underrated, Barrilito brands.

Cuba

One of the few places in the world where you won't find Bacardi is Cuba. No great surprise there, as it was Fidel Castro's nationalization of the rum industry that precipitated Bacardi's departure from the island. The revolution also meant the loss of the American holidaymakers who had been charmed by Cuba's vibrant nightlife and had fallen in love with those masterpieces of the Cuban barman's art – the Mojito and the Daiquiri.

But although the Americans still feel that this tiny island represents a threat to their national security, and have done everything in their power to bring the island to its knees for having the temerity to challenge their bully-boy tactics, the Cubans have survived, and if they haven't prospered they remain defiantly, proudly, Cuban.

These days Old Havana may be crumbling, and there may be no petrol and little food, but you can still sip a Daiquiri in its birthplace, el Floridita. It's also deeply ironic that at a time when the USA is going ga-ga over quality cigars and quality spirits, you can't (legally) puff on a Cohiba or sip a Daiquiri made from Havana Club. You can in Paris and London, though, and in these two cities Havana Club is one of the "hippest" brands.

Havana Club isn't Bacardi; it's a fine rum in its own right. It uses cane from the south of the island, a "secret" columnn-still distillation and a complex ageing in warehouses which are cooled by the sea breezes. For the three- and seven-year-old versions, this involves ageing the different distillates separately, then blending them and ageing them for a second time. It's America's loss.

Opposite: *Lew Ward, the managing director of Mount Gay rum refinery, enjoys a rum tasting in St Lucy's parish Barbados*

Martinique

Along with Guadeloupe, this is the lush heart of the finest rhums, and there are more distilleries here than on any other eastern Caribbean island. It doesn't take long to get the feeling that this is how rhum has always been made, retaining the steady, easy rhythm of the seasons. It may seem slow to a Western European, but there's an elegant tempo to life here (and on all the islands). What's the point of rushing in this heat?

You'll find ox carts, water wheels and ancient stills, but don't be fooled into thinking rhum producers are lazy; their passion for their art burns through. The best of these rhums attest that no one is taking the easy option – they are beautifully crafted spirits.

But these small distilleries are under threat. You can produce more rhum at a lower cost from multiple column stills, but you get the feeling that some of rhum's quality is being lost in the process. Efficiency and volume are important, but these commercial aims must undoubtedly be balanced by producers who believe in the old ways.

Martinique is filled with ancient distilling firms. J. M. has been distilling since 1790, Saint James since 1765 and La Mauny since 1749. Dillon, the oldest of all, was founded in 1690 by the Girardin de Montegeralde family, the most famous of whom was Josephine de Beauharnais, the mistress and wife of Napoleon. It's entirely possible that the saying: "not tonight Josephine" may have been a polite refusal of a glass of her family's rhum.

Dillon, incidentally, was an Irish Jacobin who helped the French turf the Brits out of Martinique and married into the Girardin family. These days Dillon's Vieux and Millessime rhums are among the finest examples of their style you can find.

J. M.'s Fonds Preville distillery is one of the oldest on the island. The firm still produces its range from cane grown on the 30-hectare estate and distils in the only linked column still on the island – and ages, unusually, in ex-wine barrels, for a stunning range which includes Paille, Vieux and Millessime.

J. Bally also uses estate-grown cane, but its still is akin to an alambic Armagnaçais in size – and therefore gives a lower-strength spirit for its excellent range of white, Paille, Vieux and vintages.

Guadeloupe

Cane arrived here in the seventeenth century and plantations still cover the northern part of the island, but these days there are only six distilleries. Among them is Bologne, which is notable not just for its high-quality rhum but for the fact it was the first plantation bought by a free black man. Also notable are Mon Repos, which uses cane from its own estate to produce an excellent range of beautiful hand-crafted rhums, and Damoiseau, whose aged rhums (up to 15-year-old) rival those of Martinique for complexity.

Other islands

The US Virgin Islands was a significant supplier of rum to the New England distilleries, and currently one of its two distilleries is doing sterling work in trying to convince today's US consumer that rum has flavour.

Cruzan, owned by the US-based Todhunter – but still run by the Nelthropp family, which arrived in St Croix in the late 1700s – now has a wide range, including light (aged for two years), Estate (four-year-old), two high-strength brands (Clipper and 151 Proof), a single barrel brand as well as four flavoured styles.

These very different rums all come off the same highly sophisticated linked column still – here's another distiller that's looking to the future with confidence.

The rums from the neighbouring British Virgin Islands are less commonly seen, but rum lovers should seek out Calwood, from what claims to be the oldest operating distillery in the eastern Caribbean – and one of the few "British" rums which is made from cane juice rather than molasses.

There are a few cane rums from Grenada, although you're unlikely to find a bottle on the export markets. Grenada's fertile soil has allowed a wider range of crops to be cultivated and therefore sugar and rum production have never played the central role that they have on other islands. Although the bulk of the island's fragrant rums are overproof, like River Antoine's Royale Grenadian (allegedly the strongest rum on the market), Westerhall makes a delicate, clean, aged example that's worth searching out, as is Clarke's Court.

The final island of note is beautiful (but forlorn) Haiti,

Opposite: *A bay rum still at Fort Christian, on St Thomas, U.S. Virgin Islands; distillers are enjoying more success in selling to Americans*

Bay Rum Still
Donated ... Wicks Estate

which can lay claim to be one of the oldest rhum-producing sites in the world – after all, it was here that Columbus planted the first cane. Rhum is made here in the French style by the quality-obsessed Barbancourt distillery. Its complex, aged rhums have a deservedly high reputation among aficionados, and are becoming more widely seen.

South America

Guyana is home to the rich, powerful Demerara rums, and to one of the world's great distilleries, a plant where rums of every description can be made by using pot stills, linked columns and the only remaining wooden Coffey still in the world.

The bulk of the production from Demerara Distillers is destined for blends – they make up the majority of the British brands – but the firm also releases underrated rums under the El Dorado label.

Sugar cane arrived in Venezuela in the sixteenth century and rum inevitably followed. In common with other South American rums, the Venezuelan style is lightly flavoured with delicate, fruity, aged (*anejo*) rums at the top of the tree. The first firm to age its rums in the country was Pampero, whose top brands have a graceful elegance. The other major distiller, Ocumare, produces a charcoal-filtered white and a three-year-old *anejo*, which uniquely has *guarana* added to it.

Rums from Nicaragua and Guatemala are along the same lines, though having a richer, more luxurious weight on the palate. The top Nicaraguan brand Flor de Cana is, sadly, now hard to find. You're probably more likely to chance upon the excellent Ron Botran from Guatemala.

Cachaça

It may come as a surprise to discover that the world's biggest-selling spirit style is a rum – although it isn't called that: it's known as cachaça.

Hailing from Brazil, this sugar cane juice distillate is drunk in vast quantities in its home country and is responsible for one of the world's finest cocktails, the caiparinha – the very mention of which gets knowledgeable drinkers salivating.

The cachaça market is dominated by brands such as 51, Pitu and Sao Francisco. Both are fine examples of the style. It's worth searching out the intriguing ginger-flavoured cachaça available from Dreher and, if you look hard enough, you'll find some aged pot-still examples, such as those from Ypioca.

Rum is also an important style in Mexico – indeed it's claimed that Mexicans drink more rum than they do mezcal or tequila, although here they call it *aguardiente*. Confusing? You bet.

Keep your eyes peeled for Aguardiente Juanito el Camineno from Pueblo, or mezcal/cane spirit mix El Tigre Aguardiente, which has had a short time marrying in wood. It qualifies as being an *aguardiente*, as it has more than 50 per cent cane spirit in the blend.

Rest of the world

Although rums are produced in Madagascar, Surinam and the French dependencies of Réunion and Mauritius, they are rarely found outside their home markets. More common is Bundaberg, Australia's native spirit. The distillery, situated close to the cane plantations of Queensland, has been in production since the late nineteenth century and remains an essential part of Australian life – and Australian drinking ritual. Although bottled at standard proof, "Bundy" has acquired a somewhat fearsome reputation – which is probably more to do with the way it's flung down the throat with reckless abandon than anything inherently wicked about the drink itself. Wherever Australians are gathered, a bottle of Bundy is never likely to be very far away.

So, does rum have a sense of place? Maybe not in the way that Cognac, Armagnac, bourbon and malt whisky do, but rum is part of the pulse of the Caribbean. It's not just the drink of the tourists in their protected all-inclusive compounds; it's as much the people's drink as it has always been.

Rum started life as the drink of slaves trying to seek oblivion from their hellish existence. Now it's a drink of national pride – from the shacks at the side of the road offering unmarked bottles of illicit hooch to gaudy beachfront bars, the sipping of rum remains an essential part of Caribbean life.

Rum, more than any other spirit, has an image of eternal youth. If malt whisky is rather grave, Cognac sophisticated and bourgeois, gin middle-class, then rum is the drink of sunshine, of laughter, of relaxed sociability.

The Depaz rum distillery, near Saint-Pierre on the eastern Caribbean island of Martinique; the island has more rum distilleries than any other

GIN

There are only a few lights glimmering deep in the darkness surrounding the arrival of distilling spirits in Europe that give a clue as to how it all started. One belongs to the ninth-century medical school of Salerno in Italy, which was founded by Benedictine monks. They were the first to translate the works of Greek and Arab scholars into Latin, and were distilling alcohol at some point between 1050 and 1150.

At this time spirits were used purely for their medicinal properties, with various herbs, spices, roots and viscera being macerated in spirit and distilled either in crude pot stills, or in glass jars. While we can't be sure what the brothers were making in Salerno, it's certain that they would have used the restorative herbs and spices which were already being used in so-called folk medicine – and one of these was juniper (*ginepro* in Latin), which grows well and freely across Italy.

Juniper-based elixirs only became widely used during the fourteenth century, when the Black Death arrived in Europe. One of the potions which followed in its wake like some grisly camp follower was made from juniper. The Salernan monks had already discovered that the berry was effective against bladder and kidney disease, and it was alleged to strengthen the immune system as well as curing prostate problems. If it were taken to excess, it would more than likely have caused prostrate problems. Still, with the pustulant ravages of the bubonic plague laying waste to Western Europe, what better than a patent cure-all?

The juniper drink is likely to have arrived in Flanders (then controlled by the Dutch) at some point in the late fourteenth century, although we have to wait until 1572 to find the first recorded distillation of an *eau de vie de genièvre* by one Franciscus Sylvius, a physic of Leiden. It wasn't long before *genever* (as it became known in Holland) had left the apothecaries' cellars and entered public use, not just as a health tonic but as an enjoyable intoxicant. Lucas Bols, the father of commercial gin production, built his first distillery in 1575 near Amsterdam.

Genever soon became a staple part of the Dutch/Belgian diet, used not only to cure upset stomachs but also to give soldiers a certain numbed fearlessness in battle (after all, Sir Robert Savage, the Lord of Bushmills, gave *aqua vitae* to his Irish troops in 1296). This other side-effect of *genever* was discovered (and greatly appreciated) by the regiments of English mercenaries who went to fight on the side of the Dutch in the Thirty Years' War (1618–48). On their return to England they brought tales of this "Dutch Courage", and no doubt some bottles of it as well.

It's unclear whether gin was already being produced in England at this time. In fact, it's unclear what spirits were being produced there in the period that followed the dissolution of the monasteries. Certainly large houses would have had still-houses, but commercial production wasn't in place. If England wanted spirits, it imported them.

That isn't to say that there weren't keen distillers, although they still tended to be more embroiled in alchemical research than commercial production. John Doxat in *The Gin Book* quotes the example of The Worshipful Company of Distillers who in 1653, under the leadership of alchemist Sir Theodore de Mayerne-Turquet, issued a decree that all spirits should undergo rectification (i.e. a second distillation) to generate a purer end product. This enlightened quality control sadly lasted only until 1702.

In 1663 the famous diarist Samuel Pepys records taking "strong water made of juniper" as a medicine for his upset stomach, and gin might have remained no more than a medicine and a faddish drink – the equivalent of

Opposite: *Junpier berries, long used as an ingredient in the distillation of gin*

today's tourists bringing back bottles of retsina from their holidays in Greece – if the Dutch William of Orange had not been invited to become King. One of his first acts was to ban the import of French goods, among them brandies and wines. Scottish and Irish whiskies were little known outside their own borders and rum wasn't yet established. At that time brandy was the staple tipple of the English. What else was there to drink?

Opiate of the people

Why did gin become the English spirit? The art of distillation was known, there was a surplus of grain, but no one was forced to add juniper. Quite why gin emerged triumphant is more than likely due to a number of factors. With no brandy to drink, people needed some spirit or other. Gin was being made anyway, it was also fashionable and the new king was Dutch. This combination of circumstances, fuelled by a certain new-found patriotism, made the English populace embrace the new-fangled "Hollands", or, as they eventually called it, "gin".

Certainly King Billy consumed his fair share; the Banqueting House at Hampton Court Palace became known as the gin temple.

To say that gin was an immediate success would be to make one of the greatest understatements of all time. Within a few years the major cities of England were awash with alcohol purporting to be gin, with the major ports of Bristol, Plymouth and, most importantly, London becoming distilling centres.

People living in the desperate slums of that time needed something to numb the reality of their situation, just as the soldiers needed a distraction from the horrors of the battlefield, and gin fitted the bill. The government didn't exactly stand in their way. In 1690, Parliament decreed that all you needed to do to become a distiller was to display a notice of intent in a public place for 10 days, and four years later it also raised the tax on beer, making gin the cheapest option. With gin-making easy, by 1730 one-fifth of London's houses were "gin shops", and people were swilling back 11 million gallons a year.

These amateur distillers would have been making the spirit from anything they could get their hands on, although the constants were juniper, sugar and other flavourings. Juniper was particularly useful as its strong flavour would have hidden the "off" tastes in what would have been dangerously badly distilled spirits. Never mind; they worked, and they had the desired effect – oblivion.

It's difficult to conceive how heavy the drinking was. Gin was the drink of the huddled masses in their stinking slums, their fetid homes. It was the enemy of the upper classes, the opiate of the people. Gin was singled out as the root of all evil, while beer was an acceptable drink. Absinthe suffered in the same way at the turn of the nineteenth century, while in our own times marijuana is banned but tobacco is permitted. Some things never change…

By the 1730s the government had had enough, although it tried to get to grips with the problem in the most bizarre fashion: by decreeing that "intoxicating liquors" could only be sold in a dwelling house. The reaction was swift – and obvious. Every house became a gin shop. It wasn't until 1743, when legislation was introduced licensing distilleries, that the industry we know today began to take shape. It was centred around a few reputable producers, among them Alexander Gordon, who started his Southwark distillery in 1769.

Consumption continued to rise, peaking at an astonishing 20 million gallons in 1750, before beginning to slide down to more reasonable levels as the double effect of licensed distilleries and high excise duties made cheap gin a thing of the past. Only people with sufficient capital and the ambition to succeed stuck with gin. The combined effect was an improvement in quality, and gin began to move very slowly up the social scale.

Gin, however, was far from the refined, rather bourgeois spirit it is today. It was still the drink of the poor, the desperate, the disenfranchised; the tipple of the mob, drunk in gilded and mirrored gin palaces. Not only was it a disreputable spirit, it probably didn't taste particularly great either. The most widely made style was still Old Tom, a juniper-laden drink flavoured with glycerine and sugar syrup.

Gin and gentility

How Old Tom got its name is a mystery – although it has brought various theories to light. John Doxat quotes two tales: the cat in the vat (it fell in), and the more prosaic explanation that it was named in honour of Thomas Chamberlain, an early distiller. Stephen Bayley, in his book *Gin*, prefers the more lurid legend of one Dudley Bradstreet, gin distiller and all-round wide-boy, who had a wooden tomcat outside his gin shop. People put their money in the cat's mouth and their gin trickled down its leg. You can still find Old Tom if you search hard enough, and allegedly it (or a version of it) is still made in Finland.

The first major shift in gin's fortunes happened when dry gin (the name meant "not sweet") was invented in the late eighteenth century – with Plymouth claiming to be the first distillery to produce a dry, crystal-clear gin. However, it was only when the continuous still was invented that gin began to take its first genteel steps toward respectability. As the quality of the spirit improved, so it no longer needed to be sweetened up, and this new dry style was a more sophisticated drink than Old Tom. This, Doxat argues, gave gin the leg-up it needed. Certainly, dry gin was a more acceptable style. It was lighter, drier and appealed to new drinkers. It was, to use a modern-day term, "trendy" – just like vodka became in the 1960s when it killed gin off. The Victorian middle classes could quite fairly say that they weren't drinking the same stuff as the working classes.

There was also the issue of peer pressure. The gin makers – men like Alexander Gordon, Charles Tanqueray, James Burrough and Sir Felix Booth were pillars of the community, men of substance. If the upper middle class were making it, perhaps it would be all right for the middle class to drink it as well; after all, it was miles away from the old "mother's ruin". It's an early example of the premium effect coming into play.

That's not to say it was all plain sailing. There remained some vestiges of snobbery; decanters of gin would carry neck-labels marked NIG, or White Wine. But the newly exotic, aspirational gin was becoming the drink not just of the emerging middle class; it was starting to be drunk by both sexes.

It was also embraced by the officers of the armed forces stationed in the far-flung reaches of the British Empire. Rum had been the drink of the Navy since 1687, but for some reason in the late nineteenth century, gin was embraced by the officer class. No one

can be sure quite why; it may simply have been elitism – a way to differentiate themselves from the ratings. Whatever the case, gin became the wardroom's preferred tipple.

There was a practical reason as well, a distant echo of the monks of Salerno. Gin was a perfect medium in which to mix the Angostura Bitters which the Navy drank to prevent stomach problems – so that drink of retired admirals, the pink gin, was born. Equally, lime juice (taken as a preventative against scurvy) was mixed with gin, and the gimlet arrived. Meanwhile, a purveyor of soft drinks and mineral waters, Jacob Schweppe, was devising a Tonic Water containing quinine, especially formulated for officers and gentlemen stationed in areas where malaria was rife. That, too, was added to their gin, and one of the world's great alcoholic long drinks was born.

The Navy also acted as representatives for the early brands, serving gin during the traditional drinks party on board the vessel when a ship first docked at a new port. It's no coincidence that the gin made in one of the major naval ports, Plymouth, could claim to be the most widely available gin brand in the world by the mid-nineteenth century, and was the naval officer's drink of choice.

In this way, by the turn of the century gin wasn't just acceptable, it was *de rigueur*. Cognac had temporarily disappeared thanks to *phylloxera*, and although blended Scotch whisky benefited most from this, gin wasn't that far behind it, and when the new American fashion of cocktails hit, it flourished. Gin had finally risen out of the gutter and on to a glittering stage. One of gin's greatest attributes is that its complex flavours are shown at their best when mixed. It's a classic cocktail base – after all, it's at the heart of the world's greatest cocktail, the Martini.

Gin remained the drink of fashionable London in the 1920s, and therefore became one of the main aspirational drinks in the United States of America during Prohibition. Despite the fact that bathtub gin (a concoction of industrial alcohol, juniper and glycerine that even an eighteenth-century Londoner would have thought twice about downing) was produced by bootleggers, gin managed to retain a sophisticated, almost decadent, image.

Gin came out of the restrictions imposed during the

Second World War in a remarkably fit state. While whisky distilleries had been closed and little stock had been laid down, it was relatively easy for gin distillers to get up and running again. The boom continued through the 1950s, but gin was beginning to run out of steam, and by the 1970s it had become saddled with an old-fashioned image – the sort of drink consumed only by retired brigadiers. Vodka, which had started eating into gin's share of the US market in the 1940s, became the white spirit of choice in the UK as well.

The gin producers didn't know how to react. Just like blended whisky makers, they had assumed everything would remain rosy, that people would come to their senses and "mature" into gin. No chance. Cocktails were *passé*, gin and tonic was old hat (and badly served) and the firms searched in vain for a way to market themselves out of a crisis.

The return of flavour

In the United States of America, Michel Roux invented Bombay Sapphire, a new style of high-strength premium gin in stunning packaging. In the UK they went a slightly different way. Roux had already made his name with Absolut vodka, where he tapped into the new, design-conscious drinkers and gave them a brand that not only tasted good, but looked good as well.

He felt that he could do the same with gin and took the rather tired Bombay brand, put it in a sapphire-blue bottle, emphasised the use of exotic botanicals and the delicacy of flavour and watched it take off. Sapphire was proof that not only could gin be made hip once more, but was evidence that drinkers were also beginning to think more seriously about their drinks.

In the UK they went a slightly different way. Someone at Gordon's realized that if they cut the strength from 40 per cent ABV to 37.5 per cent ABV, they would save money on excise duty which could be reinvested in promotion. You can understand the logic and, to be fair, Gordon's has remained the only British gin with a high profile during the recent slump in gin's fortunes. The trouble was that the cut in strength (which was followed by virtually every other brand with the exceptions of Tanqueray and Beefeater) had a direct effect on flavour. But more of that later.

Gin's crisis of confidence has been shared by all the

"old" spirit categories as the youth market has turned to something that their parents didn't drink. But there's a glimmer on the horizon. Premium spirits are in vogue, as are cocktails. The most significant shift is in the new passion for flavour, and if the demand is for clean spirit with complex flavours, then what's better than gin? In recent years, just as with top-quality vodka, few people in the West have taken it seriously. Perhaps its time is due again.

The Plymouth Distillery uses an unconventionally shaped still, perhaps accounting for Plymouth's characteristic richness of body

HOW IT'S MADE

There are two main ways in which to make gin: redistilling a neutral spirit which has had natural flavouring ingredients (botanicals) added to it; or adding essences of the flavouring agents and stirring them into the spirit.

This latter method, known as cold compounding, has the advantage of being cheap, but the poor-quality gin it produces is not worth the money in the first place. Most (although not all) supermarket own-label gins are made by this technique. Avoid them. Stick with a gin that is labelled "Distilled Gin".

Needless to say, each distiller has its own slight variation on the gin-making process, which starts with the spirit itself. Neutral spirit is alcohol which has undergone rectification to bring it up to around 96 per cent ABV, which is about as pure as you can go. That isn't to say that the spirit is neutral on the nose, or that it doesn't matter from which base the distillate was made. Most quality gin producers insist on (more expensive) grain spirit rather than cane (molasses), which can give a slight sweet note. Although distillers agree that the quality of cane spirit has improved, they still prefer to use the more delicate grain. Since the majority of the gin producers also own grain whisky plants, supply is not a problem, but even then the supply has to be constantly monitored to make sure that it remains consistent, not just in quality but in aroma.

For some reason though, no British gin distiller is allowed to produce its own neutral spirit on site, so it all has to be trucked in. This means that gin distilleries are strangely peaceful places to visit, even when they are distilling. There are no clouds of steam from mash tuns, no bubbling fermenters; just the quiet hiss of steam heating the large pot stills and the steady flow of clear, new spirit into the sight glass – and the aroma. Gordon's has run an advertisement which shows a man being shot into a glass of gin and tonic (a nice idea, but probably a rather sticky experience). A gin distillery intensifies that image. The smell of juniper berries is all-pervading, then you notice other subtle smells which swirl around your head, just as the spirit vapour rises in the still, capturing the flavour compounds from the botanicals, stripping them, clutching and entwining them to itself.

The stills are copper pot stills, usually with high necks, which help extract only the higher, more fragrant alcohols – the stills at Glenmorangie, which produces a delicate malt whisky, are former gin stills. The gin still at Plymouth distillery, though, has a more unconventional shape, with a relatively short neck and an exaggerated curve on the lie pipe. This could account for Plymouth's characteristic richness of body – although that distillery also makes great play of the fact that it uses spring water which has run through granite and peat to first dilute the spirit in the still. Other distilleries have to clean their water before use. (The dilution, by the way, is necessary otherwise the still would be in danger of blowing up.)

Secret recipes

But what happens inside? This is where distilleries differ widely. All have a secret recipe of botanicals;

how they put them in the still also varies. Some, such as Gordon's and Plymouth, put the botanicals in only a short time before the steam is turned on and redistillation starts. Beefeater, on the other hand, steeps them for 24 hours before distilling, while Bombay Sapphire uses a Carterhead still which contains a basket holding the botanicals. The vapour passes through the basket, stripping the flavours from the botanicals.

Of course, each distiller thinks that its approach is the correct one. Sapphire points to the delicate manner of the extraction, which gives a delicate gin (although, as we'll see, there are inherent problems with this technique).

Beefeater feels that steeping gives a gentler extraction, but builds in complexity, as it fixes the aromas in the spirit before distillation, while Plymouth counters that steeping can give harder flavours and allow certain ones to dominate.

A matter of aromatics

Distilling "fixes" the botanical flavours in the gin. But, as ever, distillation needs to be a careful process. For one thing, not all botanical aromas appear at the same time; they queue up in the still, waiting their turn to rise, mingle and be turned into flavoured spirit. After a quick foreshots run, the volatile citrus notes appear, then come juniper and coriander, then the roots such as orris, angelica and liquorice. That's not to say that one appears for a while, stops and then the next one starts; rather they blur into each other, each peaking at a different time. If you nose a distillation at regular intervals, you'll find the aromas changing continually, albeit subtly.

The speed at which the still is run is therefore of tremendous importance to the final quality of the gin. Run a still too hot and too fast, and all the botanical aromas will be pushed over at the same time, along with unwanted heavier alcohols from the end of the run. Equally, each distillery will stop collecting spirit at a slightly different strength. Although this is also a closely guarded secret, it would be fair to assume that the richest and heaviest gins, with greater evidence of rooty aromas, will have been allowed to run for longer than ones with more lifted, citric notes. Since

Beefeater relies on having a light, citric aroma, it is likely to cut at a higher strength.

But, inevitably, it's not quite as simple as that. Each distiller has his own recipe, and each handles the botanicals in a slightly different way to attain a different effect. In Bombay Sapphire's case, this involves suspending the botanicals over the rising vapour. The gin makes great play of the sheer number of botanicals it uses – including oddities like cubeb berries and grains of paradise.

The problem is that the technique seems to give too subtle an effect. The aromas don't appear to be fixed as firmly as they would if the botanicals had been placed directly into the still. Each time you nose Sapphire you will get a slightly different aroma – perhaps that's a style you like, but at times it seems too ethereal.

The aroma could also be the effect of the alcoholic strength of the gin. This may seem strange, but since different aromas come off the still at different times (i.e. at different strengths), so they are held in the gin at different points. There are bands of flavour compounds within the gin.

When you reduce the gin, initially by water to get it to bottled strength and then with, say, a mixer like tonic, there's a series of little flavour explosions as these trigger points are hit. Citric notes, since they are the most volatile, are the first ones to be released.

When Gordon's made its decision to lower the strength in the UK from 40 per cent ABV to 37.5 per cent, it saved money, but it also changed the aroma and flavour of the gin. The trigger point for the volatile citric aromas would appear to be around 40 per cent. Dilute to below that strength, and you'll kill them completely. The result is a flatter, more overtly junipery aroma and a flavour which doesn't carry all the way through on the palate. "There is clear correlation between alcoholic strength and the ability to hold botanicals," says Sean Harris, distiller at Plymouth Gin. "You can't hold light citrus flavours at low strength, which is why when you go below 40 per cent you lose them."

If this just sounds like ungentlemanly criticism of a rival brand, remember he is talking from experience. Plymouth's previous owner reduced its strength – and

quality and aroma suffered. It's worth trying out Gordon's at 37.5 per cent and comparing it to the same gin at "export strength" (which is how the rest of the world buys it). The fact that most UK gins followed the lead set by Gordon's meant that most gins in Britain suddenly lost flavour at the very time they were trying to attract new drinkers by saying that gin is full of flavour.

"Ultimately what you are doing in distilling is turning a science into an art," says Harris. "If that still was a nuclear submarine, it would be covered with dials telling us what to do. Distilling is knowing what to do intuitively and creating the spirit, not manufacturing it."

THE USE OF BOTANICALS

The defining element in gin is the use of botanicals – with juniper as the main one. Without them you have a type of vodka. It may strike us as unusual that the early distillers would have used such exotic ingredients, but you have to remember that these early gin-makers were living and working in a society where the use of spices was the norm. According to Elizabeth David in her masterly *Spices, Salts and Aromatics in the English Kitchen*, Europe from the fifteenth century onward used "lavish" amounts of spices in its cooking – particularly in the great houses of the day. "In Europe, spices were the jewels and brocades of the kitchen and the still-room," she writes.

By the time that Dr Sylvius was making his first *Genever*, Holland was beginning to exert control over the Western world's spice trade. By the end of the seventeenth century it had a virtual monopoly of the business and, through the trade done by the all-powerful Dutch East India Company and its British equivalent, spices flooded into the two countries and flavoured drinks became a craze.

This is another reason why gin became the preferred tipple of the English – it was tapping into an existing fashion. While the poor added herbs to their drinks, the rich explored the effects of different combinations of spices and aromatics in their alchemical researches. David singles out Sir Kenelm

Digby, whose recipes for the then-popular honey-based drinks meath, metheglin and hydromel were published posthumously in 1669. One of them gives precise details on making a hydromel of crushed juniper.

Not only were spices coming into the country from distant lands, but others which seem unusual today were being cultivated in England. Saffron was extensively grown in Suffolk and Cambridgeshire, while coriander – traditionally the second most heavily used gin botanical – was grown commercially in Southern England (and, in particular, Sussex).

In other words, Lucas Bols and the English alchemists/distillers who belonged to the Worshipful Company of Distillers would have had experience of using a vast range of flavouring agents in their spirits. Certainly, their gins would have borne little resemblance to today's London Dry (or Plymouth), although they do share similarities with some of the old-style gins produced in Holland and Belgium.

Made in pot stills, these gins would have used juniper for two reasons: its aromas were preserved by the alcohol, but they also hid the off-notes in the alcohol. Better production meant that the botanical flavours were used as an attribute rather than as a masking agent, but it wasn't until the dry gins came off the continuous stills that the lighter citric flavours began to emerge.

Botanicals remain the single most important element in making gin, and each brand's recipe is known to only a few people. "You could use 120 different herbs, spices and aromatics", says Hugh Williams at Gordon's, "though most use no more than ten. Only 12 people know the Gordon's recipe and, even if you did know it, you couldn't replicate the gin."

All brands use juniper and coriander, but Gordon's also uses ginger, cassia oil and nutmeg; Beefeater uses bitter orange as well as angelica root and seed; Plymouth's seven botanicals include sweet (rather than bitter) orange and cardamom; while Sapphire uses cubeb berries, cassia bark and grains of paradise. The aim is to produce a balanced, complex aroma – which doesn't necessarily mean the more botanicals, the more complex the smell. As any cook knows, flavours can end up cancelling each other out.

The combination of botanicals is also important. The roots not only give a dry, almost earthy, character but, according to Desmond Payne, distiller at Beefeater, angelica also helps to hold in the volatile orange and lemon aromas.

The distillers use some of the most exotic aromas in the world in their gins. Juniper, with its hints of heather, lavender and camphor, is from Italy and southern Germany; coriander seed, with its lemon balm notes, will come either from Eastern Europe – or, in Sapphire's case, where a peppery quality is wanted – Morocco. Musky, dry angelica comes from Saxony; orange peel comes from Spain; earthy orris root, with its hint of violet, from Italy; cinnamon and cassia bark from India; ginger from the Far East; nutmeg from Grenada; Javanese cubeb berries; and grains of paradise from West Africa.

It all starts with the juniper berries, which are hand-picked from October to March. Spice merchants either send distillers samples after the October harvest, or distillers will go to seek out their supply. Then comes a long period of assessing the quality. Each vintage will give a slightly different crop and each merchant will also have slightly different berries. The quality-conscious distillers will extract the essential oil from each of the samples, put it in neutral alcohol and then nose all the samples – perhaps up to 200 – blind. Only then will they pick the supplier(s) they wish to use. A large concern like Gordon's will choose up to 20, Beefeater perhaps four or five; a smaller producer like Plymouth picks just one. Although all the berries will also be examined for oil content, that isn't the sole criterion. What the distiller is looking for is a berry that has the same character as their gin, and which will give consistency of style.

The same system is carried out with all the botanicals, and distillers will put together a blend of the ingredients to check if the style is consistent. The recipe remains the same in principle, but it may have to be tweaked given that each of the botanicals changes each year. The aroma isn't just from the botanicals themselves, but the relation between them.

At the end of the day, the botanicals supply the fingerprint for each brand. They are what ensures that every gin is different.

THE 'BRANDS

The start of gin's climb to respectability was partly down to improved production, but was also as a result of the efforts of the gentlemen distillers of London (and Plymouth) who elevated the spirit from one drunk in the slums to the preferred choice of the bourgeoisie. This is their story...

Gordon's

Alexander Gordon established his distillery in Southwark in 1769, although it moved premises to Clerkenwell in 1786. By the end of the nineteenth century Gordon's gin was widely exported, and was one of the gins "distributed" by the Navy. The firm recalls the tale that one of the first export orders came from Australian miners who sent payment, in advance, in gold dust. By that time it had merged with Tanqueray, and both firms came under the wing of DCL (now UDU) in 1922.

Throughout Prohibition Gordon's planned how to attack the US market when it re-opened, and almost as soon as Repeal arrived it established two distilleries in the United States of America, stealing a march on its rivals and helping to make it still the best-selling gin in the world. Controversially, it cut its strength in the UK which freed up money for promotion but, as repeated blind tastings show, this damaged its quality. In its favour, though, the money has been used to build not only the brand, but also gin as a category.

Beefeater

James Burrough was a pharmacist who started distilling gin in Chelsea in 1863, on the back of gin's rise to respectability. His sons had to shift production to a new distillery in Vauxhall in 1908, and then moved to the current site in 1958. The fact that the distillery is only a well-struck "six" away from the Oval cricket ground means that two (in recent times, rather shaky) pillars of English identity now sit cheek by jowl.

Long one of the most active gins on the export markets – particularly in North America – it became part of Whitbread's brief (and disastrous) foray into spirits in the late 1980s, before being bought by Allied Distillers in 1991. Recently, a new high-strength (50 per cent ABV) brand, Crown Jewel, has been launched in the duty-free market.

This, though true to the Beefeater citric style, is an elegant refined gin which carries its high alcohol content lightly. Beefeater remains the only gin distilled in London – and one of the few British gins to stick at 40 per cent ABV.

Tanqueray

The Tanqueray family were French in origin, arriving in England at the beginning of the eighteenth century. Although the family were originally silversmiths, they turned to the Church, with three successive Tanquerays becoming rector of Tingrith, Bedfordshire. Alcohol entered the equation only in 1828 when Charles Tanqueray followed the successful examples of Felix Booth and Alexander Gordon and built his distillery in Finsbury – a part of London noted in those days for its spa water. Tanqueray has always been a premium style; even in its early days it attracted a small, prestigious clientele, and was exporting to the rich sugar planters in Jamaica by the middle of the nineteenth century.

It joined forces with Gordon's in 1898 and the two firms split the world between them, with Tanqueray taking the road to America and the Far East. It is still the most widely distributed strong gin and the first to be recognized – not because of its strength, but its complex, rich flavour – as a premium brand. Badly affected after Prohibition (when DCL pushed Gordon's at the expense of its premium sister brand), it only re-established itself on the US market in the 1950s in its now-familiar round bottle – modelled on the fire hydrants which pumped water to the original distillery. Recently it introduced a new brand, Tanqueray Malacca, a triple-distilled 40 per cent ABV gin with a different botanical recipe.

Booth's

One of the oldest gin families was started by Philip Booth, who opened his distillery in 1740 in Clerkenwell, another water-rich area. By the end of the century control had passed to Philip's son, (Sir) Felix, who became the biggest gin distiller in Britain. At one point the distillery was threatened by the anti-Catholic rioters and the workers had to be armed with muskets.

Despite reportedly losing out in the taste stakes when it cut its strength in the UK, Gordon's has succeeded in building gin as a spirits category

Sir Felix eventually became the best-known distiller on the planet, thanks to his financing of Captain John Ross's 1829 expedition to find the North West Passage (Ross's crew, incidentally, were supplied with Booth's old muskets). It didn't find the elusive way through but did discover the magnetic North Pole, and the grateful Captain Ross named the Boothia Peninsula, Felix Harbour, Cape Felix and the Gulf of Boothia after his gin-making patron. As Stephen Bayley points out in his book *Gin*: "It's quaintly touching that one of the largest pieces of ice on the planet should be named after one of the most distinguished gin distillers."

Booth's is famous for its "High & Dry" and "Dry" brands, the latter being a straw-coloured gin thanks to a period of maturation in oak casks. This was the result not of a cunning marketing ploy but, if legend is to be believed, an accident.

At one point during the nineteenth century there was a glut of Booth's, and it was laid for a short while in ex-sherry butts. The firm still has a cooperage, and its apprentice coopers still have to obey the rules laid down in the fourteenth century that they must not "contact matrimony" or "commit fornication" during their apprenticeship. Booth's, too, was cut in strength in the 1980s, to the detriment of its flavour.

Gilbey

Although their grandfather had been a publican, the brothers Gilbey, Walter and Alfred were relative latecomers to the gin aristocracy. In 1857, after serving in the Crimean War, they set themselves up as fine wine merchants, specializing in wines "from the Colonies" in premises situated in Berwick Street, Soho. Soon they had 20,000 customers on their books – allowing them to move to a rather more salubrious site in Oxford Street in 1867.

By 1872, just as gin was becoming the drink to be seen with, they had built their own distillery in Camden and had begun to produce their London Dry Gin. By the 1920s, there were distilleries producing gin to the Gilbey's recipe in Australia and Canada. This latter distillery helped Gilbey's establish a foothold in the United States of America during Prohibition (during that period it was packaged in frosted bottles to avoid imitations). These days it claims to be the second-largest-selling gin in the world, with its biggest sales in

the United States of America and the Philippines, although in the UK it has become a member of the 37.5 per cent gang. A premium brand, Antique, has recently been launched.

Plymouth

The Plymouth distillery was originally built as a monastery (although there are no records of distilling) and then was used as a meeting house; it was where the Pilgrim Fathers spent their last night in England before heading for the New World. In 1793 it was bought by the Coates family, and can therefore claim to be the oldest continually used gin distillery in England. Once the most widely distributed gin in the world, it can also lay claim to be the gin recommended in the first recorded recipe for a dry Martini (published in Stewart's *Fancy Drinks and How To Mix Them*, 1896).

It was badly hit in the aftermath of the Second World War. A combination of poor-quality spirit lowered demand, then it changed ownership, first to Schenley, then to Whitbread (the British brewer) and then to Allied Distillers. The quality of spirit was downgraded, the strength was cut, the label cheapened. Now, thankfully, it's back in private hands and is growing. Back to its original strength, it is one of the world's great gin brands.

Bombay

Bombay Dry gin first appeared on the US market in the late 1950s, when Alan Subin saw an opportunity for a new premium gin aimed at competing with Tanqueray and Beefeater. He contacted the English distiller Greenalls and, after choosing a recipe dating from 1761, launched the brand in the United States of America. Bombay was handled by Carillon Importers and later went to IDV (Grand Metropolitan). In 1987, Michel Roux, the president of Carillon – and the man who broke Absolut on the US market – saw the potential for a new brand as a way of invigorating the depressed US market, and Bombay Sapphire was born. A triumph of striking packaging and excellent marketing (which makes great play on the use of a large number of botanicals and redistillation in a Carterhead still) guaranteed it a place as one of the iconic brands of the late twentieth century.

TASTING NOTES – GIN

Beefeater (40 per cent): Soft, fine, attractive nose; lime peel and orange notes dominant, with a delicate heathery/lavender juniper edge. Positive, with good weight on the palate and a mouth-watering zestiness.

Beefeater Crown Jewel (50 per cent): Pleasant, not obviously alcoholic. Quite delicate and citric. When compared with Beefeater, the juniper is less in evidence and lighter, delicate notes predominate.

Bombay Sapphire (40 per cent): Delicate, exotic aromas which fade rather too quickly. Similar on the palate – delicate, with some juicy spiciness, but almost too fragile.

Gilbey's (37.5 per cent): Light, dry and attractive, but slightly neutral.

Gordon's (37.5 per cent): Rather flat and rooty/earthy, with a hint of sage and plenty of juniper. Lacking in subtlety.

Gordon's (40 per cent): Full juniper aromas with some orange notes and earthy hints.

Clean, lifted and juicily rich.

Plymouth (40 per cent): Intense, fragrant with angelica/juniper heatheriness surrounded by citrus blossom. A wonderful combination of smooth, rich texture with complex, delicate flavours and a great sagey kick on the end.

Tanqueray (47 per cent): Ripe, rich and pungent with plenty of coriander and juniper aromas coming across. Soft and rich on the palate with a firm, dry finish.

Bombay Sapphire, a marketing triumph from Carillon president Michel Roux

DUTCH GIN

The original distillers in Holland had a ready market for their *genever*. While Sylvius produced *genever* purely for medicinal purposes, it wasn't long before the popularity of the spirit spread out to the local populace. Lucas Bols had a distillery up and running by 1575, only three years after Sylvius's alleged "discovery". Wenneker started in 1693, while de Kuyper was established in Rotterdam (Holland's spice capital) in 1675. By that time, Diderot had described the Dutch as "living alembics, distilling themselves". Right enough, spirits and the Dutch go hand in hand, and they are behind the growth of a host of the world's great spirits. As a mercantile nation the Dutch needed spirits to preserve wines so they could survive long sea voyages, and they had already helped to establish Cognac and Jerez as centres of brandy production. Spices were also being brought back from the East and West Indies, brandy was flooding in from France (most notably, Cognac) and Spain. But while brandy was popular, *genever* remained Holland's own drink, one of the great Northern European spirits from the grain belt.

One reason for its popularity was the fact that the Dutch excise department turned a blind eye to domestically produced spirits. So, while brandy was taxed, *genever* got off scot-free. Farmers began to produce their own *genever*s from excess grain and the market exploded. Every house would have had a jar (or stone crock bottle) of *genever* – and, as Gordon Brown recounts in his *Classic Spirits of the World*, distillers had to employ jar sniffers to ensure that when people brought back the ,

empty jars for refilling, they hadn't been using them for, well, other fluids.

While crock bottles continue to be used today, there's no need for jar sniffers and *genever* remains Holland's national spirit, retaining a central place in the Dutch drinking ritual, which it has singularly failed to do in the rest of the world. The reason is difficult to nail down, but one possible angle is *genever's* symbiotic relationship with the other main Dutch tipple: beer. That said, in recent years *genever* has become unfashionable with younger drinkers, prompting innovative firms like Bokma to introduce new, lighter styles. This has increased an already vast number of brands and styles from a host of large and small producers.

HOW IT'S MADE

There are three categories of *genever*: *Oude*, the old, straw-coloured, pungently sweet style; *Jonge*, a newer style which appeared with the arrival of the continuous still, which is cleaner and more delicate; and *Korenwijn* (in Bols' case *Corenwyn*), which is a cask-aged product with a high percentage of malted spirit.

As ever, each distiller will have its own method of producing *genever* and, in general, *genever* differs from London Dry gin by being based on a heavier spirit. Traditionally this has been made from *moutwijn* (malt wine) which is a low-strength spirit made from a mash of wheat, rye and malted barley distilled in pot stills, but this will vary between distillers. The Schiedam-based firm Floryn, for example, uses pot still grain which gives a slightly lighter spirit, although one which is still more aromatic than the neutral grain spirit used by the majority of British gin distillers; while Hooghoudt produces a fine double-distilled pot-still *genever*. A distiller like Bokma, meanwhile, produces its top aged brand Vij Jahren (five years) in three component parts – a *moutwijn*, grain spirit and a botanical flavoured spirit – which are aged separately for the prescribed length of time before being blended. Its Volmout brand is a richer style, with a high *moutwijn* content.

It is often stated (wrongly) that *genever* uses only juniper. Other botanicals are used, but it's the way in which the Dutch distillers handle their flavouring ingredients which helps give *genever* its distinctive style. Bols, for example, passes the vapour in a fourth

TASTING NOTES

Bols Corenwyn (40 per cent): Light gold in colour. Very rich and malty on the nose, with deep juniper aromas mixed with red fruits and almond.

de Kuyper Genever (40 per cent): Rich and malty with oily juniper undercurrent. Rich in texture, clean nutty finish.

Bokma Royal Dark (40 per cent): More delicate than most genevers, gently junipery with a subtle smooth character.

Bokma Volmout (40 per cent): Highly malted but with a crisp attack.

Bokma Vijf Jaren (40 per cent): Rich elegant with juniper oil well in evidence. Full unctuous feel and restrained wood.

distillation over the juniper berries for its *Corenwyn*. Since triple distillation is common, juniper is normally introduced in the second distillation, with the other botanicals being added to the third (or sometimes fourth) distillation, although again this will vary between distilleries. In Schiedam, UTO's Notaris brand is first distilled, then part of it is redistilled with juniper, while a third blending component will be distilled with the other botanicals.

Newer-style brands include Bokma's Royal Dark – grain spirit aged in Limousin oak – while there are also some lower-strength flavoured *genever*s like Hooghoudt's blackcurrant, or Coebergh's *Bessenjenever* – the equivalent of a German or Austrian fruit schnapps, or an English sloe or damson gin.

The end result of combining a richer spirit and a higher percentage of juniper is a spirit which is more powerfully textured than London gin. Compare them by all means, but don't use "London" criteria to judge *genever*; just sit back with an ice-cold glass and sip contentedly.

The *jenevers* (*sic*) from Belgium are as close as you'll get to the original gin – after all, it started in Flanders. Today there are around 20 small producers, many of them still farmhouse-style distillers like Filliers, which uses rye and malted barley for its base spirit. Production, however, is a mix between England and Holland, with a Coffey still used to produce the initial spirit, which is then redistilled once in a pot still with the botanicals and then given extended ageing (up to eight years). The

closest you'll get to the original gin is Hoorbeke, which still makes a *jenever* which is distilled from juniper.

Gin is a hugely important spirit in Spain – volume-wise this isn't surprising. Anyone who has sat down and asked for a gin and tonic in a Spanish bar will confirm that the barman pours what seems to be a third of a bottle into the glass and, if there's any room, tops it up with tonic. The main brand is Larios which, despite the fact that it hails from Malaga, insists on calling itself a London Dry Gin, while its label pays homage to Gordon's. All of this rather takes away from the fact that Larios is a delicious, aromatic, off-dry gin.

If high strength is your bag, look out for the Lithuanian brand Nemunas which is 60 per cent ABV and uses juniper, lime blossom, hops and honey as its flavouring agents. No matter where you are in the world, though, you'll find a spirit purporting to be gin. There is Filipino gin which doesn't seem to taste hugely junipery, but makes a decent *caipirinha* (*see* pages 530 and 621). Then there are African gins, sometimes called banana gins, in which juniper is unknown. In Western Africa, these spirits are more often poured away as a sign of respect (and to drive away bad spirits).

Even today a Dutch brand, Steinhager, still sells massive amounts in Western Africa (*see* Schnapps – page 504) where it is used predominantly for ritual purposes. Gin is one of these categories you just know you'll never get to the end of. A feature on the war in Sudan described someone appearing "waving a bottle of Ethiopian gin". And so the search goes on.

VODKA

Vodka has enjoyed a rich and varied life. It's been drunk just about everywhere from the great houses and palaces of Poland and Russia to Shaman's altars in Siberia, not to mention every bar in the Western world. Yet how much do we actually know about this spirit? Vodka may play a part in the daily ritual in Eastern Europe, but few in the West give it a second thought.

Vodka, you would think, is vodka. It has made its name by being the perfect partner for any mixer – flavourless, but with an alcoholic kick, undemanding and malleable. It's ideally suited to a lifestyle where easy choices are the norm, where you don't have to try too hard. Why grapple with the intricacies of Proust when you can be "entertained" by Jeffrey Archer? Vodka's been a bit like that.

But look again … things are changing. A few years ago, if you walked into a bar and wanted a vodka it would be poured out of the well; if you were lucky, you might have got Smirnoff Blue. Then Absolut arrived and the world was never quite the same again; it made vodka become hip, rather than just popular. It fitted the 1980s like a glove. It was clean, pristine, designed, the drinks world's equivalent of a Donna Karan suit.

But, despite the fact that Absolut has been superbly marketed (and is a fine vodka), its success was underpinned by the same principle that had taken vodka from foreign oddity to one of the world's most popular spirits – namely, vodka tasted of, well, nothing. People were, and still are, being asked to pay large amounts of money for something that apparently claims to be flavourless. It's this paradox that lies at vodka's cool heart.

When you look at the subject, however, you find that true vodka is anything but tasteless; it has verve and subtlety. The best of the premium vodkas make you look differently at spirits – their only equivalent is, perhaps, the new wave of grappas that are coming out of Italy.

To get to grips with quality vodka requires you to open your mind to whispers of aroma, nuances of flavour. But this is miles from the image that most people have of this spirit. Only by looking at vodka's convoluted history are you able to get to grips with how this refined spirit has acquired this rather schizoid image.

Bill Samuels of Maker's Mark is fond of saying that bourbon died when Smirnoff started to be distilled in America and, to understand how vodka became the great mixable spirit, it's Smirnoff's story that you have to follow.

What the brand did, brilliantly, was to take a drink redolent with negative imagery – hard drinking, strange ritual and, remember this is during the Cold War, – and make a household brand. Smirnoff's early US advertising claimed it was "the drink that leaves you breathless", and it certainly did that in the way that it quickly scaled the heights of the US market.

Vladimir Smirnov (*sic*) had fled his homeland after the Russian Revolution, and then tried to establish Smirnov distilleries in Constantinople, Lvov and Paris (*see* below). However, by the time he got to Paris, like so many other Russian emigrants, he was broke. Enter Rudolph Kukhesh, an ex-supplier of alcohol to the Smirnovs who had moved to the USA, changed his name to Kunett and started working for Helena Rubenstein's cosmetics company.

In Paris on business, he met Smirnov who by now was down on his luck and gave him the rights and licence to sell the Smirnov portfolio in North America. Kunett changed the firm's name to Pierre Smirnoff & Fils, and started distilling in America in March 1934.

It wasn't the runaway success he had hoped for. Vodka had been drunk during Prohibition, but it was one of many spirits which emerged from that period with a battered reputation – not surprisingly, since the bulk of the "vodka" that would have been sold was made in bathtubs in the back streets of Chicago and New York.

In fact in 1937, Kunett, close to bankruptcy, sold the Smirnoff licence to John Martin, president of Heublein, who nearly lost his job as a result. That's how poor an image vodka had. Heublein had to wait until after the Second World War for its troublesome new charge to prove its worth.

Allied to some clever marketing, vodka became the spirit that the post-war market wanted. It mixed happily, it was light, it was undemanding. It was so versatile that barmen could create a huge number of new recipes for cocktails, but it was one of the first spirits that allowed you to make cocktails at home – add ginger beer and you had a Moscow Mule, a screwdriver was Smirnoff and orange juice. No matter what you threw at vodka, it accepted it quite happily. It even made Martinis!

Vodka was sophisticated, easy, fun – and it didn't make your breath smell. Within a brief time it had evolved into a different drink from the one which is still consumed in Eastern Europe.

Smirnoff began distilling in the UK, Canada, Australia, New Zealand and across America. Other vodkas followed in its wake – brands that were bland, neutral alcoholic bases for soft drinks and mixers.

By 1975, in terms of sales, vodka had become America's most popular spirit, and Smirnoff and Bacardi began slugging it out as the world's biggest spirit brand. The triumph of the neutral white spirit was complete. Russia's "little water" (vodka's original meaning) had grown up.

But while Bacardi had become a category in itself (*see* Rum) Smirnoff, though a massive brand, couldn't do the same. Vodka was the winner, but rather than being tied to one particular brand remained rather anonymous. You may have got a Smirnoff in a bar, but you wouldn't have asked for it by name.

This situation existed until Absolut swung into town with a marketing campaign that others have tried desperately to imitate but will never replicate. Absolut was right for its time. It tied itself to cutting-edge fashion and modern art. It was irreverent, weird, wacky, but it was never cheap. Rather, it was elitist and utterly, utterly hip.

Absolut, thanks to its success in educating barmen and wooing design-conscious consumers, began to be asked for by name. The way was now open for people to look at vodka in a different light.

Absolut managed to bridge a gap that Finlandia and Stolichnaya had already been working on – though without much success. It was a vodka that could be used for cocktails (and push the price of the cocktail up), but it was also promoted to be drunk as a shooter – which was something that no one would ever have thought of doing with Smirnoff. New opportunities suddenly appeared for vodka.

Then, the Iron Curtain fell. Now, finally, there was a chance for Stolichnaya, Moskovskaya, Polish vodkas and the classic flavoured styles, which had been made for centuries, to make their mark in the world.

The simple reason that these vodkas are now the driving force in the market is that "premium" equates with "imported" – whether that is Polish, Russian, Finnish, Swedish or Danish. By hailing from a vodka-producing country, these brands appeal to the new consumer who wants to drink spirits that are somehow "authentic".

In the USA, this new image has now been widened to include domestic brands, which have cunningly put a different spin on the taste of nothing by emphasizing production and quality.

These days you'll find pot-still vodka from Texas, organic vodka from Kentucky, vodka from glacier water from the Tetons. So successful has this shift upmarket been that, to grab a slice of this lucrative sector, Smirnoff has gone back to Moscow and started to produce a vodka from pot stills.

These new premiums are drunk neat or contribute to the revival of the Martini (though traditionalists still believe a Martini should be made from gin – no other spirit will do).

Just as with any quality spirit, the vodka drinker wants authenticity – although that term is a highly personal one. It means that "real" vodka has finally got the chance to show its true colours. But what actually is "real" vodka?

It's impossible to wrap up vodka's history in one neat bundle, because it has evolved differently in each of the countries where it is the national spirit. Vodka may be regarded as a commodity by the West, but in Poland, Russia and Scandinavia it is a very different beast.

POLISH VODKA

Trying to get to the bottom of Polish vodka alone is a Herculean task – with an estimated 1,000 brands available, it's a mission that would take a lifetime. Poland is the best place to start when looking at vodka's history.

It may not please Russians or Swedes, but there is convincing evidence that the secret of distilling (wine initially) filtered into Poland from the West and spread from there into Russia and the Baltic States.

Peasants in the eighth century were making a crude alcoholic spirit by freezing wine, though the first written record of a spirit made from grain comes in 1405 – pre-dating Russia. Precisely how distillation arrived in Poland is a matter of conjecture, but it is likely that the secret was brought to Poland by Italian monks (although some suggest they could have been Irish) who were, by then, well versed in the arcane subject of transforming a base material into another, far more potent, one.

As in every other country, these early spirits were initially used as medicines. In 1534, Stefan Falimirz devoted a chapter in his herbal book to distilling vodkas, but their usage was limited either to cures or: "for cleansing the chin after shaving [or] rubbed on after washing in the bath". Even in its earliest incarnation, vodka was being used as something rather stylish – an aftershave or cologne. Falimirz, however, claimed that not only did vodka make people smell nicer, but it also could be used "to increase fertility and awaken lust". Right enough, perfumes these days still allude to that latter quality.

These early vodkas wouldn't have been the clear, neat spirit we know today. They would have been spiced up with infusions of herbs, roots, spices and exotica like marzipan, almonds and sugar. The result was that, according to Marian Hanik's *History of Vodka* in Poland, the Polish pharmacies of their time were more like cafes, where people came to take their medicine and have a chat.

Vodka was given a significant boost when, in 1546, King Jan Olbracht decreed that all Poles could make alcohol – which they gleefully did, even though they had to pay tax for the privilege. Although this decree was soon restricted to the gentry, they seized on the money-making opportunity.

By the end of the sixteenth century, Poland was producing vodka in sufficient commercial quantities to start exporting – a trade that would grow in importance over the following two centuries. Production initially centred round the then capital of Cracow, and by 1580 there were 500 distilleries in Poznan, while Gdansk had by now taken over as vodka's capital – its first distillery being started by a Dutchman called Ambrosius Vermoellen.

With production rights restricted to the upper class, distilleries were springing up across the country, in towns, monasteries and in country houses and estates. "Naked" vodka was still less common than the vast range of flavoured vodkas that had appeared on the back of this distilling fever – there were medicinal vodkas, country vodkas flavoured with wild herbs, sweet vodkas (like Krupnik) for winter. Faith & Wisniewski, in their *Classic Vodka*, recount that over 100 different flavoured varieties were being produced in this period, with the Baczewski distillery alone making 123 different styles. Vodka had become part and parcel of Poland's life. Everyone drank it and, despite the legal restrictions, everyone made it, though quality differed according to your wealth. Those who could afford it produced vodka from rye, while the peasants had to make do with anything else they could get their hands on.

Hanik gives a typical example of a Polish manor house distillery in the seventeenth century – it drew water from local springs, had a malt house, a mill, cooperage and smithy; an ice house for cooling the yeast

---

TASTING NOTES

POLISH VODKA

Wyborowa Very clean and crisp. Light lime with good weight behind. Soft and full on the nose, with some creamy weight. Fine grip and a hot finish. A cracking vodka.

Zytnia Good rye zest on the very clean nose. Good crisp acidity on the palate. A dry aperitif vodka with white pepper on the finish.

Luksusowa If you need to be convinced that potatoes can make quality vodka, start here. Richly textured, almost sweet with a powerful, elegant finish. Drink neat.

and the mash; a still room and a barrel warehouse. It was a sophisticated operation, not some cobbled-together, moonshining unit. The spring water was filtered through charcoal, distillation was in copper stills and redistillation was common (though not universal).

With the arrival of triple (and, on occasion, quadruple) distillation and charcoal filtering in the eighteenth century, came a new style of vodka that was stronger and cleaner. Polish vodka became the model for quality production across Eastern Europe with equipment (and techniques) being exported to Russia and Sweden.

Vodkas would have been made from the main Polish starch crops – rye, wheat, barley and oats were all used. Potatoes, although they had arrived as an exotic ingredient in the fifteenth century, only began to be used for vodka production in the middle of the eighteenth century, becoming a major raw material a hundred years later.

The style was still following the aim of the earliest distillers, to try to produce as clean and pure a spirit as possible. Vodka by now was not only a spirit that could be drunk on its own, but one that would also provide a base for the seemingly infinite number of flavourings that had become established as an integral part of Polish vodka's style (*see* below).

The next major step towards this goal of a pure spirit came at the start of the nineteenth century, when the first three-chambered Pistorius column still was installed at General Ludowik Pac's distillery.

When steam was incorporated into the method in 1826, Polish vodka production was ready to expand once more – with higher volumes of purer spirit flooding on to the market.

Although rectifying columns didn't make their first appearance until 1871, Pistorius equipment was a major breakthrough. From here on in purity was not only the aim, it was an achievable goal.

As well as new technology appearing, as Faith & Wisniewski point out, the emergence of the first kosher vodkas in the 1830s also had a significant impact on improving distilling practice and making the production process as clean as possible.

The combination of this new technology and the planting of potatoes as a main crop meant that the beginning of the nineteenth century saw a doubling of vodka consumption and an explosion in the number of distilleries. It wasn't to last long.

The potato blight (1843–51) crippled spirits production – as it did in Ireland – while increased taxation put paid to most of the smaller distilleries. By the end of the century, rural distillers could no longer compete in terms of volume or quality.

Although they produced spirit, they were sending it off to the large plants for rectification. This spirit was then either bottled or sold on once more to producers specializing in flavoured styles. These producers were using the new Henckmann equipment, which used alcohol vapour to not only strip flavours but also speed up the process.

During the First World War, there was a further fall in the number of legal distilleries. Much of it was caused by a further rise in taxation, which in turn fuelled a rise in home distilling.

In the 1930s, 4,000 illegal stills were confiscated every year. Vodka was too important to Polish life and culture to be given up without a fight. The industry, however, consolidated further and was brought under the control of a state monopoly after the Second World War. In 1973, this body became Polmos.

Vodka remained the lifeblood of Polish society. During the shortages of the 1980s it was used as a form of currency to barter for goods, and those who wanted more than their ration made their own. Wisniewski highlights the sudden increase in the use of junior chemistry sets during this desperate time. With the arrival of democracy, the 25 distilleries controlled by Polmos were granted independent status, although they are still ostensibly government controlled.

This has produced an explosion of brands – there are an estimated 1,000 brands of Polish vodka available – with each distillery trying to find its own point of difference. It's only to the benefit of the spirits lover, as the newly liberated distilleries have gone for the top end of the market.

It is difficult to describe how important a role vodka plays in Polish and Russian culture. It's not just a neutral spirit to be diluted with a soft drink; it's a social event with its own rituals. Flavours aren't the recent invention that the West seems to think they are

In some countries drinking is seen as an act of generosity and hospitality, without the the stigma it has in the West.

– they all have their own use, their own ethos.

In Poland, drinking has long been seen as a social event, an act of generosity and hospitality. This means it's regarded in a very different light from how it is in the West (and, in particular, the USA). Hanik quotes Jedrzej Kitowicz, who wrote in 1850: "Among the Poles, nothing could be done without getting drunk... It was the host's greatest ... satisfaction when [the day after a party] he heard how none of his guests had left sober."

It was nothing new. "Among them [the Poles] getting drunk is a praiseworthy custom, certain proof of sincerity and good manners," wrote Fulvius Ruggeri to Pope Pius V in his 1568 description of distilling in Poland. The maxim was repeated 400 years later by the aristocrat Czartoryski, who wrote: "twice a year, one should get properly drunk".

It might seem reprehensible advice in these abstemious times, when the merest hint of a lack of sobriety is seen as a crime, but vodka remains a safety valve in Polish life, as well as an inherent part of the culture.

Poles, Russians and Swedes all treat vodka in the same way as the French treat wine. It's an aperitif, served with the snacks that appear before the meal, drunk as a liqueur after the meal. Children are weaned on to its charms at an early age – and end up more responsible drinkers as a result. It is not unusual for children to be given a small glass of Wisniowka (a sweet, cherry vodka) to celebrate a special occasions.

Polish vodka's inherent high quality and versatility demand to be examined more closely.

TASTING NOTES

RUSSIAN VODKA

Smirnoff Red Quite a fat nose with a sweet, grainy quality. Formless with a light tingle on the finish. No great definition, but clean.

Smirnoff Black Soft, slightly floral nose with merest lemony spice. Well rounded with good weight and a long, powerful finish. Elegant.

Stolichnaya More lifted and crisp than Smirnoff Black. Clean, with a hint of butter. Hot, peppery finish. Clean.

Scandinavian vodka

Absolut Initially dumb, in time a soft, slightly spicy, fragrance comes across. Quite oily on palate with light burn.

RUSSIAN VODKA

If Poland can lay claim to being the first vodka producer, its image is still associated with Russia. But until the mid-fifteenth century the Russian nobility were still sipping on mead and wines, while the people were drinking beer. Faith & Wisniewski argue that some distillation was taking place beforehand as an adjunct to producing pitch from pine. It's possible that alcohol was being distilled in log stills (the same thing happened in Kentucky), and it was the need to keep redistilling the alcohol to remove unwanted elements that, they argue, established vodka distillers' obsession with producing a pure spirit.

This proposition goes a long way to explaining why when other distillers across Europe were happy to retain flavouring compounds, those in Russia and Poland wanted to get rid of as many as possible. There is a further theory, but we'll come to that in a minute.

Russian vodka historian William Pokhelbin claims that vodka production was known from the mid-fifteenth century, citing the sudden degeneration of public morals and accounts of mass drunkenness and violence. This, he argues, points to a change in the type of alcohol consumed. Sadly, whether this wild depravity was caused by strong spirits or another wider social cause we cannot (yet) ascertain.

Though there is no evidence that vodka was at the root of this dissolute behaviour, records do show that a Russian delegation had visited Italian monasteries in 1430 where they were shown how to make *aqua vitae*. Given that their return coincided with a grain surplus, it is entirely possible that vodka distillation was in place by the middle of the century.

Virtually every country has tried to control spirits in some way or other. Taxation is the most common method. In Russia they went one step further. While Jan Olbrecht was allowing all Poles the right to distil, Ivan the Great had already established the world's first spirit monopoly. Ivan the Terrible took state control one stage further, decreeing that vodka could only be sold in official taverns and be produced from stills owned either by tavern owners or nobles. Vodka fitted in neatly with the age-old framework of Russian society – the landowners got rich and the poor got drunk.

Though Peter the Great (1672–1725) liberalized distillation – mainly to collect taxes – vodka production was a rich man's hobby. Peter himself invented a modified still to improve quality, and his recipe for vodka involved producing a triple-distilled spirit, flavouring it with anise and then redistilling it once more. The search for a pristine spirit was well advanced.

It could be argued that this was only to the benefit of vodka's quality. By the turn of the seventeenth century, four distillations were common, and exotic, complex flavoured vodkas were being drunk by the ruling classes. Filtering the spirit through charcoal to further clean it up arrived in the eighteenth century – at much the same time as in Poland – and is credited to Theodore Lowitz, who was working on the Tsar's request. There's every chance that it was a Russian or Polish *émigré* who took the art of charcoal filtration to America and into Tennessee. It certainly was known long before the 1880s, when Smirnoff claims to have invented the technique.

In the eighteenth century, a series of government bills restricted production still further. This effectively split production into two quality tiers. The nobility, who used their vast feudal power and wealth to make it to perfection; and the state distillers, who supplied base spirit for the poor. While the poor soaked up crude spirits to obliterate their misery, the top Russian vodkas began to acquire an international reputation. Catherine II sent vodka to the kings of Prussia and Sweden, to Voltaire and to her friend, the Swedish botanist Karl von Linne, who, suitably inspired, wrote a lengthy treatise on "vodka in the hands of a philosopher, physician and commoner".

By now, class divisions had created different vodkas for each stratum of society. The nobility drank rye and elegantly flavoured vodkas, while the poor drank rank spirit made from potato, beet and nettles bought in at low prices from Poland, Germany and from illicit stills, rather than from the state distillers.

The state was forced to take control of production once more, cut the number of distilleries in half, introduced the continuous still and, under the controlling influence of the chemist Dr Mendeleyev, set quality control standards. By the time that Piotr Smirnov started to make his own vodka in 1861, the best Russian vodkas had become the elegant, clean spirit we know today.

Smirnov's rise was inexorable. The firm built a distillery in Moscow in 1868 and was granted a Royal Warrant in 1896 – an award which didn't go down too well with the Bolsheviks. By the turn of the century, the firm was producing 3,500,000 cases a year and had an annual income of US$2 million.

Vodka was very big business and distillers were pillars of the capitalist class. Little surprise that vodka was one of the first targets of the Bolshevik government – and that Vladimir Smirnov fled to Constantinople, Lvov and Paris in his unsuccessful attempt to start all over again.

The initial reaction of the Bolshevik government was to restrict vodka's strength to 20 per cent ABV to try to reduce drunkenness – but people just kept on making stronger stuff at home.

Things changed dramatically when Stalin took power. Faith & Wisniewski make a strong case that Stalin used vodka as a means of social control. By keeping the price artificially low and making it easily available, he ensured that the Soviet Union was in a state of endemic alcoholism. Vodka was a way of suppressing dissent and, in those dark days, the drinking wasn't heroic – it was desperate.

Stalin wasn't the first to use cheap alcohol as a way of keeping people compliant. Rum was also used in this fashion in the Caribbean by planters who gave the spirit to their slaves. Brandy, too, was given to the black majority by white employers in apartheid South Africa.

Now with Communism (allegedly) overthrown, things have gone full circle, with Smirnoff now being produced in pot stills in Moscow once more. The market has opened up, allowing Stolichnaya to blast on to the world market. Then there are Moskovskaya, Kubanskaya and Ultraa from St Petersburg, and vodkas like Altai, a winter wheat vodka from Zmeinogorsk in Western Siberia. There may not be quite as many brands as there are in Poland, but the gates have been opened.

Vodka epitomizes Russia. It has kept spirits buoyant in times of desperation and obliterated misery. In the wilds of the Altai and Tuva, it is used by shamans as a libation to the spirits. In Moscow it is sipped by the new bourgeoisie.

Although Russia's future is less than clear, one thing is for certain: empires may rise and fall, but vodka will always survive.

SCANDINAVIAN VODKA

Records suggest that distillation arrived in Sweden in the fourteenth century when *brannvin* (burnt wine) was being distilled from imported wine – and domestic grain.

This was initially used as a medicine (which has echoes in later years) and also in the development of gunpowder. It was first embraced by the aristocracy, and only began to spread to the rest of the population in the seventeenth century.

As soon as it did, though, distilling became endemic. By 1756, the country could boast 180,000 stills.

Home distillation was banned in 1860, the first of many attempts by the Swedish government to exert control over consumption, and large commercial plants equipped with Coffey stills began to exert control over the market – and produce more vodka. Less than 20 years later, Sweden's most famous distiller emerged on the scene.

Lars Olsson Smith started distilling young. Unbelievably, by the time he had reached his early teens he was producing an estimated one third of Sweden's vodka. It was his creation of Sweden's first rectified spirit in 1879 that was to elevate his name to one of legend.

Smith was a stubborn individual with very fixed ideas about quality. He was so convinced that his new Absolut Rent Brannvin (Absolutely Pure Vodka) was the very best vodka on the market that he took on the might of the Stockholm monopoly.

His distillery was located in an elegant house situated on the small island of Reimersholme, conveniently just outside Stockholm's city boundaries. By providing a free ferry service to his customers he not only guaranteed high sales, but angered the other distillers to such an extent that shots were fired at the boats.

His Absolut vodka was an instant success and Smith soon needed more raw material for his new brand. Accordingly, he switched production to the far south of the country, to the wheat fields of Skåne. He went about buying up distilleries and ensured that his vodka was the best-distributed brand in the country – at one point even using the unions to boycott shops that were selling what he claimed were inferior brands.

By the end of the First World War, Sweden had a state monopoly, Vin & Spirit, in place to control the sales and production of all alcoholic beverages and immediately put up taxes to astronomical levels.

Who knows what would have happened to the fortunes of Smith's brand had it not fallen victim to Sweden's strict state control of drink?

Scandinavian governments (with the notable exception of Denmark) have long had a strange relationship with alcohol. The people drink a lot of it, but their rulers don't like them indulging and, until recently, have tried everything in their powers (Finland even tried a period of total prohibition) to make it impossible to enjoy a drink – though without any real success.

It only encouraged Swedes, Finns and Norwegians (who also have state monopolies) to go on massive drinking binges, either on the duty-free ferry routes between the countries, or in Denmark. Many people have also continued to distil at home. Even the Swedish state monopoly will admit that more than 20 per cent of the vodka drunk in Sweden is distilled privately – though the true figure in fact could be a great deal higher.

Carillon's Michel Roux has propelled Absolut from obscurity to the seventh biggest vodka brand in the world

Strangely, this tight control – which is part and parcel of the Swedish state's benign interpretation of socialism – created one of the world's biggest spirits brands. Absolut was forgotten until 1979 when V&S decided to hit the international vodka market.

The brand was distilled once more, repackaged in a replica of an old medicine bottle and went for the top end of the US market – the most competitive vodka market in the world. Carillon Importers' Michel Roux took it up and ran with it (he was later to do the same with Bombay Sapphire). It's now the seventh biggest brand in the world.

Absolut was following in the footsteps of Finlandia, which had hit the USA in 1970. Finnish vodka dates back to the sixteenth century, but it too was taken under the state's wing in the twentieth century – when the distillery was closed down to make alcohol for Molotov cocktails.

Denmark traditionally has been better known for its akvavits (see Other Spirits), but has always produced fine quality vodkas. The father of these was Isidor Henius who, in the 1850s, installed the country's first rectification column at his Aalborg distillery.

This famous site is now owned by the giant producer Danisco, home to the new wave of Danish vodkas, foremost among which is Danzka. To be strictly accurate, Danzka was originally produced by an independent distiller but, in the way of these things, was snapped up by the giant firm when it saw the potential for a high-quality brand on the export markets. The fine, ultra-clean grain vodka in its distinctively packaged silver metal bottles comes in a wide of range of flavours, including Citron and Currant. They are fine and rather attractive. The firm also produces Fris, a vodka created to be served straight from the freezer.

Norway's contribution to the growing band of Scandinavian brands is the potato vodka Vikingfjord. It's a good example of the Nordic style, flirting with neutrality, but being saved by smooth mouthfeel and delicate flavour.

Finnish industry started in earnest in the 1950s and now has one of the most technically advanced distilleries in the world making the Finlandia a by-word for Scandinavian purity.

REST OF THE WORLD

The rest of the world has always looked on vodka in a slightly different light from Scandinavia and Eastern Europe. Although you can say that vodka akvavit, korn and gin are all white spirits from the northern European grain belt, they have evolved in subtly different ways.

In vodka the prime motivator was to produce as clean a spirit as possible. This could then either be drunk neat or subtly flavoured. While cleanliness of the base spirit was important for the rest of these white spirits, their aim was to still have a dominant powerful character – juniper for gin, caraway for akvavit.

It wasn't until America recreated vodka as a neutral, mixable spirit in the 1950s (see above) that vodka began to make inroads into Western Europe. Vodka had been produced prior to this date – the Dutch firm Hooghoudt has been making vodka since the end of the nineteenth century – but it hadn't captured the public imagination. Now, with America reinforcing its role as the arbiter of global cultural taste, vodka became the latest in a chain of cultural signs like jazz, rock n' roll and the movies, which signified modernity – and "American-ness".

The vodka that Western Europe drank therefore wasn't a European creation but an American one, a drink where neutrality was the sole intent. But what's the difference between any of these commodity vodkas and Moskovskaya, Luksusowa or Belvedere? The simple answer is that the quality brands have retained subtle traces of their raw material, they have grace and elegance – and they therefore retain your interest. What you got with the Westernized versions was a spirit that, even neat, gave no offence, that was a bland, non-committal mixer. Vodka was dumbed down before the phrase was ever thought up.

It was also relatively easy to produce. Any distillery with a rectifying column can make it. Smirnoff is made across the globe, there's Suhoi from Italy, Zar from Bolivia. Things, however, are beginning to change and a new, more flavoursome premium sector is emerging. There's Skyyy and welcome innovations such as Tito's Texas Handmade and the organic Rain from the Ancient Age distillery in Kentucky, Fris and Danska from Denmark and the Dutch brands Ketel One and Royalty. The West is slowly beginning to pay attention and take note of what real vodka is all about.

HOW IT'S MADE

In technical terms, vodka is pure (usually rectified) spirit that has been diluted with water and filtered before bottling. The aim has always been to look for the purest spirit possible.

But why did Poland and Russia decide that a flavoursome grain spirit – akin to the early whiskies made in Scotland and Ireland – wasn't for them? One answer was the need to redistil the spirit from the early log stills (*see* above); another is down to the climate. Low-alcohol spirits freeze. If you were wanting to transport spirit during the bitter winters, it made sense to have as high strength a spirit as possible – and that meant redistillation.

In addition, it is worth remembering that even in the early days vodka was flavoured, and that while herbs were used as masking agents, they were also there to be tasted (the complexity of the recipes is evidence of this). The need, therefore, was for as light a spirit base as possible.

Neutral spirit can be made from anything that contains starch – in principle, vodka can be made from molasses, sugar beet, potatoes, rye, wheat, millet, maize, whey and even rectified wood alcohol.

Most basic commercial brands these days will use molasses, but premium vodkas, however, need to retain the finer qualities of their raw material – and the best are made from either grain or potato. "Vodka seems to be the simplest liquor," says Dr Boleslaw Skrzypczak, one of Poland's recognized vodka experts. "But this understanding only skims the surface. In reality a host of factors influence the quality of vodka – proper raw material and technology for producing raw spirit, the effectiveness of spirit purification and water quality."

Raw materials

The early distillers made their spirit from the most widely available source of starch. That meant wheat in Sweden, rye and potatoes in Poland, rye and wheat in Russia. Already you are looking at different styles. Of the widely available premium vodkas today, Absolut and Altai are made from winter wheat, Moskovskaya is a classic

Moscow rye (although Stolichnaya also uses wheat), while Luksusowa and Chopin are potato spirits. Rye gives bite and weight, wheat a delicacy, while potato gives a distinctive creaminess to the spirit.

The mention of the last ingredient is always liable to produce a strange reaction from Westerners. Potatoes are seen as a sign of an inferior spirit, something rustic and crude. You use potatoes to make hooch in prison, not in a distillery.

While golden fields of grain are infinitely more alluring (and photograph better), a vodka like Luksusowa proves that potatoes can result in a beautifully rich, creamy spirit that's more than a match for grain vodka. In Poland, only special high-starch varieties grown along the Vistula river and on the Baltic coast are used for vodka production – and although they give less alcohol than wheat, they are still preferred for the distinctive character of the final spirit. Dr Skrzypczak also claims that, since potatoes have fewer aromatic compounds, they are better for producing neutral rectified spirits.

Water

One distiller claims that 60 per cent of vodka's quality is down to the water used – although quite how this figure is quantified isn't specified. Water, however, is of vital importance to any spirit, and vodka is no exception.

Expert tasters agree that Moscow vodka's quality suffered when the water supply changed. Finlandia, rightly, can point to its pure water source as one of the major contributory factors in its natural clean taste. The same goes for the Siberian brand Altai, while Absolut has its own well.

Water is used twice – once for mashing, and then again at the end of the process when the spirit is diluted prior to filtration. While some distilleries can use pure spring water at this stage, others have to soften and demineralize the water in order to prevent any clouding of the spirit.

Distilled water was widely used, but it's agreed that it gives a flat flavour to the spirit and, for quality brands at least, is not used. Nothing must get in the way of the pure flavour.

Opposite: *Chopin is among the premium vodkas that are potato spirits; flavoured vodkas have been produced for over 500 years*

Distillation

That purity has been achieved by a highly controlled distillation process. Vodka distillers will point out that after ferment they have a mash that contains hundreds of flavouring compounds and different alcohols. No different from a Scotch distiller. The difference is that vodka distillers will talk of congeners as "harmful" compounds, which must be eliminated. For whisky, rum and brandy producers, they are the very things that they want to retain to give their spirit its personality.

To get to that stage of cleanliness a vodka will be distilled two, three, four or more times. While some vodkas are produced in pot stills (for example, Smirnoff Black and Ketel One), the majority are made in continuous stills with a rectification column (or columns) to remove the unwanted by-products. The difference between premium vodkas comes in the manner in which they are rectified and, later, filtered.

In the Absolut distillery, for example, the spirit passes through a number of columns, each designed to extract a different set of "impurities". One takes out solvents, another fusel oils, another methanol, while the fourth concentrates the spirit to 96 per cent ABV. Go to the Absolut lab and they'll point proudly to the chemical readouts and show that it's as close to ethanol as you'll get.

Here's the dilemma: distillation and rectification are so efficient that they have also removed the trace elements that give premium vodka its character. Absolut at this stage is indeed absolutely pure – so pure, in fact, that it tastes of nothing. What they have to do is put flavour back in by blending in a spirit that's been distilled at a lower strength, along with some vodka that has been aged in wood. That is not to say that these top vodkas will blow you away with a massive whack of the original raw material, but it will be there and you can differentiate between them.

Though most vodka producers aim for a neutral rectified spirit, Polish distillers rectify to a lower degree and attempt to retain some elements of the base material, while still achieving purity of flavour and character.

Some distillers are quite happy producing nothing more than ethyl alcohol. These vodkas are stateless drifters that have no connection with the place of their birth – but they have their uses if you are wanting to make a long drink that tastes of the mixer, not the spirit. Other distillers take the Absolut route (though few are willing to share in any aspect of production) to ensure that character and personality are evident in the final product.

Filtration

The final stage for any vodka is filtration, the aim of which is to remove the spirit's raw, aggressive edge and replace it with a mild, mellow, often sweet taste. In many ways, filtration replaces wood ageing as a method of getting smoothness to the spirit.

It's a process that distillers guard jealously – there are as many secret methods of filtration as there are of distillation. The most common method involves passing the spirit through activated charcoal. What the charcoal is made from will have an impact on the spirit – most agree that alder and birch are best – though some distillers use synthetic or bone charcoal, but the results aren't as good.

Some have a more complex filtration system. Stolichnaya and Altai, for example, are repeatedly filtered over silver-birch charcoal and pure quartz sand; Suhoi, allegedly, is filtered through diamonds, while Smirnoff is passed through seven columns packed with charcoal. Distillers can then add compounds to round out the mouthfeel.

Technical though this undoubtedly is, at the end of the day the best vodkas are only approved if they are passed by a tasting panel. Any professional spirits taster possesses a rare ability for smell. In vodka they are detecting minuscule differences.

"There are people with extraordinarily refined sensitivity," explains Dr Skrzypczak. "Before World War Two, there was a Mrs Wasikowa working at the State Spirits Monopoly Central Laboratory. Just by tasting, she could say which of the 50 or so rectification apparatuses then operating in Poland had produced a given sample, and what kind of defect the apparatus had. Another specialist was in the habit of having stiff shots of the tested beverages before starting the tasting proper."

You bow in awe.

FLAVOURED VODKA

After filtering, the vodka is either reduced and bottled or passes to another stage – flavouring. Most people these days think that flavoured vodkas are some new phenomenon. Bars have gone flavouring crazy – although they almost inevitably end up with vile home-made examples.

Some lower-end brands have also jumped on the bandwagon by adding flavour extracts to the vodka, but these clumsy attempts to replicate the classic old styles are immediately exposed when you taste them side by side. Sadly, though, not everyone has the chance to do this experiment, and these new gimmicky flavours could end up destroying one of vodka's forgotten styles.

While flavours were originally either medicinal herbs or sweetening agents used to disguise off-notes in the distillate, the intricacy of the old Polish and Russian recipes implies that flavour for its own end was an aim at an early stage in vodka's evolution.

These classic flavoured vodkas give a window into the past, lighting up the woods and fields that surrounded the early distillers.

Flavouring is added not by redistillation – like gin or akvavit – but by maceration, leaching or, in some cases, by blending in distillates of flavourings or wine. The cheapest option (which also gives the clumsiest examples) is cold compounding, where flavourings are poured into the vodka. To achieve better results you have to macerate the ingredients in the spirit for a lengthy period at room temperature. The time will vary according to the ingredients, and some of the more complex recipes will have different ingredients added at different points.

A newer method, outlined by Faith & Wisniewski, is the circulation process, which is used for styles such as Zubrowka. Here, the flavouring agents are placed on a rack inside the tank and the alcohol is passed through them at regular intervals to get an even, quick extraction. Ricard uses a similar technique for making pastis.

The end result is a vast range of flavours with extraordinary tastes – and a history that dates right back 500 years to vodka's origins. In those days the distillers would have used the ingredients around them – like Tatra vodka flavoured with the herbs from the mountains, while others give a clue to their aristocratic heritage by using the essences and contents of the manor house's spice room.

You'll find vodkas like the Polish winter warmer Krupnik, which is flavoured with honey (the oldest of all fermented drinks) and 30 other herbs and spices, including cinnamon, nutmeg and ginger; or the Russian hunter's vodka, Okhotnichaya, which combines 10 spices and herbs, including ginger, clove, juniper, anise, orange peel and port.

There are echoes of the age-old rural custom of using wild autumn fruits in Jarzebiak, made with rowan berries, or the heady languorous sweetness of wild cherry in Wisniowka. Then there are vodkas which must have originally been the preserve of the rich – lifted, effervescent Cytrynowka (using lemon

TASTING NOTES

FLAVOURED VODKA

Smirnoff Citrus Twist Confected lemon sherbet bon-bons laid on top of neutral spirit.

Cytrynowka (Polish lemon) Delicate nose that's a little spirity. Attractive, light and clean on the palate, it's a little short.

Goldwasser Bitter nose with anise and caraway dominant. Very sweet, but with a bitter lime marmalade peel drive keeping it fresh.

Absolut Kurant Intense aromas which seem artificial. Clean, dry spirit behind. Very light.

Pieprzowka (Polish pepper) Fragrant and surprisingly sweet on the nose with a mix of thyme, rosemary, cloves, cinnamon and dry pepper behind. Bone dry with a crackling mix of black pepper and chilli on the palate.

Absolut Peppar Green jalapeño/fresh dill nose. The pepper carries through with chilli seed heat burning on the finish. Tremendous, it goes for the throat with fangs bared.

Zubrowka A haunting aroma of cut grass and blossom, like a meadow after a rainstorm, the air doused with the ever-changing fragrance of herbs, grass and lavender. Very soft with a hint of sweetness and spice. Crisp, clean finish. A classic.

Krupnik A little spirity on the nose, with rounded wild herbs. On the palate it's lightly sweet with some baked apple, herbs and a lightly vegetal edge. Lovely.

peel and leaves in Poland) or Russia's equivalent Limmonaya (which only uses peel) and, most expensive of all, the rare, delicate Rose Petal.

You name the flavour, it's there. Bloody Mary aficionados can choose between crisp Pieprzowka; the softer Wyborowa pepper; the dry Absolut Peppar; or the powerful Stolichnaya Pertsovka. To put a different spin on things, there is even oak-aged vodka, Starka. In Poland this is made from a 50 per cent ABV rye spirit that is aged in Tokaji wine barrels or large vats, sometimes with a touch of Malaga fortified wine to sweeten it.

Originally, this was a feast vodka, which was made by pouring the spirit over the lees in a wine barrel and then burying it for three to four years. Starka is pretty rare, but those keen to explore them should investigate the range from Szczecin distillery – Specjalna (12-year-old), Jubileuszowa (15-year-old), Piastowska (20-year-old) and Banquet (30-year-old).

Russian Starka has apple and pear leaves, as well as a fortification of brandy and port. Unusual though it may seem to those of us brought up on naked vodka, adding wine and other distillates is common practice. In Poland the marvellous Zytnia is a strong rye vodka which has had apple and plum wine blended in.

If that leaves your mind reeling, unsure of where to start, then go straight to the top of the tree, however, and search out Zubrowka (spelt with a 'v' in Russian).

Hailing from the Bialowieska forest on the Polish/Belarus border, Zubrowka was originally a seventeenth-century regional speciality, and a particular favourite of the Polish royal family on their hunting visits to the forest.

Each bottle of Zubrowka has a blade of bison grass (*hierochloe odorata*) in it. This plant is the favourite grazing of the European bison, which still roam wild in the forest – in fact, legend has it that only grass that's been urinated on by one of the beasts can be used in the vodka.

The grass itself is high in fragrant components which impart an evocative, green scent to the vodka with a delicate vanilla touch (coming from the coumarin ester in the grass). A glorious drink.

TODAY'S MARKET

Vodka will endure, of that there's little doubt. The question is whether it can break free of its commodity image and be recognized as the classy spirit it is. There are a number of different factors at play in today's market. Almost inevitably, there has been a raft of brands that have entered the market hanging on to Absolut's coat-tails.

Here style is considerably more important than content. Fancy bottles and huge price tags can't hide the fact that there are a large number of premium vodkas on the market that are not worth the money, and hopefully someone is soon going to notice that these Emperors (or Tsars) have no clothes.

At the same time, though, there are "new" brands from Poland and Russia that deserve wider attention. Vodka lovers already appreciate the herbal lift of Stolichnaya (and its richer big brother, Cristal), Absolut's clarity and Finlandia's light dryness.

But don't pass over the lime oil richness of Wyborowa; Moskovskaya's full, elegant, rye weight; and the creamy, soft Luksusowa – or dismiss Smirnoff Black. Poland can also weigh in with the premium potato vodkas Baltic and Chopin, or the rye crunch of Belvedere. Also try and find the kosher vodkas made at the Nissebaum's plant in Bielsko-Biala or at Lancut – it's worth it.

Elsewhere you can browse among Holland's pot-still Ketel One, or Royalty, Denmark's Fris and Danska and, from the USA, Rain and Tito's Texas Handmade. Though these may all be seen as esoteric brands at the moment, they are providing the impetus for vodka's future long-term success as a serious spirit.

This shift upmarket is much needed, as the category has become increasingly bogged down with inferior, cheap products and a rather peculiar image. Vodka isn't seen as a bad spirit, but few consumers in recent years have bothered giving it a second thought. This in itself isn't surprising as, since the 1950s, the whole category has been sold on the premise that it tastes of nothing.

Well, as we have seen, times are changing and vodka is most definitely making a comeback.

Opposite: *Sean Connery, James Bond in the film* Dr No, *pours a Smirnoff vodka as part of one of his celebrated cocktails*

TEQUILA

Few contemporary spirits tap into the mythic past quite like mezcal (of which tequila is a regional speciality). Though becoming increasingly sophisticated – some would say, gentrified – at its heart this Mexican spirit, distilled from agave (not cactus!), has retained its mystery, and still embraces the ancient notion of alcohol as a gift from the gods.

Although distillation didn't arrive in Mexico until the invasion of the Spanish Conquistadors, if you want to get to the "why" of mezcal you have to examine how its fermented equivalent, pulque, was used by the indigenous inhabitants of this vast, mysterious country. According to mythology the agave plant is the incarnation of the goddess Mayahuel; the honey-like sap (aguamiel) is her blood. The secret of fermenting pulque was given to man by the trickster figure (and the first drunk) Tlacuache. It's said he still shows producers when the agave is ready to be harvested, although these days José Cuervo prefers to rely on satellite imaging.

Pulque had a dual significance. By getting drunk on pulque, the god-king Quetzalcoatl committed the sin that precipitated his leaving earth and ascending into the heavens. At the same time, though, pulque had acquired a ritual importance, with its own god (Tetzcatzoncatl) and his symbolic entourage of 400 rabbits who represented the different forms of intoxication.

Unlike in North America, the otherworldly experience induced by intoxication (either of pulque or hallucinogens) was of fundamental importance to religious ritual and culture. The agave was seen as a cosmic plant that received and dispensed energy, so pulque eventually became a powerful symbol of nature's rebirth, and was used ceremonially after the harvest to guarantee a good crop the following year. The same ritual was performed with fermented drinks across the world, from Celtic Europe to Indonesia and Crete.

In Mexico there is an established culture of producing alcoholic brews from wild ferments. Corn was used to make chicha and tesguino; wild plums were used to make obo mezcal; honey was fermented with bark to produce balche, but these were local specialities. The agave, however, grows wild in every region of Mexico, so pulque became the "national" drink, hugely important socially, economically and religiously. Myths, legends and ritual sprang up around its usage – and even today there's no other drink that has so many rituals as mezcal and tequila.

When distillation arrived, many of pulque's ancient usages were simply transferred to tequila and mezcal. The spirits are used in traditional medicine, to bless fields and new buildings and, running true to the Mexican fashion of melding Christianity with a pre-Columbian belief system, even for blessing crosses. In Oaxaca on the Day of the Dead, the last glass of mezcal in the bottle is sprinkled over the deceased relative's grave. Though for long a social drink, the spirit has stubbornly refused to relinquish its symbolic power.

"It's a special, sacred event when you take mezcal", says Ron Cooper of mezcal specialist del Maguey. "Originally, the people could only drink it on feast days – but you could consume it until you were smashed because then you were considered to be 'with the gods'."

Sources suggest that mezcal wasn't the first spirit to be produced after the Conquest in the sixteenth century. There is circumstantial evidence that aguardiente (or chinguirito) was illegally made by slaves on the Caribbean coast from molasses and sugar cane. In spite of the Conquistadors clearly being aware of pulque, they mainly drank wine or brandy, which was imported from the home country. So why didn't they make brandy in Mexico? There are three reasons. The first is that grapes cannot be grown throughout the whole of the country. The second is that distillation was, technically, not allowed – everything had to come from Spain. Thirdly, even if brandy production had been permitted, the lack of a good communications network meant that transportation was well-nigh impossible. So they, like the indigenous people before them, turned to the most ready source of fermentable sugars – the agave.

It's likely that crude distillation took place in the seventeenth century (or even before), but it wasn't until 1758 that today's industry began to emerge around the town of Tequila. The town was an important centre of the New Kingdom of Galicia, and it was near there that the King of Spain granted land to Don José Antonio Cuervo to farm agave in Jalisco province. This was the first time that permission had been granted to plant crops (other than grapes) that could be turned into alcohol. It was also the first time that producers of pulque or its distilled relative had used cultivated, rather than wild, plants.

In 1795, Don José's son (José Maria Guadeloupe Cuervo) was granted a licence to produce "mezcal wine" in his La Rojena distillery, which is still used by the firm. Agave plantations soon spread across the region and other distilleries appeared – such as Sauza's La Perseverancia, which was founded in 1873. The market expanded further when the railway arrived – an initiative by General Manuel Gonzalez, whose great-grandson went on to found the tequila producer Chinaco.

It wasn't until after the Second World War, though, that tequila began to build up a head of steam on the export markets. By that time, Mexico had acquired a heady exoticism for young Americans – writers like Jack Kerouac and William Burroughs were attracted to its image of being somehow a "lost" America.

It had a frontier spirit – there was a sense of recklessness about it, an element of danger (more wishful than real), and if it got too much you could scuttle back across the border. Tequila came back with these travellers and brought with it the essence of this heady, decadent, weird Mexican experience.

Matters improved further with the creation of the Margarita in the late 1950s and, with increased tourism and a more liberal attitude to life in the 1960s, tequila became the counter-culture drink. New rituals started up – slamming it, and drinking it with lime and salt. Tequila fuelled youth culture. Then people grew up and forgot about the joy of a well-made Margarita. Tequila remained a youthful kick, or a morally dissolute drink.

Tequila comes of age

It was all right pretending to be like Geoffrey Firmin in Lowry's *Under the Volcano* in the 1960s. In the reactionary backlash of the late 1980s, two-fisted drinking just wasn't the thing to be seen doing. But then, just as with malt whisky and bourbon, the pendulum began to swing back. There are various theories as to where it started, or who started it, but what is certain is that in the past five years or so, younger drinkers have been looking at tequila in a new light, and distilleries have responded. Many believe it started in Mexico with young, middle-class drinkers turning their backs on the white spirit that happened to be tequila and wanting something better – something that could be sipped.

Sipping tequila? That seems like a contradiction in terms. Or it did until aged tequilas from Porfidio, Herradura, el Tesoro, Tres Magueyes, Chinaco and the top brands from Cuervo and Sauza hit the scene. Martin Grassl of Porfidio recalls that when, in 1990, he decided to produce a top-quality tequila, the top product in the category was selling for $20. These days tequila aficionados don't blink at $100-plus.

The difference lay in production. In the past tequila was made to satisfy the slammin', shootin' market. To make matters worse, in the 1970s the Mexican government allowed tequila to include 49 per cent of "other fermentable sugars" (in other words, neutral cane spirit), which suited the large firms perfectly. Gold tequilas were not necessarily aged; they were usually just sweetened versions of silver.

What the new wave did was to get back to basics. The new sipping tequilas are (by and large) made from 100 per cent blue agave; they are given either a short time in wood (reposado) or aged in small barrels (anejo). As a result the full character of the spirit is finally being revealed in its subtle, often elegant, glory. Part of tequila's easy charm is down to the fact that it tastes like an overripe exotic fruit punch, with a seductive sweetness that borders on decay. These new tequilas give that quality an extra layer of complexity.

This fits in neatly with the changing American palate, which is demanding richer, fuller flavours; which is looking for genuine native cuisine; and which believes that small is beautiful.

Tighter controls are in place. The European Union has banned the production of ersatz tequila from sugar beet in Spain and Greece. Tequila has come of age.

HOW TEQUILA
IS MADE

Tequila is a distillate of the blue agave (*agave azul tequilana weber*), one of over 200 strains of this family of desert lilies which grow across Mexico. Half the size and quicker-maturing than the giant agave that produces pulque, the blue agave is the true treasure of the Sierra Madre – that high, dry, mineral-rich volcanic plain to the north-west of Guadalajara. Weighing in at between 40 and 70 kilograms when harvested, each plant has a hard, caustic centre of pure starch which, when distilled, will give roughly two-and-a-half litres of tequila.

To qualify as tequila, the blue agave must be grown in one of five designated regions – the whole of Jalisco, parts of Nayarit, Michoacan, Guanajuato and, thanks to the efforts of Chinaco's Guillermo Gonzalez, parts of Tamaulipas. Only here is the *terroir* correct for it to grow and thrive.

Agave hijuelos (babies) are collected from mother plants, and are transplanted in the rainy season (June–October) to prepared fields in the plantations. It takes eight to 10 years for the plant to reach maturity, during which time the grower will feed it, fertilize it, prune back the leaves to retain the plant's energy in its core and remove the sharp, spiny tips from the leaves. Once the agave is ripe, its lower leaves begin to turn brown and a flower spike starts to sprout. This and the leaves are macheted off, exposing the central core which, because of its appearance, is called a *piña* (pineapple). An experienced worker will be able to harvest between 130 and 150 *piñas* a day – three to five tons of agave. The leaves are ploughed back into the field, which will lie fallow for a year before being replanted.

Once in the distillery, the rock-hard *piñas* are cooked to convert their starches into sugar. There are two ways of doing this. The traditional fashion is to leave them in massive ovens at around 95°C for 36 hours. But producers such as Sauza are increasingly using pressure-cooking, which means they can complete the process in less than half the time. The end result is the same. The great, solid ball of starch has been turned into a gloopy mass of sweet, brownish sugar.

This then needs to be crushed and the juice drained off. Traditional producers (like el Tesoro) still place the cooked *piñas* in a pit and crush them with a stone wheel, while Cuervo and Sauza feed the mass into shredders and pass running water through.

The liquid (*aguamiel*) is then put into large fermenting vats made of either wood or stainless steel. Once again there's a split in production techniques, with the firms who crush traditionally putting both liquid and fibres into the vat (and ultimately into the first distillation). This, they argue, gives a richer flavour. Some firms (such as Cuervo) add their own strains of yeast to the fermenters, others add a little sugar, while it's also common for firms to add chemicals in order to produce a standardized ferment which can be whizzed through in a matter of a few hours.

The traditionalists, however, still rely on wild yeasts to trigger the ferment. Porfidio occupies a half-way house in that its new distillery is equipped with closed fermenters, but the ferment is allowed to run for up to four days.

All tequila is double-distilled in either copper or stainless steel pot stills. Once again, the exception is Porfidio whose new stills are adapted from the schnapps stills that Austrian-born owner Martin Grassl was trained on. These consist of a pot with two linked columns to concentrate and refine the distillate.

Many firms distil to a high strength and dilute immediately after, but others, such as el Tesoro and Sauza, distil to a lower strength – and the results are

TASTING NOTES

GOLD/REPOSADO

Tres Magueyes Reposado. Vanilla ice and light lime leaf.

Real Hacienda Reposado. Floral nose with hint of peppermint. A sipping tequila.

Porfidio Reposado. Fragrant ripe fruits. Elegant, restrained.

Chinaco Reposado. Waft of citric juiciness backed with ripe agave.

ANEJO

Jose Cuervo 1800. Pulpy fruit with a slightly sugared quality. Clean and smooth.

Sauza Comemorativo. Chocolatey aroma with positive agave character.

Tres Magueyes Don Julio. Ripe pears with soft orange blossom. Gentle in the mouth.

El Tesoro Anejo. Spicy, rich and profound. Subtle with exotic fruitiness. Classy.

Real Hacienda. Fragrant lemon/lime zestiness mixed with white chocolate.

Porfidio 5 year-old. Rich with assertive ripe agave nose with nutty fruit on the finish.

more pungent spirits which have retained the rich fruitiness of the agave. Sauza also claims to use a smaller central cut for its 100 per cent blue agave brands.

Silver tequila can be released after a brief period of marrying, while gold usually has some caramel added to it. However, it's the wood-aged styles – reposado (aged for between two and 11 months) and anejo (one year and over) which are turning the market around. The quality-conscious firms are experimenting with different sizes of cask and also with different woods. Traditionally ex-bourbon barrels have been used, but sherry butts are also appearing, as are ex-Cognac barrels and, in the case of Cuervo's Reserva de la Familia, new French oak and, for Porfidio, new US oak for its Cactus brand. It gives blenders more building blocks to work with – different ages, different barrel types – to assemble these new premium brands.

Traditionally, tequila has never been aged for much over five years. In essence it is a fragile spirit, and after a lengthy period in wood that character begins to disappear (some distillers believe it actually degrades) while the wood takes over. Sauza has recently tried to prove the point that tequila can cope with extended ageing by releasing Tres Generaciones which, at eight years, is claimed to be the oldest brand on the market. Fine spirit though it may be, you're hard pressed to find true blue agave character in there. Still, it is evidence of the new-found spirit of quality that's taken over the industry.

Harvested piñas *are cooked in clay ovens to convert their starches into sugar*

HOW MEZCAL IS MADE

There are many myths about Mexican spirits. Tequila being made from cactus is one of them, Mezcal making you "trip" is another. Both are untrue. Like tequila, mezcal is made from agave. In fact, technically speaking, tequila is a mezcal from a designated area. Wherever agave grows, mezcal will not be far behind – although most is from Oaxaca, it's produced across the central plains to the Chihuahuan desert, the Pacific coast and Chiapas. Each remote village will have its palenquero, or distiller.

What makes mezcal different is the result of a number of factors. The *terroir* of the region will have an effect, as will the type of agave used. While tequila can

TASTING NOTES

MEZCAL

Monte Alban. Burnt car tyres. Abrasive.

Hacienda Sotol. Peachy, citric with light smoke and earth. Very delicate. Crisp with a touch of almond essence on the finish.

Del Maguey brands

Minero. Earthy, rooty nose. Hot tiles with complex sweet fruit behind. Tart start then bitter grip before a long smoky, pear-tongued finish.

Chichicapa. Flowery, delicate, roasted pear aromas. Mouthfilling with good feel, mingling light, fragrant citric top notes with rich mouthfeel.

Luis del Rio. Plump, Germoline nose. Fruit-driven with a slight wood bark edge. Sweet start then violets, earth and fruit. Rich and complex.

Santo Domingo Albarradas. Slightly rubbery on nose which carries slightly on palate, then is blown away by overripe peach and plum flavours. A dust-dry finish.

only be made from blue agave, mezcal can be produced from a host of different strains, including the giant agave, the wild silvestre, the rare but highly prized tobala, sotol and, most commonly, espadin.

The production, with a few exceptions, remains resolutely rural and rustic. The *piñas* are harvested at around eight years old, although this will vary between species and the richness of the soil. The sotol agave, for example, is smaller than the blue agave, takes longer to mature – and requires twice as many *piñas* to make a litre of spirit.

The process is subtly different from tequila. Whereas blue agave is baked or steamed, the *piñas* for mezcal are slow-roasted for three days, either over a fire in adobe or gas-fired ovens or in a deep rock-lined pit that's sealed with leaves and earth. As the *piñas* roast, so they absorb the smoke, which gives mezcal its distinctive earthy, rich pungency.

This roasting activates the wild yeasts in the *piña* and the cooked hearts are left to start fermenting naturally before being placed in a stone ring and crushed by a horse-drawn millstone. The fibrous juice is put into open-topped fermenters with a little water and left to ferment naturally.

Once the ferment is deemed to have finished – it can take between four and 30 days – the entire contents of the vat are transferred to the pot still. These are usually copper, but can be clay, like the one used for del Maguey's single village brand Minero. After the first distillation, the fibres are cleared out of the still and the second run takes place.

In del Maguey's case, the second distillation will contain the head and heart of the first distillation with a small percentage of the tail to increase the flavour. There aren't any hydrometers in these remote villages. The palenquero (distiller) will judge when to start and stop collecting spirit by sucking up the mezcal in a bamboo pipette and spraying the liquid into a gourd. The size and density of the bubbles on the surface tell him the strength and purity of the spirit. It's distillation as it has been done for hundreds of years, by people using nothing more than local resources, intuition and soul.

Mezcal remains the drink of the rural communities. You'll find some that's been sweetened, flavoured with herbs and bark and fruit; some that's fermented in

leather and distilled once. The most unusual (and expensive) is the rarely seen Pechuga, a double-distilled mezcal which is redistilled with the addition of wild plantain, mountain apple, pineapple, plum, fruits, nuts, rice and sugar. To complete the melange of flavours a chicken breast is suspended over the alcoholic vapour.

These hand-crafted spirits are normally consumed not far from where they are made. Some are no more than crude moonshine, others are made with care and love. The few firms that do export (the most notable in quality terms being Hacienda Sotol and del Maguey) have then to try and convince people that mezcal can

Blue agave, from which tequila is distilled, in a field at Heiraduro; in the background stands Tequila mountain

be as serious a drink as one of the "new" sipping tequilas. The complex range of hand-crafted organic, single village mezcals from del Maguey are a resounding demonstration of the heights that this spirit can reach. Untainted by commercial demands, they remain the few spirits in the world which have a direct link to the past.

The trouble is that if tequila has long suffered under the image of slamming, then mezcal has to live with the legacy of the gusano worm, which some brands pop into their bottled product. In legend, because these moth larvae live in the agave, they have ingested some of its power. Therefore, the person who eats the gusano also acquires some of the spirit of the plant. That's one story. Another is that they add flavour to the drink – which is possible, but unlikely. Yet another claims that it "proves" that the mezcal is made from agave – which is a strange way to get an appellation. The most common story is that eating the worm makes you hallucinate. This comes from a basic confusion between mezcal and the unrelated psychedelic drug mescalin.

At the end of the day, the addition of the gusano worm is nothing more than a gimmick, and it's one which hasn't done mezcal any favours.

ANISE

One of the world's oldest medicinal herbs, anise (first cultivated by the Egyptians) and star anise (the fruit of a tree originally grown in the Far East) have been used as ingredients in alcohol since the dawn of distillation. With ambitious-sounding claims that anise could cure stomach contractions, aid circulation and breathing, and act as a stimulant and a diuretic, the trade in anise was already well established in Roman times.

An important ingredient in the medicines produced in Egypt, Mesopotamia and Ancient Greece – the key centres of the first experiments in distillation – anise lives on in the national drinks of these and other Mediterranean countries.

As an ingredient it is best-known as the main flavour compound in such brands as Pernod and Ricard, but it's also used in ouzo, raki, sambuca and the huge range of Spanish anise-based aperitifs and liqueurs. Peter the Great used anise as the sole flavouring for his own personal vodka (*see* Vodka), and it is still used in some flavoured vodka recipes, such as the Russian hunter's vodka, Okhotnichaya.

Anise only sloughed off its medicinal image in the sixteenth century, when it began to be used as a part of spirits such as the Italian liqueur Popula – which was made from water, *eaux-de-vie*, anise essence, cinnamon, musk and amber. It was also added to vinegars and soft drinks like early lemonades.

These days it remains the most widely drunk style of spirit in all the countries that border the Mediterranean. From Lebanon to Morocco, Greece to Italy, France and Spain, every culture has its own variant on this most ancient of drinks.

The Green fairy

These days the drinks flavoured with anise are cosmopolitan aperitifs, cloudy, light green, yellow or white, sipped in the shady squares of the Mediterranean. But the precursor of today's Pernod, Ricard and ouzo was a drink that scandalized Europe in the late nineteenth century – absinthe.

This notorious spirit first appeared in the late eighteenth century when a Dr Pierre Ordinaire fled revolutionary France and set up as a travelling physician in the area around the Swiss town of Covet. There he began peddling an elixir that was produced by the two Henriot sisters in a tiny still that sat on top of their kitchen stove.

The sisters, carrying on the old tradition of "wise women", had concocted a recipe which involved infusing star anise, fennel, hyssop, melissa, parsley, camomile, coriander, veronica, spinach and, most importantly, wormwood, in alcohol.

Wormwood (*artemisia absinthium*) itself is an ancient ingredient, and is mentioned in John French's 1651 treatise *Art of Distillation* as one of the vast number of herbs, spices and roots that went into Aqua Celestis. French also recommended adding a few drops of the essential oil of wormwood to a glass of "Rheinish" wine to make a "wormwood wine". The name, wormwood, comes from the German, wermut, meaning "preserver of the mind".

Dr Ordinaire's medicine became known as absinthe after this ingredient, and soon became a local speciality drink rather than just a cure-all. In 1787, the Henriot sisters sold their secret recipe to one Major Henri Dubeid, who promptly established his own distillery dedicated to commercial-scale production of the drink – which by now was building itself a reputation in Switzerland and the bordering regions of France. Spurred on by the success of absinthe, Dubeid's son-in-law, Henri-Louis Pernod, opened a larger distillery in Covet; eight years later he moved production back to

Opposite: The star anise has been used as an ingredient in alcohol since the beginning of distillation

France at Pontarlier, and his absinthe – now known as Pernod – began to take France by storm.

The French aperitif market offered a pretty limited choice in those days, with people having to choose between wine and one of the bitter quinine-based tonics. The arrival of this strong (between 65 and 75 per cent ABV), dry, refreshing, scented drink was the fillip the market needed.

Absinthe received its biggest boost in the 1830s when soldiers from the African Battalion returned from the continent with tales of how diluting their drinking water with absinthe had saved them from a whole host of tropical diseases like malaria. On their return home they continued to drink absinthe and, in the way people do, smart society followed. Absinthe had become the hero's drink.

With this acceptance by bourgeois society, La Fée Verte (the green fairy, so called because of the green colour it went after water was added) became France's chosen spirit. Ironically, by the 1850s, when Cognac was making its mark on the world, the French were drinking more absinthe than brandy.

Production increased. Four more distilleries opened in Pontarlier and others were started in Doubs, Haute-Savoie, Jura, the Midi and Paris, although the best absinthe was still regarded as being from Pernod's original distilleries close to the Swiss border.

By the middle of the century, absinthe drinking took another twist when it was embraced by the radical artists, writers and poets – Baudelaire, Verlaine, Huysmans and Rimbaud – who were scandalizing polite society with their flouting of morals and their radical, visionary approach to writing and painting. As well as experimenting with hashish and opium, they saw absinthe not just as a drink, but as a stimulus to creativity. In 20 years absinthe had gone from being the saviour of heroic soldiers to the equivalent of LSD. "The most delicate, the most precarious adornment, to be drunk of the magic of that herb from the glaciers, absumphe!" wrote Rimbaud in 1872.

Almost inevitably, it came under the scrutiny of the self-appointed guardians of the nation's morals, and from the late 1870s on absinthe began its rapid fall from the height of fashionability and cafe society to become the tipple of madmen and degenerates.

By the start of this century, absinthe was being blamed for all of French society's ills (a bit like the English middle classes had done with gin). Dementia, crime, TB ... you name it, absinthe took the rap.

Scientists claimed to have discovered a new mental disease called "absinthism", which could be passed on from mother to child. In *The Hyperreal Drug Archives*, Matthew Baggott relates that absinthism was allegedly "characterized by addiction, hyperexcitability, tremors, convulsions and hallucinations".

Politicians railed against the evil grip that the Green Fairy was exerting on the nation, as did the protectors of "family values" and the Press. Winemakers, seeing an opportunity to get sales moving again after *phylloxera*, joined in the free-for-all, rallying support around the less-than-catchy, but effective, slogan of "Up With Wine, Down With Absinthe". On January 7, 1915, production of absinthe was banned.

Over 80 years on, absinthe still has a sinister reputation. Even today you will hear people claiming that artists such as Toulouse-Lautrec were killed by their addiction to absinthe – although syphilis and laudanum were probably more to blame.

There is no doubt that absinthe ruined many lives, but this was more a result of its extremely high alcoholic strength, than of any weird, addictive, mind-bending poison that lurked in its opalescent depths.

It might seem strange to devote all this space to a drink that barely exists today, but absinthe still captures the imagination of all spirit lovers. It mirrors the change in Western society's attitude to spirits that emerged in the twentieth century – it also carries with it echoes of the primal spirits, the mind-altering shamanic drugs that elevate you to a different plane of reality.

But was absinthe itself addictive? Yes and no. Pernod's absinthe was 75 per cent ABV. Drink a lot of that on a regular basis, and you are liable to be flirting with alcoholism, which has remarkably similar symptoms to "absinthism". The drink was cheap, it was strong, it was widely available and it was often poorly made. There are records of unscrupulous producers making "absinthe" from a base of wood alcohol with copper sulphate being added for colour, and (the highly toxic) antimony to make it go cloudy. No great surprise, then, that it produced rather bizarre effects.

That doesn't quite address the fact that absinthe intoxication is unlike any other. The closest is achieved with Chartreuse and Calisay (*see* Liqueurs), but while they both give a certain detached, contemplative effect, absinthe is an altogether more intense experience – an absinthe-induced hangover feels as if your brain stem has been severed.

This could be entirely down to the alcoholic strength, but, intriguingly, as Baggott points out, wormwood contains thujone, part of the same chemical group that includes THC, the active ingredient in cannabis that induces hallucinations. Records also show that some absinthe producers used the mildly psychoactive calamus and nutmeg in their recipes. Perhaps there's something to it after all.

Absinthe remains banned in most of Europe, although it can be bought in Andorra, Spain, Portugal, Denmark and the Czech Republic. Sadly, given today's timid attitude to alcohol, it would seem unlikely that many spirits lovers will be able to join in Rimbaud's toast: "Long live the Absinthe Academy!"

What happened next ...

Pernod's Pontarlier distillery was closed by the ban on absinthe and France had to wait until after the First World War before a new, acceptable variant was allowed to be made.

In 1920, the various firms that had been set up by Pernod and his sons joined forces, and in 1928 the firm launched its new eponymous anise drink, sweeter, lower in alcohol and without wormwood. The French, deprived of their favourite aperitif, took to it immediately and the absinthe that had fuelled the fantastical writings of Baudelaire, Poe and Apollinaire became the more civilized Pernod, once more sipped by cafe society.

This time, though, Pernod wasn't to have the market all to itself. In 1932, 23-year-old Paul Ricard discovered a formula for an anise-based pastis, while other small producers, based in the south of the country, also started up. Ricard took Pernod on before eventually reaching an amicable agreement in 1975, when the two firms merged. By 1984, one billion bottles of Ricard had been sold. The Green Fairy had gone like the Wicked Witch of the West; the world was ready for anise once more.

An 1896 poster advertising Absinthe Robette, by Privat Livemont

HOW IT'S MADE

From elixir to fashionable drink to scourge of society and, now, once again, a distinctly classic and individual aperitif, anise-based spirits have a long, varied and colourful history in all the countries that border the Mediterranean.

Absinthe

All anise (and wormwood) drinks would have started their days as medicinal extracts obtained by either distilling or macerating herbs in alcohol. The absinthe prescribed by Dr Ordinaire was a complex infusion of

573

A street cafe in Provence, home to the pastis, where anise can again be enjoyed, even if absinthe has now disappeared

15 herbs – the main ingredients being star anise, fennel and wormwood left to steep in alcohol and bottled at around 80 per cent ABV. Though unusual these days, this high strength was quite common for medicinal extracts. Chartreuse Elixir (*see* Liqueurs) is 71 per cent ABV, and the standard Green Chartreuse is 50 per cent.

Pernod built in greater complexity to his absinthe recipe by not only adding other ingredients – hyssop, lemon balm, angelica, dittany, juniper, nutmeg and veronica – but then distilling the macerated alcohol (made from wine spirit rather than the more widely available maize or beet) and then adding more dried herbs, including an extra dose of wormwood, before diluting the mixture to the desired strength of 75 per cent ABV.

Pernod

When the firm was allowed to produce anise-based spirit again, it revamped its production methods and some of the ingredients. Until recently, all of Pernod's aniseed flavour was derived from Chinese star anise, although since 1982 the firm has also been using fennel.

You'll find Pernod's recipe varies slightly between countries – some get a spirit that's been sweetened with saccharose rather than glucose syrup, while the addition of synthetic colouring is not permitted in some countries. The strength will vary between 40 and 45 per cent ABV. If you get the choice, go for the higher strength.

Pastis is made in a significantly different fashion. While Pernod uses distillation, pastis is made solely by macerating the flavour compounds in spirit. The aniseed flavour is also obtained in a different fashion – while the colour is different.

Ricard is made in a four-step process. It, too, uses anethol, produced by rectifying star anise and fennel, but it also uses alcohol flavoured with liquorice root. The roots are crushed and placed on a screen inside a closed-circuit system through which water and neutral alcohol is forced, thereby extracting the aromatic juices, (a similar process is used to produce Zubrowka vodka). It's this particular method of extraction that gives Ricard its amber colour.

These two aromatic bases are then shipped to all of Ricard's production centres in France and abroad. There the secret collection of other dried aromatic ingredients native to Provence are mixed together. These are then placed in a mix of neutral spirit (most commonly from sugar beet), water and the two aromatic concentrates. The mix is adjusted with sugar and caramel and left to macerate for a minimum of 24 hours and a maximum of 72 hours.

The product is filtered three times and then bottled at a higher strength than Pernod, as Ricard claims that pastis has to be at a minimum of 45 per cent ABV in order to fully dissolve the anethol and make the product stable.

A smaller pastis producer, Janot, claims to use a more traditional method. For its standard pastis, the Provençal ingredients are left to macerate in neutral alcohol for a minimum of three weeks before being filtered and then bottled.

Janot's top pastis, Grand Pastis Lou Garagai, is one of the most complex on the market – having a wider selection of flavouring ingredients (including wormwood flowers), which are left to steep in higher-grade spirit for 12 weeks. The firm claims it is the only one to use this old, long maceration technique.

Pernod is built up in three main blocks. The star anise and fennel are distilled and rectified to produce an essential oil called anethol. This is then blended with neutral alcohol and the distillates of a number of aromatic plants. The firm keeps the number and nature of these a closely guarded secret. Meanwhile liquorice is macerated in alcohol and blended with another distillate of flavouring herbs. These component parts are then blended together with neutral alcohol, softened water, glucose syrup and colouring agents before being filtered, stored and bottled.

THE TASTE

Absinthe makes the heart grow fonder

The author's first meeting with absinthe was in a duty-free shop in Andorra where a bottle was bought partly for academic interest – and partly to scare his mother-in-law. It's difficult to separate fact from fiction when it comes to this spirit. Absinthe has been an unknown quantity for so long that no one quite knows what it should taste like. The initial reaction is that it is simply a more intense pastis, but there's a depth to it – partly from the alcohol.

Then there's its extraordinary colour. All anise-based drinks go cloudy when water is added because anethol forms an emulsion when it's diluted, but while Pernod turns a gentle green and pastis goes yellow, absinthe turns the colour of opal and seems to glow in the glass.

If you experience difficulty in finding a bottle, look at Degas's *The Absinthe Drinker*. Not only does the painting capture the lifeless slouch of an alcoholic, but the colour of the drink is exactly correct.

These days absinthe is also sold in the Czech Republic. It was one of the spirits that eluded the author in his global trawl, but a friend of his who visited Prague agreed to act as guinea-pig. His tasting note is worth repeating in full. "…As per your recommendation I tried the absinthe – Bloody Hell!! What is that stuff? It seemed to metamorphose in the mouth into some weird, hot substance reminiscent of something used to aid aircraft propulsion. Mind you, its blue colour was rather reminiscent of paraffin. It seemed to change to a "hot" liquid in the mouth. Not "hot" in the usual alcoholic "nippy" way, but hot as in temperature, and weird in texture, slimy?! I have tried many unusual drinks in my time, but I have to say I think this one beats them all." Quite what this blue spirit was made from is not worth investigating.

Although pastis and Pernod can be mixed with various soft drinks and cordials, the best way to sip them is to dilute them with five parts of water, see the drink change from clear to cloudy and allow the rich aniseed and liquorice aromas to rise from the glass. While Pernod smells of aniseed twists and sweet shops, pastis is refreshing, delicate and dry. Ricard is the benchmark style, but Pernod's 51 is a crisp alternative, while Janot's rich, clean mix of liquorice and wild herbs is the perfect refreshing drink for a hot, dusty climate.

Indeed the best place to drink them is in pastis's home territory, the south of France. It could be the scent of herbs in the air or just the general ambience: on ariving in Provence you'll automatically start drinking pastis. Whether you are in the midst of Marseille's chaotic anarchy or a tiny cafe in the hills, it's simply the thing to do. Pastis makes the south of France suddenly make sense.

OTHER ANISE-BASED DRINKS

Ouzo and raki

Anise-flavoured spirits have been the national spirit of the Eastern Mediterranean since the days of the Byzantine Empire, when the distillers of Greece and Smyrna were recognized as being masters of their craft. These rakitzides used copper stills produced for them by Armenian coppersmiths, and distilled spirits from the dried pomace (raki) of grapes, although occasionally figs would be used. This was then flavoured with aniseed, fennel, aromatic herbs and mastic – the aromatic resin from an evergreen tree.

The drink's height of popularity came during the Ottoman Empire; in fact, so much raki was being drunk that alcohol had to be imported from Russia and France to cope with demand.

When the Greeks were kicked out of Asia Minor in 1922, the rakitzides moved to Macedonia, by then the centre for production of Greek spirits. Rapid commercial success followed, with production and consumption growing at an extraordinary rate. The drink by now was called ouzo – allegedly after the inscription *uso* Massalia that was put on casks of the spirit that were bound for Marseille. The French, it would seem, had looked east during the dearth of home-produced anise spirits.

The arrival of mass production resulted in a drop in quality, although ouzo experts now agree that things are improving once more, with greater care being taken over distillation, and many producers reviving the old ways of producing their native spirit.

There is a variety of ways to make ouzo and its relatives. Some producers use pot stills to redistil aniseed and other flavouring agents with molasses spirit. Others, such as Mavromatis, distil anise and fennel seeds and blend it with alcohol. In general, ouzo is used to describe molasses-based alcohol with aniseed flavouring, while tsipouro and raki are made from pomace and flavoured with aniseed (although to be strictly accurate not all tsipouro are aniseedy). It's complicated.

In general ouzo is drier and more delicate than pastis, and goes a pale, milky colour when diluted. Although the standard brands – such as the top-selling "12" – tend to be at 40 per cent ABV, the best examples are stronger, confirming Ricard's belief that you need to have a strength of 45 per cent ABV or more to achieve a balanced anise drink.

Typically ouzo producers are now making in a different number of styles and strengths. The EPOM group, based in Mytilene on the island of Lesvos, make three styles – Mini (40 per cent ABV), the more delicately flavoured Fimi (42 per cent ABV) and the old-style double-distilled Lesvos (46 per cent ABV).

Raki remains an important spirit in Levantine countries like Lebanon. Although the country produces world-class wines, raki remains the drink most commonly seen on the table in restaurants – and top wine producers such as Chateau Musar and Kefraya both make excellent, delicate examples.

Every Mediterranean country has an anise-based spirit, often bridging different categories. Italy has sambuca (*see* Liqueurs), while Spain has a vast range of liqueurs and aperitifs based on anise, from the Basque speciality Pacharan (*see* Other Spirits) to Chinchon (Liqueurs) and the most widely distributed straight anise, Anis del Mono. This is made by redistilling anethol with neutral spirit, and is sold in two styles – Dulce (sweet) which has a red label, or Seco (dry) which has a green one. It is a classic Spanish anise, light and fragrant and a design classic, not just thanks to its ornate bottle – based, legend has it, on a perfume bottle that was owned by the owner's wife – but to the story attached to its bizarre label.

The firm was founded at the end of the nineteenth century by Vicente Bosch, who had gone into business with his brother, but they fell out. In fact, they fell out so acrimoniously that Bosch replaced the face of the monkey on the label with a caricature of his brother. The label features this hideous, man-faced creature to this day. Somehow such a bizarre story seems only appropriate for this age-old drink.

A wide variety of brands of Ouza on sale at a market in Iráklion, on the island of Crete

OTHER SPIRITS OF THE WORLD

These days international brands run into high numbers, yet despite the increasingly homogenous range of drinks that are available, the true spirits hound can root out the lesser-known (but in no way inferior) styles of spirits. Here are some to look out for.

OTHER BRANDIES

Every wine-producing country has a brandy industry attached, yet few reach the quality standards set in Cognac, Armagnac and Jerez. In Germany, for example, huge volumes of brandy are drunk, but the product – though pleasant enough – hardly gets your pulse racing. One reason for this is that German brandy producers have traditionally distilled from grapes sourced in the hotter south of Europe for their spirit – although some, such as Asbach, also import wine from Cognac and Armagnac.

A warm climate means that it's difficult to produce grapes that have the right balance between ripeness and acidity that's needed for brandy production. A high-sugar, low-acidity grape is deadly for quality brandy (*see* Cognac, pages 490–500), producing a fat spirit that lacks definition.

German brandy can be distilled in either column or pot stills, and additions such as caramel, boise and other flavouring agents (such as prune juice) are permitted. A brandy must spend a minimum of six months in oak before being released. Any longer than a year in cask, and it can be designated as either Uralt or Alter. The top brand is Asbach, a tasty, undemanding product – not far removed from standard VS Cognac in style.

Although Italy claims to have invented the term "brandy" (*branda* in the Piemontese dialect meant *aqua vitae*), it has never been recognized as a top-class producer. Like the German product, the style is decent enough – produced from a mix of varieties, distilled in column and pot stills, and aged in large vats and small barrels. Generally they are rather light and delicate, with Carpene Malvolti and the top-end selection from Buton (sold as Vecchia Romagna) being the finest examples. Good though they are, if you want to discover Italy's true spirit, look at grappa (*see* pages 511–513).

The further south you go in Europe, the hotter it gets. Therefore by the time you hit Greece you know that you won't be getting grapes with low ripeness and high acidity. The Greeks have got round the problem of super-ripe raw material by turning their brandies into a cross between a brandy and a liqueur. Brands such as Metaxa have herbal additives and sweetening agents blended into them. Metaxa is drunk in huge volumes by holidaymakers, but tends to be one of those bottles that sits in the back of the cupboard when you get home.

The top brandies from Eastern Europe have long been recognized as coming from Armenia. Since this country can lay claim to being one of the cradles of winemaking, there's little surprise that it has a heritage of distillation. The top examples hail from the Ararat distillery, which uses Charentais stills and ages in barrels made at the distillery's own cooperage. The finest ones, sold under the Noyac label, are world-class.

These brandies were rarely seen outside the Soviet Union during the Communist era – although they were great favourites of the Politburo and were praised by visiting brandy-loving dignitaries, including Winston Churchill.

When the Iron Curtain came down, they made an all-too-brief appearance in the West, before war disrupted the joint ventures that were aiming to secure them long-term distribution.

American brandies have been saddled with an image problem. For years the industry was quite happy churning

Opposite: *Fruit brandies* (eaux de vie) *are part of a tradition of the Germanic countries of Europe*

Apple-picking in Normandy, the spiritual home of Calvados

out basic, bottom-end stuff, predominantly from the massive plantings of Thompson Seedless grapes in California's (hot) Central Valley. Gallo – now better known for its table wines – is the biggest producer, followed by such names as Paul Masson, Korbel and Christian Brothers. However, the brandies are nothing to write home about.

There is a ray of hope, however, with the emergence of a new top-quality tier. These brandies are being produced by firms who have gone to the cooler regions of the state, and using Charentais stills. They have planted the top

Cognac and Armagnac varieties – although some also use Pinot Noir and Gamay. These firms, such as Germain-Robin (also known as Alambic), Jepson and RMS, all produce high-quality, Cognac-aligned brandies that can hold their own with VSOP and XO brands.

Perhaps surprisingly, Mexico is home to the world's biggest-selling brandy – Presidente. Made by Domecq from its own vineyards and aged in *solera*, it's light, slightly sweet, and best drunk long and mixed.

South Africa has a long history of brandy production, with distilling starting immediately after the Dutch planted vines in the Cape in the seventeenth century. The early spirit, however, was noted only for its hideous quality – and its ability to disinfect snake bites. You have to wait until the end of the ninetheenth century for quality production to start, with the arrival of a French distiller, René Santhagan.

Today most of South Africa's brandy is made from Chenin, Colombard and Folle Blanche grapes although, with growers being encouraged to push yields up to the maximum and not picking when the grapes are high in acidity, the base material is not always ideal.

Light-flavoured, mixable blends made from column and pot stills make up the bulk of production, but there are some good-quality pot still brands on the market that have been aged in Limousin oak.

Production has been dominated by the massive KWV co-op, whose top-end range of pot-still distillates is underestimated. Smaller producers such as Backsberg are producing fine, high-quality brands on a small scale by rigorously following the same principles as Cognac, while the highly eccentric Carel Nel manages to make good stuff on his Boplaas estate in the torrid heat of the Klein Karroo.

THE STYLE OF PISCO

This South American brandy deserves an entry to itself. Pisco is best known these days as a Chilean speciality – although Peru claims it was the first to make the drink, pointing out that the town of Pisco is Peruvian and took its name from the local tribe who manufactured the clay pots in which the brandy was first stored. The drink's origins date back to the early seventeenth century when Spanish settlers, having already established vineyards, started to distil the wine. These days Pisco is a major industry in Chile, Peru and Bolivia – although it is predominantly thought of as a Chilean product.

Chilean Pisco is made from three strains of Muscat along with small amounts of other aromatic varieties like Torrontel, Moscatel de Alexandria and Pedro Ximenez. Producers often give the wine a short period of skin contact to increase aromatics. The grapes are grown in the north of the country, the best region being recognized as the Elqui valley. Although daytime temperatures are high, Chile's clear night skies mean the temperature drops dramatically at night, which allows the grapes to retain acidity.

Grapes for Chilean Pisco are grown in the north of the country where the temperatures vary hugely from daytime to night

Calvados, apple brandy; is distilled mainly in Normandy, France

the others are given progressively long periods of ageing in large used barrels traditionally made from the local rauli wood, which imparts a very pale lemon/pink hue to the top brands. The most notable two brands are Capel and Control, but La Serra, RRR, de Guarda and Mistral are worth searching out.

In Peru, the different designations apply to the grapes used. You can therefore pick from single varietal Pisco Fur or Pisco Ciuvre (made from Quebranta, Quebranta Mollar or Negra Corriente), the more fragrant Aromatico (from Moscatel, Torrontel and Albilla) and the unusual Pisco Verde, which is made from partially fermented grapes. Top producers include the classy Ocucaje and Rosario de Yaura. The latter also produces a Pisco Crema, made by blending Pisco with sugar, fruit concentrate and cream.

Bolivians know the drink as Singani, which is predominantly made from a distillate of Muscat of Alexandria. San Pedro is the best-known producer, and its San Pedro de Oro Monolito is rightly regarded as the premium brand on the market.

Pisco, like all South American and Mexican spirits, has long been sneered at by Western markets, who see them all as crude firewater. This couldn't be further from the truth. Good Pisco is an excellent spirit, headily aromatic, mellow in the mouth. It's mixable and a useful cocktail base – responsible for one of the great summer cocktails, the Pisco Sour (*see* Brandy).

The higher up the scale you go, however, the more complex the aromas are and the drier the drink becomes, allowing the best Gran Pisco brands to be enjoyed in much the same way as a good grappa.

THE OTHER SPIRITS

Calvados

This apple brandy is the pride of Normandy, and is proof once more of the ability of artisanal distillers to use their skill on any ingredient that was readily to hand. The first record of Calvados production was in 1533, although as usual there is circumstantial evidence that it had been going on for some time before. Initially, Calvados producers would have used glass stills, like their Flemish colleagues (*see* Gin), but copper pot stills

Contrary to popular belief, Pisco is not made from grape pomace but from "potable" wine distilled in pot stills. After distillation, the producer can choose between four legal designations. In ascending order these are Seleccion (30 per cent ABV); Especial (35 per cent); Reservado (40 per cent); and the top designation, Gran Pisco. Seleccion is usually kept in stainless-steel tanks for a short period before being reduced and bottled, while soon took over. These days pots similar to those of Cognac, and small column stills like those used in Armagnac, are both used.

This being France, it's inevitable that Calvados has its own *appellation* (in this case, "apple-ation") rules, which govern permitted varieties, nature of distillation and ageing. Over 40 varieties of apple and pear are allowed to be used, and these are further divided into different classifications: sweet, bitter, bitter-sweet (the largest grouping) and acid.

The apples are picked (no fallen apples are used) and each distiller will have his own recipe of how to combine and blend the juices of different varieties to make his wash. Some will include pears to give a jab of acidity. The juice is fermented, usually using only natural yeasts, and then distilled. In the top region of Pays d'Auge (which has its own AOC) only pot-still distillation can be used, while the rest of the region predominantly uses column stills. In general, Pays d'Auge Calvados is also aged for longer.

Ageing usually takes place in used oak barrels or large vats, and the maturing period can last as long as 40 years. Most Calvados, however, will hit the market as a 3-Star (a minimum of two years old), but there are a number of other age descriptors. To qualify as Vieux/Reserve the Calvados has to be three years old, and VSOP/Vieux Reserve a year older. Older brands, often called Hors d'Age or Age Inconnu, are just that – old. There are also some smaller producers who release age-designated brands, and some vintages are also on the market. In other words, there's a lot to choose from – probably more than you thought.

As Calvados matures it loses its initially rather aggressive, sharp apple character and begins to mellow, picking up some character from the wood and softening into an evocative mix that brings to mind hot apple pie with hints of cinnamon, sugar and cloves.

Just as in every French region, production is dominated by the large *négociant* houses – like Busnel, which produces a well-rounded style; Père Magloire, whose brands tend to be younger and racier; and the excellent Camut, which has a house style that emphasizes richness of fruit.

The real delights, however, are to be found in the small artisan producers who distil from their own orchards. Top among these is Berneroy, whose brands are proof of how dazzling the complexity of top Calvados can be. They are delicious, multi-layered, mouth-watering spirits. If you are lucky, you may even find venerable ones from producers like Isidore Lemorton, whose pear-dominant vintage releases go back to 1926.

Rest of the world

Apple brandy, or applejack, actually predates rum as America's first native spirit. Initially made by leaving cider outside to freeze, it was a viciously strong liquor. These days, brands like Laird's or Yukon Jack are made by double distillation and aged in wood, but they haven't lost the bracing quality that those early pioneers needed to keep them going.

In England, the flag for apple bandy has been defiantly flown by Julian Temperley's Somerset Royal brand. Temperley had to fight long and hard – first to get permission to distil, and then to call his product brandy! It was worth the battle. His brandies are a match for many Calvados and, with this being a new venture and with brandies maturing quietly away, the future looks as rosy as a Cox's Pippin.

At their best these apple brandies demonstrate that what matters most in distillation is the care and attention that only a true master distiller can devote to turning any fruit into a marvellously complex drink. They also refute the idea that grapes are somehow automatically a superior raw material.

Other fruit brandies

The production of pure fruit distillates (*eaux-de-vie*) is a tradition that runs across a band of Europe stretching from Alsace through Southern Germany, Switzerland and into Austria – although these days Spain also produces huge amounts. They appear to have been relatively late arrivals in the European world of spirits, although if Calvados was being produced in the century before, it seems unlikely that no small production was being carried out – especially since they share their heartland with some of the oldest monastic distilleries.

That aside, it wasn't until the middle of the eighteenth century that *eaux-de-vie* began to be produced in what could be called commercial quantities in this part of Europe. One reason is that distillers were spoiled for choice. They had an abundance of wild and cultivated fruits – soft berries from the forests, pears and plums from the orchards – on their doorsteps. The style of the spirit gives another clue. *Eaux-de-vie*, with an emphasis on clean, pure, natural flavours and an avoidance of wood ageing, can be seen as an extension of the northern white spirits – vodka, gin and akvavit.

Although there are some large concerns, the bulk of *eaux-de-vie* is produced by small, family-owned producers from their own stills. It may be a cottage industry compared with gin or vodka, but the aim has always been high.

Production differs slightly for stone and soft fruits. Stone fruits (pears, cherries and plums) are lightly crushed, but, in general, the stones are not cracked as they are in liqueur production. Fermentation is usually left to nature, and so lasts as long as it takes. The more sugar, the longer the ferment, but the resulting "wine" is rarely above 5 per cent ABV, fairly low for spirits production.

Soft fruits are even lower in sugar, meaning that their "wine" wouldn't be sufficiently strong to be able to be distilled. To get round this problem, the fruit is macerated in alcohol before it's given a single distillation in order to concentrate the flavoured spirit.

Traditionally, double distillation in small pot stills is used for stone fruits. These are often equipped with an inner chamber to prevent the fermented fruit coming into direct contact with the outside wall of the still. Some firms have also refined this by adding a column to the pot. A number of top grappa producers in Trentino have adopted both these techniques.

The spirit is then allowed to rest and mellow in glass jars. Wood is rarely used, but when it is, old ash barrels that won't impart colour will be used.

Name the fruit and you'll find an *eau-de-vie* to match. Kirsch is probably the best known, and the top examples – usually from Germany – are elegant, rich distillates. The cherry stones are often lightly crushed, giving the spirit a delicate hint of almond. Don't confuse true kirsch with cooking stuff, which is made from kirsch essence and neutral alcohol. In fact, don't even cook with it.

Also widely seen is Poire William, although pears are noted for being difficult to get to ferment naturally and tend to be low in sugar, giving a weak "wine". This lack of guts often carries through to the spirit, which tends to be aromatic but lifeless.

A better bet is Mirabelle, a type of yellow plum which gives a charming floral *eau-de-vie*; Quetsch is from a larger mauve-coloured plum and, while not as delicate as Mirabelle, makes up with fruity weight.

The Eastern European speciality, Slivovitz, is another plum distillate. Its heartland was Yugoslavia, but you'll find Slivovitz across Central Europe – there's a proud tradition of illegal distillation of plums in Poland. The best variety for Slivovitz is considered to be Madjarka, and many brands spend a period in wood, which helps to mellow the spirit and give it an attractive, delicate colour.

The list is endless. There are *eaux-de-vie* made from cultivated fruit like raspberry, apricot, apple and quince (the last giving a robust, punchy spirit), but the most intriguing are those that use wild fruits as their base. In addition to well-known fruits like Mure (blackberry) and Myrtille (bilberry), you can find Houx, made from holly berries. It's frighteningly expensive, but has a wonderfully complex woodland aroma. Equally obscure is the piquant Gratte-Cul (it means "kiss my arse" ...) made from wild rose hips. It's a more polite drink than the name suggests.

While most of the world knows the *eaux-de-vie* from Alsace and Germany, those from Austria are unknown quantities – mainly because the Austrians drink them all. Here, under the name schnapps, they are part and parcel of civilized life, and the best schnapps are sipped neat in small glasses as a digestif. With the exception of the most rustic style, Obstler, which is made from windfall apples and pears, they are beautifully poised, pure distillates. The most intriguing include Juniper, which manages to be delicate and elegant (a tricky feat with such a pungent ingredient); Ringlottenbrand, a zesty schnapps made from greengages; while Rowan is as hard to find as Houx berry, but is regarded as one of the finest.

The most exciting aspect of *eaux-de-vie* is the often bizarre and obscure raw materials that are used. Right enough, not all are particularly pleasant – steer clear of *eaux-de-vie* made from gentian root – but you can chance upon some of the spirits world's weirder creations. It's a field made for the spirits hound.

Take Alsace distiller, J. Bertrand's Fleur de Bière. This is made by allowing an Alsace Pilsner-style beer to oxidize. The top part is then skimmed off and double distilled, and produces an astounding *eau-de-vie* with an intense perfumed aroma, with notes of cloves, orange, ginger and cinnamon and just a hint of hop flower.

If obscurity is your bag, try and find a bottle of Adlitzbeere/Elsbeer, an Austrian speciality that can lay claim to being the rarest spirit in the world. It's made from the fruit of the wild service tree, which is noted for its wood, but only Austrians value its fruit (the last recorded use of it in the UK was in the fifteenth century). The trouble is that the tree only comes into fruit when it is 15 years old, and when it does it produces a minuscule crop high up on its brittle branches. All of this adds up to a correspondingly high price (be prepared to pay over £100 for a bottle). Those who have tasted it claim it has an evocative scent reminiscent of marzipan.

At the other end of the scale is the old "scare the tourist" trick, Vipre, which contains a snake inside a bottle. Thankfully the snake doesn't seem to impart any flavour (or poison) to the spirit, but it is an alarming sight that usually induces screams and fainting fits at the table when it's brought out by the grinning patron. There is a Polish vodka variant of this, called Zminowka.

Pacharan

This Spanish Basque speciality is one of those spirits that straddles two camps – a trick that Spain seems to perform more often than any other country. Is it a liqueur, an anise, or something else?

Pacharan is made by blending together alcohol that has had sloe (blackthorn) berries macerating in it, sugar syrup, anisette and small quantities of other supporting fragrances such as vanilla or peach. Each firm will put its own spin on production. For example, Destilerias la Navarra (which makes Etxeko and La Navarra) uses *eau-de-vie* distilled from the previous year's spent sloes as the macerating alcohol, rather than the more common neutral alcohol. The month-long maceration cycle takes place in rotating vats filled with nitrogen to prevent any oxidation of the fruit.

To make matters more confusing, Pacharan comes in varying degrees of sweetness and dryness, and a range of different hues from shocking pink to dark brooding cherry. Zoco, the most widely distributed brand, is the sweetest – in fact it's sweet to the point of being confected.

Pacharan aficionados rightly dismiss the brand, preferring more traditional brands like Etxeko or La Navarra. The latter is light in colour, very fragrant and medium sweet, and packed with fruit. Etxeko is an altogether more serious proposition. Deeper in colour, it has a rich, dry, powerful flavour in which the anise is muted, allowing the heady scent of sloes to be given its fullest expression. The extra effort that goes into production pays off.

Pacharan's origins are in the farmhouse kitchen, where it would have been made like sloe gin is in the UK, although in barrels rather than bottles. You can still find "rustic" restaurants across the Basque region with barrels of home-made Pacharan in their bar. Try them. Relatively low in alcohol, Pacharan is a style that fits in perfectly with the laid-back approach to life and eating that personifies Spain – although it's so easy to drink, that it can become a dangerous addiction.

Bitters

Originally spirits were there for your health. Any thoughts of pleasure could be forgotten. While most have managed to extricate themselves from this original purpose, there is one group – bitters – that remains firmly rooted in this ancient purpose. Because of this "drink it, it will do you good" aspect (and their often alarming bitterness), they are usually regarded as an acquired taste, and are not hugely popular in the UK and the USA, where the thought of drinking something to aid digestion is a bizarre concept. While there are some brands that are so bitter that little pleasure can be got from drinking a glass, there are some cracking examples that can be drunk as aperitifs, digestifs, or used as highly effective hangover cures.

Bitters date back to the days of apothecaries, alchemists and distiller monks, and use secret amalgamations of roots, barks, herbs and peel to work their magic on your internal organs. Although you can find examples from Germany, Denmark, France, Spain and Trinidad, the country with the largest number is where it all started – Italy, where they go under the catch-all term of Amaro.

The notion of drinking something bitter to get the gastric juices going dates back to Ancient Greece – Hippocrates drank an amaro-style tonic, and there are records of a Roman patent medicine that is basically the same as a modern amaro, but without the spirit. One brand, Cinha, is still promoted as an effective laxative, which rather rules it out as a session drink.

Such was the success of amari that several Italian monasteries grew herbs purely for the drink. In time their cultivation was taken care of by a specific order of the Fatebene (do-wells) – one of whom was eventually canonized, thereby making amaro the only spirit with its own patron saint.

The bitterness is always derived from some vegetal ingredient, and brands usually include one (or more) of the following bitter substances: quinine, angelica, gentian, bitter orange, rue, *nux vomica*, artichokes, wormwood, bitter aloes and rhubarb root. The potion is given an aromatic lift by botanicals like vanilla, cloves, coriander, nutmeg, lavender and ginger, although each brand will keep the percentages and ingredients a closely guarded secret.

The best-known traditional Italian brand is Fernet Branca. The brand, which started life as a chemist's potion at the beginning of the nineteenth century, uses over 30 herbs and spices (things are always vague in bitters), including rhubarb, liquorice and *agarico bianco* (mushroom), for bitterness, and angelica, anise, lemon peel and peppermint for aroma. The ingredients are either cold-steeped (macerated) or infused (gently heated) in alcohol before being combined and aged in large vats.

One of the most bitter of the amari, Fernet Branca is a digestif in the classic mould. Powerful, explosive even, you can sense the peppermint, but the flavour is all bitter orange peel, liquorice and cloves backed up with a hefty alcoholic kick. It's not advisable to drink it in large quantities.

Averna and Montenegro are slightly less bitter thanks to the addition of sweetened wine, while Cynar is lighter and more subtle. This last brand is produced by redistilling its secret mix of alcohol and herbs before it is reduced to a gentle 16.5 per cent ABV. Rhubarb root, bitter and sweet orange peel are used, but Cynar is defiantly proud of its main bitter component – artichokes, so much so that one is on the label. It doesn't help sales in export markets.

The best-known Italian bitters is the aperitif Campari which was created by Gaspare Campari in his Milan cafe in the 1860s. There's no middle ground with Campari. It's one of those drinks that you either love or hate. It's the spirits world's equivalent of the yeast spread Marmite.

True Campari lovers have it ice-cold, neat with ice or with soda, but it is equally good with orange juice – orange peel being a main ingredient in the (secret) recipe. It's a brilliant drink that refreshes you and stimulates your appetite. It even looks good!

Martini makes a good Campari-style bitters which is slightly sweeter, Aperol is lighter, while Punt e Mes is sweeter again – in much the same frame as France's elegant aperitif Dubonnet, and great as a long drink.

Suze, France's top bitters brand, is more in line with Campari, being mainly served as an aperitif drink. Its bitterness is obtained from gentian roots, which are either distilled to get an essential oil or macerated in alcohol before being blended with other ingredients and fortified wine.

Gentian, though prized for its medicinal properties, produces a very earthy, essential oil as dry and dusty as a gnome's cave. The fact that Suze is an elegant, mouth-watering drink that shows none of this character is proof of a very skilful recipe.

Germany, however, remains firmly in the "this is good for you" camp, and the country is home to two of the most uncompromising brands of bitters – Jagermeister and Underberg. Jagermeister, whose recipe includes anise, poppy seed, juniper and ginseng, is currently attempting to relaunch itself as a versatile drink for today's clubbing generation, and is trying to get people to drink it mixed and long. In actuality, most seem to be treating it as the 1990s equivalent of the tequila slammer. Needless to say, because of Jager's relatively high alcohol content, it produces a quick hit soon followed by oblivion.

This potency is also the reason that people turn to

Underberg, which is packaged in tiny bottles wrapped in brown paper. Underberg is meant to be a digestif, but it is most commonly used as a last resort by people suffering from a crippling hangover. It works – mainly because it tops up the alcohol levels in an instant, although the firm claims that it is low in histamines and biogenic amines, which cause headaches after too much alcohol. There might be something in it after all. Strangely enough, Campari and orange has a similarly efficacious effect on hangovers.

The two most famous Eastern European bitters, Hungary's Unicum and Melnais Balzans from Latvia, are more agreeable in style. Unicum, created in 1790, uses 40 botanicals and is gently sweet with a pleasant bitterness.

Melnais Balzans is an altogether denser proposition that uses secret resins as part of its recipe – honey, mint and wormwood are also included. A richly complex mix of bitterness and dark mysterious aromas, it's an unforgettable experience.

One of the most recent bitters to appear is Denmark's Gammeldansk Bitter Dram which was launched in 1964. It's a blend of 30 different herbs, berries and essential oils – including cinnamon, star anise, rowan berries and cloves. Tawny/gold in colour, it's a soft, approachable drink, mildly herbal, slightly sweet and with only the merest bitter twang. A great introductory brand.

Altogether weirder is Catalonia's native bitters, Calisay, which is one of the bitterest of Spain's *vinos quinados*. These take their name from their main flavouring ingredient, quinine-rich bark from the chinchon tree. Calisay, specifically, uses bark from one particular type of chinchon – called, not surprisingly, calisaya – which grows only in Ecuador. A large amount of bitter orange peel is also added, along with other herbal components. They are all macerated in sweetened fortified white wine before being aged in oak. It has a bitters' signature intensity, but this is balanced with a liquorice herbal sweetness, making it seem almost like a liqueur. Like Chartreuse and absinthe, it produces a peculiarly floaty state of intoxication.

The most widely seen *vino quinado* is Chinchon, which is half-way between a bitters, an anise and a liqueur, and shares ingredients and techniques with all three styles – bitterness from the chinchon bark, anise extract and lots of sugar syrup. The legend has it that Chinchon was first produced by the seventeenth-century Marquesa de Chinchon, the wife of a governor of Peru who, when she was in South America, "discovered" the medicinal properties of quinine and gave her name to the tree from whose bark it is extracted.

South America was the original home of one of the most widely used bitters – Angostura. This powerful, aromatic brand was created by Dr Siegert, Simon Bolivar's German doctor who named it after a small town in Venezuela. It is still made to the same secret recipe, but is now produced in Trinidad. The company is fiercely protective of the recipe; all that is known is that it uses strong rum as a base and gentian root as the main bitter agent.

Angostura is such a powerful concoction that it is only used in minuscule quantities. Originally a medicine for malaria, it is now one of the most essential and versatile items behind any bar. It makes a pink gin pink, balances a Manhattan and, mixed with Campari and gin, produces the Negroni. More difficult to find, but an equally useful mixer, is Peychaud's Bitters.

Pimm's

Although bitters are not a British tradition, one of the most quintessentially English drinks comes from this field. James Pimm was the owner of an oyster bar in the City of London in the 1820s. It was the custom for these places, the fast-food joints of their day, to serve their customers either pints of stout or the same quantity of "the house cup" – a variant of the rum punches of the century before – with their oysters. Pimm's cup, which was based on the newly acceptable gin along with a secret collection of fruit extracts, liqueurs and bitter herbs, soon became noted as the finest.

Even today, only six people know the recipe, and the purchases of ingredients are staggered so no one can know the exact proportions.

By the end of the century Pimm's was being exported to officers and gentlemen in the colonies, and it has never quite relinquished this rather snooty image – in fact, it has benefited from it.

Early in the twentieth century, Pimm's was made in

Pimm's dates from the early nineteenth century; it is the quintessential English "summer garden party" drink

six styles, each with a different spirit base. No. 1 was gin; No. 2 whisky; No. 3 brandy; No. 4 rum; No. 5 rye; and No. 6 vodka. These days, only Nos 1 and 6 are available, after an all-too-brief attempt to relaunch the full range. There are Pimm's lovers in England who occasionally unearth a cache of one of the discontinued styles mouldering in the cellar of a country house. Contact your local wine merchant to see if they have recently liberated any.

Akvavit/schnapps

Akvavit is a Scandinavian variant of flavoured vodka, and is one of the great northern white spirits that are pure and delicate in aroma but still pack a decided

punch. Its home is Denmark, where distillation started in the fifteenth century, but Norway also produces some excellent brands.

Like vodka, it's produced from a rectified spirit – most commonly made from potatoes. The difference between akvavit and flavoured vodka is that, while flavoured vodkas have their flavouring agents steeped or infused in them, in akvavit they are added and the mixture is redistilled *à la* gin.

The main flavouring is caraway seeds, but you'll find brands that also use fennel, dill, cumin and bitter orange peel. These are either macerated in alcohol and redistilled, or distilled to obtain essential oils before being blended together, diluted and allowed to marry.

Slightly confusingly, although the labels will say Akvavit (Danish), or Aquavit (Norway), people refer to it as schnapps – the word coming from the Old Norse *snappen*, meaning to snatch, or gulp. That indicates how it should be drunk: ice-cold in small shot glasses as part of a meal. In Denmark it's traditional for each person on the table to stand up in turn and shout a toast (*skål*), after which everyone drinks the schnapps down in one. It makes dining out a highly entertaining, if hazardous event.

The most widely seen brand is Aalborg Akvavit, a style which was invented by Isidore Henius, a young distiller with very fixed ideas about quality, similar, in fact, to Sweden's Lars Olsson Smith (*see* Vodka, page 555). With caraway as its flavouring agent and bottled at 45 per cent ABV, Aalborg remains the benchmark style, whistle-clean but with an intriguing, delicately flavoursome bite.

The premium Aalborg line, Jubilaeums, is lower in strength and has dill and coriander in addition to caraway as flavouring. It is also aged for a short period in wood, giving it a pale gold colour.

Norway's top aquavits are Lysholm Linie and Loiten Export. Both are potato-based spirits with caraway and other flavourings added. So far, so good. What makes them stand apart from any other spirit in the world is their strange ageing process. Both brands must have been aged in casks that have travelled around the world in the cargo-hold of a ship. Strange ... but true. They are softer than their Danish counterparts, but equally clean.

Akvavit should be treated exactly the same as a premium vodka: drunk neat, with food – it's particularly good with seafood and dill-flavoured sauces, or as a base for cocktails that call for vodka.

Korn

Although most people know Germany's main white spirit style as "schnapps", German distillers dislike the term, feeling it signifies a cheap, rough spirit. They prefer to use the term Korn, which is a more accurate descriptor, as the spirit is predominantly made from grain, although potatoes are also used.

The classification is further divided into two designations: the lower-strength Korn, usually used as the base for mixed drinks; and the stronger Doppelkorn,

a double distillation of corn/grain – an easy-drinking spirit akin to a lightly malty vodka. Kornelius is a good example. The category's leading producer, Berentzen, has a premium brand, Edelkorn vom alten fass, which has been aged for three years in Limousin oak.

Recently, the market has been given a boost by the arrival of flavoured Korn, spearheaded by Berentzen's Apfelkorn. Low in strength, the Berentzen range blends the juice from fresh fruits with reduced-strength Korn. The selection now includes Saurer Apfel and peach. This last flavour is used in the British brand Archer's – a mild, dry spirit that's a versatile ingredient in cocktails.

It's unlikely that Henkes Aromatic Schnapps is much used by mixologists. A Dutch malted white spirit which, contrary to its name, has no flavourings, its main market is West Africa, where it has acquired ritual significance – in Ghana and Nigeria it is sprinkled on the ground in ceremonies associated with birth, death and marriage.

Arak

The last spirit category in this book could well have been the first one of all. Arak, after all, is claimed to have been distilled in India in 800 BC. Palm wine and fermented sugar-cane drinks were being made around this time, but sadly there is no documentary evidence that distillation was ever done.

Arak is a catch-all term that covers a multitude of spirits hailing from the East Indies, India, the Middle East and North Africa. To make matters more complicated, each country makes it in a slightly different fashion – often using completely different raw materials. In the East Indies it's produced from sugar cane and rice. In India, the name is used for a distillate of the sap of palm trees.

The name is originally Arabic (*araq*, meaning juice or sap), and it's worth speculating if the secret of distillation and the making of araq came from the East along the spice roads to the Arab seats of learning, or if the term and the secret was an Arab invention that was carried back to India and beyond.

In North Africa, Arak is made by distilling fermented figs or dates – Tunisia's Boukha is a good, if rather pungent, example of a fig-based Arak with a certain aggressive charm. The name is often confused with raki, which is an anise-flavoured spirit (*see* Pastis) made from molasses or wine skins.

LIQUEURS

Although liqueurs can lay claim to be among the earliest of all spirits, these days they remain a strange, rather disparate, grouping. They range from the classics like Chartreuse, Grand Marnier and Drambuie to modern best-sellers like Baileys and Malibu. Even though you would never mistake one for the other, they are all liqueurs.

They come in all colours, from clear to Day-Glo, they are nearly always packaged in strangely shaped bottles, and almost inevitably have a fantastical story attached to their origins. They can be used as cocktail bases or be drunk on their own. They are made from a vast range of natural products gathered from across the globe and usually assembled in a secret recipe. You'll find liqueurs made from the skins, seeds, stones, flowers, leaves and pips of fruit, vegetables, spices and herbs. Every brand has a different story to tell – and many of them don't want to tell it.

So what are liqueurs? That's a tricky question, but for simplicity's sake we'll define them as being spirits-based drinks that have been flavoured and perfumed by natural ingredients and then sweetened. After all, they get their name from the Latin *liquefacere* – meaning to melt or dissolve – and it's this liquefying of ingredients, rather than the flavours of base spirit and wood used by other categories, that liqueurs rely on for their character.

Alchemists, apothecaries and abbots
Nowhere is the alchemist's hand seen as clearly as in liqueurs. When the art of distillation changed from producing perfume to producing medicine, the research involved making spirits and adding various beneficial plants, herbs and spices to it. Some were there solely for their medicinal effects, while others were added for more mystical reasons. The original recipe for Chartreuse – old, even when it was given to the monks in 1603 – doesn't just specify what ingredients were to be used to make the elixir, but where they were to be picked and during what phase of the moon. This element of legend and mystery is still retained by these old liqueurs. Nowhere else will you find such a wall of silence when you ask how a brand is made.

The Middle Age alchemists and monks were looking for similar things, and their early results included a huge range of magical elixirs. It was a long process of trial and error that drew on folk wisdom, then-modern science and a fair amount of intuition.

The flavouring agents they used in their potions played a dual role. Not only did they mask the crude spirit (which itself was seen as a curative), but they had their own medicinal uses.

These early laboratory/distilleries were usually in monasteries (the art is generally agreed to have started in Salerno), and even today there is a religious connection with many of the most venerable liqueurs. The herbs, spices and fruit would originally have been sourced locally, either from the countryside or cultivated in the orchards and physic gardens, but as trade routes opened up between Europe and the East so more exotic ingredients began to be included in the recipes.

As the knowledge of distilling spread out from behind monastery walls, so the other guardians of folk medicine – wise women and healers – became involved. The name Strega comes from a local legend that women used to dress up as witches and make secret potions. The Henriot sisters, who made the first absinthe, were descendants of this tradition, while the secret essence that is used in Drambuie has always been made only by the women of the Mackinnon family. The past continues to live on.

Distillation was also taken up in grand houses that had huge inventories of flavouring agents in their kitchens and still-houses. They were distilling essential oils to make perfumes as well as medicinal tonics. Inevitably, there would have been some cross-experiments going on. You can imagine the woman in charge of the still-house wondering what would happen if she added rose oil to the distillate of fruits and herbs

Liqueurs come in all shades, and are made from all manner of plants, fruit, vegetables and spices

that was meant to calm her master's stomach.

In fact, stomachs play a large part in the history of liqueurs. The first recorded commercial liqueur – Lucas Bols's recipe for kümmel in 1575 – was made to aid digestion, not as a social drink.

By this time, making liqueurs had spread from its Italian heartland, thanks partly to the marriage of Catherine de Medici to Henri II, which brought Italian Renaissance culture to France, and ushered in a different approach to liqueurs. From here on, alchemists continued their researches into the mysteries of existence, apothecaries and monks made medicines and elixirs, while home distillation brought sweet, flavoured spirits to the banqueting halls.

The compounds ranged from the simple to the complex. Alchemist John French listed 64 ingredients that went into his seventeenth-century creation Aqua Celestis, including roots, seeds, flowers and fruit, amber, honey and crushed pearls.

His recipes, published in *Art of Distillation* (1651), includes "cures" for 150 ailments, from fainting to baldness to impotence, with ingredients that not only ran through the usual aromatics but included less attractice substances such as human brains, swans, snakes and horse manure. Clearly, we're not talking of an elegant, after-dinner tipple here.

While social drinking of spirits was happening, it was only when sugar began to be brought to Europe from the Caribbean colonies that widespread commercial-scale production could start, and liqueurs' image begin to change.

While there were still bitters and liqueurs used purely as aids to digestion, newer drinks were emerging that were simply there to be enjoyed – yet which retained the fruits of centuries of learning.

It wasn't just sugar that was arriving in Europe. Botanical ingredients were also flooding into Europe thanks to the Dutch spice trade. It was a godsend to liqueur and gin specialists like Bols and de Kuyper. The two firms – along with the French giant Cusenier – produced masses of brands from every exotic ingredient you could imagine: cinnamon, citrus fruit, cloves, vanilla, rose oil and coffee.

While they have rationalized their ranges in recent years, these firms can still boast ranges of drinks that look like an explosion in a tie-dye factory, and which are made from a huge range of flavourings. Their portfolios are undoubtedly a godsend to the world's barmen.

By the early to mid-nineteenth century liqueurs had got into their swing, and many of the most famous names – Cointreau, Grand Marnier, Benedictine, Amaretto Disaronno – were founded around this time. There was also a rash of strange brands, with long-forgotten names like Rose without Thorns, Illicit Love and Up Your Nightshirt, underlining the fact that they were the sweet potions that were plied on unsuspecting ladies by unscrupulous suitors.

This increase in brands was helped by the invention of the column still, which finally allowed distillers not only to produce in volume, but provided them with a neutral spirit base – which, in turn, allowed the flavours to express themselves more fully.

Liqueurs were still being sipped gingerly from small glasses by women at the end of a meal. Then the Americans got in on the scene and the market for liqueurs was turned on its head.

Barmen, on the search for new potions in the first great cocktail age, discovered a database of flavours and colours that acted as brilliant boosters to the standard spirit bases of gin and vodka. They jazzed up drinks in the jazz age, giving them extra pizzazz, sweetness and personality.

In recent times, though, liqueurs have become rather *passé*. They are still drunk, but they have lost their lustre and appeal. There are only so many times you can tell the same story; they don't have a premium sector. Furthermore, there are very few brands (Chartreuse and Grand Marnier being exceptions) that have premium versions.

The market was given a new lease of life by the arrival of Bailey's Irish Cream, in its now familiarly-shaped botttle, which introduced a whole new category to the world, but although cream liqueurs may make the figures for the liqueur market look healthy, liqueurs are very different from, say, malt whisky or vodka. If you drink a new malt or premium vodka, you're more than likely to try another brand the next time. If you like Bailey's, however, you won't necessarily become an instant convert to every single liqueur on the market.

It seemed as if they would just tick over nicely … until cocktails started up once more. Suddenly things are beginning to look brighter for these ancient brands. They may no longer be cure-alls or give insights into the workings of the universe, but they certainly make a cocktail taste good.

HOW THEY'RE MADE

It is virtually impossible to describe exactly how liqueurs are created because not only does each brand have its own technique, but many of them won't let you know how they are made anyway! Part of a liqueur's mystique, after all, is its secret recipe.

Although the possible combinations of ingredients are infinite, broad techniques are used to produce a liqueur – maceration/infusion, distillation and adding concentrates before finishing.

Maceration/infusion

Maceration is a simple enough principle. The ingredients – be they fruit, peel and/or roots – are placed in the spirit base (usually a neutral spirit) for a long period to allow their flavours to be leached out. This can take weeks or even months, depending on the raw material.

Some brands will macerate different collections of ingredients in batches, while some will continue to add ingredients throughout the macerating period – just as a chef will add spices and herbs at different points when creating a dish.

These days, some producers force the alcohol through the aromatics, while others use gentle heating (infusion) to break down the flavour compounds in the ingredients. The end result is the same: you have a flavoured base spirit.

Distillation

In broad terms, soft fruits such as raspberries, strawberries and blackberries will be left to sit in the spirit, which will be adjusted and bottled. Other brands will keep a macerated component as part of the final blend. Seeds and nuts, peel, roots and leaves, however, have to be redistilled after their period of maceration in order to release their full flavour and to fix it in the spirit (*see* Gin).

The bulk of the top liqueurs will use redistillation for all, or part, of their product, although it's up to each distiller how he or she approaches this process. Some distillers will keep their different batches of botanicals separate and distil them on their own before blending at a later stage, while others will combine them and redistil the whole lot.

Occasionally the distiller will take some of the major aromatic ingredients and distil them with some water in order to release their essential oils, which can then be used as a powerfully scented blending component. A good example is crème de menthe. It is made by combining the essential oil from mint with neutral spirit.

Concentrates

These are industrially produced additives that can be added to a base spirit, bypassing the need for maceration or redistillation.

Base spirit

The most commonly used spirit is a neutral (or high-strength) alcohol made from molasses, grain or grape. This allows the distiller to be able to show the complex way in which the flavouring agents mix and marry. There are some distillers, however, that also use a flavoured, aged spirit – for example, Grand Marnier uses Fine Champagne Cognac when assembling its blend, while Drambuie uses a blend of aged grain and malt whisky.

Finishing

It's common practice for the top brands to then age the finished blend – usually this takes place in large, used wooden vats which will mellow the spirit and allow the flavours to marry, but which won't impart woodiness or colour. Alternatively, glass or stainless-steel tanks are also used.

After the ageing process, the liqueur is sweetened – mainly with sugar syrup, but occasionally with honey – and adjusted for colour. Some brands use caramel; others, such as Sambuca, use saffron; while others use turmeric, carrot or vegetable dyes. Then the liqueur is filtered, cold stabilized and bottled. It could not be much simpler!

THE STYLES

Liqueurs are a minefield of different ingredients, techniques and flavours, but for simplicity's sake, we have divided them into eight broad camps: Herbal, Seed, Fruit, Nut, Crème, Whisk(e)y, Emulsion and Cream.

Some brands straddle two or more camps, and others seem to exist in a space all of their own, but hopefully this is a manageable way of looking at this diverse band of spirits. It will soon become clear that more legends and tall tales are involved in this family of spirits than anywhere else. Forgotten recipes, heroic acts, the hand of God, artists' models, witches – all will make an appearance. Many of the stories have to be taken with a pinch of salt, but which ones?

Herbal

This group includes some of the oldest spirits known to man and touch on ancient wisdom and arcane knowledge. They were initially created not to bring joy, but to cure illness. The only brand that has retained this link is the high-strength Elixir de Chartreuse (*see* below) the most concentrated "liqueur" of all.

Thankfully for today's social drinker, the herbal brands are now lower in strength and not only serve as elegant after-dinner drinks but also make marvellous cocktail bases. It's impossible to list all the ingredients of all the brands, but enough can be winkled out of the producers to say with a certain degree of confidence that they will contain botanicals, such as angelica, hyssop, mint, cloves, vanilla, nutmeg, saffron, thyme, wormwood, anise, aloes, orange and lemon peel, honey, gentian, quinine, caraway, cumin and almond. Some, such as Izarra, Fior d' Alpe, Argentarium and Millefiori, still only use local ingredients, but the majority will draw from the four corners of the globe for their flavourings.

Chartreuse

The story of the greatest of all liqueurs begins in the seventeenth century when the Marechal d' Estrees handed the monks in the Monastery of the Grand Chartreuse an already ancient manuscript which claimed to contain the secret formula of an elixir bestowing long life.

This drink made from this concoction of flowers, herbs, roots and spices was originally used by local people as a medicine, but as its fame spread, so the monks adapted the recipe to produce a more palatable drink for everyday drinking – and so, in 1745, Green Chartreuse was born, followed in 1840 by Yellow.

A visit to the Chartreuse distillery in Voiron is one of the stranger experiences for the spirit hound. For starters, there appears to be no-one working there and when you ask for details on how the liqueur is produced, the answer is always: "Only the Monks know the answer to that." The reason why no-one is around is that most of the day-to-day running of the distillery is done by a computer link between it and the monastery, 30km away. This means that two monks involved in producing every bottle of Chartreuse need only visit the distillery occasionally, leaving more time for prayer.

It is unlikely that any of Chartreuse's secrets will ever slip out. Only three monks know the recipe and they are only allowed to talk (to each other) once a week.

All we know is that the liqueurs are natural, their extraordinary colour coming from their ingredients and not through artificial colouring. A total of 130 are named in the complex formula, which advises where each ingredient should be harvested and when they should be picked. As for production, all that is known is that the ingredients are macerated in alcohol in different combinations before being distilled.

The Elixir still adheres to the original recipe and is the most extraordinary flavour – and at 71 per cent ABV is best taken as a drop on a sugar cube, or diluted in warm water. Green (55 per cent ABV) and sweeter Yellow (40 per cent ABV) both have distilled honey added, before being aged, like the Elixir, in casks for up to eight years. The liqueurs which have been kept in casks for longer are designated as Chartreuse VEP.

No other spirit comes close to Chartreuse's intense complexity, and Green VEP in particular is a taste that's never forgotten, an extraordinary explosion of wild flowers, honey and fruit that mixes sweetness with herbal power. All other liqueurs – and many other spirits – pale into insignificance beside it.

If legend is to be believed, the recipe for Benedictine was created in 1510 by Don Bernardo Vinvelli, a monk at the order's abbey at Fécamp in Northern France. He

A monk empties one of the distillery vats at the monastery of La Grande Chartreuse in Voiron; St Bruno founded the monastery in 1084

was so delighted with his creation that he cried out "Deo Optimo Maximo!" (Praise be to God, most good, most great!), a religious equivalent of "Eureka!". Given that Vinvelli isn't a particularly French name, it's possible that the brother had learned distillation in Italy.

The monks continued to produce the cordial until 1789, when the Revolutionary Government dissolved the monasteries and forced all religious orders into exile and the spirit disappeared for almost 100 years.

It was only revived when one of the monastery's lawyers, Alexandre le Grande, chanced upon the recipe. Liqueurs were enjoying an unprecedented boom at the time and, knowing a good thing when he saw one, he went into production in Fécamp, in the process building one of the world's most bizarre-looking distilleries – a high-camp collision between Renaissance and Gothic styles, but with more gold.

The exact recipe is a secret, but Benedictine is constructed by first assembling five separate batches of 27 botanicals (among them juniper, myrrh, angelica, cloves, cardamom, cinnamon, vanilla and tea). These are either distilled to release essential oils or macerated in neutral spirit and redistilled. The batches are then aged separately for a short period, blended together and aged again before being sweetened with honey and caramel, coloured with saffron, filtered and bottled.

It's a classic old liqueur, softly sweet without being cloying, filled with spice, some vanilla and scents of wild, remote places.

Izarra

This Basque liqueur doesn't have such religious overtones. It is produced in green and yellow styles in a small distillery in Bayonne, and dates back to the seventeenth century. Its emergence coincided with the banishment of the Carthusians and was a sensible commercial attempt to steal Chartreuse's market.

The brands are rarely found outside their Basque heartland, but within it locals will go as far as protesting that Izarra is not only better than, but predates, Chartreuse. It's advisable not to argue with them.

Izarra is produced from a mélange of 48 ingredients, including herbs, flowers and roots, sourced from the Pyrénées. Some of these are distilled to extract essential oils, while the rest are macerated in sugar beet spirit which has had a little Armagnac added to it, before being redistilled in a pot still. The two components are blended, adjusted with more Armagnac, and aged in large wooden vats. The yellow version is then sweetened and coloured with honey.

Though it sets itself up as the Basque Chartreuse, it doesn't have that drink's magnificent complexity – but is a pleasant, fairly sweet, lightly herbal drink which can be drunk either on its own or mixed.

The roots of the herbal liqueurs lie in Italian monasteries, but today the flag is flown by two relatively recent arrivals on the scene. Like most Italian herbal brands, these are sweeter and have more obvious anise components than their French counterparts and are coloured a fairly alarming yellow.

That said, Strega is obviously from the same camp as the oldest French herbal brands. The liqueur was invented in the southern Italian town of Benevento in 1860 by the Alberti family. It remained in small-scale production as the family was doing very nicely out of its main business, which was the export of wine to the north of the country and into France. However, when fortunes changed and the wine business collapsed the family turned to liqueur production, and produced a drink called Strega (witch) after a local legend of women concocting secret potions in the hills.

The liqueur is made from no fewer than 70 botanicals which are macerated in grain spirit, redistilled in small steel pot stills, and then aged in large oak and ash vats before being coloured by saffron. As a result, Strega has a gentle lifted aroma, where mint mixes with fennel leaf.

Italy's other famous herbal liqueur shares its name with the finest designer in the world and an acid jazz band. It has one of the drinks world's most distinctive bottles. Galliano was created by Arturo Vaccari, a Tuscan distiller who named his brand after a Major Giuseppe Galliano, an Italian military hero who in 1896 was placed under siege in the Abyssinian fort of Enda Jesus, a picture of which is on the label.

It's an amalgamation of over 40 Alpine herbs, roots, berries and flowers as well as fennel, star anise and vanilla, which are divided into seven component parts and distilled. The distillates are kept separate for three months in a tank before being blended, adjusted with alcohol, sugar syrup and colouring and given a second period of marrying.

Sweet with rich aromas of anise and vanilla, Galliano is too much to drink on its own but is a great cocktail ingredient – in fact it was the component which turned the Screwdriver into the Harvey Wallbanger – and made Harvey, a Californian surfer, hit the wall in the first place.

The final major European herbal liqueur is Spain's Cuarenta y Tres which, as the name suggests, contains 43 herbs in its secret recipe. Oranges, cloves and anise are the dominant aromas in what is a rather sticky experience if drunk neat.

THE USE OF FRUIT

If the herbal liqueurs are direct descendants of the old medicines and elixirs prepared by monks and alchemists, the arrival of fruit liqueurs marks the change in drinking patterns, from the drinks that were good for you to those which were made for the drinker's enjoyment. That doesn't mean that they're simple concoctions – the best share a complexity with the finest herbal liqueurs.

Opposite: *Fruit liqueurs, such as Mandarine Napoléon made from tangerines, were created for the drinker's enjoyment*

Lemons are the main ingredients of the Italian liqueur Limoncello

Oranges...

Liqueurs can be flavoured with any ingredient that comes to hand – so the range of fruit-based examples is massive. The largest and most interesting section, however, consists of those that use dried orange peel. Although most fruit-based liqueurs only arrived in the flush of new brands that first emerged in the mid- to late-nineteenth century, orange peel was first used much earlier.

Dutch firms started using it in the seventeenth century, when the merchant fleet brought back bitter oranges from the new colonies in the Caribbean and the West Indies. It is a Dutch-owned island which has become inextricably linked with this style – Curaçao.

The liqueur trade became a larger commercial enterprise around the height of the Dutch East India Company, and de Kuyper – the important liqueur and gin producer – was founded at this time. One of its most famous brands remains the liqueur that takes its name from the bitter orange peel from Curaçao.

The method of making curaçao remains the same. Bitter oranges from Curaçao, Haiti and Seville and smaller percentages of other citrus fruits, blossoms, leaves and roots are soaked in a water and alcohol mixture and redistilled to release their essential oils. This will then be blended with either neutral spirit or brandy – and often coloured. They are subtly different from triple secs, which traditionally also use some sweet orange peel. Despite their name, triple secs aren't three times as dry, but they tend to be slightly more complex.

The best-known orange-based brand is Cointreau. It was invented in 1849 by Edouard Cointreau, the son of a liqueur producer based in Angers. He had arrived at Curaçao – quite probably to find out what the Dutch liqueur firms were going on about – and immediately started shipping back peel to the family distillery. He was a quick worker, as the first bottle of Cointreau hit the market in the 1870s.

Initially it was sold as a triple sec white curaçao, but such was the success of the brand – and so many other firms put out copy-cat products – that the name was switched to Cointreau. These days it's also produced in Spain and the USA.

Cointreau is made from a blend of bitter oranges from Haiti, Brazil and Spain, sweet oranges from the south of France and other citrus ingredients. These are macerated in neutral alcohol and double distilled in pot stills, before being adjusted with refined sugar and water. Light and delicately fragranced, with a whole range of citrus aromas – there's plenty of leaf and blossom evident – it was the liqueur used in the original Margarita (*see* Tequila).

Less well-known, but well worth searching out, is Ponche, Jerez's own liqueur. It is a classic example of how producers use local ingredients – in this case, oranges, sherry and brandy. The style was first made commercially by sherry producer José de Soto who distilled local bitter oranges, almonds, vanilla and herbs, then blended the concentrate with a blend of old amontillado sherry and Brandy de Jerez. Other Ponche producers, such as Caballero and Ruiz, have their own subtle variations.

One of the most distinctive-looking brands in the world, Ponche traditionally comes packaged in an eye-catching 75cl silver bottle and remains a classic digestif – delicate, aromatic and with a refreshingly bitter finish.

Although every bar in Spain will have a bottle on the back shelf, it's one of those drinks that has found it difficult to go beyond its domestic borders. It deserves wider attention.

The same could be said for Estonia's Vana Talinn. This is one of a range of high-quality spirits, made in the Baltic States that, sadly, are rarely seen out of their homeland. Hopefully, now that independence has been restored, they'll start to find their way on to a wider market. The liqueur is a blend of the essential oils of orange and lemon peel, with a macerated extract of cinnamon and vanilla. The mixture is then blended with some high-ester Jamaican rum (*see* Rum).

Every country appears to have its own variation on the orange-peel theme. In South Africa it's called Van der Hum. This uses tangerine as well as orange peel, and macerates the two ingredients (and some nutmeg and other spices) in brandy before redistilling. It's a finely fragranced, well-balanced example of the style.

Grand Marnier, however, is something else again. The brand is owned by the Lapostolle family, a famous nineteenth-century liqueur producer who also owned the Château de Bourg in Cognac. In 1880, Louis-Alexandre Marnier-Lapostolle, like M. Cointreau before him, was in the Caribbean looking for ingredients. He came across Haiti's bitter oranges and, once home, started to create a recipe for a liqueur based on the fruit and the firm's Cognac.

What Marnier-Lapostolle did was to take basic triple sec/curaçao one step further. Most liqueurs would originally have used the local spirit as the base ingredient but, with the arrival of the continuous still, most were using neutral spirit. He reverted to the original technique and, as a result, built in another layer of flavour and complexity to his liqueur.

Bitter orange peel (no sweet oranges are used) is given a long maceration in young, high-strength brandy and then redistilled at the Château de Bourg. This is then blended with aged Fine Champagne Cognac, sugar syrup and the inevitable secret herbs, and aged for another period in cask at the firm's cellars in Neauphle-le-Château.

The firm still makes a range of brands – including Cherry Marnier, Crème de Grand Marnier and Cordon Jaune (which uses grape brandy rather than Cognac) – but Grand Marnier Cordon Rouge remains its highlight. It's a sophisticated, aristocratic liqueur that exudes orange richness with a complex mix of spice behind. The deluxe version, Cuvée de Centenaire, uses 10-year-old Fine Champagne Cognac in the blend.

The closest orange liqueur to Grand Marnier in terms of complexity is Italy's Aurum. Invented by distiller Amadeo Pomilio, it was named by the famous Italian poet Gabriel d'Annunzio. There are entirely plausible claims that it is based on an ancient recipe that originally involved the addition of flakes of gold.

It is made by a complicated procedure. Orange peel and flesh (from a local strain grown in the Abruzzi mountains) are macerated in brandy and then triple distilled. This is then blended with 10-year-old brandy, also produced by the firm, and aged again before being sweetened and coloured with saffron. Packaged in a bottle based on a flask found in Pompeii, this is a delicately coloured, complex liqueur.

The final classic peel liqueur, Mandarine Napoleon, actually uses tangerines rather than oranges. It was invented by Antoine-François de Fourcroy, and was allegedly the drink used by Napoleon in his attempt to seduce the actress Madame Mars. Records do not reveal his success.

The recipe was revived in 1892 by the Belgian distiller Louis Schmidt, and uses the essential oils of Sicilian tangerine peel blended with aged Cognac, which is then aged and sweetened. It's a fragrant, polished drink. A premium version, Millennium, packaged in a decanter, is occasionally seen.

... and lemons

These days, a citrus-peel liqueur can claim to be Italy's top-selling style. Limoncello is, quite simply, the trendiest drink to be seen with. Originally a home-made liqueur, it has its roots in the Amalfi coast. The peel from local lemons would be macerated in alcohol for around a month to extract colour and flavour, before being decanted and sweetened with sugar syrup, left to settle and bottled.

The first time the author tried it was on his honeymoon, at lunchtime in a deserted restaurant in Ravello, high in the hills above Sorrento. Nuns were playing football outside. The home-made liqueur was ice cold, the moment perfect.

Limoncello is the perfect palate cleanser, acting a bit like an alcoholic sorbet. In fact, originally it was created to be drunk, almost frozen, after a fish course, the equivalent of drinking the finger bowl. It's vibrant, brightly coloured and utterly refreshing. Sadly, as its popularity has grown, so have the number of brands on the market, some of which are a touch confected. If you can't find the real stuff, try making it at home with a good vodka, lemon peel and sugar.

Strangely enough, lemons also make up the main flavouring ingredient in the lurid purple concoction, Parfait d'Amour. An old eighteenth-century style, this is an amalgamation of macerated and distilled lemon (and other citrus fruits) with aromatic elements such as cloves, cinnamon and the all-important violet – although this doesn't give the drink its colour; that is achieved by vegetable dye.

Other fruit liqueurs and fruit brandies

The Italians also have a monopoly on high-quality cherry-based liqueurs. There are as many styles as there are types of cherry, but at the pinnacle is maraschino. Cherry liqueurs are not the same as cherry *eaux-de-vie*

(*see* Other Spirits), but they are, by and large, made by macerating skin, pulp and stones in grape spirit.

Luxardo, which has its own marasca cherry orchard, takes this simple technique to extreme lengths. The process starts with the removal and distillation of the cherry stones to capture their almost almond-flavoured essential oil. The remaining flesh of the cherries (and some elderberries) is then fermented before the ferment is arrested by the addition of alcohol. This lightly fortified spirit is only used for cherry brandy – what the maraschino producer wants is the skins, stems and yeast that are left at the bottom of the tank. This is added to the stone concentrate and left to infuse for a number of months, before being triple distilled and then aged once more – this time for three years in ash vats. It's then sweetened and bottled.

Luxardo's maraschino ends up a marvellously concentrated sweet-and-sour mix with pungent cherry notes, mixed with a refreshingly bitter twang on the finish. It can be drunk on its own, but most people find it a bit too much solo. Best to use it judiciously in cocktails – try a tiny splash in a Manhattan.

Other cherry-based liqueurs may not have maraschino's intensity, but there are some soft and rather elegant examples – such as France's Cherry Rocher, or Denmark's Heering. Originally created in 1818 by Peter Heering, a Copenhagen grocer, Heering uses Sevn cherries from its own orchards. The fruit and the stones are crushed and, along with other botanicals, are macerated in wooden vats for months, during which time they are progressively blended in a form of *solera* (*see* Brandy de Jerez). Heering's mix of intense cherry fruit with a light body has made it the integral liqueur brand used in a Singapore Sling.

Every fruit in the world can be turned either into an *eau-de-vie* or into the rather misleadingly titled fruit brandy. These aren't clear, pure fruit distillates, but are crushed fruits (often complete with their bitter stones) that have been steeped in grape spirit and sweetened. Some are wood aged, but that's uncommon, while many firms use fruit concentrate. Bols, de Kuyper and Cusenier all make good-quality, if rather simple, fruit brandies – the most commonly seen being cherry, apricot and peach, although in the 1980s, Suntory weighed in with its melon liqueur Midori.

Just to add to the confusion, you can find Poire William liqueur as well as the *eau-de-vie*. The liqueur is made by infusion rather than distillation, and is sweet and concentrated. Don't get them confused; they are quite different beasts.

The advantage with soft fruits is that you can do what people have done for centuries and make your own at home – though it's advisable not to distil your own spirit! Any soft fruit or citrus peel left in alcohol for a period will release its colour and flavour. Vodka is a good neutral base, but gin is a brilliant medium – seen in that English classic, sloe gin. This is made quite simply by steeping sloes in the gin for a few months in the dark. Sugar can be added during the maceration or after, according to taste. It's important to remove the berries after a few months, otherwise they become unpleasantly bitter. Several commercial brands are available on the market – Gordon's, Hawker's and Plymouth all make a sloe gin (Plymouth also has a damson gin) – but it's more fun to do it yourself.

THE USE OF SEEDS AND NUTS

The production of liqueurs from spice seed is a natural spin-off from the ancient herbal elixirs. Rather than relying on the impact of a large number of ingredients, these liqueurs were usually made from relatively few ingredients and dominated by one particular flavour. They heralded a change in the apothecaries' art as, rather than being cure-all cordials and tonics, they were distillates of one beneficial herb for one specific purpose.

The oldest commercial liqueur, kümmel, is a member of this small grouping, as is anisette – the liqueur equivalent of anise.

The use of caraway seeds, the main ingredient in kümmel, is a peculiarity of countries that border the North Sea and the Baltic. Quite why this particular flavouring was used is lost in time – caraway certainly wasn't an indigenous plant, although some producers like Blanckenhagen began cultivating it purely for liqueur production.

Where it originated is also open to debate. In 1575 Lucas Bols produced the first commercially produced kümmel, although Mentzendorff, the London-based fine wine importer, claims that its Latvian brand (sold as Mentzendorff or Blanckenhagen-Allasch) was the original brand, first made by the aristocratic Blanckenhagen family on their estate near Riga.

According to legend it remained a Dutch and Northern German speciality until Peter the Great arrived in Holland in the late-seventeenth century. A noted distiller (*see* Vodka), he is credited with taking the recipe back to Russia. It seems unlikely. For a start, distillers in Gdansk were producing caraway-accented Goldwasser from the sixteenth century onward (*see* below).

Whoever was first, kümmel remains a northern classic that's made by rectifying caraway seed and then blending the infusion with neutral alcohol and other flavouring ingredients (although cumin seed is not used, as is widely believed), and then sweetening the mixture. Mentzendorff includes aniseed and violet roots among its secret botanicals.

Mildly dry and slightly bitter, kümmel has moved a long way since its invention as a cure for flatulence. For some reason, it's highly regarded by senior members of English golf clubs. Whether there is a connection between the two is not known…

As well as being a main ingredient in akvavit (*see* Other Spirits), caraway crops up in the ancient Gdansk speciality vodka, Goldwasser. First made in 1598, Goldwasser contains infusions of aniseed, caraway, citrus peel, other botanicals and, most importantly, flakes of gold. The gold may originally have had a medicinal reason for its inclusion, but it's more than likely that it was used as an ostentatious way of showing that the owner of the bottle was very rich indeed.

If the northern sea ports' speciality was caraway-flavoured liquors, then their equivalents in the Mediterranean were doing the same with anise. Although the majority of these are dry to medium-dry, there are a number of liqueurs that have evolved out of this tradition – the most visible being Sambuca. Originally a Roman speciality, Sambuca is produced from infusions of elderberries, anise and other herbal flavourings. Lighter and more fragrant than anisette, it was one of the fashionable drinks of the disco era, drunk according to traditional ritual with two or three flaming coffee beans floating on its surface – a remarkably dangerous practice if tried when you were less than coherent.

Almonds are used to make the Italian liqueur Amaretto; it has made Disaronno one of the world's most famous liqueur-makers

Anisette remains the main brand in the Marie Brizard range. It is produced by macerating a concoction of 16 seeds, plants and citrus peel, and then blending in anethol and huge amounts of sugar syrup. It is chill-filtered to stop any clouding. One for people with a sweet tooth.

Nuts

The infusion of fruits, seeds and nuts in alcohol is an old rural tradition – even today in Umbria, green walnuts are gathered, taken home, quartered and placed in large jars full of either grape spirit or a simple water-and-sugar mix. It is this tradition that could well have been the origin of one of the most famous liqueur brands in the world – Amaretto Disaronno.

Legend has it that the sixteenth-century artist, Bernardino Luini, was given the recipe for Amaretto by an innkeeper's wife, whom he was using as a model for the Virgin in his fresco in the convent of Sta Maria delle Grazie in Saronno. The story goes that, overwhelmed with gratitude (this is a familiar motif in the folk tales surrounding liqueurs), she whipped up a bottle of the liqueur from the fruit of the almond trees growing in her garden. Probably she'd have had a bottle already sitting from the previous year's harvest.

Whatever the truth, it wasn't until the late eighteenth century before it was commercially produced, first by an apothecary called Reina in his store in Saronno. Although there are a number of brands on the market, the first (and best) is the

Amaretto from the Reina-owned firm Illva that's packaged in a thick rectangular bottle. A total of 17 flavouring ingredients go into this brand, the most important of which are an infusion of bitter almond oil and crushed apricot pits macerated in neutral alcohol. These combine to give the drink its distinctive, rich, marzipan aroma.

Walnuts are the main ingredient in a speciality from Madrid called Madrono. The liqueur, made by blending the essential oil from madrono nuts with alcohol, had been forgotten until the early 1980s, when a small patisserie in the working-class district of La Vapies began to use the madrono nuts in its cakes. When the cakes began to acquire a cult following with the students who lived in the area, the couple who ran the patisserie decided to revive the liqueur, and for years it was only available by the glass in this tiny shop.

The cult continued to grow, and the firm has now switched to full commercial production – and larger premises. It tastes like walnut whip concentrate with a slight bitter edge. Italy's equivalent is the richer, heavier, more serious Nocino.

Good though it is, Madrono will never be able to compete in volume terms with Malibu, one of the most successful new brands launched in the 1980s when people, mistakenly, thought cocktails were making a comeback. A blend of rectified rum and an extract made from coconut pulp and milk, Malibu has a strangely thick texture, and how much you like it depends purely on how much you like coconut and how sweet your tooth is. The Brazilian equivalent, Batida de Coco, isn't quite as fat.

If you have to drink a coconut drink, the recommendation is to stick to a flavoured rum, such as Wray & Nephew's Koko Kanu or Cruzan's Coconut, both of which are lighter and less cloying.

The French and Italians make a huge range of liqueurs from other nuts, such as Noisette, Crème de noix (hazelnut and walnut, respectively) and Crème de noyau (a mix of cherry, peach and plum stones).

The principle is the same for all the styles. The nuts are chopped up and steeped in neutral or grape spirit, filtered, sweetened and sometimes coloured. The most famous Italian nut brand is Frangelico, a sticky mix of hazelnut and herbs.

THE USE OF CRÈMES

Although closely related to fruit brandies (*see* above), crème liqueurs form their own select club. The main difference is that they don't use the stones of the fruit, and are often produced with concentrates rather than by macerating the fruit, although some brands – crème de menthe, Himbergeest and Kroatzbeere – will also use essential oils. They are also considerably sweeter, lower in alcohol and more brightly coloured than fruit brandies. Fundamentally, they are sweetened alcoholic essences of a single fruit, herb or pod. They might not be complex, but where would the cocktail barman be without them?

The three huge liqueur firms of Bols, de Kuyper and Cusenier dominate this market with vast ranges of multicoloured potions, but it's worth searching out the wild fruit crèmes from smaller liqueur producers such as Chartreuse and Izarra. Both these firms produce astonishingly concentrated examples that are hugely versatile, both in making cocktails and in cooking. Once you have tasted examples like their cassis or mure, life will never quite be the same again.

By and large, crèmes aren't intended to be drunk on their own. There are, however, two international crème brands that can quite happily be sipped with nothing more than a lump or two of ice – Kahlua and Tia Maria. These two coffee-based brands have taken the market away from the older, sweeter crème de cacaos made by Bols and de Kuyper.

Kahlua claims to hail originally from Mexico, although as ever there's some debate over the accuracy of the statement. Some feel that the brand originated in Turkey, pointing to the turban-clad figure that appeared on the original label and the continued use of a distinctly Arabic archway – although both of these might be nothing more than Andalucian nostalgia.

A rich, flavoursome blend of cane spirit, Mexican coffee and vanilla, Kahlua was one of the brands that stormed into America after Repeal and immediately made its mark with the Kahlua Sombrero, and its inclusion is essential in the making of a good Black Russian.

These days it claims to be the world's second biggest-selling liqueur brand, and is produced under licence in Mexico, Denmark and Scotland. Its only rival in the coffee-crème market is Tia Maria (which is also owned

The Blue Mountains of Jamaica which give their name to the coffee beans used to make Tia Maria

by Allied Domecq). The story of the recipe dates back to the seventeenth century, when Jamaica was caught up in the colonial wars that raged across the Caribbean. When one estate was attacked the owners had to flee, and the young daughter and her maidservant Maria got separated from the rest of the family. Maria managed to collect her mistress's possessions, along with a box containing (wait for it) the secret recipe for the family's coffee liqueur. Years later the girl gave the recipe to her daughter, who named the liqueur Tia Maria (Aunty Mary) after the servant.

The liqueur is a blend of Blue Mountain coffee beans and spices (including vanilla), which are infused in Jamaican cane spirit. A touch of chocolate is added before bottling. Tia Maria is sweeter than Kahlua, but lacks the former's body, allowing the spirit to show a little too much. It's a versatile mixer though.

This small but select band has recently been joined by Touissant, named after the Jacobin revolutionary who liberated Haiti from the French. It is made by a Trinidadian in Flensburg, Germany. Life can get pretty complicated in the world of liqueurs!

It's a great alternative to Kahlua and Tia Maria with far more coffee (and a touch of bitter chocolate) on show on the nose. It's much drier than its rivals, making it easier to drink on its own or on the rocks. Worth looking out for.

Don't get confused between crème liqueurs and cream liqueurs, such as Bailey's. They are different creations.

THE USE OF WHISKY

The vast majority of liqueurs use a neutral spirit base – Grand Marnier and Aurum are notable exceptions, as are the whisk(e)y-based specialities that include Drambuie, Glayva and Southern Comfort.

Drambuie harks back to the old herbal infusions that were made when whisky was first distilled in Scotland. In those days it was common practice for the Highland distillers to throw in heather and other aromatic plants to their *uisce beatha* and sweeten the result with heather or clover honey. Smith's 1729 work *The Compleat Book of Distilling* lists mace, cloves, nuts, cinnamon, coriander, ginger, cubeb berries and English saffron as being integral ingredients in making "Fine Usquebaugh".

It comes as no great surprise, then, that Drambuie is an ancient recipe, although the story of how the recipe came into the hands of the Mackinnon family of Skye is one of the more fanciful that litter the history of liqueurs.

According to the tale, the recipe was given by a grateful Bonnie Prince Charlie to Captain Mackinnon as a token of his gratitude for saving him from the Duke of Cumberland's troops after Culloden.

Now quite how the Prince would have had the time or the inclination to do this when his life was in danger, the legend doesn't say. It's pretty unlikely that he would have carried a recipe about his person on a long military campaign in case it came in useful. In fact, the Prince spent very little of his life in Scotland, and had virtually no experience of whisky.

What's more plausible is that the Mackinnons were already making their liqueur, and gave it to the Prince before he sailed off to exile in France.

Whatever the truth, Drambuie is a cracking liqueur.

The family kept the recipe to themselves for over 150 years until, in 1906, Malcolm Mackinnon moved from Skye to join the Edinburgh wine trade and started to sell the occasional bottle. Very occasional, in fact. In the first year only 12 cases were sold.

These days Drambuie is still made by the family in their plant at Kirkliston, just outside Edinburgh. In accordance with family tradition that only the women can make the secret recipe, Mary Mackinnon assembles the essence and then seals it in locked containers. Another employee then blends it with aged grain and malt whiskies (the oldest malt is 17 years old) before it is sweetened with heather honey. Intense on the nose with touches of clove, nutmeg and wild herbs, it's a medium-sweet liqueur that's fresh in the mouth with a dry cinnamon-stick finish. Add one measure of Drambuie to two of a good blended Scotch, and you get the delicious (but dangerous) Rusty Nail.

Scotland's other main whisky liqueur, Glayva, was invented in the post-war period. It appears to be based on similar ingredients to Drambuie – heather honey, malt whisky and wild herbs – but it has a more pronounced sweet orange-peel aroma and is generally a sweeter drink. The name comes from the Gaelic *Gle mhath!* (very good!), the Scottish secular equivalent of Don Bernardo Vinvelli's "Deo Optimo Maximo!".

Scotland has seen a mini-explosion of whisky liqueurs in recent years. Stag's Breath is a blend of malt and fermented honey; Wallace is a clean, medium-dry mix of Deanston single malt, berries and "French" herbs – which appears to include some anise; while Hebridean is more malt-accented, with touches of cinnamon on the nose and a very light, almond-paste palate.

These are mere whippersnappers compared to Southern Comfort, America's greatest contribution to the world of liqueurs. The brand's origins are rooted in New Orleans where in the 1860s a barman called Heron allegedly tried to improve the taste of the barrels of red eye he was receiving from Bourbon County, by adding spices and fruit to them. His invention was such a success that he moved to St Louis and went into commercial production.

Southern Comfort still uses American whiskey as its base spirit, but it is not – as many people still insist – a bourbon! The main flavouring agent is peach, but there are also another 100 ingredients macerating in the spirit before it is given a long period of ageing. Peach and whiskey mix well. Maker's Mark's ex-director Jimmy Conn invented the Just Peachy (bourbon, orange juice, ginger ale, peach schnapps) as a long drink – although that seems rather a waste of Maker's to many whiskey connoisseurs.

What's intriguing about Southern Comfort is the way in which it has managed to cultivate such a wild and rebellious image. Maybe it's because it was Janis Joplin's favourite tipple, maybe because spirits from the Deep South are simply always reckoned to be rebel drinks. Whatever the case, Southern Comfort is the only liqueur that's managed this considerable feat.

THE USE OF EMULSION

The drinking of the egg-yolk-based liqueur advocaat is a Dutch speciality. Its original incarnation was as a planter's drink in Holland's Brazilian enclaves, where the fruit of the abacate tree would be fermented and drunk. When the planters returned home they found that abacate trees were distinctly thin on the ground and, warping the original name to advocaat, decided to use eggs instead.

Production is dominated by Warninks, which goes though an estimated 60 million egg-yolks a year. The eggs are broken by machine, separated, and up to 70,000 yolks per hour can be mixed with the grape spirit, sugar, vanilla and an emulsifying agent. Thick, gloopy and sweet, it can be drunk on its own, diluted with lemonade or even eaten like alcoholic custard with a spoon.

Italy, inevitably, has a version of this liqueur as well. Called Vov, it's made with Marsala and is even thicker and sweeter than advocaat. One for sweet-toothed egg-lovers only.

THE USE OF CREAMS

The same cannot be said for Bailey's Irish Cream, which claims to be the single most successful new spirit launch in the last 30 years and the world's top-selling liqueur. The creation of this sassy new kid on the block started when Gilbey's in Ireland didn't know what to do with a surplus of spirit. Someone had the bright idea of trying to make a bottled Irish coffee, and in 1975 Bailey's was launched to immediate success.

Bailey's is the polar opposite to Chartreuse or Benedictine. It doesn't come from an ancient heritage of herbal knowledge; it springs from twentieth-century technology, but that's not to do it down. Bailey's is not only a great technical achievement – an alcohol/dairy product blend that doesn't have any artificial agents, and yet doesn't curdle or go off in the bottle – but it tastes good as well.

It started an explosion of cream liqueur brands – some good, like Cadbury's or Amarula (see below), but with an excess of "me-too" brands. Even established liqueur brands have tried to get in on the act – you can now buy Crème de Grand Marnier, Cointreau and Tia Maria, none of which is a patch on its original incarnation.

One of the few that may last is the South African brand Amarula Cream. This is made from the distilled fruit of the marula tree, which is given three years' maturation in oak before being blended with fresh cream. Smooth and strangely fruity/toffeeish, it allegedly has aphrodisiac qualities. Certainly, Amarula has an advantage over many of its rivals in at least being made from natural ingredients and having a story to tell.

The attraction of cream liqueurs lies in the fact that they are easy to drink, they have little or no discernible alcoholic content and they are also softly sweet. In many ways they're the drinks world's equivalent of milkshakes. Some, like Bailey's are rather good, but be careful of the cheaper brands.

The long history of liqueurs is littered with brands that jumped on a bandwagon and promptly fell off a few years later.

The great brands simply carry on. They might not occupy a central part of anyone's drinking habits, but either on their own or in a cocktail they remain some of the most fascinating spirits around – whether you believe the stories or not.

Opposite: Amarula Cream is made from the distilled fruit of the marula tree; the makers claim it has aphrodisiac qualities

COCKTAILS

Who invented the cocktail? Answer: the first person who decided to find out what two or three different ingredients would taste like when they were mixed together. Cocktails are a product of experiment, the result of satisfied curiosity. Their fortunes have ebbed and flowed as people's tastes have changed. Some have lasted the distance, becoming legendary concoctions, others have fallen by the wayside.

THE HISTORY OF COCKTAILS

Cocktails mirror the trends of their time; they are a barometer of society. They range from aristocratic concoctions to drinks of the people. They were the tipple for the "Bright Young Things" of the 1920s; the fuel that spurred Hemingway and Ian Fleming; that sharpened the wit of Dorothy Parker; that gave the disco era added froth and sparkle. Today they are cool, ironic and decidedly post-modern in attitude.

Their recipes have sealed friendships, but mostly cocktails are a matter of heated debate. No two people can agree about when they were first made, where the name came from, or even how to make them. Beware, you are entering a minefield.

The rum punches drunk in England by Boswell (*see* Rum, pages 514–531) were, in their own way, urcocktails, but the term first appeared in an American dictionary in 1806, meaning "a mixed drink of any spirit bitters and sugar".

That said, no one can agree where the name came from. Some argue it came from a horse-breeding term, referring to a horse that was part thoroughbred and known as a "cocktail" because its tail was docked. Others have a fanciful tall tale that it was the name of an Aztec princess called Xochitl.

James Fenimore Cooper preferred the convoluted history of an inn-keeper called Betsy Flanagan, who stole her neighbour's chickens and served them to some of Lafayette's volunteers. She tied the tail feathers to mugs of drink and the French soldiers raised a toast of "Vive le Cock-tail!" The most plausible, if rather prosaic, explanation remains the French term *coquetel*, meaning a mixed drink. The fact that other tales point to New Orleans using the term early in its life gives a hint that this might be the right one.

Many countries have contributed to the evolution of the cocktail, but America remains its spiritual home – the cocktail bar is the high temple, the barman a priest, the drinkers acolytes, genuflecting before the raised shaker.

The first high priest of the cult was Professor Jerry Thomas, a relentless showman and self-publicist, the Barnum of the bar, and his 1862 book *The Bar-Tender's Guide and Bon Vivant's Companion* contains the first recorded recipes of the craze that was beginning to grip America.

Thomas toured Europe, lugging £1,000 worth of silver bar equipment with him, showing off his dazzling creations such as the Blue Blazer, which would involve tossing a stream of flaming whiskey from mixing flask to mixing flask.

Cocktails have swung from sweet to dry throughout their life. In the early days, sweet was in. The main base spirit was gin, but the most common style at that time was the sweet Old Tom, rather than the dry gins that were being made by the end of the century. Bitters were also an integral part of all the early mixes – orange, Angostura and Peychaud all feature heavily in the recipes of the time, as do the sweet liqueurs that were widely drunk. So when the good professor invented the Martinez, it wasn't the Martini we know today, but a sweet mix of Old Tom, sweet vermouth, maraschino liqueur and bitters.

The best gauge of how the cocktail continued its passage into the heart of American social life can be

Cocktails – drinks of celebration – come in all colours and strengths; they are served in glasses of all shapes and sizes

charted by the number of books that appeared on the subject. Thomas's greatest rival was Harry Johnson, who in 1882 published *New And Improved Illustrated Bartender's Manual, Or How to Mix Drinks of the Present Style*, with hundreds of recipes in it. Many – most of them, even – are forgotten. Barmen have taken the ones they wanted and modified them, while ingredients and tastes have changed. Shed a tear then for the Goat's Delight, Bishop's Poker and the Hoptoad.

By the time Johnson was penning his book, the swanky hotels of the day had caught on to the craze and become cocktail laboratories. New York's Waldorf-Astoria (home of The Bronx) was typical of its day in having a cocktail created for it. In fact, the Astoria was one of the drinks edging us closer to the Martini we know today, but it has languished in the shadows as other, newer drinks have taken centre stage.

American bars had begun to spring up in the fanciest European capitals, and new creations were soon spilling out of them, like The Sidecar which was invented in Paris in 1911. In London, the Ritz, the Savoy and the RAC Club all chipped in with their own contributions to the fast-growing lexicon.

The new dry gins were at the centre of the majority of the most successful, and by bringing gin to a wider audience, cocktails were the making of the spirit as an international favourite. Gin, recognized as one of the great mixers, had found its role, and without vodka to challenge it, had the field to itself.

Despite this, gin's homeland remained a tad aloof from the phenomenon. There were cocktail bars in Britain, but it was not appropriate behaviour to be seen in one. The country had to wait until the end of the First World War for cocktails to become truly popular.

Cuba and London

The end of the war brought an eruption of relief. The corsets of the Edwardian era were removed and young people, for the first time in Britain's history, began to rebel. This coincided with America starting its long experiment with banning alcohol, and so the focus of attention switched to Cuba, London, Paris, Venice and Berlin. Cocktails, however, remained quintessentially American. This was a time when the rest of the world was first bombarded with images of America. It was the birth of the movies, the first great explosion of jazz. Cocktails were bound up in this American spirit, and Europeans recovering from war drank them because they wanted to taste some of that sense of optimism and youth.

That said, in Britain cocktails remained slightly decadent. They were drunk by a small number of young middle-class artists and students. Cocktail parties weren't held in the working-class slums. Then the Second World War came and put paid to all of that frivolity.

In Cuba, meanwhile, a revolution was brewing. Cocktails had been made since the turn of the century when the Mojito, the Daiquiri and the Cuba Libre were all invented. During Prohibition, though, America decanted itself into Old Havana – literally, in the case of a Boston barman called Donovan, who transported his entire bar to the city of Havana. And with the gangsters, movie stars and tourists came barmen, ready to learn from the recently formed Cuban Cantineros Club, an association and a school for cocktail makers.

Havana's hotels and bars were crammed with thirsty, partying Americans and the barmen responded. New recipes, like the Jai-Alai, the Ron Fizz, the Santiago, the Presidente, the Mary Pickford and the Caruso flooded out of the Inglaterra, the Pasaje and, most famous of all, el Floridita, home to the greatest barman of his day, Constante Ribailagua – the inventor of the frozen Daiquiri. "When it comes to cocktails, Cuba is ahead of us all. American, French and English barmen could learn a lot here," wrote Albert Crocket in the *Old Waldorf Astoria Bar Book* in 1935.

Meanwhile, back in America...

That isn't to say that America had taken the pledge. In fact, drinking increased during Prohibition and, though underground, the cocktail continued. The reason that so many new recipes were created during this period is conceivably because the taste of the bathtub gin and vodka that was being produced desperately needed to be masked, so fruit juices, other spirits and bitters were added. Long drinks such as the Screwdriver were born around this time, for this very reason.

Those who could get their hands on good-quality English gin were beginning to develop a taste for drier drinks. It is around this time that the Martini first begins to move from the 2:1 ratio of gin to vermouth to the drier style we know today.

After Repeal, America picked up where it had (officially) left off before Prohibition. Cocktails grew even through the Depression, the rationale perhaps being that it made more sense to have one strong drink than a lot of little ones.

If gin had had it all its own way before the Second World War, then the arrival of white whiskey (as vodka was first called) was soon to change all that. Over the years, vodka has outstripped its rival, muscling in on the Martini and dragging the title of hangover cure away from the Red Snapper made with gin and tomato juice to the Bloody Mary.

Some see vodka's rise as a triumph of no taste over flavour. It's certainly true that the vodkas that arrived in the United States and Britain after the war were miles away from the real stuff produced in Russia and Poland, but this flavourless base spirit allowed people to enjoy mixed drinks all the more. Vodka was new, it was light, it was cool. People have always looked for light flavours in cocktails. Even when the cream-laden drinks of the 1970s arrived, it was a virtually neutral base that drinkers wanted. Brown spirits, most notably bourbon, may have been the base for many classics, but light remains most people's main criterion for a great cocktail. Vodka was the lightest of them all.

In the 1960s cocktails hit a wall. They had become an acceptable part of society, the businessman's drink, the politician's. In the 1960s, if you wanted to be rebellious you wouldn't sip a Martini – you'd let your freak flag fly and drop acid instead.

Cocktails remained quiet until disco arrived in the late 1970s and everything went silly again. It was all mirror balls, creamy drinks, spangly tops and Gloria

Gaynor. The trendiest drinks were brightly coloured and had drag-queen names like Brandy Alexander and Pink Pussy.

In Britain in the late 1970s and early 1980s there was a mini-revival when post-punk people began listening to acid jazz and salsa and took to sipping classic cocktails, but it was always more of a pose than any great love of what they were actually drinking. At the same time, though, some drinks – the Piña Colada, the Black Russian, the Tequila Sunrise and the Margarita had escaped from the cocktail bar and made their way into pubs and clubs. The Wham! era of blonde highlights, tight shorts and fake suntans was defined by the irresistible rise of the Piña Colada.

In America, meanwhile, it all went badly wrong. It's Jimmy Carter who gets the blame for the downfall, with his speech complaining about the three-Martini lunch, although he was actually complaining about the tax-deductible lunch, not the Martinis!

There again, it's difficult to think of the Georgia peanut farmer being like FDR and mixing Dirty Martinis in the Oval Office every night.

This was the trigger for the Moral Majority to ride out and lynch anyone who dared to suggest drinking might not be all that anti-social. In time, cocktails became ensnared in the War Against Drugs and, as they did and people began to be scared of drinking them, so barmen tried to out-gross each other to get some attention. The names (and the drinks) got sillier – the Blow Job being a good example: a B-52 with whipped cream on the top that had to be drunk without touching the glass with your hands. Try it, and you'll see why it gets its name... If you weren't drinking dumb drinks, you were trying to pile as much alcohol in the glass as possible. Enter the Long Island Iced Tea.

Gary and Mardee Regan, in *New Classic Cocktails*, their essential guide to today's cutting-edge concoctions, define them as punk cocktails (that's the American cartoon version of punk, not the nihilistic UK one) but go on to say "without punk cocktails as an impetus we might never have seen some of these new classics... Punk cocktails smartly slapped the classicist bartenders across the face and screamed 'create, goddamn it, create'".

Then, in the mid-90s the classicists hit back. The Martini returned, with a new post-modern ironic twist along with the slice of lemon. They seem to be nostalgic for the past but, by being knowingly nostalgic, they are also detached and ironic. Much of the Martini revival, which has now reached ludicrous proportions, remains unconvincing. Gin and – at a stretch – vodka can make Martinis, but no other spirit can be used. If you want to make a tequila "Martini", go and find another name.

This isn't some purist, fundamentalist position. There are some that work brilliantly and, anyway, the whole nature of cocktails is that they change and shift with each generation.

Progress is to be encouraged, but what seems to be happening is that in the rush to create something new, many have forgotten the basic principle of any cocktail, especially a Martini, which is that the drink highlights its base spirit while being subtly enhanced by its flavourings. *There's* the art of mixing a cocktail. It's about putting a new spin on perfection. A haiku in its mixing, satori when it is sipped.

The post-modern cocktail has come about as a result of there now being a greater range of high-quality spirits than ever before. The consumer and the barman are spoiled for choice. There's reposado and anejo tequila and fine mezcal, top-quality bourbon, premium gins and vodkas, and great flavoured vodka – and by that we mean the real Polish and Russian varieties, not the ersatz confected cheapies. All of this opens up a massive new range of possibilities.

It's wonderful to see this backlash against the morality of the late 1980s and early 1990s. It might not be two-fisted drinking, but people are sick of being told that everything is bad for them.

Generation X wants to enjoy itself and, as we have seen in every chapter of this book, the desire for quality and flavour is what is driving the new push for the top end of the market. Cocktails are another manifestation of this – you can't make a great cocktail with poor-quality ingredients.

Why has it happened? Maybe it is simply because we just feel better about ourselves. After all, cocktails are drinks of celebration. Enjoy.

When you read a cocktail recipe, it all looks so simple. Three ingredients, ice and a glass. How can it go wrong? Easily, is the answer. Here are some tips to ensure you won't mess things up.

HOW TO MAKE COCKTAILS

It has been said many times before, but it's worth repeating that a cocktail is a combination of three things:
• *The base spirit, which gives the cocktail its main flavour and identity.*
• *The modifier/mixer, which melds with the base spirit and transports it on to another plane, but doesn't dominate it.*
• *The flavouring. This is the smallest element, but acts like the tiny detail that sets good clothes apart. It's the drop of bitters, the splash of coloured liqueur, the squeeze of a twist of lemon.*

Understand that, and you're on your way. Now the technical bit.

Shaking

First, an explanation of why you shake. It is to mix and also to chill the drink down, and give it a slight dilution, which helps to release flavours. The shaker, which should be made of stainless steel or glass, should never be more than half-filled with ice. Shaking actually doesn't take too long. A vigorous shake for 10 seconds will be ideal for the majority of cocktails. A simple indication is that the outside of the shaker should be freezing to the touch. If you shake for too long you'll end up diluting the drink. The contents are then strained though the strainer so that none of the ice ends up in the drink. Only use fresh ice cubes in the glass.

Stirring

There's as much written about this as any part of cocktail-making. In general, stirring is used to marry flavours that go together easily, and to prevent the cocktail becoming cloudy. Whether you shake or stir your Martini is entirely up to you. As in shaking, this is another way to chill a drink down quickly. Half-fill the stirring glass with ice and agitate (15–25 seconds should do it). Normally, stirred drinks are strained into the cocktail glass, although a few are stirred in their final resting place.

Blending

Here, ice is whizzed up with the spirit and served unstrained, although the pile of mush that is usually served up as a frozen cocktail rather ruins the point of the drink in the first place, as all you do is freeze your insides and not taste anything. The blender is also handy for zapping fruit for Daiquiris.

Muddling

This means gently pressing and mixing some ingredients in the bottom of a glass, either with a pestle or the back of a spoon. It doesn't involve pulverizing them, just making a rough purée.

Layering

The heaviest part of a layered drink goes in first; the successive layers are gently poured in over the back of a spoon.

Ice

For some reason, this ingredient is rarely given a second thought. But water has a flavour too – and chlorinated water has a flavour that is enough to turn a potentially great cocktail into a hideous undrinkable mess. If the tap water tastes of chemicals, don't use it for ice. Use filtered water or, better still, bottled water. Ice cubes are normally used in shaking and stirring. Crushed ice is colder, but it melts and leads to quicker dilution. Freezing tonic water works, or you can make vermouth-flavoured ice cubes for the Martini.

Chilling glasses

Most cocktails call for chilled glasses. The simple solution is to keep them in the freezer, but if you don't have space they can be chilled down quickly by filling them with ice and water and leaving them to stand. When you are ready to use them, shake them so the freezing water chills the outer surface, then tip all the ice and water out. Try not to pick them up by the bowl, but by the stem.

Salting the rim

Don't bury the glass rim down in a pile of salt or sugar. The intention here is to coat the outside surface of the glass, not

Opposite: *The range of equipment required to make cocktails*

the inside. Moisten with lemon or lime juice, then carefully turn the glass side on in a saucer of the salt/sugar, or sprinkle the coating on to the glass while rotating it (make sure you have some paper to catch the mess).

Fruit

Always use fresh, washed fruit. One tip is to roll limes before cutting them or using them for Caipirinhas. This allows them to start releasing their juices.

How to cut and use a twist

Pare small strips from a lemon, ensuring that some white pith is still attached. Holding the peel between your thumb and forefinger, give it a quick twist so that some oil sprays from the skin on to the drink. Run the twist round the rim of the glass and drop in. Longer strips can be tied into a knot and dropped in.

Measurements

All the recipes are in the standard accepted US ounces. The Imperial British ounce is slightly smaller, but makes virtually no difference.

If you are making cocktails at home, a US ounce is 2.8cl, an Imperial 2.5cl. For home mixing, an Imperial ounce is the equivalent of two-and-a-half tablespoons or six teaspoons.

It's worth getting a set of stainless-steel measuring spoons for teaspoons (tsp) and tablespoons (tbs). With a bit of practice, you'll end up knowing what an ounce looks like.

A dash is just what it says: the merest splash. When small additions are indicated (such as with maraschino), it's just a bit more than a dash.

Following a cocktail recipe is much the same as using a cookery book; you don't have to be restricted by the instructions.

If you prefer more lemon juice, less (or more) alcohol, a different garnish, then go ahead and satisfy your own palate. Once you have mastered the basics, the world is your oyster (or bar).

THE BARTENDER'S CHECKLIST

Fresh juice, fruit and ice are just as essential ingredients in a cocktail as quality spirits. Keep everything you need to hand. And don't skimp on the details. It's the little "extras" that make or break the final result.

ESSENTIAL INGREDIENTS
Alcoholic
Gin (keep in refrigerator)
Vodka (keep in refrigerator)
White and Gold rum
Tequila
Bourbon
Cognac
Blended Scotch
Dry and Sweet vermouth
Cointreau/Curaçao
Campari
Maraschino liqueur
Pernod/Absinthe
Drambuie

Green Chartreuse
Yellow Chartreuse
Kahlua
Champagne
Underberg (for hangovers)
Angostura bitters
Peychaud bitters
Orange bitters

The last two ingredients can be found in specialist retail outlets and are essential in any self-respecting bar.

Other
Tobasco/Worcestershire sauce
Fresh limes, oranges, lemons
Fresh fruit juice
Fresh mint
Maraschino cherries
Caster sugar
Coarse salt
Grenadine (made from pomegranates)
Rose's Lime Cordial
Mixers (soda water, tonic water, ginger ale, etc.)

SIMPLE SYRUP
This is called for in a large number of cocktails. You can buy Sirop de Gomme, but simple syrup is easy to make as its name suggests. Take equal parts of sugar and water and bring to a gentle boil, stirring occasionally. When the sugar has dissolved and the syrup is clear remove from the heat and allow to cool. Then bottle and refrigerate.

HOME-FLAVOURED SPIRITS
These are so easy to make that once you start you'll become hooked. Do not, however, fall into the trap of making all your home-made infusions from sweets and chocolate bars. You'll find savoury and fruit infusions much more versatile.

Vodka can be used for all infusions. Gin tends to work best with fruits, while tequila is good at picking up savoury flavours like jalapeno or citrus peel. Strongly flavoured herbs and pods only need a few days' steeping. Chillies need about one week, while citrus zest can take as long as a month. Check the flavour of the infusions regularly to see when they are ready to use. Vodkas can be sweetened with simple syrup.

High-strength Polish Pure Spirit is an excellent medium for maceration and extraction which can then be diluted with vodka to taste.

WHISKY-BASED COCKTAILS

The Manhattan

There is always debate as to who was the first to make any specific drink, but the Manhattan's origins seem to be pretty clear. It was created in the 1870s at the Manhattan Club in New York for Lady Jennie Churchill (Sir Winston's mother) at a celebration dinner given when William Tilden became state governor. At its heart beat the essential ingredients of nineteenth-century cocktails: sweet vermouth and bitters.

There is almost as much debate over Manhattans as there is over Dry Martinis but, while the cocktail has undoubtedly become drier over the years, it should not be a dry drink. The magnificence of the Manhattan lies in the way the bitters and sweet vermouth join in an unlikely alliance to round off the whiskey's more abrasive edges.

The original recipe calls for rye – a style that sadly is hard to find these days – so most use the sweeter bourbon. Canadian whisky is too light. But which brand? That's a matter of personal preference. Try Wild Turkey when you need a weighty belt of liquor after a tough day, or Maker's Mark for sophisticated sipping. Knob Creek is equally good, although Booker's is, perhaps, just too strong and tends to dominate the supporting flavours.

Manhattan

2 oz bourbon
1 oz sweet vermouth
3 dashes Angostura
drop of maraschino juice
maraschino cherry
Stir over ice in mixing glass and strain into cocktail glass. Garnish with cherry.

Mint Julep

If a Manhattan sparks debate, then a Mint Julep can incite war. Typically, its secret is simplicity, which is where the debate comes in. To crush or not to crush the mint, the quality of the ice, the receptacle, which bourbon to use. Every aspect causes argument.

On paper it's simple. All you need is fresh mint, ice, sugar syrup and bourbon. Ah, but if you are Bill Samuels of Maker's Mark, you pick mint only in April and use only the tenderest leaves, which you then tie up in a T-shirt, place in a container holding the whiskey, batter with a mallet and then squeeze. Before he became a distiller, Bill designed nuclear warheads…

If you are one of those Julepians who doesn't believe in bruising the leaves, try gently squeezing the leaves instead or bruise them gently with a muddler. Jim Beam's Booker Noe only uses mint to infuse his syrup, by pouring the cooled syrup over a jar filled with mint, refrigerating it and then discarding the mint.

There's also debate as to how much mint to use for the garnish. Six sprigs are about right. In his *Book of Bourbon*, Gary Regan suggests cutting the mint at the last minute and allowing some flavour to bleed from the stems into the drink.

A Mint Julep cools, refreshes and makes the world a beautiful place. Too many of them, however, and the soothing Southern experience turns into something bitter and twisted.

Mint Julep No. 1

3 oz bourbon
1 oz simple syrup
3 cups finely crushed ice
6 sprigs of mint
Fill a julep cup or glass two-thirds full with crushed ice. Add bourbon and syrup. Stir to blend. Pack the glass with more ice so it domes over the top. Garnish with the mint and insert straws. Let stand until a thin layer forms on the glass.

The Manhattan – use a bourbon if you can't find a rye whiskey

Mint Julep No. 2

3 oz bourbon

1 oz simple syrup

handful of mint leaves

3 cups freshly finely crushed ice

6 sprigs of mint

Cover leaves in bourbon for 15 minutes. Take out and put in muslin cloth and wring over the bourbon. Put bourbon and syrup in another bowl. Fill cup, glass with crushed ice so it domes over the top. Add bourbon, mint, syrup mix. Add straws and garnish. Let stand until a thin layer forms on the glass.

More Whisky-based Cocktails

Bourbon is a hugely versatile base spirit for cocktails, and it comes to life when given a dash of bitters. Try and find Peychaud bitters, it's worth the quest. The widespread use of bitters in many of these recipes points to the fact that this was one of the earliest spirits to be used in cocktails like the Old Fashioned and the Seelbach, which was only rediscovered recently when this elegant hotel was renovated. Many recipes call for rye whiskey. This refers to the true Kentucky rye, and not to Canadian whiskey. If you can't find a bottle, use bourbon instead.

Affinity

¾ oz Scotch whisky
¾ oz dry vermouth
¾ oz sweet vermouth
2 dashes Angostura
lemon twist
Shake and strain into a cocktail glass.

The Algonquin

2 oz rye
1 oz dry vermouth
1 oz pineapple juice
dash of Peychaud bitters
Shake and strain into a cocktail glass.

Brighton Punch

1 oz bourbon
3 oz brandy
¼ oz Benedictine
2 oz orange juice
¾ oz lemon juice
1 tsp sugar syrup
Shake and strain into an ice-filled Collins glass.

Brooklyn

1 oz rye
¾ oz vermouth rosso
dash maraschino liqueur
Stir and strain into a cocktail glass.

Harper Cranberry

2 oz I.W. Harper
3 oz cranberry juice
Stir into an ice-filled highball glass.

Horse's Neck

2 oz bourbon
2 dashes Angostura bitters
ginger ale
lemon twist
Coat a Collins glass with bitters. Add ice and bourbon. Stir. Add ginger ale and twist. Stir briefly.

Old Fashioned 1

2½ oz bourbon
3 dashes bitters
½ tsp sugar syrup
splash water
half orange wheel
maraschino cherry
In a highball glass muddle the sugar, water, bitters, orange and cherry, lightly mushing up the fruit. Fill the glass with ice cubes and add bourbon. Stir.

Sazerac

2½ oz bourbon
2 tsp absinthe/Pernod
½ tsp sugar syrup
3 dashes Peychaud bitters
1 lemon twist
Pour absinthe/Pernod into a highball glass, coat and discard the excess. Shake other ingredients and pour over ice into the glass.

The Seelbach Cocktail

Seelbach Hotel, Louisville, KY
1 oz Old Forester bourbon
½ oz Cointreau
7 dashes Angostura
7 dashes Peychaud bitters
5 oz Champagne
orange twist
Pour the bourbon, Cointreau and both bitters into a Champagne flute and stir. Add the Champagne and garnish with the orange twist.

Sidney

2 oz rye/bourbon
½ oz dry vermouth
splash Yellow Chartreuse
dash orange bitters
lemon twist
Stir and strain into a cocktail glass.

Rob Roy

1½ oz Scotch whisky
½ oz sweet vermouth
1 dash Angostura bitters
Stir and strain into a chilled cocktail glass.

Rusty Nail

1½ oz Scotch whisky
¾ oz Drambuie
Stir over ice in a highball glass.

Tipperary

1 oz Irish whiskey
¾ oz dry vermouth
¼ oz Green Chartreuse
Shake and strain into a cocktail glass.

BRANDY-BASED COCKTAILS

The Sidecar

Theories abound when it comes to attempting to discover who first made this cocktail. What's beyond doubt is that it is a Parisian creation, but trying to find out who was the first to put Cognac, Cointreau and lemon juice together ends up with you following clues which only lead you up some blind alley in an obscure arrondissement being pursued by a homicidal monkey. According to David Embury, author of *The Fine Art of Mixing Drinks*, it was created by a military acquaintance in Paris during the First World War who travelled to drink "his" cocktail in a motorcycle sidecar. Sadly, the friend isn't named, nor is the bar to which the sidecar travelled so regularly, lending the whole tale an apocryphal quality.

It could have been a creation of Harry's New York Bar, the famous Parisian haunt where a host of cocktails were invented, including the Bucket of Blood (*see* Vodka, page 626), but in the end no one really knows.

The minimalist beauty of the sidecar makes it a classic drink – indeed it can be regarded as the spiritual father of the Pisco Sour and the Daiquiri. The important element is to get the correct balance between the mouth-puckering acidity of fresh lemon juice (lime won't do, which is why a Sidecar isn't just a Daiquiri made with brandy) and the clean, sweet orange richness of triple sec. If these sweet and sour elements are in harmony, they provide the ideal frame for the fruity richness and kick of the Cognac.

The Sidecar

1½ oz Cognac
¾ oz Cointreau/triple sec
¾ oz lemon juice
Lemon twist
Shake and strain over ice into a chilled cocktail glass with sugared rim. Garnish with a twist of lemon.

The Pisco Sour

Sours are not normally the stuff of legend. They are one of the great workhorses of the cocktail bar. Any spirit can be combined with lemon juice and sugar to make a lip-smacking drink that wakes you up on a steamy day. The Pisco Sour is an exception to this rule. It's the national drink of Chile and Peru, and is used as a cooling glass during the hot South American summers. But behind a Pisco Sour's calming exterior beats the heart of a beast.

It's deceptively easy to drink, thanks to the aromatic, apparently benign influence of the Pisco. So, you have another – and another. All of a sudden this gentle drink turns round and belts you on the back of the neck, distorting your vision, rendering all speech into gibberish. You might feel an overwhelming urge to dance like a crazy fool, you might feel a desire to have another. Be warned, once Pisco madness is unleashed it is difficult to keep under control.

Inevitably there's some debate over how a classic Pisco Sour is assembled. Getting the Pisco right is the first task. Use a top brand like Control or Capel, and go for the top designation of Gran Pisco. This is the strongest, but it is also the driest and most flavoursome – and flavour, after all, is the whole point of the exercise.

Most arguments revolve around whether to use egg-whites or not, although it depends on the mood. Bitters can be used. If you must, try and use orange or Peychaud, rather than Angostura.

Pisco Sour

2 oz Gran Pisco
1 oz lemon juice
1 tsp caster sugar
(optional extra: dash bitters and egg-white)
Shake well in shaker – particularly if you are using egg-white – and strain into glasses.

More Brandy-based Cocktails

If whisky is unknown, then brandy remains virtually unseen.

Still, brandy is quite capable of giving an elegant fruity kick to many great cocktails, ranging from the classic Sidecar, which was invented in Paris at around the time of the First World War, to the Brandy Alexander. Brandy also makes an appearance in some of the new post-modern creations.

Be careful when using Armagnac, however, as its rich and earthy qualities tend to overpower many of these cocktails. It is better to stick to a good VS – Martell, for example. On days when you are feeling particularly extravagant, you can always push the boat out and procure a bottle of VSOP.

American Beauty

¾ oz brandy
¼ oz dry vermouth
¼ oz sweet vermouth
¾ oz orange juice
dash grenadine
port
Shake and strain into a cocktail glass and float port on top.

Brandy Alexander

1 oz brandy
1 oz brown crème de cacao
1 oz cream
2 tsp whipped cream
nutmeg
Shake first three ingredients and strain into cocktail glasses. Add whipped cream and sprinkle with nutmeg.

Corpse Reviver

¾ oz brandy
¾ oz Calvados
¾ oz sweet vermouth
Shake and strain into a cocktail glass.

Deauville

1 oz brandy
¾ oz Calvados
½ oz triple sec
¾ oz lemon juice
Shake and strain into a cocktail glass.

Prince of Wales

¾ oz brandy
¼ oz Benedictine
Champagne
dash Angostura bitters
sugar cube
orange
cherry
Put sugar cube in a highball glass and soak with Angostura. Add ice, Cognac and garnish. Stir. Add Champagne and finally Benedictine.

Sidecar

1½ oz brandy
¾ oz Cointreau
¾ oz lemon juice
twist of lemon
Shake and strain into a cocktail glass with sugared rim and garnish with twist.

Stinger

1½ oz brandy
¼ oz white crème de menthe
Shake and strain into a cocktail glass.

THE COLLINS FAMILY

The three largest groupings also make three great thirst-quenchers. Any spirit can be used to make them. Sours are aptly named, as they have a delicious, mouth-puckering effect thanks to the higher percentage of lemon juice. Fizzes, allegedly first made as a hangover cure at the RAC Club in London, are long sours and perhaps easier to take for the uninitiated. Collinses are a variant on fizzes, which are stirred rather than shaken.

A Sour contains
¾ oz lemon juice
½ tsp caster sugar
2 oz spirit
Shake and strain into a sour glass.

A Fizz contains
¾–1 oz lemon juice
1 tsp caster sugar
2 oz spirit
dash Angostura (optional)
soda
Shake and strain into a tall glass, and top up with soda.

A Collins contains
¾–1 oz lemon juice
1 tsp caster sugar
2 oz spirit
dash Angostura (optional)
soda
Place the first three ingredients in a tall glass half-filled with ice, and stir to mix. Top up with soda. Stir gently.

Tom Collins = gin
Colonel Collins = bourbon
Pierre Collins = Cognac
Joe Collins = vodka

RUM-BASED COCKTAILS

The Daiquiri

Rum's magical combination of delicate sweetness with an alcoholic kick makes it a wonderful base for cocktails, and in the 1920s the world's finest centre for their creation was unquestionably Havana.

There, in the el Floridita bar, barman Constante Ribailagua perfected a cocktail that had originally been invented in the mines in the Daiquiri mountain range in the south of the country. It was there, according to legend, that two engineers called Pagliuchi and Cox mixed together rum, lime juice, sugar and ice. Simplicity itself, but the greatest cocktails always are.

Constante gave this a further dimension by creating the frozen Daiquiri, although his original is far from the mushy slush that's decanted out of blenders today. He used crushed ice, but strained the drink rather than letting the ice cause unwanted further dilution in the glass.

His creation was to inspire Hemingway – still the most famous regular at the el Floridita – prompting Papa to launch into a beautiful, evocative and accurate description of the perfect Daiquiri in *Islands in the Stream*: "Hudson drank another frozen Daiquiri – and when he raised his glass he looked at the clear part under the crushed ice and it reminded him of the sea. The crushed-ice part was like the trail of a boat, and the clear part like when the boat cuts across its own trail when it moves over the sandy seabed in shallow water. The colour was almost the same."

All you need are the same ingredients as Pagliuchi and Cox – white rum, simple syrup or sugar and lime juice, but, as ever, balance is all-important. You have to hit that precise spot where the tart lime counter-balances the alcohol and the sweetness of the sugar.

Hemingway liked his Daiquiri cold and sour, and so to please the grumpy old devil the sugar was replaced by dash of maraschino liqueur and some unsweetened grapefruit juice.

As blending became common, so the possibilities increased, with fresh fruit being added. Try it with bananas, mango, strawberry, raspberry and, best of all, in an extension of that other Cuban classic, the Mojito – mint.

Simple Daiquiri

2 oz Cognac
Juice of 1 lime
1 tsp sugar
Lemon twist
Shake and strain over ice into cocktail glass.

Frozen Daiquiri

2 oz white rum
Juice of 1 lime
1 tsp sugar
Prepare in blender with crushed ice.

Mint Daiquiri

2 oz white rum
Juice of 1 lime
¹⁄₂ oz Cointreau
handful of mint leaves
Juice of half a lime
1 tsp caster sugar
Blend with crushed ice and strain into cocktail glass.

A simple Daiquiri, created in 1920s Havana

More Rum-based Cocktails

In recent times, rum cocktails have immediately conjured up images of badly made Piña Coladas or Daiquiris so cold that your innards were turned into a deep freeze. Naff, in other words. But rum remains a classic mixer – many of these recipes come from Havana's Golden Age, when that city was at the cutting edge of cocktail invention. The Mojito and Caipirinha are summer classics that refresh and stimulate. Both started life as people's cocktails, rather than creations of the swanky bars. Overproof white rum gives an undoubted kick that will keep you totally relaxed for the afternoon. Havana Club mixes well, while a gold rum will give extra weight and sweetness if that's what's desired. Once again, experimentation is the key. Recipes are guides, not rules.

Bee's Kiss

1½ oz white rum
1 tbs black coffee
1 tbs fresh cream
Shake well and strain into a cocktail glass.

Caipirinha

2 oz cachaça (or white rum)
1 lime, quartered
1 tsp sugar syrup
Put lime and syrup in bottom of a large highball glass. Muddle well for a minute to extract juice and lime oil. Add ice. Stir. Add Cachaça. Stir again.

Castro

1½ oz gold rum
¾ oz Calvados
1½ oz orange juice
¾ oz lime juice
¾ oz Rose's Lime Cordial
1 tsp sugar syrup
wedge of lime
Shake and strain into an ice-filled Collins glass.

Centenario

1½ oz gold rum
1 oz overproof white rum
¼ oz Kahlua
¼ oz Cointreau
juice of 1 lime
mint sprig
dash grenadine
Stir ingredients over ice in a Collins glass.

Cuban Island

(Schumann)
¾ oz white rum
¾ oz vodka
¼–¾ oz Cointreau
¾ oz lemon juice
Shake and strain into a cocktail glass.

The Floridita

1½ oz white rum
½ oz sweet vermouth
dash white crème de cacao
dash grenadine
juice of half a lime
Shake over ice cubes and strain into a cocktail glass.

Mai Tai 1

1 oz white rum
½ oz Cointreau
¼ oz Rose's Lime Cordial
1½ oz each of orange and unsweetened pineapple juice
splash grenadine
½ oz gold rum
wedge of pineapple
Shake and strain into a Collins glass half-filled with ice. Add grenadine and gold rum. Garnish with pineapple.

Mai Tai 2

2 oz gold rum
1 oz Curaçao
1½ oz Rose's Lime Cordial
1 tbs Orgeat (almond syrup)
1 tsp sugar syrup
splash grenadine
½ oz overproof
wedge of pineapple and lime
Shake and strain into a Collins glass half-filled with ice. Add grenadine and overproof. Garnish with pineapple and lime.

Mary Pickford

1½ oz white rum
dash maraschino liqueur
1½ oz unsweetened pineapple juice
dash grenadine
lime twist
Shake and strain into a cocktail glass. Add twist.

Naked Lady

1½ oz white rum
1½ oz sweet vermouth
4 dashes apricot brandy
2 dashes grenadine
4 dashes lemon/lime juice
Shake and strain into a cocktail glass.

RUM PUNCH

Rum punches are equally open to interpretation. It's the nature of the drink that every island, every bar will have its own variation on the theme, but all will be mixing sour, sweet, strong and weak components. Sourness is given by lime juice and bitters, sweetness from fruit juices, syrup and grenadine. Rum is the sole alcohol and most recipes dilute the punch with either water or ice. The end result is a gentle, soothing drink, not some confected mess. In Jamaica, Wray & Nephew dilutes lime, grenadine/syrup and overproof rum with water, and adds dashes of bitters and nutmeg. In Haiti they combine orange and passion-fruit juice as the sweet part, and use crushed ice for the dilution.

Mojito

2 oz white rum
1 tsp sugar syrup
half a lime
fresh mint leaves
soda water
sprig of mint

In a large highball glass, muddle the mint and sugar syrup. Squeeze lime into the glass and add lime half. Add rum and ice. Stir. Add soda water. Stir briefly and garnish with mint.

Presidente

2 oz white rum
¼ oz Cointreau
¾ oz dry vermouth
¾ oz sweet vermouth
dash grenadine
dash lime juice

Shake and strain into a cocktail glass.

Piña Colada

1 oz Appleton Special/Overproof
½ oz Appleton 12-year-old
2 oz unsweetened pineapple juice
¾ oz coconut cream
crushed ice

Blend the crushed ice, white rum, coconut cream and pineapple juice together, then pour into a Collins glass. Top up with the 12-year-old rum.

Ronaldo

1 oz cachaca
1 oz gold rum
½ oz crème de banane
½ oz unsweetened pineapple juice
lime juice
lime wedge

Shake and strain into a highball glass half-filled with ice. Garnish with lime.

Rum Shrub

2 oz dark rum
1 oz shrub
1 oz soda

Fill wine goblet two-thirds with ice. Add rum, shrub and soda. Stir lightly. (Shrub is an old English speciality fruit and herb syrup – most often seen in the West Country.)

September Morn

2 oz white rum
splash grenadine
1 oz lemon juice
egg white

Shake for about 30 seconds and strain into a cocktail glass.

Yellow Bird

1½ oz gold rum
½ oz overproof
¾ oz crème de banane
dash Galliano
¼ oz apricot brandy
3 oz unsweetened pineapple juice
¼ oz orange juice

Shake and strain into a highball glass half-filled with ice.

Zombie

¼ oz gold rum
2 oz dark rum
¼ oz overproof
¼ oz Cherry Heering
1¾ oz lime juice
dash grenadine
¼ oz orange juice

Shake and strain into a large highball glass half-filled with ice.

Piña Colada, a classic white-rum based cocktail

GIN-BASED COCKTAILS

Dry Martini

Gin is the original cocktail spirit, and has provided the world with its most famous and most personal example of the barman's art – the Dry Martini. Arguments rage about every aspect of this most famous of all cocktails – even its birth is a matter of debate – although most serious students of the subject agree (more or less) that it first appeared in the bar of the Knickerbocker Hotel in New York in 1911, where head barman, Martini di Arma di Taggia, mixed a cocktail of half-and-half London gin, Noilly Prat vermouth and orange bitters.

Now, ingredient-wise this is, to all intents and purposes, a gin and French. Martini's twist on the recipe was that he stirred the ingredients with lots of ice and then strained them into a chilled glass. The olive, it is said, was an addition by Knickerbocker regulars. What is certain is that the cocktail swept all before it.

The confusion arises because there was already a sweet Martinez cocktail on the market, consisting of Old Tom gin, red vermouth, maraschino and orange bitters. Indeed, one of the first bottled pre-mixes was a Martinez made along these lines by the US drinks firm Heublein in 1892. Legend has it that this was a Californian product named after a hung-over travelling salesman who asked for a pick-me-up so he could make the journey from San Francisco to Martinez.

Although vermouth is an integral part of the cocktail, there is in fact no connection with Martini & Rossi – the firm wasn't even making vermouth when di Taggia made his great invention. Ironically, though, Martini & Rossi went on to buy Noilly Prat, the firm that produces the best vermouth for a Dry Martini.

Though the recipe is apparently simple, the Dry Martini is infuriatingly complex. Every Dry Martini lover has his or her own spin on it – every element is open to contention.

Luis Bunuel described the process of adding vermouth to the gin as being similar to the Immaculate Conception, as all that should happen was that a ray of sunlight should shine through the bottle of Noilly Prat before hitting the gin. Unbelievers would call that neat gin, but true aficionados would agree that it is in fact a Dry Martini.

Never has a cocktail had such a catalogue of obsessives – all of whom are on a personal search for some Holy Grail. These days that means as dry as you can get, although the fact is that, as it has aged, so the Martini has become drier. It started life as an equal mix between gin and vermouth; these days the ration is liable to be anywhere from 4:1 to 25:1.

The aim is to get a drink that has the illusion of purity, but which has complexity. It defines cocktails, yet it is barely a cocktail at all. There's little more than one spirit and an infinitesimal amount of flavouring, so why is mixing one so difficult? Because simplicity is the

VERMOUTH

For thousands of years, people have been flavouring wines and spirits with herbs and roots. It's the basis for many liqueurs, while aromatized fortified wines like Suze, with its flavour of gentian, or Dubonnet and St Raphael, with their high percentages of quinine, are still with us. However, vermouth continues to be the best-known of the breed.

It takes its name from the German for its main flavouring compound wormwood (wermut). The Latin name for this plant is artemisia absinthium, meaning that vermouth is a second cousin to Absinthe. The difference is that vermouth uses the flowers, while absinthe uses a distillate of the leaves.

There are three broad types of vermouth: Southern French (typified by Noilly Prat), Savoie (Chambery) and Italian (Martini & Rossi, Cinzano). Southern French vermouths (the best for the Dry Martini) are the most complex, being made from dry white wine that is lightly fortified with brandy and then left outdoors in open casks for two summers and two winters to "weather". After this, some casks are fortified to 50 per cent ABV, herbs are added and left to macerate. The remaining casks are flavoured with mistelle (wine prevented from fermenting by fortification). The final product (about 18 per cent ABV) is a blend of the two.

Savoie vermouths are more delicate, having not been weathered, while the Italian examples are made from spirit infused with herbs, which is then blended with wine.

most difficult thing to achieve. Atomizer sprays, vermouth-flavoured ice cubes and vermouth-soaked olives have been used to try and achieve that moment of satori when perfection is reached.

All the ingredients must be chilled – from glasses to gin. Only use the best-quality gin – that means Tanqueray, Beefeater, Crown Jewel or Plymouth. Be single-minded. After all, you are the only person who can make the perfect example.

These days the Martini is becoming the centre of a new cult as barmen find new twists on the old theme (*see* Cocktails for recipes). Some are post-modern classics, others are a mess. What is certain is that the Dry Martini will never die.

Dry Martini

3 oz gin
1 tsp Noilly Prat
lemon twist

Place vermouth in shaker with ice. Shake and strain. Add gin. Stir and strain into pre-chilled cocktail glasses. Add lemon twist. You can vary the amount of vermouth to taste, but the principle remains the same.

The Singapore Sling

Barmen are naturally inquisitive people, always playing around with ingredients, seeing just what happens when another ingredient is added to a classic cocktail base. It was therefore inevitable that one of the oldest "simple" cocktails, the Gin Sling, would serve as the base for a whole range of outlandish experiments.

The Gin Sling itself is Tom Collins travelling under disguise and takes its name from the German *schlingen* (to swallow). So normal was this refreshing speciality of the English summer that no less a person than Mrs Beeton includes a recipe for one. It's the Victorian equivalent of Delia Smith telling you how to make a Martini.

Slings evolved into the Collins family (*see* Cocktails, page 619), but the name lives on in the Singapore Sling, which was allegedly created in 1915 by Ngiam Tong Boon, the bartender of that enduring symbol of British colonialism, Singapore's Raffles Hotel. Some gin experts (among them the doyen of gin writers, John

Doxat) disagree, claiming it dates from earlier. Certainly records show that there was a drink called a Straits Sling in existence before the Raffles recipe, which was another variant on the sling theme with Benedictine as a flavouring, but what we now know as the Singapore Sling does appear to have its origins in the Raffles' bar.

You can find some recipes for so-called Singapore Slings which still include Benedictine, just as you'll find some suggesting that you can replace the original lime juice with other, softer and sweeter, fruit juices. There is even one which fuse (or freeze) the classic Singapore Sling ingredients (replacing Heering with kirsch), and add splashes of Benedictine and Cognac, plus maraschino cherries and their juice, then whiz it all together with ice in a blender and top it off with chilled ruby port. Try variants like this by all means – part of the fun of making cocktails is improvization – but don't call the end result a Singapore Sling, call it a Phuket or Ko Samui Sling instead!

The Singapore Sling

2 oz Beefeater gin
2 oz fresh lime juice
2 tsp sugar
Dash of Angostura bitters

Pour on to crushed ice in a Collins glass. Stir. Top with soda and add ½ oz Cointreau and ½ oz Peter Heering (replace Cointreau with Benedictine for a Straits Sling).

HOW TO MAKE A GIN AND TONIC

It would be wrong to leave gin without mentioning the gin and tonic. It may have recently taken on a rather staid image, but that's more to do with the utter inability of the vast majority of bartenders in the UK to make such a simple, but utterly refreshing drink. Gordon's, thankfully, is trying to redress the balance, but here's a small contribution to give its efforts a bit of extra shove. Incidentally, if you are ever stuck for something to drink with Thai food – or even mild- to medium-spiced curries – try a G&T!

Cocktail Recipe

1 First fill a tall (preferably chilled) glass two-thirds full with clean ice. Use spring or mineral water for the ice. Cubes that have been made from chlorinated water will render the G&T undrinkable. Squeeze some lime on the ice and stir.

2 Choose your gin. Go for a brand that's over 40 per cent ABV, such as Beefeater, Plymouth, Crown Jewel or Bombay Sapphire. Pour in a generous slug.

3 Top up with fresh, good-quality, bottled tonic water (usually twice as much tonic as gin). Only use one-litre bottles if you intend to empty the bottle almost immediately.

4 Add a wedge of lime and stir. You can also pass the lime around the rim of the glass.

5 Enjoy!

More Gin-based Cocktails

It's a sad indication of how disregarded gin is that this, the greatest mixing white spirit, is most commonly found lurking at the bottom of warm gin and tonic with a flaccid lemon sulking above. Gin deserves far better than that. It is an invigorating drink, bursting with a fresh mix of citrus fruits, heather and juniper that gets the taste buds working. Indeed, it remains the cocktail spirit base *par excellence*.

Gin was the fuel for the rise of cocktails, and remains the base of many classics. The Martini has already been discussed (*see* page 623), but it is also responsible for The Bronx, the Singapore Sling (which originated in the Raffles Hotel at the turn of the century) and the Gimlet, which is tricky to master despite its simple ingredients.

As ever with any naked cocktail, the Gimlet is about hitting the right balance, allowing the gin to shine but using just enough lime to take the edge off its neat flavour and transform it altogether. If it was good enough for Philip Marlowe, it ought to be good enough for you.

Alaska
2 oz gin
splash Yellow Chartreuse
dash Angostura or orange bitters
lemon twist
Shake and strain into a cocktail glass. Garnish with the lemon twist.

Astoria
2 oz gin
½–1 oz dry vermouth
dash orange bitters
Shake and strain into a cocktail glass.

The Butterfly
2 oz gin
¼ oz Noilly Prat
¼ oz Blue curaçao
dash Poire William
Shake and strain into a cocktail glass.

Bronx
2 oz dry gin
½ oz dry vermouth
½ oz sweet vermouth
1 oz fresh orange juice
Shake and strain into a cocktail glass. Garnish with a cherry.

The Silver Bronx
2 oz dry gin
1 oz sweet vermouth
1 oz fresh orange juice
half an egg white
Shake well and strain into a cocktail glass.

Cajun Martini
Paul Prudhomme
1 fresh chilli
1 bottle dry gin
1 oz dry vermouth
Slice chilli lengthwise, but keeping it in one piece, insert into the bottle of gin. Top bottle up with vermouth. Reseal and refrigerate for up to 16 hours. Strain into clean bottle. Refrigerate until well chilled. Serve in cocktail glasses.

Caruso
1 oz gin
¼ oz dry vermouth
¼ oz green crème de menthe
Stir and strain into a cocktail glass.

Clover Club
2 oz dry gin
splash grenadine
1 oz lemon juice
egg white
Shake well for 30 seconds and strain into a cocktail glass.

Gimlet
2¼ oz dry gin
¾ oz Rose's Lime Cordial
Shake and strain into a cocktail glass.

Gloom Raiser

2 oz gin
1 oz vermouth
2 dashes grenadine
2 dashes Pernod/absinthe
Shake and strain into cocktail glasses.

Mandarine Martini

Mayflower Park Hotel

1½ oz gin
½ oz vodka
splash Mandarine Napoleon
dash Cointreau
mandarin twist
Pour liqueurs into empty shaker. Coat and
discard surplus. Add ice and other
ingredients. Shake and strain into cocktail
glass. Garnish with twist.

Martini Thyme

Ted & Linda Fondulas

3 oz gin
¼ oz Green Chartreuse
1 sprig of thyme
Stir together the gin and Chartreuse. Strain
into a cocktail glass and garnish with the
thyme.

Pink Gin

4 oz Plymouth gin
2 dashes Angostura
Coat a chilled cocktail glass with
Angostura. Discard excess. Top up with
gin.

Smoky Martini

2 oz gin
½ tsp Noilly Prat
dash to ¼ oz Scotch
Stir or shake and strain into a cocktail
glass.

Dirty Martini

2 oz gin
1 tsp Noilly Prat
splash of olive brine
Stir or shake and strain into a cocktail
glass.

Monkey Gland

2 oz gin
2 oz orange juice
dash grenadine
dash absinthe/Pernod
Stir or shake and strain into a cocktail
glass.

The Original Martinez

2 oz Old Tom gin
½ oz sweet vermouth
2 dashes maraschino liqueur
dash orange bitters/lemon
Shake and strain into a cocktail glass.

Scarborough Fair

2 oz Plymouth gin
¼ oz Chambery
sprig of thyme
sprig of rosemary
sprig of flat leaf parsley
2 fresh sage leaves
Muddle sage, parsley and Chambery in
shaker. Add gin. Shake and strain into a
cocktail glass. Garnish with rosemary and
thyme.

Singapore Gin Sling

2 oz gin
½ oz Cointreau
1½ oz fresh lime juice
1 tsp each caster sugar, sugar syrup
¼ oz Cherry Heering
lime
Shake first four and strain into Collins
glass. Top up with soda and float Cherry
Heering. Garnish with lime.

Star

1 oz dry gin
1 oz Calvados
dash Noilly Prat
dash dry vermouth
dash grapefruit
Stir and strain into a cocktail glass.

Vesper

3 oz Plymouth gin
1 oz Moskovskaya
½ oz Lillet Blanc
twist of lemon peel
Shake and strain into cocktail glasses and
garnish with twist.

White Lady

2 oz gin
¼ oz lemon juice
¼ oz Cointreau
1 tsp caster sugar
1 egg white
Shake and strain into a cocktail glass.

VODKA-BASED COCKTAILS

The Bloody Mary

As vodka started its rise to become America's favourite spirit, so it began stealing cocktails away from gin. It muscled in on the Martini action and wrestled away the Bloody Mary. Actually, it's a bit more complicated than that. The Bloody Mary started life in the 1920s in Harry's New York Bar in Paris, where a barman called Fernand Petiot mixed vodka (available in Europe) with tomato juice and called his creation "The Bucket of Blood". It wasn't a hit.

Petiot decided to try his luck in the States after Repeal and took his recipe with him. However, because he couldn't guarantee a supply of vodka, he used gin instead and re-christened his drink "The Red Snapper", which later got changed to "The Bloody Mary". Who Mary was, nobody really knows.

It was sold as a hangover cure from the start – and quite right too. It's one of the great restorative drinks, the only remedy when the world is a little too noisy, colours are too bright and all you want to do is sit and groan. It gives enough of a kick of alcohol to get you started again, but enough flavour and liquid to build you up without having to face a full cooked breakfast.

As ever, no two people can agree on what should and shouldn't go into a Bloody Mary – OK, other than vodka, tomato juice and Worcestershire sauce. The recipe here works, simply because it isn't too soupy. It also omits those irritating celery stalks that just end up disappearing up your nose or poking you in the eye. You are fragile enough – the last thing you need is a belligerent vegetable.

In Canada, they give the recipe a brilliant spin by substituting Clamato juice for tomato, adding horseradish sauce and celery salt and calling the result a Caesar. It's a great alternative – unlike the Bullshot, which uses beef bouillon (not consommé). Steer clear of mad cows.

Bloody Mary
2 oz Absolut Peppar vodka
Pour over ice in Collins glass.
In a jug, combine:
tomato juice
Worcestershire sauce
white pepper
salt
dash of celery salt
splash of fino sherry
splash of orange juice
Tabasco sauce to taste
Add mix to vodka and ice.

The Moscow Mule

Back in the 1940s when America hadn't woken up to vodka, John Martin of Heublein met in New York with Jack Morgan, the owner of the Cock 'n' Bull restaurant in Hollywood. Morgan had landed himself with a surplus of ginger beer, which was proving difficult to shift. Martin wanted to get rid of the equally slow-moving Smirnoff.

They put their heads – and their products – together, added a splosh of lime juice and created the Moscow Mule. Martin and Morgan then went a step further and ordered 500 copper mugs to be engraved with a kicking mule – now highly prized by mixologists – and marketed the items to bars.

On the back of the mule, Smirnoff's sales tripled between 1947 and 1950, and then doubled again the year after. America would never be the same again.

Moscow Mule
2 oz vodka
ginger beer
squeeze of lime juice
wedge of lime
Pour vodka over ice in a Collins glass. Add other ingredients. Stir.

More Vodka-based Cocktails

Vodka can be used in any of the gin cocktails (there again, gin can be used in all of the vodka ones as well!). We have to thank vodka for giving cocktails a new lease of life in the post-war period – even if it did hasten the decline of gin. Now with high-quality premium vodkas from Russia, Poland, Holland and the United States, the spirit has a chance to show it does have a personality after all. This mix of classic and post-modern cocktails will gain something extra as a result. The new flavoured vodkas will also pep many of them up. Experiment!

James Bond

1 oz vodka
dash Angostura
1 sugar cube
Champagne
In flute, soak sugar cube in Angostura. Add vodka and top up with Champagne.

Chambord Kamikaze

Peter Meddick
3 oz vodka
½ oz Cointreau
½ oz lemon juice
½ oz simple syrup
½ oz Chambord
½ lime, sliced
lime to garnish
Place all ingredients in large shaker with ice. Muddle violently. Strain and garnish.

Copenhagen

2 oz vodka
½ oz akvavit
slivered blanched almonds
Shake and strain into cocktail glasses and garnish with almonds.

Cosmopolitan

2 oz vodka
1 oz Cointreau
½ oz lime juice
splash cranberry juice
lime twist
Stir and strain into chilled cocktail glass with sugared rim. Garnish with lime twist.

Fortunella

Oliver's, Mayflower Park Hotel
1 oz Ketel One
¾ oz Bombay Sapphire
¾ oz Caravella
splash Cointreau
splash Campari
1 tsp candied kumquat nectar
lemon twist and kumquat
Coat shaker with the Cointreau and Campari, discard excess. Shake and strain into cocktail glasses and garnish.

French Martini

2 oz vodka
dash Chambord
dash pineapple juice
Shake and strain into a cocktail glass.

Harvey Wallbanger

1½ oz vodka
3½ oz orange juice
¼ oz Galliano
Stir vodka and orange juice and strain into a Collins glass. Float the Galliano on top.

Metropolitan

2 oz Absolut Kurant
½ oz Rose's Lime Cordial
½ oz lime juice
1 oz cranberry
lime wedge to garnish
Shake and strain into a cocktail glass and garnish with the wedge of lime.

Molotov Cocktail

3 oz Finlandia
½ oz Black Bush
½ oz Irish Mist
Shake and strain into cocktail glasses. (Finlandia, rather than Stoli, is ideal, as the distillery produced military alcohol used in Molotov cocktails during the Second World War..)

Orange Blossom

1¼ oz vodka
1¼ oz orange juice
dash orange flower water
Shake and strain into a cocktail glass. (Making this with eight parts juice to one part spirit is a Screwdriver.)

Polish Martini

1½ oz Wyborowa
½ oz Krupnik
dash apple juice
Shake and strain into a cocktail glass.

Russian Bear

1 oz vodka
1½ oz cream
¼ oz crème de cacao
1 tsp sugar
Shake and strain into a cocktail glass.

Salty Dog

2 oz vodka
2 oz grapefruit juice
Shake and strain into a salt-rimmed cocktail glass.

Seabreeze

2 oz Absolut vodka
2 oz cranberry juice
1 oz grapefruit juice
Shake and strain into a highball glass.

Vodka Martini

2 oz vodka
dash Noilly Prat
lemon twist
Shake (or stir!) and strain into cocktail glass. Garnish with twist.

Where The Buffalo Roam

2 oz Wyborowa
½ oz Zubrowka
dash Chambery
blade of bison grass
Coat shaker with Chambery and discard excess. Add ice and ingredients and shake. Garnish with blade of grass.

Yellow Fever

2 oz vodka
¼ oz lime juice
¼ oz Galliano
2 oz pineapple juice
Shake and strain into a highball glass.

TEQUILA-BASED COCKTAILS

The Margarita

The Margarita has been rather overlooked in the brave new world of the post-modern cocktail. This is partly because it was abused by unfeeling and uncaring barmen during the 1970s and 1980s, who turned it from a cracking aperitif that cleared your head and made your eyes gleam, into a glorified slush puppy.

The cocktail, in fact, has a pretty refined history before the madmen with their blenders got hold of it. Legend recounts that it was created for (or invented by) Margarita Sames, an American socialite of the 1940s, who used to serve it at parties in Acapulco. To be honest, there are rumours aplenty that a similar drink was already popular in Mexico before Margarita graciously allowed her name to be attached to it. What's certain, though, is that it was the first tequila cocktail, and a great one at that.

As so often, it's probably best to get back to basics. The first Margarita was a mix of tequila, Cointreau and lime juice. The best Margaritas still follow this basic recipe (see left). As with Daiquiris, though, as soon as the blenders began to be wielded with reckless abandon, so fruit began to be whizzed into the mix. To be fair, some are good – strawberry is a common variant, although the best I ever tasted was a blueberry one at London's Cactus Blue.

In principle there's nothing to making a Margarita. A good one doesn't mean a drink that will blow your socks

The Margarita is a mix of Tequila, Cointreau and lime juice

TEQUILA SLAMMERS

Ritual and tequila are so interlinked it is often difficult to separate fact from fiction. At one time slamming was regarded as the real way to drink tequila; before then it was the salt and lime ritual.

Slamming was often the best way to drink some of the dodgier brands on the market, while the salt and lime way is basically just a lazy Margarita – the underlying principle in both methods was to get the alcohol down your neck as quickly as possible.

In these days of sipping tequilas and mezcals a new ritual is needed. So welcome a truly Mexican way of enjoying tequila or mezcal – drinking with Sangrita. This tomato-based fruit juice with its chilli kick is served chilled in shot glasses. A sip of tequila, a sip of Sangrita. You can buy it pre-mixed or make your own. In principle, it's a Mexican Bloody Mary mix.

As always, using fresh ingredients makes all the difference. Blend together 2lb of tomatoes, the juice of three oranges and a couple of limes, some onion and fresh chillis.

Some recipes add hot pepper sauce (a Caribbean one is better than Tabasco) and use sugar, although if you need to sweeten the mix, then a splash of sherry is best.

A true taste of Mexico is the result.

off. Being too aware of the alcohol is the opposite of what you want to achieve. The aim is to intoxicate subtly.

First, use a good tequila, made from 100 per cent blue agave, such as abasic silver or reposado. Don't waste an expensive anejo brand on a Margarita. Cointreau is the best triple sec.

Use fresh limes for the juice. If the drink seems too sour, don't reduce the lime, simply add some more caster sugar.

The best Margaritas are either shaken or stirred on the rocks – blending with ice may make them good and chilled, but you run the risk of diluting the mix – and just as you don't want too much alcohol, nor do you want too little!

More Tequila-based Cocktails

The "new" reposado and anejo tequilas have opened up this branch of cocktails to a whole new world. The difference between these new tequilas and the old silver and gold brands that we had to put up with is considerable. Finally the delicate, pear and citrus flavours of blue agave are allowed to work their magic on these fine concoctions.

Chapala

1½ oz tequila
dash triple sec
¾ oz lemon juice
1½–2 oz orange juice
dash grenadine
Stir over ice in a Collins glass.

El Diablo

1½ oz reposado tequila
¾ oz crème de cassis
½ oz lime juice
ginger ale or ginger beer
wedge of lime
Stir tequila and cassis over ice in a Collins glass. Top up with ginger ale or ginger beer and add lime wedge.

Malcolm Lowry

1 oz Chicicapa Mezcal
½ oz overproof white rum
¼ oz Cointreau
lime juice
lime twist
Shake and serve in a cocktail glass and garnish with the twist.

Matador

2 oz tequila
¼ oz Cointreau
juice of half lime
1 tsp sugar syrup
pineapple chunk
Shake over crushed ice and strain into a highball glass with sugared rim.

Mexicana

1½ oz tequila
1½ oz unsweetened pineapple juice
¼ oz lime juice
dash grenadine
Shake and strain into a highball glass filled with ice.

Rosalita

¼ oz dry vermouth
¼ oz sweet vermouth
¼ oz Campari
¾ oz tequila
Shake and strain into a cocktail glass.

South of the Border

1 oz tequila
¾ oz Kahlua
½ lime
Squeeze lime over ice in highball glass. Stir before adding spirits. Stir to mix.

Tapika

Tapika, New York, NY
3½ oz Chinaco Plata
½ oz Cointreau
½ oz prickly pear cactus syrup
1 oz lime juice
lime slice
Coat cocktail glass with Cointreau and discard, ensuring rim is moistened. Sprinkle rim with salt. Shake tequila, prickly pear syrup and lime juice, strain into glass and garnish with lime.

Tequila Sunrise

2 oz tequila
3½ oz orange juice
dash grenadine
lime
Squeeze lime over ice into a large highball glass and drop into the glass. Add tequila and orange juice and slowly pour in grenadine.

Tequini

¾ oz tequila
¾ oz vodka
¾ oz Noilly Prat
dash Angostura
lemon twist
Shake and strain into a cocktail glass.

CHAMPAGNE-BASED COCKTAILS

Fizzing Americano

1 oz Campari
½ oz sweet vermouth
Prosecco/Champagne
orange wheel

Shake and pour over rocks in a highball glass. Top up with Prosecco or Champagne and garnish with orange.

Bellini

Puréed fresh white peaches
dash lemon juice
dash peach brandy
sparkling wine

Stir peach juice and brandy in a Champagne flute. Top up with sparkling wine. Adding fresh mango purée makes a Bombay Bellini.

Champagne Cocktail

Champagne
1 sugar cube
dash Angostura
twist lemon peel
orange

Place sugar cube into Champagne flute and dash with Angostura. Pour in Champagne. Add lemon twist and garnish with orange.

Due Campari

(Schumann)
¼ oz Campari
¾ oz Cordiale Campari
Champagne
¾ oz lemon juice

Shake lemon juice and Camparis and strain into Champagne flute. Fill with sparkling wine.

French 75

¾ oz gin
Champagne
¼ oz lemon juice
dash sugar syrup
dash grenadine

Shake first four, strain into flute and top with Champagne. (A French 76 is the same, but with vodka instead of gin.)

MISCELLANEOUS COCKTAILS

Long Island Iced Tea

¼ oz triple sec
¾ oz white rum
¾ oz gin
¾ oz vodka
¾ oz tequila
½ lime
¾ oz orange juice
cola

Squeeze lime into a Collins glass, add ice cubes and spirits. Stir and top up with cola. (Replacing the cola with sparkling wine produces Anita's Attitude Adjuster, while replacing the cola with cranberry gives a New England Iced Tea.)

Negroni

1½ oz gin
1½ oz sweet vermouth
1½ oz Campari
soda
orange slice

Shake and serve on the rocks in a highball glass. Top up with soda and garnish with orange.

Strawberry Cream Tea

Equal measures of:
Kahlua
Bailey's
Fraise
Vodka
Lassi

Blend and pour into an ice-filled Collins glass. Lassi is an Indian yoghurt drink. It gives this cocktail a lighter, cleaner flavour.

GLOSSARY

WINE
The Language of Bordeaux

Bordeaux Basic (often very) quality. 10 per cent alcohol for red and 10.5 per cent for white.

Bordeaux Supérieur One level above basic Bordeaux with reds at 10.5 per cent and whites at 11.5 per cent. In other words, made from riper grapes but not necessarily much "supérieur" at all.

Chai Bordeaux term for cellar/winery.

Clairet Bordeaux rosé.

Cru Bourgeois/Grand Bourgeois/Grand Bourgeois Exceptionnel Middle-class Médocs – ranked below cru classé.

Grand Premier Cru/Premier Cru/Deuxième Cru Top Sauternes classifications.

Grand Vin A château's top wine – the one sold under the château's own name.

Petit Château Unofficial name for lesser château, beneath cru bourgeois level.

Premier/Deuxième/Troisième/Quatrième/Cinquième Cru Classé Top Médoc classifications.

Premier Grand Cru Classé/Grand Cru Classé Top St Emilion classifications.

Second Vin A château's second wine – the one sold under a brand name like Pavillon Rouge du Château Margaux or under that of another château (Château Notton is the second label of Château Brane-Cantenac).

The Language of Champagne

Assemblage Mixing of base wines to create the desired blend, or cuvée.

Atmosphere 1 atmosphere = 15 pounds per square inch. The average Champagne is under 6 atmospheres of pressure – more than you'd find in the tyre of a fully laden London bus.

Autolysis The flavour-imparting process of ageing wines on their lees.

Bead The size of the bubbles.

Blanc de blancs Champagne made purely from the Chardonnay grape.

Blanc de noirs Champagne made purely from the black grapes Pinot Meunier and/or Pinot Noir. The wine itself is white.

Brut Very common sparkling wine term – literally "dry" but in practice not bone-dry.

B.O.B. "Buyer's own brand" wine.

Cuvée The assembled or blended wine.

Cuvée de prestige/deluxe The flagships of the Champagne houses. Supposed to be the finest cuvées. Sometimes very great (Roederer Cristal and Dom Pérignon) and always very expensive.

Dégorgement Removal of the yeast lees created during the second fermentation.

Dosage Wine added to top up Champagne after disgorging, setting sweetness level.

Giropalette Rémuage machine.

Grande marque Literally "great brand", a grouping of recognized producers whose names should be a guarantee of quality. Usually the name of the house or grower, but it may be a brand name.

Liqueur de tirage Mixture of sugar, yeast and wine added to still Champagne to create the sparkle.

Matriculation number This number, mandatory on all Champagne labels, reveals, by the two letters preceding it, the origins of the contents of a bottle of Champagne.

NM = négociant-manipulant; wine from all over the region was bought and blended by a commercial house.

CM = co-opérative-manipulant; a group of growers "pool" their grapes/ wine to produce a blend.

RM = récoltant-manipulant; a grower/ producer who grows, vinifies and sells his own wine.

MA = marque auxiliaire; a brand name owned by the producer or purchaser.

Microbilles *See* pille.

Mousse The effervescence of Champagne.

Non-dosage A term for wines without sugar added at dosage – also called Brut Zéro or Brut Sauvage.

Non-vintage The objective of these blends is to keep to a uniform "house" style. A blend will be based on one vintage, normally the last, plus wine from older vintage(s). "NV" accounts for over 80 per cent of the region's production.

Pille A membrane-coated yeast capsule under experimentation in Champagne.

Pupitre The racks which hold Champagne bottles on end while *rémuage* takes place.

Ratafia Liqueur made in Champagne blending grape must and marc.

Récemment dégorgé Recently disgorged. Bollinger has registered the abbreviation "RD" as a trademark.

Rémuage The "riddling" – twiddling – of bottles of Champagne undergoing the secondary fermentation to move the yeast deposit on to the corks. A laborious task by hand, it is today increasingly done by giropalettes.

Rosé Pink champagne. Uniquely in EC wine law, may be made in this region by blending white and red wines. To some, however, the best method is to use only black grapes, as with Blanc de Noirs, but allowing minimal maceration.

Vintage Wine from a single "declared" vintage. Must have more bottle-age than non-vintage, with strict quality control of the cuvée. No more than 80 per cent of the harvest can be sold as vintage.

The Language of Italy

Abboccato Semi-sweet.

Amabile Semi-sweet, but usually sweeter than *abboccato*.

Amarone Bitter.

Annato Year.

Asciutto Bone-dry.

Azienda/Azienda Agricola Estate/winery.

Azienda Vitivinicola Specialist wine estate.

Barrique Denotes ageing in new oak.

Bianco White.

Bric Piedmont term for hill.

Cantina Cellar, winery.

Cantina Sociale Co-operative winery.

Cascina Farm or estate (northern Italy).

Cérasuolo Cherry-red.

Chiaretto Somewhere between rosé and very light red.

Classico Wine from a restricted area within a DOC. Usually the central area and often the source of the best wines.

Colli Hilly area.

Consorzio Group of producers who control and promote the wines in their particular region.

Cru Vineyard.

Denominazione di Origine Controllata (DOC) Controlled wine region. The DOC system has been recognized as having many faults, notably that it patently fails to acknowledge some of the best wines in Italy and that it has been granted to some areas more for their wine tradition than for their present quality. The best guarantee of quality is the name of the producer.

Denominazione di Origine Controllata e Garantita (DOCG) Theoretically a superior classification to DOC but this was cast into doubt when the first white DOCG was granted to the undistinguished Albana di Romagna. Nevertheless, it does recognize some of the best Italian reds, for example Barolo, Barbaresco and Brunello di Montalcino. In future it should apply to specific, higher-quality sub-regions.

Dolce Very sweet.

Enoteca Literally a "wine library" – most commonly a wine shop but sometimes a local wine "institute" or regulatory body.

Fattoria Farm.

Fermentazione Naturale Natural fermentation, but can be in bottle or tank.

Flore Literally "flower", refers to the first pressing of grapes.

Frizzante Semi-sparkling.

Frizzantino Very lightly sparkling.

Gradi Percentage of alcohol by volume.

Imbottigliato Bottled.

Indicazione Geografica Tipica (IGT) New quality designation below DOC but above vino da tavola

Liquoroso Sweet and fortified, or a dry white wine high in alcohol.

Località (also **Ronco** and **Vigneto**) Single vineyard.

Metodo Classico The *méthode champenoise*.

Passito Strong, sweet wine made from semi-dried (*passito*) grapes.

Pastoso Medium-sweet.

Podere Small farm or estate.

Ramato Copper-coloured wines made from Pinot Grigio grapes briefly macerated on their skins.

Recioto (della Valpolicella, di Soave) Speciality styles of the Veneto made from semi-dried grapes. Can be dry and bitter (*amarone*), sweet (*amabile*) or an intermediate style (*amandorlato*). All are characterized by strong, concentrated flavours and high alcohol levels.

Ripasso Wine fermented on the lees of a *recioto*.

Riserva/Riserva Speciale DOC wine matured for a statutory number of years in a barrel.

Rosato Rosé.

Rosso Red.

Secco Dry.

Semi-secco Medium-dry.

Sori Piedmont term for hillside.

Spumante Fully sparkling wine.

Stravecchio Very old.

Superiore DOC wines meeting certain additional conditions, such as higher alcohol content.

Uvaggio Wine blended from a number of grape varieties.

Uvas Grapes.

Vecchio Old

Vendemmia Vintage.

Vigna Vineyard.

Vin Santo/Vino Santo Traditionally sweet – although can be dry – white from *passito* grapes stored in sealed casks that have not been topped up for several years. Literally means "holy wine", as it was traditionally picked during Holy Week before Easter.

Vini tipici Equivalent of French *vins de pays* – "country wines" with some regional character. A new designation which may or may not catch on.

Vino novello New, "nouveau-style" wine.

Vino da arrosto A robust red that is a "wine for roast meat".

Vino da pasta Ordinary "meal-time" wine.

Vino da tavola Literally means "table wine" but includes some of Italy's finest wines since the DOC laws place onerous restrictions on the use of non-traditional grape varieties and innovative methods.

The Language of Germany

Amtliche Prufungsnummer Literally means "official proof number" – and refers to the unique code given to batches of wine that have passed statutory tests for the area of origin. Usually referred to as the AP number.

Anbaugebiet Wine region, e.g. the Rheingau or Baden.

Auslese Third step on the QmP quality ladder: wine made from grapes with a high natural sugar content. The wines are usually rich and concentrated.

Beerenauslese Fourth step on the QmP quality ladder: wine made from individually selected overripe grapes with up to 16 per cent potential alcohol. Such wines are rich and very sweet.

Bereich Grouping of villages or a district within an Anbaugebiet, e.g. Bernkastel.

Bundesweinprämierung German state wine award.

Charta Organization of Rheingau estates whose members make drier (Halbtrocken) styles, observing higher standards than the legal minimum.

Deutscher Sekt Sparkling wine made from 100 per cent German grapes.

Deutscher Tafelwein Lowest grade of German wine.

Deutsches Weinsiegel Quality seal around the neck of a bottle for wines that have passed certain tasting tests.

Domäne Domaine or estate.

Edelfäule Noble rot – *botrytis cinerea*.

Einzellage "Single site" or individual vineyard, usually following name of a specific town or village: e.g. Graacher Himmelreich.

Eiswein Literally, "ice wine", made from grapes of at least Beerenauslese ripeness, picked while the water content is frozen thus leaving the concentrated sugar, acids and flavour. Eiswein is rare and expensive.

Erzeugerabfüllung Estate-bottled.

Flurbereinigung Government-assisted replanting of slopes to up-and-down rows instead of terracing.

Gemeinde Commune or parish.

Grosslage A group of neighbouring Einzellagen producing wines of similar style and character – a group site, e.g. Piesporter Michelsberg.

Halbtrocken Half-dry.

Herb German equivalent of Brut.

Hock English term for a wine from the Rhine, derived from Hochheim.

Kabinett First step on the QmP quality ladder. The equivalent of reserve wines, Kabinetts are the lightest and driest of the naturally unsugared QmP wines.

Kellerei Winery.

Landwein German equivalent of French vin de pays: Trocken or Halbtrocken wines of a higher quality than Tafelwein and produced in a specific region.

Lieblich Wine of medium sweetness, equivalent to the French moëlleux.

Oechsle German measure of the ripeness of grapes used as the basis for determining the quality level of individual wines.

Perlwein Semi-sparkling wine.

Qualitätswein bestimmter Anbaugebiete (QbA) Quality level below QmP for wines that satisfy certain controls, such as area of origin, but which have had sugar added for extra alcohol.

Qualitätswein mit Prädikat (QmP) Wines made from grapes that are ripe enough not to require any additional sugar. Meaning "a quality wine predicated by ripeness", these top wines are further classified into the categories Kabinett to Trockenbeerenauslese.

Rotling Rosé.

Rotwein Red wine.

Schaumwein Sparkling wine.

Sekt Sparkling wine, usually made by the cuve close method, which, if not prefixed by "Deutscher", can be produced from grapes grown outside Germany. Little of it is any good.

Spätlese The second step on the QmP ladder; literally means "late-picked". Sweet or dry and full-flavoured, these wines are balanced with fine acidity.

Spritz/Spritzig Light sparkle.

Süss Sweet.

Süssreserve Pure, unfermented grape juice used to sweeten basic German wines. Also used by English wine-makers.

Tafelwein Table wine that, even if bottled in Germany, may be a blend of wines from different EC countries. Deutscher Tafelwein must be 100 per cent German.

Trocken Dry.

Trockenbeerenauslese Fifth and highest step on the QmP quality ladder. Made from "shrivelled single overripe berries" affected by botrytis, these intense, complex wines are extremely rare and expensive, with a potential alcohol of at least 21.5 per cent, although only 5.5 per cent need be actual alcohol. The high level of residual sugar produces rich wine with wonderfully intense honey, raisin and caramel flavours.

Weingut Wine estate. Can only be used on labels where all the grapes are grown on that estate.

Weinkellerei Wine cellar or winery.

Weissherbst Rosé of QbA standard or above produced from a single variety of black grape.

Weisswein White wine.

Winzergenossenschaft Wine-growers' co-operative.

The Language of Spain

Abocado Medium-sweet.

Añejado por Aged by.

Año Year.

Blanco White.

Bodega Wine shop, firm or cellar.

Cepa Vine.

Clarete Very light red.

Consejo Regulador Official organization controlling each region's system of Denominación de Origen.

Cosecha Harvest, vintage.

Criada por Matured by.

Crianza A red wine with a minimum of two years in the barrel (six months for whites).

Denominación de Origen (DO) Controlled quality wine region, equivalent to France's AOC. Every such region possesses its own quality stamp.

Denominación de Origen Calificada (DOC) A superior quality level, created in 1988, and confusingly similar to Italy's DOCG. So far Rioja is the only region.

Doble Pasta A wine macerated with twice the normal proportion of grape skins to juice during fermentation.

Dulce Sweet.

Embotellado Bottled.

Espumoso Sparkling.

Elaborado por Made by.

Flor Wine yeast peculiar to sherry that is vital to the development of the fino style.

Garantia de Origen Simple wines that have received little or no oak ageing.

Generoso Fortified.

Gran Reserva The top quality level for wines. Reds must have spent two years in oak and three years in bottle, or *vice versa*. Whites must have been aged for four years with at least six months in cask.

Granvas Sparkling wine made by the cuve close method.

Joven Young wine – unwooded, fresh, fruity and modern.

Nuevo "Nouveau-style" red.

Reserva Reds matured for a minimum of three years, of which at least one is spent in cask. Whites and rosados receive two years' ageing with at least six months in cask.

Rosado Rosé.

Seco Dry.

Semi-seco Medium-dry.

Sin Crianza Without wood ageing.

Solera Traditional system of producing consistent style of sherry or Málaga whereby increasingly mature barrels are topped up – refreshed – with slightly younger wine.

Tintillo Light red (like clarete).

Tinto Red.

Vendimia Harvest, vintage.

Viejo Old.

Viña/Viñedo Vineyard.

Vino de aguja Wine with a slight sparkle.

Vino de mesa Table wine.

Vino de pasta Ordinary, inexpensive wine, usually light in style.

Vino de la Tierra Equivalent of France's vin de pays; "country wine" with some regional character.

The Language of Portugal

Adamado Sweet.

Adega Cellar, winery.

Branco White.

Carvalho Oak.

Clarete Light red wine.

Colheita Vintage.

DOC (Denominação de Origem Controlada) Portugal's new appellation system which replaced the old RD.

Dolce Sweet.

Engarrafado na Origem Estate-bottled.

Espumante Sparkling.

Garrafeira A wine made from one or more areas and matured for three years including one in bottle if red, and for one year including six months in bottle if white. Wines must bear a vintage date and have 0.5 per cent alcohol above the minimum. Often, the garrafeira is the "private reserve" of the merchant.

IPR (Indicação de Proviência Regulamentada) The second layer of Portugal's new DOC appellation system.

Licoroso Sweet fortified wine.

Maduro Matured (in vat).

Quinta Farm.

RD (Região Demarcada) Now-defunct appellation system, replaced by DOC (qv).

Reserva A wine from one or several areas from an outstanding vintage. It must contain 0.5 per cent alcohol above the minimum.

Rosado Rosé.

Seco Dry.

Tinto Red.

Velho Old. Reds must be over three years old, whites over two years old before they may use the term on the label.

Verde Young, "green" (as in Vinho Verde).

Vinho consumo Ordinary wine.

Vinho generoso Fortified aperitif or dessert wine.

Vinho de mesa Table wine.

Vinhos Regionãos Roughly equi-valent to the French vins de pays.

BEER

Abbey Commercial Belgian beers licensed by abbeys. Not to be confused with Trappist ales.

Adjuncts Materials used in place of traditional grains for cheapness or lightness of flavour. Common adjuncts are rice, maize (corn) and brewing sugar.

Ale The world's oldest beer style produced by top or warm fermentation.

Alpha acid The main component of the bittering agent in the hop flower.

Alt Literally Old in German, a top-fermenting beer mainly confined to the city of Düsseldorf.

Attenuation The extent to which brewing sugars turn to alcohol and carbon dioxide.

Beer Generic term for an alcoholic drink made from grain; includes both ale and lager.

Bitter British term for the pale, amber or copper-coloured beers that developed from the pale ales of the nineteenth century.

Bock or Bok Strong beer style of Germany and the Netherlands.

Bottle-conditioned A beer that undergoes a secondary fermentation in the bottle.

Cask-conditioned Beer that undergoes a secondary fermentation in the cask, a style closely identified with British beers. Popularly known as "real ale".

Copper Vessel used to boil the sugary wort with hops. Also known as a brew kettle.

Decoction mashing A system mainly used in lager brewing in which portions of the wort are removed from the mashing vessel, heated to a higher temperature and then returned. Improves enzymic activity and the conversion of starch to sugar in poorly modified malts.

Dry-hopping The addition of a small amount of hops to a cask of beer to improve aroma and bitterness.

Dunkel A dark lager beer in Germany, a Bavarian speciality that predated the first pale lagers.

EBC European Beer Convention that indicates the colour in malts and beers.

Entire The earliest form of porter, short for "entire butt".

Ester Flavour compounds produced by the action of yeast turning sugars into alcohol and carbon dioxide. Esters may be fruity or spicy.

Fining Substance that clarifies beer, usually made from the swim bladder of sturgeon fish; also known as isinglass.

Framboise or frambozen Raspberry-flavoured lambic beer.

Grist The coarse powder derived from malt that has been milled or "cracked" in the brewery prior to mashing.

Gueuze A blend of Belgian lambic beers.

Helles or Hell A pale Bavarian lager beer.

IBU International Units of Bitterness, scale for measuring the bitterness of beer.

Infusion Method of mashing used mainly in ale-brewing where the grains are left to soak with pure water while starches convert to sugar, usually carried out at a constant temperature.

Kölsch Top-fermenting golden beer from Cologne.

Kräusen The addition of partially-fermented wort during lagering to encourage a strong secondary fermentation.

Kriek Cherry-flavoured lambic beer.

Lager From the German meaning "store". The cold-conditioning of beer at around 0° Centigrade to encourage the yeast to settle out, increase carbonation and produce a smooth, clean-tasting beer.

Lambic Belgian beer made by spontaneous fermentation.

Lauter tun Vessel used to clarify the wort after the mashing stage.

Malt Barley or other cereals that have been partially germinated to allow starches to be converted into fermentable sugars.

Mash First stage of the brewing process, when the malt is mixed with pure hot water to extract the sugars.

Märzen Traditional Bavarian lager brewed in March and stored until autumn for the Munich Oktoberfest.

Mild Dark brown (occasionally pale) English and Welsh beer, lightly hopped. The oldest style of beer that once derived its colour from malt cured over wood fires. One of the components of the first porters.

Milk stout Stout made with the addition of lactose, which is unfermentable, producing a beer low in alcohol with a creamy, slightly sweet character.

Pilsner or Pilsener or Pils International brand name for a light-coloured lager. In the Czech Republic the term is confined to beers brewed in Pilsen or Pilzen where the style was perfected.

Porter Dark – brown or black – beer originating in London, deriving its name from its popularity with street-market porters.

Priming The addition of sugar to encourage a secondary fermentation in beer.

Reinheitsgebot Bavarian beer law of 1516 , the "Purity Pledge", that lays down that only malted grain, hops, yeast and water can be used in brewing. Now covers the whole of Germany.

Shilling Ancient method of invoicing beer in Scotland based on strength. Beers are called 60, 70 or 80 shilling.

Sparging Sprinkling or spraying the spent grains in the mash tun or lauter tun to flush out any remaining malt sugars. From the French esparger, to sprinkle.

Square A traditional open fermenting vessel.

Steam beer American beer style saved by the Anchor Brewery in San Francisco.

Stout Once an English generic term for the strongest or "stoutest" beer in a brewery; came to be identified with porter. Porter Stout eventually became modified to just stout. Now considered a quintessentially Irish style.

Trappist Ales brewed by monks of the Trappist order in Belgium and The Netherlands.

Union Method of fermentation developed in Burton-on-Trent using large oak casks.

Ur or Urtyp German for original. Urquell as in Pilsner Urquell means "original source Pilsner".

Weizen or weisse German term meaning wheat or white beer. Wit in Flemish.

Wort Liquid resulting from the mashing process, rich in malt sugars.

SPIRITS

ABV The alcoholic strength of a spirit measured as a percentage in relation to the liquid as a whole (i.e. 40% ABV is 40% alcohol, 60% water). See "Proof".

Aguard(i)ente Spanish/Portuguese term for spirit. In Spain and Portugal it refers to grape brandy, in Brazil and Mexico it is sometimes used to refer to a young sugar cane spirit.

Alambic/Alembic Old term for a pot still.

Alambic Armagnaçais Traditional small continuous still used in Armagnac.

Alambic Charentais Traditional Cognac pot still.

Alquitara Spanish term for a pot still and a pot-still distillate.

Analyser The first column of a multi-column still.

Anejo Tequila/mezcal that has been aged in the barrel for more than one year.

Agave Family of Mexican desert lilies used to produce mezcal and tequila.

Age statement The age on a bottle of spirits referring to the youngest component in the blend/vatting.

Angel's share The term given to the spirit which evaporates from warehoused barrels. Known as "Duppies' Share" in Jamaica.

Aqua vitae The original term for spirits, meaning "water of life". In Scottish Gaelic, it is *uisce beatha*; in Irish Gaelic, usquebaugh; and in Danish, akvavit.

Assemblage French term for blending.

Backset (aka setback or sour mash) In North America, the acidic residue from the first distillation which is added to the mash tub and/or the fermenter, totalling no less than 25 per cent of the overall mash. It is used to stop bacterial infection and to lower the pH in the fermenter allowing an even fermentation.

Bagasse The fibrous stalks of sugar cane, sometimes used as fuel for rum stills.

Batch distillation Another term for pot-still, or discontinuous distillation. The first distillation produces a low-strength spirit which is then redistilled and separated into three parts – heads, heart and tails – of which only the heart is retained.

Beading A simple method of assessing the strength of a spirit. When a bottle is shaken, bubbles (beads) form. The bigger they are and the longer they remain, the higher the strength.

Beer North American/Caribbean term for fermented "mash".

Beer still North American term for the first still in the distillation process.

Blending (1) Mixing different types of spirit; (2) Assembling different ages of the same spirit. In both cases the aim is to produce a consistent style.

Boise Extract of oak chips and spirit used to colour and flavour young brandies.

Botanicals The herbs, peel, etc. which flavour gin; the most important of them all being juniper.

Bouilleur French term for distiller.

Brandewijn Dutch term for grape spirit (burnt wine) which evolved into brandy.

Brouillis (aka Premier Chauffe) The spirit collected at the end of the first distillation in Cognac.

Cask strength A spirit which has not been reduced by the addition of water to the standard strength.

Chai Above-ground warehouse used for ageing Cognac and Armagnac.

Charcoal filtration Technique (used in Tennessee whiskeys and vodka production) which involves passing new spirit through vats or tanks containing granulated charcoal. This removes impurities and imparts a roundness to the spirit.

Charring The firing of the inside of a barrel. The flame opens up cracks in the surface of the oak, allowing easy penetration by the spirit, and also releases sugar compounds which aid flavouring and colouring of the spirit.

Chill filtration Filtering process done by lowering the temperature of a spirit to remove compounds which could cause clouding. It also has the effect of removing some congeners.

Condenser The equipment which turns the alcoholic vapours into liquid form. Traditionally this was a spiral of copper immersed in cold water. Today, heat exchangers are used.

Congeners Chemical compounds found in a spirit formed during fermentation, distillation and maturation. They contain many flavour-carrying elements. The higher the alcoholic strength of a spirit, the fewer congeners present.

Cold compounding Method of adding concentrates of flavours to neutral spirit. A cheaper method than maceration and infusion, giving a cruder product.

Column still (aka continuous, Coffey or beer still) The type of still most commonly used in continuous distillation. It works by forcing pressurised steam up the column where it meets the descending alcoholic wash, vaporizing the alcohol and carrying it up to be condensed.

Distillation The technique of extracting alcohol from a fermented liquid by heating it. Because alcohol boils at a lower temperature than water, the vapour can be collected and condensed, thus concentrating the strength.

Doubler North American term for the pot still used for the second distillation.

Dram Scottish, Irish and Caribbean term for a glass of spirit.

Enzymes Organic catalysts which convert non-fermentable starches into fermentable soluble sugars. Grains such as malted barley and rye contain such enzymes and are added to other cereal crops for this process of conversion or saccharification.

Esters Flavour-giving chemical compounds, produced by the reaction of alcohol and acids during fermentation and maturation, that appear soon after the start of distillation.

Eau-de-vie (1) French term for young distillate (brandy); (2) French term for spirits made from fruit.

Faibles Low-strength solution of distilled water and Cognac used to dilute maturing brandies.

Fermenters Large vessels made of either steel or wood where the mash is turned into beer or wash.

Fusel oil A heavy congener.

Fut/Fut de chêne French term for a barrel of less than 650 litres.

Heads (aka high wines/foreshots/têtes) The volatile first runnings from the still during the second distillation. They are collected and redistilled.

Heart (aka coeur/middle cut) Term for the potable central fraction of the spirit in batch distillation which the distiller keeps.

Holandas Young Spanish brandy produced from a pot still (*alquitara*).

Infusion Process of extracting flavour from ingredients by gentle heating.

Maceration The process of steeping ingredients (fruits, herbs, etc.) in alcohol to extract colour and flavour.

Malt (1) A grain, usually barley, which has been stimulated artificially into germination and then halted by drying ("Malting"). The malt is high in sugars and enzymes; (2) Common term for a single malt whisky.

Maltings The building where malting takes place.

Marrying Process where recently blended spirits are placed in a large vat before bottling. The technique allows the different distillates to homogenize.

Mash The sweet liquid produced after hot water has been flushed through the base ingredient in the mash tub/tun to extract the fermentable sugars prior to fermentation.

Mash bill North American term for the percentage make-up of ingredients (corn, wheat, rye, barley) being used in mashing.

Molasses The thick black liquid that is left after sugar has been crystallized. It can then be used to make rum, rhum industriel, or neutral alcohol.

Mouthfeel Tasting term used for the shape and texture of the spirit in the mouth.

Neutral alcohol/spirit Spirit of above 95.5% ABV containing little or no congeners.

Nose The aroma of the spirit.

Oak The most common type of wood used for casks used in maturation. Oak is a strong, watertight wood which allows light oxidation. It also imparts a range of colour and flavour components to the maturing spirit. Different types of oak will give different effects.

Overproof Rum terminology for high-strength, unaged rum.

Paille French rhum that has been aged for less than three years.

Paradis Cellar containing the oldest and rarest brandies.

Peat A soft fuel made from compressed and carbonized vegetable matter – usually heather, wood, grass and occasionally seaweed. Its smoke, known as peat reek, is very pungent and when used in drying malted barley imparts its phenolic aroma to the malt.

Piña Term used to describe ripe agave.

Pomace See Vinaccia.

Pot stills Stills, usually made from copper, used in batch distillation.

Proof American measurement of alcoholic strength. A 100° proof spirit is 50% ABV.

Rancio The rich, pungent aroma with hints of mushrooms, cheese, dried fruit and nuts, which is created by the oxidation of fatty acids during the extended maturation of a brandy. It usually appears after 20 years or more.

Rectification Purification of a distillate by redistillation, giving a high-strength distillate with very few congeners.

Reflux The process in which the shape or control of a still forces alcohol vapours to fall back down the still to be redistilled. The end result usually produces a lighter spirit.

Reposado Tequila/mezcal that has been aged in the barrel for less than eleven months.

Retort A vessel used in batch distillation containing either the heads or tails of the previous distillation. The alcoholic vapour passes through the bottom of the retort, heating the liquid and causing a second distillation.

Rhum Rum from French-governed *départements* (such as Martinique and Guadeloupe). Rhum agricole is produced from sugar cane juice; Rhum industriel is made from molasses.

Ricks The wooden frames that hold maturing American whiskey.

Solera Predominantly Spanish method of maturation and fractional blending, most commonly seen in Jerez and used for sherry and Brandy de Jerez.

Sour mash Another term for backset. A sour mash whiskey must contain 25% backset and the use of a lactic bacteria soured yeast mash which has been fermented for a minimum of 72 hours. All Kentucky and Tennessee whiskey is sour mash.

Stillage The non-alcoholic residue at the bottom of a still containing solids – which are processed for animal feed – and acidic liquid which in North America is used as backset.

Tails (aka low wines, feints) The unwanted end part of the second distillation. They are collected and redistilled.

Thumper A type of doubler containing water through which the alcoholic vapours pass.

Toasting The process of lightly heating the inside of a barrel, releasing sugars in the wood. A more gentle process than charring.

Vatting Scottish/Irish term for the mixing together of malt from one distillery. A "vatted malt" is a blend of malts from more than one distillery.

Vieux French term used for long-aged spirits like rhum or Calvados.

Vinaccia (aka pomace) The skins left after a wine has been fermented which when distilled produce grappa/marc.

Vintage Term referring to a spirit produced from a single year.

VS (aka ***) French term for the youngest grading of brandy, usually spirits which have been aged for a minimum of two and a half years.

VSOP French term for the second-quality grading of brandy, referring to a spirit which has usually been aged for a minimum of four and a half years.

Wash The fermented liquid which is ready to be distilled.

XO (aka extra, extra vieux, Napoleon, Reserve) French term for the top quality grade of a spirit which has usually been aged for a minimum of six to seven years but normally considerably longer.

Yeast A micro-organism of the fungi family which feeds on sugar converting it to alcohol and carbon dioxide. Yeast also imparts flavour compounds to the liquid.

INDEX

The publishers would like to thank the following sources for their kind permission to reproduce the pictures in this book:

Adnams & Co. Ltd. 325
Allied Distillers Ltd. 447
James L. Amos 399
the art archive ltd. 425, Detail of Inside the Winter Bierhaus,
Vienna, Wilhelm Gause 220
Balvenie Maltings 428
Beamish 338
Benton Associates 311
Berenhen 579
Brewers Imports Ltd. 247
Brooklyn 375
Dave Broom 420, 473
Brown Forman Ltd. 419
Budweiser 358
Burn Stewart Distillers plc 3, 455
CBL/Howard Shooter 255, 533, 571
Canadian Mist 484
Carlsberg Tetley 322
Castlemaine XXXX 394
Celis Golden 378
The Chivas & Glenlivet Group 445, 452-3, 482
Communications Plus 597
Corbis 13, 17, 18, 21, 83, 259, 415, 486, 563/ Paul Almasy 28,
Archivio Iconografico, S.A.285, 409, Tony Arruza 523, Neil Beer 386,
Jonathan Blair 526, 598, Michael Boys 239, Michael Busselle 30, 64,
84, 87, 88, 90-1, 99, 495, Jan Butchofsky-Houser 179, Carol Cohen
176, Dean Conger 552-3, Jerry Cooke 481, Carl Corey 259, Sergio
Dorantes 385, Reinhard Eisele 520, Macduff Everton 7t, 434, 441,
465, Peter Finger 10, Owen Franken 262, 574, Franz-Marc Frei 580,
Michelle Garrett 588, Raymond Gehman 477, Mark Gibson 529,
Todd Gipstein 61, Philip Gould 531, Roger de la Harpe; Gallo Images
4, Historical Picture Archive 573, Robert Holmes 62, 172, 182, Dave
G. Houser 48, 581, Hulton Getty 410, Wolfgang Kaehler 294,
Catherine Karnow 36, 491, 582, Bob Krist 128, George Lepp 602,
Gail Mooney 27, 32, 39, 577, Kevin R. Morris 372, Charles O'Rear
35, 51, 53, 73, 150, 200, Diego Lezama Orezzoli 134, Bryan
Pickering; Eye Ubiquitous 66, Enzo & Paolo Ragazzini 108, Vittoriani
Rastelli 101, Steve Raymer 348, 556, Reuters NewMedia Inc. 282,
Bob Rowan; Progressive Image 180, Christian Sarramon 341, 546,
591, Gregor Schmid 315, Paul A. Souders 362, Ted Streshinsky 137,
146, 149, Liba Taylor 488, Sandro Vannini 355, Patrick Ward 47,
147, Gavin Wickham; Eye Ubiquitous 604, John Wilkinson/Ecoscene
433, Adam Woolfitt 97, 298, 312, 595, Michael S. Yamashita 218,
401, Ed Young 175, Jim Zuckerman 502
Courvoisier 496
Diageo 544
George Dickel 479
Enotria Winecellars Ltd. 102, 112
Mary Evans Picture Library 223, 232, 277/Explorer 224, 515
First Drinks Brands Ltd. 607
Food Features 609, 613, 616, 620, 622, 629

Michael Freeman 271
Gettyone Stone/Sean Ellis 406, Hubertus Hamm 8b, Carin Krasner 9
Glenturret Distillery Ltd., Crieff, Perthshire 459
William Grant & Sons International Ltd. 463
Grant's Brewpub 368
GWIS@Phipps PR 120, 123, 124Hart Brewery, Seattle, WA 371
Heineken N.V. 342, 343, 393
Henninger 309
Herradura 567, 569 Jeremy Horner 518
Irish Distillers Ltd. 466
Istituto Trentino del Vino 510
Jameson Irish Whisky 430
Janneau CSPR 504
de Jerez 507
Kriek-Lambic Cantillon 266
Kona Brewing Company 405
La Chouffe 273
La Choulette 289
J.W.Lees & Co. (Brewers) Ltd., Middleton Jnc., Manchester 242, 327
John Locke & Company Ltd. 468-9
Lowenbrau 243
The Macallan Distilleries 432, 448-9
Macdonald & Muir 456-7
Marstons 248, 319
Morrison Bowmore Distillers Ltd./Eric Thorburn 439
Newcastle Breweries/Ian Dobson Photography 329
The Orkney Brewery 332
Panos Pictures/Pietro Cenini 388, Dean Chapman 489
Plymouth Gin 537
Rochefort abbey 269
The Royal Tokaji Wine Company 7b Ryan & Cox Public Relations 275
Privatbrauerei G Schneider & Sohn/Brewers Imports 304
Schutzenberger 287, 291 Seagram UK Ltd. 492
Smithwicks/Tom Brett 339
Sopexa 42, 56, 69, 75, 76, 79
Southcorp Wines Europe Ltd. 194, 203
Spaten-Franziskaner-Brau/H.G.Kaufmann 297
Summit 250, 253
The Swan Brewery, Perth, Western Australia 396
United Distillers and Vintners 542 The Upper Canada Brewing
Company 382
Hiram Walker & Sons Ltd. 485
Westbury Blake/Patrick Parenteau Photo 8t
Whyte & Mackay Group 442
Wines of Chile 6, 188, 192
Wodka Restaurants Ltd., London 559
Every effort has been made to acknowledge correctly and contact the
source and/copyright holder of each picture, and Carlton Books
Limited apologises for any unintentional errors or omissions which
will be corrected in future editions of this book.